Thomas Moore

Poetical Works

Vol. 1

Thomas Moore

Poetical Works
Vol. 1

ISBN/EAN: 9783337778019

Printed in Europe, USA, Canada, Australia, Japan

Cover: Foto ©Thomas Meinert / pixelio.de

More available books at **www.hansebooks.com**

THE POETICAL WORKS

OF

THOMAS MOORE.

WITH MEMOIR BY

DAVID HERBERT, M.A.

NEW EDITION CAREFULLY REVISED.

EDINBURGH:
W. P. NIMMO, HAY, & MITCHELL.
1887.

CONTENTS.

	PAGE
LIFE OF THOMAS MOORE,	7

LALLA ROOKH.

The Veiled Prophet of Khorassan,	54
Paradise and the Peri,	81
The Fire-Worshippers,	90
The Light of the Haram,	114

ODES OF ANACREON.

Index showing the number of each Ode in Barnes' and other Editions,	128
An Ode by the Translator,	129
Remarks on Anacreon,	ib.
1. I saw the smiling bard of pleasure,	134
2. Give me the harp of epic song,	ib.
3. Listen to the Muse's lyre,	135
4. Vulcan! hear your glorious task,	ib.
5. Grave me a cup with brilliant grace,	ib.
6. As late I sought the spangled bowers,	136
7. The women tell me every day,	ib.
8. I care not for the idle state,	ib.
9. I pray thee, by the gods above,	137
10. Tell me how to punish thee,	ib.
11. Tell me, gentle youth, I pray thee,	ib.
12. They tell how Atys, wild with love,	138
13. I will, I will; the conflict's past,	ib.
14. Count me, on the summer trees,	139
15. Tell me why, my sweetest dove,	140
16. Thou, whose soft and rosy hues,	ib.
17. And now, with all thy pencil's truth,	141
18. Now the star of day is high,	142
19. Here recline you, gentle maid,	143
20. One day the Muses twined the hands,	ib.
21. Observe when mother earth is dry,	144
22. The Phrygian rock, that braves the storm,	ib.
23. I often wish this languid lyre,	145
24. To all that breathe the airs of heaven,	ib.
25. Once in each revolving year,	146
26. Thy harp may sing of Troy's alarms,	ib.
27. We read the flying courser's name,	ib.
28. As in the Lemnian caves of fire,	ib.
29. 'T—s—loving is a painful thrill,	147
30. 'Twas in an airy dream of night,	ib.
31. Armed with hyacinthine rod,	ib.

ODES OF ANACREON—*continued.*

32. Strew me a breathing bed of leaves,	148
33. 'Twas noon of night, when round the pole,	ib.
34. Oh thou, of all creation blest,	149
35. Cupid once upon a bed,	ib.
36. If hoarded gold possessed a power,	150
37. 'Twas night, and many a circling bowl,	ib.
38. Let us drain the nectared bowl,	151
39. How I love the festive boy,	ib.
40. I know that Heaven ordains me here,	152
41. When Spring begems the dewy scene,	ib.
42. Yes, be the glorious revel mine,	ib.
43. While our rosy fillets shed,	ib.
44. Buds of roses, virgin flowers,	153
45. Within this goblet, rich and deep,	ib.
46. See, the young, the rosy Spring,	ib.
47. 'Tis true, my fading years decline,	154
48. When my thirsty soul I steep,	ib.
49. When Bacchus, Jove's immortal boy,	ib.
50. When I drink, I feel, I feel,	155
51. Fly not thus, my brow of snow,	ib.
52. Away, away, you men of rules,	ib.
53. When I behold the festive train,	156
54. Methinks the pictured bull we see,	ib.
55. While we invoke the wreathèd spring,	ib.
56. He, who instructs the youthful crew,	157
57. And whose immortal hand could shed,	158
58. When gold, as fleet as Zephyr's pinion,	ib.
59. Sabled by the solar beam,	159
60. Awake to life, my dulcet shell,	ib.
61. Golden hues of youth are fled,	160
62. Fill me, boy, as deep a draught,	161
63. To Love, the soft and blooming child,	ib.
64. Haste thee, nymph, whose wingèd spear,	ib.
65. Like some wanton filly sporting,	ib.
66. To thee, the Queen of nymphs divine,	162
67. Gentle youth! whose looks assume,	ib.
68. Rich in bliss, I proudly scorn,	ib.
69. Now Neptune's sullen month appears,	ib.
70. They wove the lotus band, to deck,	ib.
71. A broken cake, with honey sweet,	163
72. With twenty chords my lyre is hung,	ib.

A

	PAGE		PAGE
ODES OF ANACREON—*continued.*		JUVENILE POEMS—*continued.*	
73. Fare thee well, perfidious maid,	163	On the Death of a Lady,	180
74. I bloomed, awhile, a happy flower,	ib.	To Rosa,	ib.
75. Monarch Love! resistless boy,	ib.	Nature's Labels,	ib.
76. Spirit of Love! whose tresses shine,	ib.	To Julia,	181
77. Hither, gentle Muse of mine,	164	Sympathy,	ib.
78. Would that I were a tuneful lyre,	ib.	To Julia,	ib.
79. When Cupid sees my beard of snow,	ib.	To Mrs. M.——,	ib.
		Song,	ib.
FRAGMENTS.		The Ring,	182
Cupid, whose lamp has lent the ray,	ib.	Song,	184
Let me resign a wretched breath,	ib.	Song,	ib.
I know thou lov'st a brimming measure,	ib.	The Shrine,	185
I fear that love disturbs my rest,	ib.	The Catalogue,	ib.
From dread Leucadia's frowning steep,	ib.	To ——,	ib.
Mix me, child, a cup divine,	165	Song,	186
		Song,	ib.
EPIGRAMS TRANSLATED FROM ANTIPATER SIDONIUS.		Reuben and Rose,	ib.
		To a Boy with a Watch,	187
Around the tomb, oh bard divine,	ib.	Song,	ib.
Here sleeps Anacreon, in this ivied shade,	ib.	The Natal Genius,	188
Oh stranger! if Anacreon's shell,	166	Morality,	ib.
At length thy golden hours have winged their flight,	ib.	Song,	189
		Song,	ib.
		Fragments of College Exercises,	ib.
JUVENILE POEMS.		Song,	190
Preface,	171	The Shield,	ib.
Dedication,	173	The Tear,	ib.
To a Lady,	ib.	A Dream,	ib.
To the Large and Beautiful Miss ——,	ib.	To a Lady, on her Singing,	ib.
To Julia,	174	Written in a Commonplace Book, called	
Inconstancy,	ib.	'The Book of Follies,'.	191
To Julia,	ib.	To Julia, weeping,	ib.
Song,	ib.	Charity,	ib.
Imitation of Catullus,	175	At Night,	ib.
A Reflection at Sea,	ib.	To ——,	ib.
Song,	ib.	Fanny, Dearest,	192
Elegiac Stanzas,	ib.	Song,	ib.
Song,	176		
Song,	ib.	MISCELLANEOUS PIECES.	
To ——,	ib.	The Twopenny Post Bag,	195
A Night Thought,	177	Corruption: an Epistle,	210
The Kiss,	ib.	Intolerance,	215
Elegiac Stanzas,	ib.	The Sceptic: a Philosophical Satire,	2
Rondeau,	ib.	Fables for the Holy Alliance,	2
To Rosa,	ib.	Rhymes on the Road,	23
To Rosa,	ib.	M.P.; or, The Blue-Stocking,	241
Written in the Blank Leaf of a Lady's Commonplace Book,	ib.	THE LOVES OF THE ANGELS,	227
Love and Marriage,	178	THE FUDGE FAMILY IN PARIS,	269
To Rosa,	ib.		
Anacreontic,	ib.	EPISTLES, ODES, AND OTHER POEMS.	
Anacreontic,	ib.	Epistle I.— To Lord Viscount Strangford,	298
The Ballad,	ib.	Stanzas,	299
To Phillis,	179	The Tell-Tale Lyre,	300
To Miss ——,	ib.	To the Flying-Fish,	300
To Rosa,	ib.	Epistle II.—To Miss M——e,	301
To Julia, on her Birth-day,	ib.	To Cara, after an interval of absence,	302
Elegiac Stanzas,	ib.	To Cara, on the dawning of a New Year's day,	303
Nonsense,	180		
The Surprise,	ib.	To the Invisible Girl,	ib.
To Mrs. ——, on her translation of Voiture's Kiss,	ib.	Peace and Glory,	ib.

CONTENTS.

	PAGE
EPISTLES, ODES, AND OTHER POEMS—continued.	
To ——, 1801,	304
Song,	ib.
A Ballad: The Lake of the Dismal Swamp,	ib.
Epistle III.—To the Marchioness Dowager of D——ll,	305
The Genius of Harmony,	306
Epistle IV.—To George Morgan, Esq., of Norfolk, Virginia,	307
The Ring,	309
To ——, on seeing her with a white veil and a rich girdle,	ib.
The Resemblance,	310
To ——,	ib.
From the Greek of Meleager,	ib.
Lines written in a Storm at Sea,	ib.
Odes to Nea,	311
Nay, tempt me not to love again,	ib.
I pray you, let us roam no more,	ib.
You read it in my languid eyes,	ib.
A Dream of Antiquity,	312
Well—peace to thy heart, though another's it be,	313
If I were yonder wave, my dear,	ib.
The Snow Spirit,	314
I stole along the flowery bank,	ib.
I found her not—the chamber seemed,	315
A Kiss à l'Antique,	ib.
There's not a look, a word of thine,	ib.
Epistle V—To Joseph Atkinson, Esq.,	316
Love and Reason,	317
Nay, do not weep, my Fanny dear,	ib.
Aspasia,	318
The Grecian Girl's Dream of the Blessed Islands,	ib.
The Steersman's Song,	320
To Cloe,	ib.
To the Fire-Fly,	ib.
The Vase,	ib.
The Wreath and the Chain,	321
The timid girl now hung her head,	ib.
To ——,	ib.
Epistle VI.—To Lord Viscount Forbes,	322
Song,	324
Lying,	ib.
Anacreontic,	ib.
To ——'s Picture,	ib.
Fragment of a Mythological Hymn to Love	325
To his Serene Highness the Duke of Montpensier, on his Portrait of the Lady Adelaide F-rb-s,	ib.
The Philosopher Aristippus,	ib.
To Mrs. Bl—h—d, written in her Album,	327
Epistle VII.—To Thomas Hume, Esq., M.D.,	328
The Snake,	329
Lines written on leaving Philadelphia,	ib.
The Fall of Hebe,	330
To ——,	332
Anacreontic,	ib.
To Mrs. ——,	ib.

	PAGE
EPISTLES, ODES, AND OTHER POEMS—continued.	
Hymn of a Virgin of Delphi, at the Tomb of her Mother,	332
Rings and Seals,	333
To Miss Susan B-ckf—d,	ib.
Lines written at the Cohos, or Falls of the Mohawk River,	334
Chloris and Fanny,	ib.
Song of the Evil Spirit of the Woods,	ib.
To Mrs. Henry T-ghe,	335
Impromptu, upon leaving some Friends,	336
Epistle VIII.—To the Honourable W. R. Spencer,	336
A Warning,	337
To —— ——,	338
From the High Priest of Apollo to a Virgin of Delphi,	ib.
Woman,	339
Ballad Stanzas,	ib.
To —— ——,	340
A Vision of Philosophy,	ib.
To —— ——,	341
Dreams,	ib.
To Mrs. ——,	342
A Canadian Boat-Song,	ib.
Epistle IX.—To the Lady Charlotte R-wd-n,	343
Impromptu, after a visit to Mrs. —— of Montreal,	345
Written on passing Deadman's Island,	ib.
To the Boston Frigate,	ib.
To Lady H——,	346
To —— ——,	347
Extract from the 'Devil among the Scholars,'	ib.
To Sir Hudson Lowe,	350
MISCELLANEOUS POEMS.	
A Melologue upon National Music,	353
Lines on the Death of Mr. P-r—v-l,	354
Lines on the Death of Sh-r-d-n,	ib.
Lines written on hearing that the Austrians had entered Naples,	355
The Insurrection of the Papers,	356
Parody of a Celebrated Letter,	ib.
Anacreontic: To a Plumassier,	358
Extracts from the Diary of a Politician,	ib.
King Crack and his Idols,	359
Wreaths for the Ministers,	ib.
The New Costume of the Ministers,	360
Occasional Address,	361
The Sale of the Tools,	ib.
Little Man and Little Soul,	362
Reinforcements for Lord Wellington,	ib.
Lord Wellington and the Ministers,	363
Fum and Hum, the Two Birds of Royalty,	ib.
Epistle from Tom Crib to Big Ben,	364
To Lady Holland, on Napoleon's Legacy of a Snuff-box,	ib.
Correspondence between a Lady and a Gentleman,	ib
Horace, Ode XI. Lib. II.,	365
Horace, Ode XXII. Lib. I.,	ib.

CONTENTS.

MISCELLANEOUS POEMS—*continued.*

	PAGE
Horace, Ode I. Lib. III.,	366
Horace, Ode XXXVIII. Lib. I.,	ib.
To ——,	367
Impromptu: Between Adam and me,	ib.
What's my Thought like?	ib.
Epigram: What news to-day?	367
Epigram: Said his Highness to Ned,	ib.
Epigram: I want the Court-guide,	ib.
Epigram: I never give a kiss,	ib.
On a Squinting Poetess,	ib.
Epilogue,	ib.
The Sylph's Ball,	368
Remonstrance to Lord J. Russell,	369
My Birth-Day,	370
Fancy,	ib.
Love and Hymen,	ib.
Translation from Catullus,	ib.
To my Mother,	371
A Speculation,	ib.
Scepticism,	ib.
A Joke Versified,	ib.
On ——,	ib.
Fragment of a Character,	ib.
Country Dance and Quadrille,	372
Song, for the Poco-curante Society,	373
Genius and Criticism,	374

HUMOROUS POEMS.

An Amatory Colloquy between Bank and Government,	377
Ode to the Goddess Ceres,	ib.
Dialogue between a Sovereign and a One-Pound Note,	378
An Expostulation to Lord King,	379
Moral Positions,	ib.
Memorabilia of Last Week,	380
A Hymn of Welcome after the Recess,	381
All in the Family Way,	ib.
The Canonization of St. B-tt-rw-rth,	382
New Creation of Peers,	383
A Cambridge Ballad,	384
Copy of an Intercepted Despatch,	ib.
Mr. Roger Dodsworth,	385
The Millennium,	ib.
The Three Doctors,	386
Epitaph on a Tuft-Hunter,	387
The Petition of the Orangemen of Ireland,	ib.
A Vision by the author of Christabel,	388
News for Country Cousins,	ib.
An Incantation, sung by the Bubble Spirit,	389
A Dream of Turtle, by Sir W. Curtis,	390
Cotton and Corn,	ib.
The Donkey and his Panniers,	ib.
Ode to the Sublime Porte,	391
The Ghost of Miltiades,	ib.
Corn and Catholics,	392
The Periwinkles and the Locusts,	ib.
A Case of Libel,	393
Literary Advertisement,	394
The Slave,	ib.

BALLADS AND SONGS.

	PAGE
Black and Blue Eyes,	399
Cease, oh cease to tempt,	ib.
Dear Fanny,	ib.
Did Not,	ib.
Fanny, Dearest!	400
From life without freedom,	ib.
Here's the bower,	ib.
Holy be the pilgrim's sleep	ib.
I saw the moon rise clear,	401
Joys that pass away,	ib.
Light sounds the harp,	ib.
Love and the Sun-Dial,	ib.
Love and Time,	402
Love, my Mary, dwells with thee,	ib.
Love's Light Summer Cloud,	ib.
Love, wandering through the golden maze,	ib.
Merrily every bosom boundeth,	ib.
Now let the warrior,	403
Oh, Lady fair!	ib.
Oh! remember the time,	ib.
Oh! Soon return!	ib.
Oh! yes, so well,	ib.
Oh! yes, when the bloom,	404
One dear Smile,	ib.
The Day of Love,	ib.
The Song of War,	ib.
The Young Rose,	ib.
When 'midst the gay I meet,	405
When twilight dews,	ib.
Young Jessica,	ib.
Farewell, Bessy,	ib.
To-day, dearest, is ours,	ib.
When on the lip the sigh delays,	406
Here, take my heart,	ib.
Oh! call it by some better name,	ib.
Poor wounded heart!	ib.
The East Indian,	ib.
Pale broken flower!	407
The Pretty Rose-Tree,	ib.
Shine out, Stars!	ib.
The Young Muleteers of Grenada,	ib.
Tell her, oh tell her,	ib.
Nights of music,	408
Our first young love,	ib.

NATIONAL AIRS.

Advertisement,	411
A Temple to Friendship,	ib.
Flow on, thou shining river,	ib.
All that's bright must fade,	ib.
So warmly we met,	412
Those evening bells,	ib.
Should those fond hopes,	ib.
Reason, Folly, and Beauty,	ib.
Fare thee well, thou lovely one!	413
Dost thou remember?	ib.
Oh! come to me when daylight sets,	ib.
Oft, in the stilly night,	ib.
Hark! the vesper hymn is stealing,	414
Love and Hope,	ib.
There comes a time,	ib.

CONTENTS.

	PAGE
NATIONAL AIRS—*continued.*	
My harp has one unchanging theme,	414
Oh! no—not e'en when first we loved,	415
Peace be around thee,	ib.
Common Sense and Genius,	ib.
Then, fare thee well!	ib.
Gaily sounds the castanet,	416
Love is a hunter-boy,	ib.
Come, chase that starting tear away,	ib.
Joys of Youth, how fleeting!	ib.
Hear me but once,	ib.
When Love was a child,	ib.
Say, what shall be our sport to-day?	417
Bright be thy dreams!	ib.
Go, then—'tis vain,	ib.
The Crystal Hunters,	ib.
Row gently here,	ib.
Oh! days of youth,	418
When first that smile,	ib.
Peace to the slumberers!	ib.
When thou shalt wander,	ib.
Who'll buy my Love-knots?	ib.
See, the dawn from heaven,	419
Nets and Cages,	ib.
When through the Piazzetta,	ib.
Go, now, and dream,	ib.
Take hence the bowl,	420
Farewell, Theresa!	ib.
How oft, when watching stars,	ib.
When the first summer bee,	ib.
Though 'tis all but a dream,	ib.
'Tis when the cup is smiling,	421
Where shall we bury our shame?	ib.
Ne'er talk of Wisdom's gloomy schools,	ib.
Here sleeps the Bard!	ib.
IRISH MELODIES.—No. I.	
Advertisement,	425
Go where glory waits thee,	426
War Song: Remember the glories of Brien the brave,	ib.
Erin! The tear and the smile in thine eyes,	ib.
Oh! breathe not his name,	ib.
When he who adores thee,	427
The harp that once through Tara's halls,	ib.
Fly not yet,	ib.
Oh! think not my spirits are always as light,	ib.
Though the last glimpse of Erin with sorrow I see,	428
Rich and rare were the gems she wore,	ib.
As a beam o'er the face of the waters may glow,	ib.
The Meeting of the Waters,	ib.
No. II.	
St. Senanus and the Lady,	429
How dear to me the hour,	ib.
Take back the virgin page,	ib.
The Legacy,	430
How oft has the Benshee cried?	ib.
We may roam through this world,	ib.

	PAGE
IRISH MELODIES—*continued.*	
Eveleen's Bower,	431
Let Erin remember the days of old,	ib.
The Song of Fionnuala,	ib.
Come, send round the wine,	432
Sublime was the warning,	ib.
Believe me if all those endearing young charms,	ib.
No. III.	
To the Marchioness Dowager of Donegal,	ib.
Erin! oh Erin!	435
Drink to her,	ib.
Oh! blame not the bard,	436
While gazing on the moon's light,	ib.
Ill Omens,	ib.
Before the Battle,	437
After the Battle,	ib.
Oh! 'tis sweet to think,	ib.
The Irish Peasant to his Mistress,	438
On Music,	ib.
It is not the tear at this moment shed,	ib.
The Origin of the Harp,	ib.
No. IV.	
Love's Young Dream,	439
The Prince's Day,	440
Weep on, weep on,	ib.
Lesbia hath a beaming eye,	ib.
I saw thy form in youthful prime,	441
By that lake whose gloomy shore,	ib.
She is far from the land,	ib.
Nay, tell me not,	442
Avenging and bright,	ib.
What the bee is to the floweret,	ib.
Love and the Novice,	443
This life is all chequered with pleasures and woes,	ib.
No. V.	
Oh, the Shamrock!	444
At the mid hour of night,	ib.
One bumper at parting,	445
'Tis the last rose of summer,	ib.
The young May-moon,	ib.
The Minstrel Boy,	ib.
The Song of O'Ruark, Prince of Breffni,	446
Oh! had we some bright little isle of our own!	ib.
Farewell!—but whenever you welcome the hour,	ib.
Oh! doubt me not,	447
You remember Ellen,	ib.
I'd mourn the hopes,	ib.
No. VI.	
Come o'er the sea,	448
Has sorrow thy young days shaded?	ib.
No, not more welcome,	449
When first I met thee,	ib.
While History's Muse,	ib.
The time I've lost in wooing,	450
Where is the slave,	ib.

	PAGE
IRISH MELODIES—*continued.*	
Come, rest in this bosom,	450
'Tis gone, and for ever,	ib.
I saw from the beach,	451
Fill the bumper fair,	ib.
Dear harp of my country!	452

No. VII.

My gentle Harp,	ib.
As slow our ship,	453
In the morning of life,	ib.
When cold in the earth,	ib.
Remember thee!	454
Wreathe the bowl,	ib.
Whene'er I see those smiling eyes,	ib.
If thou'lt be mine,	455
To ladies' eyes,	ib.
Forget not the field,	ib.
They may rail at this life,	ib.
Oh for the swords of former time!	456

No. VIII.

Ne'er ask the hour,	ib.
Sail on, sail on,	ib.
The Parallel,	457
Drink of this cup,	ib.
The Fortune-Teller,	ib.
Oh, ye dead,	458
O'Donoghue's Mistress,	ib.
Echo,	ib.
Oh! banquet not,	459
Thee, thee, only thee,	ib.
Shall the Harp then be silent?	ib.
Oh, the sight entrancing,	460

No. IX.

Sweet Innisfallen,	ib.
'Twas one of those dreams,	461
Fairest! put on awhile,	ib.
Quick! we have but a second,	ib.
And doth not a meeting like this,	462
The Mountain Sprite,	ib.

	PAGE
IRISH MELODIES—*continued.*	
As vanquished Erin,	463
Desmond's Song,	ib.
They know not my heart,	ib.
I wish I was by that dim lake,	464
She sung of love,	ib.
Sing—sing—music was given,	ib.

SACRED SONGS.

Thou art, oh God!	467
This world is all a fleeting show,	ib.
Fallen is thy throne,	ib.
Who is the maid?	468
The bird, let loose,	ib.
Oh! Thou who dry'st the mourner's tear!	ib.
Weep not for those,	ib.
The turf shall be my fragrant shrine,	469
Sound the loud timbrel!	ib.
Go, let me weep!	470
Come not, oh Lord!	ib.
Were not the sinful Mary's tears,	ib.
As down in the sunless retreats,	ib.
But who shall see,	471
Almighty God! when round thy shrine,	ib.
Oh fair! oh purest!	ib.
Angel of Charity,	ib.
Behold the sun,	472
Lord, who shall bear that day?	ib.
Oh! teach me to love thee,	ib.
Weep, children of Israel,	ib.
Like morning, when her early breeze,	ib.
Come, ye disconsolate,	473
Awake, arise, thy light is come,	ib.
There is a bleak Desert,	ib.
Since first thy word,	474
Hark!—'tis the breeze,	ib.
Where is your dwelling, ye sainted?	ib.
How lightly mounts the Muse's wing,	ib.
Go forth to the Mount,	ib.
Is it not sweet to think, hereafter?	475
War against Babylon,	ib.

THE LIFE OF THOMAS MOORE.

THOMAS MOORE'S success in society during the entire period of his public career was more brilliant than that of any English, Irish, or Scottish poet whose life has been put on record. Burns and Byron had each his season. While in this social aspect Sir Walter Scott was eminent, Tom Moore was pre-eminent. The Irish poet rose from a humbler social grade than his Scottish contemporary; and his success in society was due to a faculty of which Scott was destitute. It was owing to his musical talent. Indeed, all Moore's distinction in life and literature is to be traced to music as its main source. His *Irish Melodies* are his *monumentum æris*—his memorial in bronze. Moore was aware of this himself. In his Diary, after expatiating on his first efforts in acting and rhyming, he adds: 'I must try the reader's patience with some account of my beginnings in music,— the only art for which, in my own opinion, I was born with a real natural love; my poetry, such as it is, having sprung out of my deep feeling for music.' Coleridge defines a poet as 'a man who has music in his soul.' This definition may, after reflection as profound as Coleridge himself was capable of, be seen to apply to all poets; but superficially it leaves entirely out of the list of laurelled brows that of many another poet besides Sir Walter Scott, and it leaves Tom Moore on a proud pre-eminence to which he would have laid no claim, and which his wise admirers make no attempt to vindicate for him. Social success and songs—both due to musical talent—these are the principal facts in the life of Thomas Moore, of which it is proposed here to give a simple record, culled mainly from Lord John Russell's *Memoirs, Journal, and Correspondence*. Thomas Moore had no pedigree to boast of, on the grounds on which such a boast is wont to be made. He was nevertheless manly enough not to be ashamed of the very few of his relations of whom he knew anything. Of his ancestry, birth, and boyhood he writes as follows in his Diary :—

'Of my ancestors on the paternal side I know little or nothing. Of the family of my mother, who was born in the town of Wexford, and whose maiden name was Codd, I can speak. My old gouty grandfather, Tom Codd, who lived in the Corn-market, Wexford, is connected with some of my earliest remembrances. Besides being engaged in the provision trade, he must also, I think (from my recollection of the machinery), have had something to do with weaving.

'It was some time in the year 1778 that Anastasia, the eldest daughter of this Thomas Codd, became the wife of my father, John Moore, and in the following year I came into the world. My father had kept a small wine store in Johnson's Court, Grafton Street, Dublin; the same court, by the way, where I afterwards went to school. On his marriage, however, having received, I rather think, some little money with my mother, he set up business in Aungier Street, No. 12, at the corner of Little Longford Street; and in that house, on the 28th of May 1779, I was born.

'At a very early age I was sent to a school kept by a man of the name of Malone, in the same street where we lived. This wild, odd fellow, of whose cocked hat I have still a very clear remembrance, used to pass the greater part of his nights in drinking at public-houses, and was hardly ever able to make his appearance in the school before noon. He would then generally whip the boys all round for disturbing his slumbers. I was myself, however, a special favourite with him, partly perhaps from being the youngest boy in the school, but chiefly, I think, from the plan which then, and ever after, my anxious mother adopted, of heaping with all sorts of kindnesses and attentions those who were in any way, whether as masters, ushers, or schoolfellows, likely to assist me in my learning.'

Moore refers to his mother in this passage in the spirit of devoted love, which never ceased to flame till his own spark of life went out. At the mature age of forty-two he wrote:

'This heart, my own dear mother, bends
With love's true instinct back to thee.'

His whole life was shaped by his mother. His delight in society was largely inherited from her. He says: 'It was from the first my poor mother's ambition, though with no undue aspirings for herself, to secure for her children an early footing in the better walks of society; and to her constant attention to this object I owe both my taste for good company, and the facility I afterwards found in adapting myself to that sphere.'

As soon as this mother's boy was considered by her old enough to hold his own at a public school, it was resolved upon to send him to the grammar school of Mr. Samuel Whyte, a teacher who at that time was at the head of his profession in Dublin, and whose reputation had not begun to fade, notwithstanding that it had endured the wear and tear of three decades of Irish pruning. Fully twenty years before Tom Moore was born, a boy was put under this gentleman's tuition whom he pronounced 'a most incorrigible dunce,' after trying for some years to birch knowledge into him. This boy was no other than the celebrated Richard Brinsley Sheridan. Mr. Whyte, however, was too good a teacher either to try to palliate or to be ashamed of his mistake in after years; for Moore tells us, that the worthy schoolmaster had the good sense often to mention the circumstance, as an instance of the difficulty and rashness of forming any judgment of the future capacity of children. In Mr. Whyte we find a second moulder of the pliable material of Moore's nature,—a nature which showed itself so susceptible of external influences. Indeed, it might almost be said, that no man of genius ever passed his whole life so much inside out as Thomas Moore,—a fact which any one will observe who spends an hour or two over his Correspondence or his Diary. He tells us the nature of the lasting impression which Mr. Whyte made on him in the following passage from his Diary :—

'The turn for recitation and acting which I had so very early manifested was the talent, of all others, which my new schoolmaster was most inclined to encourage; and it was not long before I attained the honour of being singled out by him on days of public examination, as one of his most successful and popular exhibitors,—to the no small jealousy, as may be supposed, of all other mammas, and the great glory of my own. As I looked particularly infantine for my age, the wonder was, of course, still more wonderful. "Oh, he's an old little crab," said one of the rival Cornelias, on an occasion of this kind; "he can't be less than eleven or twelve years of age." "Then, madam," said a gentleman sitting next her, who was slightly acquainted with our family, "if that is the case, he must have been four years old before he was born." This answer, which was reported to my mother, won her warm heart towards that gentleman for ever after. To the drama, and all connected with it, Mr. Whyte had been through his whole life warmly devoted, having lived in habits of intimacy with the family of Brinsley Sheridan, as well as with most of the other ornaments of the Irish stage in the middle of the last century. . . . In the direction of those private theatricals which were at that time so fashionable among the higher circles in Ireland, he had always a leading share. Besides teaching and training the young actors, he took frequently a part in the *dramatis personæ* himself; and either the prologue or epilogue was generally furnished by his pen. . . .

'In addition to his private pupils in the dilettante line of theatricals, Mr. Whyte was occasionally employed in giving lessons on elocution to persons who meant to make the stage their profession. One of these, a very pretty and interesting girl, Miss Campion, became afterwards a popular actress both in Dublin and London. She continued, I think, to take instructions of him in reading even after she had made her appearance on the stage; and one day, while she was with him, a messenger came into the school to say that "Mr. Whyte wanted Tommy Moore in the drawing-room." A summons to the master's house (which stood detached away from the school on the other side of a yard) was at all times an event; but how great was my pride, delight, and awe—for I looked upon actors then as a race of superior beings—when I found I had been summoned for no less a purpose than to be introduced to Miss Campion, and to have the high honour of reciting to her *Alexander's Feast!*

'The pride of being thought worthy of appearing before so celebrated a person took possession of all my thoughts. I felt my heart beat as I walked through the streets, not only with the expectation of meeting her, but with anxious doubts whether, if I did happen to meet her, she would condescend to recognise me; and when at last the happy moment did arrive, and she made me a gracious bow in passing, I question if a salute from Corinne, when on her way to be crowned in the Capitol, would in after days have affected me half so much.

'Whyte's connection, indeed, with theatrical people was rather against his success in the way of his profession; as many parents were apprehensive lest, being so fond of the drama himself, he might inspire too much the same taste in his pupils. As for me, it was thought hardly possible that I could escape being made an actór; and my poor mother, who, sanguinely speculating on the speedy removal of the Catholic disabilities, had destined me to the bar, was frequently doomed to hear prognostics of my devotion of myself to the profession of the stage.'

This is of interest to the student of Moore's life. Only Dickens has surpassed him among the literary men of this century in an intelligent interest in the stage. The author of *Lalla Rookh* had always an actor's eye after scenic effect.

Thomas Moore began very young to produce the verbal clink of rhyming The first instance of it he was able to recall, when he wrote his Diary, was on a subject the date of which was fixed, oddly enough, by an early foible of a man who, as the Iron Duke, was subsequently seldom suspected of ever having had any foibles at all. About the year 1789 or 1790, a certain toy, called in French a 'bandalore' and in English a 'quiz,' was all the rage in fashionable society:

'To such a ridiculous degree,' in the language of our poet, 'did the fancy for this toy pervade at that time all ranks and ages, that in the public gardens and in the streets numbers of persons, of both sexes, were playing it up and down as they walked along; or, as my own very young doggerel described it:

The ladies too, when in the streets, or walking in the GREEN,
Went quizzing on, to show their shapes and graceful mien.

'I have been enabled to mark more certainly the date of this toy's reign, from a circumstance mentioned to me by Lord Plunket concerning the Duke of Wellington, who, at the time I am speaking of, was one of the aides-de-camp of the Lord-Lieutenant of Ireland, and in the year 1790, according to Lord Plunket's account, must have been a member of the Irish House of Commons. "I remember," said Lord Plunket, "being on a committee with him; and, it is remarkable enough, Lord Edward Fitzgerald was also one of the members of it. The Duke (then Captain Wellesley, or Wesley?) was, I recollect, playing with one of those toys called quizzes, the whole time of the sitting of the committee." This trait of the Duke coincides perfectly with all that I have ever heard about this great man's apparent frivolity at that period of his life. Luttrell, indeed, who is about two years older than the Duke, and who lived on terms of intimacy with all the Castle men of those days, has the courage to own, in the face of all the Duke's present glory, that often, in speculating on the future fortunes of the young men with whom he lived, he has said to himself, in looking at Wellesley's vacant face, "Well, let who will get on in this world, *you* certainly will not." So little promise did there appear at that time of even the most ordinary success in life, in the man who has since accumulated around his name such great and lasting glory.'

After this the future musical poet was a constant rhymer. At the period of his life which we have now reached—eleven years of age—he frequently played at Lady Barrowe's private theatre in Dublin. One evening, 'An Epilogue, *A Squeeze at St. Paul's*,' formed a portion of the evening entertainment at her Ladyship's house. He informs us also, with further reference to his early amateur acting, how, as harlequin, he 'skipped, leaped, danced, and died.' Our harlequins now-a-days don't do the dying. He writes:

'Of all theatrical beings, harlequin was my idol and passion. To have been put in possession of a real and complete harlequin's dress, would have made me the happiest of mortals; and I used sometimes to dream that there appeared sometimes at my bedside a good spirit, presenting to me a full suit of the true parti-coloured raiment. But the utmost I ever attained of this desire was the possession of an old cast-off wand, which had belonged to the harlequin at Astley's, and which I viewed with as much reverence and delight as if it really possessed the wonderful powers attributed to it. Being a very active boy, I was quite as much charmed with harlequin's jumping talents as with any of his other attributes, and by constant practice over the rail of a tent-bed which stood in one of our rooms, was at last able to perform the *head-foremost* leap of my hero most successfully.'

Thus the youth of Thomas Moore was what may be fairly described as very pleasurable, and, to a nature like his, a very happy one. His mother kept a sharp eye upon his lessons; and he, in his devoted love for that parent, considered no amount of application irksome, if only he gained her approbation. At this period an attempt was made to teach him music on 'an old lumbering harpsichord,' thrown on his father's hands as part payment of a debt owing by some bankrupt customer. But the power of accompanying his own songs, by which he in later years charmed the highest in the land, was acquired at a subsequent period in the course of his education.

When the young poet and actor was about thirteen years of age, the political affairs of Ireland were in a state of very dangerous tension. The Catholic question was fast ripening into an Irish question, in which distinguished Protestants were taking an active part against the British Government. The patriotic feeling was fast neutralizing the zeal of religious partisanship. Moore tells us that some of the most violent of those who early took a part in the proceedings of the United Irishmen were among his most intimate friends. He remembered being taken by his father to a public dinner in honour of Napper Tandy, where one of the toasts, as well from its poetry as its politics, made an indelible impression on his mind: ' May the breezes of France blow our Irish Oak into verdure!' He recollected his pride, too, at the hero of the night, Napper Tandy, taking him for some minutes on his knee.

Most of these patriotic acquaintances of the Moore family were Protestants. The Catholics, to whose religious persuasion both his parents were devotedly attached, were still too timorous to come forward openly in their own cause. Let it be remembered that the Protestants of that period took the lead in the struggle for the rights of their Catholic fellow-countrymen. The disestablishment of the Irish Church is a recent illustration of what Protestants who are not Irishmen are able and willing to do for their Irish Catholic fellow-subjects.

The large measure of Catholic enfranchisement which passed in the year 1793, admitting persons of that faith to the university and the bar, gladdened the heart of Moore's mother. Her dearest wish was to have this darling son of hers a barrister. Now no time was lost in putting him under course of preparation for the university. A Latin usher—kept by Mr. Whyte, who himself only taught English, and, as seems, knew no other language—was charged with this duty. To a lad of Tommy Moore's talent, rapid progress in Latin was an easy matter. He remained at Mr. Whyte's school, under this usher, till 1794, the year he entered Dublin University.

It was in the year 1793, the year in which these school arrangements were made, that the subsequent prime favourite of poetical fame first enjoyed the honour and glory of seeing verses of his own in print. Romeo, an anagram of Moore, was the *nom de plume* he adopted in carrying on an imaginary love correspondence with an old maid named Hannah Byrne, who, being much in the poetical line, not only encouraged his youthful effusions, but wrote rhyming answers to them. To this lady was Moore's first printed composition addressed, in the *Anthologia Hibernica*, with his own proper name subscribing the epistle.

This Magazine, which Moore designates as one of the most respectable attempts at periodical literature that had ever been ventured upon in Ireland up till the time he was writing his Diary, was started by Mercier, the college bookseller, and was carried on for two years, after which it died, as all such enterprises were wont to expire at that time in that country—for the want of money and of talent; 'for,' adds Moore, 'the Irish never fight or write well on their own soil.' His pride at seeing his own name in the first list of subscribers to this publication—'Master Thomas Moore,' in full —was only surpassed by that of reading in it the mention of his name as one of its 'esteemed contributors.' He tells us: 'It was in the pages of this Magazine for the months of January and February 1793 that I first read, being then a schoolboy, Rogers' *Pleasures of Memory*, little dreaming that I should one day become the intimate friend of the author; and such an impression did it then make upon me, that the particular type in which it is there printed, and the very colour of the paper, are associated with every line of it in my memory.' In his Diary he informs us besides, that not content with his own boyish stirrings of ambition, and the attempts at literature of all kinds to which they impelled him, he contrived to inoculate Tom Ennis and Johnny Delany (his father's two clerks) with the same literary propensities. The young *littérateur* organized these two hopefuls into a debating and literary society, and elected himself its president; and this society met, unknown to his father and mother, in a little closet beyond a bedroom which was itself not very large. Such was Tom Moore before he entered Dublin University. Regarding this great step in his life—a step which a Catholic ten times as talented as Moore was could not have taken two years before—he writes:

'Though I began my college course at the commencement of the year 1795, I must have been entered, as I have already said, in the summer of the preceding year, as I recollect well my having had a long spell of holidays before the term commenced; and if I were to single out the part of my life the most happy and the most *poetical* (for all was yet in fancy and in promise with me), it would be that interval of holidays. In the first place, I was not a little proud of being a student of Trinity College, Dublin, which was in itself a sort of *status* in life; and instead of *Master* Thomas Moore, as I had been designated the year before among the "Anthologian" subscribers, I now read myself Mr. Thomas Moore, of Trinity College, Dublin. In the next place, I had passed my examinations, I believe, creditably; at least so said my old master Whyte, who, in publishing soon after, in a new edition of his works, some verses which I had addressed to him a short time before leaving school, appended to them a note of his own manufacture, stating that the author of the verses had "entered college at a very early age, with distinguished honour to himself as well as to his able and worthy preceptor." This favourable start of mine gave, of course, great pleasure to my dear father and mother, and made *me* happy in seeing *them* so.'

Though by the bill of 1793 Catholics were admitted to the university, they were yet excluded from scholarships, fellowships, and all the honours which brought emolument. This, of course, shut Thomas Moore, the Catholic son of Catholic parents, out from all those little aids in the way of money by means of which many a clever youth has worked his way through a university curriculum. The Moores were not in very affluent circumstances. It was for a short time deliberated in the family circle whether Tom should not be entered as a Protestant. His father favoured this view. His mother, who was a sincere and ardent Catholic, and, as her son says, 'even gave in to some of the old superstitions connected with that faith, in a manner remarkable for a person of her strength of mind,' would not consent to this piece of time-serving. At this period he was receiving lessons in Italian from an old friar named Father Ennis. He had also a regular French master, an intelligent *emigré*, named La Fosse, who could hardly speak a word of English. To these two teachers he was indebted for that display of French and Italian reading which he put forth about five or six years after, in the notes to his translation of Anacreon. Referring to his university life, he writes:—

'The tutor under whom I was placed on entering college was the Rev. — Burrowes, a man of considerable reputation, as well for classical acquirements as for wit and humour. There are some literary papers of his in the Transactions of the Royal Irish Academy; and he enjoyed the credit, I believe deservedly, of having been the author, in his youth, of a celebrated flash song, called "The night before Larry was *stretched*," *i.e. hanged*. Of this classical production I remember but two lines, where, on the "Dominie" (or parson) proposing to administer spiritual consolation to the hero,—

"Larry tipped him an elegant look,
And pitched his big wig to the devil."

The fame of this song (however Burrowes himself and his brother dominies might regret it) did him no harm, of course, among the younger part of our college community. Having brought with me so much reputation from school, it was expected, especially by my anxious mother, that I should distinguish myself equally at college; and in the examinations of the first year I *did* gain a premium, and I believe a certificate. But here the brief career of my college honours terminated. After some unavailing efforts (solely to please my anxious mother), and some memento of mortification on finding myself vanquished by competitors whom I knew to be dull fellows, "*intus et in cute*," and who have indeed proved themselves such through life, I resolved in the second year of my course to give up the strnggle entirely, and to confine myself to such parts of the course as fell within my own tastes and pursuits.'

This he did, and became a very accomplished classical scholar, as was proved by his translation of Anacreon, his first step on the ladder of lasting fame. In the second year of his college course, Moore wrote a short Masque, with songs, which was performed by a small party of friends in his father's drawing-room. Thus he kept practising and strengthening the poetic wing. The latter part of his college career, however, was fraught with incidents of a gloomy nature, very different from writing, or acting, or singing. He says (after recording a great many very convincing proofs of a light heart):—

'But "hæ nugæ seria ducent in mala." Most serious and awful indeed were the times which followed these gay doings. The political ferment that was abroad through Ireland soon found its way within the walls of our university; and a youth destined to act a melancholy but for ever memorable part in the troubled scenes that were fast approaching, had now begun to attract in no ordinary degree the attention both of his fellow-students and the college authorities in general. This youth was Robert Emmet, whose brilliant success in his college studies, and more particularly in the scientific portion of them, had crowned his career, as far as he had gone, with all the honours of the course; while his powers of oratory displayed at a debating society, of which about this time (1796-7) I became a member, were beginning to excite universal attention, as well from the eloquence as the political boldness of his displays. He was, I rather think by two classes, my senior, though it might have been only by one. But there was, at all events, such an interval between our standings as at that time of life makes a material difference; and when I became a member of the debating society, I found him in full fame, not only for his scientific attainments, but also for the blamelessness of his life and the grave suavity of his manners. Besides this minor society, there was also another in college, for the higher classes of students, called the Historical Society, established on the ruins of one bearing the same name, which had some years before been (on account of its politics, I believe) put down by the fellows, but continued, in defiance of them, to hold its sittings *out*side the walls.'

Of this latter association he relates that Charles Bushe, afterwards well known as a witty Chief Justice, was once one of the most turbulent as well as most eloquent members.

The political tone of these debating societies was such as might have been expected from young Irishmen, at a time of such feverish excitement in their country as was the year 1797. Robert Emmet and Moore both in due course became members of the Historical. Of it the unfortunate Emmet was the chief ornament on the liberal side. It was he who gave Moore the first hint of those formidable United Irish Societies—the Fenians of the end of last century. The following narrative, written by Moore in his Diary, will tell the upshot of all the stir of the time, as far as regarded the university career of these model Irishmen:—

'My first tutor, Burrowes, having a little before this time retired on a good living—the *euthanasia* of most of the monks of old Trinity—I was placed under a lay fellow of the name of Phipps, a civil and zealous man, though far more collegiate in mind and manners than the destined Dean[1] whom I had left. Being also, however, a much more warm-hearted person, he took a very kind and active interest in all my concerns, and showed this interest by a step which, though at the time not a little painful to me, I afterwards learned to appreciate as it deserved. Requesting a few minutes with my father and mother, he advised confidentially and strenuously that I should avoid being seen so much in public with Robert Emmet; hinting at the same time that our intimacy had been much noticed, and that there were circumstances which rendered it highly imprudent. Though not aware at that time of the extent to which Emmet was implicated in the Irish conspiracy, we knew quite enough to enable us to understand this friendly warning, though, if I recollect right, we but in a very slight degree acted upon it.

'There was now left, however, but little time either for caution or deliberation, as the fearful drama of "The Plot Discovered," in all its horrors, soon after commenced; and one of the first scenes the curtain rose upon, was that formidable Inquisition held within the walls of our college by the bitterest of all Orange politicians, the Lord Chancellor Fitzgibbon. I must say in fairness, however, that strong and harsh as then appeared the measure of setting up this sort of tribunal, with the power of examining witnesses on oath, in a place dedicated to the instruction of youth, yet the facts that came out afterwards in the course of evidence but too much justified even this inquisitorial proceeding; and to many who, like myself, were acquainted only with the general views of those engaged in the conspiracy, without knowing, except in a few instances, who those persons were, or what were their plans and resources, it was really most startling and awful to hear the disclosures which every new succeeding witness brought forth.

---

[1] Burrowes was, some time after, made a Dean.

'There were a few—and among that number were poor Robert Emmet, John Brown, and the two Corbets—whose total absence from the whole scene, as well as the dead silence that daily followed the calling out of their names, proclaimed how deep had been their share in the transactions now about to be inquired into. But there was one young friend of mine whose appearance among the suspected and examined quite as much surprised as it deeply and painfully interested me. This was Dacre Hamilton, the son of a Protestant lady, a widow, with very small means, but of highly respectable connections; and he himself, in addition to his scholarship and talents, being one of the most primitively innocent persons with whom I was acquainted; and accordingly producing often among those who were intimate with him that sort of amusement, mixed with affection, which the Parson Adams class of character is always certain to inspire. He and Emmet—both of them my seniors in the university—had long been intimate and attached friends; their congenial fondness for mathematical studies being, I think, a far stronger bond of sympathy between them than their politics. For whatever interest poor Dacre Hamilton may have taken *speculatively* in the success of the popular cause, he knew quite as little, I believe, of the definite objects of the United Irishmen, and was as innocent of the plans then at work for their accomplishment, as I can truly allege I was myself. From his being called up, however, on this first day of the inquiry—when, as it appeared, all the most important evidence was brought forward—there can be little doubt that, in addition to his intimacy with Emmet, the college authorities must have had some information which led them to suspect him of being an accomplice in the conspiracy. In the course of his examination some questions were put to him which he refused to answer (most probably from their tendency to involve or criminate others), and he was dismissed, poor fellow, with the melancholy certainty that his future prospects were all utterly blasted; it being already known that the punishment for such contumacy was to be not merely banishment from the university, but exclusion from all the learned professions.

'The proceedings, indeed, of the whole day had been such as to send me home to my anxious parents with no very agreeable feelings or prospects. I had heard evidence given compromising even the lives of some of those friends whom I had been most accustomed to regard both with affection and admiration; and what I felt even still more than their danger,—a danger ennobled at that time in my eyes by the great cause in which it had been incurred,—was the degrading spectacle exhibited by those who had appeared in evidence against them; persons who had themselves, of course, been implicated in the plot, and now came forward either as volunteer informers, or else were driven by the fear of the consequences to secure their own safety at the expense of their associates and friends. I remember well the gloom that hung over our family circle on that evening, as we talked over the events of the day, and discussed the probability of my being among those who would be called up for examination on the morrow. The deliberate conclusion to which my dear honest father and mother came was, that overwhelming as the consequences were to all their prospects and hopes for me, yet, if the questions leading to the crimination of others which had been put to almost all examined on that day, and which poor Dacro Hamilton alone refused to answer, should be put also to me, I must in the same manner, and at all risks, return a similar refusal. I forget whether I received any intimation on the following morrow that I should be one of those examined in the course of the day, but I rather think that some such notice was conveyed to me; and at last my awful turn came, and I stood in presence of the terrific tribunal. There sat the formidable Fitzgibbon, whose name I had never heard connected but with domineering insolence and cruelty; and by his side the memorable "Paddy" Duigenan, memorable, at least to all who lived in those dark times, for his eternal pamphlets sounding the tocsin of persecution against the Catholics.

'The oath was proffered to me. "I have an objection, my lord," said I in a clear, firm voice, "I have an objection to taking this oath." "What's your objection, sir?" he asked sternly. "I have no fear, my lord, that anything I might say would criminate myself, but it might tend to affect others; and I must say that I despise that person's character who could be led under any circumstances to criminate his associates." This was aimed at some of the revelations of the preceding day, and, as I learned afterwards, was so felt. "How old are you, sir?" I told him my age,—between seventeen and eighteen, though looking, I dare say, not more than fourteen or fifteen. He then turned to his assessor, Duigenan, and exchanged a few words with him in an under voice. "We cannot," he resumed, again looking towards me, "we

cannot allow any person to remain in our university who would refuse to take this oath."
"I shall then, my lord," I replied, "take the oath, still reserving to myself the power of refusing to answer any such questions as I have described." "We do not sit here to argue with you, sir," he rejoined sharply; upon which I took the oath, and seated myself in the witness's chair.

'The following were the questions and answers that then ensued; and I can pretty well pledge myself for their almost verbal accuracy, as well as for that of the conversation which preceded them. After having adverted to the proved existence of United Irish Societies in the university, he asked, "Have you ever belonged to any of these societies?" "No, my lord." "Have you ever known of any of the proceedings which took place in them?" "No, my lord." "Did you ever hear of a proposal at any of their meetings for the purchase of arms and ammunition?" "No, my lord." "Did you ever hear of a proposition made in one of those societies with respect to the expediency of assassination?" "Oh no, my lord." He then turned again to Duigenan, and after a few words with him, resumed: "When such are the answers you are able to give, pray what was the cause of your great repugnance to taking the oath?" "I have already told you, my lord, my chief reasons; in addition to which, it was the first oath I ever took, and it was, I think, a very natural hesitation." I was told afterwards that a fellow of the college, named Stokes (a man of liberal politics, who had alleged, as one of the grounds of his dislike to this inquisition, the impropriety of putting oaths to such young men), turned round, on hearing this last reply, to some one who sat next him, and said, "That's the best answer that has been given yet."

'I was now dismissed without any further questioning; and though tolerably conscious in my own mind that I had acted with becoming firmness and honesty, I yet could not feel quite assured on the subject, till I had returned among my young friends and companions in the body of the hall, and seen what sort of verdict their looks and manner would pass on my conduct. And here I had certainly every reason to feel satisfied, as all crowded around me with hearty congratulations, not so much, I could see, on my acquittal by my judges, as on the manner in which I had acquitted *myself*. Of my reception at home, after the fears entertained of so very different a result, I will not attempt any description: it was all that *such a* home alone could furnish.'

The plucky conduct of the young poet and political enthusiast on this occasion gained him the good opinion of older and wiser heads than those of his 'young friends and companions in the body of the hall.' In either 1798 or the following year he took his degree of Bachelor of Arts. Before going up for examination, he had reason to fear, from certain prevailing rumours, that the Chancellor would object to admitting to any degree some of those who, like himself, had, on the occasion of the visitation, to appear before their betters. He found out, however, that he was a distinguished exception from this list of the proscribed. Indeed, he tells us that he had afterwards good reason to believe that his conduct during the grand visitation and grave examination had left a most favourable impression on that high functionary. The Provost of Trinity, Dr. Kearney, also through many years gave gratifying proofs to Thomas Moore that he had no feelings towards him but those of esteem and respect, notwithstanding his having been one of the suspected.

So early as 1794, when he was about fifteen years of age, Moore published a paraphrase of the fifth ode of Anacreon, in the *Anthologia Hibernica*. But it was three or four years later when the idea of translating all the odes attributed to Anacreon first took firm hold of his mind; and about the time when he was compelled to appear as a creditable actor in the drama of *The Plot Discovered*, he had made considerable progress in this work. He selected about twenty of his translations, and submitted them to the perusal and judgment of Dr. Kearney. His hope was, that if the good Provost approved of the versions, he would lay them before the Board of the University, and thus secure him some substantial recognition of his merits. The selected judge gave a highly flattering account of the odes in English, but expressed his doubts as to whether such a 'Board could properly confer any public reward upon the translation of a collection of poems so amatory and convivial as the Odes of Anacreon.' The Provost advised the translator, however, to complete the work he had begun, and to offer it to the public rather than to a Board necessarily so restricted in its recognition of talent, and assured Moore that he had no doubt of his success with the wider circle of critics. He added, 'The young people will like it.' This brings under our notice a prominent third in the list of those who moulded the form of Moore's character and shaped his early career. His mother, Mr. Samuel Whyte, schoolmaster in Graftón Street, and Dr. Kearney, Provost of Trinity College, Dublin, each performed a part of these functions, all-important to their object. The publication of his Odes was what sent him to London; and as 'Anacreon Moore' he was long known in the fashionable society in which he shone so brightly, and which he loved so well. Let Dr. Kearney be remembered in this connection, and receive his due meed of praise. He is not known to general readers in any other relation whatsoever.

All this time Moore's father carried on the business which he has said was a wine merchant, but which is generally spoken of as that of a grocer —'grocer and spirit dealer' most probably. His kind parents, in their straitened circumstances, must have felt the expense of his excellent education rather heavily—as exacting, indeed, as they could well stand. Now, however, when he was nineteen years of age, and, if he had not been a songster and something of a poet, might have helped to increase the family income in some sort of way of winning wages, a more serious additional drain was to be made on their scanty resources. This was necessary to help him on in the world in the way his mother had early marked out in her fond imaginings. She had long been hoarding up every penny she could save towards the expense of his journey to London, for the purpose of his being entered a student at the Middle Temple. He left the home which he loved so well, and at which he was so dearly beloved, at the age of nineteen. He writes in his Diary:

'A part of the small sum which I took with me was in guineas, and I recollect was carefully sewed up by my mother in the waistband of my pantaloons. There was also another treasure which she had, unknown to me, sewed up in some other part of my clothes, and that was a scapular (as it is called), or a small bit of cloth blessed by the priest, which a fond superstition inclined her to believe would keep the wearer of it from harm. And thus, with this charm about me, of which I was wholly unconscious, and my little packet of guineas, of which I felt deeply the responsibility, did I for the first time start from home for the great world of London

. . . I had been consigned to an old friend of ours named Masterson, then living in Manchester Street, Manchester Square, and to reach them was my first and immediate object, notwithstanding all the persuasions of my companion, who had set his heart, he said, at our dining together at our inn (Charing Cross), and then going to one of the theatres in the evening. "You ought to see a little of London," he said, "and I'll show it you." Allowing him to remain under the impression that all this was likely to happen, I yet ventured to say that I must *first* visit those friends whom I have mentioned ; and to this he considerately acceded, saying that he would himself, after we had breakfasted, walk with me part of the way. To this, not knowing how to get rid of him, I very unwillingly assented ; and accordingly, arm-in-arm with that swindler (as I have no doubt the fellow was), I made my first appearance in the streets of London. . . . The lodging taken for me by my friends the Mastersons was a front room up two pair of stairs, at No. 44, George Street, Portman Square, for which I paid six shillings a-week.

'I had already, through the introductions I brought with me from Ireland, made several acquaintances, all of whom (being chiefly Irish) were very kind to me, and some occasionally asked me to dinner. Of this latter serviceable class was Martin Archer Shee (afterwards Sir Martin Archer Shee, President of the Royal Academy : he died in 1850) ; while his brother-in-law Nugent, an engraver, and not very prosperous, poor fellow, was always a sure card of an evening for a chat about literature and a cup of tea. There was also a Dublin apothecary, named M'Mahon, who had transported himself and gallipots to London, and whose wife at least I ought not to forget, as, on some trifling difficulty arising respecting my fees at the Middle Temple (the money I brought with me, though painfully scraped together, being insufficient for the purpose), she took me aside one evening, and telling me in confidence of a small sum she had laid by for a particular use, said it should be at my service until I was able to repay her. I got through my difficulty, however, without encroaching on her small means ; but such generous offers come too rarely in this world to allow themselves to be forgotten.'

Moore, when he wrote his Diary, had no clear recollection of the details of this his first visit to London—not even of its duration. Having gone through all the forms of initiation at the Middle Temple, and having arranged, through the mediation of one of his earliest friends, Dr. Hume, that Stockdale of Piccadilly was to be the publisher of his translation of Anacreon as soon as it was ready, he returned with delight to his 'dear Dublin home.'

It was during his second visit to England that Moore was introduced to Lord Moira. It is in his relations with this kind-hearted nobleman that he is to be seen in the light which is least agreeable to his admirers. Lord Moira did something—indeed, a great deal—for him. Lord Moira obtained for him the permission to dedicate his translation of Anacreon to the Prince of Wales. This was that start in life which thousands of men of more intense genius and extensive talent than ever Moore could pretend to never receive. Taking life as we find it, the proposition would not have too much of the improbable in it, if it were asserted, that without this introduction, Thomas Moore, the singer of *The Irish Melodies,* would not have soared into the high free sky, in which he has, lark-like, forced so many to listen to his song. Lord Moira gave him that start in life which is all that genius and industry ever need from any man. Lord Moira also procured for the father of his *protégé* a good situation, with a fair salary, —a favour which neither son, mother, nor father seem ever to have valued too highly. His Lordship did not do all that the aspiring and imaginative expectant of place and pay through his influence had set his heart upon; and on that account, in his correspondence, Moore sets Moira down as a not very clear-headed individual, who had sadly failed in his duty to him. His own account of his introduction to Lord Moira may as well be quoted. He says: 'It was, I believe, on my next visit to England, that having, through the medium of another of my earliest friends, Joe Atkinson, been introduced to Lord Moira, I was invited to pay a visit to Donington Park on my way to London. This was, of course, at that time, a great event in my life; and among the most vivid of my early recollections is that of my first night at Donington, when Lord Moira, with that high courtesy for which he was remarkable, lighted me himself to my bedroom; and there was this stately personage stalking on before me through the long lighted gallery, bearing in his hand my bed-candle, which he delivered to me at the door of my apartment. I thought it all exceedingly fine and grand, but at the same time most uncomfortable; and little I foresaw how much at home and at my ease I should one day find myself in that great house.' A letter to his mother, written most probably about this time, and with reference to this first visit, shows more fully how great was the privilege to him at the time—and how deeply he felt it—of this introduction to Lord Moira, and of that nobleman's truly kind interest in him. It is dated 'Donington Park, Dec. 31, 1800,' and reads:

'MY DEAR MOTHER,—This is from my bed-chamber at Donington Park, where I arrived at two o'clock to-day, through snow mountains deep. . . . Nothing can be more princely than the style of this place, nor anything more flatteringly polite than my reception here. Lady Charlotte told me that she regretted very much that I was not here during the Prince's stay, and that she had written to her mother to beg of her to hurry me. The Prince, too, she told me, expressed a wish that I had met him. Dearest mother! there is no fear of my not doing *everything*. Keep up your spirits, my little woman, and you'll find I'll make you as rich as a nabob. But I am now far away from you, and that is the only idea that can hang heavy on my mind; but, dear mother, be happy and contented, and then you'll be everything to us. Your *excessive* solicitude for us is the *only thing* we can blame you for. I shall not stay here more than a day or two, certainly, for I find my portmanteau tormentingly troublesome. I dread the packing of it again; and I have to *rout* into it for everything I want. Lord Moira has but this moment left me, after attending me very politely to show me my bedroom. Good-bye.
'THOMAS MOORE.'

It begins in this letter to be very apparent that Thomas Moore had a keen eye to worldly advantage and advancement. He clung to Lord Moira, in the hope of realizing these through him. He expected much, and received little, in comparison with his ardent hope; and hence evolves an aspect of Moore's character in which it is not altogether pleasant to make him a subject of contemplation. It is one aspect; and there are likeable features even in it: for he never sought wealth for his own dear sake; he was always anxious about the comfort of his parents and sisters. Well might his father say, in less than three years after this letter was written, 'Surely no parents had ever such happiness in a child.' About a year after the publication of his translation of the Odes of Anacreon, Moore brought out a volume of verses, purporting to be *The Poetical Works of the late Thomas Little*,—an assumed name which had the double reference to his own by way of contrast, and to his stature by way of resemblance. Moore was a very little man. Sir Walter Scott described him as the smallest of men who were not deformed. An admirer who wrote a very inaccurate account of him during his lifetime says: 'When Mr. Moore first came to London, his youthful appearance was such, that being at a large dinner-party, and getting up to escort the ladies to the drawing-room, a French gentleman observed, "Ah! le petit bon homme qui s'en va!" Mr. Moore's subsequent brilliant conversation, however, soon proved him to be, though little of stature, yet, like Gay, "in wit a man."'

Of the contents of this volume of poems, published in 1801, perhaps it will be best to say that they need not be spoken of in terms of unqualified condemnation. They are chiefly what is called, by a sort of euphemism, amatory; that is, they are of a loose and immoral tendency. Many sound judges blamed them severely at the time. It cannot be denied that scintillations of genius sparkle in them and from them, and the age in which they were written was not remarkably nice on such matters. The want of decency was therefore easily condoned by the felt presence of poetical ability. Moore, however, like a great many other men of genius—as our Swinburne will undoubtedly do if he lives long enough—remembered these effluences of predominant passion with feelings of shame in after years.

In 1803 Lord Moira's influence procured the little gentleman, in whom he had begun to feel a great interest, an appointment under Government, as Registrar to the Court of Admiralty at Bermuda. This is another of the not over appreciated kindnesses of that nobleman. When this situation was proposed to him, Moore wrote to his dearest mother as usual, on the 7th of August 1803, to inform her of it. In his letter he says:

'I am going to town to-morrow morning on a business which may prove as fallacious as all the rest have been, but which I think myself bound to follow up, as it will possibly in the end be productive of something, even if it be not itself a desirable object. Lord Moira told me to-day that he had had a letter from Tierney, offering him the gift of a place which Government had left at his (Tierney's) disposal. It must be something far from contemptible, as Lord M. told me in confidence, Tierney was under obligations to him, and that this was the first opportunity he had of, in any manner, repaying them. I fear, however, it is a situation not in either of these countries; and I fear it *solely* from the violence which a *wider* separation would cause to your feelings, my dearest mother. As for my *own* part, I should not consider any sacrifice of either comforts or society at all to be avoided, if it promised me a permanent subsistence, and the means of providing for those I love. I have hopes that even if it *be* necessary to leave this country, the place may be considerable enough to allow you all to accompany me. This would be delightful; but I know nothing certain of it yet. I take a letter to Tierney from Lord Moira, and the circumstances will of course be explained to me. Be assured, however, that I will do nothing without the total concurrence of your *feelings* as well as your *judgment*.

'Poor Lord Moira met with a very disagreeable accident the other evening. As he was leaving the judges' dinner at Leicester, he fell in going down stairs and hurt his back, I think, very seriously; for he has been in very great pain ever since, and cannot rise from a sofa without assistance. It is a pity that hearts like his should be perplexed by such common casualties of life, which should be only reserved for the every-day pedlars of this world. He is indeed most amiable. I hope, however, it will not long be troublesome.

'This journey is a new expense and perplexity to me, which I of course could by no means foresee. However, I am very well able for it both in purse and spirits; and God knows but it may be a "tide in my affairs" which will "lead to fortune." Fortune or not, I am still the same, your own devoted   TOM.'

The 'pity that hearts like his should be perplexed by such common casualties of life' is a rather toadying expression. The feeling which it uttered was forgotten by and by; and that about the every-day pedlars of this world is very like Tom Moore, man and boy.

To Bermuda he went. On his way, after reaching Norfolk, Virginia, he wrote home: 'Safe across the Atlantic, my darling mother, after a six weeks' passage, during which my best consolation was my thought and remembrance of home, and the dear hope that I should soon be assured of what I anxiously persuade myself—that you were all well and happy.' The side of Moore's nature which presents itself in this passage was proved through his whole life to be genuine and authentic. It is pleasant to keep turning it to those who care to read even the slightest sketch of his life. Moore did not like his situation at Bermuda. In his correspondence with those he loved he gives some very worldly reasons for this dislike. He wrote home that he could not acquire any accurate information with respect to the profits of his registrarship. One thing was *certain*, he said: a Spanish war *alone* could make it worth a very long sacrifice of other opportunities. 'Perhaps we are at this moment engaged in a Spanish war; if so, *tant mieux pour Jeannette*,' is his hopeful conclusion.

This is a study. The unamiable and the amiable were never more happily—some would say unhappily—blended. The love for the dear ones at home was as true as ever was love in the heart of an Irishman; which is saying a great deal. No subjects of Britannic Majesty love more truly than Irishmen. And yet the faithful possessor of this loving heart was longing for a Spanish war, that his income might be worth the sacrifice he had made in submitting to be so far separated from those he loved so well. Irishmen, as well as Scotchmen and Englishmen, slain by the thousand, that an affectionate son of Erin might have his salary increased for the comfort of his father, mother, and sisters! Both the love and the longing for a Spanish war were exceedingly earnest. There is here an obstinate nut for moralists to crack. The present compiler, making no pretence to the high functions professed and exercised by these excellent gentlemen, leaves the nut to them. He only remarks that the mind of man seems capable of reducing strange discords to stirring harmonies. The reason of this seems to be, that one dominant tone rules all the rest. The dominant in the mind of Thomas Moore was affection for his family at home. It subdued all feeling of the heartlessness of war. Widows, lovers, orphans, might be left desolate in his own green isle as well as among the hills and dales of Scotland, on the broad lands of England, and in the sunny regions of Spain — the best loved home of romance; but he would enjoy a better pay! Let us not dwell on it. Thomas Moore was like the most of us in this mysterious faculty of reducing savage discords to saintly harmonies.

Our poet did not like his work in Bermuda. It was slow. Two months were sufficient to convince him that the place was not suitable for him. He appointed a deputy to do the work, and share the wages; and this appointment brought him into trouble later on in life. After leaving Bermuda, Moore travelled through America. He wrote from Geneva, Tennessee County, in the State of New York,—

'I just pause a moment on my way to give one word to my dearest mother. I have been amongst the Oneida Indians, and have been amused very much by the novelty of their appearance. An old chief, Seenando, received me very courteously, and told us as well as he could by broken English and signs, that his nation consisted of 900, divided into three tribes, entitled the Wolf, the Bear, and the Turtle; poor, harmless savages! The Government of America are continually deceiving them into a surrender of the lands they occupy, and are driving them back into the woods farther and farther, till at length they will have no retreat but the ocean. This old chief's manners were extremely gentle and intelligent, and almost inclined me to be of the Frenchman's opinion, that the savages are the only well-bred gentlemen in America.'

It might have been expected, from Moore's early Republican sympathies, that he would be charmed by all he saw in the great Republic of the West. But it was not so: he did not admire the state of society in the country under its control. Alluding to his trip across the Atlantic, he says: 'Though curiosity was certainly not the motive of my voyage to America, yet it happened that the gratification of curiosity was the only advantage which I derived from it. Having remained about a week at New York,' he continues, 'I saw Madame, the half-repudiated wife of Jerome Buonaparte, and felt a slight shock of an earthquake, the only things that particularly awakened my attention.'

He recorded his sentiments regarding America in his *Odes and Epistles* like a young poet as he was, and the satire of his poetical epistles has been very much blamed. It is certainly not very pointed, but there is a good deal of Irish and youthful fervour in it. He did not think well of America. The following few lines, from a letter in rhyme to the Hon. W. R. Spencer, is a pretty fair specimen of them, and the spirit in which they were written:

'Oh! if America can yet be great,
If neither chained by choice nor damned by fate
To the mob-mania which imbrutes her now,
She yet can raise the bright but temperate brow
Of single majesty, can grandly place
An empire's pillar upon freedom's base,

> Nor fear the mighty shaft will feebler prove
> For the fair capital that flowers above !—
> If yet, released from all that vulgar throng,
> So vain of dulness and so pleased with wrong,
> Who hourly teach her, like themselves, to hide
> Folly in froth, and barrenness in pride,
> She yet can rise, can wreathe the Attic charms
> Of soft refinement round the pomp of arms,
> And see her poets flash the fires of song,
> To light her warriors' thunderbolts along !
> It is to you, to souls that favouring Heaven
> Has made like yours, the glorious task is given—
> Oh ! but for *such*, Columbia's days were done ;
> Rank without ripeness, quickened without sun,
> Crude at the surface, rotten at the core,
> Her fruits would fall before her spring was o'er ! '

After the tour through the United States—during which he attended the levee of President Jefferson, of which occurrence he observed afterwards that it was an event never to be forgotten, to see and speak with the man who drew up the Declaration of Independence—Moore visited the Falls of Niagara. This great phenomenon of nature was not so easily *done* by British tourists in those days, so long before the starting of the Cunard and Inman lines of steamers. It is interesting, therefore, to read the impression it produced on the susceptible mind of a visitor who had not learnt, and never did learn, to be so 'used up' as those victims of wealth and indolence who are not able to see anything new or wonderful in the places to which they lumber, and in which they lounge. This is Moore's letter to his mother after visiting the Falls of Niagara:—

'NIAGARA, *July* 24, 1804.

'MY DEAREST MOTHER,—I have seen the Falls, and am all rapture and amazement. I cannot give you a better idea of what I felt than by transcribing what I wrote off hastily in my journal on returning. '' Arrived at Chippewa, within three miles of the Falls, on Saturday, July 21st, to dinner. That evening walked towards the Falls, but got no farther than the Rapids, which gave us a prelibation of the grandeur we had to expect. Next day, Sunday, July 22d, went to visit the Falls. Never shall I forget the impression I felt at the first glimpse of them which we got as the carriage passed over the hill that overlooks them. We were not near enough to be agitated by the terrific effects of the scene ; but saw through the trees this mighty flow of waters descending with calm magnificence, and received enough of its grandeur to set imagination on the wing ; imagination which, even at Niagara, can outrun reality. I felt as if approaching the very residence of the Deity ; the tears started into my eyes ; and I remained, for moments after we had lost sight of the scene, in that delicious absorption which pious enthusiasm alone can produce. We arrived at the New Ladder, and descended to the bottom. Here all its awful sublimities rushed full upon me. But the former exquisite sensation was gone. I now saw all. The string that had been touched by the first impulse, and which *fancy* would have kept for ever in vibration, now rested at *reality*. Yet, though there was no more to imagine, there was much to feel. My whole heart and soul ascended towards the Divinity in a swell of devout admiration, which I never before experienced. Oh ! bring the atheist here, and he cannot return an atheist ! I pity the man who can coldly sit down to write a description of these ineffable wonders ; much more do I pity him who can submit them to the admeasurement of gallons and yards. It is impossible by pen or pencil to convey even a faint idea of their magnificence. Painting is lifeless; and the most burning words of poetry have all been lavished upon inferior and ordinary subjects. We must have new combinations of language to describe the Falls of Niagara."'

On his return to England, Moore landed at Plymouth on November 12, 1804. And from this time he was more than ever a hanger-on of Providence, so far as that supreme power might dispense any office with emolument through Lord Moira. His hopes and fears on this point are the burden of the letters which he wrote so voluminously at the time. His friend Miss Godfrey, and her sister the Marchioness of Donegal, make constant allusion to what Lord Moira might, could, should, or would, or would not do for him. That nobleman is rather disrespectfully spoken of in the course of these epistolary mutual confidences. His policy is severely criticised. He is abused for his concessions to the Prince Regent. Lord Moira was appointed to India. Moore and his friends hoped he would provide for him some splendid secretaryship in that country, or would use his influence before he left England with some of his friends to provide him with a lucrative post at home. But it all ended in disappointment. The sad announcement was wrung out of him to his mother in a letter written in the year 1812: 'I am quite sure Lord Moira will do nothing for me.' At the wind-up of long years of bowing down to Lord Moira, and begging from him anything good he might be pleased to give, he writes to Lady Donegal:

'And such is the end of my long-cherished hopes from the Earl of Moira, K.G., etc. He has certainly not done his duty by me: his *manner*, since his appointment, has been even worse than his deficiencies of *matter;* but (except to such friends as you) I shall never complain of him. He served my father when my father much wanted it, and he and his sister took my dear Bessy by the hand most cordially and seasonably; for all this I give him complete absolution; and as to disappointment, I feel but little of it, as his late conduct had taught me not to rely much upon him.'

This is rich. He absolves his best benefactor from the sin of not doing more for him!

The service to his father here alluded to was the situation of barrackmaster in Dublin, with a pay of about £300. This is the end of the Moira meanness on the part of Thomas Moore, who is forced to the sad conclusion, which he mentions to a friend, that now he must depend on his own industry. Miss Godfrey's sentence was:

'Poor Lord Moira! his good qualities have been the ruin of him.

"Que les vertus sont dangereuses
Dans un homme *sans jugement*."

'They must keep him out of the reach of all Indian *princes*, or the Company's rights will be in a bad way. A shake by the hand from a *tawny* prince-regent, and a plume of *heron's feathers* to wear upon birthdays, would go near to endanger our empire in India. This is too severe, but it is *wrung* from me by his criminal gullibility to such a —— as the Prince.'

Poor Lord Moira, indeed! He was the object of an inconvenient amount of that gratitude which is literally a lively anticipation of future favours.

But we must pause in this hurdle-race over dates. To resume with some respect to chronology: in 1806 Moore published his *Odes and Epistles*, dedicated to Lord Moira, and Jeffrey in the *Edinburgh Review* gave forth judgment without mercy on them. All the Irishman in Moore revealed himself in consequence of this review. A hostile meeting with Jeffrey— and it had a ludicrous termination—was one result. It may, perhaps, be as well to let our poet tell this part of his own story. He wrote in his Diary:—

'Though, on the first perusal of the article, the contemptuous language applied to me by the reviewer a good deal roused my Irish blood, the idea of seriously noticing the attack did not occur to me, I think, till some time after. I remember, at all events, having talked over the article with my friends, Lady Donegal and her sister, in so light and careless a tone, as to render them not a little surprised at the explosion which afterwards took place. I also well remember that, when the idea of calling out Jeffrey first suggested itself to me, the necessity I should be under of proceeding to Edinburgh for the purpose was a considerable drawback on my design, not only from the difficulty I was likely to experience in finding any one to accompany me in so Quixotic an expedition, but also from the actual and but too customary state of my finances, which rendered it doubtful whether I should be able to compass the expense of so long a journey.

'In this mood of mind I returned to London, and there, whether by *good* or *ill* luck, but in my own opinion the *former*, there was the identical Jeffrey himself just arrived, on a short visit to his London friends. From Rogers, who had met Jeffrey the day before at dinner at Lord Fincastle's, I learned that the conversation in the course of the day having happened to fall upon me, Lord F. was good enough to describe me as possessing "great amenity of manners;" on which Jeffrey said, laughingly, "I am afraid he would not show much amenity to *me*."

'The first step I took towards my hostile proceeding was to write to Woolriche, a kind and cool-headed friend of mine, begging of him to join me in town as soon as possible, and intimating in a few words the nature of the services on which I wanted him. It was plain from his answer that he considered me to be acting from the impulse of anger; which, though natural to conclude, was by no means the case; for, however boyish it might have been of me to consider myself bound to take this sort of notice of the attack, there was certainly but little if any mixture either of ill-temper or mere personal hostility with my motives. That they were equally free from a certain *Irish* predilection for such encounters, or wholly unleavened by a dash of *vanity*, I will not positively assert. But if this sort of feeling *did* mix itself with my motives, there certainly could not have been a more fitting punishment for it than the sort of result that immediately followed.

'As Woolriche's answer implied delay and deliberation, it did not suit, of course, my notions of the urgency of the occasion; and I accordingly applied to my old friend Hume, who without hesitation agreed to be the bearer of my message. It is needless to say that, feeling as I then did, I liked him all the better for his readiness; nor indeed am I at all disposed to like him a whit the less for it now. Having now secured my second, I lost no time in drawing up the challenge which he was to deliver; and as actual combat, not parley, was my object, I took care to put it out of the power of my antagonist to explain or retract, even if he was so disposed. Of the short note which I sent, the few first lines have long escaped my memory; but after adverting to some assertion contained in the article accusing me, if I recollect right, of a deliberate intention to corrupt the minds of my readers, I thus proceeded: "To this I beg leave to answer, You are a liar; yes, sir, a liar; and I choose to adopt this harsh and vulgar mode of defiance in order to prevent at once all equivocation between us, and to compel you to adopt, for your own satisfaction, that alternative which you might otherwise have hesitated in affording to mine." I am not quite sure as to the exact construction of this latter part of the note, but it was as nearly as possible, I think, in this form.

'There was of course but one kind of answer to be given to such a cartel. Hume had been referred by Jeffrey to his friend Mr. Horner, and the meeting was fixed for the following morning at Chalk Farm. Our great difficulty now was where to procure a case of pistols; for Hume, though he had been once, I think, engaged in mortal affray, was possessed of no such implements; and as for *me*, I had once nearly blown off my thumb by discharging an overloaded pistol, and that was the whole, I believe, of my previous acquaintance with fire-arms. William Spencer being the only one of all my friends whom I thought likely to furnish me with these *sine-quâ-nons*, I hastened to confide to him my wants, and request his assistance on this point. He told me if I would come to him in the evening, he would have the pistols ready for me.

' I forget where I dined, but I know it was not in company, as Hume had left to me the task of providing powder and bullets, which I bought in the course of the evening at some shop in Bond Street, and in such large quantities, I remember, as would have done for a score of duels. I then hastened to Spencer, who, in praising the pistols, as he gave them to me, said, "They are but too good." I then joined Hume, who was waiting for me in a hackney-coach, and proceeded to my lodgings. We had agreed that for every reason, both of convenience and avoidance of suspicion, it would be most prudent for me not to sleep at home; and as Hume was not the man, either then or at any other part of his life, to be able to furnish a friend with an extra pair of clean sheets, I quietly (having let myself in by my key, it being then between twelve and one at night) took the sheets off my own bed, and, huddling them up as well as I could, took them away with us in the coach to Hume's.

' I must have slept pretty well, for Hume, I remember, had to wake me in the morning; and the chaise being in readiness, we set off for Chalk Farm. Hume had also taken the precaution of providing a surgeon to be within call. On reaching the ground we found Jeffrey and his party already arrived. I say his "party;" for although Horner only was with him, there were, as we afterwards found, two or three of his attached friends (and no man, I believe, could ever boast of a greater number), who in their anxiety for his safety had accompanied him, and were hovering about the spot.[1] And then was it that, for the first time, my excellent friend Jeffrey and I met face to face. He was standing with the bag, which contained the pistols, in his hand, while Horner was looking anxiously around.

' It was agreed that the spot where we found them, which was screened on one side by large trees, would be as good for our purpose as any we could select; and Horner, after expressing some anxiety respecting some men whom he had seen suspiciously hovering about, but who now appeared to have departed, retired with Hume behind the trees, for the purpose of loading the pistols, leaving Jeffrey and myself together.

' All this had occupied but a very few minutes. We, of course, had bowed to each other on meeting; but the first words I recollect to have passed between us was Jeffrey's saying, on our being left together, "What a beautiful morning it is!" "Yes," I answered, with a slight smile, "a morning made for better purposes;" to which his only response was a sort of assenting sigh. As our assistants were not, any more than ourselves, very expert at warlike matters, they were rather slow in their proceedings; and as Jeffrey and I walked up and down together, we came once in sight of their operations: upon which I related to him, as rather *à propos* to the purpose, what Billy Egan, the Irish barrister, once said, when, as he was sauntering about in like manner while the pistols were loading, his antagonist, a fiery little fellow, called out to him angrily to keep his ground. "Don't make yourself unaisy, my dear fellow," said Egan; "sure, isn't it bad enough to take the dose, without being by at the mixing up?"

' Jeffrey had scarcely time to smile at this story, when our two friends, issuing from behind the trees, placed us at our respective posts (the distance, I suppose, having been previously measured by them), and put the pistols into our hands. They then retired to a little distance; the pistols were on both sides raised; and we waited but the signal to fire, when some police-officers, whose approach none of us had noticed, and who were within a second of being too late, rushed out from a hedge behind Jeffrey; and one of them, striking at Jeffrey's pistol with his staff, knocked it to some distance into the field, while another, running over to me, took possession also of mine. We were then replaced in our respective carriages, and conveyed, crestfallen, to Bow Street.

---

[1] One of those friends was, I think, the present worthy Lord Advocate, John Murray.

'On our way thither Hume told me, that from Horner not knowing anything about the loading of pistols, he had been obliged to help him in the operation, and in fact to take upon himself chiefly the task of loading both pistols. When we arrived at Bow Street, the first step of both parties was to despatch messengers to procure some friends to bail us; and as William Spencer was already acquainted with the transaction, to him I applied on my part, and requested that he would lose no time in coming to me. In the meanwhile we were all shown into a sitting-room, the people in attendance having first inquired whether it was our wish to be separated; but neither party having expressed any desire to that effect, we were all put together in the same room. Here conversation upon some literary subject, I forget what, soon ensued, in which I myself took only the brief and occasional share, beyond which, at any time of my life, I seldom ventured in general society. But whatever was the topic, Jeffrey, I recollect, expatiated upon it with all his peculiar fluency and eloquence; and I can now most vividly recall him to my memory, as he lay upon his back on a form which stood beside the wall, pouring volubly forth his fluent but most oddly pronounced diction, and dressing this subject out in every variety of array that an ever rich and ready wardrobe of phraseology could supply. I have been told of his saying, soon after our rencontre, that he had taken a fancy to me from the first moment of our meeting together in the field; and I can truly say that my liking for him is of the same early date.

'Though I sent for William Spencer, I am not quite sure that it was he that acted as my bail, or whether it was not Rogers that so officiated. I am, however, certain that the latter joined us at the office; and after all the usual ceremony of binding over, etc., had been gone through, it was signified to us that we were free to depart, and that our pistols should be restored to us. Whether unluckily or not, it is hardly worth while now to consider, but both Hume and myself, in quitting the office, forgot all about our borrowed pistols, and left them behind us; and as *he* set off immediately to join his wife, who was in the country, I was obliged myself to return to Bow Street, in the course of a few hours, for the purpose of getting them. To my surprise, however, the officer refused to deliver them up to me, saying, in a manner not very civil, that it appeared to the magistrate there was something unfair intended; as, on examining the pistol taken from me, there was found in it a bullet, while there had been no bullet found in that of Mr. Jeffrey.

'Recollecting what Hume had told me as to the task of loading the pistols being chiefly left to him, and observing the view taken by the officer, and, according to his account, by the magistrate, I felt the situation in which I was placed to be anything but comfortable. Nothing remained for me, therefore (particularly as Hume had taken his departure), but to go at once to Horner's lodgings and lay all the circumstances before him. This I did without a moment's delay, and was lucky enough to find him at his chambers. I then told him exactly what the officer had said as to the suspicion entertained by the magistrate that something unfair was intended; and even at this distance of time, I recollect freshly the immediate relief which it afforded me when I heard Horner (who had doubtless observed my anxiety) exclaim, in his honest and manly manner, " Don't mind what these fellows say. I myself saw your friend put the bullet into Jeffrey's pistol, and shall go with you instantly to the office to set the matter right." We both then proceeded together to Bow Street, and Horner's statement having removed the magistrate's suspicions, the officers returned to me the pistols, together with the bullet which had been found in one of them; and this very bullet, by the by, I gave afterwards to Carpenter, my then publisher, who requested it of me (as a sort of *polemic* relique, I suppose), and who, no doubt, has it still in his possession.

'The following letter, which I wrote immediately to Miss Godfrey (she and her sister Lady Donegal being among the persons whose good opinion I was most anxious about), will show, better than any words I could now employ, what were my feelings at that time:—

'TO MISS GODFREY.

'*Monday.*

'I have just time to tell you that this morning I was fool enough (as I know you will call it) to meet Mr. Jeffrey, by my own invitation, at Chalk Farm, and that just as we were ready to fire, those official and officious gentlemen, the Bow Street runners, appeared from behind a hedge and frustrated our valorous intentions, so that we are bound over to keep the peace for God knows how long. William Spencer is the cause of this very ill-judged interruption, though he had pledged his honour to keep the matter as secret as the grave. I never can forgive him; for at this moment I would rather have lost a limb than that such a circumstance had happened. And so there is all my fine sentimental letters which I wrote yesterday for posthumous delivery to your sister, you, etc. etc., all gone for nothing, and I made to feel very like a ninny indeed. Good-bye. I have not yet had time to read your letter. Best love to Lady Donegal and your sister. Ever your TOM Fool till death.

'What I asserted in this letter—namely, that it was through Spencer's means the meeting had been interrupted—was communicated to me by Rogers, and I have no doubt was perfectly correct. Spencer dined alone with the Fincastles, and after dinner told all the circumstances of the challenge, the loan of the pistols, etc., to Lord Fincastle, who (without, as it appears, communicating his purpose to Spencer) sent information that night of the intended duel to Bow Street.

'The manner in which the whole affair was misrepresented in the newspapers of the day is too well known to need any repetition here; but I have been told, and I think it not improbable, that to a countryman of my own (named Q———), who was editor of one of the evening papers, I owed the remarkable concurrence in falsehood which pervaded all the statements on the subject. The report from Bow Street was taken first (as I have heard the story) to the office of the paper in question, and contained a statement of the matter, correctly, thus:—"In the pistol of one of the parties a bullet was found, and nothing at all in the pistol of the other." Thinking it a good joke, doubtless, upon literary belligerents, my countryman changed, without much difficulty, the word "bullet" into "pellet;" and in this altered state the report passed from him to the offices of all the other evening papers.

'By another letter of my own, written on the following day, to Lady Donegal, I am enabled to give to my narrative not only authenticity, but a good deal of the freshness of the feeling of the moment to which it refers.

'TO LADY DONEGAL.

'*Tuesday.*

'You will see that I am doomed inevitably to one day's ridicule, by the unfortunate falsehood, which they have inserted in all the morning papers, about the loading of our pistols; but, of course, a contradiction will appear to-morrow, signed by our seconds, and authorized by the magistrate. This is the only mortifying *suite* that this affair could have, and Heaven knows it has given me unhappiness enough. Do not scold me, dearest Lady Donegal; if the business was to be again gone through, I should feel it my duty to do it; and all the awkwardness that results from it must be attributed to the ill-judged officiousness of the persons who were sent to interrupt us. To be sure, there cannot be a fairer subject for quizzing than an author and a critic fighting with pellets of paper. God bless you! Tell every one as industriously as you can the falsehood of to-day's statement, and stem, if possible, the tide of ridicule till our contradiction appears. Love to your dear sisters. Ever your attached,

'T. M.

'The statement announced in this letter was regularly drawn up, signed by Horner, and authorized by the magistrate; but alas! never appeared. My friend Hume (now again my friend, though his conduct on that occasion caused a severance between us for more than thirty years) took fright at the ridicule which had been brought upon the transaction; said that he did not like to expose his name; that he "did not know who Mr. Horner was;" in short, he refused to sign the paper; and the only effort made at public explanation was a short letter on the subject from myself, which of course, to those who did not know me personally, went deservedly for nothing.

'Through the kind offices of Rogers, a treaty of peace was negotiated between Jeffrey and myself; I mean those formalities of explanation which the world requires, for in every other respect we already understood each other. In the two letters that follow will be found some particulars of the final arrangement of our strife.

'TO LADY DONEGAL.
'*August* 29, 1806.

'I have been looking for a frank (like that best of all thrifty good girls, Miss J————), in order to send you back Hayley's letter, which is as pretty a specimen of the old gentleman's twaddling as I could wish to see. But the last person I asked for a frank was Humphrey Butler; and he told me if I had applied before the Union he could have given me one,—which, however satisfactory it was, made me resolve to keep Hayley's letter from you a little longer, and I shall return it the instant I get a cover, and not a soul shall see it, I assure you. Lord Moira has written to me a very kind note, in consequence of my communicating to him the explanations which I had from Jeffrey, and he assures me "he feels uncommon satisfaction that it has terminated so pleasantly." If I were just now seated upon the couch, with my legs turned up, I could show you this letter; but as I am not, I must only give you an extract from it, thus: "I feel perfectly for you how disagreeable it is to be obliged to start one's self as the butt for all the wild constructions of the public. Misrepresentation, in some way or other, is the inevitable lot of every one who stands in such a predicament; but the squibs against you were only momentary, and a *fair tribute to the spirit with which you vindicated your character will remain.*"

'This high Spanish approbation of my conduct has given me much pleasure, as I know it will to you; indeed, nothing can be more gratifying than the generous justice which every friend whose opinion I value has done to my feelings upon this occasion. I was particularly happy to hear that Horner, the other day, at Holland House, spoke warmly in praise of what he called "the mixture of feeling and fortitude which my conduct exhibited."

'I met your friend the Duke of York, and the Duke of Cambridge, in a dinner party of eight only the other day at Harry Greville's. In short, I do nothing but *dine;* yesterday at Ward's, to-day at Lord Cowper's, etc. Somebody told me, and made my heart flutter not a little, that you are coming to town before your Tunbridge trip. I believe it was Chichester that "*whispered* the flattering tale," but I am almost afraid to believe it. I should in that case see you once before I go to bury myself among my St. Chrysostoms and Origens, and to shake hands with a dearer father than whole centuries of such fathers. Carpenter is to give me forty pounds for the Sallust, and I wait but for this forty-pounder to discharge me at one single shot to Dublin.

'Best love to dear Mary (why shouldn't I call her Mary, as well as that old ridiculous Hermit?); and to sister Philippa, too, a thousand remembrances. Ever yours, most truly,
'T. M.

'TO LADY DONEGAL.
'*Monday, August* 1806.

'I have the pleasure to tell you that this morning I had a pacific meeting with Mr. Jeffrey at Rogers', and received from him the most satisfactory apologies for the intemperance of his attack upon me. He acknowledged that it is the opinion, not only of himself, but his friends, that the *Review* contained too much that was exceptionable, and that he was sincerely sorry for having written it. He has given me a statement to this purpose in his own autograph, which concludes thus: "I shall always hold myself bound to bear testimony to the fairness and spirit with which you have conducted yourself throughout the whole transaction." Is not this all pleasant! I know you will be glad to hear it. The letter which you will see in to-morrow's *Post* was a very necessary step, and will put an end to every misconstruction of the affair; so that (for the first time since I took the business into contemplation) I feel "my bosom's lord sit lightly on his throne," and the sooner I receive your congratulations upon the subject the better. Ever yours, 'T. M.'

So ends the farce of 'The Duel; or, Critic and Poet befooled.' The friendship thus begun between Moore and Jeffrey became fast, and was to the advantage of both.

It may be as well to notice here, although out of chronological order, another deep and lasting friendship—at least on Moore's side—which originated in a challenge sent by him to fight a duel. This was his friendship with Byron. In his *English Bards and Scotch Reviewers*, the great Anglo-Scottish poet could not well be expected to overlook such an incident in the life of the arch-enemy among reviewers as that just narrated. He could have at the time comparatively little reason for wishing to annoy Moore, or rather Little, as he calls him, and as Moore had ere this called himself. Accordingly he takes advantage of the incident thus:

> 'Health to great Jeffrey! Heaven preserve his life
> To flourish on the fertile shores of Fife,
> And guard it sacred in his future wars,
> Since authors sometimes seek the field of Mars!
> Can none remember that eventful day,
> That ever-glorious, almost fatal fray,
> When Little's leadless pistol met his eye,
> And Bow Street myrmidons stood laughing by!'

If a duel was at all necessary after such a bare allusion to undeniable facts, it certainly was Jeffrey's affair. But Moore seemed anxious to sign his deed of friendship with the Edinburgh editor by running another risk of his life—the former one not having been very serious. So, all aflame with friendship, and on fire for vengeance, he determined to challenge the aristocratic satirist to the final arbitrement of pistol and paces. Byron was, however, not quite so conveniently encountered as Jeffrey. He had no such steady business habits as would induce him to visit any London bookseller at a stated season. In fact, the letter in which 'Little Tommy's' vengeful challenge was wordily couched, did not reach him for months after; and then it looked in his eyes too much like the canine picture of 'Dignity and Impudence,' to be regarded as anything serious. So, instead of 'Pistols for two and coffee for one,' it resolved itself into coffee for both and no pistols at all. It was better than coffee. After easily made and accepted explanations, such a dinner as Byron could enjoy, and Moore could not refuse, soldered up the wrath which in a nature like Moore's could never issue from any very 'direful spring.' Had there been another satirist as able as Byron, he might have turned this duel also into as excellent raillery as was done with the first. These were the two duels in Moore's life. In both of them, his strongest and his weakest—his best and his worst—elements of character obtrude themselves. He had always to be aroused to a considerable pitch of excitement before he could throw off his excessively polite bearing towards any superior. When he did so, there was a bluster. The bluster over, there was never much difficulty in inducing him to be very polite again. He refers to this duel later on in life, in terms which do not much modify the feeling to which expression has just been given. In his Diary on the 29th of

November 1818, when he had reached the mature age of thirty-nine—and let every reader of this simple extract reflect a little upon it, that he may have some clear idea of Tom Moore at his prime—he enters:

'Called upon Perry. Seemed to think that the coming in of the Duke of Wellington would lead ultimately to the break-up of the present Administration. Dined to-day with Scrope Davies, to meet Jackson the boxer at my own request, as I want to pick up as much of the flash, *from authority*, as possible. Some talk with Davies before dinner, about Lord Byron and me having been so near blowing each other's brains out: told him that Lord B. had said since he never meant to fire at me. Davies was with him at the time this hostile correspondence took place, and offered to bet upon friendship against fighting as the most likely result. The event found him right. Lord B.'s conduct on this occasion was full of manliness and candour. Got very little out of Jackson; he makes, Davies tells me, more than a thousand a year by teaching sparring. Caleb Baldwin is the teacher in the city.'

Hanger-on for Government mercies, would-be boxer, and *quondam* duellist: such is our hero at about forty years of age. These words are not written with any intention to depreciate. They are meant as minor outlines of the character of the man who sang the *Irish Melodies* and the *Sacred Songs*. Thus we have two instances of life-long friendship on the part of able men, originating in each case in a challenge to fight a duel. The provocation in both instances was literary. In both cases the criticism was just. *Odes and Epistles* deserved all Jeffrey wrote against them. Byron's lines were allusions to facts which Moore himself could not deny, and Jeffrey was too wise to say much about. Are there two other such originations of friendship in the excited history of the brethren of the pen? It is to be doubted if there are. The friendship on Jeffrey's part was, and remained, undoubtedly sincere. One of the earliest uses he made of it was to try and enlist Moore in the service of the *Edinburgh Review*. The delicacy of friendship as well as the earnestness of the admiration which Jeffrey felt for him, could not be better expressed than it was in the letter which he addressed to Rogers soliciting his influence with Moore to induce him to join his staff. Rogers used his influence, and Moore responded to the invitation with two or three articles, especially one on the Christian Fathers, which made Byron exclaim: 'By God! Moore, you can do anything.' As to Byron's friendship for the little Irish poet, it was as sincere a feeling of the sort as he was capable of entertaining for any length of time. For it must never be forgotten that deeply impassioned natures are not the kind which evolve themselves into long-enduring and faithful friendships. Their impulses are too strong to live long, unless on that kind of stimulus on which passion flames out its incandescent existence. It will not be forgotten by any reader of Byron that he remembered Tom Moore to the last—of his stay in this country at least —when he wrote so beautifully:

'My boat is on the shore,
And my bark is on the sea;
But before I go, Tom Moore,
Here's a double health to thee.'

Byron himself asserts that he never felt the emotion of friendship towards any one, except Lord Clare, and 'perhaps little Moore.' He is not quite sure of the unselfishness of 'little Moore's' esteem and love. He thinks Moore admires the rank and title as much as the man. Here there is in Byron a glimmering sense of the great truth uttered by Scotland's national poet, when he wrote :

> 'The rank is but the guinea stamp,
> The man's the gowd for a' that.'

Byron cannot divest himself of this notion altogether in the case of Moore, who entertained an affection for him almost like the love of woman. More than once does he assert that 'Little Tommy dearly loves a lord.' And this is a truth of which Tommy's whole life was a demonstration, and which he would have been the last to attempt to deny. He would have resented the denial of it on his behalf, even by a lord.

In 1808 and 1809 our poet published, anonymously, three poems, entitled respectively *Corruption, Intolerance,* and *The Sceptic.* The first two are political. They were issued as 'Two Poems: Addressed by an Irishman to an Englishman.' In the former, Moore takes a peculiarly Irish view of the Revolution. He uses, towards that great event in English history, the language which was formerly common to, and became the lips of, the old English Tories; but the meaning he puts into that language is quite Irish; and Ireland, we all know, did not for a long time, if she does yet, seem to see any benefit which she owed to the Revolution. The second poem is on the want of toleration in Religion; and the third is an attempt to satirize the schoolmen of long past ages. This last attempt no Horace or Juvenal would ever have dreamed of. Satire is nothing if it does not laugh at or lash living vices. These three poems were a dead failure. An admiring biographer of Moore, a fellow-countryman too, Mr. James Burke, A.B., Barrister-at-law, says: 'These poems were not successful. The stately tone of Juvenal but ill became the light Horatian vein of Moore. He could ridicule folly with more force than he could lash vice. There is, however, another reason for the failure of Moore's serious political satires. They were written in a spirit which England could not then understand: they were neither Whig nor Tory, which was a defect in the eyes of the partisans of the age.' It has been said above that they were Irish. They should not have been addressed to an Englishman at all; indeed, they should never have been addressed to anybody. When, in the preface, their author speaks of them as 'indifferent verses' and 'stupid poetry,' his acuteness is very much to be admired, although he did not mean these phrases to be too suggestive of what the words plainly mean.

On the 25th of March, Lady-day, 1811, Moore married Miss Bessy Dyke at St. Martin's Church, London. This young Irish lady—the sister of the first wife of the late Mr. W. H. Murray, of the Theatre Royal, Edinburgh—

was an actress when she won the heart of our very susceptible poet. Of all the society he ever sought, she was perhaps the lowliest,—that is, according to Moore's own estimate of high and low in society, not in that of the writer of this meagre outline of his life. And this look around rather above himself brought greater blessings with it than all his adoration of the great. Tennyson might have been thinking of the wife of Thomas Moore when he wrote of

> 'The stately flower of female fortitude,
> Of perfect wifehood and pure lowlihead.
>   . . . . .
> Through all her placid life,
> The queen of marriage, a most perfect wife.'

It must have been a struggle to a man of Moore's nature and aspirations to marry a lady so far from aristocracy in rank. It was evidently an affair of the heart. It resulted in Moore's unalloyed happiness while he lived—thanks to his 'most perfect wife.' With almost any other woman in the world, Thomas Moore would have made as signal a shipwreck of conjugal happiness as ever did any of the rhyming fraternity: and they are only too proverbial for this feat in family arrangements. Lord John Russell hints gently at this in his preface, the best part of his biographical labours, when he writes: 'Moore's domestic life gave scope to the best parts of his character. His beautiful wife, faultless in conduct, a fond mother, a lively companion, devoted in her attachments, always ready—perhaps too ready—to sacrifice her own domestic enjoyments, that he might be admired and known, was a treasure of inestimable value to his happiness. I have said that perhaps she was too ready to sacrifice herself, because it would have been better for Mr. Moore if he had not yielded so much to the attractions of society, however dazzling and however tempting.' Allowing for the reticence of a highly bred gentleman, there is much in this passage to suggest that Bessy, the *quondam* actress on the mimic stage, acted a part on the stage of life which should set her among the heroines who have conquered happiness.

Little touches occur in his correspondence which shows a pastoral simplicity in their married love which are as good as songs. Thus, writing from Mayfield Cottage to Miss Godfrey, two years after his marriage, he says: 'We walked this evening in to Ashbourne, and brought back some peas to our supper, which Bessy carried in a little basket on her arm, as happily and prettily as any market-girl in Derbyshire.' But better still, writing from the same cottage to his mother a little later, he says: 'We dined out to-day at the Ackroyds', neighbours of ours. You would have laughed to see Bessy and me in going to dinner. We found, in the middle of our walk, that we were nearly half an hour too early for dinner; so we set to *practising country-dances*, in the middle of a retired green lane, till the time was expired.' Here is light-heartedness and love. And all this with no very reliable means of subsistence, just at the time when the sad truth was becoming clear to his mind that Lord Moira was going to prove a broken reed! Truly light-heartedness and love are better things than cynics and ascetics call them. The two allusions to Mayfield Cottage require a word of explanation. When Moore first settled down in a home out of Lord Moira's Hall, he chose Kegworth, in Leicestershire. But he did not stay there long. In the course of the same year he removed to Mayfield Cottage, near Ashbourne, in Derbyshire, that he might be near the library of Lord Moira, which was placed at his disposal.

During the year in which he was married, Moore produced an opera. The songs which were sung in it are to be found in the ordinary editions of his works under the heading—which was the title of the opera—*M.P.; or, The Blue Stocking*. There are some very pretty sentiments, verses, and lines in these songs. Any one who cares to see the leading peculiarities of Moore's mind gathered up within an hour's thoughtful reading, could not do better than spend the hour reading these lyrics. Thus, as to his faculty of developing a common proverb into a pretty verse, we see in this stanza what can be made of 'When poverty comes in at the door, love flies out at the window:'

'Alas! that Poverty's evil eye,
   Should e'er come hither,
   Such sweets to wither!
The flowers laid down their heads to die,
And Hope fell sick as the witch drew nigh.
   She came one morning,
   Ere Love had warning,
And raised the latch where the young god lay;
"Oh, ho!" said Love, "is it you? good-bye;"
So he oped the window, and flew away!'

Again, was there ever a prettier sentiment expressed than the following?

'The child who sees the dew of night
   Upon the spangled hedge at morn,
Attempts to catch the drops of light,
   But wounds his finger with the thorn.
Thus oft the brightest joys we seek
   Are lost, when touched, and turned to pain;
The flush they kindle leaves the cheek,
   The tears they waken long remain.'

Moore himself never surpassed this; and he is pre-eminently the poet of sentiment and simile. Again, his love of liberty—British, not merely Irish liberty—is beautifully worded in the following stanza:

'Farewell to the land where in childhood I wandered!
   In vain is she mighty, in vain is she brave!
Unblessed is the blood that for tyrants is squandered,
   And fame has no wreaths for the brow of the slave.

> But hail to thee, Albion! who meet'st the commotion
> Of Europe as calm as thy cliffs meet the foam!
> With no bonds but the law, and no slave but the ocean,
> Hail, Temple of Liberty! thou art my home.'

'No bonds but the law, and no *slave but the ocean!*' He was a poet of the true ring who conceived and expressed that thought on behalf of trueborn Britons. Notwithstanding—or rather, perhaps, on account of— delicate shades of beauty like these, the opera, which was first brought out in Dublin, was not a success. A few nights seemed all that were necessary to exhaust what interest it contained. When he was convinced it was to be a failure, he wrote to his friend Miss Godfrey complaints in the usual strain and tone of disappointed dramatic authors, when they feel that, having missed a great success, they have made a failure.

At the close of the letter to Miss Godfrey he writes: 'I shall now take to my poem, and do something, I hope, that will place me above the vulgar herd both of worldlings and of critics; but you shall hear from me again, when I get among the maids of Cashmere, the sparkling springs of Rochabad, and the fragrant banquets of the Peris. How much sweeter employments these than the vile jokemaking I have been at these two months past!' This was written on the 11th of September 1811. It is the first mention of an intention to write a great Oriental poem which occurs in Moore's correspondence. It is usually stated that the determination to write this poem was formed in 1812; but here we have it referred to as a work going on a year earlier. Allusions to it crop out here and there in the correspondence. Thus, writing in 1812 to Lady Donegal about a tour he and Rogers had taken from Mayfield Cottage to Matlock, he says:

> 'Rogers and I had a very pleasant tour of it, though I felt throughout it all, as I always feel with him, that the fear of *losing* his good opinion almost embitters the *possession* of it, and that though in his society one *walks upon roses*, it is with constant apprehension of the *thorns* that are among them. . . . He left me rather out of conceit with my poem *Lalla Rookh* (as his fastidious criticism generally does), and I have returned to it with rather an humbled spirit; but I have already once altered my whole plan to please him, and I will do so no more, for I should make as long a voyage of it as his own *Columbus* if I attended to all his objections. His *general* opinion, however, of what I have done is very flattering; he only finds fault with *every part* of it in detail; and this you know is the style of his criticism of characters—"an *excellent* person, *but*"'——

This 'but,' by the way, is significant, and it may as well be supplemented by what Lady Donegal writes in reply. It is this:

> 'Your description of Rogers is too like him. How vexatious it is that a man who has so much the power of pleasing and attaching people to him should mar the gifts of nature so entirely by giving way to that sickly and discontented turn of mind, which makes him dissatisfied with everything, and disappointed in all his views of life! Yet he can feel for others; and, notwithstanding this unfortunate habit he has given himself of dwelling upon the faults and follies of his friends, he really can feel attachment; and to you I am certain he is attached, though I acknowledge that the thorns sometimes make one wish to throw away the roses, and forego the pleasure to avoid the pain. But with all his faults I like him, though I know he spares me no more than any of his other dear friends.'

These gossipy remarks may be taken as letterpress descriptions of the best portrait of Rogers: the portrait, at least, with which the public is most familiar. Well, here we have *Lalla Rookh* so far in shape as to be criticised and altered in 1812. Moore must have been at work at it long before the first reference to it which crops up in his correspondence. Another question of chronology is corrected by a study of the correspondence. With reference to the sale of this poem to a publisher, the conduct of Mr. Perry of the *Morning Chronicle*—a paper which at that time divided the lead of public opinion with the *Times*—and the Messrs. Longman has been held up to wonder as one of the most marvellous instances of commercial faith—and that in a transaction between an author and a publisher!—on record. Moore himself lends countenance to the prevailing idea, which is to this effect: 'The Messrs. Longman agreed, on the representation of Mr. Perry, to pay Moore three thousand guineas for an Eastern romance, to take it for better for worse, at whatever time suited the author's convenience, and without any power to suggest changes or alterations.' It has been commonly remarked that this was certainly a most unbusiness-like bargain—on the part of the publishers at all events—but that it turned out a profitable one. Now this is itself all a bit of a romance. It is quite a romance to the English mind, the preliminary reading of which would no doubt set zest a-boiling to get hold of the Oriental story about which it was written. Well, about Mr. Perry, the Messrs. Longman, and Tom Moore's embryonic poem, these are the facts. Mr. Perry writes to Moore on July 25, 1814, a letter in which, among other things, he says:

'I have had a friendly conversation with Mr. Longman. I told him, of course, that I had no authority to enter into any negotiation with him; but that as your friend I should be happy to communicate to you any proposal that he might wish to make to you on the subject of your poem. He said that he was most desirous to treat for it, that he understood from Mr. Orme I had mentioned the sum of 3000 guineas as the price that I thought you should fix upon it, and that this sum was so large as to make him desirous of seeing the copy of the poem before he made up his mind. From long experience he conceived himself capable of judging of the probable demand that there would be for the work, and it would satisfy his mind if he could have an opportunity of forming this judgment. All that he wished to ascertain was the character and design of the fable. You will be the only judge of your conduct on this proposal. I think him quite in earnest as to his wish to treat. Of his judgment in the way of anticipating the popularity of a poem I can form no estimate. There may be a bookseller's knack; but I foresee an obvious inconvenience in this mode of treating. If, after seeing the copy, he should hesitate in giving the sum, or attempt to chaffer, he might wound your delicacy, and even injure the character of the work, by saying that he had refused it. I am not sure, therefore, my dear sir, whether I ought not to tell you my own sentiment on the matter, which is frankly to decline the previous communication.'

When Mr. Perry spoke to the Messrs. Longman, there can be little doubt that he had seen the poem, as Rogers had two years before. When they listened so eagerly to terms, it is not impossible that they heard also extracts from it, as far as Mr. Perry could reproduce them, or perhaps even read them. But all that was in the *sanctum sanctorum* of a publisher; and what was to reach the public was the sweet little tale about a bargain reminding vulgar people about something like a pig in a bag. The great poem was ready in 1816, but was, for reasons determined by the state of the bookselling market, not brought out till the next year. It was dedicated to Mr. Rogers. To give any account of its details after it has been read, since 1817 till 1871, by millions of intelligent readers, would be an impertinence. How true it is in external scenery—that is, as a panorama of the East—has been variously attested. One biographer tells us, that a brother of his who served as an officer in the 30th Regiment during the Sutlej campaign of 1846, remarked to him, that to a man who has read *Lalla Rookh*, the journey from Delhi to Lahore seems like treading familiar ground. Another writes: 'So carefully did he "coach" himself in knowledge of the manners and customs, arts and sciences, geography, natural history, and climate of the East, that a distinguished traveller observed, if the author of *Lalla Rookh* had never seen the lands he described, a person might learn as much of those countries from books as by riding on the back of a camel.' When *Lalla Rookh* was published, it was an immediate and an immense success, for that or any other time. Seven editions were demanded in the first year of its printed existence. It was a poem exactly suited to the prevailing taste of the period. It belongs to the species styled objective or panoramic. It speaks much of the light of the sun and the moon, and but little of 'the light that never was on sea or land.' It is full of sentiment—its very reflections are sentimental. There is in it little or no exercise of the creative imagination in the sense in which Tennyson's *Palace of Art*, for example, shows the working of that potent faculty of the poetical wizard. Moore was no high priest in poetry, as is Tennyson, and was Wordsworth. He was in the outer court among the worshippers, and seemed very much inclined to wield the explanatory pointing-rod, or to ask them if they didn't think the sentiment true to nature, the simile ingenious, or the reflection fine. He was hand to hand with them, and they loved him, even if they looked upon him as 'Little Tommy.' His verse is the effluence of the rich music which was in his soul. The similes and the imagery are unsurpassed. The pictures of heroic action make the pages of the poem glow. The tender pathos has melted many an eye unused to tears. The sensuous beauty often leaves a sleepy sense of languor. Lord Jeffrey wrote in the *Edinburgh Review* of November 1817: 'There is a great deal of our present poetry derived from the East, but this is the finest Orientalism we have had yet. The Land of the Sun has never shone out so brightly on the children of the North, nor the sweets of Asia been poured forth, nor her gorgeousness been displayed so profusely to the delighted senses of Europe. The beauteous forms, the dazzling splendour, the breathing odours of the East, seem at last to have found a kindred poet in the "Green Isle" of the West.'

When one reads *Lalla Rookh*, he has, till he explains the feeling to himself, a sense of familiarity with the poem in some aspect or another which is suggestive of want of originality in it. He may turn to Scott, and Byron, and Southey, but he will not find the explanation in them which he feels he is in search of. He finds it when he turns to the *Irish Melodies*. The poems in *Lalla Rookh* are four long-drawn Irish melodies. The prevailing sentiments are akin. The similes are of the same richness, and are equally profuse. The heroism is as reckless, and the love as rapturous. Moore lets us into this secret himself, if we would only listen to the explanations he is in the outer court to give us. 'The same spirit,' he says, 'which spoke in the Melodies of Ireland, found a home in the East.' But a minute knowledge of the East could not have supplied even his soul with the music which he has rolled out in this his longest poem, if he had not been the Irishman he was—familiar and sympathetic with the struggle for religious freedom which was fierce at the time in the country he loved so well, but would not live in. *The Veiled Prophet* is revolting. *The Fire-Worshippers*, admittedly the ablest of these four long Irish melodies, is a product of that mixed sentiment of patriotism and martyrdom which was fostered by the struggles of Ireland at the time. The *Light of the Haram* is that ever old, always new story of the conquering power of a faithful woman's patient love which Tennyson works out in his own very different style in the trials and triumph of *Enid*. The underlying idea of *Elaine*—a hopeless love which consumes to death—is essentially the same as that which gives life to *The Fire-Worshippers*. As to the story of Lalla Rookh and Feramorz, which runs through the whole of these four poems—if it will not be thought pushing the parallel to far—it has a happier result, no doubt; but still one is reminded of it when he reads of Sir Launcelot's being sent to bring home to the British King Arthur his bride. In each case, the lady fell terribly in love with the noble leader of her escort. In Moore's story, that leader was her lover in disguise. In Tennyson's tale, the love was similarly reciprocated, only to prove in subsequent years the ruin of both. So that Tennyson's general conception is much the more tragic of the two. These resemblances are exceedingly general, and very vague. Still they serve to remind us of the enchanted circle within which the subtlest charmers of the successive generations are constrained to move: 'Love is lord of all.' Moore's satire in the prose connectives which contain the story of Lalla Rookh and Feramorz is capital. The one character created in these belts or bands which combine wheel with wheel in the machinery of the story is Fadladeen. Fadladeen lives for ever. He is not so well rounded as Polonius. He has no opportunity of showing himself off in a variety of situations, like Hudibras. But he is a creation worthy of a younger brother in the craft of which Shakspeare and Butler were worshipful masters. Lalla Rookh herself is perhaps best as Moore intentionally placed her—passive, languid, beautiful, ruled by love and the senses, well equipped without and within to be 'The Light of the Haram.'

Moore could not afford—having a wife and family—to devote those five or six years exclusively to Lalla Rookh, the Tulip Cheek. He needed money constantly in the meantime. In 1813, accordingly,—the dedication to 'Stephen Woolriche, Esq.,' is dated the 4th of March of that year,—he published *Intercepted Letters, or the Twopenny Post Bag*. These ephemeral squibs were a satire against the Prince Regent and his ministers. Moore exposed himself to a good deal of remark for his obtrusive hostility to the Prince. It was remembered that the permission to dedicate his translation of the *Odes of Anacreon* to His Royal Highness had helped to float that book into a good market, and its author into the favourable notice which is both necessary and sufficient to give genius an advantageous start in his pursuit of fame and funds. Moore replied to this sort of quizzing rather summarily. He wrote in one of his prefaces: ' Luckily the list of benefits showered upon me from that high quarter may be despatched in a few sentences. At the request of the Earl of Moira, one of my earliest and best friends, His Royal Highness graciously permitted me to dedicate to him my translation of the Odes of Anacreon. I was twice, I think, admitted to the honour of dining at Carlton House; and when the Prince, on his being made Regent in 1811, gave his memorable *fête*, I was one of the envied—about 1500, I believe, in number—who enjoyed the privilege of being his guests on the occasion.' This was all very agreeable to Moore at the time; and his summary account of benefits received has a spice of depreciation in it which is not very admirable. These *Intercepted Letters* jumped with the humour of a large public at the time of their issue. They went through thirteen or fourteen editions in twelve months. This, of course, put money in Moore's purse. The *Times* and the *Morning Chronicle* also served as 'go-carts' for many light satirical effusions during the period of his pondering and penning *Lalla Rookh*. Even these newspaper squibs are said to have yielded the needy poet from four to five hundred pounds a year. It was at this part of his career also that he wrote the few articles in the *Edinburgh Review* which have been already referred to. About this time also, Mr. Murray the publisher offered him, through Lord Byron, several hundreds a year (the number of hundreds was not specified) to become the editor of a Review like the *Edinburgh* or the *Quarterly*. He did not give the proposal even consideration, although he knew that Jeffrey had fifteen hundred a year. He had consecrated himself to the Muses, and he continued faithful.

Thomas Moore's enduring fame is due to his *Irish Melodies*. In these songs Moore gave utterance to all that was best in him. In reading them, singing, or hearing them sung, we forget his vanity, worldliness, darling love of lords, and all the innumerable inside-outs of a favourite minstrel; and we think only of a graceful, beautiful, and beneficent being, who lived for our improvement, and sang that our hearts might be glad. The *Irish Melodies* are to Moore what a public monument is always intended to be to the man whose memory it is meant to honour. The monument is—or is meant to be—all symmetry and beauty; thus symbolizing the image in which the dead one lives on in the hearts of those who admire and love him. It is thus with Burns' beautiful cenotaph on the banks o' Bonny Doon. How unlike the character of the man while he lived, even in the eyes of those who loved him best! But death puts to the distance, which enchants, and the monument tells us that all the angles have been smoothed away, and the hidden beauties have been brought out into bold relief. So with Moore's *Irish Melodies*. The man who was honoured to pass across the isthmus of Time from the one eternity to the other, and keep strewing his path with these things of beauty, is, to those who meet his path, a joy for ever, and is well fitted to be one of the joys of the whole earth. Before he left Ireland, in the last year of the eighteenth century, he had cherished the idea which Burns expresses when he utters the aspiration:

> ' That I, for puir auld Scotland's sake,
> Some usefu' plan or beuk could make,
> Or sing a sang at least.'

In one sense, both of these poets set themselves to the same good work—to write words to the beautiful music of their native land. Burns remained in his native land, and wrote in its vocabulary the native sentiments in which that music felt itself still at home and among its kith and kin. Moore left his native land, and carried Irish music with him to London, and made London and England in his time admire it; but the words were not Irish—except here and there a forced though sweet one from the Erse Gaelic—and the sentiments were the common inheritance of all civilised nations.

About 1807 he entered into an arrangement with Mr. Power, a publisher of music in London, to furnish words for a collection of Irish melodies, most of which were supplied by himself. It was part of the bargain that Sir J. Stevenson was to set them to harmony. This engagement with Power was one of the most fortunate events of Moore's early career. In a letter to his mother in 1812 he writes: 'I don't know whether I told you before, that the Powers give me between them *five hundred* a year for my music; the agreement is for seven years, and as much longer as I choose to say.' And we see, from his correspondence, that he did not need to ask them twice for an advance of money if he was in any strait. The *Melodies* were issued in detached numbers, and their publication ranged over a period of nearly thirty years. During this time the *Sacred Songs* and the *National Airs* came out under the same happy auspices. Moore, with remarkable clearness of discernment and soundness of judgment, spoke of his *Irish Melodies* as the ' only work of his pen whose fame could boast of a chance of prolonging its existence to a day much beyond his own.' They have lived, as he foresaw, and have buoyed up, and will buoy up for generations yet to come, all else that ever he wrote. Of modern song-writers only Burns and Beranger compare with him. It would be superfluous to specify any of these melodies. They are all known to every cultivated lady and gentleman who reads the English language. The last in the list as they are usually printed—'Dear Harp of my Country'—should be compared with Sir Walter Scott's 'Harp of the North, Farewell,' at the close of the *Lady of the Lake*. The two melodies ought to be read together. 'Dear Harp of my Country' re-echoes the strains of the gentle emblem of Irish music—indeed, of Ireland; while 'Harp of the North, Farewell,' reminds us rather of another instrument, and lets us hear the pibroch through every line. One other word in honour of the songs of Moore. The greatest of his countrymen knew their meaning best. The brilliant orations of Shiell were often begemmed with quotations from them. O'Connell knew their effect on the minds of his audiences, and did not disdain to adorn his massive eloquence with the sentiments with which they abound. These lyrics had, besides this peculiar influence, also a controlling power over the political questions which agitated the public mind when they were first chanted. The apparent applicability of many of the ideas and sentiments in them to the state of Ireland, rendered Irishmen adorers of their author. Ireland inspired the *Irish Melodies*.

A great sorrow befell Moore and Bessy in the year 1817. Their eldest child, Anne Jane Barbara, died at that age—five years old—when a child is so attractive. Her death, it seems, was accelerated by a fall; but the doctors said before, that if she lived it would only be as 'an invalid, from the bad state of her inward parts.' She died at Muswell Hill, and was buried in Hornsey churchyard. They had left Mayfield in Derbyshire by this time.

The following year was a busy and an eventful one to Moore. In the spring he accompanied Rogers to the gay capital of France, and there he gathered up materials for *The Fudge Family in Paris*, a poetical satire in his favourite form of letters from the types of the parties satirized. It is not easy to peruse these effusions now, but they must have been read at the time of their publication with an eagerness which it is far less easy to imagine. Five editions of the *Fudges* were sold in less than a fortnight, and, going half and half with the Longmans, Moore's share of the profits was £350. This enabled him to pay these gentlemen the amount of money he had overdrawn on them, and left him some ready money in his purse besides. Immediately after this Moore paid a visit to Dublin; and there he was lionized to a degree which might have satisfied any heart, however greedy for public acknowledgment of distinguished merit. On the 8th of June he was entertained at dinner in Morison's hotel in that city. This social gathering was brightened by the presence of some of the most distinguished literary and political characters of Ireland at the time.

His father had the happiness of being present to behold all the glory which was shed by his son, and shed on him. Moore delivered two speeches of the carefully-got-up sort on the occasion; but it may be as well now to let them 'sleep in the shade.' In this year also he was brought into very serious trouble by his deputy at Bermuda. He had never drawn much out of the sort of sleeping partnership he held with this individual. Now he was let in for a small fortune to pay. The active partner made off with the proceeds of a ship and cargo which came under his official charge, and left Moore, the responsible partner, saddled with £6000 to answer for. There were many wealthy people, quite able to afford it, who were willing to help him out of this awkward predicament. He would not admit at first of active interference on his behalf in respect of helping him to pay. He wrote to a friend at the time: 'I need not remind you that this is not a case for interference with Sir Walter Scott, or *any one*. The thing must take its course; and any interest you have must be reserved for my *prison comforts*.' It is strange that he should have specified the name of this one man on such an occasion. By and by he, too, showed a similar spirit in a terrific commercial crash under which his great brain reeled, and ultimately staggered without being able to steady itself again. Both Moore and Scott preferred to pay off their debts by the labours of their pens. An attachment was issued against Moore's person by the Admiralty Court; and to escape it he visited Paris again in September 1819. Shortly afterwards he accompanied Lord John Russell—then twenty-six years of age—to Italy. Of this journey we have two accounts, one in prose, the other in rhyme; the former being by far the most interesting. It is headed in his Diary—'An account of my travels in Italy with Lord John Russell, Chantrey the sculptor, Jackson the painter, etc.' The account in verse is well known as *Rhymes on the Road*. Did ever mortal man turn every experience of life into rhyme as did Thomas Moore? His visit to Bermuda, his tour through America, his voyage home, his former visit to Paris, and now his journey to Italy—all reduced to verses! To be a poet, he had the business faculty largely developed. In literature the only parallel to Moore in this respect that occurs readily to mind is a greater than he—the late Charles Dickens. There are many points of resemblance between these two gentlemen. In this journey he went from Paris with Lord John Russell as far as Switzerland, and thence to Milan, where they parted. Moore visited Lord Byron at his abode, La Mira, near Tusina, and went to Venice with him. Byron was living at this time with the Countess Guiccioli, whose appearance Moore did not admire. Childe Harold had grown rather stout. He paid the husband of the Countess £1000, and for this consideration that worthy gentleman was quite agreeable that she should cast in her lot with this particular 'fat Adonis.' After his return from Italy, Moore was joined at Paris by Bessy and the children on the 1st of January 1820. Here he stayed till the Bermuda difficulty was got over. William Howitt, in his

Homes and Haunts of English Poets, tells us that 'the places in which Moore lived in and near Paris were, first, apartments in the Rue Chantereine, where they lived only six weeks, when they removed to a cottage in the Champs Elysées; after that they occupied for some time a cottage of their friends the Villamils, at La Butte Coaslin, near Sèvres. Kenney, the dramatic writer, lived near them, and Washington Irving visited them there. Thence they went back to the Allée des Venves, Champs Elysées, and then back to Sèvres. After that they had lodgings at 17 Rue d'Anjou, Paris; and finally at Passy.'

The Bermuda affair was at length arranged about the close of 1822. The claims against the luckless Registrar were reduced to a thousand guineas. Of this the defaulter's uncle paid £300; Lord John Russell paid £200; and Lord Lansdowne handed a cheque for the remainder, which Moore repaid from the money he received for his poem, *The Loves of the Angels*, which was published in 1823. In this poem, which was much read at the time of its publication, and has been little read since, Moore shadows forth, according to his own account, the fall of 'the soul from its original purity; the loss of light and happiness which it suffers in the pursuit of this world's perishable pleasures; and the punishments, both from conscience and divine justice, with which impurity, pride, and presumptuous inquiry into the awful secrets of God are sure to be visited.' It is the same style of poem, or rather the ideas hover about the same imaginary period and state of created existence, as we encounter in Byron's *Mystery of Heaven and Earth*, which is professedly founded on the text Gen. vi. 2: 'The sons of God saw the daughters of men that they were fair; and they took them wives of all which they chose.' Moore says he had been for about two years pondering his subject, which he does not profess to found on this text; and when he heard that Byron was treating it dramatically, he brought out his *Loves of the Angels* rather hurriedly. It records that, 'when the world was in its prime,'—

> 'One evening, in the time of bloom,
> On a hill's side, where hung the ray
> Of sunset, sleeping in perfume,
> Three noble youths conversing lay.'

And these three angels tell each his story. This is all the structure that is in Moore's poem, while Byron's is carefully built, and has a certain degree of dramatic movement, with its three angels, three men, and two women. Nor is Moore's poem to be compared with Byron's for power.

After returning to England, Moore took up his residence at Sloperton Cottage, near Devizes, within easy reach of Bowood, the seat of his new patron and good kind friend, Lord Lansdowne. This was done at his lordship's special request. In this cottage Moore lived for the remaining thirty years of his life.

Our poet was now a man in the prime of life—forty-three years of age

He had already carved his name on his generation. Henceforth he does a good deal of real work, while at the same time he lives as a man of fashion —dining, dancing, and singing with the great and noble of the land, and only with them.

As one wanders through the Diary of Thomas Moore, he feels the truth of Lord John Russell's remark, that the defect of this Journal is, that 'while he is at great pains to put in writing the stories and the jokes he hears, he seldom records a serious discussion, or notices the instructive portion of the conversations in which he bore a part.' If the best that Moore perpetuates contains the choicest specimens of the wit and wisdom displayed at Bowood, at Rogers' breakfast-table, or at dinner in Holland House, surely high society and high soul are separable. If any soaring intellect ever rested at these gatherings, either its wings were clipped, or Moore ignored its presence. What time and talent he must have wasted over the miserable gilding of fusionless gingerbread! Of course it would savour of profanity to allude with the remotest intention to the eminent Whig families—the Russells, the Lansdownes, and the Hollands—when one makes a remark like this. Lord John Russell is apparently touchy on this question, and he gives in his preface such an account of Lord Holland, and the hospitality he was wont to dispense, as is intended to set such a supposition aside for ever. But all the great— Society's great—are not wise. There was a rabble of the titled people whom Moore dearly loved, who looked upon him exactly as their predecessors in social rank had looked upon the fool or the jester. The Duke and Duchess of Bedford both expressed the fond wish, that 'they had some one like Mr. Moore to be agreeable when they got to their inn in the evening.' And yet the blinded little proud man was too vain to be aware of the use he was being put to. He looked down upon literary men, however eminent, if he could not recognise them as people he had met at these humiliating tables of the great. He tells us in his Diary, that he met at Dr. Bowring's house some first-rate *literati*, not one of whom he knew by name. This gives us a hint, by the way, of a miserable limit to Moore's general reading. Probably for years he read nothing but what he wrote or wrote about. He could not make the twenty-four hours any longer than another man, even by the process of taking 'a few hours from the night.' He was once disgusted, at the house of Martin the painter, to find himself in the company of mere *literati*. This is sad; and yet it was not all bad. Butterflies have their mission as well as busy bees; and, in a strange way, Moore combined the qualities of these two insects. Neither poverty nor sorrow could lessen in him the sense of the pleasure of being smiled on and flattered by individuals in that class of society to which he had consecrated the energies of his life. One effect of this moth-like fluttering about aristocratic candles is worth noting. The minstrel who sang so many songs about liberty; the man who, in his youth, had come so honourably out of that grim visitation of Trinity College; the friend and companion of Lord John Russell; the guest of the great Whig families, cordially hated the great Reform Bill. Lord John Russell remarks on how singular it was that Mr. Moore should have been one of the gloomy prophets who predicted revolution and calamity as the consequences of the Reform Act.

Little remains now to be done, in a sketchy biography like this, but to give a hasty catalogue of some of Moore's other writings. In the same year (1823) in which he published *The Loves of the Angels*, the *Fables of the Holy Alliance* were issued. *The Memoirs of Captain Rock* were brought out during the following year. This is the designation adopted by the 'Rob Roys' of Ireland. Moore's reputation as a prose writer was enhanced in 1825 by his *Biography of Richard Brinsley Sheridan*, —a work for which he had superior sources of information, and which may be regarded as the memoir of a poet by a poet, done in very poetical style. It was in this year that Moore visited Scott at Abbotsford. He came to Edinburgh on the occasion, did all the sights and celebrities, and had his vanity gratified to the fulness of his bent. He writes in his Diary: 'Went to the Courts after breakfast: found out Jeffrey, and walked about with him to see everything, being myself the greatest show of the place, and followed by crowds from Court to Court. Had the pleasure of seeing Scott sitting at his table. Jeffrey asked him to dine to meet me. I begged of Jeffrey to dine pretty early, in order that I might see the theatre. Met Scott afterwards, and told him the arrangement. "Very well," he said, " I'll order my carriage to come at eight o'clock, and I'll just step down to the playhouse with you myself."' Lockhart went with them. It is related that a man in the pit, recognising them, cried out, 'Eh! eh! yon's Sir Walter wi' Lockhart and his wife; and wha's the wee body wi' the pawky een? Wow, but it's Tam Moore just.' Moore's Diary is comparatively lengthy regarding this visit. It contains some rather improbable statements. He says Scott 'spoke of the powers of all Irishmen for oratory; the Scotch, on the contrary, cannot speak; no Scotch orator can be named; no Scotch actors.' If Scott said all this to Moore, he must have been blarneying a bit. *The Epicurean* was published in 1827. This work was one of his many meditations while he was in Paris in 1822. When he lived at La Butte Coaslin, near Sèvres, he was in the habit of strolling in the noble park of St. Cloud—alas for its nobleness now!—with his pocket-book and pencil, composing verses and pondering on the *Epicurean*. This is an Oriental tale in prose. It is a book that should be more widely known: it sends that thrill through the reader occasionally which only genius can leave lurking in the lines of a story. But by far the most valuable of his prose works is *The Letters and Journals of Lord Byron, with Notices of his Life*. This was issued in 1830. There is not a more interesting piece of biographical work in the English language. Murray the bookseller supplied a good many of the materials, and gave Moore four hundred guineas for the work when it was done. Moore took pains with this biography, amounting almost to a work of atonement. There was good reason for this. One of the few thorny controversies of his life had reference to an autobiography of himself which Byron gave Moore as a legacy about the year 1820, and which he was to publish after the noble poet's death, and the profits of this fine inheritance would of course be his own. But our poet was often in straits for money; here was something which could easily be discounted. Accordingly, he sold it to Murray for two thousand guineas. So far there is not much wrong. In Murray's hands, the autobiography was safe for the public. But when Byron died, his relatives seem to have had strange fears of disclosures from it; and they urged Moore to redeem the manuscript from Murray by paying back the two thousand guineas. He did so, and destroyed the precious inheritance. How short-sighted the policy of the friends was, we have seen in our own day. This manuscript might have prevented Mrs. Stowe from ever writing about Byron; or it might have foreclosed any reply to her strictures. A worse charge brought against Moore in our day, is that he burnt also a portion of the continuation of *Don Juan*. This can only be referred to in passing here. If it could be proved to be true, it would stamp Tom Moore indelibly as the most unfaithful snob and pretentious prig who ever was made a literary executor. In 1831 Moore entered the bookselling market afresh twice. His first venture was *A Summer Fête*, in poetry. The second was a *Memoir of Lord Edward Fitzgerald*. This latter work was peculiarly acceptable to the patriotic party in Ireland. In 1833 appeared the *Travels of an Irish Gentleman in Search of a Religion*. This work displays an amount of theological learning which would be astonishing, if we did not remember his article in the *Edinburgh Review*, long before this, on the Christian Fathers. Dr. Doyle said of it: 'If St. Augustine were more orthodox, and Scratchinbach less plausible, it is a book of which any of us might be proud.'

Regarding the religion professed by Moore during his life, Lord John Russell tells us that 'he occasionally attended the Protestant Church; he had his children baptized into that Church; and when the Head of his own Church was restored to his throne, he dreaded the consequences of that triumph to the liberty which he prized. Yet he always adhered to the Roman Catholic Church, and when in London attended the Roman Catholic chapel in Wardour Street. His answer to a person who tried to convert him to Protestantism, was nearly in these terms: "I was born and bred in the faith of my fathers, and in that faith I intend to die." In that intention he persevered to the end. Of two things all who knew him must have been persuaded: the one, his strong feelings of devotion, his aspirations, his longing for life and immortality, and his submission to the will of God; the other, his love of his neighbour, his charity, his Samaritan kindness for the distressed, his goodwill to all men. In the last days of his life he frequently repeated to his wife, "Lean upon God, Bessy; lean upon God." That God is love was the summary of his belief; that a man should love his neighbour as himself, seems to have been the rule of his life.' There is something as beautiful as it is simple in Thomas Moore's religion.

In 1835, *A History of Ireland* by our prolific author was published; and, six years later, he commenced that collection of his works which is the usual occupation of prolific authors who live to a good old age. Moore was now sixty-two years old. His poetical works, which were those included in this re-issue, extended to ten volumes. There are many more products of our poet's pen to be put down in the record of his industry, but space, in this short account of his life and works, calls a halt here. It is generally known that Swift, Southey, and Scott, each suffered, while still he existed among men on earth, an eclipse of that light from heaven which placed them among the stars which shine in the firmament. So also did Moore. In 1846 we read the following inexpressibly sad entry in the Diary of this man, who had lived a life so gay: 'I still continue to take my Diary down from Bessy's dictation, and a mournful task it now begins to be, though (such is life!) the very first item I have now to enter is a gay ball at our neighbours the Schombergs, January 1, 1846, where I was one of the guests.' He 'still continues' to write to Bessy's dictation! Was there ever such a wife? The end, which is drawing near, may as well be expressed in the gentle words of Moore's noble biographer. Lord John Russell says: 'The latter years of Moore were clouded by loss of memory, and a helplessness almost childish; yet he preserved his interest about his friends; and when I saw him for the last time, on the 20th of December 1849, he spoke rationally, agreeably, and kindly on all those subjects which were the topics of our conversation. But the death of his sister Ellen, and of his two sons, seem to have saddened his heart and obscured his intellect. The wit which sparkled so brightly, the gaiety which threw such sunshine over society, the readiness of reply, the quickness of recollection, all that marked the poet and the wit, were gone. As we left his house, Lord Lansdowne remarked that he had not seen him so well for a long time; Mrs. Moore has since made to me the same observation. But that very evening he had a fit, from the effects of which he never recovered. The light of his intellect grew still more dim; his memory failed still more; yet there never was a total extinction of that bright flame. To the last day of his life, he would inquire with anxiety about the health of his friends, and would sing, or ask his wife to sing to him, the favourite airs of his past days. Even the day before his death he "warbled," as Mrs. Moore expressed it; and a fond love of music never left him but with life. On the 26th February 1852 he expired, calmly and without pain, at Sloperton Cottage. His body was interred within the neighbouring churchyard of Bromham, where the remains of two of his children had been deposited. The funeral was quite private, as no doubt he would have desired.' The death of Moore's eldest child has been mentioned. His second daughter, Anastatia Mary, died in 1829, at nearly seventeen years of age—a fierce calamity. She was buried at Bromham, as was also her brother John Russell, Moore's second son, who died in 1842, at the age of nineteen. In that churchyard the poet and these two beloved children sleep in peace. Russell had secured a cadetship in the East India Company's Service, but he could not stand the climate of that country. It exhausted him in eighteen months. Olivia Mary, the third daughter whom Bessy bore to her idolized husband, lived only a few months. Moore's eldest son, Thomas Lansdowne Parr, was a great sorrow to him, and was the grief of his mother. This son's wildness, and his death in 1846 from consumption, at Mostaganem, a town of Algeria, where he was in the military service of Louis Philippe, after dissipation and the climate of India had rendered him incapable of discharging his duty to his own country in the East, had a terrible effect on the failing mind of the poet. Thus all his children died before him. The ages of those who did not go astray, and the errors of the one prodigal, had each an element of poignant sorrow. Moore left for the benefit of his lonely widow his *Memoirs, Journals, and Correspondence*. These, as edited by Lord John Russell, secured for the good Bessy £3000. In 1835 the Government had granted Moore a pension of £300 a year. Two years before his death a further pension of £100 a year was granted to Bessy. After his death she lived nearly fourteen years, having died on the 4th of September 1865, aged sixty-eight.

LALLA ROOKH:

AN ORIENTAL ROMANCE.

———◆———

TO

SAMUEL ROGERS, Esq.,

THIS VOLUME IS DEDICATED

BY

ITS VERY GRATEFUL AND AFFECTIONATE FRIEND,

THOMAS MOORE.

LALLA ROOKH.

IN the eleventh year of the reign of Aurungzebe, Abdalla, King of the Lesser Bucharia, a lineal descendant from the Great Zingis, having abdicated the throne in favour of his son, set out on a pilgrimage to the Shrine of the Prophet, and, passing into India through the delightful valley of Cashmere, rested for a short time at Delhi on his way. He was entertained by Aurungzebe in a style of magnificent hospitality, worthy alike of the visitor and the host, and was afterwards escorted with the same splendour to Surat, where he embarked for Arabia. During the stay of the Royal Pilgrim at Delhi, a marriage was agreed upon between the Prince, his son, and the youngest daughter of the Emperor, Lalla Rookh,[1]—a princess described by the poets of her time as more beautiful than Leila, Shirine, Dewildé, or any of those heroines whose names and loves embellish the songs of Persia and Hindostan. It was intended that the nuptials should be celebrated at Cashmere, where the young king, as soon as the cares of the empire would permit, was to meet for the first time his lovely bride, and, after a few months' repose in that enchanting valley, conduct her over the snowy hills into Bucharia.

The day of Lalla Rookh's departure from Delhi was as splendid as sunshine and pageantry could make it. The bazaars and baths were all covered with the richest tapestry; hundreds of gilded barges upon the Jumna floated with their banners shining in the water; while through the streets groups of beautiful children went strewing the most delicious flowers around, as in that Persian festival called Gul Reazee, or the Scattering of the Roses, till every part of the city was as fragrant as if a caravan of musk from Khoten had passed through it. The Princess, having taken leave of her kind father,—who at parting hung a carnelian of Yemen round her neck, on which was inscribed a verse from the Koran,—and having sent a considerable present to the Fakirs, who kept up the perpetual lamp in her sister's tomb, meekly ascended the palankeen prepared for her; and while Aurungzebe stood to take a last look from his balcony, the procession moved slowly on the road to Lahore.

Seldom had the Eastern world seen a cavalcade so superb. From the gardens in the suburbs to the imperial palace it was one unbroken line of splendour. The gallant appearance of the Rajahs and Mogul lords, distinguished by those insignia of the Emperor's favour,[2] the feathers of the egret of Cashmere in their turbans, and the small silver-rimmed kettle-drums at the bows of their saddles;—the costly armour of their cavaliers, who vied on this occasion with the guards of the great Keder Khan,[3] in the brightness of their silver battle-axes and the massiness of their maces of gold;—the glittering of the gilt pine-apples[4] on the

---

[1] 'Tulip Cheek.
[2] 'One mark of honour or knighthood bestowed by the Emperor is the permission to wear a small kettle-drum at the bows of their saddles, which at first was invented for the training of hawks, and is worn in the field by all sportsmen for that end.'—*Fryer's Travels.*
Those on whom the king has conferred the privilege must wear an ornament of jewels on the right side of the turban, surmounted by a high plume of the feathers of a kind of egret.'—*Elphinstone's Account of Caubul.*

[3] 'Khedar Khan, the Khakan, or King of Turquestan, beyond the Gihon (at the end of the eleventh century), whenever he appeared abroad, was preceded by seven hundred horsemen with silver battle-axes, and was followed by an equal number bearing maces of gold.'—*Richardson's Dissertation prefixed to his Dictionary.*
[4] 'The kubdeh, a large golden knob, generally in the shape of a pine-apple, on the top of the canopy over the litter or palanquin.'—*Scott's Notes on the Bahar-danush.*

tops of the palankeens;—the embroidered trappings of the elephants, bearing on their backs small turrets, in the shape of little antique temples, within which the ladies of Lalla Rookh lay, as it were, enshrined;—the rose-coloured veils[1] of the Princess's own sumptuous litter, at the front of which a fair young female slave sat fanning her through the curtains with feathers of the Argus pheasant's wing;—and the lovely troop of Tartarian and Cashmerian maids of honour, whom the young king had sent to accompany his bride, and who rode on each side of the litter, upon small Arabian horses;—all was brilliant, tasteful, and magnificent, and pleased even the critical and fastidious Fadladeen, Great Nazir or Chamberlain of the Haram, who was borne in his palankeen immediately after the Princess, and considered himself not the least important personage of the pageant.

Fadladeen was a judge of everything—from the pencilling of a Circassian's eyelids to the deepest questions of science and literature; from the mixture of a conserve of rose-leaves to the composition of an epic poem; and such influence had his opinion upon the various tastes of the day, that all the cooks and poets of Delhi stood in awe of him. His political conduct and opinions were founded upon that line of Sadi: 'Should the Prince at noonday say, "It is night," declare that you behold the moon and stars.' And his zeal for religion,[2] of which Aurungzebe was a munificent protector, was about as disinterested as that of the goldsmith who fell in love with the diamond eyes of the idol of Jaghernaut.[3]

During the first days of their journey, Lalla Rookh, who had passed all her life within the shadow of the royal gardens of Delhi, found enough in the beauty of the scenery through which they passed to interest her mind and delight her imagination; and when, at evening or in the heat of the day, they turned off from the high road to those retired and romantic places which had been selected for her encampments,—sometimes on the banks of a small rivulet, as clear as the waters of the Lake of Pearl;[4] sometimes under the sacred shade of a Banian tree, from which the view opened upon a glade covered with antelopes; and often in those hidden, embowered spots, described by one from the Isles of the West[5] as 'places of melancholy, delight, and safety, where all the company around was wild peacocks and turtle-doves,'—she felt a charm in these scenes, so lovely and so new to her, which for a time made her indifferent to every other amusement. But Lalla Rookh was young, and the young love variety; nor could the conversation of her ladies and the great chamberlain Fadladeen (the only persons, of course, admitted to her pavilion) sufficiently enliven those many vacant hours which were devoted neither to the pillow nor the palankeen. There was a little Persian slave who sung sweetly to the vina, and who now and then lulled the Princess to sleep with the ancient ditties of her country, about the loves of Wamak and Ezra,[6] the fair-haired Zal and his mistress Rodahver;[7] not forgetting the combat of Rustam with the terrible White

---

[1] In the poem of Zohair, in the Moallakat, there is the following lively description of 'a company of maidens seated on camels:'—
'They are mounted in carriages covered with costly awnings and with rose-coloured veils, the linings of which have the hue of crimson Andemwood.
'When they ascend from the bosom of the vale, they sit forward on the saddle-cloths with every mark of a voluptuous gaiety.
'Now, when they have reached the brink of yon blue gushing rivulet, they fix the poles of their tents like the Arabs with a settled mansion.'

[2] This hypocritical Emperor would have made a worthy associate of certain Holy Leagues. 'He held the cloak of religion,' says Dow, 'between his actions and the vulgar; and impiously thanked the Divinity for a success which he owed to his own wickedness. When he was murdering and persecuting his brothers and their families, he was building a magnificent mosque at Delhi, as an offering to God for His assistance to him in the civil wars. He acted as high priest at the consecration of this temple, and made a practice of attending divine service there, in the humble dress of a fakeer. But when he lifted one hand to the Divinity, he with the other signed warrants for the assassination of his relations.'—*History of Hindostan*, vol. iii. p. 285. See also the curious letter of Aurungzebe given in the *Oriental Collections*, vol. i. p. 320.

[3] 'The Idol at Jaghernat has two fine diamonds for eyes. No goldsmith is suffered to enter the pagoda, one having stolen one of these eyes, being locked up all night with the idol.'—*Tavernier*.

[4] 'In the neighbourhood is Notte Gill, or the Lake of Pearl, which receives this name from its pellucid water.'—*Pennant's Hindostan*.

[5] Sir Thomas Roe, ambassador from James I. to Jehanguire.

[6] 'The Romance *Wamakweazra*, written in Persian verse, which contains the loves of Wamak and Ezra, two celebrated lovers who lived before the time of Mohammed.'—*Note on the Oriental Tales*.

[7] There is much beauty in the passage which describes the slaves of Rodahver sitting on the bank of the river and throwing flowers into the stream in order to draw the attention of the young hero who is encamped on the opposite side.—*Vide Champion's Translation of the Shah Namêh of Ferdousi*.

Demon.¹ At other times she was amused by those graceful dancing girls of Delhi, who had been permitted by the Brahmins of the Great Pagoda to attend her, much to the horror of the good Mussulman Fadladeen, who could see nothing graceful or agreeable in idolaters, and to whom the very tinkling of their golden anklets² was an abomination.

But these and many other diversions were repeated till they lost all their charm, and the nights and noondays were beginning to move heavily, when at length it was recollected that, among the attendants sent by the bridegroom, was a young poet of Cashmere, much celebrated throughout the valley for his manner of reciting the stories of the East, on whom his royal master had conferred the privilege of being admitted to the pavilion of the Princess, that he might help to beguile the tediousness of the journey by some of his most agreeable recitals. At the mention of a poet, Fadladeen elevated his critical eyebrows ; and having refreshed his faculties with a dose of that delicious opium³ which is distilled from the black poppy of the Thebais, gave orders for the minstrel to be forthwith introduced into the presence.

The Princess, who had once in her life seen a poet from behind the screens of gauze in her father's hall, and had conceived from that specimen no very favourable ideas of the caste, expected but little in this new exhibition to interest her. She felt inclined, however, to alter her opinion on the very first appearance of Feramorz. He was a youth about Lalla Rookh's own age, and graceful as that idol of women, Chrishna⁴ (the Indian Apollo),—such as he appears to their young imaginations, heroic, beautiful, breathing music from his very eyes, and exalting the religion of his worshippers into love. His dress was simple, yet not without some marks of costliness ; and the ladies of the Princess were not long in discovering that the cloth which encircled his high Tartarian cap was of the most delicate kind that the shawl-goats of Tibet supply. Here and there, too, over his vest, which was confined by a flowered girdle of Kashan, hung strings of fine pearl, disposed with an air of studied negligence ; nor did the exquisite embroidery of his sandals escape the observation of these fair critics, who, however they might give way to Fadladeen upon the unimportant topics of religion and government, had the spirit of martyrs in everything relating to such momentous matters as jewels and embroidery.

For the purpose of relieving the pauses of recitation by music, the young Cashmerian held in his hand a kitar,—such as in old times the Arab maids of the west used to listen to by moonlight in the gardens of the Alhambra ; and having premised, with much humility, that the story he was about to relate was founded on the adventures of that Veiled Prophet of Khorassan,⁵ who in the year of the Hegira 163 created such alarm throughout the Eastern Empire, made an obeisance to the Princess, and thus began :—

---

¹ Rustam is the Hercules of the Persians. For the particulars of his victory over the Sepoed Deeve, or White Demon, see *Oriental Collections*, vol. ii. p. 45. Near the city of Shiraz is an immense quadrangular monument in commemoration of this combat, called the 'Kelaat-i-Deev Sepeed,' or Castle of the White Giant, which Father Angelo, in his *Gazophylacium Persicum*, p. 127, declares to have been the most memorable monument of antiquity which he had seen in Persia.—*Vide Ouseley's Persian Miscellanies.*

² 'The women of the idol, or dancing girls of the pagoda, have little golden bells fastened to their feet, the soft harmonious tinkling of which vibrates in unison with the exquisite melody of their voices.'— *Maurice's Indian Antiquities.* The Arabian princesses wear golden rings on their fingers, to which little bells are suspended, as well as in the flowing tresses of their hair, that their superior rank may be known.—*Vide Calmet's Dictionary*, art. *Bells.*

³ 'Abou-Tige, ville de la Thebaïde, où il croit beaucoup de pavot noir, dont se fait le meilleur opium.'— *D'Herbelot.*

⁴ 'He and the three Rámas are described as youths of perfect beauty; and the princesses of Hindustán were all passionately in love with rishna, who continues to this hour the darling god of the Indian women.'—*Sir W. Jones, on the Gods of Greece, Italy, and India.*

⁵ For the real history of this impostor, whose original name was Hakem ben Haschem, and who was called Mokanna from the veil of silver gauze (or, as others say, golden) which he always wore. *vide D'Herbelot.*

THE VEILED PROPHET OF KHORASSAN.[1]

In that delightful Province of the Sun,
The first of Persian lands he shines upon,
Where all the loveliest children of his beam,
Flowerets and fruits,[2] blush over every stream,
And, fairest of all streams, the Murga roves
Among Merou's[3] bright palaces and groves;—
There on that throne, to which the blind belief
Of millions raised him, sat the Prophet-Chief,
The Great Mokanna. O'er his features hung
The veil, the silver veil, which he had flung
In mercy there, to hide from mortal sight
His dazzling brow, till man could bear its light.
For, far less luminous, his votaries said,[4]
Were even the gleams miraculously shed
O'er Moussa's[5] cheek, when down the Mount he trod,
All glowing from the presence of his God!

On either side, with ready hearts and hands,
His chosen guard of bold Believers stands;
Young fire-eyed disputants, who deem their swords,
On points of faith, more eloquent than words;
And such their zeal, there's not a youth with brand
Uplifted there, but, at the Chief's command,
Would make his own devoted heart its sheath,
And bless the lips that doomed so dear a death!
In hatred to the Caliph's hue of night,[6]
Their vesture, helms and all, is snowy white;
Their weapons various—some equipp'd, for speed,
With javelins of the light Kathaian reed;[7]
Or bows of buffalo horn, and shining quiver
Filled with the stems[8] that bloom on Iran's rivers;
While some, for war's more terrible attacks,
Wield the huge mace and ponderous battle-axe;
And as they wave aloft in morning's beam
The milk-white plumage of their helms, they seem

Like a chenar-tree grove,[9] when winter throws
O'er all its tufted heads his feathering snows.

Between the porphyry pillars, that uphold
The rich moresque-work of the roof of gold,
Aloft the Haram's curtained galleries rise,
Where, through the silken network, glancing eyes
From time to time, like sudden gleams that glow
Through autumn clouds, shine o'er the pomp below.
What impious tongue, ye blushing saints, would dare
To hint that aught but Heaven hath placed you there?
Or that the loves of this light world could bind,
In their gross chain, your Prophet's soaring mind?
No—wrongful thought!—commissioned from above
To people Eden's bowers with shapes of love,
(Creatures so bright that the same lips and eyes
They wear on earth will serve in Paradise,)
There to recline among Heaven's native maids,
And crown th' Elect with bliss that never fades—
Well hath the Prophet-Chief his bidding done;
And every beauteous race beneath the sun,
From those who kneel at Brahma's burning founts,[10]
To the fresh nymphs bounding o'er Yemen's mounts;
From Persia's eyes of full and fawn-like ray,
To the small, half-shut glances of Kathay;[11]
And Georgia's bloom, and Azab's darker smiles,
And the gold ringlets of the Western Isles;
All, all are there;—each land its flower hath given,
To form that fair young nursery for Heaven!

But why this pageant now? this armed array?
What triumph crowds the rich Divan to-day

---

[1] 'Khorassan signifies, in the old Persian language, Province or Region of the Sun.'—*Sir W. Jones.*

[2] 'The fruits of Meru are finer than those of any other place; and one cannot see in any other such palaces, with groves, and streams, and gardens.'—*Ebn Haukal's Geography.*

[3] One of the royal cities of Khorassan.

[4] 'Ses disciples assuraient qu'il se couvroit le visage pour ne pas éblouir ceux qui l'approchoit par l'éclat de son visage, comme Moyse.'—*D'Herbelot.*

[5] Moses.

[6] Black was the colour adopted by the Caliphs of the House of Abbas, in their garments, turbans, and standards. 'Il faut remarquer ici touchant les habits blancs des disciples de Hakem, que la couleur des habits, des coiffures, et des étendards des Khalifes Abassides étant la noire, ce chef de rebelles ne pouvait pas choisir une que lui fût plus opposée.'—*D'Herbelot.*

[7] 'Our dark javelins, exquisitely wrought of Kathaian reeds, slender and delicate.'—*Poem of Amru.*

[8] Pichula, used anciently for arrows by the Persians. The Persians call this plant Gaz. The celebrated shaft of Isfendiar, one of their ancient heroes, was made of it. 'Nothing can be more beautiful than the appearance of this plant in flower during the rains on the banks of rivers, where it is usually interwoven with a lovely twining asclepias.'—*Sir W. Jones, Botanical Observations.*

[9] The oriental plane. 'The chenar is a delightful tree: its bole is of a fine white and smooth bark; and its foliage, which grows in a tuft at the summit, is of a bright green.'—*Morier's Travels.*

[10] The burning fountains of Brahma near Chittogong, esteemed as holy.—*Turner.*

[11] China.

With turbaned heads, of every hue and race,
Bowing before that veiled and awful face,
Like tulip-beds,¹ of different shapes and dyes,
Bending beneath th' invisible west-wind's sighs!
What new-made mystery now, for Faith to sign,
And blood to seal, as genuine and divine,—
What dazzling mimicry of God's own power,
Hath the bold Prophet plann'd to grace this hour?
Not such the pageant now, though not less
  proud;
Yon warrior youth, advancing from the crowd,
With silver bow, with belt of broidered crape,
And fur-bound bonnet ² of Bucharian shape,
So fiercely beautiful in form and eye,
Like war's wild planet in a summer sky;
That youth to-day,—a proselyte, worth hordes
Of cooler spirits and less practised swords,—
Is come to join, all bravery and belief,
The creed and standard of the Heaven-sent Chief.

Though few his years, the West already knows
Young Azim's fame;—beyond th' Olympian
  snows,
Ere manhood darkened o'er his downy cheek,
O'erwhelmed in fight, and captive to the Greek,³
He linger'd there, till peace dissolved his chains;—
Oh! who could, even in bondage, tread the
  plains
Of glorious Greece, nor feel his spirit rise
Kindling within him? who, with heart and eyes,
Could walk where Liberty had been, nor see
The shining footprints of her Deity,
Nor feel those godlike breathings in the air
Which mutely told her spirit had been there?
Not he, that youthful warrior,—no, too well
For his soul's quiet worked th' awakening spell;
And now, returning to his own dear land,
Full of those dreams of good that, vainly grand,
Haunt the young heart,—proud views of human-
  kind,
Of men to gods exalted and refined,—
False views, like that horizon's fair deceit,
Where earth and heaven but *seem*, alas, to meet!—
Soon as he heard an arm divine was raised
To right the nations, and beheld, emblazed
On the white flag, Mokanna's host unfurl'd,
Those words of sunshine, 'Freedom to the
  World,'

At once his faith, his sword, his soul obey'd
Th' inspiring summons; every chosen blade
That fought beneath that banner's sacred text
Seem'd doubly edged, for this world and the next;
And ne'er did Faith with her smooth bandage
  bind
Eyes more devoutly willing to be blind
In Virtue's cause;—never was soul inspired
With livelier trust in what it most desired,
Than his, th' enthusiast there, who kneeling, pale
With pious awe, before that silver veil,
Believes the form to which he bends his knee
Some pure, redeeming angel, sent to free
This fetter'd world from every bond and stain,
And bring its primal glories back again!

Low as young Azim knelt, that motley crowd
Of all earth's nations sunk the knee and bowed,
With shouts of 'Alla!' echoing long and loud;
While high in air, above the Prophet's head,
Hundreds of banners, to the sunbeam spread,
Waved, like the wings of the white birds that
  fan
The flying throne of star-taught Soliman.⁴
Then thus he spoke:—' Stranger, though new
  the frame
Thy soul inhabits now, I've tracked its flame
For many an age,⁵ in every chance and change
Of that existence through whose varied range,—
As through a torch-race, where, from hand to
  hand,
The flying youths transmit their shining brand,—
From frame to frame the unextinguished soul
Rapidly passes, till it reach the goal!

' Nor think 'tis only the gross spirits, warmed
With duskier fire and for earth's medium formed,
That run this course;—beings the most divine
Thus deign through dark mortality to shine.
Such was the Essence that in Adam dwelt,
To which all heaven, except the Proud One,
  knelt;⁶
Such the refined Intelligence that glowed
In Moussa's frame—and, thence descending,
  flowed
Through many a prophet's breast;⁷—in Issa ⁸
  shone,
And in Mohammed burned; till hastening on,

---

¹ 'The name of tulip is said to be of Turkish ex-
traction, and given to the flower on account of its resembling a turban.'—*Deckmann's History of Inventions*.
² 'The inhabitants of Bucharia wear a round cloth
bonnet, shaped much after the Polish fashion, having
a large fur border. They tie their kaftans about the
middle with a girdle of a kind of silk crape, several times
round the body.'—*Independent Tartary, in Pinkerton's Col.*
³ In the war of the Caliph Mahadi against the Empress Irene, for an account of which, *vide Gibbon*, vol. x.
⁴ This wonderful throne was called the 'Star of the
Genii.' When Soliman travelled, the Eastern writers
say, ' he had a carpet of green silk on which his throne
was placed, being of a prodigious length and breadth,
and sufficient for all his forces to stand upon—the men
placing themselves on his right hand, and the spirits
on his left; and that, when all were in order, the wind,

at his command, took up the carpet, and transported it,
with all that were upon it, wherever he pleased; the
army of ... at the same time flying over their heads,
and forming a kind of canopy to shade them from the
sun.'—*Sale's Koran*, vol. ii. p. 214, *note*.
⁵ 'The transmigration of souls was one of his doctrines.'
⁶ 'And when we said unto the angels, 'Worship Adam,'
they all worshipped him except Eblis (Lucifer), who
refused.—*The Koran*, chap. ii.
⁷ This is according to D'Herbelot's account of the doctrines of Mokanna:—' Sa doctrine étoit que Dieu avoit
pris une forme et figure humaine, depuis qu'il ent com-
mandé aux Anges d'adorer Adam, le premier des
hommes. Qu' après la mort d'Adam, Dieu étoit apparu

⁸ Jesus.

(As a bright river that, from fall to fall
In many a maze descending, bright through all,
Finds some fair region where, each labyrinth
 past,
In one full lake of light it rests at last),
That Holy Spirit, settling calm and free
From lapse or shadow, centres all in me!'

Again, throughout th' assembly at these words
Thousands of voices rung: the warriors' swords
Were pointed up to heaven; a sudden wind
In th' open banners played, and from behind
Those Persian hangings, that but ill could screen
The Haram's loveliness, white hands were seen
Waving embroidered scarves, whose motion gave
A perfume forth—like those the Houris wave
When beckoning to their bowers th' immortal
 brave.

'But these,' pursued the Chief, 'are truths
 sublime,
That claim a holier mood and calmer time
Than earth allows us now;—this sword must
 first
The darkling prison-house of mankind burst,
Ere Peace can visit them, or Truth let in
Her wakening daylight on a world of sin.
But then,—celestial warriors, then, when all
Earth's shrines and thrones before our banner fall;
When the glad slave shall at these feet lay down
His broken chain, the tyrant lord his crown,
The priest his book, the conqueror his wreath,
And from the lips of Truth one mighty breath
Shall, like a whirlwind, scatter in its breeze
That whole dark pile of human mockeries;—
Then shall the reign of Mind commence on earth,
And, starting fresh as from a second birth,
Man, in the sunshine of the world's new spring,
Shall walk transparent, like some holy thing!
Then, too, your Prophet from his angel brow
Shall cast the veil that hides its splendours now,
And gladdened earth shall, through her wide
 expanse,
Bask in the glories of this countenance!

'For thee, young warrior, welcome!—thou
 hast yet
Some tasks to learn, some frailties to forget,
Ere the white war-plume o'er thy brow can wave;
But, once my own, mine all till in the grave!'

The pomp is at an end; the crowds are gone;
Each ear and heart still haunted by the tone
Of that deep voice, which thrill'd like Alla's own!
The Young all dazzled by the plumes and lances,
The glittering throne, and Haram's half-caught
 glances;

The Old deep pondering on the promised reign
Of peace and truth; and all the female train
Ready to risk their eyes, could they but gaze
A moment on that brow's miraculous blaze!

But there was one, among the chosen maids,
Who blushed behind the gallery's silken shades—
One to whose soul the pageant of to-day
Has been like death;—you saw her pale dismay,
Ye wondering sisterhood, and heard the burst
Of exclamation from her lips, when first
She saw that youth, too well, too dearly known,
Silently kneeling at the Prophet's throne.

Ah, Zelica! there was a time when bliss
Shone o'er thy heart from every look of his;
When but to see him, hear him, breathe the air
In which he dwelt, was thy soul's fondest
 prayer;
When round him hung such a perpetual spell,
Whate'er he did, none ever did so well.
Too happy days! when, if he touched a flower
Or gem of thine, 'twas sacred from that hour;
When thou didst study him till every tone
And gesture and dear look became thy own,—
Thy voice like his, the changes of his face
In thine reflected with still lovelier grace,
Like echo, sending back sweet music, fraught
With twice th' aerial sweetness it had brought!
Yet now he comes—brighter than even he
E'er beamed before—but, ah! not bright for thee;
No—dread, unlooked for, like a visitant
From th' other world, he comes as if to haunt
Thy guilty soul with dreams of lost delight,
Long lost to all but memory's aching sight:—
Sad dreams! as when the spirit of our youth
Returns in sleep, sparkling with all the truth
And innocence once ours, and leads us back,
In mournful mockery, o'er the shining track
Of our young life, and points out every ray
Of hope and peace we've lost upon the way!

Once happy pair!—in proud Bokhara's groves,
Who had not heard of their first youthful loves?
Born by that ancient flood,[1] which from its
 spring
In the Dark Mountains swiftly wandering,
Enriched by every pilgrim brook that shines
With relics from Bucharia's ruby mines,
And, lending to the Caspian half its strength,
In the cold Lake of Eagles sinks at length;—
There, on the banks of that bright river born,
The flowers that hung above its wave at morn
Blessed not the waters, as they murmured by
With holier scent and lustre than the sigh
And virgin glance of first affection cast
Upon their youth's smooth current, as it passed!

---

sous la figure de plusieurs prophètes, et autres grands hommes qu'il avoit choisis, jusqu'à ce qu'il prit celle d'Abu Moslem, Prince de Khorassan, lequel professoit l'erreur de la Tenassukhiah ou Métempsychose; et qu' après la mort de ce Prince, la Divinité étoit passée et descendue en sa personne.'

[1] The Amoo, which rises in the Belur Tag, or Dark Mountains, and running nearly from east to west, splits into two branches, one of which falls into the Caspian Sea, and the other into Aral Nahr, or the Lake of Eagles.

But war disturbed this vision: far away
From her fond eyes summoned to join th' array
Of Persia's warriors on the hills of Thrace,
The youth exchanged his sylvan dwelling-place
For the rude tent and war-field's deathful clash;
His Zelica's sweet glances for the flash
Of Grecian wild-fire, and love's gentle chains
For bleeding bondage on Byzantium's plains.

Month after month, in widowhood of soul
Drooping, the maiden saw two summers roll
Their suns away—but ah how cold and dim
Even summer suns, when not beheld with him!
From time to time ill-omened rumours came,
Like spirit-tongues, muttering the sick man's name
Just ere he dies:—at length those sounds of dread
Fell withering on her soul, 'Azim is dead!'
Oh grief, beyond all other griefs, when fate
First leaves the young heart lone and desolate
In the wide world, without that only tie
For which it loved to live or feared to die;—
Lorn as the hung-up lute, that ne'er hath spoken
Since the sad day its master-chord was broken!

Fond maid, the sorrow of her soul was such,
Even reason sunk—blighted beneath its touch;
And though, ere long, her sanguine spirit rose
Above the first dead pressure of its woes,
Though health and bloom returned, the delicate chain
Of thought, once tangled, never cleared again.
Warm, lively, soft as in youth's happiest day,
The mind was still all there, but turned astray;—
A wandering bark, upon whose pathway shone
All stars of heaven, except the guiding one!
Again she smiled, nay, much and brightly smiled,
But 'twas a lustre strange, unreal, wild;
And when she sung to her lutes a touching strain,
'Twas like the notes, half ecstasy, half pain,
The bulbul[1] utters, ere her soul depart,
When, vanquished by some minstrel's powerful art,
She dies upon the lute whose sweetness broke her heart.

Such was the mood in which that mission found
Young Zelica,—that mission which around
The Eastern world, in every region blest
With woman's smile, sought out its loveliest,
To grace that galaxy of lips and eyes
Which the Veiled Prophet destined for the skies:—
And such quick welcome as a spark receives
Dropped on a bed of autumn's withered leaves,
Did every tale of these enthusiasts find
In the wild maiden's sorrow-blighted mind.
All fire, at once the maddening zeal she caught;—
Elect of Paradise! blest, rapturous thought!

Predestined bride, in Heaven's eternal dome,
Of some brave youth—ha! durst they say 'of some?'
No—of the one, one only object traced
In her heart's core too deep to be effaced;
The one whose memory, fresh as life, is twined
With every broken link of her lost mind;
Whose image lives, though reason's self be wrecked,
Safe 'mid the ruins of her intellect!

Alas, poor Zelica! it needed all
The fantasy which held thy mind in thrall
To see in that gay Haram's glowing maids
A sainted colony for Eden's shades;
Or dream that he, of whose unholy flame
Thou wert too soon the victim, shining came
From Paradise, to people its pure sphere
With souls like thine, which he hath ruined here!
No—had not reason's light totally set,
And left thee dark, thou hadst an amulet
In the loved image, graven on thy heart,
Which would have saved thee from the tempter's art,
And kept alive, in all its bloom of breath,
That purity whose fading is love's death!—
But lost, inflamed,—a restless zeal took place
Of the mild virgin's still and feminine grace;
First of the Prophet's favourites, proudly first
In zeal and charms,—too well th' Impostor nursed
Her soul's delirium, in whose active flame,
Thus lighting up a young luxuriant frame,
He saw more potent sorceries to bind
To his dark yoke the spirits of mankind,
More subtle chains than hell itself e'er twined.
No art was spared, no witchery;—all the skill
His demons taught him was employed to fill
Her mind with gloom and ecstasy by turns—
That gloom through which frenzy but fiercer burns;
That ecstasy which from the depth of sadness
Glares like the maniac's moon, whose light is madness!

'Twas from a brilliant banquet, where the sound
Of poesy and music breathed around,
Together picturing to her mind and ear
The glories of that heaven, her destined sphere,
Where all was pure, where every stain that lay
Upon the spirit's light should pass away,
And, realizing more than youthful love
E'er wished or dreamed, she should for ever rove
Through fields of fragrance by her Azim's side,
His own blessed, purified, eternal bride!—
'Twas from a scene, a witching trance like this,
He hurried her away, yet breathing bliss,
To the dim charnel-house;—through all its steams
Of damp and death, led only by those gleams
Which foul corruption lights, as with design
To show the gay and proud *she* too can shine—

---

[1] The nightingale

And, passing on through upright ranks of dead,
Which to the maiden, doubly crazed by dread,
Seemed, through the bluish death-light round
    them cast,
To move their lips in mutterings as she passed—
There, in that awful place, when each had quaffed
And pledged in silence such a fearful draught,
Such—oh! the look and taste of that red bowl
Will haunt her till she dies—he bound her soul
By a dark oath, in hell's own language framed,
Never, while earth his mystic presence claimed,
While the blue arch of day hung o'er them both,
Never, by that all-imprecating oath,
In joy or sorrow from his side to sever.
She swore, and the wide charnel echo'd, 'Never,
    never!'

From that dread hour, entirely, wildly given
To him and—she believed, lost maid!—to
    Heaven,
Her brain, her heart, her passions all inflamed,
How proud she stood, when in full Haram named
The Priestess of the Faith!—how flashed her
    eyes
With light, alas! that was not of the skies,
When round, in trances only less than hers,
She saw the Haram kneel, her prostrate wor-
    shippers.
Well might Mokanna think that form alone
Had spells enough to make the world his own:—
Light, lovely limbs, to which the spirit's play
Gave motion, airy as the dancing spray
When from its stem the small bird wings away!
Lips in whose rosy labyrinth, when she smiled,
The soul was lost; and blushes, swift and wild
As are the momentary meteors sent
Across th' uncalm but beauteous firmament.
And then her look—oh! where's the heart so
    wise
Could unbewildered meet those matchless eyes?
Quick, restless, strange, but exquisite withal,
Like those of angels just before their fall;
Now shadowed with the shames of earth—now
    crost
By glimpses of the heaven her heart had lost;
In every glance there broke, without control,
The flashes of a bright but troubled soul,
Where sensibility still wildly played,
Like lightning, round the ruins it had made!

    And such was now young Zelica—so changed
From her who, some years since, delighted
    ranged
The almond groves that shade Bokhara's tide,
All life and bliss, with Azim by her side!
So altered was she now, this festal day,
When, 'mid the proud Divan's dazzling array,
The vision of that youth whom she had loved,
Had wept as dead, before her breathed and
    moved;—
When—bright, she thought, as if from Eden's
    track
But half-way trodden, he had wandered back

Again to earth, glistening with Eden's light—
Her beauteous Azim shone before her sight.

O Reason! who shall say what spells renew,
When least we look for it, thy broken clue!
Through what small vistas o'er the darkened
    brain
Thy intellectual day-beam bursts again;
And how, like forts to which beleaguerers win
Unhoped-for entrance through some friend
    within,
One clear idea, wakened in the breast
By memory's magic, lets in all the rest!
Would it were thus, unhappy girl, with thee!
But though light came, it came but partially;
Enough to show the maze in which thy sense
Wandered about—but not to guide it thence;
Enough to glimmer o'er the yawning wave,
But not to point the harbour which might save.
Hours of delight and peace, long left behind,
With that dear form came rushing o'er her mind;
But, oh! to think how deep her soul had gone
In shame and falsehood since those moments
    shone;
And, then, her oath—*there* madness lay again,
And, shuddering, back she sunk into her chain
Of mental darkness, as if blest to flee
From light, whose every glimpse was agony!
Yet, *one* relief this glance of former years
Brought, mingled with its pain,—tears, floods of
    tears,
Long frozen at her heart, but now like rills
Let loose in spring-time from the snowy hills,
And gushing warm, after a sleep of frost, [lost.
Through valleys where their flow had long been

    Sad and subdued, for the first time her frame
Trembled with horror when the summons came
(A summons proud and rare, which all but she,
And she till now, had heard with ecstasy)
To meet Mokanna at his place of prayer,
A garden oratory, cool and fair,
By the stream's side, where still at close of day
The Prophet of the Veil retired to pray;
Sometimes alone, but oftener far with one—
One chosen nymph to share his orison.

    Of late none found such favour in his sight
As the young Priestess; and though, since that
    night
When the death-caverns echoed every tone
Of the dire oath that made her all his own,
Th' Impostor, sure of his infatuate prize,
Had more than once thrown off his soul's disguise,
And uttered such unheavenly, monstrous things,
As even across the desperate wanderings
Of a weak intellect, whose lamp was out,
Through startling shadows of dismay and
    doubt;—
Yet zeal, ambition, her tremendous vow,
The thought still haunting her of that bright brow
Whose blaze, as yet from mortal eye concealed,
Would soon, proud triumph! be to her revealed,

To her alone;—and then the hope, most dear,
Most wild of all, that her transgression here
Was but a passage through earth's grosser fire,
From which the spirit would at last aspire,
Even purer than before,—as perfumes rise
Through flame and smoke, most welcome to the skies;
And that, when Azim's fond, divine embrace
Should circle her in heaven, no darkening trace
Would on that bosom he once loved remain,
But all be bright, be pure, be *his* again!—
These were the wildering dreams, whose curst deceit
Had chained her soul beneath the tempter's feet,
And made her think even damning falsehood sweet.
But now that shape which had appalled her view,
That semblance—oh, how terrible, if true!—
Which came across her frenzy's full career
With shock of consciousness, cold, deep, severe,
As when, in northern seas, at midnight dark,
An isle of ice encounters some swift bark,
And, startling all its wretches from their sleep,
By one cold impulse hurls them to the deep;—
So came that shock not frenzy's self could bear,
And waking up each long-lulled image there,
But checked her headlong soul, to sink it in despair!

Wan and dejected, through the evening dusk,
She now went slowly to that small kiosk,
Where, pondering alone his impious schemes,
Mokanna waited her—too wrapt in dreams
Of the fair-ripening future's rich success
To heed the sorrow, pale and spiritless,
That sat upon his victim's downcast brow,
Or mark how slow her step, how altered now
From the quick, ardent Priestess, whose light bound
Came like a spirit's o'er th' unechoing ground,—
From that wild Zelica whose every glance
Was thrilling fire, whose every thought a trance!

Upon his couch the veiled Mokanna lay,
While lamps around—not such as lend their ray,
Glimmering and cold, to those who nightly pray
In holy Koom,[1] or Mecca's dim arcades,—
But brilliant, soft, such lights as lovely maids
Look loveliest in, shed their luxurious glow
Upon his mystic veil's white glittering flow.
Beside him, 'stead of beads and books of prayer,
Which the world fondly thought he mused on there,
Stood vases filled with Kishmee's[2] golden wine,
And the red weepings of the Shiraz vine;
Of which his curtained lips full many a draught
Took zealously, as if each drop they quaffed,
Like Zemzem's Spring of Holiness,[3] had power
To freshen the soul's virtues into flower!
And still he drank and pondered—nor could see
Th' approaching maid, so deep his reverie;
At length, with fiendish laugh, like that which broke
From Eblis at the fall of man, he spoke:—
'Yes, ye vile race, for hell's amusement given,
Too mean for earth, yet claiming kin with heaven;
God's images, forsooth!—such gods as he
Whom India serves, the monkey deity;[4]—
Ye creatures of a breath, proud things of clay,
To whom, if Lucifer, as grandams say,[5]
Refused, though at the forfeit of heaven's light,
To bend in worship, Lucifer was right!—
Soon shall I plant this foot upon the neck
Of your foul race, and without fear or check,
Luxuriating in hate, avenge my shame,
My deep-felt, long-nurst loathing of man's name!—
Soon at the head of myriads, blind and fierce
As hooded falcons, through the universe
I'll sweep my darkening, desolating way,
Weak man my instrument, curst man my prey!

'Ye wise, ye learned, who grope your dull way on
By the dim twinkling gleams of ages gone,
Like superstitious thieves, who think the light
From dead men's marrow guides them best at night [6]—
Ye shall have honours, wealth—yes, sages, yes—
I know, grave fools, your wisdom's nothingness;
Undazzled it can track yon starry sphere,
But a gilt stick, a bauble, blinds it here.

---

[1] 'The cities of Com (or Koom) and Kashan are full of mosques, mausoleums, and sepulchres of the descendants of Ali, the saints of Persia.'—*Chardin.*

[2] An island in the Persian Gulf, celebrated for its white wine.

[3] 'The miraculous well at Mecca; so called from the murmuring of its waters.'

[4] The good Hannaman. 'Apes are in many parts of India highly venerated, out of respect to the god Hannaman, a deity partaking of the form of that race.'—*Pennant's Hindostan.*

See a curious account in Stephen's *Persia* of a solemn embassy from some part of the Indies to Goa, when the Portuguese were there, offering vast treasures for the recovery of a monkey's tooth, which they held in great veneration, and which had been taken away upon the conquest of the kingdom of Jafanapatan.

[5] This resolution of Eblis not to acknowledge the new creature man, was, according to Mohammedan tradition, thus adopted: 'The earth (which God had selected for the materials of His work) was carried into Arabia, to a place between Mecca and Tayef, where, being first kneaded by the angels, it was afterwards fashioned by God Himself into a human form, and left to dry for the space of forty days, or, as others say, as many years; the angels in the meantime often visiting it, and Eblis (then one of the angels nearest to God's presence, afterwards the devil) among the rest; but he, not contented with looking at it, kicked it with his foot till it rung; and, knowing God designed that creature to be his superior, took a secret resolution never to acknowledge him as such.'—*Sale on the Koran.*

[6] A kind of lantern, formerly used by robbers, called the Hand of Glory; the candle for which was made of the fat of a dead malefactor. This, however, was rather a western than an eastern superstition.

How I shall laugh, when trumpeted along,
In lying speech, and still more lying song,
By these learned slaves, the meanest of the throng;
Their wits bought up, their wisdom shrunk so small,
A sceptre's puny point can wield it all!

'Ye too, believers of incredible creeds,
Whose faith enshrines the monsters which it breeds;
Who, bolder even than Nimrod, think to rise,
By nonsense heaped on nonsense, to the skies;
Ye shall have miracles, ay, sound ones too,
Seen, heard, attested, everything—but true.
Your preaching zealots, too inspired to seek
One grace of meaning for the things they speak;
Your martyrs, ready to shed out their blood
For truths too heavenly to be understood;
And your state priests, sole vendors of the lore
That works salvation;—as, on Ava's shore,
Where none *but* priests are privileged to trade
In that best marble of which gods are made;[1]—
They shall have mysteries—ay, precious stuff
For knaves to thrive by—mysterious enough;
Dark, tangled doctrines, dark as fraud can weave,
Which simple votaries shall on trust receive,
While craftier feign belief, till they believe.
A heaven too ye must have, ye lords of dust,—
A splendid Paradise,—pure souls, ye must:
That prophet ill sustains his holy call
Who finds not heavens to suit the tastes of all;
Houris for boys, omniscience for sages,
And wings and glories for all ranks and ages.
Vain things!—as lust or vanity inspires,
The heaven of each is but what each desires,
And, soul or sense, whate'er the object be,
Man would be man to all eternity!
So let him—Eblis!—grant this crowning curse,
But keep him what he is, no hell were worse.'

'Oh, my lost soul!' exclaimed the shuddering maid,
Whose ears had drunk like poison all he said.
Mokanna started—not abashed, afraid,—
He knew no more of fear than one who dwells
Beneath the tropics knows of icicles!
But, in those dismal words that reached his ear—
'Oh, my lost soul!'—there was a sound so drear,
So like that voice, among the sinful dead,
In which the legend o'er hell's gate is read,
That, new as 'twas from her, whom nought could dim
Or sink till now, it startled even him.

'Ha, my fair Priestess!'—thus, with ready wile,
Th' impostor turned to greet her—'thou whose smile

Hath inspiration in its rosy beam
Beyond th' enthusiast's hope or prophet's dream;
Light of the Faith! who twin'st religion's zeal
So close with love's, men know not which they feel,
Nor which to sigh for, in their trance of heart,
The heaven thou preachest or the heaven thou art!
What should I be without thee? without thee
How dull were power, how joyless victory!
Though borne by angels, if that smile of thine
Blessed not my banner, 'twere but half divine.
But—why so mournful, child? those eyes, that shone
All life last night—what!—is their glory gone?
Come, come—this morn's fatigue hath made them pale,
They want rekindling—suns themselves would fail
Did not their comets bring, as I to thee,
From light's own fount supplies of brilliancy.
Thou seest this cup—no juice of earth is here,
But the pure waters of that upper sphere
Whose rills o'er ruby beds and topaz flow,
Catching the gem's bright colour as they go.
Nightly my genii come and fill these urns—
Nay, drink—in every drop life's essence burns;
'Twill make that soul all fire, those eyes all light—
Come, come, I want thy loveliest smiles to-night:
There is a youth—why start?—thou sawest him then;
Looked he not nobly? such the godlike men
Thou'lt have to woo thee in the bowers above;—
Though *he*, I fear, hath thoughts too stern for love,
Too ruled by that cold enemy of bliss
The world calls Virtue—we must conquer this.
Nay, shrink not, pretty sage! 'tis not for thee
To scan the mazes of heaven's mystery:
The steel must pass through fire, ere it can yield
Fit instruments for mighty hands to wield.
This very night I mean to try the art
Of powerful beauty on that warrior's heart.
All that my Haram boasts of bloom and wit,
Of skill and charms, most rare and exquisite,
Shall tempt the boy;—young Mirzala's blue eyes,
Whose sleepy lid like snow on violets lies;
Arouya's cheeks, warm as a spring-day sun,
And lips that, like the seal of Solomon,
Have magic in their pressure; Zeba's lute,
And Lilla's dancing feet, that gleam and shoot
Rapid and white as sea-birds o'er the deep,—
All shall combine their witching powers to steep
My convert's spirit in that softening trance,
From which to heaven is but the next advance;—
That glowing, yielding fusion of the breast,
On which Religion stamps her image best.
But hear me, Priestess!—though each nymph of these
Hath some peculiar, practised power to please,

---

[1] The material of which images of Gaudma (the Birman deity) are made, is held sacred. 'Birmans may not purchase the marble in mass, but are suffered, and indeed encouraged, to buy figures of the deity ready made.'—*Syme's Ava*, vol. ii. p. 376

Some glance or step which, at the mirror tried,
First charms herself, then all the world beside;
There still wants *one*, to make the victory sure,
One who in every look joins every lure;
Through whom all beauty's beams concentred pass,
Dazzling and warm, as through love's burning-glass;
Whose gentle lips persuade without a word,
Whose words, even when unmeaning, are adored,
Like inarticulate breathings from a shrine,
Which our faith takes for granted are divine!
Such is the nymph we want, all warmth and light,
To crown the rich temptations of to-night;
Such the refined enchantress that must be
This hero's vanquisher—and thou art she!'

With her hands clasped, her lips apart and pale,
The maid had stood, gazing upon the veil
From which these words, like south-winds through a fence
Of Kerzrah flowers, came filled with pestilence;[1]
So boldly uttered, too! as if all dread
Of frowns from her—of virtuous frowns—were fled,
And the wretch felt assured that, once plunged in,
Her woman's soul would know no pause in sin!

At first, though mute she listened, like a dream
Seemed all he said: nor could her mind, whose beam
As yet was weak, penetrate half his scheme.
But when, at length, he utter'd, 'Thou art she!'
All flashed at once, and shrieking piteously,
'Oh not for worlds!' she cried—'Great God! to whom
I once knelt innocent, is this my doom?
Are all my dreams, my hopes of heavenly bliss,
My purity, my pride, then come to this—
To live, the wanton of a fiend! to be
The pander of his guilt—oh infamy!
And, sunk myself as low as hell can steep
In its hot flood, drag others down as deep!
Others—ha! yes—that youth who came to-day—
Not him I loved—not him—oh! do but say,
But swear to me this moment, 'tis not he,
And I will serve, dark fiend, will worship even thee!'

'Beware, young raving thing;—in time beware,
Nor utter what I cannot, must not bear,
Even from *thy* lips. Go—try thy lute, thy voice,
The boy must feel their magic;—I rejoice
To see those fires, no matter whence they rise,
Once more illuming my fair Priestess' eyes;

And should the youth, whom soon those eyes shall warm,
Indeed resemble thy dead lover's form,
So much the happier wilt thou find thy doom,
As one warm lover, full of life and bloom,
Excels ten thousand cold ones in the tomb.
Nay, nay, no frowning, sweet!—those eyes were made
For love, not anger: I must be obeyed.'

'Obeyed!—'tis well—yes, I deserve it all—
On me, on me Heaven's vengeance cannot fall
Too heavily; but Azim, brave and true
And beautiful, must *he* be ruined too?
Must *he* too, glorious as he is, be driven
A renegade, like me, from love and heaven?
Like me?—weak wretch, I wrong him!—not like me;
No—he's all truth and strength and purity!
Fill up your maddening hell-cup to the brim,
Its witchery, fiends, will have no charm for him!
Let loose your glowing wantons from their bowers,
He loves, he loves, and can defy their powers!
Wretch as I am, in *his* heart still I reign
Pure as when first we met, without a stain!
Though ruined, lost, my memory, like a charm
Left by the dead, still keeps his soul from harm.
Oh! never let him know how deep the brow
He kissed at parting is dishonoured now;
Ne'er tell him how debased, how sunk is she
Whom once he loved—once!—*still* loves dotingly!
Thou laugh'st, tormentor! What! thou'lt brand my name?
Do, do—in vain; he'll not believe my shame:
He thinks me true, that nought beneath God's sky
Could tempt or change me, and—so once thought I.
But this is past—though worse than death my lot,
Than hell—'tis nothing while *he* knows it not.
Far off to some benighted land I'll fly,
Where sunbeam ne'er shall enter till I die;
Where none will ask the lost one whence she came,
But I may fade and fall without a name,
And thou—curst man or fiend, whate'er thou art,
Who found'st this burning plague-spot in my heart,
And spread'st it—oh, so quick!—through soul and frame
With more than demon's art, till I became
A loathsome thing, all pestilence, all flame!—
If, when I'm gone——'

'Hold, fearless maniac, hold,
Nor tempt my rage—by Heaven, not half so bold
The puny bird, that dares with teasing hum
Within the crocodile's stretched jaws to come![2]

---

[1] 'It is commonly said in Persia, that if a man breathe in the hot south wind, which in June or July passes over that flower (the Kerzereh), it will kill him.'

[2] 'The ancient story concerning the Trochilus, or humming-bird, entering with impunity into the mouth of the crocodile, is firmly believed at Java.'—It is said to run this risk for the purpose of picking the crocodile's teeth. The same circumstance is related of the lapwing, as a fact to which he was witness, by Paul Lucas. —*Voyage faits en* 1714.

And so thou'lt fly, forsooth?—what!—give up all
Thy chaste dominion in the Haram hall,
Where, now to Love and now to Alla given,
Half mistress and half saint, thou hang'st as even
As doth Medina's tomb, 'twixt hell and heaven!
Thou'lt fly?—as easily may reptiles run
The gaunt snake once hath fixed his eyes upon;
As easily, when caught, the prey may be
Plucked from his loving folds, as thou from me.
No, no, 'tis fixed—let good or ill betide,
Thou'rt mine till death, till death Mokanna's
  bride!
Hast thou forgot thy oath?'—
    At this dread word,
The Maid, whose spirit his rude taunts had
  stirred
Through all its depths, and roused an anger there
That burst and lightened even through her
  despair,
Shrunk back, as if a blight were in the breath
That spoke that word, and staggered, pale as
  death.

'Yes, my sworn Bride; let others seek in
  bowers
Their bridal place—the charnel vault was ours!
Instead of scents and balms, for thee and me
Rose the rich steams of sweet mortality;
Gay, flickering death-lights shone while we
  were wed,
And, for our guests, a row of goodly dead
(Immortal spirits in their time, no doubt)
From reeking shrouds upon the rite looked out!
That oath thou heard'st more lips than thine
  repeat—
That cup—thou shudderest, lady—was it sweet?
That cup we pledged, the charnel's choicest wine,
Hath bound thee—ay—body and soul all mine;

Bound thee by chains that, whether blest or curst
No matter now, not hell itself shall burst!
Hence, woman, to the Haram, and look gay,
Look wild, look—anything but sad; yet stay—
One moment more—from what this night hath
  passed,
I see thou know'st me, know'st me *well* at last.
Ha! ha! and so, fond thing, thou thought'st all
  true,
And that I love mankind?—I do, I do—
As victims, love them; as the sea-dog doats
Upon the small, sweet fry that round him floats;
Or as the Nile-bird loves the slime that gives
That rank and venomous food on which she
  lives!—

' And now thou seest my *soul's* angelic hue,
'Tis time these *features* were uncurtained too;—
This brow, whose light—oh, rare celestial light!
Hath been reserved to bless thy favoured sight;
These dazzling eyes, before whose shrouded might
Thou'st seen immortal man kneel down and
  quake—
Would that they *were* Heaven's lightnings for his
  sake!
But turn and look—then wonder, if thou wilt,
That I should hate, should take revenge, by guilt,
Upon the hand whose mischief or whose mirth
Sent me thus maimed and monstrous upon earth;
And on that race who, though more vile they be
Than mowing apes, are demi-gods to me!
Here—judge if hell, with all its power to damn,
Can add one curse to the foul thing I am!'—

He raised his veil—the Maid turned slowly
  round,
Looked at him—shrieked—and sunk upon the
  ground!

On their arrival next night at the place of encampment, they were surprised and delighted to find the groves all around illuminated,—some artists of Yamtcheou having been sent on previously for the purpose. On each side of the green alley which led to the royal pavilion, artificial sceneries of bamboo work were erected, representing arches, minarets, and towers, from which hung thousands of silken lanterns,[2] painted by the most delicate pencils of Canton. Nothing could be more beautiful than the leaves of the mango-trees and acacias, shining in the light of the bamboo scenery, which shed a lustre round as soft as that of the nights of Peristan.

Lalla Rookh, however, who was too much occupied by the sad story of Zelica and her lover to give a thought to anything else, except perhaps to him who related it, hurried on through this scene of splendour to her pavilion,—greatly to the mortification of the poor artists of Yamtcheou,—and was followed with equal rapidity by the Great Chamberlain, cursing as he went that ancient Mandarin, whose parental anxiety in lighting up the shores of the lake,

---

[1] Circum easdem ripas (Nili, viz.) ales est Ibis. Ea serpentium populatur ova, gratissimamque ex his escam nidis suis refert.—*Solinus.*

[2] 'The Feast of Lanterns is celebrated at Yamtcheou with more magnificence than anywhere else; and the report goes, that the illuminations there are so splendid, that an Emperor once, not daring openly to leave his court to go thither, committed himself with the Queen and several princesses of his family into the hands of a magician, who promised to transport them thither in a trice. He made them in the night to ascend magnificent thrones that were borne up by swans, which in a moment arrived at Yamtcheou. The Emperor saw at his leisure all the solemnity, being carried upon a cloud that hovered over the city and descended by degrees; and came back again with the same speed and equipage, nobody at court perceiving his absence.'—*The Present State of China. p.* 156

where his beloved daughter had wandered and been lost, was the origin of these fantastic Chinese illuminations.[1]

Without a moment's delay young Feramorz was introduced, and Fadladeen, who could never make up his mind as to the merits of a poet till he knew the religious sect to which he belonged, was about to ask him whether he was a Shia or a Sooni, when Lalla Rookh impatiently clapped her hands for silence, and the youth, being seated upon the musnud near her, proceeded:—

Prepare thy soul, young Azim!—thou hast braved
The bands of Greece, still mighty though enslaved;
Hast faced her phalanx, armed with all its fame,
Her Macedonian pikes and globes of flame;
All this hast fronted with firm heart and brow;
But a more perilous trial waits thee now,—
Woman's bright eyes, a dazzling host of eyes
From every land where woman smiles or sighs;
Of every hue, as Love may chance to raise
His black or azure banner in their blaze;
And each sweet mode of warfare, from the flash
That lightens boldly through the shadowy lash,
To the sly, stealing splendours, almost hid,
Like swords half-sheathed, beneath the downcast lid;—
Such, Azim, is the lovely, luminous host
Now led against thee; and, let conquerors boast
Their fields of fame, he who in virtue arms
A young, warm spirit against beauty's charms,
Who feels her brightness, yet defies her thrall,
Is the best, bravest conqueror of them all.

Now, through the Haram chambers moving lights
And busy shapes proclaim the toilet's rites;—
From room to room the ready handmaids hie,
Some skilled to wreathe the turban tastefully,
Or hang the veil, in negligence of shade,
O'er the warm blushes of the youthful maid,
Who, if between the folds but *one* eye shone,
Like Seba's Queen, could vanquish with that one:[3]—
While some bring leaves of henna, to imbue
The fingers' ends with a bright roseate hue,[3]

So bright, that in the mirror's depth they seem
Like tips of coral branches in the stream;
And others mix the kohol's jetty dye,
To give that long, dark languish to the eye,[4]
Which makes the maids, whom kings are proud to cull
From fair Circassia's vales, so beautiful.
All is in motion; rings and plumes and pearls
Are shining everywhere: some younger girls
Are gone by moonlight to the garden-beds,
To gather fresh, cool chaplets for their heads;—
Gay creatures! sweet, though mournful, 'tis to see
How each prefers a garland from that tree
Which brings to mind her childhood's innocent day
And the dear fields and friendships far away.
The maid of India, blest again to hold
In her full lap the champac's leaves of gold,[5]
Thinks of the time when, by the Ganges' flood,
Her little playmates scattered many a bud
Upon her long black hair, with glossy gleam
Just dripping from the consecrated stream;
While the young Arab, haunted by the smell
Of her own mountain flowers, as by a spell—
The sweet elcaya,[6] and that courteous tree
Which bows to all who seek its canopy [7]—
Sees, called up round her by these magic scents,
The well, the camels, and her father's tents;
Sighs for the home she left with little pain,
And wishes even its sorrows back again!

Meanwhile, through vast illuminated halls,
Silent and bright, where nothing but the falls

---

[1] 'The vulgar ascribe it to an accident that happened in the family of a famous mandarin, whose daughter, walking one evening upon the shore of a lake, fell in and was drowned. This afflicted father, with his family, ran thither, and, the better to find her, he caused a great company of lanterns to be lighted. All the inhabitants of the place thronged after him with torches. The year ensuing they made fires upon the shores the same day; they continued the ceremony every year, every one lighted his lantern, and by degrees it commenced into a custom.'—*Present State of China.*

[2] 'Thou hast ravished my heart with one of thine eyes.'—*Sol. Song.*

[3] 'They tinged the ends of her fingers scarlet with henna, so that they resembled branches of coral.'

[4] 'The women blacken the inside of their eyelids with a powder named the black kohol.'

'None of these ladies,' says Shaw, 'take themselves to be completely dressed till they have tinged the hair and edges of their eyelids with the powder of lead-ore.'

Now, as this operation is performed by dipping first into the powder a small wooden bodkin of the thickness of a qalll, and then drawing it afterwards through the eyelids, over the ball of the eye, we shall have a lively image of what the prophet (Jer. iv. 30) may be supposed to mean by *renting the eyes with painting.* This practice is no doubt of great antiquity; for, besides the instance already taken notice of, we find that where Jezebel is said (2 Kings ix. 30) *to have painted her face,* the original words are, *she adjusted her eyes with the powder of lead-ore.*—*Shaw's Travels.*

[5] 'The appearance of the blossoms of the gold-coloured campac in the black hair of the Indian women has supplied the Sanscrit poets with many elegant allusions.'

[6] 'A tree famous for its perfume, and common on the hills of Yemen.'

[7] Of the genus mimosa, 'which droops its branches whenever any person approaches it, seeming as if it saluted those who retire under its shade.'

Of fragrant waters, gushing with cool sound
From many a jasper fount, is heard around,
Young Azim roams bewildered,—nor can guess
What means this maze of light and loneliness.
Here, the way leads o'er tessclated floors,
Or mats of Cairo, through long corridors,
Where, ranged in cassolets and silver urns,
Sweet wood of aloe or of sandal burns;
And spicy rods, such as illume at night
The bowers of Tibet,[1] send forth odorous light,
Like Peris' wands, when pointing out the road
For some pure spirit to its blest abode:—
And here, at once, the glittering saloon
Bursts on his sight, boundless and bright as noon;
Where, in the midst, reflecting back the rays
In broken rainbows, a fresh fountain plays
High as th' enamelled cupola, which towers
All rich with arabesques of gold and flowers:
And the mosaic floor beneath shines through
The sprinkling of that fountain's silvery dew,
Like the wet, glistening shells, of every dye,
That on the margin of the Red Sea lie.

Here, too, he traces the kind visitings
Of woman's love in those fair, living things
Of land and wave, whose fate — in bondage thrown
For their weak loveliness—is like her own!
On one side gleaming with a sudden grace
Through water, brilliant as the crystal vase
In which it undulates, small fishes shine,
Like golden ingots from a fairy mine ;
While on the other, latticed lightly in
With odoriferous woods of Comorin,[2]
Each brilliant bird that wings the air is seen ;—
Gay, sparkling loories, such as gleam between
The crimson blossoms of the coral tree
In the warm isles of India's sunny sea :
Mecca's blue sacred pigeon,[3] and the thrush
Of Hindostan,[4] whose holy warblings gush
At evening from the tall pagoda's top ;—
Those golden birds that, in the spice-time, drop
About the gardens, drunk with that sweet food[5]
Whose scent hath lured them o'er the summer flood;
And those that under Araby's soft sun
Build their high nests of budding cinnamon ;—
In short, all rare and beauteous things that fly
Through the pure element, here calmly lie

Sleeping in light, like the green birds[6] that dwell
In Eden's radiant fields of asphodel!

So on, through scenes past all imagining—
More like the luxuries of that impious king[7]
Whom Death's dark angel, with his lightning torch,
Struck down and blasted even in Pleasure's porch,
Than the pure dwelling of a Prophet sent,
Armed with Heaven's sword, for man's enfranchisement,—
Young Azim wandered, looking sternly round,
His simple garb and war-boots' clanking sound
But ill according with the pomp and grace
And silent lull of that voluptuous place.

'Is this, then,' thought the youth, 'is this the way
To free man's spirit from the deadening sway
Of worldly sloth,—to teach him, while he lives,
To know no bliss but that which virtue gives,
And, when he dies, to leave his lofty name
A light, a landmark on the cliffs of fame?
It was not so, Land of the generous thought
And daring deed, thy godlike sages taught;
It was not thus, in bowers of wanton ease,
Thy Freedom nursed her sacred energies:
Oh! not beneath the enfeebling, withering glow
Of such dull luxury did those myrtles grow
With which she wreathed her sword when she would dare
Immortal deeds; but in the bracing air
Of toil, of temperance, of that high, rare,
Ethereal virtue, which alone can breathe
Life, health, and lustre into Freedom's wreath.
Who that surveys this span of earth we press,—
This speck of life in time's great wilderness,
This narrow isthmus 'twixt two boundless seas,
The past, the future, two eternities!—
Would sully the bright spot, or leave it bare,
When he might build him a proud temple there,
A name that long shall hallow all its space,
And be each purer soul's high resting-place?
But no; it cannot be that one whom God
Has sent to break the wizard Falsehood's rod,—
A Prophet of the Truth, whose mission draws
Its rights from Heaven, should thus profane its cause
With the world's vulgar pomps: no, no; I see—
He thinks me weak—this glare of luxury

---

[1] 'Cloves are a principal ingredient in the composition of the perfumed rods which men of rank keep constantly burning in their presence.'

[2] ' C'est d'où vient le bois d'aloës, que les Arabes appellent Oud Comari, et celui du sandal, qui s'y trouve en grande quantité.'—*D'Herbelot.*

[3] 'In Mecca there are quantities of blue pigeons, which none will affright or abuse, much less kill.'

[4] 'The pagoda thrush is esteemed among the first choristers of India. It sits perched on the sacred pagodas, and from thence delivers its melodious song.'

[5] 'Birds of paradise, which at the nutmeg season come in flights from the southern isles to India; and the strength of the nutmeg so intoxicates them, that they fall dead drunk to the earth.' Tavernier adds, that while the birds of paradise lie in this intoxicated state, the emmets come and eat off their legs; and that hence it is they are said to have no feet.

[6] 'The spirits of the martyrs will be lodged in the crops of green birds.'—*Gibbon*, vol. ix. p. 421.

[7] Shedad, who made the delicious gardens of Irim, in imitation of Paradise, and was destroyed by lightning the first time he attempted to enter them.

Is but to tempt, to try the eaglet gaze
Of my young soul: shine on, 'twill stand the
    blaze!'

So thought the youth; but, even while he
    defied
This witching scene, he felt its witchery glide
Through every sense. The perfume breathing
    round,
Like a pervading spirit;—the still sound
Of falling waters, lulling as the song
Of Indian bees at sunset, when they throng
Around the fragrant Nilica, and deep
In its blue blossoms hum themselves to sleep;[1]
And music, too—dear music! that can touch
Beyond all else the soul that loves it much—
Now heard far off, so far as but to seem
Like the faint, exquisite music of a dream;—
All was too much for him, too full of bliss,
The heart could nothing feel that felt not this;
Softened he sunk upon a couch, and gave
His soul up to sweet thoughts, like wave on
    wave
Succeeding in smooth seas, when storms are
    laid;—
He thought of Zelica, his own dear maid,
And of the time when, full of blissful sighs,
They sat and looked into each other's eyes,
Silent and happy—as if God had given
Nought else worth looking at on this side heaven.

'Oh, my loved mistress, thou, whose spirit still
Is with me, round me, wander where I will—
It is for thee, for thee alone I seek
The paths of glory; to light up thy cheek
With warm approval—in that gentle look
To read my praise, as in an angel's book,
And think all toils rewarded, when from thee
I gain a smile worth immortality!
How shall I bear the moment when restored
To that young heart where I alone am lord,
Though of such bliss unworthy,—since the best
Alone deserve to be the happiest:—
When from those lips, unbreathed upon for years,
I shall again kiss off the soul-felt tears,
And find those tears warm as when last they
    started,
Those sacred kisses pure as when we parted?
O my own life!—why should a single day,
A moment, keep me from those arms away?'

While thus he thinks, still nearer on the breeze
Come those delicious, dream-like harmonies,
Each note of which but adds new, downy links
To the soft chain in which his spirit sinks.

He turns him toward the sound, and, far away
Through a long vista, sparkling with the play
Of countless lamps,—like the rich track which
    Day
Leaves on the waters, when he sinks from us,
So long the path, its light so tremulous;—
He sees a group of female forms advance,
Some chained together in the mazy dance
By fetters, forged in the green sunny bowers,
As they were captives to the King of Flowers;[2]
And some disporting round, unlinked and free,
Who seemed to mock their sisters' slavery;
And round and round them still in wheeling
    flight
Went, like gay moths about a lamp at night;
While others waked, as gracefully along
Their feet kept time, the very soul of song
From psaltery, pipe, and lutes of heavenly thrill,
Or their own youthful voices, heavenlier still.
And now they come, now pass before his eye,
Forms such as Nature moulds when she would
    vie
With Fancy's pencil, and give birth to things
Lovely beyond its fairest picturings.
Awhile they dance before him, then divide,
Breaking, like rosy clouds at eventide
Around the rich pavilion of the sun,—
Till silently dispersing, one by one,
Through many a path, that from the chamber
    leads
To gardens, terraces, and moonlight meads,
Their distant laughter comes upon the wind,
And but one trembling nymph remains behind,—
Beckoning them back in vain, for they are gone,
And she is left in all that light alone;
No veil to curtain o'er her beauteous brow
In its young bashfulness more beauteous now;
But a light golden chain-work round her hair,[3]
Such as the maids of Yezd[4] and Shiraz wear,
From which, on either side, gracefully hung
A golden amulet, in the Arab tongue
Engraven o'er with some immortal line
From Holy Writ, or bard scarce less divine;
While her left hand, as shrinkingly she stood,
Held a small lute of gold and sandal-wood,
Which, once or twice, she touched with hurried
    strain,
Then took her trembling fingers off again.
But when at length a timid glance she stole
At Azim, the sweet gravity of soul
She saw through all his features calmed her fear,
And, like a half-tamed antelope, more near,
Though shrinking still, she came;—then sat her
    down
Upon a musnud's[5] edge, and, bolder grown,

---

[1] 'My pandits assure me that the plant before us (the Nilica) is their sephalica, thus named because the bees are supposed to sleep on its blossoms.'—*Sir W. Jones.*
[2] 'They deferred it till the King of Flowers should ascend his throne of enamelled foliage.'—*Bahardanush.*
[3] 'One of the head-dresses of the Persian women is composed of a light golden chain-work, set with small pearls, with a thin gold plate pendent, about the big-

ness of a crown-piece, on which is impressed an Arabian prayer, and which hangs upon the cheek below the ear.' —*Hanway's Travels.*
[4] 'Certainly the women of Yezd are the handsomest women in Persia. The proverb is, that to live happy, a man must have a wife of Yezd, eat the bread of Yezdecas, and drink the wine of Shiraz.'—*Tavernier.*
[5] Musnuds are cushioned seats, usually reserved for persons of distinction.

E

In the pathetic mode of Isfahan[1]
Touched a preluding strain, and thus began:—

'There's a bower of roses by Bendemeer's[2] stream,
  And the nightingale sings round it all the day long;
In the time of my childhood 'twas like a sweet dream
To sit in the roses and hear the bird's song.

'That bower and its music I never forget,
  But oft when alone, in the bloom of the year,
I think—Is the nightingale singing there yet?
  Are the roses still bright by the calm Bendemeer?

'No, the roses soon withered that hung o'er the wave,
  But some blossoms were gathered while freshly they shone,
And a dew was distilled from their flowers, that gave
  All the fragrance of summer, when summer was gone.

'Thus memory draws from delight, ere it dies,
  An essence that breathes of it many a year;
Thus bright to my soul, as 'twas then to my eyes,
  Is that bower on the banks of the calm Bendemeer!'

'Poor maiden!' thought the youth, 'if thou wert sent,
With thy soft lute and beauty's blandishment,
To wake unholy wishes in this heart,
Or tempt its troth, thou little know'st the art.
For though thy lip should sweetly counsel wrong,
Those vestal eyes would disavow its song.
But thou hast breathed such purity, thy lay
Returns so fondly to youth's virtuous day,
And leads thy soul—if o'er it wandered thence—
So gently back to its first innocence,
That I would sooner stop the unchained dove,
When swift returning to its home of love,
And round its snowy wing new fetters twine,
Than turn from virtue one pure wish of thine!'

Scarce had this feeling passed, when, sparkling through
The gently opened curtains of light blue
That veiled the breezy casement, countless eyes,
Peeping like stars through the blue evening skies,
Looked laughing in, as if to mock the pair
That sat so still and melancholy there:—

And now the curtains fly apart, and in
From the cool air, 'mid showers of jessamine
Which those without fling after them in play,
Two lightsome maidens spring,—lightsome as they
Who live in the air on odours,—and around
The bright saloon, scarce conscious of the ground,
Chase one another, in a varying dance
Of mirth and languor, coyness and advance,
Too eloquently like love's warm pursuit:—
While she, who sung so gently to the lute
Her dream of home, steals timidly away,
Shrinking as violets do in summer's ray,—
But takes with her from Azim's heart that sigh
We sometimes give to forms that pass us by
In the world's crowd, too lovely to remain,
Creatures of light we never see again!

Around the white necks of the nymphs who danced
Hung carcanets of orient gems, that glanced
More brilliant than the sea-glass glittering o'er
The hills of crystal on the Caspian shore;[3]
While from their long dark tresses, in a fall
Of curls descending, bells, as musical
As those that on the golden-shafted trees
Of Eden shake in the eternal breeze,[4]
Rung round their steps, at every bound more sweet,
As 'twere the ecstatic language of their feet.
At length the chase was o'er, and they stood wreathed
Within each other's arms; while soft there breathed
Through the cool casement, mingled with the sighs
Of moonlight flowers, music that seemed to rise
From some still lake, so liquidly it rose;
And, as it swelled again at each faint close,
The ear could track through all that maze of chords
And young sweet voices these impassioned words:—

'A Spirit there is, whose fragrant sigh
Is burning now through earth and air;
Where cheeks are blushing, the Spirit is nigh;
Where lips are meeting, the Spirit is there!

'His breath is the soul of flowers like these,
And his floating eyes—oh! *they* resemble
Blue water-lilies,[5] when the breeze
Is making the stream around them tremble.

---

[1] The Persians, like the ancient Greeks, call their musical modes or Perdas by the names of different countries or cities, as the mode of Isfahan, the mode of Irak, etc.

[2] A river which flows near the ruins of Chilminar.

[3] 'To the north of us (on the coast of the Caspian, near Badku) was a mountain, which sparkled like diamonds, arising from the sea-glass and crystals with which it abounds.'—*Journey of the Russian Ambassador to Persia*, 1746.

[4] 'To which will be added the sound of the bells, hanging on the trees, which will be put in motion by the wind proceeding from the throne of God, as often as the blessed wish for music.'—*Sale*.

[5] The blue lotos, which grows in Cashmere and in Persia. 'Whose wanton eyes resemble blue water-lilies agitated by the breeze.'—*Jayadeva*.

THE VEILED PROPHET OF KHORASSAN.

'Hail to thee, hail to thee, kindling power!
Spirit of Love, Spirit of Bliss!
Thy holiest time is the moonlight hour,
And there never was moonlight so sweet as
this.

   By the fair and brave
    Who blushing unite,
   Like the sun and wave
    When they meet at night;

   By the tear that shows
    When passion is nigh,
   As the rain-drop flows
    From the heat of the sky;

'By the first love-beat
    Of the youthful heart,
By the bliss to meet,
    And the pain to part;

'By all that thou hast
    To mortals given,
Which—oh could it last,
    This earth were heaven!

We call thee hither, entrancing Power!
Spirit of Love! Spirit of Bliss!
Thy holiest time is the moonlight hour,
And there never was moonlight so sweet as
this.'

Impatient of a scene, whose luxuries stole,
Spite of himself, too deep into his soul,
And where, midst all that the young heart loves
   most,
Flowers, music, smiles, to yield was to be lost,
The youth had started up, and turned away
From the light nymphs, and their luxurious lay,
To muse upon the pictures that hung round,[1]—
Bright images that spoke without a sound,
And views like vistas into fairy ground.
But here again new spells came o'er his sense;—
All that the pencil's mute omnipotence
Could call up into life, of soft and fair,
Of fond and passionate, was glowing there;
Nor yet too warm, but touched with that fine art
Which paints of pleasure but the purer part;
Which knows even Beauty when half-veiled is
   best,
Like her own radiant planet of the west,
Whose orb when half-retired looks loveliest.[2]

There hung the history of the Genii-King,[3]
Traced through each gay, voluptuous wandering
With her from Saba's bowers,[4] in whose bright
He read that to be blest is to be wise;— [eyes
Here fond Zuleika[5] woos with open arms
The Hebrew boy, who flies from her young
   charms,
Yet, flying, turns to gaze, and, half undone,
Wishes that heaven and she could *both* be won;
And here Mohammed, born for love and guile,
Forgets the Koran in his Mary's smile;—
Then beckons some kind angel from above
With a new text to consecrate their love.[6]

With rapid step, yet pleased and lingering eye,
Did the youth pass these pictured stories by,
And hastened to a casement, where the light
Of the calm moon came in, and freshly bright
The fields without were seen, sleeping as still
As if no life remained in breeze or rill.
Here paused he, while the music, now less near,
Breathed with a holier language on his ear,
As though the distance, and that heavenly ray
Through which the sounds came floating, took
   away
All that had been too earthly in the lay.

Oh! could he listen to such sounds unmoved,
And by that light—nor dream of her he loved?
Dream on, unconscious boy! while yet thou
   mayst;
'Tis the last bliss thy soul shall ever taste.
Clasp yet awhile her image to thy heart,
Ere all the light that made it dear depart.
Think of her smiles as when thou saw'st them
   last,
Clear, beautiful, by nought of earth o'ercast;
Recall her tears, to thee at parting given,
Pure as they weep, *if* angels weep, in heaven.
Think, in her own still bower she waits thee now,
With the same glow of heart and bloom of brow,
Yet shrined in solitude—thine all, thine only
Like the one star above thee, bright and lonely.
Oh, that a dream so sweet, so long enjoyed,
Should be so sadly, cruelly destroyed!

The song is hushed, the laughing nymphs are
   flown,
And he is left, musing of bliss, alone;—
Alone?—no, not alone—that heavy sigh,
That sob of grief, which broke from some one
   nigh—,

---

[1] It has been generally supposed that the Mohammedans prohibit all pictures of animals; but Toderini shows that, though the practice is forbidden by the Koran, they are not more averse to painted figures and images than other people. From Mr. Murphy's work, too, we find that the Arabs of Spain had no objection to the introduction of figures into painting.

[2] This is not quite astronomically true. 'Dr. Halley,' says Keil, 'has shown that Venus is brightest when she is about forty degrees removed from the sun; and that then but *only a fourth part* of her lucid disk is to be seen from the earth.'

[3] For the loves of King Solomon (who was supposed to preside over the whole race of Genii) with Balkis, the Queen of Sheba or Saba, see *D'Herbelot*, and the *Notes on the Koran*, chap. ll.

[4] The Queen of Sheba or Saba.

[5] The wife of Potiphar, thus named by the Orientals.

[6] The particulars of Mahomet's amour with Mary, the Coptic girl, in justification of which he added a new chapter to the Koran, may be found in *Gagnier's Notes upon Abulfeda*, p. 151.

Whose could it be?—alas! is misery found
Here, even here, on this enchanted ground?
He turns, and sees a female form, close veiled,
Leaning, as if both heart and strength had failed,
Against a pillar near;—not glittering o'er
With gems and wreaths, such as the others wore,
But in that deep-blue, melancholy dress [1]
Bokhara's maidens wear in mindfulness
Of friends or kindred dead or far away;—
And such as Zelica had on that day
He left her,—when, with heart too full to speak,
He took away her last warm tears upon his
 cheek.

A strange emotion stirs within him—more
Than mere compassion ever waked before;
Unconsciously he opes his arms, while she
Springs forward, as with life's last energy,
But, swooning in that one convulsive bound,
Sinks, ere she reach his arms, upon the ground;—
Her veil falls off—her faint hands clasp his
 knees—
'Tis she herself!—'tis Zelica he sees!
But, ah, so pale, so changed—none but a lover
Could in that wreck of beauty's shrine discover
The once-adored divinity—even he
Stood for some moments mute, and doubtingly
Put back the ringlets from her brow, and gazed
Upon those lids, where once such lustre blazed,
Ere he could think she was *indeed* his own,
Own darling maid, whom he so long had known
In joy and sorrow, beautiful in both;
Who, even when grief was heaviest—when loth
He left her for the wars—in that worst hour
Sat in her sorrow like the sweet night-flower,[2]
When darkness brings its weeping glories out,
And spreads its sighs like frankincense about.

'Look up, my Zelica—one moment show
Those gentle eyes to me, that I may know
Thy life, thy loveliness is not all gone,
But *there*, at least, shines as it ever shone.
Come, look upon thy Azim—one dear glance,
Like those of old, were heaven! whatever chance
Hath brought thee here, oh 'twas a blessed one!
There—my loved lips—they move—that kiss
 hath run
Like the first shoot of life through every vein,
And now I clasp her, mine, all mine again!
Oh the delight—now, in this very hour
When, had the whole rich world been in my
 power,
I should have singled out thee, only thee,
From the whole world's collected treasury—
To have thee here—to hang thus fondly o'er
My own, best, purest Zelica once more!'

It was indeed the touch of those fond lips
Upon her eyes that chased their short eclipse,

And, gradual as the snow at heaven's breath
Melts off and shows the azure flowers beneath,
Her lids unclosed, and the bright eyes were seen
Gazing on his—not, as they late had been,
Quick, restless, wild, but mournfully serene;
As if to lie, even for that tranced minute,
So near his heart, had consolation in it;
And thus to wake in his beloved caress
Took from her soul one half its wretchedness.
But, when she heard him call her good and pure,
Oh, 'twas too much, too dreadful to endure!
Shuddering she broke away from his embrace,
And, hiding with both hands her guilty face,
Said, in a tone whose anguish would have riven
A heart of very marble, 'Pure!—O Heaven!'——

That tone—those looks so changed—the
 withering blight
That sin and sorrow leave where'er they light;
The dead despondency of those sunk eyes,
Where once, had he thus met her by surprise,
He would have seen himself, too happy boy,
Reflected in a thousand lights of joy;
And then the place,—that bright, unholy place,
Where vice lay hid beneath each winning grace
And charm of luxury, as the viper weaves
Its wily cowering of sweet balsam-leaves,—
All struck upon his heart, sudden and cold
As death itself;—it needs not to be told—
No, no—he sees it all, plain as the brand
Of burning shame can mark—whate'er the hand
That could from Heaven and him such bright-
 ness sever,
'Tis done—to Heaven and him she's lost for
 ever!
It was a dreadful moment; not the tears,
The lingering, lasting misery of years
Could match that minute's anguish—all the
 worst
Of sorrow's elements in that dark burst
Broke o'er his soul, and, with one crash of fate,
Laid the whole hopes of his life desolate.

'Oh! curse me not,' she cried, as wild he tossed
His desperate hand tow'rds heaven—'though I
 am lost,
Think not that guilt, that falsehood made me fall,
No, no—'twas grief, 'twas madness did it all!
Nay, doubt me not—though all thy love hath
 ceased—
I know it hath—yet, yet believe, at least,
That every spark of reason's light must be
Quenched in this brain ere I could stray from
 thee.
They told me thou wert dead—why, Azim, why
Did we not, both of us, that instant die
When we were parted?—oh! couldst thou but
 know
With what a deep devotedness of woe
I wept thy absence—o'er and o'er again
Thinking of thee, still thee, till thought grew pain,
And memory, like a drop that, night and day,
Falls cold and ceaseless, wore my heart away.

---

[1] 'Deep-blue is their mourning colour.'
[2] The sorrowful nyctanthes, which begins to spread its rich odour after sunset.

THE VEILED PROPHET OF KHORASSAN.

Didst thou but know how pale I sat at home,
My eyes still turned the way thou wert to come,
And, all the long, long night of hope and fear,
Thy voice and step still sounding in my ear—
O God! thou wouldst not wonder that, at last,
When every hope was all at once o'ercast,
When I heard frightful voices round me say,
Azim is dead!—this wretched brain gavo way,
And I became a wreck, at random driven,
Without one glimpse of reason or of Heaven—
All wild—and even this quenchless love within
Turned to foul fires to light me into sin!—
Thou pitiest me—I knew thou wouldst—that sky
Hath nought beneath it half so lorn as I.
The fiend who lured me hither—hist! come near,
Or thou too, *thou* art lost, if he should hear—
Told me such things—oh! with such devilish
  art,
As would have ruined even a holier heart—
Of thee, and of that ever-radiant sphere,
Where blessed at length, if I but served *him* here,
I should for ever live in thy dear sight,
And drink from those pure eyes eternal light.
Think, think how lost, how maddened I must be,
To hope that guilt could lead to God or thee!
Thou weep'st for me—do weep—oh that I durst
Kiss off that tear! but no—these lips are curst,
They must not touch thee;—one divine caress,
One blessed moment of forgetfulness
I've had within those arms, and *that* shall lie,
Shrined in my soul's deep memory till I die;
The last of joy's last relics here below,
The one sweet drop, in all this waste of woe,
My heart has treasured from affection's spring,
To soothe and cool its deadly withering!
But thou—yes, thou must go—for ever go;
This place is not for thee—for thee! oh no!
Did I but tell thee half, thy tortured brain
Would burn like mine, and mine go wild again!
Enough, that Guilt reigns here — that hearts,
  once good,
Now tainted, chilled, and broken, are his food.
Enough, that we are parted—that there rolls
A flood of headlong fate between our souls,
Whose darkness severs me as wide from thee
As hell from heaven, to all eternity!'

'Zelica! Zelica!' the youth exclaimed,
In all the tortures of a mind inflamed
Almost to madness—'by that sacred heaven,
Where yet, if prayers can move, thou'lt be for-
  given,
As thou art here—here, in this writhing heart,
All sinful, wild, and ruined as thou art!
By the remembrance of our once pure love,
Which, like a churchyard light, still burns above
The grave of our lost souls—which guilt in thee
Cannot extinguish, nor despair in me!
I do conjure, implore thee to fly hence—
If thou hast yet one spark of innocence,
Fly with me from this place'—
           'With thee! O bliss!
'Tis worth whole years of torment to hear this.

What! take the lost one with thee?—let her rove
By thy dear side, as in those days of love,
When we were both so happy, both so pure—
Too heavenly dream! if there's on earth a cure
For the sunk heart, 'tis this—day after day
To be the blest companion of thy way;
To hear thy angel eloquence—to see
Those virtuous eyes for ever turned on me;
And in their light re-chastened silently,
Like the stained web that whitens in the sun,
Grow pure by being purely shone upon!
And thou wilt pray for me—I know thou wilt—
At the dim vesper hour, when thoughts of guilt
Come heaviest o'er the heart, thou'lt lift thine
  eyes,
Full of sweet tears, unto the darkening skies,
And plead for me with Heaven, till I can dare
To fix my own weak, sinful glances there;—
Till the good angels, when they see me cling
For ever near thee, pale and sorrowing,
Shall for thy sake pronounce my soul forgiven,
And bid thee take thy weeping slave to heaven!
Oh yes, I'll fly with thee'——
             Scarce had she said
These breathless words, when a voice deep and
  dread
As that of Monker waking up the dead
From their first sleep—so startling 'twas to
  both—
Rung through the casement near, 'Thy oath!
  thy oath!'
O Heaven, the ghastliness of that maid's look!—
''Tis he,' faintly she cried, while terror shook
Her inmost core, nor durst she lift her eyes,
Though through the casement now nought but
  the skies
And moonlight fields were seen, calm as before—
''Tis he, and I am his—all, all is o'er—
Go—fly this instant, or thou'rt ruined too—
My oath, my oath, O God! 'tis all too true,
True as the worm in this cold heart it is—
I am Mokanna's bride—his, Azim, his—
The dead stood round us while I spoke that vow,
Their blue lips echoed it—I hear them now!
Their eyes glared on me while I pledged that
  bowl,
'Twas burning blood—I feel it in my soul!
And the Veiled Bridegroom—hist! I've seen
  to-night
What angels know not of—so foul a sight,
So horrible—oh, never may'st thou see
What *there* lies hid from all but hell and me!
But I must hence—off, off—I am not thine,
Nor Heaven's, nor Love's, nor aught that is
  divine—
Hold me not—ha! think'st thou the fiends that
  sever
Hearts cannot sunder hands?—thus, then—for
  ever!'

With all that strength which madness lends
  the weak,
She flung away his arm; and, with a shriek,—

Whose sound, though he should linger out more years
Than wretch e'er told, can never leave his ears,—

Flew up through that long avenue of light,
Fleetly as some dark, ominous bird of night
Across the sun, and soon was out of sight!

Lalla Rookh could think of nothing all day but the misery of these two young lovers. Her gaiety was gone, and she looked pensively even upon Fadladeen. She felt, too, without knowing why, a sort of uneasy pleasure in imagining that Azim must have been just such a youth as Feramorz; just as worthy to enjoy all the blessings, without any of the pangs, of that illusive passion, which too often, like the sunny apples of Istkahar, is all sweetness on one side, and all bitterness on the other.[1]

As they passed along a sequestered river after sunset, they saw a young Hindoo girl upon the bank, whose employment seemed to them so strange that they stopped their palankeens to observe her. She had lighted a small lamp, filled with oil of cocoa, and placing it in an earthen dish, adorned with a wreath of flowers, had committed it with a trembling hand to the stream, and was now anxiously watching its progress down the current, heedless of the gay cavalcade which had drawn up beside her. Lalla Rookh was all curiosity;—when one of her attendants, who had lived upon the banks of the Ganges (where this ceremony is so frequent that often, in the dusk of the evening, the river is seen glittering all over with lights, like the Oton-Tala, or Sea of Stars[2]), informed the Princess that it was the usual way in which the friends of those who had gone on dangerous voyages offered up vows for their safe return. If the lamp sank immediately, the omen was disastrous; but if it went shining down the stream, and continued to burn till entirely out of sight, the return of the beloved object was considered as certain.

Lalla Rookh, as they moved on, more than once looked back to observe how the young Hindoo's lamp proceeded; and while she saw with pleasure that it was still unextinguished, she could not help fearing that all the hopes of this life were no better than that feeble light upon the river. The remainder of the journey was passed in silence. She now, for the first time, felt that shade of melancholy which comes over the youthful maiden's heart, as sweet and transient as her own breath upon a mirror; nor was it till she heard the lute of Feramorz touched lightly at the door of her pavilion, that she waked from the reverie in which she had been wandering. Instantly her eyes were lighted up with pleasure, and, after a few unheard remarks from Fadladeen upon the indecorum of a poet seating himself in presence of a princess, everything was arranged as on the preceding evening, and all listened with eagerness, while the story was thus continued:—

Whose are the gilded tents that crowd the way,
Where all was waste and silent yesterday?
This City of War which, in a few short hours,
Hath sprung up here, as if the magic powers
Of him who, in the twinkling of a star,
Built the high pillared halls of Chilminar,[3]
Had conjured up, far as the eye can see,
This world of tents, and domes, and sun-bright armoury;—
Princely pavilions, screened by many a fold
Of crimson cloth, and topped with balls of gold;—
Steeds, with their housings of rich silver spun,
Their chains and poitrels glittering in the sun;

And camels, tufted o'er with Yemen's shells,[4]
Shaking in every breeze their light-toned bells!

But yester-eve, so motionless around,
So mute was this wide plain, that not a sound
But the far torrent, or the locust-bird[5]
Hunting among the thickets, could be heard;—
Yet hark! what discords now, of every kind,
Shouts, laughs, and screams are revelling in the wind;
The neigh of cavalry;—the tinkling throngs
Of laden camels and their drivers' songs;[6]—

---

[1] 'In the territory of Istkahar there is a kind of apple, half of which is sweet, and half sour.'—*Ebn Haukal.*

[2] 'The place where the Whango, a river of Tibet, rises, and where there are more than a hundred springs, which sparkle like stars; whence it is called Hotun-nor, that is, the Sea of Stars.'—*Description of Tibet in Pinkerton.*

[3] The edifices of Chilminar and Baalbec are supposed to have been built by the genii, acting under the orders of Jan ben Jan, who governed the world long before the time of Adam.

[4] 'A superb camel, ornamented with strings and tufts of small shells.'—*Ali Bey.*

[5] A native of Khorassan, and allured southward by means of the water of a fountain between Shiraz and Ispahan, called the Fountain of Birds, of which it is so fond that it will follow wherever that water is carried.

[6] 'Some of the camels have bells about their necks, and some about their legs, like those which our carriers put about their fore-horses' necks.'—*Pitt's Account of the Mohammedans.*

'The camel-driver follows the camels singing, and sometimes playing upon his pipe; the louder he sings and pipes, the faster the camels go. Nay, they will stand still when he gives over his music.'—*Tavernier*

Ringing of arms, and flapping in the breeze
Of streamers from ten thousand canopies;—
War-music, bursting out from time to time,
With gong and tymbalon's tremendous chime;—
Or, in the pause, when harsher sounds are mute,
The mellow breathings of some horn or flute,
That far off, broken by the eagle note
Of th' Abyssinian trumpet,[1] swell and float!

Who leads this mighty army?—ask ye 'who?'
And mark ye not those banners of dark hue,
The Night and Shadow,[2] over yonder tent?—
It is the Caliph's glorious armament.
Roused in his palace by the dread alarms,
That hourly came, of the false Prophet's arms,
And of his host of infidels, who hurled
Defiance fierce at Islam[3] and the world;—
Though worn with Grecian warfare, and behind
The veils of his bright palace calm reclined,
Yet brooked he not such blasphemy should stain,
Thus unrevenged, the evening of his reign;
But, having sworn upon the Holy Grave[4]
To conquer or to perish, once more gave
His shadowy banners proudly to the breeze,
And with an army nursed in victories
Here stands to crush the rebels that o'errun
His blest and beauteous Province of the Sun.

Ne'er did the march of Mahadi display
Such pomp before;—not even when on his way
To Mecca's temple, when both land and sea
Were spoiled to feed the pilgrim's luxury;[5]
When round him, 'mid the burning sands, he saw
Fruits of the North in icy freshness thaw,
And cooled his thirsty lip, beneath the glow
Of Mecca's sun, with urns of Persian snow:—
Nor e'er did armament more grand than that
Pour from the kingdoms of the Caliphat.
First, in the van, the People of the Rock,[6]
On their light mountain steeds of royal stock;[7]
Then Chieftains of Damascus, proud to see
The flashing of their swords' rich marquetry;[8]

Men, from the regions near the Volga's mouth,
Mixed with the rude, black archers of the South;
And Indian lancers, in white turbaned ranks,
From the far Sinde, or Attock's sacred banks,
With dusky legions from the Land of Myrrh,[9]
And many a mace-armed Moor and Mid-Sea
  Islander.

Nor less in number, though more new and rude
In warfare's school, was the vast multitude
That, fired by zeal, or by oppression wronged,
Round the white standard of the Impostor
  thronged.
Beside his thousands of Believers,—blind,
Burning, and headlong as the Samiel wind,—
Many who felt and more who feared to feel
The bloody Islamite's converting steel,
Flocked to his banner:—Chiefs of the Uzbek race,
Waving their heron crests with martial grace;[10]
Turkomans, countless as their flocks, led forth
From the aromatic pastures of the North;
Wild warriors of the turquoise hills,[11]—and those
Who dwell beyond the everlasting snows
Of Hindoo Kosh, in stormy freedom bred,
Their fort the rock, their camp the torrent's bed.
But none, of all who owned the Chief's command,
Rushed to that battle-field with bolder hand
Or sterner hate than Iran's outlawed men,
Her Worshippers of Fire[12]—all panting then
For vengeance on the accursed Saracen;
Vengeance at last for their dear country spurned,
Her throne usurped, and her bright shrines o'er-
  turned.
From Yezd's[13] eternal Mansion of the Fire,
Where aged saints in dreams of heaven expire;
From Badku, and those fountains of blue flame
That burn into the Caspian,[14] fierce they came,
Careless for what or whom the blow was sped,
So vengeance triumphed, and their tyrants bled!

Such was the wild and miscellaneous host
That high in air their motley banners tost

---

[1] 'This trumpet is often called in Abyssinia *Nesser Cano*, which signifies the Note of the Eagle.'—*Note of Bruce's Editor.*

[2] The two black standards borne before the Caliphs of the House of Abbas were called, allegorically, 'The Night and The Shadow.'

[3] The Mohammedan religion.

[4] 'The Persians swear by the Tomb of Shah Besade, who is buried at Casbin; and when one desires another to asseverate a matter, he will ask him if he dare swear by the Holy Grave.'

[5] Mahadi, in a single pilgrimage to Mecca, expended six millions of dinars of gold.

[6] 'The inhabitants of Hejaz, or Arabia Petræa, called "The People of the Rock."'

[7] 'Those horses, called by the Arabians Kochlani, of whom a written genealogy has been kept for 2000 years. They are said to derive their origin from King Solomon's steeds.'

[8] 'Many of the figures on the blades of their swords are wrought in gold or silver, or in marquetry with small gems.'

[9] Azab or Saba.

[10] 'The chiefs of the Uzbek Tartars wear a plume of white heron's feathers in their turbans.'

[11] 'In the mountains of Nishapour and Tous, in Khorassan, they find turquoises.'

[12] The Ghebers or Guebres, those original natives of Persia who adhered to their ancient faith, the religion of Zoroaster, and who, after the conquest of their country by the Arabs, were either persecuted at home or forced to become wanderers abroad.

[13] 'Yezd, the chief residence of those ancient natives who worship the Sun and the Fire, which latter they have carefully kept lighted, without being once extinguished for a moment, above 30 0 years, on a mountain near Yezd, called Ater Quedah, signifying the House or Mansion of the Fire. He is reckoned very unfortunate who dies off that mountain.'

[14] 'When the weather is hazy, the springs of naphtha (on an island near Baku) boil up the higher, and the naphtha often takes fire on the surface of the earth, and runs in a flame into the sea to a distance almost incredible.'

Around the Prophet-Chief—all eyes still bent
Upon that glittering veil, where'er it went,
That beacon through the battle's stormy flood,
That rainbow of the field, whose showers were
   blood!

Twice hath the sun upon their conflict set,
And risen again, and found them grappling yet;
While streams of carnage in his noontide blaze
Smoke up to heaven—hot as that crimson haze
By which the prostrate caravan is awed
In the red desert when the wind's abroad.
'On, Swords of God!' the panting Caliph calls,—
'Thrones for the living—heaven for him who
   falls!'—
'On, brave avengers, on,' Mokanna cries,
'And Eblis blast the recreant slave that flies!'
Now comes the brunt, the crisis of the day—
They clash—they strive—the Caliph's troops
   give way!
Mokanna's self plucks the black banner down,
And now the orient world's imperial crown
Is just within his grasp—when, hark, that shout!
Some hand hath checked the flying Moslems' rout;
And now they turn, they rally—at their head
A warrior (like those angel youths who led,
In glorious panoply of heaven's own mail,
The Champions of the Faith through Beder's
   vale),[2]
Bold as if gifted with ten thousand lives,
Turns on the fierce pursuers' blades, and drives
At once the multitudinous torrent back,
While hope and courage kindle in his track,
And, at each step, his bloody falchion makes
Terrible vistas through which victory breaks!
In vain Mokanna, 'midst the general flight,
Stands, like the red moon, on some stormy night,
Among the fugitive clouds that, hurrying by,
Leave only her unshaken in the sky,—
In vain he yells his desperate curses out,
Deals death promiscuously to all about,
To foes that charge and coward friends that fly,
And seems of *all* the great arch-enemy.
The panic spreads—'A miracle!' throughout
The Moslem ranks, 'A miracle!' they shout,
All gazing on that youth, whose coming seems
A light, a glory, such as breaks in dreams;
And every sword, true as o'er billows dim
The needle tracks the load-star, following him!

Right tow'rds Mokanna now he cleaves his
   path,
Impatient cleaves, as though the bolt of wrath
He bears from Heaven withhold its awful burst
From weaker heads, and souls but half-way curst,
To break o'er him, the mightiest and the worst!

But vain his speed—though, in that hour of
   blood,
Had all God's seraphs round Mokanna stood,
With swords of fire, ready like fate to fall,
Mokanna's soul would have defied them all;—
Yet now, the rush of fugitives, too strong
For human force, hurries even *him* along:
In vain he struggles 'mid the wedged array
Of flying thousands,—he is borne away;
And the sole joy his baffled spirit knows
In this forced flight is—murdering as he goes!
As a grim tiger, whom the torrent's might
Surprises in some parched ravine at night,
Turns, even in drowning, on the wretched flocks
Swept with him in that snow-flood from the
   rocks,
And, to the last, devouring on his way,
Bloodies the stream he hath not power to stay.

'Alla il Alla!'—the glad shout renew—
'Alla Akbar!'[3]—the Caliph's in Merou.
Hang out your gilded tapestry in the streets,
And light your shrines and chant your ziralects;[4]
The Swords of God have triumphed—on his
   throne
Your Caliph sits, and the Veiled Chief hath
   flown.
Who does not envy that young warrior now,
To whom the Lord of Islam bends his brow,
In all the graceful gratitude of power,
For his throne's safety in that perilous hour?
Who doth not wonder, when, amidst the acclaim
Of thousands, heralding to heaven his name—
'Mid all those holier harmonies of fame
Which sound along the path of virtuous souls,
Like music round a planet as it rolls,—
He turns away, coldly, as if some gloom
Hung o'er his heart no triumphs can illume;—
Some sightless grief, upon whose blasted gaze
Though glory's light may play, in vain it plays?
Yes, wretched Azim! thine is such a grief,
Beyond all hope, and terror, all relief;
A dark, cold calm, which nothing now can
   break,
Or warm, or brighten,—like that Syrian Lake[5]
Upon whose surface morn and summer shed
Their smiles in vain, for all beneath is dead!—
Hearts there have been o'er which this weight
   of woe
Came by long use of suffering, tame and slow;
But thine, lost youth! was sudden—over thee
It broke at once, when all seemed ecstasy;
When Hope looked up, and saw the gloomy past
Melt into splendour, and bliss dawn at last—
'T was then, even then, o'er joys so freshly blown,
This mortal blight of misery came down;

---

[1] Savary says—'Torrents of burning sand roll before it, the firmament is enveloped in a thick veil, and the sun appears of the colour of blood. Sometimes whole caravans are buried in it.'

[2] 'In the great victory gained by Mohammed at Beder, he was assisted by three thousand angels, led by Gabriel, mounted on his horse Hiazum.'

[3] The Tecbir, or cry of the Arabs. 'Alla Acbar!' says Ockley, 'means God is most mighty.'

[4] 'The ziraleet is a kind of chorus which the women of the East sing upon joyful occasions.'

[5] The Dead Sea, which contains neither animal nor vegetable life.

Even then, the full, warm gushings of thy heart
Were checked—like fount-drops, frozen as they
    start—
And there, like them, cold, sunless relics hang,
Each fixed and chilled into a lasting pang!

One sole desire, one passion now remains,
To keep life's fever still within his veins,
Vengeance!—dire vengeance on the wretch who
    cast
O'er him and all he loved that ruinous blast.
For this, when rumours reached him in his flight
Far, far away, after that fatal night,—
Rumours of armies, thronging to the attack
Of the Veiled Chief,—for this he winged him back,
Fleet as the vulture speeds to flags unfurled,
And, when all hope seemed desperate, wildly hurled
Himself into the scale, and saved a world.
For this he still lives on, careless of all
The wreaths that Glory on his path lets fall;
For this alone exists—like lightning-fire,
To speed one bolt of vengeance, and expire!

But safe as yet that Spirit of Evil lives;
With a small band of desperate fugitives,
The last sole stubborn fragment, left unriven,
Of the proud host that late stood fronting Heaven,
He gained Merou—breathed a short curse of blood
O'er his lost throne—then passed the Jihon's flood,[1]
And gathering all whose madness of belief
Still saw a saviour in their down-fallen Chief,
Raised the white banner within Neksheb's gates,[2]
And there, untamed, th' approaching conqueror
    waits.

Of all his Haram, all that busy hive,
With music and with sweets sparkling alive,
He took but one, the partner of his flight,
One, not for love—not for her beauty's light—
No, Zelica stood withering 'midst the gay,
Wan as the blossom that fell yesterday
From the Alma tree and dies, while overhead
To-day's young flower is springing in its stead.[3]
Oh, not for love—thus the deepest damned must be
Touched with heaven's glory, ere such fiends as he
Can feel one glimpse of Love's divinity.
But no, she is his victim:—*there* lie all
Her charms for him—charms that can never pall,
As long as hell within his heart can stir,
Or one faint trace of heaven is left in her.
To work an angel's ruin—to behold
As white a page as Virtue e'er unrolled

Blacken, beneath his touch, into a scroll
Of damning sins, sealed with a burning soul—
This is his triumph; this the joy accurst,
That ranks him among demons all but first:
This gives the victim, that before him lies
Blighted and lost, a glory in his eyes,
A light like that with which hell-fire illumes
The ghastly, writhing wretch whom it consumes!

But other tasks now wait him—tasks that need
All the deep daringness of thought and deed
With which the Dives[4] have gifted him—for
    mark,
Over yon plains, which night had else made dark,
Those lanterns, countless as the winged lights
That spangle India's fields on showery nights,[5]
Far as their formidable gleams they shed,
The mighty tents of the beleaguerer spread,
Glimmering along the horizon's dusky line,
And thence in nearer circles, till they shine
Among the founts and groves, o'er which the town
In all its armed magnificence looks down.
Yet, fearless, from his lofty battlements
Mokanna views that multitude of tents;
Nay, smiles to think that, though entoiled, beset,
Not less than myriads dare to front him yet;—
That friendless, throneless, he thus stands at
    bay,
Even thus a match for myriads such as they.
'Oh for a sweep of that dark angel's wing
Who brushed the thousands of th' Assyrian king[6]
To darkness in a moment, that I might
People hell's chambers with yon host to-night!
But, come what may, let who will grasp the
    throne,
Caliph or Prophet, man alike shall groan;
Let who will torture him, Priest—Caliph—
    King—
Alike this loathsome world of his shall ring
With victims' shrieks and howlings of the
    slave,—
Sounds that shall glad me even within my
    grave!'
Thus to himself—but to the scanty train
Still left around him, a far different strain:—
'Glorious defenders of the sacred Crown
I bear from heaven, whose light nor blood shall
    drown,
Nor shadow of earth eclipse; before whose gems
The paly pomp of this world's diadems,
The crown of Gerashid, the pillared throne[7]
Of Parviz,[8] and the heron crest that shone,[9]

---

[1] The ancient Oxus.
[2] A city of Transoxiana.
[3] 'You never can cast your eyes on this tree but you meet there either blossoms or fruit; and as the blossom-drop underneath on the ground, others come forth in their stead.'
[4] The demons of the Persian mythology.
[5] Carreri mentions the fire-flies in India during the rainy season.
[6] 'Sennacherib, called by the orientals King of Moussal.'

[7] There were said to be under this throne or palace of Khosrou Parviz a hundred vaults filled with 'treasures so immense, that some Mohammedan writers tell us, their Prophet, to encourage his disciples, carried them to a rock, which at his command opened, and gave them a prospect through it of the treasures of Khosrou.'—*Universal History.*
[8] Chosroes.
[9] 'The crown of Gerashid is cloudy and tarnished before the heron tuft of thy turban.'—From one of the elegies or songs in praise of Ali, written in characters of gold round the gallery of Abbas's tomb.

Magnificent, o'er Ali's beauteous eyes,[1]
Fade like the stars when morn is in the skies:
Warriors, rejoice—the port, to which we've passed
O'er destiny's dark wave, beams out at last!
Victory's our own—'tis written in that Book
Upon whose leaves none but the angels look,
That Islam's sceptre shall beneath the power
Of her great foe fall broken in that hour
When the moon's mighty orb, before all eyes,
From Neksheb's Holy Well portentously shall
    rise!
Now turn and see!'——

        They turned, and, as he spoke,
A sudden splendour all around them broke,
And they beheld an orb, ample and bright,
Rise from the Holy Well,[2] and cast its light
Round the rich city and the plain for miles,[3]—
Flinging such radiance o'er the gilded tiles
Of many a dome and fair-roofed imaret
As autumn suns shed round them when they
    set.
Instant from all who saw the illusive sign
A murmur broke—'Miraculous! divine!'
The Gheber bowed, thinking his idol star
Had waked, and burst impatient through the bar
Of midnight, to inflame him to the war;
While he of Moussa's creed saw in that ray
The glorious Light which, in his freedom's day,
Had rested on the Ark,[4] and now again
Shone out to bless the breaking of his chain.

'To victory!' is at once the cry of all—
Nor stands Mokanna loitering at that call;
But instant the huge gates are flung aside,
And forth, like a diminutive mountain-tide
Into the boundless sea, they speed their course
Right on into the Moslems' mighty force.
The watchmen of the camp,—who in their rounds
Had paused, and even forgot the punctual sounds
Of the small drum with which they count the
    night,[5]
To gaze upon that supernatural light,—
Now sink beneath an unexpected arm,
And in a death-groan give their last alarm.
'On for the lamps that light yon lofty screen,[6]
Nor blunt your blades with massacre so mean;
There rests the Caliph—speed—one lucky lance
May now achieve mankind's deliverance!'

Desperate the die—such as they only cast
Who venture for a world, and stake their last.
But Fate's no longer with him—blade for blade
Springs up to meet them through the glimmer-
    ing shade,
And as the clash is heard, new legions soon
Pour to the spot, like bees of Kauzeroon[7]
To the shrill timbrel's summons, till at length
The mighty camp swarms out in all its strength,
And back to Neksheb's gates, covering the plain
With random slaughter, drives the adventurous
    train;
Among the last of whom, the Silver Veil
Is seen glittering at times, like the white sail
Of some tossed vessel, on a stormy night,
Catching the tempest's momentary light!

And hath not *this* brought the proud spirit
    low?
Nor dashed his brow, nor checked his daring?
No.
Though half the wretches whom at night he led
To thrones and victory lie disgraced and dead,
Yet morning hears him, with unshrinking crest,
Still vaunt of thrones and victory to the rest;—
And they believe him!—oh, the lover may
Distrust that look which steals his soul away;—
The babe may cease to think that it can play
With heaven's rainbow;—alchymists may doubt
The shining gold their crucible gives out;
But Faith, fanatic Faith, once wedded fast
To some dear falsehood, hugs it to the last.

And well th' Impostor knew all lures and arts
That Lucifer e'er taught to tangle hearts;
Nor, 'mid these last bold workings of his plot
Against men's souls, is Zelica forgot.
Ill-fated Zelica! had reason been
Awake through half the horrors thou hast seen,
Thou never couldst have borne it—Death had
    come
At once and taken thy wrung spirit home.
But 'twas not so—a torpor, a suspense
Of thought, almost of life, came o'er the intense
And passionate struggles of that fearful night
When her last hope of peace and heaven took
    flight;
And though, at times, a gleam of frenzy broke,
As through some dull volcano's veil of smoke

---

[1] 'The beauty of Ali's eyes was so remarkable, that whenever the Persians would describe anything as very lovely, they say it is Ayn Hali, or the eyes of Ali.'

[2] We are not told more of this trick of the Impostor, than that it was 'une machine, qu'il disoit être la Lune.' According to Richardson, the miracle is perpetuated in Nekshcheb:—'Nakshab, the name of a city in Trans-oxiana, where they say there is a well in which the appearance of the moon is to be seen night and day.'

[3] 'Il amusa pendant deux mois le peuple de la ville de Nekhscheb, en faisant sortir toutes les nuits du fond d'un puits un corps lumineux semblable à la Lune, qui portoit sa lumière jusqu'à la distance de plusieurs milles.' —*D'Herbelot.* Hence he was called Sazendéhmah, or the Moonmaker.

[4] The Shechinah, called Sakinat in the Koran; *vide* Sale.

[5] 'The parts of the night are made known as well by instruments of music as by the rounds of the watchmen with cries and small drums.'

[6] 'The Serrapurda, high screens of red cloth stiffened with cane, used to enclose a considerable space round the royal tents.'
The tents of princes were generally illuminated. Norden tells us that the tent of the Bey of Girge was distinguished from the other tents by forty lanterns being suspended before it. *Vide Harmer's Observations on Job.*

[7] 'From the groves of orange-trees at Kauzerocn the bees cull a celebrated honey.'

Ominous flashings now and then will start,
Which show the fire's still busy at its heart;
Yet was she mostly wrapped in solemn gloom,—
Not such as Azim's, brooding o'er its doom,
And calm without, as is the brow of death,
While busy worms are gnawing underneath—
But in a blank and pulseless torpor, free
From thought or pain, a sealed-up apathy,
Which left her oft, with scarce one living thrill,
The cold, pale victim of her torturer's will.

Again, as in Merou, he had her decked
Gorgeously out, the Priestess of the sect;
And led her glittering forth before the eyes
Of his rude train, as to a sacrifice,—
Pallid as she, the young, devoted Bride
Of the fierce Nile, when, decked in all the pride
Of nuptial pomp, she sinks into his tide.[1]
And while the wretched maid hung down her head,
And stood, as one just risen from the dead,
Amid that gazing crowd, the fiend would tell
His credulous slaves it was some charm or spell
Possessed her now,—and from that darkened trance
Should dawn ere long their Faith's deliverance.
Or if, at times, goaded by guilty shame,
Her soul was roused, and words of wildness came,
Instant the bold blasphemer would translate
Her ravings into oracles of fate,
Would hail Heaven's signals in her flashing eyes,
And call her shrieks the language of the skies!

But vain at length his arts—despair is seen
Gathering around; and famine comes to glean
All that the sword had left unreaped:—in vain
At morn and eve across the northern plain
He looks impatient for the promised spears
Of the wild hordes and Tartar mountaineers;
They come not—while his fierce beleaguerers pour
Engines of havoc in, unknown before,[2]

And horrible as new;[3]—javelins, that fly
Enwreathed with smoky flames through the dark sky,
And red-hot globes that, opening as they mount,
Discharge, as from a kindled naphtha fount,[4]
Showers of consuming fire o'er all below;
Looking, as through th' illumined night they go,
Like those wild birds[5] that by the Magians oft,
At festivals of fire, were sent aloft
Into the air, with blazing faggots tied
To their huge wings, scattering combustion wide.
All night, the groans of wretches who expire
In agony beneath these darts of fire
Ring through the city—while, descending o'er
Its shrines, and domes, and streets of sycamore;—
Its lone bazaars, with their bright cloth of gold,
Since the last peaceful pageant left unrolled;—
Its beauteous marble baths, whose idle jets
Now gush with blood;—and its tall minarets,
That late have stood up in the evening glare
Of the red sun, unhallowed by a prayer;—
O'er each in turn the terrible flame-bolts fall,
And death and conflagration throughout all
The desolate city hold high festival!

Mokanna sees the world is his no more;—
One sting at parting, and his grasp is o'er.
'What! drooping now?'—thus, with unblushing cheek,
He hails the few who yet can hear him speak,
Of all those famished slaves around him lying,
And by the light of blazing temples dying;—
'What! drooping now?—now, when at length we press
Home o'er the very threshold of success;
When Alla from our ranks hath thinned away
Those grosser branches, that kept out his ray
Of favour from us, and we stand at length
Heirs of his light and children of his strength,
The chosen few who shall survive the fall
Of kings and thrones, triumphant over all!

---

[1] 'A custom, still subsisting at this day, seems to me to prove that the Egyptians formerly sacrificed a young virgin to the god of the Nile; for they now make a statue of earth in shape of a girl, to which they give the name of the Betrothed Bride, and throw it into the river.'—*Savary*.

[2] That they knew the secret of the Greek fire among the Mussulmans early in the eleventh century, appears from Dow's account of Mamood I.:—'When he had launched this fleet, he ordered twenty archers into each boat, and five others with fire-balls, to burn the craft of the Jits, and naphtha to set the whole river on fire.'
The *Agnee aster*, too, in Indian poems, the instrument of Fire, whose flame cannot be extinguished, is supposed to signify the Greek fire. *Vide Wilks's South of India*, vol. i. p. 471.
The mention of gunpowder as in use among the Arabians, long before its supposed discovery in Europe, is introduced by Ebn Fadhl, the Egyptian geographer, who lived in the thirteenth century. 'Bodies,' he says, 'in the form of scorpions, bound round and filled with nitrous powder, glide along, making a gentle noise; then, exploding, they lighten as it were, and burn. But there are others which, cast into the air, stretch along like a cloud, roaring horribly, as thunder roars, and on all sides vomiting out flames, burst, burn, and reduce to cinders whatever comes in their way.' The historian Ben Abdalla, in speaking of Abulualid in the year of Hegira 712, says, 'a fiery globe, by means of combustible matter, with a mighty noise suddenly emitted, strikes with the force of lightning, and shakes the citadel.' *Vide* the extracts from Casiri's *Biblioth. Arab. Hispan.* in the Appendix to Berrington's *Literary History of the Middle Ages*.

[3] The Greek fire, which was occasionally lent by the Emperors to their allies.

[4] See Hanway's *Account of the Springs of Naphtha at Baku* (which is called by Lieutenant Pottinger, Joala Mookhee, or the Flaming Mouth), taking fire, and running into the sea.

[5] 'At the great festival of fire, called the Sheb Sezé, they used to set fire to large bunches of dry combustibles, fastened round wild beasts and birds, which being then let loose, the air and earth appeared one great illumination; and as these terrified creatures naturally fled to the wood for shelter, it is easy to conceive the conflagrations they produced.'—*Richardson's Dissertation*.

Have you then lost, weak murmurers as you are,
All faith in him who was your light, your star?
Have you forgot the eye of glory, hid
Beneath this veil, the flashing of whose lid
Could, like a sun-stroke of the desert, wither
Millions of such as yonder chief brings hither?
Long have its lightnings slept—too long—but now
All earth shall feel th' unveiling of this brow!
To-night—yes, sainted men! this very night,
I bid you all to a fair festal rite,
Where—having deep refreshed each weary limb
With viands such as feast heaven's cherubim,
And kindled up your souls, now sunk and dim,
With that pure wine the dark-eyed maids above
Keep, sealed with precious musk, for those they love¹—
I will myself uncurtain in your sight
The wonders of this brow's ineffable light;
Then lead you forth, and with a wink disperse
Yon myriads, howling through the universe!'

Eager they listen—while each accent darts
New life into their chilled and hope-sick hearts;—
Such treacherous life as the cool draught supplies
To him upon the stake, who drinks and dies!
Wildly they point their lances to the light
Of the fast-sinking sun, and shout, 'To-night!'
'To-night,' their chief re-echoes in a voice
Of fiend-like mockery that bids hell rejoice.
Deluded victims!—never hath this earth
Seen mourning half so mournful as their mirth.
Here, to the few whose iron frames had stood
This racking waste of famine and of blood,
Faint, dying wretches clung, from whom the shout
Of triumph like a maniac's laugh broke out;—
There, others, lighted by the smouldering fire,
Danced, like wan ghosts about a funeral pyre,
Among the dead and dying strewed around;—
While some pale wretch looked on, and from his wound
Plucking the fiery dart by which he bled,
In ghastly transport waved it o'er his head!

'Twas more than midnight now—a fearful pause
Had followed the long shouts, the wild applause,
That lately from those royal gardens burst,
Where the veiled demon held his feast accurst,
When Zelica—alas, poor ruined heart,
In every horror doomed to bear its part!—
Was hidden to the banquet by a slave,
Who, while his quivering lip the summons gave,
Grew black, as though the shadows of the grave
Compassed him round, and, ere he could repeat
His message through, fell lifeless at her feet!

Shuddering she went—a soul-felt pang of fear,
A presage that her own dark doom was near,
Roused every feeling, and brought reason back
Once more, to writhe her last upon the rack.
All round seemed tranquil—even the foe had ceased,
As if aware of that demoniac feast,
His fiery bolts; and though the heavens looked red,
'Twas but some distant conflagration's spread.
But hark!—she stops—she listens—dreadful tone!
'Tis her Tormentor's laugh—and now, a groan,
A long death-groan comes with it;—can this be
The place of mirth, the bower of revelry?
She enters—Holy Alla, what a sight
Was there before her! By the glimmering light
Of the pale dawn, mixed with the flare of brands
That round lay burning, dropped from lifeless hands,
She saw the board, in splendid mockery spread,
Rich censers breathing—garlands overhead—
The urns, the cups, from which they late had quaffed,
All gold and gems, but—what had been the draught?
Oh! who need ask, that saw those livid guests,
With their swoln heads sunk blackening on their breasts,
Or looking pale to heaven with glassy glare,
As if they sought, but saw no mercy there;
As if they felt, though poison racked them through,
Remorse the deadlier torment of the two!
While some, the bravest, hardiest in the train
Of their false Chief, who on the battle-plain
Would have met death with transport by his side,
Here mute and helpless gasped;—but, as they died,
Looked horrible vengeance with their eyes' last strain,
And clenched the slackening hand at him in vain

Dreadful it was to see the ghastly stare,
The stony look of horror and despair,
Which some of these expiring victims cast
Upon their souls' tormentor to the last;—
Upon that mocking fiend, whose veil, now raised,
Showed them, as in death's agony they gazed,
Not the long-promised light, the brow whose beaming
Was to come forth, all-conquering, all-redeeming,
But features horribler than hell e'er traced
On its own brood;—no Demon of the Waste,²
No churchyard ghole, caught lingering in the light
Of the blest sun, e'er blasted human sight
With lineaments so foul, so fierce as those
Th' Impostor now, in grinning mockery, shows:—

---

¹ 'The righteous shall be given to drink of pure wine, sealed; the seal whereof shall be musk.'—*Koran*, chap. xxxiii.

² 'The Afghauns believe each of the numerous solitudes and deserts of their country to be inhabited by a lonely demon whom they call the Ghoolee Beeabau, or Spirit of the Waste. They often illustrate the wildness of any sequestered tribe, by saying they are wild as the Demon of the Waste.'

He sprung, and sunk as the last words were said—
Quick closed the burning waters o'er his head,
And Zelica was left—within the ring
Of those wide walls the only living thing;
The only wretched one, still cursed with breath,
In all that frightful wilderness of death!
More like some bloodless ghost—such as they tell
In the lone Cities of the Silent dwell.

Page 77.

'There, ye wise saints, behold your Light, your
    Star—
Ye *would* be dupes and victims, and ye *are*.
Is it enough? or must I, while a thrill
Lives in your sapient bosoms, cheat you still?
Swear that the burning death ye feel within
Is but the trance with which heaven's joys begin;
That this foul visage, foul as e'er disgraced
Even monstrous man, is—after God's own taste;
And that—but see!—ere I have half-way said
My greetings through, th' uncourteous souls are
    fled.
Farewell, sweet spirits! not in vain ye die,
If Eblis loves you half so well as I.—
Ha, my young bride!—'tis well—take thou thy
    seat;
Nay, come—no shuddering—didst thou never
    meet
The dead before?—they graced our wedding,
    sweet;
And these, my guests to-night, have brimmed so
    true
Their parting cups, that *thou* shalt pledge one too.
But—how is this?—all empty? all drunk up?
Hot lips have been before thee in the cup,
Young bride,—yet stay—one precious drop
    remains,
Enough to warm a gentle Priestess' veins;—
Here, drink—and should thy lover's conquering
    arms
Speed hither, ere thy lip lose all its charms,
Give him but half this venom in thy kiss,
And I'll forgive my haughty rival's bliss!

'For *me*—I too must die—but not like these
Vile, rankling things, to fester in the breeze;
To have this brow in ruffian triumph shown,
With all death's grimness added to its own,
And rot to dust beneath the taunting eyes
Of slaves, exclaiming, "There his godship lies!"
No, cursed race, since first my soul drew breath,
They've been my dupes, and *shall* be, even in
    death.
Thou seest yon cistern in the shade,—'tis filled
With burning drugs, for this last hour distilled;—
There will I plunge me, in that liquid flame—
Fit bath to lave a dying prophet's frame!—
There perish, all—ere pulse of thine shall fail—
Nor leave one limb to tell mankind the tale.
So shall my votaries, wheresoe'er they rave,
Proclaim that Heaven took back the Saint it
    gave;—
But I've but vanished from this earth a while,
To come again, with bright, unshrouded smile!
So shall they build me altars in their zeal,
Where knaves shall minister, and fools shall
    kneel;

Where Faith may mutter o'er her mystic spell,
Written in blood, and Bigotry may swell
The sail he spreads for heaven with blasts from
    hell!
So shall my banner through long ages be
The rallying sign of fraud and anarchy;—
Kings yet unborn shall rue Mokanna's name,
And, though I die, my spirit, still the same,
Shall walk abroad in all the stormy strife,
And guilt, and blood, that were its bliss in life!
But hark! their battering engine shakes the
    wall—
Why, *let* it shake—thus I can brave them all.
No trace of me shall greet them when they
    come,
And I can trust thy faith, for—thou'lt be dumb.
Now mark how readily a wretch like me
In one bold plunge commences Deity!'—

He sprung and sunk, as the last words were
    said,—
Quick closed the burning waters o'er his head,
And Zelica was left—within the ring
Of those wide walls the only living thing;
The only wretched one, still cursed with breath,
In all that frightful wilderness of death!
More like some bloodless ghost, such as, they
    tell,
In the lone Cities of the Silent [2] dwell,
And there, unseen of all but Alla, sit
Each by its own pale carcass, watching it.

But morn is up, and a fresh warfare stirs
Throughout the camp of the beleaguerers.
Their globes of fire (the dread artillery lent
By Greece to conquering Mahadi) are spent;
And now the scorpion's shaft, the quarry sent
From high balistas, and the shielded throng
Of soldiers swinging the huge ram along,—
All speak th' impatient Islamites' intent
To try, at length, if tower and battlement
And bastioned wall be not less hard to win,
Less tough to break down, than the hearts within.
First in impatience and in toil is he,
The burning Azim,—oh! could he but see
The Impostor once alive within his grasp,
Not the gaunt lion's hug, nor boa's clasp,
Could match that gripe of vengeance, or keep
    pace
With the fell heartiness of Hate's embrace!

Loud rings the ponderous ram against the
    walls;
Now shake the ramparts, now a buttress falls,
But still no breach—' Once more, one mighty
    swing
Of all your beams, together thundering!'

---

[1] 'Il donna du poison dans le vin à tous ses gens, et
se jetta lui-même ensuite dans une cuve pleine de
drogues brûlantes et consumantes, afin qu'il ne restât
rien de tous les membres de son corps, et que ceux qui
restoient de sa secte puissent croire qu'il étoit monté au
ciel, ce qui ne manqua pas d'arriver.'—*D'Herbelot*.

[2] 'They have all a great reverence for burial-grounds,
which they sometimes call by the poetical name of
Cities of the Silent, and which they people with the
ghosts of the departed, who sit each at the head of his
own grave, invisible to mortal eyes.'

There—the wall shakes—the shouting troops exult—
Quick, quick discharge your weightiest catapult
Right on that spot, and Neksheb is our own!'—
'Tis done—the battlements come crashing down,
And the huge wall, by that stroke riven in two,
Yawning like some old crater rent anew,
Shows the dim, desolate city smoking through.
But strange! no signs of life—nought living seen
Above, below—what can this stillness mean?
A minute's pause suspends all hearts and eyes—
'In through the breach,' impetuous Azim cries;
But the cool Caliph, fearful of some wile
In this blank stillness, checks the troops awhile.
Just then, a figure with slow step advanced
Forth from the ruined walls; and, as there glanced
A sunbeam over it, all eyes could see
The well-known Silver Veil!—"'Tis he, 'tis he,
Mokanna, and alone!' they shout around;
Young Azim from his steed springs to the ground—
'Mine, Holy Caliph! mine,' he cries, 'the task
To crush yon daring wretch—'tis all I ask.'
Eager he darts to meet the demon foe,
Who still across wide heaps of ruin slow
And falteringly comes, till they are near;
Then, with a bound, rushes on Azim's spear,
And, casting off the veil in falling, shows—
Oh!—'tis his Zelica's life-blood that flows!

'I meant not, Azim,' soothingly she said,
As on his trembling arm she leaned her head,
And, looking in his face, saw anguish there
Beyond all wounds the quivering flesh can bear—
'I meant not *thou* shouldst have the pain of this;
Though death, with thee thus tasted, is a bliss
Thou wouldst not rob me of, didst thou but know
How oft I've prayed to God I might die so!
But the fiend's venom was too scant and slow;—
To linger on were maddening—and I thought
If once that veil—nay, look not on it—caught
The eyes of your fierce soldiery, I should be
Struck by a thousand death-darts instantly.
But this is sweeter—oh! believe me, yes—
I would not change this sad but dear caress,
This death within thy arms I would not give,
For the most smiling life the happiest live!
All that stood dark and drear before the eye
Of my strayed soul is passing swiftly by;
A light comes o'er me from those looks of love,
Like the first dawn of mercy from above;
And if thy lips but tell me I'm forgiven,
Angels will echo the blest words in heaven!

But live, my Azim;—oh! to call thee mine
Thus once again! *my* Azim—dream divine!
Live, if thou ever lov'dst me, if to meet
Thy Zelica hereafter would be sweet,
Oh, live to pray for her—to bend the knee
Morning and night before that Deity
To whom pure lips and hearts without a stain,
As thine are, Azim, never breathed in vain,—
And pray that He may pardon her,—may take
Compassion on her soul for thy dear sake,
And, nought remembering but her love to thee,
Make her all thine, all His, eternally!
Go to those happy fields where first we twined
Our youthful hearts together—every wind
That meets thee there, fresh from the well-known flowers,
Will bring the sweetness of those innocent hours
Back to thy soul, and thou may'st feel again
For thy poor Zelica as thou didst then.
So shall thy orisons, like dew that flies
To heaven upon the morning's sunshine, rise
With all love's earliest ardour to the skies!
And should they—but alas! my senses fail—
Oh for one minute!—should thy prayers prevail,
If pardoned souls may from that World of Bliss
Reveal their joy to those they love in this,
I'll come to thee—in some sweet dream—and tell—
O Heaven!—I die—dear love! farewell, farewell!'

Time fleeted—years on years had passed away
And few of those who on that mournful day
Had stood, with pity in their eyes, to see
The maiden's death, and the youth's agony,
Were living still—when, by a rustic grave
Beside the swift Amoo's transparent wave,
An aged man, who had grown aged there
By that lone grave, morning and night in prayer,
For the last time knelt down—and, though the shade
Of death hung darkening over him, there played
A gleam of rapture on his eye and cheek
That brightened even death—like the last streak
Of intense glory on the horizon's brim,
When night o'er all the rest hangs chill and dim.
His soul had seen a vision while he slept;
She, for whose spirit he had prayed and wept
So many years, had come to him, all drest
In angel smiles, and told him she was blest!
For this the old man breathed his thanks, and died.—
And there, upon the banks of that loved tide,
He and his Zelica sleep side by side.

The story of the Veiled Prophet of Khorassan being ended, they were now doomed to hear Fadladeen's criticisms upon it. A series of disappointments and accidents had occurred to this learned chamberlain during the journey. In the first place, those couriers stationed, as in the reign of Shah Jehan, between Delhi and the western coast of India, to secure a constant supply of mangoes for the royal table, had, by some cruel irregularity, failed in their duty; and to eat any mangoes but those of Mazagong was, of course, impossible.[1] In the next place, the elephant, laden with his fine antique porcelain,[2] had, in an unusual fit of liveliness, shattered the whole set to pieces,—an irreparable loss, as many of the vessels were so exquisitely old as to have been used under the Emperors Yan and Chun, who reigned many ages before the dynasty of Tang. His Koran, too, supposed to be the identical copy between the leaves of which Mohammed's favourite pigeon used to nestle, had been mislaid by his Koran-bearer three whole days ; not without much spiritual alarm to Fadladeen, who, though professing to hold, with other loyal and orthodox Mussulmans, that salvation could only be found in the Koran, was strongly suspected of believing in his heart, that it could only be found in his own particular copy of it. When to all these grievances is added the obstinacy of the cooks, in putting the pepper of Canara into his dishes instead of the cinnamon of Serendib, we may easily suppose that he came to the task of criticism with at least a sufficient degree of irritability for the purpose.

'In order,' said he, importantly swinging about his chaplet of pearls, 'to convey with clearness my opinion of the story this young man has related, it is necessary to take a review of all the stories that have ever'—— 'My good Fadladeen!' exclaimed the Princess, interrupting him, 'we really do not deserve that you should give yourself so much trouble. Your opinion of the poem we have just heard, will, I have no doubt, be abundantly edifying, without any further waste of your valuable erudition.' 'If that be all,' replied the critic,—evidently mortified at not being allowed to show how much he knew about everything but the subject immediately before him,—' if that be all that is required, the matter is easily despatched.' He then proceeded to analyse the poem, in that strain (so well known to the unfortunate bards of Delhi) whose censures were an infliction from which few recovered, and whose very praises were like the honey extracted from the bitter flowers of the aloe. The chief personages of the story were, if he rightly understood them, an ill-favoured gentleman, with a veil over his face ; —a young lady, whose reason went and came according as it suited the poet's convenience to be sensible or otherwise ;—and a youth, in one of those hideous Bucharian bonnets, who took the aforesaid gentleman in a veil for a Divinity. 'From such materials,' said he, 'what can be expected ?—after rivalling each other in long speeches and absurdities, through some thousands of lines as indigestible as the filberts of Berdaa, our friend in the veil jumps into a tub of aquafortis ; the young lady dies in a set speech, whose only recommendation is, that it is her last ; and the lover lives on to a good old age, for the laudable purpose of seeing her ghost, which he at last happily accomplishes, and expires. This, you will allow, is a fair summary of the story ; and if Nasser, the Arabian merchant, told no better, our Holy Prophet (to whom be all honour and glory!) had no need to be jealous of his abilities for story-telling.'[3]

With respect to the style, it was worthy of the matter : it had not even those politic contrivances of structure which make up for the commonness of the thoughts by the peculiarity of the manner, nor that stately poetical phraseology by which sentiments mean in themselves, like the blacksmith's apron[4] converted into a banner, are so easily gilt and embroidered into consequence. Then as to the versification, it was, to say no worse of it, execrable ; it had neither the copious flow of Ferdosi, the sweetness of Hafez, nor the sententious march of Sadi ; but appeared to him, in the uneasy heaviness of its movements, to have been modelled upon

---

[1] 'The celebrity of Mazagong is owing to its mangoes, which are certainly the best fruit I ever tasted. The parent tree, from which all those of this species have been grafted, is honoured during the fruit season by a guard of sepoys; and in the reign of Shah Jehan, couriers were stationed between Delhi and the Mahratta coast, to secure an abundant and fresh supply of mangoes for the royal table.'—*Mrs. Graham's Journal of a Residence in India.*

[2] This old porcelain is found in digging, and 'if it is esteemed, it is not because it has acquired any new degree of beauty in the earth, but because it has retained its ancient beauty; and this alone is of great importance in China, where they give large sums for the smallest vessels which were used under the Emperors Yan and Chun, who reigned many ages before the dynasty of Tang, at which time porcelain began to be used by the Emperors' (about the year 442).—*Dunn's Collection of Curious Observations*, etc.—a bad translation of some parts of the 'Lettres Edifiantes et Curieuses' of the Missionary Jesuits.

[3] 'La lecture de ces fables plaisoit si fort aux Arabes, que, quand Mohammed les entretenoit de l'Histoire de l'Ancien Testament, ils les méprisoient, lui disant que celles que Nasser leur racontoient étoient beaucoup plus belles. Cette préférence attira à Nasser la malédiction de Mohammed et de tous ses disciples.'

[4] The blacksmith Gao, who successfully resisted the tyrant Zohak, and whose apron became the royal standard of Persia.

the gait of a very tired dromedary. The licences, too, in which it indulged were unpardonable; —for instance, this line, and the poem abounded with such:—

'Like the faint, exquisite music of a dream.'

'What critic that can count,' said Fadladeen, 'and has his full complement of fingers to count withal, would tolerate for an instant such syllabic superfluities?' He here looked round, and discovered that most of his audience were asleep; while the glimmering lamps seemed inclined to follow their example. It became necessary, therefore, however painful to himself, to put an end to his valuable animadversions for the present, and he accordingly concluded, with an air of dignified candour, thus:—' Notwithstanding the observations which I have thought it my duty to make, it is by no means my wish to discourage the young man; so far from it, indeed, that if he will but totally alter his style of writing and thinking, I have very little doubt that I shall be vastly pleased with him.'

Some days elapsed, after this harangue of the Great Chamberlain, before Lalla Rookh could venture to ask for another story. The youth was still a welcome guest in the pavilion,—to *one* heart, perhaps, too dangerously welcome; but all mention of poetry was, as if by common consent, avoided. Though none of the party had much respect for Fadladeen, yet his censures, thus magisterially delivered, evidently made an impression on them all. The Poet himself, to whom criticism was quite a new operation (being wholly unknown in that Paradise of the Indies—Cashmere), felt the shock as it is generally felt at first, till use has made it more tolerable to the patient; the ladies began to suspect that they ought not to be pleased, and seemed to conclude that there must have been much good sense in what Fadladeen said, from its having set them all so soundly to sleep; while the self-complacent chamberlain was left to triumph in the idea of having, for the hundred and fiftieth time in his life, extinguished a poet. Lalla Rookh alone—and Love knew why—persisted in being delighted with all she had heard, and in resolving to hear more as speedily as possible. Her manner, however, of first returning to the subject was unlucky. It was while they rested during the heat of noon near a fountain, on which some hand had rudely traced those well-known words from the Garden of Sadi,—' Many, like me, have viewed this fountain, but they are gone, and their eyes are closed for ever!'—that she took occasion, from the melancholy beauty of this passage, to dwell upon the charms of poetry in general. ' It is true,' she said, ' few poets can imitate that sublime bird,[1] which flies always in the air, and never touches the earth;—it is only once in many ages a genius appears, whose words, like those on the Written Mountain,[2] last for ever;—but still there are some, as delightful perhaps, though not so wonderful, who, if not stars over our head, are at least flowers along our path, and whose sweetness of the moment we ought gratefully to inhale, without calling upon them for a brightness and a durability beyond their nature. In short,' continued she, blushing, as if conscious of being caught in an oration, ' it is quite cruel that a poet cannot wander through his regions of enchantment, without having a critic for ever, like the Old Man of the Sea (Sinbad), upon his back!' Fadladeen, it was plain, took this last luckless allusion to himself, and would treasure it up in his mind as a whetstone for his next criticism. A sudden silence ensued; and the Princess, glancing a look at Feramorz, saw plainly she must wait for a more courageous moment.

But the glories of Nature, and her wild, fragrant airs, playing freshly over the current of youthful spirits, will soon heal even deeper wounds than the dull Fadladeens of this world can

---

[1] The huma, a bird peculiar to the East. It is supposed to fly constantly in the air, and never touch the ground. It is looked upon as a bird of happy omen; and that every head it overshades will in time wear a crown. —*Richardson.* In the terms of alliance made by Fuzzel Oola Khan with Hyder in 1760, one of the stipulations was, ' that he should have the distinction of two honorary attendants standing beside him, holding fans composed of the feathers of the huma, according to the practice of his family.'— *Wilks's South of India.* He adds in a note:—' The huma is a fabulous bird. The head over which its shadow once passes will assuredly be circled with a crown.'

[2] ' To the pilgrims to Mount Sinai we must attribute the inscriptions, figures, etc., on those rocks, which have from thence acquired the name of the Written Mountain.'—*Volney.* M. Gebelin and others have been at much pains to attach some mysterious and important meaning to these inscriptions; but Niebuhr, as well as Volney, thinks that they must have been executed at idle hours by the travellers to Mount Sinai, ' who were satisfied with cutting the unpolished rock with any pointed instrument; adding to their names, and the date of their journeys, some rude figures which bespeak the hand of a people but little skilled in the arts.'—*Niebuhr.*

inflict. In an evening or two after, they came to the small Valley of Gardens, which had been planted by order of the Emperor for his favourite sister Rochinara, during their progress to Cashmere, some years before; and never was there a more sparkling assemblage of sweets, since the Gulzar-e-Irem, or Rose-bower of Irem. Every precious flower was there to be found that poetry, or love, or religion has ever consecrated, from the dark hyacinth, to which Hafez compares his mistress's hair, to the *Cámalatá*, by whose rosy blossoms the heaven of Indra is scented.[1] As they sat in the cool fragrance of this delicious spot, and Lalla Rookh remarked that she could fancy it the abode of that flower-loving nymph whom they worship in the temples of Kathay, or of one of those Peris, those beautiful creatures of the air, who live upon perfumes, and to whom a place like this might make some amends for the Paradise they have lost,—the young Poet, in whose eyes she appeared, while she spoke, to be one of the bright spiritual creatures she was describing, said, hesitatingly, that he remembered a story of a Peri, which, if the Princess had no objection, he would venture to relate. 'It is,' said he, with an appealing look to Fadladeen, 'in a lighter and humbler strain than the other;' then, striking a few careless but melancholy chords on his kitar, he thus began:—

PARADISE AND THE PERI.

ONE morn a Peri at the gate
Of Eden stood, disconsolate;
And as she listened to the Springs
Of Life within, like music flowing,
And caught the light upon her wings
Through the half-open portal glowing,
She wept to think her recreant race
Should e'er have lost that glorious place!

'How happy,' exclaimed this child of air,
'Are the holy spirits who wander there,
'Mid flowers that never shall fade or fall;
Though mine are the gardens of earth and sea,
And the stars themselves have flowers for me,
One blossom of Heaven outblooms them all!

'Though sunny the Lake of cool Cashmere,
With its plane-tree Isle reflected clear,[2]
And sweetly the founts of that valley fall;
Though bright are the waters of Sing-su-hay,
And the golden floods that thitherward stray,[3]
Yet—oh 'tis only the blest can say
How the waters of Heaven outshine them all!

'Go, wing thy flight from star to star,
From world to luminous world, as far
As the universe spreads its flaming wall:
Take all the pleasures of all the spheres,
And multiply each through endless years,
One minute of Heaven is worth them all!'

The glorious Angel who was keeping
The Gates of Light beheld her weeping;
And, as he nearer drew and listened
To her sad song, a tear-drop glistened
Within his eyelids, like the spray
From Eden's fountain, when it lies
On the blue flower, which—Bramins say—
Blooms nowhere but in Paradise.[4]

'Nymph of a fair but erring line!'
Gently he said—'One hope is thine.
'Tis written in the Book of Fate,
*The Peri yet may be forgiven
Who brings to this Eternal gate
The Gift that is most dear to Heaven!*
Go, seek it, and redeem thy sin—
'Tis sweet to let the pardoned in.'

Rapidly as comets run
To the embraces of the Sun;—
Fleeter than the starry brands
Flung at night from angel-hands[5]
At those dark and daring sprites
Who would climb the empyreal heights,
Down the blue vault the Peri flies,
And, lighted earthward by a glance
That just then broke from morning's eyes,
Hung hovering o'er our world's expanse.

But whither shall the Spirit go
To find this gift for Heaven?—'I know
The wealth,' she cries, 'of every urn,
In which unnumbered rubies burn,

---

[1] 'The Cámalatá (called by Linnæus, *Ipomæa*) is the most beautiful of its order, both in the colour and form of its leaves and flowers; its elegant blossoms are "celestial rosy red, love's proper hue," and have justly procured it the name of Cámalatá, or Love's Creeper.'—*Sir W. Jones.*

'Cámalatá may also mean a mythological plant, by which all desires are granted to such as inhabit the heaven of Indra; and if ever flower was worthy of Paradise, it is our charming Ipomæa.'—*Ib.*

[2] 'Numerous small islands emerge from the Lake of Cashmere.'

[3] 'The Altan Kol or Golden River of Tibet has abundance of gold in its sands.'—*Pinkerton.*

[4] 'The Brahmins of this province insist that the blue campac flowers only in Paradise.'—*Sir W. Jones.*

[5] 'The Mohammedans suppose that falling stars are the firebrands wherewith the good angels drive away the bad when they approach too near the empyrean or verge of the heavens.'

Beneath the pillars of Chilminar;[1]
I know where the Isles of Perfume are,[2]
Many a fathom down in the sea,
To the south of sun-bright Araby;
I know, too, where the Genii hid
The jewelled cup of their King Jamshid,[3]
With Life's elixir sparkling high—
But gifts like these are not for the sky.
Where was there ever a gem that shone
Like the steps of Alla's wonderful Throne?
And the Drops of Life—oh! what would they be
In the boundless Deep of Eternity?'
While thus she mused, her pinions fanned
The air of that sweet Indian land
Whose air is balm; whose ocean spreads
O'er coral rocks and amber beds;[4]
Whose mountains, pregnant by the beam
Of the warm sun, with diamonds teem;
Whose rivulets are like rich brides,
Lovely, with gold beneath their tides;
Whose sandal groves and bowers of spice
Might be a Peri's Paradise!
But crimson now her rivers ran
With human blood—the smell of death
Came reeking from those spicy bowers,
And man, the sacrifice of man,
Mingled his taint with every breath
Upwafted from the innocent flowers.
Land of the Sun! what foot invades
Thy Pagods and thy pillared shades[5]—
Thy cavern shrines, and Idol stones,
Thy Monarchs and their thousand Thrones?[6]
'Tis He of Gazna![7]—fierce in wrath
He comes, and India's diadems
Lie scattered in his ruinous path.—
His bloodhounds he adorns with gems,
Torn from the violated necks
Of many a young and loved Sultana;[8]
Maidens within their pure Zenana,
Priests in the very fane, he slaughters,

And chokes up with the glittering wrecks
Of golden shrines the sacred waters!

Downward the Peri turns her gaze,
And, through the war-field's bloody haze
Beholds a youthful warrior stand,
Alone beside his native river,—
The red blade broken in his hand,
And the last arrow in his quiver.
'Live,' said the Conqueror, 'live to share
The trophies and the crowns I bear!'
Silent that youthful warrior stood—
Silent he pointed to the flood
All crimson with his country's blood,
Then sent his last remaining dart,
For answer, to the Invader's heart.

False flew the shaft, though pointed well;
The Tyrant lived, the Hero fell!—
Yet marked the Peri where he lay,
And, when the rush of war was past,
Swiftly descending on a ray
Of morning light she caught the last—
Last glorious drop his heart had shed,
Before its free-born spirit fled!

'Be this,' she cried, as she winged her flight,
'My welcome gift at the Gates of Light.
Though foul are the drops that oft distil
On the field of warfare, blood like this,
For Liberty shed, so holy is,[9]
It would not stain the purest rill
That sparkles among the Bowers of Bliss!
Oh if there be, on this earthly sphere,
A boon, an offering Heaven holds dear,
'Tis the last libation Liberty draws [cause
From the heart that bleeds and breaks in her

'Sweet,' said the Angel, as she gave
The gift into his radiant hand,

---

[1] 'The Forty Pillars—so the Persians call the ruins of Persepolis. It is imagined by them that this palace and the edifices at Baalbec were built by Genii, for the purpose of hiding in their subterraneous caverns immense treasures, which still remain there.'

[2] The Isles of Panchaia. Diodorus mentions the Isle of Panchaia, to the south of Arabia Felix, where there was a temple of Jupiter. This island, or rather cluster of isles, has disappeared—'sunk (says Grandpré) in the abyss made by the fire beneath their foundations.'—*Voyage to the Indian Ocean.*

[3] 'The cup of Jamshid, discovered, they say, when digging for the foundations of Persepolis.'

[4] 'Like the Sea of India, whose bottom is rich with pearls and ambergris, whose mountains on the coast are stored with gold and precious stones, whose gulfs breed creatures that yield ivory, and among the plants of whose shores are ebony, red wood, and the wood of Hairzan, aloes, camphor, cloves, sandal-wood, and all other spices and aromatics; whose parrots and peacocks are birds of the forest, and musk and civet are collected upon the lands.'—*Travels of Two Mohammedans.*

[5] 'The bended twigs take root, and daughters grow, About the mother-tree, *a pillared shade.*'—*Milton.*

[6] 'With this immense treasure Mahmoud returned to Ghizni, and in the year 400 prepared a magnificent festival, where he displayed to the people his wealth in golden thrones and other ornaments, in a great plain without the city of Ghizni.'—*Ferishta.*

[7] 'Mahmoud of Gazna, or Ghizni, who conquered India in the beginning of the eleventh century.'

[8] 'It is reported that the hunting equipage of the Sultan Mahmoud was so magnificent, that he kept four hundred greyhounds and bloodhounds, each of which wore a collar set with jewels, and a covering edged with gold and pearls.'

[9] 'Objections may be made to my use of the word liberty, in this, and more especially in the story that follows it, as totally inapplicable to any state of things that has ever existed in the East; but though I cannot, of course, mean to employ it in that enlarged and noble sense which is so well understood at the present day, and, I grieve to say, so little acted upon, yet it is no disparagement to the word to apply it to that national independence, that freedom from the interference and dictation of foreigners, without which, indeed, no liberty of any kind can exist, and for which both Hindoos and Persians fought against their Mussulman invaders with, in many cases, a bravery that deserved much better success.'

'Sweet is our welcome of the Brave
  Who die thus for their native Land.—
But see—alas!—the crystal bar
Of Eden moves not—holier far
Than even this drop the boon must be
That opes the Gates of Heaven for thee!'

Her first fond hope of Eden blighted,
  Now among Afric's Lunar Mountains,[1]
Far to the South, the Peri lighted;
  And sleeked her plumage at the fountains
Of that Egyptian tide whose birth
Is hidden from the sons of earth
Deep in those solitary woods,
Where oft the Genii of the Floods
Dance round the cradle of their Nile,
And hail the now-born Giant's smile.[2]
Thence over Egypt's palmy groves,
  Her grots, and sepulchres of Kings,[3]
The exiled Spirit sighing roves;
  And now hangs listening to the doves
In warm Rosetta's vale[4]—now loves
  To watch the moonlight on the wings
Of the white pelicans that break
The azure calm of Mœris' Lake.[5]
'Twas a fair scene—a Land more bright
  Never did mortal eye behold!
Who could have thought, that saw this night
  Those valleys and their fruits of gold
Basking in Heaven's serenest light;—
Those groups of lovely date-trees[6] bending
Languidly their leaf-crowned heads,
Like youthful maids, when sleep descending
  Warns them to their silken beds;—
Those virgin lilies, all the night
  Bathing their beauties in the lake,
That they may rise more fresh and bright,
  When their beloved Sun's awake;—
Those ruined shrines and towers that seem
The relics of a splendid dream;
  Amid whose fairy loneliness
Nought but the lapwing's cry is heard,
Nought seen but (when the shadows, flitting
Fast from the moon, unsheath its gleam,)
Some purple-winged Sultana[7] sitting
  Upon a column, motionless
And glittering like an Idol bird—
Who could have thought, that there, even there,
Amid those scenes so still and fair,

The Demon of the Plague hath cast
From his hot wing a deadlier blast,
More mortal far than ever came
From the red Desert's sands of flame!
So quick, that every living thing
Of human shape, touched by his wing,
Like plants where the Simoon hath past,
At once falls black and withering!
The sun went down on many a brow
  Which, full of bloom and freshness then,
Is rankling in the pest-house now,
  And ne'er will feel that sun again.
And oh! to see the unburied heaps
On which the lonely moonlight sleeps—
The very vultures turn away,
And sicken at so foul a prey!
Only the fierce hyæna stalks[8]
Throughout the city's desolate walks
At midnight, and his carnage plies:—
  Woe to the half-dead wretch who meets
The glaring of those large blue eyes
  Amid the darkness of the streets!

'Poor race of men!' said the pitying Spirit,
  'Dearly ye pay for your primal Fall—
Some flowerets of Eden ye still inherit,
  But the trail of the Serpent is over them all!'
She wept—the air grew pure and clear
  Around her, as the bright drops ran;
For there's a magic in each tear
  Such kindly Spirits weep for man!

Just then beneath some orange-trees,
Whose fruit and blossoms in the breeze
Were wantoning together, free,
Like age at play with infancy—
Beneath that fresh and springing bower,
Close by the Lake, she heard the moan
Of one who, at this silent hour,
Had thither stolen to die alone.
One who in life where'er he moved
  Drew after him the hearts of many;
Yet now, as though he ne'er were loved,
  Dies here unseen, unwept by any!
None to watch near him—none to slake
  The fire that in his bosom lies,
With even a sprinkle from that lake
  Which shines so cool before his eyes;

---

[1] 'The Mountains of the Moon, or the Montes Lunæ of antiquity, at the foot of which the Nile is supposed to arise.' 'Sometimes called,' says Jackson, 'Jibbel Kumrie, or the White or Lunar-coloured Mountains; so a white horse is called by the Arabians a moon-coloured horse.'
[2] 'The Nile, which the Abyssinians know by the names of Abey and Alawy, or the Giant.'
[3] *Vide* Perry's *View of the Levant* for an account of the sepulchres in Upper Thebes, and the numberless griots, covered all over with hieroglyphics, in the mountains of Upper Egypt.
[4] 'The orchards of Rosetta are filled with turtle-doves.'
[5] Savary mentions the pelicans upon Lake Mœris.
[6] 'The superb date-tree, whose head languidly reclines like that of a handsome woman overcome with sleep.'

[7] 'That beautiful bird, with plumage of the finest shining blue, with purple beak and legs, which, from the stateliness of its port as well as the brilliancy of its colours, has obtained the title of Sultana.'
[8] Jackson, speaking of the plague that occurred in West Barbary when he was there, says, 'The bi ds of the a r fled away from the abodes of men. The hyænas, on the contrary, visited the cemeteries,' etc.
'Gondar was full of hyænas from the time it turned dark till the dawn of day, seeking the different pieces of slaughtered carcases, which this cruel and unclean people expose in the streets without burial, and who firmly believe that these animals are Falashta from the neighbouring mountains, transformed by magic, and come down to eat human flesh in the dark in safety.'—*Bruce.*

No voice, well known through many a day,
  To speak the last, the parting word,
Which, when all other sounds decay,
  Is still like distant music heard ;—
That tender farewell on the shore
Of this rude world, when all is o'er,
Which cheers the spirit, ere its bark
Puts off into the unknown Dark.

Deserted youth! one thought alone
  Shed joy around his soul in death—
That she whom he for years had known,
  And loved, and might have called his own.
    Was safe from this foul midnight's breath,—
Safe in her father's princely halls,
Where the cool airs from fountain-falls,
Freshly perfumed by many a brand
Of the sweet wood from India's land,
Were pure as she whose brow they fanned.

But see—who yonder comes by stealth,
  This melancholy bower to seek,
Like a young envoy, sent by Health,
  With rosy gifts upon her cheek?
'Tis she—far off, through moonlight dim,
  He knew his own betrothed bride,
She, who would rather die with him,
  Than live to gain the world beside!—
Her arms are round her lover now,
  His livid cheek to hers she presses,
And dips, to bind his burning brow,
  In the cool lake her loosened tresses.
Ah! once, how little did he think
An hour would come when he should shrink
With horror from that dear embrace,
Those gentle arms that were to him
Holy as is the cradling place
Of Eden's infant cherubim!
And now he yields—now turns away,
Shuddering as if the venom lay
All in those proffered lips alone—
Those lips that, then so fearless grown,
Never until that instant came
Near his unasked or without shame.
'Oh! let me only breathe the air,
  The blessed air, that's breathed by thee,
And, whether on its wings it bear
  Healing or death, 'tis sweet to me!
There—drink my tears, while yet they fall—
  Would that my bosom's blood were balm,
And, well thou know'st, I'd shed it all,
  To give thy brow one minute's calm.
Nay, turn not from me that dear face—
  Am I not thine—thy own loved bride—
The one, the chosen one, whose place
  In life or death is by thy side?

Think'st thou that she, whose only light,
  In this dim world, from thee hath shone,
Could bear the long, the cheerless night,
  That must be hers when thou art gone?
That I can live, and let thee go,
  Who art my life itself?—No, no—
When the stem dies, the leaf that grew
Out of its heart must perish too!
Then turn to me, my own love, turn,
Before, like thee, I fade and burn;
Cling to these yet cool lips, and share
The last pure life that lingers there!'
She fails—she sinks—as dies the lamp
In charnel airs, or cavern-damp,
So quickly do his baleful sighs
Quench all the sweet light of her eyes.
One struggle—and his pain is past—
  Her lover is no longer living!
One kiss the maiden gives, one last
  Long kiss, which she expires in giving

'Sleep,' said the Peri, as softly she stole
The farewell sigh of that vanishing soul,
As true as e'er warmed a woman's breast—
'Sleep on, in visions of odour rest,
In balmier airs than ever yet stirred
The enchanted pile of that lonely bird[1]
Who sings at the last his own death-lay,
And in music and perfume dies away!'

Thus saying, from her lips she spread
Unearthly breathings through the place,
And shook her sparkling wreath, and shed
Such lustre o'er each paly face
That like two lovely saints they seemed,
Upon the eve of doomsday taken
From their dim graves, in odour sleeping;
While that benevolent Peri beamed
Like their good angel, calmly keeping
Watch o'er them till their souls would waken

But morn is blushing in the sky;
  Again the Peri soars above,
Bearing to Heaven that precious sigh
  Of pure, self-sacrificing love.
High throbbed her heart, with hope elate,
  The Elysian palm she soon shall win,
For the bright Spirit at the gate
  Smiled as she gave that offering in;
And she already hears the trees
  Of Eden, with their crystal bells
Ringing in that ambrosial breeze
  That from the throne of Alla swells;
And she can see the starry bowls
  That lie around that lucid lake
Upon whose banks admitted Souls
  Their first sweet draught of glory take![2]

---

[1] 'In the East they suppose the Phœnix to have fifty orifices in his bill, which are continued to his tail; and that, after living one thousand years, he builds himself a funeral pile, sings a melodious air of different harmonies through his fifty organ pipes, flaps his wings with a velocity which sets fire to the wood, and consumes himself.'

[2] On the shores of a quadrangular lake stand a thousand goblets, made of stars, out of which souls predestined to enjoy felicity drink the crystal wave.—From Chateaubriand's 'Mohammedan Paradise,' in his *Beauties of Christianity*.

But ah! even Peris' hopes are vain—
Again the Fates forbade, again
The immortal barrier closed—'Not yet,'
The Angel said, as, with regret,
He shut from her that glimpse of glory—
'True was the maiden, and her story,
Written in light o'er Alla's head,
By seraph eyes shall long be read.
But, Peri, see—the crystal bar
Of Eden moves not—holier far
Than even this sigh the boon must be
That opes the Gates of Heaven for thee.'

Now, upon Syria's land of roses [1]
Softly the light of Eve reposes,
And, like a glory, the broad sun
Hangs over sainted Lebanon;
Whose head in wintry grandeur towers,
  And whitens with eternal sleet,
While summer, in a vale of flowers,
  Is sleeping rosy at his feet.

To one who looked from upper air
O'er all the enchanted regions there,
How beauteous must have been the glow,
The life, the sparkling from below!
Fair gardens, shining streams, with ranks
Of golden melons on their banks,
More golden where the sunlight falls;—
Gay lizards glittering on the walls [2]
Of ruined shrines, busy and bright
As they were all alive with light;
And, yet more splendid, numerous flocks
Of pigeons, settling on the rocks,
With their rich restless wings, that gleam
Variously in the crimson beam
Of the warm West,—as if inlaid
With brilliants from the mine, or made
Of tearless rainbows, such as span
The unclouded skies of Peristan.
And then the mingling sounds that come,
Of shepherd's ancient reed,[3] with hum
Of the wild bees of Palestine,
  Banqueting through the flowery vales;
And, Jordan, those sweet banks of thine,
  And woods, so full of nightingales.[4]

But nought can charm the luckless Peri;
Her soul is sad—her wings are weary—
Joyless she sees the Sun look down
On that great Temple, once his own,[5]
Whose lonely columns stand sublime,
  Flinging their shadows from on high,
Like dials, which the wizard, Time,
  Had raised to count his ages by!

Yet haply there may lie concealed
  Beneath those Chambers of the Sun
Some amulet of gems, annealed
  In upper fires, some tablet sealed
With the great name of Solomon,
Which, spelled by her illumined eyes,
May teach her where, beneath the moon,
In earth or ocean, lies the boon,
The charm, that can restore so soon
  An erring Spirit to the skies.

Cheered by this hope she bends her thither;—
  Still laughs the radiant eye of Heaven,
Nor have the golden bowers of Even
  In the rich West begun to wither;—
When, o'er the vale of Baalbec winging
  Slowly, she sees a child at play,
Among the rosy wild flowers singing,
  As rosy and as wild as they;
Chasing, with eager hands and eyes,
The beautiful blue damsel-flies,[6]
That fluttered round the jasmine stems,
Like winged flowers or flying gems:—
And, near the boy, who tired with play
Now nestling 'mid the roses lay,
She saw a wearied man dismount
  From his hot steed, and on the brink
Of a small imaret's rustic fount [7]
  Impatient fling him down to drink.
Then swift his haggard brow he turned
  To the fair child, who fearless sat,
Though never yet hath day-beam burned
  Upon a brow more fierce than that,—
Sullenly fierce—a mixture dire,
Like thunder-clouds, of gloom and fire;
In which the Peri's eye could read
Dark tales of many a ruthless deed;
The ruined maid—the shrine profaned—
Oaths broken—and the threshold stained
With blood of guests!—*there* written, all,
Black as the damning drops that fall
From the denouncing Angel's pen,
Ere Mercy weeps them out again.

Yet tranquil now that man of crime
  (As if the balmy evening time
Softened his spirit) looked and lay,
Watching the rosy infant's play:—

---

[1] Richardson thinks that Syria had its name from Suri, a beautiful and delicate species of rose, for which that country has been always famous; hence Suristan, the Land of Roses.

[2] 'The number of lizards I saw one day in the great court of the Temple of the Sun at Baalbec amounted to many thousands; the ground, the walls, and stones of the ruined buildings were covered with them.'—*Bruce.*

[3] 'The syrinx, or Pan's pipe, is still a pastoral instrument in Syria.'

[4] 'The river Jordan is on both sides beset with little, thick, and pleasant woods, among which thousands of nightingales warble all together.'—*Thevenot.*

[5] The Temple of the Sun at Baalbec.

[6] 'You behold there a considerable number of a remarkable species of beautiful insects, the elegance of whose appearance, and their attire, procured for them the name of Damsels.'

[7] Imaret, 'hospice où on loge et nourrit, gratis, les pélerins pendant trois jours.'—*Toderini.*

Though still, whene'er his eye by chance
  Fell on the boy's, its lurid glance
  Met that unclouded, joyous gaze,
As torches, that have burnt all night
Through some impure and godless rite,
  Encounter morning's glorious rays.

But, hark! the vesper call to prayer,
  As slow the orb of daylight sets,
Is rising sweetly on the air,
  From Syria's thousand minarets!
The boy has started from the bed [1]
  Of flowers where he had laid his head,
And down upon the fragrant sod
  Kneels with his forehead to the south,
Lisping the eternal name of God
  From Purity's own cherub mouth,
And looking, while his hands and eyes
Are lifted to the glowing skies,
Like a stray babe of Paradise,
  Just lighted on that flowery plain,
And seeking for its home again.
Oh! 'twas a sight — that Heaven — that child—
A scene which might have well beguiled
  Even haughty Eblis of a sigh
For glories lost and peace gone by.

And how felt he, the wretched Man
Reclining there—while memory ran
O'er many a year of guilt and strife,
Flew o'er the dark flood of his life,
Nor found one sunny resting-place,
Nor brought him back one branch of grace.
'There was a time,' he said, in mild
Heart-humbled tones—'thou blessed child!
When, young and haply pure as thou,
I looked and prayed like thee—but now—'
He hung his head—each nobler aim,
  And hope, and feeling, which had slept
From boyhood's hour, that instant came
  Fresh o'er him, and he wept—he wept!

Blest tears of soul-felt penitence!
  In whose benign, redeeming flow
Is felt the first, the only sense
  Of guiltless joy that guilt can know.

'There's a drop,' said the Peri, 'that down from the moon
Falls through the withering airs of June

Upon Egypt's land,[2] of so healing a power,
So balmy a virtue, that even in the hour
That drop descends, contagion dies,
And health re-animates earth and skies!—
Oh, is it not thus, thou man of sin,
  The precious tears of repentance fall?
Though foul thy fiery plagues within,
  One heavenly drop hath dispelled them all!'

And now—behold him kneeling there
By the child's side, in humble prayer,
While the same sunbeam shines upon
  The guilty and the guiltless one,
And hymns of joy proclaim through Heaven
  The triumph of a Soul Forgiven!

'Twas when the golden orb had set,
While on their knees they lingered yet,
There fell a light more lovely far
Than ever came from sun or star,
Upon the tear that, warm and meek,
Dewed that repentant sinner's cheek
To mortal eye this light might seem
A northern flash or meteor beam—
But well the enraptured Peri knew
'Twas a bright smile the Angel threw
From Heaven's gate, to hail that tear,
Her harbinger of glory near!

'Joy, joy for ever! my task is done—
The gates are passed, and Heaven is won!
Oh! am I not happy? I am, I am—
To thee, sweet Eden! how dark and sad
Are the diamond turrets of Shadukiam,[3]
  And the fragrant bowers of Amberabad!

'Farewell, ye odours of Earth, that die,
Passing away like a lover's sigh;—
My feast is now of the Tooba Tree,[4]
Whose scent is the breath of Eternity!

'Farewell, ye vanishing flowers, that shone
  In my fairy wreath, so bright and brief;—
Oh! what are the brightest that e'er have blown,
To the lote-tree, springing by Alla's throne,[5]
  Whose flowers have a soul in every leaf?
Joy, joy for ever!—my task is done—
The Gates are passed, and Heaven is won!'

---

[1] 'Such Turks as at the common hours of prayer are on the road, or so employed as not to find convenience to attend the mosques, are still obliged to execute that duty; nor are they ever known to fail, whatever business they are then about, but pray immediately when the hour alarms them, in that very place they chance to stand on.'—*Aaron Hill's Travels.*

[2] The Nucta, or Miraculous Drop, which falls in Egypt precisely on St. John's day, in June, and is supposed to have the effect of stopping the plague.

[3] The Country of Delight—the name of a province in the kingdom of Jinnistan or Fairy Land, the capital of which is called the 'City of Jewels.' Amberabad is another of the cities of Jinnistan.

[4] The tree Tooba, that stands in Paradise, in the palace of Mohammed.—See *Sale's Prelim. Disc.* Tooba, says D'Herbelot, signifies 'beatitude,' or 'eternal happiness.'

[5] Mohammed is described, in the fifty-third chapter of the Koran, as having seen the angel Gabriel 'by the lote-tree, beyond which there is no passing: near it is the Garden of Eternal Abode.' This tree, say the commentators, stands in the seventh heaven, on the right hand of the throne of God

'And this,' said the Great Chamberlain, 'is poetry! this flimsy manufacture of the brain, which, in comparison with the lofty and durable monuments of genius, is as the gold filigree-work of Zamara beside the eternal architecture of Egypt!' After this gorgeous sentence, which, with a few more of the same kind, Fadladeen kept by him for rare and important occasions, he proceeded to the anatomy of the short poem just recited. The lax and easy kind of metre in which it was written ought to be denounced, he said, as one of the leading causes of the alarming growth of poetry in our times. If some check were not given to this lawless facility, we soon should be overrun by a race of bards as numerous and as shallow as the hundred and twenty thousand Streams of Basra.[1] They who succeeded in this style deserved chastisement for their very success; as warriors have been punished, even after gaining a victory, because they had taken the liberty of gaining it in an irregular or unestablished manner. What, then, was to be said to those who failed? to those who presumed, as in the present lamentable instance, to imitate the licence and ease of the bolder sons of song, without any of that grace or vigour which gave a dignity even to negligence; who, like them, flung the jereed[2] carelessly, but not, like them, to the mark; 'and who,' said he, raising his voice to excite a proper degree of wakefulness in his hearers, 'contrive to appear heavy and constrained in the midst of all the latitude they allow themselves, like one of those young pagans that dance before the Princess, who is ingenious enough to move as if her limbs were fettered, in a pair of the lightest and loosest drawers of Masulipatam!'

It was but little suitable, he continued, to the grave march of criticism to follow this fantastical Peri, of whom they had just heard, through all her flights and adventures between earth and heaven; but he could not help adverting to the puerile conceitedness of the Three Gifts which she is supposed to carry to the skies,—a drop of blood, forsooth, a sigh, and a tear! How the first of these articles was delivered into the Angel's 'radiant hand,' he professed himself at a loss to discover; and as to the safe carriage of the sigh and the tear, such Peris and such poets were beings by far too incomprehensible for him even to guess how they managed such matters. 'But, in short,' said he, 'it is a waste of time and patience to dwell longer upon a thing so incurably frivolous,—puny, even among its own puny race, and such as only the Banyan Hospital[3] for Sick Insects should undertake.'

In vain did Lalla Rookh try to soften this inexorable critic; in vain did she resort to her most eloquent commonplaces,—reminding him that poets were a timid and sensitive race, whose sweetness was not to be drawn forth, like that of the fragrant grass near the Ganges, by crushing and trampling upon them;[4] that severity often extinguished every chance of the perfection which it demanded; and that, after all, perfection was like the Mountain of the Talisman,—no one had ever yet reached its summit.[5] Neither these gentle axioms, nor the still gentler looks with which they were inculcated, could lower for one instant the elevation of Fadladeen's eyebrows, or charm him into anything like encouragement, or even toleration, of her poet. Toleration, indeed, was not among the weaknesses of Fadladeen: he carried the same spirit into matters of poetry and of religion, and though little versed in the beauties or sublimities of either, was a perfect master of the art of persecution in both. His zeal was the same, too, in either pursuit; whether the game before him was pagans or poetasters, worshippers of cows or writers of epics.

They had now arrived at the splendid city of Lahore, whose mausoleums and shrines,

---

[1] 'It is said that the rivers or streams of Basra were reckoned in the time of Pelai Ben Abi Bordeh, and amounted to the number of one hundred and twenty thousand streams.'

[2] 'The name of the javelin with which the Easterns exercise.'

[3] 'This account excited a desire of visiting the Banyan Hospital, as I had heard much of their benevolence to all kinds of animals that were either sick, lame, or infirm, through age or accident. On my arrival there were presented to my view many horses, cows, and oxen, in one apartment; in another, dogs, sheep, goats, and monkeys, with clean straw for them to repose on. Above stairs were depositories for seeds of many sorts, and flat, broad dishes for water, for the use of birds and insects.'—*Parsons*.

It is said that all animals know the Banyans, that the most timid approach them, and that birds will fly nearer to them than to other people.—*Vide* Grandpré.

[4] 'A very fragrant grass from the banks of the Ganges, near Heridwar, which in some places covers whole acres, and diffuses, when crushed, a strong odour.'—*Sir W. Jones on the Spikenard of the Ancients.*

[5] 'Near this is a curious hill, called Koh Talism, the "Mountain of the Talisman," because, according to the traditions of the country, no person ever succeeded in gaining its summit.'

magnificent and numberless, where Death appeared to share equal honours with Heaven, would have powerfully affected the heart and imagination of Lalla Rookh, if feelings more of this earth had not taken entire possession of her already. She was here met by messengers, despatched from Cashmere, who informed her that the King had arrived in the Valley, and was himself superintending the sumptuous preparations that were then making in the Saloons of the Shalimar for her reception. The chill she felt on receiving this intelligence—which, to a bride whose heart was free and light, would have brought only images of affection and pleasure—convinced her that her peace was gone for ever, and that she was in love, irretrievably in love, with young Feramorz. The veil had fallen off in which this passion at first disguises itself, and to know that she loved was now as painful as to love *without* knowing it had been delicious. Feramorz, too,—what misery would be his, if the sweet hours of intercourse so imprudently allowed them should have stolen into his heart the same fatal fascination as into hers; if, notwithstanding her rank, and the modest homage he always paid to it, even *he* should have yielded to the influence of those long and happy interviews, where music, poetry, the delightful scenes of nature,—all had tended to bring their hearts close together, and to waken by every means that too ready passion, which often, like the young of the desert-bird, is warmed into life by the eyes alone![1] She saw but one way to preserve herself from being culpable as well as unhappy; and this, however painful, she was resolved to adopt. Feramorz must no more be admitted to her presence. To have strayed so far into the dangerous labyrinth was wrong, but to linger in it, while the clue was yet in her hand, would be criminal. Though the heart she had to offer to the King of Bucharia might be cold and broken, it should at least be pure; and she must only endeavour to forget the short dream of happiness she had enjoyed,—like that Arabian shepherd who, in wandering into the wilderness, caught a glimpse of the Gardens of Irim, and then lost them again for ever![2]

The arrival of the young bride at Lahore was celebrated in the most enthusiastic manner. The Rajas and Omras in her train, who had kept at a certain distance during the journey, and never encamped nearer to the Princess than was strictly necessary for her safeguard, here rode in splendid cavalcade through the city, and distributed the most costly presents to the crowd. Engines were erected in all the squares, which cast forth showers of confectionery among the people; while the artisans, in chariots adorned with tinsel and flying streamers, exhibited the badges of their respective trades through the streets. Such brilliant displays of life and pageantry among the palaces and domes and gilded minarets of Lahore, made the city altogether like a place of enchantment; particularly on the day when Lalla Rookh set out again upon her journey, when she was accompanied to the gate by all the fairest and richest of the nobility, and rode along between ranks of beautiful boys and girls, who kept waving over their heads plates of gold and silver flowers,[3] and then threw them around to be gathered by the populace.

For many days after their departure from Lahore, a considerable degree of gloom hung over the whole party. Lalla Rookh, who had intended to make illness her excuse for not admitting the young minstrel, as usual, to the pavilion, soon found that to feign indisposition was unnecessary. Fadladeen felt the loss of the good road they had hitherto travelled, and was very near cursing Jehan-Guire (of blessed memory!) for not having continued his delectable alley of trees[4] at least as far as the mountains of Cashmere; while the Ladies, who had nothing now to do all day but to be fanned by peacocks' feathers and listen to Fadladeen, seemed heartily weary of the life they led, and, in spite of all the Great Chamberlain's criticisms, were so tasteless as to wish for the poet again. One evening, as they were proceeding to their place of rest for the night, the Princess, who, for the freer enjoyment of the air, had mounted her favourite Arabian palfrey, in passing by a small grove heard the notes

---

[1] 'The Arabians believe that the ostriches hatch their young by only looking at them.'—*P. Vanslebe, Relat. d'Egypte.*

[2] *Vide Sale's Koran*, note, vol. ii. p. 484.

[3] Ferishta. 'Or rather,' says Scott, upon the passage of Ferishta from which this is taken, 'small coins stamped with the figure of a flower. They are still used in India to distribute in charity, and, on occasion, thrown by the purse-bearers of the great among the populace.'

[4] The fine road made by the Emperor Jehan-Guire from Agra to Lahore, planted with trees on each side. This road is 250 leagues in length. It has 'little pyramids or turrets,' says Bernier, 'erected every half league, to mark the ways, and frequent wells to afford drink to passengers, and to water the young trees.'

of a lute from within its leaves, and a voice, which she but too well knew, singing the following words:—

> Tell me not of joys above,
> If that world can give no bliss
> Truer, happier, than the Love
> Which enslaves our souls in this.
>
> Tell me not of Houris' eyes;—
> Far from me their dangerous glow,
> If those looks that light the skies
> Wound like some that burn below.
>
> Who that feels what Love is here,
> All its falsehood—all its pain—
> Would, for even Elysium's sphere,
> Risk the fatal dream again?
>
> Who that midst a desert's heat
> Sees the waters fade away,
> Would not rather die than meet
> Streams again as false as they?

The tone of melancholy defiance in which these words were uttered went to Lalla Rookh's heart; and as she reluctantly rode on, she could not help feeling it to be a sad but still sweet certainty that Feramorz was to the full as enamoured and as miserable as herself.

The place where they encamped that evening was the first delightful spot they had come to since they left Lahore. On one side of them was a grove full of small Hindoo temples, and planted with the most graceful trees of the East; where the tamarind, the cassia, and the silken plantains of Ceylon were mingled in rich contrast with the high fan-like foliage of the Palmyra,—that favourite tree of the luxurious bird that lights up the chambers of its nest with fire-flies.[1] In the middle of the lawn where the pavilion stood there was a tank surrounded by small mangoe-trees, on the clear cold waters of which floated multitudes of the beautiful red lotus;[2] while at a distance stood the ruins of a strange and awful-looking tower, which seemed old enough to have been the temple of some religion no longer known, and which spoke the voice of desolation in the midst of all that bloom and loveliness. This singular ruin excited the wonder and conjectures of all. Lalla Rookh guessed in vain, and the all-pretending Fadladeen, who had never till this journey been beyond the precincts of Delhi, was proceeding most learnedly to show that he knew nothing whatever about the matter, when one of the ladies suggested that perhaps Feramorz could satisfy their curiosity. They were now approaching his native mountains, and this tower might perhaps be a relic of some of those dark superstitions which had prevailed in that country before the light of Islam dawned upon it. The Chamberlain, who usually preferred his own ignorance to the best knowledge that any one else could give him, was by no means pleased with this officious reference; and the Princess, too, was about to interpose a faint word of objection; but before either of them could speak, a slave was despatched for Feramorz, who in a very few minutes made his appearance before them, looking so pale and unhappy in Lalla Rookh's eyes, that she repented already of her cruelty in having so long excluded him.

That venerable tower, he told them, was the remains of an ancient Fire-temple, built by those Ghebers or Persians of the old religion who, many hundred years since, had fled hither from their Arab conquerors,[3] preferring liberty and their altars in a foreign land to the alternative of apostasy or persecution in their own. It was impossible, he added, not to feel interested in the many glorious but unsuccessful struggles which had been made by these

---

[1] The Baya, or Indian Gross-beak.—*Sir W. Jones.*
[2] 'Here is a large pagoda by a tank, on the water of which float multitudes of the beautiful red lotus: the flower is larger than that of the white water-lily, and is the most lovely of the nymphœas I have seen.'—*Mrs. Graham's Journal of a Residence in India.*

[3] 'On les voit, persécutés par les Khalifes, se retirer dans les montagnes du Kerman: plusieurs choisirent pour retraite la Tartarie et la Chine; d'autres s'arêtèrent sur les bords du Gange, à l'est Delhi.'—*M. Anquetil, Mémoires de l'Academie,* tom. xxxi. p. 346.

original natives of Persia to cast off the yoke of their bigoted conquerors. Like their own Fire in the Burning Field at Bakou, when suppressed in one place, they had but broken out with fresh flame in another; and as a native of Cashmere, of that fair and Holy Valley which had in the same manner become the prey of strangers,[1] and seen her ancient shrines and native princes swept away before the march of her intolerant invaders, he felt a sympathy, he owned, with the sufferings of the persecuted Ghebers, which every monument like this before them but tended more powerfully to awaken.

It was the first time that Feramorz had ever ventured upon so much *prose* before Fadladeen, and it may easily be conceived what effect such prose as this must have produced upon that most orthodox and most pagan-hating personage. He sat for some minutes aghast, ejaculating only at intervals, 'Bigoted conquerors!—sympathy with Fire-worshippers!'[2]—while Feramorz, happy to take advantage of this almost speechless horror of the Chamberlain, proceeded to say that he knew a melancholy story connected with the events of one of those struggles of the brave Fire-worshippers against their Arab masters, which, if the evening was not too far advanced, he should have much pleasure in being allowed to relate to the Princess. It was impossible for Lalla Rookh to refuse: he had never before looked half so animated; and when he spoke of the Holy Valley his eyes had sparkled, she thought, like the talismanic characters on the scimitar of Solomon. Her consent was therefore most readily granted; and while Fadladeen sat in unspeakable dismay, expecting treason and abomination in every line, the poet thus began his story of the Fire-worshippers:—

THE FIRE-WORSHIPPERS.

'Tis moonlight over Oman's sea;[3]
  Her banks of pearl and palmy isles
Bask in the night-beam beauteously,
  And her blue waters sleep in smiles.
'Tis moonlight in Harmozia's[4] walls;
  And through her Emir's porphyry halls,
Where, some hours since, was heard the swell
Of trumpet and the clash of zel,[5]
Bidding the bright-eyed sun farewell;—
The peaceful sun, whom better suits
  The music of the bulbul's nest,
Or the light touch of lovers' lutes,
  To sing him to his golden rest.
All hushed—there's not a breeze in motion;
The shore is silent as the ocean.
If zephyrs come, so light they come
  No leaf is stirred nor wave is driven;—
The wind-tower on the Emir's dome[6]
  Can hardly win a breath from heaven.

Even he, that tyrant Arab, sleeps
Calm, while a nation round him weeps;
While curses load the air he breathes,
And falchions from unnumbered sheaths

Are starting to avenge the shame
His race hath brought on Iran's[7] name.
Hard, heartless Chief, unmoved alike
'Mid eyes that weep, and swords that strike;—
One of that saintly, murderous brood,
  To carnage and the Koran given,
Who think through unbelievers' blood
  Lies their directest path to heaven;—
One who will pause and kneel unshod
  In the warm blood his hand hath poured,
To mutter o'er some text of God
  Engraven on his reeking sword;[8]—
Nay, who can coolly note the line,
The letter of those words divine,
To which his blade, with searching art,
Had sunk into its victim's heart!

Just Alla! what must be thy look,
  When such a wretch before thee stands
Unblushing, with thy Sacred Book,—
  Turning the leaves with blood-stained hands,
And wresting from its page sublime
His creed of lust, and hate, and crime;—

---

[1] 'Cashmere,' says its historians, 'had its own princes 4000 years before its conquest by Akbar in 1585. Akbar would have found some difficulty to reduce this paradise of the Indies, situated as it is, within such a fortress of mountains; but its monarch, Yusef Khan, was basely betrayed by his Omrahs.'—*Pennant.*

[2] Voltaire tells us that in his Tragedy, *Les Guèbres*, he was generally supposed to have alluded to the Jansenists. I should not be surprised if this story of the Fire-worshippers were found capable of a similar doubleness of application.

[3] The Persian Gulf, sometimes so called, which separates the shores of Persia and Arabia.

[4] The present Gombaroon, a town on the Persian side of the Gulf.

[5] A Moorish instrument of music.

[6] 'At Gombaroon, and other places in Persia, they have towers for the purpose of catching the wind and cooling the houses.'—*Le Bruyn.*

[7] Iran is the true general name for the empire of Persia.

[8] 'On the blades of their scimitars some verse from the Koran is usually inscribed.'

THE FIRE-WORSHIPPERS.

Even as those bees of Trebizond
  Which, from the sunniest flowers that glad
With their pure smile the gardens round,
  Draw venom forth that drives men mad.[1]

Never did fierce Arabia send
  A satrap forth more direly great;
Never was Iran doomed to bend
  Beneath a yoke of deadlier weight.
Her throne had fallen—her pride was crushed—
Her sons were willing slaves, nor blushed,
In their own land,—no more their own,—
To crouch beneath a stranger's throne.
Her towers, where Mithra once had burned,
To Moslem shrines—oh shame!—were turned,
Where slaves, converted by the sword,
Their mean, apostate worship poured,
And cursed the faith their sires adored.
Yet has she hearts, 'mid all this ill,
O'er all this wreck high-buoyant still
With hope and vengeance;—hearts that yet—
  Like gems, in darkness, issuing rays
They've treasured from the sun that's set,—
  Beam all the light of long-lost days!
And swords she hath, nor weak nor slow
  To second all such hearts can dare;
As he shall know, well, dearly know,
  Who sleeps in moonlight luxury there,
Tranquil as if his spirit lay
  Becalmed in Heaven's approving ray.
Sleep on—for purer eyes than thine
Those waves are hushed, those planets shine;
Sleep on, and be thy rest unmoved
  By the white moonbeam's dazzling power;—
None but the loving and the loved
  Should be awake at this sweet hour.

And see—where, high above those rocks
  That o'er the deep their shadows fling,
Yon turret stands;—where ebon locks,
  As glossy as a heron's wing
  Upon the turban of a king,[2]
Hang from the lattice, long and wild,—
'Tis she, that Emir's blooming child,
All truth and tenderness and grace,
Though born of such ungentle race;—

An image of Youth's radiant Fountain
Springing in a desolate mountain!

Oh what a pure and sacred thing
  Is beauty, curtained from the sight
Of the gross world, illumining
  One only mansion with her light!
Unseen by man's disturbing eye,—
  The flower that blooms beneath the sea,
Too deep for sunbeams, doth not lie
  Hid in more chaste obscurity.
So, Hinda, have thy face and mind,
Like holy mysteries, lain enshrined.
And oh, what transport for a lover
  To lift the veil that shades them o'er!—
Like those who, all at once, discover
  In the lone deep some fairy shore,
Where mortal never trod before,
And sleep and wake in scented airs
No lip had ever breathed but theirs.

Beautiful are the maids that glide,
  On summer-eves, through Yemen's[4] dales,
And bright the glancing looks they hide
  Behind their litters' roseate veils;—
And brides, as delicate and fair
As the white jasmine flowers they wear,
Hath Yemen in her blissful clime,
  Who, lulled in cool kiosk or bower,[5]
Before their mirrors count the time,[6]
  And grow still lovelier every hour;
But never yet hath bride or maid
  In Araby's gay Haram smiled
Whose boasted brightness would not fade
  Before Al Hassan's blooming child.

Light as the angel shapes that bless
  An infant's dream, yet not the less
Rich in all woman's loveliness;—
  With eyes so pure that from their ray
Dark Vice would turn abashed away,
Blinded like serpents, when they gaze
Upon the emerald's virgin blaze;[7]—
Yet filled with all youth's sweet desires,
Mingling the meek and vestal fires

---

[1] 'There is a kind of Rhododendron about Trebizond, whose flowers the bee feeds upon, and the honey thence drives people mad.'

[2] 'Their kings wear plumes of black herons' feathers upon the right side, as a badge of sovereignty.'

[3] 'The Fountain of Youth, by a Mohammedan tradition, is situated in some dark region of the East.'—*Richardson.*

[4] Arabia Felix.

[5] 'In the midst of the garden is the chiosk, that is, a large room, commonly beautified with a fine fountain in the midst of it. It is raised nine or ten steps, and enclosed with gilded lattices, round which vines, jessamines, and honeysuckles make a sort of green wall; large trees are planted round this place, which is the scene of the greatest pleasures.'—*Lady M. W. Montagu.*

[6] 'The women of the East are never without their looking-glasses. 'In Barbary,' says Shaw, 'they are so fond of their looking-glasses, which they hang upon their breasts, that they will not lay them aside, even when, after the drudgery of the day, they are obliged to go two or three miles with a pitcher or a goat's skin to fetch water.'—*Travels.*

In other parts of Asia they wear little looking-glasses on their thumbs. 'Hence (and from the lotus being considered the emblem of beauty) is the meaning of the following mute intercourse of two lovers before their parents:—

"He with salute of deference due,
  A lotus to his forehead prest;
She raised her mirror to his view,
  Then turned it inward to her breast."'
Asiatic Miscellany, vol. II.

[7] 'They say that if a snake or serpent fix his eyes on the lustre of those stones (emeralds), he immediately becomes blind.'

Of other worlds with all the bliss,
The fond, weak tenderness of this:
A soul, too, more than half divine,
   Where, through some shades of earthly
      feeling,
Religion's softened glories shine,
   Like light through summer foliage stealing,
Shedding a glow of such mild hue,
So warm, and yet so shadowy too,
As makes the very darkness there
More beautiful than light elsewhere.

Such is the maid who, at this hour,
   Hath risen from her restless sleep,
And sits alone in that high bower,
   Watching the still and shining deep.
Ah! 'twas not thus,—with tearful eyes,
   And beating heart,—she used to gaze
On the magnificent earth and skies,
   In her own land, in happier days.
Why looks she now so anxious down
Among those rocks, whose rugged frown
Blackens the mirror of the deep?
Whom waits she all this lonely night?
Too rough the rocks, too bold the steep,
For man to scale that turret's height!—

So deemed at least her thoughtful sire,
   When high, to catch the cool night air,
After the day-beam's withering fire,[1]
   He built her bower of freshness there,
And had it decked with costliest skill,
   And fondly thought it safe as fair:—
Think, reverend dreamer! think so still,
   Nor wake to learn what Love can dare;—
Love, all-defying Love, who sees
No charm in trophies won with ease;—
Whose rarest, dearest fruits of bliss
Are plucked on Danger's precipice!
Bolder than they who dare not dive
   For pearls but when the sea's at rest,
Love, in the tempest most alive,
   Hath ever held that pearl the best
He finds beneath the stormiest water.
Yes—Araby's unrivalled daughter,
Though high that tower, that rock-way rude,
   There's one who, but to kiss thy cheek,
Would climb the untrodden solitude
   Of Ararat's tremendous peak,
And think its steeps, though dark and dread,
Heaven's pathways, if to thee they led.
Even now thou seest the flashing spray,
That lights his oar's impatient way;
Even now thou hear'st the sudden shock
Of his swift bark against the rock,

And stretchest down thy arms of snow,
As if to lift him from below!
Like her to whom, at dead of night,
The bridegroom with his locks of light,[2]
Came, in the flush of love and pride,
And scaled the terrace of his bride;—
When, as she saw him rashly spring,
And midway up in danger cling,
She flung him down her long black hair,
Exclaiming, breathless, 'There, love, there!'
And scarce did manlier nerve uphold
The hero Zal in that fond hour
Than wings the youth who, fleet and bold,
   Now climbs the rocks to Hinda's bower.
See—light as up their granite steeps
   The rock-goats of Arabia clamber,[3]
Fearless from crag to crag he leaps,
   And now is in the maiden's chamber.

She loves—but knows not whom she loves,
   Nor what his race, nor whence he came;—
Like one who meets, in Indian groves,
   Some beauteous bird without a name,
Brought by the last ambrosial breeze,
From isles in the undiscovered seas,
To show his plumage for a day
To wondering eyes, and wing away!
Will *he* thus fly—her nameless lover?
Alla forbid! 'twas by a moon
As fair as this, while singing over
   Some ditty to her soft Kanoon,[4]
Alone, at this same witching hour,
   She first beheld his radiant eyes
Gleam through the lattice of the bower,
   Where nightly now they mix their sighs;
And thought some spirit of the air
(For what could waft a mortal there?)
Was pausing on his moonlight way
To listen to her lonely lay!
This fancy ne'er hath left her mind:
   And—though, when terror's swoon had past,
She saw a youth, of mortal kind,
   Before her in obeisance cast,—
Yet often since, when he hath spoken
Strange, awful words,—and gleams have broken
From his dark eyes, too bright to bear,
Oh! she hath feared her soul was given
To some unhallowed child of air,
   Some erring Spirit cast from heaven,
Like those angelic youths of old
Who burned for maids of mortal mould,
Bewildered left the glorious skies,
And lost their heaven for woman's eyes.
Fond girl! nor fiend nor angel he
Who woos thy young simplicity;

---

[1] 'At Gombaroon and the Isle of Ormus, it is sometimes so hot that the people are obliged to lie all day in the water.'—*Marco Polo.*

[2] In one of the books of the Shāh Nāmeh, when Zal (a celebrated hero of Persia, remarkable for his white hair) comes to the terrace of his mistress Rodahver at night, she lets down her long tresses to assist him in his ascent. He, however, manages it in a less romantic way, by fixing his crook in a projecting beam.—See *Champion's Ferdosi.*

[3] 'On the lofty hills of Arabia Petræa are rock-goats.' —*Niebuhr.*

[4] 'Canun, espèce de psaltérion, avec des cordes de boyaux; les dames en touchent dans le sérail, avec des décailles armées de pointes de coco.'—*Toderini, translated by Dr Cournand.*

Such is the maid who, at this hour,
  Hath risen from her restless sleep,
And sits alone in that high bower,
  Watching the still and moonlight deep.
Ah! 'twas not thus—with tearful eyes
  And beating heart—she used to gaze
On the magnificent earth and skies
  In her own land, in happier days.
Page 92.

THE FIRE-WORSHIPPERS. 93

But one of earth's impassioned sons,
  As warm in love, as fierce in ire,
As the best heart whose current runs
  Full of the Day God's living fire.

But quenched to-night that ardour seems,
  And pale his cheek, and sunk his brow;—
Never before, but in her dreams,
  Had she beheld him pale as now:
And those were dreams of troubled sleep,
From which 'twas joy to wake and weep;
Visions that will not be forgot,
  But sadden every waking scene,
Like warning ghosts, that leave the spot
  All withered where they once have been.

'How sweetly, said the trembling maid,
  Of her own gentle voice afraid,
So long had they in silence stood,
Looking upon that tranquil flood—
'How sweetly does the moon-beam smile
To-night upon yon leafy isle!
Oft, in my fancy's wanderings,
I've wished that little isle had wings,
And we, within its fairy bowers,
  Were wafted off to seas unknown,
Where not a pulse should beat but ours,
  And we might live, love, die alone!
Far from the cruel and the cold,—
  Where the bright eyes of angels only
Should come around us, to behold
  A paradise so pure and lonely.
Would this be world enough for thee?'—
Playful she turned, that he might see
  The passing smile her cheek put on;
But when she marked how mournfully
  His eyes met hers, that smile was gone;
And, bursting into heartfelt tears,
'Yes, yes,' she cried, 'my hourly fears,
My dreams have boded all too right—
We part—for ever part—to-night!
I knew, I knew it *could* not last—
'Twas bright, 'twas heavenly, but 'tis past!
Oh! ever thus, from childhood's hour,
  I've seen my fondest hopes decay;
I never loved a tree or flower,
  But 'twas the first to fade away.
I never nursed a dear gazelle,
  To glad me with its soft black eye,
But when it came to know me well,
  And love me, it was sure to die!
Now too—the joy most like divine
  Of all I ever dreamt or knew,
To see thee, hear thee, call thee mine,—
  Oh misery! must I lose *that* too?
Yet go—on peril's brink we meet;—
  Those frightful rocks—that treacherous sea—
No, never come again—though sweet,
  Though heaven, it may be death to thee.
Farewell—and blessings on thy way,
  Where'er thou go'st, beloved stranger!
Better to sit and watch that ray,

And think thee safe, though far away,
  Than have thee near me, and in danger!'

'Danger!—oh, tempt me not to boast'—
The youth exclaimed—'thou little know'st
What he can brave who, born and nurst
In Danger's paths, has dared her worst;
Upon whose ear the signal-word
Of strife and death is hourly breaking;
Who sleeps with head upon the sword
  His fevered hand must grasp in waking.
Danger!—'
          'Say on—thou fear'st not then,
And we may meet—oft meet again?'
'Oh! look not so—beneath the skies
I now fear nothing but those eyes.
If aught on earth could charm or force
My spirit from its destined course,—
If aught could make this soul forget
The bond to which its seal is set,
'Twould be those eyes;—they, only they,
Could melt that sacred seal away!
But no—'tis fixed—*my* awful doom
Is fixed—on this side of the tomb
We meet no more;—why, why did Heaven
Mingle two souls that earth has riven,
Has rent asunder wide as ours?
Oh Arab maid, as soon the Powers
Of Light and Darkness may combine
As I be linked with thee or thine!
Thy Father———'
              'Holy Alla save
His gray head from that lightning glance!
Thou know'st him not—he loves the brave;
Nor lives there under heaven's expanse
One who would prize, would worship thee
And thy bold spirit, more than he.
Oft when, in childhood, I have played
  With the bright falchion by his side,
I've heard him swear his lisping maid
  In time should be a warrior's bride.
And still, whene'er at Haram hours
I take him cool sherbets and flowers,
He tells me, when in playful mood,
  A hero shall my bridegroom be,
Since maids are best in battle wooed,
  And won with shouts of victory!
Nay, turn not from me—thou alone
Art formed to make both hearts thy own.
Go, join his sacred ranks—thou know'st
  The unholy strife these Persians wage:—
Good Heaven, that frown!—even now thou glow'st
With more than mortal warrior's rage.
Haste to the camp by morning's light,
And, when that sword is raised in fight,
Oh still remember, Love and I
Beneath its shadow trembling lie!
One victory o'er those Slaves of Fire,
Those impious Ghebers, whom my sire
Abhors———'
          'Hold, hold—thy words are death'—
The stranger cried, as wild he flung

His mantle back, and showed beneath
 The Gheber belt that round him clung.'—
'Here, maiden, look—weep—blush to see
All that thy sire abhors, in me!
Yes—*I* am of that impious race,
 Those Slaves of Fire who, morn and even,
Hail their Creator's dwelling-place
 Among the living lights of heaven:[2]
Yes—*I* am of that outcast few,
 To Iran and to vengeance true,
Who curse the hour your Arabs came
 To desolate our shrines of flame,
And swear, before God's burning eye,
 To break our country's chains or die!
Thy bigot sire—nay, tremble not—
 He who gave birth to those dear eyes,
With me is sacred as the spot
 From which our fires of worship rise!
But know—'twas he I sought that night
 When, from my watch-boat on the sea,
I caught this turret's glimmering light,
 And up the rude rocks desperately
Rushed to my prey—thou know'st the rest—
 I climbed the gory vulture's nest,
And found a trembling dove within;—
 Thine, thine the victory—thine the sin—
If Love hath made one thought his own
 That Vengeance claims first—last—alone!
Oh! had we never, never met,
 Or could this heart even now forget
How linked, how blessed we might have been,
 Had fate not frowned so dark between!
Hadst thou been born a Persian maid,
 In neighbouring valleys had we dwelt,
Through the same fields in childhood played,
 At the same kindling altar knelt,—
Then, then, while all those nameless ties
 In which the charm of Country lies
Had round our hearts been hourly spun,
 Till Iran's cause and thine were one;
While in thy lute's awakening sigh
 I heard the voice of days gone by,
And saw, in every smile of thine,
 Returning hours of glory shine;—
While the wronged Spirit of our Land [thee,—
 Lived, looked, and spoke her wrongs through
God! who could then this sword withstand?
 Its very flash were victory!

But now—estranged, divorced for ever,
 Far as the grasp of Fate can sever;
Our only ties what love has wove,—
 In faith, friends, country, sundered wide;
And then, then only, true to love
 When false to all that's dear beside!
Thy father Iran's deadliest foe—
 Thyself, perhaps, even now—but no—
Hate never looked so lovely yet!
 No—sacred to thy soul will be
The land of him who could forget
 All but that bleeding land for thee.
When other eyes shall see, unmoved,
 Her widows mourn, her warriors fall,
Thou'lt think how well one Gheber loved,
 And for *his* sake thou'lt weep for all!
But look ——'

 With sudden start he turned
 And pointed to the distant wave,
Where lights, like charnel meteors, burned
 Bluely, as o'er some seaman's grave:
And fiery darts, at intervals,[3]
 Flew up all sparkling from the main,
As if each star that nightly falls
 Were shooting back to heaven again.

'My signal lights!—I must away—
 Both, both are ruined, if I stay.
Farewell—sweet life! thou cling'st in vain—
 Now, Vengeance, I am thine again!'
Fiercely he broke away, nor stopped,
 Nor looked—but from the lattice dropped
Down 'mid the pointed crags beneath,
 As if he fled from love to death.
While pale and mute young Hinda stood,
 Nor moved, till in the silent flood
A momentary plunge below
 Startled her from her trance of woe;—
Shrieking she to the lattice flew:
 'I come—I come—if in that tide
Thou sleep'st to-night, I'll sleep there too,
 In death's cold wedlock, by thy side.
Oh! I would ask no happier bed
 Than the chill wave my love lies under:—
Sweeter to rest together dead,
 Far sweeter, than to live asunder!'

---

[1] 'They (the Ghebers) lay so much stress on their cushee or girdle, as not to dare to be an instant without it.'—*Grose's Voyage*. 'Pour se distinguer des Idolatres de l'Inde, les Guèbres se ceignent tous d'un cordon delaine, ou de poil de chameau.'—*Encyclopédie Françoise.*
D'Herbelot says this belt was generally of leather.

[2] 'They suppose the throne of the Almighty is seated in the sun, and hence their worship of that luminary.' 'As to fire, the Ghebers place the spring-head of it in that globe of fire, the sun, by them called Mythras, or Mihir, to which they pay the highest reverence, in gratitude for the manifold benefits flowing from its ministerial omniscience. But they are so far from confounding the subordination of the servant with the majesty of its Creator, that they not only attribute no sort of sense or reasoning to the sun or fire in any of its operations, but consider it as a purely passive blind instrument, directed and governed by the immediate impression on it of the will of God; but they do not even give that luminary, all-glorious as it is, more than the second rank amongst His works, reserving the first for that stupendous production of divine power, the mind of man.'—*Grose*. The false charges brought against the religion of these people by their Mussulman tyrants is but one proof among many of the truth of this writer's remark, 'that calumny is often added to oppression, if but for the sake of justifying it.'

[3] 'The Mamelukes that were in the other boat, when it was dark, used to shoot up a sort of fiery arrows into the air, which in some measure resembled lightning or falling stars.'—*Baumgarten.*

But no—their hour is not yet come—
Again she sees his pinnace fly,
Wafting him fleetly to his home,
Where'er that ill-starred home may lie;

And calm and smooth it seemed to win
Its moonlight way before the wind,
As if it bore all peace within,
Nor left one breaking heart behind!

The Princess, whose heart was sad enough already, could have wished that Feramorz had chosen a less melancholy story, as it is only to the happy that tears are a luxury. Her ladies, however, were by no means sorry that love was once more the Poet's theme; for, whenever he spoke of love, they said his voice was as sweet as if he had chewed the leaves of that enchanted tree which grows over the tomb of the musician Tan-Sein.[1]

Their road all the morning had lain through a very dreary country—through valleys covered with a low beachy jungle, where, in more than one place, the awful signal of the bamboo staff,[2] with the white flag at its top, reminded the traveller that in that very spot the tiger had made some human creature his victim. It was therefore with much pleasure that they arrived at sunset in a safe and lovely glen, and encamped under one of those holy trees whose smooth columns and spreading roofs seem to destine them for natural temples of religion. Beneath this spacious shade some pious hands had erected a row of pillars ornamented with the most beautiful porcelain,[3] which now supplied the use of mirrors to the young maidens, as they adjusted their hair in descending from the palankeens. Here, while, as usual, the Princess sat listening anxiously, with Fadladeen in one of his loftiest moods of criticism by her side, the young Poet, leaning against a branch of the tree, thus continued his story:—

The morn hath risen clear and calm,
And o'er the Green Sea[4] palely shines,
Revealing Bahrein's[5] groves of palm,
And lighting Kishma's[6] amber vines.
Fresh smell the shores of Araby,
While breezes from the Indian Sea
Blow round Selama's sainted cape,[6]
And curl the shining flood beneath,—
Whose waves are rich with many a grape
And cocoa-nut and flowery wreath,
Which pious seamen, as they passed,
Had toward that holy headland cast—
Oblations to the Genii there
For gentle skies and breezes fair.
The nightingale[7] now bends her flight
From the high trees, where all the night
She sung so sweet, with none to listen;
And hides her from the morning star
Where thickets of pomegranate glisten
In the clear dawn,—bespangled o'er
With dew, whose night-drops would not stain
The best and brightest scimitar[8]

That ever youthful Sultan wore
On the first morning of his reign

And see—the Sun himself!—on wings
Of glory up the East he springs.
Angel of Light! who from the time
Those heavens began their march sublime,
Hath first of all the starry choir
Trod in his Maker's steps of fire!
Where are the days, thou wondrous sphere,
When Irau, like a sun-flower, turned
To meet that eye where'er it burned?—
When, from the banks of Bendemeer
To the nut-groves of Samarcand,
Thy temples flamed o'er all the land?
Where are they? ask the shades of them
Who on Cadessia's[9] bloody plains,
Saw fierce invaders pluck the gem
From Iran's broken diadem,
And bind her ancient faith in chains:—
Ask the poor exile, cast alone
On foreign shores unloved, unknown,

---

[1] 'At Gualior is a small tomb to the memory of Tan-Sein, a musician of incomparable skill, who flourished at the court of Akbar. The tomb is overshadowed by a tree, concerning which a superstitious notion prevails, that the chewing of its leaves will give an extraordinary melody to the voice.'—*Journey from Agra to Ousein, by W. Hunter, Esq.*

[2] 'It is usual to place a small white triangular flag, fixed to a bamboo staff of ten or twelve feet long, at the place where a tiger has destroyed a man. The sight of these flags imparts a certain melancholy, not perhaps altogether void of apprehension.'—*Oriental Field Sports*, vol. ii.

[3] 'The Ficus Indica is called the Pagod Tree and Tree of Councils: the first, from the idols placed under its shade; the second, because meetings were held under its cool branches. In some places it is believed to be the haunt of spectres, as the ancient spreading oaks of Wales have been of fairies; in others are erected beneath the shade pillars of stone, or posts, elegantly carved, and ornamented with the most beautiful porcelain to supply the use of mirrors.'—*Pennant*.

[4] The Persian Gulf.

[5] Islands in the Gulf.

[6] Or Selemeh, the genuine name of the headland at the entrance of the Gulf, commonly called Cape Musseldom.

[7] 'The nightingale sings from the pomegranate-groves in the day-time, and from the loftiest trees at night.'—*Russel's Aleppo*.

[8] In speaking of the climate of Shiraz, Francklin says: 'The dew is of such a pure nature, that if the brightest scimitar should be exposed to it all night, it would not receive the least rust.'

[9] The place where the Persians were finally defeated by the Arabs, and their ancient monarchy destroyed.

Beyond the Caspian's Iron Gates,[1]
Or on the snowy Mossian mountains,
Far from his beauteous land of dates,
  Her jasmine bowers and sunny fountains:
Yet happier so than if he trod
His own beloved, but blighted, sod,
Beneath a despot stranger's nod!—
Oh he would rather houseless roam
  Where Freedom and his God may lead,
Than be the sleekest slave at home
  That crouches to the conqueror's creed!

Is Iran's pride then gone for ever,
  Quenched with the flame in Mithra's caves?—
No—she has sons that never—never—
  Will stoop to be the Moslem's slaves,
While heaven has light or earth has graves;—
Spirits of fire, that brood not long,
But flash resentment back for wrong;
And hearts where, slow but deep, the seeds
Of vengeance ripen into deeds,
Till, in some treacherous hour of calm,
They burst, like Zeilan's giant palm,[2]
Whose buds fly open with a sound
That shakes the pygmy forests round!

Yes, Emir! he, who scaled that tower,
  And, had he reached thy slumbering breast,
Had taught thee in a Gheber's power
  How safe even tyrant heads may rest—
Is one of many, brave as he,
Who loathe thy haughty race and thee;
Who, though they know the strife is vain,
Who, though they know the riven chain
Snaps but to enter in the heart
Of him who rends its links apart,
Yet dare the issue,—blest to be
Even for one bleeding moment free,
And die in pangs of liberty!
Thou know'st them well—'tis some moons since
  Thy turbaned troops and blood-red flags,
Thou satrap of a bigot Prince,
  Have swarmed among these Green Sea crags;
Yet here, even here, a sacred band
Ay, in the portal of that land
Thou, Arab, dar'st to call thy own,
Their spears across thy path have thrown;
Here—ere the winds half winged thee o'er—
Rebellion braved thee from the shore.

Rebellion! foul, dishonouring word,
  Whose wrongful blight so oft has stained
The holiest cause that tongue or sword
  Of mortal ever lost or gained.

How many a spirit born to bless
  Hath sunk beneath that withering name,
Whom but a day's, an hour's success
  Had wafted to eternal fame!
As exhalations, when they burst
From the warm earth, if chilled at first,
If checked in soaring from the plain,
Darken to fogs and sink again;—
But, if they once triumphant spread
Their wings above the mountain-head,
Become enthroned in upper air,
And turn to sun-bright glories there!

And who is he that wields the might
Of Freedom on the Green Sea brink,
Before whose sabre's dazzling light[3]
The eyes of Yemen's warriors wink?
Who comes, embowered in the spears
Of Kerman's hardy mountaineers?
Those mountaineers that truest, last,
Cling to their country's ancient rites,
As if that God whose eyelids cast
Their closing gleam on Iran's heights
Among her snowy mountains threw
The last light of his worship too!

'Tis Hafed—name of fear, whose sound
Chills like the muttering of a charm;—
Shout but that awful name around,
And palsy shakes the manliest arm.
'Tis Hafed, most accursed and dire
(So ranked by Moslem hate and ire)
Of all the rebel Sons of Fire;
Of whose malign, tremendous power
The Arabs, at their mid-watch hour,
Such tales of fearful wonder tell
That each affrighted sentinel
Pulls down his cowl upon his eyes,
Lest Hafed in the midst should rise!
A man, they say, of monstrous birth,
A mingled race of flame and earth,
Sprung from those old, enchanted kings[4]
Who in their fairy helms, of yore,
A feather from the mystic wings
Of the Simoorgh resistless wore;
And gifted by the Fiends of Fire,
Who groaned to see their shrines expire,
With charms that, all in vain withstood,
Would drown the Koran's light in blood!

Such were the tales that won belief,
And such the colouring Fancy gave
To a young, warm, and dauntless Chief,—
One who, no more than mortal brave,

---

[1] Derbend.—'Les Turcs appelent cette ville Demir Capi, Porte de Fer; ce sont les Caspiæ Portæ des anciens.'—*D'Herbelot.*

[2] The Talpot or Talipot tree. 'This beautiful palm-tree, which grows in the heart of the forests, may be classed among the loftiest trees, and becomes still higher when on the point of bursting forth from its leafy summit. The sheath which then envelopes the flower is very large, and, when it bursts, makes an explosion like the report of a cannon.'—*Thunberg.*

[3] 'When the bright cimitars make the eyes of our heroes wink.'—*The Moallakat, Poem of Amru.*

[4] Tahmuras, and other ancient kings of Persia, whose adventures in Fairy-land among the Peris and Dives may be found in Richardson's Dissertation. The griffin Simoorgh, they say, took some feathers from her breast for Tahmuras, with which he adorned his helmet, and transmitted them afterwards to his descendants.

Around its base the bare rocks stood,
Like naked giants in the flood,
As if to guard the gulf across;
While, on its peak, that braved the sky,
A ruin'd temple tower'd so high
That oft the sleeping albatross
Struck the wild ruins with her wings.

Page 97.

THE FIRE-WORSHIPPERS.

Fought for the land his soul adored,
For happy homes and altars free,
His only talisman the sword,
His only spell-word Liberty!
One of that ancient hero line,
Along whose glorious current shine
Names that have sanctified their blood;
As Lebanon's small mountain-flood
Is rendered holy by the ranks[1]
Of sainted cedars on its banks.[2]
'Twas not for him to crouch the knee
Tamely to Moslem tyranny;
'Twas not for him, whose soul was cast
In the bright mould of ages past,
Whose melancholy spirit, fed
With all the glories of the dead,
Though framed for Iran's happiest years,
Was born among her chains and tears!—
'Twas not for him to swell the crowd
Of slavish heads that shrinking bowed
Before the Moslem, as he passed,
Like shrubs beneath the poison-blast—
No—far he fled—indignant fled
The pageant of his country's shame;
While every tear her children shed
Fell on his soul like drops of flame;
And, as a lover hails the dawn
Of a first smile, so welcomed he
The sparkle of the first sword drawn
For vengeance and for liberty!

But vain was valour—vain the flower
Of Kerman, in that deathful hour,
Against Al Hassan's whelming power,—
In vain they met him, helm to helm,
Upon the threshold of that realm
He came in bigot pomp to sway,
And with their corpses blocked his way—
In vain—for every lance they raised,
Thousands around the conqueror blazed;
For every arm that lined their shore,
Myriads of slaves were wafted o'er,—
A bloody, bold, and countless crowd,
Before whose swarm as fast they bowed
As dates beneath the locust cloud.

There stood—but one short league away
From old Harmozia's sultry bay—

A rocky mountain, o'er the Sea
Of Oman beetling awfully;[3]
A last and solitary link
Of those stupendous chains that reach
From the broad Caspian's reedy brink
Down winding to the Green Sea beach
Around its base the bare rocks stood,
Like naked giants, in the flood,
As if to guard the Gulf across;
While, on its peak, that braved the sky,
A ruined Temple towered, so high
That oft the sleeping albatross[4]
Struck the wild ruins with her wing,
And from her cloud-rocked slumbering
Started—to find man's dwelling there
In her own silent fields of air!
Beneath, terrific caverns gave
Dark welcome to each stormy wave
That dashed, like midnight revellers, in;—
And such the strange, mysterious din
At times throughout those caverns rolled,—
And such the fearful wonders told
Of restless sprites imprisoned there,
That bold were Moslem who would dare,
At twilight hour, to steer his skiff
Beneath the Gheber's lonely cliff.[5]
On the land side, those towers sublime,
That seemed above the grasp of Time,
Were severed from the haunts of men
By a wide, deep, and wizard glen,
So fathomless, so full of gloom,
No eye could pierce the void between:
It seemed a place where Gholes might
   come
With their foul banquets from the tomb,
And in its caverns feed unseen.
Like distant thunder, from below,
The sound of many torrents came,
Too deep for ear or eye to know
If 'twere the sea's imprisoned flow,
Or floods of ever-restless flame.
For each ravine, each rocky spire
Of that vast mountain stood on fire;[6]
And, though for ever past the days
When God was worshipped in the blaze
That from its lofty altar shone,—
Though fled the priests, the votaries gone,
Still did the mighty flame burn on,[7]

---

[1] In the *Lettres Edifiantes* there is a different cause assigned for its name of holy. 'In these are deep caverns, which formerly served as so many cells for a great number of recluses, who had chosen these retreats as the only witnesses upon earth of the severity of their penance. The tears of these pious penitents gave the river of which we have just treated the name of the Holy River.'—*Vide Chateaubriand's Beauties of Christianity.*
[2] This rivulet, says Dandini, is called the Holy River from the 'cedar-saints' among which it rises.
[3] This mountain is my own creation, as the 'stupendous chain,' of which I suppose it a link, does not extend quite so far as the shores of the Persian Gulf.
[4] These birds sleep in the air. They are most common about the Cape of Good Hope.

[5] 'There is an extraordinary hill in the neighbourhood called Kohé Gubr, or the Guebre's mountain. It rises in the form of a lofty cupola, and on the summit of it, they say, are the remains of an Atush Kudu or Fire Temple. It is superstitiously held to be the residence of Deeves or Sprites, and many marvellous stories are recounted of the injury and witchcraft suffered by those who essayed in former days to ascend or explore it.'—*Pottinger's Beloochistan.*
[6] The Ghebers generally built their temples over subterraneous fires.
[7] 'At the city of Yezd in Persia, which is distinguished by the appellation of the Darûb Abadut, or Seat of Religion, the Guebres are permitted to have an Atush Kudu or Fire Temple (which they assert has had the sacred fire in it since the days of Zoroaster) in their

G

Through chance and change, through good and ill,
Like its own God's eternal will,
Deep, constant, bright, unquenchable!

Thither the vanquished Hafed led
  His little army's last remains;—
'Welcome, terrific glen!' he said,
'Thy gloom, that Eblis' self might dread,
  Is Heaven to him who flies from chains!'
O'er a dark, narrow bridge-way, known
To him and to his Chiefs alone,
They crossed the chasm and gained the towers.
'This home,' he cried, 'at least is ours;—
Here we may bleed, unmocked by hymns
  Of Moslem triumph o'er our head;
Here we may fall, nor leave our limbs
  To quiver to the Moslem's tread.
Stretched on this rock, while vultures' beaks
Are whetted on our yet warm cheeks,
Here—happy that no tyrant's eye
Gloats on our torments—we may die!'

'Twas night when to those towers they came,
And gloomily the fitful flame
That from the ruined altar broke
Glared on his features as he spoke:—
'''Tis o'er—what men could do we've done—
If Iran *will* look tamely on,
And see her priests, her warriors driven
  Before a sensual bigot's nod,
A wretch who shrines his lust in heaven,
  And makes a pander of his God;
If her proud sons, her high-born souls,
Men in whose veins—oh last disgrace!
The blood of Zal and Rustam rolls,[1]—
If they *will* court this upstart race,
And turn from Mithra's ancient ray,
To kneel at shrines of yesterday;
If they *will* crouch to Iran's foes,
Why, let them—till the land's despair
Cries out to Heaven, and bondage grows
  Too vile for even the vile to bear!
Till shame at last, long hidden burns
Their inmost core, and conscience turns
Each coward tear the slave lets fall
Back on his heart in drops of gall.
But *here*, at least, are arms unchained,
And souls that thraldom never stained;—

This spot, at least, no foot of slave
Or satrap ever yet profaned;
And though but few—though fast the wave
Of life is ebbing from our veins,
Enough for vengeance still remains.
As panthers, after set of sun,
Rush from the roots of Lebanon
Across the dark-sea robber's way,
We'll bound upon our startled prey;
And when some hearts that proudest swell
Have felt our falchions' last farewell;
When Hope's expiring throb is o'er,
And even Despair can prompt no more,
This spot shall be the sacred grave
Of the last few who, vainly brave,
Die for the land they cannot save!'

His Chiefs stood round—each shining blade
Upon the broken altar laid—
And though so wild and desolate
Those courts, where once the Mighty sate;
Nor longer on those mouldering towers
Was seen the feast of fruits and flowers
With which of old the Magi fed
The wandering Spirits of their dead;[2]
Though neither priest nor rites were there,
  Nor charmèd leaf of pure pomegranate;[3]
Nor hymn, nor censer's fragrant air,
  Nor symbol of their worshipped planet;[4]
Yet the same God that heard their sires
Heard *them*, while on that altar's fires[5]
They swore the latest, holiest deed
Of the few hearts, still left to bleed,
Should be, in Iran's injured name,
To die upon that Mount of Flame—
The last of all her patriot line,
Before her last untrampled Shrine!

Brave, suffering souls! they little knew
How many a tear their injuries drew
From one meek maid, one gentle foe,
Whom love first touched with others' woe—
Whose life, as free from thought as sin,
Slept like a lake, till Love threw in
His talisman, and woke the tide,
And spread its trembling circles wide.
Once, Emir! thy unheeding child,
'Mid all this havoc, bloomed and smiled,—
Tranquil as on some battle plain
  The Persian lily shines and towers,[6]

---

own compartment of the city; but for this indulgence they are indebted to the avarice, not the tolerance, of the Persian Government, which taxes them at twenty-five rupees each man.'—*Pottinger's Beloochistan.*

[1] Ancient heroes of Persia. 'Among the Ghebers there are some who boast their descent from Rustam.'

[2] 'Among other ceremonies the Magi used to place upon the tops of high towers various kinds of rich viands, upon which it was supposed the Peris and the spirits of their departed heroes regaled themselves.'—*Richardson.*

[3] In the ceremonies of the Ghebers round their Fire, as described by Lord, 'the Daroo,' he says, 'giveth them water to drink, and a pomegranate leaf to chew in the mouth, to cleanse them from inward uncleanness.'

[4] 'Early in the morning, they (the Parsees or Ghebers at Oulam) go in crowds to pay their devotions to the sun, to whom upon all the altars there are spheres consecrated, made by magic, resembling the circles of the sun; and when the sun rises, these orbs seem to be inflamed, and to turn round with a great noise. They have every one a censer in their hands, and offer incense to the sun.'

[5] 'Nul d'entre eux oseroit se perjurer, quand il a pris à témoin cet élement terrible et vengeur.'—*Encyclopédie François.*

[6] 'A vivid verdure succeeds the autumnal rains, and the ploughed fields are covered with the Persian lily, of a resplendent yellow colour.'—*Russel's Aleppo.*

THE FIRE-WORSHIPPERS.

Before the combat's reddening stain
 Hath fallen upon her golden flowers;
Light-hearted maid, unawed, unmoved,
 While Heaven but spared the sire she loved.
Once at thy evening tales of blood
Unlistening and aloof she stood—
And oft, when thou hast paced along
 Thy Haram halls with furious heat,
Hast thou not cursed her cheerful song,
 That came across thee, calm and sweet,
Like lutes of angels, touched so near
Hell's confines that the damned can hear!

Far other feelings Love hath brought—
 Her soul all flame, her brow all sadness,
She now has but the one dear thought,
 And thinks that o'er, almost to madness!
Oft doth her sinking heart recall
His words—'for *my* sake weep for all;'
And bitterly, as day on day
 Of rebel carnage fast succeeds,
She weeps a lover snatched away
 In every Gheber wretch that bleeds.
There's not a sabre meets her eye
 But with his life-blood seems to swim;
There's not an arrow wings the sky
 But fancy turns its point to him.
No more she brings with footstep light
Al Hassan's falchion for the fight;
And—had he looked with clearer sight,
 Had not the mists that ever rise
From a foul spirit dimmed his eyes—
He would have marked her shuddering frame
 When from the field of blood he came,
The faltering speech—the look estranged—
Voice, step, and life, and beauty changed—
He would have marked all this, and known
Such change is wrought by Love alone!

Ah! not the Love that should have blessed
So young, so innocent a breast;
Not the pure, open, prosperous Love,
That, pledged on earth and sealed above,
Grows in the world's approving eyes,
 In friendship's smile and home's caress,
Collecting all the heart's sweet ties
 Into one knot of happiness!
No, Hinda, no,—thy fatal flame
Is nursed in silence, sorrow, shame;—
 A passion, without hope or pleasure,
In thy soul's darkness buried deep,
 It lies like some ill-gotten treasure,—
Some idol, without shrine or name,
O'er which its pale-eyed votaries keep
Unholy watch, while others sleep.

Seven nights have darkened Oman's sea,
 Since last, beneath the moonlight ray,
She saw his light oar rapidly
 Hurry her Gheber's bark away,—
And still she goes, at midnight hour,
To weep alone in that high bower,
And watch, and look along the deep
For him whose smiles first made her weep;—
But watching, weeping, all was vain,
She never saw his bark again.
The owlet's solitary cry,
The night-hawk, flitting darkly by,
 And oft the hateful carrion bird,
Heavily flapping his clogged wing,
Which reeked with that day's banqueting—
 Was all she saw, was all she heard.

'Tis the eighth morn—Al Hassan's brow
 Is brightened with unusual joy—
What mighty mischief glads him now,
 Who never smiles but to destroy?
The sparkle upon Herkend's Sea,
When tossed at midnight furiously,[1]
Tells not of wreck and ruin nigh
More surely than that smiling eye!

'Up, daughter, up—the Kerna's[2] breath
Has blown a blast would waken death,
And yet thou sleep'st—up, child, and see
This blessèd day for Heaven and me,
A day more rich in Pagan blood
Than ever flashed o'er Oman's flood.
Before another dawn shall shine,
His head—heart—limbs—will all be mine;
This very night his blood shall steep
These hands all over ere I sleep!'—
'*His* blood!' she faintly screamed—her mind
Still singling *one* from all mankind.
'Yes—spite of his ravines and towers,
Hafed, my child, this night is ours.
Thanks to all-conquering treachery,
Without whose aid the links accurst
That bind these impious slaves would be
Too strong for Alla's self to burst!
That rebel fiend, whose blade has spread
My path with piles of Moslem dead,
Whose baffling spells had almost driven
Back from their course the Swords of Heaven,
This night, with all his band, shall know
How deep an Arab's steel can go,
When God and vengeance speed the blow.
And—Prophet! by that holy wreath
Thou wor'st on Ohod's field of death,[3]
I swear, for every sob that parts
In anguish from these heathen hearts,
A gem from Persia's plundered mines
Shall glitter on thy Shrine of Shrines.
But, ha!—she sinks—that look so wild—
Those livid lips—my child, my child,

---

[1] 'It is observed, with respect to the Sea of Herkend, that when it is tossed by tempestuous winds it sparkles like fire.'

[2] A kind of trumpet;—it 'was that used by Tamerlane, the sound of which is described as uncommonly dreadful, and so loud as to be heard at the distance of several miles.'—*Richardson.*

[3] 'Mohammed had two helmets, an interior and exterior one; the latter of which, called Al Mawashah, the wreathed garland, he wore at the battle of Ohod.'

This life of blood befi's not thee,
And thou must back to Araby.
  Ne'er had I risked thy timid sex
In scenes that man himself might dread,
Had I not hoped our every tread
  Would be on prostrate Persian necks—
Curst race, they offer swords instead!
But cheer thee, maid,—the wind that now
Is blowing o'er thy feverish brow,
To-day shall waft thee from the shore;
And, ere a drop of this night's gore
Have time to chill in yonder towers,
Thou'lt see thy own sweet Arab bowers!'

His bloody boast was all too true;
There lurked one wretch among the few
Whom Hafed's eagle eye could count
Around him on that Fiery Mount,—
One miscreant, who for gold betrayed
The pathway through the valley's shade
To those high towers where Freedom stood
In her last hold of flame and blood.
Left on the field that dreadful night,
When, sallying from their sacred height,
The Ghebers fought hope's farewell fight,
He lay—but died not with the brave;
That sun, which should have gilt his grave,
Saw him a traitor and a slave;—

And, while the few who thence returned
To their high rocky fortress mourned
For him among the matchless dead
They left behind on glory's bed,
He lived, and, in the face of morn,
Laughed them and Faith and Heaven to scorn.

Oh for a tongue to curse the slave
  Whose treason, like a deadly blight,
Comes o'er the councils of the brave,
  And blasts them in their hour of might!
May Life's unblessed cup for him
Be drugged with treacheries to the brim,—
  With hopes that but allure to fly,
  With joys that vanish while he sips,
Like Dead Sea fruits, that tempt the eye,
  But turn to ashes on the lips![1]
His country's curse, his children's shame,
Outcast of virtue, peace, and fame,
May he, at last, with lips of flame,
On the parched desert thirsting die,—
While lakes, that shone in mockery nigh,[2]
Are fading off, untouched, untasted,
Like the once glorious hopes he blasted!
And, when from earth his spirit flies,
  Just Prophet, let the damned-one dwell
Full in the sight of Paradise,
  Beholding heaven, and feeling hell!

Lalla Rookh had, the night before, been visited by a dream which, in spite of the impending fate of poor Hafed, made her heart more than usually cheerful during the morning, and gave her cheeks all the freshened animation of a flower that the Bid-musk has just passed over.[3] She fancied that she was sailing on that Eastern Ocean where the sea-gipsies, who live for ever on the water,[4] enjoy a perpetual summer in wandering from isle to isle, when she saw a small gilded bark approaching her. It was like one of those boats which the Maldivian islanders send adrift, at the mercy of winds and waves, loaded with perfumes, flowers, and odoriferous wood, as an offering to the Spirit whom they call King of the Sea. At first this little bark appeared to be empty, but on coming nearer—

She had proceeded thus far in relating the dream to her Ladies, when Feramorz appeared at the door of the pavilion. In his presence, of course, everything else was forgotten, and the continuance of the story was instantly requested by all. Fresh wood of aloes was set to burn in the cassolets; the violet sherbets[5] were hastily handed round, and after a short prelude on

---

[1] 'They say that there are apple-trees upon the sides of this sea, which bear very lovely fruit, but within are full of ashes.'—*Therenot*. The same is asserted of the oranges there.—*Vide Witman's Travels in Asiatic Turkey*. Lord Byron has a similar allusion to the fruits of the Dead Sea, in that wonderful display of genius—his Third Canto of *Childe Harold*.

[2] 'The Suhrab or Water of the Desert is said to be caused by the rarefaction of the atmosphere from extreme heat; and, which augments the delusion, it is most frequent in hollows, where water might be expected to lodge. I have seen bushes and trees reflected in it, with as much accuracy as though it had been the face of a clear and still lake.'—*Pottinger*. 'As to the unbelievers, their works are like a vapour in a plain, which the thirsty traveller thinketh to be water, until when he cometh thereto he findeth it to be nothing.'—*Koran*, chap. xxiv.

[3] 'A wind which prevails in February, called Bid-musk, from a small and odoriferous flower of that name.'—'The wind which blows these flowers commonly lasts till the end of the month.'—*Le Bruyn*.

[4] 'The Biajús are of two races; the one is settled on Borneo, and are a rude but warlike and industrious nation, who reckon themselves the original possessors of the island of Borneo. The other is a species of sea-gipsies or itinerant fishermen, who live in small covered boats, and enjoy a perpetual summer in the eastern ocean, shifting to leeward from island to island, with the variations of the monsoon. In some of their customs this singular race resembles the natives of the Maldivia islands. The Maldivians annually launch a small bark, loaded with perfumes, gums, flowers, and odoriferous wood, and turn it adrift at the mercy of wind and waves, as an offering to the *Spirit of the Winds*; and sometimes similar offerings are made to the spirit whom they term the *King of the Sea*. In like manner the Biajús perform their offering to the god of evil, launching a small bark, loaded with all the sins and misfortunes of the nation, which are imagined to fall on the unhappy crew that may be so unlucky as first to meet with it.'—*Dr. Leyden on the Language and Literature of the Indo-Chinese Nations*.

[5] 'The sweet-scented violet is one of the plants most

THE FIRE-WORSHIPPERS.

his lute, in the pathetic measure of Nava,[1] which is always used to express the lamentations of absent lovers, the Poet thus continued:—

The day is lowering—stilly black
Sleeps the grim wave, while heaven's rack,
Dispersed and wild, 'twixt earth and sky
Hangs like a shattered canopy.
There's not a cloud in that blue plain
But tells of storm to come or past;—
Here, flying loosely as the mane
Of a young war-horse in the blast;—
There, rolled in masses dark and swelling,
As proud to be the thunder's dwelling!
While some, already burst and riven,
Seem melting down the verge of heaven;
As though the infant storm had rent
   The mighty womb that gave him birth,
And, having swept the firmament,
   Was now in fierce career for earth.

On earth 'twas yet all calm around,
A pulseless silence, dread, profound,
More awful than the tempest's sound.
The diver steered for Ormus' bowers,
And moored his skiff till calmer hours;
The sea-birds, with portentous screech,
Flew fast to land;—upon the beach
The pilot oft had paused, with glance
Turned upward to that wild expanse;—
And all was boding, drear, and dark
As her own soul, when Hinda's bark
Went slowly from the Persian shore.—
No music timed her parting oar,
Nor friends upon the lessening strand
Lingered, to wave the unseen hand,
Or speak the farewell, heard no more;—
But lone, unheeded, from the bay
The vessel takes its mournful way,
Like some ill-destined bark that steers
In silence through the Gate of Tears.[2]

And where was stern Al Hassan then?
Could not that saintly scourge of men
From bloodshed and devotion spare
One minute for a farewell there?
No—close within, in changeful fits
Of cursing and of prayer, he sits
In savage loneliness to brood
Upon the coming night of blood,—
With that keen second-scent of death,

By which the vulture snuffs his food
In the still warm and living breath![3]
While o'er the wave his weeping daughter
Is wafted from these scenes of slaughter,—
As a young bird of Babylon,
Let loose to tell of victory won,
Flies home, with wing, ah! not unstained
By the red hands that held her chained.

And does the long-left home she seeks
Light up no gladness on her cheeks?
The flowers she nursed — the well-known
   groves,
Where oft in dreams her spirit roves—
Once more to see her dear gazelles
Come bounding with their silver bells;
Her birds' new plumage to behold,
   And the gay, gleaming fishes count,
She left, all filleted with gold,
   Shooting around their jasper fount;[4]
Her little garden mosque to see,
   And once again, at evening hour,
To tell her ruby rosary[5]
   In her own sweet acacia bower—
Can these delights, that wait her now,
Call up no sunshine on her brow?
No,—silent, from her train apart,—
As even now she felt at heart
The chill of her approaching doom,—
She sits, all lovely in her gloom
As a pale Angel of the Grave;
And o'er the wild tempestuous wave
Looks, with a shudder, to those towers
Where, in a few short awful hours,
Blood, blood, in streaming tides shall run,
Foul incense for to-morrow's sun!
'Where art thou, glorious stranger! thou,
So loved, so lost, where art thou now?
Foe—Gheber—infidel—whate'er
The unhallowed name thou'rt doomed to bear
Still glorious—still to this fond heart
Dear as its blood, whate'er thou art!
Yes—Alla, dreadful Alla! yes—
If there be wrong, be crime in this,
Let the black waves that round us roll,
Whelm me this instant, ere my soul,

---

esteemed, particularly for its great use in Sorbet, which they make of violet sugar.'—*Hasselquist.*
'The sherbet they most esteem, and which is drunk by the Grand Signor himself, is made of violets and sugar.'—*Tavernier.*

[1] 'Last of all she took a guitar, and sung a pathetic air in the measure called Nava, which is always used to express the lamentations of absent lovers.'—*Persian Tales.*

[2] 'The Gate of Tears, the straits or passage into the Red Sea, called Babelmandel. It received this name from the old Arabians, on account of the danger of the navigation, and the number of shipwrecks by which it was distinguished; which induced them to consider as dead, and to wear mourning for, all who had the boldness to hazard the passage through it into the Ethiopic ocean.'—*Richardson.*

[3] 'I have been told that, whensoever an animal falls down dead, one or more vultures, unseen before, instantly appear.'

[4] 'The Empress of Jehan-Guire used to divert herself with feeding tame fish in her canals, some of which were many years afterwards known by fillets of gold, which she caused to be put round them.'—*Harris.*

[5] 'Le Tespih, qui est un chapelet, composé de 99 petites boules d'agathe, de jaspe, d'ambre, de corall, ou d'autre matière précieuse. J'en ai vu un superbe au Seigneur Jerpos; il étoit de belles et grosses perles parfaites et égales, estimé trentee mille piastres.'—*Toderini.*

Forgetting faith—home—father—all—
Before its earthly idol fall,
Nor worship even Thyself above him—
For oh so wildly do I love him,
Thy Paradise itself were dim
And joyless, if not shared with him!'
Her hands were clasped—her eyes upturned,
  Dropping their tears like moonlight rain;
And, though her lip, fond raver! burned
  With words of passion, bold, profane,
Yet was their light around her brow,
  A holiness in those dark eyes,
Which showed—though wandering earthward now—
  Her spirit's home was in the skies.
Yes—for a spirit pure as hers
  Is always pure, even while it errs;
As sunshine broken in the rill,
  Though turned astray, is sunshine still!
So wholly had her mind forgot
All thoughts but one, she heeded not
The rising storm—the wave that cast
A moment's midnight, as it passed—
Nor heard the frequent shout, the tread
Of gathering tumult o'er her head—
Clashed swords, and tongues that seemed to vie
With the rude riot of the sky.—
But, hark!—that war-whoop on the deck—
  That crash, as if each engine there,
Mast, sails, and all, were gone to wreck,
  'Mid yells and stampings of despair!
Merciful Heaven! what *can* it be?
'Tis not the storm, though fearfully
The ship has shuddered as she rode
O'er mountain-waves—' Forgive me, God!
Forgive me '—shrieked the maid, and knelt,
Trembling all over—for she felt
As if her judgment-hour was near;
While crouching round, half dead with fear,
Her handmaids clung, nor breathed nor stirred—
When, hark!—a second crash—a third—
And now, as if a bolt of thunder
Had riven the labouring planks asunder,
The deck falls in—what horrors then!
Blood, waves, and tackle, swords and men
Come mixed together through the chasm,—
Some wretches in their dying spasm
Still fighting on—and some that call
' For God and Iran!' as they fall!

Whose was the hand that turned away
The perils of the infuriate fray,
And snatched her breathless from beneath
This wilderment of wreck and death?
She knew not—for a faintness came
Chill o'er her, and her sinking frame
Amid the ruins of that hour
Lay, like a pale and scorched flower,
Beneath the red volcano's shower.

But oh! the sights and sounds of dread
That shocked her ere her senses fled!
The yawning deck—the crowd that strove
Upon the tottering planks above—
The sail, whose fragments, shivering o'er
The strugglers' heads, all dashed with gore,
Fluttered like bloody flags—the clash
Of sabres, and the lightning's flash
Upon their blades, high tossed about
Like meteor brands[1]—as if throughout
  The elements one fury ran,
One general rage, that left a doubt
  Which was the fiercer, Heaven or Man!

Once too—but no—it could not be—
  'Twas fancy all—yet once she thought,
While yet her fading eyes could see,
  High on the ruined deck she caught
A glimpse of that unearthly form,
  That glory of her soul,—even then,
Amid the whirl of wreck and storm,
  Shining above his fellow-men,
As, on some black and troublous night,
The Star of Egypt,[2] whose proud light
Never hath beamed on those who rest
In the White Islands of the West,
Burns through the storm with looks of flame
That put Heaven's cloudier eyes to shame.
But no—'twas but the minute's dream—
  A fantasy—and ere the scream
Had half-way passed her pallid lips,
A death-like swoon, a chill eclipse
Of soul and sense, its darkness spread
Around her, and she sunk, as dead.

How calm, how beautiful comes on
The stilly hour when storms are gone;
When warring winds have died away,
And clouds, beneath the glancing ray,
Melt off, and leave the land and sea
Sleeping in bright tranquillity,—
Fresh as if Day again were born,
Again upon the lap of Morn!—
When the light blossoms, rudely torn
And scattered at the whirlwind's will,
Hang floating in the pure air still,
Filling it all with precious balm,
In gratitude for this sweet calm;—
And every drop the thunder-showers
Have left upon the grass and flowers
Sparkles, as 'twere that lightning gem[3]
Whose liquid flame is born of them!
When, 'stead of one unchanging breeze,
  There blow a thousand gentle airs,
And each a different perfume bears,
As if the loveliest plants and trees
Had vassal breezes of their own
To watch and wait on them alone,
And waft no other breath than theirs:

---

[1] The meteors that Pliny calls ' Faces.'
[2] The brilliant Canopus, unseen in European climates.
[3] A precious stone of the Indies, called by the ancients Ceraunium because it was supposed to be found in places where thunder had fallen. Tertullian says it has a glittering appearance, as if there had been fire in it; and the author of the Dissertation in *Harris's Voyages* supposes it to be the opal.

When the blue waters rise and fall,
In sleepy sunshine mantling all;
And even that swell the tempest leaves
Is like the full and silent heaves
Of lovers' hearts when newly blest,
Too newly to be quite at rest.
Such was the golden hour that broke
Upon the world when Hinda woke
From her long trance, and heard around
No motion but the water's sound
Rippling against the vessel's side,
As slow it mounted o'er the tide.—
But where is she?—her eyes are dark,
Are wildered still—is this the bark,
The same, that from Harmozia's bay
Bore her at morn—whose bloody way
The sea-dog tracked?— no — strange and new
Is all that meets her wondering view.
Upon a galliot's deck she lies,
 Beneath no rich pavilion's shade,—
No plumes to fan her sleeping eyes,
 Nor jasmine on her pillow laid.
But the rude litter, roughly spread
With war-cloaks, is her homely bed,
And shawl and sash, on javelins hung,
For awning o'er her head are flung.
Shuddering she looked around—there lay
A group of warriors in the sun,
Resting their limbs, as for that day
 Their ministry of death were done.
Some gazing on the drowsy sea,
Lost in unconscious reverie;
And some who seemed but ill to brook
That sluggish calm, with many a look
To the slack sail impatient cast,
As loose it flagged around the mast.

Blest Alla! who shall save her now?
 There's not in all that warrior band
One Arab sword, one turbaned brow
 From her own faithful Moslem land.
Their garb—the leathern belt that wraps
 Each yellow vest[1]—that rebel hue—
The Tartar fleece upon their caps[2]—
 Yes—yes—her fears are all too true,
And Heaven hath, in this dreadful hour,
Abandoned her to Hafed's power;
Hafed, the Gheber!—at the thought
 Her very heart's blood chills within;
He whom her soul was hourly taught
 To loathe, as some foul fiend of sin,
Some minister whom Hell had sent,
To spread its blast, where'er he went,
And fling, as o'er our earth he trod,
His shadow betwixt man and God!
And she is now his captive,—thrown
In his fierce hands, alive, alone;
His the infuriate band she sees,
All infidels—all enemies!

What was the daring hope that then
Crossed her like lightning, as again,
With boldness that despair had lent,
She darted through that armed crowd
A look so searching, so intent,
That even the sternest warrior bowed
Abashed, when he her glances caught,
As if he guessed whose form they sought.
But no—she sees him not—'tis gone,
The vision that before her shone
Through all the maze of blood and storm,
Is fled—'twas but a phantom form—
One of those passing, rainbow dreams,
Half light, half shade, which Fancy's beams
Paint on the fleeting mists that roll
In trance or slumber round the soul.

But now the bark, with livelier bound,
 Scales the blue wave—the crew's in motion,
The oars are out, and with light sound
 Break the bright mirror of the ocean,
Scattering its brilliant fragments round.
And now she sees—with horror sees,
Their course is toward that mountain-hold,—
Those towers that make her life-blood freeze,
Where Mecca's godless enemies
 Lie, like beleaguered scorpions rolled
In their last deadly, venomous fold!
Amid the illumined land and flood
Sunless that mighty mountain stood;
Save where, above its awful head,
There shone a flaming cloud, blood-red,
As 'twere the flag of destiny
Hung out to mark where death would be!

Had her bewildered mind the power
Of thought in this terrific hour,
She well might marvel where or how
Man's foot could scale that mountain's brow,
Since ne'er had Arab heard or known
Of path but through the glen alone.—
But every thought was lost in fear,
When, as their bounding bark drew near
The craggy base, she felt the waves
Hurry them toward those dismal caves,
That from the Deep in windings pass
Beneath that Mount's volcanic mass;—
And loud a voice on deck commands
To lower the mast and light the brands!—
Instantly o'er the dashing tide
Within a cavern's mouth they glide,
Gloomy as that eternal Porch
 Through which departed spirits go:—
Not even the flare of brand and torch
 Its flickering light could further throw
Than the thick flood that boiled below.
Silent they floated—as if each
Sat breathless, and too awed for speech
In that dark chasm, where even sound
Seemed dark,—so sullenly around

---

[1] 'The Ghebers are known by a dark yellow colour which the men affect in their clothes.'

[2] 'The Kolah, or cap, worn by the Persians, is made of the skin of the sheep of Tartary.'

The goblin echoes of the cave
Muttered it o'er the long black wave,
As 'twere some secret of the grave!

But soft—they pause—the current turns
  Beneath them from its onward track;—
Some mighty, unseen barrier spurns
  The vexèd tide, all foaming, back,
And scarce the oars' redoubled force
Can stem the eddy's whirling course;
When, hark!—some desperate foot has sprung
Among the rocks—the chain is flung—
The oars are up—the grapple clings,
And the tossed bark in moorings swings.
Just then, a day-beam through the shade
Broke tremulous—but, ere the maid
Can see from whence the brightness steals,
Upon her brow she shuddering feels
A viewless hand, that promptly ties
A bandage round her burning eyes;
While the rude litter where she lies,
Uplifted by the warrior throng,
O'er the steep rocks is borne along.

Blest power of sunshine!—genial Day,
What balm, what life is in thy ray!
To feel thee is such real bliss,
That had the world no joy but this,
To sit in sunshine calm and sweet,—
It were a world too exquisite
For man to leave it for the gloom,
The deep, cold shadow of the tomb.
Even Hinda, though she saw not where
  Or whither wound the perilous road,
Yet knew, by that awakening air
  Which suddenly around her glowed,
That they had risen from darkness then,
And breathed the sunny world again!
But soon this balmy freshness fled—
For now the steepy labyrinth led
Through damp and gloom—'mid crash of boughs,
And fall of loosened crags that rouse
The leopard from his hungry sleep,
  Who, starting, thinks each crag a prey,
And long is heard, from steep to steep,
  Chasing them down their thundering way!
The jackal's cry—the distant moan
Of the hyæna, fierce and lone—
And that eternal saddening sound
Of torrents in the glen beneath,
As 'twere the ever-dark Profound
That rolls beneath the Bridge of Death!
All, all is fearful—even to see,
  To gaze on those terrific things
She now but blindly hears, would be
  Relief to her imaginings;
Since never yet was shape so dread,
  But Fancy, thus in darkness thrown,
And by such sounds of horror fed,
  Could frame more dreadful of her own.

But does she dream? has Fear again
Perplexed the workings of her brain,
Or did a voice, all music, then

Come from the gloom, low whispering near—
'Tremble not, love, thy Gheber's here?
She *does* not dream,—all sense, all ear
She drinks the words, 'Thy Gheber's here.
'Twas his own voice—she could not err—
Throughout the breathing world's extent
There was but *one* such voice for her,
  So kind, so soft, so eloquent!
Oh sooner shall the rose of May
  Mistake her own sweet nightingale,
And to some meaner minstrel's lay
  Open her bosom's glowing veil,[1]
Than Love shall ever doubt a tone,
A breath of the beloved one!

Though blest, 'mid all her ills, to think
  She has that one beloved near,
Whose smile, though met on ruin's brink,
  Hath power to make even ruin dear,—
Yet soon this gleam of rapture, crost
By fears for him, is chilled and lost.
How shall the ruthless Hafed brook
That one of Gheber blood should look,
With aught but curses in his eye,
On her, a maid of Araby—
A Moslem maid—the child of him
  Whose bloody banner's dire success
Hath left their altars cold and dim,
  And their fair land a wilderness!
And, worse than all, that night of blood
  Which comes so fast—Oh! who shall stay
The sword that once hath tasted food
  Of Persian hearts, or turn its way?
What arm shall then the victim cover,
Or from her father shield her lover?

'Save him, my God!' she inly cries—
'Save him this night—and if Thine eyes
Have ever welcomed with delight
The sinner's tears, the sacrifice
Of sinners' hearts—guard him this night,
And here, before Thy throne, I swear
From my heart's inmost core to tear
Love, hope, remembrance, though they be
Linked with each quivering life-string there,
  And give it bleeding all to Thee!
Let him but live,—the burning tear,
The sighs, so sinful, yet so dear,
Which have been all too much his own,
Shall from this hour be Heaven's alone.
Youth passed in penitence, and age
In long and painful pilgrimage,
Shall leave no traces of the flame
That wastes me now—nor shall his name
E'er bless my lips, but when I pray
For his dear spirit, that away
Casting from its angelic ray
The eclipse of earth, he, too, may shine
Redeemed, all glorious and all Thine!

---

[1] A frequent image among the oriental poets. 'The nightingales warbled their enchanting notes, and rent the thin veils of the rose-bud and the rose.'—*Jami.*

Think—think what victory to win
One radiant soul like his from sin,—
One wandering star of virtue back
To its own native, heavenward track!

Let him but live, and both are Thine,
Together thine—for, blest or crost,
Living or dead, his doom is mine,
And, if *he* perish, both are lost!'

The next evening Lalla Rookh was entreated by her Ladies to continue the relation of her wonderful dream ; but the fearful interest that hung round the fate of Hinda and her lover had completely removed every trace of it from her mind ;—much to the disappointment of a fair seer or two in her train, who prided themselves on their skill in interpreting visions, and who had already remarked, as an unlucky omen, that the Princess, on the very morning after the dream, had worn a silk tie dyed with the blossoms of the sorrowful tree, Nilica.[1]

Fadladeen, whose indignation had more than once broken out during the recital of some parts of this heterodox poem, seemed at length to have made up his mind to the infliction ; and took his seat this evening with all the patience of a martyr, while the Poet resumed his profane and seditious story as follows :—

To tearless eyes and hearts at ease
The leafy shores and sun-bright seas,
That lay beneath that mountain's height,
Had been a fair enchanting sight.
'Twas one of those ambrosial eves
A day of storm so often leaves
At its calm setting—when the West
Opens her golden bowers of rest,
And a moist radiance from the skies
Shoots trembling down, as from the eyes
Of some meek penitent, whose last
Bright hours atone for dark ones past,
And whose sweet tears, o'er wrong forgiven
Shine, as they fall, with light from heaven!

'Twas stillness all—the winds that late
 Had rushed through Kerman's almond groves
And shaken from her bowers of date
 That cooling feast the traveller loves,[2]
Now, lulled to languor, scarcely curl
 The Green Sea wave, whose waters gleam
Limpid, as if her mines of pearl
 Were melted all to form the stream:
And her fair islets, small and bright,
 With their green shores reflected there,
Look like those Peri isles of light
 That hang by spell-work in the air.

But vainly did those glories burst
 On Hinda's dazzled eyes, when first
The bandage from her brow was taken,
And, pale and awed as those who waken
In their dark tombs—when, scowling near,
The Searchers of the Grave[3] appear,—
She shuddering turned to read her fate
In the fierce eyes that flashed around;
And saw those towers all desolate,
That o'er her head terrific frowned,

As if defying even the smile
Of that soft heaven to gild their pile.
In vain, with mingled hope and fear,
She looks for him whose voice so dear
Had come, like music, to her ear—
Strange, mocking dream! again 'tis fled.
And oh the shoots, the pangs of dread
That through her inmost bosom run,
 When voices from without proclaim
' Hafed, the Chief '—and, one by one,
 The warriors shout that fearful name!
He comes—the rock resounds his tread—
How shall she dare to lift her head,
Or meet those eyes whose scorching glare
Not Yemen's boldest sons can bear ?
In whose red beam, the Moslem tells,
Such rank and deadly lustre dwells
As in those hellish fires that light
The mandrake's charnel leaves at night.[4]
How shall she bear that voice's tone,
At whose loud battle-cry alone
Whole squadrons oft in panic ran,
Scattered like some vast caravan,
When, stretched at evening round the well,
They hear the thirsting tiger's yell ?
Breathless she stands, with eyes cast down,
Shrinking beneath the fiery frown
Which, fancy tells her, from that brow
Is flashing o'er her fiercely now,
And shuddering as she hears the tread
Of his retiring warrior band.—
Never was pause so full of dread;
Till Hafed with a trembling hand
Took hers, and leaning o'er her, said,
' Hinda ;'—that word was all he spoke,
And 'twas enough—the shriek that broke
From her full bosom told the rest.—

---

[1] ' Blossoms of the sorrowful Nyctanthes give a durable colour to silk.'—*Remarks on the Husbandry of Bengal*, p. 200. Nilica is one of the Indian names of this flower.—*Sir W. Jones.* The Persians call it Gul.—*Carreri.*

[2] ' In parts of Kerman, whatever dates are shaken from the trees by the wind, they do not touch, but leave them for those who have not any, or for travellers.'— *Ebn Haukal.*

[3] The two terrible angels, Monkir and Nakir, who are called 'the Searchers of the Grave' in the 'Creed of the orthodox Mohammedans,' given by Ockley, vol. II.

[4] 'The Arabians call the mandrake "the Devil's candle," on account of its shining appearance in the night.'—*Richardson.*

Panting with terror, joy, surprise,
The maid but lifts her wondering eyes,
  To hide them on her Gheber's breast!
'Tis he, 'tis he—the man of blood,
The fellest of the Fire-fiend's brood,
Hafed, the demon of the fight,
Whose voice unnerves, whose glances blight,—
Is her own lovèd Gheber, mild
And glorious as when first he smiled
In her lone tower, and left such beams
Of his pure eye to light her dreams,
That she believed her bower had given
Rest to some wanderer from heaven!

Moments there are, and this was one,
Snatched like a minute's gleam of sun
Amid the black Simoom's eclipse—
  Or like those verdant spots that bloom
Around the crater's burning lips,
  Sweetening the very edge of doom!
The past—the future—all that Fate
Can bring of dark or desperate
Around such hours, but makes them cast
Intenser radiance while they last!
Even he, this youth—though dimmed and gone
Each star of Hope that cheered him on—
His glories lost—his cause betrayed—
Iran, his dear-loved country, made
A land of carcases and slaves,
One dreary waste of chains and graves!—
Himself but lingering, dead at heart,
  To see the last, long struggling breath
Of Liberty's great soul depart,
  Then lay him down and share her death—
Even he, so sunk in wretchedness,
  With doom still darker gathering o'er him,
Yet, in this moment's pure caress,
  In the mild eyes that shone before him,
Beaming that blest assurance, worth
All other transports known on earth,
That he was loved—well, warmly loved—
Oh! in this precious hour he proved
How deep, how thorough-felt the glow
Of rapture kindling out of woe;—
How exquisite one single drop
Of bliss, thus sparkling to the top
Of misery's cup—how keenly quaffed,
Though death must follow on the draught!

She, too, while gazing on those eyes
  That sink into her soul so deep,
Forgets all fears, all miseries,
  Or feels them like the wretch in sleep,
Whom fancy cheats into a smile,
Who dreams of joy, and sobs the while!
The mighty Ruins where they stood,
  Upon the mount's high, rocky verge,
Lay open towards the ocean flood,
  Where lightly o'er the illumined surge
Many a fair bark that, all the day,
Had lurked in sheltering creek or bay,
Now bounded on, and gave their sails,
Yet dripping, to the evening gales;

Like eagles, when the storm is done,
Spreading their wet wings in the sun.
The beauteous clouds, though daylight's Star
Had sunk behind the hills of Lar,
Were still with lingering glories bright,—
As if, to grace the gorgeous West,
  The Spirit of departing Light
That eve had left his sunny vest
  Behind him, ere he winged his flight.
Never was scene so formed for love!
Beneath them waves of crystal move
In silent swell—Heaven glows above,
And their pure hearts, to transport given,
Swell like the wave, and glow like Heaven.

But ah! too soon that dream is past—
  Again, again her fear returns;—
Night, dreadful night, is gathering fast,
  More faintly the horizon burns,
And every rosy tint that lay
On the smooth sea hath died away.
Hastily to the darkening skies
A glance she casts—then wildly cries
'*At night*, he said—and, look, 'tis near—
Fly, fly—if yet thou lov'st me, fly—
Soon will his murderous band be here,
And I shall see thee bleed and die.—
Hush! heard'st thou not the tramp of men
Sounding from yonder fearful glen?—
Perhaps even now they climb the wood—
  Fly, fly—though still the West is bright,
He'll come—oh! yes—he wants thy blood—
I know him—he'll not wait for night!'

In terrors even to agony
  She clings around the wondering Chief;—
'Alas, poor wildered maid! to me
  Thou ow'st this raving trance of grief.
Lost as I am, nought ever grew
Beneath my shade but perished too—
My doom is like the Dead Sea air,
And nothing lives that enters there!
Why were our barks together driven
Beneath this morning's furious heaven?
Why, when I saw the prize that chance
  Had thrown into my desperate arms,—
When, casting but a single glance
  Upon thy pale and prostrate charms,
I vowed (though watching viewless o'er
  Thy safety through that hour's alarms)
To meet the unmanning sight no more—
Why have I broke that heart-wrung vow?
Why weakly, madly met thee now?—
Start not—that noise is but the shock
Of torrents through yon valley hurled—
Dread nothing here—upon this rock
We stand above the jarring world,
Alike beyond its hope—its dread—
In gloomy safety, like the Dead!
Or, could even earth and hell unite
In league to storm this Sacred Height,
Fear nothing thou—myself, to-night,

And each o'erlooking star that dwells
Near God will be thy sentinels;—
And, ere to-morrow's dawn shall glow,
Back to thy sire——'

    'To-morrow!—no—'
The maiden screamed—'thou'lt never see
To-morrow's sun—death, death will be
The night-cry through each reeking tower,
Unless we fly, ay, fly this hour!
Thou art betrayed—some wretch who knew
That dreadful glen's mysterious clue—
Nay, doubt not—by yon stars, 'tis true—
Hath sold thee to my vengeful sire;
This morning, with that smile so dire
He wears in joy, he told me all,
And stamped in triumph through our hall,
As though thy heart already beat
Its last life-throb beneath his feet!
Good Heaven, how little dreamed I then
 His victim was my own loved youth!—
Fly—send—let some one watch the glen—
By all my hopes of heaven 'tis truth!'

Oh! colder than the wind that freezes
 Founts that but now in sunshine played,
Is that congealing pang which seizes
 The trusting bosom, when betrayed.
He felt it—deeply felt—and stood,
As if the tale had frozen his blood,
So mazed and motionless was he;—
Like one whom sudden spells enchant,
Or some mute, marble habitant
Of the still Halls of Ishmonie.¹
But soon the painful chill was o'er,
And his great soul, herself once more,
Looked from his brow in all the rays
Of her best, happiest, grandest days;
Never, in moment most elate,
Did that high spirit loftier rise!—
While bright, serene, determinate,
 His looks are lifted to the skies,
As if the signal lights of Fate
 Were shining in those awful eyes!
'Tis come—his hour of martyrdom
In Iran's sacred cause is come;
And, though his life hath passed away,
Like lightning on a stormy day,
Yet shall his death-hour leave a track
 Of glory, permanent and bright,
To which the brave of after-times,
 The suffering brave, shall long look back
With proud regret,—and by its light
Watch through the hours of slavery's night
For vengeance on the oppressor's crimes.

This rock, his monument aloft,
 Shall speak the tale to many an age;
And hither bards and heroes oft
 Shall come in secret pilgrimage,
And bring their warrior sons, and tell
The wondering boys where Hafed fell;
And swear them on those lone remains
Of their lost country's ancient fanes,
Never—while breath of life shall live
Within them—never to forgive
The accursed race whose ruthless chain
Hath left on Iran's neck a stain
Blood, blood alone can cleanse again!

Such are the swelling thoughts that now
Enthrone themselves on Hafed's brow;
And ne'er did Saint of Issa² gaze
On the red wreath, for martyrs twined,
More proudly than the youth surveys
 That pile which through the gloom behind,
Half lighted by the altar's fire,
Glimmers—his destined funeral pyre!
Heaped by his own, his comrades' hands,
 Of every wood of odorous breath,
There, by the Fire-God's shrine it stands,
 Ready to fold in radiant death
The few still left of those who swore
To perish there, when hope was o'er—
The few, to whom that couch of flame,
Which rescues them from bonds and shame,
Is sweet and welcome as the bed
For their own infant Prophet spread,
When pitying Heaven to roses turned
The death-flames that beneath him burned!'³

With watchfulness the maid attends
His rapid glance, where'er it bends—
Why shoot his eyes such awful beams?
What plans he now? what thinks or dreams?
Alas! why stands he musing here,
When every moment teems with fear?
'Hafed, my own beloved Lord,'
She kneeling cries—'first, last adored!
If in that soul thou'st ever felt
Half what thy lips impassioned swore,
Here, on my knees, that never knelt
 To any but their God before,
I pray thee, as thou lov'st me, fly—
Now, now—ere yet their blades are nigh.
Oh haste—the bark that bore me hither
Can waft us o'er yon darkening sea,
East—west—alas, I care not whither,
So thou art safe, and I with thee!
Go where we will, this hand in thine,
Those eyes before me smiling thus,

---

¹ For an account of Ishmonie, the petrified city in Upper Egypt, where it is said there are many statues of men, women, etc., to be seen to this day see Perry's *View of the Levant*.
² Jesus.
³ The Ghebers say that when Abraham, their great Prophet, was thrown into the fire by order of Nimrod, the flame turned instantly into a 'bed of roses, where the child sweetly reposed.'—*Tavernier*. Of their other Prophet Zoroaster there is a story told in *Dion Prusæus*, Orat 36 that the love of wisdom and virtue leading him to a solitary life upon a mountain, he found it one day all in a flame, shining with celestial fire, out of which he came without any harm, and instituted certain sacrifices to God, who, he declared, then appeared to him.—*Vide Patrick on Exodus*, ii. 2.

Through good and ill, through storm and shine,
　The world's a world of love for us!
On some calm, blessed shore we'll dwell,
　Where 'tis no crime to love too well;—
Where thus to worship tenderly
　An erring child of light like thee
Will not be sin—or, if it be,
　Where we may weep our faults away,
Together kneeling, night and day,
　Thou, for *my* sake, at Alla's shrine,
And I—at *any* God's for thine!'

Wildly these passionate words she spoke—
　Then hung her head, and wept for shame;
Sobbing, as if a heart-string broke
　With every deep-heaved sob that came.
While he, young, warm—oh! wonder not
　If, for a moment, pride and fame,
His oath—his cause—that shrine of flame,
　And Iran's self are all forgot
For her whom at his feet he sees
　Kneeling in speechless agonies.
No, blame him not if Hope awhile
　Dawned in his soul, and threw her smile
O'er hours to come—o'er days and nights,
　Winged with those precious, pure delights
Which she, who bends all beauteous there,
　Was born to kindle and to share.
A tear or two, which, as he bowed
　To raise the suppliant, trembling stole,
First warned him of this dangerous cloud
　Of softness passing o'er his soul.
Starting, he brushed the drops away,
　Unworthy o'er that cheek to stray;—
Like one who, on the morn of fight,
　Shakes from his sword the dews of night,
That had but dimmed, not stained its light.
Yet, though subdued the unnerving thrill,
　Its warmth, its weakness, lingered still,
So touching in its look and tone,
　That the fond, fearing, hoping maid
Half counted on the flight she prayed,
　Half thought the hero's soul was grown
As soft, as yielding as her own,
　And smiled and blessed him, while he said,—
'Yes—if there be some happier sphere,
　Where fadeless truth like ours is dear,—
If there be any land of rest
　For those who love and ne'er forget,
Oh! comfort thee—for safe and blest
　We'll meet in that calm region yet!'

Scarce had she time to ask her heart
　If good or ill these words impart,
When the roused youth impatient flew
　To the tower-wall, where, high in view,
A ponderous sea-horn[1] hung, and blew
　A signal, deep and dread as those
The storm-fiend at his rising blows.—

Full well his Chieftains, sworn and true
　Through life and death, that signal know;
For 'twas the appointed warning blast,
　The alarm, to tell when hope was past,
And the tremendous death-die cast!
　And there, upon the mouldering tower,
Hath hung this sea-horn many an hour,
　Ready to sound o'er land and sea
That dirge-note of the brave and free.

They came—his Chieftains at the call
　Came slowly round, and with them all—
Alas, how few!—the worn remains
　Of those who late o'er Kerman's plains
Went gaily prancing to the clash
　Of Moorish zel and tymbalon,
Catching new hope from every flash
　Of their long lances in the sun,
And, as their coursers charged the wind,
　And the white ox-tails streamed behind,[2]
Looking as if the steeds they rode
　Were winged, and every Chief a God!
How fallen, how altered now! how wan
　Each scarred and faded visage shone
As round the burning shrine they came;—
　How deadly was the glare it cast,
As mute they paused before the flame
　To light their torches as they passed!
'Twas silence all—the youth had planned
　The duties of his soldier band;
And each determined brow declares
　His faithful Chieftains well know theirs.

But minutes speed—night gems the skies—
　And oh, how soon, ye blessed eyes
That look from heaven, ye may behold
　Sights that will turn your star-fires cold!
Breathless with awe, impatience, hope,
　The maiden sees the veteran group
Her litter silently prepare,
　And lay it at her trembling feet;—
And now the youth, with gentle care,
　Hath placed her in the sheltered seat,
And pressed her hand—that lingering press
　Of hands that for the last time sever;
Of hearts whose pulse of happiness,
　When that hold breaks, is dead for ever.
And yet to *her* this sad caress
　Gives hope—so fondly hope can err!
'Twas joy, she thought, joy's mute excess—
　Their happy flight's dear harbinger;
'Twas warmth—assurance—tenderness—
　'Twas anything but leaving her.

'Haste, haste!' she cried, 'the clouds grow dark,
　But still, ere night, we'll reach the bark;
And by to-morrow's dawn—oh bliss!
　With thee upon the sun-bright deep,

---

[1] 'The shell called Sliankos, common to India, Africa, and the Mediterranean, and still used in many parts as a trumpet for blowing alarms or giving signals: it sends forth a deep and hollow sound.'—*Pennant.*

[2] 'The finest ornament for the horses is made of six large flying tassels of long white hair, taken out of the tails of wild oxen, that are to be found in some places of the Indies.'—*Thevenot.*

Far off, I'll but remember this,
  As some dark vanished dream of sleep;
And thou ——' but ah!—he answers not—
  Good Heaven!—and does she go alone?
She now has reached that dismal spot
  Where, some hours since, his voice's tone
Had come to soothe her fears and ills, ·
Sweet as the angel Israfil's,[1]
  When every leaf on Eden's tree
Is trembling to his minstrelsy—
  Yet now—oh, now, he is not nigh.—
'Hafed! my Hafed!—if it be
Thy will, thy doom this night to die,
  Let me but stay to die with thee,
And I will bless thy lovèd name,
  Till the last life-breath leave this frame.
Oh! let our lips, our cheeks be laid
But near each other while they fade;
Let us but mix our parting breaths,
And I can die ten thousand deaths!
You too, who hurry me away
So cruelly, one moment stay—
  Oh! stay—one moment is not much—
He yet may come—for *him* I pray—
Hafed! dear Hafed!'—all the way
  In wild lamentings, that would touch
A heart of stone, she shrieked his name
  To the dark woods—no Hafed came :—
No—hapless pair—you've looked your last :—
  Your hearts should both have broken then :
The dream is o'er—your doom is cast—
  You'll never meet on earth again!

Alas for him, who hears her cries!
  Still half-way down the steep he stands,
Watching with fixed and feverish eyes
  The glimmer of those burning brands
That down the rocks, with mournful ray,
  Light all he loves on earth away!
Hopeless as they who, far at sea,
  By the cold moon hath just consigned
The corse of one, loved tenderly,
  To the bleak flood they leave behind;
And on the deck still lingering stay,
  And long look back, with sad delay,
To watch the moonlight on the wave,
That ripples o'er that cheerless grave.

But see—he starts—what heard he then?
  That dreadful shout!—across the glen
From the land-side it comes, and loud
  Rings through the chasm; as if the crowd
Of fearful things that haunt that dell,
  Its Ghoules and Dives and shapes of hell,
Had all in one dread howl broke out,
  So loud, so terrible that shout!
'They come—the Moslems come!'—he cries,
  His proud soul mounting to his eyes,—
'Now, Spirits of the Brave, who roam
Enfranchised through yon starry dome,

---

[1] 'The angel Israfil, who has the most melodious voice of all God's creatures.'—*Sale*.

Rejoice—for souls of kindred fire
Are on the wing to join your choir!'
He said—and, light as bridegrooms bound
  To their young loves, reclimbed the steep
And gained the Shrine—his Chiefs stood round—
  Their swords, as with instinctive leap,
Together, at that cry accurst,
Had from their sheaths, like sunbeams, burst.
And hark!—again—again it rings;
Near and more near its echoings
Peal through the chasm—oh! who that then
Had seen those listening warrior-men,
With their swords grasped, their eyes of flame
Turned on their Chief—could doubt the shame,
The indignant shame with which they thrill
To hear those shouts, and yet stand still?

He read their thoughts—they were his own—
'What! while our arms can wield these
      blades,
Shall we die tamely? die alone?
  Without one victim to our shades.
One Moslem heart, where, buried deep,
  The sabre from its toil may sleep?
No—God of Iran's burning skies!
Thou scorn'st the inglorious sacrifice.
No—though of all earth's hope bereft,
Life, swords, and vengeance still are left.
We'll make yon valley's reeking caves
  Live in the awe-struck minds of men,
Till tyrants shudder, when their slaves
  Tell of the Gheber's bloody glen.
Follow, brave hearts!—this pile remains
Our refuge still from life and chains;
But his the best, the holiest bed,
Who sinks entombed in Moslem dead!'

Down the precipitous rocks they sprung,
  While vigour more than human strung
Each arm and heart —The exulting foe
Still through the dark defiles below,
Tracked by his torches' lurid fire,
  Wound slow, as through Golconda's vale
The mighty serpent, in his ire,
  Glides on with glittering, deadly trail.
No torch the Ghebers need—so well
They know each mystery of the dell,
So oft have, in their wanderings,
Crossed the wild race that round them dwell,
  The very tigers from their delves
Look out, and let them pass, as things
  Untamed and fearless like themselves!

There was a deep ravine, that lay
Yet darkling in the Moslem's way;
Fit spot to make invaders rue
The many fallen before the few.
The torrents from that morning's sky
Had filled the narrow chasm breast-high,
And, on each side, aloft and wild,
Huge cliffs and toppling crags were piled,—
The guards with which young Freedom lines
The pathways to her mountain-shrines.

Here, at this pass, the scanty band
Of Iran's last avengers stand;
Here wait, in silence like the dead,
And listen for the Moslem's tread
So anxiously, the carrion bird
Above them flaps his wing unheard!

They come—that plunge into the water
Gives signal for the work of slaughter.
Now, Ghebers, now—if e'er your blades
 Had point or prowess, prove them now—
Woe to the file that foremost wades!
They come—a falchion greets each brow,
And, as they tumble, trunk on trunk,
Beneath the gory waters sunk,
Still o'er their drowning bodies press
New victims quick and numberless;
Till scarce an arm in Hafed's band,
So fierce their toil, hath power to stir,
But listless from each crimson hand
The sword hangs, clogged with massacre.
Never was horde of tyrants met
With bloodier welcome—never yet
To patriot vengeance hath the sword
More terrible libations poured!

All up the dreary, long ravine,
By the red, murky glimmer seen
Of half-quenched brands, that o'er the flood
Lie scattered round and burn in blood,
What ruin glares! what carnage swims!
Heads, blazing sabres, quivering limbs,
Lost swords that, dropped from many a hand,
In that thick pool of slaughter stand;—
Wretches who wading, half on fire
From the tossed brands that round them fly,
'Twixt flood and flame in shrieks expire;—
And some who, grasped by those that die,
Sink woundless with them, smothered o'er
In their dead brethren's gushing gore!

But vainly hundreds, thousands bleed,
Still hundreds, thousands more succeed;
Ceaseless as towards some flame at night
The North's dark insects wing their flight,
And quench or perish in its light;
To this terrific spot they pour—
Till, bridged with Moslem bodies o'er,
It bears aloft their slippery tread,
And o'er the dying and the dead,
Tremendous causeway! on they pass.—
Then, hapless Ghebers, then, alas,
What hope was left for you? for you,
Whose yet warm pile of sacrifice
Is smoking in their vengeful eyes;—
Whose swords how keen, how fierce they knew,
And burn with shame to find how few?

Crushed down by that vast multitude,
Some found their graves where first they stood;

While some with hardier struggle died,
And still fought on by Hafed's side,
Who, fronting to the foe, trod back
Towards the high towers his gory track;
And, as a lion, swept away
By sudden swell of Jordan's pride
From the wild covert where he lay,[1]
Long battles with the o'erwhelming tide,
So fought he back with fierce delay,
And kept both foes and fate at bay.

But whither now? their track is lost,
Their prey escaped—guide, torches gone—
By torrent-beds and labyrinths crost,
The scattered crowd rush blindly on—
'Curse on those tardy lights that wind,'
They panting cry, 'so far behind;
Oh for a bloodhound's precious scent,
To track the way the Gheber went!'
Vain wish—confusedly along
They rush, more desperate as more wrong:
Till, wildered by the far-off lights
Yet glittering up those gloomy heights,
Their footing, mazed and lost, they miss,
And down the darkling precipice
Are dashed into the deep abyss;
Or midway hang, impaled on rocks,
A banquet, yet alive, for flocks
Of ravening vultures,—while the dell
Re-echoes with each horrible yell.

Those sounds—the last, to vengeance dear,
That e'er shall ring in Hafed's ear,—
Now reached him, as aloft, alone,
Upon the steep way breathless thrown,
He lay beside his reeking blade,
Resigned, as if life's task were o'er,
Its last blood-offering amply paid,
And Iran's self could claim no more.
One only thought, one lingering beam
Now broke across his dizzy dream
Of pain and weariness—'twas she,
His heart's pure planet, shining yet
Above the waste of memory,
When all life's other lights were set.
And never to his mind before
Her image such enchantment wore.
It seemed as if each thought that stained
Each fear that chilled their loves was past,
And not one cloud of earth remained
Between him and her radiance cast;—
As if to charms, before so bright,
New grace from other worlds was given,
And his soul saw her by the light
Now breaking o'er itself from heaven!

A voice spoke near him—'twas the tone
Of a loved friend, the only one
Of all his warriors left with life
From that short night's tremendous strife.—

---

[1] 'In this thicket, upon the banks of the Jordan, wild beasts are wont to harbour, whose being washed out of the covert by the overflowings of the river gave occasion to that allusion of Jeremiah, "He shall come up like a lion from the swelling of Jordan."'—*Maundrell's Aleppo.*

'And must we then, my Chief, die here?
Foes round us, and the Shrine so near!'
These words have roused the last remains
Of life within him—'What! not yet
Beyond the reach of Moslem chains!'
The thought could make even Death forget
His icy bondage—with a bound
He springs, all bleeding, from the ground,
And grasps his comrade's arm, now grown
Even feebler, heavier than his own,
And up the painful pathway leads,
Death gaining on each step he treads.
Speed them, thou God, who heard'st their vow!
They mount—they bleed—oh save them now—
The crags are red they've clambered o'er,
The rock-weed's dripping with their gore;—
Thy blade too, Hafed, false at length,
Now breaks beneath thy tottering strength!
Haste, haste—the voices of the Foe
Come near and nearer from below—
One effort more—thank Heaven! 'tis past,
They've gained the topmost steep at last.
And now they touch the temple's walls,
Now Hafed sees the Fire divine—
When, lo!—his weak, worn comrade falls
Dead on the threshold of the shrine.
'Alas, brave soul, too quickly fled!
And must I leave thee withering here,
The sport of every ruffian's tread,
The mark for every coward's spear?
No, by yon altar's sacred beams!'
He cries, and, with a strength that seems
Not of this world, uplifts the frame
Of the fallen Chief, and towards the flame
Bears him along;—with death-damp hand
The corpse upon the pyre he lays,
Then lights the consecrated brand,
And fires the pile, whose sudden blaze
Like lightning bursts o'er Oman's Sea.—
'Now, Freedom's God! I come to Thee,'
The youth exclaims, and with a smile
Of triumph vaulting on the pile,
In that last effort, ere the fires
Have harmed one glorious limb, expires!

What shriek was that on Oman's tide?
It came from yonder drifting bark,
That just hath caught upon her side
The death-light—and again is dark.
It is the boat—ah, why delayed?—
That bears the wretched Moslem maid;
Confided to the watchful care
Of a small veteran band, with whom
Their generous Chieftain would not share
The secret of his final doom,
But hoped when Hinda, safe and free,
Was rendered to her father's eyes,
Their pardon, full and prompt, would be
The ransom of so dear a prize.—
Unconscious, thus, of Hafed's fate,
And proud to guard their beauteous freight,
Scarce had they cleared the surfy waves
That foam around those frightful caves,

When the curst war-whoops, known so well,
Came echoing from the distant dell.
Sudden each oar, upheld and still,
Hung dripping o'er the vessel's side,
And, driving at the current's will,
They rocked along the whispering tide;
While every eye, in mute dismay,
Was toward that fatal mountain turned,
Where the dim altar's quivering ray
As yet all lone and tranquil burned.

Oh! 'tis not, Hinda, in the power
Of Fancy's most terrific touch
To paint thy pangs in that dread hour—
Thy silent agony—'twas such
As those who feel could paint too well,
But none e'er felt and lived to tell!
'Twas not alone the dreary state
Of a lorn spirit, crushed by fate,
When, though no more remains to dread,
The panic chill will not depart;—
When, though the inmate Hope be dead,
Her ghost still haunts the mouldering heart;
No—pleasures, hopes, affections gone,
The wretch may bear, and yet live on,
Like things within the cold rock found
Alive, when all's congealed around.
But there's a blank repose in this,
A calm stagnation, that were bliss
To the keen, burning, harrowing pain,
Now felt through all thy breast and brain;—
That spasm of terror, mute, intense,
That breathless, agonized suspense,
From whose hot throb, whose deadly aching,
The heart hath no relief but breaking!

Calm is the wave—heaven's brilliant lights
Reflected dance beneath the prow;—
Time was when, on such lovely nights,
She who is there, so desolate now,
Could sit all cheerful, though alone,
And ask no happier joy than seeing
That star-light o'er the waters thrown—
No joy but that, to make her blest,
And the fresh, buoyant sense of Being
Which bounds in youth's yet careless breast,—
Itself a star, not borrowing light,
But in its own glad essence bright.
How different now!—but, hark, again
The yell of havoc rings—brave men!
In vain, with beating hearts, ye stand
On the bark's edge—in vain each hand
Half draws the falchion from its sheath;
All's o'er—in rust your blades may lie:—
He at whose word they've scattered death,
Even now, this night, himself must die!
Well may ye look to yon dim tower,
And ask, and wondering guess what means
The battle-cry at this dead hour—
Ah! she could tell you—she, who leans
Unheeded there, pale, sunk, aghast,
With brow against the dew-cold mast;—
Too well she knows—her more than life,

Her soul's first idol and its last,
 Lies bleeding in that murderous strife.

But see—what moves upon the height?
Some signal!—'tis a torch's light.
What bodes its solitary glare?
In gasping silence toward the Shrine
All eyes are turned—thine, Hinda, thine
Fix their last fading life-beams there.
'Twas but a moment—fierce and high
The death-pile blazed into the sky,
And far away, o'er rock and flood
 Its melancholy radiance sent;
While Hafed like a vision stood
Revealed before the burning pyre,
Tall, shadowy, like a Spirit of Fire
 Shrined in its own grand element!
"'Tis he!'—the shuddering maid exclaims,—
But, while she speaks, he's seen no more;
High burst in air the funeral flames,
 And Iran's hopes and hers are o'er.

One wild, heart-broken shriek she gave;
Then sprung, as if to reach that blaze,
Where still she fixed her dying gaze,
And, gazing, sunk into the wave,—
Deep, deep,—where never care or pain
Shall reach her innocent heart again!

Farewell—farewell to thee, Araby's daughter!
(Thus warbled a Peri beneath the dark sea,)
No pearl ever lay, under Oman's green water,
 More pure in its shell than thy Spirit in thee.

Oh! fair as the sea-flower close to thee growing,
 How light was thy heart till Love's witchery came,
Like the wind of the south[1] o'er a summer lute blowing,
 And hushed all its music, and withered its frame!

But long, upon Araby's green sunny highlands,
 Shall maids and their lovers remember the doom

Of her who lies sleeping among the Pearl Islands,
 With nought but the sea-star[2] to light up her tomb.

And still, when the merry date-season is burning,
 And calls to the palm-groves the young and the old,
The happiest there, from their pastime returning
 At sunset, will weep when thy story is told.

The young village-maid, when with flowers she dresses
 Her dark flowing hair for some festival day,
Will think of thy fate till, neglecting her tresses,
 She mournfully turns from the mirror away.

Nor shall Iran, beloved of her Hero! forget thee—
 Though tyrants watch over her tears as they start,
Close, close by the side of that Hero she'll set thee,
 Embalmed in the innermost shrine of her heart.

Farewell—be it ours to embellish thy pillow
 With everything beauteous that grows in the deep;
Each flower of the rock, and each gem of the billow
 Shall sweeten thy bed and illumine thy sleep.

Around thee shall glisten the loveliest amber
 That ever the sorrowing sea-bird has wept;[3]
With many a shell, in whose hollow-wreathed chamber
 We, Peris of Ocean, by moonlight have slept.

We'll dive where the gardens of coral lie darkling,
 And plant all the rosiest stems at thy head;
We'll seek where the sands of the Caspian[4] are sparkling,
 And gather their gold to strew over thy bed.

Farewell—farewell—until Pity's sweet fountain
 Is lost in the hearts of the fair and the brave,
They'll weep for the Chieftain who died on that mountain,
 They'll weep for the Maiden who sleeps in this wave.

The singular placidity with which Fadladeen had listened, during the latter part of this obnoxious story, surprised the Princess and Feramorz exceedingly, and even inclined towards him the hearts of these unsuspicious young persons, who little knew the source of a complacency so marvellous. The truth was, he had been organizing, for the last few days, a most notable plan of persecution against the poet, in consequence of some passages that had fallen from him on the second evening of recital,—which appeared to this worthy Chamberlain to contain language and principles for which nothing short of the summary criticism of the Chabuk[5] would be advisable. It was his intention, therefore, immediately on their arrival at

---

[1] 'This wind (the Samoor) so softens the strings of lutes, that they can never be tuned while it lasts.'—*Stephen's Persia.*

[2] 'One of the greatest curiosities found in the Persian Gulf is a fish which the English call Star-fish. It is circular, and at night very luminous, resembling the full moon surrounded by rays.'—*Mirza Abu Taleb.*

[3] Some naturalists have imagined that amber is a concretion of the tears of birds.—See *Trevoux, Chambers.*

[4] 'The bay Kieselarke, which is otherwise called the Golden Bay, the sand whereof shines as fire.'

[5] 'The application of whips or rods.'

Cashmere, to give information to the King of Bucharia of the very dangerous sentiments of his minstrel; and if, unfortunately, that monarch did not act with suitable vigour on the occasion (that is, if he did not give the Chabuk to Feramorz, and a place to Fadladeen), there would be an end, he feared, of all legitimate government in Bucharia. He could not help, however, auguring better both for himself and the cause of potentates in general; and it was the pleasure arising from these mingled anticipations that diffused such unusual satisfaction through his features, and made his eyes shine out like poppies of the desert, over the wide and lifeless wilderness of that countenance.

Having decided upon the Poet's chastisement in this manner, he thought it but humanity to spare him the minor tortures of criticism. Accordingly, when they assembled the following evening in the pavilion, and Lalla Rookh was expecting to see all the beauties of her bard melt away, one by one, in the acidity of criticism, like pearls in the cup of the Egyptian queen, he agreeably disappointed her, by merely saying, with an ironical smile, that the merits of such a poem deserved to be tried at a much higher tribunal; and then suddenly passed off into a panegyric upon all Mussulman sovereigns, more particularly his august and imperial master, Aurungzebe—the wisest and best of the descendants of Timur—who, among other great things he had done for mankind, had given to him, Fadladeen, the very profitable posts of Betel-carrier, and Taster of Sherbets to the Emperor, Chief Holder of the Girdle of Beautiful Forms,[1] and Grand Nazir, or Chamberlain of the Haram.

They were now not far from that Forbidden River[2] beyond which no pure Hindoo can pass, and were reposing for a time in the rich valley of Hussun Abdaul, which had always been a favourite resting-place of the Emperors in their annual migrations to Cashmere. Here often had the Light of the Faith, Jehan-Guire, been known to wander with his beloved and beautiful Nourmahal; and here would Lalla Rookh have been happy to remain for ever, giving up the throne of Bucharia and the world, for Feramorz and love in this sweet lonely valley. But the time was now fast approaching when she must see him no longer,—or, what was still worse, behold him with eyes whose every look belonged to another; and there was a melancholy preciousness in these last moments, which made her heart cling to them as it would to life. During the latter part of the journey, indeed, she had sunk into a deep sadness, from which nothing but the presence of the young minstrel could awake her. Like those lamps in tombs, which only light up when the air is admitted, it was only at his approach that her eyes became smiling and animated. But here, in this dear valley, every moment appeared an age of pleasure; she saw him all day, and was therefore all day happy,—resembling, she often thought, that people of Zinge,[3] who attribute the unfading cheerfulness they enjoy to one genial star that rises nightly over their heads.[4]

The whole party, indeed, seemed in their liveliest mood during the few days they passed in this delightful solitude. The young attendants of the Princess, who were here allowed a much freer range than they could safely be indulged with in a less sequestered place, ran wild among the gardens and bounded through the meadows lightly as young roes over the aromatic plains of Tibet; while Fadladeen, in addition to the spiritual comfort derived by him from a pilgrimage to the tomb of the saint from whom the valley is named, had also opportunities of indulging in a small way his taste for victims, by putting to death some hundreds of those unfortunate little lizards[5] which all pious Mussulmans make it a point to kill,—taking for granted that the manner in which the creature hangs its head is meant as a mimicry of the attitude in which the Faithful say their prayers.

---

[1] Kempfer mentions such an officer among the attendants of the King of Persia, and calls him *formæ corporis estimator*. His business was at stated periods to measure the ladies of the Haram by a sort of regulation-girdle, whose limits it was not thought graceful to exceed. If any of them outgrew this standard of shape, they were reduced by abstinence till they came within proper bounds.

[2] The Attock.

[3] 'Akbar on his way ordered a fort to be built upon the Nilab, which he called Attock, which means in the Indian language Forbidden; for, by the superstition of the Hindoos, it was held unlawful to cross that river.'—*Dow's Hindostan*.

[4] 'The inhabitants of this country (Zinge) are never affected with sadness or melancholy. On this subject the Sheikh Abu-al-Kheir-Azhari has the following distich:—
'"Who is the man without care or sorrow (tell), that I may rub my hand to him?
'"(Behold) the Zinglans, without care or sorrow, frolicksome with tipsiness and mirth."'

[5] The star Suhell, or Canopus.

[6] 'The lizard Stellio. The Arabs call it Hardun. The Turks kill it; for they imagine that, by declining the head, it mimics them when they say their prayers.'—*Hasselquist*.

About two miles from Hussun Abdaul were those Royal Gardens which had grown beautiful under the care of so many lovely eyes, and were beautiful still, though those eyes could see them no longer. This place, with its flowers and its holy silence, interrupted only by the dipping of the wings of birds in its marble basins filled with the pure water of those hills, was to Lalla Rookh all that her heart could fancy of fragrance, coolness, and almost heavenly tranquillity. As the Prophet said of Damascus, 'it was too delicious;'[1] and here, in listening to the sweet voice of Feramorz, or reading in his eyes what yet he never dared to tell her, the most exquisite moments of her whole life were passed. One evening, when they had been talking of the Sultana Nourmahal, the Light of the Haram,[2] who had so often wandered among these flowers, and fed with her own hands in those marble basins the small shining fishes of which she was so fond, the youth, in order to delay the moment of separation, proposed to recite a short story, or rather rhapsody, of which this adored Sultana was the heroine. It related, he said, to the reconcilement of a sort of lovers' quarrel which took place between her and the Emperor during a Feast of Roses at Cashmere; and would remind the Princess of that difference between Haroun-al-Raschid and his fair mistress Marida, which was so happily made up by the soft strains of the musician Moussali. As the story was chiefly to be told in song, and Feramorz had unluckily forgotten his own lute in the valley, he borrowed the vina of Lalla Rookh's little Persian slave, and thus began:—

THE LIGHT OF THE HARAM.

Who has not heard of the Vale of Cashmere,
  With its roses the brightest that earth ever
    gave,[3]
Its temples, and grottos, and fountains as clear
  As the love-lighted eyes that hang over their
    wave?
Oh! to see it at sunset,—when warm o'er the
    Lake
  Its splendour at parting a summer eve throws,
Like a bride, full of blushes, when lingering to
    take
  A last look of her mirror at night ere she
    goes!—
When the shrines through the foliage are
    gleaming half shown,
And each hallows the hour by some rites of its own.
Here the music of prayer from a minaret swells,
  Here the Magian his urn, full of perfume, is
    swinging,
And here, at the altar, a zone of sweet bells
  Round the waist of some fair Indian dancer
    is ringing.
Or to see it by moonlight,—when mellowly
    shines
The light o'er its palaces, gardens, and shrines;
When the water-falls gleam, like a quick fall of
    stars,
And the nightingale's hymn from the Isle of
    Chenars

Is broken by laughs and light echoes of feet
From the cool, shining walks where the young
    people meet,—
Or at morn, when the magic of daylight awakes
A new wonder each minute, as slowly it
    breaks,
Hills, cupolas, fountains, called forth every one
Out of darkness, as if but just born of the Sun.
When the Spirit of Fragrance is up with the
    day,
From his Haram of night-flowers stealing away;
And the wind, full of wantonness, woos like a
    lover
The young aspen-trees, till they tremble all over.
When the East is as warm as the light of first
    hopes,
  And Day, with his banner of radiance un-
    furled,
Shines in through the mountainous portal[4] that
    opes,
Sublime, from that Valley of bliss to the world.

But never yet, by night or day,
  In dew of spring or summer's ray,
  Did the sweet Valley shine so gay
As now it shines— all love and light,
  Visions by day and feasts by night!
A happier smile illumes each brow,
  With quicker spread each heart uncloses.

---

[1] 'As you enter at that Bazar without the gate at Damascus, you see the Green Mosque, so called because it hath a steeple faced with green glazed bricks, which render it very resplendent; it is covered at the top with a pavilion of the same stuff. The Turks say this mosque was made in that place because Mohammed, being come so far, would not enter the town, saying it was too delicious.'—*Thevenot*.

[2] Nourmahal signifies Light of the Haram. She was afterwards called Nourjehan, or the Light of the World.
[3] 'The Rose of Cashmere, for its brilliancy and delicacy of odour, has long been proverbial in the East.'
[4] 'The Tuckt Suliman, the name bestowed by the Mohammedans on this hill, forms one side of a grand portal to the Lake.'—*Forster*.

And all is ecstasy,—for now
 The Valley holds its Feast of Roses;[1]
The joyous Time, when pleasures pour
 Profusely round, and, in their shower,
Hearts open, like the Season's Rose,
 The floweret of a hundred leaves,[2]
Expanding while the dew-fall flows,
 And every leaf its balm receives.

'Twas when the hour of evening came
 Upon the Lake, serene and cool,
When Day had hid his sultry flame
 Behind the palms of Baramoule,
When maids began to lift their heads,
 Refreshed from their embroidered beds,
Where they had slept the sun away,
 And waked to moonlight and to play.
All were abroad—the busiest hive
On Bela's hills is less alive,
When saffron-beds are full in flower,[3]
Than looked the Valley in that hour.
A thousand restless torches played
Through every grove and island shade;
A thousand sparkling lamps were set
On every dome and minaret;
And fields and pathways, far and near,
Were lighted by a blaze so clear
That you could see, in wandering round,
The smallest rose-leaf on the ground.
Yet did the maids and matrons leave
Their veils at home, that brilliant eve;
And there were glancing eyes about,
And cheeks that would not dare shine out
In open day, but thought they might
Look lovely then, because 'twas night.
And all were free, and wandering,
 And all exclaimed to all they met
That never did the summer bring
 So gay a Feast of Roses yet;—
The moon had never shed a light
So clear as that which blessed them there;
The roses ne'er shone half so bright,
 Nor they themselves looked half so fair.

And what a wilderness of flowers!
It seemed as though from all the bowers
And fairest fields of all the year
The mingled spoil were scattered here.

The Lake, too, like a garden breathes,
 With the rich buds that o'er it lie,—
As if a shower of fairy wreaths
 Had fallen upon it from the sky!
And then the sounds of joy,—the beat
Of tabors and of dancing feet;—
The minaret-crier's chaunt of glee
Sung from his lighted gallery,[4]
And answered by a ziraleet
From neighbouring Haram, wild and sweet;—
The merry laughter, echoing
From gardens, where the silken swing[5]
Wafts some delighted girl above
The top leaves of the orange-grove;
Or from those infant groups at play
Among the tents that line the way,
Flinging, unawed by slave or mother,
Handfuls of roses at each other.—

Then, the sounds from the Lake,—the low whispering in boats,
As they shoot through the moonlight;—the dipping of oars,
And the wild, airy warbling that everywhere floats,
Through the groves, round the islands, as if all the shores,
Like those of Kathay, uttered music, and gave
An answer in song to the kiss of each wave.[6]
But the gentlest of all are those sounds, full of feeling,
That soft from the lute of some lover are stealing,—
Some lover, who knows all the heart-touching power
Of a lute and a sigh in this magical hour.
Oh! best of delights as it everywhere is
To be near the loved *One*,—what a rapture is his
Who in moonlight and music thus sweetly may glide
O'er the Lake of Cashmere, with that *One* by his side!
If woman can make the worst wilderness dear,
Think, think what a Heaven she must make of Cashmere!

So felt the magnificent Son of Acbar,[7]
When from power and pomp and the trophies of war

---

[1] 'The Feast of Roses continues the whole time of their remaining in bloom.'—See *Pietro de la Valle*.
[2] 'Gul sad berk, the Rose of a hundred leaves. I believe a particular species.'—*Ouseley*.
[3] Mentioned in the *Toozek Jehangeery*, or 'Memoirs of Jehan-Guire,' where there is an account of the beds of saffron flowers about Cashmere.
[4] 'It is the custom among the women to employ the Maazeen to chaunt from the gallery of the nearest minaret, which on that occasion is illuminated, and the women assembled at the house respond at intervals with a ziraleet or joyous chorus.'—*Russel*.
[5] 'The swing is a favourite pastime in the East, as promoting a circulation of air, extremely refreshing in those sultry climates.'—*Richardson*. 'The swings are adorned with festoons. This pastime is accompanied with music of voices and of instruments, hired by the masters of the swings.'—*Thevenot*.
[6] 'An old commentator of the Chou-King says, the ancients, having remarked that a current of water made some of the stones near its banks send forth a sound, they detached some of them, and being charmed with the delightful sound they emitted, constructed King or musical instruments of them.'—*Grosier*.
This miraculous quality has been attributed also to the shore of Attica. 'Hujus littus, ait Capella, concentum musicum illisis terræ undis reddere, quod propter tantam eruditionis vim puto dictum.'—*Ludov. Vives in Augustin. de Civitat. Dei*, lib. xviii. c. 8.
[7] Jehan-Guire was the son of the Great Acbar.

He flew to that Valley, forgetting them all
With the Light of the Haram, his young Nour-
    mahal.
When free and uncrowned as the Conqueror
    roved
By the banks of that lake, with his only beloved,
He saw, in the wreaths she would playfully
    snatch
From the hedges, a glory his crown could not
    match,
And preferred in his heart the least ringlet that
    curled
Down her exquisite neck to the throne of the
    world.

There's a beauty, for ever unchangingly bright,
Like the long, sunny lapse of a summer-day's
    light,
Shining on, shining on, by no shadow made
    tender,
Till Love falls asleep in its sameness of splendour.
This *was* not the beauty—oh nothing like this,
That to young Nourmahal gave such magic of
    bliss!
But that loveliness, ever in motion, which plays
Like the light upon autumn's soft shadowy days,
Now here and now there, giving warmth as it
    flies
From the lip to the cheek, from the cheek to the
    eyes;
Now melting in mist and now breaking in gleams,
Like the glimpses a saint hath of Heaven in his
    dreams.
When pensive, it seemed as if that very grace,
That charm of all others, was born with her
    face!
And when angry,—for even in the tranquillest
    climes
Light breezes will ruffle the blossoms sometimes—
The short, passing anger but seemed to awaken
New beauty, like flowers that are sweetest when
    shaken.
If tenderness touched her, the dark of her eye
At once took a darker, a heavenlier dye,
From the depth of whose shadow, like holy re-
    vealings
From innermost shrines, came the light of her
    feelings.
Then her mirth—oh! 'twas sportive as ever took
    wing
From the heart with a burst, like the wild-bird
    in spring;
Illumed by a wit that would fascinate sages,
Yet playful as Peris just loosed from their cages.[1]
While her laugh, full of life, without any control
But the sweet one of gracefulness, rung from her
    soul;

And where it most sparkled no glance could dis-
    cover,
In lip, cheek, or eyes, for she brightened all
    over —
Like any fair lake that the breeze is upon.
When it breaks into dimples, and laughs in the
    sun.
Such, such were the peerless enchantments that
    gave
Nourmahal the proud Lord of the East for her
    slave:
And though bright was his Haram,—a living
    parterre
Of the flowers[2] of this planet,—though treasures
    were there,
For which Soliman's self might have given all
    the store
That the navy from Ophir e'er winged to his
    shore,
Yet dim before *her* were the smiles of them all,
And the Light of his Haram was young Nour-
    mahal!

But where is she now, this night of joy,
When bliss is every heart's employ?—
When all around her is so bright,
So like the visions of a trance,
That one might think, who came by chance
Into the vale this happy night,
He saw that City of Delight[3]
In Fairy-land, whose streets and towers
Are made of gems and light and flowers!
Where is the loved Sultana? where?
When mirth brings out the young and fair,
Does she, the fairest, hide her brow,
In melancholy stillness now?

Alas!—how light a cause may move
Dissension between hearts that love!
Hearts that the world in vain had tried,
And sorrow but more closely tied;
That stood the storm when waves were rough,
Yet in a sunny hour fall off,
Like ships that have gone down at sea,
When heaven was all tranquillity!
A something, light as air—a look,
    A word unkind or wrongly taken—
Oh! love, that tempests never shook,
    A breath, a touch like this, hath shaken.
And ruder words will soon rush in
To spread the breach that words begin;
And eyes forgot the gentle ray
They wore in courtship's smiling day;
And voices lose the tone that shed
A tenderness round all they said;
Till fast declining, one by one,
The sweetnesses of love are gone,

---

[1] In the wars of the Dives with the Peris, whenever the former took the latter prisoners, 'they shut them up in iron cages, and hung them on the highest trees. Here they were visited by their companions, who brought them the choicest odours.'—*Richardson.*

[2] In the Malay language, the same word signifies women and flowers.

[3] The capital of Shadukiam.

THE LIGHT OF THE HARAM.

And hearts, so lately mingled, seem
Like broken clouds,—or like the stream
That smiling left the mountain's brow
  As though its waters ne'er could sever,
Yet, ere it reach the plain below,
  Breaks into floods, that part for ever.

Oh you that have the charge of Love,
  Keep him in rosy bondage bound,
As in the Fields of Bliss above
  He sits, with flowerets fettered round;[1]
Loose not a tie that round him clings,
Nor ever let him use his wings;
For even an hour, a minute's flight,
Will rob the plumes of half their light:
Like that celestial bird,—whose nest
  Is found beneath far Eastern skies,—
Whose wings, though radiant when at rest,
  Lose all their glory when he flies![2]
Some difference, of this dangerous kind,—
By which, though light, the links that bind
The fondest hearts may soon be riven;
Some shadow in Love's summer heaven,
Which, though a fleecy speck at first,
May yet in awful thunder burst;—
Such cloud it is, that now hangs over
The heart of the Imperial Lover,
And far hath banished from his sight
His Nourmahal, his Haram's Light!
Hence is it, on this happy night,
When Pleasure through the fields and groves
Has let loose all her world of loves,
And every heart has found its own,
He wanders, joyless and alone,
And weary as that bird of Thrace,
Whose pinion knows no resting-place.[3]

In vain the loveliest cheeks and eyes
This Eden of the Earth supplies
Come crowding round—the cheeks are pale,
The eyes are dim:—though rich the spot
With every flower this earth has got.
  What is it to the nightingale.
If there his darling rose is not?[4]
In vain the Valley's smiling throng
Worship him, as he moves along;
He heeds them not—one smile of hers
Is worth a world of worshippers.
They but the Star's adorers are,
She is the Heaven that lights the Star!

Hence is it, too, that Nourmahal,
  Amid the luxuries of this hour,
Far from the joyous festival,
  Sits in her own sequestered bower,
With no one near, to soothe or aid,
But that inspired and wondrous maid,
Namouna, the Enchantress;—one,
O'er whom his race the golden sun
For unremembered years has run,
Yet never saw her blooming brow
Younger or fairer than 'tis now.
Nay, rather,—as the west wind's sigh
Freshens the flower it passes by,—
Time's wing but seemed, in stealing o'er,
To leave her lovelier than before.
Yet on her smiles a sadness hung,
And when, as oft, she spoke or sung
Of other worlds, there came a light
From her dark eyes so strangely bright,
That all believed nor man nor earth
Were conscious of Namouna's birth!
All spells and talismans she knew,
  From the great Mantra,[5] which around
The Air's sublimer Spirits drew,
  To the gold gems[6] of Afric, bound
Upon the wandering Arab's arm,
To keep him from the Siltim's[7] harm.
And she had pledged her powerful art,—
Pledged it with all the zeal and heart
Of one who knew, though high her sphere,
What 'twas to lose a love so dear,—
To find some spell that should recall
Her Selim's[8] smile to Nourmahal!

'Twas midnight—through the lattice, wreathed
With woodbine, many a perfume breathed
From plants that wake when others sleep,
From timid jasmine buds, that keep
Their odour to themselves all day,
But, when the sunlight dies away,
Let the delicious secret out
To every breeze that roams about;—
When thus Namouna:—''Tis the hour
That scatters spells on herb and flower,
And garlands might be gathered now,
That, twined around the sleeper's brow,
Would make him dream of such delights,
Such miracles and dazzling sights,
As Genii of the Sun behold,
At evening, from their tents of gold

---

[1] See the representation of the Eastern Cupid, pinioned closely round with wreaths of flowers, in *Picart's Cérémonies Religieuses*.

[2] 'Among the birds of Tonquin is a species of goldfinch, which sings so melodiously that it is called the Celestial Bird. Its wings, when it is perched, appear variegated with beautiful colours, but when it flies they lose all their splendour.'—*Grosier*.

[3] 'As these birds on the Bosphorus are never known to rest, they are called by the French "les âmes damnées."'—*Dalloway*.

[4] 'You may place a hundred handfuls of fragrant herbs and flowers before the nightingale, yet he wishes not, in his constant heart, for more than the sweet breath of his beloved rose.'—*Jami*.

[5] 'He is said to have found the great *Mantra*, spell or talisman, through which he ruled over the elements and spirits of all denominations.'—*Wilford*.

[6] 'The gold jewels of Jinnie, which are called by the Arabs El Herrez, from the supposed charm they contain.'—*Jackson*.

[7] 'A demon, supposed to haunt woods, etc., in a human shape.'—*Richardson*.

[8] The name of Jehan-Guire before his accession to the throne.

Upon the horizon—where they play
Till twilight comes, and, ray by ray,
Their sunny mansions melt away.
Now, too, a chaplet might be wreathed
Of buds o'er which the moon has breathed,
Which, worn by her whose love has strayed,
  Might bring some Peri from the skies,
Some sprite whose very soul is made
  Of flowerets' breaths and lovers' sighs,
And who might tell ——'
          'For me, for me,'
Cried Nourmahal impatiently,—
'Oh! twine that wreath for me to-night.'
Then, rapidly, with foot as light
As the young musk-roe's, out she flew,
To cull each shining leaf that grew
Beneath the moonlight's hallowing beams,
For this enchanted Wreath of Dreams.
Anemones and Seas of Gold,[1]
  And new-blown lilies of the river,
And those sweet flowerets that unfold
  Their buds on Camadeva's quiver;[2]—
The tuberose, with her silvery light,
  That in the Gardens of Malay
Is called the Mistress of the Night,[3]
  So like a bride, scented and bright,
She comes out when the sun's away;—
Amarantha, such as crown the maids
That wander through Zamara's shades;[4]
And the white moon-flower, as it shows,
On Serendib's high crags, to those
Who near the isle at evening sail,
Scenting her clove-trees in the gale;
In short, all flowerets and all plants,
  From the divine Amrita tree,[5]
That blesses heaven's inhabitants
  With fruits of immortality,
Down to the basil tuft,[6] that waves
Its fragrant blossom over graves,
  And to the humble rosemary,
Whose sweets so thanklessly are shed
To scent the desert[7] and the dead:—
All in that garden bloom, and all
Are gathered by young Nourmahal,
Who heaps her basket with the flowers
  And leaves, till it can hold no more;

Then to Namouna flies, and showers
  Upon her lap the shining store.

With what delight the Enchantress views
So many buds, bathed with the dews
And beams of that blessed hour!—her glance
  Spoke something, past all mortal pleasures,
As, in a kind of holy trance,
  She hung above those fragrant treasures,
Bending to drink their balmy airs,
As if she mixed her soul with theirs.
And 'twas, indeed, the perfume shed
From flowers and scented flame that fed
Her charmed life—for none had e'er
Beheld her taste of mortal fare,
Nor ever in aught earthly dip,
But the morn's dew, her roseate lip.
Filled with the cool, inspiring smell,
The Enchantress now begins her spell,
Thus singing as she winds and weaves
In mystic form the glittering leaves:—

'I know where the winged visions dwell
  That around the night-bed play,
I know each herb and floweret's bell,
  Where they hide their wings by day.
    Then hasten we, maid,
    To twine our braid,—
To-morrow the dreams and flowers will fade.

'The image of love, that nightly flies
  To visit the bashful maid,
Steals from the jasmine flower, that sighs
  Its soul, like her, in the shade.
The dream of a future, happier hour,
  That alights on misery's brow,
Springs out of the silvery almond flower,
  That blooms on a leafless bough.[8]
    Then hasten we, maid,
    To twine our braid,—
To-morrow the dreams and flowers will fade.

'The visions, that oft to worldly eyes
  The glitter of mines unfold,
Inhabit the mountain-herb,[9] that dyes
  The tooth of the fawn like gold.[10]

---

[1] 'Hemasagara, or the Sea of Gold, with flowers of the brightest gold colour.'—*Sir W. Jones.*

[2] 'This tree (the Nagacesara) is one of the most delightful on earth, and the delicious odour of its blossoms justly gives them a place in the quiver of Camadeva, or the God of Love.'—*Sir W. Jones.*

[3] 'The Malayans style the tube-rose (*Polianthes tuberosa*) "Sandal Malam," or the Mistress of the Night.'

[4] 'The people of the Batta country in Sumatra (of which Zamara is one of the ancient names), 'when not engaged in war, lead an idle, inactive life, passing the day in playing on a kind of flute, crowned with garlands of flowers, among which the globe-amaranthus, a native of the country, mostly prevails.'—*Marsden.*

[5] 'The largest and richest sort (of the Jambu, or roseapple) is called Amrita, or immortal, and the mythologists of Tibet apply the same word to a celestial tree, bearing ambrosial fruit.'—*Sir W. Jones.*

[6] Sweet bazil, called Rayhan in Persia, and generally found in churchyards.

'The women in Egypt go, at least two days in the week, to play and weep at the sepulchres of the dead; and the custom then is to throw upon the tombs a sort of herb which the Arabs call *rihan*, and which is our sweet basil.'—*Maillet, Letter 10.*

[7] 'In the Great Desert are found many stalks of lavender and rosemary.'

[8] 'The almond-tree, with white flowers, blossoms on the bare branches.'

[9] An herb on Mount Libanus, which is said to communicate a yellow golden hue to the teeth of the goats and other animals that graze upon it.

[10] Niebuhr thinks this may be the herb which the Eastern alchymists look to as a means of making gold. 'Most of those alchymical enthusiasts think themselves sure of success if they could but find out the herb which

The phantom shapes—oh touch not them—
That appal the murderer's sight,
Lurk in the fleshly mandrake's stem,
That shrieks, when plucked at night!
　　Then hasten we, maid,
　　To twine our braid,—
To-morrow the dreams and flowers will fade.

'The dream of the injured, patient mind,
That smiles with the wrongs of men,
Is found in the bruised and wounded rind
Of the cinnamon, sweetest then.
　　Then hasten we, maid,
　　To twine our braid,—
To-morrow the dreams and flowers will fade.'

No sooner was the flowery crown
Placed on her head, than sleep came down,
Gently as nights of summer fall,
Upon the lids of Nourmahal ;—
And, suddenly, a tuneful breeze,
As full of small, rich harmonies
As ever wind that o'er the tents
Of Azab[1] blew was full of scents,
Steals on her ear, and floats and swells,
Like the first air of morning creeping
Into those wreathy Red Sea shells
Where Love himself, of old, lay sleeping ;[2]
And now a Spirit formed, 'twould seem,
Of music and of light,—so fair,
So brilliantly his features beam,
And such a sound is in the air
Of sweetness when he waves his wings,—
Hovers around her, and thus sings :

'From Chindara's[3] warbling fount I come,
　　Called by that moonlight garland's spell ;
From Chindara's fount, my fairy home,
　　Where in music, morn and night, I dwell.
Where lutes in the air are heard about,
　　And voices are singing the whole day long,
And every sigh the heart breathes out
　　Is turned, as it leaves the lips, to song !
　　　Hither I come
　　　From my fairy home ;

And if there's a magic in Music's strain,
　　I swear by the breath
　　Of that moonlight wreath,
Thy Lover shall sigh at thy feet again.

'For mine is the lay that lightly floats,
And mine are the murmuring, dying notes,
That fall as soft as snow on the sea,
And melt in the heart as instantly :—
And the passionate strain that, deeply going,
　　Refines the bosom it trembles through,
As tho musk-wind, over the water blowing,
　　Ruffles the wave, but sweetens it too.

'Mine is the charm whose mystic sway
The Spirits of past Delight obey ;—
Let but the tuneful talisman sound,
And they come, like Genii, hovering round.
And mine is the gentle song that bears
　　From soul to soul the wishes of love,
As a bird that wafts through genial airs
　　The cinnamon-seed from grove to grove.[4]

'"Tis I that mingle in one sweet measure
The past, the present, and future of pleasure ;[5]
When Memory links the tone that is gone
With the blissful tone that's still in the ear ;
And Hope from a heavenly note flies on
To a note more heavenly still that is near.

'The warrior's heart, when touched by me,
Can as downy soft and as yielding be
As his own white plume that high amid death
Through the field has shone—yet moves with a
　　breath !
And oh how the eyes of Beauty glisten,
　　When Music has reached her inward soul,
Like the silent stars, that wink and listen
　　While Heaven's eternal melodies roll !
　　　So, hither I come
　　　From my fairy home,
And if there's a magic in Music's strain,
　　I swear by the breath
　　Of that moonlight wreath,
Thy lover shall sigh at thy feet again.'

---

gilds the teeth and gives a yellow colour to the flesh of the sheep that eat it.' Father Jerome Dandini, however, asserts that the teeth of the goats at Mount Libanus are of a *silver* colour ; and adds, 'This confirms me that which I observed in Candia ; to wit, that the animals that live on Mount Ida eat a certain herb which renders their teeth of a golden colour ; which, according to my judgment, cannot otherwise proceed than from the mines which are under ground.'—*Dandini, Voyage to Mount Libanus.*

[1] The myrrh country.

[2] 'This idea (of deities living in shells) was not unknown to the Greeks, who represent the young Nerites, one of the Cupids, as living in shells on the shores of the Red Sea.'—*Wilford.*

[3] 'A fabulous fountain, where instruments are said to be constantly playing.'—*Richardson.*

[4] 'The Pompadour pigeon, by carrying the fruit of the cinnamon to different places, is a great disseminator of this valuable tree.'

[5] 'Whenever our pleasure arises from a succession of sounds, it is a perception of complicated nature, made up of a *sensation* of the present sound or note, and an *idea* or remembrance of the foregoing, while their mixture and concurrence produce such a mysterious delight as neither could have produced alone. And it is often heightened by an anticipation of the succeeding notes. Thus sense, memory, and imagination, are conjunctively employed.'—*Gerard on Taste.* Madame de Staël accounts upon the same principle for the gratification we derive from *rhyme :*—' Elle est l'image de l'espérance et du souvenir. Un son nous fait désirer celui qui doit lui répondre, et quand le second retentit, il nous rappelle celui que vient de nous échapper.'

'Tis dawn—at least that earlier dawn,
Whose glimpses are again withdrawn,[1]
As if the morn had waked, and then
Shut close her lids of light again.
And Nourmahal is up, and trying
The wonders of her lute, whose strings—
Oh bliss!—now murmur like the sighing
From that ambrosial Spirit's wings.
And then, her voice—'tis more than human—
Never, till now. had it been given
To lips of any mortal woman
To utter notes so fresh from heaven;
Sweet as the breath of angel sighs,
When angel sighs are most divine.—
'Oh! let it last till night,' she cries,
'And he is more than ever mine.'
And hourly she renews the lay,
So fearful lest its heavenly sweetness
Should, ere the evening, fade away,—
For things so heavenly have such fleetness!
But, far from fading, it but grows
Richer, diviner as it flows;
Till rapt she dwells on every string,
And pours again each sound along,
Like Echo, lost and languishing,
In love with her own wondrous song.

That evening, (trusting that his soul
Might be from haunting love released
By mirth, by music, and the bowl,)
The Imperial Selim held a feast
In his magnificent Shalimar:[2]—
In whose Saloons, when the first star
Of evening o'er the waters trembled,
The Valley's loveliest all assembled;
All the bright creatures that, like dreams,
Glide through its foliage, and drink beams
Of beauty from its founts and streams;[3]
And all those wandering minstrel-maids
Who leave—how can they leave!—the shades

Of that dear Valley, and are found
Singing in gardens of the South
Those songs that ne'er so sweetly sound
As from a young Cashmerian's mouth.

There, too, the Haram's inmates smile;—
Maids from the West, with sun-bright hair,
And from the Garden of the Nile,
Delicate as the roses there;[4]—
Daughters of Love from Cyprus' rocks,
With Paphian diamonds in their locks;[5]—
Light Peri forms, such as they are
On the gold meads of Candahar;[6]
And they before whose sleepy eyes,
In their own bright Kathaian bowers,
Sparkle such rainbow butterflies[7]
That they might fancy the rich flowers
That round them in the sun lay sighing
Had been by magic all set flying.

Everything young, everything fair,
From East and West is blushing there,
Except— except—oh Nourmahal!
Thou loveliest, dearest of them all,
The one whose smile shone out alone,
Amidst a world the only one;
Whose light, among so many lights,
Was like that star, on starry nights,
The seaman singles from the sky,
To steer his bark for ever by!
Thou wert not there—so Selim thought,
And everything seemed drear without thee;
But ah! thou wert, thou wert,—and brought
Thy charm of song all fresh about thee.
Mingling unnoticed with a band
Of lutanists from many a land,
And veiled by such a mask as shades
The features of young Arab maids,[8]—
A mask that leaves but one eye free,
To do its best in witchery,—

---

[1] 'The Persians have two mornings, the Soobhi Kazim and the Soobhi Sadig, the false and the real daybreak. They account for this phenomenon in a most whimsical manner. They say that as the sun rises from behind the Kohi Qaf (Mount Caucasus), it passes a hole perforated through that mountain, and that darting its rays through it, it is the cause of the Soobhi Kazim, or this temporary appearance of daybreak. As it ascends, the earth is again veiled in darkness, until the sun rises above the mountain, and brings with it the Soobhi Sadig, or real morning.'—*Scott Waring.* He thinks Milton may allude to this, when he says,—

'Ere the blabbing Eastern scout,
The nice morn on the Indian steep,
From her cabined loophole peep.'

[2] 'In the centre of the plain, as it approaches the Lake, one of the Delhi Emperors, I believe Shah Jehan, constructed a spacious garden called the Shalimar, which is abundantly stored with fruit-trees and flowering shrubs. Some of the rivulets which intersect the plain are led into a canal at the back of the garden, and flowing through its centre, or occasionally thrown into a variety of water-works, compose the chief beauty of the Shalimar. To decorate this spot the Mogul Princes of India have displayed an equal magnificence and taste; especially Jehan Gheer, who, with the enchanting Noor Mahl, made Kashmire his usual residence during the summer months.'—*Forster.*

[3] 'The waters of Cachemir are the more renowned from its being supposed that the Cachemirians are indebted for their beauty to them.'—*Ali Yesdi.*

[4] 'The roses of the Jinan Nile, or Garden of the Nile (attached to the Emperor of Morocco's palace), are unequalled, and mattresses are made of their leaves for the men of rank to recline upon.'—*Jackson.*

[5] 'On the side of a mountain near Paphos there is a cavern which produces the most beautiful rock-crystal. On account of its brilliancy it has been called the Paphian diamond.'—*Mariti.*

[6] 'There is a part of Candahar called Peria, or Fairy Land.'—*Thevenot.* In some of those countries to the north of India, vegetable gold is supposed to be produced.

[7] 'Butterflies, which are called, in the Chinese language, "Flying Leaves."'

[8] 'The Arabian women wear black masks with little clasps, prettily ordered.'—*Carreri.* Niebuhr mentions their showing but one eye in conversation.

THE LIGHT OF THE HARAM.

She roved, with beating heart, around,
    And waited, trembling, for the minute
When she might try if still the sound
    Of her loved lute had magic in it.

The board was spread with fruits and wine;
With grapes of gold, like those that shine
On Casbin's hills;—pomegranates full
    Of melting sweetness, and the pears,
And sunniest apples that Caubul
    In all its thousand gardens bears;—
Plantains, the golden and the green,
Malaya's nectared mangusteen;[1]
Prunes of Bokhara, and sweet nuts
    From the far groves of Samarcand,
And Basra dates, and apricots,
    Seed of the Sun,[2] from Iran's land;—
With rich conserve of Visna cherries,[3]
Of orange flowers, and of those berries
That, wild and fresh, the young gazelles
Feed on in Erac's rocky dells.
All these in richest vases smile,
    In baskets of pure santal-wood.
And urns of porcelain from that isle[4]
    Sunk underneath the Indian flood,
Whence oft the lucky diver brings
Vases to grace the halls of kings.
Wines, too, of every clime and hue,
Around their liquid lustre threw;
Amber Rosolli,—the bright dew
From vineyards of the Green-Sea gushing;[5]
And Shiraz wine, that richly ran
    As if that jewel, large and rare,
The ruby for which Kublai-Khan
Offered a city's wealth,[6] was blushing,
    Melted within the goblets there!

And amply Selim quaffs of each,
And seems resolved the flood shall reach
His inward heart,—shedding around
A genial deluge, as they run,
That soon shall leave no spot undrowned,
For Love to rest his wings upon.
He little knew how well the boy
    Can float upon a goblet's streams,
Lighting them with his smile of joy;—
    As bards have seen him in their dreams

Down the blue Ganges laughing glide
    Upon a rosy lotus wreath,[7]
Catching new lustre from the tide
    That with his image shone beneath.

But what are cups, without the aid
    Of song to speed them as they flow?
And see—a lovely Georgian maid,
    With all the bloom, the freshened glow
Of her own country maidens' looks,
    When warm they rise from Teflis' brooks;[8]
And with an eye whose restless ray,
    Full, floating, dark—oh he who knows
His heart is weak of Heaven should pray
    To guard him from such eyes as those!—
With a voluptuous wildness flings
Her snowy hand across the strings
Of a syrinda,[9] and thus sings:—

' Come hither, come hither—by night and by day,
    We linger in pleasures that never are gone;
Like the waves of the summer, as one dies away,
    Another as sweet and as shining comes on.
And the love that is o'er, in expiring, gives birth
    To a new one as warm, as unequalled in bliss;
And, oh! if there be an Elysium on earth,
            It is this, it is this.[10]

' Here maidens are sighing, and fragrant their sigh
    As the flower of the Amra just oped by a bee;
And precious their tears as that rain from the sky[11]
    Which turns into pearls as it falls in the sea.
Oh! think what the kiss and the smile must be worth
    When the sigh and the tear are so perfect in bliss,
And own if there be an Elysium on earth,
            It is this, it is this.

' Here sparkles the nectar, that, hallowed by love,
    Could draw down those angels of old from their sphere,
Who for wine of this earth[12] left the fountains above,
    And forgot heaven's stars for the eyes we have here.

---

[1] 'The mangosteen, the most delicate fruit in the world; the pride of the Malay Islands.'

[2] 'A delicious kind of apricot, called by the Persians "Tokm-ek-shems," signifying sun's seed.'

[3] 'Sweetmeats in a crystal cup, consisting of rose-leaves in conserve, with lemon or Visna cherry, orange flowers,' etc.

[4] 'Mauri-ga-Sima, an island near Formosa, supposed to have been sunk in the sea for the crimes of its inhabitants. The vessels which the fishermen and divers bring up from it are sold at an immense price in China and Japan.'

[5] The white wine of Kishma.

[6] 'The King of Zeilan is said to have the very finest ruby that was ever seen. Kublai-Khan sent and offered the value of a city for it, but the king answered he would not give it for the treasure of the world.'—*Marco Polo.*

[7] The Indians feign that Cupid was first seen floating down the Ganges on the Nymphæa Nelumbo.—See *Pennant.*

[8] Teflis is celebrated for its natural warm baths.—See *Ebn Haukal.*

[9] 'The Indian Syrinda, or guitar.'—*Symes.*

[10] 'Around the exterior of the Dewan Khafs (a building of Shah Allum's), in the cornice, are the following lines in letters of gold upon a ground of white marble—"If there be a paradise upon earth, it is this, it is this."'—*Franklin.*

[11] 'The Nisan or drops of spring rain, which they believe to produce pearls if they fall into shells.'—*Richardson.*

[12] For an account of the share which wine had in the fall of the angels, see *Mariti.*

And, blessed with the odour our goblet gives forth,
What Spirit the sweets of his Eden would miss?
For, oh! if there be an Elysium on earth,
    It is this, it is this.'

The Georgian's song was scarcely mute,
  When the same measure, sound for sound,
Was caught up by another lute,
  And so divinely breathed around
That all stood hushed and wondering,
  And turned and looked into the air,
As if they thought to see the wing
  Of Israfil,[1] the Angel, there;—
So powerfully on every soul
  That now, enchanted measure stole.
While now a voice, sweet as the note
  Of the charmed lute, was heard to float
Along its chords, and so entwine
  Its sounds with theirs that none knew whether
The voice or lute was most divine,
  So wondrously they went together:—

There's a bliss beyond all that the minstrel has told,
When two, that are linked in one heavenly tie,
With heart never changing, and brow never cold,
  Love on through all ills, and love on till they die!
One hour of a passion so sacred is worth
  Whole ages of heartless and wandering bliss;
And, oh! if there be an Elysium on earth,
    It is this, it is this.'

'Twas not the air, 'twas not the words,
  But that deep magic in the chords
And in the lips, that gave such power
  As Music knew not till that hour.
At once a hundred voices said,
  'It is the masked Arabian maid!'
While Selim, who had felt the strain
  Deepest of any, and had lain
Some minutes wrapt, as in a trance,
  After the fairy sounds were o'er,
Too inly touched for utterance,
  Now motioned with his hand for more:—

'Fly to the desert, fly with me,
  Our Arab tents are rude for thee;
But, oh! the choice what heart can doubt,
  Of tents with love, or thrones without?

'Our rocks are rough, but smiling there
  The acacia waves her yellow hair,
Lonely and sweet, nor loved the less
  For flowering in a wilderness.

'Our sands are bare, but down their slope
  The silvery-footed antelope
As gracefully and gaily springs
  As o'er the marble courts of kings.

'Then come—thy Arab maid will be
The loved and lone acacia-tree,
The antelope, whose feet shall bless
With their light sound thy loneliness.

'Oh! there are looks and tones that dart
An instant sunshine through the heart,—
As if the soul that minute caught
Some treasure it through life had sought;

'As if the very lips and eyes,
Predestined to have all our sighs,
And never be forgot again,
Sparkled and spoke before us then!

'So came thy every glance and tone
When first on me they breathed and shone,
New, as if brought from other spheres,
Yet welcome as if loved for years.

'Then fly with me,—if thou hast known
No other flame, nor falsely thrown
A gem away that thou hadst sworn
Should ever in thy heart be worn.

'Come, if the love thou hast for me
Is pure and fresh as mine for thee,—
Fresh as the fountain under ground
When first 'tis by the lapwing found.[2]

'But if for me thou dost forsake
Some other maid, and rudely break
Her worshipped image from its base,
To give to me the ruined place;—

'Then, fare thee well—I'd rather make
My bower upon some icy lake
When thawing suns begin to shine,
Than trust to love so false as thine!'

There was a pathos in this lay,
  That, even without enchantment's art,
Would instantly have found its way
  Deep into Selim's burning heart;
But, breathing, as it did, a tone
  To earthly lutes and lips unknown;
With every chord fresh from the touch
  Of Music's Spirit,—'twas too much!

Starting, he dashed away the cup,—
  Which, all the time of this sweet air,
His hand had held, untasted, up,
  As if 'twere fixed by magic there,—
And naming her, so long unnamed,
So long unseen, wildly exclaimed,
  'Oh Nourmahal! oh Nourmahal!
Hadst thou but sung this witching strain,
I could forget—forgive thee all,
  And never leave those eyes again.'

---

[1] 'The Angel of Music, who has the most melodious voice of all God's creatures.'—*Sale.*

[2] The Hudhud, or Lapwing, is supposed to have the power of discovering water under ground.

THE LIGHT OF THE HARAM.

The mask is off—the charm is wrought—
And Selim to his heart has caught,
In blushes, more than ever bright,
His Nourmahal, his Haram's Light!
And well do vanished frowns enhance
The charm of every brightened glance;
And dearer seems each dawning smile
For having lost its light awhile:
And, happier now for all her sighs,
As on his arm her head reposes,
She whispers him, with laughing eyes,
'Remember, love, the Feast of Roses!'

Fadladeen, at the conclusion of this light rhapsody, took occasion to sum up his opinion of the young Cashmerian's poetry, of which he trusted they had that evening heard the last. Having recapitulated the epithets 'frivolous,' 'inharmonious,' 'nonsensical,' he proceeded to say that, viewing it in the most favourable light, it resembled one of those Maldivian boats to which the Princess had alluded in the relation of her dream,—a slight, gilded thing, sent adrift without rudder or ballast, and with nothing but vapid sweets and faded flowers on board. The profusion, indeed, of flowers and birds, which this poet had ready on all occasions —not to mention dews, gems, etc.—was a most oppressive kind of opulence to his hearers; and had the unlucky effect of giving to his style all the glitter of the flower garden without its method, and all the flutter of the aviary without its song. In addition to this, he chose his subjects badly, and was always most inspired by the worst parts of them. The charms of paganism, the merits of rebellion,—these were the themes honoured with his particular enthusiasm; and in the poem just recited, one of his most palatable passages was in praise of that beverage of the Unfaithful, wine;—'being perhaps,' said he, relaxing into a smile, as conscious of his own character in the Haram on this point, 'one of those bards whose fancy owes all its illumination to the grape, like that painted porcelain,[1] so curious and so rare, whose images are only visible when liquor is poured into it.' Upon the whole, it was his opinion, from the specimens which they had heard, and which, he begged to say, were the most tiresome part of the journey, that—whatever other merits this well-dressed young gentleman might possess—poetry was by no means his proper avocation; 'and, indeed,' concluded the critic, 'from his fondness for flowers and for birds, I would venture to suggest that a florist or a bird-catcher is a much more suitable calling for him than a poet.'

They had now begun to ascend those barren mountains which separate Cashmere from the rest of India; and as the heats were intolerable, and the time of their encampments limited to the few hours necessary for refreshment and repose, there was an end to all their delightful evenings, and Lalla Rookh saw no more of Feramorz. She now felt that her short dream of happiness was over, and that she had nothing but the recollection of its few blissful hours, like the one draught of sweet water that serves the camel across the wilderness, to be her heart's refreshment during the dreary waste of life that was before her. The blight that had fallen upon her spirits soon found its way to her cheek, and her Ladies saw with regret—though not without some suspicion of the cause—that the beauty of their mistress, of which they were almost as proud as of their own, was fast vanishing away at the very moment of all when she had most need of it. What must the King of Bucharia feel, when, instead of the lively and beautiful Lalla Rookh, whom the poets of Delhi had described as more perfect than the divinest images in the house of Azor,[2] he should receive a pale and inanimate victim, upon whose cheek neither health nor pleasure bloomed, and from whose eyes Love had fled—to hide himself in her heart?

If anything could have charmed away the melancholy of her spirits, it would have been the fresh airs and enchanting scenery of that Valley which the Persians so justly called the Unequalled. But neither the coolness of its atmosphere, so luxurious after toiling up those bare and burning mountains,—neither the splendour of the minarets and pagodas, that shone out from the depth of its woods, nor the grottos, hermitages, and miraculous fountains[3] which

---

[1] 'The Chinese had formerly the art of painting on the sides of porcelain vessels, fish and other animals, which were only perceptible when the vessel was full of some liquor. They call this species Kia-tsin, that is, *azure is put in press*, on account of the manner in which the azure is laid on.'—'They are every now and then trying to recover the art of this magical painting, but to no purpose.'—*Dunn*.

[2] An eminent carver of idols, said in the Koran to be father to Abraham. 'I have such a lovely idol as is not to be met with in the house of Azor.'—*Hafiz*.

[3] 'The pardonable superstition of the sequestered inhabitants has multiplied the places of worship of Mahadeo, of Beschan, and of Brama. All Cashmere is holy land, and miraculous fountains abound.'—*Major Rennell's Memoirs of a Map of Hindostan*.

make every spot of that region holy ground,—neither the countless waterfalls, that rush into the Valley from all those high and romantic mountains that encircle it, nor the fair city on the Lake, whose houses, roofed with flowers,[1] appeared at a distance like one vast and variegated parterre;—not all these wonders and glories of the most lovely country under the sun could steal her heart for a minute from those sad thoughts which but darkened and grew bitterer every step she advanced.

The gay pomps and processions that met her upon her entrance into the Valley, and the magnificence with which the roads all along were decorated, did honour to the taste and gallantry of the young King. It was night when they approached the city, and for the last two miles they had passed under arches, thrown from hedge to hedge, festooned with only those rarest roses from which the Attar Gul, more precious than gold, is distilled, and illuminated in rich and fanciful forms with lanterns of the triple-coloured tortoise-shell of Pegu.[2] Sometimes from a dark wood by the side of the road a display of fireworks would break out, so sudden and so brilliant that a Brahmin might fancy he beheld that grove in whose purple shade the God of Battles was born, bursting into a flame at the moment of his birth ; while, at other times, a quick and playful irradiation continued to brighten all the fields and gardens by which they passed, forming a line of dancing lights along the horizon, like the meteors of the north as they are seen by those hunters who pursue the white and blue foxes on the confines of the Icy Sea.

These arches and fireworks delighted the Ladies of the Princess exceedingly ; and with their usual good logic, they deduced, from his taste for illuminations, that the King of Bucharia would make the most exemplary husband imaginable. Nor, indeed, could Lalla Rookh herself help feeling the kindness and splendour with which the young bridegroom welcomed her ; but she also felt how painful is the gratitude which kindness from those we cannot love excites ; and that their best blandishments come over the heart with all that chilling and deadly sweetness which we can fancy in the cold, odoriferous wind[3] that is to blow over this earth in the last days.

The marriage was fixed for the morning after her arrival, when she was for the first time to be presented to the monarch in that Imperial Palace beyond the Lake, called the Shalimar. Though never before had a night of more wakeful and anxious thought been passed in the Happy Valley, yet, when she rose in the morning, and her Ladies came around her to assist in the adjustment of the bridal ornaments, they thought they had never seen her look half so beautiful. What she had lost of the bloom and radiancy of her charms was more than made up by that intellectual expression, that soul beaming forth from the eyes, which is worth all the rest of loveliness. When they had tinged her fingers with the Henna leaf, and placed upon her brow a small coronet of jewels of the shape worn by the ancient Queens of Bucharia, they flung over her head the rose-coloured bridal veil, and she proceeded to the barge that was to convey her across the lake—first kissing, with a mournful look, the little amulet of carnelian which her father at parting had hung about her neck.

The morning was as fresh and fair as the maid on whose nuptials it rose ; and the shining lake all covered with boats, the minstrels playing upon the shores of the islands, and the crowded summer-houses on the green hills around, with shawls and banners waving from their roofs, presented such a picture of animated rejoicing as only she who was the object of it all did not feel with transport. To Lalla Rookh alone it was a melancholy pageant ; nor could she have even borne to look upon the scene, were it not for a hope that, among the crowds around, she might once more perhaps catch a glimpse of Feramorz. So much was her imagination haunted by this thought, that there was scarcely an islet or boat she passed on the way at

---

[1] 'On a standing roof of wood is laid a covering of fine earth, which shelters the building from the great quantity of snow that falls in the winter season. This fence communicates an equal warmth in winter, as a refreshing coolness in the summer season, when the tops of the houses, which are planted with a variety of flowers, exhibit at a distance the spacious view of a beautifully-chequered parterre.'—*Forster.*

[2] 'Two hundred slaves there are who have no other office than to hunt the woods and marshes for triple-coloured tortoises for the King's Vivary. Of the shells of these also lanterns are made.'—*Vincent le Blanc's Travels.*

[3] This wind, which is to blow from Syria Damascena, is, according to the Mohammedans, one of the signs of the Last Day's approach. Another of the signs is, ' Great distress in the world, so that a man when he passes by another's grave shall say, Would to God I were in his place.'—*Sale's Preliminary Discourse.*

which her heart did not flutter with the momentary fancy that he was there. Happy, in her eyes, the humblest slave upon whom the light of his dear looks fell! In the barge immediately after the Princess sat Fadladeen, with his silken curtains thrown widely apart, that all might have the benefit of his august presence, and with his head full of the speech he was to deliver to the King, 'concerning Feramorz, and literature, and the Chabuk, as connected therewith.'

They now had entered the canal which leads from the Lake to the splendid domes and saloons of the Shalimar, and went gliding on through the gardens that ascended from each bank, full of flowering shrubs that made the air all perfume; while from the middle of the canal rose jets of water, smooth and unbroken, to such a dazzling height, that they stood like tall pillars of diamond in the sunshine. After sailing under the arches of various saloons, they at length arrived at the last and most magnificent, where the monarch awaited the coming of his bride; and such was the agitation of her heart and frame, that it was with difficulty she could walk up the marble steps which were covered with cloth of gold for her ascent from the barge. At the end of the hall stood two thrones, as precious as the Cerulean Throne of Koolburga,[1] on one of which sat Aliris, the youthful King of Bucharia; and on the other was, in a few minutes, to be placed the most beautiful Princess in the world. Immediately upon the entrance of Lalla Rookh into the saloon, the monarch descended from his throne to meet her; but scarcely had he time to take her hand in his when she screamed with surprise, and fainted at his feet. It was Feramorz himself that stood before her!—Feramorz was himself the Sovereign of Bucharia, who in this disguise had accompanied his young bride from Delhi, and, having won her love as an humble minstrel, now amply deserved to enjoy it as a king.

The consternation of Fadladeen at this discovery was, for the moment, almost pitiable. But change of opinion is a resource too convenient in courts for this experienced courtier not to have learned to avail himself of it. His criticisms were all, of course, recanted instantly; he was seized with an admiration of the King's verses, as unbounded as, he begged him to believe, it was disinterested; and the following week saw him in possession of an additional place, swearing by all the Saints of Islam that never had there existed so great a poet as the Monarch Aliris, and, moreover, ready to prescribe his favourite regimen of the Chabuk for every man, woman, and child that dared to think otherwise.

Of the happiness of the King and Queen of Bucharia, after such a beginning, there can be but little doubt; and among the lesser symptoms, it is recorded of Lalla Rookh, that to the day of her death, in memory of their delightful journey, she never called the King by any other name than Feramorz.

---

[1] 'On Mohammed Shaw's return to Koolbarga (the capital of Dekkan), he made a great festival, and mounted this throne with much pomp and magnificence, calling it Firozeh or Cerulean. I have heard some old persons, who saw the throne Firozeh in the reign of Sultan Mamood Bhamenee, describe it. They say that it was in length nine feet, and three in breadth: made of ebony, covered with plates of pure gold, and set with precious stones of immense value. Every prince of the house of Bhamenee, who possessed this throne, made a point of adding to it some rich stones, so that when in the reign of Sultan Mamood it was taken to pieces, to remove some of the jewels to be set in vases and cups, the jewellers valued it at one corore of oons (nearly four millions sterling). I learned also that it was called Firozeh from being partly enamelled of a sky-blue colour, which was in time totally concealed by the number of jewels.'—*Ferishta.*

ODES OF ANACREON.

DEDICATION.

TO HIS ROYAL HIGHNESS
THE PRINCE OF WALES.

SIR,—In allowing me to dedicate this work to your Royal Highness, you have conferred upon me an honour which I feel very sensibly; and I have only to regret that the pages which you have thus distinguished are not more deserving of such illustrious patronage.

   Believe me,
     SIR,
   With every sentiment of respect,
    Your Royal Highness's
   Very grateful and devoted Servant,
     THOMAS MOORE.

It may be necessary to mention that, in arranging the Odes, the Translator has adopted the order of the Vatican MS. For those who wish to refer to the original, he has prefixed an Index which marks the number of each ode in Barnes and the other editions.

INDEX.

ODE	BARNES.	ODE	BARNES
1. ΑΝΑΚΡΕΩΝ ιδων μι,	63	36. Ὁ πλουτος ειγι χρυσον,	23
2. Δοτι μοι λυρην Ὁμηρου,	48	37. Δια νυκτων εγκαθιυδων,	8
3. Αγι, ζωγραφων αριστι,	49	38. Λιαρον πιωμεν οινον,	41
4. Τον αργυρον τοριυον,	17	39. Φιλω γεροντα τερπνον,	47
5. Καλητιχνα τορινον,	18	40. Επιδη βροτος ετυχθην,	24
6. Στιφος πλικων ποτ' ιυρον,	59	41. Τι καλον ιστι βαδιζειν,	66
7. Λιγουσιν αἱ γυναικις,	11	42. Ποθιω μεν Διονυσου,	42
8. Ου μοι μιλει τα Γυγου,	15	43. Στιφανους μεν κροταφοισι,	6
9. Αφις μι τους θιους σοι,	31	44. Το ῥοδον το των ἑρωτων,	5
10. Τι σοι θιλεις ποιησω,	12	45. Ὁταν πινω τον οινον,	25
11. Ερωτα κηριον τις,	10	46. Ιδε, πως ιαρος φανιντος,	37
12. Οἱ μεν καλην Κυβηβην,	13	47. Εγω γερων μεν ειμι,	38
13. Θιλω, θιλω φιλησαι,	14	48. Ὁταν ὁ Βακχος εισιλθη,	26
14. Ει φυλλα παντα δινδρων,	32	49. Του Διος ὁ παις Βακχος,	27
15. Ερασμιη πιλεια,	9	50. Ὁτ' εγω πιω τον οινον,	39
16. Αγι, ζωγραφων αριστι,	28	51. Μη μι φυγης ερωσα,	34
17. Γραφι μοι Βαβυλλον οὑτω,	29	52. Τι μι τους νομους διδασκεις;	36
18. Δοτι μοι, δοτι, γυναικις,	21	53. Ὁτ' εγω νεων ὁμιλον,	54
19. Παρα την σκιην Βαβυλλου,	22	54. Ὁ ταυρος οὑτος, ω παι,	35
20. Αἱ Μουσαι τον Ερωτα,	30	55. Στιφανηφορου μιτ' Ηρος,	53
21. Ἡ γι μιλαινα πινει,	19	56. Ὁ τον εν πονοις ατειρι,	50
22. Ἡ Ταντάλου ποτ' ἑστη,	20	57. Αρα τις τορινει πονηον,	51
23. Θιλω λιγειν Ατρειδας,	1	58. Ὁ δραπιτας μ' ὁ χρυσος,	65
24. Φυσις κιρατα ταυροις,	2	59. Τον μιλανοχρωτα βοτρυν,	52
25. Συ μεν φιλη χιλιδων,	33	60. Ανα βαρβιτον δονησω,	64
26. Συ μεν λιγεις τα Θηβης,	16		
27. Ει ισχιοις μεν ιπποι,	55	61. Πολιαι μεν ἡμιν ἡδι,	56
28. Ὁ ανηρ ὁ της Κυθηρης,	45	62. Αγε δη, φιβ ἡμιν, ω παι,	57
29. Χαλιπον το μη φιλησαι,	46	63. Τον Ερωτα γαρ τον ἁβρον,	58
30. Εδοκουν οναρ τριχαζειν,	44	64. Γουνουμαι σ' ιλαφηβολι,	60
31. Ταχινθινη μι ῥαβδῳ,	7	65. Πωλι Θρηκιη, τι δη μι,	61
32. Επι μυρσιναις τιρειναις,	4	66. Θιαων ανασσα, Κυπρι,	62
33. Μισονυκτιοις ποτ' ὡραις,	2	67. Ω παι παρθενιον βλεπων,	67
34. Μακαριζομεν σε, τιττιξ,	43	68. Εγω δ' οὐτ' αν Αμαλθιης,	68
35. Ερως ποτ' εν ῥοδοισι,	40	For the order of the rest, see the Notes.	

AN ODE BY THE TRANSLATOR.

Επι ῥοδινοις ταπησι,
Τηίος ποτ᾽ ὁ μιλιστης
Ἱλαρος γιλων ικιιτο,
Μιθυων τι και λυριζων·
Αμφι αυτον οἱ δ᾽ ερωτις
Ἁπαλοι συνιχοριυσαν·
Ὁ βιλη τα της Κυθηρης
Εποιιι, ψυχης οἰστους·
Ὁ δι λιυκα ποφυροισι
Κρινα συν ῥοδοισι πλιξας,
Εφιλιι στιφων γιροντα·
Ἡ δι Θιαων αιασσα,
ΣΟΦΙΗ ποτ᾽ ιξ Ολυμπου
Εσορωσ᾽ Ανακριοντα,
Εσορωσα τους ερωτας,
Ὑπομιιδιασσας ιιπι·
Σοφι, δ᾽ ὡς Ανακριοντα
Τον σοφωτατον ἁπαντων,
Καλιουσιν οἱ σοφισται,
Τι, γιρων, τιον βιον μιν
Τοις ερωσι, τῳ Λυαιῳ,

Κ᾽ ουκ ιμοι κρατιιν ιδωκας;
Τι φιλημα της Κυθηρης,
Τι κυπιλλα του Λυαιου,
Αιιι γ᾽ ιτρυφησας ᾀδων,
Ουκ ιμους νομους διδασκων,
Ουκ ιμοι λαχων αωτον;
Ὁ δι Τηίος μιλιστης
Μητι δυσχιραινι, φησι,
Ὁτι, θια, σου γ᾽ ανιυ μιν,
Ὁ σοφωτατος ἁπαντων
Παρα των σοφων καλουμαι·
Φιλιω, πιω, λυριζω,
Μιτα των καλων γυναικων
Αφιλως δι τιρπνα παιζω,
Ὡς λυρη γαρ, ιμον ητορ
Αναπυι μονους ερωτας·
Ὡδι βιοτου γαληνην
Φιλιων μαλιστα παντων,
Ου σοφος μιλῳδος ιιμι;
Τις σοφωτιρος μιν ιστι;

REMARKS ON ANACREON.

THERE is very little known with certainty of the life of Anacreon. Chamæleon Heracleotes, who wrote upon the subject, has been lost in the general wreck of ancient literature. The editors of the poet have collected the few trifling anecdotes which are scattered through the extant authors of antiquity; and supplying the deficiency of materials by fictions of their own imagination, they have arranged what they call a life of Anacreon. These specious fabrications are intended to indulge that interest which we naturally feel in the biography of illustrious men; but it is rather a dangerous kind of illusion, as it confounds the limits of history and romance,[1] and is too often supported by unfaithful citation.[2]

Our poet was born in the city of Téos, in the delicious region of Ionia, where everything respired voluptuousness.[3] The time of his birth appears to have been in the sixth century

---

[1] The History of Anacreon by Gacon (*le poëte sans fard*) is professedly a romance; nor does Mademoiselle Scuderi, from whom he borrowed the idea, pretend to historical veracity in her account of Anacreon and Sappho. These, then, are allowable; but how can Barnes be forgiven, who, with all the confidence of a biographer, traces every wanderi.g of the poet, and settles him in his old age at a country villa near Téos?

[2] The learned Bayle has detected some infidelities of quotation in Le Fevre. *Dictionnaire Historique*, etc. Madame Dacier is not more accurate than her father; they have almost made Anacreon prime minister to the monarch of Samos.

[3] The Asiatics were as remarkable for genius as for luxury. 'Ingenia Asiatica inclyta per gentes fecere poetæ, Anacreon, inde Mimnermus et Antimachus,' etc —*Solinus.*

before Christ,[1] and he flourished at that remarkable period when, under the polished tyrants Hipparchus and Polycrates, Athens and Samos were the rival asylums of genius. The name of his father is doubtful, and therefore cannot be very interesting. His family was perhaps illustrious; but those who discover in Plato that he was a descendant of the monarch Codrus, exhibit, as usual, more zeal than accuracy.[2]

The disposition and talents of Anacreon recommended him to the monarch of Samos, and he was formed to be the friend of such a prince as Polycrates. Susceptible only to the pleasures, he felt not the corruptions of the court; and while Pythagoras fled from the tyrant, Anacreon was celebrating his praises on the lyre. We are told, too, by Maximus Tyrius, that by the influence of his amatory songs he softened the mind of Polycrates into a spirit of benevolence towards his subjects.

The amours of the poet and the rivalship of the tyrant[3] I shall pass over in silence; and there are few, I presume, who will regret the omission of most of those anecdotes, which the industry of some editors has not only promulged, but discussed. Whatever is repugnant to modesty and virtue is considered in ethical science, by a supposition very favourable to humanity, as impossible; and this amiable persuasion should be much more strongly entertained where the transgression wars with nature as well as virtue. But why are we not allowed to indulge in the presumption? Why are we officiously reminded that there have been such instances of depravity?

Hipparchus, who now maintained at Athens the power which his father Pisistratus had usurped, was one of those elegant princes who have polished the fetters of their subjects. He was the first, according to Plato, who edited the poems of Homer, and commanded them to be sung by the rhapsodists at the celebration of the Panathenæa. As his court was the galaxy of genius, Anacreon should not be absent. Hipparchus sent a barge for him; the poet embraced the invitation, and the muses and the loves were wafted with him to Athens.[4]

The manner of Anacreon's death was singular. We are told that in the eighty-fifth year of his age he was choked by a grape-stone;[5] and however we may smile at their enthusiastic partiality, who pretend that it was a peculiar indulgence of Heaven, which stole him from the world by this easy and characteristic death, we cannot help admiring that his fate should be so emblematic of his disposition. Cœlius Calcagninus alludes to this catastrophe in the following epitaph on our poet:

'Then, hallowed sage, those lips which poured along
The sweetest lapses of the cygnet's song,
A grape has closed for ever!
Here let the ivy kiss the poet's tomb,
Here let the rose he loved with laurels bloom,
In bands that ne'er shall sever!

But far be thou, oh! far, unholy vine,
By whom the favourite minstrel of the Nine
Expired his rosy breath;
Thy God himself now blushes to confess,
Unholy vine! he feels he loves thee less,
Since poor Anacreon's death!'[6]

---

[1] I have not attempted to define the particular Olympiad, but have adopted the idea of Bayle, who says, 'Je n'ai point marqué d'Olympiade; car, pour un homme qui a vécu 85 ans, il me semble que l'on ne doit point s'enfermer dans des bornes si étroites.'

[2] This mistake is founded on a false interpretation of a very obvious passage in Plato's Dialogue on Temperance; it originated with Madame Dacier, and has been received implicitly by many. Gail, a late editor of Anacreon, seems to claim to himself the merit of detecting this error; but Bayle had observed it before him.

[3] In the romance of Clelia, the anecdote to which I allude is told of a young girl, with whom Anacreon fell in love while she personated the god Apollo in a mask. But here Mademoiselle Scuderi consulted nature more than truth.

[4] There is a very interesting French poem founded upon this anecdote, imputed to Desyveteaux, and called Anacreon Citoyen.

[5] Fabricius appears not to trust very implicitly in this story. It must be confessed that Lucian, who tells us that Sophocles was choked by a grape-stone, in the very same treatise mentions the longevity of Anacreon, and yet is silent on the manner of his death. Could he have been ignorant of such a remarkable coincidence, or knowing, could he have neglected to remark it? See Regnier's Introduction to his Anacreon.

[6] At te, sancte senex, acinus sub tartara misit;
Cygneæ clausit qui tibi vocis iter.
Vos, hederæ, tumulum, tumulum vos, cingite mauri;
Hoc rosa perpetuo vernet odora loco;

According to some authorities, Anacreon and Sappho were contemporaries; and any thought of an interchange between hearts so congenial in warmth of passion and delicacy of genius gives such play to the imagination, that the mind loves to indulge in it. But the vision dissolves before historical truth; and Chamæleon and Hermesianax, who are the source of the supposition, are considered as having merely indulged in a poetical anachronism.[1]

To infer the moral dispositions of a poet from the tone of sentiment which pervades his works, is sometimes a very fallacious analogy; but the soul of Anacreon speaks so unequivocally through his odes, that we may consult them as the faithful mirrors of his heart.[2] We find him there the elegant voluptuary, diffusing the seductive charm of sentiment over passions and propensities at which rigid morality must frown. His heart, devoted to indolence, seems to think that there is wealth enough in happiness, but seldom happiness enough in wealth; and the cheerfulness with which he brightens his old age is interesting and endearing: like his own rose, he is fragrant even in decay. But the most peculiar feature of his mind is that love of simplicity which he attributes to himself so very feelingly, and which breathes characteristically through all that he has sung. In truth, if we omit those vices in our estimate which ethnic religion not only connived at, but consecrated, we shall say that the disposition of our poet was amiable; his morality was relaxed, but not abandoned; and Virtue with her zone loosened may be an emblem of the character of Anacreon.[3]

Of his person and physiognomy time has preserved such uncertain memorials, that perhaps it were better to leave the pencil to fancy; and few can read the Odes of Anacreon without imagining the form of the animated old bard, crowned with roses, and singing to the lyre.

After the very enthusiastic eulogiums bestowed by the ancients and moderns upon the poems of Anacreon,[4] we need not be diffident in expressing our raptures at their beauty, nor hesitate to pronounce them the most polished remains of antiquity. They are all beauty, all enchantment.[5] He steals us so insensibly along with him, that we sympathize even in his excesses. In his amatory odes there is a delicacy of compliment not to be found in any other ancient poet. Love at that period was rather an unrefined emotion; and the intercourse of the sexes was animated more by passion than sentiment. They knew not those little tendernesses which form the spiritual part of affection; their expression of feeling was therefore rude and

---

At vitis procul hinc, procul hinc odiosa facessat,
  Quæ causam diræ protulit, uva, necis,
Creditur ipse minus vitem jam Bacchus amaro,
  In vatem tantum quæ fuit ausa nefas.

[1] Barnes is convinced of the synchronism of Anacreon and Sappho, but very gratuitously. In citing his authorities, it is strange that he neglected the line which Fulvius Ursinus has quoted, as from Anacreon, among the testimonies to Sappho:

Εμμ λαβων ιιοαρας Σαπφω παρθενον αδυφωνον.

Fabricius thinks that they might have been contemporary, but considers their amour as a tale of imagination. Vossius rejects the idea entirely; as also Olaus Borrichius, etc. etc.

[2] An Italian poet, in some verses on Bellean's translation of Anacreon, pretends to imagine that our bard did not feel as he wrote:

Lyæum, Venerem, Cupidinemque
Senex lusit Anacreon poeta,
Sed quo tempore nec capaciores
Rogabat cyathos, nec inquietis
Urebatur amoribus, sed ipsis
Tantum versibus et jocis amabat,
Nullum præ se habitum gerens amantis.

To Love and Bacchus, ever young,
  While sage Anacreon touched the lyre,
He neither felt the loves he sung,
  Nor filled his bowl to Bacchus higher.
Those flowery days had faded long,
  When youth could act the lover's part;

And passion trembled in his song,
  But never, never reached his heart.

[3] Anacreon's character has been variously coloured. Barnes lingers on it with enthusiastic admiration; but he is always extravagant, if not sometimes even profane. Baillet, who is in the opposite extreme, exaggerates too much the testimonies which he has consulted; and we cannot surely agree with him when he cites such a compiler as Athenæus, as 'un des plus savans critiques de l'antiquité.'—*Jugement des Savans, M.C.V.*

Barnes could not have read the passage to which he refers, when he accuses Le Fevre of having censured our poet's character in a note on Longinus: the note in question is manifest irony, in allusion to some reprehension which Le Fevre had suffered for his Anacreon; and it is evident that praise rather than censure is intimated.

[4] Besides those which are extant, he wrote hymns, elegies, epigrams, etc. Some of the epigrams still exist. Horace alludes to a poem of his upon the rivalry of Circe and Penelope in the affections of Ulysses, lib. i. od. 17. The scholiast upon Nicander cites a fragment from a poem upon sleep by Anacreon, and attributes to him likewise a medicinal treatise. Fulgentius mentions a work of his upon the war between Jupiter and the Titans, and the origin of the consecration of the eagle.

[5] 'We may perceive,' says Vossius, 'that the iteration of his words conduces very much to the sweetness of his style.' Henry Stephen remarks the same beauty in a note on the forty-fourth ode. This figure of iteration is his most appropriate grace. The modern writers of Juvenilia and Basia have adopted it to an excess which destroys the effect.

unvaried, and the poetry of Love deprived of its most captivating graces. Anacreon, however, attained some ideas of this gallantry; and the same delicacy of mind which led him to this refinement prevented him from yielding to the freedom of language which has sullied the pages of all the other poets. His descriptions are warm; but the warmth is in the ideas, not the words. He is sportive without being wanton, and ardent without being licentious. His poetic invention is most brilliantly displayed in those allegorical fictions which so many have endeavoured to imitate, because all have confessed them to be inimitable. Simplicity is the distinguishing feature of these odes, and they interest by their innocence while they fascinate by their beauty: they are, indeed, the infants of the Muses, and may be said to lisp in numbers.

I shall not be accused of enthusiastic partiality by those who have read and felt the original; but to others I am conscious that this should not be the language of a translator, whose faint reflection of these beauties can but little justify his admiration of them.

In the age of Anacreon music and poetry were inseparable. These kindred talents were for a long time associated, and the poet always sung his own compositions to the lyre. It is probable that they were not set to any regular air, but rather a kind of musical recitation, which was varied according to the fancy and feelings of the moment.[1] The poems of Anacreon were sung at banquets as late as the time of Aulus Gellius, who tells us that he heard one of the odes performed at a birthday entertainment.[2]

The singular beauty of our poet's style, and perhaps the careless facility with which he appears to have trifled, have induced, as I remarked, a number of imitations. Some have succeeded with wonderful felicity, as may be discerned in the few odes which are attributed to writers of a later period. But none of his emulators have been so dangerous to his fame as those Greek ecclesiastics of the early ages, who, conscious of inferiority to their prototypes, determined on removing the possibility of comparison, and, under a semblance of moral zeal, destroyed the most exquisite treasures of antiquity. Sappho and Alcæus were among the victims of this violation; and the sweetest flowers of Grecian literature fell beneath the rude hand of ecclesiastical presumption. It is true they pretended that this sacrifice of genius was canonized by the interests of religion, but I have already assigned the most probable motive;[3] and if Gregorius Nazianzenus had not written Anacreontics, we might now perhaps have the works of the Teian unmutilated, and be empowered to say exultingly with Horace,

'Nec si quid olim lusit Anacreon
Delevit ætas.'

The zeal by which these bishops professed to be actuated gave birth more innocently, indeed, to an absurd species of parody, as repugnant to piety as it is to taste, where the poet of voluptuousness was made a preacher of the gospel, and his muse, like the Venus in armour at Lacedæmon, was arrayed in all the severities of priestly instruction. Such was the *Anacreon Recantatus*, by Carolus de Aquino, a Jesuit, published 1701, which consisted of a series of palinodes to the several songs of our poet. Such, too, was the Christian Anacreon of Patrignanus, another Jesuit, who preposterously transferred to a most sacred subject all that Anacreon had sung to festivity.

His metre has been very frequently adopted by the modern Latin poets. Scaliger, Taubmannus, Barthius,[4] and others, have evinced that it is by no means uncongenial with that

---

[1] In the Paris edition there are four of the original odes set to music, by citizens Le Sueur, Gossec, Mehul, and Cherubini. 'On chante du Latin et de l'Italien,' says Gail, 'quelquefois même sans les entendre; qui empêche que nous ne chantions des odes Grecques?' The chromatic learning of these composers is very unlike what we are told of the simple melody of the ancients; and they have all mistaken the accentuation of the words.

[2] The Parma commentator is rather careless in referring to this passage of Aulus Gellius (lib. xix. cap. 9).—The ode was not sung by the rhetorician Julianus, as he says, but by the minstrels of both sexes, who were introduced at the entertainment.

[3] We may perceive by the beginning of the first hymn of Bishop Synesius, that he made Anacreon and Sappho his models of composition:

Αγε μοι, λιγυα φορμιγξ,
Μετα Τηΐαν αοιδαν,
Μετα Λεσβίαν τε μολπαν.

Marginius and Damascenus were likewise authors of pious Anacreontics.

[4] I have seen somewhere an account of the mss. of Barthius, written just after his death, which mentions many more Anacreontics of his than I believe have ever been published.

language.¹ The Anacreontics of Scaliger, however, scarcely deserve the name: they are glittering with conceits, and, though often elegant, are always laboured. The beautiful fictions of Angerianus² have preserved more happily than any the delicate turn of those allegorical fables which, frequently passing through the mediums of version and imitation, have generally lost their finest rays in the transmission. Many of the Italian poets have sported on the subjects and in the manner of Anacreon. Bernardo Tasso first introduced the metre which was afterwards polished and enriched by Chabriera and others. If we may judge by the references of Degen, the German language abounds in Anacreontic imitations; and Hagedorn is one among many who have assumed him as a model. La Farre, Chaulieu, and the other light poets of France, have professed, too, to cultivate the muse of Téos; but they have attained all her negligence, with little of the grace that embellishes it. In the delicate bard of Schiras³ we find the kindred spirit of Anacreon: some of his gazelles, or songs, possess all the character of our poet.

We come now to a retrospect of the editions of Anacreon. To Henry Stephen we are indebted for having first recovered his remains from the obscurity in which they had reposed for so many ages. He found the seventh ode, as we are told, on the cover of an old book, and communicated it to Victorius, who mentions the circumstance in his *Various Readings*. Stephen was then very young, and this discovery was considered by some critics of that day as a literary imposition.⁴ In 1554, however, he gave Anacreon to the world,⁵ accompanied with Annotations and a Latin version of the greater part of the odes. The learned still hesitated to receive them as the relics of the Teian bard, and suspected them to be the fabrication of some monks of the sixteenth century. This was an idea from which the classic muse recoiled.; and the Vatican manuscript, consulted by Scaliger and Salmasius, confirmed the antiquity of most of the poems. A very inaccurate copy of this MS. was taken by Isaac Vossius, and this is the authority which Barnes has followed in his collation; accordingly, he misrepresents almost as often as he quotes; and the subsequent editors, relying upon him, have spoken of the manuscript with not less confidence than ignorance. The literary world has at length been gratified with this curious memorial of the poet, by the industry of the Abbé Spaletti, who in 1781 published at Rome a fac-simile of the pages of the Vatican manuscript, which contained the odes of Anacreon.⁶

Monsieur Gail has given a catalogue of all the editions and translations of Anacreon. I find their number to be much greater than I could possibly have had an opportunity of consulting. I shall therefore content myself with enumerating those editions only which I have been able to collect; they are very few, but I believe they are the most important:—

The edition by Henry Stephen, 1554, at Paris; the Latin version is, by Colomesius, attributed to John Dorat.

The old French translations, by Ronsard and Belleau—the former published in 1555, the latter in 1556. It appears that Henry Stephen communicated his manuscript of Anacreon to Ronsard before he published it, by a note of Muretus upon one of the sonnets of that poet.

The edition by Le Fevre, 1660.

---

¹ Thus, too, Albertus, a Danish poet:
Fidit tui minister
Gaudebo semper esse
Gaudebo semper illi
Litare thure muleo;
Gaudebo semper illum
Laudare pumillilis
Anacreonticillis.
See the Danish Poets collected by Rostgaard. These pretty littlenesses defy translation. There is a very beautiful Anacreontic by Hugo Grotius. See lib. I. *Farraginis*.

² From Angerianus Prior has taken his most elegant mythological subjects.

³ See Toderini on the learning of the Turks, as translated by De Cournard. Prince Cantemir has made the Russians acquainted with Anacreon. See his Life, prefixed to a translation of his Satires, by the Abbé de Guasco.

⁴ Robertellus, in his work *De Ratione corrigendi*, pronounces these verses to be triflings of some insipid Græcist.

⁵ Ronsard commemorates this event
Je vay boire à Henri Etienne
Qui des enfers nous a rendu,
Du vieil Anacreon perdu,
La douce lyre Teïenne.—Ode xv. book 4.

⁶ I fill the bowl to Stephen's name,
Who rescued from the gloom of night
The Teian bard of festive fame,
And brought his living lyre to light.

⁶ This manuscript, which Spaletti thinks as old as the tenth century, was brought from the Palatine into the Vatican Library; it is a kind of anthology of Greek epigrams.

The edition by Madame Dacier, 1681, with a prose translation.[1]
The edition by Longepierre, 1684, with a translation in verse.
The edition by Baxter ; London, 1695.
A French translation by La Fosse, 1704.
L'Histoire des Odes d'Anacréon, by Monsieur Gacon ; Rotterdam, 1712.
A translation in English verse, by several hands, 1713, in which the odes by Cowley are inserted.
The edition by Barnes ; London, 1721.
The edition by Dr. Trapp, 1733, with a Latin version in elegiac metre.
A translation in English verse, by John Addison, 1735.
A collection of Italian translations of Anacreon, published at Venice, 1736, consisting of those by Corsini, Regnier, Salvini, Marchetti, and one by several anonymous authors.
A translation in English verse, by Fawkes and Doctor Broome, 1760.[2]
Another, anonymous, 1768.
The edition by Spaletti, at Rome, 1781 ; with the fac-simile of the Vatican MS.
The edition by Degen, 1786, who published also a German translation of Anacreon, esteemed the best.
A translation in English verse, by Urquhart, 1787.
The edition by Citoyen Gail, at Paris, seventh year, 1799, with a prose translation.

ODES OF ANACREON.

ODE I.[3]

I saw the smiling bard of pleasure,
The minstrel of the Teian measure ;
'Twas in a vision of the night,
He beamed upon my wandering sight :
I heard his voice, and warmly pressed
The dear enthusiast to my breast.
His tresses wore a silvery dye,
But beauty sparkled in his eye ;
Sparkled in his eyes of fire,
Through the mist of soft desire.[4]
His lip exhaled, whene'er he sighed,
The fragrance of the racy tide ;
And, as with weak and reeling feet,
He came my cordial kiss to meet,
An infant of the Cyprian band
Guided him on with tender hand.

Quick from his glowing brows he drew
His braid, of many a wanton hue ;
I took the braid of wanton twine,
It breathed of him and blushed with wine
I hung it o'er my thoughtless brow,
And ah ! I feel its magic now ![5]
I feel that even his garland's touch
Can make the bosom love too much !

ODE II.

Give me the harp of epic song,
Which Homer's finger thrilled along ;
But tear away the sanguine string,
For war is not the theme I sing.

---

[1] The author of *Nouvelles de la Repub. des Lett.* praises this translation very liberally. I have always thought it vague and spiritless.

[2] This is the most complete of the English translations.

[3] This ode is the first of the series in the Vatican manuscript, which attributes it to no other poet than Anacreon. They who assert that the manuscript imputes it to Basilius have been misled by the words in the margin, which are merely intended as a title to the following ode. Whether it be the production of Anacreon or not, it has all the features of ancient simplicity, and is a beautiful imitation of the poet's happiest manner.

[4] The eyes that are humid and fluctuating show a propensity to pleasure and love ; they bespeak, too, a mind of integrity and beneficence, a generosity of disposition, and a genius for poetry.

Baptista Portæ tells us some strange opinions of the ancient physiognomists on this subject, their reasons for which were curious, and perhaps not altogether fanciful — *Vide Physiognom. Johan. Baptist. Portæ.*

[5] This idea, as Longepierre remarks, is in an epigram of the seventh book of the *Anthologia :*

Εξοτι μοι τιοντι συνιστασυσα Χαριχλω
Λαθρη τους ιδιους αμφιβαλι στιζανους,
Πυρ ολοον δατ ρυ μι.

While I unconscious quaffed my wine,
'Twas then thy fingers slyly sto'e
Upon my brow that wreath of thine,
Which since has maddened all my soul!

Proclaim the laws of festal rite,[1]
I'm monarch of the board to-night;
And all around shall brim as high,
And quaff the tide as deep as I!
And when the cluster's mellowing dews
Their warm, enchanting balm infuse,
Our feet shall catch the elastic bound,
And reel us through the dance's round.
Oh Bacchus! we shall sing to thee,
In wild but sweet ebriety!
And flash around such sparks of thought,
As Bacchus could alone have taught!
Then give the harp of epic song,
Which Homer's finger thrilled along;
But tear away the sanguine string,
For war is not the theme I sing!

But let not o'er its simple frame
Your mimic constellations flame;
Nor grave upon the swelling side
Orion, scowling o'er the tide.
I care not for the glittering wane,
Nor yet the weeping sister train.
But oh! let vines luxuriant roll
Their blushing tendrils round the bowl.
While many a rose-lipped bacchant maid[4]
Is culling clusters in their shade.
Let sylvan gods, in antic shapes,
Wildly press the gushing grapes;
And flights of loves, in wanton ringlets
Flit around on golden winglets;
While Venus, to her mystic bower,
Beckons the rosy vintage-Power.

ODE III.[2]

Listen to the Muse's lyre,
Master of the pencil's fire!
Sketched in painting's bold display,
Many a city first portray;
Many a city, revelling free,
Warm with loose festivity.
Picture then a rosy train,
Bacchants straying o'er the plain;
Piping, as they roam along,
Roundelay or shepherd-song.
Paint me next, if painting may
Such a theme as this portray,
All the happy heaven of love,
These elect of Cupid prove.

ODE IV.[3]

Vulcan! hear your glorious task;
I do not from your labours ask
In gorgeous panoply to shine,
For war was ne'er a sport of mine.
No—let me have a silver bowl,
Where I may cradle all my soul;

ODE V.[5]

Grave me a cup with brilliant grace,
Deep as the rich and holy vase,
Which on the shrine of Spring reposes,
When shepherds hail that hour of roses.
Grave it with themes of chaste design,
Formed for a heavenly bowl like mine.
Display not there the barbarous rites
In which religious zeal delights;
Nor any tale of tragic fate,
Which history trembles to relate!
No—cull thy fancies from above,
Themes of heaven and themes of love.
Let Bacchus, Jove's ambrosial boy,
Distil the grape in drops of joy;
And while he smiles at every tear,
Let warm-eyed Venus, dancing near,
With spirits of the genial bed,
The dewy herbage deftly tread.
Let Love be there, without his arms,
In timid nakedness of charms;
And all the Graces linked with Love,
Blushing through the shadowy grove
While rosy boys, disporting round,
In circlets trip the velvet ground;
But ah! if there Apollo toys,
I tremble for my rosy boys![6]

---

[1] The ancients prescribed certain laws of drinking at their festivals, for an account of which see the commentators. Anacreon here acts the symposiarch, or master of the festival.

[2] La Fosse has thought proper to lengthen this poem by considerable interpolations of his own, which he thinks are indispensably necessary to the completion of the description.

[3] This is the ode which Aulus Gellius tells us was performed by minstrels at an entertainment where he was present.

[4] I have given this according to the Vatican manuscript, in which the ode concludes with the following lines, not inserted accurately in any of the editions:

Ποιησον αμπελους μοι
Και βοτρυας κατ' αυτων
Και μαιναδας τρυγωσας,
Πινει δε ληνον οινου,

Ληνοβατας σατυντας,
Τους σατυρους γιλωντας,
Και χρυσους τους ερωτας,
Και Κυθερην γελωσαν,
'Ομου καλω Λυαιω,
Ερωτα κ' Αφροδιτην.

[5] Degen thinks that this ode is a more modern imitation of the preceding. There is a poem by Cælius Calcagninus, in the manner of both, where he gives instructions about the making of a ring:

Tornabis annulum mihi
Et fabre, et apte, et commode, etc. etc.

[6] An allusion to the fable that Apollo had killed his beloved boy Hyacinth while playing with him at quoits. 'This,' says La Fosse, 'is assuredly the sense of the text, and it cannot admit of any other.'
The Italian translators, to save themselves the trouble

ODE VI.[1]

As late I sought the spangled bowers,
To cull a wreath of matin flowers,
Where many an early rose was weeping,
I found the urchin Cupid sleeping.[2]
I caught the boy, a goblet's tide
Was richly mantling by my side,
I caught him by his downy wing,
And whelm'd him in the racy spring.
Oh! then I drank the poisoned bowl,
And Love now nestles in my soul!
Yes, yes, my soul is Cupid's nest,
I feel him fluttering in my breast.

ODE VII.[3]

THE women tell me every day
That all my bloom has passed away.

'Behold,' the pretty wantons cry,
'Behold this mirror with a sigh;
The locks upon thy brow are few,
And, like the rest, they're withering too!
Whether decline has thinned my hair,
I'm sure I neither know nor care;[4]
But this I know, and this I feel,
As onward to the tomb I steal,
That still as death approaches nearer,
The joys of life are sweeter, dearer;[5]
And had I but an hour to live,
That little hour to bliss I'd give!

ODE VIII.[6]

I CARE not for the idle state
Of Persia's king, the rich, the great![7]
I envy not the monarch's throne,
Nor wish the treasured gold my own.
But oh! be mine the rosy braid,
The fervour of my brows to shade;

---

of a note, have taken the liberty of making Anacreon explain this fable. Thus Salvini, the most literal of any of them:

Ma con lor non giuochi Apollo;
Che in fiero risco
Col duro disco
A Giacinto fiaccò il collo.

[1] The Vatican MS. pronounces this beautiful fiction to be the genuine offspring of Anacreon. It has all the features of the parent:

et facile inscils
Noscitetur ab omnibus.

The commentators, however, have attributed it to Julian, a royal poet.

[2] This idea is prettily imitated in the following epigram by Andreas Naugerius:

Florentes dum forte vagans mea Hyella per hortos
Texit odoratis lilia cana rosis,
Ecce rosas inter latitantem invenit amorem
Et simul annexis floribus implicuit.
Luctatur primo, et contra nitentibus alis
Indomitus tentat solvere vincla puer,
Mox ubi lacteolas et dignas matre papillas
Vidit et ora ipsos nota movere Deos.
Impositosque comæ ambrosios ut sentit odores
Quosque legit diti messe beatus Arabs;
'I (dixit) mea, quære novum tibi mater amorem,
Imperio sedes hæc erit apta meo.'

As fair Hyella, through the bloomy grove,
A wreath of many mingled flowerets wove,
Within a rose a sleeping love she found,
And in the twisted wreaths the baby bound.
Awhile he struggled, and impatient tried
To break the rosy bonds the virgin tied;
But when he saw her bosom's milky swell,
Her features, where the eye of Jove might dwell;
And caught the ambrosial odours of her hair,
Rich as the breathings of Arabian air;
'Oh! mother Venus' (said the raptured child
By charms, of more than mortal bloom, beguiled),
'Go, seek another boy, thou'st lost thine own,
Hyella's bosom shall be Cupid's throne!'

This epigram of Naugerius is imitated by Lodovico Dolce, in a poem beginning:

Montre raccoglie hor uno, hor altro fiore
Vicina a un rio di chiare et lucid' onde,
Lidia, etc. etc.

[3] Alberti has imitated this ode, in a poem beginning
Nisa mi dice e Clori
Tirsi, tu se' pur veglio.

[4] Henry Stephen very justly remarks the elegant negligence of expression in the original here:

Εγω δε τας κομας μου
Ειτ' εισιν, ιτ' απηλθον
Ουκ' οιδα.

And Longepierre has adduced from Catullus what he thinks a similar instance of this simplicity of manner:

Ipse quis sit, utrum sit, an non sit, id quoque nescit.

Longepierre was a good critic, but perhaps the line which he has selected is a specimen of a carelessness not very elegant; at the same time, I confess that none of the Latin poets have ever appeared to me so capable of imitating the graces of Anacreon as Catullus, if he had not allowed a depraved imagination to hurry him so often into vulgar licentiousness.

[5] Pontanus has a very delicate thought upon the subject of old age:

Quid rides, Matrona? senem quid temnis amantem?
Quisquis amat nulla est conditione senex.

Why do you scorn my want of youth,
And with a smile my brow behold?
Lady, dear! believe this truth,
That he who loves cannot be old.

[6] 'The German poet Lessing has imitated this ode. Vol. i. p. 24.'—*Degen.* Gail de Editionibus.
Baxter conjectures that this was written upon the occasion of our poet's returning the money to Policrates, according to the anecdote in Stobæus.

[7] There is a fragment of Archilochus in Plutarch, 'De tranquillitate animi,' which our poet has very closely imitated here: it begins,

Ου μοι τα Γυγεω του πολυχρυσου μελει,—*Barnes.*

In one of the monkish imitators of Anacreon we find the same thought:

Ψυχην εμην ερωτω,
Τι σοι θιλις γενισθαι;
Θιλις Γυγεω, τα και τα·

Be mine the odours, richly sighing,
Amidst my hoary tresses flying.[1]
To-day I'll haste to quaff my wine,
As if to-morrow ne'er should shine;
But if to-morrow comes, why then—
I'll haste to quaff my wine again.
And thus while all our days are bright,
Nor time has dimmed their bloomy light,
Let us the festal hours beguile
With mantling cup and cordial smile;
And shed from every bowl of wine
The richest drop on Bacchus' shrine!
For death may come with brow unpleasant,
May come when least we wish him present,
And beckon to the sable shore,
And grimly bid us—drink no more!

ODE IX.[2]

I PRAY thee, by the gods above,
Give me the mighty bowl I love,
And let me sing, in wild delight,
'I will—I will be mad to-night!'
Alcmæon once, as legends tell,
Was frenzied by the fiends of hell;
Orestes too, with naked tread,
Frantic paced the mountain-head;
And why ?—a murdered mother's shade
Before their conscious fancy played;
But I can ne'er a murderer be,
The grape alone shall bleed by me;
Yet can I rave, in wild delight,
'I will—I will be mad to-night.'
The son of Jove, in days of yore,
Imbrued his hands in youthful gore,
And brandished, with a maniac joy,
The quiver of the expiring boy:

And Ajax, with tremendous shield,
Infuriate scoured the guiltless field.
But I, whose hands no quiver hold,
No weapon but this flask of gold,
The trophy of whose frantic hours
Is but a scattered wreath of flowers
Yet, yet can sing with wild delight.
'I will—I will be mad to-night!'

ODE X.[3]

TELL me how to punish thee,
For the mischief done to me!
Silly swallow! prating thing,[4]
Shall I clip that wheeling wing?
Or, as Tereus did of old[5]
(So the fabled tale is told),
Shall I tear that tongue away,
Tongue that uttered such a lay?
How unthinking hast thou been!
Long before the dawn was seen,
When I slumbered in a dream,
(Love was the delicious theme!)
Just when I was nearly blest,
Ah! thy matin broke my rest!

ODE XI.[6]

'TELL me, gentle youth, I pray thee,
What in purchase shall I pay thee
For this little waxen toy,
Image of the Paphian boy?'
Thus I said, the other day,
To a youth who passed my way.

---

[1] On account of this idea of perfuming the beard, Cornelius de Pauw pronounces the whole ode to be the spurious production of some lascivious monk, who was nursing his beard with unguents. But he should have known that this was an ancient Eastern custom, which, if we may believe Savary, still exists. 'Vous voyez, Monsieur (says this traveller), que l'usage antique de se parfumer la tête et la barbe, célébré par le prophète Roi, subsiste encore de nos jours.'—Lettre 12. Savary likewise cites this very ode of Anacreon. Angerianus has not thought the idea inconsistent; he has introduced it in the following lines:

Hæc mihi cura, rosis et cingere tempora myrto,
Et curas multo dilapidare mero.
Hæc mihi cura, comas et barbam tingere succo
Assyrio et dulces continuare jocos.

This be my care to twine the rosy wreath,
And drench my sorrows in the ample bowl;
To let my beard the Assyrian unguent breathe,
And give a loose to levity of soul!

[2] The poet here is in a frenzy of enjoyment, and it is, indeed, 'amabilis insania.'

Furor di poesia,
Di lascivia, e di vino,
Triplicato furore,
Bacco, Apollo, et Amore.
Ritratti del Cavalier Marino.

This is, as Scaliger expresses it,
Insanire dulce,
Et sapidum furere furorem.

[3] This ode is addressed to a swallow. I find from Degen and from Gail's Index, that the German poet Weisse has imitated it, Scherz Lieder, lib. ii. carm. 5; that Ramler also has imitated it, Lyr. Blumenlese, lib. iv. p. 335 ; and some others.—See Gail de Editionibus. We are referred by Degen to that stupid book, the Epistles of Alciphron, tenth epistle, third book, where Iophon complains to Eraston of being wakened, by the crowing of a cock, from his vision of riches.

[4] The loquacity of the swallow was proverbialized; thus Nicostratus:

Ει το συνεχως και πολλα και ταχεως λαλειν
Ην του φρονειν παρασημον. αι χελιδονες
Ελεγοντ' αν ημων σωφρονεστεραι πολυ.

If in prating from morning till night,
A sign of our wisdom there be,
The swallows are wiser by right,
For they prattle much faster than we.

[5] Modern poetry has confirmed the name of Philomel upon the nightingale; but many very respectable ancients assigned this metamorphose to Progne, and made Philomel the swallow, as Anacreon does here.

[6] It is difficult to preserve with any grace the narrative simplicity of this ode, and the humour of the turn with which it concludes. I feel that the translation

'Sir' (he answered, and the while
Answered all in Doric style),
'Take it, for a trifle take it;
Think not yet that I could make it;
Pray believe it was not I;
No—it cost me many a sigh,
And I can no longer keep
Little gods who murder sleep!'
'Here, then, here,' I said, with joy,
'Here is silver for the boy:
He shall be my bosom guest,
Idol of my pious breast!'
Little Love! thou now art mine,
Warm me with that torch of thine;
Make me feel as I have felt,
Or thy waxen frame shall melt.
I must burn with warm desire,
Or thou, my boy, in yonder fire!

ODE XII.

They tell how Atys, wild with love,
Roams the mount and haunted grove;
Cybele's name he howls around,[1]
The gloomy blast returns the sound!
Oft too by Claros' hallowed spring,[2]
The votaries of the laurelled king
Quaff the inspiring magic stream,
And rave in wild prophetic dream.
But frenzied dreams are not for me,
Great Bacchus is my deity!
Full of mirth, and full of him,
While waves of perfume round me swim;
While flavoured bowls are full supplied,
And you sit blushing by my side,
I will be mad and raving too—
Mad, my girl! with love for you!

ODE XIII.

I will, I will; the conflict's past,
And I'll consent to love at last.
Cupid has long, with smiling art,
Invited me to yield my heart;
And I have thought that peace of mind
Should not be for a smile resigned;
And I've repelled the tender lure,
And hoped my heart should sleep secure
But slighted in his boasted charms,
The angry infant flew to arms;
He slung his quiver's golden frame,
He took his bow, his shafts of flame,
And proudly summoned me to yield,
Or meet him on the martial field.
And what did I unthinking do?
I took to arms, undaunted too:[3]—
Assumed the corslet, shield, and spear,
And, like Pelides, smiled at fear.
Then (hear it, all you Powers above!)
I fought with Love! I fought with Love.
And now his arrows all were shed—
And I had just in terror fled—
When, heaving an indignant sigh,
To see me thus unwounded fly,
And having now no other dart,
He glanced himself into my heart![4]

---

must appear very vapid, if not ludicrous, to an English reader.

[1] I have adopted the accentuation which Elias Andreas gives to Cybele:

In montibus Cybelen
Magno sonans boatu.

[2] This fountain was in a grove, consecrated to Apollo, and situated between Colophon and Lebedos, in Ionia. The god had an oracle there. Scaliger has thus alluded to it in his Anacreontica:

Semel ut concitus œstro,
Veluti qui Clarias aquas
Ebibere loquaces,
Quo plus canunt, plura volunt.

[3] Longepierre has quoted an epigram from the *Anthologia*, in which the poet assumes Reason as the armour against Love:

'Ωπλισμαι προς ερωτα περι στερνοισι λογισμον,
Ουδε με νικησει, μονος εων προς ενα.
Θνατος δ' αθανατω συνελευσομαι, ην δε βοηθον
Βακχον εχη, τι μονος προς δυ' εγω δυναμαι;

With Reason I cover my breast as a shield,
And fearlessly meet little Love in the field;
Thus fighting his godship, I'll ne'er be dismayed;
But if Bacchus should ever advance to his aid,
Alas! then, unable to combat the two,
Unfortunate warrior! what should I do?

This idea of the irresistibility of Cupid and Bacchus united, is delicately expressed in an Italian poem, which is so very Anacreontic, that I may be pardoned for introducing it. Indeed, it is an imitation of our poet's sixth ode:

Lavossi Amore in quel vicino fiume
Ove giuro (Pastor) che bevend 'io
Bevei le fiamme, anzi l' istesso Dio,
C' hor con l' humide piume
Lascivetto mi scherza al cor intorno.
Ma che sarci s' io lo bevessi un giorno.
Bacco, nel tuo liquore?
Sarei, piu che non sono ebro d'Amore.

The urchin of the bow and quiver
Was bathing in a neighbouring river,
Where, as I drank on yester-eve
(Shepherd-youth! the tale believe),
'Twas not a cooling crystal draught,
'Twas liquid flame I madly quaffed;
For Love was in the rippling tide,
I felt him to my bosom glide;
And now the wily wanton minion
Plays o'er my heart with resiless pinion.
This was a day of fatal star,
But were it not more fatal far,
If, Bacchus, in thy cup of fire,
I found this flattering, young desire?
Then, then indeed my soul should prove
Much more than ever, drunk with love!

[4] Dryden has parodied this thought in the following extravagant lines:

I'm all o'er Love;
Nay, I am Love; Love shot, and shot so fast
He shot himself into my breast at last.

My heart—alas the luckless day!
Received the god, and died away.
Farewell, farewell, my faithless shield!
Thy lord at length was forced to yield.
Vain, vain is every outward care,
My foe's within, and triumphs there.

ODE XIV.[1]

Count me, on the summer trees,
Every leaf that courts the breeze;[2]
Count me, on the foamy deep,
Every wave that sinks to sleep;
Then, when you have numbered these
Billowy tides and leafy trees,
Count me all the flames I prove,
All the gentle nymphs I love.
First, of pure Athenian maids,
Sporting in their olive shades,
You may reckon just a score;
Nay, I'll grant you fifteen more.
In the sweet Corinthian grove,
Where the glowing wantons rove,[3]

Chains of beauties may be found,
Chains by which my heart is bound;
There indeed are girls divine,
Dangerous to a soul like mine;[4]
Many bloom in Lesbos' isle;
Many in Ionia smile;
Rhodes a pretty swarm can boast;
Caria too contains a host.
Sum these all—of brown and fair
You may count two thousand there!
What, you gaze! I pray you, peace!
More I'll find before I cease.
Have I told you all my flames
'Mong the amorous Syrian dames?
Have I numbered every one
Glowing under Egypt's sun?
Or the nymphs who, blushing sweet,
Deck the shrine of love in Crete;
Where the god, with festal play,
Holds eternal holiday?
Still in clusters, still remain
Gades' warm desiring train;[5]
Still there lies a myriad more
On the sable India's shore;
These, and many far removed,
All are loving—all are loved!

---

[1] The poet, in this catalogue of his mistresses, means nothing more than, by a lively hyperbole, to tell us that his heart, unfettered by any one object, was warm with devotion towards the sex in general. Cowley is indebted to this ode for the hint of his ballad called *The Chronicle*; and the learned Menage has imitated it in a Greek Anacreontic, of which the following is a translation:—

Tell the foliage of the woods,
Tell the billows of the floods,
Number midnight's starry store,
And the sands that crowd the shore;
Then, my Bion, thou may'st count
Of my loves the vast amount!
I've been loving, all my days,
Many nymphs, in many ways,
Virgin, widow, maid, and wife—
I've been doting all my life.
Naiads, Nereids, nymphs of fountains,
Goddesses of groves and mountains,
Fair and sable, great and small,
Yes—I swear I've loved them all!
Every passion soon was over,
I was but a moment's lover;
Oh! I'm such a roving elf,
That the Queen of Love herself,
Though she practised all her wiles,
Rosy blushes, golden smiles,
All her beauty's proud endeavour
Could not chain my heart for ever!

[2] This figure is very frequently made use of in poetry. The amatory writers have exhausted a world of imagery by it, to express the infinity of kisses which they require from the lips of their mistresses: in this Catullus led the way.

—quam sidera multa, cum tacet nox,
Furtivos hominum vident amores;
Tam te basia multa basiare,
Vesano satis, et super Catullo est:

Quæ nec pernumerare curiosi
Possint, nec mala fascinare lingua.—Carm. 7.

As many stellar eyes of light,
As through the silent waste of night,
Gazing upon this world of shade,
Witness some secret youth and maid,
Who, fair as thou, and fond as I,
In stolen joys enamoured lie!
So many kisses, ere I slumber,
Upon those dew-bright lips I'll number;
So many vermil, honeyed kisses,
Envy can never count our blisses.
No tongue shall tell the sum but mine;
No lips shall fascinate but thine!

[3] Corinth was very famous for the beauty and the number of its courtezans. Venus was the deity principally worshipped by the people, and prostitution in her temple was a meritorious act of religion. Conformable to this was their constant and solemn prayer, that the gods would increase the number of their courtezans.

[4] 'With justice has the poet attributed beauty to the women of Greece.'—*Degen.*

[5] The Gaditanian girls were like the Baladières of India, whose dances are thus described by a French author: 'Les danses sont presque toutes des pantomimes d'amour; le plan, le dessin, les attitudes, les mesures, les sons, et les cadences de ces ballets, tout respire cette passion et en exprime les voluptés et les fureurs.' *Histoire du Commerce des Europ. dans les deux Indes.—Raynal.*

The music of the Gaditanian females had all the voluptuous character of their dancing, as appears from Martial:

Cantica qui Nili, qui Gaditana susurrat.
—Lib. iii. epig. 63

Lodovico Ariosto had this ode of our bard in his mind, when he wrote his poem 'De diversis amoribus.' See the *Anthologia Italorum.*

ODE XV.

TELL me why, my sweetest dove,[1]
Thus your humid pinions move,
Shedding through the air, in showers,
Essence of the balmiest flowers?
Tell me whither, whence you rove,
Tell me all, my sweetest dove?
Curious stranger! I belong
To the bard of Teian song;
With his mandate now I fly
To the nymph of azure eye;
Ah! that eye has maddened many,
But the poet more than any!
Venus, for a hymn of love
Warbled in her votive grove[2]
('Twas, in sooth, a gentle lay),
Gave me to the bard away.
See me now, his faithful minion,
Thus, with softly-gliding pinion,
To his lovely girl I bear
Songs of passion through the air.
Oft he blandly whispers me,
'Soon, my bird, I'll set you free.'
But in vain he'll bid me fly,
I shall serve him till I die.
Never could my plumes sustain
Ruffling winds and chilling rain,
O'er the plains, or in the dell,
On the mountain's savage swell;
Seeking in the desert wood
Gloomy shelter, rustic food
Now I lead a life of ease,
Far from such retreats as these;
From Anacreon's hand I eat
Food delicious, viands sweet;
Flutter o'er his goblet's brim,
Sip the foamy wine with him.
Then I dance and wanton round
To the lyre's beguiling sound;
Or with gently-fanning wings
Shade the minstrel while he sings:
On his harp then sink in slumbers,
Dreaming still of dulcet numbers!
This is all—away—away—
You have made me waste the day.
How I chattered! prating crow
Never yet did chatter so.

ODE XVI.[3]

THOU, whose soft and rosy hues
Mimic form and soul infuse;[4]
Best of painters! come, portray
The lovely maid that's far away.[5]
Far away, my soul! thou art,
But I've thy beauties all by heart.
Paint her jetty ringlets straying,
Silky twine in tendrils playing;[6]

---

[1] The dove of Anacreon, bearing a letter from the poet to his mistress, is met by a stranger, with whom this dialogue is imagined.
  The ancients made use of letter-carrying pigeons, when they went any distance from home, as the most certain means of conveying intelligence back. That tender domestic attachment, which attracts this delicate little bird through every danger and difficulty, till it settles in its native nest, affords to the elegant author of *The Pleasures of Memory* a fine and interesting exemplification of his subject:

  Led by what chart, transports the timid dove
  The wreaths of conquest, or the vows of love?

See the poem. Daniel Heinsius has a similar sentiment, speaking of Dousa, who adopted this method at the siege of Leyden:

  Quo patriæ non tendit amor? Mandata referre
  Postquam hominem nequiit mittere, misit avem.

Fuller tells us that, at the siege of Jerusalem, the Christians intercepted a letter tied to the legs of a dove, in which the Persian Emperor promised assistance to the besieged. See *Fuller's Holy War*, cap. 24, book 1.
[2] 'This passage is invaluable, and I do not think that anything so beautiful or so delicate has ever been said. What an idea does it give of the poetry of the man from whom Venus herself, the mother of the Graces and the Pleasures, purchases a little hymn with one of her favourite doves!'—*Longepierre*.
  De Pauw objects to the authenticity of this ode, because it makes Anacreon his own panegyrist; but poets have a licence for praising themselves, which with some indeed may be considered as comprised under their general privilege of fiction.
[3] This ode and the next may be called companion pictures; they are highly finished, and give us an ex-

cellent idea of the taste of the ancients in beauty. Franciscus Junius quotes them in his third book, *De Pictura Veterum*.
  This ode has been imitated by Ronsard, Giuliano Goselini, etc. etc. Scaliger alludes to it thus in his *Anacreontica*:

  Olim lepore blando,
  Litis versibus
  Candidus Anacreon
  Quam pingeret Amicus
  Descripsit Venerem suam.

  The Teian bard, of former days,
  Attuned his sweet descriptive lays,
  And taught the painter's hand to trace
  His fair beloved's every grace!

In the dialogue of Caspar Barlæus, entitled *An formosa sit ducenda*, the reader will find many curious ideas and descriptions of beauty.
[4] 'I have followed the reading of the Vatican MS. Painting is called 'the rosy art,' either in reference to colouring, or as an indefinite epithet of excellence, from the association of beauty with that flower. Salvini has adopted this reading in his literal translation:

  Della rosea arte signore.

[5] If the portrait of this beauty be not merely ideal, the omission of her name is much to be regretted. Meleager, in an epigram on Anacreon, mentions 'the golden Eurypyle' as his mistress:

  Βαβλληκως χρυσεης χαιρες ισ' Ευρυπυλης.

[6] The ancients have been very enthusiastic in their praises of hair. Apuleius, in the second book of his Milesiacs, says that Venus herself, if she were bald, though surrounded by the Graces and the Loves, could not be pleasing even to her husband Vulcan.
  To this passage of our poet Selden alluded in a note

And, if painting hath the skill
To make the spicy balm distil,[1]
Let every little lock exhale
A sigh of perfume on the gale.
Where her tresses' curly flow
Darkles o'er the brow of snow,
Let her forehead beam to light,
Burnished as the ivory bright.
Let her eyebrows sweetly rise
In jetty arches o'er her eyes,
Gently in a crescent gliding,
Just commingling, just dividing.
But hast thou any sparkles warm,
The lightning of her eyes to form?
Let them effuse the azure ray
With which Minerva's glances play,
And give them all that liquid fire
That Venus' languid eyes respire.[2]
O'er her nose and cheek be shed
Flushing white and mellow red;
Gradual tints, as when there glows
In snowy milk the bashful rose.
Then her lip, so rich in blisses!
Sweet petitioner for kisses![3]
Pouting nest of bland persuasion,
Ripely suing Love's invasion.
Then beneath the velvet chin,
Whose dimple shades a Love within,[4]

Mould her neck with grace descending,
In a heaven of beauty ending;
While airy charms, above, below,
Sport and flutter on its snow.
Now let a floating, lucid veil
Shadow her limbs, but not conceal;[5]
A charm may peep, a hue may beam,
And leave the rest to Fancy's dream.
Enough—'tis she! 'tis all I seek;
It glows, it lives, it soon will speak!

ODE XVII.[6]

AND now, with all thy pencil's truth,
Portray Bathyllus, lovely youth!
Let his hair, in lapses bright,
Fall like streaming rays of light;[7]
And there the raven's dye confuse
With the yellow sunbeam's hues.
Let not the braid, with artful twine,[8]
The flowing of his locks confine;
But loosen every golden ring,
To float upon the breeze's wing.
Beneath the front of polished glow,
Front as fair as mountain snow,
And guileless as the dews of dawn,
Let the majestic brows be drawn,

*n the *Polyolbion* of Drayton, song the second; where, observing that the epithet ' black-haired ' was given by some of the ancients to the goddess Isis, he says: ' Nor will I swear but that Anacreon (a man very judicious in the provoking motives of wanton love), intending to bestow on his sweet mistress that one of the titles of woman's special ornament, well-haired, thought of this when he gave his painter direction to make her blackhaired.'

[1] Thus Philostratus, speaking of a picture: ' I admire the dewiness of these roses, and could say that their very smell was painted.'

[2] Tasso has painted the eyes of Armida, as La Fosse remarks:

Qual raggio in onda le scintilla un riso
Négli umidi occhi tremulo e lascivo.

Within her humid, melting eyes
A brilliant ray of laughter lies,
Soft as the broken solar beam
That trembles in the azure stream.

The mingled expression of dignity and tenderness, which Anacreon requires the painter to infuse into the eyes of his mistress, is more amply described in the subsequent ode. Both descriptions are so exquisitely touched, that the artist must have been great indeed, if he did not yield in painting to the poet.

[3] The 'lip, provoking kisses,' in the original, is a strong and beautiful expression. Achilles Tatius speaks of ' lips soft and delicate for kissing.' A grave old commentator, Dionysius Lambinus, in his notes upon Lucretius, tells us, with all the authority of experience, that girls who have large lips kiss infinitely sweeter than others! ' Suavius viros osculantur puellæ labiosæ, quum quæ sunt brevibus labris.' And Æneas Sylvius, in his tedious, uninteresting story of the adulterous loves of Euryalus and Lucretia, where he particularizes the beauties of the heroine (in a very false and laboured style of latinity), describes her lips as exquisitely adapted

for biting: ' Os parvnm decensque, labia corallini coloris ad morsum aptissima.'—*Epist.* 114, lib. 1.

[4] Madame Dacier has quoted here two pretty lines of Varro:

Sigilla in mento impressa Amoris digitulo
Vestigio demonstrant mollitudinem.

In her chin is a delicate dimple,
By the finger of Cupid imprest;
There Softness, bewitchingly simple,
Has chosen her innocent nest.

[5] This delicate art of description, which leaves imagination to complete the picture, has been seldom adopted in the imitations of this beautiful poem. Ronsard is exceptionably minute; and Politianus, in his charming portrait of a girl, full of rich and exquisite diction, has lifted the veil rather too much. The 'questo che tu m'intendi' should be always left to fancy.

[6] The reader who wishes to acquire an accurate idea of the judgment of the ancients in beauty, will be indulged by consulting Junius, *De Pictura Veterum,* ninth chapter, third book, where he will find a very curious selection of descriptions and epithets of personal perfections; he compares this ode with a description of Theodoric, king of the Goths, in the second epistle, first book of Sidonius Apollinaris.

[7] He here describes the sunny hair, the ' flava coma,' which the ancients so much admired. The Romans gave this colour artificially to their hair. See *Stanisl Kobiensyck de Luxu Romanorum.*

[8] If the original were, which is particularly beautiful, can admit of any additional value, that value is conferred by Gray's admiration of it. See his Letters to West.
Some annotators have quoted on this passage the description of Photis's hair in Apuleius; but nothing can be more distant from the simplicity of our poet's manner than that affectation of richness which distinguishes the style of Apuleius

Of ebon dyes, enriched by gold,
Such as the scaly snakes unfold.
Mingle in his jetty glances
Power that awes, and love that trances;[1]
Steal from Venus bland desire,
Steal from Mars the look of fire,
Blend them in such expression here,
That we, by turns, may hope and fear!
Now from the sunny apple seek
The velvet down that spreads his cheek!
And there let Beauty's rosy ray
In flying blushes richly play;—
Blushes of that celestial flame
Which lights the cheek of virgin shame.
Then for his lips, that ripely gem—
But let thy mind imagine them!
Paint, where the ruby cell uncloses,
Persuasion sleeping upon roses;[2]
And give his lip that speaking air,
As if a word was hovering there![3]
His neck of ivory splendour trace,
Moulded with soft but manly grace;
Fair as the neck of Paphia's boy,
Where Paphia's arms have hung in joy.
Give him the wingèd Hermes' hand,[4]
With which he waves his snaky wand;
Let Bacchus then the breast supply,
And Leda's son the sinewy thigh.
But oh! suffuse his limbs of fire
With all that glow of young desire.[5]

Which kindles when the wishful sigh
Steals from the heart, unconscious why.
Thy pencil, though divinely bright,
Is envious of the eye's delight,
Or its enamoured touch would show
His shoulder, fair as sunless snow,
Which now in veiling shadow lies,
Removed from all but Fancy's eyes.
Now, for his feet—but, hold—forbear—
I see a godlike portrait there;[6]
So like Bathyllus!—sure there's none
So like Bathyllus but the Sun!
Oh, let this pictured god be mine,
And keep the boy for Samos' shrine;
Phœbus shall then Bathyllus be,
Bathyllus then the deity!

ODE XVIII.

Now the star of day is high,
Fly, my girls, in pity fly,
Bring me wine in brimming urns,
Cool my lip, it burns, it burns!
Sunned by the meridian fire,
Panting, languid, I expire!
Give me all those humid flowers,
Drop them o'er my brow in showers.
Scarce a breathing chaplet now
Lives upon my feverish brow;

---

[1] Tasso similarly describes the eyes of Clorinda:
Lampeggiar gli occhi, e folgorar gli sguardi
Dolci ne l' ira.

Her eyes were glowing with a heavenly heat,
Emaning fire, and e'en in anger sweet!

The poetess Veronica Cambara is more diffuse upon this variety of expression:

Occhi lucenti et belli
Come esser puo ch' in un medesmo istante
Nascan de voi sì nove forme et tante?
Lieti, mesti, superbi, humili' altieri
Vi mostrate in un punto, ondi di sperma,
Et di timor de empiete, etc. etc.

Oh! tell me, brightly-beaming eye,
Whence in your little orbit lie
So many different traits of fire,
Expressing each a new desire?
Now with angry scorn you darkle,
Now with tender anguish sparkle,
And we, who view the various mirror,
Feel at once both hope and terror.

Chevreau, citing the lines of our poet, in his critique on the poems of Malherbe, produces a Latin version of them from a manuscript which he had seen, entitled *Joan Falconis Anacreontici Lusus.*

[2] It was worthy of the delicate imagination of the Greeks to deify Persuasion, and give her the lips for her throne. We are reminded of a very interesting fragment of Anacreon, preserved by the scholiast upon Pindar, and supposed to belong to a poem reflecting with some severity on Simonides, who was the first, we are told, that ever made a hireling of his muse:

Ουδ' αργυρην ποτ' ελαμψε Πιιθω.

Nor yet had fair Persuasion shone
In silver splendours, not her own.

[3] In the original, λαλων σιωπη. The mistress of Petrarch ' parla con silentio,' which is perhaps the best method of female eloquence.

[4] In Shakspeare's *Cymbeline* there is a similar method of description:

This is his hand,
His foot Mercurial, his martial thigh
The brawns of Hercules.

We find it likewise in *Hamlet.* Longepierre thinks that the hands of Mercury are selected by Anacreon on account of the graceful gestures which were supposed to characterize the god of eloquence; but Mercury was also the patron of thieves, and may perhaps be praised as a light-fingered deity.

[5] I have taken the liberty here of somewhat veiling the original. Madame Dacier, in her translation, has hung out lights (as Sterne would call it) at this passage. It is very much to be regretted that this substitution of asterisks has been so much adopted in the popular interpretations of the Classics; it serves but to bring whatever is exceptionable into notice, ' claramque facem præferre pudendis.'

[6] This is very spirited, but it requires explanation. While the artist is pursuing the portrait of Bathyllus, Anacreon, we must suppose, turns round and sees a picture of Apollo, which was intended for an altar at Samos: he instantly tells the painter to cease his work; that this picture will serve for Bathyllus; and that, when he goes to Samos, he may make an Apollo of the portrait of the boy which he had begun.

'Bathyllus (says Madame Dacier) could not be more elegantly praised, and this one passage does him more honour than the statue, however beautiful it might be, which Polycrates raised to him.'

Every dewy rose I wear
Sheds its tears, and withers there.[1]
But for you, my burning mind![2]
Oh! what shelter shall I find?
Can the bowl, or floweret's dew,
Cool the flame that scorches you?

Hark! they whisper, as they roll,
Calm persuasion to the soul;
Tell me, tell me, is not this
All a stilly scene of bliss?
Who, my girl, would pass it by?
Surely neither you nor I![4]

ODE XIX.

Here recline you, gentle maid,
Sweet is this imbowering shade;[2]
Sweet the young, the modest trees,
Ruffled by the kissing breeze;
Sweet the little founts that weep,
Lulling bland the mind to sleep;

ODE XX.

One day the Muses twined the hands[2]
Of baby Love, with flowery bands;
And to celestial Beauty gave
The captive infant as her slave.
His mother comes with many a toy,
To ransom her beloved boy;[3]—

---

[1] There are some beautiful lines, by Angerianus, upon a garland, which I cannot resist quoting here:

Ante fores madidæ sic sic pendete corollæ,
Mane orto imponet Cælia vos capiti;
At cum per niveam cervicem influxerit humor,
Dicite, non roris sed pluvia hæc lacrimæ.

By Cælia's arbour all the night
Hung, humid wreath, the lover's vow;
And haply, at the morning light,
My love shall twine thee round her brow.

Then, if upon her bosom bright
Some drops of dew shall fall from thee,
Tell her, they are not drops of night,
But tears of sorrow shed by me!

In the poem of Mr. Sheridan, 'Uncouth is this moss-covered grotto of stone,' there is an idea very singularly coincident with this of Angerianus, in the stanza which begins,

And thou, stony grot, in thy arch may'st preserve.

[2] The transition here is peculiarly delicate and impassioned; but the commentators have perplexed the sentiment by a variety of readings and conjectures.

[3] The description of this bower is so natural and animated, that we cannot help feeling a degree of coolness and freshness while we read it. Longepierre has quoted from the first book of the *Anthologia* the following epigram, as somewhat resembling this ode:

Ερχεο, και κατ' εμαν ιζευ πιτυν, α τε μελιχρον
Προς μαλακους ηχει κεκλιμενα ζεφυρους.
Ηνιδε και κρουνισμα μελιστογες, ενθα μελισδων
Ἡδυν ερημαιαις ὑπνον αγω καλαμοις.

Come, sit by the shadowy pine
That covers my sylvan retreat,
And see how the branches incline
The breathing of Zephyr to meet.

See the fountain, that, flowing, diffuses
Around me a glittering spray;
By its brink, as the traveller muses,
I soothe him to sleep with my lay!

[4] What a finish he gives to the picture by the simple exclamation of the original! In these delicate turns he is inimitable; and yet hear what a French translator says on the passage. This conclusion appeared to me too trifling after such a description, and I thought proper to add somewhat to the strength of the original.'

[5] By this allegory of the Muses making Cupid the prisoner of Beauty, Anacreon seems to insinuate the softening influence which a cultivation of poetry has over the mind, in making it peculiarly susceptible to the impressions of beauty; though in the following epigram, by the philosopher Plato, which is found in the third book of Diogenes Laertius, the Muses are made to disavow all the influence of Love:

Ἁ Κυπρις Μουσαισι, κορασια ταν Ἀφροδιταν
Τιματ' η τον Ερωτα ὑμμιν εφοπλισομαι.
Αἱ Μουσαι ποτι Κυπριν. Αρει τα στωμυλα ταυτα
Ἡμιν ου πετεται τουτο το παιδαριον.

'Yield to my gentle power, Parnassian maids;'
Thus to the Muses spoke the Queen of Charms—
'Or Love shall flutter in your classic shades,
And make your grove the camp of Paphian arms!'

'No,' said the virgins of the tuneful bower,
' We scorn thine own and all thy urchin's art;
Though Mars has trembled at the infant's power,
His shaft is pointless o'er a Muse's heart!'

There is a sonnet by Benedetto Guidi, the thought of which was suggested by this ode.

Love, wandering through the golden maze
  Of my beloved's hair,
Traced every lock with fond delays,
  And, doting, lingered there.
And soon he found 'twere vain to fly,
  His heart was close confined;
And every curlet was a tie,
  A chain by Beauty twined.

Now Venus seeks her boy's release,
  With ransom from above:
But, Venus! let thy efforts cease,
  For Love's the slave of love.
And, should we loose his golden chain,
  The prisoner would return again!

[6] Venus thus proclaims the reward for her fugitive child in the first Idyl of Moschius:

Ὁ μανυτας γερας ἑξει,
Μισθος τοι, το φιλαμα το Κυπριδος, ην δ' αγαγης νιν,
Ου γυμνον το φιλαμα, τυ δ' ω ξενε, και πλιον ἑξεις.

On him, who the haunts of my Cupid can show,
A kiss of the tenderest stamp I'll bestow;
But he who can bring me the wanderer here,
Shall have something more rapturous, something more dear.

This 'something more' is the 'quidquid post oscula dulce' of Secundus.

After this ode, there follow in the Vatican MS. these extraordinary lines:

His mother sues, but all in vain !
He ne'er will leave his chains again.
Nay, should they take his chains away,
The little captive still would stay.
'If this,' he cries, 'a bondage be,
Who could wish for liberty?'

Then, hence with all your sober thinking!
Since Nature's holy law is drinking;
I'll make the laws of Nature mine,
And pledge the universe in wine!

ODE XXI.[1]

Observe when mother earth is dry,
She drinks the droppings of the sky;
And then the dewy cordial gives
To every thirsty plant that lives.
The vapours, which at evening weep,
Are beverage to the swelling deep;
And when the rosy sun appears,
He drinks the ocean's misty tears.
The moon, too, quaffs her paly stream
Of lustre from the solar beam.

ODE XXII.[2]

The Phrygian rock, that braves the storm,
Was once a weeping matron's form;
And Progne, hapless, frantic maid,
Is now a swallow in the shade.
Oh! that a mirror's form were mine,
To sparkle with that smile divine;
And, like my heart, I then should be
Reflecting thee, and only thee!
Or were I, love, the robe which flows
O'er every charm that secret glows,
In many a lucid fold to swim,
And cling and grow to every limb!

'Ηδυμελης Ανακρεων
'Ηδυμελης δε Σαπφω
Πινδαρικον το δε μοι μελος
Συγκερασας τις εγχεει
Τα τρια ταυτα μοι δοκει
Και Διονυσος εισελθων
Και Παφιη παραχροος
Και αυτος Ερως καν εμοιν.

These lines, which appear to me to have as little sense as metre, are most probably the interpolation of the transcriber.

[1] The commentators who have endeavoured to throw the chains of precision over the spirit of this beautiful trifle, require too much from Anacreontic philosophy. One of the Capilupi has imitated this ode in an epitaph on a drunkard:

Dum vixi sino fine bibi, sic imbrifer arcus,
Sic tellus pluvias solo perusta bibit.
Sic bibit assidue fontes et flumina Pontus,
Sic semper sitiens Sol maris haurit aquas.
Ne te igitur jactes plus me, Sileno, bibiasse;
Et mihi da victas tu quoque, Bacche, manus.
—*Hippolytus Capilupus.*

While life was mine, the little hour
In drinking still unvaried flew;
I drank as earth imbibes the shower,
Or as the rainbow drinks the dew;
As ocean quaffs the rivers up,
Or flushing sun inhales the sea;
Silenus trembled at my cup,
And Bacchus was outdone by me!

[2] Ogilvie, in his *Essay on the Lyric Poetry of the Ancients*, in remarking upon the *Odes of Anacreon*, says: 'In some of his pieces there is exuberance and even wildness of imagination; in that particularly which is addressed to a young girl, where he wishes alternately to be transformed to a mirror, a coat, a stream, a bracelet, and a pair of shoes, for the different purposes which he recites; this is mere sport and wantonness.'

It is the wantonness, however, of a very graceful muse; *ludit amabiliter.* The compliment of this ode is exquisitely delicate, and so singular for the period in which Anacreon lived, when the scale of love had not yet been graduated into all its little progressive refine-

ments, that if we were inclined to question the authenticity of the poem, we should find a much more plausible argument in the features of modern gallantry which it bears, than in any of those fastidious conjectures upon which some commentators have presumed so far. Degen thinks it spurious, and De Pauw pronounces it to be miserable. Longepierre and Barnes refer us to several imitations of this ode, from which I shall only select an epigram of Dionysius:

Ειθ' ανεμος γενομην, συ δε γε στειχουσα παρ' αυγας,
Στηθεα γυμνωσαις, και με πνεοντα λαβοις.
Ειθε ροδον γενομην ὑποπορφυρον, οφρα με χερσιν
Αραμενη, κομισαις στηθεσι χιονεοις.
Ειθι κρινον γενομην λευκεχροον, οφρα με χερσιν
Αραμενη, μαλλον σης χροτιης κοριεσης.

I wish I could like zephyr steal
To wanton o'er thy mazy vest;
And thou would'st ope thy bosom veil,
And take me panting to thy breast!

I wish I might a rosebud grow,
And thou would'st cull me from the bower,
And place me on that breast of snow,
Where I should bloom, a wintry flower!

I wish I were the lily's leaf,
To fade upon that bosom warm;
There I should wither, pale and brief,
The trophy of thy fairer form!

Allow me to add, that Plato has expressed as fanciful a wish in a distich preserved by Laertius:

Αστερας εισαθρεις, αστηρ εμος· ειθε γενοιμην
Ουρανος, ὡς πολλοις ομμασιν εις σε βλεπω.

TO STELLA.

Why dost thou gaze upon the sky?
Oh! that I were that spangled sphere,
And every star should be an eye
To wonder on thy beauties here!

Apuleius quotes this epigram of the divine philosopher to justify himself for his verses on Critias and Charinus. See his *Apology*, where he also adduces the example of Anacreon : 'Fecero tamen et alii talia, et si vos ignoratis, apud Græcos Teius quidam,' etc. etc.

Oh! could I as the streamlet's wave,
Thy warmly-mellowing beauties lave,
Or float as perfume on thine hair,
And breathe my soul in fragrance there!
I wish I were the zone[1] that lies
Warm to thy breast, and feels its sighs!
Or like those envious pearls that show
So faintly round that neck of snow;
Yes, I would be a happy gem,
Like them to hang, to fade like them.
What more would thy Anacreon be?
Oh! anything that touches thee.
Nay, sandals for those airy feet[2]—
Thus to be pressed by thee were sweet!

ODE XXIII.

I often wish this languid lyre,
This warbler of my soul's desire,
Could raise the breath of song sublime,
To men of fame, in former time.
But when the soaring theme I try,
Along the chords my numbers die,
And whisper, with dissolving tone,
'Our sighs are given to Love alone!'
Indignant at the feeble lay,
I tore the panting chords away,
Attuned them to a nobler swell,
And struck again the breathing shell;
In all the glow of epic fire,
To Hercules I wake the lyre!
But still its fainting sighs repeat,
'The tale of Love alone is sweet!'[3]

Then fare thee well, seductive dream,
That mad'st me follow Glory's theme;
For thou, my lyre, and thou, my heart,
Shall never more in spirit part;
And thou the flame shalt feel as well
As thou the flame shalt sweetly tell!

ODE XXIV.[4]

To all that breathe the airs of heaven,
Some boon of strength has Nature given.
When the majestic bull was born,
She fenced his brow with wreathed horn.
She armed the courser's foot of air,
And winged with speed the panting hare.
She gave the lion fangs of terror,
And, on the ocean's crystal mirror,
Taught the unnumbered scaly throng
To trace their liquid path along;
While for the umbrage of the grove,
She plumed the warbling world of love.
To man she gave the flame refined,
The spark of heaven—a thinking mind![5]
And had she no surpassing treasure
For thee, oh woman! child of pleasure?
She gave thee beauty—shaft of eyes,
That every shaft of war outflies!
She gave thee beauty—blush of fire,
That bids the flames of war retire!
Woman! be fair, we must adore thee;
Smile, and a world is weak before thee![6]

---

[1] This was a riband, or band, called by the Romans *fuscia* and *strophium*, which the women wore for the purpose of restraining the exuberance of the bosom.—*Vide Polluc. Onomast.* Thus Martial:

Fascia crescentes dominæ compesce papillas.

The women of Greece not only wore this zone, but condemned themselves to fasting, and made use of certain drugs and powders for the same purpose. To these expedients they were compelled, in consequence of their inelegant fashion of compressing the waist into a very narrow compass, which necessarily caused an excessive tumidity in the bosom.—See Dioscorides, lib. v.

[2] The sophist Philostratus, in one of his love-letters, has borrowed this thought: 'Oh lovely feet! oh excellent beauty! oh! thrice happy and blessed should I be, if you would but tread on me!' In Shakspeare, Romeo desires to be a glove:

Oh that I were a glove upon that hand,
That I might kiss that cheek!

And, in his *Passionate Pilgrim*, we meet with an idea somewhat like that of the thirteenth line:

He, spying her, bounced in, where as he stood,
'O Jove!' quoth she, 'why was not I a flood?'

[3] The word αντιφωνει, in the original, may imply that kind of musical dialogue practised by the ancients, in which the lyre was made to respond to the questions proposed by the singer.

[4] Henry Stephens has imitated the idea of this ode in the following lines of one of his poems:—

Provida dat cunctis Natura animantibus arma,
Et sua fœmineum possidet arma genus,
Ungulaque at defendit equum, atque ut cornua taurum,
Armata est forma fœmina pulchra sua.

And the same thought occurs in those lines, spoken by Corisca in *Pastor Fido*:

Cosi noi la bellezza
Che 'è vertu nostra cosi propria, come
La forza del leone
E l' ingegno de l' huomo.

The lion boasts his savage powers,
   And lordly man his strength of mind;
But beauty's charm is solely ours,
   Peculiar boon, by Heaven assigned!

[5] In my first attempt to translate this ode, I had interpreted οφρυνημα, with Baxter and Barnes, as implying courage and military virtue; but I do not think that the gallantry of the idea suffers by the import which I have now given to it. For why need we consider this possession of wisdom as exclusive? and in truth, as the design of Anacreon is to estimate the treasure of beauty, above all the rest which Nature has distributed, it is perhaps even refining upon the delicacy of the compliment, to prefer the radiance of female charms to the cold illumination of wisdom and prudence; and to think that women's eyes are

the books, the academies,
From whence doth spring the true Promethean fire.

[6] Longepierre's remark here is very ingenious: 'The

ODE XXV.

Once in each revolving year,
Gentle bird! we find thee here,
When Nature wears her summer-vest,
Thou comest to weave thy simple nest;
But when the chilling winter lowers,
Again thou seek'st the genial bowers
Of Memphis, or the shores of Nile,
Where sunny hours of verdure smile.
And thus thy wing of freedom roves,
Alas! unlike the plumèd loves,
That linger in this hapless breast,
And never, never change their nest![1]
Still every year, and all the year,
A flight of loves engender here;
And some their infant plumage try,
And on a tender winglet fly;
While in the shell, impregn'd with fires,
Cluster a thousand more desires;
Some from their tiny prisons peeping,
And some in formless embryo sleeping.
My bosom, like the vernal groves,
Resounds with little warbling loves;
One urchin imps the other's feather,
Then twin-desires they wing together,
And still as they have learned to soar,
The wanton babies teem with more.
But is there then no kindly art,
To chase these Cupids from my heart?
No, no! I fear, alas! I fear
They will for ever nestle here!

ODE XXVI.

Thy harp may sing of Troy's alarms,
Or tell the tale of Theban arms;

With other wars my soul shall burn,
For other wounds my harp shall mourn.
'Twas not the crested warrior's dart
Which drank the current of my heart;
Nor naval arms, nor mailèd steed,
Have made this vanquished bosom bleed;
No—from an eye of liquid blue
A host of quivered Cupids flew;[2]
And now my heart all bleeding lies
Beneath this army of the eyes!

ODE XXVII.[3]

We read the flying courser's name
Upon his side, in marks of flame;
And, by their turbaned brows alone,
The warriors of the East are known.
But in the lover's glowing eyes,
The inlet to his bosom lies;[4]
Through them we see the small faint mark,
Where Love has dropped his burning spark

ODE XXVIII.

As in the Lemnian caves of fire,
The mate of her who nursed desire
Moulded the glowing steel, to form
Arrows for Cupid, thrilling warm;
While Venus every barb imbues
With droppings of her honeyed dews;
And Love (alas! the victim-heart)
Tinges with gall the burning dart;[5]
Once, to this Lemnian cave of flame,
The crested Lord of battles came;

Romans,' says he, 'were so convinced of the power of beauty, that they used a word implying strength in the place of the epithet beautiful. Thus Plautus, Act ii. Scene 2, Bacchid.

Sed Bacchis etiam fortis tibi visa.

"Fortis, id est formosa," say Servius and Nonius.'

[1] Thus Love is represented as a bird, in an epigram cited by Longepierre from the *Anthologia:*

'Tis Love that murmurs in my breast,
And makes me shed the secret tear;
Nor day nor night my heart has rest,
For night and day his voice I hear.
A wound within my heart I find,
And oh! 'tis plain where Love has been;
For still he leaves a wound behind,
Such as within my heart is seen.
Oh bird of Love! with song so drear,
Make not my soul the nest of pain;
Oh! let the wing which brought thee here,
In pity waft thee hence again!

[2] Longepierre has quoted part of an epigram from the seventh book of the *Anthologia*, which has a fancy something like this:

Ου μα λιληθας,
Τοξοτα, Ζηνοφιλας ομμασι κρυπτομενος.
Archer Love! though slyly creeping,
Well I know where thou dost lie;

I saw thee through the curtain peeping,
That fringes Zenuphelia's eye.

The poets abound with conceits on the archery of the eyes, but few have turned the thought so naturally as Anacreon. Ronsard gives to the eyes of his mistress 'un petit camp d'amours.'

[3] This ode forms a part of the preceding in the Vatican MS., but I have conformed to the editions in translating them separately.

[4] 'We cannot see into the heart,' says Madame Dacier. But the lover answers:

Il cor ne gli occhi e ne la fronte ho scritto.

La Fosse has given the following lines, as enlarging on the thought of Anacreon:

Lorsque je vois un amant,
Il cache en vain son tourment,
A le trahir tout conspire,
Sa langueur, son embarras,
Tout ce qu'il peut faire ou dire,
Même ce qu'il ne dit pas.
'n vain the lover tries to veil
The flame which in his bosom lies;
His cheek's confusion tells the tale,
We read it in his languid eyes:
And though his words the heart betray,
His silence speaks e'en more than they.

[5] Thus Claudian:

Labuntur gemini fontes, hic dulcis, amarus

'Twas from the ranks of war he rushed,
His spear with many a life-drop blushed!
He saw the mystic darts, and smiled
Derision on the archer-child.
'And dost thou smile?' said little Love;
'Take this dart, and thou may'st prove,
That though they pass the breeze's flight,
My bolts are not so feathery light.'
He took the shaft—and, oh! thy look,
Sweet Venus! when the shaft he took—
He sighed, and felt the urchin's art;
He sighed, in agony of heart,
'It is not light—I die with pain!
Take—take thy arrow back again.'
'No,' said the child, 'it must not be,
That little dart was made for thee!'

ODE XXIX.

Yes—loving is a painful thrill,
And not to love more painful still;[1]
But surely 'tis the worst of pain,
To love and not be loved again!
Affection now has fled from earth,
Nor fire of genius, light of birth,
Nor heavenly virtue, can beguile
From beauty's cheek one favouring smile.
Gold is the woman's only theme,
Gold is the woman's only dream.
Oh! never be that wretch forgiven—
Forgive him not, indignant Heaven!—
Whose grovelling eyes could first adore,
Whose heart could pant for sordid ore.

Since that devoted thirst began,
Man has forgot to feel for man;
The pulse of social life is dead,
And all its fonder feelings fled!
War too has sullied Nature's charms,
For gold provokes the world to arms!
And oh! the worst of all its art,
I feel it breaks the lover's heart!

ODE XXX.[2]

'Twas in an airy dream of night,
I fancied, that I winged my flight
On pinions fleeter than the wind,
While little Love, whose feet were twined
(I know not why) with chains of lead,
Pursued me as I trembling fled;
Pursued—and could I e'er have thought?—
Swift as the moment I was caught!
What does the wanton Fancy mean
By such a strange, illusive scene?
I fear she whispers to my breast,
That you, my girl, have stolen my rest;
That though my fancy, for a while,
Has hung on many a woman's smile,
I soon dissolved the passing vow,
And ne'er was caught by Love till now!

ODE XXXI.[3]

Armed with hyacinthine rod
(Arms enough for such a god),

Alter, et infusis corrumpit mella venenis,
Unde Cupidineus armavit fama sagittas.
In Cypras' isle two rippling fountains fall,
And one with honey flows, and one with gall;
In these, if we may take the tale from fame,
The son of Venus dips his darts of flame.

See the ninety-first emblem of Alciatus, on the close connection which subsists between sweets and bitterness. 'Apes ideo pungunt,' says Petronius, 'quia ubi dulce, ibi et acidum invenies.'
The allegorical description of Cupid's employment, in Horace, may vie with this before us in fancy, though not in delicacy:

ferus et Cupido
Semper ardentes acuens sagittas
Cote cruenta.

And Cupid, sharpening all his fiery darts
Upon a whetstone stained with blood of hearts.

Secundus has borrowed this, but has somewhat softened the image by the omission of the epithet 'cruenta.'
Fallor an ardentes acuebat cote sagittas.—Eleg. 1.

[1] Menage enforces the necessity of loving in an Anacreontic, of which the following is a translation:—

TO PETER DANIEL HUETT.

Thou! of tuneful bards the first,
Thou! by all the Graces nursed;
Friend! each other friend above,
Come with me, and learn to love.
Loving is a simple lore,
Graver men have learned before;
Nay, the boast of former ages,
Wisest of the wisest sages,

Sophroniscus' prudent son,
Was by Love's illusion won.
Oh! how heavy life would move,
If we knew not how to love!
Love's a whetstone to the mind;
Thus 'tis pointed, thus refined.
When the soul dejected lies,
Love can waft it to the skies;
When in languor sleeps the heart,
Love can wake it with his dart;
When the mind is dull and dark,
Love can light it with his spark!
Come, oh! come then, let us haste
All the bliss of love to taste;
Let us love both night and day,
Let us love our lives away!
And when hearts, from loving free
(If indeed such hearts there be),
Frown upon our gentle flame,
And the sweet delusion blame;
This shall be my only curse,
(Could I, could I wish them worse?)
May they ne'er the rapture prove,
Of the smile from lips we love!

[2] Barnes imagines from this allegory, that our poet married very late in life. I do not perceive anything in the ode which seems to allude to matrimony, except it be the lead upon the feet of Cupid; and I must confess that I agree in the opinion of Madame Dacier, in her life of the poet, that he was always too fond of pleasure to marry.

[3] The design of this little fiction is to intimate, that much greater pain attends insensibility than can ever

Cupid bade me wing my pace,
And try with him the rapid race.
O'er the wild torrent, rude and deep,
By tangled brake and pendent steep,
With weary foot I panting flew,
My brow was chill with drops of dew.
And now my soul, exhausted, dying,
To my lip was faintly flying;[1]
And now I thought the spark had fled,
When Cupid hovered o'er my head,
And, fanning light his breezy plume,
Recalled me from my languid gloom;[2]
Then said, in accents half-reproving,
'Why hast thou been a foe to loving?'

ODE XXXII.[3]

STREW me a breathing bed of leaves
Where lotus with the myrtle weaves;
And, while in luxury's dream I sink,
Let me the balm of Bacchus drink!
In this delicious hour of joy
Young Love shall be my goblet-boy;
Folding his little golden vest,
With cinctures, round his snowy breast,
Himself shall hover by my side,
And minister the racy tide!
Swift as the wheels that kindling roll,
Our life is hurrying to the goal:
A scanty dust to feed the wind,
Is all the trace 'twill leave behind.
Why do we shed the rose's bloom
Upon the cold, insensate tomb!
Can flowery breeze, or odour's breath,
Affect the slumbering chill of death?
No, no; I ask no balm to steep
With fragrant tears my bed of sleep:
But now, while every pulse is glowing,
Now let me breathe the balsam flowing;
Now let the rose with blush of fire
Upon my brow its scent expire;
And bring the nymph with floating eye,
Oh! she will teach me how to die!
Yes, Cupid! ere my soul retire,
To join the blest Elysian choir,
With wine, and love, and blisses dear,
I'll make my own Elysium here!

ODE XXXIII.[4]

'TWAS noon of night, when round the pole
The sullen Bear is seen to roll;
And mortals, wearied with the day,
Are slumbering all their cares away:
An infant, at that dreary hour,
Came weeping to my silent bower,
And waked me with a piteous prayer,
To save him from the midnight air!

---

result from the tenderest impressions of love. Longepierre has quoted an ancient epigram (I do not know where he found it), which has some similitude to this ode:

Lecto compositus, vix prima silentia noctis
Carpebam, et somno lumina victa dabam;
Cum me sævus Amor prensum, sursumque capillis
Excitat, et lacerum pervigilare jubet.
Tu famulus meus, inquit, ames cum mille puellas,
Solus Io, solus, dure jacere potes?
Exilio et pedibus nudis, tunicaque soluta,
Omne iter impedio, nullum iter expedio.
Nunc propero, nunc ire piget; rursumque redire
Pœnitet; et pudor est stare via media.
Ecce tacent voces hominum, strepitusque ferarum,
Et volucrum cantus, turbaque fida canum.
Solus ego ex cunctis paveo somnumque torumque,
Et sequor imperium, sæve Cupido, tuum.

Upon my couch I lay, at night profound,
My languid eyes in magic slumber bound,
When Cupid came and snatched me from my bed,
And forced me many a weary way to tread.
'What!' said the god, 'shall you, whose vows are known,
Who love so many nymphs, thus sleep alone?'
I rise and follow, all the night I stray,
Unsheltered, trembling, doubtful of my way;
Tracing with naked foot the painful track,
Loth to proceed, yet fearful to go back.
Yes, at that hour, when Nature seems interred,
Nor warbling birds nor lowing flocks are heard;
I, I alone, a fugitive from rest,
Passion my guide, and madness in my breast,
Wander the world around, unknowing where,
The slave of love, the victim of despair!

'In the original, he says his heart flew to his nose; but our manner more naturally transfers it to the lips Such is the effect that Plato tells us he felt from a kiss, in a distich, quoted by Aulus Gellius:

Την ψυχην, Αγαθωνα φιλων, επι χειλεσιν εσχον,
Ηλθε γαρ η τλημων ως διαβησομενη.

Whene'er thy nectared kiss I sip,
And drink thy breath, in melting twine,
My soul then flutters to my lip,
Ready to fly and mix with thine.

[2] 'The facility with which Cupid recovers him, signifies that the sweets of love make us easily forget any solicitudes which he may occasion.'—La Fosse.

[3] We here have the poet, in his true attributes, reclining upon myrtles, with Cupid for his cup-bearer. Some interpreters have ruined the picture by making Ερως the name of his slave. None but Love should fill the goblet of Anacreon. Sappho has assigned this office to Venus, in a fragment which may be thus paraphrased:

Hither, Venus! queen of kisses,
This shall be the night of blisses!
This the night, to friendship dear,
Thou shalt be our Hebe here.
Fill the golden brimmer high,
Let it sparkle like thine eye!
Bid the rosy current gush,
Let it mantle like thy blush!
Venus! hast thou e'er above
Seen a feast so rich in love?
Not a soul that is not mine!
Not a soul that is not thine!

[4] Anacreon appears to have been a voluptuary even in dreaming, by the lively regret which he expresses at being disturbed from his visionary enjoyments. See the Odes x. and xxxvii.

'And who art thou,' I waking cry,
'That bid'st my blissful visions fly?'
'O gentle sire!' the infant said,
'In pity take me to thy shed;
Nor fear deceit: a lonely child
I wander o'er the gloomy wild.
Chill drops the rain, and not a ray
Illumes the drear and misty way!'
I hear the baby's tale of woe;
I hear the bitter night-winds blow;
And, sighing for his piteous fate,
I trimmed my lamp, and oped the gate.
'Twas Love! the little wandering sprite,[1]
His pinion sparkled through the night!
I knew him by his bow and dart;
I knew him by my fluttering heart!
I take him in, and fondly raise
The dying embers' cheering blaze;
Press from his dank and clinging hair
The crystals of the freezing air,
And in my hand and bosom hold
His little fingers thrilling cold.
And now the embers' genial ray
Had warmed his anxious fears away;
'I pray thee,' said the wanton child
(My bosom trembled as he smiled),
'I pray thee let me try my bow,
For through the rain I've wandered so,
That much I fear the ceaseless shower
Has injured its elastic power.'
The fatal bow the urchin drew;
Swift from the string the arrow flew;
Oh! swift it flew as glancing flame,
And to my very soul it came!
'Fare thee well,' I heard him say,
As laughing wild he winged away;
'Fare thee well, for now I know
The rain has not relaxed my bow;
It still can send a maddening dart,
As thou shalt own with all thy heart!'

ODE XXXIV.[2]

Oh thou, of all creation blest,
Sweet insect! that delight'st to rest
Upon the wild wood's leafy tops,
To drink the dew that morning drops,
And chirp thy song with such a glee.[3]
That happiest kings may envy thee!
Whatever decks the velvet field,
Whate'er the circling seasons yield,
Whatever buds, whatever blows,
For thee it buds, for thee it grows.
Nor yet art thou the peasant's fear,
To him thy friendly notes are dear;
For thou art mild as matin dew,
And still, when summer's flowery hue
Begins to paint the bloomy plain,
We hear thy sweet prophetic strain;
Thy sweet prophetic strain we hear,
And bless the notes and thee revere!
The Muses love thy shrilly tone;
Apollo calls thee all his own;
'Twas he who gave that voice to thee,
'Tis he who tunes thy minstrelsy.
Unworn by age's dim decline,
The fadeless blooms of youth are thine.
Melodious insect! child of earth![4]
In wisdom mirthful, wise in mirth;
Exempt from every weak decay,
That withers vulgar frames away;
With not a drop of blood to stain
The current of thy purer vein;
So blest an age is passed by thee,
Thou seem'st a little deity!

ODE XXXV.[5]

Cupid once upon a bed
Of roses laid his weary head;

---

[1] See the beautiful description of Cupid, by Moschus in his first Idyl.

[2] Father Rapin, in a Latin ode addressed to the grasshopper, has preserved some of the thoughts of our author:

O quæ virenti graminis in toro,
Cicada, blande sidis, et herbidos
    Saltus obcrras, otiosos
    Ingeniosa ciere cantus.
Seu forte adultis floribus incubas,
Cœli caducis ebria fletibus, etc.

Oh thou, that on the grassy bed
Which Nature's vernal hand has spread,
Reclinest soft, and tun'st thy song,
The dewy herbs and leaves among!
Whether thou liest on springing flowers,
Drunk with the balmy morning-showers,
    Or, etc.

See what Licetus says about grasshoppers, cap. 93 and 185.

[3] 'Some authors have affirmed (says Madame Dacier) that it is only male grasshoppers which sing, and that the females are silent; and on this circumstance is founded a bon-mot of Xenarchus, the comic poet, who says, "Are not the grasshoppers happy in having dumb wives?"' This note is originally Henry Stephens'; but I chose rather to make Madame Dacier my authority for it.

[4] Longepierre has quoted the two first lines of an epigram of Antipater from the first book of the *Anthologia*, where he prefers the grasshopper to the swan:

Αρκει τεττιγας μεθυσαι δροσος, αλλα πιοντες
Αιδων κυκνων ισι γηγωνοτεροι.

In dew, that drops from morning's wings,
    The gay Cicada sipping floats;
And, drunk with dew, his matin sings
    Sweeter than any cygnet's notes.

[5] Theocritus has imitated this beautiful ode in his nineteenth Idyl, but is very inferior, I think, to his original, in delicacy of point and *naïveté* of expression. Spenser, in one of his smaller compositions, has sported more diffusely on the same subject. The poem to which I allude begins thus:

Upon a day, as Love lay sweetly slumbering
All in his mother's lap,
A gentle bee, with his loud trumpet murmuring,
About him flew by hap, etc.

In Almeloveen's collection of epigrams, there is one by Luxorius, correspondent somewhat with the turn of

Luckless urchin not to see
Within the leaves a slumbering bee!
The bee awaked—with anger wild
The bee awaked and stung the child.
Loud and piteous are his cries;
To Venus quick he runs, he flies!
'Oh mother!—I am wounded through—
I die with pain—in sooth I do!
Stung by some little angry thing,
Some serpent on a tiny wing—
A bee it was—for once, I know,
I heard a rustic call it so.'
Thus he spoke, and she the while
Heard him with a soothing smile;
Then said, ' My infant, if so much
Thou feel the little wild bee's touch,
How must the heart, ah, Cupid! be,
The hapless heart that's stung by thee!'

ODE XXXVI.[1]

If hoarded gold possessed a power
To lengthen life's too fleeting hour,
And purchase from the hand of death
A little span, a moment's breath,

How I would love the precious ore!
And every day should swell my store;
That when the Fates would send their minion,
To waft me off on shadowy pinion,
I might some hours of life obtain,
And bribe him back to hell again.
But, since we ne'er can charm away
The mandate of that awful day,
Why do we vainly weep at fate,
And sigh for life's uncertain date?
The light of gold can ne'er illume
The dreary midnight of the tomb!
And why should I then pant for treasures?
Mine be the brilliant round of pleasures;
The goblet rich, the board of friends,
Whose flowing souls the goblet blends![2]
Mine be the nymph whose form reposes
Seductive on that bed of roses;
And oh! be mine the soul's excess,
Expiring in her warm caress!

ODE XXXVII.[3]

'TWAS night, and many a circling bowl
Had deeply warmed my swimming soul;

Anacreon, where Love complains to his mother of being wounded by a rose.

The ode before us is the very flower of simplicity. The infantine complainings of the little god, and the natural and impressive reflections which they draw from Venus, are beauties of inimitable grace. I hope I shall be pardoned for introducing another Greek Anacreontic of Menage, not for its similitude to the subject of this ode, but for some faint traces of this natural simplicity, which it appears to me to have preserved:

Ερως ποτ' εν χορωαις
Των παρθενων αυτος
Την μοι φιλην Κορινναν
'Ως ειδεν, ως προς αυτην
Ηροσεδραμε τραχηλω
Διδυμας τι χηρας απτων
Φιλει μοι, μητειρ, ωπι.
Καλουμενη Κοριννα
Μητερ, ερυθριαζει,
Ος παρθενος μεν ουσα.
Κ' αυτος δε δυσχεραινον,
'Ως ομμασι πλανηθεις,
Ερως ερυθριαζει.
Εγω δε οι παροντες,
Μη δυσχεραινε, φημι.
Κυπρις τε και Κοριννα
Διαγνωσαι ουκ ιχουσι
Και οι βλεποντες οξυ.

As dancing o'er the enamelled plain,
The floweret of the virgin train,
My soul's Corinna, lightly played,
Young Cupid saw the graceful maid;
He saw, and in a moment flew,
And round her neck his arms he threw;
And said, with smiles of infant joy,
'Oh! kiss me, mother, kiss thy boy!'
Unconscious of a mother's name,
The modest virgin blushed with shame!
And angry Cupid, scarce believing
That vision could be so deceiving,

Thus to mistake his Cyprian dame,
The little infant blushed with shame.
'Be not ashamed, my boy,' I cried,
For I was lingering by his side;
'Corinna and thy lovely mother,
Believe me, are so like each other,
That clearest eyes are oft betrayed,
And take thy Venus for the maid.'

Zitto, in his *Cappricciosi Pensieri*, has translated this ode of Anacreon.

[1] Fontenelle has translated this ode, in his dialogue between Anacreon and Aristotle in the shades, where he bestows the prize of wisdom upon the poet.

[2] This communion of friendship, which sweetened the bowl of Anacreon, has not been forgotten by the author of the following scholium, where the blessings of life are enumerated with proverbial simplicity:

Of mortal blessings here, the first is health,
And next, those charms by which the eye we move;
The third is wealth, unwounding, guiltless wealth,
And then, an intercourse with those we love!

[3] 'Compare with this ode the beautiful poem, *der Traum of Us.*'—Degen. Le Fevre, in a note upon this ode, enters into an elaborate and learned justification of drunkenness; and this is probably the cause of the severe reprehension which I believe he suffered for his Anacreon. ' Fuit olim fateor (says he, in a note upon Longinus), cum Sapphonem amabam. Sed ex quo illa me perditissima fœmina pene miserum perdidit cum sceleratissimo suo congerrone (Anacreontem dico, si nescis Lector), noli sperare,' etc. etc. He adduces on this ode the authority of Plato, who allowed ebriety, at the Dionysian festivals, to men arrived at their fortieth year. He likewise quotes the following line from Alexis, which he says no one, who is not totally ignorant of the world, can hesitate to confess the truth of:

Ουδεις φιλοποτης εστιν ανθρωπος κακος.

'No lover of drinking was ever a vicious man.'

As lulled in slumber I was laid,
Bright visions o'er my fancy played!
With virgins, blooming as the dawn,
I seemed to trace the opening lawn;
Light, on tiptoe bathed in dew,
We flew, and sported as we flew!
Some ruddy striplings, young and sleek,
With blush of Bacchus on their cheek,
Saw me trip the flowery wild
With dimpled girls, and slyly smiled—
Smiled indeed with wanton glee;
But ah! 'twas plain they envied me.
And still I flew—and now I caught
The panting nymphs, and fondly thought
To kiss—when all my dream of joys,
Dimpled girls and ruddy boys,
All were gone![1] 'Alas!' I said,
Sighing for the illusions fled,
'Sleep! again my joys restore,
Oh! let me dream them o'er and o'er!'[2]

ODE XXXVIII.

LET us drain the nectared bowl,
Let us raise the song of soul
To him, the god who loves so well
The nectared bowl, the choral swell!
Him, who instructs the sons of earth
To thrid the tangled dance of mirth;
Him, who was nursed with infant Love,
And cradled in the Paphian grove;
Him, that the snowy Queen of Charms
Has fondled in her twining arms.
From him that dream of transport flows,
Which sweet intoxication knows;

[1] Nonnus says of Bacchus, almost in the same words that Anacreon uses:

Εγρομενος δε
Παρθενον ουκ ιαιχηει, και ηθελεν αυθις ιαυειν.

Waking, he lost the phantom's charms,
He found no beauty in his arms;
Again to slumber he essayed,
Again to clasp the shadowy maid!
—*Longepierre.*

[2] Doctor Johnson, in his preface to Shakspeare, animadverting upon the commentators of that poet, who pretended in every little coincidence of thought to detect an imitation of some ancient poet, alludes in the following words to the line of Anacreon before us: 'I have been told that when Caliban, after a pleasing dream, says, "I tried to sleep again," the author imitates Anacreon, who had, like any other man, the same wish on the same occasion.'

[3] The brevity of life allows arguments for the voluptuary as well as the moralist. Among many parallel passages which Longepierre has adduced, I shall content myself with this epigram from the *Anthologia*:

Λουσαμενοι, Προδικη, συκασωμεθα, και τον ακρατον
Ελκωμεν, κυλικας μειζονας αιρομενοι.
'Ραιος ο χαιροντων εστι βιος· ειτα τα λοιπα
Γηρας κωλυσει, και το τελος θανατος·

Of which the following is a loose paraphrase:

With him the brow forgets to darkle,
And brilliant graces learn to sparkle.
Behold! my boys a goblet bear,
Whose sunny foam bedews the air.
Where are now the tear, the sigh?
To the winds they fly, they fly!
Grasp the bowl; in nectar sinking,
Man of sorrow, drown thy thinking!
Oh! can the tears we lend to thought
In life's account avail us aught?
Can we discern, with all our lore,
The path we're yet to journey o'er?
No, no, the walk of life is dark,
'Tis wine alone can strike a spark![3]
Then let me quaff the foamy tide,
And through the dance meandering glide;
Let me imbibe the spicy breath
Of odours chafed to fragrant death;
Or from the kiss of love inhale
A more voluptuous, richer gale!
To souls that court the phantom Care,
Let him retire and shroud him there;
While we exhaust the nectared bowl,
And swell the choral song of soul
To him, the god who loves so well
The nectared bowl, the choral swell!

ODE XXXIX.

How I love the festive boy,
Tripping with the dance of joy!
How I love the mellow sage,
Smiling through the veil of age!
And whene'er this man of years
In the dance of joy appears,
Age is on his temples hung,
But his heart—his heart is young![4]

Fly, my beloved, to yonder stream,
We'll plunge us from the noontide beam!
Then cull the rose's humid bud,
And dip it in our goblet's flood.
Our age of bliss, my nymph, shall fly
As sweet, though passing, as that sigh
Which seems to whisper o'er your lip,
'Come, while you may, of rapture sip.'
For age will steal the rosy form,
And chill the pulse, which trembles warm!
And death—alas! that hearts, which thrill
Like yours and mine, should e'er be still!

[4] Saint Pavin makes the same distinction in a sonnet to a young girl:

Je sais bien que les destinées
Ont mal compassé nos années;
Ne regardez que mon amour.
Peut-être en serez vous émue:
Il est jeune, et n'est que du jour,
Belle Iris, que je vous ai vue.

Fair and young, thou bloomest now,
And I full many a year have told;
But read the heart and not the brow,
Thou shalt not find my love is old.

My love's a child; and thou canst say
How much his little age may be,
For he was born the very day
That first I set my eyes on thee!

ODE XL.

I know that Heaven ordains me here
To run this mortal life's career;
The scenes which I have journeyed o'er
Return no more—alas! no more;
And all the path I've yet to go
I neither know nor ask to know.
Then surely, Care, thou canst not twine
Thy fetters round a soul like mine;
No, no, the heart that feels with me
Can never be a slave to thee!¹
And oh! before the vital thrill,
Which trembles at my heart, is still,
I'll gather joy's luxurious flowers,
And gild with bliss my fading hours;
Bacchus shall bid my winter bloom,
And Venus dance me to the tomb!²

ODE XLI.

When Spring begems the dewy scene,
How sweet to walk the velvet green,
And hear the Zephyr's languid sighs,
As o'er the scented mead he flies!
How sweet to mark the pouting vine,
Ready to fall in tears of wine;
And with the maid whose every sigh
Is love and bliss, entranced to lie³
Where the embowering branches meet—
Oh! is not this divinely sweet?

ODE XLII.⁴

Yes, be the glorious revel mine,
Where humour sparkles from the wine!

Around me let the youthful choir
Respond to my beguiling lyre;
And while the red cup circles round,
Mingle in soul as well as sound!
Let the bright nymph, with trembling eye,
Beside me all in blushes lie;
And, while she weaves a frontlet fair
Of hyacinth to deck my hair,
Oh! let me snatch her sidelong kisses,
And that shall be my bliss of blisses!
My soul, to festive feeling true,
One pang of envy never knew;
And little has it learned to dread
The gall that Envy's tongue can shed.
Away—I hate the slanderous dart,
Which steals to wound the unwary heart;
And oh! I hate, with all my soul,
Discordant clamours o'er the bowl,
Where every cordial heart should be
Attuned to peace and harmony.
Come, let us hear the soul of song
Expire the silver harp along;
And through the dance's ringlet move,
With maidens mellowing into love;
Thus simply happy, thus at peace,
Sure such a life should never cease!

ODE XLIII.

While our rosy fillets shed
Blushes o'er each fervid head,
With many a cup and many a smile
The festal moments we beguile.
And while the harp, impassioned, flings
Tuneful rapture from the strings,⁵

---

¹ Longepierre quotes an epigram here from the *Anthologia*, on account of the similarity of a particular phrase. It is by no means Anacreontic, but has an interesting simplicity which induced me to paraphrase it, and may atone for its intrusion:

At length to Fortune, and to you,
Delusive Hope! a last adieu.
The charm that once beguiled is o'er,
And I have reached my destined shore!
Away, away, your flattering arts
May now betray some simpler hearts,
And you will smile at their believing,
And they shall weep at your deceiving!

² The same commentator has quoted an epitaph, written upon our poet by Julian, where he makes him give the precepts of good fellowship even from the tomb:

This lesson oft in life I sung,
And from my grave I still shall cry,
'Drink, mortal! drink, while time is young,
Ere death has made thee cold as I.'

³ Thus Horace:
    Quid habes illius, illius
    Quæ spirabat amores,
    Quæ me surpuerat mihi.

And does there then remain but this,
And hast thou lost each rosy ray

Of her, who breathed the soul of bliss,
And stole me from myself away?

⁴ The character of Anacreon is here very strikingly depicted. His love of social, harmonized pleasures is expressed with a warmth, amiable and endearing. Among the epigrams imputed to Anacreon is the following; it is the only one worth translation, and it breathes the same sentiments with this ode:

Ου φιλος, ὁς κρητηρι παρα πλιω οινοποταζων,
Νεικεα και πολεμον δακρυοεντα λιγει.
Αλλ' ὁστις Μουσεων τε, και αγλαα δωρ' Αφροδιτης
Ευμμισγων, ἐρατης μνησκεται ευφροσυνης.

When to the lip the brimming cup is pressed,
And hearts are all afloat upon the stream,
Then banish from my board the unpolished guest
Who makes the feats of war his barbarous theme.

But bring the man, who o'er his goblet wreathes
The Muse's laurel with the Cyprian flower:
Oh! give me him whose heart expansive breathes
All the refinements of the social hour.

⁵ On the barbiton a host of authorities may be collected, which, after all, leave us ignorant of the nature of the instrument. There is scarcely any point upon which we are so totally uninformed as the music of the ancients. The authors ex'ant upon the subject are, I imagine, little understood; but certainly, if one of

Some airy nymph, with fluent limbs,
Through the dance luxuriant swims,
Waving, in her snowy hand,
The leafy Bacchanalian wand,
Which, as the tripping wanton flies,
Shakes its tresses to her sighs!
A youth, the while, with loosened hair
Floating on the listless air,
Sings, to the wild harp's tender tone,
A tale of woes, alas! his own;
And then, what nectar in his sigh,
As o'er his lip the murmurs die!¹
Surely never yet has been
So divine, so blest a scene!
Has Cupid left the starry sphere,
To wave his golden tresses here?²
Oh yes! and Venus, queen of wiles,
And Bacchus, shedding rosy smiles,
All, all are here, to hail with me
The Genius of Festivity!³

ODE XLIV.⁴

Buds of roses, virgin flowers,
Culled from Cupid's balmy bowers,
In the bowl of Bacchus steep,
Till with crimson drops they weep!
Twine the rose, the garland twine,
Every leaf distilling wine;
Drink and smile, and learn to think
That we were born to smile and drink.
Rose! thou art the sweetest flower
That ever drank the amber shower;
Rose! thou art the fondest child
Of dimpled Spring, the wood-nymph wild!
Even the gods, who walk the sky,
Are amorous of thy scented sigh.

Cupid too, in Paphian shades,
His hair with rosy fillet braids,
When, with the blushing naked Graces,
The wanton winding dance he traces.
Then bring me showers of roses, bring,
And shed them round me while I sing;
Great Bacchus! in thy hallowed shade,
With some celestial, glowing maid,
While gales of roses round me rise,
In perfume sweetened by her sighs,
I'll bill and twine in early dance,
Commingling soul with every glance!

ODE XLV.

Within this goblet, rich and deep,
I cradle all my woes to sleep.
Why should we breathe the sigh of fear,
Or pour the unavailing tear?
For Death will never heed the sigh,
Nor soften at the tearful eye;
And eyes that sparkle, eyes that weep,
Must all alike be sealed in sleep:
Then let us never vainly stray,
In search of thorns, from pleasure's way;
Oh! let us quaff the rosy wave
Which Bacchus loves, which Bacchus gave;
And in the goblet, rich and deep,
Cradle our crying woes to sleep!

ODE XLVI.⁵

See, the young, the rosy Spring,
Gives to the breeze her spangled wing;

their moods was a progression by quarter-tones, which we are told was the nature of the enharmonic scale, simplicity was by no means the characteristic of their melody; for this is a nicety of progression of which modern music is not susceptible.

The invention of the barbiton is, by Athenæus, attributed to Anacreon. Neanthes of Cyzicus, as quoted by Gyraldus, asserts the same. *Vide Chabot. in Horat.* on the words 'Lesboum barbiton,' in the first ode.

¹ Longepierre has quoted here an epigram from the *Anthologia*, of which the following may give some idea:

The kiss that she left on my lip
Like a dew-drop shall lingering lie;
'Twas nectar she gave me to sip,
'Twas nectar I drank in her sigh!

The dew that distilled in that kiss,
To my soul was voluptuous wine;
Ever since it is drunk with the bliss,
And feels the delirium divine!

² The introduction of these deities to the festival is merely allegorical. Madame Dacier thinks that the poet describes a masquerade, where these deities were personated by the company in masks. The translation will conform with either idea.

³ Κωμος, the deity or genius of mirth. Philostratus, in the third of his pictures (as all the annotators have observed), gives a very beautiful description of this god.

⁴ This spirited poem is a eulogy on the rose; and again, in the fifty-fifth ode, we shall find our author rich in the praises of that flower. In a fragment of Sappho, in the romance of Achilles Tatius, to which Barnes refers us, the rose is very elegantly styled 'the eye of flowers;' and the same poetess, in another fragment, calls the favours of the Muse 'the roses of Pieria.' See the notes on the fifty-fifth ode.

⁵ The fastidious affectation of some commentators has denounced this ode as spurious. Degen pronounces the four last lines to be the putchwork of some miserable versificator, and Brunck condemns the whole ode. It appears to me to be elegantly graphical; full of delicate expressions and luxuriant imagery. Barnes conjectures, in his Life of our poet, that this ode was written after he had returned from Athens, to settle in his paternal seat at Teos: there, in a little villa at some distance from the city, which commanded a view of the Ægean Sea and the islands, he contemplated the beauties of nature, and enjoyed the felicities of retirement. *Vide Barnes, in Anac. vita,* sec. xxxv. This supposition, however unauthenticated, forms a pleasant association, which makes the poem more interesting.

While virgin Graces, warm with May,
Fling roses o'er her dewy way!
The murmuring billows of the deep
Have languished into silent sleep;
And mark! the flitting sea-birds lave
Their plumes in the reflecting wave;
While cranes from hoary winter fly
To flutter in a kinder sky.
Now the genial star of day
Dissolves the murky clouds away;
And cultured field, and winding stream,
Are sweetly tissued by his beam.
Now the earth prolific swells
With leafy buds and flowery bells;
Gemming shoots the olive twine,
Clusters ripe festoon the vine;
All along the branches creeping,
Through the velvet foliage peeping,
Little infant fruits we see
Nursing into luxury!

ODE XLVII.

'Tis true, my fading years decline,
Yet I can quaff the brimming wine
As deep as any stripling fair
Whose cheeks the flush of morning wear;
And if, amidst the wanton crew,
I'm called to wind the dance's clue,
Thou shalt behold this vigorous hand
Not faltering on the bacchant's wand,
But brandishing a rosy flask,¹
The only thyrsus e'er I'll ask!²
Let those who pant for Glory's charms
Embrace her in the field of arms;
While my inglorious, placid soul
Breathes not a wish beyond the bowl.
Then fill it high, my ruddy slave,
And bathe me in its honeyed wave!
For, though my fading years decay,
And though my bloom has passed away,
Like old Silenus, sire divine,
With blushes borrowed from my wine,
I'll wanton 'mid the dancing train,
And live my follies all again!

ODE XLVIII.

When my thirsty soul I steep,
Every sorrow's lulled to sleep.
Talk of monarchs! I am then
Richest, happiest, first of men;
Careless o'er my cup I sing,
Fancy makes me more than king;
Gives me wealthy Crœsus' store,
Can I, can I, wish for more?
On my velvet couch reclining,
Ivy leaves my brow entwining,³
While my soul dilates with glee,
What are kings and crowns to me?
If before my feet they lay,
I would spurn them all away!
Arm you, arm you, men of might,
Hasten to the sanguine fight;⁴
Let me, oh, my budding vine!
Spill no other blood than thine.
Yonder brimming goblet see,
That alone shall vanquish me;
Oh! I think it sweeter far
To fall in banquet than in war!

ODE XLIX.⁵

When Bacchus, Jove's immortal boy,
The rosy harbinger of joy,
Who, with the sunshine of the bowl,
Thaws the winter of our soul;
When to my inmost core he glides,
And bathes it with his ruby tides,
A flow of joy, a lively heat,
Fires my brain, and wings my feet!
'Tis surely something sweet, I think,
Nay, something heavenly sweet, to drink!
Sing, sing of love, let Music's breath
Softly beguile our rapturous death,
While, my young Venus, thou and I
To the voluptuous cadence die!
Then waking from our languid trance,
Again we'll sport, again we'll dance.

---

¹ Αρνος was a kind of leathern vessel for wine, very much in use, as should seem by the proverb αρνος και θυλακος, which was applied to those who were intemperate in eating and drinking. This proverb is mentioned in some verses quoted by Athenæus from the *Ilusions* of Alexis.

² Phornutus assigns as a reason for the consecration of the thyrsus to Bacchus, that inebriety often renders the support of a stick very necessary.

³ 'The ivy was consecrated to Bacchus (says Montfaucon), because he formerly lay hid under that tree, or, as others will have it, because its leaves resemble those of the vine.' Other reasons for its consecration, and the use of it in garlands at banquets, may be found in Longepierre, Barnes, etc. etc.

⁴ I have adopted the interpretation of Regnier and others:

Altri segua Marte fero;
Che sol Bacco è 'l mio conforto.

⁵ This, the preceding ode, and a few more of the same character, are merely *chansons à boire*. Most likely they were the effusions of the moment of conviviality, and were sung, we imagine, with rapture in Greece; but that interesting association, by which they always recalled the convivial emotions that produced them, can be very little felt by the most enthusiastic reader; and much less by a phlegmatic grammarian, who sees nothing in them but dialects and particles.

ODE L.[1]

When I drink, I feel, I feel,
Visions of poetic zeal![2]
Warm with the goblet's freshening dews,
My heart invokes the heavenly Muse.
When I drink, my sorrow's o'er;
I think of doubts and fears no more;
But scatter to the railing wind
Each gloomy phantom of the mind!
When I drink, the jesting boy,
Bacchus himself, partakes my joy;
And, while we dance through breathing bowers,
Whose every gale is rich with flowers,
In bowls he makes my senses swim,
Till the gale breathes of nought but him!
When I drink, I deftly twine
Flowers begemmed with tears of wine;
And, while with festive hand I spread
The smiling garland round my head,
Something whispers in my breast,
How sweet it is to live at rest!
When I drink, and perfume stills
Around me all in balmy rills,
Then as some beauty, smiling roses,
In languor on my breast reposes,
Venus! I breathe my vows to thee,
In many a sigh of luxury!
When I drink, my heart refines,
And rises as the cup declines,—
Rises in the genial flow
That none but social spirits know,
When youthful revellers, round the bowl,
Dilating, mingle soul with soul![3]
When I drink, the bliss is mine,—
There's bliss in every drop of wine!
All other joys that I have known,
I've scarcely dared to call my own;
But this the Fates can ne'er destroy,
Till Death o'ershadows all my joy!

ODE LI.[4]

Fly not thus, my brow of snow,
Lovely wanton! fly not so.
Though the wane of age is mine,
Though the brilliant flush is thine,
Still I'm doomed to sigh for thee,
Blest, if thou could'st sigh for me!
See, in yonder flowery braid,
Culled for thee, my blushing maid,[5]
How the rose, of orient glow,
Mingles with the lily's snow;
Mark how sweet their tints agree,
Just, my girl, like thee and me!

ODE LII.[6]

Away, away, you men of rules,
What have I to do with schools?
They'd make me learn, they'd make me think,
But would they make me love and drink?

---

[1] Faber thinks this spurious; but I believe he is singular in his opinion. It has all the spirit of our author. Like the wreath which he presented in the dream, 'it smells of Anacreon.'
The form of this ode in the original is remarkable. It is a kind of song of seven quatrain stanzas, each beginning with the line:

'Οτ' εγω πιω τον οινον.

The first stanza alone is incomplete, consisting but of three lines.

[2] 'Anacreon is not the only one (says Longepierre) whom wine has inspired with poetry. There is an epigram in the first book of the *Anthologia*, which begins thus:

Οινος τοι χαριεντι μεγας πελει ιππος αοιδω,
'Τδωρ δι πινων, καλον ου τιξαις εποι.'

If with water you fill up your glasses,
You'll never write anything wise;
For wine is the horse of Parnassus,
Which hurries a bard to the skies!

[3] Subjoined to Gail's edition of Anacreon, there are some curious letters upon the Θιασοι of the ancients, which appeared in the French journals. At the opening of the Odeon, in Paris, the managers of the spectacle requested Professor Gail to give them some uncommon name for the fêtes of this institution. He suggested the word 'Thiase,' which was adopted; but the *literati* of Paris questioned the propriety of it, and addressed their criticisms to Gail, through the medium of the public prints. Two or three of the letters he has inserted in his edition, and they have elicited from him some learned research on the subject.

[4] Alberti has imitated this ode; and Capilupus, in the following epigram, has given a version of it:

Cur, Lalage, mea vita, meos contemnis amores?
 Cur fugis e nostro pulchra puella sinu?
Ne fugias, sint sparsa licet mea tempora canis,
 Inque tuo roseus fulgeat ore color.
Aspice ut intextas deceant quoque flore corollas
 Candida purpureis lilia mixta rosis.

Oh! why repel my soul's impassioned vow,
And fly, beloved maid, these longing arms?
Is it that wintry time has strewed my brow,
 And thine are all the summer's roseate charms?

See the rich garland, culled in vernal weather,
Where the young rosebud with the lily glows;
In wreaths of love we thus may twine together,
 And I will be the lily, thou the rose!

[5] 'In the same manner that Anacreon pleads for the whiteness of his locks, from the beauty of the colour in garlands, a shepherd, in Theocritus, endeavours to recommend his black hair:

Και το ιον μελαν εστι, και ά γραπτα υακινθος
Αλλ' ιμπας εν τοις στιφανοις τα πρωτα λεγονται.'
— *Longepierre, Barnes*, etc.

[6] This is doubtless the work of a more modern poet than Anacreon; for at the period when he lived rhetoricians were not known.—*Degen.*
Though the antiquity of this ode is confirmed by the Vatican manuscript, I am very much inclined to agree in this argument against its authenticity; for, though the dawnings of rhetoric might already have appeared

Teach me this, and let me swim
My soul upon the goblet's brim;
Teach me this, and let me twine
My arms around the nymph divine![1]
Age begins to blanch my brow,
I've time for nought but pleasure now.
Fly, and cool my goblet's glow
At yonder fountain's gelid flow;
I'll quaff, my boy, and calmly sink
This soul to slumber as I drink!
Soon, too soon, my jocund slave,
You'll deck your master's grassy grave;
And there's an end—for ah! you know,
They drink but little wine below![2]

ODE LIII.

WHEN I behold the festive train
Of dancing youth, I'm young again!
Memory wakes her magic trance,
And wings me lightly through the dance.
Come, Cybeba, smiling maid!
Cull the flower and twine the braid;
Bid the blush of summer's rose
Burn upon my brow of snows;[3]
And let me, while the wild and young
Trip the mazy dance along,
Fling my heap of years away,
And be as wild, as young as they.

Hither haste, some cordial soul!
Give my lips the brimming bowl;
Oh! you will see this hoary sage
Forget his locks, forget his age.
He still can chaunt the festive hymn,
He still can kiss the goblet's brim;[4]
He still can act the mellow raver,
And play the fool as sweet as ever!

ODE LIV.[5]

METHINKS the pictured bull we see
Is amorous Jove—it must be he!
How fondly blest he seems to bear
The fairest of Phœnician fair!
How proud he breasts the foamy tide,
And spurns the billowy surge aside!
Could any beast of vulgar vein
Undaunted thus defy the main?
No: he descends from climes above,
He looks the god, he breathes of Jove![6]

ODE LV.[7]

WHILE we invoke the wreathèd spring,
Resplendent rose! to thee we'll sing;
Resplendent rose! the flower of flowers,
Whose breath perfumes Olympus' bowers;

---

the first who gave it any celebrity was Corax of Syracuse, and he flourished in the century after Anacreon.
Our poet anticipated the ideas of Epicurus, in his aversion to the labours of learning as well as his devotion to voluptuousness. Πασαι παιδειαι μακαριε φευγετε, said the philosopher of the garden in a letter to Pythocles.

[1] By χρυσης Αφροδιτης here, I understand some beautiful girl; in the same manner that Αναιοε is often used for wine. 'Golden' is frequently an epithet of beauty. Thus in Virgil, 'Venus aurea,' and in Propertius, 'Cynthia aurea.' Tibullus, however, calls an old woman 'golden.'

[2] Thus the witty Mainard:

La Mort nous guette; et quand ses lois
Nous ont enfermés une fois
Au sein d'une fosse profonde,
Adieu bons vins et bons repas,
Ma science ne trouve pas
Des cabarets en l'autre monde.

[3] 'It appears that wreaths of flowers were adapted for poets and revellers at banquets, but by no means became those who had pretensions to wisdom and philosophy.' On this principle, in his 152d chapter, Licetus discovers a refinement in Virgil, describing the garland of the poet Silenus as fallen off; which distinguishes, he thinks, the divine intoxication of Silenus from that of common drunkards, who always wear their crowns while they drink. This, indeed, is the 'labor ineptisrum' of commentators.

[4] Wine is prescribed by Galen as an excellent medicine for old men, 'Quod frigidos et humoribus expletos calefaciat,' etc.; but nature was Anacreon's physician.
There is a proverb in Eriphus, as quoted by Athenæus,

which says, 'that wine makes an old man dance whether he will or not.'

Λογος ιστ' αρχαιος, ου κακως ιχων,
Οινον λιγουσι τους γιροντας, ω πατιρ,
Πιιθιιν χορευιν ου θιλοντας.

[5] 'This ode is written upon a picture which represented the rape of Europa.'—*Madame Dacier.*
It may perhaps be considered as a description of one of those coins which the Sidonians struck off in honour of Europa, representing a woman carried across the sea by a bull. Thus *Natalis Comes,* lib. viii. cap. 23: 'Sidonii numismata cum fœmina tauri dorso insidente ac mare transfretante, cudorunt in ejus honorem.' In the little treatise upon the goddess of Syria, attributed very falsely to Lucian, there is mention of this coin, and of a temple dedicated by the Sidonians to Astarte, whom some, it appears, confounded with Europa. Moschus has written a very beautiful idyl on the story of Europa.

[6] Thus Moschus:

Κρυψι θιον και τρεψι διμας και γινιτο ταυρος.

The God forgot himself, his heaven, for love,
And a bull's form belied the almighty Jove.

[7] This ode is a brilliant panegyric on the rose. 'All antiquity (says Barnes) has produced nothing more beautiful.'
From the idea of peculiar excellence which the ancients attached to this flower, arose a pretty proverbial expression, used by Aristophanes, according to Suidas, ῥοδα μ' ιιρηκας, 'You have spoken roses,' a phrase somewhat similar to the 'dire des fleurettes' of the French. In the same idea of excellence originated, I doubt not, a very curious application of the word ῥοδον, for which the inquisitive reader may consult

Whose virgin blush, of chastened dye,
Enchants so much our mortal eye.
When Pleasure's bloomy season glows,
The Graces love to twine the rose;
The rose is warm Dione's bliss,
And flushes like Dione's kiss!
Oft has the poet's magic tongue
The rose's fair luxuriance sung;
And long the Muses, heavenly maids,
Have reared it in their tuneful shades.
When, at the early glance of morn,
It sleeps upon the glittering thorn,
'Tis sweet to dare the tangled fence,
To cull the timid floweret thence,
And wipe, with tender hand, away
The tear that on its blushes lay!
'Tis sweet to hold the infant stems,
Yet dropping with Aurora's gems,
And fresh inhale the spicy sighs
That from the weeping buds arise.
When revel reigns, when mirth is high,
And Bacchus beams in every eye,
Our rosy fillets scent exhale,
And fill with balm the fainting gale!
Oh, there is nought in nature bright,
Where roses do not shed their light!
When morning paints the orient skies,
Her fingers burn with roseate dyes;[1]
The nymphs display the rose's charms,
It mantles o'er their graceful arms;
Through Cytherea's form it glows,
And mingles with the living snows.
The rose distils a healing balm,
The beating pulse of pain to calm;
Preserves the cold inurned clay,[2]
And mocks the vestige of decay:

And when, at length, in pale decline,
Its florid beauties fade and pine,
Sweet as in youth, its balmy breath
Diffuses odour e'en in death!
Oh! whence could such a plant have sprung?
Attend—for thus the tale is sung.
When, humid, from the silvery stream,
Effusing beauty's warmest beam,
Venus appeared, in flushing hues,
Mellowed by Ocean's briny dews;
When, in the starry courts above,
The pregnant brain of mighty Jove
Disclosed the nymph of azure glance,
The nymph who shakes the martial lance!
Then, then, in strange eventful hour,
The earth produced an infant flower,
Which sprung, with blushing tinctures dressed,
And wantoned o'er its parent breast.
The gods beheld this brilliant birth,
And hailed the Rose, the boon of earth!
With nectar drops, a ruby tide,
The sweetly orient buds they dyed,[3]
And bade them bloom, the flowers divine
Of him who sheds the teeming vine;
And bade them on the spangled thorn
Expand their bosoms to the morn.

ODE LVI.[4]

HE, who instructs the youthful crew
To bathe them in the brimmer's dew,
And taste, uncloyed by rich excesses,
All the bliss that wine possesses!

Gaulminus upon the epithalamium of our poet, where it is introduced in the romance of Theodorus. Muretus, in one of his elegies, calls his mistress his rose:

Jam te igitur rursus teneo, formosula, jam te
(Quid trepidas?) teneo; jam, rosa, te teneo.—*Eleg.* 8.

Now I again embrace thee, dearest,
(Tell me, wanton, why thou fearest?)
Again my longing arms infold thee,
Again, my rose, again I hold thee.

This, like most of the terms of endearment in the modern Latin poets, is taken from Plautus: they were vulgar and colloquial in his time, and they are among the elegances of the modern Latinists.

[1] In the original here, he enumerates the many epithets of beauty, borrowed from roses, which were used by the poets, ϰαρα τον ϱοδων. We see that poets were dignified in Greece with the title of sages; even the careless Anacreon, who lived but for love and voluptuousness, was called by Plato the wise Anacreon. *Fuit hæc sapientia quondam.*

[2] He here alludes to the use of the rose in embalming, and perhaps (as Barnes thinks) to the rosy unguent with which Venus anointed the corpse of Hector. It may likewise regard the ancient practice of putting garlands of roses on the dead, as in Statius, *Theb.* lib. x. 782:

Hi sertis, hi veris honore soluto
Accumulant artus patriaque in sede reponunt
Coryms odoratum,—

where 'veris honor,' though it means every kind of flowers, may seem more particularly to refer to the rose. We read, in the Hieroglyphics of Pierius, lib. iv., that some of the ancients used to order in their wills, that roses should be annually scattered on their tombs, and he has adduced some sepulchral inscriptions to this purpose.

[3] The author of the *Pervigilium Veneris* (a poem attributed to Catullus, the style of which appears to me to have all the laboured luxuriance of a much later period) ascribes the tincture of the rose to the blood from the wound of Adonis—

Rosæ
Fusæ aprino de cruore—

according to the emendation of Lipsius. In the following epigram this hue is differently accounted for:

Illa quidem studiosa suum defendere Adonim,
Gradivus stricto quem petit ense ferox,
Affixit duris vestigia cæca rosetis,
Albaque divino picta cruore rosa est.

While the enamoured queen of joy
Flies to protect her lovely boy,
On whom the jealous war-god rushes;
She treads upon a thornèd rose,
And while the wound with crimson flows,
The snowy floweret feels her blood, and blushes!

[4] This appears to be one of the hymns which were sung at the anniversary festival of the vintage; one of the *ευιληνιοι υμνοι*, as our poet hints if terms them in the

He, who inspires the youth to glance
In wingèd circlets through the dance!
Bacchus, the god, again is here,
And leads along the blushing year;
The blushing year with rapture teems,
Ready to shed those cordial streams
Which, sparkling in the cup of mirth,
Illuminate the sons of earth![1]
And when the ripe and vermil wine,
Sweet infant of the pregnant vine,
Which now in mellow clusters swells,
Oh! when it bursts its rosy cells,
The heavenly stream shall mantling flow,
To balsam every mortal woe!
No youth shall then be wan or weak,
For dimpling health shall light the cheek;
No heart shall then desponding sigh,
For wine shall bid despondence fly!
Thus—till another autumn's glow
Shall bid another vintage flow!

ODE LVII.[2]

AND whose immortal hand could shed
Upon this disk the ocean's bed?[3]
And, in a frenzied flight of soul,
Sublime as Heaven's eternal pole,
Imagine thus, in semblance warm,
The Queen of Love's voluptuous form,
Floating along the silvery sea
In beauty's naked majesty?
Oh! he has given the raptured sight
A witching banquet of delight;
And all those sacred scenes of Love,
Where only hallowed eyes may rove,[4]
Lie faintly glowing, half-concealed.
Within the lucid billows veiled.
Light as the leaf that summer's breeze
Has wafted o'er the glassy seas,
She floats upon the ocean's breast,
Which undulates in sleepy rest,
And stealing on, she gently pillows
Her bosom on the amorous billows.
Her bosom, like the humid rose,
Her neck, like dewy-sparkling snows,
Illume the liquid path she traces,
And burn within the stream's embraces!
In languid luxury soft she glides,
Encircled by the azure tides,
Like some fair lily, faint with weeping,
Upon a bed of violets sleeping!
Beneath their queen's inspiring glance,
The dolphins o'er the green sea dance,
Bearing in triumph young Desire,
And baby Love with smiles of fire!
While, sparkling on the silver waves,
The tenants of the briny caves
Around the pomp in eddies play,
And gleam along the watery way.

ODE LVIII.[5]

WHEN gold, as fleet as Zephyr's pinion,
Escapes like any faithless minion,[6]
And flies me (as he flies me ever),[7]
Do I pursue him? never, never!

---

fifty-ninth ode. We cannot help feeling a peculiar veneration for these relics of the religion of antiquity. Horace may be supposed to have written the nineteenth ode of his second book and the twenty-fifth of the third for some bacchanalian celebration of this kind.

[1] Madame Dacier thinks that the poet here had the nepenthé of Homer in his mind.—*Odyssey*, lib. iv. This nepenthé was a something of exquisite charm, infused by Helen into the wine of her guests, which had the power of dispelling every anxiety. A French writer, with very elegant gallantry, conjectures that this spell, which made the bowl so beguiling, was the charm of Helen's conversation. See de Meré, quoted by Bayle, art. Helène.

[2] This ode is a very animated description of a picture of Venus on a discus, which represented the goddess in her first emergence from the waves. About two centuries after our poet wrote, the pencil of the artist Apelles embellished this subject, in his famous painting of the Venus Anadyomené, the model of which, as Pliny informs us, was the beautiful Campaspe, given to him by Alexander; though, according to Natalis Comes, lib. vii. cap. 16, it was Phryne who sat to Apelles for the face and breast of this Venus.

There are a few blemishes in the reading of the ode before us, which have influenced Faber, Heyne, Brunck, etc., to denounce the whole poem as spurious. *Non ego paucis offendar maculis.* I think it is beautiful enough to be authentic.

[3] The abruptness of αρα τις ταρουσι ποντον is finely expressive of sudden admiration, and is one of those beauties which we cannot but admire in their source, though by frequent imitation they are now become languid and unimpressive.

[4] The picture here has all the delicate character of the semi-reducta Venus, and is the sweetest emblem of what the poetry of passion ought to be; glowing but through a veil, and stealing upon the heart from concealment. Few of the ancients have attained this modesty of description, which is, like the golden cloud that hung over Jupiter and Juno, impervious to every beam but that of fancy.

[5] I have followed Barnes' arrangement of this ode; it deviates somewhat from the Vatican MS., but it appeared to me the more natural order.

[6] There is a kind of pun in these words, as Madame Dacier has already remarked; for Chrysos, which signifies gold, was also a frequent name for a slave. In one of Lucian's dialogues there is, I think, a similar play upon the word, where the followers of Chrysippus are called golden fishes. The puns of the ancients are in general even more vapid than our own; some of the best are those recorded of Diogenes.

[7] Αν δ', και μι φυγη. This grace of iteration has already been taken notice of. Though sometimes merely a playful beauty, it is peculiarly expressive of impassioned sentiment, and we may easily believe that it was one of the many sources of that energetic sensibility which breathed through the style of Sappho. See Gyrald. Vet. Poet. Dial. 9. It will not be said that this is a mechanical ornament by any one who can feel

No, let the false deserter go,
For who would court his direst foe?
But when I feel my lightened mind
No more by ties of gold confined,
I loosen all my clinging cares,
And cast them to the vagrant airs.
Then, then I feel the Muse's spell,
And wake to life the dulcet shell;
The dulcet shell to beauty sings,
And love dissolves along the strings!
Thus, when my heart is sweetly taught
How little gold deserves a thought,
The wingèd slave returns once more,
And with him wafts delicious store
Of racy wine, whose balmy art
In slumber seals the anxious heart!
Again he tries my soul to sever
From love and song, perhaps for ever!
Away, deceiver! why pursuing
Ceaseless thus my heart's undoing?
Sweet is the song of amorous fire;
Sweet are the sighs that thrill the lyre;
Oh! sweeter far than all the gold
The waftage of thy wings can hold.
I well remember all thy wiles;
They withered Cupid's flowery smiles,
And o'er his harp such garbage shed,
I thought its angel breath was fled!
They tainted all his bowl of blisses,
His bland desires and hallowed kisses.[1]
Oh! fly to haunts of sordid men,
But rove not near the bard again;
Thy glitter in the Muse's shade
Scares from her bower the tuneful maid;
And not for worlds would I forego
That moment of poetic glow,
When my full soul, in Fancy's stream,
Pours o'er the lyre its swelling theme.
Away, away! to worldlings hence,
Who feel not this diviner sense,
And, with thy gay fallacious blaze,
Dazzle their unrefinèd gaze.

ODE LIX.[2]

Sabled by the solar beam,
Now the fiery clusters teem,
In osier baskets, borne along
By all the festal vintage throng

Of rosy youths and virgins fair,
Ripe as the melting fruits they bear.
Now, now they press the pregnant grapes,
And now the captive stream escapes,
In fervid tide of nectar gushing,
And for its bondage proudly blushing!
While, round the vat's impurpled brim,
The choral song, the vintage hymn
Of rosy youths and virgins fair,
Steals on the cloyed and panting air.
Mark, how they drink, with all their eyes,
The orient tide that sparkling flies;
The infant balm of all their fears,
The infant Bacchus, born in tears!
When he, whose verging years decline
As deep into the vale as mine,
When he inhales the vintage spring,
His heart is fire, his foot's a wing;
And, as he flies, his hoary hair
Plays truant with the wanton air!
While the warm youth, whose wishing soul
Has kindled o'er the inspiring bowl,
Impassioned seeks the shadowy grove,
Where, in the tempting guise of love,
Reclining sleeps some witching maid,
Whose sunny charms, but half displayed,
Blush through the bower, that, closely twined,
Excludes the kisses of the wind!
The virgin wakes, the glowing boy
Allures her to the embrace of joy;
Swears that the herbage heaven has spread
Was sacred as the nuptial bed;
That laws should never bind desire,
And love was nature's holiest fire!
The virgin weeps, the virgin sighs;
He kissed her lips, he kissed her eyes;
The sigh was balm, the tear was dew,
They only raised his flame anew,
And, oh! he stole the sweetest flower
That ever bloomed in any bower!

Such is the madness wine imparts,
Whene'er it steals on youthful hearts.

ODE LX.[3]

Awake to life, my dulcet shell,
To Phœbus all thy sighs shall swell;

Its charm in those lines of Catullus, where he complains of the infidelity of his mistress, Lesbia:

Cœli, Lesbia nostra, Lesbia illa,
Illa Lesbia, quam Catullus unam,
Plus quam se atque suos amavit omnes,
Nunc, etc.

Si sic omnia dixisset! but the rest does not bear citation.
[1] Original:

Φιλημάτων δε κιδνων,
Ποθων κυπελλα κιρνας.

Horace has, 'Desiderique temperare poculum;' not figuratively, however, like Anacreon. but importing the love-philtres of the witches. By 'cups of kisses' our poet may allude to a favourite gallantry among the ancients, of drinking when the lips of their mistresses had touched the brim:

'Or leave a kiss within the cup,
And I'll not ask for wine.'

[2] Degen, in the true spirit of literary scepticism, doubts that this ode is genuine, without assigning any reason for such a suspicion. 'Non amo te, Sabidi, nec possum dicere quare;' but this is far from satisfactory criticism.

[3] This hymn to Apollo is supposed not to have been written by Anacreon. and it certainly is rather a

And though no glorious prize be thine,
No Pythian wreath around thee twine,
Yet every hour is glory's hour,
To him who gathers wisdom's flower!
Then wake thee from thy magic slumbers,
Breathe to the soft and Phrygian numbers,
Which, as my trembling lips repeat,
Thy chords shall echo back as sweet.
The cygnet thus, with fading notes,
As down Cayster's tide he floats,
Plays with his snowy plumage fair
Upon the wanton murmuring air,
Which amorously lingers round,
And sighs responsive sound for sound!
Muse of the Lyre! illume my dream,
Thy Phœbus is my fancy's theme;
And hallowed is the harp I bear,
And hallowed is the wreath I wear,
Hallowed by him, the god of lays,
Who modulates the choral maze!
I sing the love which Daphne twined
Around the godhead's yielding mind;
I sing the blushing Daphne's flight
From this ætherial youth of light;
And how the tender, timid maid
Flew panting to the kindly shade,
Resigned a form, too tempting fair,
And grew a verdant laurel there;
Whose leaves, with sympathetic thrill,
In terror seemed to tremble still!
The god pursued, with winged desire;
And when his hopes were all on fire,
And when he thought to hear the sigh
With which enamoured virgins die,
He only heard the pensive air
Whispering amid her leafy hair!

But oh, my soul! no more—no more!
Enthusiast, whither do I soar?
This sweetly maddening dream of soul
Has hurried me beyond the goal.
Why should I sing the mighty darts
Which fly to wound celestial hearts,
When sure the lay, with sweeter tone,
Can tell the darts that wound my own?
Still be Anacreon, still inspire
The descant of the Teian lyre:
Still let the nectared numbers float,
Distilling love in every note!
And when the youth, whose burning soul
Has felt the Paphian star's control,
When he the liquid lays shall hear
His heart will flutter to his ear,
And drinking there of song divine,
Banquet on intellectual wine![1]

ODE LXI.[2]

GOLDEN hues of youth are fled;
Hoary locks deform my head.
Bloomy graces, dalliance gay,
All the flowers of life decay.[3]
Withering age begins to trace
Sad memorials o'er my face;
Time has shed its sweetest bloom,
All the future must be gloom!
This awakes my hourly sighing;
Dreary is the thought of dying![4]
Pluto's is a dark abode,
Sad the journey, sad the road:

---

sublimer flight than the Teian wing is accustomed to soar. But we ought not to judge from this diversity of style, in a poet of whom time has preserved such partial relics. If we knew Horace but as a satirist, should we easily believe there could dwell such animation in his lyre? Suidas says that our poet wrote hymns, and this perhaps is one of them. We can perceive in what an altered and imperfect state his works are at present, when we find a scholiast upon Horace citing an ode from the third book of Anacreon.

[1] Here ends the last of the odes in the Vatican MS., whose authority confirms the genuine antiquity of them all, though a few have stolen among the number which we may hesitate in attributing to Anacreon. In the little essay prefixed to this translation, I observed that Barnes had quoted this manuscript incorrectly, relying upon an imperfect copy of it, which Isaac Vossius had taken; I shall just mention two or three instances of this inaccuracy, the first which occur to me. In the ode of the Dove, on the words Πτεροισι συγκαλυψω, he says, 'Vatican MS. συκιαζων, etiam Presciano invito,' though the MS. reads συγκαλυψω, with συκιαζω interlined. Degen, too, on the same line, is somewhat in error. In the twenty-second ode of this series, line thirteenth, the MS. has τυσι with αι interlined, and Barnes imputes to it the reading of τυιδη. In the fifty-seventh, line twelfth, he professes to have preserved the reading of the MS. Αλωλημενη δ' ισ' αυτη, while the latter has αλωλημενος δ' ισ' αυτα. Almost all the other annotators have transplanted these errors from Barnes.

[2] The intrusion of this melancholy ode among the careless levities of our poet, has always reminded me of the skeletons which the Egyptians used to hang up in their banquet-rooms, to inculcate a thought of mortality even amidst the dissipations of mirth. If it were not for the beauty of its numbers, the Teian Muse should disown this ode. *Quid habet illius, illius quæ spirabat amores?*

To Stobæus we are indebted for it.

[3] Horace often, with feeling and elegance, deplores the fugacity of human enjoyments. See book ii. ode 11; and thus in the second epistle, book ii. :

Singula de nobis anni prædantur euntes,
Eripuere jocos, venerem, convivia, ludum.

The wing of every passing day
Withers some blooming joy away;
And wafts from our enamoured arms
The banquet's mirth, the virgin's charms.

[4] Regnier, a libertine French poet, has written some sonnets on the approach of death, full of gloomy and trembling repentance. Chaulieu, however, supports more consistently the spirit of the Epicurean philosopher. See his poem, addressed to the Marquis La Farre:

Plus j'approche du terme et moins je le redoute, etc.

I shall leave it to the moralist to make his reflections here: it is impossible to be very Anacreontic on such a subject.

And, the gloomy travel o'er,
Ah! we can return no more!¹

ODE LXII.²

FILL me, boy, as deep a draught
As e'er was filled, as e'er was quaffed;
But let the water amply flow,
To cool the grape's intemperate glow;³
Let not the fiery god be single,
But with the nymphs in union mingle;
For, though the bowl's the grave of sadness,
Oh! be it ne'er the birth of madness!
No, banish from our board to-night
The revelries of rude delight!
To Scythians leave these wild excesses,
Ours be the joy that soothes and blesses!
And while the temperate bowl we wreathe,
Our choral hymns shall sweetly breathe,
Beguiling every hour along
With harmony of soul and song!

ODE LXIII.⁴

To Love, the soft and blooming child,
I touch the harp in descant wild;
To Love, the babe of Cyprian bowers,
The boy, who breathes and blushes flowers!
To Love, for heaven and earth adore him,
And gods and mortals bow before him!

ODE LXIV.⁵

HASTE thee, nymph, whose wingèd spear
Wounds the fleeting mountain deer!
Dian, Jove's immortal child,
Huntress of the savage wild!
Goddess with the sun-bright hair!
Listen to a people's prayer.
Turn, to Lethe's river turn,
There thy vanquished people mourn!⁶
Come to Lethe's wavy shore,
There thy people's peace restore.
Thine their hearts, their altars thine;
Dian! must they—must they pine?

ODE LXV.⁷

LIKE some wanton filly sporting,
Maid of Thrace! thou fly'st my courting.
Wanton filly! tell me why
Thou trip'st away, with scornful eye,
And seem'st to think my doting heart
Is novice in the bridling art?
Believe me, girl, it is not so;
Thou 'lt find this skilful hand can throw
The reins upon that tender form,
However wild, however warm!
Thou 'lt own that I can tame thy force,
And turn and wind thee in the course.
Though wasting now thy careless hours,
Thou sport'st amid the herbs and flowers,
Thou soon shalt feel the rein's control,
And tremble at the wished-for goal!

---

¹ Scaliger, upon Catullus' well-known lines, 'Qui nunc it per iter,' etc., remarks that Acheron, with the same idea, is called ἀνεξόδος by Theocritus, and δυσικδρομος by Nicander.

² This ode consists of two fragments, which are to be found in Athenæus, book x., and which Barnes, from the similarity of their tendency, has combined into one. I think this a very justifiable liberty, and have adopted it in some other fragments of our poet. Degen refers us here to verses of Uz, lib. iv. der Trinker.

³ It was Amphictyon who first taught the Greeks to mix water with their wine; in commemoration of which circumstance they erected altars to Bacchus and the nymphs. On this mythological allegory the followin epigram is founded:—

   Ardentem ex utero Semeles lavere Lyæum
    Naiades, extincto fulminis igne sacri;
   Cum nymphis igitur tractabilis, at sine nymphis
    Candenti rursus fulmine corripitur.
          —*Pierius Valerianus.*

Which is, *non verbum verbo,*

   While heavenly fire consumed his Theban dame,
   A Naiad caught young Bacchus from the flame,
   And dipped him burning in her purest lymph;
   Still, still he loves the sea-maid's crystal urn,
   And when his native fires infuriate burn,
   He bathes him in the fountain of the nymph.

⁴ 'This fragment is preserved in Clemens Alexandrinus, *Strom* lib. vi., and in Arsenius, *Collect. Græc.*'

⁵ —*Barnes.* It appears to have been the opening of a hymn in praise of Love.

⁶ This hymn to Diana is extant in Hephæstion. There is an anecdote of our poet, which has led to some doubt whether he ever wrote any odes of this kind. It is related by the Scholiast upon Pindar (*Isthmionic.* od. II. v. 1, as cited by Barnes). Anacreon being asked why he addressed all his hymns to women, and none to the deities, answered, 'Because women are my deities.' I have assumed the same liberty in reporting this anecdote which I have done in translating some of the odes; and it were to be wished that these little infidelities were always considered pardonable in the interpretation of the ancients; thus, when nature is forgotten in the original, in the translation, 'tamen usque recurret.'

⁶ Lethe, a river of Ionia, according to Strabo, falling into the Meander. Near to it was situated the town Magnesia, in favour of whose inhabitants our poet is supposed to have addressed this supplication to Diana. It was written (as Madame Dacier conjectures) on the occasion of some battle, in which the Magnesians had been defeated.

⁷ This ode, which is addressed to some Thracian girl, exists in Heraclides, and has been imitated very frequently by Horace, as all the annotators have remarked. Madame Dacier rejects the allegory, which runs so obviously throughout it, and supposes it to have been addressed to a young mare belonging to Polycrates. There is more modesty than ingenuity in the lady's conjecture. Pierius, in the fourth book of his Hieroglyphics, cites this ode, and informs us that the horse was the hieroglyphical emblem of pride.

L.

ODE LXVI.[1]

To thee, the Queen of nymphs divine,
Fairest of all that fairest shine;
To thee, thou blushing young Desire,
Who rul'st the world with darts of fire!
And oh! thou nuptial Power, to thee
Who bear'st of life the guardian key;
Breathing my soul in fragrant praise,
And weaving wild my votive lays,
For thee, O Queen! I wake the lyre,
For thee, thou blushing young Desire!
And oh! for thee, thou nuptial Power,
Come, and illume this genial hour.
Look on thy bride, luxuriant boy!
And while thy lambent glance of joy
Plays over all her blushing charms,
Delay not, snatch her to thine arms,
Before the lovely, trembling prey,
Like a young birdling, wing away!
Oh! Stratocles, impassioned youth!
Dear to the Queen of amorous truth,
And dear to her, whose yielding zone
Will soon resign her all thine own;
Turn to Myrilla, turn thine eye,
Breathe to Myrilla, breathe thy sigh!
To those bewitching beauties turn;
For thee they mantle, flush, and burn!
Not more the rose, the queen of flowers,
Outblushes all the glow of bowers,
Than she unrivalled bloom discloses,
The sweetest rose, where all are roses!
Oh! may the sun, benignant, shed
His blandest influence o'er thy bed;
And foster there an infant tree,
To blush like her, and bloom like thee!

ODE LXVII.[2]

GENTLE youth! whose looks assume
Such a soft and girlish bloom,
Why repulsive, why refuse
The friendship which my heart pursues?
Thou little know'st the fond control
With which thy virtue reins my soul!

Then smile not on my locks of gray,
Believe me oft with converse gay;
I've chained the years of tender age,
And boys have loved the prattling sage!
For mine is many a soothing pleasure,
And mine is many a soothing measure;
And much I hate the beamless mind,
Whose earthly vision, unrefined,
Nature has never formed to see
The beauties of simplicity!
Simplicity, the flower of heaven,
To souls elect, by Nature given!

ODE LXVIII.[3]

RICH in bliss, I proudly scorn
The stream of Amalthea's horn!
Nor should I ask to call the throne
Of the Tartessian prince my own;[4]
To totter through his train of years,
The victim of declining fears.
One little hour of joy to me
Is worth a dull eternity!

ODE LXIX.[5]

Now Neptune's sullen month appears,
The angry night-cloud swells with tears;
And savage storms, infuriate driven,
Fly howling in the face of heaven!
Now, now, my friends, the gathering gloom
With roseate rays of wine illume:
And while our wreaths of parsley spread
Their fadeless foliage round our head,
We'll hymn the almighty power of wine,
And shed libations on his shrine!

ODE LXX.[6]

THEY wove the lotus band, to deck
And fan with pensile wreath their neck;

---

[1] This ode is introduced in the romance of Theodorus Prodromus, and is that kind of epithalamium which was sung like a scholium at the nuptial banquet.
Among the many works of the impassioned Sappho, of which time and ignorant superstition have deprived us, the loss of her epithalamiums is not one of the least that we deplore. A subject so interesting to an amorous fancy was warmly felt, and must have been warmly described, by such a soul and such an imagination. The following lines are cited as a relic of one of her epithalamiums:

Ολβιε γαμβρε, σοι μεν δη γαμος ας αραο,
Εκτετελεστ', εχεις δε παρθενον αν αραο.

—See Scaliger, in his *Poetics*, on the Epithalamium.
[2] I have formed this poem of three or four different fragments, which is a liberty that perhaps may be justi- fied by the example of Barnes, who has thus complied the 57th of his edition, and the little ode beginning ειπ' ύδωρ, ειπ' οινον, ω παι, which he has subjoined to the epigrams. The fragments combined in this ode are the 67th, 96th, 97th, and 100th of Barnes' edition, to which I refer the reader for the names of the authors by whom they are preserved.
[3] This fragment is preserved in the third book of Strabo.
[4] He here alludes to Arganthonius, who lived, according to Lucian, a hundred and fifty years; and reigned, according to Herodotus, eighty.—See Barnes.
[5] This is composed of two fragments, the 70th and 81st in Barnes. They are both found in Eustathius.
[6] Three fragments form this little ode, all of which are preserved in Athenæus. They are the 82d, 75th, and 83d in Barnes.

And every guest, to shade his head,
Three little breathing chaplets spread;[1]
And one was of Egyptian leaf,
The rest were roses, fair and brief!
While from a golden vase profound,
To all on flowery beds around,
A goblet-nymph, of heavenly shape,
Poured the rich weepings of the grape!

ODE LXXI.[2]

A BROKEN cake, with honey sweet,
Is all my spare and simple treat;
And while a generous bowl I crown,
To float my little banquet down,
I take the soft, the amorous lyre,
And sing of love's delicious fire!
In mirthful measures, warm and free,
I sing, dear maid, and sing for thee!

ODE LXXII.[3]

WITH twenty chords my lyre is hung,
And while I wake them all for thee,
Thou, O virgin! wild and young,
Disport'st in airy levity.

The nursling fawn, that in some shade
Its antlered mother leaves behind,[4]
Is not more wantonly afraid,
More timid of the rustling wind!

ODE LXXIII.[5]

FARE thee well, perfidious maid!
My soul, too long on earth delayed,
Delayed, perfidious girl! by thee,
Is now on wing for liberty.
I fly to seek a kindlier sphere,
Since thou hast ceased to love me here.

ODE LXXIV.[6]

I BLOOMED, awhile, a happy flower,
Till love approached, one fatal hour,
And made my tender branches feel
The wounds of his avenging steel.
Then, then I feel like some poor willow
That tosses on the wintry billow!

ODE LXXV.[7]

MONARCH Love! resistless boy,
With whom the rosy Queen of Joy,
And nymphs, that glance ethereal blue,
Disporting tread the mountain-dew;
Propitious, oh! receive my sighs,
Which, burning with entreaty, rise;
That thou wilt whisper, to the breast
Of her I love, thy soft behest;
And counsel her to learn from thee
The lesson thou hast taught to me.
Ah! if my heart no flattery tell,
Thou't own I've learned that lesson well!

ODE LXXVI.[8]

SPIRIT of Love! whose tresses shine
Along the breeze, in golden twine,
Come, within a fragrant cloud,
Blushing with light, thy votary shroud;

---

[1] Longepierre, to give an idea of the luxurious estimation in which garlands were held by the ancients, relates an anecdote of a courtezan, who, in order to gratify three lovers, without leaving cause for jealousy with any of them, gave a kiss to one, let the other drink after her, and put a garland on the brow of the third; so that each was satisfied with his favour, and flattered himself with the preference.
This circumstance is extremely like the subject of one of the tensons of Savari de Mauléon, a troubadour. See l'Histoire Littéraire des Troubadours. The recital is a curious picture of the puerile gallantries of chivalry.

[2] This poem is compiled by Barnes, from Athenæus, Hephæstion, and Arsenius. See Barnes, 80.

[3] This I have formed from the 84th and 85th of Barnes' edition. The two fragments are found in Athenæus.

[4] In the original:
'Ος εν ὑλη κεροεσσης
Απολειφθεις ὑπο μητρος.

'Horned' here undoubtedly seems a strange epithet. Madame Dacier, however, observes that Sophocles, Callimachus, etc., have all applied it in the very same manner; and she seems to agree in the conjecture of the scholiast upon Pindar, that perhaps horns are not always peculiar to the males. I think we may with more ease conclude it to be a licence of the poet, 'jussit habere puellam cornua.'

[5] This fragment is preserved by the scholiast upon Aristophanes, and is the 87th in Barnes.

[6] This is to be found in Hephæstion, and is the 89th of Barnes' edition.
I must here apologize for omitting a very considerable fragment imputed to our poet, Ξανθη δ' Ευρυπυλη μελει, etc., which is preserved in the twelfth book of Athenæus, and is the 91st in Barnes. If it was really Anacreon who wrote it, nil fuit unquam sic impar sibi. It is in a style of gross satire, and is full of expressions which never could be gracefully translated.

[7] This fragment is preserved by Dion. Chrysostom, Orat. II. de Regno.—See Barnes, 93.

[8] This fragment, which is extant in Athenæus (Barnes, 101), is supposed, on the authority of Chamæleon, to have been addressed to Sappho. We have also a stanza attributed to her, which some romancers have supposed to be her answer to Anacreon. ''Mais par

And, on those wings that sparkling play,
Waft, oh! waft me hence away!
Love! my soul is full of thee,
Alive to all thy luxury.
But she, the nymph for whom I glow,
The pretty Lesbian, mocks my woe;
Smiles at the hoar and silvered hues
Which Time upon my forehead strews.
Alas! I fear she keeps her charms
In store for younger, happier arms!

ODE LXXVII.[1]

HITHER, gentle Muse of mine,
Come and teach thy votary old
Many a golden hymn divine,
For the nymph with vest of gold.

Pretty nymph, of tender age,
Fair thy silky locks unfold:
Listen to a hoary sage,
Sweetest maid with vest of gold!

ODE LXXVIII.[2]

WOULD that I were a tuneful lyre,
Of burnished ivory fair,
Which in the Dionysian choir
Some blooming boy should bear!

Would that I were a golden vase,
And then some nymph should hold
My spotless frame with blushing grace,
Herself as pure as gold!

ODE LXXIX.[3]

WHEN Cupid sees my beard of snow,
Which blanching time has taught to flow,
Upon his wing of golden light
He passes with an eaglet's flight,
And, flitting on, he seems to say,
'Fare thee well, thou'st had thy day!'

CUPID, whose lamp has lent the ray
Which lightens our meandering way—
Cupid, within my bosom stealing,
Excites a strange and mingled feeling,
Which pleases, though severely teasing,
And teases, though divinely pleasing![4]

LET me resign a wretched breath,
Since now remains to me
No other balm than kindly death,
To soothe my misery![5]

I KNOW thou lov'st a brimming measure,
And art a kindly, cordial host;
But let me fill and drink at pleasure,
Thus I enjoy the goblet most.[6]

I FEAR that love disturbs my rest,
Yet feel not love's impassioned care;
I think there's madness in my breast,
Yet cannot find that madness there![7]

FROM dread Leucadia's frowning steep
I'll plunge into the whitening deep,
And there I'll float, to waves resigned,
For love intoxicates my mind![8]

---

malheur (as Bayle says) Sapho vint au monde environ cent on six vingts ans avant Anacréon.' *Nouvelles de la Rép. des Lett.* tom. ii. de Novembre 1684. The following is her fragment, the compliment of which is very finely imagined; she supposes that the Muse has dictated the verses of Anacreon:

Κεινον, ω χρυσοθρονι Μουσ', ενισπες
Ὑμνον, εκ της καλλιγυναικος εσθλας
Τηιος χωρας ὁ αοιδι τερπνως
Πρισβυς αγαυος.

Oh Muse! who sitt'st on golden throne,
Full many a hymn of dulcet tone
The Teian sage is taught by thee;
But, goddess, from thy throne of gold,
The sweetest hymn thou'st ever told,
He lately learned and sang for me.

[1] This is formed of the 124th and 119th fragments in Barnes, both of which are to be found in Scaliger's *Poetics*.
De Pauw thinks that those detached lines and couplets, which Scaliger has adduced as examples in his *Poetics*, are by no means authentic, but of his own fabrication.

[2] This is generally inserted among the remains of Alcæus. Some, however, have attributed it to Anacreon. See our poet's 22d ode, and the notes.

[3] See Barnes, 173. This fragment, to which I have taken the liberty of adding a turn not to be found in the original, is cited by Lucian in his little essay on the Gallic Hercules.

[4] Barnes, 125. This, if I remember right, is in Scaliger's *Poetics*. Gail has omitted it in his collection of fragments.

[5] This fragment is extant in Arsenius and Hephæstion. See Barnes (69), who has arranged the metre of it very elegantly.

[6] Barnes, 72. This fragment, which is quoted by Athenæus, is an excellent lesson for the votaries of Jupiter Hospitalis.

[7] This fragment is in Hephæstion. See Barnes, 95. Catullus expresses something of this contrariety of feelings:

Odi et amo; quare id faciam fortasse requiris;
Nescio: sed fieri sentio, et excrucior.—*Carm.* 53.

I love thee and hate thee, but if I can tell
The cause of my love and my hate, may I die!
I can feel it, alas! I can feel it too well,
That I love thee and hate thee, but cannot tell why.

[8] This also is in Hephæstion, and perhaps is a fragment of some poem in which Anacreon had commemorated the fate of Sappho. It is the 123d of Barnes.

ODES OF ANACREON.

Mix me, child, a cup divine,
Crystal water, ruby wine:
Weave the frontlet, richly flushing,
O'er my wintry temples blushing.

Mix the brimmer—love and I
Shall no more the gauntlet try,
Here—upon this holy bowl,
I surrender all my soul![1]

Among the Epigrams of the *Anthologia* there are some panegyrics on Anacreon, which I had translated, and originally intended as a kind of Coronis to the work; but I found, upon consideration, that they wanted variety: a frequent recurrence of the same thought, within the limits of an epitaph, to which they are confined, would render a collection of them rather uninteresting. I shall take the liberty, however, of subjoining a few, that I may not appear to have totally neglected those elegant tributes to the reputation of Anacreon. The four epigrams which I give are imputed to Antipater Sidonius. They are rendered, perhaps, with too much freedom; but, designing a translation of all that are on the subject, I imagined it was necessary to enliven their uniformity by sometimes indulging in the liberties of paraphrase.

Αντιπατρου Σιδωνιου, εις Ανακριοντα.

Θαλλοι τετρακορυμβος, Ανακριον, αμφι σε κισσος
  'Αβρα τε λειμωνων πορφυριων πεταλα·
Πηγαι δ' αργινοεντος αναβλιβοιντο γαλακτος,
  Ευωδες δ' απο γης ηδυ χεοιτο μεθυ,
Οφρα κε τοι σποδιη τε και οστεα τερψιν αρηται,
  Ει δη τις φθιμενοις χριμπτεται ευφροσυνα,
Ω το φιλον στερξας, φιλε, βαρβιτον, ω συν αοιδα
  Παντα διαπλωσας και συν ερωτι βιον.

Around the tomb, oh bard divine!
Where soft thy hallowed brow reposes,
Long may the deathless ivy twine,
And Summer pour her waste of roses!

And many a fount shall there distil,
And many a rill refresh the flowers;
But wine shall gush in every rill,
And every fount be milky showers.

Who gave to love his warmest thought,
Who gave to love his fondest measure!

Thus, after death, if spirits feel,
Thou mayst, from odours round thee streaming,
A pulse of past enjoyment steal,
And live again in blissful dreaming!

Του αυτου, εις τον αυτον.

Τυμβος Ανακρειοντος. ὁ Τηϊος ενθαδε κυκνος
  Ευδει, χη παιδων ζωροτατη μανιη.
Ακμην λειριοεντι μελιζεται αμφι Βαθυλλω
  'Ιμερα· και κισσου λευκος οδωδε λιθος.
Ουδ' Αϊδης σοι ερωτας απεσβεσεν· εν δ' Αχεροντος
  Ων, ὁλος ωδινεις Κυπριδι θερμοτερη.

Here sleeps Anacreon, in this ivied shade;
Here, mute in death, the Teian swan is laid.[2]
Cold, cold the heart, which lived but to respire
All the voluptuous frenzy of desire!
And yet, oh bard! thou art not mute in death,
Still, still we catch thy lyre's delicious breath;[3]

---

[1] This fragment is collected by Barnes from Demetrius Phalereus and Eustathius, and is subjoined in his edition to the epigrams attributed to our poet. And here is the last of those little scattered flowers which I thought I might venture with any grace to transplant. I wish it could be said of the garland which they form, Το δ' ωζ' Ανακρεοντος.

[2] Thus Horace of Pindar:

  Multa Dircæum levat aura cycnum.

A swan was the hieroglyphical emblem of a poet. Anacreon has been called the swan of Teos by another of his eulogists:

  Εν τοις μελιχροις 'Ιμεροισι συντροφον
  Λυαιος Ανακριοντα, Τηϊον κυκνον,
  Εσφηλας υγρη νεκταρος μελῃδονη.
      Ευγενους, Ανθολογ.

God of the grape! thou hast betrayed,
  In wine's bewildering dream,
The fairest swan that ever played
  Along the Muse's stream!
The Teian, nursed with all those honeyed boys,
The young Desires, light Loves, and rose-lipped Joys!

[3] Thus Simonides, speaking of our poet:

  Μολπης δ' ου ληθη μελιτερπεος, αλλ' ετι κεινο
  Βαρβιτον ουδε θανων ευνασεν εν αϊδη.
      Σιμωνιδου, Ανθολογ.

Nor yet are all his numbers mute,
  Though dark within the tomb he lies;
But living still, his amorous lute
  With sleepless animation sighs!

This is the famous Simonides, whom Plato styled 'divine,' though Le Fevre, in his *Poëtes Grecs*, supposes that the epigrams under his name are all falsely imputed. The most considerable of his remains is a satirical poem upon women, preserved by Stobæus, ψογος γυναικων.

We may judge from the lines I have just quoted, and the import of the epigram before us, that the works of Anacreon were perfect in the times of Simonides and Antipater. Obsopœus the commentator here appears to exult in their destruction; and telling us they were burned by the bishops and patriarchs, he adds, 'nec sane id necquicquam fecerunt,' attributing to this outrage an effect which it could never produce.

And still thy songs of soft Bathylla bloom,
Green as the ivy round the mouldering tomb!
Nor yet has death obscured thy fire of love,
Still, still it lights thee through the Elysian grove:
And dreams are thine that bless the elect alone,
And Venus calls thee, even in death, her own!

Του αυτου, εις τον αυτον.

Ειπε, ταφον παρα λιτον Ανακρειοντος αμειβων
Ετ τι τοι εκ βιβλων ηλθεν εμων οφελος,
Σπεισον εμη σποδιη, σπεισον γανος, οφρα κεν οινῳ·
Οστεα γηθησε ταμα νοτιζομενα,
Ως ὁ Διονυσου μεμελημενος ουασι κωμος
Ὡς ὁ φιλακρητου συντροφος ἁρμονιης,
Μηδε καταφθιμενος Βακχου διχα τουτον ὑποισω
Τον γενεῃ μεροπων χωρον οφειλομενον.

Oh stranger![1] if Anacreon's shell
Has ever taught thy heart to swell[2]
With passion's throb or pleasure's sigh,
In pity turn, as wandering nigh,
And drop thy goblet's richest tear,[3]
In exquisite libation here!
So shall my sleeping ashes thrill
With visions of enjoyment still.
I cannot even in death resign
The festal joys that once were mine.

---

[1] The spirit of Anacreon utters these verses from the tomb, somewhat 'mutatus ab illo,' at least in simplicity of expression.

[2] We may guess from the words εκ βιβλων εμων, that Anacreon was not merely a writer of billets-doux, as some French critics have called him. Amongst these, Le Fevre, with all his professed admiration, has given our poet a character by no means of an elevated cast:—

Aussi c'est pour cela que la postérité
L'a toujours justement d'âge en âge chanté
Comme un franc goguenard, ami de goinfrerie,
Ami de billets-doux et de badinerie.

See the verses prefixed to his *Poëtes Grecs*. This is unlike the language of Theocritus, to whom Anacreon is indebted for the following simple eulogium:

Εις Ανακρεοντος ανδριαντα.

Θασαι τον ανδριαντα τουτον, ω ξενε,
Σπουδᾳ, και λεγ', επαν ες οικον ελθῃς,
Ανακρεοντος εικον' ειδον εν Τεῳ,
Των προσθ' ει τι περισσον ῳδοποιων.
Προσθεις δε χ' ὁτι τοις νεοισιν ἁδετο,
Ερεις ατρεκεως ὁλον τον ανδρα.

UPON THE STATUE OF ANACREON.

Stranger! who near this statue chance to roam,
Let it awhile your studious eyes engage;
And you may say, returning to your home,
' I've seen the image of the Teian sage,
Best of the bards who deck the Muse's page.'
Then, if you add, 'That striplings loved him well,'
You tell them all he was, and aptly tell.

The simplicity of this inscription has always delighted me: I have given it, I believe, as literally as a verse translation will allow.

[3] Thus Simonides, in another of his epitaphs on our poet:

When Harmony pursued my ways,
And Bacchus wantoned to my lays.[4]
Oh! if delight could charm no more,
If all the goblet's bliss were o'er,
When Fate had once our doom decreed,
Then dying would be death indeed!
Nor could I think, unblest by wine,
Divinity itself divine!

Του αυτου, εις τον αυτον.

Ευδεις εν φθιμενοισιν, Ανακρεον, εσθλα πονησας,
Ευδει δ' ἡ γλυκερη νυκτιλαλος κιθαρα,
Ευδει και Σμερδις, το Ποθων εαρ, ῳ συ μελισδων
Βαρβιτ', ανεκρουον νεκταρ εναρμονιον.
Ηϊθεων γαρ Ερωτος εφυς σκοπος· εις δε σε μουνον
Τοξα τε και σκολιας ειχεν εκηβολιας.

At length thy golden hours have winged their flight,
And drowsy death that eyelid steepeth;
Thy harp, that whispered through each lingering night,[5]
Now mutely in oblivion sleepeth!

She, too, for whom that heart profusely shed
The purest nectar of its numbers,[6]
She, the young spring of thy desires, has fled,[7]
And with her blest Anacreon slumbers!

Και μεν και τεγγει νοτερη δροσος, ἡς ὁ γεραιος
Λαροτερον μαλακων επνεεν εκ στοματων.

Let vines, in clustering beauty wreathed,
Drop all their treasures on his head,
Whose lips a dew of sweetness breathed,
Richer than vine hath ever shed!

[4] The original here is corrupted; the line ὡς ὁ Διονυσου is unintelligible.

Brunck's emendation improves the sense, but I doubt if it can be commended for elegance. He reads the line thus:

ὡς ὁ Διονυσοιο λιλασμενος ουποτι κωμον.

See *Brunck, Analecta Veter. Poet. Græc.* vol. ii.

[5] In another of these poems, 'the nightly-speaking lyre' of the bard is not allowed to be silent even after his death.

'Ως ὁ φιλακρητος τε και οινοβαρης φιλοκωμος
Παννυχιος κρουει * της φιλοπαιδα χελυν.
            Σιμωνιδου, εις Ανακρεοντα.

To beauty's smile and wine's delight,
To joys he loved on earth so well,
Still shall his spirit, all the night,
Attune the wild aërial shell!

[6] Thus, says Brunck, in the prologue of the Satires of Persius:

Cantare credas Pegaseium nectar.

'Melos' is the usual reading in this line, and Casaubon has defended it; but 'nectar,' I think, is much more spirited.

[7] The original, το Ποθων εαρ, is beautiful. We regret that such praise should be lavished so preposterously,

* Brunck has κρουει; but κρουσι, the common reading, better suits a detached quotation.

Farewell! thou hadst a pulse for every dart That Love could scatter from his quiver;	And every woman found in thee a heart,[1] Which thou, with all thy soul, didst give her!

and feel that the poet's mistress, Eurypyle, would have deserved it better. Her name has been told us by Meleager, as already quoted, and in another epigram by Antipater:

Τυρω δι δερκομενοισιν εν ομμασιν ουλον αιδως,
Αιθυσσων λιπαρης ανθος υπερθι κομης,
Η προς Ευρυπυλην τετραμμενος . . .

Long may the nymph around thee play,
  Eurypyle, thy soul's desire!
Basking her beauties in the ray
  That lights thine eyes' dissolving fire!

Sing of her smile's bewitching power,
  Her every grace that warms and blesses;
Sing of her brow's luxuriant flower,
  The beaming glory of her tresses.

The expression here, ανθος κομης, 'the flower of the hair,' is borrowed from Anacreon himself, as appears by a fragment of the poet preserved in Stobæus: Απεκειρας δ' απαλης αμωμον ανθος.

[1] This couplet is not otherwise warranted by the ori-ginal, than as it dilates the thought which Antipater has figuratively expressed:

Του δι γυναικιων μελιων πλιξαντα ποτ' ᾠδας,
Ηδυν Ανακριοντα,ª Τιως εις 'Ελλαδ' ανηγιν,
Συμποσιων ερεθισμα, γυναικων ηπεροπευμα.

Critias, of Athens, pays a tribute to the legitimate gallantry of Anacreon, calling him, with elegant concisoness, γυναικων ηπεροπευμα.

Teos gave to Greece her treasure,
  Sage Anacreon, sage in loving;
Fondly weaving lays of pleasure
  For the maids who blushed approving!

Oh! in nightly banquets sporting,
  Where's the guest could ever fly him?
Oh! with love's seduction courting,
  Where's the nymph could e'er deny him?

ª Thus Scaliger, in his dedicatory verses to Ronsard:
  Blandus, suaviloquus, dulcis Anacreon.

JUVENILE POEMS.

PREFACE BY THE EDITOR.

The Poems which I take the liberty of publishing were never intended by the Author to pass beyond the circle of his friends. He thought, with some justice, that what are called Occasional Poems must be always insipid and uninteresting to the greater part of their readers. The particular situations in which they were written ; the character of the author and of his associates ;—all these peculiarities must be known and felt before we can enter into the spirit of such compositions. This consideration would have always, I believe, prevented Mr. Little from submitting these trifles of the moment to the eye of dispassionate criticism ; and if their posthumous introduction to the world be injustice to his memory, or intrusion on the public, the error must be imputed to the injudicious partiality of friendship.

Mr. Little died in his one-and-twentieth year ; and most of these Poems were written at so early a period, that their errors may claim some indulgence from the critic: their author, as unambitious as indolent, scarce ever looked beyond the moment of composition ; he wrote as he pleased, careless whether he pleased as he wrote. It may likewise be remembered, that they were all the productions of an age when the passions very often give a colouring too warm to the imagination ; and this may palliate, if it cannot excuse, that air of levity which pervades so many of them. The 'aurea legge, s' ei piace ei lice,' he too much pursued, and too much inculcates. Few can regret this more sincerely than myself; and if my friend had lived, the judgment of riper years would have chastened his mind, and tempered the luxuriance of his fancy.

Mr. Little gave much of his time to the study of the amatory writers. If ever he expected to find in the ancients that delicacy of sentiment and variety of fancy which are so necessary to refine and animate the poetry of love, he was much disappointed. I know not any one of them who can be regarded as a model in that style : Ovid made love like a rake, and Propertius like a schoolmaster. The mythological allusions of the latter are called erudition by his commentators ; but such ostentatious display, upon a subject so simple as love, would be now esteemed vague and puerile, and was, even in his own times, pedantic. It is astonishing that so many critics have preferred him to the pathetic Tibullus ; but I believe the defects which a common reader condemns have been looked upon rather as beauties by those erudite men, the commentators, who find a field for their ingenuity and research in his Grecian learning and quaint obscurities.

Tibullus abounds with touches of fine and natural feeling. The idea of his unexpected return to Delia, 'Tunc veniam subito,' etc., is imagined with all the delicate ardour of a lover ; and the sentiment of 'nec te posse carere velim,' however colloquial the expression may have been, is natural and from the heart. But, in my opinion, the poet of Verona possessed more genuine feeling than any of them. His life was, I believe, unfortunate ; his associates were wild and abandoned ; and the warmth of his nature took too much advantage of the latitude which the morals of those times so criminally allowed to the passions. All this depraved his imagination, and made it the slave of his senses ; but still a native sensibility is often very warmly perceptible, and when he touches on pathos he reaches the heart immediately. They who have felt the sweets of return to a home from which they have long been absent, will confess the beauty of those simple, unaffected lines :

'O quid solutis est beatius curis?
Cum mens onus reponit, ac peregrino
Labore fessi venimus Larem ad nostrum
Desideratoque acquiescimus lecto.'—Carm. xxxii.

His sorrows on the death of his brother are the very tears of poesy; and when he complains of the ingratitude of mankind, even the inexperienced cannot but sympathize with him. I wish I were a poet; I should endeavour to catch, by translation, the spirit of those beauties which I admire[1] so warmly.

It seems to have been peculiarly the fate of Catullus, that the better and more valuable part of his poetry has not reached us; for there is confessedly nothing in his extant works to authorize the epithet 'doctus,' so universally bestowed upon him by the ancients. If time had suffered the rest to escape, we perhaps should have found among them some more purely amatory; but of those we possess, can there be a sweeter specimen of warm, yet chastened description, than his loves of Acme and Septimius? and the few little songs of dalliance to Lesbia are distinguished by such an exquisite playfulness, that they have always been assumed as models by the most elegant modern Latinists. Still I must confess, in the midst of these beauties,

'Medio de fonte leporum
Surgit amari aliquid, quod in ipsis floribus angat.'[2]

It has often been remarked, that the ancients knew nothing of gallantry; and we are told there was too much sincerity in their love to allow them to trifle with the semblance of passion. But I cannot perceive that they were anything more constant than the moderns: they felt all the same dissipation of the heart, though they knew not those seductive graces by which gallantry almost teaches it to be amiable. Watton, the learned advocate for the moderns, deserts them in considering this point of comparison, and praises the ancients for their ignorance of such a refinement; but he seems to have collected his notions of gallantry from the insipid *fadeurs* of the French romances, which are very unlike the sentimental levity, the 'grata protervitas,' of a Rochester or a Sedley.

From what I have had an opportunity of observing, the early poets of our own language were the models which Mr. Little selected for imitation. To attain their simplicity (*ævo rarissima nostro simplicitas*) was his fondest ambition. He could not have aimed at a grace more difficult of attainment,[3] and his life was of too short a date to allow him to perfect such a taste; but how far he was likely to have succeeded, the critic may judge from his productions.

I have found among his papers a novel, in rather an imperfect state, which, as soon as I have arranged and collected it, shall be submitted to the public eye.

Where Mr. Little was born, or what is the genealogy of his parents, are points in which very few readers can be interested. His life was one of those humble streams which have scarcely a name in the map of life, and the traveller may pass it by without inquiring its source or direction. His character was well known to all who were acquainted with him; for he had too much vanity to hide its virtues, and not enough of art to conceal its defects. The lighter traits of his mind may be traced perhaps in his writings; but the few for which he was valued live only in the remembrance of his friends.

T. M.

---

[1] In the following Poems there is a translation of one of his finest Carmina; but I fancy it is only a schoolboy's essay, and deserves to be praised for little more than the attempt.

[2] Lucretius.

[3] It is a curious illustration of the labour which simplicity requires, that the Ramblers of Johnson, elaborate as they appear, were written with fluency, and seldom required revision; while the simple language of Rousseau, which seems to come flowing from the heart, was the slow production of painful labour, pausing on every word, and balancing every sentence.

TO J. ATK—NS—N, ESQ.

MY DEAR SIR,
           I feel a very sincere pleasure in dedicating to you the Second Edition of our friend Little's Poems. I am not unconscious that there are many in the collection which perhaps it would be prudent to have altered or omitted; and, to say the truth, I more than once revised them for that purpose. But, I know not why, I distrusted either my heart or my judgment; and the consequence is, you have them in their original form:

        'Non possunt nostros multæ, Faustine, lituræ
        Emendare jocos; una litura potest.'

I am convinced, however, that though not quite a *casuiste reláché*, you have charity enough to forgive such inoffensive follies: you know the pious Beza was not the less revered for those sportive *juvenilia* which he published under a fictitious name; nor did the levity of Bembo's poems prevent him from making a very good cardinal.

        Believe me, my dear friend,
            With the truest esteem,
                Yours,
                      T. M.

April 19, 1802.

POEMS, ETC.

TO A LADY,
WITH SOME MANUSCRIPT POEMS.
ON LEAVING THE COUNTRY.

WHEN, casting many a look behind,
  I leave the friends I cherish here—
Perchance some other friends to find,
  But surely finding none so dear—

Haply the little simple page,
  Which votive thus I've traced for thee,
May now and then a look engage,
  And steal a moment's thought for me.

But, oh! in pity let not those
  Whose hearts are not of gentle mould,
Let not the eye, that seldom flows
  With feeling tear, my song behold.

For, trust me, they who never melt
  With pity, never melt with love;
And they will frown at all I've felt,
  And all my loving lays reprove.

But if, perhaps, some gentler mind,
  Which rather loves to praise than blame,
Should in my page an interest find,
  And linger kindly on my name;

Tell him,—or, oh! if gentler still,
  By female lips my name be blest:
Ah! where do all affections thrill
  So sweetly as in woman's breast?—

Tell her, that he whose loving themes
  Her eye indulgent wanders o'er,
Could sometimes wake from idle dreams,
  And bolder flights of fancy soar;

That glory oft would claim the lay,
  And friendship oft his numbers move;
But whisper then, that, 'sooth to say,
  His sweetest song was given to LOVE!'

TO THE LARGE AND BEAUTIFUL
MISS ———.
IN ALLUSION TO SOME PARTNERSHIP IN A LOTTERY SHARE.

IMPROMPTU.
Ego pars.—*Virg.*

IN wedlock a species of lottery lies,
  Where in blanks and in prizes we deal;
But how comes it that you, such a *capital prize*,
  Should so long have *remained in the wheel?*

If ever, by Fortune's indulgent decree,
　To me such a ticket should roll,
A *sixteenth*, Heaven knows! were sufficient for me;
　For what could I do with the *whole?*

TO JULIA.

IN ALLUSION TO SOME ILLIBERAL CRITICISMS.

Why, let the stingless critic chide
　With all that fume of vacant pride
　Which mantles o'er the pedant fool,
　Like vapour on a stagnant pool!
Oh! if the song, to feeling true,
　Can please the elect, the sacred few,
　Whose souls, by Taste and Nature taught,
　Thrill with the genuine pulse of thought—
If some fond feeling maid like thee,
　The warm-eyed child of Sympathy,
　Shall say, while o'er my simple theme
　She languishes in Passion's dream,
' He was, indeed, a tender soul—
　No critic law, no chill control,
　Should ever freeze, by timid art,
　The flowings of so fond a heart!'
Yes! soul of Nature! soul of Love!
　That, hovering like a snow-winged dove,
　Breathed o'er my cradle warblings wild,
　And hailed me Passion's warmest child!
Grant me the tear from Beauty's eye,
From Feeling's breast the votive sigh;
Oh! let my song, my memory, find
　A shrine within the tender mind;
　And I will scorn the critic's chide,
　And I will scorn the fume of pride
　Which mantles o'er the pedant fool,
　Like vapour on a stagnant pool!

INCONSTANCY.

And do I then wonder that Julia deceives me,
　When surely there's nothing in nature more common?
She vows to be true, and while vowing she leaves me—
　But could I expect any more from a woman?

Oh, woman! your heart is a pitiful treasure;
　And Mahomet's doctrine was not too severe,
When he thought you were only materials of pleasure,
　And reason and thinking were out of your sphere.

By your heart, when the fond sighing lover can win it,
　He thinks that an age of anxiety's paid;
But, oh! while he's blest, let him die on the minute—
　If he live but a *day*, he'll be surely betrayed.

TO JULIA.

Though Fate, my girl, may bid us part,
　Our souls it cannot, shall not, sever;
The heart will seek its kindred heart,
　And cling to it as close as ever.

But must we, must we part indeed?
　Is all our dream of rapture over?
And does not Julia's bosom bleed
　To leave so dear, so fond a lover?

Does *she* too mourn?—Perhaps she may;
　Perhaps she weeps our blisses fleeting:
But why is Julia's eye so gay,
　If Julia's heart like mine is beating?

I oft have loved the brilliant glow
　Of rapture in her blue eye streaming—
But can the bosom bleed with woe,
　While joy is in the glances beaming."

No, no!—Yet, love, I will not chide,
　Although your heart *were* fond of roving:
Nor that, nor all the world beside,
　Could keep your faithful boy from loving.

You'll soon be distant from his eye,
　And, with you, all that's worth possessing
Oh! then it will be sweet to die,
　When life has lost its only blessing!

SONG.

Sweet seducer! blandly smiling;
Charming still, and still beguiling!
Oft I swore to love thee never,
Yet I love thee more than ever!

Why that little wanton blushing,
Glancing eye, and bosom flushing?
Flushing warm, and wily glancing—
All is lovely, all entrancing!

Turn away those lips of blisses—
I am poisoned by thy kisses!
Yet, again, ah! turn them to me:
Ruin's sweet, when they undo me!

Oh! be less, be less enchanting;
Let some little grace be wanting;
Let my eyes, when I'm expiring,
Gaze awhile without admiring!

IMITATION OF CATULLUS.[1]

TO HIMSELF.

Miser Catulle, desinas ineptire, etc.

Cease the sighing fool to play;
Cease to trifle life away;
Nor vainly think those joys thine own,
Which all, alas! have falsely flown!
What hours, Catullus, once were thine,
How fairly seemed thy day to shine,
When lightly thou didst fly to meet
The girl, who smiled so rosy sweet—
The girl thou lovedst with fonder pain
Than e'er thy heart can feel again!
You met—your souls seemed all in one—
Sweet little sports were said and done—
Thy heart was warm enough for both,
And hers indeed was nothing loath.
Such were the hours that once were thine;
But, ah! those hours no longer shine!
For now the nymph delights no more
In what she loved so dear before;
And all Catullus now can do
Is to be proud and frigid too;
Nor follow where the wanton flies,
Nor sue the bliss that she denies.
False maid! he bids farewell to thee,
To love, and all love's misery.
The heyday of his heart is o'er,
Nor will he court one favour more;
But soon he'll see thee droop thy head,
Doomed to a lone and loveless bed,
When none will seek the happy night,
Or come to traffic in delight!
Fly, perjured girl!—but whither fly?
Who now will praise thy cheek and eye?
Who now will drink the syren tone,
Which tells him thou art all his own?
Who now will court thy wild delights,
Thy honey kiss, and turtle bites?
Oh! none.—And he who loved before
Can never, never love thee more!

A REFLECTION AT SEA.

See how, beneath the moonbeam's smile,
  Yon little billow heaves its breast,
And foams and sparkles for a while,
  And murmuring then subsides to rest.

Thus man, the sport of bliss and care,
  Rises on Time's eventful sea;
And, having swelled a moment there,
  Thus melts into eternity!

---

[1] Few poets knew better than Catullus what a French writer calls
    **la délicatesse
    D'un voluptueux sentiment;**
but his passions too often obscured his imagination.

SONG.

If I swear by that eye, you'll allow
  Its look is so shifting and new,
That the oath I might take on it now
  The very next glance would undo!

Those babies that nestle so sly,
  Such different arrows have got,
That an oath, on the glance of an eye
  Such as yours, may be off in a shot!

Should I swear by the dew on your lip,
  Though each moment the treasure renews,
If my constancy wishes to trip,
  I may kiss off the oath when I choose!

Or a sigh may disperse from that flower
  The dew and the oath that are there!
And I'd make a new vow every hour,
  To lose them so sweetly in air!

But clear up that heaven of your brow,
  Nor fancy my faith is a feather;
On my heart I will pledge you my vow,
  And they both must be broken together!

ELEGIAC STANZAS,

**SUPPOSED TO BE WRITTEN BY JULIA ON THE
DEATH OF HER BROTHER.**

Though sorrow long has worn my heart;
  Though every day I've counted o'er
Has brought a new and quickening smart
  To wounds that rankled fresh before;

Though in my earliest life bereft
  Of many a link by nature tied;
Though hope deceived, and pleasure left;
  Though friends betrayed, and foes belied;

I still had hopes—for hope will stay
  After the sunset of delight;
So like the star which ushers day,
  We scarce can think it heralds night!

I hoped that, after all its strife,
  My weary heart at length should rest,
And, fainting from the waves of life,
  Find harbour in a brother's breast.

That brother's breast was warm with truth,
  Was bright with honour's purest ray;
He was the dearest, gentlest youth—
  Oh! why then was he torn away?

He should have stayed, have lingered here,
  To calm his Julia's every woe;
He should have chased each bitter tear,
  And not have caused those tears to flow.

We saw his youthful soul expand
In blooms of genius, nursed by taste;
While Science, with a fostering hand,
Upon his brow her chaplet placed.

We saw his gradual opening mind
Enriched by all the graces dear;
Enlightened, social, and refined,
In friendship firm, in love sincere.

Such was the youth we loved so well;
Such were the hopes that fate denied—
We loved, but, ah! we could not tell
How deep, how dearly, till he died!

Close as the fondest links could strain,
Twined with my very heart he grew;
And by that fate which breaks the chain,
The heart is almost broken too!

SONG.

Sweetest love! I'll not forget thee;
Time shall only teach my heart,
Fonder, warmer, to regret thee,
Lovely, gentle as thou art!—
   Farewell, Bessy!

Yet, oh! yet again we'll meet, love,
And repose our hearts at last:
Oh! sure 'twill then be sweet, love,
Calm to think on sorrows past.—
   Farewell, Bessy!

Yes, my girl, the distant blessing
Mayn't be always sought in vain;
And the moment of possessing—
Will't not, love, repay our pain?—
   Farewell, Bessy!

Still I feel my heart is breaking,
When I think I stray from thee,
Round the world that quiet seeking,
Which I fear is not for me!—
   Farewell, Bessy!

Calm to peace thy lover's bosom—
Can it, dearest! must it be?
Thou within an hour shalt lose him,
He for ever loses thee!—
   Farewell, Bessy!

SONG.

Come tell me where the maid is found
Whose heart can love without deceit,
And I will range the world around,
To sigh one moment at her feet.

Oh! tell me where's her sainted home,
What air receives her blessed sigh;

A pilgrimage of years I'll roam
To catch one sparkle of her eye!

And, if her cheek be rosy bright,
While truth within her bosom lies,
I'll gaze upon her, morn and night,
Till my heart leave me through my eyes!

Show me on earth a thing so rare,
I'll own all miracles are true;
To make one maid sincere and fair,
Oh! 'tis the utmost Heaven can do!

TO ——.

With all my soul, then, let us part,
Since both are anxious to be free;
And I will send you home your heart,
If you will send back mine to me.

We've had some happy hours together,
But joy must often change its wing;
And spring would be but gloomy weather,
If we had nothing else but spring.

'Tis not that I expect to find
A more devoted, fond, and true one,
With rosier cheek or sweeter mind—
Enough for me that she's a new one.

Thus let us leave the bower of love,
Where we have loitered long in bliss;
And you may down *that* pathway rove,
While I shall take my way through *this*.

Our hearts have suffered little harm
In this short fever of desire;
You have not lost a single charm,
Nor I one spark of feeling fire.

My kisses have not stained the rose
Which Nature hung upon your lip;
And still your sigh with nectar flows
For many a raptured soul to sip.

Farewell! and when some other fair
Shall call your wanderer to her arms,
'Twill be my luxury to compare
Her spells with your remembered charms.

'This cheek,' I'll say, 'is not so bright
As one that used to meet my kiss;
This eye has not such liquid light
As one that used to talk of bliss!'

Farewell! and when some future lover
Shall claim the heart which I resign,
And in exulting joys discover
All the charms that once were mine;

I think I should be sweetly blest,
If, in a soft imperfect sigh,
You'd say, while to his bosom prest,
He loves not half so well as I!

A NIGHT THOUGHT.

How oft a cloud, with envious veil,
 Obscures yon bashful light,
Which seems so modestly to steal
 Along the waste of night!

'Tis thus the world's obtrusive wrongs
 Obscure with malice keen
Some timid heart, which only longs
 To live and die unseen!

THE KISS.

Grow to my lip, thou sacred kiss,
 On which my soul's beloved swore
That there should come a time of bliss
 When she would mock my hopes no more;
And fancy shall thy glow renew,
 In sighs at morn, and dreams at night,
And none shall steal thy holy dew
 Till thou'rt absolved by rapture's rite.
Sweet hours that are to make me blest,
 Oh! fly, like breezes, to the goal,
And let my love, my more than soul,
 Come panting to this fevered breast;
And while in every glance I drink
 The rich o'erflowings of her mind,
Oh! let her all impassioned sink,
 In sweet abandonment resigned,
Blushing for all our struggles past,
And murmuring, 'I am thine at last!'

ELEGIAC STANZAS.
Sic juvat perire.

When wearied wretches sink to sleep,
 How heavenly soft their slumbers lie!
How sweet is death to those who weep,
 To those who weep and long to die!

Saw you the soft and grassy bed,
 Where flowerets deck the green earth's breast?
'Tis there I wish to lay my head,
 'Tis there I wish to sleep at rest!

Oh! let not tears embalm my tomb,
 None but the dews by twilight given!
Oh! let not sighs disturb the gloom,
 None but the whispering winds of Heaven!

RONDEAU.

'Good night! good night!'—and is it so?
And must I from my Rosa go?
Oh, Rosa! say 'Good night!' once more,
And I'll repeat it o'er and o'er,
Till the first glance of dawning light
Shall find us saying still, 'Good night!'
And still 'Good night!' my Rosa say—
But whisper still, 'A minute stay;'
And I will stay, and every minute
Shall have an age of rapture in it.
We'll kiss and kiss in quick delight,
And murmur, while we kiss, 'Good night!'

'Good night!' you'll murmur with a sigh,
And tell me it is time to fly;
And I will vow to kiss no more,
Yet kiss you closer than before;
Till slumber seal our weary sight—
And then, my love! my soul! 'Good night!'

TO ROSA.

Like him who trusts to summer skies,
 And puts his little bark to sea,
Is he who, lured by smiling eyes,
 Consigns his simple heart to thee:
For fickle is the summer wind,
 And sadly may the bark be tossed;
For thou art sure to change thy mind,
 And then the wretched heart is lost!

TO ROSA.

Oh! why should the girl of my soul be in tears
 At a meeting of rapture like this,
When the glooms of the past, and the sorrow of years,
 Have been paid by a moment of bliss?

Are they shed for that moment of blissful delight
 Which dwells on her memory yet?
Do they flow, like the dews of the amorous night,
 From the warmth of the sun that has set?

Oh! sweet is the tear on that languishing smile,
 That smile which is loveliest then;
And if such are the drops that delight can beguile,
 Thou shalt weep them again and again!

WRITTEN IN THE BLANK LEAF OF A LADY'S COMMON-PLACE BOOK.

Here is one leaf reserved for me,
From all thy sweet memorials free;
And here my simple song might tell
The feelings thou must guess so well.
But could I thus, within thy mind,
One little vacant corner find,
Where no impression yet is seen,
Where no memorial yet has been,
Oh! it should be my sweetest care
To *write my name* for ever *there!*

LOVE AND MARRIAGE.

Eque brevi verbo ferro perenne malum.
Secundus, Eleg. vii.

STILL the question I must parry,
   Still a wayward truant prove:
Where I love, I must not marry,
   Where I marry, cannot love.

Were she fairest of creation,
   With the least presuming mind;
Learned without affectation;
   Not deceitful, yet refined;

Wise enough, but never rigid;
   Gay, but not too lightly free;
Chaste as snow, and yet not frigid;
   Warm, yet satisfied with me: .

Were she all this, ten times over,
   All that Heaven to earth allows,
I should be too much her lover
   Ever to become her spouse.

Love will never bear enslaving;
   Summer garments suit him best:
Bliss itself is not worth having,
   If we're by compulsion blest.

TO ROSA.

WRITTEN DURING ILLNESS.

THE wisest soul, by anguish torn,
   Will soon unlearn the lore it knew;
And when the shining casket's worn,
   The gem within will tarnish too.

But love's an essence of the soul,
   Which sinks not with this chain of clay—
Which throbs beyond the chill control
   Of withering pain or pale decay.

And surely when the touch of death
   Dissolves the spirit's mortal ties,
Love still attends the soaring breath,
   And makes it purer for the skies!

Oh, Rosa! when, to seek its sphere,
   My soul shall leave this orb of men,
That love it found so blissful here
   Shall be its best of blisses then!

And, as in fabled dreams of old,
   Some airy genius, child of time,
Presided o'er each star that rolled,
   And tracked it through its path sublime;

So thou, fair planet, not unled,'
   Shalt through thy mortal orbit stray;
Thy lover's shade, divinely wed,
   Shall linger round thy wandering way.

Let other spirits range the sky,
   And brighten in the solar gem;
I'll bask beneath that lucid eye,
   Nor envy worlds of suns to them!

And oh! if airy shapes may steal
   To mingle with a mortal frame,
Then, then, my love!—but drop the veil!
   Hide, hide from Heaven the unholy flame.

No!—when that heart shall cease to beat,
   And when that breath at length is free;
Then, Rosa, soul to soul we'll meet,
   And mingle to eternity.

ANACREONTIC.

FRIEND of my soul! this goblet sip,
   'Twill chase that pensive tear;
'Tis not so sweet as woman's lip,
   But, oh! 'tis more sincere.
Like her delusive beam,
   'Twill steal away thy mind;
But, like affection's dream,
   It leaves no sting behind!

Come, twine the wreath, thy brows to shade;
   These flowers were culled at noon;—
Like woman's love the rose will fade,
   But ah! not half so soon!
For though the flower's decayed,
   Its fragrance is not o'er;
But once when love's betrayed,
   The heart can bloom no more!

ANACREONTIC.

In lacrymas verterat omne merum.
Tib. lib. i. eleg. 5.

PRESS the grape, and let it pour
Around the board its purple shower;
And while the drops my goblet steep,
I'll think—in *woe* the clusters weep.
Weep on, weep on, my pouting vine!
Heaven grant no tears but tears of wine.
Weep on; and, as thy sorrows flow,
I'll taste the *luxury of woe!*

THE BALLAD.[1]

THOU hast sent me a flowery band,
   And told me 'twas fresh from the field;

---

[1] This ballad was probably suggested by the following Epigram in Martial:
   Intactas quare mittis mihi, Polla, coronas,
   A te vexatas malo tenere rosas.
            Epig. xc. lib. 11.—E.

That the leaves were untouched by the hand,
   And the purest of odours would yield.

And indeed it was fragrant and fair;
   But, if it were handled by thee,
It would bloom with a livelier air,
   And would surely be sweeter to me!

Then take it, and let it entwine
   Thy tresses, so flowing and bright;
And each little floweret will shine
   More rich than a gem to my sight.

Let the odorous gale of thy breath
   Embalm it with many a sigh;
Nay, let it be withered to death
   Beneath the warm noon of thine eye.

And instead of the dew that it bears,
   The dew dropping fresh from the tree,
On its leaves let me number the tears
   That affection has stolen from thee!

TO PHILLIS.

PHILLIS, you little rosy rake,
   That heart of yours I long to rifle:
Come, give it me, and do not make
   So much ado about a *trifle!*

TO MISS ——.

ON HER ASKING THE AUTHOR WHY SHE HAD SLEEPLESS NIGHTS.

I'LL ask the sylph who round thee flies,
   And in thy breath his pinion dips,
Who suns him in thy lucent eyes,
   And faints upon thy sighing lips:

I'll ask him where's the veil of sleep
   That used to shade thy looks of light;
And why those eyes their vigil keep,
   When other suns are sunk in night.

And I will say—her angel breast
   Has never throbbed with guilty sting;
Her bosom is the sweetest nest
   Where Slumber could repose his wing!

And I will say—her cheeks of flame,
   Which glow like roses in the sun,
Have never felt a blush of shame,
   Except for what her eyes have done!

Then tell me, why, thou child of air!
   Does Slumber from her eyelids rove?
What is her heart's impassioned care?—
   Perhaps, oh sylph! perhaps 'tis *love!*

TO ROSA.

A far conserva, e cumulo d' amanti.—*Past. Fid.*

AND are you then a thing of art,
   Seducing all and loving none?
And have I strove to gain a heart
   Which every coxcomb thinks his own?

And do you, like the dotard's fire,
   Which, powerless of enjoying any,
Feeds its abortive sick desire,
   By trifling impotent with many?

Do you thus seek to flirt a number,
   And through a round of danglers run,
Because your heart's insipid slumber
   Could never wake to *feel* for *one?*

Tell me at once if this be true,
   And I shall calm my jealous breast;
Shall learn to join the dangling crew,
   And share your simpers with the rest.

But if your heart be not so free,—
   Oh! if another share that heart,
Tell not the damning tale to me,
   But mingle mercy with your art.

I'd rather think you black as hell,
   Than find you to be all divine,
And know that heart could love so well,
   Yet know that heart would *not* be mine!

TO JULIA.

ON HER BIRTH-DAY.

WHEN Time was entwining the garland of years,
   Which to crown my beloved was given,
Though some of the leaves might be sullied with tears,
   Yet the flowers were all gathered in heaven!

And long may this garland be sweet to the eye,
   May its verdure for ever be new!
Young Love shall enrich it with many a sigh,
   And Pity shall nurse it with dew!

ELEGIAC STANZAS.[1]

How sweetly could I lay my head
   Within the cold grave's silent breast;
Where Sorrow's tears no more are shed,
   No more the ills of life molest!

For, ah! my heart, how very soon
   The glittering dreams of youth are past!
And, long before it reach its noon,
   The sun of life is overcast.

---

[1] This poem, and some others of the same pensive cast, we may suppose, were the result of the *few* melancholy moments which a life so short and so pleasant as that of the author could have allowed.—E.

NONSENSE.

Good reader! if you e'er have seen,
  When Phœbus hastens to his pillow,
The mermaids, with their tresses green,
  Dancing upon the western billow:
If you have seen, at twilight dim,
  When the lone spirit's vesper hymn
Floats wild along the winding shore:
If you have seen, through mist of eve,
The fairy train their ringlets weave,
Glancing along the spangled green;—
  If you have seen all this, and more,
God bless me! what a deal you've seen!

THE SURPRISE.

Chloris, I swear, by all I ever swore,
That from this hour I shall not love thee more.—
'What! love no more? Oh! why this altered
  vow?'
Because I *cannot* love thee *more*—than *now!*

TO MRS. ——

ON HER BEAUTIFUL TRANSLATION OF VOITURE'S KISS.

Mon ame sur ma lèvre était lors toute entière,
Pour savourer le miel qui sur la vôtre était;
Mais en me retirant, elle resta derrière,
Tant de ce doux plaisir l'amorce l'arrêtoit!—*Voit.*

How heavenly was the poet's doom,
  To breathe his spirit through a kiss;
And lose within so sweet a tomb
  The trembling messenger of bliss!

And, ah! his soul returned to feel
  That it *again* could ravished be;
For in the kiss that thou didst steal,
  His life and soul have fled to thee!

ON THE DEATH OF A LADY.

Sweet spirit! if thy airy sleep
  Nor sees my tears, nor hears my sighs,
Oh! I will weep, in luxury weep,
  Till the last heart's-drop fills mine eyes.

But if thy sainted soul can feel,
  And mingles in our misery,
Then, then, my breaking heart I'll seal—
  Thou shalt not hear one sigh from me!

The beam of morn was on the stream,
  But sullen clouds the day deform:
Thou wert, indeed, that morning beam,
  And death, alas! that sullen storm.

Thou wert not formed for living here,
  For thou wert kindred with the sky;
Yet, yet we held thee all so dear,
  We thought thou wert not formed to die!

TO ROSA.

Does the harp of Rosa slumber?
Once it breathed the sweetest number!
Never does a wilder song
Steal the breezy lyre along,
When the wind, in odours dying,
Woos it with enamoured sighing.

Does the harp of Rosa cease?
Once it told a tale of peace
To her lover's throbbing breast—
Then he was divinely blest!
Ah! but Rosa loves no more,
Therefore Rosa's song is o'er;
And her harp neglected lies;
And her boy forgotten sighs.
Silent harp—forgotten lover—
Rosa's love and song are over!

NATURE'S LABELS.

A FRAGMENT.

In vain we fondly strive to trace
The soul's reflection in the face;
In vain we dwell on lines and crosses,
Crookèd mouth, or short proboscis;
Boobies have looked as wise and bright
As Plato or the Stagyrite:
And many a sage and learned skull
Has peeped through windows dark and dull!
Since then, though art do all it can,
We ne'er can reach the inward man,
Nor inward woman, from without
(Though, ma'am, you *smile*, as if in doubt),
I think 'twere well if Nature could
(And Nature could, if Nature would)
Some pretty short descriptions write,
In tablets large, in black and white,
Which she might hang about our throttles,
Like labels upon physic-bottles.
There we might read of all—But stay—
As learned dialectics say,
The argument most apt and ample
For common use, is the example.
For instance, then, if Nature's care
Had not arranged those traits so fair,
Which speak the soul of Lucy L—nd—n,
This is the label she'd have pinned on.

LABEL FIRST.

Within this vase there lies enshrined
The purest, brightest gem of mind!
Though Feeling's hand may sometimes throw
Upon its charms the shade of woe,

The lustre of the gem, when veiled,
Shall be but mellowed, not concealed.

Now, sirs, imagine, if you're able,
That Nature wrote a second label,
They're her own words—at least suppose so—
And boldly pin it on Pomposo.

LABEL SECOND.

When I composed the fustian brain
Of this redoubted Captain Vain,
I had at hand but few ingredients,
And so was forced to use expedients.
I put therein some small discerning,
A grain of sense, a grain of learning;
And when I saw the void behind,
I filled it up with—froth and wind!

* * * * * * *

TO JULIA.

Mock me no more with love's beguiling dream,
  A dream, I find, illusory as sweet:
One smile of friendship, nay, of cold esteem,
  Is dearer far than passion's bland deceit!

I've heard you oft eternal truth declare;
  Your heart was only mine, I once believed.
Ah! shall I say that all your vows were air?
  And must I say, my hopes were all deceived?

Vow, then, no longer that our souls are twined,
  That all our joys are felt with mutual zeal:
Julia! 'tis pity, pity makes you kind;
  You know I love, and you would seem to feel.

But shall I still go revel in those arms
  On bliss in which affection takes no part?
No, no! farewell! you give me but your charms,
  When I had fondly thought you gave your heart.

SYMPATHY.

TO JULIA.

Sine me sit nulla Venus.—Sulpicia.

Our hearts, my love, were doomed to be
The genuine twins of Sympathy:
  They live with one sensation:
In joy or grief, but most in love,
Our heart-strings musically move,
  And thrill with like vibration.

How often have I heard thee say,
Thy vital pulse shall cease to play
  When mine no more is moving!
Since, now, to feel a joy *alone*
Were worse to thee than feeling none:
  Such sympathy in loving!

TO JULIA.

I saw the peasant's hand unkind
  From yonder oak the ivy sever;
They seemed in very being twined;
  Yet now the oak is fresh as ever.

Not so the widowed ivy shines:
  Torn from its dear and only stay,
In drooping widowhood it pines,
  And scatters all its blooms away!

Thus, Julia, did our hearts entwine,
  Till Fate disturbed their tender ties:
Thus gay indifference blooms in thine,
  While mine, deserted, droops and dies!

TO MRS. M———.

Sweet lady! look not thus again:
  Those little pouting smiles recall
A maid remembered now with pain,
  Who was my love, my life, my all!

Oh! while this heart delirious took
  Sweet poison from her thrilling eye,
Thus would she pout, and lisp, and look,
  And I would hear, and gaze, and sigh!

Yes, I did love her—madly love—
  She was the sweetest, best deceiver!
And oft she swore she'd never rove!
  And I was destined to believe her!

Then, lady, do not wear the smile
  Of her whose smile could thus betray:
Alas! I think the lovely wile
  Again might steal my heart away.

And when the spell that stole my mind
  On lips so pure as thine I see,
I fear the heart which she resigned
  Will err again, and fly to thee!

SONG.

When Time, who steals our years away,
  Shall steal our pleasures too,
The memory of the past will stay,
  And half our joys renew.

Then, Chloe, when thy beauty's flower
  Shall feel the wintry air,
Remembrance will recall the hour
  When thou alone wert fair!

Then talk no more of future gloom;
  Our joys shall always last;
For hope shall brighten days to come,
  And memory gild the past.

Come, Chloe, fill the genial bowl,
  I drink to love and thee:
Thou never canst decay in soul,
  Thou'lt still be young for me.

And as thy lips the tear-drop chase,
  Which on my cheek they find,
So hope shall steal away the trace
  Which sorrow leaves behind!

Then fill the bowl—away with gloom!
  Our joys shall always last;
For hope shall brighten days to come,
  And memory gild the past!

But mark, at thought of future years,
  When love shall lose its soul,
My Chloe drops her timid tears,
  They mingle with my bowl!

How like this bowl of wine, my fair,
  Our loving life shall fleet;
Though tears may sometimes mingle there,
  The draught will still be sweet!

Then fill the bowl—away with gloom!
  Our joys shall always last;
For hope will brighten days to come,
  And memory gild the past!

THE RING.[1]

A TALE.

Annulus ille viri.—Ovid. *Amor.* lib. ii. eleg. 15.

THE happy day at length arrived
  When Rupert was to wed
The fairest maid in Saxony,
  And take her to his bed.

As soon as morn was in the sky,
  The feast and sports began;
The men admired the happy maid,
  The maids the happy man.

In many a sweet device of mirth
  The day was passed along;
And some the featly dance amused,
  And some the dulcet song.

The younger maids with Isabel
  Disported through the bowers,
And decked her robe, and crowned her head
  With motley bridal flowers.

The matrons all in rich attire,
  Within the castle walls,
Sat listening to the choral strains
  That echoed through the halls.

Young Rupert and his friends repaired
  Unto a spacious court,
To strike the bounding tennis-ball
  In feat and manly sport.

The bridegroom on his finger had
  The wedding-ring so bright,
Which was to grace the lily hand
  Of Isabel that night.

And fearing he might break the gem,
  Or lose it in the play,
He looked around the court, to see
  Where he the ring might lay.

Now in the court a statue stood,
  Which there full long had been;
It was a heathen goddess, or
  Perhaps a heathen queen.

Upon its marble finger then
  He tried the ring to fit;
And, thinking it was safest there,
  Thereon he fastened it.

And now the tennis sports went on,
  Till they were wearied all,
And messengers announced to them
  Their dinner in the hall.

Young Rupert for his wedding-ring
  Unto the statue went;
But, oh! how was he shocked to find
  The marble finger bent!

The hand was closed upon the ring
  With firm and mighty clasp;
In vain he tried, and tried, and tried,
  He could not loose the grasp!

How sore surprised was Rupert's mind,—
  As well his mind might be;
'I'll come,' quoth he, 'at night again,
  When none are here to see.'

He went unto the feast, and much
  He thought upon his ring;
And much he wondered what could mean
  So very strange a thing!

The feast was o'er, and to the court
  He went without delay,

---

[1] I should be sorry to think that my friend had any serious intentions of frightening the nursery by this story: I rather hope—though the manner of it leads me to doubt—that his design was to ridicule that distempered taste which prefers those monsters of the fancy to the 'speciosa miracula' of true poetic imagination.

I find, by a note in the manuscript, that he met with this story in a German author, Fromman upon *Fascination*, book iii. part vi. chap. 18. On consulting the work, I perceive that Fromman quotes it from Beluacensis, among many other stories equally diabolical and interesting.—E.

Resolved to break the marble hand,
 And force the ring away!

But mark a stranger wonder still—
 The ring was there no more;
Yet was the marble hand ungrasped,
 And open as before!

He searched the base, and all the court,
 And nothing could he find,
But to the castle did return
 With sore bewildered mind.

Within he found them all in mirth,
 The night in dancing flew;
The youth another ring procured,
 And none the adventure knew.

And now the priest has joined their hands,
 The hours of love advance!
Rupert almost forgets to think
 Upon the morn's mischance.

Within the bed fair Isabel
 In blushing sweetness lay,
Like flowers half-opened by the dawn,
 And waiting for the day.

And Rupert, by her lovely side,
 In youthful beauty glows,
Like Phœbus, when he bends to cast
 His beams upon a rose!

And here my song should leave them both,
 Nor let the rest be told,
But for the horrid, horrid tale
 It yet has to unfold!

Soon Rupert, 'twixt his bride and him,
 A death-cold carcase found;
He saw it not, but thought he felt
 Its arms embrace him round.

He started up, and then returned,
 But found the phantom still;
In vain he shrunk, it clipped him round,
 With damp and deadly chill!

And when he bent, the earthy lips
 A kiss of horror gave;
'Twas like the smell from charnel vaults,
 Or from the mouldering grave!

Ill-fated Rupert, wild and loud
 Thou criedst to thy wife,
'Oh! save me from this horrid fiend,
 My Isabel! my life!'

But Isabel had nothing seen,
 She looked around in vain;
And much she mourned the mad conceit
 That racked her Rupert's brain.

At length from this invisible
 These words to Rupert came;
(Oh God! while he did hear the words,
 What terrors shook his frame!)

'Husband! husband! I've the ring
 Thou gav'st to-day to me;
And thou'rt to me for ever wed,
 As I am wed to thee!'

And all the night the demon lay
 Cold-chilling by his side,
And strained him with such deadly grasp,
 He thought he should have died!

But when the dawn of day was near,
 The horrid phantom fled,
And left the affrighted youth to weep
 By Isabel in bed.

All, all that day a gloomy cloud
 Was seen on Rupert's brows;
Fair Isabel was likewise sad,
 But strove to cheer her spouse.

And, as the day advanced, he thought
 Of coming night with fear:
Ah! that he must with terror view
 The bed that should be dear!

At length the second night arrived,
 Again their couch they pressed;
Poor Rupert hoped that all was o'er,
 And looked for love and rest.

But oh! when midnight came, again
 The fiend was at his side,
And, as it strained him in its grasp,
 With howl exulting cried,—

'Husband! husband! I've the ring,
 The ring thou gav'st to me;
And thou'rt to me for ever wed,
 As I am wed to thee!'

In agony of wild despair,
 He started from the bed;
And thus to his bewildered wife
 The trembling Rupert said:

'Oh Isabel! dost thou not see
 A shape of horrors here,
That strains me to the deadly kiss,
 And keeps me from my dear?'

'No, no, my love! my Rupert, I
 No shape of horrors see;
And much I mourn the phantasy
 That keeps my dear from me!'

This night, just like the night before,
 In terrors passed away,
Nor did the demon vanish thence
 Before the dawn of day.

Says Rupert then, 'My Isabel,
  Dear partner of my woe,
To Father Austin's holy cave
  This instant will I go.'

Now Austin was a reverend man,
  Who acted wonders maint,
Whom all the country round believed
  A devil or a saint!

To Father Austin's holy cave
  Then Rupert went full straight,
And told him all, and asked him how
  To remedy his fate.

The father heard the youth, and then
  Retired awhile to pray;
And, having prayed for half an hour,
  Returned, and thus did say:

'There is a place where four roads meet,
  Which I will tell to thee;
Be there this eve, at fall of night,
  And list what thou shalt see.

Thou'lt see a group of figures pass
  In strange disordered crowd,
Travelling by torchlight through the roads,
  With noises strange and loud.

And one that's high above the rest,
  Terrific towering o'er,
Will make thee know him at a glance,
  So I need say no more.

To him from me these tablets give,
  They'll soon be understood;
Thou need'st not fear, but give them straight,
  I've scrawled them with my blood!'

The nightfall came, and Rupert all
  In pale amazement went
To where the cross-roads met, and he
  Was by the father sent.

And lo! a group of figures came
  In strange disordered crowd,
Travelling by torchlight through the roads,
  With noises strange and loud.

And as the gloomy train advanced,
  Rupert beheld from far
A female form of wanton mien
  Seated upon a car.

And Rupert, as he gazed upon
  The loosely-vested dame,
Thought of the marble statue's look,
  For hers was just the same.

Behind her walked a hideous form,
  With eyeballs flashing death;
Whene'er he breathed, a sulphured smoke
  Came burning in his breath!

He seemed the first of all the crowd
  Terrific towering o'er;
'Yes, yes,' said Rupert, 'this is he,
  And I need ask no more.'

Then slow he went, and to this fiend
  The tablets trembling gave,
Who looked and read them with a yell
  That would disturb the grave.

And when he saw the blood-scrawled name,
  His eyes with fury shine;
'I thought,' cries he, 'his time was out,
  But he must soon be mine!'

Then darting at the youth a look,
  Which rent his soul with fear,
He went unto the female fiend,
  And whispered in her ear.

The female fiend no sooner heard,
  Than, with reluctant look,
The very ring that Rupert lost
  She from her finger took;

And, giving it unto the youth,
  With eyes that breathed of hell,
She said in that tremendous voice
  Which he remembered well:

'In Austin's name take back the ring,
  The ring thou gav'st to me;
And thou'rt to me no longer wed,
  Nor longer I to thee.'

He took the ring, the rabble passed,
  He home returned again;
His wife was then the happiest fair,
  The happiest he of men.

SONG.

Think on that look of humid ray,
  Which for a moment mixed with mine,
And for that moment seemed to say,
  'I dare not, or I would be thine!'

Think, think on every smile and glance,
  On all thou hast to charm and move;
And then forgive my bosom's trance,
  And tell me 'tis not sin to love!

Oh! *not* to love thee were the sin;
  For sure, if Heaven's decrees be done,
Thou, thou art destined still to win,
  As I was destined to be won!

SONG.

Fly from the world, O Bessy! to me,
  Thou'lt never find any sincerer;

I'll give up the world, O Bessy! for thee,
I can never meet any that's dearer!
Then tell me no more, with a tear and a sigh,
That our loves will be censured by many;
All, all have their follies, and who will deny
That ours is the sweetest of any?

When your lip has met mine, in abandonment sweet,
Have we felt as if virtue forbid it?—
Have we felt as if Heaven denied them to meet?—
No, rather 'twas Heaven that did it!
So innocent, love! is the pleasure we sip,
So little of guilt is there in it,
That I wish all my errors were lodged on your lip,
And I'd kiss them away in a minute!

Then come to your lover, oh! fly to his shed,
From a world which I know thou despisest;
And slumber will hover as light on our bed,
As e'er on the couch of the wisest!
And when o'er our pillow the tempest is driven,
And thou, pretty innocent! fearest,
I'll tell thee, it is not the chiding of Heaven,
'Tis only our lullaby, dearest!

And, oh! when we lie on our death-bed, my love!
Looking back on the scene of our errors,
A sigh from my Bessy shall plead then above,
And Death be disarmed of his terrors!
And each to the other embracing will say,
'Farewell! let us hope we're forgiven!'
Thy last fading glance will illumine the way,
And a kiss be our passport to heaven!

THE SHRINE.

TO ——.

My fates had destined me to rove
A long, long pilgrimage of love;
And many an altar on my way
Has lured my pious steps to stay;
For, if the saint was young and fair,
I turned and sung my vespers there.
This, from a youthful pilgrim's fire,
Is what your pretty saints require:
To pass, nor tell a single bead,
With them would be *profane indeed!*
But, trust me, all this young devotion,
Was but to keep my zeal in motion;
And, every *humbler altar* past,
I now have reached THE SHRINE at last!

THE CATALOGUE.

'COME, tell me,' says Rosa, as, kissing and kissed,
One day she reclined on my breast;
'Come, tell me the number, repeat me the list
Of the nymphs you have loved and caressed.'

Oh, Rosa! 'twas only my fancy that roved,
My heart at the moment was free;
But I'll tell thee, my girl, how many I've loved,
And the number shall finish with thee!

My tutor was Kitty; in infancy wild
She taught me the way to be blest;
She taught me to love her, I loved like a child,
But Kitty could fancy the rest.
This lesson of dear and enrapturing lore
I have never forgot, I allow;
I have had it *by rote* very often before,
But never *by heart* until now!

Pretty Martha was next, and my soul was all flame,
But my head was so full of romance,
That I fancied her into some chivalry dame,
And I was her knight of the lance!
But Martha was not of this fanciful school,
And she laughed at her poor little knight;
While I thought her a goddess, she thought me a fool,
And I'll swear *she* was most in the right.

My soul was now calm, till, by Cloris's looks,
Again I was tempted to rove;
But Cloris, I found, was so learned in books,
That she gave me more logic than love!
So I left this young Sappho, and hastened to fly
To those sweeter logicians in bliss,
Who argue the point with a soul-telling eye,
And convince us at once with a kiss!

Oh! Susan was then all the world unto me,
But Susan was piously given;
And the worst of it was, we could never agree
On the road that was shortest to heaven!
'Oh, Susan!' I've said, in the moments of mirth
'What's devotion to thee or to me?
I devoutly believe there's a heaven on earth,
And believe that *that* heaven's in *thee!*'

* * * * *

TO ——.

REMEMBER him thou leav'st behind,
Whose heart is warmly bound to thee,
Close as the tenderest links can bind
A heart as warm as heart can be.

Oh! I had long in freedom roved,
Though many seemed my soul to share;
'Twas passion when I thought I loved,
'Twas fancy when I thought them fair.

E'en she, my Muse's early theme,
Beguiled me only while she warmed;
'Twas young desire that fed the dream,
And reason broke what passion formed.

But thou—ah! better had it been
If I had still in freedom roved,

If I had ne'er thy beauties seen,
  For then I never should have loved!

Then all the pain which lovers feel
  Had never to my heart been known;
But, ah! the joys which lovers steal,
  Should they have ever been my own?

Oh! trust me, when I swear thee this,
  Dearest! the pain of loving thee,
The very pain, is sweeter bliss
  Than passion's wildest ecstasy!

That little cage I would not part,
  In which my soul is prisoned now,
For the most light and wingèd heart
  That wantons on the passing vow.

Still, my beloved! still keep in mind,
  However far removed from me,
That there is one thou leav'st behind,
  Whose heart respires for only thee!

And though ungenial ties have bound
  Thy fate unto another's care,
That arm, which clasps thy bosom round,
  Cannot confine the heart that's there.

No, no! that heart is only mine,
  By ties all other ties above,
For I have wed it at a shrine
  Where we have had no priest but Love!

SONG.

A CAPTIVE thus to thee, my girl,
  How sweetly shall I pass my age,
Contented, like the playful squirrel,
  To wanton up and down my cage!

When Death shall envy joy like this,
  And come to shade our sunny weather,
Be our last sigh the sigh of bliss,
  And both our souls exhaled together!

SONG.

WHERE is the nymph, whose azure eye
  Can shine through rapture's tear?
The sun has sunk, the moon is high,
  And yet she comes not here!

Was that her footstep on the hill—
  Her voice upon the gale?—
No; 'twas the wind, and all is still:
  Oh, maid of Marlivale!

Come to me, love, I've wandered far,
  'Tis past the promised hour:
Come to me, love, the twilight star
  Shall guide thee to my

REUBEN AND ROSE.

A TALE OF ROMANCE.

THE darkness which hung upon Willumberg's walls
  Has long been remembered with awe and dismay!
For years not a sunbeam had played in its halls,
  And it seemed as shut out from the regions of day:

Though the valleys were brightened by many a beam,
  Yet none could the woods of the castle illume;
And the lightning which flashed on the neighbouring stream
  Flew back, as if fearing to enter the gloom!

'Oh! when shall this horrible darkness disperse?'
  Said Willumberg's lord to the seer of the cave.
'It can never dispel,' said the wizard of verse,
  'Till the bright star of chivalry's sunk in the wave!'

And who was the bright star of chivalry then?
  Who could be but Reuben, the flower of the age?
For Reuben was first in the combat of men,
  Though Youth had scarce written his name on her page.

For Willumberg's daughter his bosom had beat,
  For Rose, who was bright as the spirit of dawn,
When with wand dropping diamonds, and silvery feet,
  It walks o'er the flowers of the mountain and lawn!

Must Rose, then, from Reuben so fatally sever?
  Sad, sad were the words of the man in the cave,
That darkness should cover the castle for ever,
  Or Reuben be sunk in the merciless wave!

She flew to the wizard—'And tell me, oh tell!
  Shall my Reuben no more be restored to my eyes?'—
'Yes, yes—when a spirit shall toll the great bell
  Of the mouldering abbey, your Reuben shall rise!'

Twice, thrice he repeated, 'Your Reuben shall rise!'
  And Rose felt a moment's release from her pain;
She wiped, while she listened, the tears from her eyes,
  And she hoped she might yet see her hero again!

Her hero could smile at the terrors of death,
  When he felt that he died for the sire of his Rose!
To the Oder he flew, and there plunging beneath,
  In the lapse of the billows soon found his

How strangely the order of destiny falls!
　Not long in the waters the warrior lay,
When a sunbeam was seen to glance over the
　　walls,
　And the castle of Willumberg basked in the ray!

All, all but the soul of the maid was in light,
　There sorrow and terror lay gloomy and blank:
Two days did she wander, and all the long night,
　In quest of her love on the wide river's bank.

Oft, oft did she pause for the toll of the bell,
　And she heard but the breathings of night in
　　the air;
Long, long did she gaze on the watery swell,
　And she saw but the foam of the white billow
　　there.

And often as midnight its veil would undraw,
　As she looked at the light of the moon in the
　　stream,
She thought 'twas his helmet of silver she saw,
　As the curl of the surge glittered high in the
　　beam.

And now the third night was begemming the sky,
　Poor Rose on the cold dewy margent reclined,
There wept till the tear almost froze in her eye,
　When,—hark!—'twas the bell that came deep
　　in the wind!

She startled, and saw, through the glimmering
　　shade,
　A form o'er the waters in majesty glide;
She knew 'twas her love, though his cheek was
　　decayed,
　And his helmet of silver was washed by the
　　tide.

Was this what the seer of the cave had fore-
　　told?—
Dim, dim through the phantom the moon shot
　　a gleam;
'Twas Reuben, but ah! he was deathly and cold,
　And flitted away like the spell of a dream!

Twice, thrice did he rise, and as often she thought
　From the bank to embrace him, but never, ah!
　　never!
Then springing beneath, at a billow she caught,
　And sunk to repose on its bosom for ever!

TO A BOY WITH A WATCH.

WRITTEN FOR A FRIEND.

Is it not sweet, beloved youth,
　To rove through erudition's bowers,
And cull the golden fruits of truth,
　And gather fancy's brilliant flowers?

And is it not more sweet than this
　To feel thy parents' hearts approving,

And pay them back in sums of bliss
　The dear, the endless debt of loving?

It must be so to thee, my youth;
　With this idea toil is lighter;
This sweetens all the fruits of truth,
　And makes the flowers of fancy brighter!

The little gift we send thee, boy,
　May sometimes teach thy soul to ponder,
If indolence or syren joy
　Should ever tempt that soul to wander.

'Twill tell thee that the wingèd day
　Can ne'er be chained by man's endeavour;
That life and time shall fade away,
　While heaven and virtue bloom for ever!

SONG.
ON THE BIRTHDAY OF MRS. ——.

WRITTEN IN IRELAND.

Of all my happiest hours of joy,—
　And even I have had my measure,
When hearts were full and every eye
　Has kindled with the beams of pleasure!—

Such hours as this I ne'er was given,
　So dear to friendship, dear to blisses;
Young Love himself looks down from heaven,
　To smile on such a day as this is!

Then, oh! my friends, this hour improve,
　Let's feel as if we ne'er could sever!
And may the birth of her we love
　Be thus with joy remembered ever!

Oh! banish every thought to-night,
　Which could disturb our soul's communion
Abandoned thus to dear delight,
　We'll e'en for once forget the Union!

On that let statesmen try their powers,
　And tremble o'er the rights they'd die for;
The union of the soul be ours,
　And every union else we sigh for!

Then, oh! my friends, this hour improve,
　Let's feel as if we ne'er could sever;
And may the birth of her we love
　Be thus with joy remembered ever!

In every eye around I mark
　The feelings of the heart o'erflowing,
From every soul I catch the spark
　Of sympathy in friendship glowing!

Oh! could such moments ever fly;
　Oh! that we ne'er were doomed to lose 'em
And all as bright as Charlotte's eye,
　And all as pure as Charlotte's bosom.

But oh! my friends, this hour improve,
  Let's feel as if we ne'er could sever;
And may the birth of her we love
  Be thus with joy remembered ever!

For me—whate'er my span of years,
  Whatever sun may light my roving;
Whether I waste my life in tears,
  Or live, as now, for mirth and loving—

This day shall come with aspect kind,
  Wherever Fate may cast your rover;
He'll think of those he left behind,
  And drink a health to bliss that's over!

Then, oh! my friends, this hour improve,
  Let's feel as if we ne'er could sever;
And may the birth of her we love
  Be thus with joy remembered ever!

THE NATAL GENIUS.
A DREAM.
TO ——, THE MORNING OF HER BIRTHDAY.

In witching slumbers of the night,
  I dreamed I was the airy sprite
    That on thy natal moment smiled;
And thought I wafted on my wing
Those flowers which in Elysium spring,
    To crown my lovely mortal child.

With olive-branch I bound thy head,
Heart's-ease along thy path I shed,
  Which was to bloom through all thy years;
Nor yet did I forget to bind
Love's roses, with his myrtle twined,
  And dewed by sympathetic tears.

Such was the wild but precious boon,
Which Fancy, at her magic noon,
    Bade me to Nona's image pay—
Oh! were I, love, thus doomed to be
Thy little guardian deity,
    How blest around thy steps I'd play!

Thy life should softly steal along,
Calm as some lonely shepherd's song
  That's heard at distance in the grove;
No cloud should ever shade thy sky,
No thorns along thy pathway lie,
  But all be sunshine, peace, and love!

The wing of Time should never brush
  Thy dewy lip's luxuriant flush,
    To bid its roses withering die;

Nor age itself, though dim and dark,
Should ever quench a single spark
  That flashes from my Nona's eye!

MORALITY.
A FAMILIAR EPISTLE.
ADDRESSED TO J. AT—NS—N, ESQ., M.R.I.A.[1]

Though long at school and college, dozing
On books of rhyme and books of prosing,
And copying from their moral pages
Fine recipes for forming sages;
Though long with those divines at school,
Who think to make us good by rule,
Who, in methodic forms advancing,
Teaching morality like dancing,
Tell us, for Heaven or money's sake,
What *steps* we are through life to take:
Though thus, my friend, so long employed,
And so much midnight oil destroyed,
I must confess, my searches past,
I only learned to *doubt* at last.

I find the doctors and the sages
Have differed in all climes and ages,
And two in fifty scarce agree
On what is pure morality!
'Tis like the rainbow's shifting zone
And every vision makes its own.

The doctors of the Porch advise,
As modes of being great and wise,
That we should cease to own or know
The luxuries that from feeling flow.

'Reason alone must claim direction,
And Apathy's the soul's perfection.
Like a dull lake the heart must lie;
Nor passion's gale nor pleasure's sigh,
Though heaven unseal the breeze, the breath supplied,
Must curl the wave or swell the tide!'

Such was the rigid Zeno's plan
To form his philosophic man;
Such were the modes he taught mankind
To weed the garden of the mind;
They tore away *some weeds*, 'tis true,
But all the *flowers* were ravished too!

Now listen to the wily strains,
Which, on Cyrené's sandy plains,
When Pleasure, nymph with loosened zone,
Usurped the philosophic throne;
Hear what the courtly sage's tongue[2]
To his surrounding pupils sung:

'Pleasure's the only noble end
To which all human powers should tend,

---

[1] The gentleman to whom this poem is addressed is the author of some esteemed works, and was Mr. Little's most particular friend. I have heard Mr. Little very frequently speak of him as one in whom the 'elements were so mixed,' that neither in his head nor heart had nature left any deficiency.—E.

[2] Aristippus.

And Virtue gives her heavenly lore,
But to make Pleasure please us more!
Wisdom and she were both designed
To make the senses more refined,
That man might revel, free from cloying,
Then most a sage, when most enjoying!'

Is this morality?—Oh, no!
E'en I a wiser path could show.
The flower within this vase confined,
The pure, the unfading flower of mind,
Must not throw all its sweets away
Upon a mortal mould of clay;
No, no! its richest breath should rise
In virtue's incense to the skies!

But thus it is, all sects, we see,
Have watchwords of morality:
Some cry out Venus, others Jove;
Here 'tis religion, there 'tis love!
But while they thus so widely wander,
While mystics dream, and doctors ponder,
And some, in dialectics firm,
Seek virtue in a middle term;
While thus they strive, in Heaven's defiance,
To chain morality with science;
The plain good man, whose actions teach
More virtue than a sect can preach,
Pursues his course, unsagely blest,
His tutor whispering in his breast:
Nor could he act a purer part,
Though he had Tully all by heart;
And when he drops the tear on woe,
He little knows or cares to know
That Epictetus blamed that tear,
By Heaven approved, to virtue dear!

Oh! when I've seen the morning beam
Floating within the dimpled stream,
While Nature, wakening from the night,
Has just put on her robes of light,
Have I, with cold optician's gaze,
Explored the *doctrine* of those rays?
No, pedants, I have left to you
Nicely to separate hue from hue:
Go, give that moment up to art,
When Heaven and Nature claim the heart;
And dull to all their best attraction,
Go—measure *angles of refraction!*
While I, in feeling's sweet romance,
Look on each day-beam as a glance
From the great eye of Him above,
Wakening his world with looks of love!

SONG.

Why does azure deck the sky?
  'Tis to be like thy looks of blue;
Why is red the rose's dye?
  Because it is thy blushes' hue.
All that's fair, by Love's decree,
Has been made resembling thee!

Why is falling snow so white,
  But to be like thy bosom fair?
Why are solar beams so bright?
  That they may seem thy golden hair!
All that's bright, by Love's decree,
Has been made resembling thee!

Why are Nature's beauties felt?
  Oh! 'tis thine in her we see!
Why has music power to melt?
  Oh! because it speaks like thee.
All that's sweet, by Love's decree,
Has been made resembling thee!

SONG.[1]

Mary, I believed thee true,
  And I was blest in thus believing;
But now I mourn that e'er I knew
  A girl so fair and so deceiving!

Few have ever loved like me,—
  Oh! I have loved thee too sincerely!
And few have e'er deceived like thee,—
  Alas! deceived me too severely!

Fare thee well! yet think awhile
  On one whose bosom bleeds to doubt thee;
Who now would rather trust that smile,
  And die with thee, than live without thee!

Fare thee well! I'll think of thee,
  Thou leav'st me many a bitter token;
For see, distracting woman! see,
  My peace is gone, my heart is broken!—
Fare thee well!

FRAGMENTS OF COLLEGE EXERCISES.

Nobilitas sola est atque unica virtus.—*Juv.*

Mark those proud boasters of a splendid line,
Like gilded ruins, mouldering while they shine,
How heavy sits that weight of alien show,
Like martial helm upon an infant's brow;
Those borrowed splendours, whose contrasting light
Throws back the native shades in deeper night.

Ask the proud train who glory's shade pursue,
Where are the arts by which that glory grew?
The genuine virtues that with eagle-gaze
Sought young Renown in all her orient blaze?
Where is the heart by chymic truth refined,
The exploring soul, whose eye had read mankind?
Where are the links that twined with heavenly art
His country's interest round the patriot's heart?

[1] I believe these words were adapted by Mr. Little to the pathetic Scotch air 'Gala Water.'—E.

Where is the tongue that scattered words of fire?
The spirit breathing through the poet's lyre?
Do these descend with all that tide of fame
Which vainly waters an unfruitful name?

. . . . .

*Justum bellum quibus necessarium, et pia arma
quibus nulla nisi in armis relinquitur spes.—Liv.*

. . . . .

Is there no call, no consecrating cause,
Approved by Heaven, ordained by Nature's laws,
Where justice flies the herald of our way,
And truth's pure beams upon the banners play?

Yes, there's a call, sweet as an angel's breath
To slumbering babes, or innocence in death;
And urgent as the tongue of heaven within,
When the mind's balance trembles upon sin.

Oh! 'tis our country's voice, whose claims should meet
An echo in the soul's most deep retreat;
Along the heart's responding string should run,
Nor let a tone there vibrate—but the one!

SONG.

Have not you seen the timid tear
  Steal trembling from mine eye?
Have you not marked the flush of fear,
  Or caught the murmured sigh?
And can you think my love is chill,
  Nor fixed on you alone?
And can you rend, by doubting still,
  A heart so much your own?

To you my soul's affections move
  Devoutly, warmly true;
My life has been a task of love,
  One long, long thought of you.
If all your tender faith is o'er,
  If still my truth you'll try;
Alas! I know but *one* proof more,—
  I'll bless your name, and die!

THE SHIELD.[1]

Oh! did you not hear a voice of death?
  And did you not mark the paly form
Which rode on the silver mist of the heath,
  And sung a ghostly dirge in the storm?

Was it a wailing bird of the gloom,
  Which shrieks on the house of woe all night?
Or a shivering fiend that flew to a tomb,
  To howl and to feed till the glance of light?

[1] This poem is perfectly in the taste of the present day—'his nam plebecula gaudet.'—E.

'Twas *not* the death-bird's cry from the wood,
  Nor shivering fiend that hung in the blast;
'Twas the shade of Helderic—man of blood—
  It screams for the guilt of days that are past!

See how the red, red lightning strays,
  And scares the gliding ghosts of the heath!
Now on the leafless yew it plays,
  Where hangs the shield of this son of death!

That shield is blushing with murderous stains·
  Long has it hung from the cold yew's spray;
It is blown by storms and washed by rains,
  But neither can take the blood away!

Oft by that yew, on the blasted field,
  Demons dance to the red moon's light;
While the damp boughs creak, and the swinging shield
  Sings to the raving spirit of night!

THE TEAR.

On beds of snow the moonbeam slept,
  And chilly was the midnight gloom,
When by the damp grave Ellen wept—
  Sweet maid! it was her Lindor's tomb!

A warm tear gushed, the wintry air
  Congealed it as it flowed away;
All night it lay an ice-drop there,
  At morn it glittered in the ray!

An angel, wandering from her sphere,
  Who saw this bright, this frozen gem,
To dew-eyed Pity brought the tear,
  And hung it on her diadem!

A DREAM.

I thought this heart consuming lay
  On Cupid's burning shrine:
I thought he stole thy heart away,
  And placed it near to mine.

I saw thy heart begin to melt,
  Like ice before the sun;
Till both a glow congenial felt,
  And mingled into one!

TO A LADY.

ON HER SINGING.

Thy song has taught my heart to feel
  Those soothing thoughts of heavenly love,
Which o'er the sainted spirits steal
  When listening to the spheres above!

At night, when all is still around,
How sweet to hear the distant sound
 Of footstep, coming soft and light !
What pleasure in the anxious beat
With which the bosom flies to meet
 That foot that comes so soft at night !
Page 191.

When, tired of life and misery,
 I wish to sigh my latest breath,
Oh, Emma! I will fly to thee,
 And thou shalt sing me into death!

And if along thy lip and cheek
 That smile of heavenly softness play,
Which,—ah! forgive a mind that's weak,—
 So oft has stolen my mind away;

Thou'lt seem an angel of the sky,
 That comes to charm me into bliss:
I'll gaze and die—who would not die,
 If death were half so sweet as this?

WRITTEN IN A COMMON-PLACE BOOK,
CALLED 'THE BOOK OF FOLLIES;'

In which every one that opened it should contribute something.

TO THE BOOK OF FOLLIES.

This tribute's from a wretched elf,
Who hails thee emblem of himself!
The book of life, which I have traced,
Has been, like thee, a motley waste
Of follies scribbled o'er and o'er,
One folly bringing hundreds more.
Some have indeed been writ so neat,
In characters so fair, so sweet,
That those who judge not too severely
Have said they loved such follies dearly!
Yet still, O book! the allusion stands;
For these were penned by *female* hands;
The rest,—alas! I own the truth,—
Have all been scribbled so uncouth,
That prudence, with a withering look,
Disdainful flings away the book.
Like thine, its pages here and there
Have oft been stained with blots of care;
And sometimes hours of peace, I own,
Upon some fairer leaves have shown,
White as the snowings of that Heaven
By which those hours of peace were given.
But now no longer—such, oh! such
The blast of Disappointment's touch!
No longer now those hours appear;
Each leaf is sullied by a tear:
Blank, blank is every page with care,
Not e'en a folly brightens there.
Will they yet brighten?—Never, never!
Then *shut the book*, O God, for ever!

TO JULIA.
WEEPING.

Oh! if your tears are given to care,
 If real woe disturbs your peace,
Come to my bosom, weeping fair!
 And I will bid your weeping cease

But if with Fancy's visioned fears,
 With dreams of woe your bosom thrill;
You look so lovely in your tears,
 That I must bid you drop them still!

CHARITY.

'Neither do I condemn thee: go, and sin no more.'—
 ST. JOHN, chap. viii.

O WOMAN! if by simple wile
 Thy soul has strayed from honour's track,
'Tis mercy only can beguile,
 By gentle ways, the wanderer back.

The stain that on thy virtue lies,
 Washed by thy tears, may yet decay;
As clouds that sully morning skies
 May all be wept in showers away.

Go, go—be innocent, and live—
 The tongues of men may wound thee sore;
But Heaven in pity can forgive,
 And bids thee 'go, and sin no more!

AT NIGHT.

At night, when all is still around,
How sweet to hear the distant sound
 Of footstep, coming soft and light!
What pleasure in the anxious beat,
With which the bosom flies to meet
 That foot that comes so soft at night!

And then, at night, how sweet to say
''Tis late, my love!' and chide delay,
 Though still the western clouds are bright;
Oh! happy too the silent press,
The eloquence of mute caress,
 With those we love exchanged at night!

At night, what dear employ to trace,
In fancy, every glowing grace
 That's hid by darkness from the sight!
And guess, by every broken sigh,
What tales of bliss the shrouded eye
 Is telling from the soul, at night!

TO ———.

'Moria pur quando vuol, non è bisogna mutar ni faccia
 ni voce per esser un Angelo.'

Die when you will, you need not wear
 At heaven's court a form more fair
Than beauty here on earth has given;
 Keep but the lovely looks we see—
The voice we hear—and you will be
 An angel *ready-made* for heaven!

FANNY, DEAREST.

Oh! had I leisure to sigh and mourn,
  Fanny, dearest, for thee I'd sigh;
And every smile on my cheek should turn
  To tears when thou art nigh.

But between love, and wine, and sleep,
  So busy a life I live,
That even the time it would take to weep
  Is more than my heart can give.

Then bid me not to despair and pine,
  Fanny, dearest of all the dears!
The Love that's ordered to bathe in wine
  Would be sure to take cold in tears.

Reflected bright in this heart of mine,
  Fanny, dearest, thy image lies;
But oh, the mirror would cease to shine,
  If dimmed too often with sighs.

They lose the half of beauty's light,
  Who view it through sorrow's tear;
And 'tis but to see thee truly bright
  That I keep my eye-beam clear.

Then wait no longer till tears shall flow,
  Fanny, dearest—the hope is vain;
If sunshine cannot dissolve thy snow,
  I shall never attempt it with rain.

SONG.

I NE'ER on that lip for a minute have gazed,
  But a thousand temptations beset me,
And I've thought, as the dear little rubies you raised,
  How delicious 'twould be—if you'd let me!

Then be not so angry for what I have done,
  Nor say that you've sworn to forget me;
They were buds of temptation too pouting to shun,
  And I thought that—you could not but let me!

When your lip with a whisper came close to my cheek,
  Oh think how bewitching it met me!
And, plain as the eye of a Venus could speak,
  Your eye seemed to say—you would let me!

Then forgive the transgression, and bid me remain,
  For, in truth, if I go, you'll regret me;
Or, oh!—let me try the transgression again,
  And I'll do all you wish—will you let me?

MISCELLANEOUS PIECES.

THE TWOPENNY POST BAG.
CORRUPTION AND INTOLERANCE.
THE SCEPTIC.
FABLES FOR THE HOLY ALLIANCE.
RHYMES ON THE ROAD.
M.P.; OR, BLUE STOCKING.

THE TWOPENNY POST BAG.

E lapsæ manibus cecidêre tabellæ.—*Ovid.*

DEDICATION.

To ST——N W——LR——E, Esq.

MY DEAR W——E,—It is now about seven years since I promised (and I grieve to think it is almost as long since we met) to dedicate to you the very first book, of whatever size or kind, I should publish. Who could have thought that so many years would elapse without my giving the least signs of life upon the subject of this important promise? Who could have imagined that a volume of doggerel, after all, would be the first offering that Gratitude would lay upon the shrine of Friendship?

If, however, you are as interested about me and my pursuits as formerly, you will be happy to hear that doggerel is not my only occupation; but that I am preparing to throw my name to the Swans of the Temple of Immortality,[1] leaving it, of course, to the said Swans to determine whether they ever will take the trouble of picking it from the stream.

In the meantime, my dear W——e, like a pious Lutheran, you must judge of me rather by my *faith* than my *works*; and however trifling the tribute which I offer, never doubt the fidelity with which I am, and always shall be,

Your sincere and attached friend,

THE AUTHOR.

March 4, 1813.

PREFACE.

THE Bag from which the following Letters are selected was dropped by a Twopenny Postman about two months since, and picked up by an emissary of the Society for the S—pp—ss—n of Vice, who, supposing it might materially assist the private researches of that institution, immediately took it to his employers, and was rewarded handsomely for his trouble. Such a treasury of secrets was worth a whole host of informers; and accordingly, like the Cupids of the poet (if I may use so profane a simile), who 'fell at odds about the sweet-bag of a bee,'[2] those venerable suppressors almost fought with each other for the honour and delight of first ransacking the Post Bag. Unluckily, however, it turned out, upon examination, that the discoveries of profligacy which it enabled them to make, lay chiefly in those upper regions of society which their well-bred regulations forbid them to molest or meddle with. In conse-

---

[1] Ariosto, canto 35.   [2] Herrick.

quence, they gained but very few victims by their prize; and after lying for a week or two under Mr. H—tch—d's counter, the Bag, with its violated contents, was sold for a trifle to a friend of mine.

It happened that I had been just then seized with an ambition (having never tried the strength of my wing but in a newspaper) to publish something or other in the shape of a book; and it occurred to me that, the present being such a letter-writing era, a few of these twopenny post epistles, turned into easy verse, would be as light and popular a task as I could possibly select for a commencement. I did not think it prudent, however, to give too many Letters at first, and accordingly have been obliged (in order to cke out a sufficient number of pages) to reprint some of those trifles which had already appeared in the public journals. As, in the battles of ancient times, the shades of the departed were sometimes seen among the combatants, so I thought I might remedy the thinness of my ranks by conjuring up a few dead and forgotten ephemerons to fill them.

Such are the motives and accidents that led to the present publication; and as this is the first time my Muse has ever ventured out of the go-cart of a newspaper, though I feel all a parent's delight at seeing little Miss go alone, I am also not without a parent's anxiety, lest an unlucky fall should be the consequence of the experiment; and I need not point out the many living instances there are of Muses that have suffered severely in their heads, from taking too early and rashly to their feet. Besides, a book is so very different a thing from a newspaper! In the former, your doggerel, without either company or shelter, must stand shivering in the middle of a bleak white page by itself; whereas in the latter it is comfortably backed by advertisements, and has sometimes even a Speech of Mr. St—ph—n's, or something equally warm, for a *chauffe-pié*,—so that, in general, the very reverse of 'laudatur et alget' is its destiny.

Ambition, however, must run some risks, and I shall be very well satisfied if the reception of these few Letters should have the effect of sending me to the Post Bag for more.

PREFACE TO THE FOURTEENTH EDITION.

BY A FRIEND OF THE AUTHOR.

In the absence of Mr. Brown, who is at present on a tour through ———, I feel myself called upon, as his friend, to notice certain misconceptions and misrepresentations to which this little volume of Trifles has given rise.

In the first place, it is not true that Mr. Brown has had any accomplices in the work. A note, indeed, which has hitherto accompanied his Preface, may very naturally have been the origin of such a supposition; but that note, which was merely the coquetry of an author, I have in the present edition taken upon myself to remove, and Mr. Brown must therefore be considered (like the mother of that unique production the Centaur, μονα και μονον) as alone responsible for the whole contents of the volume.

In the next place, it has been said that, in consequence of this graceless little book, a certain distinguished Personage prevailed upon another distinguished Personage to withdraw from the author that notice and kindness with which he had so long and so liberally honoured him. There is not one syllable of truth in this story. For the magnanimity of the *former* of these persons I would, indeed, in no case answer too rashly; but of the conduct of the *latter* towards my friend, I have a proud gratification in declaring that it has never ceased to be such as he must remember with indelible gratitude,—a gratitude the more cheerfully and warmly paid, from its not being a debt incurred solely on his own account, but for kindness shared with those nearest and dearest to him.

To the charge of being an Irishman poor Mr. Brown pleads guilty; and I believe it must also be acknowledged that he comes of a Roman Catholic family: an avowal which, I am aware, is decisive of his utter reprobation in the eyes of those exclusive patentees of Christianity, so worthy to have been the followers of a certain enlightened bishop, Donatus,[1] who held 'that God is in Africa, *and not elsewhere.*' But from all this it does not necessarily follow that Mr. Brown is a Papist; and, indeed, I have the strongest reasons for suspecting that they who say so are totally mistaken. Not that I presume to have ascertained his opinions upon such subjects: all I know of his orthodoxy is, that he has a Protestant wife, and two or three little Protestant children, and that he has been seen at church every Sunday for a whole year together, listening to the sermons of his truly reverend and amiable friend Dr. ———, and behaving there as well and as orderly as most people.

There are a few more mistakes and falsehoods about Mr. Brown, to which I had intended with all becoming gravity to advert; but I begin to think the task is altogether as useless as it is tiresome. Calumnies and misrepresentations of this sort are, like the arguments and statements of Dr. Duigenan, not at all the less vivacious or less serviceable to their fabricators for having been refuted and disproved a thousand times over: they are brought forward again as good as new, whenever malice or stupidity is in want of them, and are as useful as the old broken lantern, in Fielding's *Amelia*, which the watchman always keeps ready by him, to produce, in proof of riot, against his victims. I shall therefore give up the fruitless toil of vindication, and would even draw my pen over what I have already written, had I not promised to furnish the Publisher with a Preface, and know not how else I could contrive to eke it out.

I have added two or three more trifles to this edition, which I found in the *Morning Chronicle*, and knew to be from the pen of my friend.[2] The rest of the volume remains[3] in its original state.

April 20, 1814.

---

[1] Bishop of Casæ Nigræ in the fourth century.
[2] The Trifles here alluded to, and others which have since appeared, will be found in this edition.—*Publisher*.
[3] A new reading has been suggested in the original of the Ode of Horace, freely translated by Lord Eld-n. In the line 'Sive per Syrteis iter æstuosas,' it is proposed by a very trifling alteration to read '*Surtees*' instead of '*Syrteis*,' which brings the Ode, it is said, more home to the noble translator, and gives a peculiar force and aptness to the epithet 'æstuosas.' I merely throw out this emendation for the learned, being unable myself to decide upon its merits.

INTERCEPTED LETTERS, ETC.

LETTER I.

FROM THE PR—NC—SS CH———E OF W———S TO THE LADY B—RD—A A—SHL—Y.[1]

My dear Lady Bab, you'll be shocked, I'm afraid,
When you hear the sad rumpus your ponies have made;
Since the time of horse-consuls (now long out of date)
No nags ever made such a stir in the State!

Lord Eld—n first heard—and as instantly prayed he
To God and his King—that a Popish young lady
(For though you've bright eyes, and twelve thousand a year,
It is still but too true you're a Papist, my dear)
Had insidiously sent, by a tall Irish groom,
Two priest-ridden ponies, just landed from Rome,
And so full, little rogues, of pontifical tricks,
That the dome of St. Paul's was scarce safe from their kicks!

Off at once to papa, in a flurry, he flies—
For papa always does what these statesmen advise,
On condition that they'll be, in turn, so polite
As in no case whate'er to advise him *too right*—
'Pretty doings are here, sir (he angrily cries,
While by dint of dark eyebrows he strives to look wise);
'Tis a scheme of the Romanists, so help me God!
To ride over your most Royal Highness roughshod—
Excuse, sir, my tears, they're from loyalty's source—
Bad enough 'twas for Troy to be sacked by a *Horse*,
But for us to be ruined by *Ponies*, still worse!'

Quick a council is called—the whole cabinet sits—
The Archbishops declare, frightened out of their wits,

That if vile Popish ponies should eat at my manger,
From that awful moment the Church is in danger!
As give them but stabling, and shortly no stalls
Will suit their proud stomachs but those of St. Paul's.

The Doctor, and he, the devout man of Leather,
V—ns—tt—t, now laying their saint-heads together,
Declare that these skittish young a-bominations
Are clearly foretold in chap. vi. Revelations—
Nay, they verily think they could point out the one
Which the Doctor's friend Death was to canter upon!

Lord H—rr—by, hoping that no one imputes
To the Court any fancy to persecute brutes,
Protests, on the word of himself and his cronies,
That had these said creatures been Asses, not Ponies,
The Court would have started no sort of objection,
As Asses were, *there*, always sure of protection.

'If the Pr—nc—ss *will* keep them (says Lord C—stl—r—gh),
To make them quite harmless, the only true way
Is (as certain Chief-Justices do with their wives)
To flog them within half an inch of their lives—
If they've any bad Irish blood lurking about,
This (he knew by experience) would soon draw it out.'
Or—if this be thought cruel—his Lordship proposes
'The new *Veto*-snaffle to bind down their noses—
A pretty contrivance, made out of old chains,
Which appears to indulge, while it doubly restrains;
Which, however high-mettled, their gamesomeness checks
(Adds his Lordship humanely), or else breaks their necks!'

This proposal received pretty general applause
From the statesmen around — and the neckbreaking clause

---

[1] This young lady, who is a Roman Catholic, has lately made a present of some beautiful ponies to the Pr—nc—ss.

Had a vigour about it, which soon reconciled
Even Eld—n himself to a measure so mild.
So the snaffles, my dear, were agreed to nem. con.,
And my Lord C—stl—r—gh, having so often
    shone
In the *fettering* line, is to buckle them on.

I shall drive to your door in these *Vetos* some day,
But, at present, adieu!—I must hurry away
To go see my mamma, as I'm suffered to meet her
For just half-an-hour by the Qu—n's best re-
    peater.
                                C——E.

LETTER II.

FROM COLONEL M'M—H—N TO G—LD FR—NC—S
L—CKIE, ESQ.

DEAR Sir, I've just had time to look
Into your very learned book,[1]
Wherein—as plain as man can speak,
Whose English is half modern Greek—
You prove that we can ne'er intrench
Our happy isles against the French,
Till Royalty in England's made
A much more independent trade—
In short, until the House of Guelph
Lays Lords and Commons on the shelf,
And boldly sets up for itself!

All, that can be well understood
In this said book, is vastly good;
And, as to what's incomprehensible,
I dare be sworn 'tis full as sensible.

But, to your work's immortal credit,
The P——e, good sir,—the P——e has read it.
(The only book, himself remarks,
Which he has read since Mrs. Clarke's.)
Last levee-morn he looked it through
During that awful hour or two
Of grave tonsorial preparation,
Which, to a fond admiring nation,
Sends forth, announced by trump and drum,
The best-wigged P——e in Christendom!

He thinks, with you, the imagination
Of *partnership* in legislation
Could only enter in the noddles
Of dull and ledger-keeping twaddles,
Whose heads on *firms* are running so,
They even must have a King and Co.,
And hence, too, eloquently show forth
On *checks* and *balances*, and so forth.

But now, he trusts, we are coming near a
Better and more royal era;

When England's monarch need but say,
'Whip me those scoundrels, C—stl—r—gh!'
Or—'Hang me up those Papists, Eld—n,'
And 'twill be done—ay, faith, and well done.

With view to which, I've his command
To beg, sir, from your travelled hand
(Round which the foreign graces swarm)
A plan of radical reform;
Compiled and chosen, as best you can,
In Turkey or at Ispahan,
And quite upturning, branch and root,
Lords, Commons, and Burdett to boot!

But, pray, whate'er you may impart, write
Somewhat more brief than Major C—rtwr—ght;
Else, though the P——e be long in rigging,
'Twould take, at least, a fortnight's wigging—
Two wigs to every paragraph—
Before he well could get through half.

You'll send it, also, speedily—
As, truth to say, 'twixt you and me,
His Highness, heated by your work,
Already thinks himself Grand Turk!
And you'd have laughed, had you seen how
He scared the Ch—nc—ll—r just now,
When (on his Lordship's entering puffed) he
Slapped his back and called him 'Mufti!'

The tailors, too, have got commands
To put directly into hands
All sorts of dulimans and pouches,
With sashes, turbans, and pabouches
(While Y—rm—th's sketching out a plan
Of new *moustaches à l'Ottomane*),
And all things fitting and expedient
To *Turkify* our gracious R—g—nt!

You therefore have no time to waste—
So send your system.—
                    Yours, in haste.

POSTSCRIPT.

Before I send this scrawl away,
I seize a moment, just to say
There's some parts of the Turkish system
So vulgar, 'twere as well you missed 'em.
For instance in *Seraglio* matters—
Your Turk, whom girlish fondness flatters,
Would fill his Haram (tasteless fool!)
With tittering, red-cheeked things from school—
But *here* (as in that fairy land,
Where Love and Age went hand in hand;[2]
Where lips till sixty shed no honey,
And Grandams were worth any money)
Our Sultan has much riper notions—
So, let your list of *she*-promotions

---

[1] See the *Edinburgh Review*, No. xl.
[2] The learned Colonel must allude here to a description of the Mysterious Isle, in the History of Abdalla, Son of Hanif, where such inversions of the order of nature are said to have taken place.—' A score of old women and the same number of old men played here and there in the court, some at chuck-farthing, others at tip-cat or at cockles.'—And again, 'There is nothing, believe me, more engaging than those lovely wrinkles,' etc. etc.—See *Tales of the East*, vol. iii. pp. 607, 609.

Include those only, plump and sage,
Who've reached the *regulation*-age;
That is—as near as one can fix
From Peerage dates—full fifty-six.

This rule's for *favourites*—nothing more—
For, as to *wives*, a Grand Signor,
Though not decidedly *without* them,
Need never care one curse about them!

LETTER III.

FROM G. R. TO THE E—— OF Y——.[1]

WE missed you last night at the 'hoary old sinner's,'
Who gave us, as usual, the cream of good dinners—
His soups scientific—his fishes quite *prime*—
His pâtés superb—and his cutlets sublime!
In short, 'twas the snug sort of dinner to stir a
Stomachic orgasm in my Lord E———gh,
Who *set-to*, to be sure, with miraculous force,
And exclaimed, between mouthfuls, 'A *He*-cook, of course!—
While you live—(what's there under that cover? pray, look)—
While you live—(I'll just taste it)—ne'er keep a She-cook.
'Tis a sound Salic law—(a small bit of that toast)—
Which ordains that a female shall ne'er rule the roast;
For Cookery's a secret—(this turtle's uncommon)—
Like Masonry, never found out by a woman!'

The dinner, you know, was in gay celebration
Of *my* brilliant triumph and H——nt's condemnation;
A compliment too to his Lordship the J——e
For his speech to the J——y,—and zounds! who would grudge
Turtle-soup, though it came to five guineas a bowl,
To reward such a loyal and complaisant soul!
We were all in high gig—Roman Punch and Tokay
Travelled round, till our heads travelled just the same way,—
And we cared not for Juries or Libels—no—dam'me! nor
Even for the threats of last Sunday's Examiner!

More good things were eaten than said—but Tom T——rrh——t
In quoting Joe Miller, you know, has some merit,
And, hearing the sturdy Justiciary Chief
Say—sated with turtle—'I'll now try the beef'—

Tommy whispered him (giving his Lordship a sly hit),
'I fear 'twill be *hung*-beef, my Lord, if you try it!'

And C——md——n was there, who, that morning, had gone
To fit his new Marquis's coronet on;
And the dish set before him—oh dish well-devised!—
Was, what old Mother Glasse calls, 'a calf's head surprised!'
The *brains* were near ——; and *once* they'd been fine,
But of late they had lain so long soaking in wine,
That, however we still might in courtesy call
Them a fine dish of brains, they were no brains at all.

When the dinner was over, we drank, every one
In a bumper, 'the venial delights of Crim. Con.'
At which H——d——t with warm reminiscences gloated,
And E——b'r——h chuckled to hear himself quoted.

Our next round of toasts was a fancy quite new,
For we drank—and you'll own 'twas benevolent too—
To those well-meaning husbands, cits, parsons, or peers,
Whom we've any time honoured by kissing their dears:
This museum of wittols was comical rather;
Old H——d——t gave M——y, and *I* gave ——.

In short, not a soul till this morning would budge—
We were all fun and frolic!—and even the J——e
Laid aside, for the time, his juridical fashion,
And through the whole night was *not once* in a passion!

I write this in bed, while my whiskers are airing,
And M——c has a sly dose of jalap preparing
For poor T——mmy T——rr——t at breakfast to quaff;
As I feel I want something to give me a laugh,
And there's nothing so good as old T——mmy, kept close
To his Cornwall accounts, after taking a dose!

LETTER IV.

**FROM THE RIGHT HON. P——TR——CK D——G——N——N
TO THE RIGHT HON. SIR J——HN N——CH——L.**

Dublin.[2]

LAST week, dear N——ch——l, making merry
At dinner with our Secretary,

---

[1] This letter, as the reader will perceive, was written the day after a dinner given by the M—— of H——d——t.
[2] This letter, which contained some very heavy enclosures, seems to have been sent to London by a private hand, and then put into the Twopenny Post-Office, to save trouble. See the Appendix.

When all were drunk, or pretty near
(The time for doing business here),
Says he to me, 'Sweet Bully Bottom!
These Papist dogs—hiccup—od rot 'em!
Deserve to be bespattered—hiccup—
With all the dirt even *you* can pick up—
But, as tho P——e—(here's to him—fill—
Hip, hip, hurra!)—is trying still
To humbug them with kind professions,
And as you deal in *strong* expressions—
" *Rogue* "—" *traitor* "—hiccup—and all that—
You must be muzzled, Doctor Pat!—
You must indeed—hiccup—that's flat.'

Yes—'muzzled' was the word, Sir John—
These fools have clapped a muzzle on
The boldest mouth that e'er ran o'er
With slaver of the times of yore!¹—
Was it for this that back I went
As far as Lateran and Trent,
To prove that they, who damned us then,
Ought now, in turn, be damned again!—
The silent victim still to sit
Of Gr—tt—n's fire and C—nn—g's wit,
To hear even noisy M—th—w gabble on,
Nor mention once the W—e of Babylon!
Oh! 'tis too much—who now will be
The Nightman of No-Popery?
What Courtier, Saint, or even Bishop,
Such learned filth will ever fish up?
If there among our ranks be one
To take my place, 'tis *thou*, Sir John—
Thou—who, like me, art dubbed Right Hon.,
Like me, too, art a Lawyer Civil
That wishes Papists at the devil!

To whom, then, but to thee, my friend,
Should Patrick ² his portfolio send?
Take it—'tis thine—his learned portfolio,
With all its theologic olio
Of Bulls, half Irish and half Roman—
Of Doctrines now believed by no man—
Of Councils, held for men's salvation,
Yet always ending in damnation—
(Which shows that since the world's creation,
Your Priests, whate'er their gentle shamming,
Have always had a taste for damning);
And many more such pious scraps,
To prove (what we've long proved perhaps)
That, mad as Christians used to be
About the Thirteenth Century,
There's *lots* of Christians to be had
In this, the Nineteenth, just as mad!

Farewell—I send with this, dear N—ch—ll
A rod or two I've had in pickle,
Wherewith to trim old Gr—tt—n's jacket.—
The rest shall go by Monday's packet.
P. D.

Among the enclosures in the foregoing Letter was the following ' Unanswerable Argument against the Papists.'

⁕ ⁕ ⁕ ⁕ ⁕ ⁕

We're told the ancient Roman nation
Made use of spittle in lustration.³—
(Vide Lactantium ap. Gallæum ⁴—
I.e. you need not *read* but *see* 'em).
Now, Irish Papists (fact surprising!)
Make use of spittle in baptizing,
Which proves them all, O'Finns, O'Fagans,
Connors, and Tooles, all downright Pagans!
This fact's enough—let no one tell us
To free such sad, *salivous* fellows—
No—no—the man baptized with spittle
Hath no truth in him—not a tittle!

⁕ ⁕ ⁕ ⁕ ⁕ ⁕

LETTER V.

FROM THE COUNTESS DOWAGER OF C——— TO LADY ———.

My dear Lady ———! I've been just sending out
About five hundred cards for a snug little Rout—
(By-the-bye, you've seen *Rokeby ?*—this moment got mine—
The Mail-Coach Edition ⁵—prodigiously fine!)
But I can't conceive how, in this very cold weather,
I'm ever to bring my five hundred together;
As, unless the thermometer's near boiling heat,
One can never .get half of one's hundreds to meet—
(*Apropos*—you'd have laughed to see Townsend, last night,
Escort to their chair, with his staff so polite,
The ' three maiden Miseries,' all in a fright!
Poor Townsend, like Mercury, filling two posts,
Supervisor of *thieves*, and chief-usher of *ghosts!*)
But, my dear Lady ———, can't you hit on some notion,
At least for one night to set London in motion?
As to having the R—g—nt—*that* show is gone by—
Besides, I've remarked that (between you and I)

---

¹ In sending this sheet to the Press, however, I learn that the 'muzzle' has been taken off, and the Right Hon. Doctor let loose again.

² This is a bad name for poetry; but D—gen—n is worse. — As Prudentius says, upon a very different subject—

    torquetur Apollo
    Nomine percussus.

³ . . . . . lustralibus ante salivis
    Explat.—*Pers. Sat.* 2.

⁴ I have taken the trouble of examining the Doctor's reference here, and find him, for once, correct. The following are the words of his indignant referee Gallæus: 'Asserere non veremur sacrum baptismum a Papistis profanari, et spoti usum in peccatorum expiatione a Paganis non a Christianis *manasse.*'

⁵ See Mr. Murray's advertisement about the Mail-Coach copies of *Rokeby.*

The Marchesa and he, inconvenient in more ways,
Have taken much lately to whispering in doorways;
Which—considering, you know, dear, the *size* of the two—
Makes a block that one's company *cannot* get through;
And a house such as mine is, with doorways so small,
Has no room for such cumbersome love-work at all!—
(*Apropos*, though, of love-work—you've heard it, I hope,
That Napoleon's old Mother's to marry the Pope,—
What a comical pair!)—But, to stick to my Rout,
'Twill be hard if some novelty can't be struck out.
Is there no Algerine, no Kamchatkan arrived?
No Plenipo Pacha, three-tailed and ten-wived?
No Russian, whose dissonant consonant name
Almost rattles to fragments the trumpet of fame?

I remember the time, three or four winters back,
When—provided their wigs were but decently black—
A few Patriot monsters, from Spain, were a sight
That would people one's house for one, night after night.
But—whether the Ministers *pawed* them too much—
(And you know how they spoil whatever they touch),
Or, whether Lord G—rge (the young man about town)
Has by dint of bad poetry written them down—
One has certainly lost one's *Peninsular* rage,
And the only stray Patriot seen for an age
Has been at such places (think how the fit cools)
As old Mrs. V——n's or Lord L—v—rp—l's!

But in short, my dear, names like Wintztschits-topschiuzoudhoff
Are the only things now make an evening go smooth off—
So get me a Russian—till death I'm your debtor—
If he brings the whole Alphabet, so much the better:

And—Lord! if he would but *in character*, sup
Off his fish-oil and candles, he'd quite set me up!

Au revoir, my sweet girl—I must leave you in haste—
Little Gunter has brought me the Liqueurs to taste.

POSTSCRIPT.

By-the-bye, have you found any friend that can construe
That Latin account, t'other day, of a Monster?[1]
If we can't get a Russian, and *that thing* in Latin
Be not *too* improper, I think I'll bring that in.

LETTER VI.

FROM ABDALLAH[2] IN LONDON, TO MOHASSAN IN ISPAHAN.

Whilst thou, Mohassan (happy thou!),
Dost daily bend thy loyal brow
Before our King—our Asia's treasure!
Nutmeg of Comfort! Rose of Pleasure!—
And bear'st as many kicks and bruises
As the said Rose and Nutmeg chooses;—
Thy head still near the bowstring's borders,
And but left on till further orders!
Through London streets, with turban fair,
And caftan floating to the air,
I saunter on—the admiration
Of this short-coated population—
This sewed-up race—this buttoned nation—
Who, while they boast their laws so free,
Leave not one limb at liberty,
But live, with all their lordly speeches,
The slaves of buttons and tight breeches.
Yet, though they thus their knee-pans fetter
(They're Christians, and they know no better),[3]
In *some* things they're a thinking nation—
And, on Religious Toleration,
I own I like their notions *quite*,
They are so Persian and so right!
You know our Sunnites,[4] hateful dogs!
Whom every pious Shiite flogs,
Or longs to flog[5]—'tis true, they pray
To God, but in an ill-bred way;
With neither arms, nor legs, nor faces
Stuck in their right, canonic places![6]

---

[1] Alluding, I suppose, to the Latin advertisement of a *Lusus Naturæ* in the newspapers lately.

[2] I have made many inquiries about this Persian gentleman, but cannot satisfactorily ascertain who he is. From his notions of Religious Liberty, however, I conclude that he is an importation of Ministers; and he has arrived just in time to assist the P——e and Mr. L—ck—e in their new Oriental Plan of Reform. See the second of these Letters.—How Abdallah's epistle to Ispahan found its way into the Twopenny Post Bag is more than I can pretend to account for.

[3] ' C'est un honnête homme,' said a Turkish governor of de Ruyter; ' c'est grand dommage qu'il soit Chrétien.'

[4] *Sunnites* and *Shiites* are the two leading sects into which the Mohammedan world is divided; and they have gone on cursing and persecuting each other, without any intermission, for about eleven hundred years. The *Sunni* is the established sect in Turkey, and the *Shia* in Persia; and the differences between them turn chiefly upon those important points which our pious friend Abdallah, in the true spirit of Shiite ascendency, reprobates in this Letter.

[5] ' Les Sunnites, qui étaient comme les catholiques de Musulmanisme.'—*D'Herbelot*.

[6] 'In contradistinction to the Sounis, who in their prayers cross their hands on the lower part of the breast,

'Tis true, they worship Ali's name!—
Their heaven and *ours* are just the same—
(A Persian's heaven is easily made,
'Tis but—black eyes and lemonade).
Yet, though we've tried for centuries back,
We can't persuade the stubborn pack,
By bastinadoes, screws, or nippers,
To wear the established pea-green slippers!²
Then—only think—the libertines!
They wash their toes, they comb their chins,³
With many more such deadly sins!
And (what's the worst, though last I rank it)
Believe the Chapter of the Blanket!

Yet, spite of tenets so flagitious,
(Which *must* at bottom be seditious;
As no man living would refuse
Green slippers, but from treasonous views;
Nor wash his toes, but with intent
To overturn the government!)
Such is our mild and tolerant way,
We only curse them twice a-day
(According to a form that's set),
And, far from torturing, only let
All orthodox believers beat 'em,
And twitch their beards, where'er they meet 'em.

As to the rest, they're free to do
Whate'er their fancy prompts them to,
Provided they make nothing of it
Towards rank or honour, power or profit;
Which things, we naturally expect,
Belong to us, the Established sect,
Who disbelieve (the Lord be thankèd!)
The aforesaid Chapter of the Blanket.

The same mild views of Toleration
Inspire, I find, this buttoned nation,
Whose Papists (full as given to rogue,
And only Sunnites with a brogue)
Fare just as well, with all their fuss,
As rascal Sunnites do with us.

The tender Gazel I enclose
Is for my love, my Syrian Rose—
Take it, when night begins to fall,
And throw it o'er her mother's wall.

GAZEL.

Rememberest thou the hour we past?
That hour, the happiest and the last!—

Oh! not so sweet the Siha thorn
To summer bees at break of morn,
Not half so sweet, through dale and dell,
To camels' ears the tinkling bell,
As is the soothing memory
Of that one precious hour to me!

How can we live, so far apart?
Oh! why not rather heart to heart
United live and die?—
Like those sweet birds that fly together,
With feather always touching feather,
Linked by a hook and eye!⁴

LETTER VII.

FROM MESSRS. L—CK—GT—N AND CO.

TO ———— ————, ESQ.⁵

PER POST, Sir, we send your MS.—looked it through—
Very sorry—but can't undertake—'twouldn't do.
Clever work, Sir!—would *get up* prodigiously well—
Its only defect is—it never would sell!
And though *Statesmen* may glory in being *un-bought*,
In an *Author* we think, Sir, that's *rather* a fault.

Hard times, Sir,—most books are too dear to be read—
Though the *gold* of Good-sense and Wit's *small-change* are fled,
Yet the *paper* we publishers pass, in their stead,
Rises higher each day, and ('tis frightful to think it)
Not even such names as F—tzg—r—d's can sink it!
However, Sir—if you're for trying again,
And at somewhat that's vendible—we are your men.

Since the Chevalier C—rr took to marrying lately,
The Trade is in want of a *Traveller* greatly—
No job, Sir, more easy—your *Country* once planned,
A month aboard ship and a fortnight on land
Puts your Quarto of Travels clean out of hand.

---

the Schiahs drop their arms in straight lines; and as the Sounis, at certain periods of the prayer, press their foreheads on the ground or carpet, the Schiahs,' etc. etc.—*Forster's Voyage.*

¹ ' Les Turcs ne détestent pas Ali réciproquement; au contraire ils le reconnaissent,' etc. etc.—*Chardin.*

² ' The Shiites wear green slippers, which the Sunnites consider as a great abomination.'—*Maritt.*

³ For these points of difference, as well as for the Chapter of the Blanket, I must refer the reader (not having the book by me) to *Picart's Account of the Mahometan Sects.*

⁴ This will appear strange to an English reader, but it is literally translated from Abdallah's Persian; and the curious bird to which he alludes is the *Juftak*, of which I find the following account in Richardson:—' A sort of bird that is said to have but one wing, on the opposite side to which the male has a hook and the female a ring, so that, when they fly, they are fastened together.'

⁵ From motives of delicacy, and indeed of *fellow-feeling*, I suppress the name of the author whose rejected manuscript was enclosed in this letter.—See the Appendix.

An East-India pamphlet's a thing that would tell—
And a lick at the Papists is *sure* to sell well.
Or—supposing you have nothing *original* in you—
Write Parodies, Sir, and such fame it will win you,
You'll get to the Blue-stocking Routs of Alb—n—a![1]
(Mind—*not* to her *dinners*—a *second-hand* Muse
Mustn't think of aspiring to *mess* with the *Blues*.)
Or—in case nothing else in this world you can do—
The deuce is in't, Sir, if you cannot *review!*

Should you feel any touch of *poetical* glow,
We've a scheme to suggest—Mr. Sc—tt, you must know
(Who, we're sorry to say it, now works for *the Row*[2]),
Having quitted the Borders to seek new renown,
Is coming, by long Quarto stages, to Town;
And beginning with Rokeby (the job's sure to pay),
Means to do all the Gentlemen's Seats on the way.
Now, the Scheme is (though none of our hackneys can beat him)
To start a fresh Poet through Highgate to *meet* him;
Who, by means of quick proofs—no revises—long coaches—
May do a few Villas before Sc—tt approaches—
Indeed, if our Pegasus be not curst shabby,
He'll reach, without foundering, at least Woburn Abbey.

Such, Sir, is our plan—if you're up to the freak,
'Tis a match! and we'll put you in *training*, next week—
At present, no more—in reply to this Letter, a Line will oblige very much

Yours, et cetera.
Temple of the Muses.

LETTER VIII.

FROM COLONEL TH—M—S TO ———

———, ESQ.

COME to our Fête,[3] and bring with thee
Thy newest, best embroidery!
Come to our Fête, and show again
That pea-green coat, thou pink of men!
Which charmed all eyes that last surveyed it,
When B———l's self inquired 'who made it?'—
When Cits came wondering from the East,
And thought thee Poet Pye, *at least!*

Oh! come—(if haply 'tis thy week
For looking pale)—with paly cheek;
Though more we love thy roseate days,
When the rich rouge-pot pours its blaze
Full o'er thy face, and, amply spread,
Tips even thy whisker-tops with red—
Like the last tints of dying Day
That o'er some darkling grove delay!

Bring thy best lace, thou gay Philander!
(That lace, like H—rry Al—x—nd—r,
Too precious to be washed)—thy rings,
Thy seals—in short, thy prettiest things!
Put all thy wardrobe's glories on,
And yield, in frogs and fringe, to none
But the great R—g—t's self alone!
Who, by particular desire,
For that night only, means to hire
A dress from Romeo C—tes, Esquire—
Something between ('twere sin to hack it)
The Romeo robe and Hobby jacket!
Hail, first of Actors![4] best of R—g—ts!
Born for each other's fond allegiance!
Both gay Lotharios—both good dressers—
Of Serious Farce *both* learned Professors—
Both circled round, for use or show,
With cocks'-combs, wheresoe'er they go!

Thou know'st the time, thou man of lore!
It takes to chalk a ball-room floor—
Thou know'st the time, too, well-a-day!
It takes to dance that chalk away.[5]
The ball-room opens—far and nigh
Comets and suns beneath us lie;
O'er snowy moons and stars we walk,
And the floor seems a sky of chalk!
But soon shall fade the bright deceit,
When many a maid, with busy feet
That sparkle in the Lustre's ray,
O'er the white path shall bound and play
Like Nymphs along the Milky Way!—
At every step a star is fled,
And suns grow dim beneath their tread!
So passeth life—(thus Sc—tt would write,
And spinsters read him with delight)—

---

[1] This alludes, I believe, to a curious correspondence which is said to have passed lately between Alb—n—a, Countess of B—ck—gh—ms—e, and a certain ingenious Parodist.

[2] Paternoster Row.

[3] This Letter enclosed a Card for the Grand Fête on the 5th of February.

[4] Quem tu, Melpomene, semel
Nascentem *placido lumine*, **videris**, etc.—*Horat.*
The Man, upon whom thou hast deigned to look funny,
Thou great Tragic Muse! at the hour of his birth—
Let them say what they will, that's the man for *my* money,
Give others thy tears, but let *me* have thy mirth!
The assertion that follows, however, is not verified in the instance before us:

Illum . . . . .
. . . non equus impiger
Curru ducet *Achaico.*

[5] To those who neither go to balls nor read the *Morning Post*, it may be necessary to mention that the floors of ball-rooms, in general, are chalked, for safety and for ornament, with various fanciful devices.

Hours are not feet, yet hours trip on,
Time is not chalk, yet time's soon gone![1]

But, hang this long digressive flight!
I meant to say, thou'lt see, that night,
What falsehood rankles in their hearts,
Who say the P——e neglects the arts—
Neglects the arts!—no, St——g! no;
Thy Cupids answer ' 'tis not so;'
And every floor, that night, shall tell
How quick thou daubest, and how well!
Shine as thou may'st in French vermilion,
Thou'rt *best*—beneath a French cotillion;
And still com'st off, whate'er thy faults,
With *flying colours* in a Waltz!
Nor need'st thou mourn the transient date
To thy best works assigned by Fate—
While *some* chefs-d'œuvre live to weary one,
Thine boast a short life and a merry one;
Their hour of glory past and gone
With 'Molly, put the kettle on!'

But, bless my soul! I've scarce a leaf
Of paper left—so, must be brief.

This festive Fête, in fact, will be
The former Fête's *fac-simile;*[2]
The same long Masquerade of Rooms,
Tricked in such different, quaint costumes
(These, P—rt—r, are thy glorious works!)
You'd swear Egyptians, Moors, and Turks,
Bearing Good-Taste some deadly malice,
Had clubbed to raise a Pic-Nic Palace;
And each, to make the oglio pleasant,
Had sent a State-Room as a present;—
The same *fauteuils* and girondoles—
The same gold Asses,[3] pretty souls!
That, in this rich and classic dome,
Appear so perfectly at home!
The same bright river 'mongst the dishes,
But *not*—ah! not the same dear fishes—
Late hours and claret killed the old ones!
So, 'stead of silver and of gold ones
(It being rather hard to raise
Fish of that *specie* now-a-days),
Some sprats have been, by Y—rm—th's wish,
Promoted into *Silver* Fish,
And Gudgeons (so V—ns—tt—t told
The B—g—t) are as good as *Gold!*

E'n, pr'ythee, come—our Fête will be
But half a Fête, if wanting thee!   J. T.

---

[1] Hearts are not flint, yet flints are rent,
Hearts are not steel, yet steel is bent.

After all, however, Mr. Sc—tt may well say to the Colonel (and, indeed, to much better wags than the Colonel), *μισω μνημονα ἡ μνημονας.*

[2] 'C—rl—t—n H——e will exhibit a complete *fac-simile*, in respect to interior ornament, to what it did at the last Fête. The same splendid draperies,' etc. etc.— *Morning Post.*

APPENDIX.

LETTER IV. Page 200.

AMONG the papers enclosed in Dr. D—g—n—n's Letter, there is an Heroic Epistle in Latin verse, from Pope Joan to her Lover, of which, as it is rather a curious document, I shall venture to give some account. This female Pontiff was a native of England (or, according to others, of Germany), who at an early age disguised herself in male attire, and followed her lover, a young ecclesiastic, to Athens, where she studied with such effect, that upon her arrival at Rome she was thought worthy of being raised to the Pontificate. This Epistle is addressed to her Lover (whom she had elevated to the dignity of Cardinal), soon after the fatal *accouchement*, by which her Fallibility was betrayed.

She begins by reminding him very tenderly of the time when they were in Athens—when

' By Ilissus' stream
We whispering walked along, and learned to speak
The tenderest feelings in the purest Greek;
Ah! then how little did we think or hope,
Dearest of men! that I should e'er be Pope![4]
That I—the humble Joan—whose housewife art
Seemed just enough to keep thy house and heart
(And those, alas! at sixes and at sevens),
Should soon keep all the keys of all the Heavens!'

Still less (she continues to say) could they have foreseen that such a catastrophe as had happened in Council would befall them—that she

' Should thus surprise the Conclave's grave decorum,
And let a *little Pope* pop out before 'em—
Pope *Innocent!* alas, the only one
That name should ever have been fixed upon!'

She then very pathetically laments the downfall of her greatness, and enumerates the various treasures to which she is doomed to bid farewell for ever.

' But oh! more dear, more precious ten times over—
Farewell, my Lord, my Cardinal, my Lover!
I made *thee* Cardinal—thou mad'st *me*—oh!
Thou mad'st the Papa[5] of the World—Mamma!'

---

[3] The salt-cellars on the P——e's *own* table were in the form of an ass with panniers.

[4] Spanheim attributes the unanimity with which Joan was elected, to that innate and irresistible charm by which her sex, though latent, operated upon the instinct of the Cardinals: 'Non vi aliqua, sed concorditer, omnium in se converso desiderio, quæ sunt blandientis sexus artes, latentes in hac quanquam!'

[5] This is an anachronism, for it was not till the eleventh century that the Bishop of Rome took the title of Papa, or Universal Father.

I have not time now to translate any more of this Epistle; but I presume the argument which the Right Hon. Doctor and his friends mean to deduce from it, is (in their usual convincing strain) that Romanists must be unworthy of Emancipation *now*, because they had a Petticoat Pope in the Ninth Century—Nothing can be more logically clear, and I find that Horace had exactly the same views upon the subject:

Romanus (eheu posteri, negabitis!)
  Emancipatus Fœminæ
    Fert vallum!—

LETTER VII. Page 203.

The Manuscript, which I found in the Bookseller's Letter, is a Melodrama, in two Acts, entitled, 'The Book,' of which the Theatres, of course, had had the refusal, before it was presented to Messrs. L—ck—ngt—n and Co. This rejected Drama, however, possesses considerable merit, and I shall take the liberty of laying a sketch of it before my Readers.

The first Act opens in a very awful manner:— *Time*, three o'clock in the morning—*Scene*, the Bourbon Chamber[2] in C—r—lt—n House—Enter the P——e R—g—t solus.—After a few broken sentences, he thus exclaims:

Away—away—
Thou haunt'st my fancy so, thou devilish Book!
I meet thee—trace thee, wheresoe'er I look.
I see thy damned *ink* in Eld—n's brows—
I see thy *foolscap* on my H—rtf—d's Spouse—
V—ns—t—t's head recalls thy *leathern case*,
And all thy *blank-leaves* stare from R—d—r's face!
While, turning here [*laying his hand on his heart*],
  I find, ah wretched elf!
Thy *List* of dire *Errata* in myself.
  [*Walks the stage in considerable agitation.*]
Oh Roman Punch! oh potent Curaçoa!
Oh Mareschino! Mareschino oh!
Delicious drams! why have you not the art
To kill this gnawing *Book-worm* in my heart?

He is here interrupted in his Soliloquy by perceiving some scribbled fragments of paper on the ground, which he collects, and 'by the light of two magnificent candelabras' discovers the following unconnected words—'*Wife neglected*'—'*the Book*'—'*Wrong Measures*'—'*the Queen*'—'*Mr. Lambert*'—'*the R—g—t.*'

Ha! treason in my House!—Curst words, that wither
My princely soul [*shaking the papers violently*], what Demon brought you hither?
'My wife!'—'the Book,' too!—stay—a nearer look—
  [*Holding the fragments closer to the Candelabras*]
Alas! too plain, B, double O, K, Book—
Death and destruction!

He here rings all the bells, and a whole legion of Valets enter—A scene of cursing and swearing (very much in the German style) ensues, in the course of which messengers are despatched in different directions for the L—rd Ch—nc—l—l—r, the D—e of C—b—l—d, etc. etc.—The intermediate time is filled up by another Soliloquy, at the conclusion of which the aforesaid Personages rush on alarmed—the D—e with his stays only half-laced, and the Ch—nc—llor with his wig thrown hastily over an old red night-cap, 'to maintain the becoming splendour of his office.'[3] The R—g—t produces the appalling fragments, upon which the Ch—nc—ll—r breaks out into exclamations of loyalty and tenderness, and relates the following portentous dream:—

'Tis scarcely two hours since
I had a fearful dream of thee, my P——e!—
Methought I heard thee, midst a courtly crowd,
Say from thy throne of gold, in mandate loud,
'Worship my whiskers!'—[*weeps*] not a knee was there
But bent and worshipped the Illustrious Pair
That curled in conscious majesty! [*pulls out his handkerchief*]—while cries
Of 'Whiskers! whiskers!' shook the echoing skies!—
Just in that glorious hour, methought, there came,
With looks of injured pride, a Princely Dame,
And a young maiden clinging to her side,
As if she feared some tyrant would divide
The hearts that nature and affection tied!
The Matron came—within her *right* hand glowed
A radiant torch; while from her *left* a load
Of Papers hung—[*wipes his eyes*]—collected in her veil—
The venal evidence, the slanderous tale,
The wounding hint, the current lies that pass
From *Post* to *Courier*, formed the motley mass;

---

[1] There was a mysterious Book, in the 16th century, which employed all the anxious curiosity of the learned of that day—every one spoke of it; many wrote against it; though it does not appear that anybody had ever seen it; and, indeed, Grotius is of opinion that no such book ever existed. It was entitled *Liber de tribus Impostoribus*. (See Morhof. Cap. de Libris damnatis.)—Our more modern mystery of the 'Book' resembles this in many particulars; and if the number of lawyers employed in drawing it up be stated correctly, a slight alteration of the title into '*à tribus impostoribus*' would produce a coincidence altogether very remarkable.

[2] The chamber, I suppose, which was prepared for the reception of the Bourbons at the first Grand Fête, and which was ornamented (all 'for the deliverance of Europe') with *fleurs de lys*.

[3] 'To enable the individual who holds the office of Chancellor to maintain it in becoming splendour.' (*A loud laugh.*)—Lord *Castlereagh's Speech upon the Vice-Chancellor's Bill.*

Which, with disdain, before the Throne she throws,
And lights the Pile beneath thy princely nose.
[*Weeps.*]
Heavens, how it blazed!—I'd ask no livelier fire
[*with animation*] To roast a Papist by, my gracious Sire!—
But ah! the Evidence—[*weeps again*]—I mourned to see—
Cast, as it burned, a deadly light on thee!
And Tales and Hints their random sparkles flung,
And hissed and crackled like an old maid's tongue;
While *Post* and *Courier*, faithful to their fame,
Made up in stink for what they lacked in flame!
When, lo, ye Gods!—the fire, ascending brisker,
Now singes *one*, now lights the *other* whisker—
Ah! where was then the Sylphid, that unfurls
Her fairy standard in defence of curls?
Throne, Whiskers, Wig, soon vanished into smoke,
The watchman cried 'past One,' and—I awoke.

Here his Lordship weeps more profusely than ever, and the R—g—t (who has been very much agitated during the recital of the dream), by a movement as characteristic as that of Charles XII. when he was shot, claps his hands to his whiskers to feel if all be really safe. A Privy Council is held — all the Servants, etc. are examined, and it appears that a Tailor, who had come to measure the R—g—t for a Dress (which takes three whole pages of the best superfine *clinquant* in describing), was the only person who had been in the Bourbon Chamber during the day. It is accordingly determined to seize the Tailor, and the Council breaks up with a unanimous resolution to be vigorous.

The commencement of the Second Act turns chiefly upon the Trial and Imprisonment of two Brothers; but as this forms the *under* plot of the Drama, I shall content myself with extracting from it the following speech, which is addressed to the two brothers, as they 'exeunt severally' to Prison:

Go to your prisons—though the air of Spring
No mountain coolness to your cheeks shall bring;
Though summer flowers shall pass unseen away,
And all your portion of the glorious day
May be some solitary beam that falls,
At morn or eve, upon your dreary walls—
Some beam that enters, trembling as if awed,
To tell how gay the young world laughs abroad!
Yet go—for thoughts, as blessed as the air
Of Spring or Summer flowers, await you there;
Thoughts, such as He, who feasts his courtly crew
In rich conservatories, *never* knew!
Pure self-esteem—the smiles that light within—
The Zeal, whose circling charities begin

With the few loved-ones Heaven has placed it near,
Nor cease, till all Mankind are in its sphere!—
The Pride, that suffers without vaunt or plea,
And the fresh Spirit, that can warble free.
Through prison-bars, its hymn to Liberty!

The Scene next changes to a Tailor's Workshop, and a fancifully-arranged group of these Artists is discovered upon the Shop-board—Their task evidently of a *royal* nature, from the profusion of gold-lace, frogs, etc. that lie about—They all rise and come forward, while one of them sings the following Stanzas, to the tune of 'Derry Down:'

My brave brother Tailors, come, straighten your knees,
For a moment, like gentlemen, stand up at ease,
While I sing of our P——e (and a fig for his railers),
The Shop-board's delight! the Mæcenas of Tailors!
Derry down, down, down derry down.

Some monarchs take roundabout ways into note,
But His short cut to fame is—the cut of his coat;
Philip's Son thought the World was too small for his Soul,
While our R—g—t's finds room in a laced button-hole!
Derry down, etc.

Look through all Europe's Kings—at least those who go loose—
Not a King of them all's such a friend to the Goose.
So, God keep him increasing in size and renown,
Still the fattest and best-fitted P—e about town!
Derry down, etc.

During the 'Derry down' of this last verse, a messenger from the S—c—t—y of S——e's Office rushes on, and the singer (who, luckily for the effect of the scene, is the very Tailor suspected of the mysterious fragments) is interrupted in the midst of his laudatory exertions, and hurried away, to the no small surprise and consternation of his comrades. The plot now hastens rapidly in its development—the management of the Tailor's examination is highly skilful, and the alarm which he is made to betray is natural without being ludicrous. The explanation, too, which he finally gives, is not more simple than satisfactory. It appears that the said fragments formed part of a self-exculpatory note which he had intended to send to Colonel M'M——n upon subjects purely professional; and the corresponding bits (which still lie luckily in his pocket) being produced, and skilfully laid beside the others, the following billet-doux is the satisfactory result of their juxtaposition:

Honoured Colonel—my Wife, who's the Queen of all slatterns,
Neglected to put up the Book of new Patterns.
She sent the wrong Measures too—shamefully wrong—
They're the same used for poor Mr. Lambert, when young;

But, bless you! they wouldn't go half round tue R—g—t,
So, hope you'll excuse yours till death, most obedient.

This fully explains the whole mystery—the R—g—t resumes his wonted smiles, and the Drama terminates, as usual, to the satisfaction of all parties.

CORRUPTION AND INTOLERANCE.

TWO POEMS.

———◆———

PREFACE.

THE practice which has lately been introduced into literature, of writing very long notes upon very indifferent verses, appears to me rather a happy invention ; for it supplies us with a mode of turning stupid poetry to account ; and as horses too dull for the saddle may serve well enough to draw lumber, so poems of this kind make excellent beasts of burden, and will bear notes, though they may not bear reading. Besides, the comments in such cases are so little under the necessity of paying any servile deference to the text, that they may even adopt that Socratic dogma, ' Quod supra nos nihil ad nos.'

In the first of the following poems I have ventured to speak of the Revolution in language which has sometimes been employed by Tory writers, and which is therefore neither very new nor popular. But, however an Englishman may be reproached with ingratitude, for appreciating the merits and results of a measure which he is taught to regard as the source of his liberties,—however ungrateful it might be in Alderman Birch to question for a moment the purity of that glorious era to which he is indebted for the seasoning of so many orations,—yet an Irishman, who has none of these obligations to acknowledge, to whose country the Revolution brought nothing but injury and insult, and who recollects that the book of Molyneux was burned, by order of William's Whig Parliament, for daring to extend to unfortunate Ireland those principles on which the Revolution was professedly founded—an Irishman *may* venture to criticise the measures of that period, without exposing himself either to the imputation of ingratitude, or the suspicion of being influenced by any Popish remains of Jacobitism. No nation, it is true, was ever blessed with a more golden opportunity of establishing and securing its liberties for ever, than the conjuncture of Eighty-eight presented to the people of Great Britain. But the disgraceful reigns of Charles and James had weakened and degraded the national character. The bold notions of popular right, which had arisen out of the struggles between Charles the First and his Parliament, were gradually supplanted by those slavish doctrines for which Lord H—kesb—ry eulogizes the churchmen of that period ; and as the Reformation had happened too soon for the purity of religion, so the Revolution came too late for the spirit of liberty. Its advantages accordingly were for the most part specious and transitory, while the evils which it entailed are still felt and still increasing. By rendering unnecessary the frequent exercise of prerogative, that unwieldy power which cannot move a step without alarm, it limited the only interference of the Crown which is singly and independently exposed before the people, and whose abuses are therefore obvious to their senses and capacities : like the myrtle over a certain statue in Minerva's temple at Athens, it skilfully veiled from their sight the only obtrusive feature of royalty. At the same time, however, that the Revolution abridged this unpopular attribute, it amply compensated by the substitution of a new power, as much more potent in its effect as it is more secret in its operations. In the disposal of an immense revenue, and the extensive patronage annexed to it, the first foundations of this power of the Crown were laid ; the innovation of a standing army at once increased and strengthened it ; and the few slight barriers which the Act of Settlement opposed to its progress have all been gradually removed during the Whiggish reigns that succeeded, till at length this spirit of influence is become the vital principle of the state, whose agency, subtle and unseen, pervades every part of the constitution, lurks under all its forms, and regulates all its movements; and, like the invisible sylph or grace which presides over the motions of beauty,

'Illam, quicquid agit, quoquo vestigia flectit,
Componit furtim subsequiturque.'

The cause of liberty and the Revolution are so habitually associated by Englishmen, that probably, in objecting to the latter, I may be thought hostile or indifferent to the former; but nothing can be more unjust than such a suspicion. The very object which my humble animadversions would attain is, that in the crisis to which I think England is hastening, and between which and foreign subjugation she may soon be compelled to choose, the errors and omissions of 1688 may be remedied, and that, as she then had a Revolution without a Reform, she may now seek a Reform without a Revolution.

In speaking of the parties which have so long agitated England, it will be observed that I lean as little to the Whigs as to their adversaries. Both factions have been equally cruel to Ireland, and perhaps equally insincere in their efforts for the liberties of England. There is one name, indeed, connected with Whiggism, of which I can never think but with veneration and tenderness. As justly, however, might the light of the sun be claimed by any particular nation, as the sanction of that name be assumed by any party whatever: Mr. Fox belonged to mankind, and they have lost in him their ablest friend.

With respect to the few lines upon Intolerance which I have subjoined, they are but the imperfect beginning of a long series of Essays, with which I here menace my readers, upon the same important subject. I shall look to no higher merit in the task, than that of giving a new form to claims and remonstrances which have often been much more eloquently urged, and which would long ere now have produced their effect, but that the minds of some men, like the pupil of the eye, contract themselves the more, the stronger light there is shed upon them.

CORRUPTION

AN EPISTLE.

Νυν δ' άπανθ' ώσπερ εξ αγορας εκπεπραται ταυτα· αντεισηκται δε αντι τουτων, ύφ' ών απολωλε και νενοσηκεν ή Έλλας. Ταυτα δ' εστι τι; ζηλος, ει τις ειληφε τι· γελως αν ομολογη· συγγνωμη τοις ελεγχομενοις· μισος, αν τουτοις τις επιτιμα· ταλλα, παντα, όσα εκ του δωροδοκειν ηρτηται.
Demosth. Philipp. III.

Boast on, my friend—though, stript of all beside,
Thy struggling nation still retains her pride:
That pride which once in genuine glory woke,
When Marlborough fought, and brilliant St. John spoke;
That pride which still, by time and shame unstung,
Outlives e'en Wh-tel-cke's sword and H-wks-b'ry's tongue!
Boast on, my friend, while in this humbled isle,
Where honour mourns and freedom fears to smile,
Where the bright light of England's fame is known
But by the baleful shadow she has thrown

On all our fate—where, doomed to wrongs and slights,
We hear you talk of Britain's glorious rights,
As weeping slaves, that under hatches lie,
Hear those on deck extol the sun and sky!
Boast on, while wandering through my native haunts,
I coldly listen to thy patriot vaunts,
And feel, though close our wedded countries twine,
More sorrow for my own than pride from thine.

Yet pause a moment—and if truths severe
Can find an inlet to that courtly ear

Which loves no politics in rhyme but P—e's,
And hears no news but W—rd's gazetted lies;
If aught can please thee but the good old saws
Of 'Church and State,' and 'William's matchless laws,'
And 'Acts and Rights of glorious Eighty-eight,'—
Things which, though now a century out of date,
Still serve to ballast, with convenient words,
A few crank arguments for speeching Lords—
Turn, while I tell how England's freedom found,
Where most she looked for life, her deadliest wound;
How brave she struggled, while her foe was seen,
How faint since Influence lent that foe a screen;
How strong o'er James and Popery she prevailed,
How weakly fell, when Whigs and gold assailed.
While Kings were poor, and all those schemes unknown
Which drain the People, but enrich the Throne;
Ere yet a yielding Commons had supplied
Those chains of gold by which themselves are tied;
Then proud Prerogative, untaught to creep
With Bribery's silent foot on Freedom's sleep,[1]
Frankly avowed his bold enslaving plan,
And claimed a right from God to trample man!
But Luther's light had too much warmed mankind
For Hampden's truths to linger long behind;
Nor then, when king-like Popes had fallen so low,
Could pope-like Kings[2] escape the levelling blow.

That ponderous sceptre (in whose place we bow
To the light talisman of influence now),
Too gross, too visible to work the spell
Which Modern Power performs, in fragments fell:
In fragments lay, till, patched and painted o'er
With fleurs-de-lys, it shone and scourged once more!
'Twas then, my friend, thy kneeling nation quaffed
Long, long and deep, the churchman's opiate draught
Of tame obedience—till her sense of right
And pulse of glory seemed extinguished quite,
And Britons slept so sluggish in their chain,
That wakening Freedom called almost in vain!
Oh England! England! what a chance was thine,
When the last tyrant of that ill-starred line
Fled from his sullied crown, and left thee free
To found thy own eternal liberty!
How bright, how glorious in that sunshine hour,
Might patriot hands have raised the triple tower[3]
Of British freedom on a rock divine,
Which neither force could storm nor treachery mine!
But no—the luminous, the lofty plan,
Like mighty Babel, seemed too bold for man;
The curse of jarring tongues again was given
To thwart a work which raised men near to Heaven!
While Tories marred what Whigs had scarce begun,[4]
While Whigs undid what Whigs themselves had done,[5]

---

[1] Though the Kings of England were most unroyally harassed and fettered in all their pursuits by pecuniary difficulties, before the provident enactments of William's reign had opened to the Crown its present sources of wealth, yet we must not attribute to the Revolutionary Whigs the credit altogether of inventing this art of government. Its advantages had long been understood by ministers and favourites, though the limits of the royal revenue prevented them from exercising it with effect. In the reign of Mary, indeed, the gold of Spain, being added to the usual resources of the Throne, produced such a spirit of ductility in her Parliaments that the price for which each member had sold himself was publicly ascertained; and if Charles the First could have commanded a similar supply, it is not too much to suppose that the Commonwealth never would have existed. But it was during the reign of the second Charles that the nearest approaches were made to that pecuniary system which our debt, our funds, and our taxes have since brought to such perfection; and Clifford and Danby would not disgrace even the present times of political venality. Still, however, the experiment was but partial and imperfect, and attended with scarcely any other advantage than that of suggesting the uses to which the power of the purse has been since converted, just as the fulminating dust of the chemists may have prepared the way for the invention of gunpowder.

[2] The drivelling correspondence between James I. and his 'dog Steenie' (the Duke of Buckingham), which we find among the Hardwicke Papers, sufficiently shows, if we wanted such illustration, into what doting, idiotic brains the plan of arbitrary power may enter.

[3] Tacitus has expressed his opinion, in a passage very frequently quoted, that such a distribution of power as the theory of the British constitution exhibits is merely a subject of bright speculation—'a system more easily praised than practised, and which, even could it happen to exist, would certainly not prove permanent;' and, in truth, if we reflect on the English history, we shall feel very much inclined to agree with Tacitus. We shall find that at no period whatever has this balance of the three estates existed; that the nobles predominated till the policy of Henry VII. and his successor reduced their weight by breaking up the feudal system of property; that the power of the Crown became then supreme and absolute, till the bold encroachments of the Commons subverted the fabric altogether; that the alternate ascendency of prerogative and privilege distracted the period which followed the Restoration; and that, lastly, the Acts of 1688, by laying the foundation of an unbounded court influence, have secured a preponderance to the Throne which every succeeding year increases. So that the British constitution has never perhaps existed but in theory.

[4] 'Those two thieves (says Ralph) between whom the nation was crucified.'—*Use and Abuse of Parliaments*, page 164.

[5] The monarchs of Great Britain can never be sufficiently grateful for that generous spirit which led the Revolutionary Whigs to give away the Crown, without imposing any of those restraints or stipulations which other men might have taken advantage of such a

The time was lost, and William, with a smile,
Saw Freedom weeping o'er the unfinished pile!
Hence all the ills you suffer, hence remain
Such galling fragments of that feudal chain,[1]
Whose links, around you by the Norman flung,
Though loosed and broke so often, still have clung.
Hence sly Prerogative, like Jove of old,
Has turned his thunder into showers of gold,
Whose silent courtship wins securer joys,[2]
Taints by degrees, and ruins without noise.

While Parliaments, no more those sacred things
Which make and rule the destiny of Kings,
Like loaded dice by ministers are thrown,
And each new set of sharpers cog their own!
Hence the rich oil that from the Treasury steals,
And drips o'er all the Constitution's wheels,
Giving the old machine such pliant play,[3]
That Court and Commons jog one joltless way,
While Wisdom trembles for the crazy car,
So gilt, so rotten, carrying fools so far!
And the duped people, hourly doomed to pay
The sums that bribe their liberties away,[4]

moment to enforce, and in framing of which they had so good a model to follow as the limitations proposed by the Lords Essex and Halifax in the debate upon the Exclusion Bill. They not only condescended, however, to accept of places, but they took care that these dignities should be no impediment to their 'voice potential' in affairs of legislation; and though an Act was after many years suffered to pass, which by one of its articles disqualified placemen from serving as members of the House of Commons, yet it was not allowed to interfere with the influence of the reigning monarch, nor indeed with that of his successor Anne, as the purifying clause was not to take effect till after the decease of the latter sovereign, and she very considerately repealed it altogether. So that, as representation has continued ever since, if the King were simple enough to send to foreign courts ambassadors who were most of them in the pay of those courts, he would be just as faithfully represented as his people. It would be endless to enumerate all the favours which were conferred upon William by those 'apostate Whigs.' They complimented him with the first suspension of the Habeas Corpus Act which had been hazarded since the confirmation of that privilege; and this example of our deliverer's reign has not been lost upon any of his successors. They promoted the establishment of a standing army, and circulated in its defence the celebrated 'Balancing Letter,' in which it is insinuated that England, even then, in her boasted hour of regeneration, was arrived at such a pitch of faction and corruption that nothing could keep her in order but a Whig ministry and a standing army. They refused, as long as they could, to shorten the duration of Parliaments; and though the declaration of rights acknowledged the necessity of such a reform, they were able, by arts not unknown to modern ministers, to brand those as traitors and republicans who urged it. But the grand and distinguishing trait of their measures was the power which they gave to the Crown of annihilating the freedom of elections, of muddying for ever that stream of representation which had, even in the most agitated times, reflected some features of the people, but which then for the first time became the Pactolus of the Court, and grew so darkened with sands of gold that it served for the people's mirror no longer. We need but consult the writings of that time to understand the astonishment then excited by measures which the practice of a century has rendered not only familiar, but necessary. See a pamphlet called *The Danger of Mercenary Parliaments*, 1698; *State Tracts*, Will. III. vol. ii. p. 638; and see also *Some Paradoxes presented as a New Year's Gift* (*State Poems*, vol. iii. p. 327).

[1] The last great wound given to the feudal system was the Act of the 12th of Charles II., which abolished the tenure of knight's service *in capite*, and which Blackstone compares, for its salutary influence upon property, to the boasted provisions of Magna Charta itself. Yet even in this Act we see the effects of

that counteracting spirit, that Arimanius, which has weakened every effort of the English nation towards liberty, which allowed but half the errors of Popery to be removed at the Reformation, and which planted more abuses than it suffered to be rooted out at the Revolution. The exclusion of copyholders from their share of elective rights was permitted to remain as a brand of feudal servitude, and as an obstacle to the rise of that strong counterbalance which an equal representation of property would oppose to the weight of the Crown. If the managers of the Revolution had been sincere in their wishes for reform, they would not only have taken this fetter off the rights of election, but they would have renewed the mode adopted in Cromwell's time of increasing the number of knights of the shire, to the exclusion of those rotten insignificant boroughs which have tainted the whole mass of the constitution. Lord Clarendon calls this measure of Cromwell's 'an alteration fit to be more warrantably made, and in a better time.' It formed part of Mr. Pitt's plan in 1783; but Mr. Pitt's plan of reform was a kind of dramatic piece, about as likely to be acted as Mr. Sheridan's *Foresters*.

[2] . . . Fore enim tutum iter et patens,
Converso in pretium Deo.
Aurum per medios ire satellites,
Et perrumpere amat saxa, potentius
Ictu fulmineo.
—*Horat.* lib. iii. od. 16.

The Athenians considered seduction so much more dangerous than force, that the penalty for a rape was merely a pecuniary fine, while the guilt of seduction was punished with death. And though it must be owned that during the reign of that ravisher Prerogative, the poor Constitution was treated like Miss Cunegund among the Bulgarians; yet I agree with the principle of the Athenian law, that her present state of willing self-abandonment is much more hopeless and irreclaimable, and calls for a more signal vengeance upon her seducers.

[3] 'They drove so fast (says Welwood of the ministers of Charles I.), that it was no wonder that the wheels and chariot broke.'—*Memoirs*, p. 35. But this fatal accident, if we may judge from experience, is to be imputed less to the folly and impetuosity of the drivers than to the want of that suppling oil from the Treasury which has been found so necessary to make a government like that of England run smoothly. If Charles had been as well provided with this article as his successors have been since the happy Revolution, his Commons would never have merited from the Throne the harsh appellation of 'seditious vipers,' but would have been (as they are now, and I trust always will be) 'dutiful Commons,' 'loyal Commons,' etc. etc., and would have given him ship-money or any other sort of money he might take a fancy to.

[4] The period that immediately succeeds a coronation

Like a young eagle, who has lent his plume
To fledge the shaft by which he meets his doom,
See their own feathers plucked, to wing the dart
Which rank corruption destines for their heart!
But soft! my friend—I hear thee proudly say,
' What! shall I listen to the impious lay,
That dares, with Tory licence, to profane
The bright bequests of William's glorious reign?
Shall the great wisdom of our patriot sires,
Whom H—wk—sb—y quotes and savoury B–rch admires,
Be slandered thus? shall honest St—le agree
With virtuous R—se to call us pure and free,
Yet fail to prove it? Shall our patent pair
Of wise State-Poets waste their words in air,
And P—e unheeded breathe his prosperous strain,
And C—nn—ng *take the people's sense* in vain?'

The people!—ah! that Freedom's form should stay
Where Freedom's Spirit long hath passed away!
That a false smile should play around the dead,
And flush the features where the soul has fled![1]
When Rome had lost her virtue with her rights,
When her foul tyrant sat on Capreæ's heights

Amid his ruffian spies, and doomed to death
Each noble name they blasted with their breath!
Even then (in mockery of that golden time,
When the Republic rose revered, sublime,
And her free sons, diffused from zone to zone,
Gave kings to every country but their own),
Even then the Senate and the Tribunes stood,
Insulting marks, to show how Freedom's flood
Had dared to flow, in glory's radiant day,
And how it ebbed, for ever ebbed away!
Oh! look around—though yet a tyrant's sword
Nor haunts your sleep nor trembles o'er your board,
Though blood be better drawn by modern quacks
With Treasury leeches than with sword or axe;
Yet say, could even a prostrate Tribune's power,
Or a mock Senate, in Rome's servile hour,
Insult so much the rights, the claims of man,
As doth that fettered mob, that free divan,
Of noble tools and honourable knaves,
Of pensioned patriots and privileged slaves?
That party-coloured mass, which nought can warm
But quick Corruption's heat—whose ready swarm

---

has been called very aptly the honeymoon of a reign; and if we suppose the Throne to be the wife, and the People the husband, I know no better model of a matrimonial transaction, nor one that I would sooner recommend to a woman of spirit, than that which the arrangements of 1688 afford. In the first place, she must not only obtain from her husband an allowance of pin-money or civil list establishment sufficient to render her independent of his caprice, but she must also prevail on him to make her the steward of his estates, and to entrust her with the management of all his pecuniary concerns. I need not tell a woman of sense to what spirited uses she may turn such concessions. He will soon become so tame and docile under her hands, that she may make him play the strangest and most amusing tricks, such as quarrelling with his nearest and dearest relations about a dish of tea, a turban, or a wafer; preparing his house for defence against robbers, by putting fetters and handcuffs on two-thirds of its inmates; employing C—nn—g and P—rc—v—l in his sickest moments to read to him alternately *Joe Miller* and the *Catechism*, with a thousand other diverting inconsistencies. If her spouse have still enough of sense remaining to grumble at the ridiculous exhibition which she makes of him, let her withhold from him now and then the rights of the Habeas Corpus Act (a mode of proceeding which the women of Athens once adopted); and if the good man loves such privileges, the interruption will soon restore him to submission. If his former wife were a Papist, or had any tendency that way, I would advise my fair Sovereign, whenever he begins to argue with her unpleasantly, to shout out, 'No Popery! no Popery!' as loud as she can into his ears, and it is astonishing what an effect it will have in disconcerting all his arguments. This method was tried lately by an old woman at Northampton, and with much success. Seriously, this convenient bugbear of Popery is by no means the least among the numberless auxiliaries which the Revolution has marshalled on the side of the Throne. Those unskilful tyrants, Charles and James, instead of profiting wisely by that useful subserviency which has always

distinguished the ministers of our religious establishment, were blind enough to plan the ruin of this best bulwark of their power, and connected their designs upon the Church so closely with their attacks upon the Constitution, that they identified in the minds of the people the interests of their religion and their liberties. During those times, therefore, 'No Popery' was the watchword of freedom, and served to keep the public spirit awake against the invasions of bigotry and prerogative. The Revolution, however, by removing this object of jealousy, has produced a reliance on the orthodoxy of the Throne, of which the Throne has not failed to take every possible advantage; and the cry of 'No Popery' having by this means lost its power of alarming the people against the encroachments of the Crown, has served ever since the very different purpose of strengthening the Crown against the claims and struggles of the people. The danger of the Church from Papists and Pretenders was the chief pretext for the repeal of the Triennial Bill, for the adoption of a standing army, for the numerous suspensions of the Habeas Corpus Act, and, in short, for all those spirited infractions of the constitution by which the reigns of the last century were so eminently distinguished. We have seen too, very lately, how the same scarecrow alarm has enabled the Throne to select its ministers from men whose servility is their only claim to elevation, and who are pledged (if such an alternative *could* arise) to take part with the scruples of the King against the salvation of the empire.

[1] 'It is a scandal (said Sir Charles Sedley in William's reign) that a Government so sick at heart as ours is should look so well in the face;' and Edmund Burke has said, in the present reign, 'When the people conceive that laws and tribunals, and even popular assemblies, are perverted from the ends of their institution, they find in these names of degenerated establishments only new motives to discontent. Those bodies which, when full of life and beauty, lay in their arms and were their joy and comfort, when dead and putrid become more loathsome from remembrance of former endearments.'—*Thoughts on the present Discontents*, 1770.

Spread their light wings in Bribery's golden sky,
Buzz for a period, lay their eggs, and die!
That greedy vampire, which from Freedom's tomb
Comes forth with all the mimicry of bloom
Upon its lifeless cheek, and sucks and drains
A people's blood to feed its putrid veins!—
'Heavens, what a picture!'—yes, my friend, 'tis dark—
'But can *no* light be found, no genuine spark
Of former fire to warm us? Is there none
To act a Marvell's part?'[1]—I fear, not one.
To place and power all public spirit tends,
In place and power all public spirit ends;[2]
Like hardy plants, that love the air and sky,
When *out*, 'twill thrive, but taken *in*, 'twill die!

Not bolder truths of sacred freedom hung
From Sidney's pen or burned on Fox's tongue,
Than upstart Whigs produce each market-night,
While yet their conscience, as their purse, is light;
While debts at home excite their care for those
Which, dire to tell, their much-loved country owes,
And loud and upright, till their price be known,
They thwart the King's supplies to raise their own—
But bees, on flowers alighting, cease their hum—
So, settling upon places, Whigs grow dumb!
And though I feel as if indignant Heaven
Must think that wretch too foul to be forgiven,
Who basely hangs the bright, protecting shade
Of Freedom's ensign o'er Corruption's trade,
And makes the sacred flag he dares to show
His passport to the market of her foe!—
Yet, yet I own, so venerably dear
Are Freedom's grave old anthems to my ear,
That I enjoy them, though by rascals sung,
And reverence Scripture even from Satan's tongue.

Nay, when the Constitution has expired,
I'll have such men, like Irish wakers, hired
To sing old Habeas Corpus by its side,
And ask, in purchased ditties, why it died?[3]

See that smooth Lord, whom nature's plastic pains
Seemed to have destined for those Eastern reigns
When eunuchs flourished, and when nerveless things
That men rejected were the chosen of Kings.
Even *he*, forsooth (oh, mockery accurst!)
Dared to assume the patriot's name at first—
Thus Pitt began, and thus begin his apes;
Thus devils, when *first* raised, take pleasing shapes—
But oh, poor Ireland! if revenge be sweet
For centuries of wrong, for dark deceit
And withering insult—for the Union thrown
Into thy bitter cup, when that alone
Of slavery's draught was wanting—if for this
Revenge be sweet, thou *hast* that demon's bliss;
For oh! 'tis more than hell's revenge to see
That England trusts the men who've ruined thee!
That, in these awful days, when every hour
Creates some new or blasts some ancient power,
When proud Napoleon, like the burning shield
Whose light compelled each wondering foe to yield,
With baleful lustre blinds the brave and free,
And dazzles Europe into slavery!
That, in this hour, when patriot zeal should guide,
When Mind should rule, and—Fox should *not* have died,
All that devoted England can oppose
To enemies made fiends, and friends made foes,
Is the rank refuse, the despised remains [4]
Of that unpitying power, whose whips and chains

---

[1] Andrew Marvell, the honest opposer of the Court during the reign of Charles the Second, and the last member of Parliament who, according to the ancient mode, took wages from his constituents. How very much the Commons have changed their paymasters!—See the *State Poems* for some rude but spirited effusions of Andrew Marvell.

[2] The following artless speech of Sir Francis Winnington, in the reign of Charles the Second, will amuse those who are fully aware of the perfection which we have attained in that system of Government whose humble beginnings seem to have astonished the worthy Baronet so much: 'I did observe (says he) that all those who had pensions, and most of those who had offices, voted all of a side, as they were directed by some great officer, exactly as if their business in this House had been to preserve their pensions and offices, and not to make laws for the good of them who sent them here.'—He alludes to that Parliament which was called, *par excellence*, the Pensionary Parliament! a distinction, however, which it has long lost, and which we merely give it from old custom, just as we say, *The Irish Rebellion*.

[3] I believe it is in following the corpse to the grave, and not at the wakes (as we call the watching of the dead), that this elegiac howl of my countrymen is performed. Spenser says, that our howl 'is heathenish, and proceeds from a despair of salvation.' If so, I think England may join in chorus with us at present.—The Abbé de Motraye tells us that the Jews in the East address their dead in a similar manner, and say, 'Hu! Hu! Hu! why did you die? Hadn't you a wife? Hadn't you a long pipe?' etc. etc. (See his *Travels*.) I thought for a long time with Vallancey, that we were a colony of Carthaginians; but from this passage of de Motraye, and from the way in which Mr. P-rc-v-l would have us treated, I begin to suspect we are no better than Jews.

[4] When the Duke of Buckingham was assassinated, Charles the First, as a tribute to his memory, continued all his creatures in the same posts and favours which they had enjoyed under their patron; and much in the same manner do we see the country sacrificed to the manes of a Minister at present.

It is invidious perhaps to look for parallels in the reign of Charles the First; but the expedient of threatening the Commons with dissolution, which has lately been played off with so much *éclat*, appears to have been

Made Ireland first, in wild, adulterous trance,
Turn false to England's bed and whore with
    France!—
Those hacked and tainted tools, so foully fit
For the grand artisan of mischief, P—tt,

So useless ever but in vile employ,
So weak to save, so vigorous to destroy!
Such are the men that guard thy threatened
    shore,
Oh England! sinking England! boast no more.

INTOLERANCE.

'This clamour, which pretends to be raised for the safety of Religion, has almost worn out the very appearance of it, and rendered us not only the most divided, but the most immoral people upon the face of the earth.'—*Addison, Freeholder*, No. 37.

START not, my Friend, nor think the Muse will
    stain
Her classic fingers with the dust profane
Of Bulls, Decrees, and fulminating scrolls,
That took such freedom once with royal souls,
When Heaven was yet the Pope's exclusive trade,
And Kings were *damned* as fast as now they're
    made!
No, no—let D—gen-n search the Papal chair
For fragrant treasures long forgotten there;
And, as the witch of sunless Lapland thinks
That little swarthy gnomes delight in stinks,
Let sallow P-rc-v-l snuff up the gale
Which wizard D—gen-n's gathered sweets ex-
    hale!
Enough for me, whose heart has learned to scorn
Bigots alike in Rome or England born,
Who loathe the venom, whencesoe'er it springs,
From Popes or Lawyers, Pastry-cooks or Kings;
Enough for me to laugh and weep by turns,
As mirth provokes, or indignation burns,
As C-nn-ng vapours, or as France succeeds,
As H-wk-sb'ry proses, or as Ireland bleeds!

And thou, my Friend—if, in these headlong
    days,
When bigot Zeal her drunken antics plays
So near a precipice, that men the while
Look breathless on and shudder while they
    smile—
If, in such fearful days, thou'lt dare to look
To hapless Ireland, to this rankling nook
Which Heaven has freed from poisonous things
    in vain
While G-ff-rd's tongue and M-sgr-ve's pen
    remain—

If thou hast yet no golden blinkers got
To shade thine eyes from this devoted spot,
Whose wrongs, though blazoned o'er the world
    they be,
Placemen alone are privileged *not* to see—
Oh! turn awhile, and, though the shamrock
    wreathes
My homely harp, yet shall the song it breathes
Of Ireland's slavery, and of Ireland's woes,
Live, when the memory of her tyrant foes
Shall but exist, all future knaves to warn,
Embalmed in hate and canonized by scorn!
When C-stl-r—gh, in sleep still more profound
Than his own opiate tongue now deals around,
Shall wait the impeachment of that awful day
Which even *his* practised hand can't bribe away!
And oh! my friend, wert thou but near me now,
To see the spring diffuse o'er Erin's brow
Smiles that shine out, unconquerably fair,
Even through the blood-marks left by C—md-n
    there!
Couldst thou but see what verdure paints the sod
Which none but tyrants and their slaves have
    trod,
And didst thou know the spirit, kind and brave,
That warms the soul of each insulted slave,
Who, tired with struggling, sinks beneath his
    lot,
And seems by all but watchful France forgot!—
Thy heart would burn—yes, even thy Pittite
    heart
Would burn, to think that such a blooming part
Of the world's garden, rich in Nature's charms,
And filled with social souls and vigorous arms,
Should be the victim of that canting crew,
So smooth, so godly, yet so devilish too,

---

frequently resorted to at that period. In one instance Hume tells us, that the King sent his Lord Keeper (*not his Jester*) to menace the House, that unless they despatched a certain Bill for subsidies, they must expect to sit no longer. By similar threats the excise upon beer and ale was carried in Charles the Second's reign. It is edifying to know, that though Mr. C-nn-ng despises Puffendorf, he has no objection to precedents derived from the Courts of the Stuarts.

[1] The example of toleration which Bonaparte has given will produce, I fear, no other effect than that of determining the British Government to persist, from the very spirit of opposition, in their own old system of intolerance and injustice; just as the Siamese blacken their teeth, 'because,' as they say, 'the devil has white ones.'

Who, armed at once with prayer-books and with whips,
Blood on their hands, and Scripture on their lips,
Tyrants by creed, and torturers by text,
Make *this* life hell, in honour of the *next!*
Your R-desd-les, P-rc-v-ls — oh, gracious Heaven!
If I'm presumptuous, be my tongue forgiven,
When here I swear, by my soul's hope of rest,
I'd rather have been born, ere man was blest
With the pure dawn of Revelation's light,
Yes!—rather plunge me back in Pagan night,
And take my chance with Socrates for bliss,[1]
Than be the Christian of a faith like this,
Which builds on heavenly cant its earthly sway,
And in a convert mourns to lose a prey;
Which, binding polity in spiritual chains,
And tainting piety with temporal stains,[2]
Corrupts both State and Church, and makes an oath
The knave and atheist's passport into both—
Which, while it dooms dissenting souls to know
Nor bliss above nor liberty below,

Adds the slave's suffering to the sinner's fear,
And, lest he 'scape hereafter, racks him here!
But no—far other faith, far milder beams
Of heavenly justice warm the Christian's dreams,
His creed is writ on Mercy's page above,
By the pure hands of all-atoning Love!
He weeps to see his soul's Religion twine
The tyrant's sceptre with her wreath divine,
And *he*, while round him sects and nations raise
To the one God their varying notes of praise,
Blesses each voice, whate'er its tone may be,
That serves to swell the general harmony!
Such was the spirit, grandly, gently bright,
That filled, oh Fox! thy peaceful soul with light;
While blandly spreading, like that orb of air
Which folds our planet in its circling care,
The mighty sphere of thy transparent mind
Embraced the world, and breathed for all mankind!
Last of the great, farewell!—yet *not* the last—
Though Britain's sunshine hour with thee be past,
Ierne still one gleam of glory gives,
And feels but half thy loss while Grattan lives.

APPENDIX.

THE following is part of a Preface which was intended by a friend and countryman of mine for a collection of Irish airs, to which he had adapted English words. As it has never been published, and is not inapplicable to my subject, I shall take the liberty of subjoining it here.

. . . .

'Our history, for many centuries past, is creditable neither to our neighbours nor ourselves, and ought not to be read by any Irishman who wishes either to love England or to feel proud of Ireland. The loss of independence very early debased our character; and our feuds and

---

[1] There is a singular work 'upon the Souls of the Pagans,' by one Franciscus Collius, in which he discusses, with much coolness and erudition, all the probable chances of salvation upon which a heathen philosopher may calculate. He damns without much difficulty Socrates, Plato, etc., and the only one at whose fate he seems to hesitate is Pythagoras, in consideration of his golden thigh, and the many miracles which he performed; but having balanced his claims a little, and finding reason to father all these miracles on the devil, he at length, in the twenty-fifth chapter, decides upon damning him also (*De Animis Paganorum*, lib. iv. cap. 20 and 25).—Dante compromises the matter with the Pagans, and gives them a neutral territory or limbo of their own, where their employment, it must be owned, is not very enviable—'Senza speme vivemo in desio.' Cant. iv.—Among the many errors imputed to Origen, he is accused of having denied the eternity of future punishment; and if he never advanced a more irrational doctrine, we may forgive him. He went so far, however, as to include the devil himself in the general he'l-delivery which he supposed would one day or other take place, and in this St. Augustin thinks him rather too merciful—'Misericordior profecto fuit Origenes, qui et ipsum diabolum,' etc. (*De Civitat. Dei*, lib. xxi. cap. 17). —St. Jerom says that, according to Origen, 'the devil, after a certain time, will be as well off as the angel Gabriel'—'Id ipsum fore Gabrielem quod diabolum.' (See his *Epistle to Pammachius*.) But Halloix, in his *Defence of Origen*, denies that he had any of this misplaced tenderness for the devil.—I take the liberty of recommending these *notitiæ* upon damnation to the particular attention of the learned Chancellor of the Exchequer.

[2] Mr. Fox, in his speech on the Repeal of the Test Act (1790), condemns the intermixture of religion with the political constitution of a state. 'What purpose (he asks) can it serve, except the baleful purpose of communicating and receiving contamination? Under such an alliance corruption must alight upon the one, and slavery overwhelm the other.'

Locke, too, says of the connection between Church and State: 'The boundaries on both sides are fixed and immoveable. He jumbles heaven and earth together the things most remote and opposite, who mixes these two societies, which are in their original, end, business, and in everything, perfectly distinct and infinitely different from each other.'—*First Letter on Toleration.*

The corruptions of Christianity may be dated from the period of its establishment under Constantine, nor could all the splendour which it then acquired atone for the peace and purity which it lost.

rebellions, though frequent and ferocious, but seldom displayed that generous spirit of enterprise with which the pride of an independent monarchy so long dignified the struggles of Scotland. It is true this island has given birth to heroes who, under more favourable circumstances, might have left in the hearts of their countrymen recollections as dear as those of a Bruce or a Wallace ; but success was wanting to consecrate resistance ; their cause was branded with the disheartening name of treason ; and their oppressed country was such a blank among nations, that, like the adventures of those woods which Rinaldo wished to explore, the fame of their actions was lost in the obscurity of the place where they achieved them.

> Errando in quelli boschi
> Trovar potria strane avventure e molte,
> Ma come i luoghi i fatti ancor son foschi,
> Che non se'n ha notizia le più volte.

'Hence it is that the annals of Ireland, through a long lapse of six hundred years, exhibit not one of those shining names, not one of those themes of national pride, from which poetry borrows her noblest inspiration ; and that history, which ought to be the richest garden of the Muse, yields nothing to her here but weeds and cypress. In truth, the poet who would embellish his song with allusions to Irish names and events, must be content to seek them in those early periods when our character was yet unalloyed and original, before the impolitic craft of our conquerors had divided, weakened,.and disgraced us ; and the only traits of heroism which he can venture at this day to commemorate, with safety to himself, or perhaps with honour to the country, are to be looked for in those times when the native monarchs of Ireland displayed and fostered virtues worthy of a better age ; when our Malachies wore collars of gold which they had won in single combat from the invader,[1] and our Briens deserved the blessings of a people by all the most estimable qualities of a king. It may be said, indeed, that the magic of tradition has shed a charm over this remote period to which it is in reality but little entitled, and that most of the pictures, which we dwell on so fondly, of days when this island was distinguished amidst the gloom of Europe, by the sanctity of her morals, the spirit of her knighthood, and the polish of her schools, are little more than the inventions of national partiality, that bright but spurious offspring which vanity engenders upon ignorance, and with which the first records of every people abound. But the sceptic is scarcely to be envied who would pause for stronger proofs than we already possess of the early glories of Ireland ; and were even the veracity of all these proofs surrendered, yet who would not fly to such flattering fictions from the sad degrading truths which the history of later times presents to us ?

'The language of sorrow, however, is in general best suited to our music, and with themes of this nature the poet may be amply supplied. There is not a page of our annals which cannot afford him a subject ; and while the national Muse of other countries adorns her temple with trophies of the past, in Ireland her altar, like the shrine of Pity at Athens, is to be known only by the tears that are shed upon it ; "*lacrymis altaria sudant.*"[2]

'There is a well-known story, related of the Antiochians under the reign of Theodosius, which is not only honourable to the powers of music in general, but which applies so peculiarly to the mournful melodies of Ireland, that I cannot resist the temptation of introducing it here: The piety of Theodosius would have been admirable, if it had not been stained with intolerance ; but his reign affords, I believe, the first example of a disqualifying penal code enacted by Christians against Christians.[3] Whether his interference with the religion of the Antiochians had any share in the alienation of their loyalty, is not expressly ascertained by historians ; but severe edicts, heavy taxation, and the rapacity and insolence of the men whom he sent to govern them, sufficiently account for the discontents of a warm and susceptible people. Repentance soon followed the crimes into which their impatience had hurried them ;

---

[1] See Warner's *History of Ireland*, vol. 1. book ix.
[2] Statius, *Thebaid.* lib. xii.
[3] 'A sort of civil excommunication (says Gibbon), which separated them from their fellow-citizens by a peculiar brand of infamy; and this declaration of the supreme magistrate tended to justify, or at least to excuse, the insults of a fanatic populace. The sectaries were gradually disqualified for the possession of honourable or lucrative employments; and Theodosius was satisfied with his own justice, when he decreed that, as the Ennomians distinguished the nature of the Son from that of the Father, they should be incapable of making their wills, or of receiving any advantage from testamentary donations.'

but the vengeance of the Emperor was implacable, and punishments of the most dreadful nature hung over the city of Antioch, whose devoted inhabitants, totally resigned to despondence, wandered through the streets and public assemblies, giving utterance to their grief in dirges of the most touching lamentation.[1] At length Flavianus, their bishop, whom they sent to intercede with Theodosius, finding all his entreaties coldly rejected, adopted the expedient of teaching these songs of sorrow, which he had heard from the lips of his unfortunate countrymen, to the minstrels who performed for the Emperor at table. The heart of Theodosius could not resist this appeal; tears fell fast into his cup while he listened, and the Antiochians were forgiven. Surely, if music ever spoke the misfortunes of a people, or could ever conciliate forgiveness for their errors, the music of Ireland ought to possess those powers!'

---

[1] Μέλη τινα ελεφυριων πληρη και συμπαθιας συνθιμενοι, ταις μελωδιαις εψηδον.—*Nicephor.* lib. xii. cap. 43. This story is also in Sozomen, lib. vii. cap. 23; but unfortunately Chrysostom says nothing whatever about it, and he not only had the best opportunities of information, but was too fond of music, as appears by his praises of psalmody (Exposit. in Psal. xli.) to omit such a flattering illustration of its powers. He imputes their reconciliation to the interference of the Antiochian solitaries, while Zozimus attributes it to the remonstrances of the sophist Libanius.—Gibbon, I think, does not even allude to the story of the musicians.

THE SCEPTIC:

A PHILOSOPHICAL SATIRE.

ΝΟΜΟΝ ΠΑΝΤΩΝ ΒΑΣΙΛΕΑ.—*Pindar, ap. Herodot.* lib. 3.

PREFACE.

The sceptical philosophy of the ancients has been as much misrepresented as the Epicurean. Pyrrho, perhaps, may have carried it to an irrational excess (though we must not believe, with Beattie, all the absurdities imputed to this philosopher); but it appears to me that the doctrines of the school, as stated by Sextus Empiricus, are much more suited to the frailty of human reason, and more conducive to the mild virtues of humility and patience, than any of those systems which preceded the introduction of Christianity. The Sceptics held a middle path between the Dogmatists and Academicians, the former of whom boasted that they had attained the truth, while the latter denied that any attainable truth existed. The Sceptics, however, without asserting or denying its existence, professed to be modestly and anxiously in search of it; as St. Augustin expresses it, in his liberal tract against the Manicheans, 'nemo nostrum dicat jam se invenisse veritatem; sic eam quæramus quasi ab utrisque nesciatur.' From this habit of impartial investigation, and the necessity which they imposed upon themselves of studying, not only every system of philosophy, but every art and science which pretended to lay its basis in truth, they necessarily took a wider range of erudition, and were more travelled in the regions of philosophy than those whom conviction or bigotry had domesticated in any particular system. It required all the learning of dogmatism to overthrow the dogmatism of learning; and the Sceptics, in this respect, resembled that ancient incendiary, who stole from the altar the fire with which he destroyed the temple. This advantage over all the other sects is allowed to them even by Lipsius, whose treatise on the miracles of the Virgo Hallensis will sufficiently save him from all suspicion of scepticism. 'Labore, ingenio, memoria supra omnes pene philosophos fuisse.—Quid nonne omnia aliorum secta tenere debuerunt et inquirere, si poterunt refellere? res dicit. Nonne orationes varias, raras, subtiles inveniri ad tam receptas, claras, certas (ut videbatur) sententias evertendas?' etc. etc.—*Manuduct. ad Philosoph. Stoic.* Diss. 4.

The difference between the scepticism of the ancients and the moderns is, that the former doubted for the purpose of investigating, as may be exemplified by the third book of Aristotle's *Metaphysics*, while the latter investigate for the purpose of doubting, as may be seen through most of the philosophical works of Hume. Indeed, the Pyrrhonism of latter days is not only more subtle than that of antiquity, but, it must be confessed, more dangerous in its tendency. The happiness of a Christian depends so much upon his belief, that it is natural he should feel alarm at the progress of doubt, lest it steal by degrees into the region from which he is most interested in excluding it, and poison at last the very spring of his consolation and hope. Still, however, the abuses of doubting ought not to deter a philosophical mind from indulging mildly and rationally in its use; and there is nothing, I think, more consistent with the humble spirit of Christianity, than the scepticism of him who professes not to extend his distrust beyond the circle of human pursuits and the pretensions of human knowledge. A philosopher of this kind is among the readiest to admit the claims of Heaven upon his faith and adoration:

It is only to the wisdom of this weak world that he refuses, or at least delays, his assent ; it is only in passing through the shadow of earth that his mind undergoes the eclipse of scepticism. No follower of Pyrrho has ever spoken more strongly against the dogmatists than St. Paul himself, in the First Epistle to the Corinthians ; and there are passages in Ecclesiastes and other parts of Scripture which justify our utmost diffidence in all that human reason originates. Even the sceptics of antiquity refrained from the mysteries of theology, and, in entering the temples of religion, laid aside their philosophy at the porch. Sextus Empiricus thus declares the acquiescence of his sect in the general belief of a superintending Providence : Τῳ μεν βιῳ κατακολουθουντες αδοξαστως φαμεν ειναι θεους και ευβεμεν θεους και προνοειν αυτους φαμεν.—Lib. iii. cap. 1. In short, it appears to me that this rational and well-regulated scepticism is the only daughter of the schools that can be selected as a handmaid for piety : he who distrusts the light of reason will be the first to follow a more luminous guide ; and if, with an ardent love for truth, he has sought her in vain through the ways of this life, he will turn with the more hope to that better world, where all is simple, true, and everlasting : for there is no parallax at the zenith—it is only near our troubled horizon that objects deceive us into vague and erroneous calculations.

THE SCEPTIC.

As the gay tint that decks the vernal rose,[1]
Not in the flower, but in our vision glows ;
As the ripe flavour of Falernian tides,
Not in the wine, but in our taste resides ;
So when, with heartfelt tribute, we declare
That Marco's honest and that Susan's fair,
'Tis in our minds, and not in Susan's eyes
Or Marco's life, the worth or beauty lies :
For she, in flat-nosed China, would appear
As plain a thing as Lady Anne is here ;
And one light joke at rich Loretto's dome
Would rank good Marco with the damned at Rome.

There's no deformity so vile, so base,
That 'tis not somewhere thought a charm, a grace ;

No foul reproach that may not steal a beam
From other suns, to bleach it to esteem !
Ask, who is wise ?—you'll find the self-same man
A sage in France, a madman in Japan ;
And *here* some head beneath a mitre swells,
Which *there* had tingled to a cap and bells :
Nay, there may yet some monstrous region be,
Unknown to Cook, and from Napoleon free,
Where C—stl—r—gh would for a patriot pass,
And mouthing M—lgr—ve scarce be deemed an ass !

'List not to reason,' Epicurus cries,
But trust the senses, *there* conviction lies : '[2]—
Alas ! *they* judge not by a purer light,
Nor keep their fountains more untinged and bright :

[1] 'The particular bulk, number, figure, and motion of the parts of fire or snow are really in them, whether any one perceive them or not, and therefore they may be called real qualities, because they really exist in those bodies ; but light, heat, whiteness, or coldness, are no more really in them than sickness or pain is in manna. Take away the sensation of them ; let not the eye see light or colours, nor the ear hear sounds, let the palate not taste, nor the nose smell, and all colours, tastes, odours, and sounds, as they are such particular ideas, vanish and cease.'—*Locke*, book ii. chap. 8.

Bishop Berkeley, it is well known, extended this doctrine even to primary qualities, and supposed that matter itself has but an ideal existence. How shall we apply the bishop's theory to that period which preceded the formation of man, when our system of sensible things was produced, and the sun shone, and the waters flowed, without any sentient being to witness them ? The spectator, whom Whiston supplies, will scarcely solve the difficulty : 'To speak my mind freely,' says he, 'I believe that the Messias was there actually present.'—See *Whiston, Of the Mosaic Creation*.

[2] This was also the creed of those modern Epicureans whom Ninon de l'Enclos collected around her in the

Rue des Tournelles, and whose object seems to have been to decry the faculty of reason, as tending only to embarrass our use of pleasures, without enabling us in any degree to avoid their abuse. Madame des Houlières, the fair pupil of Des Barreaux in the arts of poetry and voluptuousness, has devoted most of her verses to this laudable purpose, and is such a determined foe to reason, that in one of her pastorals she congratulates her sheep on the want of it. St. Evremont speaks thus upon the subject :

' Un mélange incertain d'esprit et de matière
Nous fait vivre avec trop ou trop peu de lumière.

Nature, élève-nous à la clarté des anges,
Ou nous abaise au sens des simples animaux.'

Which sentiments I have thus ventured to paraphrase :

Had man been made, at nature's birth,
Of only flame or only earth,
Had he been formed a perfect whole
Of purely *that*, or grossly *this*,
Then sense would ne'er have clouded soul,
Nor soul restrained the sense's bliss.

Habit so mars them, that the Russian swain
Will sigh for train-oil while he sips champagne;
And health so rules them, that a fever's heat
Would make even Sh—r—d—n think water
    sweet!

Just as the mind the erring sense believes,
The erring mind, in turn, the sense deceives;
And cold disgust can find but wrinkles there,
Where passion fancies all that's smooth and
    fair.
——, who sees, upon his pillow laid,
A face for which ten thousand pounds were paid,
Can tell, how quick before a jury flies
The spell that mocked the warm seducer's eyes!

Self is the medium least refined of all
Through which opinion's searching beam can
    fall;
And, passing there, the clearest, steadiest ray
Will tinge its light and turn its line astray.
The Ephesian smith a holier charm espied
In Dian's toe, than all his heaven beside;
And true religion shines not half so true
On *one* good living as it shines on *two*.
Had W—lc—t first been pensioned by the Throne,
Kings would have suffered by his praise alone;
And P—ine perhaps, for something snug per ann.,
Had laughed, like W—ll—sly, at all Rights of
    Man!

But 'tis not only individual minds
That habit tinctures, or that interest blinds;
Whole nations, fooled by falsehood, fear, or pride,
Their ostrich-heads in self-illusion hide:
Thus England, hot from Denmark's smoking
    meads,
Turns up her eyes at Gallia's guilty deeds;
Thus, selfish still, the same dishonouring chain
She binds in Ireland, she would break in Spain;
While praised at distance, but at home forbid,
'Rebels in Cork are patriots at Madrid!

Oh! trust me, Self can cloud the brightest cause,
Or gild the worst;—and then, for nations' laws!
Go, good civilian, shut thy useless book,
In force alone for laws of nations look.
Let shipless Danes and whining Yankees dwell
On naval rights, with Grotius and Vattel,
While C—bb—t's¹ pirate code alone appears
Sound moral sense to England and Algiers!

Woe to the Sceptic, in these party days,
Who burns on neither shrine the balm of praise!
For him no pension pours its annual fruits,
No fertile sinecure spontaneous shoots;
Not *his* the meed that crowned Don H—kh—m's
    rhyme,
Nor sees he e'er, in dreams of future time,
Those shadowy forms of sleek reversions rise,
So dear to Scotchmen's second-sighted eyes!
Yet who, that looks to Time's accusing leaf,
Where Whig and Tory, thief opposed to thief,
On either side in lofty shame are seen,
While Freedom's form hangs crucified between—
Who, B—rd—tt, who such rival rogues can see,
But flies from *both* to honesty and thee?

If, giddy with the world's bewildering maze,²
Hopeless of finding, through its weedy ways,
One flower of truth, the busy crowd we shun,
And to the shades of tranquil learning run,
How many a doubt pursues! how oft we sigh,
When histories charm, to think that histories
    lie!
That all are grave romances at the best,
And M—sgr—ve's but more clumsy than the
    rest!
By Tory Hume's seductive page beguiled,
We fancy Charles was just and Strafford mild;
And Fox himself, with party pencil, draws
Monmouth a hero 'for the good old cause!'³

Then, rights are wrongs, and victories are defeats,
As French or English pride the tale repeats;

Oh happy! had his light been strong,
    Or had he never shared a light,
Which burns enough to show he's wrong,
    Yet not enough to lead him right!

¹ With most of this writer's latter politics I confess I feel a most hearty concurrence. and perhaps, if I were an Englishman, my pride might lead me to acquiesce in that system of lawless, unlimited sovereignty which he claims so boldly for his country at sea; but viewing the question somewhat more disinterestedly, and as a friend to the common rights of mankind, I cannot help thinking that the doctrines which he maintained upon the Copenhagen expedition and the differences with America, would establish a species of maritime tyranny, as discreditable to the character of England as it would be galling and unjust to the other nations of the world.

² The agitation of the ship is one of the chief difficulties which impede the discovery of the longitude at sea; and the tumult and hurry of life are equally unfavourable to that calm level of mind which is necessary to an inquirer after truth.

³ That flexibility of temper and opinion which the habits of scepticism are so calculated to produce are

thus pleaded for by Mr. Fox, in the very sketch of Monmouth to which I allude; and this part of the picture the historian may be thought to have drawn for himself. 'One of the most conspicuous features in his character seems to have been a remarkable, and, as some think, a culpable degree of flexibility. That such a disposition is preferable to its opposite extreme will be admitted by all who think that modesty, even in excess, is more nearly allied to wisdom than conceit and self-sufficiency. He who has attentively considered the political, or indeed the general, concerns of life, may possibly go still further, and may rank a willingness to be convinced, or in some cases even without conviction, to concede our own opinion to that of other men, among the principal ingredients in the composition of practical wisdom.' The sceptic's readiness of concession, however, arises more from uncertainty than conviction, more from a suspicion that his own opinion may be wrong than from any persuasion that the opinion of his adversary is right. 'It may be so,' was the courteous and sceptical formula with which the Dutch were accustomed to reply to the statements of ambassadors.—See *Lloyd's State Worthies*, art. Sir Thomas Wiat.

And when they tell Corunna's story o'er,
They'll disagree in all but honouring Moore!
Nay, future pens, to flatter future courts,
May cite perhaps the Park-guns' gay reports,
To prove that England triumphed on the morn
Which found her Junot's jest and Europe's
 scorn!

In science too—how many a system, raised
Like Neva's icy domes, awhile hath blazed
With lights of fancy and with forms of pride,
Then, melting, mingled with the oblivious
 tide!
Now Earth usurps the centre of the sky,
Now Newton puts the paltry planet by;
Now whims revive beneath Descartes' pen,
Which *now*, assailed by Locke's, expire again:
And when, perhaps, in pride of chemic powers,
We think the keys of Nature's kingdom ours,
Some Davy's magic touch the dream unsettles,
And turns at once our alkalis to metals!

Or, should we roam, in metaphysic maze,
Through fair-built theories of former days,
Some Dr—mm—d from the north, more ably
 skilled,
Like other Goths, to ruin than to build,
Tramples triumphant through our fanes o'er-
 thrown,
Nor leaves one grace, one glory of his own!

Oh Learning! Learning! whatsoe'er thy boast,
Unlettered minds have taught and charmed us
 most:

The rude, unread Columbus was our guide
To worlds which learned Lactantius had denied,
And one wild Shakspeare, following Nature's
 lights,
Is worth whole planets filled with Stagyrites!

See grave Theology, when once she strays
From Revelation's path, what tricks she plays!
How many various heavens hath Fancy's wing
Explored or touched from Papias down to King![1]
And hell itself, in India nought but smoke,[2]
In Spain's a furnace, and in France—a joke.

Hail, modest ignorance! thou goal and prize,
Thou last, best knowledge of the humbly wise!
Hail, sceptic ease! when error's waves are past,
How sweet to reach thy tranquil port at last,
And, gently rocked in undulating doubt,
Smile at the sturdy winds which war without!
There gentle Charity, who knows how frail
The bark of virtue, even in summer's gale,
Sits by the nightly fire, whose beacon glows
For all who wander, whether friends or foes!
There Faith retires, and keeps her white sail
 furled,
Till called to spread it for a purer world;
While Patience lingers o'er the weedy shore,
And, mutely waiting till the storm be o'er,
Turns to young Hope, who still directs his eye
To some blue spot, just breaking in the sky!

These are the mild, the blest associates given
To him who doubts, and trusts in nought but
 Heaven!

---

[1] King, in his *Morsels of Criticism*, vol. i., supposes the sun to be the receptacle of blessed spirits.
[2] The Indians call hell 'the House of Smoke.' See Picart upon the *Religion of the Banians*. The reader who is curious about infernal matters may be edified by consulting *Rusca de Inferno*, particularly lib. ii. cap. 7, 8, where he will find the precise sort of fire ascertained in which wicked spirits are to be burned here-after.

FABLES FOR THE HOLY ALLIANCE.

> Tu Regibus alas
> Eripe.—VIRGIL, *Georg.* lib. iv.
>
> Clip the wings
> Of these high-flying, arbitrary Kings.—DRYDEN's *Translation.*

TO LORD BYRON.

DEAR LORD BYRON,—Though this Volume should possess no other merit in your eyes than that of reminding you of the short time we passed together at Venice, when some of the trifles which it contains were written, you will, I am sure, receive the dedication of it with pleasure, and believe that I am, my dear Lord, ever faithfully yours,

T. B.

PREFACE.

THOUGH it was the wish of the Members of the Poco-curante Society (who have lately done me the honour of electing me their Secretary) that I should prefix my name to the following Miscellany, it is but fair to them and to myself to state that, except in the 'painful pre-eminence' of being employed to transcribe their lucubrations, my claim to such a distinction in the title-page is not greater than that of any other gentleman who has contributed his share to the contents of the volume.

I had originally intended to take this opportunity of giving some account of the origin and objects of our Institution, the names and characters of the different members, etc. etc.; but as I am at present preparing for the press the First Volume of the 'Transactions of the Poco-curante Society,' I shall reserve for that occasion all further details upon the subject; and content myself here with referring, for a general insight into our tenets, to a Song which will be found at the end of this work, and which is sung to us on the first day of every month, by one of our oldest members, to the tune of (as far as I can recollect, being no musician) either 'Nancy Dawson' or 'He stole away the Bacon.'

It may be as well also to state, for the information of those critics who attack with the hope of being answered, and of being thereby brought into notice, that it is the rule of this Society to return no other answer to such assailants than is contained in three words, 'Non curat Hippoclides' (meaning, in English, 'Hippoclides does not care a fig'), which were spoken two thousand years ago by the first founder of Poco-curantism, and have ever since been adopted as the leading *dictum* of the sect.

THOMAS BROWN.

FABLE I.

THE DISSOLUTION OF THE HOLY ALLIANCE.

A Dream.

I'VE had a dream that bodes no good
Unto the Holy Brotherhood.
I may be wrong, but I confess—
  As far as it is right or lawful
For one, no conjurer, to guess—
  It seems to me extremely awful.

Methought, upon the Neva's flood
A beautiful Ice Palace stood ;
A dome of frost-work, on the plan
Of that once built by Empress Anne,[1]
Which shone by moonlight—as the tale is—
Like an aurora borealis.

In this said palace—furnished all
  And lighted as the best on land are—
I dreamed there was a splendid ball,
  Given by the Emperor Alexander,
To entertain, with all due zeal,
  Those holy gentlemen who've shown a
Regard so kind for Europe's weal,
  At Troppau, Laybach, and Verona.

The thought was happy, and designed
To hint how thus the human mind
May—like the stream imprisoned there—
Be checked and chilled till it can bear
The heaviest Kings, that ode or sonnet
E'or yet be-praised, to dance upon it.

And all were pleased, and cold, and stately,
Shivering in grand illumination—
Admired the superstructure greatly,
Nor gave one thought to the foundation.
Much too the Czar himself exulted,
  To all plebeian fears a stranger,
As Madame Krudener, when consulted,
  Had pledged her word there was no danger.
So, on he capered, fearless quite,
  Thinking himself extremely clever,
And waltzed away with all his might,
  As if the frost would last for ever.

Just fancy how a bard like me,
  Who reverence monarchs, must have trembled,
To see that goodly company
  At such a ticklish sport assembled.

Nor were the fears, that thus astounded
My loyal soul, at all unfounded ;
For, lo! ere long, those walls so massy
  Were seized with an ill-omened dripping,
And o'er the floors, now growing glassy,
  Their Holinesses took to slipping.

The Czar, half through a Polonaise,
  Could scarce get on for downright stumbling ;
And Prussia, though to slippery ways
  So used, was cursedly near tumbling.

Yet still 'twas who could stamp the floor most,
Russia and Austria 'mong the foremost.
And now, to an Italian air,
  This precious brace would hand in hand go ;
Now—while old . . . . from his chair,
  Intreated them his toes to spare—
  Called loudly out for a fandango.

And a fandango, 'faith, they had,
At which they all set to like mad—
Never were Kings (though small the expense is
Of wit among their Excellencies)
So out of all their princely senses.

But, ah! that dance—that Spanish dance—
  Scarce was the luckless strain begun,
When, glaring red—as 'twere a glance
  Shot from an angry southern sun—
A light through all the chambers flamed,
  Astonishing old Father Frost,
Who, bursting into tears, exclaimed,
  'A thaw, by Jove!—we're lost, we're lost!
Run, F———! a second *Waterloo*
Is come to drown you—*sauve qui peut !* '

Why, why will monarchs caper so
  In palaces without foundations?
Instantly all was in a flow :
Crowns, fiddles, sceptres, decorations:
Those royal arms, that looked so nice,
Cut out in the resplendent ice ;
Those eagles, handsomely provided
  With double heads for double dealings—
How fast the globes and sceptres glided
  Out of their claws on all the ceilings!
Proud Prussia's double bird of prey,
Tame as a spatch-cock, slunk away ;
While—just like France herself, when she
  Proclaims how great her naval skill is—
Poor . . . drowning *fleurs-de-lys*
  Imagined themselves *water-lilies.*
And not alone rooms, ceilings, shelves,
  But—still more fatal execution—
The Great Legitimates themselves
  Seemed in a state of dissolution.
The indignant Czar—when just about
  T'o issue a sublime Ukase—
' Whereas, all light must be kept out '—
  Dissolved to nothing in its blaze.
Next Prussia took his turn to melt,
  And, while his lips illustrious felt
The influence of this southern air,
  Some word like ' Constitution,' long
Congealed in frosty silence there,
  Came slowly thawing from his tongue.

---

[1] 'It is well known that the Empress Anne built a palace of ice on the Neva in 1740, which was fifty-two feet in length, and when illuminated had a surprising effect.'—*Pinkerton.*

FABLES FOR THE HOLY ALLIANCE.

While ——, lapsing by degrees,
 And sighing out a faint adieu
To truffles, salmis, toasted cheese,
 And smoking *fondus*, quickly grew
 Himself into a *fondu* too;—
Or, like that goodly King they make
Of sugar, for a twelfth-night cake,
When in some urchin's mouth, alas,
It melts into a shapeless mass!

In short, I scarce could count a minute
Ere the bright dome, and all within it—
Kings, Fiddlers, Emperors—all were gone!
 And nothing now was seen or heard
But the bright river, rushing on,
 Happy as an enfranchised bird,
 And prouder of that natural ray,
Shining along its chainless way—
More proudly happy thus to glide
 In simple grandeur to the sea,
Than when in sparkling fetters tied,
 And decked with all that kingly pride
Could bring to light its slavery!

Such is my dream—and, I confess,
I tremble at its awfulness.
That Spanish dance—that southern beam—
But I say nothing—there's my dream—
And Madame Krudener, the she-prophet,
May make just what she pleases of it.

FABLE II.

THE LOOKING-GLASSES.

Proem.

WHERE Kings have been by mob-elections
Raised to the throne, 'tis strange to see
What different and what odd perfections
Men have required in royalty.
Some, liking monarchs large and plumpy,
 Have chosen their Sovereigns by the weight;
Some wished them tall; some thought your
 dumpy,
 Dutch-built the true Legitimate.[1]
The Easterns, in a Prince, 'tis said,
Prefer what's called a jolter-head;[2]
The Egyptians weren't at all partic'lar,
 So that their Kings had not red hair—
This fault not even the greatest stickler
 For the blood-royal well could bear.
A thousand more such illustrations
Might be adduced from various nations;
But, 'mong the many tales they tell us,
 Touching the acquired or natural right
Which some men have to rule their fellows,
 There's one which I shall here recite :—

Fable.

THERE was a land—to *name* the place
 Is neither now my wish nor duty—
Where reigned a certain royal race,
 By right of their superior beauty.

What was the cut legitimate
 Of these great persons' chins and noses,
By right of which they ruled the state,
 No history I have seen discloses.

But so it was—a settled case—
 Some act of Parliament, passed snugly,
Had voted them a beauteous race,
 And all their faithful subjects ugly.

As rank, indeed, stood high or low,
 Some change it made in visual organs;
Your Peers were decent—Knights, so-so—
 But all your *common* people gorgons!

Of course, if any knave but hinted
 That the King's nose was turned awry,
Or that the Queen (God save us!) squinted—
 The judges doomed that knave to die.

But rarely things like this occurred:
 The people to their King were duteous,
And took it, on his royal word,
 That they were frights and he was beauteous.

The cause whereof, among all classes,
 Was simply this :—These island elves
Had never yet seen looking-glasses,
 And therefore did not *know themselves*.

Sometimes, indeed, their neighbours' faces
 Might strike them as more full of reason,
More fresh than those in certain places—
 But, Lord! the very thought was treason!

Besides, howe'er we love our neighbour,
 And take his face's part, 'tis known
We never half so earnest labour,
 As when the face attacked 's our own.

So, on they went—the crowd believing
 (As crowds well governed always do);
Their rulers, too, themselves deceiving—
 So old the joke they thought it true.

But jokes, we know, if they too far go,
 Must have an end; and so, one day,
Upon that coast there was a cargo
 Of looking-glasses cast away.

'Twas said some Radicals, somewhere,
 Had laid their wicked heads together,
And forced that ship to founder there—
 While some believe it was the weather.

---

[1] The Goths had a law to choose always a short thick man for their king.—*Munster, Cosmog.* lib. iii. p. 164.

[2] 'In a Prince, a jolter-head is invaluable.'—*Oriental Field Sports.*

However this might be, the freight
　Was landed without fees or duties;
And from that hour historians date
　The downfall of the race of beauties.

The looking-glasses got about,
　And grew so common through the land,
That scarce a tinker could walk out
　Without a mirror in his hand.

Comparing faces, morning, noon,
　And night, their constant occupation—
By dint of looking-glasses, soon
　They grew a most reflecting nation.

In vain the Court, aware of errors
　In all the old-established mazards,
Prohibited the use of mirrors,
　And tried to break them at all hazards:

In vain—their laws might just as well
　Have been waste paper on the shelves;
That fatal freight had broke the spell;
　People had looked—and knew themselves.

If chance a Duke, of birth sublime,
　Presumed upon his ancient face
(Some calf-head, ugly from all time),
　They popped a mirror to his Grace—

Just hinting, by that gentle sign,
　How little Nature holds it true,
That what is called an ancient line
　Must be the line of Beauty too.

From Dukes they passed to regal phizzes,
　Compared them proudly with their own,
And cried, 'How *could* such monstrous quizzes
　In Beauty's name usurp the throne?'

They then wrote essays, pamphlets, books,
　Upon cosmetical economy,
Which made the King try various looks,
　But none improved his physiognomy.

And satires at the Court they levelled,
　And small lampoons, so full of slynesses,
That soon, in short, they quite be-devilled
　Their Majesties and Royal Highnesses.

At length—but here I drop the veil,
　To spare some loyal folks' sensations:
Besides, what follows is the tale
　Of all such late-enlightened nations;

Of all to whom old Time discloses
　A truth they should have sooner known—
That Kings have neither rights nor noses
　A whit diviner than their own.

FABLE III.

THE TORCH OF LIBERTY.

I SAW it all in Fancy's glass—
　Herself, the fair, the wild magician,
Who bid this splendid day-dream pass,
　And named each gliding apparition.

'Twas like a torch-race—such as they
　Of Greece performed, in ages gone,
When the fleet youths, in long array,
　Passed the bright torch triumphant on.

I saw the expectant nations stand,
　To catch the coming flame in turn;—
I saw, from ready hand to hand,
　The clear, though struggling, glory burn.

And oh, their joy, as it came near,
　'Twas in itself a joy to see;—
While Fancy whispered in my ear,
　'That torch they pass is Liberty!'

And each, as she received the flame,
　Lighted her altar with its ray;
Then, smiling to the next who came,
　Speeded it on its sparkling way.

From Albion first, whose ancient shrine
　Was furnished with the fire already,
Columbia caught the boon divine,
　And lit a flame, like Albion's, steady.

The splendid gift then Gallia took,
　And, like a wild Bacchante, raising
The brand aloft, its sparkles shook,
　As she would set the world a-blazing!

And when she fired her altar high,
　It flashed into the reddening air
So fierce, that Albion, who stood nigh,
　Shrunk, almost blinded by the glare!

Next, Spain, so new was light to her,
　Leaped at the torch—but, ere the spark
That fell upon her shrine could stir,
　'Twas quenched—and all again was dark.

Yet, no—*not* quenched—a treasure, worth
　So much to mortals, rarely dies:
Again her living light looked forth,
　And shone, a beacon, in all eyes.

Who next received the flame? alas,
　Unworthy Naples—shame of shames,
That ever through such hands should pass
　That brightest of all earthly flames!

Scarce had her fingers touched the torch,
　When, frighted by the sparks it shed,
Nor waiting even to feel the scorch,
　She dropped it to the earth—and fled

And fallen it might have long remained!
But Greece, who saw her moment now,
Caught up the prize, though prostrate, stained,
And waved it round her beauteous brow.

And Fancy bade me mark where, o'er
Her altar, as its flame ascended,
Fair, laurelled spirits seemed to soar,
Who thus in song their voices blended:

'Shine, shine for ever, glorious Flame,
Divinest gift of gods to men!
From Greece thy earliest splendour came,
To Greece thy ray returns again.

'Take, Freedom, take thy radiant round,
When dimmed, revive—when lost, return—
Till not a shrine through earth be found,
On which thy glories shall not burn!'

FABLE IV

THE FLY AND THE BULLOCK.

Proem.

Of all that, to the sage's survey,
This world presents of topsy-turvey,
There's nought so much disturbs his patience
As little minds in lofty stations.
'Tis like that sort of painful wonder
Which slight and pigmy columns under
Enormous arches give beholders;
Or those poor Caryatides,
Condemned to smile and stand at ease,
With a whole house upon their shoulders.

If, as in some few royal cases,
Small minds are *born* into such places—
If they are there by right Divine,
Or any such sufficient reason,
Why—Heaven forbid we should repine!—
To wish it otherwise were treason;
Nay, even to see it in a vision,
Would be what lawyers call *misprision.*

Sir Robert Filmer says—and he,
Of course, knew all about the matter—
'Both men and beasts love monarchy;'
Which proves how rational—the latter.
Sidney, indeed, we know, had quite
A different notion from the knight;
Nay, hints a King may lose his head
By slipping awkwardly his bridle:
But this is Jacobin, ill-bred,
And (now-a-days, when Kings are led
In patent snaffles) downright idle.

No, no—it isn't foolish Kings
(Those fixed, inevitable things—
Bores paramount, by right of birth)
That move my wrath, but your pretenders,

Your mushroom rulers, sons of earth,
Who, not like t'others, *crowned* offenders
(Regular *gratia Dei* blockheads,
Born with three kingdoms in their pockets),
Nor leaving, on the scale of mind,
These royal Zeros far behind,
Yet, with a brass that nothing stops,
Push up into the loftiest stations,
And, though too dull to manage shops,
Presume, the dolts, to manage nations!

This class it is that moves my gall,
And stirs up spleen, and bile, and all.
While other senseless things appear
To know the limits of their sphere—
While not a cow on earth romances
So much as to conceit she dances—
While the most jumping Frog we know of,
Would scarce at Astley's hope to show off—
Your ——s and ——s dare,
Pigmy as are their minds, to set them
To *any* business, *any* where,
At *any* time that fools will let them.
But leave we here these upstart things—
My business is, just now, with Kings;
To whom, and to their right-line glory,
I dedicate the following story:

Fable.

The wise men of Egypt were secret as dummies;
And, even when they most condescended to teach,
They packed up their meaning, as they did their mummies,
In so many wrappers, 'twas out of one's reach.

They were also, good people, much given to Kings—
Fond of monarchs and crocodiles, monkeys and mystery,
Bats, hieraphants, blue-bottle flies, and such things—
As will partly appear in this very short history.

A Scythian philosopher (nephew, they say,
To that other great traveller, young Anacharsis)
Stepped into a temple of Memphis one day,
To have a short peep at their mystical farces.

He saw a brisk blue-bottle Fly on an altar,[1]
Made much of, and worshipped as something divine;
While a large handsome Bullock, led there in a halter,
Before it lay stabbed at the foot of the shrine.

Surprised at such doings, he whispered his teacher—
'If 'tisn't impertinent, may I ask why

---

[1] According to Ælian, it was in the Island of Leucadia they practised this ceremony—θυσι βουν ταις μυιαις— *De Animal.* lib. ii. cap. 8.

Should a Bullock, that useful and powerful
   creature,
Be thus offered up to a blue-bottle fly?'

'No wonder,' said t'other, 'you stare at the sight,
But *we* as a symbol of monarchy view it:
That Fly on the shrine is Legitimate Right,
And that Bullock the people that's sacrificed
   to it.'

FABLE V.

CHURCH AND STATE.

Proem.

'The moment any religion becomes national, or established, its purity must certainly be lost, because it is then impossible to keep it unconnected with men's interests; and, if connected, it must evidently be perverted by them.'—*Soame Jenyns.*

Thus did Soame Jenyns—though a Tory,
   A Lord of Trade and the Plantations
Feel how Religion's simple glory
   Is stained by State associations.

When Catherine, after murdering Poles,
   Appealed to the benign Divinity,
Then cut them up in protocols,
Made fractions of their very souls![1]—
All in the name of the blessed Trinity;
Or when her grandson, Alexander,
That mighty northern salamander,
Whose icy touch, felt all about,
Puts every fire of Freedom out—
When he, too, winds up his Ukases
With God and the Panagia's praises—
When he, of royal saints the type,
In holy water dips the sponge,
With which, at one imperial wipe,
He would all human rights expunge!
When —— (whom, as King and eater,
Some name ——, and some ——)
Calls down 'Saint Louis' God' to witness
The right, humanity, and fitness
Of sending eighty thousand Solons—
   Sages with muskets and laced coats—
To cram instruction, *nolens volens*,
   Down the poor struggling Spaniards' throats—
I can't help thinking (though to Kings
   I must, of course, like other men, bow)
That when a Christian monarch brings
Religion's name to gloss these things,
   Such blasphemy out-Benbows Benbow!

Or—not so far for facts to roam,
Having a few much nearer home—
When we see churchmen, who, if asked,
'Must Ireland's slaves be tithed and tasked,

And driven, like negroes or Croats,
   That *you* may roll in wealth and bliss?'
Look from beneath their shovel hats
   With all due pomp, and answer 'Yes!'
But then, if questioned, 'Shall the brand
Intolerance flings throughout that land,
Betwixt her palaces and hovels,
   Suffering nor peace nor love to grow,
Be ever quenched?'—from the same shovels
   Look grandly forth, and answer 'No!'
Alas, alas! have *these* a claim
   To merciful Religion's name?

If more you want, go, see a bevy
Of bowing parsons at a levee
(Choosing your time, when straw's before
Some apoplectic bishop's door):
There, if thou canst with life escape
That sweep of lawn, that press of crape,
Just watch their reverences and graces,
Shouldering their way on, at all risks,
And say, if those round ample faces
   To heaven or earth most turn their disks?

This, this it is—Religion, made,
'Twixt Church and State, a truck, a trade—
This most ill-matched unholy Co.
From whence the ills we witness flow—
The war of many creeds with one,
The extremes of *too* much faith, and none—
The qualms, the fumes of sect and sceptic,
And all that Reason, grown dyspeptic
By swallowing forced or noxious creeds,
From downright indigestion breeds;
Till, 'twixt old bigotry and new,
'Twixt Blasphemy and Cant—the two
Rank ills with which this age is cursed—
We can no more tell *which* is worst,
Than erst could Egypt, when so rich
In various plagues, determine which
She thought most pestilent and vile—
Her frogs, like Benbow and Carlile,
Croaking their native mud-notes loud,
Or her fat locusts, like a cloud
Of pluralists, obesely lowering,
At once benighting and devouring!

This—this it is—and here I pray
Those sapient wits of the Reviews,
Who make us poor, dull authors say,
   Not what we mean, but what they choose;
Who to our most abundant shares
Of nonsense add still more of theirs,
And are to poets just such evils
   As caterpillars find those flies,[2]
That, not content to sting like devils,
   Lay eggs upon their backs likewise—
To guard against such foul deposits,
Of others' meanings in my rhymes

---

[1] Ames, demi-ames, e'c.

[2] 'The greatest number of the ichneumon tribe are seen settling upon the back of the caterpillar, and darting at different intervals their stings into its body —at every dart they depose an egg.'—*Goldsmith.*

(A thing more needful here, because it's
  A subject ticklish in these times),
I here to all such wits make known,
  Monthly and weekly, Whig and Tory,
'Tis *this* Religion—this alone—
  I aim at in the following story:

Fable.

WHEN Royalty was young and bold,
  Ere, touched by Time, he had become—
If 'tis not civil to say *old*—
  At least, a *ci-devant jeune homme.*

One evening, on some wild pursuit,
  Driving along, he chanced to see
Religion, passing by on foot,
  And took him in his *vis-à-vis.*

This said Religion was a friar,
  The humblest and the best of men,
Who ne'er had notion or desire
  Of riding in a coach till then.

'I say'—quoth Royalty, who rather
  Enjoyed a masquerading joke—
'I say, suppose, my good old father,
  You lend me, for a while, your cloak.'

The friar consented—little knew
  What tricks the youth had in his head;
Besides, was rather tempted, too,
  By a laced coat he got instead.

Away ran Royalty, slap-dash,
  Scampering like mad about the town;
Broke windows—shivered lamps to smash,
  And knocked whole scores of watchmen down.

While nought could they whose heads were broke,
  Learn of the 'why' or the 'wherefore,'
Except that 'twas Religion's cloak
  The gentleman who cracked them wore.

Meanwhile, the friar, whose head was turned
  By the laced coat, grew frisky too—
Looked big—his former habits spurned—
  And stormed about as great men do—

Dealt much in pompous oaths and curses—
  Said 'Damn you' often, or as bad—
Laid claim to other people's purses—
  In short, grew either knave or mad.

As work like this was unbefitting,
  And flesh and blood no longer bore it,
The Court of Common Sense, then sitting,
  Summoned the culprits both before it.

Where, after hours in wrangling spent
  (As courts must wrangle to decide well),
Religion to Saint Luke's was sent,
  And Royalty packed off to Bridewell:

With this proviso—Should they be
  Restored in due time to their senses,
They both must give security
  In future, against such offences—

Religion ne'er to *lend his cloak,*
  Seeing what dreadful work it leads to;
And Royalty to crack his joke—
  But *not* to crack poor people's heads, too.

FABLE VI.

THE LITTLE GRAND LAMA.

Proem.

NOVELLA, a young Bolognese,
  The daughter of a learned law doctor,[1]
Who had with all the subtleties
  Of old and modern jurists stocked her,
Was so exceeding fair, 'tis said,
  And over hearts held such dominion,
That when her father, sick in bed,
  Or busy, sent her, in his stead,
To lecture on the Code Justinian,
  She had a curtain drawn before her,
Lest, if her charms were seen, the students
  Should let their young eyes wander o'er her,
  And quite forget their jurisprudence.[2]
Just so it is with Truth—when *seen,*
  Too fair and bright—'tis from behind
A light, thin allegoric screen,
  She thus can safest teach mankind.

Fable.

IN Thibet once there reigned, we're told,
  A little Lama, one year old—
Raised to the throne, that realm to bless,
  Just when his little Holiness
Had cut—as near as can be reckoned—
  Some say his *first* tooth, some his *second.*
Chronologers and verses vary,
  Which proves historians should be wary.
We only know the important truth—
  His Majesty *had* cut a tooth.[3]

And much his subjects were enchanted,
  As well all Lamas' subjects may be,
And would have given their heads, if wanted,
  To make tee-totums for the baby.

---

[1] Andreas.

[2] Quand il étoit occupé d'aucune essoine, il envoyait Novelle, sa fille, en son lieu lire aux escholes en charge, et, afin que la biaîtié d'elle n'empêchât la pensée des oyants, elle avoit une petite courtine devant elle.—*Christ. de Pise, Cité des Dames,* p. 11, chap. 36.

[3] See Turner's *Embassy to Thibet* for an account of his interview with the Lama. 'Teshoo Lama (he says) was at this time eighteen months old. Though he was unable to speak a word, he made the most expressive signs, and conducted himself with astonishing *dignity* and decorum.'

As he was there by Right Divine
  (What lawyers call *Jure Divino*,
Meaning a right to yours, and mine,
  And everybody's goods and rhino)—
Of course his faithful subjects' purses
  Were ready with their aids and succours—
Nothing was seen but pensioned nurses,
  And the land groaned with bibs and tuckers.

Oh! had there been a Hume or Bennet
  Then sitting in the Thibet Senate,
Ye Gods, what room for long debates
  Upon the Nursery Estimates!
What cutting down of swaddling-clothes
  And pin-a-fores in nightly battles!
What calls for papers to expose
  The waste of sugar-plums and rattles!
But no—if Thibet *had* M.Ps.,
  They were far better bred than these;
Nor gave the slightest opposition,
  During the Monarch's whole dentition.

But short this calm; for just when he
  Had reached the alarming age of three,
When royal natures—and, no doubt,
  Those of *all* noble beasts—break out,
The Lama, who till then was quiet,
  Showed symptoms of a taste for riot;
And, ripe for mischief, early, late,
  Without regard for Church or State,
Made free with whosoe'er came nigh—
  Tweaked the Lord Chancellor by the nose,
Turned all the Judges' wigs awry,
  And trod on the old Generals' toes—
Pelted the Bishops with hot buns,
  Rode cock-horse on the City maces,
And shot, from little devilish guns,
  Hard peas into his subjects' faces.
In short, such wicked pranks he played,
  And grew so mischievous (God bless him!)
That his chief Nurse—though with the aid
  Of an Archbishop—was afraid,
When in these moods, to comb or dress him;
  And even the persons most inclined
For Kings, through thick and thin, to stickle,
  Thought him (if they'd but speak their mind,
Which they did *not*) an odious pickle.

At length, some patriot lords—a breed
  Of animals they have in Thibet,
Extremely rare, and fit, indeed,
  For folk like Pidcock to exhibit—
Some patriot lords, seeing the length
  To which things went, combined their strength,
And penned a manly, plain and free
  Remonstrance to the Nursery;
In which, protesting that they yielded
  To none, that ever went before 'em,
In loyalty to him who wielded
  The hereditary pap-spoon o'er 'em—
That, as for treason, 'twas a thing
  That made them almost sick to think of—
That they and theirs stood by the King,
  Throughout his measles and his chin-cough,

When others, thinking him consumptive,
  Had ratted to the Heir Presumptive'—
But, still—though much admiring Kings
  (And chiefly those in leading-strings)—
They saw, with shame and grief of soul,
  There was no longer now the wise
And constitutional control
  Of *birch* before their ruler's eyes;
But that, of late, such pranks, and tricks,
  And freaks occurred the whole day long,
As all, but men with bishopricks,
  Allowed, in even a King, were wrong—
Wherefore it was they humbly prayed
  That Honourable Nursery,
That such reforms be henceforth made,
  As all good men desired to see;—
In other words (lest they might seem
  Too tedious), as the gentlest scheme
For putting all such pranks to rest,
  And in its bud the mischief nipping—
They ventured humbly to suggest
  His Majesty should have a whipping!

When this was read, no Congreve rocket,
  Discharged into the Gallic trenches,
E'er equalled the tremendous shock it
  Produced upon the Nursery Benches.
The Bishops, who of course had votes,
  By right of age and petticoats,
Were first and foremost in the fuss—
  'What, whip a Lama!—Suffer birch
To touch his sacred —— infamous!
  Deistical!—assailing thus
The fundamentals of the Church!
  No—no—such patriot plans as these
(So help them Heaven—and their sees!)
  They held to be rank blasphemies.'

The alarm thus given, by these and other
  Grave ladies of the Nursery side,
Spread through the land, till, such a pother,
  Such party squabbles, far and wide,
Never in history's page had been
  Recorded, as were then between
The Whippers and Non-whippers seen.
  Till, things arriving at a state
Which gave some fears of revolution,
  The patriot lords' advice, though late,
Was put at last in execution.
  The Parliament of Thibet met—
The little Lama, called before it,
  Did, then and there, his whipping get,
And (as the Nursery Gazette
  Assures us) like a hero bore it.

And though 'mong Thibet Tories, some
  Lament that Royal Martyrdom
(Please to observe, the letter D
  In this last word's pronounced like B),
Yet to the example of that Prince
  So much is Thibet's land a debtor,
'Tis said, her little Lamas since
  Have all behaved themselves *much* better.

FABLE VII.

THE EXTINGUISHERS.

Proem.

Though soldiers are the true supports,
The natural allies of Courts,
Woe to the Monarch who depends
Too *much* on his red-coated friends;
For even soldiers sometimes think—
  Nay Colonels have been known to *reason*,—
And reasoners, whether clad in pink,
Or red, or blue, are on the brink
  (Nine cases out of ten) of treason.

Not many soldiers, I believe, are
  As fond of liberty as Mina;
Else—woe to Kings, when Freedom's fever
  Once turns into a *Scarletina!*
For then—but hold—'tis best to veil
My meaning in the following tale:—

Fable.

A LORD of Persia, rich and great,
Just come into a large estate,
Was shocked to find he had, for neighbours,
Close to his gate, some rascal Ghebers,
Whose fires, beneath his very nose,
In heretic combustion rose.
But lords of Persia can, no doubt,
Do what they will—so, one fine morning,
He turned the rascal Ghebers out,
  First giving a few kicks for warning.
Then, thanking Heaven most piously,
  He knocked their temple to the ground,
Blessing himself for joy to see
  Such Pagan ruins strewed around.
But much it vexed my lord to find,
  That, while all else obeyed his will,
The fire these Ghebers left behind—
  Do what he would—kept burning still.
Fiercely he stormed, as if his frown
Could scare the bright insurgent down;
But, no—such fires are headstrong things,
And care not much for lords or kings.
Scarce could his lordship well contrive
  The flashes in *one* place to smother,
Before—hey, presto!—all alive,
  They sprung up freshly in another.

At length, when, spite of prayers and damns,
'Twas found the sturdy flame defied him,
His stewards came, with low *salams*,
  Offering, by *contract*, to provide him
Some large extinguishers (a plan
Much used, they said, at Ispahan,
Vienna, Petersburgh—in short,
Wherever light's forbid at court)—
Machines no lord should be without,
Which would, at once, put promptly out

Fires of all kinds—from staring stark
Volcanos to the tiniest spark—
Till all things slept as dull and dark
As, in a great lord's neighbourhood,
'Twas right and fitting all things should.

Accordingly, some large supplies
  Of these extinguishers were furnished
(All of the true, imperial size),
  And there, in rows, stood black and burnished,
Ready, where'er a gleam but shone
Of light or fire, to be clapped on.

But, ah! how lordly wisdom errs
In trusting to extinguishers!
One day, when he had left all sure
  (At least *believed* so), dark, secure—
The flame, at all its exits, entries,
  Obstructed to his heart's content,
And black extinguishers, like sentries,
  Placed upon every dangerous vent—
Ye Gods! imagine his amaze,
  His wrath, his rage, when, on returning,
He found not only the old blaze,
  Brisk as before, crackling and burning—
Not only new, young conflagrations,
Popping up round in various stations—
But, still more awful, strange, and dire,
The extinguishers themselves on fire!![1]
They, they—those trusty, blind machines
  His lordship had so long been praising,
As, under Providence, the means
  Of keeping down all lawless blazing,
Were now themselves—alas, too true
The shameful fact!—turned blazers too,
And, by a change as odd as cruel,
Instead of dampers, served for fuel!

Thus, of his only hope bereft,
  'What,' said the great man, 'must be done?'
All that, in scrapes like this, is left
  To great men is—to cut and run.
So run he did; while to their grounds
  The banished Ghebers blessed returned;
And, though their fire had broke its bounds,
  And all abroad now wildly burned,
Yet well could they, who loved the flame,
  Its wandering, its excess reclaim;
And soon another, fairer dome
  Arose to be its sacred home,
Where, cherished, guarded, not confined,
  The living glory dwelt enshrined,
And, shedding lustre, strong but even,
Though born of earth, grew worthy Heaven.

Moral.

The moral hence my Muse infers
  Is—that such lords are simple elves,
In trusting to extinguishers
  That are combustible themselves.

---

[1] The idea of this fable was caught from one of those brilliant *mots* which abound in the conversation of my friend, the author of the *Letters to Julia*—a production which contains some of the happiest specimens of playful poetry that have appeared in this or any age.

RHYMES ON THE ROAD,

EXTRACTED FROM THE JOURNAL

OF A

TRAVELLING MEMBER OF THE POCOCURANTE SOCIETY, 1819.

THE Gentleman from whose Journal the following extracts are taken, tells the reader in his Introduction that the greater part of these poems were written or composed in an old *calèche*, for the purpose of beguiling the ennui of solitary travelling; and as verses made by a gentleman in his sleep have lately been called '*a psychological* curiosity,' it is to be hoped that verses made by a gentleman to keep himself awake may be honoured with some appellation equally Greek.

INTRODUCTORY RHYMES.

Different Attitudes in which Authors compose.—Bayes, Henry Stephens, Herodotus, etc.—Writing in Bed—in the Fields.—Plato and Sir Richard Blackmore.—Fiddling with Gloves and Twigs.—Madame de Staël.—Rhyming on the Road, in an old Calèche.

WHAT various attitudes, and ways,
 And tricks, we authors have in writing!
While some write sitting, some, like Bayes,
 Usually stand while they're inditing.
Poets there are, who wear the floor out,
 Measuring a line at every stride;
While some, like Henry Stephens, pour out
 Rhymes by the dozen, while they ride.[1]

Herodotus wrote most in bed;
 And Richerand, a French physician,
Declares the clock-work of the head
 Goes best in that reclined position.
If you consult Montaigne[2] and Pliny on
 The subject, 'tis their joint opinion
That Thought its richest harvest yields
 Abroad, among the woods and fields;
That bards, who deal in small retail,
 At home may, at their counters, stop;
But that the grove, the hill, the vale,
 Are Poesy's true wholesale shop.

And truly I suspect they're right—
 For, many a time, on summer eves,
Just at that closing hour of light,
 When, like an eastern Prince, who leaves
For distant war his Haram bowers,
 The Sun bids farewell to the flowers,
Whose heads are sunk, whose tears are flowing
 'Mid all the glory of his going—
Even *I* have felt beneath those beams,
 When wandering through the fields alone,
Thoughts, fancies, intellectual gleams,
 That, far too bright to be my own,
Seemed lent me by the Sunny Power,
 That was abroad at that still hour.

If thus I've felt, how must *they* feel,
 The few whom genuine Genius warms,
And stamps upon their soul his seal,
 Graven with Beauty's countless forms;—
The few upon this earth who seem
 Born to give truth to Plato's dream,
Since in their souls, as in a glass,
 Shadows of things divine appear—
Reflections of bright forms that pass
 Through fairer worlds beyond our sphere!

---

[1] Pleraque sua carmina equitans composuit.—*Parasitis. Singular.*

[2] Mes pensées dorment, si je les assis.—*Montaigne.* Animus eorum, qui in aperto aëre ambulant, attollitur.—*P*

But this reminds me I digress;—
For Plato, too, produced, 'tis said
(As one indeed might almost guess),
    His glorious visions all in bed.[1]
'Twas in his carriage the sublime
Sir Richard Blackmore used to rhyme;
And (if the wits don't do him wrong),
'Twixt death and epics passed his time,
    Scribbling and killing all day long—
Like Phœbus in his car, at ease,
    Now warbling forth a lofty song,
    Now murdering the young Niobes.

There was a hero 'mong the Danes,
Who wrote, we're told, 'mid all the pains
    And horrors of exenteration,
Nine charming odes, which, if you look,
    You'll find preserved, with a translation,
By Bartholinus in his book.[2]
In short, 'twere endless to recite
The various modes in which men write.
Some wits are only in the mind
    When beaux and belles are round them prating;
Some, when they dress for dinner, find
    Their muse and valet both in waiting,
And manage, at the self-same time,
To adjust a neckcloth and a rhyme.

Some bards there are who cannot scribble
Without a glove, to tear or nibble,
Or a small twig to whisk about—
    As if the hidden founts of Fancy,
Like those of water, were found out
    By mystic tricks of rhabdomancy.

Such was the little feathery wand[3]
That, held for ever in the hand
Of her who won and wore the crown
    Of female genius in this age,
Seemed the conductor, that drew down
    Those words of lightning on her page.

As for myself—to come at last
    To the odd way in which *I* write—
Having employed these few months past
    Chiefly in travelling, day and night,
I've got into the easy mode,
You see, of rhyming on the road—
Making a way-bill of my pages,
Counting my stanzas by my stages—
'Twixt lays and re-lays no time lost—
In short, in two words, *writing post*.
My verses, I suspect, not ill
Resembling the crazed vehicle
(An old *calèche*, for which a villain
Charged me some twenty Naps at Milan)
In which I wrote them—patched-up things,
On weak, but rather easy, springs,
Jingling along, with little in 'em,
    And (where the road is not so rough,
Or deep, or lofty, as to spin 'em,
    Down precipices) safe enough.—
Too ready to take fire, I own,
And *then*, too, nearest a break-down;
But, for my comfort, hung so low,
I haven't, in falling, far to go,—
With all this, light, and swift, and airy,
And carrying (which is best of all)
But little for the *Doganieri*[4]
    Of the Reviews to overhaul.

RHYMES ON THE ROAD.

EXTRACT I.

Geneva.

View of the Lake of Geneva from the Jura.[5]—*Anxious to reach it before the Sun went down.—Obliged to proceed on Foot.—Alps.—Mont Blanc.—Effect of the Scene.*

'Twas late—the sun had almost shone
His last and best, when I ran on,
Anxious to reach that splendid view
Before the day-beams quite withdrew;
And feeling as all feel, on first
    Approaching scenes where, they are told,
Such glories on their eyes shall burst
    As youthful bards in dreams behold.
'Twas distant yet, and, as I ran,
    Full often was my wistful gaze
Turned to the sun, who now began
    To call in all his outpost rays,
And form a denser march of light,
Such as beseems a hero's flight.
Oh, how I wished for Joshua's power,
To stay the brightness of that hour!

---

[1] The only authority I know for imputing this practice to Plato and Herodotus, is a Latin poem by M. de Valois on his Bed, in which he says:

   Lucifer Herodotum vidit vesperque cubantem;
       Desedit totos hic Plato sæpo dies.

[2] Eadem cura nec minores inter cruciatus animam infelicem agentl fuit Asbiorno Prudæ Danico heroi, cum Biuso ipsum, intestina extrahens, immaniter torqueret, tunc enim novem carmina cecinit, etc.—*Bartholin. de causis contempt. mort.*

[3] Made of paper, twisted up like a fan or feather.

[4] Custom-house officers.

[5] Between Vattay and Gex.

But no—the sun still less became,
　Diminished to a speck, as splendid
And small as were those tongues of flame
　That on the Apostles' heads descended!

'Twas at this instant—while there glowed
　This last, intensest gleam of light—
Suddenly, through the opening road,
　The valley burst upon my sight!
That glorious valley, with its lake,
　And Alps on Alps in clusters swelling,
Mighty, and pure, and fit to make
　The ramparts of a Godhead's dwelling!

I stood entranced and mute—as they
　Of Israel think the assembled world
Will stand upon that awful day,
　When the Ark's Light, aloft unfurled,
Among the opening clouds shall shine,
　Divinity's own radiant sign!
Mighty Mont Blanc! thou wert to me,
　That minute, with thy brow in Heaven,
As sure a sign of Deity
　As e'er to mortal gaze was given.
Nor ever, were I destined yet
　To live my life twice o'er again,
Can I the deep-felt awe forget—
　The ecstasy that thrilled me then!

'Twas all that consciousness of power,
　And life, beyond this mortal hour,—
Those mountings of the soul within
　At thoughts of Heaven—as birds begin
By instinct in the cage to rise,
　When near their time for change of skies—
That proud assurance of our claim
　To rank among the Sons of Light,
Mingled with shame—oh, bitter shame!—
　At having risked that splendid right,
For aught that earth, through all its range
　Of glories, offers in exchange!
'Twas all this, at the instant brought,
　Like breaking sunshine, o'er my thought—
'Twas all this, kindled to a glow
　Of sacred zeal, which, could it shine
Thus purely ever, man might grow,
　Even upon earth, a thing divine,
And be once more the creature made
　To walk unstained the Elysian shade!

No—never shall I lose the trace
　Of what I've felt in this bright place.
And should my spirit's hope grow weak;
　Should I, oh God! e'er doubt thy power,
This mighty scene again I'll seek,
　At the same calm and glowing hour,
And here, at the sublimest shrine
　That Nature ever reared to Thee,

'Rekindle all that hope divine,
　And *feel* my immortality!

EXTRACT II.

VENICE.

The Fall of Venice not to be lamented.—Former Glory. — Expedition against Constantinople. — Giustinianis.—Republic —Characteristics of the old Government. — Golden Book. — Brazen Mouths.—Spies.—Dungeons.—Present Desolation.

MOURN not for Venice—let her rest
　In ruin, 'mong those States unblessed,
Beneath whose guilded hoofs of pride,
　Where'er they trampled, Freedom died.
No—let us keep our tears for them,
　Where'er they pine, whose fall hath been
Not from a blood-stained diadem,
　Like that which decked this ocean-queen,
But from high daring in the cause
　Of human Rights—the only good
And blessed strife, in which man draws
　His powerful sword on land or flood.

Mourn not for Venice—though her fall
　Be awful, as if Ocean's wave
Swept o'er her—she deserves it all,
　And Justice triumphs o'er her grave.
Thus perish every King and State
　That run the guilty race she ran,
Strong but in fear, and only great
　By outrage against God and man!

True, her high spirit is at rest,
　And all those days of glory gone,
When the world's waters, east and west,
　Beneath her white-winged commerce shone;
When with her countless barks she went
　To meet the Orient Empire's might,[1]
And the Giustinianis sent
　Their hundred heroes to that fight.[2]

Vanished are all her pomps, 'tis true,
　But mourn them not—for, vanished too
(Thanks to that Power who, soon or late,
　Hurls to the dust the guilty Great)
Are all the outrage, falsehood, fraud,
　The chains, the rapine, and the blood,
That filled each spot, at home, abroad,
　Where the Republic's standard stood!

Desolate Venice! when I track
　Thy haughty course through centuries back,—
Thy ruthless power, obeyed but cursed,—
　The stern machinery of thy State,

---

[1] Under the Doge Michaeli, in 1171.
[2] 'La famille entière des Justiniani, l'une des plus illustres de Venise, voulut marcher toute entière dans cette expedition; elle fournit cent combattans; c'était renouveler l'exemple d'une illustre famille de Rome; le même malheur les attendait.'—*Histoire de Venise, par Daru.*

Which hatred would, like steam, have burst,
　Had stronger fear not chilled even hate;
Thy perfidy, still worse than aught
　Thy own unblushing Sarpi¹ taught,—
Thy friendship, which, o'er all beneath
　Its shadow, rained down dews of death,²—
Thy Oligarchy's Book of Gold,
　Shut against humble Virtue's name,³
But opened wide for slaves who sold
　Their native land to thee and shame,⁴—
Thy all-pervading host of spies,
　Watching o'er every glance and breath,
Till men looked in each other's eyes,
　To read their chance of life or death,—
Thy laws, that made a mart of blood,
　And legalized the assassin's knife,³—
Thy sunless cells beneath the flood,
　And racks, and leads⁶ that burn out life;—
When I review all this, and see
　What thou art sunk and crushed to now;
Each harpy maxim, hatched by thee,
　Returned to roost on thy own brow,—
Thy Nobles towering once aloft,
　Now sunk in chains—in chains, that have
Not even that borrowed grace, which oft
　The master's fame sheds o'er the slave,
But are as mean as e'er were given
　To stiff-necked Pride by angry Heaven—
I feel the moral vengeance sweet,
And, smiling o'er the wreck, repeat—
'Thus perish every King and State,
　That tread the steps which Venice trod,
Strong but in fear, and only great
　By outrage against man and God!'

EXTRACT III.

VENICE.

*L——d B——'s Memoirs, written by himself.—
Reflections, when about to read them.*

LET me, a moment—ere with fear and hope
Of gloomy, glorious things, these leaves I ope—
As one, in fairy tale, to whom the key
Of some enchanter's secret halls is given,
Doubts, while he enters, slowly, tremblingly,
　If he shall meet with shapes from hell or
　　heaven—
Let me, a moment, think what thousands live
O'er the wide earth this instant, who would
　give,
Gladly, whole sleepless nights to bend the brow
Over these precious leaves, as I do now.
How all who know—and where is he unknown?
To what far region have his songs not flown,
Like Psaphon's birds,⁷ speaking their master's
　name
In every language syllabled by Fame?—
How all, who've felt the various spells combined
Within the circle of that splendid mind,
Like powers, derived from many a star, and met
Together in some wondrous amulet,
Would burn to know when first the light awoke
In his young soul,—and if the gleams that broke
From that Aurora of his genius, raised
More bliss or pain in those on whom they
　blazed—
Would love to trace the unfolding of that power,
Which hath grown ampler, grander, every hour;
And feel, in watching o'er its first advance,
As did the Egyptian traveller,⁸ when he stood
By the young Nile, and fathomed with his lance
　The first small fountains of that mighty flood.

They, too, who 'mid the scornful thoughts that
　dwell
In his rich fancy, tinging all its streams,
As if the Star of Bitterness which fell
　On earth of old, and touched them with its
　　beams,
Can track a spirit, which, though driven to hate,
From Nature's hands came kind, affectionate;
And which, even now, struck as it is with
　blight,
Comes out, at times, in love's own native light—
How gladly all, who've watched these struggling
　rays
Of a bright, ruined spirit through his lays,
Would here inquire, as from his own frank lips,
　What desolating grief, what wrongs had
　　driven

---

¹ The celebrated Fra Paolo. The collection of maxims which this bold monk drew up, at the request of the Venetian Government, for the guidance of the Secret Inquisition of State, are so atrocious as to seem rather an over-charged satire upon despotism, than a system of policy seriously inculcated, and but too readily and constantly pursued.

² Conduct of Venice towards her allies and dependencies, particularly to unfortunate Padua.—Fate of Francesco Carrara, for which see Daru, vol. ii. p. 141.

³ 'A l'exception des trente citadins admis au grand conseil pendant la guerre de Chiozzi, il n'est pas arrivé une seule fois que les talens ou les services aient paru à cette noblesse orgueilleuse des titres suffisans pour s'asseoir avec elle.'—*Daru.*

⁴ Among those admitted to the honour of being inscribed in the *Libro d'Oro* were some families of Brescia, Treviso, and other places whose only claim to that distinction was the zeal with which they prostrated themselves and their country at the feet of the republic.

⁵ By the infamous statutes of the State Inquisition not only was assassination recognised as a regular mode of punishment, but this secret power over life was delegated to their minions at a distance, with nearly as much facility as a licence is given under the game laws of England. The only restriction seems to have been the necessity of applying for a new certificate after every individual exercise of the power.

⁶ ' Les prisons des plombs; c'est-à-dire ces fournaises ardentes qu'on avait distribuées en petites cellules sous les terrasses qui couvrent le palais.'

⁷ Psaphon, in order to attract the attention of the world, taught multitudes of birds to speak his name, and then let them fly away in various directions: whence the proverb, *Psaphonis aves.*

⁸ Bruce.

That noble nature into cold eclipse—
  Like some fair orb that, once a sun in Heaven,
And born, not only to surprise, but cheer
With warmth and lustre all within its sphere,
Is now so quenched, that, of its grandeur, lasts
Nought but the wide cold shadow which it casts!

Eventful volume! whatsoe'er the change
Of scene and clime—the adventures, bold and
    strange—
The griefs—the frailties, but too frankly told—
The loves, the feuds thy pages may unfold;
If truth with half so prompt a hand unlocks
  His virtues as his failings, we shall find
The record there of friendships, held like rocks,
  And enmities, like sun-touched snow, re-
    signed—
Of fealty, cherished without change or chill,
In those who served him young, and serve him
    still—
Of generous aid, given with that noiseless art
Which wakes not pride, to many a wounded
    heart—
Of acts—but, no—*not* from himself must aught
Of the bright features of his life be sought.
While they who court the world, like Milton's
    cloud,[1]
'Turn forth their silver lining' on the crowd,
This gifted Being wraps himself in night,
And, keeping all that softens, and adorns,
And gilds his social nature, hid from sight,
  Turns but its darkness on a world he scorns.

EXTRACT IV.

VENICE.

The English to be met with everywhere.—Alps and Threadneedle Street.—The Simplon and the Stocks.—Rage for Travelling.—Blue Stockings among the Wahabees.—Parasols and Pyramids. —Mrs. Hopkins and the Wall of China.

AND is there then no earthly place
  Where we can rest, in dream Elysian,
Without some cursed, round English face,
  Popping up near, to break the vision?

'Mid northern lakes, 'mid southern vines,
  Unholy cits we're doomed to meet;
Nor highest Alps nor Apennines
  Are sacred from Threadneedle Street!

If up the Simplon's path we wind,
  Fancying we leave this world behind,
Such pleasant sounds salute one's ear
As—'Baddish news from 'Change, my dear—

'The Funds—(phew, curse this ugly hill!)
Are lowering fast—(what! higher still?)

And—(zooks, we're mounting up to heaven!)—
Will soon be down to sixty-seven'

Go where we may, rest where we will,
Eternal London haunts us still.
The trash of Almack's or Fleet-Ditch—
And scarce a pin's head difference *which*—
Mixes, though even to Greece we run,
With every rill from Helicon!
And, if this rage for travelling lasts,
If Cockneys, of all sects and castes,
Old maidens, aldermen, and squires,
Will leave their puddings and coal fires,
To gape at things in foreign lands
No soul among them understands—
If Blues desert their coteries,
To show off 'mong the Wahabees—
If neither sex nor age controls,
  Nor fear of Mamelukes forbids
Young ladies, with pink parasols,[2]
  To glide among the pyramids—
Why, then, farewell all hope to find
A spot that's free from London-kind!
Who knows, if to the West we roam,
But we may find some *Blue* 'at home'
Among the *Blacks* of Carolina—
Or, flying to the Eastward, see
Some Mrs. Hopkins, taking tea
And toast upon the Wall of China!

EXTRACT V.

FLORENCE.

No—'tis not the region where love's to be
    found—
  They have bosoms that sigh, they have glances
    that rove,
They have language a Sappho's own lip might
    resound,
  When she warbled her best—but they've
    nothing like Love.

Nor is it that *sentiment* only they want,
  Which Heaven for the pure and the tranquil
    hath made—
Calm, wedded affection, that home-rooted plant,
  Which sweetens seclusion, and smiles in the
    shade;

That feeling which, after long years are gone
    by,
  Remains like a portrait we've sat for in youth,
Where, even though the flush of the colours may
    fly,
  The features still live in their first smiling
    truth;

That union, where all that in Woman is kind,
  With all that in man most ennoblingly towers,

---

[1] 'Did a sable cloud
Turn forth her silver lining on the night.'—*Comus.*

[2] It was pink *spencers*, I believe, that the imagination of the French traveller conjured up.

Grow wreathed into one—like the column, combined
Of the *strength* of the shaft and the capital's *flowers*.

Of this—bear ye witness, ye wives, everywhere,
By the Arno, the Po, by all Italy's streams—
Of this heart-wedded love, so delicious to share,
Not a husband hath even one glimpse in his dreams.

But it *is* not this only—born, full of the light
Of a sun, from whose fount the luxuriant festoons
Of these beautiful valleys drink lustre so bright,
That, beside him, our suns of the north are but moons!

We might fancy, at least, like their climate they burned,
And that Love, though unused, in this region of spring,
To be thus to a tame Household Deity turned,
Would yet be all soul, when abroad on the wing.

And there *may* be, there *are* those explosions of heart,
Which burst, when the senses have first caught the flame;
Such fits of the blood as those climates impart,
Where Love is a sunstroke that maddens the frame.

But that Passion, which springs in the depth of the soul,
Whose beginnings are virginly pure as the source
Of some mountainous rivulet, destined to roll
As a torrent, ere long, losing peace in its course—

A course, to which Modesty's struggle but lends
A more headlong descent, without chance of recall;
But which Modesty even to the last edge attends,
And, at length, throws a halo of tears round its fall!

This exquisite Passion—ay, exquisite, even
In the ruin its madness too often hath made,
As it keeps, even then, a bright trace of the heaven,
The heaven of Virtue, from which it has strayed—

This entireness of love, which can only be found
Where Woman, like something that's holy,
watched over,
And fenced, from her childhood, with purity round,
Comes, body and soul, fresh as Spring, to a lover!

Where not an eye answers, where not a hand presses,
Till spirit with spirit in sympathy move;
And the Senses, asleep in their sacred recesses,
Can only be reached through the Temple of Love!

This perfection of Passion—how *can* it be found,
Where the mysteries Nature hath hung round the tie
By which souls are together attracted and bound,
Are laid open, for ever, to heart, ear, and eye—

Where nought of those innocent doubts can exist,
That ignorance, even than knowledge, more bright,
Which circles the young, like the morn's sunny mist,
And curtains them round in their own native light—

Where Experience leaves nothing for Love to reveal,
Or for Fancy, in visions, to gleam o'er the thought,
But the truths which alone we would die to conceal
From the maiden's young heart, are the *only* ones taught—

Oh no—'tis not here, howsoever we're given,
Whether purely to Hymen's *one* planet we pray,
Or adore, like Sabœans, each light of Love's heaven,
Here *is* not the region to fix or to stray;

For, faithless in wedlock, in gallantry gross,
Without honour to guard, or reserve to restrain,
What have they a husband can mourn as a loss?—
What have they a lover can prize as a gain?

EXTRACT VI.

ROME.

Reflections on reading Du Cerceau's Account of the Conspiracy of Rienzi in 1347.—The Meeting of the Conspirators on the night of the 19th of May.—Their Procession in the Morning to the Capitol.—Rienzi's Speech.

'Twas a proud moment—even to hear the words
Of Truth and Freedom 'mid these temples breathed,
And see, once more, the Forum shine with swords,
In the Republic's sacred name unsheathed—
That glimpse, that vision of a brighter day
For his dear Rome, must to a Roman be,
Short as it was, worth ages past away
In the dull lapse of hopeless slavery.

'Twas on a night of May—beneath that moon
Which had through many an age seen Time
  untune
The strings of this Great Empire, till it fell
From his rude hands, a broken, silent shell—
The sound of the church clock,[1] near Adrian's
  Tomb,
Summoned the warriors, who had risen for Rome,
To meet unarmed, with naught to watch them
  there
But God's own eye, and pass the night in prayer.
Holy beginning of a holy cause,
When heroes, girt for Freedom's combat, pause
Before high Heaven, and, humble in their might,
Call down its blessing on that awful fight.

At dawn, in arms, went forth the patriot band,
And as the breeze, fresh from the Tiber, fanned
Their gilded gonfalons, all eyes could see
  The palm-tree there, the sword, the keys of
    Heaven—
Types of the justice, peace, and liberty,
  That were to bless them when their chains
    were riven.
On to the Capitol the pageant moved,
While many a Shade of other times, that still
Around that grave of grandeur sighing roved,
  Hung o'er their footsteps up the Sacred Hill,
And heard its mournful echoes, as the last
High-minded heirs of the Republic passed.
'Twas then that thou, their Tribune (name which
  brought
Dreams of lost glory to each patriot's thought),
Didst, from a spirit Rome in vain shall seek
To call up in her sons again, thus speak:—

'Romans! look round you—on this sacred place
  There once stood shrines, and gods, and god-
    like men—
What see you now? what solitary trace
  Is left of all that made Rome's glory then?
The shrines are sunk, the Sacred Mount beroft
Even of its name—and nothing now remains
But the deep memory of that glory, left
To whet our pangs and aggravate our chains!
But *shall* this be?—our sun and sky the same,
Treading the very soil our fathers trod,
What withering curse hath fallen on soul and
  frame,
What visitation hath there come from God,
To blast our strength and rot us into slaves,
Here, on our great forefathers' glorious graves?

It cannot be—rise up, ye Mighty Dead,
  If we, the living, are too weak to crush
These tyrant priests, that o'er your empire tread,
  Till all but Romans at Rome's tameness blush!

'Happy Palmyra! in thy desert domes,
  Where only date-trees sigh and serpents hiss;
And thou, whose pillars are but silent homes
  For the stork's brood, superb Persepolis!
Thrice happy both that your extinguished race
Have left no embers—no half-living trace—
No slaves, to crawl around the once proud spot,
Till past renown in present shame's forgot;
While Rome, the Queen of all, whose very
  wrecks,
If lone and lifeless through a desert hurled,
Would wear more true magnificence than decks
  The assembled thrones of all the existing
    world—
Rome, Rome alone, is haunted, stained, and
  cursed,
Through every spot her princely Tiber laves,
By living human things—the deadliest, worst,
  This earth engenders — tyrants and their
    slaves!
And we?—oh shame!—we, who have pondered
  o'er
The patriot's lesson and the poet's lay;
Have mounted up the streams of ancient lore,
  Tracking our country's glories all the way—
Even *we* have tamely, basely kissed the ground
Before that Papal Power, that Ghost of Her,
The World's Imperial Mistress—sitting, crowned
  And ghastly, on her mouldering sepulchre!
But this is past—too long have lordly priests
  And priestly lords led us, with all our pride
Withering about us, like devoted beasts,
  Dragged to the shrine, with faded garlands
    tied.
'Tis o'er—the dawn of our deliverance breaks!
  Up from his sleep of centuries awakes
The Genius of the Old Republic, free
As first he stood, in chainless majesty,
And sends his voice through ages yet to come,
Proclaiming Rome, Rome, Rome, Eternal Rome!'

EXTRACT VII.

ROME.

*Mary Magdalen.—Her Story.—Numerous Pictures
  of her.—Correggio.—Guido.—Raphael, etc.—*

---

[1] It is not easy to discover what church is meant by Du Cerceau here: 'Il fit crier dans les rues de Rome, à son de trompe, que chacun eût à se trouver, sans armes, la nuit du lendemain, dix-neuvième, dans l'église du château de Saint-Ange au son de la cloche, afin de pourvoir au Bon Etat.'

[2] The fine Canzone of Petrarch, beginning 'Spirto gentil,' is supposed, by Voltaire and others, to have been addressed to Rienzi; but there is much more evidence of its having been written, as Ginguené asserts, to the young Stephen Colonna, on his being created a Senator of Rome. That Petrarch, however, was filled with high and patriotic hopes by the first measures of this extraordinary man, appears from one of his letters, quoted by Du Cerceau, where he says, 'Pour tout dire, en un mot, j'atteste, non comme lecteur, mais comme témoin oculaire, qu'il nous a ramené la justice, la paix, la bonne foi, la sécurité, et toutes les autres vestiges de l'âge d'or.'

Canova's two exquisite Statues.—The Somariva Magdalen.—Chantrey's Admiration of Canova's Works.

No wonder, Mary, that thy story
  Touches all hearts; for there we see
The soul's corruption and its glory,
  Its death and life, combined in thee.
From the first moment, when we find
  Thy spirit, haunted by a swarm
Of dark desires, which had enshrined
  Themselves, like demons, in thy form,
Till when, by touch of Heaven set free,
  Thou camest, with those bright locks of gold
(So oft the gaze of Bethany),
  And, covering in their precious fold
Thy Saviour's feet, didst shed such tears
  As paid, each drop, the sins of years!—
Thence on, through all thy course of love
  To Him, thy Heavenly Master,—Him
Whose bitter death-cup from above,
  Had yet this sweetening round the brim,
That woman's faith and love stood fast
  And fearless by Him to the last!
Till—blessed reward for truth like thine!—
  Thou wert, of all, the chosen one,
Before whose eyes that Face Divine,
  When risen from the dead, first shone,
That thou mightst see how, like a cloud,
  Had passed away its mortal shroud,
And make that bright revealment known
  To hearts less trusting than thy own—
All is affecting, cheering, grand;
  The kindliest record ever given,
Even under God's own kindly hand,
  Of what Repentance wins from Heaven!

No wonder, Mary, that thy face,
  In all its touching light of tears,
Should meet us in each holy place,
  Where Man before his God appears,
Hopeless—were he not taught to see
  All hope in Him who pardoned thee!
No wonder that the painter's skill
  Should oft have triumphed in the power
Of keeping thee most lovely still
  Throughout thy sorrow's bitterest hour—
That soft Correggio should diffuse
  His melting shadows round thy form;
That Guido's pale unearthly hues
  Should, in portraying thee, grow warm;
That all—from the ideal, grand,
  Inimitable Roman hand,
Down to the small, enamelling touch
  Of smooth Carlino—should delight
In picturing her who 'loved so much,'
  And was, in spite of sin, so bright!

But, Mary, 'mong the best essays
  Of Genius and of Art to raise
A semblance of those weeping eyes—
  A vision, worthy of the sphere
Thy faith has given thee in the skies,
  And in the hearts of all men here—
Not one hath equalled, hath come nigh
  Canova's fancy; oh, not one
Hath made thee feel, and live, and die
  In tears away, as *he* hath done,
In those bright images, more bright
  With true expression's breathing light
Than ever yet beneath the stroke
  Of chisel into life awoke!
The one,[1] portraying what thou wert
  In thy first grief, while yet the flower
Of those young beauties was unhurt
  By sorrow's slow consuming power,
And mingling earth's luxurious grace
  With Heaven's subliming thoughts so well,
We gaze, and know not in *which* place
  Such beauty most was formed to dwell!—
The other, as thou lookedst when years
  Of fasting, penitence, and tears
Had worn thee down—and ne'er did Art
  With half such mental power express
The ruin which a breaking heart
  Spreads, by degrees, o'er loveliness!
Those wasted arms, that keep the trace,
  Even now, of all their youthful grace;
Those tresses, of thy charms the last
  Whose pride forsook thee, wildly cast—
Those features, even in fading worth
  The freshest smiles to others given,
And those sunk eyes, that see not earth,
  But whose last looks are full of Heaven!

Wonderful artist! praise like mine—
  Though springing from a soul that feels
Deep worship of those works divine,
  Where Genius all his light reveals—
Is little to the words that came
  From him, thy peer in art and fame,
Whom I have known, by day, by night,
  Hang o'er thy marble with delight,
And, while his lingering hand would steal
  O'er every grace the taper's rays,[2]
Give thee, with all the generous zeal
  Such master-spirits only feel,
That best of fame—a rival's praise!

EXTRACT VIII.

LES CHARMETTES.

A Visit to the House where Rousseau lived with Madame de Warens. — Their Ménage. — Its

---

[1] This statue is one of the last works of Canova, and was not yet in marble when I left Rome. The other, which seems to prove, in contradiction to very high authority, that expression of the intensest kind is fully within the sphere of sculpture, was executed many years ago, and is in the possession of the Count Somariva, at Paris.

[2] Canova always shows his fine statue, the Venere Vincitrice, by the light of a small candle.

Grossness.—Claude Anet.—Reverence with which the Spot is now visited.—Absurdity of this blind Devotion to Fame. — Feelings excited by the Beauty and Seclusion of the Scene.—Disturbed by its Associations with Rousseau's History.— Impostures of Men of Genius.—Their Power of mimicking all the best Feelings, Love, Independence, etc.

STRANGE power of Genius, that can throw
O'er all that's vicious, weak, and low,
Such magic lights, such rainbow dyes,
As dazzle even the steadiest eyes!

. . . . . .
. . . . . .

'Tis too absurd—'tis weakness, shame,
This low prostration before Fame—
This casting down beneath the car
Of idols, whatsoe'er they are,
Life's purest, holiest decencies,
To be careered o'er, as they please.
No—let triumphant Genius have
All that his loftiest wish can crave.
If he be worshipped, let it be
   For attributes, his noblest, first—
Not with that base idolatry,
   Which sanctifies his last and worst.

I may be cold—may want that glow
Of high romance, which bards should know;
That holy homage, which is felt
In treading where the great have dwelt —
This reverence, whatsoe'er it be,
   I fear, I feel, I have it not,
For here, at this still hour, to me
   The charms of this delightful spot—
Its calm seclusion from the throng,
   From all the heart would fain forget—
This narrow valley, and the song
   Of its small murmuring rivulet—
The flitting to and fro of birds,
   Tranquil and tame as they were once
In Eden, ere the startling words
   Of man disturbed their orisons!—
Those little, shadowy paths, that wind
   Up the hill-side, with fruit-trees lined,
And lighted only by the breaks
   The gay wind in the foliage makes,
Or vistas here and there, that ope
   Through weeping willows, like the snatches
Of far-off scenes of light, which Hope,
   Even through the shade of sadness, catches!—
All this, which—could I once but lose
The memory of those vulgar ties,
Whose grossness all the heavenliest hues
Of Genius can no more disguise,
Than the sun's beams can do away
The filth of fens o'er which they play—
This scene, which would have filled my heart
   With thoughts of all that happiest is—
Of Love, where self hath only part,
   As echoing back another's bliss—

Of solitude, secure and sweet,
Beneath whose shade the Virtues meet;
Which, while it shelters, never chills
   Our sympathies with human woe,
But keeps them, like sequestered rills,
   Purer and fresher in their flow—
Of happy days, that share their beams
   'Twixt quiet mirth and wise employ—
Of tranquil nights, that give in dreams
   The moonlight of the morning's joy!—
All this my heart could dwell on here,
But for those hateful memories near,
Those sordid truths, that cross the track
Of each sweet thought, and drive them back
Full into all the mire, and strife,
And vanities of that man's life,
Who, more than all that e'er have glowed
   With Fancy's flame (and it was *his*,
If ever given to mortal) showed
   What an impostor Genius is—
How with that strong, mimetic art,
   Which is its life and soul, it takes
All shapes of thought, all hues of heart,
   Nor feels, itself, one throb it wakes—
How like a gem its light may smile
   O'er the dark path, by mortals trod,
Itself as mean a worm, the while,
   As crawls along the sullying sod—
What sensibility may fall
From its false lip, what plans to bless,
While home, friends, kindred, country, all,
   Lie waste beneath its selfishness—
How, with the pencil hardly dry
   From colouring up such scenes of love
And beauty, as make young hearts sigh,
   And dream, and think through Heaven they rove,
They, who can thus describe and move,
   The very workers of these charms,
Nor seek, nor ask a Heaven, above
   Some Maman's or Theresa's arms!

How all, in short, that makes the boast
Of their false tongues, they want the most;
And while, with Freedom on their lips,
   Sounding her timbrels, to set free
This bright world, labouring in the eclipse
   Of priestcraft and of slavery,
They may, themselves, be slaves as low
   As ever lord or patron made,
To blossom in his smile, or grow,
   Like stunted brushwood, in his shade?

Out on the craft—I'd rather be
One of those hinds that round me tread,
With just enough of sense to see
The noon-day sun that's o'er my head,
Than thus, with high-built genius cursed,
That hath no heart for its foundation,
Be all, at once, that's brightest—worst—
Sublimest—meanest in creation!

M.P.; OR, THE BLUE-STOCKING.

SONG.
SUSAN.

YOUNG Love lived once in an humble shed,
  Where roses breathing
  And woodbines wreathing
Around the lattice their tendrils spread,
As wild and sweet as the life he led.
  His garden flourished,
  For young Hope nourished
The infant buds with beams and showers;
But lips, though blooming, must still be fed,
And not even Love can live on flowers.

Alas! that Poverty's evil eye
  Should e'er come hither,
  Such sweets to wither!
The flowers laid down their heads to die,
And Hope fell sick as the witch drew nigh.
  She came one morning,
  Ere Love had warning,
And raised the latch, where the young god lay;
'Oh ho!' said Love—'is it you? good-bye;'
So he oped the window, and flew away!

To sigh, yet feel no pain,
To weep, yet scarce know why;
To sport an hour with Beauty's chain,
  Then throw it idly by;
To kneel at many a shrine,
  Yet lay the heart on none;
To think all other charms divine,
  But those we just have won;
This is love, careless love,
Such as kindleth hearts that rove.

To keep one sacred flame,
  Through life unchilled, unmoved,
To love in wintry age the same
  As first in youth we loved;
To feel that we adore
  To such refined excess,
That though the heart would break with *more*,
  We could not live with *less;*
This is love, faithful love,
Such as saints might feel above.

SPIRIT of Joy, thy altar lies
  In youthful hearts that hope like mine;
And 'tis the light of laughing eyes
  That leads us to thy fairy shrine.
There if we find the sigh, the tear,
  They are not those to sorrow known;
But breathe so soft, and drop so clear,
  That bliss may claim them for her own.
Then give me, give me, while I weep,
  The sanguine hope that brightens woe,
And teaches even our tears to keep
  The tinge of pleasure as they flow.

The child who sees the dew of night
  Upon the spangled hedge at morn,
Attempts to catch the drops of light,
  But wounds his finger with the thorn.
Thus oft the brightest joys we seek,
  Are lost when touched, and turned to pain
The flush they kindle leaves the cheek,
  The tears they waken long remain.
    But give me, give me, etc. etc.

WHEN Leila touched the lute,
  Not *then* alone 'twas felt,
But when the sounds were mute,
  In memory still they dwelt.
Sweet lute! in nightly slumbers
Still we heard thy morning numbers.

Ah, how could she, who stole
  Such breath from simple wire,
Be led, in pride of soul,
  To string with gold her lyre?
Sweet lute! thy chords she breaketh;
Golden now the strings she waketh!

But where are all the tales
  Her lute so sweetly told?
In lofty themes she fails,
  And soft ones suit not gold.
Rich lute! we see thee glisten,
But, alas! no more we listen!

BOAT GLEE.

The song that lightens the languid way,
  When brows are glowing,
  And faint with rowing,
Is like the spell of Hope's airy lay,
To whose sound through life we stray;
The beams that flash on the oar a while,
  As we row along through waves so clear,
Illume its spray, like the fleeting smile
  That shines o'er sorrow's tear.

Nothing is lost on him who sees
  With an eye that feeling gave;—
For him there's a story in every breeze,
  And a picture in every wave.
Then sing to lighten the languid way;
  When brows are glowing,
  And faint with rowing,
'Tis like the spell of Hope's airy lay,
To whose sound through life we stray.

Oh think, when a hero is sighing,
  What danger in such an adorer!
What woman can dream of denying
  The hand that lays laurels before her?
No heart is so guarded around,
  But the smile of a victor would take it;
No bosom can slumber so sound,
  But the trumpet of glory will wake it.

Love sometimes is given to sleeping,
  And woe to the heart that allows him;
For oh, neither smiling nor weeping
  Has power at those moments to rouse him.
But though he was sleeping so fast,
  That the life almost seemed to forsake him,
Even then, one soul-thrilling blast
  From the trumpet of glory would wake him.

CUPID'S LOTTERY.

A Lottery, a Lottery,
  In Cupid's court there used to be;
    Two roguish eyes
    The highest prize
  In Cupid's scheming Lottery;
    And kisses, too,
    As good as new,
  Which weren't very hard to win,
    For he who won
    The eyes of fun
  Was sure to have the kisses in
    A Lottery, a Lottery, etc.

This Lottery, this Lottery,
  In Cupid's court went merrily,
    And Cupid played
    A Jewish trade
  In this his scheming Lottery;
For hearts, we're told,
In *shares* he sold
  To many a fond believing drone,
  And cut the hearts
  In sixteen parts
  So well, each thought the whole his own.
    Chor.—A Lottery, a Lottery, etc.

SONG.

Though sacred the tie that our country entwineth,
  And dear to the heart her remembrance remains,
Yet dark are the ties where no liberty shineth,
  And sad the remembrance that slavery stains.
O thou who wert born in the cot of the peasant,
  But diest of languor in luxury's dome,
Our vision, when absent — our glory, when present—
  Where thou art, O Liberty! there is my home.

Farewell to the land where in childhood I've wandered!
  In vain is she mighty, in vain is she brave!
Unblessed is the blood that for tyrants is squandered,
  And fame has no wreaths for the brow of the slave.
But hail to thee, Albion! who meet'st the commotion
  Of Europe as calm as thy cliffs meet the foam!
With no bonds but the law, and no slave but the ocean,
  Hail, Temple of Liberty! thou art my home.

When Charles was deceived by the maid he loved,
  We saw no cloud his brow o'ercasting,
But proudly he smiled, as if gay and unmoved,
  Though the wound in his heart was deep and lasting.
And oft at night, when the tempest rolled,
  He sung as he paced the dark deck over—
'Blow, wind, blow! thou art not so cold
  As the heart of a maid that deceives her lover.'

Yet he lived with the happy, and seemed to be gay,
  Though the wound but sunk more deep for concealing;
And fortune threw many a thorn in his way,
  Which, true to one anguish, he trod without feeling!
And still, by the frowning of fate unsubdued,
  He sung, as if sorrow had placed him above her—
'Frown, fate, frown! thou art not so rude
  As the heart of a maid that deceives her lover.'

Yet who would not turn with a fonder emotion
   To gaze on the life-boat, though rugged and worn,
Which often hath wafted o'er hills of the ocean,
   The lost light of hope to the seaman forlorn!
Oh! grant that of those who in life's sunny slumber
   Around us like summer-barks idly have play'd;
When storms are abroad we may find in the number
   One friend, like the life-boat, to fly to our aid.

Page 243.

At length his career found a close in death,
The close he long wished to his cheerless roving,
For victory shone on his latest breath,
And he died in a cause of his heart's approving.
But still he remembered his sorrow,—and still
He sung till the vision of life was over—
'Come, death, come! thou art not so chill
As the heart of a maid that deceives her lover.'

When life looks lone and dreary,
  What light can expel the gloom?
When Time's swift wing grows weary,
  What charm can refresh his plume?
'Tis woman, whose sweetness beameth
  O'er all that we feel or see;
And if man of heaven e'er dreameth,
  'Tis when he thinks purely of thee,
    O woman!

Let conquerors fight for glory,
  Too dearly the meed they gain;
Let patriots live in glory—
  Too often they die in vain;
Give kingdoms to those who choose 'em,
  This world can offer to me
No throne like beauty's bosom,
  No freedom like serving thee,
    O woman!

Mr. Orator Puff had two tones in his voice,
The one squeaking thus, and the other down so!
In each sentence he uttered he gave you your choice,
For one was B alt, and the rest G below.
  Oh! oh! Orator Puff!
  One voice for one orator's surely enough.

But he still talked away spite of coughs and of frowns,
So distracting all ears with his ups and his downs,
That a wag once, on hearing the orator say,
My voice is for war, asked him, Which of them, pray?
  Oh! oh! etc.

Reeling homewards one evening, top-heavy with gin,
And rehearsing his speech on the weight of the crown,
He tripped near a sawpit, and tumbled right in,
'Sinking Fund,' the last words as his noddle came down.
  Oh! oh! etc.

'Help! help!' he exclaimed, in his he and she tones,
'Help me out! help me out—I have broken my bones!'
'Help you out?' said a Paddy who passed,
  'what a bother!
Why, there's two of you there, can't you help one another?'
  Oh! oh! etc.

Dear aunt, in the olden time of love,
  When women like slaves were spurned,
A maid gave her heart, as she would her glove,
  To be teased by a fop, and returned!
But women grow wiser as men improve,
  And, though beaux, like monkeys, amuse us,
Oh! think not we'd give such a delicate gem
  As the heart, to be played with or sullied by them;
    No, dearest aunt, excuse us.

We may know by the head on Cupid's seal
  What impression the heart will take;
If shallow the head, oh! soon we feel
  What a poor impression 'twill make!
Though plagued, Heaven knows! by the foolish zeal
  Of the fondling fop who pursues me,
Oh, think not I'd follow their desperate rule,
  Who get rid of the folly, by wedding the fool;
    No, dearest aunt! excuse us.

'Tis sweet to behold, when the billows are sleeping,
Some gay-coloured bark moving gracefully by;
No damp on her deck but the even-tide's weeping,
No breath in her sails but the summer-wind's sigh.

Yet who would not turn with a fonder emotion,
To gaze on the life-boat, though rugged and worn,
Which often hath wafted o'er hills of the ocean
The lost light of hope to the seaman forlorn!

Oh! grant that of those who in life's sunny slumber
Around us like summer-barks idly have played,
When storms are abroad we may find in the number
One friend, like the life-boat, to fly to our aid.

THE LOVES OF THE ANGELS.

THE LOVES OF THE ANGELS.

PREFACE.

This Poem, somewhat different in form, and much more limited in extent, was originally designed as an episode for a work about which I have been, at intervals, employed during the last two years. Some months since, however, I found that my friend Lord Byron had, by an accidental coincidence, chosen the same subject for a drama; and as I could not but feel the disadvantage of coming after so formidable a rival, I thought it best to publish my humble sketch immediately, with such alterations and additions as I had time to make, and thus, by an earlier appearance in the literary horizon, give myself the chance of what astronomers call an *Heliacal rising*, before the luminary, in whose light I was to be lost, should appear.

As objections may be made, by persons whose opinions I respect, to the selection of a subject of this nature from the Scripture, I think it right to remark that, in point of fact, the subject is *not* scriptural—the notion upon which it is founded (that of the love of angels for women) having originated in an erroneous translation by the LXX. of that verse in the sixth chapter of Genesis, upon which the sole authority for the fable rests.[1] The foundation of my story, therefore, has as little to do with Holy Writ as have the dreams of the later Platonists, or the reveries of the Jewish divines; and, in appropriating the notion thus to the uses of poetry, I have done no more than establish it in that region of fiction, to which the opinions of the most rational Fathers, and of all other Christian theologians, have long ago consigned it.

In addition to the fitness of the subject for poetry, it struck me also as capable of affording an allegorical medium, through which might be shadowed out (as I have endeavoured to do in the following stories) the fall of the soul from its original purity—the loss of light and happiness which it suffers, in the pursuit of this world's perishable pleasures—and the punishments, both from conscience and divine justice, with which impurity, pride, and presumptuous inquiry into the awful secrets of God, are sure to be visited. The beautiful story of Cupid and Psyche owes its chief charm to this sort of 'veiled meaning,' and it has been my wish (however I may have failed in the attempt) to communicate the same *moral* interest to the following pages.

---

[1] The error of these interpreters (and, it is said, of the old Italic version also) was in making it οἱ Ἄγγελοι τοῦ Θεοῦ, 'the *Angels* of God,' instead of 'the *Sons*'—a mistake which, assisted by the allegorizing comments of Philo, and the rhapsodical fictions of the Book of Enoch, was more than sufficient to affect the imaginations of such half-Pagan writers as Clemens Alexandrinus, Tertullian, and Lactantius, who, chiefly among the Fathers, have indulged themselves in fanciful reveries upon the subject. The greater number, however, have rejected the fiction with indignation. Chrysostom, in his twenty-second Homily upon Genesis, earnestly exposes its absurdity; and Cyril accounts such a supposition as ἐγγὺς μωρίας, 'bordering on folly.' According to these Fathers (and their opinion has been followed by all the theologians, down from St. Thomas to Caryl and Lightfoot), the term 'Sons of God' must be understood to mean the descendants of Seth, by Enos—a family peculiarly favoured by Heaven, because with them men first began to 'call upon the name of the Lord'—while, by 'the daughters of men' they suppose that the corrupt race of Cain is designated. The probability, however, is, that the words in question ought to have been translated 'the sons of the nobles or great men,' as we find them interpreted in the Targum of Onkelos (the most ancient and accurate of all the Chaldaic paraphrases), and as, it appears from Cyril, the version of Symmachus also rendered them. This translation of the passage removes all difficulty, and at once relieves the Sacred History of an extravagance, which, however it may suit the imagination of the poet, is inconsistent with all our notions, both philosophical and religious.

THE LOVES OF THE ANGELS.

'TWAS when the world was in its prime,
  When the fresh stars had just begun
Their race of glory, and young Time
  Told his first birthdays by the sun;
When, in the light of Nature's dawn
  Rejoicing, men and angels met
On the high hill and sunny lawn,—
Ere Sorrow came, or Sin had drawn
  'Twixt man and Heaven her curtain yet!
When earth lay nearer to the skies
  Than in those days of crime and woe,
And mortals saw, without surprise,
  In the mid air, angelic eyes
    Gazing upon this world below.

Alas, that passion should profane,
  Even then, the morning of the earth!
That, sadder still, the fatal stain
  Should fall on hearts of heavenly birth—
And that from woman's love should fall
So dark a stain, most sad of all!

One evening, in that time of bloom,
  On a hill's side, where hung the ray
Of sunset, sleeping in perfume,
  Three noble youths conversing lay;
And as they looked, from time to time,
  To the far sky, where Daylight furled
His radiant wing, their brows sublime
  Bespoke them of that distant world—
Creatures of light, such as still play,
  Like motes in sunshine, round the Lord,
And through their infinite array
  Transmit each moment, night and day,
The echo of his luminous word![1]

Of heaven they spoke, and, still more oft,
  Of the bright eyes that charmed them thence;
Till, yielding gradual to the soft
  And balmy evening's influence—
The silent breathing of the flowers—
  The melting light that beamed above,
As on their first fond erring hours,
  Each told the story of his love,
The history of that hour unblest,
  When, like a bird, from its high nest
Won down by fascinating eyes,
For woman's smile he lost the skies.

The first who spoke was one, with look
  The least celestial of the three—

A Spirit of light mould, that took
  The prints of earth most yieldingly;
Who, even in heaven, was not of those
  Nearest the throne, but held a place
Far off, among those shining rows
  That circle out through endless space,
And o'er whose wings the light from Him
  In Heaven's centre falls most dim.

Still fair and glorious, he but shone
  Among those youths the unheavenliest one—
A creature to whom light remained
  From Eden still, but altered, stained,
And o'er whose brow not Love alone
  A blight had, in his transit, sent,
But other, earthlier joys had gone,
  And left their foot-prints as they went.

Sighing, as through the shadowy Past,
  Like a tomb-searcher, Memory ran,
Lifting each shroud that time had cast
  O'er buried hopes, he thus began:—

FIRST ANGEL'S STORY.

'TWAS in a land, that far away
  Into the golden orient lies,
Where Nature knows not Night's delay,
  But springs to meet her bridegroom, Day,
    Upon the threshold of the skies.
One morn, on earthly mission sent,
  And midway choosing where to light,
I saw from the blue element—
  Oh beautiful, but fatal sight!—
One of earth's fairest womankind,
  Half veiled from view, or rather shrined
In the clear crystal of a brook;[2]
  Which, while it hid no single gleam
Of her young beauties, made them look
  More spirit-like, as they might seem
Through the dim shadowing of a dream.

Pausing in wonder, I looked on,
  While, playfully around her breaking
The waters, that like diamonds shone,
  She moved in light of her own making.
At length, as slowly I descended
  To view more near a sight so splendid,

---

[1] Dionysius (*De Cœlest. Hierarch.*) is of opinion that when Isaiah represents the Seraphim as crying out 'one unto the other,' his intention is to describe those communications of the divine thought and will, which are continually passing from the higher orders of the angels to the lower.

[2] This is given upon the authority, or rather according to the fancy, of some of the Fathers, who suppose that the women of earth were first seen by the angels in this situation; and St. Basil has even made it the serious foundation of rather a rigorous rule for the toilet of his fair disciples; adding, ἱκανον γαρ εστι παρα γυμνουμενον καλλος και νιους Θεου προς ἡδονην γοητευσαι, και ὡς ανθρωπους δια ταυτην ασθηνεκωστας, θνητους αποδειξαι. —*De Vera Virginitat.* tom. i. p. 747. edit. Paris, 1618.

The tremble of my wings all o'er
  (For through each plume I felt the thrill)
Startled her, as she reached the shore
  Of that small lake—her mirror still—
Above whose brink she stood, like snow
  When rosy with a sunset glow.
Never shall I forget those eyes!—
  The shame, the innocent surprise
Of that bright face, when in the air
  Uplooking, she beheld me there.
It seemed as if each thought, and look,
  And motion were that minute chained
Fast to the spot, such root she took,
  And—like a sunflower by a brook,
    With face upturned—so still remained!

In pity to the wondering maid,
  Though loth from such a vision turning,
Downward I bent, beneath the shade
  Of my spread wings, to hide the burning
Of glances which—I well could feel—
  For me, for her, too warmly shone;
But ere I could again unseal
  My restless eyes, or even steal
One side-long look, the maid was gone—
  Hid from me in the forest leaves,
Sudden as when, in all her charms
  Of full-blown light, some cloud receives
The moon into his dusky arms.
'Tis not in words to tell the power,
  The despotism, that, from that hour,
Passion held o'er me—day and night
  I sought around each neighbouring spot,
And, in the chase of this sweet light,
  My task, and Heaven, and all forgot—
All but the one, sole, haunting dream
  Of her I saw in that bright stream.

Nor was it long, ere by her side
  I found myself whole happy days,
Listening to words, whose music vied
  With our own Eden's seraph lays,
When seraph lays are warmed by love,
  But wanting *that*, far, far above!—
And looking into eyes where, blue
  And beautiful, like skies shone through
The sleeping wave, for me there shone
  A heaven more worshipped than my own.
Oh what, while I could hear and see
  Such words and looks, was heaven to me?
Though gross the air on earth I drew,
  'Twas blessed, while she breathed it too;
Though dark the flowers, though dim the sky,
  Love lent them light, while she was nigh.
Throughout creation I but knew
  Two separate worlds—the *one*, that small,
    Beloved, and consecrated spot

Where Lea *was*—the other, all
  The dull wide waste, where she was *not!*

But vain my suit, my madness vain;
  Though gladly, from her eyes to gain
One earthly look, one stray desire,
  I would have torn the wings that hung
Furled at my back, and o'er that Fire
  Unnamed in heaven their fragments flung;—
'Twas hopeless all—pure and unmoved
  She stood, as lilies in the light
Of the hot noon but look more white;—
  And though she loved me, deeply loved,
'Twas not as man, as mortal—no,
  Nothing of earth was in that glow—
She loved me but as one, of race
  Angelic, from that radiant place
She saw so oft in dreams—that heaven,
  To which her prayers at morn were sent,
And on whose light she gazed at even,
  Wishing for wings that she might go
Out of this shadowy world below,
  To that free glorious element!

Well I remember by her side
  Sitting at rosy eventide,
When,—turning to the star, whose head
  Looked out, as from a bridal bed,
At that mute blushing hour,—she said,
  'Oh! that it were my doom to be
The spirit of yon beauteous star,¹
  Dwelling up there in purity,
Alone, as all such bright things are;—
  My sole employ to play and shine,
To light my censer at the sun,
  And cast its fire towards the shrine
  Of Him in Heaven, the Eternal One!'

So innocent the maid—so free
  From mortal taint in soul and frame,
Whom 'twas my crime—my destiny—
  To love, ay, burn for, with a flame
To which earth's wildest fires are tame.
  Had you but seen her look, when first
From my mad lips the avowal burst!
  Not angry—no—the feeling had
No touch of anger, but most sad—
  It was a sorrow, calm as deep,
A mournfulness that could not weep,
  So filled the heart was to the brink,
So fixed and frozen there—to think
  That angel natures—even I,
Whose love she clung to, as the tie
  Between her spirit and the sky—
Should fall thus headlong from the height
  Of such pure glory into sin.

---

¹ It is the opinion of Kircher, Ricciolus, etc. (and was, I believe, to a certain degree, that of Origen), that the stars are moved and directed by intelligences or angels who preside over them. Among other passages from Scripture in support of this notion, they cite those words of the Book of Job, 'When the morning stars sang together;' upon which Kircher remarks, 'Non de materialibus intelligitur.'—*Itin. i. Isagog. Astronom.* See also Caryl's most wordy commentary on the same text.

That very night—my heart had grown
Impatient of its inward burning;
The term, too, of my stay was flown,
And the bright Watchers[1] near the throne
Already, if a meteor shone
Between them and this nether zone,
  Thought 'twas their herald's wing returning;—
Oft did the potent spell-word, given
  To envoys hither from the skies,
To be pronounced, when back to heaven
It is their hour or wish to rise,
Come to my lips that fatal day;
  And once, too, was so nearly spoken,
That my spread plumage in the ray
And breeze of heaven began to play—
  When my heart failed, the spell was broken,
The word unfinished died away,
And my checked plumes, ready to soar,
Fell slack and lifeless as before.

How could I leave a world which she,
Or lost or won, made all to me?
No matter where my wanderings were,
  So there she looked, moved, breathed about—
Woe, ruin, death, more sweet with her,
Than all heaven's proudest joys without!

But, to return—that very day
A feast was held, where, full of mirth,
Came, crowding thick as flowers that play
In summer winds, the young and gay
And beautiful of this bright earth.
And she was there, and 'mid the young
And beautiful stood first, alone;
Though on her gentle brow still hung
  The shadow I that morn had thrown—
The first that ever shame or woe
Had cast upon its vernal snow.

My heart was maddened—in the flush
  Of the wild revel I gave way
To all that frantic mirth, that rush
  Of desperate gaiety, which they
Who never felt how pain's excess
Can break out thus, think happiness—
Sad mimicry of mirth and life,
Whose flashes come but from the strife
Of inward passions, like the light
Struck out by clashing swords in fight.

Then, too, that juice of earth, the bane[2]
And blessing of man's heart and brain—
That draught of sorcery, which brings
Phantoms of fair, forbidden things—
Whose drops, like those of rainbows, smile
  Upon the mists that circle man,
Brightening not only earth, the while,
  But grasping heaven, too, in their span!—
Then first the fatal wine-cup rained[3]
  Its dews of darkness through my lips,
Casting whate'er of light remained
  To my lost soul into eclipse,
And filling it with such wild dreams,
Such fantasies and wrong desires,
As in the absence of heaven's beams,
Haunt us for ever, like wild-fires
That walk this earth when day retires.

Now hear the rest—our banquet done,
  I sought her in the accustomed bower,
Where late we oft, when day was gone,
And the world hushed, had met alone,
  At the same silent moonlight hour.
I found her—oh, so beautiful!
Why, why have hapless angels eyes?[4]
Or why are there not flowers to cull,
As fair as woman, in yon skies?

---

[1] 'The watchers, the offspring of Heaven.'—*Book of Enoch.* In Daniel also the angels are called watchers: 'And behold, a watcher and an holy one came down from heaven.'—iv. 13.

[2] For all that relates to the nature and attributes of angels, the time of their creation, the extent of their knowledge, and the power which they possess, or can occasionally assume, of performing such human functions as eating, drinking, etc. etc., I shall refer those who are inquisitive upon the subject to the following works:—The *Treatise upon the Celestial Hierarchy*, written under the name of Dionysius the Areopagite, in which, among much that is heavy and trifling, there are some sublime notions concerning the agency of these spiritual creatures; the questions *de Cognitione Angelorum* of St. Thomas, where he examines most prolixly into such puzzling points as 'whether angels illuminate each other,' 'whether they speak to each other,' etc. etc.; the *Thesaurus* of Coccelus, containing extracts from almost every theologian that has written on the subject; the 9th, 10th, and 11th chapters, sixth book, of *l'Histoire des Juifs*, where all the extraordinary reveries of the Rabbins about angels and demons are enumerated; the questions attributed to St. Athanasius; the treatise of Bonaventure *upon the Wings of the Seraphim*; and, lastly, the ponderous folio of Suarez de *Angelis*, where the reader will find all that has ever been fancied or reasoned, upon a subject which only *such* writers could have contrived to render so dull.

[3] Some of the circumstances of this story were suggested to me by the Eastern legend of the two angels, Harut and Marut, as it is given by Mariti, who says that the author of the Taalim founds upon it the Mahometan prohibition of wine. The Baharadanush tells the story differently.

[4] Tertullian imagines that the words of St. Paul, 'Woman ought to have a veil on her head, *on account of the angels,*' have an evident reference to the fatal effects which the beauty of women once produced upon those spiritual beings. See the strange passage of this Father *(de Virgin. Ve'andi.)*, beginning, 'Si enim propter angelos,' etc., where his editor Pamelius endeavours to save his morality, at the expense of his Latinity, by substituting the word 'excussat' for 'excusat.' Such instances of indecorum, however, are but too common throughout the Fathers; in proof of which I need only refer to some passages in the same writer's treatise, *De Anima*, to the Second and Third Books of the *Pædagogus* of Clemens Alexandrinus, and to the instances which La Mothe le Vayer has adduced from Chrysostom in his *Hexameron Rustique*, Journée 5me.

Still did her brow, as usual, turn
To her loved star, which seemed to burn
Purer than ever on that night;
While she, in looking, grew more bright,
As though that planet were an urn
From which her eyes drank liquid light.

There was a virtue in that scene,
A spell of holiness around,
Which would have—had my brain not been
Thus poisoned, maddened—held me bound,
As though I stood on God's own ground.
Even as it was, with soul all flame,
And lips that burned in their own sighs,
I stood to gaze, with awe and shame—
The memory of Eden came
Full o'er me when I saw those eyes;
And though too well each glance of mine
To the pale shrinking maiden proved
How far, alas, from aught divine,
Aught worthy of so pure a shrine,
Was the wild love with which I loved,
Yet must she, too, have seen—oh yes,
'Tis soothing but to *think* she saw—
The deep, true, soul-felt tenderness,
The homage of an angel's awe
To her, a mortal, whom pure love
Then placed above him—far above—
And all that struggle to repress
A sinful spirit's mad excess,
Which worked within me at that hour,
When—with a voice, where Passion shed
All the deep sadness of her power,
Her melancholy power—I said,
' Then be it so—if back to heaven
I must unloved, unpitied fly,
Without one blest memorial given
To soothe me in that lonely sky—
One look like those the young and fond
Give when they're parting, which would be,
Even in remembrance, far beyond
All heaven hath left of bliss for me!

'Oh, but to see that head recline
A minute on this trembling arm,
And those mild eyes look up to mine
Without a dread, a thought of harm!
To meet but once the thrilling touch
Of lips that are too fond to fear me,
Or, if that boon be all too much,
Even thus to bring their fragrance near me!

Nay, shrink not so—a look—a word—
Give them but kindly and I fly;
Already, see, my plumes have stirred,
And tremble for their home on high.
Thus be our parting—cheek to cheek—
One minute's lapse will be forgiven,
And thou, the next, shalt hear me speak
The spell that plumes my wing for heaven!'

While thus I spoke, the fearful maid,
Of me and of herself afraid,
Had shrinking stood, like flowers beneath
The scorching of the south wind's breath;
But when I named—alas, too well
I now recall, though wildered then,—
Instantly, when I named the spell,
Her brow, her eyes uprose again,
And, with an eagerness that spoke
The sudden light that o'er her broke,
'The spell, the spell!—oh, speak it now,
And I will bless thee!' she exclaimed.
Unknowing what I did, inflamed,
And lost already, on her brow
I stamped one burning kiss, and named
The mystic word, till then ne'er told
To living creature of earth's mould!
Scarce was it said, when, quick as thought,
Her lips from mine, like echo, caught
The holy sound—her hands and eyes
Were instant lifted to the skies,
And thrice to heaven she spoke it out,
With that triumphant look Faith wears
When not a cloud of fear or doubt,
A vapour from this vale of tears,
Between her and her God appears!

That very moment her whole frame
All bright and glorified became,
And at her back I saw unclose
Two wings magnificent as those
That sparkle round the eternal throne,
Whose plumes, as buoyantly she rose
Above me, in the moonbeam shone
With a pure light, which—from its hue,
Unknown upon this earth—I knew
Was light from Eden, glistening through!
Most holy vision! ne'er before
Did aught so radiant—since the day
When Lucifer, in falling, bore
The third of the bright stars away [1]—
Rise, in earth's beauty, to repair
That loss of light and glory there! [2]

---

[1] 'And his tail drew the third part of the stars of heaven, and did cast them to the earth.' Rev. xii. 4.—'Docent sancti (says Suarez) supremum angelum traxisse secum tertiam partem stellarum.'—Lib. 7. cap. 7.

[2] The idea of the Fathers was, that the vacancies occasioned in the different orders of angels by the fall were to be filled up from the human race. There is, however, another opinion, backed by papal authority, that it was only the tenth order of the Celestial Hierarchy that fell, and that, therefore, the promotions which occasionally take place from earth are intended for the completion of that *grade* alone; or, as it is explained by Salonius (*Dial. in Eccl.*)—'Decem sunt ordines angelorum, sed unus cecidit per superbiam, et idcirco boni angeli semper laborant, ut de hominibus numerus adimpleatur, et proveniat ad perfectum numerum, id est, denarium.' According to some theologians, virgins alone are admitted 'ad collegium angelorum;' but the author of the *Speculum Peregrinarum Quæstionum* rather questions this exclusive privilege:—' Hoc non videtur verum, quia multi, non virgines, ut Petrus et Magdalena. multis etiam virginibus eminentiores sunt.'—*Decad.* 2, cap. 10.

But did I tamely view her flight?
Did not I, too, proclaim out thrice
The powerful words that were, that night,—
Oh, even for Heaven too much delight!—
Again to bring us eyes to eyes,
And soul to soul in Paradise?
I did—I spoke it o'er and o'er—
I prayed, I wept, but all in vain;
For me the spell had power no more,
There seemed around me some dark chain,
Which still, as I essayed to soar,
Baffled, alas! each wild endeavour;
Dead lay my wings, as they have lain
Since that sad hour, and will remain—
So wills the offended God—for ever!

It was to yonder star I traced
Her journey up the illumined waste—
That isle in the blue firmament,
To which so oft her fancy went
In wishes and in dreams before,
And which was now—such, Purity,
Thy blest reward—ordained to be
Her home of light for evermore!
Once—or did I but fancy so?—
Even in her flight to that fair sphere,
'Mid all her spirit's new-felt glow,
A pitying look she turned below
On him who stood in darkness here;
Him whom, perhaps, if vain regret
Can dwell in heaven, she pities yet;
And oft, when looking to this dim
And distant world, remembers him.

But soon that passing dream was gone;
Farther and farther off she shone,
Till lessened to a point as small
As are those specks that yonder burn—
Those vivid drops of light, that fall
The last from day's exhausted urn.
And when at length she merged, afar,
Into her own immortal star,
And when at length my straining sight
Had caught her wing's last fading ray,
That minute from my soul the light
Of heaven and love both passed away;
And I forgot my home, my birth,
Profaned my spirit, sunk my brow,
And revelled in gross joys of earth,
Till I became—what I am now!

The Spirit bowed his head in shame;
A shame that of itself would tell—
Were there not even those breaks of flame,
Celestial, through his clouded frame—
How grand the height from which he fell!
That holy Shame which ne'er forgets
The unblenched renown it used to wear;
Whose blush remains, when Virtue sets,
To show her sunshine *has* been there.
Once only, while the tale he told,
Were his eyes lifted to behold
That happy stainless star, where she
Dwelt in her bower of purity!
One minute did he look, and then—
As though he felt some deadly pain
From its sweet light through heart and brain—
Shrunk back, and never looked again.

Who was the Second Spirit?—he
With the proud front and piercing glance,
Who seemed, when viewing heaven's expanse,
As though his far-sent eye could see
On, on into the Immensity
Behind the veils of that blue sky,
Where God's sublimest secrets lie?—
His wings, the while, though day was gone,
Flashing with many a various hue
Of light they from themselves alone,
Instinct with Eden's brightness, drew?
'Twas Rubi[1]—once among the prime
And flower of those bright creatures, named
Spirits of Knowledge,[2] who o'er Time
And Space and Thought an empire claimed,
Second alone to Him, whose light
Was, even to theirs, as day to night—
'Twixt whom and them was distance far
And wide, as would the journey be
To reach from any island star
The vague shores of Infinity!

'Twas Rubi, in whose mournful eye
Slept the dim light of days gone by;
Whose voice, though sweet, fell on the ear
Like echoes in some silent place,
When first awaked for many a year;
And when he smiled—if o'er his face
Smile ever shone—'twas like the grace
Of moonlight rainbows, fair, but wan,
The sunny life, the glory gone.

---

[1] I might have chosen, perhaps, some better name; but it is meant (like that of Zaraph in the following story) to define the particular class of spirits to which the angel belonged. The author of the Book of Enoch, who estimates at 200 the number of angels that descended upon Mount Hermon, for the purpose of making love to the women of earth, has favoured us with the names of their leader and chiefs—Samyaza, Urakabarameel, Akibeel, Tamiel, etc. etc.

In that heretical worship of angels, which prevailed to a great degree during the first ages of Christianity, to *name* them seems to have been one of the most important ceremonies; for we find it expressly forbidden in one of the canons (35th) of the Council of Laodicea, ονομαζειν τους αγγελους. Josephus, too, mentions, among the religious rites of the Essenes, their 'swearing to preserve the names of the angels,'—συντηρησιν τα των αγγελων ονοματα.—*Bell. Jud.* lib. 2, cap. 8. See upon this subject Van Dale, *de Orig. et Progress. Idololat.* cap. 9.

[2] The word cherub signifies knowledge— το γνωστικον αυτων και θεωρικον, says Dionysius. Hence it is that Ezekiel, to express the abundance of their knowledge, represents them as 'full of eyes.'

Even o'er his pride, though still the same,
A softening shade from sorrow came;
And though at times his spirit knew
 The kindlings of disdain and ire,
Short was the fitful glare they threw—
Like the last flashes, fierce but few,
 Seen through some noble pile on fire!

Such was the Angel who now broke
 The silence that had come o'er all,
When he, the Spirit that last spoke,
 Closed the sad history of his fall;
And, while a sacred lustre, flown
 For many a day, relumed his cheek,
Beautiful as in days of old;
And not those eloquent lips alone,
But every feature seemed to speak—
Thus his eventful story told:

SECOND ANGEL'S STORY.

You both remember well the day
 When unto Eden's new-made bowers,
He, whom all living things obey,
 Summoned his chief angelic powers,[1]
To witness the one wonder yet,
 Beyond man, angel, star, or sun,
He must achieve, ere He could set
 His seal upon the world as done—
To see that last perfection rise,
 That crowning of creation's birth,
When, 'mid the worship and surprise
Of circling angels, Woman's eyes
 First opened upon heaven and earth;
And from their lids a thrill was sent,
That through each living spirit went,
Like first light through the firmament!

Can you forget how gradual stole
 The fresh awakened breath of soul
Throughout her perfect form—which seemed
 To grow transparent, as there beamed
That dawn of mind within, and caught
New loveliness from each new thought?
Slow as o'er summer seas we trace
 The progress of the noon-tide air,
Dimpling its bright and silent face
Each minute into some new grace,
 And varying heaven's reflections there—
Or, like the light of evening, stealing
 O'er some fair temple, which all day
Hath slept in shadow, slow revealing
 Its several beauties, ray by ray,
Till it shines out, a thing to bless,
All full of light and loveliness.

Can you forget her blush, when round
Through Eden's lone enchanted ground

She looked—and at the sea, the skies,
 And heard the rush of many a wing,
 By God's command then vanishing,
And saw the last few angel eyes,
Still lingering—mine among the rest,—
 Reluctant leaving scene so blest?
From that miraculous hour, the fate
 Of this new glorious Being dwelt
For ever, with a spell-like weight,
 Upon my spirit—early, late,
 Whate'er I did, or dreamed, or felt,
The thought of what might yet befall
That splendid creature mixed with all.—
Nor she alone, but her whole race
 Through ages yet to come—whate'er
Of feminine, and fond, and fair,
 Should spring from that pure mind and face,
 All waked my soul's intensest care:
Their forms, souls, feelings, still to me
God's most disturbing mystery!

It was my doom—even from the first,
 When summoned with my cherub peers,
To witness the young vernal burst
 Of nature through those blooming spheres,
Those flowers of light, that sprung beneath
 The first touch of the Eternal's breath—
It was my doom still to be haunted
 By some new wonder, some sublime
And matchless work, that, for the time,
Held all my soul enchained, enchanted,
And left me not a thought, a dream,
A word, but on that only theme!

The wish to know—that endless thirst,
 Which even by quenching is awaked,
And which becomes or blessed or cursed,
 As is the fount whereat 'tis slaked—
Still urged me onward, with desire
Insatiate, to explore, inquire—
Whate'er the wondrous things might be,
That waked each new idolatry—
 Their cause, aim, source from whence they
  sprung,
Their inmost powers, as though for me
 Existence on that knowledge hung.

Oh what a vision were the stars,
 When first I saw them burn on high,
Rolling along, like living cars
 Of light, for gods to journey by!
They were my heart's first passion—days
And nights, unwearied, in their rays
Have I hung floating, till each sense
Seemed full of their bright influence.
Innocent joy! alas, how much
 Of misery had I shunned below,
Could I have still lived blest with such;
 Nor, proud and restless, burned to know
The knowledge that brings guilt and woe!
Often—so much I loved to trace
The secrets of this starry race—

---

[1] St. Augustin, upon Genesis, seems rather inclined to admit that the angels had some share (*aliquod ministerium*) in the creation of Adam and Eve.

Have I at morn and evening run
 Along the lines of radiance spun,
Like webs, between them and the sun,
Untwisting all the tangled ties
 Of light into their different dyes—
Then fleetly winged I off, in quest
 Of those, the farthest, loneliest,
That watch, like winking sentinels,
 The void, beyond which Chaos dwells,
And there, with noiseless plume, pursued
 Their track through that grand solitude,
Asking intently all and each
 What soul within their radiance dwelt,
And wishing their sweet light were speech,
 That they might tell me all they felt.

Nay, oft, so passionate my chase
 Of these resplendent heirs of space,
Oft did I follow—lest a ray
 Should 'scape me in the farthest night—
Some pilgrim Comet, on his way
 To visit distant shrines of light;
And well remember how I sung
 Exulting out, when on my sight
New worlds of stars, all fresh and young,
 As if just born of darkness, sprung!

Such was my pure ambition then,
 My sinless transport, night and morn,
Ere this still newer world of men,
 And that most fair of stars was born,
Which I, in fatal hour, saw rise
 Among the flowers of Paradise!
Thenceforth my nature all was changed,
 My heart, soul, senses turned below;
And he, who but so lately ranged
 Yon wonderful expanse, where glow
Worlds upon worlds, yet found his mind
 Even in that luminous range confined,
Now blest the humblest, meanest sod
 Of the dark earth where Woman trod!
In vain my former idols glistened
 From their far thrones; in vain these ears
To the once thrilling music listened,
 That hymned around my favourite spheres—
To earth, to earth each thought was given,
 That in this half-lost soul had birth;

Like some high mount, whose head's in heaven,
 While its whole shadow rests on earth!

Nor was it Love, even yet, that thralled
 My spirit in his burning ties;
And less, still less could it be called
 That grosser flame, round which Love flies
 Nearer and nearer, till he dies—
No, it was wonder, such as thrilled
 At all God's works my dazzled sense;
The same rapt wonder, only filled
 With passion, more profound, intense,—
A vehement, but wandering fire,
Which, though nor love, nor yet desire,
 Though through all womankind it took
 Its range, as vague as lightnings run,
Yet wanted but a touch, a look,
 To fix it burning upon *One*.

Then, too, the ever-restless zeal,
 The insatiate curiosity
To know what shapes, so fair, must feel—
To look, but once, beneath the seal
 Of so much loveliness, and see
What souls belonged to those bright eyes—
 Whether, as sunbeams find their way
Into the gem that hidden lies,
 Those looks could inward turn their ray,
 To make the soul as bright as they!
All this impelled my anxious chase,
 And still the more I saw and knew
Of Woman's fond, weak, conquering race,
 The intenser still my wonder grew.

I had beheld their First, their Eve,[1]
 Born in that splendid Paradise,
Which God made solely to receive
 The first light of her waking eyes.
I had seen purest angels lean
 In worship o'er her from above;
And man—oh, yes—had envying seen
 Proud man possessed of all her love.

I saw their happiness, so brief,
 So exquisite—her error, too,[2]
That easy trust, that prompt belief
 In what the warm heart wishes true;

---

[1] Whether Eve was created *in* Paradise or not is a question that has been productive of much doubt and controversy among the theologians. With respect to Adam, it is agreed on all sides that *he* was created *outside*; and it is accordingly asked, with some warmth, by one of the commentators, 'why should woman, the ignobler creature of the two, be created *within?*' Others, on the contrary, consider this distinction as but a fair tribute to the superior beauty and purity of women; and some, in their zeal, even seem to think that, if the scene of her creation was not already Paradise, it became so, immediately upon that event, in compliment to her. Josephus is one of those who think that Eve was formed outside; Tertullian, too, among the Fathers; and, among the Theologians, Rupertus, who, to do him justice, never misses an opportunity of putting on record his ill-will to the sex. Pererius however (and his opinion seems to be considered the most orthodox), thinks it more consistent with the order of the Mosaic narration, as well as with the sentiments of Basil and other Fathers, to conclude that Eve was created *in* Paradise.

[2] The comparative extent of Eve's delinquency, and the proportion which it bears to that of Adam, is another point which has exercised the tiresome ingenuity of the commentators; and they seem generally to agree (with the exception always of Rupertus) that, as she was not yet created when the prohibition was issued, and therefore could not have heard it (a conclusion remarkably confirmed by the inaccurate way in which she reports it to the serpent), her share in the crime of disobedience is considerably lighter than that of Adam. In corroboration of this view of the matter, Pererius remarks that it is to Adam alone the Deity addresses his reproaches

That faith in words, when kindly said,
By which the whole fond sex is led—
Mingled with (what I durst not blame,
For 'tis my own) that wish to *know*,
Sad, fatal zeal, so sure of woe;
Which, though from Heaven all pure it came,
Yet stained, misused, brought sin and shame
On her, on me, on all below!

I had seen this; had seen Man—armed
As his soul is with strength and sense—
By her first words to ruin charmed;
His vaunted reason's cold defence,
Like an ice-barrier in the ray
Of melting summer, smiled away!
Nay—stranger yet—spite of all this—
    Though by her counsels taught to err,
    Though driven from Paradise for her
(And *with* her—*that*, at least, was bliss),
Had I not heard him, ere he crossed
The threshold of that earthly heaven,
Which by her wildering smile he lost—
So quickly was the wrong forgiven—
Had I not heard him, as he pressed
The frail fond trembler to a breast
Which she had doomed to sin and strife,
Call her—think what—his Life! his Life![1]
Yes—such the love-taught name—the first
    That ruined Man to Woman gave,
Even in his outcast hour, when curst,
By her fond witchery, with that worst
And earliest boon of love—the grave!
She, who brought death into the world,
There stood before him, with the light
Of their lost Paradise still bright
Upon those sunny locks, that curled
Down her white shoulders to her feet—
So beautiful in form, so sweet
In heart and voice, as to redeem
The loss, the death of all things dear,
Except herself—and make it seem
Life, endless life, while she was near!
Could I help wondering at a creature,
Enchanted round with spells so strong—

One, to whose every thought, word, feature,
    In joy and woe, through right and wrong,
Such sweet omnipotence Heaven gave,
To bless or ruin, curse or save?

Nor did the marvel cease with her—
    New Eves in all her daughters came,
As strong to charm, as weak to err,
As sure of man through praise and blame,
    Whate'er they brought him, pride or shame,
Their still unreasoning worshipper—
    And, wheresoe'er they smiled, the same
    Enchantresses of soul and frame,
Into whose hands, from first to last,
This world, with all its destinies,
Devotedly by Heaven seems cast,
To save or damn it as they please!
Oh, 'tis not to be told how long,
How restlessly I sighed to find
Some *one* from out that shining throng,
Some abstract of the form and mind
Of the whole matchless sex, from which,
In my own arms beheld, possessed,
I might learn all the powers to witch,
To warm, and (if my fate unblessed
Would have it) ruin, of the rest!
Into whose inward soul and sense
I might descend, as doth the bee
Into the flower's deep heart, and thence
Rifle, in all its purity,
The prime, the quintessence, the whole
Of wondrous Woman's frame and soul!

At length, my burning wish, my prayer
(For such—oh, what will tongues not dare,
When hearts go wrong?—this lip preferred)—
At length my ominous prayer was heard—
But whether heard in heaven or hell,
Listen—and thou wilt know *too* well.

There was a maid, of all who move
Like visions o'er this orb, most fit
To be a bright young angel's love,
Herself so bright, so exquisite!

---

for having eaten of the forbidden tree, because to Adam alone the order had been originally promulgated. So far, indeed, does the gallantry of another commentator, Hugh de St. Victor, carry him, that he looks upon the words, 'I will put enmity between thee and the woman,' as a proof that the sex was from that moment enlisted into the service of Heaven, and the chief foe and obstacle which the Spirit of Evil would have to contend with in his inroads on this world:—' Si deinceps Eva inimica Diabo'o, ergo fuit grata et amica Deo.'

[1] Chavah (or, as it is in the Latin version, Eva) has the same signification as the Greek, Zoe.

Epiphanius, among others, is not a little surprised at the application of such a name to Eve, so immediately, too, after that awful denunciation of death, 'Dust thou art,' etc. etc. Some of the commentators think that it was meant as a sarcasm, and spoken by Adam, in the first bitterness of his heart,—in the same spirit of irony (says Pererius) as that of the Greeks in calling their Friues, Eumenidus, or Gentle. But the Bishop of Chalon rejects this supposition:—' Explodend! sane qui id nominis ab Adamo per Ironiam inditum uxori suæ putant; atque quod mortis causa esset, amaro joco vitam appellasse.'

With a similar feeling of spleen against women, some of these 'distillateurs des Saintes Lettres' (as Bayle calls them), in rendering the text 'I will make him a help *meet for him*,' translate these last words '*against* or *contrary* to him' (a meaning which, it appears, the original will bear), and represent them as prophetic of those contradictions and perplexities which men experience from women in this life.

It is rather strange that these two instances of perverse commentatorship should have escaped the researches of Bayle, in his curious article upon Eve. He would have found another subject of discussion, equally to his taste, in Gataker's whimsical dissertation upon Eve's knowledge of the *πχρι ὑρανταν*, and upon the notion of Epiphanius, that it was taught her in a special revelation from heaven.—*Miscellan.* lib. ii. cap. 3, p. 200

The pride, too, of her step, as light
  Along the unconscious earth she went,
Seemed that of one born with a right
  To walk some heavenlier element,
And tread in places where her feet
  A star at every step should meet.
'Twas not alone that loveliness
  By which the wildered sense is caught—
Of lips whose very breath could bless—
  Of playful blushes, that seemed nought
But luminous escapes of thought—
Of eyes that, when by anger stirred,
  Were fire itself, but, at a word
Of tenderness, all soft became,
As though they could, like the sun's bird,
  Dissolve away in their own flame—
Of form, as pliant as the shoots
  Of a young tree in vernal flower;
Yet round and glowing as the fruits
  That drop from it in summer's hour—
'Twas not alone this loveliness
  That falls to loveliest woman's share,
Though even here her form could spare
From its own beauty's rich excess
  Enough to make all others fair—
But 'twas the Mind, sparkling about
Through her whole frame—the soul brought out
To light each charm, yet independent
  Of what it lighted, as the sun
That shines on flowers, would be resplendent
  Were there no flowers to shine upon—
'Twas this, all this in one combined,
  The unnumbered looks and arts that form
The glory of young womankind
  Taken in their first fusion, warm,
Ere time had chilled a single charm,
And stamped with such a seal of Mind,
  As gave to beauties, that might be
Too sensual else, too unrefined,
  The impress of divinity!

'Twas this—a union, which the hand
  Of Nature kept for her alone,
Of everything most playful, bland,
Voluptuous, spiritual, grand,
  In angel-natures and her own—
Oh! this it was that drew me nigh
One who seemed kin to Heaven as I,
  My bright twin sister of the sky—
One in whose love, I felt, were given
  The mixed delights of either sphere,
All that the spirit seeks in heaven,
  And all the senses burn for here!

Had we—but hold—hear every part
  Of our sad tale, spite of the pain
Remembrance gives, when the fixed dart
  Is stirred thus in the wound again—
Hear every step, so full of bliss,
  And yet so ruinous, that led
Down to the last dark precipice,
  Where perished both—the fallen, the dead!

From the first hour she caught my sight,
I never left her—day and night
Hovering unseen around her way,
  And 'mid her loneliest musings near,
I soon could track each thought that lay
  Gleaming within her heart, as clear
As pebbles within brooks appear;
And there, among the countless things
  That keep young hearts for ever glowing,
Vague wishes, fond imaginings,
  Love-dreams, as yet no object knowing—
Light, winged hopes, that come when bid,
  And rainbow joys that end in weeping,
And passions among pure thoughts hid,
  Like serpents under flowerets sleeping—
'Mong all these feelings, felt where'er
  Young hearts are beating, I saw there
Proud thoughts, aspirings high—beyond
Whate'er yet dwelt in soul so fond—
Glimpses of glory, far away
Into the bright vague future given,
And fancies free and grand, whose play,
  Like that of eaglets, is near heaven!
With this, too—what a soul and heart
To fall beneath the tempter's art!—
A zeal for knowledge, such as ne'er
Enshrined itself in form so fair,
Since that first fatal hour when Eve,
  With every fruit of Eden blessed,
Save only *one*, rather than leave
  That one unknown, lost all the rest.

It was in dreams that first I stole
  With gentle mastery o'er her mind—
In that rich twilight of the soul,
  When Reason's beam, half hid behind
The clouds of sense, obscurely gilds
Each shadowy shape that Fancy builds—
'Twas then, by that soft light, I brought
  Vague, glimmering visions to her view—
Catches of radiance, lost when caught,
  Bright labyrinths that led to nought,
And vistas with a void seen through—
Dwellings of bliss, that opening shone,
  Then closed, dissolved, and left no trace—
All that, in short, could tempt Hope on,
  But give her wing no resting-place;
Myself the while, with brow as yet
Pure as the young moon's coronet,
Through every dream still in her sight,
  The enchanter of each mocking scene
Who gave the hope, then brought the blight,
Who said, 'Behold yon world of light!'
  Then sudden dropped a veil between.

At length, when I perceived each thought,
Waking or sleeping, fixed on nought
But these illusive scenes, and me,
The phantom, who thus came and went,
In half revealments, only meant
  To madden curiosity—
When by such various arts I found
Her fancy to its utmost wound,

One night—'twas in a holy spot,
Which she for prayer had chosen—a grot
Of purest marble, built below
Her garden beds, through which a glow
From lamps invisible then stole,
   Brightly pervading all the place—
Like that mysterious light the soul,
   Itself unseen, sheds through the face—
There, at her altar while she knelt,
And all that woman ever felt,
   When God and man both claimed her sighs—
Every warm thought that ever dwelt,
   Like summer clouds, 'twixt earth and skies,
Too pure to fall, too gross to rise,
   Spoke in her gestures, tones, and eyes,
Then, as the mystic light's soft ray
Grew softer still, as though its ray
Was breathed from her, I heard her say:—

'Oh, idol of my dreams! whate'er
   Thy nature be—human, divine,
Or but half heavenly [1]—still too fair,
   Too heavenly to be ever mine!

Wonderful Spirit, who dost make
   Slumber so lovely that it seems
No longer life to live awake,
   Since Heaven itself descends in dreams.

Why do I ever lose thee? why—
   When on thy realms and thee I gaze—
Still drops that veil, which I could die,
   Oh gladly, but one hour to raise?

Long ere such miracles as thou
   And thine came o'er my thoughts, a thirst
For light was in this soul, which now
   Thy looks have into passion nursed.

There's nothing bright above, below,
   In sky—earth—ocean, that this breast
Doth not intensely burn to know,
   And thee, thee, thee, o'er all the rest!

Then come, oh Spirit, from behind
   The curtains of thy radiant home,
Whether thou wouldst as God be shrined,
   Or loved and clasped as mortal, come!

Bring all thy dazzling wonders here,
   That I may waking know and see;
Or waft me hence to thy own sphere,
   Thy heaven or—ay, even *that* with thee!

Demon or God, who hold'st the book
   Of knowledge spread beneath thine eye,
Give me, with thee, but one bright look
   Into its leaves, and let me die!

By those ethereal wings, whose way
   Lies through an element, so fraught
With floating Mind, that, as they play,
   Their every movement is a thought!

By that most precious hair, between
   Whose golden clusters the sweet wind
Of Paradise so late hath been,
   And left its fragrant soul behind!

By those impassioned eyes, that melt
   Their light into the inmost heart,
Like sunset in the waters, felt
   As molten fire through every part,—

I do implore thee, oh most bright
   And worshipped Spirit, shine but o'er
My waking wondering eyes this night,
   This one blest night—I ask no more!'

Exhausted, breathless, as she said
These burning words, her languid head
Upon the altar's steps she cast,
As if that brain-throb were its last—
Till, startled by the breathing, nigh,
Of lips, that echoed back her sigh,
Sudden her brow again she raised,
   And there, just lighted on the shrine,
Behold me—not as I had blazed
   Around her, full of light divine,
In her late dreams, but softened down
Into more mortal grace—my crown
Of flowers, too radiant for this world,
   Left hanging on yon starry steep;
My wings shut up, like banners furled,
   When Peace hath put their pomp to sleep;
Or like autumnal clouds, that keep
Their lightnings sheathed, rather than mar
The dawning hour of some young star—

---

[1] In an article upon the Fathers, which appeared some years since in the *Edinburgh Review* (No. xlvii.), and of which I have made some little use in these notes (having that claim over it—as 'quiddam notum *propriumque*'—which Lucretius gives to the cow over the calf), there is the following remark: 'The belief of an intercourse between angels and women, founded upon a false version of a text in Genesis, is one of those extravagant notions of St. Justin and other Fathers, which show how little they had yet purified themselves from the grossness of heathen mythology, and in how many respects their heaven was but Olympus with other names. Yet we can hardly be angry with them for this one error, when we recollect that possibly to their enamoured angels we owe the fanciful world of sylphs and gnomes, and that at this moment we might have wanted Pope's most exquisite poem, if the version of the LXX. had translated the Book of Genesis correctly.'

The following is one among many passages which may be adduced from the Comte de Gabalis, in confirmation of this remark:—' Ces enfans du ciel engendrèrent les géans fameux, s'étant fait aimer aux filles des hommes; et les mauvais cabalistes Joseph et Philo (comme tous les Juifs sont ignorans), et après eux tous les auteurs que j'ai nommés tont à l'heure, ont dit que c'étoit des anges, et n'ont pas su que c'étaits les sylphes et les autres peuples des élémens, qui, sous le nom d'enfans d'Eloïm, sont distingués des enfans des hommes.'— See Entret. Second.

And nothing left but what beseemed
    The accessible, though glorious mate
Of mortal woman—whose eyes beamed
    Back upon hers, as passionate:
Whose ready heart brought flame for flame,
Whose sin, whose madness was the same,
And whose soul lost, in that one hour,
    For her and for her love—oh more
Of Heaven's light than even the power
    Of Heaven itself could now restore!

And yet that hour!—

                    The Spirit here
Stopped in his utterance, as if words
Gave way beneath the wild career
Of his then rushing thoughts—like chords,
Midway in some enthusiast's song,
Breaking beneath a touch too strong—
While the clenched hand upon the brow
Told how remembrance throbbed there now!
But soon 'twas o'er—that casual blaze
From the sunk fire of other days,
That relic of a flame, whose burning
Had been too fierce to be relumed,
Soon passed away, and the youth, turning
To his bright listeners, thus resumed:—

Days, months elapsed, and, though what most
    On earth I sighed for was mine, all,—
Yet—was I happy? God, thou know'st
    Howe'er they smile, and feign, and boast,
    What happiness is theirs, who fall!
'Twas bitterest anguish—made more keen
Even by the love, the bliss, between
Whose throbs it came, like gleams of hell
    In agonizing cross-light given
Athwart the glimpses they who dwell
    In purgatory catch of heaven!
The only feeling that to me
Seemed joy, or rather my sole rest
From aching misery, was to see
My young, proud, blooming Lilis blest—
She, the fair fountain of all ill
To my lost soul—whom yet its thirst
Fervidly panted after still,
And found the charm fresh as at first!—
To see *her* happy—to reflect
Whatever beams still round me played
Of former pride, of glory wrecked,
On her, my Moon, whose light I made,
And whose soul worshipped even my shade—

This was, I own, enjoyment—this
My sole, last lingering glimpse of bliss.
And proud she was, bright creature!—proud,
    Beyond what even most queenly stirs
In woman's heart, nor would have bowed
    That beautiful young brow of hers
To aught beneath the First above,
So high she deemed her Cherub's love!

Then, too, that passion, hourly growing
    Stronger and stronger—to which even
Her love, at times, gave way—of knowing
    Everything strange in earth and heaven;
Not only what God loves to show,
But all that He hath sealed below
In darkness for man *not* to know—
Even this desire, alas, ill-starred
    And fatal as it was, I sought
To feed each minute, and unbarred
    Such realms of wonder on her thought,
As ne'er, till then, had let their light
Escape on any mortal's sight!
In the deep earth—beneath the sea—
    Through caves of fire—through wilds of air—
Wherever sleeping Mystery
    Had spread her curtain, we were there—
Love still beside us, as we went,
At home in each new element,
And sure of worship everywhere!

Then first was Nature taught to lay
    The wealth of all her kingdoms down
At woman's worshipped feet, and say,
    'Bright creature, this is all thine own!'
Then first were diamonds caught—like eyes
Shining in darkness—by surprise,
And made to light the conquering way
Of proud young Beauty with their ray.

Then, too, the pearl from out its shell,
    Unsightly in the sunless sea
(As 'twere a spirit forced to dwell
    In form unlovely), was set free,
And round the neck of woman throw
A light it lent and borrowed too.
For never did this maid, whate'er
    The ambition of the hour, forget
Her sex's pride in being fair,
Nor that adornment, tasteful, rare,
    Which makes the mighty magnet, set
In Woman's form,[2] more mighty yet.

---

[1] Tertullian traces all the chief luxuries of female attire, the necklaces, armlets, rouge, and the black powder for the eye-lashes, to the researches of these fallen angels into the inmost recesses of nature, and the discoveries they were in consequence enabled to make of all that could embellish the beauty of their earthly favourites. The passage is so remarkable that I shall give it entire:—' Nam et illi qui ea constituerant, damnati in pœnam mortis deputantur: illi scilicet angeli, qui ad filias hominum de cœlo ruerunt, ut hæc quoque ignominia fœminæ accedat. Nam cum et materias quasdam bene occultas et artes plerasque non bene revelatas, sæculo multo magis imperito prodidissent (siquidem et metallorum opera nudaverant, et herbarum ingenia traduxerant et incantationum vires provulgaverant, et omnem curiositatem usque ad stellarum interpretationem designaverant) proprie et quasi peculiariter fœminis instrumentum istud muliebris gloriæ contulerunt: lumina lapillorum quibus monilia variantur, et circulos ex auro quibus brachia arctantur; et medicamenta ex fuco, quibus lanæ colorantur, et illum ipsum nigrum pulvereum, quo oculorum exordia producuntur.' *De Habitu Mulieb*. cap. 2.—See him also, *De Cultu Fœm*. cap. 10.

[2] The same figure, as applied to female attractions, occurs in a singular passage of St. Basil, of which the

Nor was there aught within the range
  Of my swift wing in sea or air,
Of beautiful, or grand, or strange,
  That, quickly as her wish could change,
  I did not seek with such fond care,
That when I've seen her look above
  At some bright star admiringly,
I've said, 'Nay, look not there, my love,
  Alas, I *cannot* give it thee!'[1]

But not alone the wonders found
  Through Nature's realm — the unveiled, material,
Visible glories that hang round,
Like lights, through her enchanted ground—
But whatsoe'er unseen, ethereal,
Dwells far away from human sense,
Wrapped in its own intelligence—
The mystery of that Fountainhead,
  From which all vital spirit runs,
All breath of life where'er 'tis shed,
  Through men or angels, flowers or suns—
The workings of the Almighty Mind,
When first o'er Chaos he designed
The outlines of this world; and through
That spread of darkness—like the bow,
Called out of rain-clouds, hue by hue—
  Saw the grand gradual picture grow!—
The covenant with human-kind
Which God has made—the chains of Fate
He round himself and them hath twined,
  Till his high task he consummate—
Till good from evil, love from hate,
Shall be worked out through sin and pain,
And Fate shall loose her iron chain,
And all be free, be bright again!

Such were the deep-drawn mysteries,
  And some, perhaps, even more profound,
More wildering to the mind than these,
  Which—far as woman's thought could sound,
Or a fallen outlawed spirit reach—
  She dared to learn, and I to teach.
Till—filled with such unearthly lore,
  And mingling the pure light it brings
With much that Fancy had, before,
  Shed in false tinted glimmerings—
The enthusiast girl spoke out, as one
  Inspired, among her own dark race,
Who from their altars, in the sun
Left standing half adorned, would run
  To gaze upon her holier face.

And, though but wild the things she spoke,
  Yet, 'mid that play of error's smoke
Into fair shapes by fancy curled,
Some gleams of pure religion broke—
Glimpses that have not yet awoke,
  But startled the still dreaming world!
Oh! many a truth, remote, sublime,
  Which God would from the minds of men
Have kept concealed, till his own time,
  Stole out in these revealments then—
Revealments dim, that have fore-run,
By ages, the bright, Saving One![2]
Like that imperfect dawn, or light
  Escaping from the Zodiac's signs,
Which makes the doubtful east half bright
  Before the real morning shines!

Thus did some moons of bliss go by—
  Of bliss to her, who saw but love
And knowledge throughout earth and sky;
  To whose enamoured soul and eye,
I seemed, as is the sun on high,
  The light of all below, above,
The spirit of sea, land, and air,
  Whose influence, felt everywhere,
Spread from its centre, her own heart,
Even to the world's extremest part—
While through that world her reinless mind
  Had now careered so fast and far,
That earth itself seemed left behind,
  And her proud fancy, unconfined,
  Already saw heaven's gates ajar!

Happy enthusiast! still, oh still,
Spite of my own heart's mortal chill,
Spite of that double-fronted sorrow,
  Which looks at once before and back,
Beholds the yesterday, the morrow,
  And sees both comfortless, both black—
Spite of all this, I could have still
In her delight forgot all ill;
Or, if pain *would* not be forgot,
At least have borne and murmured not.
When thoughts of an offended Heaven,
  Of sinfulness, which I—even I,
While down its steep most headlong driven,—
  Well knew could never be forgiven,
Came o'er me with an agony
Beyond all reach of mortal woe,—
A torture kept for those who know,
Know everything, and, worst of all,
Know and love virtue while they fall!—

---

following is the conclusion:—Διὰ τῶν τοιούτων κατὰ τοῦ ἀρρένος αὐτῆς φυσικήν δυναστείαν, ὡς εὔμορφος, φησὶ, παρθενικῆ μαγνήτις, τοῦτο πρός ἑαυτὸν μαγγανεῦει.—*De Vera Virginitat.* tom. i. p. 727. It is but fair, however, to add, that Hermant, the biographer of Basil, has pronounced this most unsanctified treatise to be spurious.

[1] I am aware that this happy saying of Lord Albemarle's loses much of its grace and playfulness by being put into the mouth of any but a human lover.

[2] It is the opinion of some of the Fathers, that the knowledge which the heathens possessed of the providence of God, a future state, and other sublime doctrines of Christianity, was derived from the premature revelations of these fallen angels to the women of earth. Clemens Alexandrinus is one of those who suppose that the knowledge of such sublime doctrines was derived from the disclosure of the angels.—*Stromat.* lib. v. p. 48. To the same source Cassianus and others trace all impious and daring sciences, such as magic, alchemy, etc. 'From the fallen angels (says Zosimus) came all that miserable knowledge which is of no use to the soul.'—Πάντα τὰ πονηρὰ καὶ μηδὲν ὠφελοῦντα τὴν ψυχήν.—*Ap. Photium.*

THE LOVES OF THE ANGELS.

Even then her presence had the power
  To soothe, to warm,—nay, even to bless—
If ever bliss could graft its flower
  On stem so full of bitterness—
Even then her glorious smile to me
Brought warmth and radiance, if not balm,
Like moonlight on a troubled sea,
  Brightening the storm it cannot calm.

Oft, too, when that disheartening fear,
  Which all who love beneath yon sky
Feel, when they gaze on what is dear—
  The dreadful thought that it must die!
That desolating thought, which comes
Into men's happiest hours and homes;
Whose melancholy boding flings
Death's shadow o'er the brightest things,
Sicklies the infant's bloom, and spreads
The grave beneath young lovers' heads!
This fear, so sad to all—to me
Most full of sadness, from the thought
That I must still live on, when she
Would, like the snow that on the sea
  Fell yesterday, in vain be sought—
That Heaven to me the final seal
  Of all earth's sorrow would deny,
And I eternally must feel
  The death-pang, without power to die!
Even this, her fond endearments—fond
As ever twisted the sweet bond
'Twixt heart and heart—could charm away:
Before her look no clouds would stay,
Or, if they did, their gloom was gone,
Their darkness put a glory on!
There seemed a freshness in her breath,
Beyond the reach, the power of death!
And then, her voice—oh, who could doubt
That 'twould for ever thus breathe out
A music, like the harmony
Of the tuned orbs, too sweet to die!
While in her lip's awakening touch
There thrilled a life ambrosial—such
As mantles in the fruit steeped through
With Eden's most delicious dew—
Till I could almost think, though known
And loved as human, they had grown
By bliss, celestial as my own!
But 'tis not, 'tis not for the wrong,
The guilty, to be happy long;
And she, too, now, had sunk within
The shadow of a tempter's sin—
  Too deep for even *her* soul to shun
The desolation it brings down!

Listen, and if a tear there be
Left in your hearts, weep it for me.

'Twas on the evening of a day,
Which we in love had dreamed away;
In that same garden, where, beneath
The silent earth, stripped of my wreath,
And furling up those wings, whose light
For mortal gaze were else too bright,
I first had stood before her sight;

And found myself—oh, ecstasy,
  Which even in pain I ne'er forget—
Worshipped as only God should be,
  And loved as never man was yet!
In that same garden we were now,
  Thoughtfully side by side reclining,
Her eyes turned upward, and her brow
  With its own silent fancies shining.

It was an evening bright and still
  As ever blushed on wave or bower,
Smiling from Heaven, as if nought ill
  Could happen in so sweet an hour.
Yet, I remember, both grew sad
In looking at that light—even she,
Of heart so fresh, and brow so glad,
Felt the mute hour's solemnity,
And thought she saw, in that repose,
  The death-hour not alone of light,
But of this whole fair world—the close
  Of all things beautiful and bright—
The last grand sunset, in whose ray
Nature herself died calm away!

At length, as if some thought, awaking
  Suddenly, sprung within her breast—
Like a young bird, when daylight breaking
  Startles him from his dreamy nest—
She turned upon me her dark eyes,
  Dilated into that full shape
They took in joy, reproach, surprise,
  As if to let more soul escape,
And, playfully as on my head
Her white hand rested, smiled and said:—

'I had, last night, a dream of thee,
  Resembling those divine ones, given,
Like preludes to sweet minstrelsy,
  Before thou cam'st, thyself, from heaven.

The same rich wreath was on thy brow,
  Dazzling as if of starlight made;
And these wings, lying darkly now,
  Like meteors round thee flashed and played

All bright as in those happy dreams
  Thou stood'st, a creature to adore
No less than love, breathing out beams,
  As flowers do fragrance, at each pore!

Sudden I felt thee draw me near
  To thy pure heart, where, fond'y placed,
I seemed within the atmosphere
  Of that exhaling light embraced;

And, as thou held'st me there, the flame
  Passed from thy heavenly soul to mine,
Till—oh, too blissful!—I became,
  Like thee, all spirit, all divine.

Say, why did dream so bright come o'er me,
  If, now I wake, 'tis faded, gone?
When will my Cherub shine before me
  Thus radiant, as in heaven he shone?

When shall I, waking, be allowed
  To gaze upon those perfect charms,
And hold thee thus, without a cloud,
  A chill of earth, within my arms?

Oh what a pride to say, This, this
  Is my own Angel—all divine,
And pure, and dazzling as he is,
  And fresh from heaven, he's mine, he's mine!

Think'st thou, were Lilis in thy place,
  A creature of yon lofty skies,
She would have hid one single grace,
  One glory from her lover's eyes?

No, no: then, if thou lov'st like me,
  Shine out, young Spirit, in the blaze
Of thy most proud divinity,
  Nor think thou'lt wound this mortal gaze.

Too long have I looked doating on
  Those ardent eyes, intense even thus—
Too near the stars themselves have gone,
  To fear aught grand or luminous.

Then doubt me not—oh, who can say
  But that this dream may yet come true,
And my blest spirit drink thy ray
  Till it becomes all heavenly too?

Let me this once but feel the flame
  Of those spread wings, the very pride
Will change my nature, and this frame
  By the mere touch be deified!'

Thus spoke the maid, as one not used
  To be by man or God refused—
As one, who felt her influence o'er
  All creatures, whatsoe'er they were,
And, though to heaven she could not soar,
  At least would bring down heaven to her!

Little did she, alas, or I—
  Even I, whose soul, but half-way yet
Immerged in sin's obscurity,
  Was as the planet where we lie,
O'er half whose disk the sun is set—
Little did we foresee the fate,
  The dreadful—how can it be told?
Oh God! such anguish to relate
  Is o'er again to feel, behold!
But, charged as 'tis, my heart must speak
  Its sorrow out, or it will break!
Some dark misgivings had, I own,
  Passed for a moment through my breast—
Fears of some danger, vague, unknown,
  To one, or both—something unblessed
  To happen from this proud request.
But soon these boding fancies fled;
  Nor saw I ought that could forbid
My full revealment, save the dread
  Of that first dazzle, that unhid
  And bursting glory on a lid

Untried in heaven—and even this glare
  She might, by love's own nursing care,
  Be, like young eagles, taught to bear.
For well I knew the lustre shed
From my rich wings, when proudliest spread,
  Was, in its nature, lambent, pure,
    And innocent as is the light
  The glow-worm hangs out to allure
    Her mate to her green bower at night.
Oft had I, in the mid-air, swept
Through clouds in which the lightning slept,
  As in his lair, ready to spring,
  Yet waked him not—though from my wing
  A thousand sparks fell glittering!
Oft too when round me from above
  The feathered snow (which, for its whiteness,
  In my pure days I used to love)
Fell like the moultings of Heaven's Dove,—
  So harmless, though so full of brightness,
Was my brow's wreath, that it would shake
From off its flowers each downy flake
  As delicate, unmelted, fair,
  And cool as they had fallen there!

Nay even with Lilis—had I not
  Around her sleep in splendour come—
Hung o'er each beauty, nor forgot
  To print my radiant lips on some?
And yet, at morn, from that repose,
  Had she not waked, unscathed and bright,
As doth the pure, unconscious rose,
  Though by the fire-fly kissed all night?
Even when the rays I scattered stole
Intensest to her dreaming soul,
No thrill disturbed the insensate frame—
So subtle, so refined that flame,
  Which, rapidly as lightnings melt
  The blade within the unharmed sheath,
  Can, by the outward form unfelt,
  Reach and dissolve the soul beneath!

Thus having (as, alas, deceived
By my sin's blindness, I believed)
No cause for dread, and those black eyes
  There fixed upon me, eagerly
As if the unlocking of the skies
  Then waited but a sign from me—
  How was I to refuse? how say
  One word that in her heart could stir
A fear, a doubt, but that each ray
  I brought from heaven belonged to her?
Slow from her side I rose, while she
Stood up, too, mutely, tremblingly,
But not with fear—all hope, desire,
  She waited for the awful boon,
Like priestesses, with eyes of fire
  Watching the rise of the full moon,
  Whose beams—they know, yet cannot shun—
  Will madden them when looked upon!

Of all my glories, the bright crown,
  Which, when I last from heaven came down,
  I left—see, where those clouds afar
  Sail through the west—there hangs it yet,

Shining remote, more like a star
  Than a fallen angel's coronet—
Of all my glories, this alone
  Was wanting; but the illumined brow,
The curls, like tendrils that had grown
  Out of the sun—the eyes, that now
Had love's light added to their own,
  And shed a blaze, before unknown
Even to themselves—the unfolded wings,
  From which, as from two radiant springs,
Sparkles fell fast around, like spray—
  All I could bring of heaven's array,
Of that rich panoply of charms
  A cherub moves in, on the day
Of his best pomp, I now put on;
  And, proud that in her eyes I shone
Thus glorious, glided to her arms,
  Which still (though) at a sight so splendid
Her dazzled brow had instantly
Sunk on her breast) were wide extended
  To clasp the form she durst not see!

Great God! how *could* thy vengeance light
So bitterly on one so bright?
How could the hand, that gave such charms,
Blast them again, in love's own arms?
Scarce had I touched her shrinking frame,
  When—oh most horrible!—I felt
That every spark of that pure flame—
  Pure, while among the stars I dwelt—
Was now by my transgression turned
Into gross, earthly fire, which burned,
Burned all it touched, as fast as eye
  Could follow the fierce ravening flashes,
Till there—oh God, I still ask why
  Such doom was hers?—I saw her lie
Blackening within my arms to ashes!
Those cheeks, a glory but to see—
  Those lips, whose touch was what the first
Fresh cup of immortality
  Is to a new-made angel's thirst!
Those arms, within whose gentle round,
My heart's horizon, the whole bound
Of its hope, prospect, heaven was found!
  Which, even in this dread moment, fond
As when they first were round me cast,
Loosed not in death the fatal bond,
  But, burning, held me to the last—
That hair, from under whose dark veil,
  The snowy neck, like a white sail
At moonlight seen 'twixt wave and wave,
  Shone out by gleams—that hair, to save
But one of whose long glossy wreaths,
I could have died ten thousand deaths!—
All, all, that seemed, one minute since,
So full of love's own redolence,
  Now, parched and black, before me lay,
Withering in agony away;
  And mine, oh misery! mine the flame,
From which this desolation came—
  And I the fiend, whose foul caress
Had blasted all that loveliness!

'Twas maddening, 'twas—but hear even worse—
  Had death, death only, been the curse
I brought upon her—had the doom
  But ended here, when her young bloom
Lay in the dust, and did the spirit
No part of that fell curse inherit,
'Twere not so dreadful—but, come near—
  Too shocking 'tis for earth to hear—
Just when her eyes, in fading, took
  Their last, keen, agonized farewell,
And looked in mine with—oh, that look!
  Avenging Power, whate'er the hell
Thou may'st to human souls assign,
  The memory of that look is mine!—
In her last struggle, on my brow
  Her ashy lips a kiss impressed,
So withering!—I feel it now—
  'Twas fire—but fire, even more unblessed
Than was my own, and like that flame,
  The angels shudder but to name,
Hell's everlasting element!
  Deep, deep it pierced into my brain,
Maddening and torturing as it went,
  And here—see here, the mark, the stain
It left upon my front—burnt in
  By that last kiss of love and sin—
A brand, which even the wreathèd pride
Of these bright curls, still forced aside
By its foul contact, cannot hide!

But is it thus, dread Providence—
  Can it, indeed, be thus, that she,
Who, but for one proud, fond offence,
  Had honoured Heaven itself, should be
Now doomed—I cannot speak it—no,
  Merciful God! it *is* not so—
Never could lips divine have said
  The fiat of a fate so dread.
And yet, that look—that look, so fraught
  With more than anguish, with despair—
That new, fierce fire, resembling nought
  In heaven or earth—this scorch I bear!—
Oh,—for the first time that these knees
  Have bent before thee since my fall,
Great Power, if ever thy decrees
  Thou couldst for prayer like mine re-
    call,
Pardon that spirit, and on me,
  On me, who taught her pride to err,
Shed out each drop of agony
  Thy burning phial keeps for her!
See, too, where low beside me kneel
  Two other outcasts, who, though gone
And lost themselves, yet dare to feel
  And pray for that poor mortal one.
Alas, too well, too well they know
  The pain, the penitence, the woe
That Passion brings down on the best,
  The wisest and the loveliest.—
Oh, who is to be saved, if such
  Bright erring souls are not forgiven?
So loth they wander, and so much
  Their very wanderings lean towards heaven!

Again I cry, Just God, transfer
  That creature's sufferings all to me—
  Mine, mine the guilt, the torment be—
  To save one minute's pain to her,
    Let mine last all eternity!

———

He paused, and to the earth bent down
  His throbbing head; while they, who felt
That agony as 'twere their own,
  Those angel youths, beside him knelt,
And, in the night's still silence there,
While mournfully each wandering air
Played in those plumes, that never more
To their lost home in heaven must soar,
Breathed inwardly the voiceless prayer,
Unheard by all but Mercy's ear—
And which if Mercy *did not* hear,
Oh, God would not be what this bright
  And glorious universe of his,
This world of beauty, goodness, light,
  And endless love, proclaims He *is!*

Not long they knelt, when, from a wood
  That crowned that airy solitude,
They heard a low, uncertain sound,
  As from a lute, that just had found
Some happy theme, and murmured round
The new-born fancy—with fond tone,
Like that of ringdove o'er her brood—
Scarce thinking aught so sweet its own!
Till soon a voice that matched as well
  That gentle instrument, as suits
The sea-air to an ocean-shell
  (So kin its spirit to the lute's),
Tremblingly followed the soft strain,
Interpreting its joy, its pain,
  And lending the light wings of words
To many a thought that else had lain
Unfledged and mute among the chords.

All started at the sound—but chief
  The third young Angel, in whose face,
Though faded like the others, grief
  Had left a gentler, holier trace;
As if, even yet, through pain and ill,
Hope had not quit him—as if still
  Her precious pearl in sorrow's cup,
  Unmelted at the bottom lay,
To shine again, when, all drunk up,
  The bitterness should pass away.
Chiefly did he, though in his eyes
There shone more pleasure than surprise,
Turn to the wood, from whence that sound
Of solitary sweetness broke,
Then listening, looked delighted round
  To his bright peers, while thus it spoke:—

'Come, pray with me, my seraph love,
  My angel-lord, come pray with me;
In vain to-night my lip hath strove
  To send one holy prayer above—

The knee may bend, the lip may move,
  But pray I cannot without thee!
I've fed the altar in my bower
  With droppings from the incense-tree;
I've sheltered it from wind and shower,
  But dim it burns the livelong hour,
As if, like me, it had no power
  Of life or lustre, without thee!

'A boat at midnight sent alone
  To drift upon the moonless sea,
A lute, whose leading chord is gone,
  A wounded bird, that hath but one
Imperfect wing to soar upon,
  Are like what I am without thee!

'Then ne'er, my spirit-love, divide,
  In life or death, thyself from me;
But when again, in sunny pride,
  Thou walk'st through Eden, let me glide,
A prostrate shadow, by thy side—
  Oh, happier thus than without thee!'

The song had ceased, when from the wood—
  Where curving down that airy height,
It reached the spot on which they stood—
  There suddenly shone out a light
From a clear lamp, which, as it blazed
Across the brow of one who raised
The flame aloft (as if to throw
  Its light upon that group below),
Displayed two eyes, sparkling between
The dusky leaves, such as are seen
  By fancy only, in those faces,
  That haunt a poet's walk at even,
Looking from out their leafy places
  Upon his dreams of love and heaven.
'Twas but a moment—the blush, brought
O'er all her features at the thought
  Of being seen thus late, alone,
By any but the eyes she sought,
  Had scarcely for an instant shone
Through the dark leaves when she was gone—
  Gone, like a meteor that o'erhead
Suddenly shines, and, ere we've said,
'Look, look, how beautiful!'—'tis fled.

Yet, ere she went, the words, 'I come,
  I come, my Nama,' reached her ear,
  In that kind voice, familiar, dear,
Which tells of confidence, of home,—
Of habit, that hath drawn hearts near,
  Till they grow *one*—of faith sincere,
And all that Love most loves to hear!
A music, breathing of the past,
  The present, and the time to be,
Where Hope and Memory, to the last,
  Lengthen out life's true harmony!

Nor long did he, whom call so kind
  Summoned away, remain behind;
Nor did there need much time to tell
  What they—alas, more fallen than he

From happiness and heaven—knew well,
His gentler love's short history!

Thus did it run—*not* as he told
The tale himself, but as 'tis graved
Upon the tablets that, of old,
By Cham were from the deluge saved,
All written over with sublime
And saddening legends of the unblest
But glorious spirits of that time,
And this young Angel's 'mong the rest.

THIRD ANGEL'S STORY.

AMONG the Spirits, of pure flame,
That round the Almighty Throne abide—
Circles of light, that from the same
Eternal centre sweeping wide,
Carry its beams on every side
(Like spheres of air that waft around
The undulations of rich sound),
Till the far-circling radiance be
Diffused into infinity!
First and immediate near the Throne,
As if peculiarly God's own,
The Seraphs stand——this burning sign
Traced on their banner, 'Love Divine!'
Their rank, their honours, far above
Even those to high-browed Cherubs given,
Though knowing all—so much doth Love
Transcend all knowledge, even in heaven!

'Mong these was Zaraph once—and none
E'er felt affection's holy fire,
Or yearned towards the Eternal One,
With half such longing, deep desire.
Love was to his impassioned soul
Not, as with others, a mere part
Of its existence, but the whole—
The very life-breath of his heart!
Often, when from the Almighty brow
A lustre came too bright to bear,
And all the seraph ranks would bow
Their heads beneath their wings, nor dare
To look upon the effulgence there—
This Spirit's eyes would court the blaze
(Such pride he in adoring took),
And rather lose, in that one gaze,
The power of looking than *not* look!
Then, too, when angel voices sung
The mercy of their God, and strung
Their harps to hail, with welcome sweet,
The moment, watched for by all eyes,
When some repentant sinner's feet
First touched the threshold of the skies,
Oh then how clearly did the voice
Of Zaraph above all rejoice!
Love was in every buoyant tone,
Such love as only could belong
To the blest angels, and alone
Could, even from angels, bring such song!

Alas, that it should e'er have been
The same in heaven as it is here,
Where nothing fond or bright is seen,
But it hath pain and peril near—
Where right and wrong so close resemble,
That what we take for virtue's thrill
Is often the first downward tremble
Of the heart's balance into ill—
Where Love hath not a shrine so pure,
So holy, but the serpent, Sin,
In moments even the most secure,
Beneath his altar may glide in!

So was it with that Angel—such
The charm that sloped his fall along
From good to ill, from loving much,
Too easy lapse, to loving wrong.—
Even so that amorous Spirit, bound
By beauty's spell, where'er 'twas found,
From the bright things above the moon,
Down to earth's beaming eyes descended,
Till love for the Creator soon
In passion for the creature ended!

'Twas first at twilight, on the shore
Of the smooth sea, he heard the lute
And voice of her he loved steal o'er
The silver waters, that lay mute,
As loth, by even a breath, to stay
The pilgrimage of that sweet lay;
Whose echoes still went on and on,
Till lost among the light that shone
Far off beyond the ocean's brim—
There, where the rich cascade of day
Had, o'er the horizon's golden rim,
Into Elysium rolled away!
Of God she sung, and of the mild
Attendant Mercy, that beside
His awful throne for ever smiled,
Ready with her white hand, to guide
His bolts of vengeance to their prey—
That she might quench them on the way!
Of Peace—of that Atoning Love,
Upon whose star, shining above
This twilight world of hope and fear,
The weeping eyes of Faith are fixed
So fond, that with her every tear
The light of that love-star is mixed!—
All this she sung, and such a soul
Of piety was in that song,
That the charmed Angel, as it stole
Tenderly to his ear, along
Those lulling waters, where he lay
Watching the day-light's dying ray,
Thought 'twas a voice from out the wave,
An echo that some spirit gave
To Eden's distant harmony,
Heard faint and sweet beneath the sea!

Quickly, however, to its source,
Tracking that music's melting course,
He saw upon the golden sand
Of the sea-shore a maiden stand,

Before whose feet the expiring waves
Flung their last tribute with a sigh—
As, in the East, exhausted slaves
Lay down the far-brought gift, and die—
And, while her lute hung by her, hushed,
As if unequal to the tide
Of song, that from her lips still gushed,
She raised, like one beatified,
Those eyes, whose light seemed rather given
To be adored than to adore—
Such eyes as may have looked *from* heaven,
But ne'er were raised to it before!

Oh Love, Religion, Music—all
That's left of Eden upon earth—
The only blessings, since the fall
Of our weak souls, that still recall
A trace of their high glorious birth—
How kindred are the dreams you bring!
How Love, though unto earth so prone,
Delights to take Religion's wing,
When time or grief hath stained his own!
How near to Love's beguiling brink,
Too oft, entranced Religion lies!
While Music, Music is the link
They *both* still hold by to the skies,
The language of their native sphere,
Which they had else forgotten here.

How then could Zaraph fail to feel
That moment's witcheries?—one so fair
Breathing out music that might steal
Heaven from itself, and rapt in prayer
That seraphs might be proud to share!
Oh, he *did* feel it—far too well—
With warmth that much too dearly cost;
Nor knew he, when at last he fell,
To which attraction, to which spell,
Love, Music, or Devotion, most
His soul in that sweet hour was lost.

Sweet was the hour, though dearly won,
And pure, as aught of earth could be,
For then first did the glorious sun
Before Religion's altar see
Two hearts in wedlock's golden tie
Self-pledged, in love to live and die—
Then first did woman's virgin brow
That hymeneal chaplet wear,
Which, when it dies, no second vow
Can bid a new one bloom out there—
Blest union! by that angel wove,
And worthy from such hands to come;
Safe, sole asylum, in which Love,
When fallen or exiled from above,
In this dark world can find a home.

And, though the Spirit had transgressed,
Had, from his station 'mong the blessed,
Won down by woman's smile, allowed
Terrestrial passion to breathe o'er
The mirror of his heart, and cloud
God's image, there so bright before—

Yet never did that God look down
On error with a brow so mild;
Never did justice launch a frown
That, ere it fell, so nearly smiled.
For gentle was their love, with awe
And trembling like a treasure kept,
That was not theirs by holy law,
Whose beauty with remorse they saw,
And o'er whose preciousness they wept.
Humility, that low, sweet root,
From which all heavenly virtues shoot,
Was in the hearts of both—but most
In Nama's heart, by whom alone
Those charms, for which a heaven was lost,
Seemed all unvalued and unknown;
And when her Seraph's eyes she caught,
And hid hers glowing on his breast,
Even bliss was humbled by the thought,
'What claim have I to be so blessed?'
Still less could maid so meek have nursed
Desire of knowledge—that vain thirst
With which the sex hath all been cursed,
From luckless Eve to her who near
The Tabernacle stole, to hear
The secrets of the Angels—no—
To love as her own seraph loved,
With Faith, the same through bliss and woe—
Faith that, were even its light removed,
Could, like the dial, fixed remain,
And wait till it shone out again—
With Patience that, though often bowed
By the rude storm, can rise anew,
And Hope that, even from Evil's cloud,
Sees sunny Good half breaking through!
This deep, relying Love, worth more
In heaven than all a cherub's lore—
This Faith, more sure than aught beside,
Was the sole joy, ambition, pride,
Of her fond heart—the unreasoning scope
Of all its views, above, below—
So true she felt it that to *hope*,
To *trust*, is happier than to *know*.

And thus in humbleness they trod,
Abashed, but pure before their God;
Nor e'er did earth behold a sight
So meekly beautiful as they,
When, with the altar's holy light
Full on their brows, they knelt to pray,
Hand within hand, and side by side,
Two links of love, awhile untied
From the great chain above, but fast
Holding together to the last—
Two fallen Splendors from that tree
Which buds with such eternally,
Shaken to earth, yet keeping all
Their light and freshness in the fall.

Their only punishment (as wrong,
However sweet, must bear its brand),
Their only doom was this—that, long
As the green earth and ocean stand,

They both shall wander here—the same
Throughout all time, in heart and frame—
Still looking to that goal sublime,
  Whose light, remote but sure, they see,
Pilgrims of Love, whose way is Time,
  Whose home is in Eternity!
Subject, the while, to all the strife
True love encounters in this life—
The wishes, hopes, he breathes in vain;
  The chill, that turns his warmest sighs
  To earthly vapour, ere they rise;
The doubt he feeds on, and the pain
  That in his very sweetness lies.
Still worse, the illusions that betray
  His footsteps to their shining brink;
That tempt him, on his desert way
  Through the bleak world, to bend and drink,
Where nothing meets his lips, alas,
But he again must sighing pass
On to that far-off home of peace,
In which alone his thirst will cease.

All this they bear, but, not the less,
Have moments rich in happiness—
Blest meetings, after many a day
Of widowhond past far away,
When the loved face again is seen
Close, close, with not a tear between—
Confidings frank, without control,
Poured mutually from soul to soul;
As free from any fear or doubt
  As is that light from chill or stain,
The sun into the stars sheds out,
  To be by them shed back again!—
That happy minglement of hearts,
  Where, changed as chymic compounds are,
Each with its own existence parts,
  To find a new one, happier far!
Such are their joys—and, crowning all,
That blessed hope of the bright hour,

When, happy and no more to fall,
  Their spirits shall, with freshened power,
Rise up rewarded for their trust
  In Him, from whom all goodness springs,
And, shaking off earth's soiling dust
  From their emancipated wings,
Wander for ever through those skies
Of radiance, where Love never dies!

In what lone region of the earth
  These pilgrims now may roam or dwell,
God and the Angels, who look forth
  To watch their steps, alone can tell.
But should we, in our wanderings,
  Meet a young pair, whose beauty wants
But the adornment of bright wings
  To look like heaven's inhabitants—
Who shine where'er they tread, and yet
  Are humble in their earthly lot,
As is the wayside violet,
  That shines unseen, and were it not
For its sweet breath would be forgot—
Whose hearts in every thought are one,
  Whose voices utter the same wills,
Answering as Echo doth, some tone
  Of fairy music 'mong the hills,
So like itself, we seek in vain
Which is the echo, which the strain—
Whose piety is love—whose love,
  Though close as 'twere their souls' embrace,
Is not of earth, but from above—
  Like two fair mirrors, face to face,
Whose light, from one to the other thrown,
Is heaven's reflection, not their own—
Should we e'er meet with aught so pure,
So perfect here, we may be sure
There is but *one* such pair below;
And, as we bless them on their way
Through the world's wilderness, may say,
  ' There Zaraph and his Nama go.'

THE FUDGE FAMILY IN PARIS.

THE FUDGE FAMILY IN PARIS.

EDITED BY
THOMAS BROWN, THE YOUNGER,
AUTHOR OF THE TWOPENNY POST BAG.

Le Leggi della Maschera richiedono che una persona mascherata non sia salutata per nome da uno che la conosce malgrado il suo travestimento.—*Castiglione.*

PREFACE.

In what manner the following Epistles came into my hands, it is not necessary for the public to know. It will be seen by Mr. Fudge's Second Letter, that he is one of those gentlemen whose *Secret Services* in Ireland, under the mild ministry of my Lord C——gh, have been so amply and gratefully remunerated. Like his friend and associate, Thomas Reynolds, Esq., he had retired upon the reward of his honest industry; but has lately been induced to appear again in active life, and superintend the training of that *Delatorian Cohort* which Lord S—dm—th, in his wisdom and benevolence, has organized.

Whether Mr. Fudge himself has yet made any discoveries, does not appear from the following pages; but much may be expected from a person of his zeal and sagacity; and, indeed, to *him*, Lord S—dm—th, and the Greenland-bound ships, the eyes of all lovers of *discoveries* are now most anxiously directed.

I regret that I have been obliged to omit Mr. Bob Fudge's Third Letter, concluding the adventures of his Day with the Dinner, Opera, etc. etc.; but in consequence of some remarks upon Marinette's thin drapery, which it was thought might give offence to certain well-meaning persons, the manuscript was sent back to Paris for his revision, and had not returned when the last sheet was put to press.

It will not, I hope, be thought presumptuous if I take this opportunity of complaining of a very serious injustice I have suffered from the public. Dr. King wrote a treatise to prove that Bentley 'was not the author of his own book;' and a similar absurdity has been asserted of *me*, in almost all the best informed literary circles. With the name of the real author staring them in the face, they have yet persisted in attributing my works to other people; and the fame of the *Twopenny Post Bag*—such as it is—having hovered doubtfully over various persons, has at last settled upon the head of a certain little gentleman, who wears it, I understand, as complacently as if it actually belonged to him, without even the honesty of avowing, with his own favourite author (he will excuse the pun),

Εγω δ' 'Ο ΜΩΡΟΣ αρας
Εδησαμην μιτωτῳ.

I can only add, that if any lady or gentleman, curious in such matters, will take the trouble of calling at my lodgings, 245, Piccadilly, I shall have the honour of assuring them, *in propria persona*, that I am—his, or her,

Very obedient and very humble servant,

THOMAS BROWN, THE YOUNGER.

April 17, 1818.

THE FUDGE FAMILY IN PARIS.

LETTER I.

**FROM MISS BIDDY FUDGE TO MISS DOROTHY ——,
OF CLONSKILTY, IN IRELAND.**

Amiens.

DEAR DOLL, while the tails of our horses are plaiting,
The trunks tying on, and Papa, at the door,
Into very bad French is, as usual, translating
His English resolve not to give a *sou* more,
I sit down to write you a line—only think!—
A letter from France, with French pens and French ink,
How delightful! though—would you believe it, my dear?—
I have seen nothing yet *very* wonderful here;
No adventure, no sentiment, far as we've come,
But the corn-fields and trees quite as dull as at home;
And, *but* for the post-boy, his boots and his queue,
I might *just* as well be at Clonskilty with you!
In vain, at Dessein's, did I take from my trunk
That divine fellow, Sterne, and fall reading *The Monk!*
In vain did I think of his charming dead Ass,
And remember the crust and the wallet—alas!
No monks can be had now for love or for money
(All owing, Pa says, to that infidel Boney);
And, though *one* little Neddy we saw in our drive
Out of classical Nampont, the beast was alive!

By the by, though, at Calais, Papa had a touch
Of romance on the pier, which affected me much.
At the sight of that spot, where our darling
Set the first of his own dear legitimate foot [1]
(Modelled out so exactly, and—God bless the mark!—
'Tis a foot, Dolly, worthy so *Grand* a *M—que*),
He exclaimed, 'Oh mon R—!' and, with tear-dropping eye,
Stood to gaze on the spot—while some Jacobin, nigh,
Muttered out with a shrug (what an insolent thing!)
'Ma foi, he be right—'tis de Englishman's K—g;
And dat *gros pied de cochon*—begar, me vil say,
Dat de foot look mosh better, if turned toder way.'
There's the pillar, too—Lord! I had nearly forgot—
What a charming idea! raised close to the spot;
The mode being now (as you've heard, I suppose)
To build tombs over legs, and raise pillars to toes.

This is all that's occurred sentimental as yet;
Except, indeed, some little flower-nymphs we've met,
Who disturb one's romance with pecuniary views,
Flinging flowers in your path, and then bawling for *sous!*
And some picturesque beggars, whose multitudes seem
To recall the good days of the *ancien régime*,
All as ragged and brisk, you'll be happy to learn,
And as thin, as they were in the time of dear Sterne.

Our party consists, in a neat Calais job,
Of Papa and myself, Mr. Connor and Bob.
You remember how sheepish Bob looked at Kilrandy,
But Lord! he's quite altered—they've made him a Dandy,
A thing, you know, whiskered, great-coated, and laced,
Like an hour-glass, exceedingly small in the waist;
Quite a new sort of creatures, unknown yet to scholars,
With heads so immoveably stuck in shirt-collars,
That seats like our music-stools soon must be found them,
To twirl, when the creatures may wish to look round them!
In short, dear, 'a Dandy' describes what I mean,
And Bob's far the best of the *genus* I've seen:
An improving young man, fond of learning, ambitious,
And goes now to Paris to study French dishes,
Whose names—think, how quick!—he already knows pat,
A la braise, petits pâtés, and—what d'ye call that
They inflict on potatoes? oh! *maître d'hôtel*—
I assure you, dear Dolly, he knows them as well
As if nothing but these all his life he had ate,
Though a bit of them Bobby has never touched yet;
But just knows the names of French dishes and cooks,
As dear Pa knows the titles of authors and books.

As to Pa, what d'ye think?—mind it's all *entre nous*,
But you know, love, I never keep secrets from you—
Why, he's writing a book—what! a tale? a romance?
No, ye Gods, would it were!—but his Travels in France;
At the special desire (he let out t'other day)
Of his friend and his patron, my Lord C—stl—r—gh,

---

[1] To commemorate the landing of —— —— ——
from England, the impression of his foot is marked on the pier at Calais, and a pillar with an inscription raised opposite to the spot.

Who said, 'My dear Fudge ——,' I forget th'
  exact words,
And, it's strange, no one ever remembers my
  Lord's;
But 'twas something to say, that, as all must
  allow,
A good orthodox work is much wanting just now,
To expound to the world the new—thingummie
  —science,
Found out by the—what's-its-name—Holy A——ce,
And prove to mankind that their rights are but
  folly,
Their freedom a joke (which it *is*, you know,
  Dolly);
'There's none,' said his Lordship, 'if *I* may be
  judge,
Half so fit for this great undertaking as Fudge!'

The matter's soon settled—Pa flies to *the Row*
(The *first* stage your tourists now usually go),
Settles all for his quarto — advertisements,
  praises—
Starts post from the door, with his tablets—
  French phrases—
'Scott's Visit,' of course—in short, everything
  he has
An author can want, except words and ideas:—
And, lo! the first thing in the spring of the year,
Is Phil. Fudge at the front of a Quarto, my dear!

But, bless me, my paper's near out, so I'd better
Draw fast to a close:—this exceeding long letter
You owe to a *déjeûner à la Fourchette*,
Which Bobby would have, and is hard at it yet.—
What's next? oh, the tutor, the last of the party,
Young Connor:—they say he's so like Bon—te,
His nose and his chin,—which Papa rather
  dreads,
As the D——ns, you know, are suppressing all
  heads
That resemble old Nap's, and who knows but
  their honours
May think, in their fright, of suppressing poor
  Connor's?
Au reste (as we say), the young lad's well
  enough,
Only talks much of Athens, Rome, virtue, and
  stuff;
A third cousin of ours, by the way—poor as Job
(Though of royal descent by the side of
  Mamma),
And for charity made private tutor to Bob—
Entre nous, too, a Papist—how liberal of Pa!

This is all, dear—forgive me for breaking off
  thus;
But Bob's *déjeûner's* done, and Papa's in a fuss.
                                B. F.

P.S.
How provoking of Pa! he will not let me stop
Just to run in and rummage some milliner's
  shop;
And my *début* in Paris, I blush to think on it,
Must now, Doll, be made in a hideous low
  bonnet.
But Paris, dear Paris—oh, *there* will be joy,
And romance, and high bonnets, and Madame
  le Roi!'

LETTER II.

FROM PHIL. FUDGE, ESQ., TO THE LORD VISCOUNT
           C———H.
                                       Paris.

AT length, my Lord, I have the bliss
To date to you a line from this
'Demoralized' metropolis;
Where, by plebeians low and scurvy,
The throne was turned quite topsy-turvy,
And Kingship, tumbled from its seat,
'Stood prostrate' at the people's feet;
Where (still to use your Lordship's tropes)
The *level* of obedience *slopes*
Upward and downward, as the *stream*
Of *hydra* faction *kicks the beam!*²
Where the poor palace changes masters
Quicker than a snake its skin,
And —— is rolled out on castors
While ——'s borne on shoulders in:
But where, in every change, no doubt,
One special good your Lordship traces,—
That 'tis the *Kings* alone turn out,
The *Ministers* still keep their places.

How oft, dear Viscount C———gh,
I've thought of thee upon the way,
As in my *job* (what place could be
More apt to wake a thought of thee?)
Or, oftener far, when gravely sitting
Upon my dickey (as is fitting
For him who writes a Tour, that he
May more of men and manners see),
I've thought of thee and of thy glories,
Thou guest of Kings, and King of Tories!
Reflecting how thy fame has grown
And spread, beyond man's usual share,
At home, abroad, till thou art known,
Like Major Semple, everywhere!
And marvelling with what powers of breath
Your Lordship, having speeched to death
Some hundreds of your fellow-men,
Next speeched to Sovereigns' ears,—and when
All sovereigns else were dozed, at last
Speeched down the Sovereign³ of Belfast.

---

¹ A celebrated mantua-maker in Paris.
² This excellent imitation of the noble Lord's style shows how deeply Mr. Fudge must have studied his great original. Irish oratory, indeed, abounds with such startling peculiarities. Thus the eloquent Coun-sellor B——, in describing some hypocritical pretender to charity, said: 'He put his hand in his breeches pocket, like a crocodile, and,' etc. etc.
³ The title of the chief magistrate of Belfast, before whom his Lordship (with the 'studium immane loquendi'

Oh! 'mid the praises and the trophies
Thou gain'st from Morosophs and Sophis,
'Mid all the tributes to thy fame,
   There's *one* thou shouldst be chiefly pleased at—
That Ireland gives her snuff thy name,
   And C———gh's the thing now sneezed at!

But hold, my pen!—a truce to praising—
Though even your Lordship will allow
The theme's temptations are amazing;
   But time and ink run short, and now
(As *thou* wouldst say, my guide and teacher
   In these gay metaphoric fringes),
I must *embark* into the *feature*
   On which this letter chiefly *hinges;*[1]—
My Book, the Book that is to prove—
And *will*, so help ye Sprites above,
That sit on clouds, as grave as judges,
Watching the labours of the Fudges!—
Will prove that all the world, at present,
Is in a state extremely pleasant:
That Europe—thanks to royal swords
And bayonets, and the Duke commanding—
Enjoys a peace which, like the Lord's,
   Passeth all human understanding:
That F———ce prefers her go-cart ——
   To such a coward scamp as ——:
Though round, with each a leading-string,
   There standeth many a R—y—l crony,
For fear the chubby, tottering thing
   Should fall, if left there *loney-poney:*
That England, too, the more her debts,
The more she spends, the richer gets;
And that the Irish, grateful nation!
Remember when by *thee* reigned over,
And bless thee for their flagellation,
   As Heloisa did her lover!
That Poland, left for Russia's lunch,
   Upon the sideboard, snug reposes;
While Saxony's as pleased as Punch,
   And Norway 'on a bed of roses!'
That, as for some few million souls,
Transferred by contract, bless the clods!
If half were strangled—Spaniards, Poles,
   And Frenchmen—'twouldn't make much odds,
So Europe's goodly Royal ones
Sit easy on their sacred thrones;
So Ferdinand embroiders gaily,[2]
   And —— eats his *salmi* daily;
So time is left to Emperor Sandy
To be *half* Cæsar and *half* Dandy;

And G—ge the R—g—t (who'd forget
That doughtiest chieftain of the set?)
Hath wherewithal for trinkets new,
   For dragons, after Chinese models,
And chambers where Duke Ho and Soo
   Might come and nine times knock their noddles!—
All this my Quarto 'll prove—much more
Than Quarto ever proved before—
In reasoning with the *Post* I'll vie,
My facts the *Courier* shall supply,
My jokes V—ns—t, P—le my sense,
And thou, sweet Lord, my eloquence!

My Journal, penned by fits and starts,
   On Biddy's back or Bobby's shoulder
(My son, my Lord, a youth of parts,
   Who longs to be a small place-holder),
Is—though I say't that shouldn't say—
Extremely good; and, by the way,
One extract from it—*only* one—
To show its spirit, and I've done.

'*Jul. thirty-first.* Went, after snack,
   To the cathedral of St. Denny;
Sighed o'er the kings of ages back,
   And—gave the old concierge a penny!
(*Mem.*—Must see *Rheims*, much famed, 'tis said,
For making kings and gingerbread.)
Was shown the tomb where lay, so stately,
A little B—bon, buried lately,
Thrice high and puissant, we were told,
Though only twenty-four hours old![3]
Hear this, thought I, ye Jacobins;
Ye Burdetts tremble in your skins!
If R—alty, but aged a day,
Can boast such high and puissant sway,
What impious hand its power would fix,
Full fledged and wigged,[4] at fifty-six?'

The argument's quite new, you see,
And proves exactly Q. E. D.—
So now, with duty to the R—g—t,
I am, dear Lord,
       Your most obedient,
                    P. F.

Hotel Breteuil, Rue Rivoli.
Neat lodgings—rather dear for me;
But Biddy said she thought 'twould look
Genteeler thus to date my book,
And Biddy's right—besides, it curries
Some favour with our friends at Murray's,

---

attributed by Ovid to that chattering and rapacious class of birds, the pies) delivered sundry long and self-gratulatory orations, on his return from the Continent. It was at one of these Irish dinners that his gallant brother, Lord S., proposed the health of 'The best cavalry officer in Europe—the Regent!'

[1] Verbatim from one of the noble Viscount's speeches: 'And now, sir, I must embark into the feature on which this question chiefly hinges.'

[2] It would be an edifying thing to write a history of the private amusements of sovereigns, tracing them down from the fly-sticking of Domitian, the mole-catching of Artabanus, the hog-mimicking of Parmenides, the horse-currying of Aretas, to the petticoat embroidering of Ferdinand, and the patience-playing of the P———e R———t.

[3] So described on the coffin: 'Très-haute et puissante Princesse, âgée d'un jour.'

[4] There is a fulness and breadth in this portrait of Royalty which remind us of what Pliny says in speaking of Trajan's great qualities: '*Nouns longe lateque Principem ostentant?*'

THE FUDGE FAMILY IN PARIS.

Who scorn what any man can say,
That dates from Rue St. Honoré.[1]

LETTER III.

FROM MR. BOB FUDGE TO RICHARD ———, ESQ.

O Dick! you may talk of your writing and reading,
Your logic and Greek, but there's nothing like feeding;
And *this* is the place for it, Dicky, you dog,
Of all places on earth—the headquarters of prog.
Talk of England,—her famed Magna Charta, I swear, is
A humbug, a flam, to the Carte[2] at old Véry's;
And as for your Juries—*who* would not cet o'er 'em
A jury of tasters,[3] with woodcocks before em?
Give Cartwright his parliaments fresh every year—
But those friends of *short Commons* would never do here;
And let Romilly speak as he will on the question,
No digest of law 's like the laws of digestion!

By the by, Dick, *I* fatten—but *n'importe* for that,
'Tis the mode—your legitimates always get fat;
There's the R—g—t, there's ———'s—and B—n—y tried too,
But, though somewhat imperial in paunch, 'twouldn't do:
He improved, indeed, much in this point when he wed,
But he ne'er grew right r-y-lly fat *in the head*.

Dick, Dick, what a place is this Paris!—but stay—
As my raptures may bore you, I'll just sketch a day,

As we pass it, myself and some comrades I've got,
All thorough-bred *Gnostics*, who know what is what.

After dreaming some hours of the land of Cocaigne,[4]
That Elysium of all that is *friand* and nice,
Where for hail they have *bons-bons*, and claret for rain,
And the skaters in winter show off on cream-ice;
Where so ready all nature its cookery yields,
Macaroni au parmesan grows in the fields;
Little birds fly about with the true pheasant taint,
And the geese are all born with a liver complaint![5]
I rise—put on neckcloth—stiff, tight as can be—
For, a lad who *goes into the world*, Dick, like me,
Should have his neck tied up, you know—there's no doubt of it—
Almost as tight as *some* lads who *go out of* it.
With whiskers well oiled, and with boots that 'hold up
The mirror to nature'—so bright you could sup
Off the leather like china; with coat, too, that draws
On the tailor, who suffers, a martyr's applause!—
With head bridled up, like a four-in-hand leader,
And stays—devil's in them—too tight for a feeder,
I strut to the old Café Hardy, which yet
Beats the field at a *déjeûner à la fourchette*.
There, Dick, what a breakfast!—oh, not like your ghost
Of a breakfast in England, your curst tea and toast;[6]
But a sideboard, you dog, where one's eye roves about,
Like a Turk's in the harem, and thence singles out

---

[1] See the *Quarterly Review* for May 1810, where Mr. Hobhouse is accused of having written his book 'in a back street of the French capital.'

[2] The bill of fare.—Véry, a well-known restaurateur.

[3] Mr. Bob a'ludes particularly, I presume, to the famous Jury Dégustateur which used to assemble at the hotel of M. Grimod de la Reynière, and of which this modern Archestratus has given an account in his *Almanach des Gourmands*, cinquième année, p. 78.

[4] The fairy-land of cookery and *gourmandise*: 'Pays, où le ciel offre les viandes toutes cuites, et où, comme on parle, les alouettes tombent toutes roties. Du Latin, coquere.'—*Dachat.*

[5] The process by which the liver of the unfortunate goose is enlarged, in order to produce that richest of all dainties, the *foie gras*, of which such renowned *pâtés* are made at Strasbourg and Toulouse, is thus described in the *Cours Gastronomique:* 'On déplume l'estomac des oies; on attache ensuite ces animaux aux chenets d'une cheminée, et on les nourrit devant le feu. La captivité et la chaleur donnent à ces volatiles une maladie hépatique, qui fait gonfler leur foie,' etc.—P. 206.

[6] Is Mr. Bob aware that his contempt for *tea* renders him liable to a charge of *atheism?* Such, at least, is the opinion cited in *Christian. Falster. Amœnitat. Philolog.: '*Atheum interpretabatur hominem ab herba The aversum.' He would not, I think, have been so irreverent to this beverage of scholars, if he had read *Peter Petit's* Poem in prai-e of Tea, addressed to the learned *Huet;* or the Epigraph which *Pechlinus* wrote for an altar he meant to dedicate to this herb; or the Anacreontics of *Peter Francius*, in which he calls tea

Θεαν, θεην, θεαιναν.

The following passage from one of these Anacreontics will, I have no doubt, be gratifying to all true Theistas

Θειης, θεων τι πατρι
Εν χρυσεοις σκυφοισι
Διδοι τo νεκταρ Ἡβη.
Σι μοι διακονειτω
Σκυφοις τε μυρρινοισι,
Τῳ καλλει πρισκοισι
Καλαις χερεσσι κουραι.

Which may be thus translated:

One's *pâté* of larks, just to tune up the throat,
One's small limbs of chickens, done *en papillote*,
One's erudite cutlets, drest all ways but plain,
Or one's kidneys—imagine, Dick—done with champagne!
Then some glasses of *Beaune* to dilute — or, mayhap,
Chambertin,¹ which, you know, 's the pet tipple of Nap,
And which Dad, by the by, that legitimate stickler,
Much scruples to taste, but *I'm* not so partic'lar.—
Your coffee comes next, by prescription; and then, Dick, 's
The coffee's ne'er-failing and glorious appendix—
(If books had but such, my old Grecian, depend on't
I'd swallow even W—tk—n's, for sake of the end on't)—
A neat glass of *parfait-amour*, which one sips
Just as if bottled velvet tipped over one's lips!
This repast being ended, and *paid for*—(how odd! Till a man's used to paying there's something so queer in't)—
The sun now well out, and the girls all abroad,
And the world enough aired for us, Nobs, to appear in't,
We lounge up the Boulevards, where—oh Dick, the phizzes, ·
The turn-outs, we meet—what a nation of quizzes!
Here toddles along some old figure of fun,
With a coat you might date Anno Domini One;
A laced hat, worsted stockings, and—noble old soul!—
A fine ribbon and cross in his best button-hole;
Just such as our Pr—e, who nor reason nor fun dreads,
Inflicts, without even a court-martial, on hundreds.²
Here trips a *grisette*, with a fond, roguish eye
(Rather eatable things these *grisettes* by the by);
And there an old *demoiselle*, almost as fond,
In a silk that has stood since the time of the Fronde.
There goes a French dandy—ah, Dick! unlike some ones
We've seen about White's—the Mounseers are but rum ones;
Such hats!—fit for monkeys—I'd back Mrs. Draper
To cut neater weather-boards out of brown paper:

And coats—how I wish, if it wouldn't distress 'em,
They'd club for old B—m—l, from Calais, to dress 'em!
The collar sticks out from the neck such a space,
That you'd swear 'twas the plan of this head-lopping nation,
To leave there behind them a snug little place
For the head to drop into, on decapitation!
In short, what with mountebanks, Counts, and friseurs,
Some mummers by trade, and the rest amateurs—
What with captains in new jockey boots and silk breeches,
Old dustmen with swinging great opera hats,
And shoeblacks reclining by statues in niches,
There never was seen such a race of Jack Sprats.

From the Boulevards—but hearken!—yes—as I'm a sinner,
The clock is just striking the half-hour for dinner:
So *no* more at present—short time for adorning—
My day must be finished some other fine morning.
Now, hey for old Beauvilliers'³ larder, my boy!
And, once *there*, if the goddess of beauty and joy
Were to write 'Come and kiss me, dear Bob!'
I'd not budge—
Not a step, Dick, as sure as my name is
R. FUDGE.

LETTER IV.

FROM PHELIM CONNOR TO ———.

'RETURN!'—no, never, while the withering hand
Of bigot power is on that hapless land;
While for the faith my fathers held to God,
Even in the fields where free those fathers trode
I am proscribed, and—like the spot left bare
In Israel's halls, to tell the proud and fair
Amidst their mirth that slavery had been there⁴—
On all I love,—home, parents, friends,—I trace
The mournful mark of bondage and disgrace!
No!—let *them* stay, who in their country's pangs
See nought but food for factious and harangues;
Who yearly kneel before their masters' doors,
And hawk their wrongs as beggars do their sores;

Yes, let Hebe, ever young,
High in heaven her nectar hold,
And to Jove's immortal throng
Pour the tide in cups of gold.—
I'll not envy heaven's princes,
While, with snowy hands, for me,
Kate the china tea-cup rinses,
And pours out her best Bohea!

¹ The favourite wine of Napoleon.
² It was said by Wicquefort, more than a hundred

years ago, 'Le Roi d'Angleterre fait seul plus de chevaliers que tous les autres Rois de la Chrétienté ensemble.' What would he say now?

³ A celebrated restaurateur.

⁴ 'They used to leave a yard square of the wall of the house unplastered, on which they write, in large letters, either the fore-mentioned verse of the Psalmist ("If I forget thee, O Jerusalem," etc.), or the words, "The memory of the desolation."'—*Leo y Modena*.

Still let your¹ . . . . . .
. . . .
Still hope and suffer, all who can!—but I,
Who durst not hope, and cannot bear, must fly.

But whither?—everywhere the scourge pursues—
Turn where he will, the wretched wanderer views,
In the bright, broken hopes of all his race,
Countless reflections of the oppressor's face!
Everywhere gallant hearts, and spirits true,
Are served up victims to the vile and few;
While E———, everywhere—the general foe
Of truth and freedom, wheresoe'er they glow—
Is first, when tyrants strike, to aid the blow!

O E———! could such poor revenge atone
For wrongs that well might claim the deadliest one;
Were it a vengeance, sweet enough to sate
The wretch who flies from thy intolerant hate,
To hear his curses, on such barbarous sway,
Echoed where'er he bends his cheerless way;—
Could *this* content him, every lip he meets
Teems for his vengeance with such poisonous sweets;
Were *this* his luxury, never is thy name
Pronounced, but he doth banquet on thy shame;
Hears maledictions ring from every side
Upon that grasping power, that selfish pride,
Which vaunts its own, and scorns all rights beside;
That low and desperate envy which, to blast
A neighbour's blessings, risks the few thou hast;—
That monster, self, too gross to be concealed,
Which ever lurks behind thy proffered shield;
That faithless craft, which, in thy hour of need,
Can court the slave, can swear he shall be freed,
Yet basely spurns him, when thy point is gained,
Back to his masters, ready gagged and chained!
Worthy associate of that band of kings,
That royal, ravening flock, whose vampire wings
O'er sleeping Europe treacherously brood,
And fan her into dreams of promised good,
Of hope, of freedom—but to drain her blood!
If *thus* to hear thee branded be a bliss
That vengeance loves, there's yet more sweet than this,—
That 'twas an Irish head, an Irish heart,
Made thee the fallen and tarnished thing thou art;
That, as the Centaur gave the infected vest,
In which he died, to rack his conqueror's breast,
We sent thee C———gh:—as heaps of dead
Have slain their slayers by the pest they spread,

So hath our land breathed out—thy fame to dim,
Thy strength to waste, and rot thee, soul and limb—
Her worst infections all condensed in him!

. . . .

When will the world shake off such yokes! oh, when
Will that redeeming day shine out on men,
That shall behold them rise, erect and free
As Heaven and Nature meant mankind should be!
When reason shall no longer blindly bow
To the vile pagod things, that o'er her brow,
Like him of Jaghernaut, drive trampling now;
Nor Conquest dare to desolate God's earth;
Nor drunken Victory, with a Nero's mirth,
Strike her lewd harp amidst a people's groans;—
But, built on love, the world's exalted thrones
Shall to the virtuous and the wise be given—
Those bright, those sole legitimates of Heaven.

When will this be?—or, oh! is it in truth,
But one of those sweet day-break dreams of youth,
In which the Soul, as round her morning springs,
'Twixt sleep and waking, sees such dazzling things!
And must the hope, as vain as it is bright,
Be all given up?—and are *they* only right,
Who say this world of thinking souls was made
To be by kings partitioned, trucked, and weighed
In scales that, ever since the world begun,
Have counted millions but as dust to one?
Are *they* the only wise, who laugh to scorn
The rights, the freedom to which man was born;
Who . . . .

Who, proud to kiss each separate rod of power,
Bless, while he reigns, the minion of the hour;
Worship each would-be God, that o'er them moves,
And take the thundering of his brass for Jove's!
If *this* be wisdom, then farewell, my books,
Farewell, ye shrines of old, ye classic brooks,
Which fed my soul with currents, pure and fair,
Of living truth, that now must stagnate there!—
Instead of themes that touch the lyre with light,
Instead of Greece, and her immortal fight
For Liberty, which once awaked my strings,
Welcome the Grand Conspiracy of Kings,
The High L-git—ates, the Holy Band,
Who, bolder even than he of Sparta's land,
Against whole millions, panting to be free,
Would guard the pass of right-line tyranny!
Instead of him, the Athenian bard, whose blade
Had stood the onset which his pen portrayed,
Welcome . . . .

---

¹ I have thought it prudent to omit some parts of Mr. Phelim Connor's letter. He is evidently an intemperate young man, and has associated with his cousins, the Fudges, to very little purpose.

And, 'stead of Aristides—woe the day
Such names should mingle!—welcome C——gh!

Here break we off, at this unhallowed name,[1]
Like priests of old, when words ill-omened came.
My next shall tell thee, bitterly shall tell,
Thoughts that . . . . .
Thoughts that — could patience hold — 'twere wiser far
To leave still hid and burning where they are!

LETTER V.

FROM MISS BIDDY FUDGE TO MISS DOROTHY ——.

WHAT a time since I wrote!—I'm a sad naughty girl—
Though, like a tee-totum, I'm all in a twirl,
Yet even (as you wittily say) a tee-totum
Between all its twirls gives a *letter* to note 'em.
But, Lord, such a place! and then, Dolly, my dresses,
My gowns, so divine!—there's no language expresses,
Except just the *two* words 'superbe,' 'magnifique,'
The trimmings of that which I had home last week!
It is called—I forget—à la—something which sounded
Like *alicampane*—but, in truth, I'm confounded
And bothered, my dear, 'twixt that troublesome boy's
(Bob's) cookery language, and Madame Le Roi's:
What with fillets of roses, and fillets of veal,
Things *garni* with lace, and things *garni* with eel,
One's hair and one's cutlets both *en papillote*,
And a thousand more things I shall ne'er have by rote,
I can scarce tell the difference, at least as to phrase,
Between beef *à la Psyché* and curls *à la braise*.—
But, in short, dear, I'm tricked out quite *à la française*,
With my bonnet—so beautiful!—high up and poking,
Like things that are put to keep chimneys from smoking.

Where *shall* I begin with the endless delights
Of this Eden of milliners, monkeys, and sights—
This dear busy place, where there's nothing transacting,
But dressing and dinnering, dancing and acting?

Imprimis, the Opera—mercy, my ears!
Brother Bobby's remark t'other night was a true one;
'This *must* be the music,' said he, 'of the *spears*,
For I'm curst if each note of it doesn't run through one!'
Pa says (and you know, love, his book's to make out
'Twas the Jacobins brought every mischief about)
That this passion for roaring has come in of late,
Since the rabble all tried for a *voice* in the State.
What a frightful idea, one's mind to o'erwhelm!
What a chorus, dear Dolly, would soon be let loose of it!
If, when of age, every man in the realm
Had a voice like old Lais,[2] and chose to make use of it!
No—never was known in this riotous sphere
Such a breach of the peace as their singing, my dear.
So bad, too, you'd swear that the god of both arts,
Of Music and Physic, had taken a frolic
For setting a loud fit of asthma in parts,
And composing a fine rumbling base to a colic!

But, the dancing—*ah parlez moi*, Dolly, *de ça*—
There, indeed, is a treat that charms all but Papa.
Such beauty—such grace—oh ye sylphs of romance!
Fly, fly to Titania, and ask her if *she* has
One light-footed nymph in her train, that can dance
Like divine Bigottini and sweet Fanny Bias!
Fanny Bias in Flora—dear creature!—you'd swear,
When her delicate feet in the dance twinkle round,
That her steps are of light, that her home is the air,
And she only *par complaisance* touches the ground.
And when Bigottini in Psyche dishevels
Her black flowing hair, and by dæmons is driven,
Oh! who does not envy those rude little devils,
That hold her and hug her, and keep her from heaven?

---

[1] The late Lord C., of Ireland, had a curious theory about names; he held that every man with *three* names was a Jacobin. His instances in Ireland were numerous: viz. Archibald Hamilton Rowan, Theobald Wolfe Tone, James Napper Tandy, John Philpot Curran, etc. etc.; and, in England, he produced as examples Charles James Fox, Richard Brinsley Sheridan, John Horne Tooke, Francis Burdett Jones, etc. etc.

The Romans called a thief ' homo trium literarum:'

Tun' trium literarum homo
Me vituperas! Fur.[a]
—*Plautus, Aulular*, Act II. Scene 4.

[2] The oldest, most celebrated, and most noisy of the singers at the French Opera.

[a] *Dusaulteus* supposes this word to be a *glossema*; that is, he thinks ' Fur' has made his escape from the margin into the text.

Then, the music—so softly its cadences die,
So divinely—oh, Dolly! between you and I,
It's as well for my peace that there's nobody nigh
To make love to me then—*you've* a soul, and can judge
What a crisis 'twould be for your friend Biddy Fudge!

The next place (which Bobby has near lost his heart in),
They call it the Play-house—I think—of Saint Martin;[1]
Quite charming—and *very* religious—what folly
To say that the French are not pious, dear Dolly,
When here one beholds, so correctly and rightly,
The Testament turned into melodrames nightly;[2]
And, doubtless, so fond they're of scriptural facts,
They will soon get the Pentateuch up in five acts.
Here Daniel, in pantomime,[3] bids bold defiance
To Nebuchadnezzar and all his stuffed lions,
While pretty young Israelites dance round the Prophet,
In very thin clothing, and *but* little of it;—
Here Bégrand,[4] who shines in this scriptural path,
As the lovely Susanna, without even a relic
Of drapery round her, comes out of the bath
In a manner that, Bob says, is quite *Eve-angelic!*

But, in short, dear, 'twould take me a month to recite
All the exquisite places we're at, day and night;
And, besides, ere I finish, I think you'll be glad
Just to hear one delightful adventure I've had.

Last night, at the Beaujon,[5] a place where—I doubt
If I well can describe—there are cars, that set out
From a lighted pavilion, high up in the air,
And rattle you down, Doll—you hardly know where.

These vehicles, mind me, in which you go through
This delightfully dangerous journey, hold *two*.
Some cavalier asks, with humility, whether
You'll venture down with him—you smile—
'tis a match;
In an instant you're seated, and down both together
Go thundering, as if you went post to old Scratch![6]
Well, it was but last night, as I stood and remarked
On the looks and odd ways of the girls who embarked,
The impatience of some for the perilous flight,
The forced giggle of others, 'twixt pleasure and fright,
That there came up—imagine, dear Doll, if you can—
A fine sallow, sublime, sort of Werter-faced man,
With mustachios that gave (what we read of so oft)
The dear Corsair expression, half savage, half soft,
As hyænas in love may be fancied to look, or
A something between Abelard and old Blucher!
Up he came, Doll, to me, and uncovering his head,
(Rather bald, but so warlike!) in bad English said,
'Ah! my dear—if Ma'mselle vil be so very good—
Just for von little course'—though I scarce understood
What he wished me to do, I said, thank him, I would.
Off we set—and, though 'faith, dear, I hardly knew whether
My head or my heels were the uppermost then,
For 'twas like heaven and earth, Dolly, coming together,—
Yet, spite of the danger, we dared it again.
And oh! as I gazed on the features and air
Of the man, who for me all this peril defied,
I could fancy almost he and I were a pair
Of unhappy young lovers, who thus, side by side,
Were taking, instead of rope, pistol, or dagger, a
Desperate dash down the falls of Niagara!

---

[1] The Théâtre de la Porte St. Martin, which was built when the Opera House in the Palais Royal was burned down, in 1781. A few days after this dreadful fire, which lasted more than a week, and in which several persons perished, the Parisian *élégantes* displayed flame-coloured dresses, 'couleur feu de l'Opéra!'—*Dulaure, Curiosités de Paris.*

[2] 'The Old Testament,' says the theatrical critic in the *Gazette de France*, 'is a mine of gold for the managers of our small playhouses. A multitude crowd round the Théâtre de la Gaîté every evening to see the Passage of the Red Sea.'
In the playbill of one of these sacred melodrames at Vienna, we find '*The Voice of G-d*, by Mr. Schwartz.'

[3] A piece very popular last year, called 'Daniel, ou la Fosse aux Lions.' The following scene will give an idea of the daring sublimity of these scriptural pantomimes. '*Scène 20.*—La fournaise devient un berceau de nuages azurés, au fond duquel est un groupe de nuages plus lumineux, et au milieu "Jéhovah" au centre d'un cercle de rayons brillans, qui annonce la présence de l'Eternel.'

[4] Madame Bégrand, a finely-formed woman, who acts in *Susanna and the Elders, L'Amour et la Folie*, etc. etc.

[5] The Promenades Aériennes, or French Mountains.—See a description of this singular and fantastic place of amusement, in a pamphlet, truly worthy of it, by F. F. Cotterel, Médecin, Docteur de la Faculté de Paris, etc. etc.

[6] According to Dr. Cotterel, the cars go at the rate of forty-eight miles an hour.

This achieved, through the gardens[1] we sauntered about,
Saw the fireworks, exclaimed 'Magnifique!' at each cracker,
And when 'twas all o'er, the dear man saw us out
With the air, I *will* say, of a prince, to our *fiacre*.

Now, hear me—this stranger—it may be mere folly—
But *who* do you think we all think it is, Dolly?
Why, bless you, no less than the great King of Prussia,
Who's here now incog.[2]—he, who made such a fuss, you
Remember, in London, with Blucher and Platoff,
When Sal was near kissing old Blucher's cravat off!
Pa says he's come here to look after his money
(Not taking things now as he used under Boney),
Which suits with our friend, for Bob saw him, he swore,
Looking sharp to the silver received at the door.
Besides, too, they say that his grief for his Queen
(Which was plain in this sweet fellow's face to be seen)
Requires such a stimulant dose as this car is,
Used three times a day with young ladies in Paris.
Some Doctor, indeed, has declared that such grief
Should—unless 'twould to utter despairing its folly push—
Fly to the Beaujon, and there seek relief
By rattling, as Bob says, 'like shot through a holly-bush.'

I must now bid adieu—only think, Dolly, think
If this *should* be the King—I have scarce slept a wink
With imagining how it will sound in the papers,
And how all the Misses my good luck will grudge,
When they read that Count Ruppin, to drive away vapours,
Has gone down the Beaujon with Miss Biddy Fudge.

Nota Bene.—Papa's almost certain 'tis he—
For he knows the Legitimate cut, and could see,
In the way he went poising, and managed to tower
So erect in the car, the true *Balance of Power.*

---

[1] In the Café attached to these gardens there are to be (as Dr. Cottorel informs us) 'douze nègres, très-alertes, qui contrasteront, par l'ébène de leur peau avec la teint de lis et de roses de nos belles. Les glaces et les sorbets servis par une main bien noire, fera davantage ressortir l'albâtre des bras arrondis de celles-ci.'—P. 22.

[2] His Majesty, who was at Paris under the travelling name of Count Ruppin, is known to have gone down the Beaujon very frequently.

LETTER VI.

FROM PHIL. FUDGE, ESQ., TO HIS BROTHER TIM FUDGE, ESQ., BARRISTER-AT-LAW.

YOURS of the 12th received just now—
Thanks for the hint, my trusty brother!
'Tis truly pleasing to see how
We Fudges stand by one another.
But never fear—I know my chap,
And he knows *me*, too—*verbum sap.*
My Lord and I are kindred spirits,
Like in our ways as two young ferrets;
Both fashioned, as that supple race is,
To twist into all sorts of places;—
Creatures lengthy, lean, and hungering,
Fond of blood and *burrow*-mongering.

As to my Book in 91,
Called 'Down with Kings, or, Who'd have thought it?'
Bless you, the Book's long dead and gone,—
Not even th' Attorney-General bought it.
And, though some few seditious tricks
I played in 95 and 6,
As you remind me in your letter,
His Lordship likes me all the better;
We, proselytes, that come with news full,
Are, as he says, so vastly useful!

Reynolds and I—(you know Tom Reynolds—
Drinks his claret, keeps his chaise—
Lucky the dog that first unkennels
Traitors and Luddites now-a-days;
Or who can help to *bag* a few,
When S—d——th wants a death or two);
Reynolds and I, and some few more,
All men like us of *information*,
Friends, whom his Lordship keeps in store,
As *under*-saviours of the nation[3]—
Have formed a Club this season, where
His Lordship sometimes takes the chair,
And gives us many a bright oration
In praise of our sublime vocation;
Tracing it up to great King Midas,
Who, though in fable typified as
A royal ass, by grace divine
And right of ears, most asinine,
Was yet no more, in fact historical,
Than an exceeding well-bred tyrant;
And these, his *ears*, but allegorical,
Meaning Informers, kept at high rent[4]—
Gemmen, who touched the Treasury glisteners,
Like us, for being trusty listeners;

---

[3] Lord C.'s tribute to the character of his friend, Mr. Reynolds, will long be remembered with equal credit to both.

[4] This interpretation of the fable of Midas' ears seems the most probable of any, and is thus stated in Hoffman: 'Hac allegoria significatum, Midam, utpote tyrannum, subauscultatores dimittere solitum, per quos, quæcunque per omnem regionem vel fierent, vel dicerentur, cognosceret, nimirum illis utens aurium vice.'

And picking up each tale and fragment,
For royal Midas's green bag meant.
'And wherefore,' said this best of Peers,
'Should not the R—g—t too have ears,¹
To reach as far, as long and wide as
Those of his model, good King Midas?'
This speech was thought extremely good,
And (rare for him) was understood—
Instant we drank 'The R—g—t's Ears,'
With three times three illustrious cheers,
    That made the room resound like thunder—
'The R—g—t's Ears, and may he ne'er
From foolish shame, like Midas, wear
    Old paltry *wigs* to keep them under!'²
This touch at our old friends, the Whigs,
Made us as merry all as grigs.
In short (I'll thank you not to mention
    These things again) we get on gaily;
And, thanks to pension and Suspension,
    Our little Club increases daily.
Castles, and Oliver, and such,
Who don't as yet full salary touch,
Nor keep their chaise and pair, nor buy
Houses and lands, like Tom and I,
Of course don't rank with us, *salvators*,³
But merely serve the Club as waiters.
Like Knights, too, we've our *collar* days
(For *us*, I own, an awkward phrase),
When, in our new costume adorned,—
The R—g—t's buff-and-blue coats *turned*—
We have the honour to give dinners
    To the chief Rats in upper stations;⁴
Your W—ys, V—ns—half-fledged sinners,
    Who shame us by their imitations;
Who turn, 'tis true—but what of that?
Give me the useful *peaching* Rat;
Not things as mute as Punch, when bought,
Whose wooden heads are all they've brought;
Who, false enough to shirk their friends,
But too faint-hearted to betray,
Are, after all their twists and bends,
But souls in Limbo, damned half-way.
No, no,—we nobler vermin are
A *genus* useful as we're rare;

'Midst all the things miraculous
Of which your natural histories brag,
The rarest must be Rats like us,
Who *let the cat out of the bag*.
Yet still these Tyros in the cause
Deserve, I own, no small applause;
And they're by us received and treated
With all due honours—only seated
In the inverse scale of their reward,
The merely *promised* next my Lord;
Small pensions then, and so on, down,
Rat after rat, they graduate
Through job, red ribbon, and silk gown,
    To Chancellorship and Marquisate.
This serves to nurse the ratting spirit;
The less the bribe, the more the merit.

Our music's good, you may be sure;
My Lord, you know, 's an amateur⁵—
Takes every part with perfect ease,
    Though to the Base by nature suited,
And, formed for all, as best may please,
    For whips and bolts, or chords and keys,
Turns from his victims to his glees,
    And has them both well *executed*.⁶
H—t—d, who, though no rat himself,
    Delights in all such liberal arts,
Drinks largely to the House of Guelph,
    And superintends the *Corni* parts.
While C—nn—g,⁷ who'd be *first* by choice,
Consents to take an *under* voice;
And G—s,⁸ who well that signal knows,
Watches the *Volti Subitos*.⁹

In short, as I've already hinted,
    We take, of late, prodigiously;
But as our Club is somewhat stinted
    For *Gentlemen*, like Tom and me,
We'll take it kind if you'll provide
A few *Squireens*¹⁰ from t' other side;—
Some of those loyal, cunning elves
(We often tell the tale with laughter)
Who used to hide the pikes themselves,
Then hang the fools who found them after.

---

¹ Drossette, in a note on this line of Boileau,
    'Midas, le roi Midas a des oreilles d'anc,'
tells us that ' M. Perrault le Médecin voulut faire à notre auteur un crime d'état de ce vers, comme d'une maligne allusion au Roi.' I trust, however, that no one will suspect the line in the text of any such indecorous allusion.

² It was not under wigs, but tiaras, that King Midas endeavoured to conceal these appendages:
    Tempora purpureis tentat velare tiaris.—*Ovid.*
The noble giver of the toast, however, had evidently, with his usual clearness, confounded King Midas, Mr. Liston, and the P—ce R—g—t together.

³ Mr. Fudge and his friends should go by this name—as the man who, some years since, saved the late Right Hon. George Rose from drowning, was ever after called *Salvator Rosa.*

⁴ This intimacy between the Rats and Informers is just as it should be—*esse dulce sodalitium.*

⁵ His Lordship, during one of the busiest periods of his Ministerial career, took lessons three times a week from a celebrated music-master in glee-singing.

⁶ How amply these two propensities of the noble Lord would have been gratified among that ancient people of Etruria, who, as Aristotle tells us, used to whip their slaves once a year to the sound of flutes!

⁷ This Right Hon. gentleman ought to give up his present alliance with Lord C., if upon no other principle than that which is inculcated in the following arrangement between two ladies of fashion:—

Says Clarinda, 'Though tears it may cost,
    It is time we should part, my dear Sue;
For *your* character's totally lost,
    And *I* have not sufficient for *two!*'

⁸ The rapidity of this Noble Lord's transformation, at the same instant, into a Lord of the Bed-chamber and an opponent of the Catholic Claims was truly miraculous.

⁹ *Turn instantly*—a frequent direction in music books

¹⁰ The Irish diminutive of *Squire.*

I doubt not you could find us, too,
Some Orange Parsons that would do;
Among the rest, we've heard of one,
The Reverend—something—Hamilton,
Who stuffed a figure of himself
   ·(Delicious thought!) and had it shot at,
To bring some Papists to the shelf,
   That couldn't otherwise be got at—
If *he*'ll but join the Association,
We'll vote him in by acclamation.

And now, my brother, guide, and friend,
This somewhat tedious scrawl must end.
I've gone into this long detail,
   Because I saw your nerves were shaken
With anxious fears lest I should fail
   In this new, *loyal*, course I've taken.
But, bless your heart! you need not doubt—
We Fudges know what we're about.
Look round, and say if you can see
A much more thriving family.
There's Jack, the Doctor—night and day
   Hundreds of patients so besiege him,
You'd swear that all the rich and gay
   Fell sick on purpose to oblige him.
And while they think, the precious ninnies,
   He's counting o'er their pulse so steady,
The rogue but counts how many guineas
   He's fobbed, for that day's work, already.
I'll ne'er forget the old maid's alarm,
   When, feeling thus Miss Sukey Flirt, he
Said, as he dropped her shrivelled arm,
   ' Damn'd bad this morning—only thirty ! '

Your dowagers, too, every one,
   So generous are, when they call him in,
That he might now retire upon
   The rheumatisms of three old women.
Then, whatsoe'er your ailments are,
   He can so learnedly explain ye 'em—
Your cold, of course, is a *catarrh*,
   Your headache is a *hemi-cranium :—*
His skill, too, in young ladies' lungs,
   The grace with which, most mild of men,
He begs them to put out their tongues,
   Then bids them—put them in again !
In short, there's nothing now like Jack ;—
   Take all your doctors, great and small,
Of present times and ages back,
   Dear Doctor Fudge is worth them all.

So much for physic—then, in law too,
   Counsellor Tim! to thee we bow ;
Not one of us gives more *éclat* to
   The immortal name of Fudge than thou.
Not to expatiate on the art
   With which you played the patriot's part,
Till something good and snug should offer ;—
   Like one, who, by the way he acts
The *enlightening* part of candle-snuffer,
   The manager's keen eye attracts,
And is promoted thence by him
To strut in robes, like thee, my Tim !

Who shall describe thy powers of face,
   Thy well-fee'd zeal in every case,
Or wrong or right—but ten times warmer
   (As suits thy calling) in the former—
Thy glorious, lawyer-like delight
   In puzzling all that's clear and right,
Which, though conspicuous in thy youth,
   Improves so with a w'g and band on,
That all thy pride's to waylay Truth,
   And leave her not a leg to stand on.—
Thy patent, prime, morality,—
   Thy cases, cited from the Bible—
Thy candour, when it falls to thee
   To help in trouncing for a libel :—
' God knows, I, from my soul, profess
   To hate all bigots and benighters !
God knows, I love, to even excess,
   The sacred Freedom of the Press,
My only aim's to—crush the writers.
These are the virtues, Tim, that draw
   The briefs into thy bag so fast ;
And these, oh Tim—if Law be Law—
   Will raise thee to the Bench at last.

I blush to see this letter's length,
   But 'twas my wish to prove to thee
How full of hope, and wealth, and strength,
   Are all our precious family.
And, should affairs go on as pleasant
   As, thank the Fates, they do at present—
Should we but still enjoy the sway
Of S—dm—h and of C———gh,
I hope, ere long, to see the day
When England's wisest statesmen, judges,
Lawyers, peers, will all be—Fudges !

Good-bye—my paper's out so nearly,
I've only room for
                  Yours sincerely.

LETTER VII.

FROM PHELIM CONNOR TO ————.

Before we sketch the Present—let us cast
A few short rapid glances to the Past.

When he, who had defied all Europe's strength,
Beneath his own weak rashness sunk at length ;—
When loosed, as if by magic, from a chain
That seemed like Fate's, the world was free
   again,
And Europe saw, rejoicing in the sight,
The cause of Kings, *for once*, the cause of Right ;
Then was, indeed, an hour of joy to those
Who sighed for justice—liberty—repose,
And hoped the fall of *one* great vulture's nest
Would ring its warning round, and scare the
   rest.
And all was bright with promise ;—Kings began
To own a sympathy with suffering Man.

And Man was grateful—Patriots of the South
Caught wisdom from a Cossack Emperor's mouth,
And heard, like accents thawed in Northern air,
Unwonted words of freedom burst forth there!

Who did not hope in that triumphant time,
When monarchs, after years of spoil and crime,
Met round the shrine of Peace, and Heaven looked on,
Who did not hope the lust of spoil was gone ;—
That that rapacious spirit, which had played
The game of Pilnitz o'er so oft, was laid,
And Europe's Rulers, conscious of the past,
Would blush, and deviate into right at last?
But no—the hearts that nursed a hope so fair
Had yet to learn what men on thrones can dare;
Had yet to know, of all earth's ravening things,
The only *quite* untameable are K—gs!
Scarce had they met when, to its nature true,
The instinct of their race broke out anew ;
Promises, treaties, charters, all were vain,
And 'Rapine!—rapine!' was the cry again.
How quick they carved their victims, and how well,
Let Saxony, let injured Genoa tell,—
Let all the human stock that, day by day,
Was at the Royal slave-mart trucked away,—
The million souls that, in the face of Heaven,
Were split to fractions,[1] bartered, sold, or given
To swell some despot power, too huge before,
And weigh down Europe with one Mammoth more!
How safe the faith of K—gs let F——ce decide ;—
Her charter broken, ere its ink had dried—
Her Press enthralled—her Reason mocked again
With all the monkery it had spurned in vain—
Her crown disgraced by one, who dared to own
He thanked not F——ce but E——d for his throne—
Her triumphs cast into the shade by those
Who had grown old among her bitterest foes,
And now returned, beneath her conquerors' shields,
Unblushing slaves! to claim her heroes' fields,
To tread down every trophy of her fame,
And curse that glory which to them was shame !—
Let these—let all the damning deeds, that then
Were dared through Europe, cry aloud to men,
With voice like that of crashing ice that rings
Round Alpine huts, the perfidy of K—gs;
And tell the world, when hawks shall harmless bear
The shrinking dove, when wolves shall learn to spare
The helpless victim for whose blood they lusted,
Then, and then only, monarchs may be trusted!

It could not last—these horrors *could* not last—
F——ce would herself have risen, in might, to cast
The insulters off—and oh! that then, as now,
Chained to some distant islet's rocky brow,
N—ol—n ne'er had come to force, to blight,
Ere half matured, a cause so proudly bright ;—
To palsy patriot hearts with doubt and shame,
And write on Freedom's flag a despot's name,
To rush into the lists, unasked, alone,
And make the stake of *all* the game of *one !*
Then would the world have seen again what power
A people can put forth in Freedom's hour ;
Then would the fire of F——ce once more have blazed ;
For every single sword, reluctant raised
In the stale cause of an oppressive throne,
Millions would then have leaped forth in her own ;
And never, never had the unholy stain
Of B——b—n feet disgraced her shores again !

But Fate decreed not so—the Imperial Bird,
That, in his neighbouring cage, unfeared, unstirred,
Had seemed to sleep with head beneath his wing,
Yet watched the moment for a daring spring ;—
Well might he watch, when deeds were done that made
His own transgressions whiten in their shade;
Well might he hope a world, thus trampled o'er
By clumsy tyrants, would be his once more :
Forth from its cage that eagle burst to light,
From steeple on to steeple winged its flight,
With calm and easy grandeur, to that throne
From which a royal craven just had flown ;
And resting there, as in its aerie, furled
Those wings, whose very rustling shook the world!

What was your fury then, ye crowned array,
Whose feast of spoil, whose plundering holiday
Was thus broke up in all its greedy mirth,
By one bold chieftain's stamp on G—ll—c earth!
Fierce was the cry and fulminant the ban,—
' Assassinate, who will—enchain, who can,
The vile, the faithless, outlawed, low-born man!'
' Faithless ! '—and this from *you*—from *you,* forsooth,
Ye pious K—gs, pure paragons of truth,
Whose honesty all knew, for all had tried ;
Whose true Swiss zeal had served on every side;
Whose fame for breaking faith so long was known,
Well might ye claim the craft as all your own,

---

[1] ' Whilst the Congress was reconstructing Europe—not according to rights, natural affinces, language, habits, or laws, but by tables of finance, which divided and subdivided her population into *souls, demi-souls,* and even *fractions,* according to a scale of the direct duties or taxes which could be levied by the acquiring state,' etc.—*Sketch of the Military and Political Power of Russia.*—The words on the protocol are *ames, demi-ames,*

And lash your lordly tails, and fume to see
Such low-born apes of royal perfidy!
Yes—yes—to you alone did it belong
To sin for ever, and yet ne'er do wrong—
The frauds, the lies of lords legitimate
Are but fine policy, deep strokes of state;
But let some upstart dare to soar so high
In k—gly craft, and 'outlaw' is the cry!
What, though long years of mutual treachery
Had peopled full your diplomatic shelves
With ghosts of treaties, murdered 'mong your-
   selves;
Though each by turns was knave and dupe—
   what then?
A Holy League would set all straight again;
Like Juno's virtue, which a dip or two
In some blest fountain made as good as new!
Most faithful Russia—faithful to whoe'er
Could plunder best, and give him amplest share;
Who, even when vanquished, sure to gain his
   ends,
For want of *foes* to rob, made free with *friends*,[1]
And, deepening still by amiable gradations,
When foes are stript of all, then fleeced re-
   lations![2]
Most mild and saintly Prussia—steeped to the
   ears
In persecuted Poland's blood and tears,
And now, with all her harpy wings outspread
O'er severed Saxony's devoted head!
Pure Austria too,—whose history nought repeats
But broken leagues and subsidized defeats;
Whose faith, as Prince, extinguished Venice
   shows,
Whose faith, as man, a widowed daughter
   knows!
And thou, oh England!—who, though once as shy
As cloistered maids, of shame or perfidy,
Art now *broke in*, and, thanks to C———gh,
In all that's worst and falsest lead'st the way!

Such was the pure divan, whose pens and wits
The escape from E—a frightened into fits;
Such were the saints who doomed N—ol—n's
   life,
In virtuous frenzy, to the assassin's knife!
Disgusting crew!—*who* would not gladly fly
To open, downright, bold-faced tyranny,
To honest guilt, that dares do all but lie,
From the false, juggling craft of men like these,
Their canting crimes and varnished villanies;—
These Holy Leaguers, who then loudest boast
Of faith and honour, when they've stained them
   most;

From whose affection men should shrink as loth
As from their hate, for they'll be fleeced by both;
Who, even while plundering, forge Religion's
   name
To frank their spoil, and, without fear or shame,
Call down the Holy Trinity[3] to bless
Partition leagues, and deeds of devilishness!
But hold—enough—soon would this swell of
   rage
O'erflow the boundaries of my scanty page,—
So, here I pause—farewell—another day
Return we to those Lords of prayer and prey
Whose loathsome cant, whose frauds by right
   divine
Deserve a lash—oh! weightier far than mine!

LETTER VIII.

FROM MR. BOB FUDGE TO RICHARD ———, ESQ.

DEAR DICK, while old Donaldson's[2] mending my
   stays,—
Which I *knew* would go smash with me one of
   these days,
And, at yesterday's dinner, when, full to the
   throttle,
We lads had begun our dessert with a bottle
Of neat old Constantia, on *my* leaning back
Just to order another, by Jove I went crack!
Or, as honest Tom said, in his nautical phrase,
'D—n my eyes, Bob, in *doubling* the *Cape* you've
   missed stays.'[5]
So, of course, as no gentleman's seen out with-
   out them,
They're now at the Schneider's;[6] and, while
   he's about them,
Here goes for a letter, post-haste, neck and
   crop—
Let us see—in my last I was—where did I stop?
Oh, I know—at the Boulevards, as motley a
   road as.
Man ever would wish a day's lounging upon;
With its cafés and gardens, hotels and pagodas,
Its founts, and old Counts sipping beer in the
   sun:
With its houses of all architectures you please,
From the Grecian and Gothic, Dick, down by
   degrees
To the pure Hottentot, or the Brighton Chinese;
Where in temples antique you may breakfast or
   dinner it,
Lunch at a mosque, and see Punch from a
   minaret.

---

[1] At the Peace of Tilsit, where he abandoned his ally, Prussia, to France, and received a portion of her territory.
[2] The seizure of Finland from his relative of Sweden.
[3] The usual preamble of these flagitious compacts. In the same spirit, Catherine, after the dreadful massacre of Warsaw, ordered a solemn 'thanksgiving to God, in all the churches, for the blessings conferred upon the Poles;' and commanded that each of them should 'swear fidelity and loyalty to her, and to shed in her defence the last drop of their blood, as they should answer for it to God, and his terrible judgment, kissing the holy word and cross of their Saviour!'
[4] An English tailor at Paris.
[5] A ship is said to miss stays when she does not obey the helm in tacking.
[6] The dandy term for a tailor.

Then, Dick, the mixture of bonnets and bowers,
Of foliage and frippery, *fiacres* and flowers,
Greengrocers, green gardens—one hardly knows
  whether
'Tis country or town, they're so messed up to-
  gether!
And there, if one loves the romantic, one sees
Jew clothes-men, like shepherds, reclined under
  trees;
Or Quidnuncs, on Sunday, just fresh from the
  barber's,
Enjoying their news and *groseille*[1] in those
  arbours,
While gaily their wigs, like the tendrils, are
  curling,
And founts of red currant-juice[2] round them are
  purling.

Here, Dick, arm in arm, as we chattering stray,
And receive a few civil 'God-dems' by the way,—
For 'tis odd, these Mounseers,—though we've
  wasted our wealth
And our strength, till we've thrown ourselves
  into a phthisic,
To cram down their throats an old K—g for
  their health,
As we whip little children to make them take
  physic;—
Yet, spite of our good-natured money and
  slaughter,
They hate us, as Beelzebub hates holy water!
But who the deuce cares, Dick, as long as they
  nourish us
Neatly as now, and good cookery flourishes—
Long as, by bayonets protected, we Natties
May have our full fling at their *salmis* and *pâtés?*
And, truly, I always declared 'twould be pity
To burn to the ground such a choice-feeding city:
Had *Dad* but his way, he'd have long ago blown
The whole batch to Old Nick—and the *people*,
  I own,
If for no other cause than their curst monkey
  looks,
Well deserve a blow-up—but then, damn it, their
  cooks!
As to Marshals, and Statesmen, and all their
  whole lineage,
For aught that *I* care, you may knock them to
  spinage;
But think, Dick, their cooks—what a loss to
  mankind!
What a void in the world would their art leave
  behind!

Their chronometer spits — their intense sala-
  manders—
Their ovens—their pots, that can soften old
  ganders,
All vanished for ever—their miracles o'er,
And the *Marmite Perpétuelle* bubbling no more!

Forbid it, forbid it, ye Holy Allies,
  Take whatever ye fancy—take statues, take
    money—
But leave them, oh leave them their Périgueux
  pies,
  Their glorious goose-livers, and high-pickled
    tunny?[3]
Though many, I own, are the evils they've
  brought us,
Though R—al-y's here on her very last legs,
Yet, who can help loving the land that has
  taught us
Six hundred and eighty-five ways to dress
  eggs?'[4]

You see, Dick, in spite of their cries of 'God-
  dem,'
'Coquin Anglais,' et cætera, how generous I
  am!
And now (to return, once again, to my ' Day,'
Which will take us all night to get through in
  this way)
From the Boulevards we saunter through many
  a street,
Crack jokes on the natives — mine, all very
  neat—
Leave the Signs of the Times to political fops,
And find twice as much fun in the Signs of the
  Shops;—
Here, a L—s D—x—h—t—*there*, a Martinmas goose
(Much in vogue since your eagles are gone out
  of use)—
Henri Quatres in shoals, and of Gods a great
  many,
But Saints are the most on hard duty of any:—
St. Tony, who used all temptations to spurn,
Here hangs o'er a beershop, and tempts in his
  turn;
While *there* St. Venecia[5] sits hemming and
  frilling her
Holy *mouchoir* o'er the door of some milliner;—
St. Austin's the 'outward and visible sign
Of an inward' cheap dinner and pint of small
  wine;

---

[1] 'Lemonade and *eau-de-groseille* are measured out at every corner of every street, from fantastic vessels, jingling with bells, to thirsty tradesmen or wearied messengers.' See Lady Morgan's lively description of the streets of Paris, in her very amusing work upon France, book vi.

[2] These gay, portable fountains, from which the groseille-water is administered, are among the most characteristic ornaments of the streets of Paris.

[3] Le thon mariné, one of the most favourite and indigestible hors-d'œuvres. This fish is taken chiefly in the Golfe de Lyon. 'La tête et le dessous du ventre sont les parties le plus recherchées des gourmets.'— *Cours Gastronomique*, p. 252.

[4] 'The exact number mentioned by M. de la Reynière —'On connoît en France 685 manières différentes d'accommoder les œufs; sans compter celles que nos savans imaginent chaque jour.'

[5] Veronica, the Saint of the Holy Handkerchief, is also, under the name of Veniise or Venecia, the tutelary saint of milliners.

While St. Denis hangs out o'er some hatter of *ton*,
And possessing, good bishop, no head of his own,[1]
Takes an interest in Dandies, who've got—next to none.
Then we stare into shops—read the evening's *affiches*—
Or, if some, who're Lotharios in feeling, should wish
Just to flirt with a luncheon (a devilish bad trick,
As it takes off the bloom of one's appetite, Dick),
To the *Passage des*—what d'ye call't—*des Panoramas*,[2]
We quicken our pace, and there heartily cram up
Seducing young *pâtés*, as ever could cozen
One out of one's appetite, down by the dozen.
We vary, of course—*petits pâtés* do *one* day,
The *next* we've our lunch with the Gauffrier Hollandais,[3]
That popular artist, who brings out, like Sc—tt,
His delightful productions so quick, hot and hot;
Not the worse for the exquisite comment that follows,
Divine *maresquino*, which — Lord, how one swallows!

Once more, then, we saunter forth after our snack, or
Subscribe a few francs for the price of a *fiacre*,
And drive far away to the old Montagues Russes,
Where we find a few twirls in the car of much use
To regenerate the hunger and thirst of us sinners,
Who've lapsed into snacks — the perdition of dinners.
And here, Dick—in answer to one of your queries,
About which we Gourmands have had much discussion—

I've tried all these mountains, Swiss, French, and Ruggieri's,
And think, for *digestion*,[4] there's none like the Russian;
So equal the motion—so gentle, though fleet—
It, in short, such a light and salubrious scamper is,
That take whom you please—take old L——D——
And stuff him—ay, up to the neck — with stewed lampreys,[5]
So wholesome these Mounts, such a *solvent* I've found them,
That, let me but rattle the Monarch well down them,
The fiend, Indigestion, would fly far away,
And the regicide lampreys[6] be foiled of their prey!

Such, Dick, are the classical sports that content us,
Till five o'clock brings on that hour so momentous,[7]
That epoch———but woa! my lad—here comes the Schneider,
And, curse him, has made the stays three inches wider—
Too wide by an inch and a half—what a Guy!
But, no matter—'twill all be set right by and by—
As we've Massinot's[8] eloquent *carte* to eat still up,
An inch and a half's but a trifle to fill up.

So—not to lose time, Dick—here goes for the task;
Au revoir, my old boy—of the Gods I but ask,
That my life, like 'the Leap of the German,'[9] may be,
'Du lit à la table, de la table au lit!'

R. F.

---

[1] St. Denis walked three miles after his head was cut off. The *mot* of a woman of wit upon this legend is well known: 'Je le crois bien; en pareil cas, il n'y a que le premier pas qui coûte.'

[2] Off the Boulevards Italiens.

[3] In the Palais Royal; successor, I believe, to the Flamand, so long celebrated for the *moëlleux* of his Gauffres.

[4] Doctor Cotterel recommends, for this purpose, the Beaujon, or French mountains, and calls them 'une médecine aérienne, couleur de rose;' but I own I prefer the authority of Mr. Bob, who seems, from the following note found in his own handwriting, to have studied all these mountains very carefully:

Memoranda.—The Swiss little notice deserves,
While the fall at Ruggieri's is death to weak nerves:
And (whate'er Doctor Cotterel may write on the question)
The turn at the Beaujon's too sharp for digestion.

I doubt whether Mr. Bob is quite correct in accenting the second syllable of Ruggieri.

[5] A dish so indigestible, that a late novelist, at the end of his book, could imagine no more summary mode of getting rid of all his heroes and heroines than by a hearty supper of stewed lampreys.

[6] Lampreys, indeed, seem to have been always a favourite dish with Kings—whether from some congeniality between them and that fish, I know not; but Dio Cassius tells us that Pollio fattened his lampreys with human blood. St. Louis of France was particularly fond of them. See the anecdote of Thomas Aquinas eating up his majesty's lamprey, in a note upon *Rabelais*, liv. 3, chap. 2.

[6] They killed Henry I. of England—'a food (says Hume, gravely) which always agreed better with his palate than his constitution.'

[7] Had Mr. Bob's *Dinner* Epistle been inserted, I was prepared with an abundance of learned matter to illustrate it, for which, as indeed for all my *scientia popinæ*, I am indebted to a friend in the Dublin University, whose faculty formerly lay in the *magic* line; but in consequence of the Provost's enlightened alarm at such studies, he has taken to the authors *de re cibaria* instead; and has left Bodin, Remigius, Agrippa, and his little dog Filiolus, for Apicius, Nonius, and that most learned and savoury Jesuit, Bulengerus.

[8] A famous restaurateur—now Dupont.

[9] An old French saying: 'Faire le saut de l'Allemand, du lit à la table, et de la table au lit.'

LETTER IX.

FROM PHIL. FUDGE, ESQ., TO THE LORD
VISCOUNT C—ST——GH.

My Lord, the Instructions, brought to-day,
'I shall in all my best obey.'
Your Lordship talks and writes so sensibly!
And—whatsoe'er some wags may say—
Oh! not at *all* incomprehensibly.

I feel the inquiries in your letter
 About my health and French most flattering;
Thank ye, my French, though somewhat better,
 Is, on the whole, but weak and smattering:
Nothing, of course, that can compare
With his who made the Congress stare
(A certain Lord we need not name),
Who, even in French, would have his trope,
And talk of '*bâtir* un système
 Sur l'*équilibre* de l'Europe!'
Sweet metaphor!—and then the epistle
Which bid the Saxon King go whistle,
That tender letter to 'Mon Prince,'[1]
Which showed alike thy French and sense;—
Oh, no, my Lord, there's none can do
Or say *un-English* things like you;
And, if the schemes that fill thy breast
Could but a vent congenial seek,
And use the tongue that suits them best,
 What charming Turkish wouldst thou speak!
But as for *me*, a Frenchless grub,
 At Congress never born to stammer,
Nor learn, like thee, my Lord, to snub
 Fallen monarchs, out of Chamband's grammar.—
Bless you, you do not, *cannot* know
How far a little French will go!
For all one's stock, one need but draw
 On some half-dozen words like these—
Comme ça—par-là—là-bas—ah! ah!
 They'll take you all through France with ease.
Your Lordship's praises of the scraps
 I sent you from my journal lately,
(Enveloping a few laced caps
 For Lady C.) delight me greatly.
Her flattering speech—'what pretty things
 One finds in Mr. Fudge's pages!'
Is praise which (as some poet sings)
 Would pay one for the toils of ages.

Thus flattered, I presume to send
 A few more extracts by a friend;
And I should hope they'll be no less
 Approved of than my last MS.—
The former ones, I fear, were creased,
 As Biddy round the caps *would* pin them;
But these will come to hand, at least
 Unrumpled, for—there's nothing in them.

---

*Extracts from Mr. Fudge's Journal, addressed to
Lord C.*

Aug. 10.

Went to the Mad-house—saw the man[2]
 Who thinks, poor wretch, that, while the Fiend
Of Discord here full riot ran,
 He like the rest was guillotined;—
But that when, under Boney's reign
 (A more discreet, though quite as strong one),
The heads were all restored again,
 He in the scramble got a *wrong one*.
Accordingly, he still cries out
 This strange head fits him most unpleasantly;
And always runs, poor devil, about,
 Inquiring for his own incessantly!

While to his case a tear I dropped,
 And sauntered home, thought I—ye gods!
How many heads might thus be swopped,
 And, after all, not make much odds!
For instance, there's V—s—tt—t's head—
 ('Tam *carum*' it may well be said)
If by some curious chance it came
 To settle on Bill Soames's[3] shoulders,
The effect would turn out much the same
 On all respectable cash-holders:
Except that while in its *new* socket,
 The head was planning schemes to win
A *zigzag* way into one's pocket,
 The hands would plunge *directly* in.

Good Viscount S—dm—h, too, instead
 Of his own grave respected head,
Might wear (for aught I see that bars)
 Old Lady Wilhelmina Frump's—
So, while the band signed *Circulars*,
 The head might lisp out 'What is trumps?'—
The R—g—t's brains could we transfer
 To some robust man-milliner,
The shop, the shears, the lace, and ribbon,
 Would go, I doubt not, quite as glib on;
And, *vice versa*, take the pains
 To give the P—ce the shopman's brains,
One only change from thence would flow—
 Ribbons would not be wasted so!

'Twas thus I pondered on, my Lord;
 And, even at night, when laid in bed,
I found myself, before I snored,
 Thus chopping, swopping head for head.

---

[1] The celebrated letter to Prince Hardenburgh (written, however, I believe, originally in English), in which his Lordship, professing to see 'no moral or political objection' to the dismemberment of Saxony, denounced the unfortunate king as 'not only the most devoted, but the most favoured, of Buonaparte's vassals.'

[2] This extraordinary madman is, I believe, in the Bicêtre. He imagines, exactly as Mr. Fudge states it, that, when the heads of those who had been guillotined were restored, he by mistake got some other person's instead of his own.

[3] A celebrated pickpocket.

At length I thought, fantastic elf!
How such a change would suit *myself.*
'Twixt sleep and waking, one by one,
  With various pericraniums saddled,
At last I tried your Lordship's on,
  And then I grew completely addled—
Forgot all other heads, od rot 'em!
And slept, and dreamt that I was—Bottom.

Aug. 21.
Walked out with daughter Bid—was shown
The House of Commons and the Throne,
Whose velvet cushion's just the same[1]
N—pol—n sat on—what a shame!
Oh, can we wonder, best of speechers!
  When L——s seated thus we see,
That France's 'fundamental features'
  Are much the same they used to be?
However, God preserve the throne,
  And *cushion* too, and keep them free
From accidents which *have* been known
  To happen even to Royalty![2]

Aug. 23.
Read, at a stall (for oft one pops
On something at these stalls and shops,
That does to *quote,* and gives one's book
A classical and knowing look.—
Indeed I've found, in Latin, lately,
A course of stalls improves me greatly).
'Twas thus I read, that, in the East,
  A monarch's *fat* 's a serious matter;
And once in every year, at least,
  He's weighed—to see if he gets fatter:[3]
Then, if a pound or two he be
Increased, there's quite a jubilee![4]

Suppose, my Lord,—and far from me
To treat such things with levity—
But just suppose the R—g—t's weight
Were made thus an affair of state;
And, every sessions, at the close,—
'Stead of a speech, which, all can see, is
Heavy and dull enough, God knows—
  We were to try how heavy *he* is.
Much would it glad all hearts to hear
  That, while the Nation's Revenue

Loses so many pounds a year,
  The P——e, God bless him! *gains* a few.
With bales of muslins, chintzes, spices,
  I see the Easterns weigh their kings;—
But, for the R—g—t, my advice is,
  We should throw in much *heavier* things:
For instance ——'s quarto volumes,
Which, though not spices, serve to wrap them,
Dominie St—dd—t's daily columns,
  'Prodigious!'—in, of course, we'd clap them—
Letters, that C—rtw—t's pen indites,
  In which, with logical confusion,
The *Major* like a *Minor* writes,
  And never comes to a *conclusion :*—
Lord S—m—rs' pamphlet—or his head—
(Ah, *that* were worth its weight in lead!)
Along with which we *in* may whip, sly,
The Speeches of Sir John C—x H—pp—sly;
That Baronet of many words,
Who loves so, in the House of Lords,
To whisper Bishops—and so nigh
  Unto their wigs in whispering goes,
That you may always know him by
  A patch of powder on his nose!—
If this won't do, we in must cram
The 'Reasons' of Lord B—ck—gh—m;
(A book his Lordship means to write,
Entitled *Reasons for my Ratting :*)
Or, should these prove too small and light,
  His ——'s a host—we'll bundle *that* in!
And, *still* should all these masses fail
  To stir the R—g—t's ponderous scale,
Why then, my Lord, in Heaven's name,
  Pitch in, without reserve or stint,
The whole of R—gl—y's beauteous Dame—
  If *that* won't raise him, devil's in't!

Aug. 31
Consulted Murphy's *Tacitus*
  About those famous spies at Rome,[5]
Whom certain Whigs—to make a fuss—
Describe as much resembling us,[6]
Informing gentlemen, at home.
But, bless the fools, they *can't* be serious,
To say Lord S—dm—th's like Tiberius!
What! *he,* the Peer, that injures no man,
Like that severe bloodthirsty Roman!—

---

[1] The only change, if I recollect right, is the substitution of lilies for bees. This war upon the bees is, of course, universal: 'Exitium misere apibus,' like the angry nymphs in Virgil:—but may not *new swarms* arise out of the *victims* of Legitimacy yet?

[2] I am afraid that Mr. Fudge alludes here to a very awkward accident, which is well known to have happened to poor L—s le D—s—é, some years since, at one of the R—g—t's fêtes. He was sitting next our gracious Queen at the time.

[3] 'The third day of the feast the King causeth himself to be weighed with great care.'—*F. Bernier's Voyage to Surat,* etc.

[4] 'I remember,' says Bernier, 'that all the Omrahs expressed great joy that the King weighed two pounds more now than the year preceding.'—Another author tells us that 'Fatness, as well as a very large head, is considered throughout India as one of the most precious gifts of Heaven. An enormous skull is absolutely revered, and the happy owner is looked up to as a superior being. To a *Prince* a joulter-head is invaluable.'—*Oriental Field Sports.*

[5] The name of the first worthy who set up the trade of Informer at Rome (to whom our Olivers and Castleses ought to erect a statue) was Romanus Hispo: 'Qui formam vitæ iniit, quam postea celebrem miseriæ temporum et audaciæ hominum fecerunt.'—*Tacit. Annal.* l. 74.

[6] They certainly possessed the same art of *instigating* their victims which the report of the Secret Committee attributes to Lord Sidmouth's agents: '*Socius* (says Tacitus of one of them) libidinum et necessitatum, *quæ pluribus indiciis illigaret.*'

'Tis true, the Tyrant lent an ear to
All sorts of spies—so doth the Peer, too.
'Tis true, my Lord's Elect tell fibs,
And deal in perjury—*ditto* Tib's.
'Tis true the Tyrant screened and hid
His rogues from justice!—*ditto* Sid.
'Tis true, the Peer is grave and glib
At moral speeches—*ditto* Tib.[2]
'Tis true, the feats the Tyrant did
Were in his dotage—*ditto* Sid.

So far, I own, the parallel
'Twixt Tib. and Sid. goes vastly well;
But there are points in Tib. that strike
My humble mind as much more like
Yourself, my dearest Lord, or him
Of the India Board—that soul of whim!
Like him, Tiberius loved his joke,
On matters, too, where few can bear one;
E.g. a man, cut up, or broke
Upon the wheel—a devilish fair one!
Your common fractures, wounds, and fits,
Are nothing to such wholesale wits;
But, let the sufferer gasp for life,
The joke is then worth any money;
And, if he writhe beneath a knife,—
Oh dear, that's something *quite* too funny.
In this respect, my Lord, you see
The Roman wag and ours agree:
Now, as to *your* resemblance—mum—
This parallel we need not follow;[3]
Though 'tis, in Ireland, said by some
Your Lordship beats Tiberius hollow;
Whips, chains,—but these are things too serious
For me to mention or discuss;
Whene'er your Lordship acts Tiberius,
Phil. Fudge's part is *Tacitus!*

Sept. 2.

Was thinking, had Lord S—dm—th got
Up any decent kind of plot
Against the winter-time—if not,
Alas, alas, our ruin's fated;
All done up, and *spifticated!*
Ministers and all their vassals,
Down from C—tl——gh to Castles,—
Unless we can kick up a riot,
Ne'er can hope for peace or quiet.

What's to be done?—Spa-Fields was clever;
But even *that* brought gibes and mockings

Upon our heads—so, *mem.*—must never
 Keep ammunition in old stockings;
For fear some wag should in his curst head
 Take it to say our force was *worsted.*
Mem. too—when Sid. an army raises,
 It must not be 'incog.' like *Bayes's:*
Nor must the General be a hobbling
 Professor of the art of Cobbling;
Lest men, who perpetrate such puns,
 Should say, with Jacobitic grin,
He felt, from *soleing Wellingtons*,[4]
 A *Wellington's* great *soul* within!
Nor must an old apothecary
 Go take the Tower, for lack of pence,
With (what these wags would call, so merry)
 Physical force and *phial*-ence!
No—no—our Plot, my Lord, must be
 Next time contrived more skilfully.
John Bull, I grieve to say, is growing
 So troublesomely sharp and knowing,
So wise—in short, so Jacobin—
 'Tis monstrous hard to *take him in.*

Sept. 6.

Heard of the fate of our ambassador
 In China, and was sorely nettled;
But think, my Lord, we should not pass it o'er
 Till all this matter's fairly settled;
And here's the mode occurs to *me:*
 As none of our nobility
(Though for their *own* most gracious King
 They would kiss hands, or—any thing)
Can be persuaded to go through
 This farce-like trick of the *Ko-tou;*
And as these Mandarins *won't* bend,
 Without some mumming exhibition,
Suppose, my Lord, you were to send
 Grimaldi to them on a mission:
As *Legate*, Joe could play his part,
 And if, in diplomatic art,
The *volto sciolto*[5] 's meritorious,
 Let Joe but grin, he has it, glorious!

A *title* for him's easily made;
 And, by the by, one Christmas time,
If I remember right, he played
 Lord Morley in some pantomime;[6]—
As Earl of M—rl—y, then, gazette him,
 If *t'other* Earl of M—rl—y 'll let him.
(And why should not the world be blest
 With *two* such stars, for East and West?)

---

[1] 'Neque tamen id Sereno noxæ fuit, *quem odium publicum tutiorem fuciebat. Nam ut quis districtior accusator velut sacrosanctus erat.'—Annal.* lib. 4. 36. Or, as it is translated by Mr. Fudge's friend, Murphy: 'This daring accuser had the *curses* of the *people*, and the *protection* of the *Emperor. Informers*, in proportion as they rose in guilt, *became sacred characters.*'

[2] Murphy even confers upon one of his speeches the epithet 'constitutional.' Mr. Fudge might have added to his parallel, that Tiberius was a *good private* character: 'Egregium vita famaque quoad privatus.'

[3] There is one point of resemblance between Tiberius and Lord C. which Mr. Fudge *might* have mentioned—*'suspensa semper et obscura verba.'*

[4] Short boots, so called.

[5] The *open countenance*, recommended by Lord Chesterfield.

[6] Mr. Fudge is a little mistaken here. It was *not* Grimaldi, but some very inferior performer, who played this part of *Lord Morley* in the pantomime,—so much to the horror of the distinguished Earl of that name. The expostulatory letters of the noble Earl to Mr. H—rr—ls, upon this vulgar profanation of his spic-and-span-new title, will, I trust, some time or other be given to the world.

Then, when before the Yellow Screen
He's brought—and, sure, the very essence
Of etiquette would be that scene
Of Joe in the Celestial Presence!—
He thus should say: 'Duke Ho and Soo,
I'll play what tricks you please for you,
If you'll, in turn, but do for me
A few small tricks you now shall see.
If I consult *your* Emperor's liking,
At least you'll do the same for *my* King.
He then should give them nine such grins
As would astound even Mandarins;
And throw such somersets before
The picture of King George (God bless him!)
As, should Duke Ho but try them o'er,
Would, by Confucius, *much* distress him!

I start this merely as a hint,
But think you'll find some wisdom in't;
And, should you follow up the job,
My son, my Lord (you *know* poor Bob),
Would in the suite be glad to go,
And help his Excellency Joe;—
At least, like noble Amh—rst's son,
The lad will do to *practise* on.¹

LETTER X.

FROM MISS BIDDY FUDGE TO MISS DOROTHY ——.

WELL, it *isn't* the King, after all, my dear
creature!
But *don't* you go laugh, now—there's nothing
to quiz in't—
For grandeur of air and for grimness of feature,
He *might* be a King, Doll, though, hang him,
he isn't.
At first I felt hurt, for I wished it, I own,
If for no other cause than to vex Miss Malone,—
(The great heiress, you know, of Shandangan,
who's here,
Showing off with *such* airs and a real Cashmere,²
While mine's but a paltry old-rabbit skin, dear!)
But says Pa, after deeply considering the thing,
'I am just as well pleased it should *not* be the
King;
As I think for my Biddy, so *gentille* and *jolie*,
Whose charms may their price in an *honest*
way fetch,
That a Brandenburg—(what *is* a Brandenburg,
Dolly?)—
Would be, after all, no such very great catch.
If the R—g—t, indeed—' added he, looking
sly—
(You remember that comical squint of his eye)

¹ See Mr. Ellis's account of the Embassy.
² See Lady Morgan's *France* for the anecdote, told her by Madame de Genlis, of the young gentleman whose love was cured by finding that his mistress wore a *shawl* 'peau de lapin.'
³ The cars, on the return, are dragged up slowly by a chain.

But I stopped him, 'La, Pa, how *can* you say so,
When the R—g—t loves none but old women,
you know!'
Which is fact, my dear Dolly—we, girls of
eighteen,
And so slim—Lord, he'd think us not fit to be
seen!
And would like us much better as old—ay, as old
As that Countess of Desmond, of whom I've
been told
That she lived to much more than a hundred
and ten,
And was killed by a fall from a cherry-tree then!
What a frisky old girl! but—to come to my lover,
Who, though not a king, is a *hero* I'll swear,—
You shall hear all that's happened just briefly
run over,
Since that happy night, when we whisked
through the air!

Let me see—'twas on Saturday—yes, Dolly,
yes—
From that evening I date the first dawn of my
bliss;
When we both rattled off in that dear little car-
riage,
Whose journey, Bob says, is so like love and
marriage,
'Beginning gay, desperate, dashing down-hilly;
And ending as dull as a six-inside Dilly!'³
Well, scarcely a wink did I sleep the night
through,
And, next day, having scribbled my letter to you,
With a heart full of hope this sweet fellow to
meet,
Set out with Papa, to see L—— D——
Make his bow to some half-dozen women and
boys,
Who get up a small concert of shrill *Vive
le* ——:
And how vastly genteeler, my dear, even this is,
Than vulgar Pall-Mall's oratorio of hisses!
The gardens seemed full—so, of course, we
walked o'er 'em,
'Mong orange-trees, clipped into town-bred
decorum,
And Daphnes, and vases, and many a statue
There staring, with not even a stitch on them,
at you!
The ponds, too, we viewed—stood awhile on
the brink
To contemplate the play of those pretty gold
fishes—
'*Live bullion*,' says merciless Bob, 'which I think
Would, if *coined*, with a little *mint* sauce, be
delicious!'⁴

⁴ Mr. Bob need not be ashamed of his cookery jokes, when he is kept in countenance by such men as Cicero, St. Augustine, and that jovial bishop, Venantius Fortunatus. The pun of the great orator upon the 'jus Verrinum,' which he calls bad *hog broth*, from a play upon both the words, is well known; and the Saint's puns upon the conversion of Lot's wife into salt are

But what, Dolly, what is the gay orange-grove,
Or gold fishes, to her that's in search of her love?
In vain did I wildly explore every chair
Where a thing *like* a man was—no lover sat
    there!
In vain my fond eyes did I eagerly cast
At the whiskers, mustachios, and wigs that went
    past,
To obtain, if I could, but a glance at that curl,
But a glimpse of those whiskers, as sacred, my
    girl,
As the lock that, Pa says,[1] is to Mussulmen
    given,
For the angel to hold by that 'lugs them to
    heaven!'
Alas, there went by me full many a quiz,
And mustachios in plenty, but nothing like his!
Disappointed, I found myself sighing out 'well-
    a-day,'
Thought of the words of T--m M--re's Irish
    melody,
Something about the 'green spot of delight,'[2]
(Which, you know, Captain Macintosh sung to
    us one day):
Ah, Dolly! my 'spot' was that Saturday night,
And its verdure, how fleeting, had withered
    by Sunday!

We dined at a tavern—La, what do I say?
If Bob was to know!—a *Restaurateur's*, dear;
Where your *properest* ladies go dine every day,
And drink Burgundy out of large tumblers,
    like beer.
Fine Bob (for he's really grown *super*-fine)
Condescended, for once, to make one of the
    party;
Of course, though but three, we had dinner for
    nine,
And, in spite of my grief, love, I own I ate
    hearty.

Indeed, Doll, I know not how 'tis, but in grief,
I have always found eating a wondrous relief;
And Bob, who's in love, said he felt the same
    quite—
'My sighs,' said he, 'ceased with the first glass
    I drank you;
The *lamb* made me tranquil, the *puffs* made me
    light,
And now that's all o'er—why, I'm—pretty
    well, thank you!'

To *my* great annoyance, we sat rather late;
For Bobby and Pa had a furious debate
About singing and cookery,—Bobby, of course,
Standing up for the latter Fine Art in full
    force;[3]
And Pa saying, 'God only knows which is
    worst,
The French singers or cooks, but I wish us
    well over it—
What with old Laïs and Very, I'm curst
If my head or my stomach will ever recover it!'
'Twas dark when we got to the Boulevards to
    stroll,
And in vain did I look 'mong the street
    Macaronis,
When sudden it struck me—last hope of my
    soul—
That some angel might take the dear man to
    Tortoni's![4]
We entered—and scarcely had Bob, with an air,
For a *grappe à la jardinière* called to the
    waiters,
When, oh! Doll, I saw him—my hero was there
(For I knew his white small-clothes and brown
    leather gaiters),
A group of fair statues from Greece smiling o'er
    him,[5]
And lots of red currant juice sparkling before
    him!

---

equally ingenious: 'In salem conversa hominibus
fidelibus quoddam præstitit *condimentum*, quo *sapiant*
aliquid, unde illud caveatur exemplum.'—*De Civitat.*
Dei, lib. 16, cap. 30.—The jokes of the pious favourite
of Queen Radagunda, the convivial Bishop Venantius,
may be found among his poems, in some lines against
a cook who had robbed him. The following is similar
to Cicero's pun:

Plus juscella Coci quam mea jura valet.

See his poems, *Corpus Poetar. Latin.* tom. 2, p. 1732.
—Of the same kind was Montmaur's joke when a dish
was spilt over him—'summum jus, summa injuria;'
and the same celebrated parasite, in ordering a sole to
be placed before him, said,

Eligi cui dicas, tu mihi sola places.

The reader may likewise see, among a good deal of
kitchen erudition, the learned Lipsius' jokes on cutting
up a capon, in his *Saturnal. Sermon.* lib. 2, cap. 2.

[1] For this scrap of knowledge 'Pa' was, I suspect,
indebted to a note upon *Volney's Ruins,*—a book which
usually forms part of a Jacobin's library, and with
which Mr. Fudge must have been well acquainted at the
time when he wrote his 'Down with Kings,' etc. The

note in Volney is as follows:—'It is by this tuft of
hair (on the crown of the head), worn by the majority
of Mussulmans, that the Angel of the Tomb is to take
the elect and carry them to Paradise.'

[2] The young lady, whose memory is not very correct,
must allude, I think, to the following lines:

Oh! that fairy form is ne'er forgot,
  Which First Love traced:
Still it lingering haunts the greenest spot
  On Memory's waste!

[3] Cookery has been dignified by the researches of a
Bacon (see his *Natural History, Receipts,* etc.), and
takes its station as one of the Fine Arts in the following passage of Mr. Dugald Stewart:—'Agreeably to this
view of the subject, *sweet* may be said to be *intrinsically*
pleasing, and *bitter* to be relatively pleasing; which
both are, in many cases, equally essential to those
effects which, in the art of cookery, correspond to that
composite beauty which is the object of the painter and
of the poet to create.'—*Philosophical Essays.*

[4] A fashionable *café glacier* on the Italian Boulevards.

[5] 'You eat your ice at Tortoni's,' says Mr. Scott,
'under a Grecian group.'

Oh Dolly, these heroes—what creatures they are!
In the *boudoir* the same as in fields full of slaughter;
As cool in the Beaujon's precipitous car
As when safe at Tortoni's, o'er iced currant-water!
He joined us—imagine, dear creature, my ecstasy—
Joined by the man I'd have broken ten necks to see!
Bob wished to treat him with punch *à la glace*,
But the sweet fellow swore that my *'beauté*, my *grace*,
And my *je-ne-sais-quoi* (then his whiskers he twirled)
Were, to *him*, 'on de top of all ponch in de vorld.'—
How pretty!—though oft (as, of course, it must be)
Both his French and his English are Greek, Doll, to me.
But, in short, I felt happy as ever fond heart did;
And, happier still, when 'twas fixed, ere we parted,
That, if the next day should be *pastoral* weather,
We all would set off in French buggies, together,
To see *Montmorency*—that place which, you know,
Is so famous for cherries and Jean Jacques Rousseau.
His card then he gave us—the *name*, rather creased—
But 'twas Calicot — something — a colonel, at least!
After which—sure there never was hero so civil —he
Saw us safe home to our door in *Rue Rivoli*,
Where his *last* words, as, at parting, he threw
A soft look o'er his shoulders, were—'How do you do!'[1]

But, lord,—there's Papa for the post—I'm so vexed—
Montmorency must now, love, be kept for my next.
That dear Sunday night!—I was charmingly dressed,
And—*so* providential—was looking my best;
Such a sweet muslin gown, with a flounce—and my frills,
You've no notion how rich—(though Pa has by the bills)—
And you'd smile had you seen, when we sat rather near,
Colonel Calicot eyeing the cambric, my dear.
Then the flowers in my bonnet—but, la, it's in vain—
So, good-bye, my sweet Doll—I shall soon write again.
B. F.

Nota Bene—Our love to all neighbours about—
Your papa in particular—how is his gout?

P.S.—I've just opened my letter to say,
In your next you must tell me (now *do*, Dolly, pray,
For I hate to ask Bob, he's so ready to quiz)
What sort of a thing, dear, a *Brandenburgh* is.

LETTER XI.

FROM PHELIM CONNOR TO ———.

YES—'twas a cause, as noble and as great
As ever hero died to vindicate—
A nation's right to speak a nation's voice,
And own no power but of the nation's choice!
Such was the grand, the glorious cause that now
Hung trembling on N—p—l—n's single brow;
Such the sublime arbitrement, that poured,
In patriot eyes, a light around his sword,
A glory then, which never, since the day
Of his young victories, had illumed its way!

Oh 'twas not then the time for tame debates,
Ye men of Gaul, when chains were at your gates;
When he who fled before your chieftain's eye,
As geese from eagles on Mount Taurus fly![2]
Denounced against the land that spurned his chain,
Myriads of swords to bind it fast again—
Myriads of fierce invading swords, to track
Through your best blood his path of vengeance back;
When Europe's kings, that never yet combined
But (like those upper stars, that, when conjoined,
Shed war and pestilence) to scourge mankind,
Gathered around, with hosts from every shore,
Hating N—p—l—n much, but freedom more,
And, in that coming strife, appalled to see
The world yet left one chance for liberty!—
No, 'twas not then the time to weave a net
Of bondage round your chief; to curb and fret
Your veteran war-horse, pawing for the fight,
When every hope was in his speed and might—
To waste the hour of action in dispute,
And coolly plan how Freedom's *boughs* should shoot
When your invader's axe was at the *root!*
No, sacred Liberty! that God, who throws
Thy light around, like his own sunshine, knows
How well I love thee, and how deeply hate
All tyrants, upstart and legitimate—
Yet in that hour, were F——ce my native land,
I would have followed, with quick heart and hand,

---

[1] Not an unusual mistake with foreigners.
[2] See *Ælian*, lib. 5, cap. 29, who tells us that these geese, from a consciousness of their own loquacity, always cross Mount Taurus with stones in their bills, to prevent any unlucky cackle from betraying them to the eagles—διαπιπτουσι σιωπωντες.

N—p—l—on, Nero—ay, no matter whom—
To snatch my country from that damning doom,
That deadliest curse that on the conquered waits—
A conqueror's satrap, throned within her gates!

True, he was false—despotic—all you please—
Had trampled down man's holiest liberties—
Had, by a genius formed for nobler things
Than lie within the grasp of *vulgar* kings,
But raised the hopes of men—as eaglets fly
With tortoises aloft into the sky—
To dash them down again more shatteringly!
All this I own—but still [1] . . .

LETTER XII.

FROM MISS BIDDY FUDGE TO MISS DOROTHY ——.

At last, Dolly,—thanks to a potent emetic
Which Bobby and Pa, with grimace sympathetic,
Have swallowed this morning, to balance the bliss
Of an eel *matelote* and a *bisque d'écrevisses*—
I've a morning at home to myself, and sit down
To describe you our heavenly trip out of town.
How agog you must be for this letter, my dear!
Lady Jane, in the novel, less languished to hear
If that elegant cornet she met at Lord Neville's
Was actually dying with love or—blue devils.
But love, Dolly, love is the theme *I* pursue;
With blue devils, thank heaven, I've nothing to do—
Except, indeed, dear Colonel Calicot spies
Any imps of that colour in *certain* blue eyes,
Which he stares at till *I*, Doll, at *his* do the same;
Then he simpers—I blush—and would often exclaim,
If I knew but the French for it, 'Lord, Sir, for shame!'

Well, the morning was lovely—the trees in full dress
For the happy occasion—the sunshine *express*—
Had we ordered it, dear, of the best poet going,
It scarce could be furnished more golden and glowing.
Though late when we started, the scent of the air
Was like Gattie's rose-water—and, bright, here and there,
On the grass an odd dew-drop was glittering yet,
Like my aunt's diamond pin on her green tabbinet!
And the birds seem to warble as blest, on the boughs,
As if *each* a plumed Calicot had for her spouse,

And the grapes were all blushing and kissing in rows,
And—in short, need I tell you, wherever one goes
With the creature one loves, 'tis all *couleur de rose*;
And ah, I shall ne'er, lived I ever so long, see
A day such as that at divine Montmorency!
There was but *one* drawback—at first when we started,
The Colonel and I were inhumanly parted;
How cruel—young hearts of such moments to rob!
He went in Pa's buggy, and I went with Bob;
And, I own, I felt spitefully happy to know
That Papa and his comrade agreed but *so-so*.
For the Colonel, it seems, is a stickler for Boney's—
Served with him, of course—nay, I'm sure they were cronies—
So martial his features! dear Doll, you can trace
Ulm, Austerlitz, Lodi, as plain in his face
As you do on that pillar of glory and brass [2]
Which the poor Duc de B—ri must hate so to pass!
It appears, too, he made—as most foreigners do—
About English affairs an odd blunder or two.
For example—misled by the names, I dare say—
He confounded Jack Castles with Lord C——gh;
And—such a mistake as no mortal hit ever on—
Fancied the *present* Lord C—md—n the *clever one*!

But politics ne'er were the sweet fellow's trade;
'Twas for war and the ladies my Colonel was made.
And, oh, had you heard, as together we walked
Through that beautiful forest, hów sweetly he talked,
And how perfectly well he appeared, Doll, to know
All the life and adventures of Jean Jacques Rousseau!—
'"Twas there,' said he—not that his *words* I can state—
'Twas a gibberish that Cupid alone could translate;—
But 'there,' said he (pointing where, small and remote,
The dear Hermitage rose), 'there his Julie he wrote,—
Upon paper gilt-edged, without blot or erasure;
Then sanded it over with silver and azure,
And—oh, what will genius and fancy not do?—
Tied the leaves up together with *nompareille* blue!' [3]

---

[1] Somebody (Fontenelle, I believe) has said, that if he had his hand full of truths, he would open but one finger at a time; and I find it necessary to use the same sort of reserve with respect to Mr. Phelim Connor's very plain-spoken letters. The remainder of this Epistle is so full of unsafe matter-of-fact, that it must, for the present at least, be withheld from the public.
[2] The column in the Place Vendôme.
[3] 'Employant pour cela le plus beau papier doré, séchant l'écriture avec de la poudre d'azur et d'argent.

What a trait of Rousseau! what a crowd of
  emotions
From sand and blue ribbons are conjured up
  here!
Alas, that a man of such exquisite[1] notions
Should send his poor brats to the Foundling,
  my dear!
"'Twas here, too, perhaps,' Colonel Calicot
  said—
As down the small garden he pensively led—
(Though once I could see his sublime forehead
  wrinkle
With rage not to find there the loved peri-
  winkle[2])
' 'Twas here he received from the fair D'Epinay,
(Who called him so sweetly *her Bear*, every
  day),
That dear flannel petticoat, pulled off to form
A waistcoat to keep the enthusiast warm!'

Such, Doll, were the sweet recollections we
  pondered,
As, full of romance, through that valley we
  wandered,
The flannel (one's train of ideas, how odd it is!)
Led us to talk about other commodities,
Cambric, and silk, and I ne'er shall forget,
For the sun was then hastening in pomp to its
  set,
And full on the Colonel's dark whiskers shone
  down,
When he asked me, with eagerness,—who made
  my gown?
The question confused me; for, Doll, you must
  know,
And I *ought* to have told my best friend long ago,
That, by Pa's strict command, I no longer
  employ[3]
That enchanting *couturière*, Madame le Roi,
But am forced, dear, to have Victorine, who—
  deuce take her!—
It seems is, at present, the King's mantua-
  maker—
I mean *of his party*—and, though much the
  smartest,
Le Roi is condemned as a rank B-n-pa-t-st.[4]

Think, Doll, how confounded I looked—so well
  knowing
The Colonel's opinions—my cheeks were quite
  glowing;

I stammered out something — nay, even half
  named
The *legitimate* sempstress, when, loud, he ex-
  claimed,
'Yes, yes, by the stitching 'tis plain to be seen
It was made by that B-rb-n-t- b—b, Victorine!'
What a word for a hero! but heroes *will* err,
And I thought, dear, I'd tell you things *just as*
  they were.
Besides, though the word on good manners in-
  trench,
I assure you 'tis not *half* so shocking in French.

But this cloud, though embarrassing, soon passed
  away,
And the bliss altogether, the dreams of that day,
The thoughts that arise when such dear fellows
  woo us,—
The *nothings* that then, love, are *everything* to
  us—
That quick correspondence of glances and sighs,
And what Bob calls the ' Twopenny Post of the
  Eyes'—
Ah Doll! though I *know* you've a heart, 'tis in
  vain
To a heart so unpractised these things to ex-
  plain.
They can only be felt in their fulness divine
By her who has wandered, at evening's decline,
Through a valley like that, with a Colonel like
  mine!

But here I must finish—for Bob, my dear Dolly,
Whom physic, I find, always makes melancholy,
Is seized with a fancy for churchyard reflections;
And full of all yesterday's rich recollections,
Is just setting off for Montmartre—'for *there* is,'
Said he, looking solemn, 'the tomb of the
  Vérys!'[5]
Long, long have I wished, as a votary true,
O'er the grave of such talents to utter my
  moans;
And to-day, as my stomach is not in good cue
For the *flesh* of the Vérys, I'll visit their
  bones!'
He insists upon *my* going with him—how teazing!
This letter, however, dear Dolly, shall lie
Unsealed in my drawer, that, if anything pleasing
Occurs while I'm out, I may tell you—Good-
  bye.
                                          B. F.

---

et cousant mes cahiers avec de la nompareille bleue.'—
Les Confessions, Part 2, liv. 9.

[1] This word 'exquisite' is evidently a favourite of
Miss Fudge's; and I understand she was not a little
angry when her brother Bob committed a pun on the
last two syllables of it in the following couplet:

  'I'd fain praise your poem—but tell me, how is it,
    When *I* cry out " Exquisite," *Echo* cries " *Quis it!*"'

[2] The flower which Rousseau brought into such
fashion among the Parisians, by exclaiming, one day,
'Ah, voila de la pervenche!'

[3] Miss Biddy's notions of French pronunciation may
be perceived in the rhymes which she always selects for
'*Le Roi*.'

[4] Le Roi, who was the *Couturière* of the Empress Maria
Louisa, is at present, of course, out of fashion, and is
succeeded in her station by the Royalist mantua-maker,
Victorine.

[5] It is the *brother* of the present excellent restaurateur who lies entombed so magnificently in the Cime-
tière Montmartre. The inscription on the column at
the head of the tomb concludes with the following
words: 'Toute sa vie fut consacrée aux *arts utiles*.'

THE FUDGE FAMILY IN PARIS.

Four o'Clock.

Oh Dolly, dear Dolly, I'm ruined for ever—
I ne'er shall be happy again, Dolly, never!
To think of the wretch—what a victim was I!
'Tis too much to endure—I shall die, I shall die—
My brain's in a fever—my pulses beat quick—
I shall die, or, at least, be exceedingly sick!
Oh what do you think? after all my romancing,
My visions of glory, my sighing, my glancing,
T'his Colonel—I scarce can commit it to paper—
This Colonel's no more than a vile linen-draper!!
'Tis true as I live—I had coaxed brother Bob so
(You'll hardly make out what I'm writing, I sob so)
For some little gift on my birthday—September
The thirtieth, dear, I'm eighteen, you remember—
That Bob to a shop kindly ordered the coach
(Ah, little I thought who the shopman would prove)
To bespeak me a few of those *mouchoirs de poche*,
Which, in happier hours, I have sighed for, my love—
(The most beautiful things—two Napoleons the price—
And one's name in the corner embroidered so nice!)
Well, with heart full of pleasure, I entered the shop,
But—ye Gods, what a phantom!—I thought I should drop—
There he stood, my dear Dolly—no room for a doubt—
There, behind the vile counter, these eyes saw him stand,
With a piece of French cambric before him rolled out,
And that horrid yard-measure upraised in his hand!

Oh—Papa, all along, knew the secret, 'tis clear—
'Twas *a shopman* he meant by a 'Brandenburgh,' dear!
The man, whom I fondly had fancied a king,
And, when *that* too delightful illusion was past,
As a hero had worshipped—vile treacherous thing—
To turn out but a low linen-draper at last!
My head swam around—the wretch smiled, I believe,
But his smiling, alas! could no longer deceive—
I fell back on Bob—my whole heart seemed to wither—
And, pale as a ghost, I was carried back hither!
I only remember that Bob, as I caught him,
With cruel facetiousness said, 'Curse the Kiddy!
A staunch Revolutionist always I've thought him,
But now I find out he's a *Counter* one, Biddy!'

Only think, my dear creature, if this should be known
To that saucy, satirical thing, Miss Malone!
What a story 'twill be at Shandangan for ever!
What laughs and what quizzing she'll have with the men!
It will spread through the country—and never, oh never
Can Biddy be seen at Kilrandy again!
Farewell—I shall do something desperate, I fear—
And, ah! if my fate ever reaches your ear,
One tear of compassion my Doll will not grudge
To her poor, broken-hearted, young friend,
BIDDY FUDGE.

Nota Bene.—I'm sure you will hear, with delight,
That we're going, all three, to see Brunet tonight.
A laugh will revive me—and kind Mr. Cox
(Do you know him?) has got us the Governor's box!

EPISTLES, ODES, AND OTHER POEMS.

EPISTLES, ODES, AND OTHER POEMS.

TO FRANCIS, EARL OF MOIRA,

GENERAL IN HIS MAJESTY'S FORCES, MASTER-GENERAL OF THE ORDNANCE,
CONSTABLE OF THE TOWER, ETC.

My LORD,—It is impossible to think of addressing a Dedication to your Lordship without calling to mind the well-known reply of the Spartan to a rhetorician who proposed to pronounce an eulogium on Hercules. 'On Hercules!' said the honest Spartan, 'who ever thought of blaming Hercules?' In a similar manner, the concurrence of public opinion has left to the panegyrist of your Lordship a very superfluous task. I shall therefore be silent on the subject, and merely entreat your indulgence to the very humble tribute of gratitude which I have here the honour to present. I am, my Lord,

With every feeling of attachment and respect,

Your Lordship's very devoted servant,

THOMAS MOORE.

27, Bury Street, St. James's, April 10, 1806.

PREFACE.

THE principal poems in the following Collection were written during an absence of fourteen months from Europe. Though curiosity was certainly not the motive of my voyage to America, yet it happened that the gratification of curiosity was the only advantage which I derived from it. Finding myself in the country of a new people, whose infancy had promised so much, and whose progress to maturity has been an object of such interesting speculation, I determined to employ the short period of time, which my plan of return to Europe afforded me, in travelling through a few of the States, and acquiring some knowledge of the inhabitants.

The impression which my mind received from the character and manners of these republicans, suggested the Epistles which are written from the city of Washington and Lake Erie.[1] How far I was right, in thus assuming the tone of a satirist against a people whom I viewed but as a stranger and a visitor, is a doubt which my feelings did not allow me time to investigate. All I presume to answer for is the fidelity of the picture which I have given; and though prudence might have dictated gentler language, truth, I think, would have justified severer

I went to America with prepossessions by no means unfavourable, and, indeed, rather indulged in many of those illusive ideas with respect to the purity of the government, and the primitive happiness of the people, which I had early imbibed in my native country, where,

---

[1] Epistles VI., VII., and VIII.

unfortunately, discontent at home enhances every distant temptation, and the western world has long been looked to as a retreat from real or imaginary oppression, as the elysian Atlantis, where persecuted patriots might find their visions realized, and be welcomed by kindred spirits to liberty and repose. I was completely disappointed in every flattering expectation which I had formed, and was inclined to say to America, as Horace says to his mistress, 'intentata nites.' Brissot, in the preface to his Travels, observes, that 'freedom in that country is carried to so high a degree as to border upon a state of nature ;' and there certainly is a close approximation to savage life, not only in the liberty which they enjoy, but in the violence of party spirit and of private animosity which results from it. This illiberal zeal embitters all social intercourse ; and though I scarcely could hesitate in selecting the party whose views appeared the more pure and rational, yet I was sorry to observe that, in asserting their opinions, they both assume an equal share of intolerance ; the Democrats, consistently with their principles, exhibiting a vulgarity of rancour which the Federalists too often are so forgetful of their cause as to imitate.

The rude familiarity of the lower orders, and, indeed, the unpolished state of society in general, would neither surprise nor disgust if they seemed to flow from that simplicity of character, that honest ignorance of the gloss of refinement, which may be looked for in a new and inexperienced people. But when we find them arrived at maturity in most of the vices and all the pride of civilisation, while they are still so remote from its elegant characteristics, it is impossible not to feel that this youthful decay, this crude anticipation of the natural period of corruption, represses every sanguine hope of the future energy and greatness of America.

I am conscious that, in venturing these few remarks, I have said just enough to offend, and by no means sufficient to convince ; for the limits of a preface will not allow me to enter into a justification of my opinions, and I am committed on the subject as effectually as if I had written volumes in their defence. My reader, however, is apprised of the very cursory observation upon which these opinions are founded, and can easily decide for himself upon the degree of attention or confidence which they merit.

With respect to the poems in general which occupy the following pages, I know not in what manner to apologize to the public for intruding upon their notice such a mass of unconnected trifles, such a world of epicurean atoms, as I have here brought in conflict together. To say that I have been tempted by the liberal offers of my bookseller, is an excuse which can hope for but little indulgence from the critic ; yet I own that, without this seasonable inducement, these poems very possibly would never have been submitted to the world. The glare of publication is too strong for such imperfect productions : they should be shown but to the eye of friendship, in that dim light of privacy, which is as favourable to poetical as to female beauty, and serves as a veil for faults, while it enhances every charm which it displays. Besides, this is not a period for the idle occupations of poetry, and times like the present require talents more active and more useful. Few have now the leisure to read such trifles, and I sincerely regret that I have had the leisure to write them.

EPISTLES, ODES, AND OTHER POEMS.

EPISTLE I.
TO LORD VISCOUNT STRANGFORD.
ABOARD THE PHAETON FRIGATE, OFF THE AZORES, BY MOONLIGHT.

SWEET moon! if like Crotona's sage,[1]
By any spell my hand could dare
To make thy disk its ample page,
And write my thoughts, my wishes there ;

How many a friend, whose careless eye
Now wanders o'er that starry sky,
Should smile, upon thy orb to meet
The recollection, kind and sweet,
The reveries of fond regret,
The promise never to forget,
And all my heart and soul would send
To many a dear-loved, distant friend!

Oh, Strangford! when we parted last,
I little thought the times were past,
For ever past, when brilliant joy
Was all my vacant heart's employ :

[1] Pythagoras, who was supposed to have a power of writing upon the moon by the means of a magic mirror. See Bayle, art. *Pythag.*

When, fresh from mirth to mirth again,
 We thought the rapid hours too few,
Our only use for knowledge then
 To turn to rapture all we knew!
Delicious days of whim and soul!
 When, mingling lore and laugh together,
We leaned the book on pleasure's bowl,
 And turned the leaf with folly's feather!
I little thought that all were fled,
 That, ere that summer's bloom was shed,
My eye should see the sail unfurled
 That wafts me to the western world.

And yet 'twas time—in youthful days,
 To cool the season's burning rays,
The heart may let its wanton wing
 Repose awhile in pleasure's spring,
But, if it wait for winter's breeze,
 The spring will dry, the heart will freeze!
And then, that Hope, that fairy Hope,
 Oh! she awaked such happy dreams,
And gave my soul such tempting scope
 For all its dearest, fondest schemes,
That not Verona's child of song,
 When flying from the Phrygian shore,
With lighter hopes could bound along,
 Or pant to be a wanderer more![1]

Even now delusive hope will steal
 Amid the dark regrets I feel,
Soothing as yonder placid beam
 Pursues the murmurs of the deep,
And lights them with consoling gleam,
 And smiles them into tranquil sleep!
Oh! such a blessed night as this,
 I often think, if friends were near,
How we should feel, and gaze with bliss
 Upon the moon-bright scenery here!
The sea is like a silvery lake,
 And o'er its calm the vessel glides
Gently, as if it feared to wake
 The slumber of the silent tides!
The only envious cloud that lowers,
 Hath hung its shade on Pico's height,[2]
Where dimly, 'mid the dusk, he towers,
 And, scowling at this Heaven of light,
Exults to see the infant storm
 Cling darkly round his giant form!

Now, could I range those verdant isles
 Invisible, at this soft hour,
And see the looks, the melting smiles,
 That brighten many an orange bower;

And could I lift each pious veil,
 And see the blushing cheek it shades,
Oh! I should have full many a tale
 To tell of young Azorian maids.[3]

Dear Strangford! at this hour, perhaps,
 Some faithful lover (not so blest
As they who in their ladies' laps
 May cradle every wish to rest)
Warbles, to touch his dear one's soul,
 Those madrigals, of breath divine,
Which Camoens' harp from rapture stole,
 And gave, all glowing warm, to thine![4]
Oh! could the lover learn from thee,
 And breathe them with thy graceful tone,
Such dear beguiling minstrelsy
 Would make the coldest nymph his own.

But, hark!—the boatswain's pipings tell
 'Tis time to bid my dream farewell:
Eight bells—the middle watch is set;
 Good night, my Strangford!—ne'er forget
That far beyond the western sea[5]
 Is one whose heart remembers thee!

STANZAS.

Θυμος δε ποτ' εμος . . . .
. . . . . μι προςφωνει ταδε
Γινωσκε τ'ανθρωπεια μη σιβειν αγαν.
 Æschyl. Fragment.

A BEAM of tranquillity smiled in the west,
 The storms of the morning pursued us no more,
And the wave, while it welcomed the moment of rest,
 Still heaved, as remembering ills that were o'er!

Serenely my heart took the hue of the hour,
 Its passions were sleeping, were mute as the dead,
And the spirit becalmed but remembered their power,
 As the billow the force of the gale that was fled!

I thought of the days, when to pleasure alone
 My heart ever granted a wish or a sigh;
When the saddest emotion my bosom had known
 Was pity for those who were wiser than I!

---

[1] Alluding to these animated lines in the 44th Carmen of this poet:

Jam mens prætrepidans avet vagari,
Jam læti studio pedes vigescunt!

[2] Pico is a very high mountain on one of the Azores, from which the island derives its name. It is said by some to be as high as the Peak of Teneriffe.

[3] I believe it is Guthrie who says, that the inhabitants of the Azores are much addicted to gallantry.

This is an assertion in which even Guthrie may be credited.

[4] These Islands belong to the Portuguese.

[5] From Captain Cockburn, who commanded the Phaeton, I received such kind attentions as I must ever remember with gratitude. As some of the journalists have gravely asserted that I went to America to speculate in lands, it may not be impertinent to state, that the object of this voyage across the Atlantic was my appointment to the office of Registrar of the Vice-Admiralty Court of Bermuda.

I felt how the pure intellectual fire
  In luxury loses its heavenly ray;
How soon, in the lavishing cup of desire,
  The pearl of the soul may be melted away!

And I prayed of that Spirit who lighted the flame,
  That pleasure no more might its purity dim,
And that sullied but little, or brightly the same,
  I might give back the gem I had borrowed from him!

The thought was ecstatic! I felt as if Heaven
  Had already the wreath of eternity shown;
As if, passion all chastened and error forgiven,
  My heart had begun to be purely its own!

I looked to the west, and the beautiful sky
  Which morning had clouded, was clouded no more:
'Oh! thus,' I exclaimed, 'can a heavenly eye
  Shed light on the soul that was darkened before!'

THE TELL-TALE LYRE.

I'VE heard, there was in ancient days
  A Lyre of most melodious spell;
'Twas Heaven to hear its fairy lays,
  If half be true that legends tell.

'Twas played on by the gentlest sighs,
  And to their breath it breathed again
In such entrancing melodies
  As ear had never drunk till then!

Not harmony's serenest touch
  So stilly could the notes prolong;
They were not heavenly song so much
  As they were dreams of heavenly song!

If sad the heart, whose murmuring air
  Along the chords in languor stole,
The soothings it awakened there
  Were eloquence from pity's soul!

Or if the sigh, serene and light,
  Was but the breath of fancied woes,
The string, that felt its airy flight,
  Soon whispered it to kind repose!

And oh! when lovers talked alone,
  If 'mid their bliss the Lyre was near,
It made their murmurs all its own,
  And echoed notes that Heaven might hear!

There was a nymph, who long had loved,
  But dared not tell the world how well;
The shades, where she at evening roved,
  Alone could know, alone could tell.

'Twas there, at twilight time, she stole
  So oft, to make the dear one blest,
Whom love had given her virgin soul.
  And nature soon gave all the rest!

It chanced that in the fairy bower
  Where they had found their sweetest shed,
This Lyre, of strange and magic power,
  Hung gently whispering o'er their head.

And while, with eyes of mingling fire,
  They listened to each other's vow,
The youth full oft would make the Lyre
  A pillow for his angel's brow!

And while the melting words she breathed
  On all its echoes wantoned round,
Her hair, amid the strings enwreathed,
  Through golden mazes charmed the sound.

Alas! their hearts but little thought,
  While thus entranced they listening lay,
That every sound the Lyre was taught
  Should linger long, and long betray!

So mingled with its tuneful soul
  Were all their tender murmurs grown,
That other sighs unanswered stole,
  Nor changed the sweet, the treasured tone.

Unhappy nymph! thy name was sung
  To every passing lip that sighed:
The secrets of thy gentle tongue
  On every ear in murmurs died!

The fatal Lyre, by Envy's hand
  Hung high amid the breezy groves,
To every wanton gale that fanned
  Betrayed the mystery of your loves!

Yet, oh!—not many a suffering hour,
  Thy cup of shame on earth was given:
Benignly came some pitying power,
  And took the Lyre and thee to heaven!

There, as thy lover dries the tear
  Yet warm from life's malignant wrongs,
Within his arms, thou lov'st to hear
  The luckless Lyre's remembered songs!

Still do your happy souls attune
  The notes it learned, on earth, to move;
Still breathing o'er the chords, commune
  In sympathies of angel love!

TO THE FLYING-FISH.[1]

WHEN I have seen thy snowy wing
  O'er the blue wave at evening spring,

---

[1] It is the opinion of St. Austin, upon Genesis, and I believe of nearly all the Fathers, that birds, like fish, were originally produced from the waters; in defence of which idea they have collected every fanciful cir-

'Twas there, at twilight time, she stole
So oft, to make the dear one blest,
Whom love had given her virgin soul,
And nature soon gave all the rest!
It chanced that in the fairy bower
Where they had found their sweetest shed,
This Lyre, of strange and magic power,
Hung gently whispering o'er their head.
Page 300.

And give those scales, of silver white,
So gaily to the eye of light,
As if thy frame were formed to rise,
And live amid the glorious skies;
Oh! it has made me proudly feel,
How like thy wing's impatient zeal
Is the pure soul, that scorns to rest
Upon the world's ignoble breast,
But takes the plume that God has given,
And rises into light and Heaven!

But when I see that wing, so bright,
Grow languid with a moment's flight,
Attempt the paths of air in vain,
And sink into the waves again:
Alas! the flattering pride is o'er;
Like thee, awhile, the soul may soar,
But erring man must blush to think,
Like thee, again, the soul may sink!

Oh virtue! when thy clime I seek,
Let not my spirit's flight be weak:
Let me not, like this feeble thing,
With brine still dropping from its wing,
Just sparkle in the solar glow,
And plunge again to depths below;
But when I leave the grosser throng
With whom my soul hath dwelt so long,
Let me, in that aspiring day,
Cast every lingering stain away,
And, panting for thy purer air,
Fly up at once and fix me there!

EPISTLE II.

TO MISS M——E.

FROM NORFOLK, IN VIRGINIA, NOVEMBER 1803.

In days, my Kate, when life was new,
When, lulled with innocence and you,
I heard, in home's belovèd shade,
The din the world at distance made;
When every night my weary head
Sunk on its own unthorned bed,
And, mild as evening's matron hour
Looks on the faintly shutting flower,
A mother saw our eyelids close,
And blessed them into pure repose!
Then, haply if a week, a day,
I lingered from your arms away,
How long the little absence seemed!
How bright the look of welcome beamed,
As mute you heard, with eager smile,
My tales of all that passed the while!
Yet now, my Kate, a gloomy sea
Rolls wide between that home and me;
The moon may thrice be born and die,
Ere even your seal can reach mine eye;

And oh! even then, that darling seal
(Upon whose print I used to feel
The breath of home, the cordial air
Of lovèd lips, still freshly there!)
Must come, alas! through every fate
Of time and distance, cold and late,
When the dear hand whose touches filled
The leaf with sweetness may be chilled!
But hence that gloomy thought! At last,
Belovèd Kate! the waves are passed:
I tread on earth securely now,
And the green cedar's living bough
Breathes more refreshment to my eyes
Than could a Claude's divinest dyes!
At length I touch the happy sphere
To Liberty and Virtue dear,
Where man looks up, and, proud to claim
His rank within the social frame,
Sees a grand system round him roll,
Himself its centre, sun, and soul!
Far from the shocks of Europe; far
From every wild, elliptic star
That, shooting with a devious fire,
Kindled by Heaven's avenging ire,
So oft hath into chaos hurled
The systems of the ancient world!

The warrior here, in arms no more,
Thinks of the toil, the conflict o'er,
And glorying in the rights they won
For hearth and altar, sire and son,
Smiles on the dusky webs that hide
His sleeping sword's remembered pride
While Peace, with sunny cheeks of toil,
Walks o'er the free unlorded soil,
Effacing with her splendid share
The drops that War had sprinkled there!
Thrice happy land! where he who flies
From the dark ills of other skies,
From scorn, or want's unnerving woes,
May shelter him in proud repose!
Hope sings along the yellow sand
His welcome to a patriot land;
The mighty wood, with pomp, receives
The stranger in its world of leaves,
Which soon their barren glory yield
To the warm shed and cultured field;
And he, who came, of all bereft,
To whom malignant Fate had left
Nor home nor friends nor country dear,
Finds home and friends and country here.

Such is the picture, warmly such,
That long the spell of Fancy's touch
Hath painted to my sanguine eye
Of man's new world of liberty!
Oh! ask me not if truth will seal
The reveries of Fancy's zeal,
If yet my charmed eyes behold
These features of an age of gold—

---

cumstance which can tend to prove a kindred similitude between them: ενγγινιαν τοις εινομενοις προς τα πρατα. With this thought in our minds when we first see the Flying-Fish, we could almost fancy that we are present at the moment of creation, and witness the birth of the first bird from the waves.

No—yet, alas! no gleaming trace![1]
Never did youth, who loved a face
From portrait's rosy, flattering art,
Recoil with more regret of heart,
To find an owlet eye of gray,
Where painting poured the sapphire's ray,
Than I have felt, indignant felt,
To think the glorious dreams should melt,
Which oft, in boyhood's witching time,
Have wrapt me to this wondrous clime!

But, courage yet, my wavering heart!
Blame not the temple's meanest part,[2]
Till you have traced the fabric o'er:—
As yet, we have beheld no more
Than just the porch to Freedom's fane,
And, though a sable drop may stain
The vestibule, 'tis impious sin
To doubt there's holiness within!
So here I pause—and now, my Kate,
To you (whose simplest ringlet's fate
Can claim more interest in my soul
Than all the Powers from pole to pole)
One word at parting—in the tone
Most sweet to you, and most my own.
The simplest notes I send you here,[3]
Though rude and wild, would still be dear,
If you but knew the trance of thought
In which my mind their murmurs caught.
'Twas one of those enchanting dreams,
That lull me oft, when Music seems
To pour the soul in sound along,
And turn its every sigh to song!
I thought the according lays
Respired the breath of happier days;
Warmly in every rising note
I felt some dear remembrance float,
Till, led by Music's fairy chain,
I wandered back to home again!
Oh! love the song, and let it oft
Live on your lip, in warble soft!
Say that it tells you, simply well,
All I have bid its murmurs tell,
Of memory's glow, of dreams that shed
The tinge of joy when joy is fled,
And all the heart's illusive hoard
Of love renewed and friends restored!
Now, sweet, adieu—this artless air,
And a few rhymes, in transcript fair,
Are all the gifts I yet can boast
To send you from Columbia's coast;
But when the sun, with warmer smile,
Shall light me to my destined Isle,

You shall have many a cowslip-bell
Where Ariel slept, and many a shell
In which the gentle spirit drew
From honey flowers the morning dew!

TO CARA,

AFTER AN INTERVAL OF ABSENCE.

CONCEALED within the shady wood
  A mother left her sleeping child,
And flew to cull her rustic food,
  The fruitage of the forest wild.

But storms upon her pathway rise,
  The mother roams, astray and weeping,
Far from the weak appealing cries
  Of him she left so sweetly sleeping.

She hopes, she fears—a light is seen,
  And gentler blows the night-wind's breath;
Yet no—'tis gone—the storms are keen,
  The baby may be chilled to death!

Perhaps his little eyes are shaded
  Dim by Death's eternal chill—
And yet, perhaps, they are not faded;
  Life and love may light them still.

Thus, when my soul with parting sigh,
  Hung on thy hand's bewildering touch,
And, timid, asked that speaking eye,
  If parting pained thee half so much:

I thought, and, oh! forgive the thought,
  For who, by eyes like thine inspired,
Could e'er resist the flattering fault
  Of fancying what his soul desired?

Yes—I *did* think, in Cara's mind,
  Though yet to Cara's mind unknown,
I left one infant wish behind,
  One feeling, which I called my own!

Oh blest! though but in fancy blest,
  How did I ask of pity's care,
To shield and strengthen in thy breast
  The nursling I had cradled there.

And, many an hour beguiled by pleasure,
  And many an hour of sorrow numbering,

---

[1] Such romantic works as *The American Farmer's Letters*, and the *Account of Kentucky*, by Imlay, would seduce us into a belief that innocence, peace, and freedom had deserted the rest of the world, for Martha's Vineyard and the banks of the Ohio. The French travellers, too, almost all from revolutionary motives, have contributed their share to the diffusion of this flattering misconception. A visit to the country is, however, quite sufficient to correct even the most enthusiastic prepossession.

[2] Norfolk, it must be owned, is an unfavourable specimen of America. The characteristics of Virginia in general are not such as can delight either the politician or the moralist, and at Norfolk they are exhibited in their least attractive form. At the time when we arrived the yellow fever had not yet disappeared, and every odour that assailed us in the streets very strongly accounted for its visitation.

[3] A trifling attempt at musical composition accompanied this Epistle.

I ne'er forgot the new-born treasure
I left within thy bosom slumbering.

Perhaps indifference has not chilled it,
Haply it yet a throb may give—
Yet no - perhaps a doubt has killed it!
Oh, Cara!—*does* the infant live?

TO CARA,

ON THE DAWNING OF A NEW YEAR'S DAY.

When midnight came to close the year,
We sighed to think it thus should take
The hours it gave us—hours as dear
As sympathy and love could make
Their blessed moments! every sun
Saw us, my love, more closely one!

But, Cara, when the dawn was nigh
Which came another year to shed,
The smile we caught from eye to eye
Told us those moments were not fled;
Oh no!—we felt, some future sun
Should see us still more closely one!

Thus may we ever, side by side,
From happy years to happier glide;
And still, my Cara, may the sigh
We give to hours that vanish o'er us,
Be followed by the smiling eye
That Hope shall shed on scenes before us!

TO THE INVISIBLE GIRL.

They try to persuade me, my dear little sprite,
That you are not a daughter of ether and light,
Nor have any concern with those fanciful forms
That dance upon rainbows and ride upon storms;
That, in short, you're a woman; your lip and your breast
As mortal as ever were tasted or pressed!
But I will not believe them—no, Science! to you
I have long bid a last and a careless adieu:
Still flying from Nature to study her laws,
And dulling delight by exploring its cause,
You forget how superior, for mortals below,
Is the fiction they dream to the truth that they know.
Oh! who, that has ever had rapture complete,
Would ask how we feel it, or why it is sweet;
How rays are confused, or how particles fly
Through the medium refined of a glance or a sigh!
Is there one, who but once would not rather have known it,
Than written, with Harvey, whole volumes upon it?
No, no—but for you, my invisible love,
I will swear you are one of those spirits that rove
By the bank where at twilight the poet reclines,
When the star of the west on his solitude shines,
And the magical fingers of Fancy have hung
Every breeze with a sigh, every leaf with a tongue!
Oh! whisper him then, 'tis retirement alone
Can hallow his harp or ennoble its tone;
Like you, with a veil of seclusion between,
His song to the world let him utter unseen,
And like you, a legitimate child of the spheres,
Escape from the eye to enrapture the ears!
Sweet spirit of mystery! how I should love,
In the wearisome ways I am fated to rove,
To have you for ever invisibly nigh,
Inhaling for ever your song and your sigh!
'Mid the crowds of the world and the murmurs of care,
I might sometimes converse with my nymph of the air,
And turn with disgust from the clamorous crew,
To steal in the pauses one whisper from you.

Oh! come and be near me, for ever be mine,
We shall hold in the air a communion divine,
As sweet as of old was imagined to dwell
In the grotto of Numa, or Socrates' cell.
And oft, at those lingering moments of night,
When the heart is weighed down and the eyelid is light,
You shall come to my pillow and tell me of love,
Such as angel to angel might whisper above!
Oh spirit!—and then, could you borrow the tone
Of that voice, to my ear so bewitchingly known,
The voice of the one upon earth, who has twined
With her essence for ever my heart and my mind!
Though lonely and far from the light of her smile,
And exile and weary and hopeless tho while,
Could you shed for a moment that voice on my ear,
I will think at that moment my Cara is near,
That she comes with consoling enchantment to speak,
And kisses my eyelid and sighs on my cheek,
And tells me the night shall go rapidly by,
For the dawn of our hope, of our heaven is nigh!
Sweet spirit! if such be your magical power,
It will lighten the lapse of full many an hour;
And let Fortune's realities frown as they will,
Hope, Fancy, and Cara may smile for me still!

PEACE AND GLORY.

WRITTEN AT THE COMMENCEMENT OF THE PRESENT WAR.

Where is now the smile that lightened
Every hero's couch of rest?
Where is now the hope that brightened
Honour's eye and Pity's breast?
Have we lost the wreath we braided
For our weary warrior men?

Is the faithless olive faded?
  Must the bay be plucked again?

Passing hour of sunny weather,
  Lovely in your light awhile,
Peace and Glory, wed together,
  Wandered through the blessed isle.
And the eyes of Peace would glisten,
  Dewy as a morning sun,
When the timid maid would listen
  To the deeds her chief had done.

Is the hour of dalliance over?
  Must the maiden's trembling feet
Waft her from her warlike lover
  To the desert's still retreat?
Fare you well! with sighs we banish
  Nymph so fair and guest so bright;
Yet the smile, with which you vanish,
  Leaves behind a soothing light!

Soothing light! that long shall sparkle
  O'er your warrior's sanguine way,
Through the field where horrors darkle,
  Shedding Hope's consoling ray!
Long the smile his heart will cherish,
  To its absent idol true,
While around him myriads perish,
  Glory still will sigh for you!

TO ———, 1801.

To be the theme of every hour
The heart devotes to Fancy's power,
When her soft magic fills the mind
With friends and joys we've left behind,
And joys return and friends are near,
And all are welcomed with a tear!
In the mind's purest seat to dwell,
To be remembered oft and well
By one whose heart, though vain and wild,
By passion led, by youth beguiled,
Can proudly still aspire to know
The feeling soul's divinest glow!
If thus to live in every part
Of a lone weary wanderer's heart;
If thus to be its sole employ
Can give thee one faint g'eam of joy,
Believe it, Mary! oh! believe
A tongue that never can deceive,
When passion doth not first betray
And tinge the thought upon its way!
In pleasure's dream or sorrow's hour,
In crowded hall or lonely bower,
The business of my life shall be,
For ever, to remember thee!
And though that heart be dead to mine,
Since love is life and wakes not thine,
I'll take thy image as the form
Of something I should long to warm,
Which, though it yield no answering thrill,
Is not less dear, is lovely still!

I'll take it, wheresoe'er I stray,
The bright, cold burthen of my way!
To keep this semblance fresh in bloom,
My heart shall be its glowing tomb,
And love shall lend his sweetest care,
With memory to embalm it there!

———

SONG.

Take back the sigh, thy lips of art
  In passion's moment breathed to me;
Yet, no—it must not, will not part,
  'Tis now the life-breath of my heart,
And has become too pure for thee!

Take back the kiss, that faithless sigh
  With all the warmth of truth imprest;
Yet, no—the fatal kiss may lie,
Upon *thy* lip its sweets would die,
  Or bloom to make a rival blest!

Take back the vows that, night and day,
  My heart received, I thought, from thine;
Yet, no—allow them still to stay,
They might some other heart betray,
  As sweetly as they've ruined mine!

———

A BALLAD.
THE LAKE OF THE DISMAL SWAMP.
WRITTEN AT NORFOLK IN VIRGINIA.

'They tell of a young man who lost his mind upon the death of a girl he loved, and who, suddenly disappearing from his friends, was never afterwards heard of. As he had frequently said, in his ravings, that the girl was not dead, but gone to the Dismal Swamp, it is supposed he had wandered into that dreary wilderness, and had died of hunger, or been lost in some of its dreadful morasses.'—*Anon.*

La Poésie a ses monstres comme la Nature.—*D'Alembert.*

'They made her a grave, too cold and damp
  For a soul so warm and true;
And she's gone to the Lake of the Dismal Swamp,[1]
  Where, all night long, by a fire-fly lamp,
She paddles her white canoe.

'And her fire-fly lamp I soon shall see,
  And her paddle I soon shall hear;
Long and loving our life shall be,
And I'll hide the maid in a cypress tree,
  When the footstep of Death is near!'

Away to the Dismal Swamp he speeds—
  His path was rugged and sore,
Through tangled juniper, beds of reeds,
Through many a fen, where the serpent feeds,
  And man never trod before!

[1] The Great Dismal Swamp is ten or twelve miles distant from Norfolk, and the Lake in the middle of it (about seven miles long) is called Drummond's Pond.

And when on the earth he sunk to sleep,
  If slumber his eyelids knew,
He lay where the deadly vine doth weep
  Its venomous tear, and nightly steep
The flesh with blistering dew!

And near him the she-wolf stirred the brake,
  And the copper-snake breathed in his ear,
Till he starting cried, from his dream awake,
  'Oh! when shall I see the dusky Lake,
And the white canoe of my dear?'

He saw the Lake, and a meteor bright
  Quick over its surface played—
'Welcome,' he said, ' my dear-one's light!'
  And the dim shore echoed, for many a night,
The name of the death-cold maid!

Till he hollowed a boat of the birchen bark,
  Which carried him off from shore;
Far he followed the meteor spark,
The wind was high and the clouds were dark,
  And the boat returned no more.

But oft, from the Indian hunter's camp,
  This lover and maid so true
Are seen, at the hour of midnight damp,
To cross the lake by a fire-fly lamp,
  And paddle their white canoe!

EPISTLE III.

TO THE
MARCHIONESS DOWAGER OF D——LL.

FROM BERMUDA, JANUARY 1804.

Lady, where'er you roam, whatever beam
Of bright creation warms your mimic dream;
Whether you trace the valley's golden meads,
Where mazy Linth his lingering current leads;[1]
Enamoured catch the mellow hues that sleep,
At eve, on Meillerie's immortal steep;
Or, musing o'er the Lake, at day's decline,
Mark the last shadow on the holy shrine,[2]
Where, many a night, the soul of Tell complains
Of Gallia's triumph and Helvetia's chains;
Oh! lay the pencil for a moment by,
Turn from the tablet that creative eye,
And let its splendour, like the morning ray
Upon a shepherd's harp, illume my lay!

Yet, Lady! no—for song so rude as mine,
Chase not the wonders of your dream divine;
Still, radiant eye! upon the tablet dwell;
Still, rosy finger! weave your pictured spell;
And, while I sing the animated smiles
Of fairy nature in these sun-born isles,
Oh! might the song awake some bright design,
Inspire a touch, or prompt one happy line,
Proud were my soul to see its humble thought
On painting's mirror so divinely caught,
And woundering genius, as he leaned to trace
The faint conception kindling into grace,
Might love my numbers for the spark they threw,
And bless the lay that lent a charm to you!

Have you not oft, in nightly vision, strayed
To the pure isles of ever-blooming shade,
Which bards of old, with kindly magic, placed
For happy spirits in the Atlantic waste?
There, as eternal gales, with fragrance warm,
Breathed from Elysium through each shadowy form
In eloquence of eye, and dreams of song,
They charmed their lapse of nightless hours along!
Nor yet in song that mortal ear may suit,
For every spirit was itself a lute,
Where Virtue wakened, with elysian breeze,
Pure tones of thought and mental harmonies!
Believe me, Lady, when the zephyrs bland
Floated our bark to this enchanted land,
These leafy isles upon the ocean thrown,
Like studs of emerald o'er a silver zone;
Not all the charm that ethnic fancy gave
To blessed arbours o'er the western wave,
Could wake a dream more soothing or sublime,
Of bowers ethereal and the spirit's clime!

The morn was lovely, every wave was still,
When the first perfume of a cedar-hill
Sweetly awaked us, and with smiling charms
The fairy harbour wooed us to its arms.[3]
Gently we stole before the languid wind,
Through plantain shades that like an awning twined,
And kissed on either side the wanton sails,
Breathing our welcome to these vernal vales;
While far reflected, o'er the wave serene,
Each wooded island sheds so soft a green,
That the enamoured keel, with whispering play,
Through liquid herbage seemed to steal its way!
Never did weary bark more sweetly glide,
Or rest its anchor in a lovelier tide!
Along the margin many a brilliant dome,
White as the palace of a Lapland gnome,
Brightened the wave; in every myrtle grove
Secluded bashful, like a shrine of love,
Some elfin mansion sparkled through the shade;
And, while the foliage interposing played,

---

[1] Lady D., I supposed, was at this time still in Switzerland, where the powers of her pencil must have been frequently awakened.
[2] The chapel of William Tell, on the Lake of Lucerne.
[3] Nothing can be more romantic than the little harbour of St. George. The number of beautiful islets, the singular clearness of the water, and the animated play of the graceful little boats, gliding for ever between the islands, and seeming to sail from one cedar-grove into another, form altogether the sweetest miniature of nature that can be imagined.

Wreathing the structure into various grace,
Fancy would love in many a form to trace
The flowery capital, the shaft, the porch,[1]
And dream of temples, till her kindling torch
Lighted me back to all the glorious days
Of Attic genius; and I seemed to gaze
On marble, from the rich Pentelic mount,
Gracing the umbrage of some Naiad's fount.

Sweet airy being![2] who, in brighter hours,
Lived on the perfume of these honeyed bowers,
In velvet buds, at evening loved to lie,
And win with music every rose's sigh!
Though weak the magic of my humble strain
To charm your spirit from its orb again,
Yet, oh! for her, beneath whose smile I sing,
For her (whose pencil, if your rainbow wing
Were dimmed or ruffled by a wintry sky,
Could smooth its feather and relume its dye),
A moment wander from your starry sphere,
And if the lime-tree grove that once was dear,
The sunny wave, the bower, the breezy hill,
The sparkling grotto, can delight you still,
Oh! take their fairest tint, their softest light,
Weave all their beauty into dreams of night,
And, while the lovely artist slumbering lies,
Shed the warm picture o'er her mental eyes;
Borrow for sleep her own creative spells,
And brightly show what song but faintly tells!

THE GENIUS OF HARMONY.

AN IRREGULAR ODE.

Ad harmoniam canere mundum.
—*Cicero, De Nat. Deor.* lib. 3.

THERE lies a shell beneath the waves
In many a hollow winding wreathed,
Such as of old,
Echoed the breath that warbling sea-maids breathed;
This magic shell
From the white bosom of a syren fell,
As once she wandered by the tide that laves
Sicilia's sand of gold.
It bears
Upon its shining side, the mystic notes
Of those entrancing airs[3]
The Genii of the deep were wont to swell,
When Heaven's eternal orbs their midnight
music rolled!
Oh! seek it, wheresoe'er it floats;
And, if the power
Of thrilling numbers to thy soul be dear,
Go, bring the bright shell to my bower,
And I will fold thee in such downy dreams,
As lap the spirit of the seventh sphere,
When Luna's distant tone falls faintly on his
ear![4]
And thou shalt own,
That, through the circle of creation's zone,
Where matter darkles or where spirit beams;
From the pellucid tides,[5] that whirl
The planets through their maze of song,
To the small rill, that weeps along
Murmuring o'er beds of pearl;
From the rich sigh
Of the sun's arrow through an evening sky,[6]
To the faint breath the tuneful osier yields
On Afric's burning fields;[7]
Oh! thou shalt own this universe divine
Is mine!
That I respire in all and all in me,
One mighty mingled soul of boundless harmony!

Welcome, welcome, mystic shell!
Many a star has ceased to burn,[8]
Many a tear has Saturn's urn

---

[1] This is an allusion which, to the few who are fanciful enough to indulge in it, renders the scenery of Bermuda particularly interesting. In the short but beautiful twilight of their spring evenings, the white cottages scattered over the islands, and but partially seen through the trees that surround them, assume often the appearance of little Grecian temples, and fancy may embellish the poor fisherman's hut with columns which the pencil of Claude might imitate. I had one favourite object of this kind in my walks, which the hospitality of its owner robbed me of, by asking me to visit him. He was a plain good man, and received me well and warmly, but I never could turn his house into a Grecian temple again.

[2] Ariel. Among the many charms which Bermuda has for a poetic eye, we cannot for an instant forget that it is the scene of Shakspeare's *Tempest*, and that here he conjured up the 'delicate Ariel,' who alone is worth the whole heaven of ancient mythology.

[3] In the *Histoire naturelle des Antilles* there is an account of some curious shells, found at Curaçoa, on the back of which were lines filled with musical characters so distinct and perfect, that, the writer assures us, a very charming trio was sung from one of them.

[4] According to Cicero, and his commentator Macrobius, the lunar tone is the gravest and faintest on the planetary heptachord.

Leone Hebreo, pursuing the idea of Aristotle, that the heavens are animal, attributes their harmony to perfect and reciprocal love. This 'reciproco amore' of Leone is the φιλότης of the ancient Empedocles, who seems, in his Love and Hate of the Elements, to have given a glimpse of the principles of attraction and repulsion.

[5] Leucippus, the atomist, imagined a kind of vortices in the heavens, which he borrowed from Anaxagoras and possibly suggested to Descartes.

[6] Heraclides, upon the allegories of Homer, conjectures that the idea of the harmony of the spheres originated with this poet, who, in representing the solar beams as arrows, supposes them to emit a peculiar sound in the air.

[7] In the account of Africa which d'Ablancourt has translated, there is mention of a tree in that country, whose branches when shaken by the hand produce very sweet sounds.

[8] Alluding to the extinction, or at least the disappearance, of some of those fixed stars which we are taught to consider as suns, attended each by its system. Descartes thought that our earth might formerly have been

O'er the cold bosom of the ocean wept,
    Since thy aerial spell
    Hath in the waters slept!
        I fly,
With the bright treasure to my choral sky,
    Where she, who waked its early swell,
    The syren, with a foot of fire,
Walks o'er the great string of my Orphic Lyre,
    Or guides around the burning pole
    The wingèd chariot of some blissful soul!
        While thou!
Oh, son of earth! what dreams shall rise for thee;
    Beneath Hispania's sun,
    Thou'lt see a streamlet run,
Which I have warmed with dews of melody;
    Listen!—when the night wind dies
Down the still current, like a harp it sighs!
A liquid chord is every wave that flows,
An airy plectrum every breeze that blows!
    There, by that wondrous stream,
    Go, lay thy languid brow,
And I will send thee such a god-like dream,
Such—mortal! mortal! hast thou heard of him,[1]
Who, many a night, with his primordial lyre,[2]
    Sate on the chill Pangæan mount,[3]
And, looking to the orient dim,
Watched the first flowing of that sacred fount,
    From which his soul had drunk its fire!
Oh! think what visions, in that lonely hour,
    Stole o'er his musing breast!
    What pious ecstasy [4]
Wafted his prayer to that eternal Power,
    Whose seal upon this world imprest [5]
    The various forms of bright divinity!

Or, dost thou know what dreams I wove,
    'Mid the deep horror of that silent bower,[6]
Where the rapt Samian slept his holy slumber?
        When, free
    From every earthly chain,
From wreaths of pleasure and from bonds of pain,
    His spirit flew through fields above,
Drank at the source of Nature's fontal number,[7]
And saw, in mystic choir, around him move
The stars of song, Heaven's burning minstrelsy!
    Such dreams, so heavenly bright,
    I swear
    By the great diadem that twines my hair,
    And by the seven gems that sparkle there,[8]
    Mingling their beams
In a soft Iris of harmonious light,
Oh, mortal! such shall be thy radiant dreams!

EPISTLE IV.

TO GEORGE MORGAN, ESQ,

OF NORFOLK, VIRGINIA.[9]

FROM BERMUDA, JANUARY 1804.

ΚΕΙΝΗ Δ' ΗΝΕΜΟΕΣΣΑ ΚΑΙ ΑΤΡΟΠΟΣ, Ο'ΙΑ
Θ'ΑΛΙΠΛΗΞ, ΑΙΘΤΙΗΣ ΚΑΙ ΜΑΛΛΟΝ ΕΠΙ-
ΔΡΟΜΟΣ ΗΕΠΕΡ, 'ΙΠΠΟΙΣ, ΠΟΝΤΩ ΕΝΕΣ-
ΤΗΡΙΚΤΑΙ.
    Callimach. Hymn. in Del. v. 11.

Oh what a tempest whirled us hither![10]
Winds, whose savage breath could wither

---

[1] a sun, which became obscured by a thick incrustation over its surface. This probably suggested the idea of a central fire.

[2] Orpheus.

[3] They call his lyre ἀρχαιότερον ἑπταχορδον Ὀρφεως. See a curious work by a professor of Greek at Venice, entitled *Hebdomades, sive septem de septenario libri,* lib. 4, cap. 3, p. 177.

[4] Eratosthenes, telling the extreme veneration of Orpheus for Apollo, says that he was accustomed to go to the Pangæan mountain at daybreak, and there wait the rising of the sun, that he might be the first to hail its beams.

[5] There are some verses of Orpheus preserved to us, which contain sublime ideas of the unity and magnificence of the Deity. As those which Justin Martyr has produced:

Οὗτος μὰν χαλκειος ἰς οὐρανον ἰστηρικται
Χρυσιω τνι θρονω, κ.τ.λ.—*Ad Græc. cohortat.*

It is thought by some, that these are to be reckoned amongst the fabrications which were frequent in the early times of Christianity. Still it appears doubtful to whom we should impute them; they are too pious for the Pagans, and too poetical for the Fathers.

[6] In one of the Hymns of Orpheus, he attributes a figured seal to Apollo, with which he imagines that deity to have stamped a variety of forms upon the universe.

[7] Alluding to the cave near Samos, where Pythagoras devoted the greater part of his days and nights to meditation and the mysteries of his philosophy. *Jamblich. de Vit.* This, as Holstenius remarks, was in imitation of the Magi.

[8] The tetractys, or sacred number of the Pythagoreans, on which they solemnly swore, and which they called παγαν αιναου φυσιος, 'the fountain of perennial nature.' Lucian has ridiculed this religious arithmetic very finely in his *Sale of Philosophers.*

[9] This diadem is intended to represent the analogy between the notes of music and the prismatic colours. We find in Plutarch a vague intimation of this kindred harmony in colours and sounds. Οψις τε και ακοη, μετα φωνης τε και φωτος την ἁρμονιαν επιφαινουσι.—*De Musica.* Cassiodorus, whose idea I may be supposed to have borrowed, says, in a letter upon music to Boetius : ' Ut diademate oculis, varia luce gemmarum, sic cythara diversitate soni, blanditur auditui.' This is indeed the only tolerable thought in the letter. Lib. 2. *Variar.*

[9] This gentleman is attached to the British consulate at Norfolk. His talents are worthy of a much higher sphere; but the excellent dispositions of the family with whom he resides, and the cordial repose he enjoys amongst some of the kindest hearts in the world, should be almost enough to atone to him for the worst caprices of fortune. The consul himself, Colonel Hamilton, is one among the very few instances of a man, ardently loyal to his king, and yet beloved by the Americans. His house is the very temple of hospitality, and I sincerely pity the heart of that stranger who, warm from the welcome of such a board, and with the taste of such Madeira still upon his lips—' col dolce in bocca '—could sit down to write a libel on 1 is host, in the true spirit of a modern philosophist. See the *Travels* of the Duke de la Rochefoucault Liancourt, vol. ii.

[10] We were seven days on our passage from Norfolk to Bermuda, during three of which we were forced to

All the light and languid flowers
That bloom in Epicurus' bowers!
Yet think not, George, that Fancy's charm
Forsook me in this rude alarm.
When close they reefed the timid sail,
  When, every plank complaining loud,
We laboured in the midnight gale,
  And even our haughty main-mast bowed!
The muse, in that unlovely hour,
Benignly brought her soothing power,
And, 'midst the war of waves and wind,
In songs elysian lapped my mind!
She opened, with her golden key,
The casket where my memory lays
Those little gems of poesy,
  Which time has saved from ancient days!
Take one of these, to Lais sung,
I wrote it while my hammock swung,
As one might write a dissertation
Upon 'suspended animation!'

SWEETLY[1] you kiss, my Lais dear!
But, while you kiss, I feel a tear,
Bitter as those when lovers part,
In mystery from your eyelid start!
Sadly you lean your head to mine,
And round my neck in silence twine,
Your hair along my bosom spread,
All humid with the tears you shed!
Have I not kissed those lids of snow?
Yet still, my love, like founts they flow,
Bathing our cheeks, whene'er they meet—
Why is it thus? do tell me, sweet!
Ah, Lais! are my bodings right?
Am I to lose you? is to-night
Our last—go, false to Heaven and me!
Your very tears are treachery.

Such, while in air I floating hung,
Such was the strain, Morgante mio!

The muse and I together sung,
With Boreas to make out the trio.
But, bless the little fairy isle!
How sweetly, after all our ills,
We saw the dewy morning smile
Serenely o'er its fragrant hills!
And felt the pure elastic flow
Of airs, that round this Eden blow
With honey freshness, caught by stealth
Warm from the very lips of health?

Oh! could you view the scenery dear,
That now beneath my window lies,
You'd think that Nature lavished here
Her purest wave, her softest skies,
To make a heaven for Love to sigh in,
For bards to live and saints to die in!
Close to my wooded bank below,
In glassy calm the waters sleep,
And to the sunbeam proudly show
The coral rocks they love to steep![2]
The fainting breeze of morning fails,
The drowsy boat moves slowly past,
And I can almost touch its sails
That languish idly round the mast.
The sun has now profusely given
The flashes of a noontide heaven,
And, as the wave reflects his beams,
Another heaven its surface seems!
Blue light and clouds of silvery tears
So pictured o'er the waters lie,
That every languid bark appears
To float along a burning sky!
Oh! for the boat the angel gave[3]
To him, who in his heavenward flight,
Sailed, o'er the Sun's ethereal wave,
To planet-isles of odorous light!
Sweet Venus, what a clime he found
Within thy orb's ambrosial round![4]
There spring the breezes, rich and warm,
That pant around thy twilight car;

---

lay-to in a gale of wind. The *Driver* sloop of war, in which I went, was built at Bermuda of cedar, and is accounted an excellent sea-boat. She was then commanded by my very regretted friend Captain Compton, who in July last was killed aboard the *Lilly*, in an action with a French privateer. Poor Compton! he fell a victim to the strange impolicy of allowing such a miserable thing as the *Lilly* to remain in the service; so small, crank, and unmanageable, that a well-manned merchantman was at any time a match for her.

[1] This epigram is by Paulus Silentiarius, and may be found in the *Analecta* of Brunck, vol. iii. p. 72. But as the reading there is somewhat different from what I have followed in this translation, I shall give it as I had it in my memory at the time, and as it is in Heinsius, who, I believe, first produced the epigram. See his *Poemata*.

Ἡδύ μέν ἐστι φίλημα τὸ Λαΐδος· ἡδὺ δὲ αὐτῶν
Ἡσιοδινητῶν δάκρυ χέεις βλεφάρων,
Καὶ πολὺ μιχλίζουσα φαθεῖς ἐυβοστρυχον αἰγλην
Ἡμίτερα κεφαλῇ δηρόν ἐρεισαμένη.

Μυρομένη δ᾽ ἐφιλησεν· τα δ᾽ ὡς δροσέρης ἀπό σμηγής,
Δάκρυα μιγνυμένων πίπτει κατὰ στομάτων·

Ἐπι δ᾽ ἀνυρομενη, τινός οὐνεκα δακρυα λειβεις;
Δειδια μη μα λιπης· ἐστι γαρ ὁρκαπαται.

[2] The water is so clear around the island, that the rocks are seen beneath to a very great depth; and as we entered the harbour, they appeared to us so near the surface, that it seemed impossible we should not strike on them. There is no necessity, of course, for heaving the lead; and the negro pilot, looking down at the rocks from the bow of the ship, takes her through this difficult navigation with a skill and confidence which seem to astonish some of the oldest sailors.

[3] In Kircher's *Ecstatic Journey to Heaven*, Cosmiel, the genius of the world, gives Theodidactus a boat of asbestos, with which he embarks into the regions of the sun. 'Vides (says Cosmiel) hanc asbestinam naviculam commoditati tuæ præparatam.'—*Itinerar*. i. dial. l. cap. 5. There are some very strange fancies in this work of Kircher.

[4] When the genius of the world and his fellow-traveller arrive at the planet Venus, they find an island of loveliness, full of odours and intelligences, where angels preside, who shed the cosmetic influence of this planet over the earth; such being, according to astrologers, the 'vis influxiva' of Venus. When they are in

There angels dwell, so pure of form,
  That each appears a living star!
These are the sprites, oh radiant queen!
  Thou send'st so often to the bed
Of her I love, with spell unseen,
  Thy planet's brightening balm to shed;
To make the eye's enchantment clearer,
  To give the cheek one rosebud more,
And bid that flushing lip be dearer,
  Which had been, oh! too dear before!

But, whither means the muse to roam?
  'Tis time to call the wanderer home.
Who could have ever thought to search her
  Up in the clouds with Father Kircher?
So, health and love to all your mansion!
  Long may the bowl that pleasures bloom in,
The flow of heart, the soul's expansion,
  Mirth, and song, your board illumine!
Fare you well—remember too,
  When cups are flowing to the brim,
That here is one who drinks to you,
  And, oh! as warmly drink to him.

THE RING.

TO ——— ———, 1801.

No—lady! lady! keep the ring;
  Oh! think how many a future year,
Of placid smile and downy wing,
  May sleep within its holy sphere!

Do not disturb their tranquil dream,
  Though love hath ne'er the mystery warmed,
Yet Heaven will shed a soothing beam,
  To bless the bond itself hath formed.

But then, that eye, that burning eye!
  Oh! it doth ask, with magic power,
If Heaven can ever bless the tie
  Where Love inwreaths no genial flower!

Away, away, bewildering look!
  Or all the boast of Virtue's o'er;
Go—hie thee to the sage's book,
  And learn from him to feel no more!

I cannot warn thee! every touch,
  That brings my pulses close to thine,
Tells me I want thy aid as much,
  Oh! quite as much, as thou dost mine!

Yet stay, dear love—one effort yet—
  A moment turn those eyes away,
And let me, if I can, forget
  The light that leads my soul astray!

Thou say'st that we were born to meet,
  That our hearts bear one common seal,—

Oh, lady! think, how man's deceit
  Can seem to sigh and feign to feel!

When o'er thy face some gleam of thought,
  Like day-beams through the morning air,
Hath gradual stole, and I have caught
  The feeling ere it kindled there:

The sympathy I then betrayed,
  Perhaps was but the child of art;
The guile of one who long hath played
  With all these wily nets of heart.

Oh! thou hast not my virgin vow!
  Though few the years I yet have told,
Canst thou believe I lived till now,
  With loveless heart or senses cold?

No—many a throb of bliss and pain,
  For many a maid, my soul hath proved;
With some I wantoned wild and vain,
  While some I truly, dearly loved!

The cheek to thine I fondly lay,
  To theirs hath been as fondly laid;
The words to thee I warmly say,
  To them have been as warmly said.

Then scorn at once a languid heart,
  Which long hath lost its early spring;
Think of the pure bright soul thou art,
  And—keep the ring, oh! keep the ring.

Enough—now, turn thine eyes again;
  What, still that look and still that sigh!
Dost thou not feel my counsel then?
  Oh! no, beloved!—nor do I.

While thus to mine thy bosom lies,
  While thus our breaths commingling glow,
'Twere more than woman to be wise,
  'Twere more than man to wish thee so!

Did we not love so true, so dear,
  This lapse could never be forgiven;
But hearts so fond and lips so near—
  Give me the ring, and now—Oh heaven!

TO ——— ———,

ON SEEING HER WITH A WHITE VEIL AND A
RICH GIRDLE.

ΜΑΡΓΑΡΙΤΑΙ ΔΗΛΟΥΣΙ ΔΑΚΡΥΩΝ ΡΟΟΝ.
  Ap. Nicephor, in Oneirocritico

Put off the vestal veil, nor, oh!
  Let weeping angels view it;
Your cheeks belie its virgin snow,
  And blush repenting through it.

---

this part of the heavens, a casuistical question occurs to Theodidactus, and he asks 'Whether baptism may be performed with the waters of Venus?'—'An aquis globi Veneris baptismus institui possit?'—to which the genius answers, 'Certainly.'

THE RESEMBLANCE.

.... vo cercand' io
Donna, quant' e possibile, in altrui
La desiata vostra forma vera.
Petrarc. Sonett. 14.

YES, if 'twere any common love
That led my pliant heart astray,
I grant, there's not a power above
Could wipe the faithless crime away!

But, 'twas my doom to err with one
In every look so like to thee,
That, oh! beneath the blessed sun,
So fair there are but thou and she!

Whate'er may be her angel birth,
She was thy lovely perfect twin,
And wore the only shape on earth
That could have charmed my soul to sin!

Your eyes!—the eyes of languid doves
Were never half so like each other!
The glances of the baby loves
Resemble less their warm-eyed mother!

Her lip!—oh, call me not false-hearted,
When such a lip I fondly pressed;
'Twas Love some melting cherry parted,
Gave thee one half and her the rest!

And when, with all thy murmuring tone,
They sued, half open, to be kissed,
I could as soon resist thine own—
And them, Heaven knows! I ne'er resist.

Then, scorn me not, though false I be,
'Twas love that waked the dear excess;
My heart had been more true to thee,
Had mine eye prized thy beauty less!

TO ——— ———.

WHEN I loved you, I can't but allow
I had many an exquisite minute;
But the scorn that I feel for you now
Hath even more luxury in it!

Thus, whether we're on or we're off,
Some witchery seems to await you;
To love you is pleasant enough,
And, oh! 'tis delicious to hate you!

FROM THE GREEK OF MELEAGER.

FILL high the cup with liquid flame,
And speak my Heliodora's name!
Repeat its magic o'er and o'er,
And let the sound my lips adore!
Sweeten the breeze, and mingling swim
On every bowl's voluptuous brim!

Give me the wreath that withers there,
It was but last delicious night
It hung upon her wavy hair,
And caught her eyes' reflected light!
Oh! haste, and twine it round my brow;
It breathes of Heliodora now!

The loving rose-bud drops a tear,
To see the nymph no longer here,
No longer, where she used to lie,
Close to my heart's devoted sigh!

LINES,

WRITTEN IN A STORM AT SEA.

THAT sky of clouds is not the sky
To light a lover to the pillow
Of her he loves—
The swell of yonder foaming billow,
Resembles not the happy sigh
That rapture moves.

Yet do I feel more tranquil now
Amid the gloomy wilds of ocean,
In this dark hour,
Than when, in transport's young emotion,
I've stolen, beneath the evening star,
To Julia's bower.

Oh! there's a holy calm profound
In awe like this, that ne'er was given
To rapture's thrill;
'Tis as a solemn voice from heaven,
And the soul, listening to the sound,
Lies mute and still!

'Tis true, it talks of danger nigh,
Of slumbering with the dead to-morrow
In the cold deep,
Where pleasure's throb or tears of sorrow
No more shall wake the heart or eye,
But all must sleep!

Well!—there are some, thou stormy bed,
To whom thy sleep would be a treasure:
Oh! most to him,
Whose lip hath drained life's cup of pleasure,
Nor left one honey-drop to shed
Round misery's brim.

Yes—*he* can smile serene at death:
Kind Heaven! do thou but chase the weeping
Of friends who love him;
Tell them that he lies calmly sleeping,
Where sorrow's sting or envy's breath
No more shall move him.

ODES TO NEA.

WRITTEN AT BERMUDA.

NEA TYPANNEI.
Euripid. Medea, v. 967.

NAY, tempt me not to love again:
There was a time when love was sweet;
Dear Nea! had I known thee then,
Our souls had not been slow to meet!
But, oh! this weary heart hath run
So many a time the rounds of pain,
Not even for thee, thou lovely one!
Would I endure such pangs again.

If there be climes where never yet
The print of Beauty's foot was set,
Where man may pass his loveless nights
Unfevered by her false delights—
Thither my wounded soul would fly,
Where rosy cheek or radiant eye
Should bring no more their bliss, their pain,
Or fetter me to earth again!
Dear absent girl! whose eyes of light,
Though little prized when all my own,
Now float before me, soft and bright
As when they first enamouring shone!
How many hours of idle waste,
Within those witching arms embraced,
Unmindful of the fleeting day,
Have I dissolved life's dream away!
O bloom of time profusely shed!
O moments! simply, vainly fled,
Yet sweetly too—for love perfumed
The flame which thus my life consumed;
And brilliant was the chain of flowers
In which he led my victim hours!

Say, Nea dear! couldst thou, like her,
When warm to feel and quick to err,
Of loving fond, of roving fonder,
My thoughtless soul might wish to wander—
Couldst thou, like her, the wish reclaim,
Endearing still, reproaching never,
Till all my heart should burn with shame,
And be thy own more fixed than ever?
No, no—on earth there's only one
Could bind such faithless folly fast:
And sure on earth 'tis I alone
Could make such virtue false at last!

Nea! the heart which she forsook,
For thee were but a worthless shrine—
Go, lovely girl, that angel look
Must thrill a soul more pure than mine.

Oh! thou shalt be all else to me,
That heart can feel or tongue can feign;
I'll praise, admire, and worship thee,
But must not, dare not, love again.

. . . . Tale iter omne cave.
Propert. lib. iv. eleg. 8.

I PRAY you, let us roam no more
Along that wild and lonely shore,
Where late we thoughtless strayed;
'Twas not for us, whom Heaven intends
To be no more than simple friends,
Such lonely walks were made.

That little bay where, winding in
From Ocean's rude and angry din
(As lovers steal to bliss),
The billows kiss the shore, and then
Flow calmly to the deep again,
As though they did not kiss!

Remember, o'er its circling flood
In what a dangerous dream we stood—
The silent sea before us,
Around us, all the gloom of grove,
That e'er was spread for guilt or love,
No eye but Nature's o'er us!

I saw you blush, you felt me tremble,
In vain would formal art dissemble
All that we wished and thought;
'Twas more than tongue could dare reveal,
'Twas more than virtue ought to feel,
But all that passion ought!

I stooped to cull, with faltering hand,
A shell that, on the golden sand,
Before us faintly gleamed;
I raised it to your lips of dew,
You kissed the shell, I kissed it too—
Good Heaven! how sweet it seemed!

Oh! trust me, 'twas a place, an hour,
The worst that e'er temptation's power
Could tangle me or you in!
Sweet Nea! let us roam no more
Along that wild and lonely shore,
Such walks will be our ruin!

You read it in my languid eyes,
And there alone should love be read;
You hear me say it all in sighs,
And thus alone should love be said.

Then dread no more; I will not speak;
Although my heart to anguish thrill,
I'll spare the burning of your cheek,
And look it all in silence still!

Heard you the wish I dared to name,
 To murmur on that luckless night,
When passion broke the bonds of shame,
 And love grew madness in your sight?

Divinely through the graceful dance,
 You seemed to float in silent song,
Bending to earth that beamy glance,
 As if to light your steps along!

Oh! how could others dare to touch
 That hallowed form with hand so free,
When but to look was bliss too much,
 Too rare for all but Heaven and me!

With smiling eyes, that little thought
 How fatal were the beams they threw,
My trembling hands you lightly caught,
 And round me, like a spirit, flew.

Heedless of all, I wildly turned,
 My soul forgot—nor, oh! condemn,
That when such eyes before me burned,
 My soul forgot all eyes but them!

I dared to speak in sobs of bliss,
 Rapture of every thought bereft me,
I would have clasped you—oh, even this!—
 But, with a bound, you blushing left me.

Forget, forget that night's offence;
 Forgive it, if, alas! you can;
'Twas love, 'twas passion—soul and sense—
 'Twas all the best and worst of man!

That moment did the mingled eyes
 Of heaven and earth my madness view,
I should have seen, through earth and skies,
 But you alone, but only you!

Did not a frown from you reprove,
 Myriads of eyes to me were none;
I should have—oh, my only love!
 My life! what should I *not* have done?

A DREAM OF ANTIQUITY.

I JUST had turned the classic page,
 And traced that happy period over,
When love could warm the proudest sage,
 And wisdom grace the tenderest lover!
Before I laid me down to sleep,
 Upon the bank awhile I stood,
And saw the vestal planet weep
 Her tears of light on Ariel's flood.

My heart was full of Fancy's dream,
 And as I watched the playful stream,
Entangling in its net of smiles
 So fair a group of elfin isles,
I felt as if the scenery there
 Were lighted by a Grecian sky—
As if I breathed the blissful air
 That yet was warm with Sappho's sigh!

And now the downy hand of rest
 Her signet on my eyes imprest,
And still the bright and balmy spell,
 Like star-dew, o'er my fancy fell!
I thought that, all enrapt, I strayed
 Through that serene luxurious shade,[1]
Where Epicurus taught the Loves
 To polish Virtue's native brightness,
Just as the beak of playful doves
 Can give to pearls a smoother whiteness![2]
'Twas one of those delicious nights
 So common in the climes of Greece,
When day withdraws but half its lights,
 And all is moonshine, balm, and peace!
And thou wert there, my own beloved!
 And dearly by thy side I roved
Through many a temple's reverend gloom,
 And many a bower's seductive bloom,
Where beauty blushed and wisdom taught,
 Where lovers sighed and sages thought,
Where hearts might feel or heads discern,
 And all was formed to soothe or move,
To make the dullest love to learn,
 To make the coldest learn to love!

And now the fairy pathway seemed
 To lead us through enchanted ground,
Where all that bard has ever dreamed
 Of love or luxury bloomed around!
Oh! 'twas a bright bewildering scene—
 Along the alley's deepening green,
Soft lamps, that hung like burning flowers,
 And scented and illumed the bowers,
Seemed, as to him, who darkling roves
 Amid the lone Hercynian groves,
Appear the countless birds of light
 That sparkle in the leaves at night,
And from their wings diffuse a ray
 Along the traveller's weary way!
'Twas light of that mysterious kind,
 Through which the soul is doomed to roam
When it has left this world behind,
 And gone to seek its heavenly home!
And, Nea, thou didst look and move,
 Like any blooming soul of bliss,
That wanders to its home above
 Through mild and shadowy light like this!

---

[1] Gassendi thinks that the gardens which Pausanias mentions in his first book were those of Epicurus: and Stuart says, in his *Antiquities of Athens:* 'Near this convent (the convent of Hagios Assomatos) is the place called at present Kepoi, or the Gardens; and Ampelos Kepos, or the Vineyard Garden: these were probably the gardens which Pausanias visited.'—Chap. ii. vol. 1.

[2] This method of polishing pearls, by leaving them awhile to be played with by doves, is mentioned by the fanciful Cardanus, *de Rerum Varietat.* lib. vii. cap 34.

But now, methought, we stole along
  Through halls of more voluptuous glory
Than ever lived in Teian song,
  Or wantoned in Milesian story![1]
And nymphs were there, whose very eyes
  Seemed almost to exhale in sighs;
Whose every little ringlet thrilled,
  As if with soul and passion filled!
Some flew, with amber cups, around,
  Shedding the flowery wines of Crete,[2]
And, as they passed with youthful bound,
  The onyx shone beneath their feet![3]
While others, waving arms of snow
  Entwined by snakes of burnished gold,[4]
And showing limbs, as loth to show,
  Through many a thin Tarentian fold,
Glided along the festal ring
  With vases, all respiring spring,
Where roses lay, in languor breathing,
  And the young bee-grape, round them wreathing,
Hung on their blushes warm and meek,
  Like curls upon a rosy cheek!

Oh, Nea! why did morning break
  The spell that so divinely bound me?
Why did I wake? how *could* I wake,
  With thee my own and Heaven around me!

WELL—peace to thy heart, though another's it
    be,
And health to thy cheek, though it bloom not
    for me!
To-morrow I sail for those cinnamon groves,
  Where nightly the ghost of the Carribee roves,
And, far from thine eye, oh! perhaps I may yet
  Its seduction forgive and its splendour forget!
Farewell to Bermuda,[5] and long may the bloom
Of the lemon and myrtle its valleys perfume;
May spring to eternity hallow the shade,
Where Ariel has warbled and Waller[6] has
    strayed!

And thou—when, at dawn, thou shalt happen to
    roam
Through the lime-covered alley that leads to thy
    home,
Where oft, when the dance and the revel were
    done,
And the stars were beginning to fade in the sun,
I have led thee along, and have told by the way
What my heart all the night had been burning
    to say—
Oh! think of the past—give a sigh to those times,
And a blessing for me to that alley of limes!

IF I were yonder wave, my dear,
  And thou the isle it clasps around,
I would not let a foot come near
  My land of bliss, my fairy ground!

If I were yonder couch of gold,
  And thou the pearl within it placed,
I would not let an eye behold
  The sacred gem my arms embraced!

If I were yonder orange-tree,
  And thou the blossom blooming there,
I would not yield a breath of thee,
  To scent the most imploring air!

Oh! bend not o'er the water's brink,
  Give not the wave that rosy sigh,
Nor let its burning mirror drink
  The soft reflection of thine eye.

That glossy hair, that glowing cheek,
  Upon the billows pour their beam
So warmly, that my soul could seek
  Its Nea in the painted stream.

The painted stream my chilly grave
  And nuptial bed at once may be;
I'll wed thee in that mimic wave,
  And die upon the shade of thee!

---

[1] The Milesiacs, or Milesian fables, had their origin in Miletus, a luxurious town of Ionia. Aristides was the most celebrated author of these licentious fictions. See Plutarch (in Crasso), who calls them αχολαστα βιβλια.

[2] 'Some of the Cretan wines, which Athenæus calls οινος ανθοσμιας, from their fragrancy resembling that of the finest flowers.'—*Barry on Wines*, chap. vii.

[3] It appears that, in very splendid mansions, the floor or pavement was frequently of onyx. Thus Martial: 'Calcatusque tuo sub pede lucet onyx.'—*Epig.* 50, lib. xii.

[4] Bracelets of this shape were a favourite ornament among the women of antiquity. Οι επικαρπιοι οφεις και οι χρυσοι εἰδει Θαιδος και Αριστιγορας και Λαιδος φαρμακα.—Philostrat. epist. xl. Lucian, too, tells of the βραχιονι δρακοντι. See his *Amores*, where he describes the dressing-room of a Grecian lady, and we find the 'silver vase,' the rouge, the tooth-powder, and all the mystic order' of a modern toilet.

[5] The inhabitants pronounce the name as if it were written Bermooda. See the commentators on the words 'still-vexed Bermoothes,' in the *Tempest*.—I wonder it did not occur to some of those all-reading gentlemen, that possibly the discoverer of this 'island of hogs and devils' might have been no less a personage than the great John Bermudez, who about the same period (the beginning of the sixteenth century) was sent Patriarch of the Latin Church to Ethiopia, and has left us most wonderful stories of the Amazons and the Griffins which he encountered.—*Travels of the Jesuits*, vol. i. vol. ii. I am afraid, however, it would take the Patriarch rather too much out of his way.

[6] Johnson does not think that Waller was ever at Bermuda; but the *Account of the European Settlements in America* affirms it confidently (vol. ii.). I mention this work, however, less for its authority than for the pleasure I feel in quoting an unacknowledged production of the great Edmund Burke.

Behold the leafy mangrove bending
  O'er the waters blue and bright,
Like Nea's silky lashes, lending
  Shadow to her eyes of light!

Oh, my beloved! where'er I turn,
  Some trace of thee enchants mine eyes;
In every star thy glances burn,
  Thy blush on every floweret lies.

But then thy breath!—not all the fire
  That lights the lone Semenda's death
In eastern climes, could e'er respire
  An odour like thy dulcet breath!

I pray thee, on those lips of thine
  To wear this rosy leaf for me,
And breathe of something not divine,
  Since nothing human breathes of thee!

All other charms of thine I meet
  In nature, but thy sigh alone;
Then take, oh! take, though not so sweet,
  The breath of roses for thine own!

So while I walk the flowery grove,
  The bud that gives, through morning dew,
The lustre of the lips I love,
  May seem to give their perfume too!

THE SNOW SPIRIT.

Tu potes insolitas, Cynthia, ferre nives?
—Propert. lib. 1. eleg. 8.

No, ne'er did the wave in its element steep
  An island of lovelier charms;
It blooms in the giant embrace of the deep,
  Like Hebe in Hercules' arms!
The tint of your bowers is balm to the eye,
  Their melody balm to the ear;
But the fiery planet of day is too nigh,
  And the Snow Spirit never comes here!

The down from his wing is as white as the pearl
  Thy lips for their cabinet stole,
And it falls on the green earth as melting, my girl,
  As a murmur of thine on the soul!
Oh! fly to the clime, where he pillows the death,
  As he cradles the birth of the year;
Bright are your bowers and balmy their breath,
  But the Snow Spirit cannot come here!

How sweet to behold him when, borne on the gale,
  And brightening the bosom of morn,
He flings, like the priest of Diana, a veil
  O'er the brow of each virginal thorn!
Yet think not the veil he so chillingly casts
  Is the veil of a vestal severe;
No, no—thou wilt see what a moment it lasts,
  Should the Snow Spirit ever come here!

But fly to his region—lay open thy zone,
  And he'll weep all his brilliancy dim,
To think that a bosom, as white as his own,
  Should not melt in the day-beam like him!
Oh! lovely the print of those delicate feet
  O'er his luminous path will appear—
Fly! my beloved! this island is sweet,
  But the Snow Spirit cannot come here!

Ἐνταῦθα δὲ καθωρμισται ἡμῖν, καὶ ὁ, τι μὲν ονομα
τῇ νησῳ ουκ οιδα· χρυση δ' αν πρς γε ιμου
ονομαζοιτε.
        Philostrat. Icon. 17, lib. 2.

I STOLE along the flowery bank,
  While many a bending sea-grape[1] drank
The sprinkle of the feathery oar
  That winged me round this fairy shore!

'Twas noon; and every orange bud
  Hung languid o'er the crystal flood,
Faint as the lids of maiden eyes
  Beneath a lover's burning sighs!
Oh for a Naiad's sparry bower,
  To shade me in that glowing hour!

A little dove, of milky hue,
  Before me from a plantain flew,
And, light along the water's brim,
  I steered my gentle bark by him;
For Fancy told me Love had sent
  This snowy bird of blandishment,
To lead me, where my soul should meet—
  I know not what, but something sweet!

Blest be the little pilot dove!
  He had indeed been sent by Love,
To guide me to a scene so dear
  As Fate allows but seldom here:
One of those rare and brilliant hours,
  Which, like the aloe's lingering flowers,
May blossom to the eye of man
  But once in all his weary span!

Just where the margin's opening shade
  A vista from the waters made,
My bird reposed his silver plume
  Upon a rich banana's bloom.
Oh, vision bright! oh, spirit fair!
  What spell, what magic raised her there?
'Twas Nea! slumbering calm and mild,
  And bloomy as the dimpled child
Whose spirit in Elysium keeps
  Its playful sabbath while he sleeps!

The broad banana's green embrace
  Hung shadowy round each tranquil grace;
One little beam alone could win
  The leaves to let it wander in,

---

[1] The sea-side or mangrove grape, a native of the West Indies.

And stealing over all her charms,
From lip to cheek, from neck to arms,
It glanced around a fiery kiss,
All trembling, as it went, with bliss!

Her eyelid's black and silken fringe
Lay on her cheek, of vermil tinge,
Like the first ebon cloud that closes
Dark on Evening's Heaven of roses!
Her glances, though in slumber hid,
Seemed glowing through their ivory lid;
And o'er her lip's reflecting dew
A soft and liquid lustre threw,
Such as, declining dim and faint,
The lamp of some beloved saint
Doth shed upon a flowery wreath,
Which pious hands have hung beneath.

Was ever witchery half so sweet!
Think, think how all my pulses beat,
As o'er the rustling bank I stole—
Oh! you that know the lover's soul,
It is for you to dream the bliss,
The tremblings of an hour like this!

I FOUND her not—the chamber seemed
Like some divinely haunted place,
Where fairy forms had lately beamed,
And left behind their odorous trace!

It felt as if her lips had shed
A sigh around her, ere she fled,
Which hung, as on a melting lute,
When all the silver chords are mute,
There lingers still a trembling breath
After the note's luxurious death,
A shade of song, a spirit air
Of melodies which had been there!

I saw the web, which, all the day,
Had floated o'er her cheek of rose
I saw the couch, where late she lay
In languor of divine repose!

And I could trace the hallowed print
Her limbs had left, as pure and warm
As if 'twere done in rapture's mint,
And Love himself had stamped the form!

Oh, Nea! Nea! where wert thou?
In pity fly not thus from me;
Thou art my life, my essence now,
And my soul dies of wanting thee!

A KISS A L'ANTIQUE.

BEHOLD, my love, the curious gem
Within this simple ring of gold;
'Tis hallowed by the touch of them
Who lived in classic hours of old.

Some fair Athenian girl, perhaps,
Upon her hand this gem displayed,
Nor thought that time's eternal lapse
Should see it grace a lovelier maid!

Look, darling, what a sweet design!
The more we gaze, it charms the more:
Come,—closer bring that cheek to mine,
And trace with me its beauties o'er.

Thou seest, it is a simple youth
By some enamoured nymph embraced—
Look, Nea, love! and say, in sooth,
Is not her hand most dearly placed?

Upon his curled head behind
It seems in careless play to lie,[1]
Yet presses gently, half inclined
To bring his lip of nectar nigh!

Oh happy maid! too happy boy!
The one so fond and faintly loth,
The other yielding slow to joy—
Oh, rare indeed, but blissful both!

Imagine, love, that I am he,
And just as warm as he is chilling;
Imagine too that thou art she,
But quite as cold as she is willing:

So may we try the graceful way
In which their gentle arms are twined,
And thus, like her, my hand I lay
Upon thy wreathèd hair behind:

And thus I feel thee breathing sweet,
As slow to mine thy head I move;
And thus our lips together meet,
And—thus I kiss thee—oh, my love!

. . . λιβανοτῳ τικασιν, ότι απολλυμενον ευφραινει.
Aristot. Rhetor. lib. iii. cap. 4.

THERE'S not a look, a word of thine,
My soul hath e'er forgot;
Thou ne'er hast bid a ringlet shine,
Nor given thy locks one graceful twine,
Which I remember not!

---

* Somewhat like the symplegma of Cupid and Psyche at Florence, in which the position of Psyche's hand is finely expressive of affection. See the *Museum Florentinum*, tom. ii. tab. 43, 44. I know of very few subjects in which poetry could be more interestingly employed, than in illustrating some of the ancient statues and gems.

There never yet a murmur fell
  From that beguiling tongue,
Which did not, with a lingering spell,
  Upon my charmèd senses dwell,
    Like something Heaven had sung!

Ah! that I could at once forget
  All, all that haunts me so—
And yet, thou witching girl!—and yet,
To die were sweeter, than to let
    The loved remembrance go!

No, if this slighted heart must see
  Its faithful pulse decay,
Oh! let it die, remembering thee,
And, like the burnt aroma, be
    Consumed in sweets away!

EPISTLE V.

TO JOSEPH ATKINSON, ESQ.

FROM BERMUDA.[1]

March.

'THE daylight is gone—but, before we depart,
One cup shall go round to the friend of my heart,
To the kindest, the dearest—oh! judge by the tear,
That I shed while I name him, how kind and how dear!'

'Twas thus, by the shade of a calabash-tree,
With a few who could feel and remember like me,
The charm, that to sweeten my goblet I threw,
Was a tear to the past and a blessing on you!

Oh! say, do you thus, in the luminous hour
Of wine and of wit, when the heart is in flower
And shoots from the lip, under Bacchus's dew,
In blossoms of thought ever springing and new!
Do you sometimes remember, and hallow the brim
Of your cup with a sigh, as you crown it to him,
Who is lonely and sad in these valleys so fair,
And would pine in Elysium, if friends were not there?

Last night, when we came from the calabash-tree,
When my limbs were at rest and my spirit was free,
The glow of the grape and the dreams of the day
Put the magical springs of my fancy in play,
And oh!—such a vision as haunted me then
I could slumber for ages to witness again!
The many I like, and the few I adore,
The friends, who were dear and beloved before,
But never till now so beloved and dear,
At the call of my fancy surrounded me here!
Soon, soon did the flattering spell of their smile
To a paradise brighten the blest little isle;
Serener the wave, as they looked on it, flowed,
And warmer the rose, as they gathered it, glowed!
Not the valleys Hermæan (though watered by rills
Of the pearliest flow, from those pastoral hills,[2]
Where the song of the shepherd, primeval and wild,
Was taught to the nymphs by their mystical child)

---

[1] Pinkerton has said that 'a good history and description of the Bermudas might afford a pleasing addition to the geographical library;' but there certainly are not materials for such a work. The island, since the time of its discovery, has experienced so very few vicissitudes, the people have been so indolent, and their trade so limited, that there is but little which the historian could amplify into importance; and, with respect to the natural productions of the country, the few which the inhabitants can be induced to cultivate are so common in the West Indies, that they have been described by every naturalist who has written any account of those islands.

It is often asserted by the transatlantic politicians, that this little colony deserves more attention from the mother-country than it receives; and it certainly possesses advantages of situation, to which we should not be long insensible if it were once in the hands of an enemy. I was told by a celebrated friend of Washington, at New York, that they had formed a plan for its capture towards the conclusion of the American War, 'with the intention (as he expressed himself) of making it a nest of hornets for the annoyance of British trade in that part of the world.' And there is no doubt it lies so fairly in the track to the West Indies, that an enemy might with ease convert it into a very harassing impediment.

The plan of Bishop Berkeley for a college at Bermuda, where American savages might be converted and educated, though concurred in by the Government of the day, was a wild and useless speculation. Mr. Hamilton, who was governor of the island some years since, proposed, if I mistake not, the establishment of a marine academy for the instruction of those children of West Indians who might be intended for any nautical employment. This was a more rational idea, and for something of this nature the island is admirably calculated. But the plan should be much more extensive, and embrace a general system of education, which would entirely remove the alternative in which the colonists are involved at present, of either sending their sons to England for instruction, or entrusting them to colleges in the States of America, where ideas by no means favourable to Great Britain are very sedulously inculcated.

The women of Bermuda, though not generally handsome, have an affectionate languor in their look and manner, which is always interesting. What the French imply by their epithet *aimante* seems very much the character of the young Bermudian girls—that predisposition to loving, which, without being awakened by any particular object, diffuses itself through the general manner in a tone of tenderness that never fails to fascinate. The men of the island, I confess, are not very civilised; and the old philosopher, who imagined that, after this life, men would be changed into mules, and women into turtle-doves, would find the metamorphosis in some degree anticipated at Bermuda.

[2] Mountains of Sicily, upon which Daphnis, the first inventor of bucolic poetry, was nursed by the nymphs.

Could display such a bloom of delight, as was given
By the magic of love to this miniature Heaven!

Oh, magic of love! unembellished by you,
Has the garden a blush or the herbage a hue?
Or blooms there a prospect in nature or art,
Like the vista that shines through the eye to the heart?

Alas! that a vision so happy should fade!
That, when morning around me in brilliancy played,
The rose and the stream I had thought of at night
Should still be before me, unfadingly bright;
While the friends, who had seemed to hang over the stream,
And to gather the roses, had fled with my dream!

But see, through the harbour, in floating array,
The bark that must carry these pages away [1]
Impatiently flutters her wing to the wind,
And will soon leave the bowers of Ariel behind!
What billows, what gales is she fated to prove,
Ere she sleep in the lea of the land that I love!
Yet pleasant the swell of those billows would be,
And the sound of those gales would be music to me!
Not the tranquillest air that the winds ever blew,
Not the silvery lapse of the summer-eve dew,
Were as sweet as the breeze, or as bright as the foam
Of the wave that would carry your wanderer home!

LOVE AND REASON.

'Quand l'homme commence à raisonner, il cesse de sentir.'—*J. J. Rousseau.*

'TWAS in the summer-time so sweet,
 When hearts and flowers are both in season,
That—who, of all the world, should meet,
 One early dawn, but Love and Reason!

Love told his dream of yesternight,
 While Reason talked about the weather;
The morn, in sooth, was fair and bright,
 And on they took their way together.

The boy in many a gambol flew,
 While Reason like a Juno stalked,
And from her portly figure threw
 A lengthened shadow as she walked.

No wonder Love, as on they passed,
 Should find that sunny morning chill,
For still the shadow Reason cast
 Fell on the boy, and cooled him still.

In vain he tried his wings to warm,
 Or find a pathway not so dim,
For still the maid's gigantic form
 Would pass between the sun and him!

'This must not be,' said little Love—
 'The sun was made for more than you.'
So, turning through a myrtle grove,
 He bid the portly nymph adieu!

Now gaily roves the laughing boy
 O'er many a mead, by many a stream;
In every breeze inhaling joy,
 And drinking bliss in every beam.

From all the gardens, all the bowers,
 He culled the many sweets they shaded,
And ate the fruits and smelt the flowers,
 Till taste was gone and odour faded!

But now the sun, in pomp of noon,
 Looked blazing o'er the parchèd plains;
Alas! the boy grew languid soon,
 And fever thrilled through all his veins!

The dew forsook his baby brow,
 No more with vivid bloom he smiled—
Oh! where was tranquil Reason now,
 To cast her shadow o'er the child?

Beneath a green and aged palm,
 His foot at length for shelter turning,
He saw the nymph reclining calm,
 With brow as cool as his was burning!

'Oh! take me to that bosom cold,'
 In murmurs at her feet he said;
And reason oped her garment's fold,
 And flung it round his fevered head.

He felt her bosom's icy touch,
 And soon it lulled his pulse to rest;
For, ah! the chill was quite too much,
 And Love expired on Reason's breast!

NAY, do not weep, my Fanny dear,
 While in these arms you lie;
The world hath not a wish, a fear,
 That ought to claim one precious tear
From that beloved eye!

The world!—ah, Fanny! Love must shun
 The path where many rove;
One bosom to recline upon,
One heart, to be his only one,
 Are quite enough for Love!

---

[1] A ship, ready to sail for England.

What can we wish, that is not here
Between your arms and mine?
Is there on earth a space so dear,
As that within the blessed sphere
Two loving arms entwine?

For me, there's not a lock of jet
Along your temples curled,
Within whose glossy, tangling net,
My soul doth not, at once, forget
All, all the worthless world!

'Tis in your eyes, my sweetest love!
My only worlds I see;
Let but *their* orbs in sunshine move,
And earth below and skies above
May frown or smile for me!

ASPASIA.

'Twas in the fair Aspasia's bower,
That Love and Learning many an hour
In dalliance met, and Learning smiled
With rapture on the playful child,
Who wanton stole to find his nest
Within a fold of Learning's vest!

There, as the listening statesman hung
In transport on Aspasia's tongue,
The destinies of Athens took
Their colour from Aspasia's look.
Oh, happy time! when laws of state,
When all that ruled the country's fate,
In glory, quiet, or alarms,
Was planned between two snowy arms!

Sweet times! you could not always last—
And yet, oh! yet, you *are* not past;
Though we have lost the sacred mould
In which their men were cast of old,
Woman, dear woman, still the same,
While lips are balm and looks are flame,
While man possesses heart or eyes,
Woman's bright empire never dies!

Fanny, my love, they ne'er shall say
That beauty's charm hath passed away;
No—give the universe a soul
Attuned to woman's soft control,
And Fanny hath the charm, the skill,
To wield a universe at will!

THE GRECIAN GIRL'S DREAM OF THE
BLESSED ISLANDS.[1]

TO HER LOVER.

. . . . . . χι τι καλοι
Πυθαγορης, ιασοι τε χοροι στηριξαν ερωτος.
Απολλων περι Πλωτινου.
—*Oracul. Metric. a Joan. Opsop. collecta.*

Was it the moon, or was it morning's ray,
That called thee, dearest, from these arms away?
I lingered still, in all the murmuring rest,
The languor of a soul too richly blest!
Upon my breath thy sigh yet faintly hung;
Thy name yet died in whispers o'er my tongue;
I heard thy lyre, which thou hadst left behind,
In amorous converse with the breathing wind;
Quick to my heart I pressed the shell divine,
And, with a lip yet glowing warm from thine,
I kissed its every chord, while every kiss
Shed o'er the chord some dewy print of bliss.
Then soft to thee I touched the fervid lyre,
Which told such melodies, such notes of fire,
As none but chords that drank the burning dews
Of kisses dear as ours could e'er diffuse!
Oh love! how blissful is the bland repose
That soothing follows upon rapture's close,
Like a soft twilight, o'er the mind to shed
Mild melting traces of the transport fled!

While thus I lay, in this voluptuous calm,
A drowsy languor steeped my eyes in balm,
Upon my lap the lyre in murmurs fell,
While, faintly wandering o'er its silver shell,
My fingers soon their own sweet requiem played,
And slept in music which themselves had made:
Then, then, my Theon, what a heavenly dream!
I saw two spirits on the lunar beam,
Two wingèd boys, descending from above,
And gliding to my bower with looks of love,
Like the young genii, who repose their wings
All day in Amatha's luxurious springs,[2]
And rise at midnight, from the tepid rill,
To cool their plumes upon some moonlight hill!
Soft o'er my brow, which kindled with their sighs,
Awhile they played; then gliding through my
    eyes
(Where the bright babies for a moment hung,
Like those thy lip hath kissed, thy lyre hath
    sung),
To that dim mansion of my breast they stole,
Where, wreathed in blisses, lay my captive
    soul.
Swift at their touch dissolved the ties that clung
So sweetly round her, and aloft she sprung!

---

[1] It was imagined by some of the ancients that there is an ethereal ocean above us, and that the sun and moon are two floating luminous islands, in which the spirits of the blessed reside. Accordingly, we find that the word Ωκεανος was sometimes synonymous with αηρ, and that death was not unfrequently called Ωκεανοιο πορος, or 'the passage of the ocean.'

[2] Eunaplus, in his *Life of Jamblichus*, tells us of two beautiful little spirits or loves, which Jamblichus raised by enchantment from the warm springs at Gadara; 'dicens astantibus (says the author of the *Dii Fatidi i*, p. 160) illos esse loci Genios:' which words, however, are not in Eunaplus.

I find from Cellarius, that Amatha, in the neighbourhood of Gadara, was also celebrated for its warm springs, and I have preferred it as a more poetical name than Gadara.

Exulting guides, the little genii flew
'Larough paths of light, refreshed with starry dew,
And fanned by airs of that ambrosial breath,
On which the free soul banquets after death!

Thou know'st, my love, beyond our clouded skies,
As bards have dreamed, the spirits' kingdom lies.
Through that fair clime a sea of ether rolls,
Gemmed with bright islands, where the hallowed souls,
Whom life hath wearied in its race of hours,
Repose for ever in unfading bowers!
That very orb, whose solitary light
So often guides thee to my arms at night,
Is no chill planet, but an isle of love,
Floating in splendour through those seas above!
Thither, I thought, we winged our airy way,
Mild o'er its valleys streamed a silvery day,
While all around, on lily beds of rest,
Reclined the spirits of the immortal Blest![1]
Oh! there I met those few congenial maids,
Whom love hath warmed, in philosophic shades;
There still Leontium,[2] on her sage's breast,
Found lore and love, was tutored and caressed;
And there the twine of Pythias'[3] gentle arms
Repaid the zeal which deified her charms!
The Attic Master,[4] in Aspasia's eyes,
Forgot the toil of less endearing ties;
While fair Theano,[5] innocently fair,
Played with the ringlets of her Samian's hair,[6]
Who, fixed by love, at length was all her own,
And passed his spirit through her lips alone!

Oh Samian sage! whate'er thy glowing thought
Of mystic Numbers hath divinely wrought,
The One that's formed of Two who dearly love,
Is the best number Heaven can boast above!

But think, my Theon, how this soul was thrilled,
When near a fount, which o'er the vale distilled,
My fancy's eye beheld a form recline,
Of lunar race, but so resembling thine,
That, oh!—'twas but fidelity in me,
To fly, to clasp, and worship it for thee!
No aid of words the unbodied soul requires
To waft a wish, or embassy delivers;
But, by a throb to spirits only given,
By a mute impulse, only felt in heaven,
Swifter than meteor shaft through summer skies,
From soul to soul the glanced idea flies!

We met—like thee the youthful vision smiled;
But not like thee, when passionately wild,
Thou wak'st the slumbering blushes of my cheek,
By looking things thyself would blush to speak!
No; 'twas the tender, intellectual smile,
Flushed with the past, and yet serene the while,
Of that delicious hour when, glowing yet,
Thou yield'st to nature with a fond regret,
And thy soul, waking from its wildered dream,
Lights in thine eye a mellower, chaster beam!

Oh, my belovèd! how divinely sweet
Is the pure joy, when kindred spirits meet!
The Elean god,[7] whose faithful waters flow,
With love their only light, through caves below,

---

[1] There were various opinions among the ancients with respect to their lunar establishment: some made it an elysium, and others a purgatory; while some supposed it to be a kind of *entrepôt* between heaven and earth, where souls which had left their bodies, and those that were on their way to join them, were deposited in the valleys of Hecate, and remained till further orders. Ταις περι σεληνην αερι λεγου αυτας κατοικειν, και απ' αυτης κατω χωρειν εις την περιγειον γενεσιν.—*Stob.* lib. I *Eclog. Physic.*

[2] The pupil and mistress of Epicurus, who called her his 'dear little Leontium' (Λεοντραριον), as appears by a fragment of one of his *Letters* in Laertius. This Leontium was a woman of talent; 'she had the impudence (says Cicero) to write against Theophrastus;' and, at the same time, Cicero gives her a name which is neither polite nor translateable. 'Meretricula etiam Leontium contra Theophrastum scribere ausa est.'—*De Na'ur. Deor.* She left a daughter, called Danae, who was just as rigid an Epicurean as her mother; something like Wieland's *Danae in Agathon.*

It would sound much better, I think, if the name were Leontia, as it occurs the first time in Laertius; but M. Menage will not hear of this reading.

[3] Pythias was a woman whom Aristotle loved, and to whom, after her death, he paid divine honours, solemnizing her memory by the same sacrifices which the Athenians offered to the goddess Ceres. For this impious gallantry the philosopher was of course censured. It would be well, however, if some of our modern Stagyrites had a little of this superstition about the memory of their mistresses.

[4] Socrates, who used to console himself in the society of Aspasia for those 'less endearing ties' which he found at home with Xantippe. For an account of this extraordinary creature, Aspasia, and her school of erudite luxury at Athens, see *L'Histoire de l'Académie*, etc., tom. xxxi. p. 69. Ségur rather fails on the subject of Aspasia. *Les Femmes*, tom. l. p. 122.

The author of the *Voyage du Monde de Descartes* has also placed those philosophers in the moon, and has allotted Seigneuries to them, as well as to the astronomers (part 2, p. 143); but he ought not to have forgotten their wives and mistresses; 'curæ non ipsa in morte relinquunt.'

[5] There are some sensible letters extant under the name of this fair Pythagorean. They are addressed to her female friends upon the education of children, the treatment of servants, etc. One, in particular, to Nicostrata, whose husband had given her reasons for jealousy, contains such truly considerate and rational advice, that it ought to be translated for the edification of all married ladies. See *Gale's Opuscul. Myth. Phys.* p. 741.

[6] Pythagoras was remarkable for fine hair, and Dr. Thiers (in his *Histoire des Perruques*) seems to take for granted it was all his own, as he has not mentioned him among those ancients who were obliged to have recourse to the 'coma apposititia.'—*L'Hist. des Perruques*, chap. 1.

[7] The river Alpheus, which flowed by Pisa or Olympia, and into which it was customary to throw offerings of different kinds during the celebration of the Olympic games. In the pretty romance of *Clitophon and Leucippe*,

Wafting in triumph all the flowery braids,
And festal rings, with which Olympic maids
Have decked their billow, as an offering meet
To pour at Arethusa's crystal feet!
Think, when he mingles with his fountain-bride,
What perfect rapture thrills the blended tide!
Each melts in each, till one pervading kiss
Confound their currents in a sea of bliss!
'Twas thus—
       But, Theon, 'tis a weary theme,
And thou delight'st not in my lingering dream.
Oh! that our lips were, at this moment, near,
And I would kiss thee into patience, dear!
And make thee smile at all the magic tales
Of star-light bowers and planetary vales,
Which my fond soul, inspired by thee and love,
In slumber's loom hath exquisitely wove.
But no; no more—soon as to-morrow's ray
O'er soft Ilissus shall dissolve away,
I'll fly, my Theon, to thy burning breast,
And there in murmurs tell thee all the rest:
Then, if too weak, too cold the vision seems,
Thy lip shall teach me something more than
    dreams!

THE STEERSMAN'S SONG.

WRITTEN ABOARD THE BOSTON FRIGATE,
28TH APRIL.[1]

When freshly blows the northern gale,
  And under courses snug we fly;
When lighter breezes swell the sail,
  And royals proudly sweep the sky;
'Longside the wheel, unwearied still
  I stand, and as my watchful eye
Doth mark the needle's faithful thrill,
  I think of her I love, and cry,
        Port, my boy! port.

When calms delay, or breezes blow
  Right from the point we wish to steer;
When by the wind close-hauled we go,
  And strive in vain the port to near;
I think 'tis thus the Fates defer
  My bliss with one that's far away;
And while remembrance springs to her,
  I watch the sails, and sighing say,
        Thus, my boy! thus.

But see the wind draws kindly aft,
  All hands are up the yards to square,
And now the floating stu'n-sails waft
  Our stately ship through waves and air.

Oh! then I think that yet for me
  Some breeze of Fortune thus may spring
Some breeze to waft me, love, to thee!
  And in that hope I smiling sing,
        Steady, boy! so.

TO CLOE.

IMITATED FROM MARTIAL.

I could resign that eye of blue,
  Howe'er it burn, howe'er it thrill me;
And though your lip be rich with dew,
  To lose it, Cloe, scarce would kill me.

That snowy neck I ne'er should miss,
  However warm I've twined about it!
And though your bosom beat with bliss,
  I think my soul could live without it.

In short, I've learned so well to fast,
  That, sooth my love, I know not whether
I might not bring myself at last
  To—do without you altogether!

TO THE FIRE-FLY.[2]

This morning, when the earth and sky
  Were burning with the blush of spring,
I saw thee not, thou humble fly!
  Nor thought upon thy gleaming wing.

But now the skies have lost their hue,
  And sunny lights no longer play,
I see thee, and I bless thee too
  For sparkling o'er the dreary way.

Oh! let me hope that thus for me,
  When life and love shall lose their bloom,
Some milder joys may come, like thee,
  To light, if not to warm the gloom!

THE VASE.

There was a vase of odour lay
  For many an hour on Beauty's shrine,
So sweet that love went every day
  To banquet on its breath divine.

And not an eye had ever seen
  The fragrant charm the vase concealed;

---

the river is supposed to carry these offerings as bridal gifts to the fountain Arethusa.

[1] I left Bermuda in the *Boston*, about the middle of April, in company with the *Cambrian* and *Leander*, aboard the latter of which was the Admiral, Sir Andrew Mitchell, who divides his year between Halifax and Bermuda, and is the very soul of society and good-fellowship to both. We separated in a few days, and the *Boston* after a short cruise proceeded to New York.

[2] The lively and varying illumination with which these fire-flies light up the woods at night gives quite an idea of enchantment. 'Puis ces mouches se développant de l'obscurité de ces arbres et s'approchant de nous, nous les voyi ns sur les orangers voisins, qu'ils mettaient tout en feu, nous rendant la vue de leurs beaux fruits dorés que la nuit avait ravie,' etc. etc.—See *l'Histoire des Antilles*, art. 2, chap. 4, liv. I.

Oh Love! how happy 'twould have been,
 If thou hadst ne'er that charm revealed!

But Love, like every other boy,
 Would know the spell that lurks within;
He wished to break the crystal toy,
 But Beauty murmured "'twas a sin!"

He swore, with many a tender plea,
 That neither Heaven nor Earth forbad it;
She told him, Virtue kept the key,
 And looked as if—she wished he had it!

He stole the key when Virtue slept
 (Even she can sleep, if Love but ask it),
And Beauty sighed, and Beauty wept,
 While silly Love unlocked the casket.

Oh dulcet air that vanished then!
 Can Beauty's sigh recall thee ever?
Can Love himself inhale again
 A breath so precious?—never, never!

Go, maiden, weep—the tears of woe
 By Beauty to repentance given,
Though bitterly on earth they flow,
 Shall turn to fragrant balm in Heaven!

THE WREATH AND THE CHAIN.

I bring thee, love, a golden chain,
 I bring thee too a flowery wreath;
The gold shall never wear a stain,
 The flowerets long shall sweetly breathe!
Come, tell me which the tie shall be
To bind thy gentle heart to me.

The Chain is of a splendid thread,
 Stolen from Minerva's yellow hair,
Just when the setting sun had shed
 The sober beam of evening there.
The Wreath's of brightest myrtle wove,
 With brilliant tears of bliss among it,
And many a rose-leaf, culled by Love,
 To heal his lip when bees have stung it!
Come, tell me which the tie shall be
To bind thy gentle heart to me.

Yes, yes, I read that ready eye,
 Which answers when the tongue is loth,
Thou lik'st the form of either tie,
 And hold'st thy playful hands for both.
Ah! if there were not something wrong,
 The world would see them blended oft;
The Chain would make the Wreath so strong!
 The Wreath would make the Chain so soft!
Then might the gold, the flowerets be
Sweet fetters for my love and me!

But, Fanny, so unblest they twine,
 That (Heaven alone can tell the reason)
When mingled thus they cease to shine,
 Or shine but for a transient season!
Whether the Chain may press too much,
 Or that the Wreath is slightly braided,
Let but the gold the flowerets touch,
 And all their glow, their tints, are faded!
Sweet Fanny, what would Rapture do,
 When all her blooms had lost their grace?
Might she not steal a rose or two
 From other wreaths, to fill their place?—
Oh! better to be always free,
Than thus to bind my love to me.

The timid girl now hung her head,
 And, as she turned an upward glance,
I saw a doubt its twilight spread
 Along her brow's divine expanse.
Just then the garland's dearest rose
 Gave one of its seducing sighs—
Oh! who can ask how Fanny chose,
 That ever looked in Fanny's eyes!
'The wreath, my life, the wreath shall be
The tie to bind my soul to thee!'

TO —— ——.

And hast thou marked the pensive shade,
 That many a time obscures my brow,
'Midst all the blisses, darling maid,
 Which thou canst give, and only thou?

Oh! 'tis not that I then forget
 The endearing charms that round me twine—
There never throbbed a bosom yet
 Could feel their witchery, like mine!

When bashful on my bosom hid,
 And blushing to have felt so blest,
Thou dost but lift thy languid lid,
 Again to close it on my breast!

Oh! these are minutes all thine own,
 Thine own to give, and mine to feel,
Yet, even in them, my heart has known
 The sigh to rise, the tear to steal.

For I have thought of former hours,
 When he who first thy soul possessed,
Like me awaked its witching powers,
 Like me was loved, like me was blest!

Upon *his* name thy murmuring tongue
 Perhaps hath all as sweetly dwelt;
For him that snowy lid hath hung
 In ecstasy, as purely felt!

For him—yet why the past recall
 To wither blooms of present bliss?
Thou'rt now my own, I clasp thee all,
 And Heaven can grant no more than this!

Forgive me, dearest, oh! forgive;
 I would be first, be sole to thee;
Thou shouldst but have begun to live
 The hour that gave thy heart to me.

Thy book of life till then effaced,
 Love should have kept that leaf alone,
On which he first so dearly traced
 That thou wert, soul and all, my own!

EPISTLE VI.

TO LORD VISCOUNT FORBES.

FROM THE CITY OF WASHINGTON.

ΚΑΙ ΜΗ ΘΑΥΜΑΣΗΙΣ ΜΗΤ' ΕΙ ΜΑΚΡΟΤΕΡΑΝ
ΓΕΓΡΑΦΑ ΤΗΝ ΕΠΙΣΤΟΛΗΝ, ΜΗΔ' ΕΙ ΤΙ
ΠΕΡΙΕΡΓΟΤΕΡΟΝ Η ΠΡΕΣΒΥΤΙΚΩΤΕΡΟΝ
ΕΙΡΗΚΑΜΕΝ ΕΑΥΤΗ.
—*Isocrat.* Epist. iv.

If former times had never left a trace
Of human frailty in their shadowy race,
Nor o'er their pathway written, as they ran,
One dark memorial of the crimes of man;
If every age, in new unconscious prime,
Rose, like a phœnix, from the fires of time,
To wing its way unguided and alone,
The future smiling and the past unknown;
Then ardent man would to himself be new,
Earth at his foot and heaven within his view;
Well might the novice hope, the sanguine scheme
Of full perfection prompt his daring dream,
Ere cold experience, with her veteran lore,
Could tell him, fools had dreamed as much before!
But tracing, as we do, through age and clime,
The plans of virtue 'midst the deeds of crime,
The thinking follies and the reasoning rage
Of man, at once the idiot and the sage,
When still we see, through every varying frame
Of arts and polity, his course the same,
And know that ancient fools but died to make
A space on earth for modern fools to take;
'Tis strange, how quickly we the past forget;
That Wisdom's self should not be tutored yet,
Nor tire of watching for the monstrous birth
Of pure perfection 'midst the sons of earth!
Oh! nothing but that soul which God has given,
Could lead us thus to look on earth for heaven;
O'er dross without to shed the flame within,
And dream of virtue while we gaze on sin!

Even here, beside the proud Potowmac's stream,
Might sages still pursue the flattering theme
Of days to come, when man shall conquer Fate,
Rise o'er the level of his mortal state,
Belie the monuments of frailty past,
And stamp perfection on this world at last!
'Here,' might they say, 'shall Power's divided reign
Evince that patriots have not bled in vain.
Here godlike Liberty's herculean youth,
Cradled in peace, and nurtured up by truth
To full maturity of nerve and mind,
Shall crush the giants that bestride mankind!'[1]
Here shall Religion's pure and balmy draught,
In form no more from cups of state be quaffed,
But flow for all, through nation, rank, and sect,
Free as that heaven its tranquil waves reflect.
Around the columns of the public shrine
Shall growing arts their gradual wreath entwine,
Nor breathe corruption from their flowering braid,
Nor mine that fabric which they bloom to shade.
No longer here shall Justice bound her view,
Or wrong the many, while she rights the few;
But take her range through all the social frame,
Pure and pervading as that vital flame
Which warms at once our best and meanest part,
And thrills a hair while it expands a heart!'

Oh, golden dream! what soul that loves to scan
The brightness rather than the shades of man,
That owns the good, while smarting with the ill,
And loves the world with all its frailty still—
What ardent bosom does not spring to meet
The generous hope with all that heavenly heat,
Which makes the soul unwilling to resign
The thoughts of growing, even on earth, divine!
Yes, dearest Forbes, I see thee glow to think
The chain of ages yet may boast a link
Of purer texture than the world has known,
And fit to bind us to a Godhead's throne!

But, is it thus? doth even the glorious dream
Borrow from truth that dim uncertain gleam,
Which bids us give such dear delusion scope,
As kills not reason, while it nurses hope?
No, no, believe me, 'tis not so—even now,
While yet upon Columbia's rising brow
The showy smile of young presumption plays,
Her bloom is poisoned, and her heart decays!
Even now, in dawn of life, her sickly breath
Burns with the taint of empires near their death,
And, like the nymphs of her own withering clime,
She's old in youth, she's blasted in her prime![2]

---

[1] Thus Morse: 'Here the sciences and the arts of civilised life are to receive their highest improvements; here civil and religious liberty are to flourish, unchecked by the cruel hand of civil or ecclesiastical tyranny; here genius, aided by all the improvements of former ages, is to be exerted in humanizing mankind, in expanding and enriching their minds with religious and philosophical knowledge,' etc. etc.—P. 569.

[2] 'What will be the old age of this government, if it is thus early decrepit!' Such was the remark of Fauchet, the French minister at Philadelphia, in that famous despatch to his government which was intercepted by one of our cruisers in the year 1794. This curious memorial may be found in Porcupine's works, vol. L. p. 279. It remains a striking monument of republican intrigue on one side, and republican profligacy

Already has the child of Gallia's school,
The foul Philosophy that sins by rule,
With all her train of reasoning, damning arts,
Begot by brilliant heads or worthless hearts,
Like things that quicken after Nilus' flood,
The venomed birth of sunshine and of mud!
Already has she poured her poison here
O'er every charm that makes existence dear,
Already blighted, with her blackening trace,
The opening bloom of every social grace,
And all those courtesies that love to shoot
Round Virtue's stem, the flowerets of her fruit!

Oh! were these errors but the wanton tide
Of young luxuriance or unchastened pride;
The fervid follies and the faults of such
As wrongly feel, because they feel too much;
Then might experience make the fever less,
Nay, graft a virtue on each warm excess;
But no; 'tis heartless, speculative ill,
All youth's transgression with all age's chill,
The apathy of wrong, the bosom's ice,
A slow and cold stagnation into vice!

Long has the love of gold, that meanest rage
And latest folly of man's sinking age,
Which, rarely venturing in the van of life,
While nobler passions wage their heated strife,
Comes skulking last, with selfishness and fear,
And dies, collecting lumber in the rear!
Long has it palsied every grasping hand
And greedy spirit through this bartering land;
Turned life to traffic, set the demon Gold
So loose abroad, that Virtue's self is sold,
And conscience, truth, and honesty, are made
To rise and fall, like other wares of trade!

Already in this free, this virtuous state,
Which, Frenchmen tell us, was ordained by Fate,
To show the world what high perfection springs
From rabble senators and merchant kings—
Even here already patriots learn to steal
Their private perquisites from public weal,
And, guardians of the country's sacred fire,
Like Afric's priests, they let the flame for hire!
Those vaunted demagogues, who nobly rose
From England's debtors to be England's foes,[1]
Who could their monarch in their purse forget,
And break allegiance but to cancel debt,[2]

Have proved at length the mineral's tempting hue,
Which makes a patriot, can unmake him too.[3]
Oh! Freedom, Freedom, how I hate thy cant!
Not Eastern bombast, nor the savage rant
Of purpled madmen, were they numbered all
From Roman Nero down to Russian Paul,
Could grate upon my ear so mean, so base,
As the rank jargon of that factious race,
Who, poor of heart and prodigal of words,
Born to be slaves and struggling to be lords,
But pant for licence, while they spurn control,
And shout for rights, with rapine in their soul!
Who can, with patience, for a moment see
The medley mass of pride and misery,
Of whips and charters, manacles and rights,
Of slaving blacks and democratic whites,[4]
And all the piebald polity that reigns
In free confusion o'er Columbia's plains?
To think that man, thou just and gentle God!
Should stand before thee, with a tyrant's rod
O'er creatures like himself, with soul from thee,
Yet dare to boast of perfect liberty:
Away, away—I'd rather hold my neck
By doubtful tenure from a sultan's beck.
In climes where liberty has scarce been named,
Nor any right but that of ruling claimed,
Than thus to live, where bastard freedom waves
Her fustian flag in mockery over slaves;
Where (motley laws admitting no degree
Betwixt the vilely slaved and madly free)
Alike the bondage and the licence suit,
The brute made ruler and the man made brute!

But, oh my Forbes! while thus, in flowerless song,
I feebly paint what yet I feel so strong—
The ills, the vices of the land, where first
Those rebel fiends that rack the world were nurst!
Where treason's arm by royalty was nerved,
And Frenchmen learned to crush the throne they served —
Thou, gently lulled in dreams of classic thought,
By bards illumined and by sages taught,
Pant'st to be all, upon this mortal scene,
That bard hath fancied or that sage hath been!
Why should I wake thee? why severely chase
The lovely forms of virtue and of grace,
That dwell before thee, like the pictures spread
By Spartan matrons round the genial bed,

---

on the other; and I would recommend the perusal of it to every honest politician who may labour under a moment's delusion with respect to the purity of American patriotism.

[1] I trust I shall not be suspected of a wish to justify those arbitrary steps of the English Government which the Colonies found it so necessary to resist; my only object here is to expose the selfish motives of some of the leading American demagogues.

[2] The most persevering enemy to the interests of this country, amongst the politicians of the western world, has been a Virginian merchant, who, finding it easier to settle his conscience than his debts, was one of the first to raise the standard against Great Britain, and has ever since endeavoured to revenge upon the whole country the obligations which he lies under to a few of its merchants.

[3] See *Porcupine's Account of the Pennsylvania Insurrection in 1794*.

[4] In Virginia the effects of this system begin to be felt rather seriously. While the master raves of liberty, the slave cannot but catch the contagion, and accordingly there seldom elapses a month without some alarm of insurrection amongst the negroes. The accession of Louisiana, it is feared, will increase this embarrassment; as the numerous emigrations which are expected to take place from the Southern States to this newly-acquired territory will considerably diminish the white population, and thus strengthen the proportion of negroes to a degree which must ultimately be ruinous

Moulding thy fancy, and with gradual art
Brightening the young conceptions of thy heart!

Forgive me, Forbes—and should the song destroy
One generous hope, one throb of social joy,
One high pulsation of the zeal for man,
Which few can feel, and bless that few who can!
Oh! turn to him, beneath whose kindred eyes
Thy talents open and thy virtues rise,
Forget where Nature has been dark or dim,
And proudly study all her lights in him!
Yes, yes, in him the erring world forget,
And feel that man may reach perfection yet!

SONG.

The wreath you wove, the wreath you wove
  Is fair—but oh! how fair,
If Pity's hand had stolen from Love
  One leaf to mingle there!

If every rose with gold were tied,
  Did gems for dew-drops fall,
One faded leaf where Love had sighed
  Were sweetly worth them all!

The wreath you wove, the wreath you wove
  Our emblem well may be;
Its bloom is yours, but hopeless love
  Must keep its tears for me!

LYING.

Che con le lor bugie pajon divini.
    —*Mauro d'Arcano.*

I do confess, in many a sigh
My lips have breathed you many a lie,
And who, with such delights in view,
Would lose them for a lie or two?

Nay—look not thus, with brow reproving,
Lies are, my dear, the soul of loving!
If half we tell the girls were true,
If half we swear to think and do,
Were aught but lying's bright illusion,
The world would be in strange confusion!
If ladies' eyes were, every one,
As lovers swear, a radiant sun,
Astronomy should leave the skies,
To learn her lore in ladies' eyes!
Oh no!—believe me, lovely girl,
When Nature turns your teeth to pearl,
Your neck to snow, your eyes to fire,
Your yellow locks to golden wire,
Then, only then, can Heaven decree
That you should live for only me,
Or I for you, as, night and morn,
We've swearing kissed, and kissing sworn!

And now, my gentle hints to clear,
For once, I'll tell you truth, my dear!
Whenever you may chance to meet
A loving youth, whose love is sweet,
Long as you're false and he believes you,
Long as you trust and he deceives you,
So long the blissful bond endures;
And while he lies, his heart is yours:
But, oh! you've wholly lost the youth
The instant that he tells you truth!

ANACREONTIC.

I filled to thee, to thee I drank,
  I nothing did but drink and fill;
The bowl by turns was bright and blank,
  'Twas drinking, filling, drinking still!

At length I bid an artist paint
  Thy image in this ample cup,
That I might see the dimpled saint
  To whom I quaffed my nectar up.

Behold, how bright that purple lip
  Is blushing through the wave at me!
Every roseate drop I sip
  Is just like kissing wine from thee!

But, oh! I drink the more for this;
  For, ever when the draught I drain,
Thy lip invites another kiss,
  And in the nectar flows again!

So, here's to thee, my gentle dear!
  And may that eye for ever shine
Beneath as soft and sweet a tear
  As bathes it in this bowl of mine!

TO ———'S PICTURE.

Go, then, if she whose shade thou art
  No more will let thee soothe my pain—
Yet tell her, it has cost this heart
  Some pangs, to give thee back again!

Tell her, the smile was not so dear
  With which she made thy semblance mine,
As bitter is the burning tear,
  With which I now the gift resign!

Yet go—and could she still restore,
  As some exchange for taking thee,
The tranquil look which first I wore,
  When her eyes found me wild and free.

Could she give back the careless flow,
  The spirit which my fancy knew—
Yet, ah! 'tis vain—go, picture, go—
  Smile at me once, and then—adieu!

FRAGMENT OF A MYTHOLOGICAL HYMN TO LOVE.[1]

Blest infant of eternity!
Before the day-star learned to move,
In pomp of fire, along his grand career,
Glancing the beamy shafts of light
From his rich quiver to the farthest sphere,
Thou wert alone, oh Love!
Nestling beneath the wings of ancient night,
Whose horrors seemed to smile in shadowing thee!

No form of beauty soothed thine eye,
As through the dim expanse it wandered wide;
No kindred spirit caught thy sigh,
As o'er the watery waste it lingering died!

Unfelt the pulse, unknown the power,
That latent in his heart was sleeping;
Oh Sympathy! that lonely hour
Saw Love himself thy absence weeping!

But look what glory through the darkness beams!
Celestial airs along the water glide:
What spirit art thou, moving o'er the tide
So lovely? art thou but the child
Of the young godhead's dreams,
That mock his hope with fancies strange and wild?
Or were his tears, as quick they fell,
Collected in so bright a form,
Till, kindled by the ardent spell
Of his desiring eyes,
And all impregnate with his sighs,
They spring to life in shape so fair and warm?

'Tis she!
Psyche, the first-born spirit of the air,
To thee, oh Love! she turns,
On thee her eye-beam burns:
Blest hour of nuptial ecstasy!
They meet—
The blooming god—the spirit fair—
Oh! sweet, oh heavenly sweet!
Now, Sympathy, the hour is thine;
All nature feels the thrill divine,
The veil of Chaos is withdrawn,
And their first kiss is great Creation's dawn!

. . . .
. . . .

TO HIS SERENE HIGHNESS THE DUKE OF MONTPENSIER,

ON HIS PORTRAIT OF THE LADY ADELAIDE F—RR—S.

Donington Park, 1802.

To catch the thought, by painting's spell,
Howe'er remote, howe'er refined
And o'er the magic tablet tell
The silent story of the mind;

O'er Nature's form to glance the eye,
And fix, by mimic light and shade,
Her morning tinges ere they fly,
Her evening blushes ere they fade!

These are the pencil's grandest theme,
Divinest of the powers divine
That light the Muse's flowery dream,
And these, oh Prince! are richly thine!

Yet, yet, when Friendship sees thee trace,
In emanating soul expressed,
The sweet memorial of a face
On which her eye delights to rest;

While o'er the lovely look serene,
The smile of peace, the bloom of youth,
The cheek that blushes to be seen,
The eye that tells the bosom's truth;

While o'er each line, so brightly true,
Her soul with fond attention roves,
Blessing the hand whose various hue
Could imitate the form it loves;

She feels the value of thy art,
And owns it with a purer zeal,
A rapture, nearer to her heart
Than critic taste can ever feel!

THE PHILOSOPHER ARISTIPPUS.[2]

TO A LAMP WHICH WAS GIVEN HIM BY LAIS.

Dulcis conscia lectuli lucerna.
—*Martial*, lib. xiv. epig 39.

'Oh! love the Lamp (my mistress said),
The faithful lamp that, many a night,

---

[1] Love and Psyche are here considered as the active and passive principles of creation, and the universe is supposed to have received its first harmonizing impulse from the nuptial sympathy between these two powers. A marriage is generally the first step in cosmogony. Timæus held Form to be the father, and Matter the mother of the World; Elion and Beroüth, I think, are Sanchoniatho's first spiritual lovers, and Manco-capac and his wife introduced creation amongst the Peruvians. In short, Harlequin seems to have studied cosmogonies, when he said, 'tutto il mondo è fatto come la nostra famiglia.'

[2] It was not very difficult to become a philosopher amongst the ancients. A moderate store of learning, with a considerable portion of confidence, and wit enough to produce an occasional apophthegm, were all the necessary qualifications for the purpose. The principles of moral science were so very imperfectly understood, that the founder of a new sect, in forming his ethical code, might consult either fancy or temperament, and adapt it to his own passions and propensities; so that Mahomet, with a little more learning, might have flourished as a philosopher in those days, and would have required but the polish of the schools to become the rival of Aristippus in morality. In the science of nature, too, though they discovered some valuable

Beside thy Lais' lonely bed
Has kept its little watch of light!

'Full often has it seen her weep,
And fix her eye upon its flame,
Till, weary, she has sunk to sleep,
Repeating her beloved's name!

'Oft has it known her cheek to burn
With recollections, fondly free,
And seen her turn, impassioned turn,
To kiss the pillow, love! for thee,
And, in a murmur, wish thee there,
That kiss to feel, that thought to share!

'Then love the Lamp—'twill often lead
Thy step through Learning's sacred way;
And, lighted by its happy ray,
Whene'er those darling eyes shall read
Of things sublime, of Nature's birth,
Of all that's bright in heaven or earth,
Oh! think that she, by whom 'twas given,
Adores thee more than earth or heaven!'

Yes, dearest Lamp! by every charm
On which thy midnight beam has hung;[1]
The neck reclined, the graceful arm
Across the brow of ivory flung;

The heaving bosom, partly hid,
The severed lips' delicious sighs,
The fringe, that from the snowy lid
Along the cheek of roses lies:

By these, by all that bloom untold,
And long as all shall charm my heart,
I'll love my little Lamp of gold,
My Lamp and I shall never part!

And often, as she smiling said,
In fancy's hour, thy gentle rays
Shall guide my visionary tread
Through poesy's enchanting maze!

Thy flame shall light the page refined,
Where still we catch the Chian's breath,
Where still the bard, though cold in death,
Has left his burning soul behind!
Or, o'er thy humbler legend shine,
Oh man of Ascra's dreary glades![2]

To whom the nightly-warbling Nine
A wand of inspiration gave,
Plucked from the greenest tree that shades
The crystal of Castalia's wave.
Then, turning to a purer lore,
We'll cull the sages' heavenly store,
From Science steal her golden clue,
And every mystic path pursue,
Where Nature, far from vulgar eyes,
Through labyrinths of wonder flies!

'Tis thus my heart shall learn to know
The passing world's precarious flight,
Where all that meets the morning glow
Is changed before the fall of night!

I'll tell thee, as I trim the fire,
'Swift, swift the tide of being runs;
And Time, who bids thy flame expire,
Will also quench yon heaven of suns!'

Oh then, if earth's united power
Can never chain one feathery hour;
If every print we leave to-day
To-morrow's wave shall steal away;
Who pauses to inquire of Heaven
Why were the fleeting treasures given,
The sunny days, the shady nights,
And all their brief but dear delights,
Which Heaven has made for man to use,
And man should think it guilt to lose?
Who that has culled a weeping rose
Will ask it why it breathes and glows,
Unmindful of the blushing ray,
In which it shines its soul away;
Unmindful of the scented sigh
On which it dies and loves to die?

Pleasure! thou only good on earth![3]
One little hour resigned to thee—
Oh! by my Lais' lip, 'tis worth
The sage's immortality!

Then far be all the wisdom hence,
And all the lore, whose tame control
Would wither joy with chill delays!
Alas! the fertile fount of sense,
At which the young, the panting soul
Drinks life and love, too soon decays!

Sweet Lamp! thou wert not formed to shed
Thy splendour on a lifeless page—

---

truths, yet they seemed not to know they were truths, or at least were as well satisfied with errors; and Xenophanes, who asserted that the stars were igneous clouds, lighted up every night and extinguished again in the morning, was thought and styled a philosopher, as generally as he who anticipated Newton in developing the arrangement of the universe.

[1] The ancients held their lucernæ cubiculariæ, or bedchamber lamps, which, as the Emperor Gallenus said, nil cras meminere;' and with the same commendation of secrecy, Praxagora addresses her lamp, in Aristophanes, Εκκλησ. We may judge how fanciful they were in the use and embellishment of their lamps, from the famous symbolic Lucerna which we find in the *Romanum Museum Mich. Ang. Caussei*, p. 127.

[2] Hesiod, who tells us in melancholy terms of his father's flight to the wretched village of Ascra. Εργ. και Ἡμερ. v. 251.

[3] Aristippus considered motion as the principle of happiness, in which idea he differed from the Epicureans, who looked to a state of repose as the only true voluptuousness, and avoided even the too lively agitations of pleasure, as a violent and ungraceful derangement of the senses.

Whate'er my blushing Lais said
  Of thoughtful lore and studies sage,
'Twas mockery all—her glance of joy
  Told me thy dearest, best employ!

And, soon as night shall close the eye
  Of Heaven's young wanderer in the west;
When seers are gazing on the sky,
  To find their future orbs of rest;
Then shall I take my trembling way,
  Unseen, but to those worlds above,
And, led by thy mysterious ray,
  Glide to the pillow of my love.
Calm be her sleep, the gentle dear!
  Nor let her dream of bliss so near,
Till o'er her cheek she thrilling feel
  My sighs of fire in murmur steal,
And I shall lift the locks that flow
  Unbraided o'er her lids of snow,
And softly kiss those sealèd eyes,
  And wake her into sweet surprise!

Or if she dream, oh! let her dream
  Of those delights we both have known,
And felt so truly, that they seem
  Formed to be felt by us alone!
And I shall mark her kindling cheek,
  Shall see her bosom warmly move,
And hear her faintly, lowly speak
  The murmured sounds so dear to love!

Oh! I shall gaze till even the sigh
  That wafts her very soul be nigh,
And, when the nymph is all but blest,
  Sink in her arms and share the rest!
Sweet Lais! what an age of bliss
  In that one moment waits for me!
Oh sages!—think on joy like this,
  And where's your boast of apathy?

TO MRS. BL——H——D.

WRITTEN IN HER ALBUM.

Ταυτα δε τι εστι τα ποταπι πλασμ, ιφη.
—*Cebetis Tabula.*

They say that Love had once a book
  (The urchin likes to copy you),
Where all who came the pencil took,
  And wrote, like us, a line or two.

'Twas Innocence, the maid divine,
  Who kept this volume bright and fair,
And saw that no unhallowed line,
  Or thought profane, should enter there.

And sweetly did the pages fill
  With fond device and loving lore,
And every leaf she turned was still
  More bright than that she turned before!

Beneath the touch of Hope, how soft,
  How light the magic pencil ran!
Till Fear would come, alas! as oft,
  And trembling close what Hope began.

A tear or two had dropped from Grief,
  And Jealousy would, now and then,
Ruffle in haste some snowy leaf,
  Which Love had still to smooth again!

But, oh! there was a blooming boy,
  Who often turned the pages o'er,
And wrote therein such words of joy,
  As all who read still sighed for more!

And Pleasure was this spirit's name,
  And though so soft his voice and look,
Yet Innocence, whene'er he came,
  Would tremble for her spotless book!

For still she saw his playful fingers
  Filled with sweets and wanton toys;
And well she knew the stain that lingers
  After sweets from wanton boys!

And so it chanced, one luckless night
  He let his honey goblet fall
O'er the dear book so pure, so white,
  And sullied lines, and marge and all!

In vain he sought, with eager lip,
  The honey from the leaf to drink;
For still the more the boy would sip,
  The deeper still the blot would sink!

Oh! it would make you weep, to see
  The traces of this honey flood
Steal o'er a page, where Modesty
  Had freshly drawn a rose's bud!

And Fancy's emblems lost their glow,
  And Hope's sweet lines were all defaced,
And Love himself could scarcely know
  What Love himself had lately traced!

At length the urchin Pleasure fled,
  (For how, alas! could Pleasure stay?)
And Love, while many a tear he shed,
  In blushes flung the book away!

The index now alone remains,
  Of all the pages spoiled by Pleasure;
And though it bears some honey stains,
  Yet Memory counts the leaf a treasure!

And oft, they say, she scans it o'er,
  And oft, by this memorial aided
Brings back the pages now no more,
  And thinks of lines that long have faded!

I know not if this tale be true,
  But thus the simple facts are stated;
And I refer their truth to you,
  Since Love and you are near related!

EPISTLE VII.

TO THOMAS HUME, ESQ., M.D.

FROM THE CITY OF WASHINGTON.

ΔΙΗΓΗΣΟΜΑΙ ΔΙΗΓΗΜΑΤΑ ΙΣΩΣ ΑΠΙΣΤΑ,
ΚΟΙΝΩΝΑ ΩΝ ΠΕΠΟΝΘΑ ΟΥΚ ΕΧΩΝ.

Xenophont. Ephes. Ephesiac. lib. v.

'Tis evening now; the heats and cares of day
In twilight dews are calmly wept away.
The lover now, beneath the western star,
Sighs through the medium of his sweet segar,
And fills the ears of some consenting she
With puffs and vows, with smoke and constancy!
The weary statesman for repose hath fled
From halls of council to his negro's shed,
Where blest he woos some black Aspasia's grace,
And dreams of freedom in his slave's embrace![1]

In fancy now beneath the twilight gloom,
Come, let me lead thee o'er this modern Rome![2]
Where tribunes rule, where dusky Davi bow,
And what was Goose Creek once is Tiber now![3]—
This famed metropolis, where Fancy sees
Squares in morasses, obelisks in trees;
Which travelling fools and gazetteers adorn
With shrines unbuilt and heroes yet unborn,
Though nought but wood[4] and —— they see,
Where streets should run, and sages *ought* to be!

And look, how soft in yonder radiant wave,
The dying sun prepares his golden grave!—
Oh great Potowmac! oh you banks of shade!
You mighty scenes, in Nature's morning made,
While still, in rich magnificence of prime,
She poured her wonders, lavishly sublime,
Nor yet had learned to stoop, with humbler care,
From grand to soft, from wonderful to fair!
Say, were your towering hills, your boundless floods,
Your rich savannas and majestic woods,
Where bards should meditate and heroes rove,
And woman charm and man deserve her love!

Oh! was a world so bright but born to grace
Its own half-organized, half-minded race[5]
Of weak barbarians, swarming o'er its breast,
Like vermin gendered on the lion's crest?
Were none but brutes to call that soil their home,
Where none but demi-gods should dare to roam?
Or, worse, thou mighty world! oh! doubly worse,
Did Heaven design thy lordly land to nurse
The motley dregs of every distant clime,
Each blast of anarchy and taint of crime
Which Europe shakes from her perturbèd sphere,
In full malignity to rankle here?
But hush!—observe that little mount of pines,
Where the breeze murmurs and the fire-fly shines,
There let thy fancy raise, in bold relief,
The sculptured image of that veteran chief,[6]
Who lost the rebel's in the hero's name,
And stepped o'er prostrate loyalty to fame;
Beneath whose sword Columbia's patriot train
Cast off their monarch, that their mob might reign!

How shall we rank thee upon Glory's page?
Thou more than soldier and just less than sage!
Too formed for peace to act a conqueror's part,
Too trained in camps to learn a statesman's art,
Nature designed thee for a hero's mould,
But, ere she cast thee, let the stuff grow cold!

While warmer souls command, nay, make their fate,
Thy fate made thee and forced thee to be great.
Yet Fortune, who so oft, so blindly sheds
Her brightest halo round the weakest heads,
Found *thee* undazzled, tranquil as before;
Proud to be useful, scorning to be more;
Less prompt at glory's than at duty's claim,—
Renown the meed, but self-applause the aim;
All thou hast been reflects less fame on thee,
Far less, than all thou hast forborne to be!

Now turn thine eye where faint the moonlight falls
On yonder dome—and in those princely halls,

---

[1] The 'black Aspasia' of the present —— of the United States, 'inter Avernales haud ignotissima nymphas,' has given rise to much pleasantry among the anti-democrat wits in America.

[2] 'On the original location of the ground now allotted for the seat of the Federal City (says Mr. Weld), the identical spot on which the Capitol now stands was called Rome. This anecdote is related by many as a certain prognostic of the future magnificence of this city, which is to be, as it were, a second Rome.'—*Weld's Travels,* Letter iv.

[3] A little stream runs through the city, which, with intolerable affectation, they have styled the Tiber. It was originally called Goose Creek.

[4] 'To be under the necessity of going through a deep wood for one or two miles, perhaps, in order to see a next-door neighbour and in the same city, is a curious, and I believe a novel, circumstance.'—*Weld,* Letter iv.

[5] The picture which Buffon and De Pauw have drawn of the American Indian, though very humiliating, is, as far as I can judge, much more correct than the flattering representations which Mr. Jefferson has given us. See the *Notes on Virginia,* where this gentleman endeavours to disprove in general the opinion maintained so strongly by some philosophers, that nature (as Mr. Jefferson expresses it) *belittles* her imperfections of animal life in America to the ravages of a very recent deluge, from whose effects upon its soil and atmosphere it has not yet sufficiently recovered.—See his *Recherches sur les Américains,* part 1 tom i. p. 102.

[6] On a small hill near the Capitol, there is to be an equestrian statue of General Washington.

If thou canst hate, as, oh! that soul must hate,
Which loves the virtuous and reveres the great,
If thou canst loathe and execrate with me
That Gallic garbage of philosophy,
That nauseous slaver of these frantic times,
With which false liberty dilutes her crimes!
If thou hast got, within thy free-born breast,
One pulse that beats more proudly than the rest,
With honest scorn for that inglorious soul
Which creeps and winds beneath a mob's control,
Which courts the rabble's smile, the rabble's nod,
And makes, like Egypt, every beast its god!
There, in those walls—but, burning tongue, forbear!
Rank must be reverenced, even the rank that's there:
So here I pause—and now, my Hume! we part;
But oh! full oft in magic dreams of heart,
Thus let us meet, and mingle converse dear
By Thames at home, or by Potowmac here!
O'er lake and marsh, through fevers and through fogs,
Midst bears and yankees, democrats and frogs,
Thy foot shall follow me, thy heart and eyes
With me shall wonder, and with me despise![1]
While I, as oft, in witching thought shall rove
To thee, to friendship, and that land I love,
Where, like the air that fans her fields of green,
Her freedom spreads, unfevered and serene;
Where sovereign man can condescend to see
The throne and laws more sovereign still than he!

THE SNAKE.
1801.

My love and I, the other day,
Within a myrtle arbour lay,
When near us, from a rosy bed,
A little snake put forth its head.

'See,' said the maid, with laughing eyes—
'Yonder the fatal emblem lies!
Who could expect such hidden harm
Beneath the rose's velvet charm?'

Never did moral thought occur
In more unlucky hour than this;
For oh! I just was leading her
To talk of love and think of bliss.

I rose to kill the snake, but she
In pity prayed it might not be.

'No,' said the girl—and many a spark
Flashed from her eyelid, as she said it—
'Under the rose, or in the dark,
One might perhaps have cause to dread it;
But when its wicked eyes appear,
And when we know for what they wink so,
One must be very simple, dear,
To let it sting one—don't you think so?'

LINES
WRITTEN ON LEAVING PHILADELPHIA.

τῇδε τῆς πόλιν φίλαις
Ειπων ιταξια γαρ.—*Sophocl. Œdip. Colon.* v. 758.

Alone by the Schuylkill a wanderer roved,
And bright were its flowery banks to his eye;
But far, very far were the friends that he loved,
And he gazed on its flowery banks with a sigh!

Oh Nature! though blessed and bright are thy rays,
O'er the brow of creation enchantingly thrown,
Yet faint are they all to the lustre that plays
In a smile from the heart that is dearly our own!

Nor long did the soul of the stranger remain
Unblest by the smile he had languished to meet;
Though scarce did he hope it would soothe him again,
Till the threshold of home had been kissed by his feet!

But the lays of his boyhood had stolen to their ear,
And they loved what they knew of so humble a name;
And they told him, with flattery welcome and dear,
That they found in his heart something sweeter than fame!

Nor did woman—oh woman! whose form and whose soul
Are the spell and the light of each path we pursue;

---

[1] In the ferment which the French Revolution excited among the democrats of America, and the licentious sympathy with which they shared in the wildest excesses of Jacobinism, we may find one source of that vulgarity of vice, that hostility to all the graces of life, which distinguishes the present demagogues of the United States, and has become, indeed, too generally the characteristic of their countrymen. But there is another cause of the corruption of private morals, which, encouraged as it is by the Government, and identified with the interests of the community, seems to threaten the decay of all honest principle in America. I allude to those fraudulent violations of neutrality to which they are indebted for the most lucrative part of their commerce, and by which they have so long infringed and counteracted the maritime rights and advantages of this country. This unwarrantable trade is necessarily abetted by such a system of collusion, imposture, and perjury, as cannot fail to spread rapid contamination around it.

Whether sunned in the tropics or chilled at the
　　pole,
If woman be there, there is happiness too!—
Nor did she her enamouring magic deny,
　　That magic his heart had relinquished so long,
Like eyes he had loved was *her* eloquent eye,
　　Like them did it soften and weep at his song.

Oh! blest be the tear, and in memory oft
　　May its sparkle be shed o'er his wandering
　　　　dream!
Oh! blest be that eye, and may passion as soft,
　　As free from a pang, over mellow its beam!

The stranger is gone—but he will not forget,
　　When at home he shall talk of the toil he has
　　　　known,
To tell with a sigh what endearments he met,
　　As he strayed by the wave of the Schuylkill
　　　　alone!

THE FALL OF HEBE.

A DITHYRAMBIC ODE.[1]

'TWAS on a day
When the immortals at their banquet lay ;
　　The bowl
Sparkled with starry dew,
The weeping of those myriad urns of light,
Within whose orbs, the almighty Power,
　　At Nature's dawning hour,
Stored the rich fluid of ethereal soul![2]
　　Around,
Soft odorous clouds, that upward wing their flight
　　From eastern isles
(Where they have bathed them in the orient ray,
And with fine fragrance all their bosoms filled),
In circles flew, and, melting as they flew,
A liquid daybreak o'er the board distilled !
　　All, all was luxury !

All *must* be luxury, where Lyæus smiles !
　　His locks divine
　　Were crowned
　　With a bright meteor-braid,
Which, like an ever-springing wreath of vine,
　　Shot into brilliant leafy shapes,
And o'er his brow in lambent tendrils played !

While 'mid the foliage hung,
　　Like lucid grapes,
A thousand clustering blooms of light,
Culled from the gardens of the galaxy!
Upon his bosom Cytherea's head
Lay lovely, as when first the Syrens sung
　　Her beauty's dawn,
And all the curtains of the deep, undrawn,
Revealed her sleeping in its azure bed.
　　The captive deity
　　Languished upon her eyes and lip,
　　　　In chains of ecstasy!
　　　　Now in his arm,
　　In blushes she reposed,
And, while her zone resigned its every charm,
To shade his burning eyes her hand in dalliance
　　　　stole,
And now she raised her rosy mouth to sip
　　　　The nectared wave
Lyæus gave,
And from her eyelids, gently closed,
　　Shed a dissolving gleam,
Which fell, like sun-dew, in the bowl!
While her bright hair, in mazy flow
　　Of gold descending
Along her cheek's luxurious glow,
　　Waved o'er the goblet's side,
And was reflected by its crystal tide
　　Like a sweet crocus flower,
Whose sunny leaves, at evening hour,
　　With roses of Cyrene blending,[3]
Hang o'er the mirror of a silver stream!

　　The Olympian cup
　　Burned in the hands
Of dimpled Hebe, as she winged her feet
　　　　Up
　　The empyreal mount,
To drain the soul-drops at their stellar fount;[4]
　　　　And still,
　　As the resplendent rill
Flamed o'er the goblet with a mantling heat,
　　Her graceful care
　　Would cool its heavenly fire
In gelid waves of snowy-feathered air,
Such as the children of the pole respire,
　　In those enchanted lands[5]
Where life is all a spring and north winds never
　　blow!

---

[1] Though I call this a Dithyrambic Ode, I cannot presume to say that it possesses in any degree the characteristics of that species of poetry. The nature of the ancient Dithyrambic is very imperfectly known. According to M. Burette, a licentious irregularity of metre, an extravagant research of thought and expression, and a rude embarrassed construction, are among its most distinguishing features.

[2] This is a Platonic fancy: the philosopher supposes, in his *Timæus*, that when the Deity had formed the soul of the world, he proceeded to the composition of other souls; in which process, says Plato, he made use of the same cup, though the ingredients he mingled were not quite so pure as for the former; and having refined the mixture with a little of his own essence, he distributed it among the stars, which served as reservoirs of the fluid. Ταυτ' ειπε και παλιν επι τον προτερον κρατηρα εν ᾡ την του παντος ψυχην κεραννυς εμισγε, κ.τ.λ.

[3] We learn from Theophrastus that the roses of Cyrene were particularly fragrant. Ευοσμοτατα τα δε τα εν Κυρηνη ῥοδα.

[4] Heraclitus (Physicus) held the soul to be a spark of the stellar essence. 'Scintilla stellaris essentiæ.'—*Macrobius, in Somn. Scip.* lib. I. cap. 14.

[5] The country of the Hyperboreans: they were supposed to be placed so far north, that the north wind could not affect them; they lived longer than any other mortals, passed their whole time in music and dancing, etc. etc. But the most extravagant fiction related of them is that to which the two lines preceding allude.

But oh!
Sweet Hebe, what a tear
And what a blush were thine,
When, as the breath of every Grace
Wafted thy fleet career
Along the studded sphere,
With a rich cup for Jove himself to drink,
Some star, that glittered in the way,
Raising its amorous head
To kiss so exquisite a tread,
Checked thy impatient pace!
And all Heaven's host of eyes
Saw those luxuriant beauties sink
In lapse of loveliness, along the azure skies![1]
Upon whose starry plain they lay,
Like a young blossom on our meads of gold,
Shed from a vernal thorn
Amid the liquid sparkles of the morn!
Or, as in temples of the Paphian shade,
The myrtled votaries of the queen behold
An image of their rosy idol, laid
Upon a diamond shrine!
The wanton wind,
Which had pursued the flying fair,
And sweetly twined
Its spirit with the breathing rings
Of her ambrosial hair,
Soared as she fell, and on its ruffling wings
(Oh wanton wind!)
Wafted the robe whose sacred flow
Shadowed her kindling charms of snow,
Pure, as an Eleusinian veil
Hangs o'er the mysteries![2]

. . . .

* the brow of Juno flushed—
Love blessed the breeze!
The Muses blushed,
And every cheek was hid behind a lyre,
While every eye was glancing through the strings.
Drops of ethereal dew,
That burning gushed,
As the great goblet flew
From Hebe's pearly fingers through the sky!
Who was the spirit that remembered Man
In that voluptuous hour?

And with a wing of Love
Brushed off your scattered tears,
As o'er the spangled heaven they ran,
And sent them floating to our orb below?
Essence of immortality!
The shower
Fell glowing through the spheres,
While all around, new tints of bliss,
New perfumes of delight,
Enriched its radiant flow!
Now, with a humid kiss,
It thrilled along the beamy wire
Of heaven's illumined lyre,
Stealing the soul of music in its flight!
And now, amid the breezes bland
That whisper from the planets as they roll,
The bright libation, softly fanned
By all their sighs, meandering stole!
They who, from Atlas' height,
Beheld the rill of flame
Descending through the waste of night,
Thought 'twas a planet whose stupendous frame
Had kindled as it rapidly revolved
Around its fervid axle, and dissolved
Into a flood so bright!

The child of day,
Within his twilight bower,
Lay sweetly sleeping
On the flushed bosom of a lotos-flower;[3]
When round him, in profusion weeping,
Dropped the celestial shower,
Steeping
The rosy clouds that curled
About his infant head,
Like myrrh upon the locks of Cupid shed!
But, when the waking boy
Waved his exhaling tresses through the sky,
O morn of joy!
The tide divine,
All glittering with the vermeil dye
It drank beneath his orient eye,
Distilled in dews upon the world,
And every drop was wine, was heavenly wine!

Blest be the sod, the floweret blest,
That caught upon their hallowed breast

---

[1] It was imagined that, instead of our vulgar atmosphere, the Hyperboreans breathed nothing but feathers! According to Herodotus and Pliny, this idea was suggested by the quantity of snow which was observed to fall in those regions.
Mr. O'Halloran, and some other Irish antiquarians, have been at great expense of learning to prove that the strange country, where they took snow for feathers, was Ireland, and that the famous Abaris was an Irish Druid. Mr Rowland, however, will have it that Abaris was a Welshman, and that his name is only a corruption of Ap Rees!
I believe it is Servius who mentions this unlucky trip which Hebe made in her occupation of cup-bearer; and Hoffman tells it after him: 'Cum Hebo pocula Jovi administrans, perque lubricum minus caute incedens, cecidisset, revolutisque vestibus'—in short, she fell in a very awkward manner; and though (as the Encyclo- pédistes think) it would have amused Jove at any other time, yet, as he happened to be out of temper on that day, the poor girl was dismissed from her employment.
[2] The arcane symbols of this ceremony were deposited in the cista, where they lay religiously concealed from the eyes of the profane. They were generally carried in the procession by an ass; and hence the proverb, which one may so often apply in the world, 'asinus portat mysteria.'—See the *Divine Legation*, book ii. sec. 4.
[3] The Egyptians represented the dawn of day by a young boy seated upon a lotos. Observing that the lotos showed its head above water at sunrise, and sank again at his setting, they conceived the idea of consecrating it to Osiris, or the sun.
This symbol of a youth sitting upon a lotos is very frequent on the Abraxases, or Basilidian stones.—See MONTFAUCON, tom. ii. planche 158; and the *Supplément*, etc. tom. ii. lib. vii. chap. 5.

The nectared spray of Jove's perennial springs!
Less sweet the floweret, and less sweet the sod,
O'er which the Spirit of the rainbow flings
The magic mantle of her solar god![1]

TO ——.

That wrinkle, when first I espied it,
 At once put my heart out of pain,
Till the eye that was glowing beside it
 Disturbed my ideas again!

Thou art just in the twilight at present,
 When woman's declension begins,
When, fading from all that is pleasant,
 She bids a good night to her sins!

Yet thou still art so lovely to me,
 I would sooner, my exquisite mother!
Repose in the sunset of thee
 Than bask in the noon of another!

ANACREONTIC.

'She never looked so kind before—
 Yet why the wanton's smile recall?
I've seen this witchery o'er and o'er,
 'Tis hollow, vain, and heartless all!'

Thus I said, and sighing sipped
 The wine which she had lately tasted;
The cup where she had lately dipped
 Breath, so long in falsehood wasted.

I took the harp, and would have sung
 As if 'twere not of her I sang;
But still the notes on Lamia hung—
 On whom but Lamia *could* they hang?

That kiss for which, if worlds were mine,
 A world for every kiss I'd give her;
Those floating eyes, that floating shine
 Like diamonds in an eastern river!

That mould, so fine, so pearly bright,
 Of which luxurious Heaven hath cast her,
Through which her soul doth beam as white
 As flame through lamps of alabaster!

Of these I sung, and notes and words
 Were sweet as if 'twas Lamia's hair

That lay upon my lute for chords,
 And Lamia's lip that warbled there!

But when, alas! I turned the theme,
 And when of vows and oaths I spoke,
Of truth and hope's beguiling dream—
 The chord beneath my finger broke!

False harp! false woman!—such, oh! such
 Are lutes too frail and maids too willing;
Every hand's licentious touch
 Can learn to wake their wildest thrilling!

And when that thrill is most awake,
 And when you think Heaven's joys await you,
The nymph will change, the chord will break—
 Oh Love, oh Music! how I hate you!

TO MRS. ——,
ON SOME CALUMNIES AGAINST HER CHARACTER.

Is not thy mind a gentle mind?
Is not thy heart a heart refined?
Hast thou not every blameless grace,
That man should love or Heaven can trace?
And oh! art *thou* a shrine for Sin
To hold her hateful worship in?

No, no, be happy—dry that tear—
Though some thy heart hath harboured near
May now repay its love with blame;
Though man, who ought to shield thy fame,
Ungenerous man, be first to wound thee;
Though the whole world may freeze around thee,
Oh! thou'lt be like that lucid tear[2]
Which, bright, within the crystal's sphere
In liquid purity was found,
Though all had grown congealed around;
Floating in frost, it mocked the chill,
Was pure, was soft, was brilliant still!

HYMN OF A VIRGIN OF DELPHI,
AT THE TOMB OF HER MOTHER.

Oh! lost, for ever lost!—no more
 Shall Vesper light our dewy way
Along the rocks of Crissa's shore,
 To hymn the fading fires of day!
No more to Tempé's distant vale
 In holy musings shall we roam,
Through summer's glow and winter's gale,
 To bear the mystic chaplets home![3]

---

[1] The ancients esteemed those flowers and trees the sweetest upon which the rainbow had appeared to rest; and the wood they chiefly burned in sacrifices was that which the smile of Iris had consecrated.

[2] This alludes to a curious gem, upon which Claudian has left us some pointless epigrams. It was a drop of pure water enclosed within a piece of crystal.—See *Claudian, Epigram. de Chrystall, cui aqua inerat.* Addison mentions a curiosity of this kind at Milan;

he also says: 'It is such a rarity as this that I saw at Vendôme in France, which they there pretend is a tear that our Saviour shed over Lazarus, and was gathered up by an angel, who put it in a little crystal vial, and made a present of it to Mary Magdalen.'—*Addison's Remarks on several parts of Italy.*

[3] The laurel, for the common uses of the temple, for adorning the altars and sweeping the pavement, was supplied by a tree near the fountain of Castalia; but

'T was then my soul's expanding zeal,
  By Nature warmed and led by thee,
In every breeze was taught to feel
  The breathings of a deity!
Guide of my heart! to memory true,
  Thy looks, thy words, are still my own—
I see thee raising from the dew
Some laurel, by the wind o'erthrown,
And hear thee say, 'This humble bough
  Was planted for a doom divine,
And, though it weep in languor now,
  Shall flourish on the Delphic shrine!
Thus in the vale of earthly sense,
  Though sunk a while the spirit lies,
A viewless hand shall cull it thence,
  To bloom immortal in the skies!'

Thy words had such a melting flow,
  And spoke of truth so sweetly well,
They dropped like heaven's serenest snow,
  And all was brightness where they fell!
Fond soother of my infant tear!
  Fond sharer of my infant joy!
Is not thy shade still lingering here?
  Am I not still thy soul's employ?
And oh! as oft at close of day,
  When meeting on the sacred mount,
Our nymphs awaked the choral lay,
  And danced around Cassotis' fount;
As then, 'twas all thy wish and care
  That mine should be the simplest mien,
My lyre and voice the sweetest there,
  My foot the lightest o'er the green;
So still, each little grace to mould,
  Around my form thine eyes are shed,
Arranging every snowy fold,
  And guiding every mazy tread!
And when I lead the hymning choir,
  Thy spirit still, unseen and free,
Hovers between my lip and lyre,
  And weds them into harmony!
Flow, Plistus, flow; thy murmuring wave
  Shall never drop its silvery tear
Upon so pure, so blest a grave,
  To memory so divinely dear!

RINGS AND SEALS.

'Ωσπερ σφραγιδες τα φιληματα.
—*Achilles Tatius*, lib. II.

' Go!' said the angry, weeping maid,
' The charm is broken!—once betrayed,

Oh! never can my heart rely
  On word or look, on oath or sigh.
Take back the gifts, so sweetly given,
  With promised faith and vows to Heaven;
That little ring which, night and morn,
  With wedded truth my hand hath worn;
That seal which oft, in moments blest,
  Thou hast upon my lip imprest,
And sworn its dewy spring should be
  A fountain sealed¹ for only thee!
Take, take them back, the gift and vow,
  All sullied, lost, and hateful now!'

I took the ring—the seal I took,
  While, oh! her every tear and look
Were such as angels look and shed,
  When man is by the world misled!
Gently I whispered, 'Fanny, dear!
  Not half thy lover's gifts are here:
Say, where are all the seals he gave
  To every ringlet's jetty wave,
And where is every one he printed
  Upon that lip so ruby-tinted—
Seals of the purest gem of bliss,
  Oh! richer, softer far than this!

' And then the ring—my love! recall
  How many rings, delicious all,
His arms around that neck have twisted,
  Twining warmer far than this did!
Where are they all, so sweet, so many?
  Oh! dearest, give back all, if any!'

While thus I murmured, trembling too
  Lest all the nymph had vowed was true,
I saw a smile relenting rise
  'Mid the moist azure of her eyes,
Like daylight o'er a sea of blue
  While yet the air is dim with dew!
She let her cheek repose on mine,
  She let my arms around her twine—
Oh! who can tell the bliss one feels
  In thus exchanging rings and seals!

TO MISS SUSAN B——CKF——D.

I MORE than once have heard, at night,
  A song like those thy lips have given;
And it was sung by shapes of light,
  Who seemed, like thee, to breathe of Heaven!

But this was all a dream of sleep,
  And I have said, when morning shone,

---

upon all important occasions they sent to Tempé for their laurel. We find in Pausanias that this valley supplied the branches of which the temple was originally constructed; and Plutarch says, in his *Dialogue on Music*, 'The youth who brings the Temple laurel to Delphi is always attended by a player on the flute.' Αλλα μην και τω κατακομιζοντι παιδι την Τεμπικην δαφνην ως Διλφους παρομαρτει αυλητης.

¹ 'There are gardens, supposed to be those of King Solomon, in the neighbourhood of Bethlehem. The friars show a foun'ain which, they say, is the "sealed fountain" to which the holy spouse in the Canticles is compared; and they pretend a tradition, that Solomon shut up these springs and put his signet upon the door, to keep them for his own drinking.'—*Maundrell's Travels*. See also the *Notes to Mr. Good's Translation of the Song of Solomon*.

'Oh! why should fairy Fancy keep
 These wonders for herself alone?'

I knew not then that Fate had lent
 Such tones to one of mortal birth;
I knew not then that Heaven had sent
 A voice, a form, like thine on earth!

And yet, in all that flowery maze
 Through which my life has loved to tread,
When I have heard the sweetest lays
 From lips of dearest lustre shed;

When I have felt the warbled word
 From Beauty's mouth of perfume sighing,
Sweet as music's hallowed bird
 Upon a rose's bosom lying!

Though form and song at once combined
 Their loveliest bloom and softest thrill,
My heart hath sighed, my heart hath pined
 For something softer, lovelier still!

Oh! I have found it all, at last,
 In thee, thou sweetest living lyre,
Through which the soul hath ever passed
 Its harmonizing breath of fire!

All that my best and wildest dream,
 In Fancy's hour, could hear or see
Of Music's sigh or Beauty's beam,
 Are realized at once in thee!

LINES,

WRITTEN AT THE COHOS, OR FALLS OF THE
 MOHAWK RIVER.[1]

*Gia era in loco ove s'udia 'l rimbombo
 Dell' acqua.*—Dante.

From rise of morn till set of sun,
 I've seen the mighty Mohawk run;
And as I marked the woods of pine
 Along his mirror darkly shine,
Like tall and gloomy forms that pass
 Before the wizard's midnight glass;
And as I viewed the hurrying pace
 With which he ran his turbid race,
Rushing, alike untired and wild,
 Through shades that frowned and flowers
  that smiled,
Flying by every green recess
 That wooed him to its calm caress,

Yet, sometimes turning with the wind,
 As if to leave one look behind!
Oh! I have thought, and thinking sighed—
 How like to thee, thou restless tide!
May be the lot, the life of him,
 Who roams along thy water's brim!
Through what alternate shades of woe
 And flowers of joy my path may go!
How many an humble, still retreat
 May rise to court my weary feet,
While still pursuing, still unblest,
 I wander on, nor dare to rest!
But, urgent as the doom that calls
 Thy water to its destined falls,
I see the world's bewildering force
 Hurry my heart's devoted course
From lapse to lapse, till life be done,
 And the lost current cease to run!
Oh! may my falls be bright as thine!
 May Heaven's forgiving rainbow shine
Upon the mist that circles me,
 As soft as now it hangs o'er thee!

CLORIS AND FANNY.

Cloris! if I were Persia's king,
 I'd make my graceful queen of thee;
While Fanny, wild and artless thing,
 Should but thy humble handmaid be.

There is but *one* objection in it—
 That, verily, I'm much afraid
I should, in some unlucky minute,
 Forsake the mistress for the maid!

SONG

OF THE EVIL SPIRIT OF THE WOODS.[2]

Qua via difficilis, quaque est via nulla.
 —Ovid. Metam. lib. iii. v. 227.

Now the vapour, hot and damp,
 Shed by day's expiring lamp,
Through the misty ether spreads
 Every ill the white man dreads:
Fiery fever's thirsty thrill,
 Fitful ague's shivering chill!

Hark! I hear the traveller's song,
 As he winds the woods along:

---

[1] There is a dreary and savage character in the country immediately above these falls, which is much more in harmony with the wildness of the scene than the cultivated lands in the neighbourhood of Niagara. See the drawing of them in Mr. Weld's book. According to him, the perpendicular height of the Cohos Fall is fifty feet; but the Marquis de Chastellux makes it seventy-six.

The fine rainbow, which is continually forming and dissolving as the spray rises into the light of the sun, is perhaps the most interesting beauty which these wonderful cataracts exhibit.

[2] The idea of this poem occurred to me in passing through the very dreary wilderness between Batavia, a new settlement in the midst of the woods, and the little village of Buffalo, upon Lake Erie. This is the most fatiguing part of the route in travelling through the Genesee country to Niagara.

Christian! 'tis the song of fear;
Wolves are round thee, night is near,
And the wild thou dar'st to roam—
Oh! 'twas once the Indian's home.[1]

Hither, sprites, who love to harm,
Wheresoe'er you work your charm,
By the creeks, or by the brakes,
Where the pale witch feeds her snakes,
And the cayman[2] loves to creep,
Torpid, to his wintry sleep;
Where the bird of carrion flits,
And the shuddering murderer sits[3]
Lone beneath a roof of blood,
While upon his poisoned food,
From the corpse of him he slew,
Drops the chill and gory dew!

Hither bend you, turn you hither
Eyes that blast and wings that wither!
Cross the wandering Christian's way,
Lead him, ere the glimpse of day,
Many a mile of maddening error
Through the maze of night and terror,
Till the morn behold him lying
O'er the damp earth, pale and dying!
Mock him, when his eager sight
Seeks the cordial cottage light;
Gleam then like the lightning-bug,
Tempt him to the den that's dug
For the foul and famished brood
Of the she-wolf, gaunt for blood!
Or, unto the dangerous pass
O'er the deep and dark morass,
Where the trembling Indian brings
Belts of porcelain, pipes, and rings,
Tributes, to be hung in air
To the Fiend presiding there![4]
Then, when night's long labour past,
'Vildered, faint he falls at last,
Sinking where the causeway's edge
Moulders in the slimy sedge,
There let every noxious thing
Trail its filth and fix its sting;

Let the bull-toad taint him over,
Round him let musquitoes hover,
In his ears and eyeballs tingling,
With his blood their poison mingling,
Till, beneath the solar fires,
Rankling all, the wretch expires!

TO MRS. HENRY T—GHE,

ON READING HER 'PSYCHE.'

1802.

TELL me the witching tale again,
  For never has my heart or ear
Hung on so sweet, so pure a strain,
  So pure to feel, so sweet to hear!

Say, Lovo! in all thy spring of fame,
  When the high Heaven itself was thine;
When piety confessed the flame,
  And even thy errors were divine!

Did ever Muse's hand so fair
  A glory round thy temple spread?
Did ever lip's ambrosial air
  Such perfume o'er thy altars shed?

One maid there was, who round her lyre
  The mystic myrtle wildly wreathed—
But all *her* sighs were sighs of fire,
  The myrtle withered as she breathed!

Oh! you that Love's celestial dream
  In all its purity would know,
Let not the senses' ardent beam
  Too strongly through the vision glow!

Love sweetest lies concealed in night,
  The night where Heaven has bid him lie,
Oh! shed not there unhallowed light,
  Or, Psyche knows, the boy will fly![5]

---

[1] 'The Five Confederated Nations (of Indians) were settled along the banks of the Susquehannah and the adjacent country, until the year 1779, when General Sullivan, with an army of 4000 men, drove them from their country to Niagara, where, being obliged to live on salted provisions, to which they were unaccustomed, great numbers of them died. Two hundred of them, it is said, were buried in one grave, where they had encamped.'—*Morse's American Geography.*

[2] The alligator, who is supposed to lie in a torpid state all the winter in the bank of some creek or pond, having previously swallowed a large number of pine knots, which are his only sustenance during the time.

[3] This was the mode of punishment for murder (as Father Charlevoix tells us) among the Hurons. 'They laid the dead body upon poles at the top of a cabin, and the murderer was obliged to remain several days together, and to receive all that dropped from the carcase, not only on himself but on his food.'

[4] 'We find also collars of porcelain, tobacco, ears of maize, skins, etc., by the side of difficult and dangerous ways, on rocks, or by the side of the falls; and these are so many offerings made to the spirits which preside in these places.'—See *Charlevoix's Letter* on *the Traditions and the Religion of the Savages of Canada.*

Father Hennepin, too, mentions this ceremony; he also says: 'We took notice of one barbarian, who made a kind of sacrifice upon an oak at the Cascade of St. Antony of Padua, upon the river Mississippi.'—See *Hennepin's Voyage into North America.*

[5] See the story in Apuleius. With respect to this beautiful allegory of Love and Psyche, there is an ingenious idea suggested by the senator Buonarotti, in his *Osservazioni sopra alcuni frammenti di vasi antichi.* He thinks the fable is taken from some very occult mysteries, which had long been celebrated in honour of Love; and he accounts, upon this supposition, for the silence of the more ancient authors upon the subject, as it was not till towards the decline of pagan superstition that writers could venture to reveal or discuss such ceremonies. Accordingly, he observes, we find Lucian and Plutarch treating, without reserve, of the

Dear Psyche! mauy a charmed hour,
  Through many a wild and magic waste,
To the fair fount and blissful bower
  Thy mazy foot my soul hath traced!

Where'er thy joys are numbered now,
  Beneath whatever shades of rest,
The Genius of the starry brow[1]
  Has chained thee to thy Cupid's breast;

Whether above the horizon dim,
  Along whose verge our spirits stray
(Half sunk within the shadowy brim,
  Half brightened by the eternal ray),[2]

Thou risest to a cloudless pole!
  Or, lingering here, dost love to mark
The twilight walk of many a soul
  Through sunny good and evil dark;

Still be the song to Psyche dear,
  The song, whose dulcet tide was given
To keep her name as fadeless here
  As nectar keeps her soul in Heaven!

IMPROMPTU,
UPON LEAVING SOME FRIENDS.

O dulces comitum valete cœtus!—Catullus.

No, never shall my soul forget
  The friends I found so cordial-hearted;
Dear shall be the day we met,
  And dear shall be the night we parted!

Oh! if regrets, however sweet,
  Must with the lapse of time decay,
Yet still, when thus in mirth you meet,
  Fill high to him that's far away!

Long be the flame of memory found
  Alive within your social glass;
Let that be still the magic round
  O'er which oblivion dares not pass!

EPISTLE VIII.
TO THE HONOURABLE W. R. SPENCER.

Nec venit ad duros musa vocata Getas.
—*Ovid. ex Ponto*, lib. 1. ep. 5.

FROM BUFFALO, UPON LAKE ERIE.

Thou oft hast told me of the fairy hours
Thy heart has numbered, in those classic bowers
Where fancy sees the ghost of ancient wit
'Mid cowls and cardinals profanely flit,
And pagan spirits, by the Pope unlaid,
Haunt every stream and sing through every shade!
There still the bard, who (if his numbers be
His tongue's light echo) must have talked like thee,
The courtly bard, from whom thy mind has caught
Those playful, sunshine holidays of thought,
In which the basking soul reclines and glows,
Warm without toil and brilliant in repose.
There still he roves, and laughing loves to see
How modern monks with ancient rakes agree;
How mitres hang where ivy wreaths might twine,
And heathen Massic's damned for stronger wine!
There too are all those wandering souls of song
With whom thy spirit hath communed so long,
Whose rarest gems are every instant hung
By memory's magic on thy sparkling tongue.
But here, alas! by Erie's stormy lake,
As far from thee my lonely course I take,
No bright remembrance o'er the fancy plays,
No classic dream, no star of other days
Has left that visionary glory here,
That relic of its light, so soft, so dear,
Which gilds and hallows even the rudest scene,
The humblest shed, where genius once has been!

All that creation's varying mass assumes
Of grand or lovely, here aspires and blooms;
Bold rise the mountains, rich the gardens glow,
Bright lakes expand, and conquering[3] rivers flow;
Mind, mind alone, without whose quickening ray,
The world's a wilderness, and man but clay,
Mind, mind alone, in barren, still repose,
Nor blooms, nor rises, nor expands, nor flows!
Take Christians, Mohawks, Democrats, and all
From the rude wigwam to the congress-hall,
From man the savage, whether slaved or free,
To man the civilised, less tame than he!
'Tis one dull chaos, one uufertile strife
Betwixt half-polished and half-barbarous life;
Where every ill the ancient world can brew
Is mixed with every grossness of the new;
Where all corrupts, though little can entice,
And nothing's known of luxury but vice!

Syria, and Isis and Osiris; and Apuleius, who has given us the story of Cupid and Psyche, has also detailed some of the mysteries of Isis.—See the *Giornale di Litterati d'Italia*, tom. xxvii. articol. 1. See also the *Observations upon the Ancient Gems in the Museum Florentinum*, vol. i. p. 156.

[1] Constancy.

[2] By this image the Platonists expressed the middle state of the soul between sensible and intellectual existence.

[3] This epithet was suggested by Charlevoix's striking description of the confluence of the Missouri with the Mississippi:—'I believe this is the finest confluence in the world. The two rivers are much of the same breadth, each about half a league; but the Missouri is by far the most rapid, and seems to enter the Mississippi like a conqueror, through which it carries its white waves to the opposite shore without mixing them: afterwards it gives its odour to the Mississippi, which it never loses again, but carries quite down to the sea.'— Letter xxvii.

Is this the region, then, is this the clime
For golden fancy? for those dreams sublime,
Which all their miracles of light reveal
To heads that meditate and hearts that feel?
No, no—the Muse of inspiration plays
O'er every scene; she walks the forest-maze,
And climbs the mountain; every blooming spot
Burns with her step, yet man regards it not!
She whispers round, her words are in the air,
But lost, unheard, they linger freezing there,
Without one breath of soul, divinely strong,
One ray of heart to thaw them into song!

Yet, yet forgive me, oh you sacred few!
Whom late by Delaware's green banks I knew;
Whom, known and loved through many a social
  eve,
'Twas bliss to live with, and 'twas pain to
  leave![1]
Less dearly welcome were the lines of yore
The exile saw upon the sandy shore,
When his lone heart but faintly hoped to find
One print of man, one blessed stamp of mind!
Less dearly welcome than the liberal zeal,
The strength to reason, and the warmth to feel,
The manly polish and the illumined taste,
Which, 'mid the melancholy, heartless waste
My foot has wandered, oh you sacred few!
I found by Delaware's green banks with you.
Long may you hate the Gallic dross that runs
O'er your fair country and corrupts its sons;
Long love the arts, the glories which adorn
Those fields of freedom where your sires were
  born.
Oh! if America can yet be great,
If, neither chained by choice, nor damned by
  fate
To the mob-mania which imbrutes her now,
She yet can raise the bright but temperate brow
Of single majesty, can grandly place
An empire's pillar upon Freedom's base,
Nor fear the mighty shaft will feebler prove
For the fair capital that flowers above!—
If yet, released from all that vulgar throng,
So vain of dulness and so pleased with wrong,
Who hourly teach her, like themselves, to hide
Folly in froth, and barrenness in pride,
She yet can rise, can wreathe the attic charms
Of soft refinement round the pomp of arms,
And see her poets flash the fires of song,
To light her warriors' thunderbolts along!
It is to you, to souls that favouring Heaven
Has made like yours, the glorious task is
  given—
Oh! but for *such*, Columbia's days were done;
Rank without ripeness, quickened without sun,

Crude at the surface, rotten at the core,
Her fruits would fall before her spring were
  o'er!

Believe me, Spencer, while I winged the hours
Where Schuylkill undulates through banks of
  flowers,
Though few the days, the happy evenings few,
So warm with heart, so rich with mind they
  flew,
That my full soul forgot its wish to roam,
And rested there, as in a dream of home!
And looks I met, like looks I loved before,
And voices too, which, as they trembled o'er
The chord of memory, found full many a tone
Of kindness there in concord with their own!
Oh! we had nights of that communion free,
That flush of heart, which I have known with
  thee
So oft, so warmly; nights of mirth and mind,
Of whims that taught, and follies that refined:
When shall we both renew them? when, re-
  stored
To the pure feast and intellectual board,
Shall I once more enjoy with thee and thine
Those whims that teach, those follies that
  refine?
Even now, as, wandering upon Erie's shore,
I hear Niagara's distant cataract roar,
I sighed for England—oh! these weary feet
Have many a mile to journey ere we meet!

Ω ΠΑΤΡΙΣ, ΩΣ ΣΟΥ ΚΑΡΤΑ ΝΥΝ ΜΝΕΙΑΝ ΕΧΩ.

A WARNING.

TO —— ——

Oh! fair as Heaven and chaste as light!
Did Nature mould thee all so bright,
That thou shouldst ever learn to weep
O'er languid Virtue's fatal sleep,
O'er shame extinguished, honour fled,
Peace lost, heart withered, feeling dead?

No, no! a star was born with thee,
Which sheds eternal purity!
Thou hast within those sainted eyes
So fair a transcript of the skies,
In lines of fire such heavenly lore,
That man should read them and adore!
Yet have I known a gentle maid
Whose early charms were just arrayed
In Nature's loveliness like thine,
And wore that clear, celestial sign,

---

[1] In the society of Mr. Dennie and his friends at Philadelphia, I passed the few agreeable moments which my tour through the States afforded me. Mr. Dennie has succeeded in diffusing through this elegant little circle that love for good literature and sound politics which he feels so zealously himself, and which is so very rarely the characteristic of his countrymen. They will not, I trust, accuse me of illiberality for the picture which I have given of the ignorance and corruption that surround them. If I did not hate as I ought the rabble to which they are opposed, I could not value as I do the spirit with which they defy it; and in learning from them what Americans *can be*, I but see with the more indignation what Americans *are*.

Which seems to mark the brow that's fair
For Destiny's peculiar care!
Whose bosom, too, was once a zone
Where the bright gem of virtue shone;
Whose eyes were talismans of fire
Against the spell of man's desire!
Yet, hapless girl, in one sad hour
Her charms have shed their radiant flower;
The gem has been beguiled away;
Her eyes have lost their chastening ray;
The simple fear, the guiltless shame,
The smiles that from reflection came,
All, all have fled, and left her mind
A faded monument behind!
Like some wave-beaten, mouldering stone,
To memory raised by hands unknown,
Which, many a wintry hour, has stood
Beside the ford of Tyra's flood,
To tell the traveller, as he crossed,
That there some lovèd friend was lost;
Oh! 'twas a sight I wept to see—
Heaven keep the lost one's fate from thee!

TO —— ——.

'Tis time, I feel, to leave thee now,
While yet my soul is something free;
While yet those dangerous eyes allow
One moment's thought to stray from thee!

Oh! thou art every instant dearer—
Every chance that brings me nigh thee,
Brings my ruin nearer, nearer;
I am lost, unless I fly thee!

Nay, if thou dost not scorn and hate me,
Wish me not so soon to fall,
Duties, fame, and hopes await me,
Oh! that eye would blast them all!

Yes, yes, it would—for thou'rt as cold
As ever yet allured or swayed,
And wouldst, without a sigh, behold
The ruin which thyself had made!

Yet—*could* I think that, truly fond,
That eye but once would smile on me,
Good Heaven! how much, how far beyond
Fame, duty, hope, that smile would be!

Oh! but to win it, night and day,
Inglorious at thy feet reclined,
I'd sigh my dreams of fame away,
The world for thee forgot, resigned!

But no, no, no—farewell—we part,
Never to meet, no, never, never—
Oh woman! what a mind and heart
Thy coldness has undone for ever!

FROM

THE HIGH PRIEST OF APOLLO

TO

A VIRGIN OF DELPHI.[1]

Cum digno digna . . .
—*Julxi la.*

'Who is the maid, with golden hair,
With eyes of fire and feet of air,
Whose harp around my altar swells,
The sweetest of a thousand shells?'

'Twas thus the deity, who treads
The arch of Heaven, and grandly sheds
Day from his eyelids!—thus he spoke,
As through my cell his glories broke:

'Who is the maid, with golden hair,
With eyes of fire and feet of air,
Whose harp around my altar swells,
The sweetest of a thousand shells?'

Aphelia is the Delphic fair,
With eyes of fire and golden hair,
Aphelia's are the airy feet,
And hers the harp divinely sweet;

For foot so light has never trod
The laurelled caverns of the god,
Nor harp so soft has ever given
A strain to earth or sigh to Heaven!

'Then tell the virgin to unfold,
In looser pomp, her locks of gold,
And bid those eyes with fonder fire
Be kindled for a god's desire;
Since He, who lights the path of years—
Even from the fount of morning's tears,

---

[1] This poem requires a little explanation. It is well known that, in the ancient temples, whenever a reverend priest, like the supposed author of the invitation before us, was inspired with a tender inclination towards any fair visitor of the shrine, and at the same time felt a diffidence in his own powers of persuasion, he had but to proclaim that the god himself was enamoured of her, and had signified his divine will that she should sleep in the interior of the temple. Many a pious husband connived at this divine assignation, and even declared himself proud of the selection with which his family had been distinguished by the deity. In the temple of Jupiter Belus there was a splendid bed for these occasions. In Egyptian Thebes the same mockery was practised; and at the oracle of Patara in Lycia, the priestess never could prophesy till an interview with the deity was allowed her. The story which we read in *Josephus* (lib. xviii. cap. 3), of the Roman matron Paulina, whom the priests of Isis, for a bribe, betrayed in this manner to Mundus, is a singular instance of the impudent excess to which credulity suffered these impostures to be carried. This story has been put into the form of a little novel, under the name of *La Pudicitia Schernita*, by the licentious and unfortunate Pallavicino. See his *Opere Scelte*, tom. i. I have made my priest here prefer a cave to the temple.

To where his setting splendours burn
Upon the western sea-maid's urn—
Cannot, in all his course, behold
Such eyes of fire, such hair of gold!
Tell her he comes in blissful pride,
His lip yet sparkling with the tide
That mantles in Olympian bowls,
The nectar of eternal souls!
For her, for her he quits the skies,
And to her kiss from nectar flies.
Oh! he would hide his wreath of rays,
And leave the world to pine for days,
Might he but pass the hours of shade
Imbosomed by his Delphic maid—
She, more than earthly woman blest,
He, more than god on woman's breast!'

There is a cave beneath the steep,[1]
Where living rills of crystal weep
O'er herbage of the loveliest hue
That ever spring begemmed with dew,
There oft the green bank's glossy tint
Is brightened by the amorous print
Of many a faun and Naiad's form,
That still upon the dew is warm
When virgins come at peep of day
To kiss the sod where lovers lay!
'There, there,' the god, impassioned, said,
'Soon as the twilight tinge is fled,
And the dim orb of lunar souls
Along its shadowy pathway rolls—
There shall we find our bridal bed,
And ne'er did rosy rapture spread,
Not even in Jove's voluptuous bowers,
A bridal bed so blest as ours!

'Tell the imperial God, who reigns
Sublime in oriental fanes,
Whose towering turrets paint their pride
Upon Euphrates' pregnant tide;
Tell him, when to his midnight loves
In mystic majesty he moves,
Lighted by many an odorous fire,
And hymned by all Chaldæa's choir—
Oh! tell the godhead to confess,
The pompous joy delights him less
(Even though his mighty arms enfold
A priestess on a couch of gold)
Than when in love's unholier prank,
By moonlight cave or rustic bank,
Upon his neck some wood-nymph lies,
Exhaling from her lip and eyes
The flame and incense of delight,
To sanctify a dearer rite,
A mystery, more divinely warmed
Than priesthood ever yet performed!'

Happy the maid, whom Heaven allows
To break for Heaven her virgin vows!

---

[1] The Corycian Cave, which Pausanias mentions. The inhabitants of Parnassus held it sacred to the Corycian nymphs, who were children of the river Plistus.

Happy the maid!—her robe of shame
Is whitened by a heavenly flame,
Whose glory, with a lingering trace,
Shines through and deifies her race!

Oh, virgin! what a doom is thine!
To-night, to-night a lip divine
In every kiss shall stamp on thee
A seal of immortality!
Fly to the cave, Aphelia, fly;
There lose the world and wed the sky!
There all the boundless rapture steal
Which gods can give or woman feel!

WOMAN.

Away, away—you're all the same,
A fluttering, smiling, jilting throng!
Oh! by my soul, I burn with shame,
To think I've been your slave so long!

Slow to be warmed and quick to rove,
From folly kind, from cunning loth,
Too cold for bliss, too weak for love,
Yet feigning all that's best in both.

Still panting o'er a crowd to reign,
More joy it gives to woman's breast
To make ten frigid coxcombs vain,
Than one true, manly lover blest!

Away, away,—your smile's a curse—.
Oh! blot me from the race of men,
Kind pitying Heaven! by death or worse
Before I love such things again!

BALLAD STANZAS.

I knew by the smoke, that so gracefully curled
  Above the green elms, that a cottage was near;
And I said, 'If there's peace to be found in the world,
  A heart that was humble might hope for it here!'

It was noon, and on flowers that languished around
  In silence reposed the voluptuous bee;
Every leaf was at rest, and I heard not a sound
  But the woodpecker tapping the hollow beech-tree.

And 'Here in this lone little wood,' I exclaimed,
  'With a maid who was lovely to soul and to eye.
Who would blush when I praised her, and weep if I blamed,
  How blest could I live, and how calm could I die!

'By the shade of yon sumach, whose red berry dips
In the gush of the fountain, how sweet to recline,
And to know that I sighed upon innocent lips,
Which had never been sighed on by any but mine!'

TO ———— ————.

NOΣEI TA ΦIΛTATA.—*Euripides.*

1803.

COME, take the harp—'tis vain to muse
Upon the gathering ills we see;
Oh! take the harp, and let me lose
All thoughts of ill in hearing thee!

Sing to me, Love! though death were near,
Thy song could make my soul forget—
Nay, nay, in pity, dry that tear,
All may be well, be happy yet!

Let me but see that snowy arm
Once more upon the dear harp lie,
And I will cease to dream of harm,
Will smile at fate, while thou art nigh!

Give me that strain, of mournful touch,
We used to love long, long ago,
Before our hearts had known as much
As now, alas! they bleed to know!

Sweet notes! they tell of former peace,
Of all that looked so rapturous then,
Now withered, lost—oh! pray thee, cease,
I cannot bear those sounds again!

Art thou too wretched? yes, thou art;
I see thy tears flow fast with mine—
Come, come to this devoted heart,
'Tis breaking, but it still is thine!

A VISION OF PHILOSOPHY.

'TWAS on the Red Sea coast, at morn we met
The venerable man:[1] a virgin bloom
Of softness mingled with the vigorous thought
That towered upon his brow; as when we see
The gentle moon and the full radiant sun
Shining in heaven together. When he spoke,
'Twas language sweetened into song—such holy sounds
As oft the spirit of the good man hears,
Prelusive to the harmony of heaven,
When death is nigh![2] and still, as he unclosed
His sacred lips, an odour, all as bland
As ocean-breezes gather from the flowers
That blossom in Elysium, breathed around!
With silent awe we listened while he told
Of the dark veil which many an age had hung
O'er Nature's form, till by the touch of Time
The mystic shroud grew thin and luminous,
And half the goddess beamed in glimpses through it!
Of magic wonders, that were known and taught
By him (or Cham or Zoroaster named)
Who mused, amid the mighty cataclysm,
O'er his rude tablets of primeval lore,[3]
Nor let the living star of science[4] sink
Beneath the waters which engulfed the world!—
Of visions, by Calliope revealed
To him[5] who traced upon his typic lyre
The diapason of man's mingled frame,
And the grand Doric heptachord of Heaven!
With all of pure, of wondrous and arcane,
Which the grave sons of Mochus, many a night
Told to the young and bright-haired visitant
Of Carmel's sacred mount![6]—Then, in a flow

---

[1] *In Plutarch's Essay on the Decline of the Oracles,* Cleombrotus, one of the interlocutors, describes an extraordinary man whom he had met with, after long research, upon the banks of the Red Sea. Once in every year this supernatural personage appeared to mortals, and conversed with them: the rest of his time he passed among the Genii and the Nymphs. Περι της ερυθραν θαλασσαν ιδρυν, ανθρωποις απα παι ετος απαξ συντυγχανοντα, ταλλα δε συν ταις νυμφαις, νομασι και δαιμοσι, ως εφασκε. He spoke in a tone not far removed from singing. and whenever he opened his lips a fragrance filled the place: φθεγγομενου δε του τοπου ιωιδια κατειχε, του στοματος εδιστυν αποτνιοντος. From him Cleombrotus learned the doctrine of a plurality of worlds.

[2] The celebrated Janus Dousa, a little before his death, imagined that he heard a strain of music in the air. See the poem of Heinsius, 'In harmoniam quam paulo ante obitum audire sibi visus est Dousa.' Page 501.

[3] Cham, the son of Noah, is supposed to have taken with him into the ark the principal doctrines of magical, or rather of natural, science, which he had inscribed upon some very durable substances, in order that they might resist the ravages of the deluge, and transmit the secrets of antediluvian knowledge to his posterity.—See the extracts made by Bayle in his article Cham. The identity of Cham and Zoroaster depends upon the authority of Berosus, or the impostor Annius, and a few more such respectable testimonies. See *Naudé's Apologie pour les Grands Hommes,* etc., chap. 8, where he takes more trouble than is necessary in refuting this gratuitous supposition.

[4] Chamum à posteris hujus artis admiratoribus Zoroastrum, seu vivum astrum, propterea fuisse dictum et pro Deo habitum.—*Bochart. Geograph. Sacr.* lib. iv. cap. 1.

[5] Orpheus.—Paulinus, in his *Hebdomades,* cap. 2, lib. iii., has endeavoured to show, after the Platonists, that man is a diapason, made up of a diatesseron, which is his soul, and a diapente, which is his body. Those frequent allusions to music, by which the ancient philosophers illustrated their sublime theories, must have tended very much to elevate the character of the art, and to enrich it with associations of the grandest and most interesting nature.

[6] Pythagoras is represented in Jamblichus as descending with great solemnity from Mount Carmel, for which reason the Carmelites have claimed him as one of their

Of calmer converse, he beguiled us on
Through many a maze of garden and of porch,
Through many a system, where the scattered light
Of heavenly truth lay, like a broken beam
From the pure sun, which, though refracted all
Into a thousand hues, is sunshine still,[1]
And bright through every change!—he spoke of Him,
The lone Eternal One, who dwells above,
And of the soul's untraceable descent
From that high fount of spirit, through the grades
Of intellectual being, till it mix
With atoms vague, corruptible, and dark;
Nor even then, though sunk in earthly dross,
Corrupted all, nor its ethereal touch
Quite lost, but tasting of the fountain still!
As some bright river, which has rolled along
Through meads of flowery light and mines of gold,
When poured at length into the dusky deep,
Disdains to mingle with its briny taint,
But keeps awhile the pure and golden tinge,
The balmy freshness of the fields it left![2]

And here the old man ceased—a wingèd train
Of nymphs and genii led him from our eyes.
The fair illusion fled! and, as I waked,
I knew my visionary soul had been
Among that people of aerial dreams
Who live upon the burning galaxy!

TO ———— ————.

THE world had just begun to steal
  Each hope that led me lightly on,
I felt not as I used to feel,
  And life grew dark and love was gone!

No eye to mingle sorrow's tear,
  No lip to mingle pleasure's breath,
No tongue to call me kind and dear—
  'Twas gloomy, and I wished for death!

But when I saw that gentle eye,
  Oh! something seemed to tell me then
That I was yet too young to die,
  And hope and bliss might bloom again!

With every beamy smile that crossed
  Your kindling cheek, you lighted home
Some feeling which my heart had lost,
  And Peace, which long had learned to roam!

'Twas then indeed so sweet to live,
  Hope looked so new, and love so kind,
That, though I weep, I still forgive
  The ruin which they've left behind!

I could have loved you—oh, so well;—
  The dream that wishing boyhood knows,
Is but a bright beguiling spell,
  Which only lives while passion glows:

But, when this early flush declines,
  When the heart's vivid morning fleets,
You know not then how close it twines
  Round the first kindred soul it meets!

Yes, yes, I could have loved, as one
  Who, while his youth's enchantments fall,
Finds something dear to rest upon,
  Which pays him for the loss of all!

. . . .
. . . .

DREAMS.

TO ———— ————.

IN slumber, I prithee how is it
That souls are oft taking the air,
And paying each other a visit,
While bodies are—Heaven knows where?

Last night, 'tis in vain to deny it,
  Your soul took a fancy to roam;
For I heard her, on tiptoe so quiet,
  Come ask, whether mine was at home.

And mine let her in with delight.
  And they talked and they kissed the time through;
For when souls come together at night.
  There is no knowing what they mayn't do!

And *your* little soul, Heaven bless her!
  Had much to complain and to say,
Of how sadly you wrong and oppress her,
  By keeping her prisoned all day.

'If I happen,' said she, 'but to steal
  For a peep now and then to her eye,
Or, to quiet the fever I feel,
  Just venture abroad on a sigh;

'In an instant, she frightens me in,
  With some phantom of prudence or terror,

---

fraternity. This Mochus or Moschus, with the descendants of whom Pythagoras conversed in Phœnicia, and from whom he derived the doctrines of atomic philosophy, is supposed by some to be the same with Moses.

[1] Lactantius asserts that all the truths of Christianity may be found dispersed through the ancient philosophical sects, and that any one who would collect these scattered fragments of orthodoxy might form a code in no respect differing from that of the Christian. 'Si extitisset aliquis, qui veritatem sparsam per singulos per sectasque diffusam colligeret in unum, ac redigeret in corpus, is profecto non dissentiret a nobis.'—*Inst.* lib. vi. c. 7.

[2] This fine Platonic image I have taken from a passage in Father Bouchet's letter upon the Metempsychosis, inserted in *Picart's Cérém. Relig.* tom. iv.

For fear I should stray into sin,
 Or, what is still worse, into error!

'So, instead of displaying my graces,
 Thro' look, and thro' words, and thro' mien,
I am shut up in corners and places,
 Where truly I blush to be seen!'

Upon hearing this piteous confession,
 My soul, looking tenderly at her,
Declared, as for grace and discretion,
 He did not know much of the matter;

'But, to-morrow, sweet spirit!' he said,
 'Be at home after midnight, and then
I will come when your lady's in bed,
 And we'll talk o'er the subject again.'

So she whispered a word in his ear,
 I suppose to her door to direct him,
And—just after midnight, my dear,
 Your polite little soul may expect him.

TO MRS. —— ——.

To see thee every day that came,
And find thee every day the same,
In pleasure's smile or sorrow's tear
The same benign consoling dear!
To meet thee early, leave thee late,
Has been so long my bliss, my fate,
That life, without this cheering ray,
Which came like sunshine every day,
And all my pain, my sorrow chased,
Is now a lone and loveless waste.—
Where are the chords she used to touch?
Where are the songs she loved so much?
The songs are hushed, the chords are still,
And so, perhaps, will every thrill

Of friendship soon be lulled to rest,
Which late I waked in Anna's breast!
Yet no—the simple notes I played,
On memory's tablet soon may fade;
The songs which Anna loved to hear
May all be lost on Anna's ear;
But friendship's sweet and fairy strain
Shall ever in her heart remain;
Nor memory lose nor time impair
The sympathies which tremble there!

A CANADIAN BOAT-SONG.

WRITTEN ON THE RIVER ST. LAWRENCE.[1]

Et remigem cantus hortatur.
—*Quintilian.*

FAINTLY as tolls the evening chime,
Our voices keep tune and our oars keep time.
Soon as the woods on shore look dim,
We'll sing at St. Ann's our parting hymn.[2]
Row, brothers, row, the stream runs fast,
The Rapids are near, and the daylight's past!

Why should we yet our sail unfurl?
There is not a breath the blue wave to curl!
But when the wind blows off the shore,
Oh! sweetly we'll rest our weary oar.
Blow, breezes, blow, the stream runs fast,
The Rapids are near, and the daylight's past!

Utawas' tide! this trembling moon
Shall see us float over thy surges soon.
Saint of this green Isle! hear our prayers,
Oh! grant us cool heavens and favouring airs.
Blow, breezes, blow, the stream runs fast,
The Rapids are near, and the daylight's past!

---

[1] I wrote these words to an air which our boatmen sung to us very frequently. The wind was so unfavourable that they were obliged to row all the way, and we were five days in descending the river from Kingston to Montreal, exposed to an intense sun during the day, and at night forced to take shelter from the dews in any miserable hut upon the banks that would receive us. But the magnificent scenery of the St. Lawrence repays all these difficulties.
  Our *voyageurs* had good voices, and sung perfectly in tune together. The original words of the air, to which I adapted these stanzas, appeared to be a long incoherent story, of which I could understand but little, from the barbarous pronunciation of the Canadians. It begins:

  Dans mon chemin j'ai rencontré
  Deux cavaliers très-bien montés;

And the *refrain* to every verse was:

  A l'ombre d'un bois je m'en vais jouer,
  A l'ombre d'un bois je m'en vais danser.

I ventured to harmonize this air, and have published it. Without that charm which association gives to every little memorial of scenes or feelings that are past, the melody may perhaps be thought common and trifling; but I remember when we have entered, at sunset, upon one of those beautiful lakes, into which the St. Lawrence so grandly and unexpectedly opens, I have heard this simple air with a pleasure which the finest compositions of the first masters have never given me; and now there is not a note of it which does not recall to my memory the dip of our oars in the St. Lawrence, the flight of our boat down the Rapids, and all those new and fanciful impressions to which my heart was alive during the whole of this very interesting voyage.
  The above stanzas are supposed to be sung by those *voyageurs* who go to the Grande Portage by the Utawas River. For an account of this wonderful undertaking, see Sir Alexander Mackenzie's *General History of the Fur Trade*, prefixed to his *Journal*.

[2] 'At the Rapid of St. Ann they are obliged to take out part, if not the whole, of their lading. It is from this spot the Canadians consider they take their departure, as it possesses the last church on the island, which is dedicated to the tutelar saint of voyagers.'—*Mackenzie's General History of the Fur Trade.*

EPISTLE IX.

TO THE LADY CHARLOTTE R—WD—N.

FROM THE BANKS OF THE ST. LAWRENCE.

Not many months have now been dreamed away
Since yonder sun (beneath whose evening ray
We rest our boat among these Indian isles)
Saw me, where mazy Trent serenely smiles
Through many an oak, as sacred as the groves
Beneath whose shade the pious Persian roves,
And hears the soul of father or of chief,
Or lovèd mistress, sigh in every leaf![1]
There listening, Lady! while thy lip hath sung
My own unpolished lays, how proud I've hung
On every mellowed number! proud to feel
That notes like mine should have the fate to steal,
As o'er thy hallowing lip they sighed along,
Such breath of passion and such soul of song.
Oh! I have wondered, like the peasant boy
Who sings at eve his Sabbath strains of joy,
And when he hears the rude, luxuriant note
Back to his ear on softening echoes float,
Believes it still some answering spirit's tone,
And thinks it all too sweet to be his own!
I dreamed not then that, ere the rolling year
Had filled its circle, I should wander here
In musing awe; should tread this wondrous world,
See all its store of inland waters hurled
In one vast volume down Niagara's steep,[2]
Or calm behold them, in transparent sleep,
Where the blue hills of old Toronto shed
Their evening shadows o'er Ontario's bed!—
Should trace the grand Cadaraqui, and glide
Down the white Rapids of his lordly tide
Through massy woods, through islets flowering fair,
Through shades of bloom, where the first sinful pair

For consolation might have weeping trod,
When banished from the garden of their God!
Oh, Lady! these are miracles which man,
Caged in the bounds of Europe's pigmy plan,
Can scarcely dream of: which his eye must see,
To know how beautiful this world can be!
But soft!—the tinges of the west decline,
And night falls dewy o'er these banks of pine.
Among the reeds, in which our idle boat
Is rocked to rest, the wind's complaining note
Dies, like a half-breathed whispering of flutes;
Along the wave the gleaming porpoise shoots,
And I can trace him, like a watery star,[3]
Down the steep current, till he fades afar
Amid the foaming breaker's silvery light,
Where yon rough Rapids sparkle through the night!
Here, as along this shadowy bank I stray,
And the smooth glass-snake,[4] gliding o'er my way,
Shows the dim moonlight through his scaly form,
Fancy, with all the scene's enchantment warm,
Hears in the murmur of the nightly breeze,
Some Indian Spirit warble words like these:

From the clime of sacred doves,[5]
Where the blessed Indian roves,
Through the air on wing, as white
As the spirit-stones of light,[6]
Which the eye of morning counts
On the Apallachian mounts!
Hither oft my flight I take
Over Huron's lucid lake,
Where the wave, as clear as dew,
Sleeps beneath the light canoe,
Which, reflected, floating there,
Looks as if it hung in air![7]

Then, when I have strayed a while
Through the Manataulin isle,[8]

---

[1] 'Avendo essi per costume di avere in veneratione gli alberi grandi ed antichi, quasi che siano spesso ricettacoli di anime beate.'—*Pietro della Valle*, Part. Second. Lettera 16 da i giardini di Sciraz.

[2] When I arrived at Chippewa, within three miles of the Falls, it was too late to think of visiting them that evening, and I lay awake all night with the sound of the cataract in my ears. The day following I consider as a kind of era in my life, and the first glimpse which I caught of those wonderful Falls gave me a feeling which nothing in this world can ever excite again.
To Colonel Brock, of the 49th, who commanded at the Fort, I am particularly indebted for his kindness to me during the fortnight I remained at Niagara. Among many pleasant days which I passed with him and his brother officers, that of our visit to the Tuscarora Indians was not the least interesting. They received us in all their ancient costume: the young men exhibited, for our amusement, in the race, the bat-game, etc.; while the old and the women sat in groups under the surrounding trees, and the picture altogether was as beautiful as it was new to me.

[3] Anburey, in his *Travels*, has noticed this shooting illumination which porpoises diffuse at night through the St. Lawrence.—Vol. i. p. 29.

[4] The glass-snake is brittle and transparent.

[5] 'The departed spirit goes into the Country of Souls, where, according to some, it is transformed into a dove.'—Charlevoix, upon the *Traditions and the Religion of the Savages of Canada.* See the curious *Fable of the American Orpheus* in Lafitau, tom. i. p. 402.

[6] 'The mountains appeared to be sprinkled with white stones, which glistened in the sun, and were called by the Indians "manetoe asenlah," or spirit-stones.'—*Mackensie's Journal.*

[7] I was thinking here of what Carver says so beautifully in his description of one of these lakes: 'When it was calm, and the sun shone bright, I could sit in my canoe, where the depth was upwards of six fathoms, and plainly see huge piles of stone at the bottom, of different shapes, some of which appeared as if they had been hewn: the water was at this time as pure and transparent as air, and my canoe seemed as if it hung suspended in that element. It was impossible to look attentively through this limpid medium, at the rocks below, without finding, before many minutes were elapsed, your head swim and your eyes no longer able to behold the dazzling scene.'

[8] Manataulin signifies a Place of Spirits, and this Island in Lake Huron is held sacred by the Indians.

Breathing all its holy bloom,
Swift upon the purple plume
Of my Wakon-Bird¹ I fly
Where, beneath a burning sky,
O'er the bed of Erie's lake,
Slumbers many a water-snake,
Basking in the web of leaves
Which the weeping lily weaves!²

Then I chase the floweret-king
Through his bloomy wild of spring;
See him now, while diamond hues
Soft his neck and wings suffuse,
In the leafy chalice sink,
Thirsting for his balmy drink;
Now behold him all on fire,
Lovely in his looks of ire,
Breaking every infant stem,
Scattering every velvet gem,
Where his little tyrant lip
Had not found enough to sip!

Then my playful hand I steep
Where the gold-thread³ loves to creep,
Cull from thence a tangled wreath,
Words of magic round it breathe,
And the sunny chaplet spread
O'er the sleeping fly-bird's head,⁴
Till, with dreams of honey blessed,
Haunted in his downy nest
By the garden's fairest spells,
Dewy buds and fragrant bells,
Fancy all his soul embowers
In the fly-bird's heaven of flowers!

Oft, when hoar and silvery flakes
Melt along the ruffled lakes;
When the gray moose sheds his horns,
When the track at evening warns
Weary hunters of the way
To the wigwam's cheering ray,
Then, aloft through freezing air,
With the snow-bird⁵ soft and fair
As the fleece that heaven flings
O'er his little pearly wings,
Light above the rocks I play,
Where Niagara's starry spray,
Frozen on the cliff, appears
Like a giant's starting tears!

There, amid the Island-sedge,
Just upon the cataract's edge,
Where the foot of living man
Never trod since time began,
Lone I sit, at close of day,
While, beneath the golden ray,
Icy columns gleam below,
Feathered round with falling snow,
And an arch of glory springs,
Brilliant as the chain of rings
Round the neck of virgins hung,—
Virgins⁶ who have wandered young
O'er the waters of the west
To the land where spirits rest!

Thus have I charmed, with visionary lay,
The lonely moments of the night away;
And now, fresh daylight o'er the water beams!
Once more embarked upon the glittering streams,
Our boat flies light along the leafy shore,
Shooting the falls, without a dip of oar
Or breath of zephyr, like the mystic bark
The poet saw, in dreams divinely dark,
Borne, without sails, along the dusky flood,
While on its deck a pilot angel stood,
And, with his wings of living light unfurled,
Coasted the dim shores of another world!

Yet oh! believe me in this blooming maze
Of lovely nature, where the fancy strays
From charm to charm, where every floweret's
  hue
Hath something strange, and every leaf is new!
I never feel a bliss so pure and still,
So heavenly calm, as when a stream or hill,
Or veteran oak, like those remembered well,
Or breeze or echo, or some wild-flower's smell
(For, who can say what small and fairy ties
The memory flings o'er pleasure as it flies!)
Reminds my heart of many a sylvan dream
I once indulged by Trent's inspiring stream;
Of all my sunny morns and moonlight nights
On Donington's green lawns and breezy
  heights!

Whether I trace the tranquil moments o'er,
When I have seen thee cull the blooms of lore,
With him, the polished warrior, by thy side,
A sister's idol and a nation's pride!

---

¹ 'The Wakon-Bird, which probably is of the same species with the Bird of Paradise, receives its name from the ideas the Indians have of its superior excellence; the Wakon-Bird being, in their language, the Bird of the Great Spirit.'—*Morse.*

² The islands of Lake Erie are surrounded to a considerable distance by the large pond-lily, whose leaves spread thickly over the surface of the lake, and form a kind of bed for the water-snakes in summer.

³ 'The gold-thread is of the vine kind, and grows in swamps. The roots spread themselves just under the surface of the morasses, and are easily drawn out by handfuls. They resemble a large entangled skein of silk, and are of a bright yellow.'—*Morse.*

⁴ 'L'oiseau mouche, gros comme un hanneton, est de toutes couleurs, vives et changeantes: il tire sa subsistence des fleurs comme les abeilles; son nid est fait d'un coton très-fin suspendu à une branche d'arbre.'—*Voyages aux Indes Occidentales*, par M. Bossu. Second part, lett. xx.

⁵ Emberiza hyemalis.—See *Imlay's Kentucky*, p 230.

⁶ Lafitau wishes to believe, for the sake of his theory, that there was an order of vestals established among the Iroquois Indians; but I am afraid that Jacques Carthier, upon whose authority he supports himself, meant anything but vestal institutions by the 'cabanes publiques' which he met with at Montreal.—See *Lafitau, Mœurs des Sauvages Américains*, etc., tom. i. p. 173.

With triumph this morning, O Boston! I hail
The stir of thy deck and the spread of thy sail;
For they tell me I soon shall be wafted in thee
To the flourishing isle of the brave and the free,
And that chill Nova Scotia's unpromising strand
Is the last I shall tread of American land.
. . . .
But see!—the bent top-sails are ready to swell—
To the boat—I am with thee—Columbia farewell!

Page 345.

When thou hast read of heroes, trophied high
In ancient fame, and I have seen thine eye
Turn to the living hero, while it read,
For pure and brightening comments on the dead!
Or whether memory to my mind recalls
The festal grandeur of those lordly halls,
When guests have met around the sparkling
  board,
And welcome warmed the cup that luxury
  poured;
When the bright future star of England's throne
With magic smile hath o'er the banquet shone,
Winning respect, nor claiming what he won,
But tempering greatness, like an evening sun
Whose light the eye can tranquilly admire,
Glorious but mild, all softness yet all fire!
Whatever hue my recollections take,
Even the regret, the very pain they wake
Is dear and exquisite!—but oh! no more—
Lady! adieu—my heart has lingered o'er
These vanished times, till all that round me lies,
Stream, banks, and bowers, have faded on my
  eyes!

IMPROMPTU,

AFTER A VISIT TO MRS. ———, OF MONTREAL.

'TWAS but for a moment—and yet in that time
She crowded the impressions of many an hour:
Her eye had a glow, like the sun of her clime,
  Which waked every feeling at once into
  flower!

Oh! could we have stolen but one rapturous
  day,
To renew such impressions again and again,
The things we could look, and imagine, and say,
  Would be worth all the life we had wasted till
  then!

What we had not the leisure or language to
  speak,
We should find some more exquisite mode of
  revealing,
And, between us, should feel just as much in a
  week,
As others would take a millennium in feeling!

WRITTEN
ON PASSING DEADMAN'S ISLAND,[1]

IN THE GULF OF ST. LAWRENCE,

LATE IN THE EVENING, SEPTEMBER 1804.

SEE you, beneath yon cloud so dark,
Fast gliding along, a gloomy bark!
Her sails are full, though the wind is still,
And there blows not a breath her sails to fill!

Oh! what doth that vessel of darkness bear?
The silent calm of the grave is there,
Save now and again a death-knell rung,
And the flap of the sails with night-fog hung!

There lieth a wreck on the dismal shore
Of cold and pitiless Labrador;
Where, under the moon, upon mounts of frost,
Full many a mariner's bones are tossed!

Yon shadowy bark hath been to that wreck,
And the dim blue fire that lights her deck
Doth play on as pale and livid a crew,
As ever yet drank the churchyard dew!

To Deadman's Isle, in the eye of the blast,
To Deadman's Isle she speeds her fast;
By skeleton shapes her sails are furled,
And the hand that steers is not of this world!

Oh! hurry thee on—oh! hurry thee on,
Thou terrible bark! ere the night be gone,
Nor let morning look on so foul a sight
As would blanch for ever her rosy light!

TO THE *BOSTON* FRIGATE.[2]

ON LEAVING HALIFAX FOR ENGLAND,
OCTOBER 1804.

ΝΟΣΤΟΥ ΠΡΟΦΑΣΙΣ ΓΛΥΚΕΡΟΤ.
— *Pindar. Pyth.* 4.

WITH triumph this morning, oh *Boston!* I hail
The stir of thy deck and the spread of thy sail;
For they tell me I soon shall be wafted, in thee,
To the flourishing isle of the brave and the free,
And that chill Nova Scotia's unpromising strand[3]
Is the last I shall tread of American land.

---

[1] This is one of the Magdalen Islands, and, singularly enough, is the property of Sir Isaac Coffin. The above lines were suggested by a superstition very common among sailors, who call this ghost-ship, I think, 'the flying Dutchman.'

We were thirteen days on our passage from Quebec to Halifax, and I had been so spoiled by the very splendid hospitality with which my friends of the *Phaeton* and *Boston* had treated me, that I was but ill prepared to encounter the miseries of a Canadian ship. The weather, however, was pleasant, and the scenery along the river delightful. Our passage through the Gut of Canso, with a bright sky and a fair wind, was particularly striking and romantic.

[2] Commanded by Captain J. E. Douglas, with whom I returned to England, and to whom I am indebted for many, many kindnesses. In truth, I should but offend the delicacy of my friend Douglas, and at the same time do injustice to my own feelings of gratitude, did I attempt to say how much I owe to him.

[3] Sir John Wentworth, the Governor of Nova Scotia, very kindly allowed me to accompany him on his visit to the college which they have lately established at Windsor, about forty miles from Halifax, and I was indeed most pleasantly surprised by the beauty and fertility of the country which opened upon us after the bleak and rocky wilderness by which Halifax is surrounded. I was told that, in travelling onwards, we should find the soil and the scenery improve, and it gave me much pleasure to know that the worthy Governor has by no means such an 'inamabile regnum' as I was at first sight inclined to believe.

Well—peace to the land! may the people, at length,
Know that freedom is bliss, but that honour is strength;
That though man have the wings of the fetterless wind,
Of the wantonest air that the north can unbind,
Yet if health do not sweeten the blast with her bloom,
Nor virtue's aroma its pathway perfume,
Unblest is the freedom and dreary the flight,
That but wanders to ruin and wantons to blight!

Farewell to the few I have left with regret,
May they sometimes recall, what I cannot forget,
That communion of heart, and that parley of soul,
Which has lengthened our nights and illumined our bowl,
When they've asked me the manners, the mind, or the mien
Of some bard I had known, or some chief I had seen,
Whose glory, though distant, they long had adored,
Whose name often hallowed the juice of their board!
And still as, with sympathy humble but true,
I told them each luminous trait that I knew,
They have listened, and sighed that the powerful stream
Of America's empire should pass, like a dream,
Without leaving one fragment of genius, to say
How sublime was the tide which had vanished away!
Farewell to the few—though we never may meet
On this planet again, it is soothing and sweet
To think that, whenever my song or my name
Shall recur to their ear, they'll recall me the same
I have been to them now, young, unthoughtful, and blest,
Ere hope had deceived me or sorrow depressed!

But, Douglas! while thus I endear to my mind
The elect of the land we shall soon leave behind,
I can read in the weather-wise glance of thine eye,
As it follows the rack flitting over the sky,
That the faint coming breeze will be fair for our flight,
And shall steal us away ere the falling of night.
Dear Douglas, thou knowest, with thee by my side,
With thy friendship to soothe me, thy courage to guide,
There's not a bleak isle in those summerless seas,
Where the day comes in darkness, or shines but to freeze,
Not a tract of the line, not a barbarous shore,
That I could not with patience, with pleasure explore!

Oh! think then how happy I follow thee now,
When hope smooths the billowy path of our prow,
And each prosperous sigh of the west-springing wind
Takes me nearer the home where my heart is enshrined;
Where the smile of a father shall meet me again,
And the tears of a mother turn bliss into pain;
Where the kind voice of sisters shall steal to my heart,
And ask it, in sighs, how we ever could part!—

But see!—the bent top-sails are ready to swell—
To the boat—I am with thee—Columbia, farewell!

TO LADY H——,

ON AN OLD RING FOUND AT TUNBRIDGE-WELLS.

'Tunnebrige est à la même distance de Londres que Fontainebleau l'est de Paris. Ce qu'il y a de beau et de galant dans l'un et dans l'autre sexe s'y rassemble au temps des eaux. La compagnie,' etc. etc.—See *Mémoires de Grammont*, seconde part. chap. iii.

TUNBRIDGE-WELLS, *August* 1805.

WHEN Grammont graced these happy springs,
And Tunbridge saw, upon her Pantiles,
The merriest wight of all the kings
That ever ruled these gay gallant isles;

Like us, by day they rode, they walked,
At eve they did as we may do,
And Grammont just like Spencer talked,
And lovely Stewart smiled like you!

The only different trait is this,
That woman then, if man beset her,
Was rather given to saying 'yes,'
Because as yet she knew no better!

Each night they held a coterie,
Where, every fear to slumber charmed,
Lovers were all they ought to be,
And husbands not the least alarmed!

They called up all their school-day pranks,
Nor thought it much their sense beneath
To play at riddles, quips, and cranks,
And lords showed wit, and ladies teeth.

As—'Why are husbands like the Mint?'
Because, forsooth, a husband's duty
Is just to set the name and print
That give a currency to beauty.

'Why is a garden's wildered maze
Like a young widow, fresh and fair?'
Because it wants some hand to raise
The weeds, which 'have no business there!'

And thus they missed, and thus they hit,
And now they struck, and now they parried,
And some lay-in of full-grown wit,
While others of a pun miscarried.

'Twas one of those facetious nights
That Grammont gave this forfeit ring,
For breaking grave conundrum rites,
Or punning ill, or—some such thing;

From whence it can be fairly traced
Through many a branch and many a bough,
From twig to twig, until it graced
The snowy hand that wears it now.

All this I'll prove, and then to you,
Oh Tunbridge! and your springs ironical,
I swear by H—tho—te's eye of blue,
To dedicate the important chronicle.

Long may your ancient inmates give
Their mantles to your modern lodgers,
And Charles' loves in H—the—te live,
And Charles' bards revive in Rogers!

Let no pedantic fools be there,
For ever be those fops abolished,
With heads as wooden as thy ware,
And, Heaven knows! not half so polished.

But still receive the mild, the gay,
The few, who know the rare delight
Of reading Grammont every day,
And acting Grammont every night!

TO —— ——.

Never mind how the pedagogue proses,
You want not antiquity's stamp,
The lip that's so scented by roses,
Oh! never must smell of the lamp.

Old Cloe, whose withering kisses
Have long set the loves at defiance,
Now, done with the science of blisses,
May fly to the blisses of science!

Young Sappho, for want of employments,
Alone o'er her Ovid may melt,
Condemned but to read of enjoyments
Which wiser Corinna had felt.

But for *you* to be buried in books—
Oh, Fanny! they're pitiful sages,
Who could not in *one* of your looks
Read more than in millions of pages!

Astronomy finds in your eye
Better light than she studies above,
And music must borrow your sigh
As the melody dearest to love.

In Ethics—'tis you that can check,
In a minute, their doubts and their quarrels;
Oh! show but that mole on your neck,
And 'twill soon put an end to their morals

Your Arithmetic only can trip
When to kiss and to count you endeavour;
But eloquence glows on your lip
When you swear that you'll love me for ever.

Thus you see what a brilliant alliance
Of arts is assembled in you—
A course of more exquisite science
Man never need wish to go through!

And, oh!—if a fellow like me
May confer a diploma of hearts,
With my lip thus I seal your degree,
My divine little Mistress of Arts!

EXTRACT FROM

'THE DEVIL AMONG THE SCHOLARS.'[1]

ΤΙ ΚΑΚΟΝ Ο ΓΕΛΩΣ;
—*Chrysost. Homil. in Epist. ad Hebræos.*

. . . .

But whither have these gentle ones,
The rosy nymphs and black-eyed nuns,
With all of Cupid's wild romancing,
Led my truant brains a-dancing?
Instead of wise encomiastics
Upon the Doctors and Scholastics,
Polymaths, and Polyhistors,
Polyglots and—all their sisters,
The instant I have got the whim in,
Off I fly with nuns and women,
Like epic poets, ne'er at ease
Until I've stolen 'in medias res!'
So have I known a hopeful youth
Sit down, in quest of lore and truth,
With tomes sufficient to confound him,
Like Tohu Bohu, heaped around him—
Mamurra stuck to Theophrastus,
And Galen tumbling o'er Bombastus![2]
When lo! while all that's learned and wise
Absorbs the boy, he lifts his eyes,

---

[1] I promised that I would give the remainder of this poem; but as my critics do not seem to relish the sublime learning which it contains, they shall have no more of it. With a view, however, to the edification of these gentlemen, I have prevailed on an industrious friend of mine, who has read a great number of unnecessary books, to illuminate the extract with a little of his precious erudition.

[2] Bombastus was one of the names of that great scholar and quack Paracelsus. 'Philippus Bombastus latet sub splendido tegmine Aureoli Theophrasti Paracelsi,' says Stadelius de circumforanea Literatorum vanitate.—He used to fight the devil every night with a broad-sword, to the no small terror of his pupil Oporinus, who has recorded the circumstance. Paracelsus had but a poor opinion of Galen. 'My very beard (says he in his *Paragranum*) has more learning in it than either Galen or Avicenna.'

348   EPISTLES, ODES, AND OTHER POEMS.

And through the window of his study
Beholds a virgin, fair and ruddy,
With eyes as brightly turned upon him as
The angel's[1] were on Hieronymus,
Saying, 'twas just as sweet to kiss her—oh!
Far more sweet than reading Cicero!
Quick fly the folios, widely scattered,
Old Homer's laurelled brow is battered,
And Sappho's skin to Tully's leather,
All are confused and tossed together!
Raptured he quits each dozing sage,
Oh woman! for thy lovelier page:
Sweet book! unlike the books of art,
Whose errors are thy fairest part;
In whom the dear errata column
Is the best page in all the volume![2]
But, to begin my subject rhyme—
'Twas just about this devilish time,
When scarce there happened any frolics
That were not done by Diabolics,
A cold and loveless son of Lucifer,
Who woman scorned, nor knew the use of her,
A branch of Dagon's family
(Which Dagon, whether He or She,

Is a dispute that vastly better is
Referred to Scaliger[3] et cæteris),
Finding that, in this cage of fools,
The wisest sots adorn the schools,
Took it at once his head Satanic in,
To grow a great scholastic mannikin,
A doctor, quite as learned and fine as
Scotus John or Tom Aquinas,[4]
Lully, Hales irrefragabilis,
Or any doctor of the rabble is!
In languages,[5] the Polyglots,
Compared to him, were Babel sots;
He chattered more than ever Jew did,
Sanhedrim and Priest included;
Priest and holy Sanhedrim
Were one-and-seventy fools to him!
But chief the learned demon felt a
Zeal so strong for gamma, delta,
That, all for Greek and learning's glory,[6]
He nightly tippled 'Græco more,'
And never paid a bill or balance
Except upon the Grecian Kalends,
From whence your scholars, when they want tick,
Say, to be At-tick's to be on tick!

---

[1] The angel who scolded St. Jerome for reading Cicero, as Gratian tells the story, in his *concordantia discordantium Canonum*, and says that for this reason bishops were not allowed to read the classics. 'Episcopus Gentilium libros non legat.'—*Distinct.* 37. But Gratian is notorious for lying; besides, angels have got no tongues, as the illustrious pupil of Pantenus assures us: Ουχ' ὡς ἡμιν τα ωτα, ουτως εκεινοις ἡ γλωττα· ουδ' αν οργανα τις δεη φωνης αγγελοις.—*Clem. Alexand. Stromat.* Now, how an angel could scold without a tongue, I shall leave the angelic Mrs. —— to determine.

[2] The idea of the Rabbins about the origin of woman is singular. They think that man was originally formed with a tail, like a monkey, but that the Deity cut off this appendage behind, and made woman of it. Upon this extraordinary supposition the following reflection is founded:—

If such is the tie between women and men,
 The ninny who weds is a pitiful elf;
For he takes to his tail, like an idiot, again,
 And he makes a deplorable ape of himself.
Yet, if we may judge as the fashions prevail,
 Every husband remembers the original plan;
And knowing his wife is no more than his tail,
 Why he—leaves her behind him as much as he can.

[3] Scaliger, *de Emendat. Tempor.*—Dagon was thought by others to be a certain sea-monster, who came every day out of the Red Sea to teach the Syrians husbandry.—See Jacques Gaffarel's *Curiosités inouïes*, chap. 1. He says he thinks this story of the sea-monster 'carries little show of probability with it.'

[4] I wish it were known with any degree of certainty whether the *Commentary on Boethius*, attributed to Thomas Aquinas, be really the work of this angelic Doctor. There are some bold assertions hazarded in it: for instance, he says that Plato kept school in a town called Academia, and that Alcibiades was a very beautiful woman whom some of Aristotle's pupils fell in love with: 'Alcibiades mulier fuit pulcherrima, quam videntes quidam discipuli Aristotelis,' etc.—See *Freytag Adparat. Lit'erar.* art. 80, tom. 1.

[5] The following compliment was paid to Laurentius Valla, upon his accurate knowledge of the Latin language:

Nunc postquam manes defunctus Valla petivit,
 Non audet Pluto verba Latina loqui.
Since Val arrived in Pluto's shade,
 His nouns and pronouns all so pat in,
Pluto himself would be afraid
 To ask even 'what's o'clock?' in Latin!

These lines may be found in the *Auctorum Censio* of Du Verdier (page 29), an excellent critic, if he could have either felt or understood any one of the works which he criticises.

[6] It is much to be regretted that Martin Luther, with all his talents for reforming, should yet be vulgar enough to laugh at Camerarius for writing to him in Greek. 'Master Joachim (says he) has sent me some dates and some raisins, and has also written me two letters in Greek. As soon as I am recovered, I shall answer them in Turkish, that he too may have the pleasure of reading what he does not understand.'—Græca sunt, legi non possunt,' is the ignorant speech attributed to Accursius, but very unjustly. Far from asserting that Greek coud not be read, that worthy juris-consult says, 'Græcæ literæ possunt intell.gi et legi' (*Vide Nov. Libror. Rarior. Collection. Fasciculi IV.*)—Scipio Carteromachus seems to think that there is no salvation out of the pale of Greek literature: 'Via prima salutis Graia pandetur ab urbe.' And the zeal of Laurentius Rhodomannus cannot be sufficiently admired, when he exhorts his countrymen, 'per gloriam Christi, per salutem patriæ, per reipublicæ decus et emolumentum,' to study the Greek language. Nor must we forget Phavorinus, the excellent Bishop of Nocera, who, careless of all the usual commendations of a Christian, required no further eulogium on his tomb than 'Here lieth a Greek Lexicographer.'

EPISTLES, ODES, AND OTHER POEMS. 349

In logics, he was quite Ho Panu! [1]
Knew as much as ever man knew.
He fought the combat syllogistic
With so much skill and art eristic,
That though you were the learned Stagyrite,
At once upon the hip he had you right!
Sometimes indeed his speculations
Were viewed as dangerous innovations.
As thus—the Doctor's house did harbour a
Sweet blooming girl, whose name was Barbara;
Oft, when his heart was in a merry key,
He taught this maid his esoterica,
And sometimes, as a cure for hectics,
Would lecture her in dialectics.
How far their zeal let him and her go
Before they came to scaling Ergo,
Or how they placed the medius terminus,
Our chronicles do not determine us;
But so it was—by some confusion
In this their logical prælusion,
The Doctor wholly spoiled, they say,
The figure [2] of young Barbara;
And thus, by many a snare sophistic,
And enthymeme paralogistic,
Beguiled a maid, who could not give,
To save her life, a negative.[3]
In music, though he had no ears
Except for that amongst the spheres
(Which most of all, as he averred it,
He dearly loved, 'cause no one heard it),
Yet aptly he, at sight, could read
Each tuneful diagram in Bede,
And find, by Euclid's corollaria,
The ratios of a jig or aria.
But, as for all your warbling Delias,
Orpheuses and Saint Cecilias,
He owned he thought them much surpassed
By that redoubted Hyaloclast,[4]
Who still contrived, by dint of throttle,
Where'er he went to crack a bottle!

Likewise to show his mighty knowledge, he,
On things unknown in physiology,
Wrote many a chapter to divert us,
Like that great little man Albertus,

Wherein he showed the reason why,
When children first are heard to cry,
If boy the baby chance to be,
He cries, OA!—if girl, OE!—
They are, says he, exceeding fair hints
Respecting their first sinful parents;
'Oh Eve!' exclaimeth little madam,
While little master cries, 'Oh Adam!'[5]

In point of science astronomical,
It seemed to him extremely comical
That, once a year, the frolic sun
Should call at Virgo's house for fun,
And stop a month and blaze around her,
Yet leave her Virgo, as he found her!
But, 'twas in Optics and Dioptrics,
Our demon played his first and top tricks:
He held that sunshine passes quicker
Through wine than any other liquor;
That glasses are the best utensils
To catch the eye's bewildered pencils;
And, though he saw no great objection
To steady light and pure reflection,
He thought the aberrating rays
Which play about a bumper's blaze,
Were by the Doctors looked, in common, on,
As a more rare and rich phenomenon!
He wisely said that the sensorium
Is for the eyes a great emporium,
To which these noted picture stealers
Send all they can, and meet with dealers.
In many an optical proceeding,
The brain, he said, showed great good breeding;
For instance, when we ogle women
(A trick which Barbara tutored him in),
Although the dears are apt to get in a
Strange position on the retina;
Yet instantly the modest brain
Doth set them on their legs again![6]

Our doctor thus with 'stuffed sufficiency
Of all omnigenous omnisciency,
Began (as who would not begin
That had like him, so much within?)

---

[1] 'O ΠΑΝΤ.—The introduction of this language into English poetry has a good effect, and ought to be more universally adopted. A word or two of Greek in a stanza would serve as ballast to the most 'light o' love' verses. Ausonius, among the ancients, may serve as a model:

Ου γαρ μοι θιμις ιστιν in hac regione μυνειν
Αξιον ab nostris ινιδινια esse χαμηναις.

Ronsard, the French poet, has enriched his sonnets and odes with many an exquisite morsel from the Lexicon. His *Chère Entelechie*, in addressing his mistress, is admirable, and can be only matched by Cowley's *Antiperistasis*.

[2] The first figure of simple syllogisms, to which Barbara belongs, together with Celarent, Darii, and Ferio.

[3] Because the three propositions in the mood of Barbara are universal affirmatives.—The poet borrowed this equivoque upon Barbara from a curious Epigram which Menckenius gives in a note upon his *Essays de Charlataneria Eruditorum*. In the *Nuptiæ Peripateticæ* of Caspar Barlæus, the reader will find some facetious applications of the terms of logic to matrimony. Crambe's *Treatise on Syllogisms*, in Martinus Scriblerus, is borrowed chiefly from the *Nuptiæ Peripateticæ* of Barlæus.

[4] Or Glass Breaker.—Morhofius has given an account of this extraordinary man, in a work published 1682. 'De vitreo csypho fracto,' etc.

[5] This is translated almost literally from a passage in *Albertus de Secretis*, etc.—I have not the book by me, or I would transcribe the words.

[6] Alluding to that habitual act of the judgment, by which, notwithstanding the inversion of the image upon the retina, a correct impression of the object is conveyed to the sensorium.

To let it out in books of all sorts,
Folios, quartos, large and small sorts;
Poems, so very deep and sensible,
That they were quite incomprehensible;[1]
Prose which had been at learning's Fair,
And bought up all the trumpery there,
The tattered rags of every vest,
In which the Greeks and Romans dressed,
And o'er her figure, swoln and antic,
Scattered them all with airs so frantic,
That those who saw the fits she had,
Declared unhappy Prose was mad!
Epics he wrote, and scores of rebusses,
All as neat as old Turnebus's;
Eggs and altars, cyclopædias,
Grammars, prayer-books—oh! 'twere tedious,
Did I but tell the half, to follow me;
Not the scribbling bard of Ptolemy,
No—nor the hoary Trismegistus
(Whose writings all, thank Heaven! have missed us),
E'er filled with lumber such a wareroom
As this great 'porcus literarum!'

* * * * * * *

---

[1] Under this description, I believe, '*The Devil among the Scholars*' may be included. Yet Leibnitz found out the uses of incomprehensibility, when he was appointed secretary to a society of philosophers at Nuremberg, merely for his merit in writing a cabalistical letter, one word of which neither they nor himself could interpret. See the *Eloge Historique de M. de Leibnitz, l'Europe Savante*. People in all ages have loved to be puzzled. We find Cicero thanking Atticus for having sent him a work of Sarapion, 'ex quo (says he) quidem ego (quod 'uter nos liceat dicere) millesimam partem vix intelligo.'—Lib. 2, epist. 4. And we know that Avicen, the learned Arabian, read *Aristotle's Metaphysics* forty times over, for the supreme pleasure of being able to inform the world that he could not comprehend one syllable throughout them.—*Nicolas Massa in Vit. Avicen.*

TO SIR HUDSON LOWE.

*Effare causam nominis,
Utrum ne mores hoc tui
Nomen dedere, an nomen hoc
Secuta morum regula.*
—*Ausonius.*

SIR HUDSON LOWE, Sir Hudson *Low*
(By name, and ah! by nature so),
As thou art fond of persecutions,
Perhaps thou'st read, or heard repeated,
How Captain Gulliver was treated,
When thrown among the Lilliputians.

They tied him down—these little men did—
And having valiantly ascended
Upon the Mighty Man's protuberance,
They did so strut!—upon my soul,
It must have been extremely droll
To see their pigmy pride's exuberance!

And how the doughty mannikins
Amused themselves with sticking pins
And needles in the great man's breeches;
And how some *very* little things,
That passed for Lords, on scaffoldings
Got up and worried him with speeches.

Alas, alas! that it should happen
To mighty men to be caught napping!—
Though different, too, these persecutions;
For Gulliver, *there*, took the nap,
While, *here*, the *Nap*, oh sad mishap,
Is taken by the Lilliputians!

MISCELLANEOUS POEMS.

MISCELLANEOUS POEMS.

A MELOLOGUE

UPON NATIONAL MUSIC.

These verses were written for a Benefit at the Dublin Theatre, and were spoken by Miss Smith, with a degree of success, which they owed solely to her admirable manner of reciting them. I wrote them in haste; and it very rarely happens that poetry which has cost but little labour to the writer, is productive of any great pleasure to the reader. Under this impression, I should not have published them if they had not found their way into some of the newspapers, with such an addition of errors to their own original stock, that I thought it but fair to limit their responsibility to those faults alone which really belong to them.

With respect to the title which I have invented for this Poem, I feel even more than the scruples of the Emperor Tiberius, when he humbly asked pardon of the Roman senate for using 'the outlandish term *monopoly*.' But the truth is, having written the Poem with the sole view of serving a Benefit, I thought that an unintelligible word of this kind would not be without its attraction for the multitude, with whom, 'if 'tis not sense, at least 'tis Greek.' To some of my readers, however, it may not be superfluous to say, that by 'Melologue' I mean that mixture of recitation and music which is frequently adopted in the performance of Collins's *Ode on the Passions*, and of which the most striking example I can remember is the prophetic speech of Joad in the *Athalie* of Racine.

T. M.

There breathes a language, known and felt
Far as the pure air spreads its living zone;
Wherever rage can rouse, or pity melt,
That language of the soul is felt and known.
From those meridian plains,
Where oft, of old, on some high tower,
The soft Peruvian poured his midnight strains,
And called his distant love with such sweet power,[1]

That, when she heard the lonely lay,
Not worlds could keep her from his arms away;
To the bleak climes of polar night,
Where, beneath a sunless sky,
The Lapland lover bids his reindeer fly,
And sings along the lengthening waste of snow,
As blithe as if the blessed light
Of vernal Phœbus burned upon his brow.
Oh music! thy celestial claim
Is still resistless, still the same;
And, faithful as the mighty sea
To the pale star that o'er its realm presides,
The spell-bound tides
Of human passion rise and fall for thee!

Greek Air.

List! 'tis a Grecian maid that sings,
While, from Ilyssus' silvery springs,
She draws the cool lymph in her graceful urn;
And by her side, in music's charm dissolving,
Some patriot youth, the glorious past revolving,
Dreams of bright days that never can return!
When Athens nursed her olive-bough,
With hands by tyrant power unchained,
And braided for the muses' brow
A wreath by tyrant touch unstained.
When heroes trod each classic field
Where coward feet now faintly falter;
When every arm was Freedom's shield,
And every heart was Freedom's altar!

Flourish of Trumpet.

Hark! 'tis the sound that charms
The war-steed's wakening ears!—
Oh! many a mother folds her arms
Round her boy-soldier when that call she hears;
And, though her fond heart sink with fears,
Is proud to feel his young pulse bound
With valour's fever at the sound!
See! from his native hills afar
The rude Helvetian flies to war;
Careless for what, for whom he fights,
For slave or despot, wrongs or rights;

---

[1] 'A certain Spaniard, one night late, met an Indian woman in the streets of Cozco, and would have taken her to his home; but she cried out, "For God's sake, Sir, let me go; for that pipe which you hear in yonder tower calls me with great passion, and I cannot refuse the summons; for love constrains me to go, that I may be his wife, and he my husband."'—*Garcilasso de la Vega*, in Sir Paul Rycaut's translation.

A conqueror oft—a hero never—
  Yet lavish of his life-blood still,
As if 'twere like his mountain rill,
  And gushed for ever!

Oh Music! here, even here,
  Amid this thoughtless, wild career,
Thy soul-felt charm asserts its wondrous power.
There is an air, which oft among the rocks
Of his own loved land, at evening hour,
  Is heard, when shepherds homeward pipe their flocks;
Oh! every note of it would thrill his mind
  With tenderest thoughts—would bring around his knees
The rosy children whom he left behind,
  And fill each little angel eye
With speaking tears, that ask him why
He wandered from his hut for scenes like these?
Vain, vain is then the trumpet's brazen roar;
Sweet notes of home—of love—are all he hears;
And the stern eyes, that looked for blood before,
Now melting, mournful, lose themselves in tears!

Swiss Air—'Ranz des Vaches.'

But, wake the trumpet's blast again,
  And rouse the ranks of warrior men!
Oh War! when Truth thy arm employs,
And Freedom's spirit guides the labouring storm,
'Tis then thy vengeance takes a hallowed form,
  And, like Heaven's lightning, sacredly destroys!
Nor, Music! through thy breathing sphere,
Lives there a sound more grateful to the ear
  Of Him who made all harmony,
Than the blessed sound of fetters breaking,
And the first hymn that man, awaking
From Slavery's slumber, breathes to Liberty!

Spanish Chorus.

Hark! from Spain, indignant Spain,
Bursts the bold, enthusiast strain,
Like morning's music on the air!
And seems, in every note, to swear
  By Saragossa's ruined streets,
By brave Gerona's deathful story,
That, while *one* Spaniard's life-blood beats,
  That blood shall stain the conqueror's glory!

Spanish Air—'Ya Desperto.'

But ah! if vain the patriot's zeal,
If neither valour's force nor wisdom's light
Can break or melt that blood-cemented seal
Which shuts so close the book of Europe's right—
  What song shall then in sadness tell
Of broken pride, of prospects shaded,
Of buried hopes, remembered well,
Of ardour quenched, and honour faded?
  What Muse shall mourn the breathless brave,
  In sweetest dirge at Memory's shrine?
What harp shall sigh o'er Freedom's grave?
  Oh Erin! thine!

LINES

ON THE DEATH OF MR. P—n—v—l.

In the dirge we sung o'er him no censure was heard,
  Unembittered and free did the tear-drop descend;
We forgot in that hour how the statesman had erred,
  And wept, for the husband, the father and friend.

Oh! proud was the meed his integrity won,
  And generous indeed were the tears that we shed,
When in grief we forgot all the ill he had done,
  And, though wronged by him living, bewailed him when dead.

Even now, if one harsher emotion intrude,
  'Tis to wish he had chosen some lowlier state—
Had known what he was, and, content to be *good*,
  Had ne'er for our ruin aspired to be *great*.

So, left through their own little orbit to move,
  His years might have rolled inoffensive away;
His children might still have been blessed with his love,
  And England would ne'er have been cursed with his sway.

LINES

ON THE DEATH OF SH—R—D—N.

Principibus placuisse viris.—*Hor.*

Yes, grief will have way—but the fast-falling tear
  Shall be mingled with deep execrations on those
Who could bask in that spirit's meridian career,
  And yet leave it thus lonely and dark at its close:—

Whose vanity flew round him only while fed
  By the odour his fame in its summer-time gave;
Whose vanity now, with quick scent for the dead,
  Like the ghole of the East, comes to feed at his grave!

Oh! it sickens the heart to see bosoms so hollow
  And spirits so mean in the great and high-born;
To think what a long line of titles may follow
  The relics of him who died—friendless and lorn!

How proud they can press to the funeral array
  Of one whom they shunned in his sickness and sorrow:—
How bailiffs may seize his last blanket to-day,
  Whose pall shall be held up by nobles to-morrow!

And thou, too, whose life, a sick epicure's dream,
  Incoherent and gross, even grosser had passed,
Were it not for that cordial and soul-giving beam
  Which his friendship and wit o'er thy nothing-
    ness cast;

No, not for the wealth of the land that supplies
    thee
  With millions to heap upon foppery's shrine;—
No, not for the riches of all who despise thee,
  Though this would make Europe's whole
    opulence mine;—

Would I suffer what—even in the heart that
    thou hast,
  All mean as it is—must have consciously
    burned,
When the pittance, which shame had wrung from
    thee at last,
  And which found all his wants at an end, was
    returned![1]

'Was *this*, then, the fate'—future ages will say,
  When *some* names shall live but in history's
    curse;
When Truth will be heard, and these lords of a day
  Be forgotten as fools, or remembered as worse—

'Was this, then, the fate of that high-gifted man,
  The pride of the palace, the bower, and the hall,
The orator—dramatist—minstrel,—who ran
  Through each mode of the lyre, and was
    master of all!

'Whose mind was an essence, compounded with
    art
  From the finest and best of all other men's
    powers—
Who ruled, like a wizard, the world of the heart,
  And could call up its sunshine, or bring down
    its showers!

'Whose humour, as gay as the fire-fly's light,
  Played round every subject, and shone as it
    played—
Whose wit, in the combat, as gentle as bright,
  Ne'er carried a heart-stain away on its blade;—

'Whose eloquence—brightening whatever it tried,
  Whether reason or fancy, the gay or the grave—
Was as rapid, as deep, and as brilliant a tide
  As ever bore Freedom aloft on its wave!'

Yes—such was the man, and so wretched his
    fate;—
  And thus, sooner or later, shall all have to
    grieve,

Who waste their morn's dew in the beams of the
    Great,
  And expect 'twill return to refresh them at eve!

In the woods of the North there are insects that
    prey
  On the brain of the elk till his very last sigh;[2]
Oh, Genius! thy patrons, more cruel than they,
  First feed on thy brains, and then leave thee
    to die!

LINES

WRITTEN ON HEARING THAT THE AUSTRIANS HAD
ENTERED NAPLES.

Carbone Notati!

AY—down to the dust with them, slaves as they
    are—
  From this hour, let the blood in their dastardly
    veins,
That shrunk at the first touch of Liberty's war,
  Be sucked out by tyrants, or stagnate in chains!

On, on, like a cloud, through their beautiful vales,
  Ye locusts of tyranny, blasting them o'er—
Fill, fill up their wide sunny waters, ye sails
  From each slave-mart of Europe, and poison
    their shore!

Let their fate be a mock-word—let men of all
    lands
  Laugh out, with a scorn that shall ring to the
    poles,
When each sword that the cowards let fall from
    their hands
  Shall be forged into fetters to enter their souls!

And deep and more deep as the iron is driven,
  Base slaves! may the whet of their agony be,
To think—as the damned haply think of that
    heaven
  They had once in their reach—that they might
    have been free!

Shame, shame, when there was not a bosom,
    whose heat
  Ever rose o'er the ZERO of ———'s heart,
That did not, like echo, your war-hymn repeat,
  And send all its prayers with your liberty's
    start—

When the world stood in hope—when a spirit,
    that breathed
  The fresh air of the olden time, whispered
    about,

---

[1] The sum was two hundred pounds—*offered* when Sh-r-d-n could no longer take any sustenance, and declined for him by his friends.

[2] Naturalists have observed that, upon dissecting an elk, there were found in its head some *large* flies, with its brain almost eaten away by them.—*History of Poland.*

And the swords of all Italy, half-way unsheathed,
But waited one conquering cry to flash out!

When around you, the shades of your mighty in fame,
Filicajas and Petrarchs, seemed bursting to view,
And their words and their warnings — like tongues of bright flame
Over Freedom's apostles—fell kindling on you!

Good God! that in such a proud moment of life,
Worth the history of ages—when, had you but hurled
One bolt at your bloody invader, that strife
Between freemen and tyrants had spread through the world—

That then—oh disgrace upon manhood! even then,
You should falter, should cling to your pitiful breath,
Cower down into beasts, when you might have stood men,
And prefer the slave's life of damnation to death!

It is strange—it is dreadful;—shout, tyranny, shout,
Through your dungeons and palaces, 'Freedom is o'er!'—
If there lingers one spark of her light, tread it out,
And return to your empire of darkness once more.

For if such are the braggarts that claim to be free,
Come, Despot of Russia, thy feet let me kiss—
Far nobler to live the brute bondman of thee,
Than to sully even chains by a struggle like this!

Paris, 1821.

THE INSURRECTION OF THE PAPERS.

A DREAM.

'It would be impossible for His Royal Highness to disengage his person from the accumulating pile of papers that encompassed it.'—*Lord Castlereagh's Speech upon Colonel M'Mahon's Appointment.*

LAST night I tossed and turned in bed,
But could not sleep—at length I said,
'I'll think of Viscount C-stl-r—gh,
And of his speeches—that's the way.'
And so it was, for instantly
I slept as sound as sound could be;
And then I dreamed—oh, frightful dream!
Fuseli has no such theme;

—— never wrote or borrowed
Any horror half so horrid!

Methought the P——e, in whiskered state,
Before me at his breakfast sate:
On one side lay unread petitions,
On t'other, hints from five physicians;
Here tradesmen's bills, official papers,
Notes from my Lady, drams for vapours—
There plans of saddles, tea and toast,
Death-warrants and the Morning Post.

When lo! the Papers, one and all,
As if at some magician's call,
Begun to flutter of themselves
From desk and table, floor and shelves,
And, cutting each some different capers,
Advanced—oh jacobinic papers!—
As though they said, 'Our soul design is
To suffocate his Royal Highness!'
The leader of this vile sedition
Was a huge Catholic Petition:
With grievances so full and heavy,
It threatened worst of all the bevy.
Then Common-Hall Addresses came
In swaggering sheets, and took their aim
Right at the R-g-nt's well-dressed head,
As if *determined* to be read!
Next Tradesmen's Bills began to fly—
And tradesmen's bills, we know, mount high;
Nay, even death-warrants thought they'd best
Be lively too, and join the rest.

But oh.—the basest of defections!
His letter about 'predilections'—
His own dear letter, void of grace,
Now flew up in its parent's face!
Shocked with this breach of filial duty,
He just could murmur, '*Et tu Brute!*'
Then sunk, subdued, upon the floor,
At Fox's bust, to rise no more!

I waked—and prayed, with lifted hand,
'Oh! never may this dream prove true
Though paper overwhelms the land,
Let it not crush the Sovereign too!'

PARODY OF A CELEBRATED LETTER.

AT length, dearest Freddy, the moment is nigh,
When, with P-rc-v-l's leave, I may throw my chains by;
And, as time now is precious, the first thing I do
Is to sit down and write a wise letter to you.
. . . .
I meant before now to have sent you this letter,
But Y-rm—th and I thought perhaps 'twould be better

To wait till the Irish affairs were decided—
That is, till both Houses had prosed and divided,
With all due appearance of thought and digestion—
For though H–rtf–rd House had long settled the question,
I thought it but decent, between me and you,
That the two *other* Houses should settle it too.

I need not remind you how cursedly bad
Our affairs were all looking when Father went mad;
A strait-waistcoat on him, and restrictions on me,—
A more *limited* monarchy could not well be.
I was called upon then, in that moment of puzzle,
To choose my own minister—just as they muzzle
A playful young bear, and then mock his disaster
By bidding him choose out his own dancing-master.

I thought the best way, as a dutiful son,
Was to do as old Royalty's self would have done.
So I sent word to say I would keep the whole batch in,
The same chest of tools, without cleansing or patching—
For tools of this kind, like Martinus's sconce,¹
Would lose all their beauty if purified once;
And think—only think—if our Father should find,
Upon graciously coming again to his mind,
That improvement had spoiled any favourite adviser—
That R-se was grown honest, or W-stm-rel-nd wiser—
That R-d-r was, even by one twinkle, the brighter—
Or L-v-r-p-l's speeches but half a pound lighter—
What a shock to his old royal heart it would be!
No!—far were such dreams of improvement from me,
And it pleased me to find at the house where, you know,
There's such good mutton-cutlets and strong curaçoa,²
That the Marchioness called me a duteous old boy,
And my Y-rm—th's red whiskers grew redder for joy!

You know, my dear Freddy, how oft, if I *would*,
By the law of last Sessions, I *might* have done good.
I *might* have withheld these political noodles
From knocking their heads against hot Yankee Doodles;

---

¹ The antique shield of Martinus Scriblerus, which, upon scouring, turned out to be only an old sconce.
² The letter-writer's favourite luncheon.

I *might* have told Ireland I pitied her lot,
Might have soothed her with hope—but you know I did not.
And my wish is, in truth, that the best of old fellows
Should not, on recovering, have cause to be jealous,
But find that, while he has been laid on the shelf,
We've been all of us nearly as mad as himself.
You smile at my hopes, but the doctors and I
Are the last that can think the K–ng *ever* will die!

A new era's arrived—though you'd hardly believe it—
And all things, of course, must be new to receive it,
New villas, new fêtes (which even Waithman attends)—
New saddles, new helmets, and—why not *new friends?*

. . . .
. . . .

I repeat it, 'new friends'—for I cannot describe
The delight I am in with this P–rc–v–l tribe.
Such capering—such vapouring!—such rigour
—such vigour!
North, South, East, and West, they have out such a figure,
That soon they will bring the whole world round our ears,
And leave us no friends—but Old Nick and Algiers.
When I think of the glory they've beamed on my chains,
'Tis enough quite to turn my illustrious brains;
It's true we are bankrupts in commerce and riches,
But think how we furnish our Allies with breeches!
We've lost the warm hearts of the Irish, 'tis granted,
But then we've got Java, an island much wanted,
To put the last lingering few who remain
Of the Walcheren warriors out of their pain.
Then, how Wellington fights! and how squabbles his brother!
For papists the one, and *with* papists the other;
One crushing Napoleon by taking a city,
While t'other lays waste a whole Catholic Committee!
Oh, deeds of renown! shall I baggle or flinch,
With such prospects before me?—by Jove, not an inch.
No—let *England's* affairs go to rack if they will,
We'll look after the affairs of the *Continent* still,
And, with nothing at home but starvation and riot,
Find Lisbon in bread, and keep Sicily quiet.
I am proud to declare I have no predilections.—
My heart is a sieve, where some scattered affections

Are just danced about for a moment or two,
And the *finer* they are, the more sure to run through:
Neither have I resentments, nor wish there should come ill
To mortal—except (now I think on't) Beau Br—mm—l,
Who threatened, last year, in a superfine passion,
To cut *me*, and bring the old K—ng into fashion.
This is all I can lay to my conscience at present.
When such is my temper, so neutral, so pleasant,
So royally free from all troublesome feelings,
So little encumbered by faith in my dealings
(And, that I'm consistent, the world will allow,—
What I was at Newmarket, the same I am now)—
When such are my merits (you know I hate cracking),
I hope, like the vender of best Patent Blacking,
'To meet with the generous and kind approbation
Of a candid, enlightened, and liberal nation.'

By the by, ere I close this magnificent letter
(No man except Pole could have writ you a better),
'Twould please me if those, whom I've humbugged so long
With the notion (good men!) that I knew right from wrong.
Would a few of them join me—mind, only a few—
To let *too* much light in on me never would do;
But even Grey's brightness shan't make me afraid,
While I've C—md—n and Eld—n to fly to for shade;
Nor will Holland's clear intellect do us much harm,
While there's W—stm—rel—nd near him to weaken the charm.
As for Moira's high spirit, if aught can subdue it,
Sure joining with H—rtf—rd and Y—rm—th will do it!
Between R—d—r and Wh—rt—n let Sheridan sit,
And their fogs will soon quench even Sheridan's wit;
And against all the pure public feeling that glows
Even in Whitbread himself we've a host in G—rge R—se!
So, in short, if they wish to have places, they may,
And I'll thank you to tell all these matters to Grey,
Who, I doubt not, will write (as there's no time to lose)
By the twopenny post, to tell Grenville the news;
And now, dearest Fred (though I've no predilection),
Believe me yours always with truest affection.

P. S.—A copy of this is to P—rc—v—l going—
Good Lord! how St. Stephen's will ring with his crowing!

ANACREONTIC.

TO A PLUMASSIER.

Fine and feathery artisan!
Best of Plumists, if you can
With your art so far presume,
Make for me a P——e's plume—
Feathers soft and feathers rare,
Such as suits a P——e to wear!

First, thou downiest of men!
Seek me out a fine pea-hen;
Such a hen, so tall and grand,
As by Juno's side might stand,
If there were no cocks at hand!
Seek her feathers, soft as down,
Fit to shine on P——e's crown;
If thou canst not find them, stupid!
Ask the way of Prior's Cupid.

Ranging these in order due,
Pluck me next an old cuckoo;
Emblem of the happy fates
Of easy, kind, cornuted mates!
Pluck him well—be sure you do—
Who wouldn't be an old cuckoo,
Thus to have his plumage blest,
Beaming on a r—y—l crest?

Bravo, Plumist!—now what bird
Shall we find for plume the third?
You must get a learned owl,
Blackest of black-letter fowl—
Bigot bird that hates the light,
Foe to all that's fair and bright!
Seize his quills (so formed to pen
Books that shun the search of men,—
Books that far from every eye,
In 'sweltered venom sleeping' lie!)
Stick them in, between the two,
Proud pea-hen and old cuckoo!

Now you have the triple feather,
Bind the kindred stems together
With a silken tie whose hue
Once was brilliant buff and blue;
Sullied now—alas! how much!—
Only fit for Y—rm—th's touch.
There—enough—thy task is done;
Present worthy G——ge's son!
Now beneath, in letters neat,
Write 'I SERVE,' and all's complete.

EXTRACTS

FROM THE DIARY OF A POLITICIAN.

Wednesday.

Through M—nch—st—r Square took a canter just now—
Met the *old yellow chariot*, and made a low bow

This I did, of course, thinking 'twas loyal and civil,
But got such a look—oh, 'twas black as the devil!
How unlucky!—*incog.* he was travelling about,
And I, like a noodle, must go find him out!

Mem.—When next by the old yellow chariot I ride,
To remember there *is* nothing princely inside.

Thursday.

At Levee to-day made another sad blunder—
What *can* be come over me lately, I wonder?
The P——e was as cheerful as if, all his life,
He had never been troubled with Friends or a Wife—
'Fine weather,' says he—to which I, who *must* prate,
Answered, 'Yes, Sir, but *changeable* rather, of late.'
He took it, I fear, for he looked rather gruff,
And handled his new pair of whiskers so rough,
That before all the courtiers I feared they'd come off,
And then, Lord! how Geramb would triumphantly scoff!

Mem.—To buy for son Dicky some unguent or lotion
To nourish his whiskers—sure road to promotion![1]

Saturday.

Last night a concert—vastly gay—
Given by Lady C-stl-r-gh.
My Lord loves music, and, we know,
Has two strings always to his bow.
In choosing songs, the R-g-nt named
'Had I a heart for falsehood framed.'
While gentle H-rtf-rd begged and prayed
For '*Young I am, and sore afraid.*'

KING CRACK[2] AND HIS IDOLS.

WRITTEN AFTER THE LATE NEGOTIATION FOR
A NEW M-N-STRY.

KING CRACK was the best of all possible kings
(At least so his courtiers would swear to you gladly),
But Crack now and then would do het'rodox things,
And, at last, took to worshipping *Images* sadly.

Some broken-down Idols, that long had been placed
In his Father's old *Cabinet*, pleased him so much
That he knelt down and worshipped, though—
such was his taste!—
They were monsters to look at and rotten to touch!

And these were the beautiful Gods of King Crack!—
Till his people, disdaining to worship such things,
Cried aloud, one and all, 'Come, your Godships must pack—
You will not do for *us*, though you *may* do for *Kings*.'

Then trampling the gross Idols under their feet,
They sent Crack a petition, beginning, 'Great Cæsar!
We are willing to worship, but only entreat
That you'll find us some *decenter* Godhead than these are.'

'I'll try,' says King Crack—then they furnished him models
Of better shaped Gods, but he sent them all back;
Some were chiselled too fine, some had heads 'stead of noddles,
In short, they were all *much* too godlike for Crack!

So he took to his darling old Idols again,
And, just mending their legs and new bronzing their faces,
In open defiance of gods and of men,
Set the monsters up grinning once more in their places!

WREATHS FOR THE MINISTERS.

AN ANACREONTIC.

HITHER, Flora, Queen of Flowers!
Haste thee from old Brompton's bowers—

---

[1] England is not the only country where merit of this kind is noticed and rewarded. 'I remember,' says Tavernier, 'to have seen one of the King of Persia's porters, whose mustachios were so long that he could tie them behind his neck, for which reason he had a double pension.'

[2] One of those antediluvian princes with whom Manetho and Whiston seem so intimately acquain'ed. If we had the Memoirs of Thoth, from which Manetho compiled his history, we should find, I dare say, that Crack was only a Regent, and that he perhaps succeeded Typhon, who (as Whiston says) was the last king of the antediluvian dynasty.

Or (if sweeter that abode)
From the King's well-odoured Road,
Where each little nursery bud
Breathes the dust and quaffs the mud!
Hither come, and gaily twine
Brightest herbs and flowers of thine
Into wreaths for those who rule us—
Those who rule and (some say) fool us:
Flora, sure, will love to please
England's HOUSEHOLD DEITIES![1]

First you must then, willy-nilly,
Fetch me many an orange lily—
Orange of the darkest dye
Irish G-ff-rd can supply!
Choose me out the longest sprig,
And stick it in old Eld-n's wig!

Find me next a poppy-posy,
Type of his harangues so dozy,
Garland gaudy, dull and cool,
For the head of L-v-rp—l!—
'Twill console his brilliant brows
For that loss of laurel boughs
Which they suffered (what a pity!)
On the road to Paris City.

Next, our C-stl-r—gh to crown,
Bring me, from the County Down,
Withered shamrocks, which have been
Gilded o'er to hide the green—
(Such as H—df—t brought away
From Pall-Mall last Patrick's Day.)[2]
Stitch the garland through and through
With shabby threads *of every hue*—
And as, Goddess!—*entre nous*—
His Lordship loves (though best of men)
A little *torture* now and then,
Crimp the leaves, thou first of syrens!
Crimp them with thy curling-irons.

That's enough—away, away—
Had I leisure, I could say
How the *oldest rose* that grows
Must be plucked to deck Old R-se,—
How the Doctor's brow should smile
Crowned with leaves of camomile!
But time presses.—To thy taste
I leave the rest; so, prithee, haste!

THE NEW COSTUME OF THE MINISTERS.

Nova monstra creavit.—*Ovid. Met.* lib. i. ver. 437.

HAVING sent off the troops of brave Major Camac,
With a swinging horse-tail at each valorous back,
And such helmets— God bless us!— as never decked any
Male creature before, except Signor Giovanni—
'Let's see,' said the R-g-nt (like Titus, perplexed
With the duties of empire), 'whom *shall* I dress next?'
He looks in the glass—but perfection is there,
Wig, whiskers, and chin-tufts, all right to a hair;[3]
Not a single *ex*-curl on his forehead he traces—
For curls are like Ministers, strange as the case is,
The *falser* they are, the more firm in their places.

His coat he next views—but the coat who could doubt?
For his Y-rm—th's own Frenchified hand cut it out;
Every pucker and seam were made matters of state,
And a grand Household Council was held on each plait!

Then whom shall he dress? Shall the new rig his brother,
Great C-mb-rl-nd's Duke, with some kickshaw or other?
And kindly invent him more Christian-like shapes
For his feather-bed neckcloths and pillory capes?
Ah! no—here his ardour would meet with delays,
For the Duke had been lately packed up in new Stays,
So complete for the winter, he saw very plain
'Twould be devilish hard work to *un*pack him again!

So what's to be done?—there's the Ministers, bless 'em!—
As he *made* the puppets, why shouldn't he *dress* 'em?

---

[1] The ancients, in like manner, crowned their lares, or household gods. See *Juvenal, Sat.* 9, v. 138. Plutarch, too, tells us that household gods were then, as they are now, 'much given to war and penal statutes:' ερινυωδεις και ποινιμους δαιμονας.

[2] Certain tinsel imitations of the Shamrock, which are distributed by the servants of C——n House every Patrick's Day.

[3] That model of princes, the Emperor Commodus, was particularly luxurious in the dressing and ornamenting of his hair. His conscience, however, would not suffer him to trust himself with a barber, and he used, accordingly, to burn off his beard. 'Timore tonsoris,' says Lampridius.—(*Hist. August. Scriptor.*) The dissolute Ælius Verus, too, was equally attentive to the decoration of his wig.—(See *Jul. Capitolin.*) Indeed, this was not the *only* princely trait in the character of Verus, as he had likewise a most hearty and dignified contempt for his wife.—See his insulting answer to her in *Spartianus*.

'An excellent thought!—call the tailors — be nimble—
Let Cum bring his spy-glass, and H-rtf-rd her thimble;
While Y-rm—th shall give us, in spite of all quizzers,
The last Paris cut with his true Gallic scissors.'

So saying, he calls C-stl-r—gh, and the rest
Of his heaven-born statesmen, to come and be dressed.
While Y-r-m—th, with snip-like and brisk expedition,
Cuts up, all at once, a large Catholic Petition
In long tailors' measures (the P——e crying,
'Well done!')
And first *puts in hand* my Lord Chancellor Eld-n.

* * * * * *

———.

OCCASIONAL ADDRESS,

For the Opening of the New Theatre of St. St-ph-n, intended to have been spoken by the Proprietor, in full Costume, on the 24th of November.

This day a New House, for your edification,
We open, most thinking and right-headed nation!
Excuse the materials—though rotten and bad,
They're the best that for money just now could be had;
And, if *echo* the charm of such houses should be,
You will find it shall echo my speech to a T.

As for actors, we've got the old Company yet,
The same motley, odd, tragi-comical set:
Aud, considering they all were but clerks t'other day,
It is truly surprising how well they can play.
Our Manager (he who in Ulster was nursed,
And sung *Erin go Brogh* for the galleries first,
But, on finding *Pitt*-interest a much better thing,
Changed his note, of a sudden, to—*God save the King!*)
Still wise as he's blooming, and fat as he's clever,
Himself and his speeches as *lengthy* as ever,
Here offers you still the full use of his breath,
Your devoted and long-winded proser till death!

You remember, last season, when things went perverse on,
We had to engage (as a block to rehearse on)
One Mr. V-ns-tt-rt, a good sort of person,
Who's also employed for this season to play
In 'Raising the Wind,' and 'The Devil to Pay.'
We expect too—at least we've been plotting and planning—
To get that great actor from Liverpool, C-nn-ng;

And, as at the Circus there's nothing attracts
Like a good *single combat* brought in 'twixt the acts,
If the Manager should, with the help of Sir P-ph-m,
Get up new *diversions*, and C-nn-ng should stop 'em,
Who knows but we'll have to announce in the papers,
'Grand fight — second time — with additional capers!'
Be your taste for the ludicrous, humdrum, or sad,
There is plenty of each in this House to be had;
Where our Manager ruleth, there weeping will be,
For a *dead hand at tragedy* always was he;
And there never was dealer in dagger and cup,
Who so *smilingly* got all his tragedies up.
His powers poor Ireland will never forget,
And the widows of Walcheren weep o'er them yet.

So much for the actors.—For secret machinery,
Traps, and deceptions, and shifting of scenery,
Y-rm—th and Cum are the best we can find
To transact all that trickery business behind.
The former's employed too to teach us French jigs,
Keep the whiskers in curl, and look after the wigs.

In taking my leave, now I've only to say
A few *Seats in the House*, not as yet sold away,
May be had of the Manager, Pat C-stl-r—gh.

———

THE SALE OF THE TOOLS.

Instrumenta regni.—*Tacitus.*

Here's a choice set of Tools for you, Gemmen and Ladies,
They'll fit you quite handy, whatever your trade is,
(Except it be *Cabinet-making*—I doubt
In that delicate service they are rather worn out;
Though their owner—bright youth!—if he'd had his own will,
Would have bungled away with them joyously still).
You can see they've been pretty well *hacked*—and, slack!
What tool is there job after job will not back?
Their edge is but dullish, it must be confessed,
And their temper, like Ell-nb'r—gh's, none of the best;
But you'll find them good hard-working Tools, upon trying—
Were it but for their *brass*, they are well worth the buying;
They are famous for making *blinds, sliders,* and *screens,*
And they're, some of them, excellent *turning machines!*

The first Tool I'll put up (they call it a *Chancellor*)
Heavy concern to both purchaser and seller.—
Though made of pig-iron, yet (worthy of note 'tis)
'Tis ready to melt at a half-minute's notice.
Who bids? Gentle buyer! 'twill turn as thou shapest—
'Twill make a good thumb-screw to torture a Papist;
Or else a cramp-iron, to stick in the wall
Of some church that old women are fearful will fall;
Or better, perhaps (for I'm guessing at random),
A heavy *drag chain* for some Lawyer's old *Tandem!*
Will nobody bid? It is cheap, I am sure, Sir—
Once, twice—going, going—thrice—gone!—It is yours, Sir.
To pay ready money you sha'n't be distressed,
As a *bill* at *long date* suits the Chancellor best.

Come, where's the next Tool?—Oh! 'tis here in a trice—
This implement, Gemmen! at first was a *Vice*—
(A tenacious and close sort of Tool, that will let
Nothing out of its grasp it once happens to get)—
But it since has received a new coating of *Tin*,
Bright enough for a Prince to behold himself in!
Come, what shall we say for it?—briskly! bid on,
We'll the sooner get rid of it—going—quite gone!
God be with it! Such Tools, if not quickly knocked down,
Might at last cost their owner—how much?—why, a *Crown!*

The next Tool I'll set up has hardly had handsel or
Trial as yet, and is *also* a Chancellor—
Such dull things as these should be sold by the gross;
Yet, dull as it is, 'twill be found to *shave close*,
And, *like* other close shavers, some courage to gather,
This *blade* first began by a flourish on *leather!*
You shall have it for nothing—then, marvel with me
At the terrible *tinkering* work there must be,
Where a Tool, such as this is (I'll leave you to judge it)
Is placed by ill luck at the top of *the Budget!*

LITTLE MAN AND LITTLE SOUL.

A Ballad to the Tune of 'There was a little Man, and he wooed a little Maid,' dedicated to the Right Hon. Ch—rl—s Abb—t.

Arcades ambo
Et cant-are pares.

1813.

There was a little Man, and he had a little Soul,
And he said, 'Little Soul, let us try, try, try,
Whether it's within our reach
To make up a little speech,
Just between little you and little I, I, I,
Just between little you and little I I!'

Then said his little Soul,
Peeping from her little hole,
'I protest, little Man, you are stout, stout, stout,
But, if 'tis not uncivil,
Pray tell me, what the devil
Must our little, little speech be about, bout, bout,
Must our little, little speech be about?'

The little Man looked big,
With the assistance of his wig,
And he called his little Soul to order, order, order,
Till she feared he'd make her jog in
To jail, like Thomas Croggan,
(As she wasn't duke or earl) to reward her, ward her, ward her,
As she wasn't duke or earl, to reward her.

The little Man then spoke:
'Little Soul, it is no joke,
For, as sure as J—cky F—ll—r loves a sup, sup, sup,
I will tell the Prince and People
What I think of Church and Steeple,
And my little patent plan to prop them up, up, up,
And my little patent plan to prop them up.'

Away then, cheek by jowl,
Little Man and little Soul
Went, and spoke their little speech to a tittle, tittle, tittle,
And the world all declare
That this priggish little pair
Never yet in all their lives looked so little, little, little,
Never yet in all their lives looked so little.

REINFORCEMENTS FOR LORD WELLINGTON.

Suosque tibi commendat Troja penates,
Hos cape fatorum comites.—*Virgil.*

1813.

As recruits in these times are not easily got,
And the Marshal *must* have them—pray, why should we not,
As the last and, I grant it, the worst of our loans to him,
Ship off the Ministry, body and bones, to him?
There's not in all England, I'd venture to swear,
Any men we could half so conveniently spare;
And, though they've been helping the French for years past,
We may thus make them useful to England at last.
C—stl—r—gh in our sieges might save some disgraces,
Being used to the *taking* and *keeping* of *places;*

And Volunteer C—nn—ng, still ready for joining,
Might show off his talent for sly *undermining*.
Could the Household but spare us its glory and pride,
Old H—df—t at *horn-works* again might be tried,
And the Ch—f J—st—ce make a *bold charge* at his side!
While V—ns—tt—rt could victual the troops *upon tick*,
And the Doctor look after the baggage and sick.

Nay, I do not see why the great R—g—nt himself
Should, in times such as these, stay at home on the shelf:—
Though through narrow defiles he's not fitted to pass,
Yet who could resist if he bore down *en masse?*
And though oft, of an evening, perhaps he might prove,
Like our brave Spanish Allies, 'unable to move;'[1]
Yet there's *one* thing in war, of advantage unbounded,
Which is, that he could not with ease be *surrounded!*

In my next I shall sing of their arms and equipment.
At present no more but—good luck to the shipment!

LORD WELLINGTON AND THE MINISTERS.
1813.

So gently in peace Alcibiades smiled,
While in battle he shone forth so terribly grand,
That the emblem they graved on his seal was a child,
With a thunderbolt placed in its innocent hand.

Oh, Wellington! long as such Ministers wield
Your magnificent arm, the same emblem will do;
For, while they're in the Council and you in the Field,
We've the *babies* in *them*, and the *thunder* in *you!*

To the Editor of the Morning Chronicle.

Sir,—In order to explain the following fragment, it is necessary to refer your readers to a late florid description of the Pavilion at Brighton, in the apartments of which, we are told, ' Fum, The Chinese Bird of Royalty,' is a principal ornament.

I am, Sir, yours, etc.

Mum.

FUM AND HUM,
THE TWO BIRDS OF ROYALTY.

One day the Chinese Bird of Royalty, Fum,
Thus accosted our own Bird of Royalty, Hum,
In that Palace or China-shop (Brighton—which is it?)
Where Fum had just come to pay Hum a short visit.—
Near akin are these Birds, though they differ in nation
(The breed of the Hums is as old as creation),
Both full-crawed Legitimates—both birds of prey,
Both cackling and ravenous creatures, half way
'Twixt the goose and the vulture, like Lord C—stl—r—gh;
While Fum deals in Mandarins, Bonzes, Bohea—
Peers, Bishops, and Punch, Hum, are sacred to thee!.
So congenial their tastes, that, when Fum first did light on
The floor of that grand China-warehouse at Brighton,
The lanterns, and dragons, and things round the dome
Were so like what he left, 'Gad,' says Fum,
'I'm at home.'—
And when, turning, he saw Bishop L———ge,
' Zooks, it is,'
Quoth the Bird, 'Yes—I know him—a Bonze, by his phiz—
And that jolly old idol he kneels to so low
Can be none but our roundabout godhead, fat Fo!'
It chanced, at this moment, the Episcopal Prig
Was imploring the P———e to dispense with his wig,[2]
Which the Bird, overhearing, flew high o'er his head,
And some Tobit-like marks of his patronage shed,
Which so dimmed the poor Dandy's idolatrous eye,
That while Fum cried 'Oh Fo!' all the Court cried ' Oh fie!'

But, a truce to digression.—These Birds of a feather
Thus talked, t'other night, on State matters together—
(The P———e just in bed, or about to depart for't,
His legs full of gout, and his arms full of ———);
'I say, Hum,' says Fum—Fum, of course, spoke Chinese;
But, bless you, that's nothing—at Brighton one sees
Foreign lingoes and Bishops *translated* with ease—
'I say, Hum, how fares it with Royalty now?
Is it *up?* is it *prime?* is it *spooney*—or how?'

---

[1] The character given to the Spanish soldier in Sir John Murray's memorable despatch.
[2] In consequence of an old promise that he should be allowed to wear his own hair, whenever he might be elevated to a bishoprick by His R———l H———ss.

(The Bird had just taken a flash man's degree
Under B——e, Y——th, and young Master
    L——.
'As for us in Pekin'——here a devil of a din
From the bed-chamber came, where that long
    Mandarin,
C–stl–r–gh (whom Fum calls the *Confucius* of
    prose),
Was rehearsing a speech upon Europe's repose,
To the deep, double-bass of the fat idol's nose!

(*Nota Bene.*—His Lordship and L–v–rp–l come,
In collateral lines, from the old Mother Hum,—
C–stl–r–gh a Hum-bug—L–v–rp–l a Hum-
    drum.)
The speech being finished, out rushed
    C–stl–r–gh,
Saddled Hum in a hurry, and whip, spur, away!
Through the regions of air, like a Snip on his
    hobby,
Ne'er paused till he lighted in St. Stephen's lobby.

⁕ ⁕ ⁕ ⁕ ⁕

EPISTLE FROM TOM CRIB TO BIG BEN.

CONCERNING SOME FOUL PLAY IN A LATE
TRANSACTION.[1]

'Ah! mio Ben!'—*Metastasio.*[2]

WHAT! Ben, my old hero, is this your renown?
Is *this* the new *go?*—kick a man when he's
    down!
When the foe has knocked under, to tread on him
    then—
By the fist of my father, I blush for thee, Ben!
'Foul! foul!' all the lads of the fancy exclaim—
Charley Shock is electrified— Belcher spits
    flame—
And Molyneux—ay, even Blacky, cries 'Shame!'
Time was, when John Bull little difference spied
'Twixt the foe at his feet and the friend at his
    side;
When he found (such his humour in fighting and
    eating)
His foe, like his beefsteak, the sweeter for beat-
    ing—
But this comes, Master Ben, of your cursed
    foreign notions,
Your trinkets, wigs, thingumbobs, gold lace, and
    lotions;
Your noyaus, curaçoas, and the devil knows
    what—
(One swig of *Blue Ruin*[3] is worth the whole
    lot!)—
Your great and small *crosses*—(my eyes, what a
    brood!

A cross-buttock from me would do some of them
    good!)
Which have spoiled you, till hardly a drop, my
    old porpoise,
Of pure English *claret* is left in your *corpus*,
And (as Jim says) the only one trick, good or bad,
Of the fancy you're up to, is *fibbing*, my lad!
Hence it comes,—Boxiana, disgrace to thy
    page!—
Having floored, by good luck, the first *swell* of
    the age,
Having conquered the *prime one*, that *milled* us
    all round,
You kicked him, old Ben, as he gasped on the
    ground!
Ay—just at the time to show spunk, if you'd got
    any—
Kicked him, and jawed him, and *lagged*[4] him to
    Botany!
Oh, shade of the *Cheesemonger!*[5] you who, alas!
Doubled *up*, by the dozen, those Mounseers in
    brass,
On that great day of *milling*, when blood lay in
    lakes,
When Kings held the bottle and Europe the
    stakes,
Look down upon Ben—see him *dunghill* all o'er,
Insult the fallen foe that can harm him no more.
Out, cowardly *spooney!*—again and again,
By the fist of my father, I blush for thee, Ben.
To *show the white feather* is many men's doom,
But, What of *one* feather?—Ben shows a *whole
    Plume.*

TO LADY HOLLAND.

ON NAPOLEON'S LEGACY OF A SNUFF-BOX.

GIFT of the Hero, on his dying day,
    To her, whose pity watched, for ever nigh;
Oh! could he see the proud, the happy ray,
    This relic lights up on her generous eye,
Sighing, he'd feel how easy 'tis to pay
    A friendship all his kingdoms could not buy.

CORRESPONDENCE

BETWEEN A LADY AND A GENTLEMAN, UPON THE
ADVANTAGE OF (WHAT IS CALLED) 'HAVING
LAW ON ONE'S SIDE.'

'LEGGE AUREA,
S' el piace, el lice.'

THE GENTLEMAN'S PROPOSAL.

COME, fly to these arms, nor let beauties so bloomy
To one frigid owner be tied;

---

[1] Written soon after B—n–p–rte's transportation to
St. Helena.
[2] Tom, I suppose, was 'assisted' to this motto by Mr.
Jackson, who, it is well known, keeps the most learned
company going.
[3] Gin.
[4] Transported.
[5] A Life-Guardsman, one of *the Fancy*, who distinguished himself, and was killed in the memorable
set-to at Waterloo.

Your prudes may revile, and your old ones look
    gloomy,
But, dearest! we've Law on our side.

Oh! think the delight of two lovers congenial,
    Whom no dull decorums divide ;
Their error how sweet, and their raptures how
    venial,
When once they've got Law on their side!

'Tis a thing that in every King's reign has been
    done, too :
Then why should it now be decried ?
If the Father has done it, why shouldn't the Son
    too ?
For so argues Law on our side!

And, even should our sweet violation of duty
    By cold-blooded jurors be tried,
They can *but* bring it in 'a misfortune,' my
    beauty!
As long as we've Law on our side.

THE LADY'S ANSWER.

Hold, hold, my good Sir! go a little more slowly ;
For, grant me so faithless a bride,
Such sinners as we are a little *too lowly,*
To hope to have Law on our side.

Had you been a great Prince, to whose star shin-
    ing o'er 'em
The People should look for their guide,
Then your Highness (and welcome!) might kick
    down decorum—
You'd always have Law on your side.

Were you even an old Marquis, in mischief
    grown hoary,
Whose heart, though it long ago died
To the *pleasures* of vice, is alive to its *glory*—
You still would have Law on your side!

But for *you,* Sir, crim. con. is a path full of
    troubles ;
By *my* advice therefore abide,
And leave the pursuit to those Princes and Nobles
Who have *such* a Law on their side!

HORACE, ODE XI. LIB. II.
FREELY TRANSLATED BY G. R.

COME, Y-rm—th, my boy, never trouble your
    brains
About what your old croney,
The Emperor Boney,
Is doing or brewing on Muscovy's plains:
Nor tremble, my lad, at the state of our gran-
    aries ;—
Should there come famine,
Still plenty to cram in
You always shall have, my dear Lord of the
    Stannaries!

Brisk let us revel, while revel we may ;
For the gay bloom of fifty soon passes away,
    And then people get fat,
    And infirm, and—all that,
And a wig (I confess it) so clumsily sits,
That it frightens the little Loves out of their
    wits.

Thy whiskers, too, Y-rm—th!—alas, even they,
    Though so rosy they burn,
    Too quickly must turn
(What a heart-breaking change for thy whiskers!)
    to Grey.
Then why, my Lord Warden! oh! why should
    you fidget
Your mind about matters you don't under-
    stand ?
Or why should you write yourself down for an
    idiot,
Because '*you,*' forsooth, '*have the pen in your
    hand!* '
Think, think how much better
Than scribbling a letter
(Which both you and I
Should avoid, by the by)—
How much pleasanter 'tis to sit under the bust
Of old Charley, my friend here, and drink like
    a new one ;
While Charley looks sulky, and frowns at me,
    just
As the ghost in the pantomime frowns at Don
    Juan !
To crown us, Lord Warden !
In C—mb-rl-nd's garden
Grows plenty of *monk's-hood* in venomous sprigs ;
    While Otto of Roses,
    Refreshing all noses,
Shall sweetly exhale from our whiskers and
    wigs.
What youth of the Household will cool our
    noyau
    In that streamlet delicious,
    That, down 'midst the dishes,
    All full of good fishes
    Romantic doth flow ?—
    Or who will repair
    Unto M——— Sq———e,
And see if the gentle *Marchesa* be there?
    Go—bid her haste hither,
    And let her bring with her
The newest No-Popery Sermon that's going—
Oh! let her come with her dark tresses flowing,
All gentle and juvenile, curly and gay,
In the manner of Ackermann's Dresses for
    May!

HORACE, ODE XXII. LIB. I.
FREELY TRANSLATED BY LORD ELD-N.

THE man who keeps a conscience pure
    (If not his own, at least his Prince's),

Through toil and danger walks secure,
 Looks big, and black, and never winces!

No want has he of sword or dagger,
 Cocked hat or ringlets of Geramb;
Though Peers may laugh, and Papists swagger,
 He does not care one single d—mn!

Whether 'midst Irish chairmen going,
 Or through St. Giles's alleys dim,
'Mid drunken Sheelahs, blasting, blowing,
 No matter—'tis all one to him.

[1] For instance, I, one evening late,
 Upon a gay vacation sally,
Singing the praise of Church and State,
 Got (God knows how) to Cranbourne-Alley.

When lo! an Irish Papist darted
 Across my path, gaunt, grim, and big—
I did but frown, and off he started,
 Scared at me, even without my wig!

[2] Yet a more fierce and raw-boned dog
 Goes not to mass in Dublin City,
Nor shakes his brogue o'er Allen's Bog,
 Nor spouts in Catholic Committee!

[3] Oh! place me 'midst O'Rourkes, O'Tooles,
 The ragged royal blood of Tara;
Or place me where Dick M—rt—n rules,
 The houseless wilds of Connemara;

[4] Of Church and State I'll warble still,
 Though even Dick M—rt—n's self should grumble;
Sweet Church and State, like Jack and Jill,
[5] So lovingly upon a hill—
 Ah! ne'er like Jack and Jill to tumble!

---

[1] Namque me sylva lupus in Sabina,
 Dum meam canto Lalagen, et ultra
 Terminum curis vagor expeditus,
 Fugit inermem.

I cannot help calling the reader's attention to the peculiar ingenuity with which these lines are paraphrased. Not to mention the happy conversion of the wolf into a papist (seeing that Romulus was suckled by a wolf, that Rome was founded by Romulus, and that the Pope has always reigned at Rome), there is something particularly neat in supposing '*ultra terminum*' to mean vacation-time; and then the modest consciousness with which the noble and learned translator has avoided touching upon the words '*curis expeditus*' (or, as it has been otherwise read, '*causis expeditus*'), and the felicitous idea of his being '*inermis*' when '*without his wig*,' are altogether the most delectable specimens of paraphrase in our language.

[2] Quale portentum neque militaris
 Daunia in latis alit æsculetis,
 Nec Jubæ tellus generat, leonum
 Arida nutrix.

HORACE, ODE I. LIB. III.
A FRAGMENT.

Odi profanum vulgus et arceo.
Favete linguis: carmina non prius
 Audita, Musarum sacerdos,
 Virginibus, puerisque canto.
Regum tremendorum in proprios greges,
Reges in ipsos imperium est Jovis.

1813.

I HATE thee, oh Mob! as my lady hates delf,
 To Sir Francis I'll give up thy claps and thy hisses,
Leave old Magna Charta to shift for itself,
 And, like G—dw—n, write books for young masters and misses.
Oh! it is not high rank that can make the heart merry,
 Even monarchs themselves are not free from mishap;
Though the Lords of Westphalia must quake before Jerry,
 Poor Jerry himself has to quake before Nap.

  . . . . .

HORACE, ODE XXXVIII. LIB. I.
A FRAGMENT.
TRANSLATED BY A TREASURY CLERK WHILE WAITING DINNER FOR THE RIGHT HON. G—RGE R—SE.

Persicos odi, puer, apparatus:
Displicent nexæ philyra coronæ.
Mitte sectari Rosa *quo locorum.*
 Sera moretur.

Boy, tell the Cook that I hate all nick-nackeries,
Fricassees, vol-au-vents, puffs, and gim-crackeries,—
Six by the Horse Guards!—old Georgy is late—
But come—lay the table-cloth—zounds! do not wait,
Nor stop to inquire, while the dinner is staying,
At which of his places Old R—se is delaying![3]

---

[3] Pone me pigris ubi nulla campis
 Arbor æstiva recreatur aura:
 Quod latus mundi, nebulæ, malusque
 Jupiter urget.

I must here remark, that the said Dick M—rt—n being a very good fellow, it was not at all fair to make a 'malus Jupiter' of him.

[4] Dulce ridentem Lalagen amabo,
 Dulce loquentem.

[5] There cannot be imagined a more happy illustration of the inseparability of Church and State, and their (what is called) 'standing and falling together,' than this ancient apologue of Jack and Jill. Jack, of course, represents the State in this ingenious little allegory:

 Jack fell down,
  And broke his *Crown*,
 And Jill came tumbling after.

[6] The literal closeness of the version here cannot but be admired. The translator has added a long, erudite, and flowery note upon *Rosa*, of which I can merely

TO ———.

Moria pur quando vuoi, non è bisogna mutar ni faccia
ni voce per esser un Angelo.[1]

DIE when you will, you need not wear
At Heaven's court a form more fair
Than beauty here on earth has given;
Keep but the lovely looks we see—
The voice we hear—and you will be
An angel *ready-made* for Heaven!

IMPROMPTU.

UPON BEING OBLIGED TO LEAVE A PLEASANT
PARTY, FROM THE WANT OF A PAIR OF
BREECHES TO DRESS FOR DINNER IN.

1810.

BETWEEN Adam and me the great difference is,
Though a paradise each has been forced to resign,
That he never wore breeches till turned out of his,
While, for want of my breeches, I'm banished from mine.

WHAT'S MY THOUGHT LIKE?

Quest.—Why is a Pump like Viscount C—st—r—gh?
Answ.—Because it is a slender thing of wood,
That up and down its awkward arm doth sway,
And coolly spout, and spout, and spout away,
In one weak, washy, everlasting flood!

EPIGRAM.

'WHAT news to-day?'—'Oh! worse and worse—
M—e is the Pr—ce's Privy Purse!'
The Pr—ce's *Purse!* no, no, you fool,
You mean the Prince's *Ridicule!*

EPIGRAM.

DIALOGUE BETWEEN A CATHOLIC DELEGATE AND
HIS R—Y—L HIGHNESS THE D—KE OF C—B—RL—ND.

SAID his Highness to Ned, with that grim face of his,
'Why refuse us the *Veto*, dear Catholic Neddy?'—
'Because, Sir,' said Ned, looking full in his phiz,
'You're *forbidding* enough, in all conscience, already!'

EPIGRAM.

DIALOGUE BETWEEN A DOWAGER AND HER MAID
ON THE NIGHT OF LORD Y—RM—TH'S FÊTE.

'I WANT the Court-Guide,' said my lady 'to look
If the house, Seymour Place, be at 30 or 20'—
'We've lost the *Court-Guide*, Ma'am, but here's the *Red Book*,
Where you'll find, I daresay, *Seymour* PLACES in plenty!'

EPIGRAM.

FROM THE FRENCH.

'I NEVER give a kiss,' says Prue,
'To naughty man, for I abhor it.'
She will not *give* a kiss, 'tis true—
She'll *take* one, though, and thank you for it.

ON A SQUINTING POETESS.

To no *one* Muse does she her glance confine,
But has an eye, at once, to *all the Nine!*

EPILOGUE.

LAST night, as lonely o'er my fire I sat,
Thinking of cues, starts, exits, and—all that,
And wondering much what little knavish sprite
Had put it first in women's heads to write:—

---

give a specimen at present. In the first place, he ransacks the *Rosarium Politicum* of the Persian poet Sadi, with the hope of finding some *Political* Roses, to match the gentleman in the text—but in vain. He then tells us that Cicero accused Verres of reposing upon a cushion '*Melitensi rosa fartum*,' which, from the odd mixture of words, he supposes to be a kind of *Irish* bed of Roses, like Lord Castlereagh's. The learned clerk next favours us with some remarks upon a well-known punning epitaph on fair Rosamond, and expresses a most loyal hope that, if '*Rosa munda*' mean 'a Rose with clean hands,' it may be found applicable to the Right Honourable Rose in question. He then dwells at some length upon the '*Rosa aurea*,' which, though descriptive in one sense of the old Treasury Statesman, yet, as being consecrated and worn by the Pope, must of course not be brought into the same atmosphere with him. Lastly, in reference to the words '*old* Rose,' he winds up with the pathetic lamentation of the poet, '*consenuisse Rosas.*' The whole note, indeed, shows a knowledge of Roses that is quite edifying.

[1] The words addressed by Lord Herbert of Cherbury to the beautiful nun at Murano.—See his *Life.*

Sudden I saw, as in some witching dream,
A bright-blue glory round my bookcase beam,
From whose quick-opening folds of azure light
Out flew a tiny form, as small and bright
As Puck the Fairy, when he pops his head,
Some sunny morning, from a violet bed.
'Bless me!' I starting cried, 'what imp are you?'—
'A small he-devil, Ma'am—my name Bas Bleu—
A bookish sprite, much given to routs and reading;
'Tis I who teach your spinsters of good breeding
The reigning taste in chemistry and caps,
The last new bounds of tuckers and of maps,
And, when the waltz has twirled her giddy brain,
With metaphysics twirl it back again!'

I viewed him, as he spoke—his hose were blue,
His wings—the covers of the last Review—
Cerulean, bordered with a jaundice hue,
And tinselled gaily o'er, for evening wear,
Till the next quarter brings a new-fledged pair.
'Inspired by me—(pursued this waggish Fairy)—
That best of wives and Sapphos, Lady Mary,
Votary alike of Crispin and the Muse,
Makes her own splay-foot epigrams and shoes.
For me the eyes of young Camilla shine,
And mingle Love's blue brilliances with mine;
For me she sits apart, from coxcombs shrinking,
Looks wise—the pretty soul!—and *thinks* she's thinking.
By my advice Miss Indigo attends
Lectures on Memory, and assures her friends,
"'Pon honour!—(*mimics*)—nothing can surpass the plan
Of that professor—(*trying to recollect*)—psha! that memory-man—
That—what's his name?—him I attended lately—
'Pon honour, he improved *my* memory greatly."'

Here, curtseying low, I asked the blue-legged sprite
What share he had in this our play to-night.
'Nay, there—(he cried)—there I am guiltless quite—
What! choose a heroine from that Gothic time,
When no one waltzed, and none but monks could rhyme;
When lovely woman, all unschooled and wild,
Blushed without art, and without culture smiled—
Simple as flowers, while yet unclassed they shone,
Ere Science called their brilliant world her own,
Ranged the wild rosy things in learned orders,
And filled with Greek the garden's blushing borders?—
No, no—your gentle Inas will not do—
To-morrow evening, when the lights burn blue,
I'll come—(*pointing downwards*)—you understand
—till then adieu!'

And *has* the sprite been here? No—jests apart—
Howe'er man rules in science and in art,
The sphere of woman's glories is the heart.
And, if our Muse have sketched with pencil true
The wife—the mother—firm, yet gentle too—
Whose soul, wrapped up in ties itself hath spun,
Trembles, if touched in the remotest one;
Who loves—yet dares even Love himself disown,
When honour's broken shaft supports his throne:
If such our Ina, she may scorn the evils,
Dire as they are, of Critics and—Blue Devils.

THE SYLPH'S BALL.

A Sylph, as gay as ever sported
Her figure through the fields of air,
By an old swarthy Gnome was courted,
And, strange to say, he won the fair.

The annals of the oldest witch
A pair so sorted could not show—
But how refuse?—the Gnome was rich,
The Rothschild of the world below;

And Sylphs, like other pretty creatures,
Learn from their mammas to consider
Love as an auctioneer of features,
Who knocks them down to the best bidder.

Home she was taken to his mine—
A palace, paved with diamonds all—
And, proud as Lady Gnome to shine,
Sent out her tickets for a ball.

The *lower* world, of course, was there,
And all the best; but of the *upper*
The sprinkling was but shy and rare—
A few old Sylphids who loved supper.

As none yet knew the wondrous lamp
Of Davy, that renowned Aladdin,
And the Gnome's halls exhaled a damp,
Which accidents from fire were bad in;

The chambers were supplied with light
By many strange but safe devices:—
Large fire-flies, such as shine at night
Among the Orient's flowers and spices:

Musical flint-mills—swiftly played
By elfin hands—that, flashing round,
Like some bright glancing minstrel maid,
Gave out, at once, both light and sound;

Bologna-stones, that drink the sun;
And water from that Indian sea,
Whose waves at night like wild-fire run,
Corked up in crystal carefully.

Glow-worms, that round the tiny dishes,
Like little lighthouses, were set up;

And pretty phosphorescent fishes,
  That by their own gay light were eat up.

'Mong the few guests from Ether, came
  That wicked Sylph, whom Love we call—
My Lady knew him but by name,
  My Lord, her husband, not at all.

Some prudent Gnomes, 'tis said, apprised
  That he was coming, and no doubt
Alarmed about his torch, advised
  He should by all means be kept out.

But others disapproved this plan,
  And, by his flame though somewhat frighted,
Thought Love too much a gentleman,
  In such a dangerous place to light it.

However, *there* he was—and dancing
  With the fair Sylph, light as a feather:
They looked like two young sunbeams, glancing,
  At daybreak, down to earth together.

And all had gone off safe and well,
  But for that plaguy torch—whose light,
Though not yet kindled, who could tell
  How soon, how devilishly it *might?*

And so it chanced—which in those dark
  And fireless halls was quite amazing,
Did we not know how small a spark
  Can set the torch of Love a-blazing.

Whether it came, when close entangled
  In the gay waltz, from her bright eyes,
Or from the *lucciole*, that spangled
  Her locks of jet—is all surmise.

Certain it is, the ethereal girl
  Did drop a spark, at some odd turning,
Which, by the waltz's windy whirl,
  Was fanned up into actual burning.

Oh for that lamp's metallic gauze—
  That curtain of protecting wire—
Which Davy delicately draws
  Around illicit, dangerous fire!—

The wall he sets 'twixt flame and air
  (Like that which barred young Thisbe's bliss),
Through whose small holes this dangerous pair
  May see each other, but not kiss.[1]

At first the torch looked rather bluely—
  A sign, they say, that no good boded—
Then quick the gas became unruly,
  And, crack! the ball-room all exploded.

Sylphs, Gnomes, and fiddlers, mixed together,
  With all their aunts, sons, cousins, nieces,

Like butterflies, in stormy weather,
  Were blown—legs, wings, and tails—to pieces;

While, 'mid these victims of the torch,
  The Sylph, alas! too, bore her part—
Found lying with a livid scorch,
  As if from lightning, o'er her heart!

'Well done!' a laughing goblin said,
  Escaping from this gaseous strife;
"Tis not the *first* time Love has made
  A *blow-up* in connubial life.'

REMONSTRANCE.

AFTER A CONVERSATION WITH L—D J—— R——,
IN WHICH HE HAD INTIMATED SOME IDEA OF
GIVING UP ALL POLITICAL PURSUITS.

WHAT! *thou*, with thy genius, thy youth, and
    thy name—
  Thou, born of a Russell—whose instinct to run
The accustomed career of thy sires, is the same
  As the eaglet's to soar with his eyes on the sun!

Whose nobility comes to thee, stamped with a
    seal,
  Far, far more ennobling than monarch e'er set;
With the blood of thy race offered up for the weal
  Of a nation that swears by that martyrdom
    yet!

Shalt *thou* be faint-hearted and turn from the
    strife,
  From the mighty arena where all that is grand,
And devoted, and pure, and adorning in life,
  Is for high-thoughted spirits, like thine, to
    command?

Oh no, never dream it—while good men despair
  Between tyrants and traitors, and timid men
    bow,
Never think for an instant thy country can spare
  Such a light from her darkening horizon as
    thou!

With a spirit as meek as the gentlest of those
  Who in life's sunny valley lie sheltered and
    warm;
Yet bold and heroic as ever yet rose
  To the top cliffs of Fortune, and breasted her
    storm;

With an ardour for liberty, fresh as in youth,
  It first kindles the bard, and gives life to his
    lyre;
Yet mellowed, even now, by that mildness of
    truth
  Which tempers, but chills not, the patriot fire;

With an eloquence—not like those rills from a
    height,
  Which sparkle, and foam, and in vapour are
    o'er;

---

[1] Partique dedere
Oscula quisque suæ non pervenientia contra.—*Ovid.*

But a current that works out its way into light
　Through the filt'ring recesses of thought and
　　of lore.

Thus gifted, thou never canst sleep in the shade;
　If the stirrings of genius, the music of fame,
　And the charms of thy cause have not power to
　　persuade,
　Yet think how to freedom thou'rt pledged by
　　thy name.

Like the boughs of that laurel, by Delphi's decree,
　Set apart for the fane and its service divine,
　All the branches that spring from the old Russell
　　tree,
　Are by Liberty *claimed* for the use of her shrine.

MY BIRTH-DAY.

'My birth-day!'—What a different sound
　　That word had in my youthful ears!
And how, each time the day comes round,
　　Less and less white its mark appears!

When first our scanty years are told,
　　It seems like pastime to grow old;
And, as youth counts the shining links
　　That time around him binds so fast,
Pleased with the task, he little thinks
　　How hard that chain will press at last.

Vain was the man, and false as vain,
　　Who said, 'were he ordained to run
His long career of life again,
　　He would do all that he *had* done.'—
Ah! 'tis not thus the voice that dwells
　In sober birth-days speaks to me;
Far otherwise—of time it tells
　Lavished unwisely, carelessly—
Of counsel mocked—of talents, made
　Haply for high and pure designs,
But oft, like Israel's incense, laid
　Upon unholy, earthly shrines—
Of nursing many a wrong desire—
　Of wandering after Love too far,
And taking every meteor fire
　That crossed my pathway for his star!
All this it tells, and, could I trace
　　The imperfect picture o'er again,
With power to add, retouch, efface
　　The lights and shades, the joy and pain,
How little of the past would stay!
How quickly all should melt away—
All—but that freedom of the mind
　Which hath been more than wealth to me;
Those friendships in my boyhood twined,
　And kept till now unchangingly;
And that dear home, that saving ark,
　Where Love's true light at last I've found,
Cheering within, when all grows dark,
　And comfortless, and stormy round!

FANCY.

The more I've viewed this world, tho more I've
　　found
　That, filled as 'tis with scenes and creatures
　　rare,
Fancy commands, within her own bright round,
　A world of scenes and creatures far more fair.
Nor is it that her power can call up there
　A single charm that's not from Nature won,
No more than rainbows, in their pride, can wear
　A single tint unborrowed from the sun—
But 'tis the mental medium it shines through,
　That lends to beauty all its charm and hue;
As the same light, that o'er the level lake
　One dull monotony of lustre flings,
Will, entering in the rounded rain-drop, make
　Colours as gay as those on angels' wings!

LOVE AND HYMEN.

Love had a fever—ne'er could close
　His little eyes till day was breaking;
And whimsical enough, Heaven knows,
　The things he raved about while waking.

To let him pine so were a sin—
　One to whom all the world's a debtor—
So Doctor Hymen was called in,
　And Love that night slept rather better.

Next day the case gave further hope yet,
　Though still some ugly fever latent;—
'Dose, as before'—a gentle opiate,
　For which old Hymen has a patent.

After a month of daily call,
　So fast the dose went on restoring,
That Love, who first ne'er slept at all,
　Now took, the rogue! to downright snoring.

TRANSLATION FROM CATULLUS.

Sweet Sirmio! thou, the very eye
　Of all peninsulas and isles
That in our lakes of silver lie,
　Or sleep, enwreathed by Neptune's smiles,

How gladly back to thee I fly!
　Still doubting, asking *can* it be
That I have left Bithynia's sky,
　And gaze in safety upon thee?

Oh! what is happier than to find
　Our hearts at ease, our perils past;
When, anxious long, the lightened mind
　Lays down its load of care at last?—

When, tired with toil on land and deep,
　Again we tread the welcome floor

Of our own home, and sink to sleep
On the long-wished-for bed once more?

This, this it is that pays alone
The ills of all life's former track—
Shine out, my beautiful, my own
Sweet Sirmio—greet thy master back.

And thou, fair lake, whose water quaffs
The light of heaven, like Lydia's sea,
Rejoice, rejoice—let all that laughs
Abroad, at home, laugh out for me!

TO MY MOTHER.

WRITTEN IN A POCKET-BOOK, 1822.

They tell us of an Indian tree
Which, howsoe'er the sun and sky
May tempt its boughs to wander free,
And shoot and blossom, wide and high,
Far better loves to bend its arms
Downward again to that dear earth
From which the life, that fills and warms
Its grateful being, first had birth.

'Tis thus, though wooed by flattering friends,
And fed with fame (*if* fame it be),
This heart, my own dear mother, bends,
With love's true instinct, back to thee!

A SPECULATION.

Of all speculations the market holds forth,
The best that I know for a lover of pelf
Is, to buy —— up, at the price he is worth,
And then sell him at that which he sets on himself.

SCEPTICISM.

Ere Psyche drank the cup that shed
Immortal life into her soul,
Some evil spirit poured, 'tis said,
One drop of doubt into the bowl—

Which, mingling darkly with the stream,
To Psyche's lips—she knew not why—
Made even that blessed nectar seem
As though its sweetness soon would die.

Oft, in the very arms of Love,
A chill came o'er her heart—a fear
That death would, even yet, remove
Her spirit from that happy sphere.

'Those sunny ringlets,' she exclaimed,
Twining them round her snowy fingers—
'That forehead, where a light, unnamed,
Unknown on earth, for ever lingers—

'Those lips, through which I feel the breath
Of heaven itself, whene'er they sever—
Oh! are they mine beyond all death—
Mine own, hereafter and for ever?

'Smile not—I know that starry brow,
Those ringlets and bright lips of thine,
Will always shine as they do now—
But shall *I* live to *see* them shine?'

In vain did Love say, 'Turn thine eyes
On all that sparkles round thee here—
Thou'rt now in heaven, where nothing dies,
And in these arms—what *canst* thou fear?'

In vain—the fatal drop, that stole
Into that cup's immortal treasure,
Had lodged its bitter near her soul,
And gave a tinge to every pleasure.

And though there ne'er was rapture given
Like Psyche's with that radiant boy,
Hers is the only face in heaven
That wears a cloud amid its joy.

A JOKE VERSIFIED.

'Come, come,' said Tom's father, 'at your time of life,
There's no longer excuse for thus playing the rake—
It is time you should think, boy, of taking a wife.'—
'Why, so it is, father,—whose wife shall I take?'

ON ——.

Like a snuffers, this loving old dame,
By a destiny grievous enough,
Though so oft she has snapped at the flame,
Hath never caught more than the snuff.

FRAGMENT OF A CHARACTER.

Here lies Factotum Ned at last:
Long as he breathed the vital air,
Nothing throughout all Europe passed
In which he hadn't some small share.

Whoe'er was *in*, whoe'er was *out*—
Whatever statesman did or said—
If not exactly brought about,
Was all at least contrived by Ned.

With Nap if Russia went to war,
'Twas owing, under Providence,
To certain hints Ned gave the Czar—
(*Vide* his pamphlet—price sixpence).

If France was beat at Waterloo—
As all but Frenchmen think she was—
To Ned, as Wellington well knew,
Was owing half that day's applause.

Then for his news—no envoy's bag
E'er passed so many secrets through it—
Scarcely a telegraph could wag
Its wooden finger, but Ned knew it.

Such tales he had of foreign plots,
With foreign names one's ear to buzz in—
From Russia che*f*s and o*f*s in lots,
From Poland *owskis* by the dozen.

When George, alarmed for England's creed,
Turned out the last Whig ministry,
And men asked, Who advised the deed?
Ned modestly confessed 'twas he.

For though, by some unlucky miss,
He had not downright *seen* the King,
He sent such hints through Viscount *This*,
To Marquis *That*, as clenched the thing.

The same it was in science, arts,
The drama, books, ms. and printed—
Kean learned from Ned his cleverest parts,
And Scott's last work by him was hinted.

Childe Harold in the proofs he read,
And here and there infused some soul in't;
Nay, Davy's lamp, till seen by Ned,
Had—odd enough—a dangerous hole in't.

'Twas thus, all doing and all knowing,
Wit, statesman, boxer, chemist, singer,
Whatever was the best pie going,
In *that* Ned—trust him—had his finger.

. . . . . .

COUNTRY-DANCE AND QUADRILLE.

ONE night, the nymph called Country-Dance—
Whom folks of late have used so ill,
Preferring a coquette from France,
A mincing thing, *Mamselle* Quadrille—

Having been chased from London down
To that last, humblest haunt of all
She used to grace—a country-town—
Went smiling to the New Year's ball.

'Here, here, at least,' she cried, 'though driven
From London's gay and shining tracks—
Though, like a Peri cast from Heaven,
I've lost, for ever lost, Almack's—

'Though not a London Miss alive
Would now for her acquaintance own me;
And spinsters, even of forty-five,
Upon their honours ne'er have known me:

'Here, here, at least, I triumph still,
And—spite of some few dandy lancers,
Who vainly try to preach Quadrille—
See nought but *true-blue* country-dancers.

'Here still I reign, and, fresh in charms,
My throne, like Magna Charta, raise
'Mong sturdy, free-born legs and arms,
That scorn the threatened *chaîne Anglaise*.

'Twas thus she said, as, 'mid the din
Of footmen, and the town sedan,
She 'lighted at the King's Head Inn,
And up the stairs triumphant ran.

The squires and their squiresses all,
With young squirinas just *come out*,
And my lord's daughters from the Hall
(Quadrillers in their hearts no doubt),

Already, as she tripped up stairs,
She in the cloak-room saw assembling—
When, hark! some new outlandish airs,
From the first fiddle, set her trembling.

She stops—she listens—*can* it be?
Alas! in vain her ears would 'scape it—
It is 'Di tanti palpiti,'
As plain as English bow can scrape it.

'Courage!' however, in she goes,
With her best sweeping country grace;
When, ah! too true, her worst of foes,
Quadrille, there meets her, face to face.

Oh for the lyre, or violin,
Or kit of that gay Muse, Terpsichore,
To sing the rage these nymphs were in,
Their looks and language, airs and trickery

There stood Quadrille, with cat-like face
(The *beau idéal* of French beauty),
A band-box thing, all art and lace,
Down from her nose-tip to her shoe-tie.

Her flounces, fresh from *Victorine*—
From *Hippolyte* her rouge and hair—
Her poetry, from *Lamartine*—
Her morals from—the Lord knows where.

And when she danced—so slidingly,
So near the ground she plied her art,
You'd swear her mother-earth and she
Had made a compact ne'er to part.

Her face the while, demure, sedate,
No signs of life or motion showing,
Like a bright *pendule's* dial-plate—
So still, you'd hardly think 'twas *going*.

Full fronting her stood Country-Dance—
A fresh, frank nymph, whom you would know
For English, at a single glance—
English all o'er, from top to toe.

A little *gauche*, 'tis fair to own,
  And rather given to skips and bounces;
Endangering thereby many a gown,
  And playing oft the devil with flounces.

Unlike *Mamselle*—who would prefer
  (As morally a lesser ill)
A thousand flaws in character,
  To one vile rumple of a frill.

No rouge did she of Albion wear;
  Let her but run that two-heat race
She calls a *Set*—not Dian e'er
  Came rosier from the woodland chase.

And such the nymph, whose soul had in't
  Such anger now—whose eyes of blue
(Eyes of that bright victorious tint
  Which English maids call '*Waterloo*'),

Like summer lightnings, in the dusk
  Of a warm evening, flashing broke,
While, to the tune of 'Money Musk,'[1]
  Which struck up now, she proudly spoke:—

'Heard you that strain—that joyous strain?
  'Twas such as England loved to hear,
Ere thou, and all thy frippery train,
  Corrupted both her foot and ear—

'Ere Waltz, that rake from foreign lands,
  Presumed, in sight of all beholders,
To lay his rude licentious hands
  On virtuous English backs and shoulders—

'Ere times and morals both grew bad,
  And, yet unfleeced by funding blockheads,
Happy John Bull not only *had*,
  But danced to, "Money in both pockets."[2]

'Alas, the change!—oh, ———!
  Where is the land could 'scape disasters,
With *such* a Foreign Secretary,
  Aided by foreign dancing-masters?

Woe to ye, men of ships and shops,
  Rulers of day-books and of waves!
Quadrilled on one side into fops,
  And drilled on t'other into slaves!

'Ye, too, ye lovely victims! seen,
  Like pigeons trussed for exhibition,
With elbows *à la cropaudine*,
  And feet in—God knows what position.

Hemmed in by watchful *chaperons*,
  Inspectors of your airs and graces,
Who intercept all signal tones,
  And read all telegraphic faces,

'Unable with the youth adored,
  In that grim *cordon* of mammas,
To interchange one loving word,
  Though whispered but in *queue-de-chats*.

'Ah, did you know how blest we ranged,
  Ere vile Quadrille usurped the fiddle—
What looks in *setting* were exchanged,
  What tender words in *down the middle!*

'How many a couple, like the wind,
  Which nothing in its course controls,
Left time and *chaperons* far behind,
  And gave a loose to legs and souls!

'How matrimony throve—ere stopped
  By this cold, silent, foot-coquetting—
How charmingly one's partner popped
  The important question in *poussette-ing!*

'While now, alas, no sly advances—
  No marriage hints—all goes on badly:
'Twixt Parson Malthus and French dances,
  We girls are at a discount sadly.

'Sir William Scott (now Baron Stowell)
  Declares not half so much is made
By licences—and *he* must know well—
  Since vile Quadrilling spoiled the trade.'

She ceased—tears fell from every Miss—
  She now had touched the true pathetic:—
One such authentic fact as this,
  Is worth whole volumes theoretic.

Instant the cry was 'Country-Dance!'
  And the maid saw, with brightening face,
The steward of the night advance,
  And lead her to her birthright place.

The fiddles, which awhile had ceased,
  Now tuned again their summons sweet,
And for one happy night at least
  Old England's triumph was complete.

SONG.

FOR THE POCO-CURANTE SOCIETY.

To those we love we've drank to-night;
  But now attend, and stare not,
While I the ampler lists recite
  Of those for whom—*we care not*.

For royal men, howe'er they frown,
  If on their fronts they bear not
That noblest gem that decks a crown—
  The People's Love—*we care not*.

For slavish men who bend beneath
  A despot yoke, and dare not
Pronounce the will, whose very breath
  Would rend its links—*we care not*.

---

[1] An old English country-dance.
[2] Another old English country-dance.

For priestly men who covet sway
 And wealth, though they declare not;
Who point, like finger-posts, the way
 They never go—*we care not.*

For martial men who on their sword,
 Howe'er it conquers, wear not
The pledges of a soldier's word,
 Redeemed and pure—*we care not.*

For legal men who plead for wrong,
 And, though to lies they swear not,
Are not more honest than the throng
 Of those who do—*we care not.*

For courtly men who feed upon
 The land like grubs, and spare not
The smallest loaf where they can sun
 Their reptile limbs—*we care not.*

For wealthy men who keep their mines
 In darkness hid, and share not
The paltry ore with him who pines
 In honest want—*we care not.*

For prudent men who keep the power
 Of Love aloof, and bare not
Their hearts in any guardless hour
 To Beauty's shaft—*we care not.*

For secret men who, round the bowl
 In friendship's circle, tear not
The cloudy curtain from their soul,
 But draw it close—*we care not.*

For all, in short, on land and sea,
 In court and camp, who are not,
Who never were, nor e'er will be
 Good men and true—*we care not.*

GENIUS AND CRITICISM.

Scripsit quidem fata, sed sequitur.—Seneca.

Of old, the Sultan Genius reigned—
 As Nature meant—supreme, alone;
With mind unchecked, and hands unchained,
 His views, his conquests were his own.

But power like his, that digs its grave
 With its own sceptre, could not last;
So Genius' self became the slave
 Of laws that Genius' self had passed.

As Jove, who forged the chain of Fate,
 Was ever after doomed to wear it;
His nods, his struggles, all too late—
 ' *Qui semel jussit, semper paret.*'

To check young Genius' proud career,
 The slaves, who now his throne invaded,

Made Criticism his Prime Vizir,
 And from that hour his glories faded.

Tied down in Legislation's school,
 Afraid of even his own ambition,
His very victories were by rule,
 And he was great but by permission.

His most heroic deeds—the same
 That dazzled, when spontaneous actions—
Now, done by law, seemed cold and tame,
 And shorn of all their first attractions.

If he but stirred to take the air,
 Instant the Vizir's Council sat—
' Good Lord! your Highness can't go there—
 Bless us! your Highness can't do that.'

If, loving pomp, he chose to buy
 Rich jewels for his diadem—
' The taste was bad—the price was high—
 A flower were simpler than a gem.'

To please them if he took to flowers—
 ' What trifling, what unmeaning things!
Fit for a woman's toilet hours,
 But not at all the style for kings.'

If, fond of his domestic sphere,
 He played no more the rambling comet—
' A dull, good sort of man, 'twas clear;
 But as for great or brave—far from it.'

Did he then look o'er distant oceans,
 For realms more worthy to enthrone him?—
' Saint Aristotle, what wild notions!
 Serve a " *Ne exeat regno* " on him.'

At length—their last and worst to do—
 They round him placed a guard of watchmen—
Reviewers, knaves in brown, or blue
 Turned up with yellow—chiefly Scotchmen—

To dog his footsteps all about,
 Like those in Longwood's prison-grounds,
Who at Napoleon's heels rode out
 For fear the Conqueror should break bounds.

Oh, for some champion of his power,
 Some *ultra* spirit, to set free,
As erst in Shakspeare's sovereign hour,
 The thunders of his royalty!—

To vindicate his ancient line,
 The first, the true, the only one
Of Right eternal and divine
 That rules beneath the blessed sun!—

To crush the rebels, that would cloud
 His triumphs with restraint or blame,
And, honouring even his faults, aloud
 Re-echo ' *Vive le Roi! quand même*——'

HUMOROUS POEMS.

HUMOROUS POEMS.

AN AMATORY COLLOQUY BETWEEN BANK AND GOVERNMENT.

BANK.

Is all then forgotten?—those amorous pranks
You and I, in our youth, my dear Government, played—
When you called me the fondest, the truest of Banks,
And enjoyed the endearing *advances* I made.

When—left to do all, unmolested and free,
That a dashing, expensive young couple should do,
A law against *paying* was laid upon me,
But none against *owing*, dear helpmate, on you?

And is it then vanished?—that 'hour (as *Othello*
So happily calls it) of Love and *Direction*;'
And must we, like other fond doves, my dear fellow,
Grow good in our old age, and cut the connexion?

GOVERNMENT.

Even so, my beloved Mrs. Bank, it must be,—
This paying in cash plays the devil with wooing—
We've both had our swing, but I plainly foresee
There must soon be a stop to our *bill*-ing and cooing.

Propagation in reason—a small child or two—
Even Reverend Malthus himself is a friend to:
The issue of some folks is moderate and few—
But *ours*, my dear corporate Bank, there's no end to!

So,—hard as it is on a pair who've already
Disposed of so many pounds, shillings, and pence;
And, in spite of that pink of prosperity, Freddy,
Who'd even in famine cry, 'D——n the expense!'—

The day is at hand, my Papyria¹ Venus,
When, high as we once used to carry our capers,
Those soft *billets-doux* we're now passing between us
Will serve but to keep Mrs. C—tts in curl-papers;

And when—if we still must continue our love
After all that is past—our amour, it is clea
(Like that which Miss Danaë managed with Jove),
Must all be transacted in *bullion*, my dear!

ODE TO THE GODDESS CERES.

BY SIR T——S L——E.

'Legiferæ Cereri Phœboque.'—*Virgil.*

DEAR Goddess of Corn, whom the ancients, we know
(Among other odd whims of those comical bodies),
Adorned with somniferous poppies, to show
Thou wert always a true Country-gentleman's Goddess!

Behold, in his best shooting-jacket, before thee,
An eloquent 'Squire, who most humbly beseeches,
Great Queen of Mark Lane (if the thing doesn't bore thee),
Thou'lt read o'er the last of his—never-last speeches.

Ah! Ceres, thou knowest not the slander and scorn
Now heaped upon England's 'Squirearchy so boasted,
Improving on Hunt's scheme, instead of the Corn,
'Tis now the Corn-growers, alas! that are *roasted!*

---

¹ To distinguish her from the 'Aurea.'

In speeches, in books, in all shapes they attack
    us,—
Reviewers, economists—fellows, no doubt,
That you, my dear Ceres, and Venus, and
    Bacchus,
And Gods of high fashion, know little about.

There's B—nth—m, whose English is all his own
    making,—
Who thinks just as little of settling a nation
As he would of smoking his pipe, or of taking
    (What he himself calls) his 'post-prandial
    vibration.'[1]

There are two Mr. M——s, too, whom those that
    like reading
Through all that's unreadable, call very
    clever;—
And, whereas M—— Senior makes war on *good*
    breeding,
M—— Junior makes war on all *breeding* what-
    ever!

In short, my dear Goddess, Old England's
    divided
Between *ultra* blockheads and superfine
    sages;—
With which of these classes we landlords have
    sided,
Thou'lt find in my Speech, if thou'lt read a few
    pages.

For therein I've proved, to my own satisfaction,
And that of all 'Squires I've the honour of
    meeting,
That 'tis the most senseless and foul-mouthed
    detraction,
To say that poor people are fond of cheap
    eating.

On the contrary, such the *chaste* notions of food
That dwell in each pale manufacturer's heart,
They would scorn any law, be it ever so good,
That would make thee, dear Goddess, less dear
    than thou art!

And, oh! for Monopoly what a blest day,
When the Land and the Silk shall, in fond
    combination,
(Like *Sulky* and *Silky*, that pair in the play),
Cry out, with one voice, for High Rents and
    Starvation![2]

Long life to the Minister!—no matter who,
Or how dull he may be, if, with dignified
    spirit, he

Keeps the ports shut—and the people's mouths,
    too,—
We shall all have a long run of Freddy's
    prosperity.

As for myself, who've, like Hannibal, sworn
    To hate the whole crew who would take our
    rents from us,
Had England but *One* to stand by thee, Dear
    Corn,
That last honest Uni-corn[3] would be—Sir
    Th——s!

DIALOGUE BETWEEN A SOVEREIGN AND A ONE-POUND NOTE.

'O ego non felix, quam tu fugis, ut pavet acres
Agna lupos, capreæque leones.'—*Hor.*

Said a Sovereign to a Note,
    In the pocket of my coat,
Where they met, in a neat purse of leather,
    'How happens it, I prithee,
    That though I'm wedded with thee,
Fair Pound, we can never live together?

    'Like your sex, fond of *change*,
    With silver you can range,
And of lots of young sixpences be mother;
    While with *me*—on my word,
    Not my Lady and my Lord
Of W——th see so little of each other!'

    The indignant Note replied
    (Lying crumpled by his side),
'Shame, shame, it is yourself that roam, Sir—
    One cannot look askance,
    But, whip! you're off to France,
Leaving nothing but old rags at home, Sir.

    'Your scampering began
    From the moment Parson Van,
Poor man, made us *one* in Love's fetter.
    "For better or for worse"
    Is the usual marriage curse:
But ours is all "worse" and no "better."

    'In vain are laws passed,
    There's nothing holds you fast.
Though you know, sweet Sovereign, I adore you—
    At the smallest hint in life,
    You forsake your lawful wife,
As *other* Sovereigns did before you.

    'I flirt with Silver, true—
    But what can ladies do,
When disowned by their natural protectors?

---

[1] The venerable Jeremy's phrase for his after-dinner walk.

[2] '*Road to Ruin.*'
Dicta Famos Cereris (quamvis contraria semper
Illius est operi) peragit.—*Ovid.*

[3] This is meant not so much for a pun, as in allusion to the natural history of the unicorn, which is supposed to be something between the Bos and the Asinus, and, as Rees' *Cyclopædia* tells us, has a particular liking for anything chaste.

And as to falsehood, stuff!
I shall soon be *false* enough,
When I get among those wicked Bank Directors.'

The Sovereign, smiling on her,
Now swore, upon his honour,
To be henceforth domestic and loyal;
But, within an hour or two,
Why—I sold him to a Jew,
And he's now at No. 10, Palais Royal.

AN EXPOSTULATION TO LORD KING.

'Quem das finem, Rex magne, laborum?'—*Virgil*.

How *can* you, my Lord, thus delight to torment all
The Peers of the realm about cheapening their corn,[1]
When you know, if one hasn't a very high rental,
'Tis hardly worth while being very high born!

Why bore them so rudely, each night of your life,
On a question, my Lord, there's so much to abhor in?
A question—like asking one, 'How is your wife?'—
At once so confounded domestic and foreign.

As to weavers, no matter how poorly they feast,
But Peers, and such animals fed up for show,
(Like the well-physicked elephant, lately deceased),
Take a wonderful quantum of cramming, you know.

You might see, my dear Baron, how bored and distrest
Were their high noble hearts by your merciless tale,
When the force of the agony wrung even a jest
From the frugal Scotch wit of my Lord L—d——le![2]

Bright Peer! to whom Nature and Berwickshire gave
A humour, endowed with effects so provoking,
That, when the whole House looks unusually grave,
You may always conclude that Lord L—d—le's joking!

And then, those unfortunate weavers of Perth—
Not to know the vast difference Providence dooms

Between weavers of Perth and Peers of high birth,
'Twixt those who have *heir*-looms, and those who've but looms!

To talk *now* of starving, as great At—l said [3]—
(And the nobles all cheered, and the bishops all wondered)
When, some years ago, he and others had fed
Of these same hungry devils about fifteen hundred!

It follows from hence—and the Duke's very words
Should be published wherever poor rogues of this craft are—
That weavers, *once* rescued from starving by Lords,
Are bound to be starved by said Lords ever after.

When Rome was uproarious, her knowing patricians
Made 'Bread and the Circus' a cure for each row;
But not so the plan of *our* noble physicians,
'No Bread and the Tread-mill's' the regimen now.

So cease, my dear Baron of Ockham, your prose,
As I shall my poetry—*neither* convinces;
And all we have spoken and written but shows,
When you tread on a nobleman's corn,[4] how he winces.

MORAL POSITIONS.

A DREAM.

'His Lordship said that it took a long time for a moral position to find its way across the Atlantic. He was sorry that its voyage had been so long,' etc.—*Speech of Lord Dudley and Ward on Colonial Slavery*, March 8.

T'OTHER night, after hearing Lord Dudley's oration
(A treat that comes once in the year, as Mayday does),
I dreamt that I saw—what a strange operation!—
A 'moral position' shipped off for Barbadoes.

The whole Bench of Bishops stood by, in grave attitudes,
Packing the article tidy and neat;—

---

[1] See the proceedings of the Lords, Wednesday, March 1, when Lord King was severely reproved by several of the noble Peers for making so many speeches against the Corn Laws.
[2] This noble Earl said, that 'when he heard the petition came from ladies' boot and shoe makers, he thought it must be against "the corns which they inflicted on the fair sex."'

[3] The Duke of Athol said, that 'at a former period, when these weavers were in great distress, the landed interest of Perth had supported 1500 of them. It was a poor return for these very men now to petition against the persons who had fed them.'
[4] An improvement, we flatter ourselves, on Lord L.'s joke.

As their Reverences know, that in southerly latitudes
'Moral positions' don't keep very sweet.

There was B-th—st arranging the custom-house pass;
And, to guard the frail package from tousing and routing,
There stood my Lord Eld-n, endorsing it 'Glass,'
Though—as to *which* side should lie uppermost —doubting.

The freight was, however, stowed safe in the hold;
The winds were polite, and the moon looked romantic,
While off in the good ship 'the *Truth*' we were rolled,
With our ethical cargo, across the Atlantic.

Long, dolefully long, seemed the voyage we made;—
For 'the *Truth*,' at all times but a very slow sailer,
By friends, near as much as by foes, is delayed,
And few come aboard her, though so many hail her.

At length, safe arrived, I went through 'tare and tret'—
Delivered my goods in the primest condition—
And next morning read, in the *Bridgetown Gazette*,
'Just arrived, by "the *Truth*," a new Moral Position;

'The Captain'——here, startled to find myself named
As 'the Captain' (a thing which, I own it with pain,
I through life have avoided), I woke — looked ashamed—
Found I *wasn't* a Captain, and dozed off again.

MEMORABILIA OF LAST WEEK.

MONDAY, MARCH 13.

THE Budget—quite charming and witty—no hearing,
For plaudits and laughs, the good things that were in it;—
Great comfort to find, though the Speech isn't cheering,
That all its gay auditors *were*, every minute.

What, *still* more prosperity!—mercy upon us,
'This boy'll be the death of me'—oft as, already,
Such smooth Budgeteers have genteelly undone us,
For *Ruin made easy* there's no one like Freddy.

TUESDAY.

Much grave apprehension expressed by the Peers,
Lest—as in the times of the Peachums and Lockitts—
The large stock of gold we're to have in three years,
Should all find its way into highwaymen's pockets![1]

A Petition presented (well timed, after this)
Throwing out a sly hint to Grandees, who are hurled
In their coaches about, that 'twould not be amiss
If they'd just throw a *little* more light on the world.[2]

A plan for transporting half Ireland to Canada,[3]
Which (briefly the clever transaction to state) is
Forcing John Bull to pay high for what, any day,
N-rb—ry, bless the old wag, would do *gratis*.

Keeping always (said Mr. Sub. Horton) in mind,
That while we thus draw off the claims on potatoes,
We make it a point that the Pats left behind
Should get no *new* claimants to fill the *hiatus*.[4]

Sub. Horton then read a long letter, just come
From the Canada Paddies, to say that these elves
Have already grown 'prosp'rous'—as *we* are, at home—
And have e'en got 'a surplus,' poor devils, like ourselves![5]

WEDNESDAY.

Little doing—for sacred, oh Wednesday, thou art
To the seven o'clock joys of full many a table,—
When *the Members* all meet, to make much of the part,
With which they so rashly fell out, in the Fable.

It appeared, though, to-night, that—as church-wardens yearly
Eat up a small baby—those cormorant sinners,

---

[1] 'Another objection to a metallic currency was, that it produced a greater number of highway robberies.'—*Debate in the Lords.*

[2] Mr. Estcourt presented a petition, praying that all persons should be compelled to have lamps in their carriages.

[3] Mr. W. Horton's motion on the subject of Emigration.

[4] 'The money expended in transporting the Irish to Canada would be judiciously laid out, provided measures were taken to prevent the gap they left in the population from being filled up again. *Government had always made that a condition.*'—*Mr. W. Horton's Speech.*

[5] 'The hon. gentleman then read a letter, which mentioned the prosperous condition of the writer; that he had on hand a considerable surplus of corn,' etc.

The Bankrupt-Commissioners, *bolt* very nearly
A moderate-sized bankrupt, *tout chaud*, for
 their dinners!¹

Nota Bene.—A rumour to-day, in the city,
'Mr. R-b-ns-n just has resigned'—what a pity!
The Bulls and the Bears all fell a-sobbing,
When they heard of the fate of poor Cock *Robin*,
While thus, to the nursery-tune, so pretty,
A murmuring *Stock*-dove breathed her ditty:—

Alas, poor *Robin*, he crowed as long
And as sweet as a prosperous cock could crow;
But his *note* was *small*, and the *gold*-finch's song
 Was a pitch too high for Poor Robin to go.
  Who'll make his shroud?

'I,' said the Bank, 'though he played me a prank,
 While I have a rag poor *Rob* shall be rolled in't;
With many a pound I'll paper him round,
 Like a plump rouleau—*without* the gold in't.'

. . . .

A HYMN OF WELCOME AFTER THE RECESS.

'Animas sapientiores fieri quiescendo.'

AND now—cross-buns and pancakes o'er—
Hail, Lords and Gentlemen, once more!
 Thrice hail and welcome, Houses T'wain!
The short eclipse of April-day
Having (God grant it!) passed away,
 Collective Wisdom, shine again!

Come, Ayes and Noes, through thick and thin,
With Paddy H—mes for whipper-in;
 Whate'er the job, prepared to back it;
Come, voters of Supplies—bestowers
Of jackets upon trumpet-blowers,
 At eighty mortal pounds the jacket!²

Come—free, at length, from Joint-Stock cares—
Ye Senators of many Shares,
 Whose dreams of premium knew no bound'ry;
So fond of aught like *Company*,
That you would e'en have taken *tea*
 (Had you been asked) with Mr. Goundry!³

Come, matchless country gentlemen;
Come, wise Sir Thomas, wisest then
 When creeds and corn-laws are debated!
Come, rival even the Harlot Red,
And show how wholly into bread
 A 'Squire is transubstantiated.

Come, L——e, and tell the world,
That—surely as thy scratch is curled,
 As never scratch was curled before—
Cheap eating does more harm than good,
And working-people, spoiled by food,
 The less they eat, will work the more.

Come, G—lb-rn, with thy glib defence
(Which thou'dst have made for Peter's Pence)
 Of Church-Rates, worthy of a halter;—
Two pipes of port (*old* port 'twas said
By honest *Newport*) bought and paid
 By Papists for the Orange Altar!⁴

Come, H-rt-n, with thy plan so merry,
For peopling Canada from Kerry—
 Not so much rendering Ireland quiet,
As grafting on the dull Canadians
That liveliest of earth's contagions,
 The *bull*-pock of Hibernian riot!

Come all, in short, ye wondrous men
Of wit and wisdom, come again;
 Though short your absence, all deplore it—
Oh, come and show, whate'er men say,
That you can, *after* April-day,
 Be just as—sapient as *before* it.

ALL IN THE FAMILY WAY.

A NEW PASTORAL BALLAD.

(Sung in the character of Britannia.)

'The Public Debt was due from ourselves to ourselves, and resolved itself into a Family Account.'—*Sir Robert Peel's Letter.*

TUNE—*My banks are all furnished with bees.*

My banks are all furnished with rags,
 So thick—even Fred cannot thin 'em!
I've torn up my old money-bags,
 Having nothing worth while to put in 'em.
My tradesmen are smashing by dozens,
 But this is all nothing, they say;
For bankrupts, since Adam, are cousins,
 So it's all in the family way.

My Debt not a penny takes from me,
 As sages the matter explain;—
Bob owes it to Tom, and then Tommy
 Just owes it to Bob back again.
Since all have thus taken *to owing*,
 There's nobody left that can *pay*;
And this is the way to keep going,
 All quite in the family way.

---

¹ Mr. Abercromby's statement of the enormous tavern bills of the Commissioners of Bankrupts.
² An item of expense which Mr. Hume in vain endeavoured to get rid of. Trumpeters, like the men of All-Souls, must be '*bene vestiti.*'
³ The gentleman lately before the public, who kept his *Joint*-Stock Tea Company all to himself, singing '*Te solum adoro.*'

⁴ This charge of two pipes of port for the sacramental wine is a precious specimen of the sort of rates levied upon their Catholic fellow-parishioners by the Irish Protestants.

'The thirst that from the soul doth rise
 Doth ask a drink divine.'

My senators vote away millions,
   To put in Prosperity's budget;
And though it were billions or trillions,
   The generous rogues wouldn't grudge it.
'Tis all but a family *hop*,
   'Twas Pitt began dancing the hay;
Hands round!—why the deuce should we stop?
   'Tis all in the family way.

My labourers used to eat mutton,
   As any great man of the state does;
And now the poor devils are put on
   Small rations of tea and potatoes.
But cheer up, John, Sawney, and Paddy,
   The King is your father, they say:
So, even if you starve for your daddy,
   'Tis all in the family way.

My rich manufacturers tumble,
   My poor ones have little to chew;
And even if themselves do not grumble,
   Their stomachs undoubtedly do.
But coolly to fast *en famille*
   Is as good for the soul as to pray;
And famine itself is genteel,
   When one starves in a family way.

I have found out a secret for Freddy,
   A secret for next Budget-day;
Though perhaps he may know it already;
   As *he*, too, 's a sage in his way.
When next for the Treasury scene he
   Announces 'the Devil to pay,'
Let him write on the bills—' *Nota bene*,
   'Tis all in the family way.'

THE CANONIZATION OF ST.
B—TT—RW—RTH.

'A Christian of the best edition.'—*Rabelais.*

CANONIZE him!—yea, verily, we'll canonize him;
   Though Cant is his hobby, and meddling his bliss,
Though sages may pity and wits may despise him,
   He'll ne'er make a *bit* the worse Saint for all this.

Descend, all ye spirits that ever yet spread
   The dominion of Humbug o'er land and o'er sea,
Descend on our B—tt-rw—rth's biblical head,
   Thrice-Great, Bibliopolist, Saint and M.P.!

Come, shade of Joanna, come down from thy sphere,
   And bring little Shiloh—if 'tisn't too far—

Such a sight will to B—ti—rw—rth's bosom be dear,
   His conceptions and *thine* being much on a par.

Nor blush, Saint Joanna, once more to behold
   A world thou hast honoured by cheating so many;
Thou'lt find still among us one Personage old,
   Who also by tricks and *the Seals*¹ makes a penny.

Thou, too, of the Shakers, divine Mother Lee!²
   Thy smiles to beatified B—tt—rw—rth deign;
Two 'lights of the Gentiles' art thou, Anne, and he,
   One hallowing Fleet Street, and *t'other* Toad Lane!³

The heathen, we know, made their gods out of wood,
   And saints, too, are framed of as handy materials;—
Old women and B—tt—rw—rths make just as good
   As any the Pope ever *booked*, as Ethereals.

Stand forth, Man of Bibles—not Mahomet's pigeon,
   When, perched on the Koran, he dropped there, they say,
Strong marks of his faith, ever shed o'er religion
   Such glory as B—tt—rw—rth sheds every day.

Great Galen of souls, with what vigour he crams
   Down Erin's idolatrous throats, till they crack again,
Bolus on bolus, good man!—and then damns
   Both their stomachs and souls, if they dare cast them back again.

Ah, well might his shop—as a type representing
   The creed of himself and his sanctified clan—
On its counter exhibit 'the Art of Tormenting,'
   Bound neatly, and lettered 'Whole Duty of Man.'

As to politics—*there*, too, so strong his digestion,
   Having learned from the law-books, by which he's surrounded,
To cull all that's worst on all sides of the question,
   His black dose of politics thus is compounded—

The rinsing of any old Tory's dull noddle,
   Made radical-hot, and then mixed with some grains
Of that gritty Scotch gabble, that virulent twaddle,
   Which Murray's New Series of Blackwood contains.

---

¹ A great part of the income of Joanna Southcott arose from the Seals of the Lord's protection which she sold to her followers.
² Mrs. Anne Lee, the 'chosen vessel' of the Shakers, and 'Mother of all the children of regeneration.'
³ Toad Lane in Manchester, where Mother Lee was born. In her *Address to Young Believers*, she says that 'it is a matter of no importance with them from whence the means of their deliverance come, whether from a stable in Bethlehem, or from Toad Lane, Manchester.'

Canonize him!—by Judas, we *will* canonize him;
For Cant is his hobby and twaddling his bliss.
And though wise men may pity and wits may
    despise him,
He'll make but the better shop-saint for all this.

Call quickly together the whole tribe of Canters,
  Convoke all the *serious* Tag-rag of the nation;
Bring Shakers and Snufflers and Jumpers and
    Ranters,
To witness their B-tt-rw-rth's Canonization!

Yes, humbly I've ventured his merits to paint,
  Yea, feebly have tried all his gifts to portray;
And they form a sum-total for making a saint,
  That the Devil's own Advocate could not
    gainsay.

Jump high, all ye Jumpers! ye Ranters, all roar!
  While B-tt-rw-rth's spirit, sublimed from your
    eyes,
Like a kite made of fool's-cap, in glory shall soar,
  With a long tail of rubbish behind, to the skies!

NEW CREATION OF PEERS.

BATCH THE FIRST.

'His 'prentice han'
He tried on man,
And then he made the lasses.'

'AND now,' quoth the minister (eased of his
    panics,
  And ripe for each pastime the summer affords),
'Having had our full swing at destroying
    mechanics,
  By way of *set-off*, let us make a few Lords.

''Tis pleasant — while nothing but mercantile
  fractures,
Some simple, some *compound*, is dinned in our
    ears—
To think that, though robbed of all coarse manu-
    factures,
  We still keep our fine manufacture of Peers;—

'Those *Gobelin* productions, which Kings take
    a pride
  In engrossing the whole fabrication and trade
    of;
Choice tapestry things, very grand on *one* side,
  But showing on t'other what rags they are
    made of.'

The plan being fixed, raw material was sought,
  No matter how middling, so Tory the creed
    be;'

And first—to begin with—Squire W-rt-y, 'twas
    thought,
  For a Lord was as raw a material as need be.

Next came, with his *penchant* for painting and
    pelf,
  The tasteful Sir Ch-rl-s, so renowned, far and
    near,
For purchasing pictures, and selling himself,—
  And *both* (as the public well knows) very dear.

Beside him comes L-c-st-r, with equal *éclát*,
    in;—
  Stand forth, chosen pair, while for titles we
    measure ye;
Both connoisseur baronets, both fond of *drawing*,
  Sir John after nature, Sir Charles on the
    Treasury.

But, bless us!—behold a new candidate come—
  In his hand he upholds a prescription, new
    written;
He poiseth a pill-box 'twixt finger and thumb,
  And he asketh a seat 'mong the Peers of Great
    Britain!

'Forbid it,' cried Jenky, 'ye Viscounts, ye
    Earls!—
Oh Rank, how thy glories would fall disen-
    chanted,
If coronets glistened with pills 'stead of pearls,
  And the strawberry-leaves were by rhubarb
    supplanted!

'No—ask it not, ask it not, dear Doctor H-lf-rd—
  If nought but a Peerage can gladden thy life,
And if young Master H-lf-rd as yet is too small
    for't,
  Sweet Doctor, we'll make a *she* Peer of thy
    wife.

'Next to bearing a coronet on our *own* brows,
  Is to bask in its light from the brows of an-
    other;
And grandeur o'er thee shall reflect from thy
    spouse,
As o'er Vesey Fitzgerald 'twill shine through
    his mother.'[1]

Thus ended the *First* Batch—and Jenky, much
    tired,
  (It being no joke to make Lords by the heap),
Took a large dram of ether—the same that in-
    spired
  His speech against Papists—and prosed off to
    sleep.

---

[1] Among the persons mentioned as likely to be raised to the Peerage are the mother of Mr. Vesey Fitzgerald, &c.

A CAMBRIDGE BALLAD.

'I authorized my Committee to take the step which they did, of proposing a fair comparison of strength, upon the understanding that whichever of the two should prove to be the weakest, should give way to the other.'—*Extract from Mr. W. J. Bankes's Letter to Mr. Goulburn.*

Νικα μεν ουδ' αλλοι, αι ΑΣΣαται δ' εγινοντο.
—*Theocritus.*

B—NKES is weak, and G—lb-rn too,
  No one e'er the fact denied;—
Which is '*weakest*' of the two,
  Cambridge can alone decide.
Choose between them, Cambridge, pray;
Which is weakest, Cambridge, say.

G—lb-rn of the Pope afraid is,
  B-nkes as much afraid as he;
Never yet did two old ladies
  On this point so well agree.
Choose between them, Cambridge, pray;
Which is weakest, Cambridge, say.

Each a different mode pursues,
  Each the same conclusion reaches;
B-nkes is foolish in Reviews,
  G—lb-rn foolish in his speeches.
Choose between them, Cambridge, pray;
Which is weakest, Cambridge, say.

Each a different foe doth damn,
  When his own affairs have gone ill;
B-nkes he damneth Buckingham,
  G—lb-rn damneth Dan. O'Connel.
Choose between them, Cambridge, pray;
Which is weakest, Cambridge, say.

B-nkes, accustomed much to roam,
  Plays with Truth a traveller's pranks;
G—lb-rn, though he stays at home,
  Travels thus as much as B-nkes.
Choose between them, Cambridge, pray;
Which is weakest, Cambridge, say.

Once, we know, a horse's neigh
  Fixed the election to a throne;
So, whichever first shall *bray*,
  Choose him, Cambridge, for thy own
Choose him, choose him by his bray;
Thus elect him, Cambridge, pray.

COPY OF AN INTERCEPTED DESPATCH.

FROM HIS EXCELLENCY DON STREPITOSO DIABOLO, ENVOY EXTRAORDINARY TO HIS SATANIC MAJESTY.

      St. James' Street, July 1.

GREAT Sir, having just had the good luck to catch
  An official young Demon, preparing to go,
Ready booted and spurred, with a black-leg despatch,
  From the Hell here, at Cr-ckf-rd's, to *our* Hell below—

I write these few lines to your Highness Satanic,
  To say that, first having obeyed your directions,
And done all the mischief I could in 'the Panic,'
  My next special care was to help the Elections.

Well knowing how dear were those times to thy soul,
  When every good Christian tormented his brother,
And caused in thy realm such a saving of coal,
  From their all coming down, ready grilled by each other;

Remembering, besides, how it pained thee to part
  With the old Penal Code,—that *chef-d'œuvre* of Law,
In which (though to own it too modest thou art)
  We could plainly perceive the fine touch of thy claw;

I thought, as we ne'er can those good times revive
  (Though Eld-n, with help from your Highness, would try),
'Twould still keep a taste for Hell's music alive,
  Could we get up a thundering No-Popery cry;—

That yell which, when chorused by laics and clerics,
  So like is to *ours*, in its spirit and tone,
That I often nigh laugh myself into hysterics,
  To think that Religion should make it her own.

So, having sent down for the original notes
  Of the chorus, as sung by your Majesty's choir,
With a few pints of lava, to gargle the throats
  Of myself and some others, who sing it 'with fire,'¹

Thought I, 'if the Marseillois Hymn could command
  Such audience, though yelled by a *Sans-culotte* crew,
What wonders shall *we* do, who've men in our band,
  That not only wear breeches, but petticoats too!'

Such *then* were my hopes; but, with sorrow, your Highness,
I'm forced to confess—be the cause what it will,

---

¹ *Con fuoco*—a music-book direction.

Whether fewness of voices, or hoarseness, or shyness,—
Our Beelzebub Chorus has gone off but ill.

The truth is, no placeman now knows his right key,
The Treasury pitch-pipe of late is so various;
And certain *base* voices, that looked for a fee
At the *York* music meeting, now think it precarious.

Even some of our Reverends *might* have been warmer—
But one or two capital roarers we've had;
Doctor Wise[1] is, for instance, a charming performer,
And *Huntingdon* Maberly's yell was not bad.

Altogether, however, the thing was not hearty;—
Even Eld—n allows we got on but so-so;
And when next we attempt a No-Popery party,
We *must*, please your Highness, recruit *from below*.

But, hark, the young Black-leg is cracking his whip—
Excuse me, Great Sir—there's no time to be civil;—
The next opportunity shan't be let slip,
But, till then,

    I'm, in haste, your most dutiful
               DEVIL.

MR. ROGER DODSWORTH.

To the Editor of the Times.

SIR,—Living in a remote part of Scotland, and having but just heard of the wonderful resurrection of Mr. Roger Dodsworth from under an *avalanche*, where he had remained, *bien frappé*, it seems, for the last 166 years, I hasten to impart to you a few reflections on the subject.

    Yours, etc.,

        LAUDATOR TEMPORIS ACTI.

WHAT a lucky turn-up!—just as Eld—n's withdrawing,
To find thus a gentleman, frozen in the year Sixteen hundred and sixty, who only wants thawing
To serve for *our* times quite as well as the Pear;—

To bring thus to light, not the wisdom alone
Of our ancestors, such as we find it on shelves,
But, in perfect condition, full-wigged and full-grown,
To shovel up one of those wise bucks themselves!

Oh thaw Mr. Dodsworth and send him safe hone,—
Let him learn nothing useful or new on the way;
With his wisdom kept snug from the light let him come,
And our Tories will hail him with 'Hear' and 'Hurra!'

What a God-send to them—a good, obsolete man,
Who has never of Locke or Voltaire been a reader;—
Oh thaw Mr. Dodsworth as fast as you can,
And the L—nsd—les and H—rtf—rds shall choose him for leader.

Yes, sleeper of ages, thou *shalt* be their Chosen;
And deeply with thee will they sorrow, good men,
To think that all Europe has, since thou wert frozen,
So altered, thou hardly canst know it again.

And Eld—n will weep o'er each sad innovation
Such oceans of tears, thou wilt fancy that he
Has been also laid up in a long congelation,
And is only now thawing, dear Roger, like thee.

THE MILLENNIUM.

SUGGESTED BY THE LATE WORK OF THE REVEREND MR. IRV—NG 'ON PROPHECY.'

A MILLENNIUM at hand!—I'm delighted to hear it—
As matters, both public and private, now go,
With multitudes round us all starving, or near it,
A good rich Millennium will come *à propos*.

Only think, Master Fred, what delight to behold,
Instead of thy bankrupt old City of Rags,
A bran-new Jerusalem, built all of gold,
Sound bullion throughout, from the roof to the flags—

A city, where wine and cheap corn[2] shall abound,—
A celestial *Cocaigne*, on whose buttery shelves
We may swear the best things of this world will be found,
As your saints seldom fail to take care of themselves!

---

[1] This reverend gentleman distinguished himself at the Reading election.

[2] 'A measure of wheat for a penny, and three measures of barley for a penny.'—REV. c. 6.

Thanks, reverend expounder of raptures elysian,[1]
  Divine Squintifobus, who, placed within reach
Of two opposite worlds, by a twist of your vision
  Can cast, at the same time, a sly look at each;—

Thanks, thanks for the hope thou hast given us,
    that we
  May, even in our own times, a jubilee share,
Which so long has been promised by prophets
    like thee,
  And so often has failed, we began to despair.

There was Whiston,[2] who learnedly took Prince
    Eugene
  For the man who must bring the Millennium
    about;
There's Faber, whose pious predictions have been
  All belied, ere his book's first edition was out;—

There was Counsellor Dobbs, too, an Irish M.P.,
  Who discoursed on the subject with signal *éclât*,
And each day of his life, sat expecting to see
  A Millennium break out in the town of Ar-
    magh![3]

There was also—but why should I burden my lay
  With your Brothereas, Southcotes, and names
    less deserving,
When all past Millenniums henceforth must give
    way
  To the last new Millennium of Orator Irv-ng?

Go on, mighty man,—doom them all to the shelf—
  And, when next thou with Prophecy troublest
    thy sconce,
Oh forget not, I pray thee, to prove that thyself
  Art the Beast (chapter 4) that sees nine ways
    at once!

THE THREE DOCTORS.

Doctoribus lætamur tribus.

Though many great Doctors there be,
  There are three that all Doctors o'ertop,—
Dr. Eady, that famous M.D.,
  Dr. S—they, and dear Doctor Slop.

The purger—the proser—the bard—
  All quacks in a different style;
Dr. S—they writes books by the yard,
  Dr. Eady writes puffs by the mile.

Dr. Slop, in no merit outdone
  By his scribbling or physicking brother,
Can dose us with stuff like the one,
  Ay, and *doze* us with stuff like the other.

Dr. Eady good company keeps
  With 'No-Popery' scribes on the walls;
Dr. S—they as gloriously sleeps
  With 'No-Popery' scribes, on the stalls.

Dr. Slop, upon subjects divine,
  Such bedlamite slaver lets drop,
That if Eady should take the *mad* line,
  He'll be sure of a patient in Slop.

Seven millions of Papists, no less,
  Dr. S—they attacks like a Turk;[4]
Dr. Eady, less bold, I confess,
  Attacks but his maid of all work.[5]

Dr. S—they, for *his* grand attack,
  Both a laureate and senator is;
While poor Dr. Eady, alack,
  Has been *had up* to Bow Street, for his!

And truly, the law does so blunder,
  That, though little blood has been spilt, he
May probably suffer as, under
  The *Chalking* Act, *known* to be guilty.

So much for the merits sublime
  (With whose catalogue ne'er should I stop)
Of the three greatest lights of our time,
  Drs. Eady and S—they and Slop!

Should you ask me, to *which* of the three
  Great Doctors the preference should fall,
As a matter of course, I agree
  Dr. Eady must go *to the wall*.

But as S—they with laurels is crowned,
  And Slop with a wig and a tail is,
Let Eady's bright temples be bound
  With a swinging 'Corona *Muralis!*'[6]

---

[1] See the oration of this reverend gentleman, where he describes the connubial joys of paradise, and paints the angels hovering around 'each happy fair.'

[2] When Whiston presented to Prince Eugene the Essay in which he attempted to connect his victories over the Turks with revelation, the Prince is said to have replied that 'he was not aware he had ever had the honour of being known to St John.'

[3] Mr. Dobbs was a Member of the Irish Parliament, and on all other subjects but the Millennium a very sensible person. He chose Armagh as the scene of the Millennium, on account of the name Armageddon, mentioned in Revelation!

[4] This Seraphic Doctor, in the preface to his last work (*Vindiciæ Ecclesiæ Anglicanæ*), is pleased to anathematize not only all Catholics, but all advocates of Catholics:—'They have for their immediate allies (he says) every faction that is banded against the State, every demagogue, every irreligious and seditious journalist, every open and every insidious enemy to Monarchy and to Christianity.'

[5] See the late accounts in the newspapers of the appearance of this gentleman at one of the police-offices, in consequence of an alleged assault upon his 'maid of all work.'

[6] A crown granted as a reward among the Romans to persons who performed any extraordinary exploits upon *walls*—such as scaling them, battering them, etc. No doubt, writing upon them, to the extent that Dr. Eady does, would equally establish a claim to the honour

EPITAPH ON A TUFT-HUNTER.

Lament, lament, Sir Isaac Heard,
Put mourning round thy page, Debrett,
For here lies one who ne'er preferred
A Viscount to a Marquis yet.

Beside him place the God of Wit,
Before him Beauty's rosiest girls;
Apollo for a *star* he'd quit,
And Love's own sister for an Earl's.

Did niggard Fate no peers afford,
He took, of course, to peers' relations;
And, rather than not sport a lord,
Put up with even the last creations.

Even Irish names, could he but tag 'em
With 'Lord' and 'Duke,' were sweet to call;
And, at a pinch, Lord Ballyraggum
Was better than no Lord at all.

Heaven grant him now some noble nook,
For, rest his soul, he'd rather be
Genteelly damned beside a Duke,
Than saved in vulgar company.

THE PETITION

OF THE ORANGEMEN OF IRELAND.

To the people of England, the humble Petition
Of Ireland's disconsolate Orangemen, show-
ing—
That sad, very sad, is our present condition;—
That our jobs are all gone, and our noble selves
going;

That, forming one seventh—within a few fractions—
Of Ireland's seven millions of hot heads and
hearts,
We hold it the basest of all base transactions
To keep us from murdering the other six
parts;—

That, as to laws made for the good of the many,
We humbly suggest there is nothing less true;
As all human laws (and our own more than any)
Are made *by* and *for* a particular few;—

That much it delights every true Orange brother
To see you, in England, such ardour evince,

In discussing *which* sect most tormented the other,
And burned with most *gusto*, some hundred
years since;—

That we love to behold, while Old England grows
faint,
Messrs. Southey and Butler near coming to
blows,
To decide whether Dunstan, that strong-bodied
saint,
Ever truly and really pulled the devil's nose;

Whether t'other saint, Dominic, burnt the devil's
paw—
Whether Edwy intrigued with Elgiva's old
mother [1]—
And many such points, from which Southey doth
draw
Conclusions most apt for our hating each other.

That 'tis very well known this devout Irish
nation
Has now for some ages gone happily on,
Believing in two kinds of Substantiation,
One party in *Trans*, and the other in *Con*; [2]

That we, your petitioning *Cons*, have, in right
Of the said monosyllable, ravaged the lands,
And embezzled the goods, and annoyed, day and
night,
Both the bodies and souls of the sticklers for
Trans;—

That we trust to Peel, Eldon, and other such
sages,
For keeping us still in the same state of mind;
Pretty much as the world used to be in those
ages,
When still smaller syllables maddened mankind;—

When the words *ex* and *per*[3] served as well, to
annoy
One's neighbours and friends with, as *con* and
trans now;
And Christians, like Southey, who stickled
for *oi*,
Cut the throats of all Christians who stickled
for *ou*.[4]

That, relying on England, whose kindness
already
So often has helped us to play the game o'er,
We have got our red coats and our carabines
ready,
And wait but the word to show sport, as
before.

---

[1] To such important discussions as these the greater part of Dr. Southey's *Vindiciæ Ecclesiæ Anglicanæ* is devoted.

[2] Consubstantiation — the true reformed belief; at least the belief of Luther, and, as Mosheim asserts, of Melancthon also.

[3] When John of Ragusa went to Constantinople (at the time this dispute between 'ex' and 'per' was going on), he found the Turks, we are told, 'laughing at the Christians for being divided by two such insignificant particles.'

[4] 'The Arian controversy. — Before that time, says Hooker, 'In order to be a sound believing Christian, men were not curious what syllables or particles of speech they used.'

That, as to the expense—the few millions, or
 so,
Which for all such diversions John Bull has to
 pay—
'Tis, at least, a great comfort to John Bull to
 know
That to Orangemen's pockets 'twill all find its
 way.

For which your petitioners ever will pray,
 etc. etc. etc. etc. etc.

A VISION.

BY THE AUTHOR OF CHRISTABEL.

'Up!' said the Spirit, and, ere I could pray
One hasty orison, whirled me away
To a limbo, lying—I wist not where—
Above or below, in earth or air;
All glimmering o'er with a *doubtful* light,
One couldn't say whether 'twas day or night;
And crossed by many a mazy track,
One didn't know how to get on or back;
And I felt like a needle that's going astray
(With its *one* eye out) through a bundle or nay;
When the Spirit he grinned, and whispered me,
'Thou'rt now in the Court of Chancery!'
Around me flitted unnumbered swarms
Of shapeless, bodiless, tailless forms;
(Like bottled-up babes that grace the room
Of that worthy knight, Sir Everard Home)—
All of them things half-killed in rearing;
Some were lame—some wanted *hearing;*
Some had through half-a-century run,
Though they hadn't a leg to stand upon.
Others, more merry, as just beginning,
Around on a *point of law* were spinning;
Or balanced aloft, 'twixt *Bill* and *Answer,*
Lead at each end—like a tight-rope dancer.—
Some were so *cross,* that nothing could please
 'em;—
Some gulped down *affidavits* to ease 'em;—
All were in motion, yet never a one,
Let it *move* as it might, could ever move on.
'These,' said the Spirit, 'you plainly see,
Are what are called Suits in Chancery!'

I heard a loud screaming of old and young,
Like a chorus by fifty Velutis sung;
Or an Irish Dump ('the words by Moore')
At an amateur concert screamed in score:—
So harsh on my ear that wailing fell
Of the wretches who in this Limbo dwell!
It seemed like the dismal symphony
Of the shapes Æneas in hell did see;
Or those frogs, whose legs a barbarous cook
Cut off, and left the frogs in the brook,
To cry all night, till life's last dregs,
'Give us our legs!—give us our legs!'
Touched with the sad and sorrowful scene,
I asked what all this yell might mean?
When the Spirit replied, with a grin of glee,
'"Tis the cry of the suitors in Chancery!'

I looked, and I saw a wizard rise,
With a wig like a cloud before men's eyes.
In his agèd hand he held a wand,
Wherewith he beckoned his embryo band,
And they moved, and moved, as he waved it
 o'er,
But they never got on one inch the more;
And still they kept limping to and fro,
Like Ariels round old Prospero—
Saying, 'Dear Master, let us go;'
But still old Prospero answered, 'No.'
And I heard the while, that wizard elf,
Muttering, muttering spells to himself,
While over as many old papers he turned,
As Hume ere moved for, or Omar burned.
He talked of his Virtue, though some, less nice,
(He owned with a sigh) preferred his *Vice*—
And he said, 'I think'—'I doubt'—'I hope,'
Called God to witness, and damned the Pope·
With many more sleights of tongue and hand
I couldn't, for the soul of me, understand.
Amazed and posed, I was just about
To ask his name, when the screams without,
The merciless clack of the imps within,
And that conjuror's mutterings, made such a
 din,
That, startled, I woke—leaped up in my bed—
Found the Spirit, the imps, and the conjuror
 fled,
And blessed my stars, right pleased to see
That I wasn't as yet in Chancery.

NEWS FOR COUNTRY COUSINS.

Dear Coz, as I know neither you nor Miss
 Draper,
When Parliament's up, ever take in a paper,
But trust for your news to such stray odds and
 ends
As you chance to pick up from political friends—
Being one of this well-informed class, I sit
 down,
To transmit you the last newest news that's
 in town.

As to Greece and Lord Cochrane, things couldn't
 look better—
 His Lordship (who promises now to fight
 faster)
Has just taken Rhodes, and despatched off a
 letter
 To Daniel O'Connel, to make him Grand
 Master;
Engaging to change the old name, if he can,
From the Knights of St. John to the Knights of
 St. Dan—
Or, if Dan should prefer, as a still better whim,
Being made the Colossus, 'tis all one to him.

From Russia the last accounts are, that he
 Czar—
Most generous and kind, as all sovereigns are,

And whose first princely act (as you know, I
  suppose)
Was to give away all his late brother's old
  clothes—
Is now busy collecting, with brotherly care,
The late Emperor's night-caps, and thinks of
  bestowing
One night-cap apiece (if he has them to spare)
On all the distinguished old ladies now going.
(While I write, an arrival from Riga—'the
  Brothers'—
Having night-caps on board for Lord Eld-n and
  others.)

Last advices from India—Sir Archy, 'tis
  thought,
Was near catching a Tartar (the first ever
  caught
In N. lat. 21)—and his Highness Burmese,
Being very hard pressed to shell out the rupees,
But not having much ready rhino, they say,
  meant
To pawn his august golden foot[1] for the pay-
  ment.—
(How lucky for monarchs, that can, when they
  choose,
Thus establish a *running account* with the
  Jews!)
The security being what Rothschild calls 'goot,'
A loan will be forthwith, of course, set on
  foot;—
The parties are Rothschild—A. Baring and Co.,
And three other great pawnbrokers—each takes
  a toe,
And engages (lest Gold-foot should give us leg
  bail,
As he did once before) to pay down *on the nail.*

This is all for the present—what vile pens and
  paper!
Yours truly, dear Cousin—best love to Miss
  Draper.

AN INCANTATION.

SUNG BY THE BUBBLE SPIRIT.

AIR—'Come with me, and we will go
  Where the rocks of coral grow.'

COME with me, and we will blow
Lots of bubbles, as we go;
Bubbles, bright as ever Hope
Drew from fancy—or from soap;

Bright as e'er the South Sea sent
From its frothy element!
Come with me, and we will blow
Lots of bubbles as we go.

Mix the lather, Johnny W-lks,
Thou who rhym'st so well to 'bilks;'[2]
Mix the lather—who can be
Fitter for such task than thee,
Great M.P. for *Sudsbury!*

Now the frothy charm is ripe,
Puffing Peter, bring thy pipe,—
Thou, whom ancient Coventry
Once so dearly loved, that she
Knew not which to her was sweeter,
Peeping Tom or puffing Peter—

Puff the bubbles high in air,
Puff thy best to keep them there.
Bravo, bravo, Peter M-re!
Now the rainbow humbugs[3] soar,
Glittering all with golden hues,
Such as haunt the dreams of Jews—
Some, reflecting mines that lie
Under Chili's glowing sky;
Some, those virgin pearls that sleep
Cloistered in the southern deep;
Others, as if lent a ray
From the streaming Milky Way,
Glistening o'er with curds and whey
From the cows of Alderney!

Now's the moment—who shall first
Catch the bubbles ere they burst?
Run, ye squires, ye viscounts, run,
Br-gd-n, T-ynh-m, P-lm-rst-n;—
John W-lks, junior, runs beside ye,
Take the good the knaves provide ye![4]
See, with upturned eyes and hands,
Where the *Chare*man,[5] Br-gd-n, stands,
Gaping for the froth to fall
Down his swallow—*lye* and all!
See!—

But, hark, my time is out—
Now, like some great waterspout,
Scattered by the cannon's thunder,
Burst, ye bubbles, all asunder!

[*Here the stage darkens—a discordant crash is
heard from the orchestra—the broken bubbles
descend in a saponaceous but uncleanly mist over
the heads of the Dramatis Personæ, and the
scene drops, leaving the bubble-hunters—all in
the suds.*]

---

[1] This Potentate styles himself the Monarch of the Golden Foot.
[2] Strong indications of character may be sometimes traced in the rhymes to names. Marvell thought so, when he wrote;
  'Sir Edward Sutton,
  The foolish knight who rhymes to mutton.'
[3] An humble imitation of one of our modern poets, who, in a poem against war, after describing the splendid habiliments of the soldier, apostrophizes him: '·Thou rainbow ruffian!'
[4] 'Lovely Thais sits beside thee,
  Take the good the Gods provide thee.'
[5] So called by a sort of Tuscan dulcification of the *ch* in the word 'Chairman.'

A DREAM OF TURTLE.

BY SIR W. CURTIS.

'TWAS evening time, in the twilight sweet
I was sailing along, when — whom should I meet,
But a turtle journeying o'er the sea,
'On the service of his Majesty!'

When I spied him first, in the twilight dim,
I did not know what to make of him;
But said to myself — as slow he plied
His fins, and rolled from side to side,
Conceitedly over the watery path —
"'Tis my Lord of St-w-ll taking a bath;
And I hear him now, among the fishes,
Quoting Vatel and Burgerdiscius!"

But, no — 'twas, indeed, a turtle, wide
And plump as ever these eyes descried;
A turtle, juicy as ever yet
Glued up the lips of a baronet!
Ah, much did it grieve my soul to see
That an animal of such dignity,
Like an absentee, abroad should roam,
When he *ought* to stay and be ate at home.

But now 'a change came o'er my dream,'
Like the magic lantern's shifting slider; —
I looked, and saw by the evening beam,
On the back of that turtle sate a rider, —
A goodly man, with an eye so merry,
I knew 'twas our Foreign Secretary,
Who there, at his ease, did sit and smile,
Like Waterton on his crocodile;
Cracking such jokes, at every motion,
As made the turtle squeak with glee,
And own that they gave him a lively notion
Of what his own *forced*-meat balls would be.

So on the Sec., in his glory, went
Over that briny element,
Waving his hand, as he took farewell,
With a graceful air, and bidding me tell
Inquiring friends that the turtle and he
Were gone on a foreign embassy —
To soften the heart of a *Diplomate*,
Who is known to doat upon verdant fat,
And to let admiring Europe see,
That *calipash* and *calipee*
Are the English forms of Diplomacy!

COTTON AND CORN.
A DIALOGUE.

SAID Cotton to Corn t'other day,
As they met, and exchanged a salute —
(Squire Corn in his cabriolet,
Poor Cotton, half famished, on foot) —

'Great Squire, if it isn't uncivil
To hint at starvation before you,
Look down on a hungry poor devil,
And give him some bread, I implore you!'

Quoth Corn then, in answer to Cotton,
Perceiving he meant to make *free*, —
'Low fellow, you've surely forgotten
The distance between you and me!

'To expect that we, peers of high birth,
Should waste our illustrious acres
For no other purpose on earth
Than to fatten curst calico-makers! —

'That bishops to bobbins should bend, —
Should stoop from their bench's sublimity,
Great dealers in *lawn*, to befriend
Your contemptible dealers in dimity!

'No — vile manufacture! ne'er harbour
A hope to be fed at our boards; —
Base offspring of Arkwright the barber,
What claim canst *thou* have upon lords?

'No — thanks to the taxes and debt,
And the triumph of paper o'er guineas,
Our race of Lord Jemmys, as yet,
May defy your whole rabble of *Jennys!*'

So saying, whip, crack, and away
Went Corn in his cab through the throng,
So madly, I heard them all say
Squire Corn would be *down* before long.

THE DONKEY AND HIS PANNIERS.
A FABLE.

Fessus jam sudat asellus,
Parce illi; vestrum deliclum est asinus. — *Virgil. Copa.*

A DONKEY, whose talent for burdens was wondrous,
So much that you'd swear he rejoiced in a load,
One day had to jog under panniers so pond'rous,
That — down the poor donkey fell, smack on the road.

His owners and drivers stood round in amaze —
What! Neddy, the patient, the prosper-us Neddy,
So easy to drive through the dirtiest ways,
For every description of job-work so ready!

One driver (whom Ned might have 'hailed' as a 'brother')[1]
Had just been proclaiming his donkey's renown,
For vigour, for spirit, for one thing or other, —
When, lo, 'mid his praises, the donkey came down!

---

[1] Alluding to an early poem of Mr. Coleridge's addressed to an ass, and beginning, 'I hail thee, brother!'

But, how to upraise him?—one shouts, t'other whistles,
While Jenky the conjuror, wisest of all,
Declared that an 'over-production' of thistles[1]—
(Here Ned gave a stare)—was the cause of his fall.

Another wise Solomon cries, as he passes,—
'There, let him alone, and the fit will soon cease;
The beast has been fighting with other jackasses,
And this is his mode of "*transition to peace*."'

Some looked at his hoofs, and, with learned grimaces,
Pronounced that too long without shoes he had gone—
'Let the blacksmith provide him a *sound metal basis,*
(The wiseacres said), and he's sure to jog on.'

But others who gabbled a jargon half Gaelic,
Exclaimed, 'Hoot awa, mon, you're a' gane astray,'—
And declared that, 'whoe'er might prefer the *metallic,*
They'd shoe their *own* donkeys with *papier maché.*'

Meanwhile the poor Neddy, in torture and fear,
Lay under his panniers, scarce able to groan,
And—what was still dolefuller—lending an ear
To advisers whose ears were a match for his own.

At length, a plain rustic, whose wit went so far
As to see others' folly, roared out, as he passed—
'Quick—off with the panniers, all dolts as ye are,
Or your prosperous Neddy will soon kick his last!'

ODE TO THE SUBLIME PORTE.

GREAT Sultan, how wise are thy state compositions!
And oh, above all, I admire that decree,
In which thou command'st that all *she* politicians
Shall forthwith be strangled and cast in the sea.

'Tis my fortune to know a lean Benthamite spinster—
A maid, who her faith in old Jeremy puts;
Who talks, with a lisp, of 'the last new Westminster,'
And hopes you're delighted with 'Mill upon Gluts;'

Who tells you how clever one Mr. F-nbl-nque is,
How charming his Articles 'gainst the Nobility;—
And assures you, that even a gentleman's rank is,
In Jeremy's school, of no sort of *utility*.

To see her, ye Gods, a new Number devouring—
Art. 1, 'On the *Needle's* variations,' by Snip;
Art. 2, 'On the *Bondage* of Greece,' by John B—r—ng
(That eminent dealer in scribbling and scrip);

Art. 3, 'Upon Fallacies,' Jeremy's own
(The chief fallacy being his hope to find readers);
Art. 4, 'Upon Honesty'—author unknown;
Art. 5 (by the young Mr. M——), 'Hints to Breeders.'

Oh Sultan, oh Sultan, though oft for the bag
And the bowstring, like thee, I am tempted to call—
Though drowning's too good for each blue-stocking hag,
I would bag this *she* Benthamite first of them all!

Ay, and—lest she should ever again lift her head
From the watery bottom, her clack to renew,—
As a clog, as a sinker, far better than lead,
I would hang round her neck her own darling Review.

THE GHOST OF MILTIADES.

Ah quoties dubius Scriptis exarsit amator!—Ovid.

THE ghost of Miltiades came at night,
And he stood by the bed of the Benthamite;
And he said in a voice that thrilled the frame,
'If ever the sound of Marathon's name
Hath fired thy blood, or flushed thy brow,
Lover of liberty, rouse thee now!'

The Benthamite, yawning, left his bed—
Away to the Stock Exchange he sped,
And he found the scrip of Greece so high,
That it fired his blood, it flushed his eye;
And oh! 'twas a sight for the ghost to see,
For there never was Greek more Greek than he!
And still, as the premium higher went,
His ecstasy rose—so much *per cent.*

---

[1] A certain country gentleman having said in the House, 'that we must return at last to the food of our ancestors,' somebody asked Mr. T. 'what food the gentleman meant?'—'Thistles, I suppose,' answered Mr. T.

(As we see, in a glass that tells the weather,
The heat and the *silver* rise together),
And Liberty sung from the patriot's lip,
While a voice from his pocket whispered 'Scrip!'

The ghost of Miltiades came again;—
He smiled, as the pale moon shines through rain,
For his soul was glad at that patriot strain;
(And, poor dear ghost, how little he knew
The jobs and tricks of the Philhellene crew!)
'Blessings and thanks!' was all he said,
Then melting away, like a night dream, fled!

The Benthamite hears—amazed that ghosts
Could be such fools—and away he posts,
A patriot still! Ah no, ah no—
Goddess of Freedom, thy scrip is low,
And, warm and fond as thy lovers are,
Thou triest their passion when under *par*.
The Benthamite's ardour fast decays,
By turns he weeps, and swears, and prays,
And wishes the d——l had crescent and cross,
Ere *he* had been forced to sell at a loss.
They quote him the stock of various nations,
But, spite of his classic associations,
Lord! how he loathes the Greek *quotations!*
'Who'll buy my scrip? Who'll buy my scrip?'
Is now the theme of the patriot's lip,
As he runs to tell how hard his lot is
To Messrs. Orlando and Luriottis,
And says, 'Oh Greece, for liberty's sake,
Do buy my scrip, and I vow to break
Those dark, unholy *bonds* of thine—
If you'll only consent to buy up *mine!*'

The ghost of Miltiades came once more;—
His brow, like the night, was lowering o'er;
And he said, with a look that flashed dismay,
'Of liberty's foes the worst are they
Who turn to a trade her cause divine,
And gamble for gold on Freedom's shrine!'
Thus saying, the ghost, as he took his flight,
Gave a parting kick to the Benthamite,
Which sent him, whimpering, off to Jerry—
And vanished away to the Stygian ferry!

CORN AND CATHOLICS.

Utrum horum
Dirius borum?—*Incerti Auctores.*

WHAT! *still* those two infernal questions,
That with our meals, our slumbers mix—
That spoil our tempers and digestions—
Eternal Corn and Catholics!

Gods! were there ever two such bores?
Nothing else talked of, night or morn—
Nothing *in* doors, or *out* of doors,
But endless Catholics and Corn!

Never was such a brace of pests—
While Ministers, still worse than either,

Skilled but in feathering their nests,
Bore us with both, and settle neither.

So addled in my cranium meet
Popery and Corn, that oft I doubt'
Whether, this year, 'twas bonded wheat
Or bonded papists they let out.

Here landlords, here polemics, nail you,
  Armed with all rubbish they can rake up;
Prices and *texts* at once assail you—
  From Daniel *these*, and *those* from Jacob.

And when you sleep, with head still torn
  Between the two, their shapes you mix,
Till sometimes Catholics seem Corn,—
  Then Corn again seem Catholics.

Now Dantzic wheat before you floats—
  Now, Jesuits from California—
Now Ceres, linked with Titus *Oats*,
  Comes dancing through the 'Porta *Cornea.*

Oft, too, the Corn grows animate,
  And a whole crop of heads appears,
Like Papists, *bearding* Church and State—
  Themselves together *by the ears!*

While, leaders of the wheat, a row
  Of Poppies, gaudily declaiming,
Like Counsellor O'Bric and Co.,
  Stand forth, somniferously flaming!

In short, their torments never cease;
  And oft I wish myself transferred off
To some far, lonely land of peace,
  Where Corn or Papists ne'er were heard of.

Oh waft me, Parry, to the Pole;
  For—if my fate is to be chosen
'Twixt bores and icebergs—on my soul,
  I'd rather, of the two, be frozen!

THE PERIWINKLES AND THE LOCUSTS.

A SALMAGUNDIAN HYMN.

'To Panurge was assigned the Lairdship of Salmagundi, which was yearly worth 6,789,106,789 ryals, besides the revenue of the *Locusts* and *Periwinkles*, amounting one year with another to the value of 2,425,768,' etc. etc.—*Rabelais.*

'HURRA! Hurra!' I heard them say,
  And they cheered and shouted all the way,
As the Laird of Salmagundi went
  To open in state his Parliament.

The Salmagundians once were rich,
Or *thought* they were—no matter which—
For, every year, the Revenue [1]
From their periwinkles larger grew;

[1] Accented as in Swift's line—
' Not so a nation's revenues are paid.'

And their rulers, skilled in all the trick,
And legerdemain of arithmetic,
Knew how to place 1, 2, 3, 4,
   5, 6, 7, 8, and 9 and 10,
Such various ways, behind, before,
That they made a unit seem a score,
   And proved themselves most wealthy men!

So, on they went, a prosperous crew,
   The people wise, the rulers clever,—
And God help those, like me and you,
Who dared to doubt (as some now do)
That the Periwinkle Revenue
   Would thus go flourishing on for ever.

'Hurra! hurra!' I heard them say,
And they cheered and shouted all the way,
As the Great Panurge in glory went
To open his own dear Parliament.

But folks at length began to doubt
What all this conjuring was about;
For, every day, more deep in debt
They saw their wealthy rulers get:—
'Let's look (said they) the items through,
And see if what we're told be true
Of our Periwinkle Revenue.'
But, lord, they found there wasn't a tittle
   Of truth in aught they heard before;
For they gained by Periwinkles little,
   And lost by Locusts ten times more!
These Locusts are a lordly breed
Some Salmagundians love to feed.
Of all the beasts that ever were born,
Your Locust most delights in *corn;*
And though his body be but small,
To fatten him takes the devil and all!

Nor this the worst, for, direr still,
   Alack, alack, and well-a-day!
Their Periwinkles—once the stay
And prop of the Salmagundian till—
For want of feeding, all fell ill!
And still, as they thinned and died away,
The Locusts, ay, and the Locusts' Bill,
   Grew fatter and fatter every day!

'Oh fie! oh fie!' was now the cry,
As they saw the gaudy show go by,
And the Laird of Salmagundi went
To open his Locust Parliament!

A CASE OF LIBEL.

A CERTAIN old Sprite, who dwells below
   ('Twere a libel, perhaps, to mention where),
Came up *incog.,* some winters ago,
   To try, for a change, the London air.

So well he looked, and dressed, and talked,
   And hid his tail and his horns so handy,
You'd hardly have known him, as he walked,
   From ———, or any other Dandy.

(*N.B.*—His horns, they say, unscrew;
   So he has but to take them out of the socket,
And—just as some fine husbands do—
   Conveniently clap them into his pocket.)

In short, he looked extremely natty,
   And even contrived—to his own grea wonder—
By dint of sundry scents from Gattie,
   To keep the sulphurous *hogo* under.

And so my gentleman hoofed about,
   Unknown to all but a chosen few
At White's and Crockford's, where, no doubt,
   He had many *post-obits* falling due.

Alike a gamester and a wit,
   At night he was seen with Crockford's crew;
At morn with learned dames would sit—
   So passed his time 'twixt *black* and *blue.*

Some wished to make him an M.P.;
   But, finding W-lks was also one, he
Was heard to say 'he'd be d———d if he
   Would ever sit in one house with Johnny.'

At length, as secrets travel fast,
   And devils, whether he or she,
Are sure to be found out at last,
   The affair got wind most rapidly.

The press, the impartial press, that snubs
   Alike a fiend's or an angel's capers—
Miss Paton's soon as Beelzebub's—
   Fired off a squib in the morning papers:

'We warn good men to keep aloof
   From a grim old Dandy, seen about,
With a fire-proof wig and a cloven hoof,
   Through a neat-cut Hoby smoking out.'

Now, the Devil being a gentleman,
   Who piques himself on his well-bred dealings,
You may guess, when o'er these lines he ran,
   How much they hurt and shocked his feelings.

Away he posts to a man of law,
   And oh, 'twould make you laugh to 've seen 'em,
As paw shook hand, and hand shook paw,
   And 'twas 'Hail, good fellow, well met,' between 'em.

Straight an indictment was preferred—
   And much the Devil enjoyed the jest,
When, looking among the judges, he heard
   That, of all the batch, his own was *Best.*

In vain Defendant proffered proof
   That Plaintiff's self was the Father of Evil—
Brought Hoby forth to swear to the hoof,
   And Stultz to speak to the tail of the Devil.

The Jury—saints, all snug and rich,
   And readers of virtuous Sunday papers—

Found for the Plaintiff; on hearing which
   The Devil gave one of his loftiest capers.

For oh, it was nuts to the father of lies
   (As this wily fiend is named in the Bible),
To find it settled by laws so wise,
   That the greater the truth, the worse the libel!

LITERARY ADVERTISEMENT.

WANTED—Authors of all-work, to job for the
      season,
   No matter which party, so faithful, to
      neither:—
Good hacks, who, if posed for a rhyme or a reason,
   Can manage, like ——, to do without either.

If in gaol, all the better for out-o'-door topics;
   Your gaol is for travellers a charming retreat;
They can take a day's rule for a trip to the
      Tropics,
   And sail round the world, at their ease, in the
      Fleet.

For Dramatists, too, the most useful of schools—
   They may study high life in the King's Bench
      community:
Aristotle could scarce keep them more *within
      rules*,
   And of *place* they're at least taught to stick
      to the *unity*.

Any lady or gentleman come to an age
   To have good 'Reminiscences' (threescore, or
      higher),
Will meet with encouragement—so much *per
      page*,
   And the spelling and grammar both found by
      the buyer.

No matter with *what* their remembrance is
      stocked,
   So they'll only remember the *quantum* desired;—
Enough to fill handsomely Two Volumes, *oct.*,
   Price twenty-four shillings, is all that's required.

They may treat us, like Kelly, with old *jeux-
      d'esprits*,
   Like Reynolds, may boast of each mountebank
      frolic,
Or kindly inform us, like Madame Genlis,[1]
   That gingerbread cakes always give them the
      colic.

There's nothing at present so popular growing
   As your Autobiographers—fortunate elves,

Who manage to know all the best people going,
   Without having ever been heard of themselves!

Wanted, also, a new stock of Pamphlets on Corn,
   By 'Farmers' and 'Landholders'—(*gemmen*,
      whose lands·
Enclosed all in bow-pots, their attics adorn,
   Or whose share of the soil may be seen on their
      hands).

No-Popery Sermons, in ever so dull a vein,
   Sure of a market;—should they, too, who pen
      'em,
Be renegade Papists, like Murtagh O'S–ll–v–n,[2]
   Something *extra* allowed for the additional
      venom.

Funds, Physic, Corn, Poetry, Boxing, Romance,
   All excellent subjects for turning a penny;—
To write upon *all* is an author's sole chance
   For attaining, at last, the least knowledge of
      any.

Nine times out of ten, if his title be good,
   His matter within of small consequence is;—
Let him only write fine, and, if not understood,
   Why,—that's the concern of the reader, not his.

N.B.—A learned Essay, now printing, to show
   That Horace (as clearly as words could express it)
Was for taxing the Fundholders, ages ago,
   When he wrote thus—'Quodcunque *in Fund
      is, assess it*.'[3]

THE SLAVE.

I HEARD, as I lay, a wailing sound,
   'He is dead—he is dead,' the rumour flew;
And I raised my chain, and turned me round,
   And asked, through the dungeon window,
      'Who?'

I saw my livid tormentors pass;
   Their grief 'twas bliss to hear and see!
For never came joy to them, alas,
   That didn't bring deadly bane to me.

Eager I looked through the mist of night,
   And asked, 'What foe of my race hath died?
Is it he—that Doubter of law and right,
   Whom nothing but wrong could e'er decide—

'Who, long as he sees but wealth to win,
   Hath never yet felt a qualm or doubt
What suitors for justice he'd keep in,
   Or what suitors for freedom he'd shut out—

---

[1] This lady, in her *Memoirs*, also favours us with the address of those apothecaries who have from time to time given her pills that agreed with her; always desiring that the pills should be ordered '*comme pour elle*.'
[2] A gentleman who distinguished himself by his evidence before the Irish Committees.
[3] According to the common reading, '*Quodcunque infundis, accescit*.'

'Who, a clog for ever on Truth's advance,
　Stifles her (like the Old Man of the Sea
Round Sinbad's neck¹), nor leaves a chance
　Of shaking him off—is't he? is't he?'

Ghastly my grim tormentors smiled,
　And thrusting me back to my den of woe,
With a laughter even more fierce and wild
　Than their funeral howling, answered 'No.'

But the cry still pierced my prison gate,
　And again I asked, 'What scourge is gone?
Is it he—that Chief, so coldly great,
　Whom Fame unwillingly shines upon—

'Whose name is one of the ill-omened words
　They link with hate on his native plains;
And why?—they lent him hearts and swords,
　And he gave, in return, scoffs and chains!

'Is it he? is it he?' I loud inquired,
　When, hark!—there sounded a royal knell;
And I knew what spirit had just expired,
　And, slave as I was, my triumph fell.

---

¹ 'You fell,' said they, 'into the hands of the old man of the sea, and are the first who ever escaped strangling by his malicious tricks.'—*Story of Sinbad*.

He had pledged a hate unto me and mine,
　He had left to the future nor nope nor choice,
But sealed that hate with a name divine,
　And he now was dead, and—I *couldn't* rejoice!

He had fanned afresh the burning brands
　Of a bigotry waxing cold and dim;
He had armed anew my torturers' hands,
　And *them* did I curse—but sighed for him

For *his* was the error of head, not heart,
　And—oh, how beyond the ambushed foe,
Who to enmity adds the traitor's part,
　And carries a smile, with a curse below!

If ever a heart made bright amends
　For the fatal fault of an erring head—
Go, learn *his* fame from the lips of friends,
　In the orphan's tear be his glory read.

A prince without pride, a man without guile,
　To the last unchanging, warm, sincere,
For worth he had ever a hand and smile,
　And for misery ever his purse and tear.

Touched to the heart by that solemn toll,
　I calmly sunk in my chains again;
While, still as I said, 'Heaven rest his soul!'
　My mates of the dungeon sighed, 'Amen!'

BALLADS AND SONGS.

BALLADS AND SONGS.

BLACK AND BLUE EYES.

The brilliant black eye
May in triumph let fly
All its darts, without caring who feels 'em;
But the soft eye of blue,
Though it scatter wounds too,
Is much better pleased when it heals 'em.
Dear Fanny! dear Fanny!
The soft eye of blue,
Though it scatter wounds too,
Is much better pleased when it heals 'em, dear
Fanny!

The black eye may say,
'Come and worship my ray,—
By adoring, perhaps you may move me!'
But the blue eye, half hid,
Says, from under its lid,
'I love, and I'm yours if you love me!'
Dear Fanny! dear Fanny!
The blue eye, half hid,
Says, from under its lid,
'I love, and am yours if you love me!' dear
Fanny!

Then tell me, oh! why,
In that lovely eye,
Not a charm of its tint I discover;
Or why should you wear
The only blue pair
That ever said 'No' to a lover?
Dear Fanny! dear Fanny!
Oh! why should you wear
The only blue pair
That ever said 'No' to a lover, dear Fanny?

CEASE, OH CEASE TO TEMPT!

Cease, oh cease to tempt
My tender heart to love!
It never, never can
So wild a flame approve.
All its joys and pains
To others I resign;
But be the vacant heart,
The careless bosom mine.

Then cease, oh cease to tempt
My tender heart to love!
It never, never can
So wild a flame approve.

Say, oh say no more
That lovers' pains are sweet!
I never, never can
Believe the fond deceit.
Weeping day and night,
Consuming life in sighs,—
This is the lover's lot,
And this I ne'er could prize.
Then say, oh say no more
That lovers' pains are sweet!
I never, never can
Believe the fond deceit.

DEAR FANNY.

She has beauty, but still you must keep your
heart cool;
She has wit, but you must not be caught so;
Thus Reason advises, but Reason's a fool,
And 'tis not the first time I have thought so,
Dear Fanny.

'She is lovely!' Then love her, nor let the bliss
fly;
'Tis the charm of youth's vanishing season:
Thus love has advised me, and who will deny
That Love reasons much better than Reason,
Dear Fanny?

DID NOT.

'Twas a new feeling—something more
Than we had dared to own before,
Which then we hid not, which then we hid not
We saw it in each other's eye,
And wished, in every murmured sigh,
To speak, but did not; to speak, but did not.

She felt my lips' impassioned touch—
'Twas the first time I dared so much,

And yet she chid not, and yet she chid not;
But whispered o'er my burning brow,
'Oh! do you doubt I love you now?'
Sweet soul! I did not; sweet soul! I did not.

Warmly I felt her bosom thrill,
I pressed it closer, closer still,
Though gently bid not, though gently bid not;
Till—oh! the world hath seldom heard
Of lovers, who so nearly erred,
And yet who did not, and yet who did not.

FANNY, DEAREST!

Oh! had I leisure to sigh and mourn,
Fanny, dearest! for thee I'd sigh;
And every smile on my cheek should turn
To tears, when thou art nigh.
But, between love, and wine, and sleep,
So busy a life I live,
That even the time it would take to weep
Is more than my heart can give.
Then bid me not to despair and pine,
Fanny, dearest of all the dears!
The love, that's ordered to bathe in wine,
Would be sure to take cold in tears.

Reflected bright in this heart of mine,
Fanny, dearest! thy image lies;
But, oh! the mirror would cease to shine,
If dimmed too oft with sighs.
They lose the halt of beauty's light,
Who view it through sorrow's tear;
And 'tis but to see thee truly bright
That I keep my eye-beam clear.
Then wait no longer till tears shall flow—
Fanny, dearest! the hope is vain;
If sunshine cannot dissolve thy snow,
I shall never attempt it with rain.

Viver en Cadenas.
FROM LIFE WITHOUT FREEDOM.

From life without freedom, oh! who would not fly?
For one day of freedom, oh! who would not die?
Hark!—hark! 'tis the trumpet! the call of the brave,
The death-song of tyrants and dirge of the slave.
Our country lies bleeding—oh! fly to her aid;
One arm that defends is worth hosts that invade.
From life without freedom, oh! who would not fly?
For one day of freedom, oh! who would not die?

In death's kindly bosom our last hope remains—
The dead fear no tyrants, the grave has no chains!
On, on to the combat! the heroes that bleed
For virtue and mankind are heroes indeed.

And oh! even if Freedom from this world be driven,
Despair not—at least we shall find her in heaven.
In death's kindly bosom our last hope remains—
The dead fear no tyrants, the grave has no chains.

HERE'S THE BOWER.

Here's the bower she loved so much,
And the tree she planted;
Here's the harp she used to touch—
Oh! how that touch enchanted!
Roses now unheeded sigh;
Where's the hand to wreathe them?
Songs around neglected lie,
Where's the lip to breathe them?
Here's the bower she loved so much,
And the tree she planted;
Here's the harp she used to touch—
Oh! how that touch enchanted!

Spring may bloom, but she we loved
Ne'er shall feel its sweetness!
Time, that once so fleetly moved,
Now hath lost its fleetness.
Years were days, when here she strayed,
Days were moments near her;
Heaven ne'er formed a brighter maid,
Nor Pity wept a dearer!
Here's the bower she loved so much,
And the tree she planted;
Here's the harp she used to touch—
Oh! how that touch enchanted!

HOLY BE THE PILGRIM'S SLEEP.

Holy be the Pilgrim's sleep,
From the dreams of terror free;
And may all, who wake to weep,
Rest to-night as sweet as he!
Hark! hark! did I hear a vesper swell!
No, no—it is my lovèd Pilgrim's prayer:
No, no—'twas but the convent bell,
That tolls upon the midnight air.
Holy be the Pilgrim's sleep!
Now, now again the voice I hear;
Some holy man is wandering near.

O Pilgrim! where hast thou been roaming?
Dark is the way, and midnight's coming.
Stranger, I've been o'er moor and mountain,
To tell my beads at Agnes' fountain.
And, Pilgrim, say, where art thou going?
Dark is the way, the winds are blowing.
Weary with wandering, weak, I falter,
To breathe my vows at Agnes' altar.
Strew, then, oh! strew his bed of rushes;
Here he shall rest till morning blushes.

Peace to them whose days are done,
   Death their eyelids closing ;
Hark ! the burial-rite's begun—
   'Tis time for our reposing.

Here, then, my Pilgrim's course is o'er :
'Tis my master! 'tis my master! Welcome here
   once more ;
Come to our shed—all toil is over ;
Pilgrim no more, but knight and lover.

I SAW THE MOON RISE CLEAR.

I saw the moon rise clear
   O'er hills and vales of snow,
Nor told my fleet reindeer
   The track I wished to go.
But quick he bounded forth ;
   For well my reindeer knew
I've but one path on earth—
   The path which leads to you.

The gloom that winter cast
   How soon the heart forgets!
When summer brings, at last,
   The sun that never sets.
So dawned my love for you ;
   Thus chasing every pain,
Than summer sun more true,
   'Twill never set again.

JOYS THAT PASS AWAY.

Joys that pass away like this,
   Alas! are purchased dear,
If every beam of bliss
   Is followed by a tear.
Fare thee well! oh, fare thee well!
Soon, too soon thou'st broke the spell.
Oh! I ne'er can love again
   The girl whose faithless art
Could break so dear a chain,
   And with it break my heart.

Once, when truth was in those eyes,
   How beautiful they shone!
But now that lustre flies,
   For truth, alas! is gone.
Fare thee well! oh, fare thee well!
How I've loved my hate shall tell.
Oh! how lorn, how lost would prove
   Thy wretched victim's fate,
If, when deceived in love,
   He could not fly to hate!

LIGHT SOUNDS THE HARP.

Light sounds the harp when the combat is
   over—
When heroes are resting, and joy is in bloom—
When laurels hang loose from the brow of the
   lover,
And Cupid makes wings of the warrior's plume.
   But when the foe returns,
   Again the hero burns ;
High flames the sword in his hand once more ;
   The clang of mingling arms
   Is then the sound that charms,
And brazen notes of war, by thousand trumpets
   roar.
Oh! then comes the harp, when the combat is
   over—
When heroes are resting, and joy is in bloom—
When laurels hang loose from the brow of the
   lover,
And Cupid makes wings of the warrior's plume.

Light went the harp when the War-God, re-
   clining,
Lay lulled on the white arm of Beauty to
   rest—
When round his rich armour the myrtle hung
   twining,
And flights of young doves made his helmet
   their nest.
   But when the battle came,
   The hero's eye breathed flame :
Soon from his neck the white arm was flung ;
   While to his wakening ear
   No other sounds were dear,
But brazen notes of war, by thousand trumpets
   sung.
But then came the light harp, when danger was
   ended,
And beauty once more lulled the War-God to
   rest ;
When tresses of gold with his laurels lay
   blended,
And flights of young doves made his helmet
   their nest.

LOVE AND THE SUN-DIAL.

Young Love found a Dial once, in a dark shade,
Where man ne'er had wandered nor sunbeam
   played ;
'Why thus in darkness lie?' whispered young
   Love,
'Thou, whose gay hours should in sunshine
   move.'
'I ne'er,' said the Dial, 'have seen the warm sun,
So noonday and midnight to me, Love, are one.'

Then Love took the Dial away from the shade,
And placed her where Heaven's beam warmly
   played.
There she reclined, beneath Love's gazing eye,
While, all marked with sunshine, her hours flew
   by.
'Oh! how,' said the Dial, 'can any fair maid,
That's born to be shone upon, rest in the
   shade ?'

But night now comes on, and the sunbeam's
  o'er,
And Love stops to gaze on the Dial no more.
Then cold and neglected, while bleak rain and
  winds
Are storming around her, with sorrow she finds
That Love had but numbered a few sunny hours,
And left the remainder to darkness and showers!

LOVE AND TIME.

'Tis said—but whether true or not
Let bards declare who've seen 'em—
That Love and Time have only got
One pair of wings between 'em.
In courtship's first delicious hour,
The boy full oft can spare 'em.
So, loitering in his lady's bower,
He lets the gray-beard wear 'em.
  Then is Time's hour of play;
  Oh! how he flies away!

But short the moments, short as bright,
When he the wings can borrow;
If Time to-day has had his flight,
Love takes his turn to-morrow.
Ah! Time and Love! your change is then
The saddest and most trying,
When one begins to limp again,
And t'other takes to flying.
  Then is Love's hour to stray;
  Oh! how he flies away!

But there's a nymph—whose chains I feel,
And bless the silken fetter—
Who knows—the dear one!—how to deal
With Love and Time much better.
So well she checks their wanderings,
So peacefully she pairs 'em,
That Love with her ne'er thinks of wings,
And Time for ever wears 'em.
  This is Time's holiday;
  Oh! how he flies away!

LOVE, MY MARY, DWELLS WITH THEE.

Love, my Mary, dwells with thee;
On thy cheek his bud I see.
No—that cheek is pale with care;
Love can find no roses there.
'Tis not on the cheek of rose
Love can find the best repose:
In my heart his home thou'lt see;
There he lives, and lives for thee.

Love, my Mary, ne'er can roam,
While he makes that eye his home.
No—the eye with sorrow dim
Ne'er can be a home for him.

Yet, 'tis not in beaming eyes
Love for ever warmest lies:
In my heart his home thou'lt see;
There he lives, and lives for thee.

LOVE'S LIGHT SUMMER CLOUD.

Pain and sorrow shall vanish before us—
Youth may wither, but feeling will last;
All the shadow that e'er shall fall o'er us,
Love's light summer-cloud sweetly shall cast.
  Oh! if to love thee more
  Each hour I number o'er—
  If this a passion be
  Worthy of thee,
Then be happy, for thus I adore thee.
Charms may wither, but feeling shall last:
All the shadow that e'er shall fall o'er thee,
Love's light summer-cloud sweetly shall cast.

Rest, dear bosom! no sorrows shall pain thee,
Sighs of pleasure alone shalt thou steal;
Beam, bright eyelid! no weeping shall stain thee,
Tears of rapture alone shalt thou feel.
  Oh! if there be a charm
  In love, to banish harm—
  If pleasure's truest spell
  Be to love well,
Then be happy, for thus I adore thee.
Charms may wither, but feeling shall last;
All the shadow that e'er shall fall o'er thee,
Love's light summer-cloud sweetly shall cast.

LOVE, WANDERING THROUGH THE GOLDEN MAZE.

Love, wandering through the golden maze
Of my beloved's hair,
Traced every lock with fond delays,
And, doting, lingered there.
And soon he found 'twere vain to fly;
His heart was close confined,
And every curlet was a tie—
A chain by beauty twined.

MERRILY EVERY BOSOM BOUNDETH

THE TYROLESE SONG OF LIBERTY.

Merrily every bosom boundeth,
  Merrily, oh! merrily, oh!
Where the Song of Freedom soundeth,
  Merrily, oh! merrily, oh!
    There the warrior's arms
    Shed more splendour,
    There the maiden's charms
    Shine more tender—
Every joy the land surroundeth,
  Merrily, oh! merrily, oh!

Wearily every bosom pineth,
　Wearily, oh! wearily, oh!
Where the bond of slavery twineth,
　Wearily, oh! wearily, oh!
　　There the warrior's dart
　　Hath no fleetness,
　　There the maiden's heart
　　Hath no sweetness—
Every flower of life declineth,
　Wearily, oh! wearily, oh!

Cheerily then from hill and valley,
　Cheerily, oh! cheerily, oh!
Like your native fountains sally
　Cheerily, oh! cheerily, oh!
　　If a glorious death,
　　Won by bravery,
　　Sweeter be than breath
　　Sighed in slavery,
Round the flag of Freedom rally,
　Cheerily, oh! cheerily, oh!

NOW LET THE WARRIOR.

Now let the warrior plume his steed,
　And wave his sword afar;
For the men of the East this day shall bleed,
　And the sun shall blush with war.
Victory sits on the Christian's helm
　To guide her holy band:
The Knight of the Cross this day shall whelm
　The men of the Pagan land.
　　Oh! blessed who in the battle dies!
　　God will enshrine him in the skies!

OH, LADY FAIR!

Oh, Lady fair! where art thou roaming?
The sun has sunk, the night is coming.
Stranger, I go o'er moor and mountain,
To tell my beads at Agnes' fountain.
And who is the man, with his white locks flowing?
Oh, Lady fair! where is he going?
A wandering Pilgrim, weak, I falter,
To tell my beads at Agnes' altar.
Chill falls the rain, night winds are blowing,
Dreary and dark's the way we're going.

Fair Lady! rest till morning blushes—
I'll strew for thee a bed of rushes.
Oh! stranger! when my beads I'm counting,
I'll bless thy name at Agnes' fountain.
Then, Pilgrim, turn, and rest thy sorrow;
Thou'lt go to Agnes' shrine to-morrow.
Good stranger, when my beads I'm telling,
My saint shall bless thy leafy dwelling.
Strew, then, oh! strew our bed of rushes;
Here we must rest till morning blushes.

OH! REMEMBER THE TIME.

THE CASTILIAN MAID.

Oh! remember the time, in La Mancha's shades,
　When our moments so blissfully flew;
When you called me the flower of Castilian maids,
　And I blushed to be called so by you.
When I taught you to warble the gay seguadilla,
　And to dance to the light castanet;
Oh! never, dear youth, let you roam where you will,
　The delight of those moments forget.

They tell me, you lovers from Erin's green isle
　Every hour a new passion can feel,
And that soon, in the light of some lovelier smile,
　You'll forget the poor maid of Castile.
But they know not how brave in the battle you are,
　Or they never could think you would rove;
For 'tis always the spirit most gallant in war
　That is fondest and truest in love!

OH! SOON RETURN!

The white sail caught the evening ray,
　The wave beneath us seemed to burn,
When all my weeping love could say
　Was, 'Oh! soon return!'
Through many a clime our ship was driven,
　O'er many a billow rudely thrown;
Now chilled beneath a northern heaven,
　Now sunned by summer's zone:
Yet still, where'er our course we lay,
　When evening bid the west wave burn,
I thought I heard her faintly say,
　'Oh! soon return!—Oh! soon return!'

If ever yet my bosom found
　Its thoughts one moment turned from thee,
'Twas when the combat raged around,
　And brave men looked to me.
But though 'mid battle's wild alarm
　Love's gentle power might not appear,
He gave to glory's brow the charm
　Which made even danger dear.
And then, when victory's calm came o'er
　The hearts where rage had ceased to burn,
I heard that farewell voice once more,
　'Oh! soon return!—Oh! soon return!'

OH! YES, SO WELL.

Oh! yes, so well, so tenderly
　Thou'rt loved, adored by me,
Fame, fortune, wealth, and liberty,
　Were worthless without thee.
Though, brimmed with blisses, pure and rare,
　Life's cup before me lay,

Unless thy love were mingled there,
I'd spurn the draught away.
Oh! yes, so well, so tenderly
Thou'rt loved, adored by me,
Fame, fortune, wealth, and liberty,
Are worthless without thee.

Without thy smile how joylessly
All glory's meeds I see!
And even the wreath of victory
Must owe its bloom to thee.
Those worlds, for which the conqueror sighs,
For me have now no charms;
My only world's thy radiant eyes—
My throne those circling arms!
Oh! yes, so well, so tenderly
Thou'rt loved, adored by me
Whole realms of light and liberty
Were worthless without thee.

OH! YES, WHEN THE BLOOM.

Oh! yes, when the bloom of Love's boyhood is o'er,
He'll turn into friendship that feels no decay;
And though Time may take from him the wings he once wore,
The charms that remain will be bright as before,
And he'll lose but his young trick of flying away.

Then let it console thee, if Love should not stay,
That Friendship our last happy moments will crown:
Like the shadows of morning, Love lessens away,
While Friendship, like those at the closing of day,
Will linger and lengthen as Life's sun goes down.

ONE DEAR SMILE.

Couldst thou look as dear as when
First I sighed for thee;
Couldst thou make me feel again
Every wish I breathed thee then,
Oh! how blissful life would be!
Hopes, that now beguiling leave me,
Joys, that lie in slumber cold—
All would wake, couldst thou but give me
One dear smile like those of old.

Oh! there's nothing left us now,
But to mourn the past;
Vain was every ardent vow—
Never yet did Heaven allow
Love so warm, so wild, to last.
Not even hope could now deceive me—
Life itself looks dark and cold:
Oh! thou never more canst give me
One dear smile like those of old.

THE DAY OF LOVE.

The beam of morning trembling
Stole o'er the mountain brook,
With timid ray resembling
Affection's early look.
Thus love begins—sweet morn of love!

The noontide ray ascended,
And o'er the valley stream
Diffused a glow as splendid
As passion's riper dream.
Thus love expands—warm noon of love!

But evening came, o'ershading
The glories of the sky,
Like faith and fondness fading
From Passion's altered eye.
Thus love declines—cold eve of love!

THE SONG OF WAR.

The song of war shall echo through our mountains,
Till not one hateful link remains
Of slavery's lingering chains—
Till not one tyrant tread our plains,
Nor traitor lip pollute our fountains.
No! never till that glorious day
Shall Lusitania's sons be gay,
Or hear, oh Peace! thy welcome lay
Resounding through her sunny mountains.

The song of war shall echo through our mountains,
Till Victory's self shall, smiling, say,
'Your cloud of foes hath passed away,
And Freedom comes with new-born ray,
To gild your vines and light your fountains.'
Oh! never till that glorious day
Shall Lusitania's sons be gay,
Or hear, oh Peace! thy welcome lay
Resounding through her sunny mountains.

THE YOUNG ROSE.

The young rose which I give thee, so dewy and bright,
Was the floweret most dear to the sweet bird of night,
Who oft by the moon o'er her blushes hath hung,
And thrilled every leaf with the wild lay he sung.

Oh! take thou this young rose, and let her life be
Prolonged by the breath she will borrow from thee!
For while o'er her bosom thy soft notes shall thrill,
She'll think the sweet night-bird is courting her still!

WHEN 'MIDST THE GAY I MEET.

When 'midst the gay I meet
  That blessed smile of thine,
Though still on me it turns most sweet,
  I scarce can call it mine:
But when to me alone
  Your secret tears you show,
Oh! then I feel those tears my own,
  And claim them as they flow.
Then still with bright looks bless
  The gay, the cold, the free;
Give smiles to those who love you less,
  But keep your tears for me.

The snow on Jura's steep
  Can smile with many a beam,
Yet still in chains of coldness sleep,
  How bright soe'er it seem.
But when some deep-felt ray,
  Whose touch is fire, appears,
Oh! then the smile is warmed away,
  And, melting, turns to tears.
Then still with bright looks bless
  The gay, the cold, the free!
Give smiles to those who love you less,
  But keep your tears for me.

WHEN TWILIGHT DEWS.

When twilight dews are falling soft
  Upon the rosy sea, love!
I watch the star whose beam so oft
  Has lighted me to thee, love!
And thou too, on that orb so clear,
  Ah! dost thou gaze at even,
And think, though lost for ever here,
  Thou'lt yet be mine in heaven?

There's not a garden walk I tread,
  There's not a flower I see, love!
But brings to mind some hope that's fled,
  Some joy I've lost with thee, love!
And still I wish that hour was near,
  When, friends and foes forgiven,
The pains, the ills, we've wept through here,
  May turn to smiles in heaven!

YOUNG JESSICA.

Young Jessica sat all the day,
  In love-dreams languishingly pining,
Her needle bright neglected lay,
  Like truant genius idly shining.
Jessy, 'tis in idle hearts
  That love and mischief are most nimble;
The safest shield against the darts
  Of Cupid, is Minerva's thimble.

A child who with a magnet played,
  And knew its winning ways so wily,
The magnet near the needle laid,
  And laughing said, 'We'll steal it slyly.'
The needle, having nought to do,
  Was pleased to let the magnet wheedle,
Till closer still the tempter drew,
  And off at length eloped the needle.

Now, had this needle turned its eye
  To some gay *Ridicule's* construction,
It ne'er had strayed from duty's tie,
  Nor felt a magnet's sly seduction.
Girls, would you keep tranquil hearts,
  Your snowy fingers must be nimble;
The safest shield against the darts
  Of Cupid, is Minerva's thimble.

FAREWELL, BESSY.

Sweetest love! I'll not forget thee,
  Time shall only teach my heart
Fonder, warmer, to regret thee,
  Lovely, gentle as thou art!
    Farewell, Bessy!
    We may meet again.

Yes, oh yes! again we meet, love!
  And repose our hearts at last;
Oh, sure 'twill then be sweet, love!
  Calm to think on sorrows past.
    Farewell, Bessy!
    We may meet again.

Yet I feel my heart is breaking
  When I think I stray from thee,
Round the world that quiet seeking
  Which I fear is not for me.
    Farewell, Bessy!
    We may meet again.

Calm to peace thy lover's bosom—
  Can it, dearest! must it be?
Thou within an hour shalt lose him,
  He for ever loses thee!
    Farewell, Bessy!
    Yet oh! not for ever.

TO-DAY, DEAREST! IS OURS.

To-day, dearest! is ours;
  Why should Love carelessly lose it?
This life shines or lowers
  Just as we, weak mortals, use it.
'Tis time enough, when its flowers decay,
  To think of the thorns of Sorrow;
And Joy, if left on the stem to-day,
  May wither before to-morrow.

Then why, dearest! so long
  Let the sweet moments fly over?
Though now, blooming and young,
  Thou hast me devoutly thy lover,

Yet time from both, in his silent lapse,
  Some treasure may steal or borrow ;
Thy charms may be less in bloom, perhaps,
  Or I less in love to-morrow.

WHEN ON THE LIP THE SIGH DELAYS.

When on the lip the sigh delays,
  As if 'twould linger there for ever ;
When eyes would give the world to gaze,
  Yet still look down, and venture never ;
When, though with fairest nymphs we rove,
  There's one we dream of more than any—
If all this is not real love,
  'Tis something wondrous like it, Fanny!

To think and ponder, when apart,
  On all we've got to say at meeting ;
And yet when near, with heart to heart,
  Sit mute, and listen to their beating :
To see but one bright object move,
  The only moon, where stars are many—
If all this is not downright love,
  I prithee say what *is*, my Fanny!

When Hope foretells the brightest, best,
  Though Reason on the darkest reckons ;
When Passion drives us to the west,
  Though prudence to the eastward beckons ;
When all turns round, below, above,
  And our own heads the most of any—
If this is not stark, staring love,
  Then you and I are sages, Fanny.

HERE, TAKE MY HEART.

Here, take my heart, 'twill be safe in thy keeping,
  While I go wandering o'er land and o'er sea ;
Smiling or sorrowing, waking or sleeping,
  What need I care, so my heart is with thee ?

If, in the race we are destined to run, love,
  They who have light hearts the happiest be—
Happier still must be they who have none, love,
  And that will be *my* case when mine is with thee ?

No matter where I may now be a rover,
  No matter how many bright eyes I see ;
Should Venus' self come and ask me to love her,
  I'd tell her I could not—my heart is with thee !

There let it lie, growing fonder and fonder—
  And should Dame Fortune turn truant to me,
Why,—let her go—I've a treasure beyond her,
  As long as my heart's out at interest with thee !

OH! CALL IT BY SOME BETTER NAME.

Oh ! call it by some better name,
  For Friendship is too cold,
And Love is now a worldly flame,
  Whose shrine must be of gold ;
And passion, like the sun at noon,
  That burns o'er all he sees,
Awhile as warm, will set as soon,—
  Oh ! call it none of these.

Imagine something purer far,
  More free from stain of clay,
Than Friendship, Love, or Passion are,
  Yet human still as they :
And if thy lip, for love like this,
  No mortal word can frame,
Go, ask of angels what it is,
  And call it by that name !

POOR WOUNDED HEART!

Poor wounded heart !
Poor wounded heart, farewell !
  Thy hour is come,
  Thy hour of rest is come ;
Thou soon wilt reach thy home,
Poor wounded heart, farewell !
The pain thou'lt feel in breaking
  Less bitter far will be,
Than that long, deadly course of aching,
  This life has been to thee—
Poor breaking heart, poor breaking heart, farewell !

There—broken heart,
Poor broken heart, farewell !
  The pang is o'er—
  The parting pang is o'er,
Thou now wilt bleed no more,
Poor broken heart, farewell !
No rest for thee but dying,
  Like waves whose strife is past,
On death's cold shore thus early lying,
  Thou sleep'st in peace at last—
Poor broken heart, poor broken heart, farewell

THE EAST INDIAN.

Come May, with all thy flowers,
  Thy sweetly-scented thorn,
Thy cooling evening showers,
  Thy fragrant breath at morn :
When May-flies haunt the willow,
  When May-buds tempt the bee,
Then o'er the shining billow
  My love will come to me.

From Eastern Isles she's winging
  Through watery wilds her way,

And on her cheek is bringing
The bright sun's orient ray:
Oh! come and court her hither,
Ye breezes mild and warm—
One winter's gale would wither
So soft, so pure a form.

The fields where she was straying
Are blest with endless light,
With zephyrs always playing
Through gardens always bright.
Then now, oh May! be sweeter
Than e'er thou'st been before;
Let sighs from roses meet her
When she comes near our shore.

PALE BROKEN FLOWER!

PALE broken flower! what art can now recover
thee?
Torn from the stem that fed thy rosy breath—
In vain the sunbeams seek
To warm that faded cheek!
The dews of heaven, that once like balm fell
over thee,
Now are but tears, to weep thy early death!

So droops the maid whose lover hath forsaken
her;
Thrown from his arms, as lone and lost as
thou;
In vain the smiles of all
Like sunbeams round her fall—
The only smile that could from death awaken
her,
That smile, alas! is gone to others now.

THE PRETTY ROSE-TREE.

BEING weary of love, I flew to the grove,
And chose me a tree of the fairest;
Saying, 'Pretty Rose-tree, thou my mistress
shalt be,
I'll worship each bud that thou bearest.
For the hearts of this world are hollow,
And fickle the smiles we follow;
And 'tis sweet, when all their witcheries pall,
To have a pure love to fly to:
So, my pretty Rose-tree, thou my mistress shalt
be,
And the only one now I shall sigh to.'

When the beautiful hue of thy cheek through
the dew
Of morning is bashfully peeping,
'Sweet tears,' I shall say (as I brush them away),
'At least there's no art in this weeping.'
Although thou shouldst die to-morrow,
'Twill not be from pain or sorrow,

And the thorns of thy stem are not like them
With which hearts wound each other:
So, my pretty Rose-tree, thou my mistress shalt
be,
And I'll ne'er again sigh to another.

SHINE OUT, STARS!

SHINE out, Stars! let Heaven assemble
Round us every festal ray,
Lights that move not, lights that tremble,
All to grace this eve of May.
Let the flower-beds all lie waking,
And the odours shut up there,
From their downy prisons breaking,
Fly abroad through sea and air.

And would Love, too, bring his sweetness,
With our other joys to weave,
Oh, what glory, what completeness,
Then would crown this bright May eve!
Shine out, Stars! let night assemble
Round us every festal ray,
Lights that move not, lights that tremble,
To adorn this eve of May.

THE YOUNG MULETEERS OF GRENADA.

OH! the joys of our evening posada,
When, resting at close of the day,
We, young Muleteers of Grenada,
Sit and sing the last sunshine away!
So blithe, that even the slumbers
Which hung around us seem gone,
Till the lute's soft drowsy numbers
Again beguile them on.

Then, as each to his favourite sultana
In sleep is still breathing the sigh,
The name of some black-eyed Tirana
Half breaks from our lips as we lie.
Then, with morning's rosy twinkle,
Again we're up and gone—
While the mule-bell's drowsy tinkle
Beguiles the rough way on.

TELL HER, OH TELL HER.

TELL her, oh tell her, the lute she left lying
Beneath the green arbour, is still lying there;
Breezes, like lovers, around it are sighing,
But not a soft whisper replies to their prayer.

Tell her, oh tell her, the tree that, in going,
Beside the green arbour she playfully set,
Lovely as ever is blushing and blowing,
And not a bright leaflet has fallen from it yet.

So while away from that arbour forsaken,
  The maiden is wandering, oh! let her be
True as the lute that no sighing can waken,
  And blooming for ever unchanged as the tree!

NIGHTS OF MUSIC.

Nights of music, nights of loving,
  Lost too soon, remembered long,
When we went by moonlight roving,
  Hearts all love and lips all song.
When this faithful lute recorded
  All my spirit felt to thee,
And that smile the song rewarded,
  Worth whole years of fame to me!

Nights of song and nights of splendour,
  Filled with joys too sweet to last—
Joys that, like your star-light tender,
  While they shone no shadow cast:
Though all other happy hours
  From my fading memory fly,
Of that star-light, of those bowers,
  Not a beam, a leaf, shall die!

OUR FIRST YOUNG LOVE.

Our first young love resembles
  That short but brilliant ray,
Which smiles, and weeps, and trembles
  Through April's earliest day.
No, no—all life before us,
  Howe'er its lights may play,
Can shed no lustre o'er us
  Like that first April ray.

Our summer sun may squander
  A blaze serener, grander,
Our autumn beam may, like a dream
  Of heaven, die calm away:
But no—let life before us
  Bring all the light it may,
'Twill shed no lustre o'er us
  Like that first trembling ray.

NATIONAL AIRS.

NATIONAL AIRS.

ADVERTISEMENT.

It is Cicero, I believe, who says, '*Natura ad modos ducimur ;*' and the abundance of wild indigenous airs which almost every country except England possesses, sufficiently proves the truth of his assertion. The lovers of this simple but interesting kind of music are here presented with the first number of a collection, which I trust their contributions will enable us to continue. A pretty air without words resembles one of those *half* creatures of Plato, which are described as wandering, in search of the remainder of themselves, through the world. To supply this other half, by uniting with congenial words the many fugitive melodies which have hitherto had none, or only such as are unintelligible to the generality of their hearers, is the object and ambition of the present work. Neither is it our intention to confine ourselves to what are strictly called National Melodies ; but wherever we meet with any wandering and beautiful air, to which poetry has not yet assigned a worthy home, we shall venture to claim it as an *estray* swan, and enrich our humble Hippocrene with its song.

. . . .

T. M.

A TEMPLE TO FRIENDSHIP.

Spanish Air.

'A temple to Friendship,' said Laura, enchanted,
'I'll build in this garden—the thought is divine!'
Her temple was built, and she now only wanted
An image of Friendship to place on the shrine.
She flew to a sculptor, who set down before her
A Friendship, the fairest his art could invent,
But so cold and so dull, that the youthful adorer
Saw plainly this was not the idol she meant.

'Oh! never,' she cried, ' could I think of enshrining
An image whose looks are so jealous and dim!
But yon little god upon roses reclining,
We'll make, if you please, Sir, a Friendship of him.'
So the bargain was struck; with the little god laden
She joyfully flew to her shrine in the grove :
Farewell,' said the sculptor, 'you're not the first maiden
Who came but for Friendship, and took away Love.'

FLOW ON, THOU SHINING RIVER.

Portuguese Air.

Flow on, thou shining river;
But ere thou reach the sea,
Seek Ella's bower, and give her
The wreaths I fling o'er thee.
And tell her thus, if she'll be mine,
The current of our lives shall be,
With joys along their course to shine,
Like those sweet flowers on thee.

But if, in wandering thither,
Thou find'st she mocks my prayer,
Then leave those wreaths to wither
Upon the cold bank there.
And tell her—thus, when youth is o'er,
Her lone and loveless charms shall be
Thrown by upon life's weedy shore,
Like those sweet flowers from thee.

ALL THAT'S BRIGHT MUST FADE.

Indian Air.

All that's bright must fade,—
The brightest still the fleetest ;

All that's sweet was made
But to be lost when sweetest.
Stars that shine and fall;—
The flower that drops in springing;—
These, alas! are types of all
To which our hearts are clinging.
All that's bright must fade,—
The brightest still the fleetest;
All that's sweet was made
But to be lost when sweetest!

Who would seek or prize
Delights that end in aching?
Who would trust to ties
That every hour are breaking?
Better far to be
In utter darkness lying,
Than be blest with light and see
That light for ever flying.
All that's bright must fade,—
The brightest still the fleetest;
All that's sweet was made
But to be lost when sweetest!

SO WARMLY WE MET.

Hungarian Air.

So warmly we met and so fondly we parted,
That which was the sweeter even I could not tell—
That first look of welcome her sunny eyes darted,
Or that tear of passion which blessed our farewell.
To meet was a heaven, and to part thus another,—
Our joy and our sorrow seemed rivals in bliss;
Oh! Cupid's two eyes are not liker each other
In smiles and in tears, than that moment to this.

The first was like day-break—new, sudden, delicious,
The dawn of a pleasure scarce kindled up yet—
The last was that farewell of daylight, more precious,
More glowing and deep, as 'tis nearer its set.
Our meeting, though happy, was tinged by a sorrow
To think that such happiness could not remain;
While our parting, though sad, gave a hope that to-morrow
Would bring back the blest hour of meeting again.

THOSE EVENING BELLS.

Air—*The Bells of St. Petersburgh.*

Those evening bells! those evening bells!
How many a tale their music tells,
Of youth, and home, and that sweet time,
When last I heard their soothing chime!

Those joyous hours are past away!
And many a heart that then was gay
Within the tomb now darkly dwells,
And hears no more those evening bells!

And so 'twill be when I am gone;
That tuneful peal will still ring on,
While other bards shall walk these dells,
And sing your praise, sweet evening bells!

SHOULD THOSE FOND HOPES.

Portuguese Air.

Should those fond hopes e'er forsake thee,[1]
Which now so sweetly thy heart employ;
Should the cold world come to wake thee
From all thy visions of youth and joy;
Should the gay friends, for whom thou wouldst banish
Him who once thought thy young heart his own,
All like spring birds, falsely vanish,
And leave thy winter unheeded and lone;—
Oh! 'tis then he thou hast slighted
Would come to cheer thee, when all seemed o'er;
Then the truant, lost and blighted,
Would to his bosom be taken once more.
Like that dear bird we both can remember,
Who left us while summer shone round,
But, when chilled by bleak December,
Upon our threshold a welcome still found.

REASON, FOLLY, AND BEAUTY.

Italian Air.

Reason, Folly, and Beauty, they say,
Went on a party of pleasure one day:
  Folly played
  Around the maid,
The bell of his cap rung merrily out;
  While Reason took
  To his sermon-book—
Oh! which was the pleasanter no one need doubt.

Beauty, who likes to be thought very sage,
Turned for a moment to Reason's dull page,
  Till Folly said,
  'Look here, sweet maid!'—
The sight of his cap brought her back to herself;
  While Reason read
  His leaves of lead,
With no one to mind him, poor sensible elf!

---

[1] The metre of the words is here necessarily sacrificed to the air.

Then Reason grew jealous of Folly's gay cap;
Had he that on, he her heart might entrap—
　'There it is,'
　Quoth Folly, 'old quiz!'
But Reason the head-dress so awkwardly wore,
That Beauty now liked him still less than before;
　While Folly took
　Old Reason's book,
And twisted the leaves in a cap of such *Ton*,
　That Beauty vowed
　(Though not aloud),
She liked him still better in that than his own!

FARE THEE WELL, THOU LOVELY ONE!
Sicilian Air.

FARE thee well, thou lovely one!
　Lovely still, but dear no more;
Once his soul of truth is gone,
　Love's sweet life is o'er.
Thy words, whate'er their flattering spell,
　Could scarce have thus deceived;
But eyes that acted truth so well
　Were sure to be believed.
Then fare thee well, thou lovely one!
　Lovely still, but dear no more;
Once his soul of truth is gone,
　Love's sweet life is o'er.

Yet those eyes look constant still,
　True as stars they keep their light;
Still those cheeks their pledge fulfil
　Of blushing always bright.
'Tis only on thy changeful heart
　The blame of falsehood lies;
Love lives in every other part,
　But there, alas! he dies.
Then fare thee well, thou lovely one!
　Lovely still, but dear no more;
Once his soul of truth is gone,
　Love's sweet life is o'er.

DOST THOU REMEMBER?
Portuguese Air.

DOST thou remember that place so lonely,
　A place for lovers and lovers only,
Where first I told thee all my secret sighs?
When, as the moonbeam, that trembled o'er thee,
Illumed thy blushes, I knelt before thee,
　And read my hope's sweet triumph in those eyes!
Then, then, while closely heart was drawn to heart,
Love bound us—never, never more to part!

And when I called thee by names the dearest[1]
That love could fancy, the fondest, nearest—
　'My life, my only life!' among the rest;

[1] The thought in this verse is borrowed from the original Portuguese words.

In those sweet accents that still enthral me,
Thou saidst, 'Ah! wherefore thy life thus call me?
　Thy soul, thy soul's the name that I love best;
For life soon passes, but how blest to be
That soul which never, never parts from thee!'

OH! COME TO ME WHEN DAYLIGHT SETS.
Venetian Air.

OH! come to me when daylight sets;
　Sweet! then come to me,
When smoothly go our gondolets
　O'er the moonlight sea.
When Mirth's awake, and Love begins,
　Beneath that glancing ray,
With sound of lutes and mandolins,
　To steal young hearts away.
Oh! come to me when daylight sets;
　Sweet! then come to me,
When smoothly go our gondolets
　O'er the moonlight sea.

Oh! then's the hour for those who love,
　Sweet! like thee and me;
When all's so calm below, above,
　In heaven and o'er the sea.
When maidens sing sweet barcarolles,
　And Echo sings again
So sweet, that all with ears and souls
　Should love and listen then.
So, come to me when daylight sets;
　Sweet! then come to me,
When smoothly go our gondolets
　O'er the moonlight sea.

OFT, IN THE STILLY NIGHT.
Scotch Air.

OFT, in the stilly night,
　Ere Slumber's chain has bound me,
Fond Memory brings the light
　Of other days around me;
　　The smiles, the tears,
　　Of boyhood's years,
　The words of love then spoken;
　　The eyes that shone,
　　Now dimmed and gone,
　The cheerful hearts now broken!
Thus, in the stilly night,
　Ere Slumber's chain has bound me,
Sad Memory brings the light
　Of other days around me.

When I remember all
　The friends, so linked together,
I've seen around me fall,
　Like leaves in wintry weather;

I feel like one
Who treads alone
Some banquet-hall deserted,
Whose lights are fled,
Whose garland's dead,
And all but he departed!
Thus, in the stilly night,
Ere Slumber's chain has bound me,
Sad Memory brings the light
Of other days around me.

HARK! THE VESPER HYMN IS STEALING.

Russian Air.

HARK! the vesper hymn is stealing
O'er the waters, soft and clear;
Nearer yet and nearer pealing,
  Jubilate, Amen.
Farther now, now farther stealing,
Soft it fades upon the ear,
  Jubilate, Amen.

Now, like moonlight waves retreating
To the shore, it dies along;
Now, like angry surges meeting,
Breaks the mingled tide of song.
  Jubilate, Amen.
Hush! again, like waves, retreating
To the shore, it dies along,
  Jubilate, Amen.

LOVE AND HOPE.

Swiss Air.

AT morn, beside yon summer sea,
  Young Hope and Love reclined;
But scarce had noontide come, when he
Into his bark leaped smilingly,
  And left poor Hope behind.

'I go,' said Love, 'to sail a while
  Across this sunny main;'
And then so sweet his parting smile,
That Hope, who never dreamed of guile,
  Believed he'd come again.

She lingered there till evening's beam
  Along the waters lay,
And o'er the sands, in thoughtful dream,
Oft traced his name, which still the stream
  As often washed away.

At length a sail appears in sight,
  And toward the maiden moves!
'Tis wealth that comes, and gay and bright,
His golden bark reflects the light,
  But ah! it is not Love's.

Another sail—'twas Friendship showed
Her night-lamp o'er the sea;
And calm the light that lamp bestowed:
But Love had lights that warmer glowed,
And where, alas! was he?

Now fast around the sea and shore
Night threw her darkling chain,
The sunny sails were seen no more,
Hope's morning dreams of bliss were o'er—
Love never came again!

THERE COMES A TIME.

German Air.

THERE comes a time, a dreary time,
  To him whose heart hath flown
O'er all the fields of youth's sweet prime,
  And made each flower its own.
'Tis when his soul must first renounce
  Those dreams so bright, so fond;
Oh! then's the time to die at once,
  For life has nought beyond.
    There comes a time, etc.

When sets the sun on Afric's shore,
  That instant all is night;
And so should life at once be o'er,
  When Love withdraws his light—
Nor, like our northern day, gleam on
  Through twilight's dim delay,
The cold remains of lustre gone,
  Of fire long passed away.
    Oh! there comes a time, etc.

MY HARP HAS ONE UNCHANGING THEME.

Swedish Air.

MY harp has one unchanging theme,
  One strain that still comes o'er
Its languid chord, as 'twere a dream
  Of joy that's now no more.
In vain I try, with livelier air,
  To wake the breathing string;
That voice of other times is there,
  And saddens all I sing.

Breathe on, breathe on, thou languid strain,
  Henceforth be all my own;
Though thou art oft so full of pain,
  Few hearts can bear thy tone.
Yet oft thou'rt sweet, as if the sigh,
  The breath that Pleasure's wings
Gave out, when last they wantoned by,
  Were still upon thy strings.

OH! NO—NOT E'EN WHEN FIRST WE LOVED.

Cashmerian Air.

Oh! no—not e'en when first we loved,
　Wert thou as dear as now thou art;
Thy beauty then my senses moved,
　But now thy virtues bind my heart.
What was but Passion's sigh before,
　Has since been turned to Reason's vow;
And though I then might love thee more,
　Trust me, I love thee better now!

Although my heart in earlier youth
　Might kindle with more wild desire,
Believe me, it has gained in truth
　Much more than it has lost in fire.
The flame now warms my inmost core,
　That then but sparkled o'er my brow;
And though I seemed to love thee more,
　Yet, oh! I love thee better now.

PEACE BE AROUND THEE.

Scotch Air.

Peace be around thee, wherever thou rovest;
　May life be for thee one summer's day,
And all that thou wishest, and all that thou lovest,
　Come smiling around thy sunny way!
If sorrow e'er this calm should break,
　May even thy tears pass off so lightly;
Like spring-showers, they'll only make
　The smiles that follow shine more brightly!

May Time, who sheds his blight o'er all,
　And daily dooms some joy to death,
O'er thee let years so gently fall,
　They shall not crush one flower beneath!
As half in shade and half in sun,
　This world along its path advances,
May that side the sun's upon
　Be all that e'er shall meet thy glances!

COMMON SENSE AND GENIUS.

French Air.

While I touch the string,
　Wreathe my brows with laurel,
For the tale I sing
　Has, for once, a moral.
Common Sense, one night,
　Though not used to gambols,
Went out by moonlight,
　With Genius on his rambles.
　　While I touch the string, etc.

Common Sense went on,
　'Many wise things saying,
While the light that shone
　Soon set Genius straying.
One his eye ne'er raised
　From the path before him,
T' other idly gazed
　On each night-cloud o'er him.
　　While I touch the string, etc.

So they came at last
　To a shady river;
Common Sense soon passed,
　Safe, as he doth ever;
While the boy, whose look
　Was in heaven that minute,
Never saw the brook,
　But tumbled headlong in it!
　　While I touch the string, etc.

How the wise one smiled,
　When safe o'er the torrent,
At that youth, so wild,
　Dripping from the current!
Sense went home to bed;
　Genius, left to shiver
On the bank, 'tis said,
　Died of that cold river!
　　While I touch the string, etc.

THEN, FARE THEE WELL.

Old English Air.

Then, fare thee well! my own dear love,
　This world has now for us
No greater grief, no pain above
　The pain of parting thus, dear love! the pain of parting thus!

Had we but known, since first we met,
　Some few short hours of bliss,
We might, in numbering them, forget
　The deep, deep pain of this, dear love! the deep, deep pain of this!

But no, alas! we've never seen
　One glimpse of pleasure's ray,
But still there came some cloud between,
　And chased it all away, dear love! and chased it all away!

Yet, e'en could those sad moments last,
　Far dearer to my heart
Were hours of grief, together past,
　Than years of mirth apart, dear love! than years of mirth apart!

Farewell! our hope was born in fears,
　And nursed 'mid vain regrets!
Like winter suns, it rose in tears,
　Like them in tears it sets, dear love! like them in tears it sets!

GAILY SOUNDS THE CASTANET.
Maltese Air.

GAILY sounds the castanet,
Beating time to bounding feet,
When, after daylight's golden set,
Maids and youths by moonlight meet.
Oh! then, how sweet to move
Through all that maze of mirth,
Lighted by those eyes we love
Beyond all eyes on earth!

Then, the joyous banquet spread
On the cool and fragrant ground,
With night's bright eye-beams overhead,
And still brighter sparkling round.
Oh! then, how sweet to say
Into the loved one's ear,
Thoughts reserved through many a day
To be thus whispered here!

When the dance and feast are done,
Arm in arm as home we stray,
How sweet to see the dawning sun
O'er her cheeks' warm blushes play!
Then, then the farewell kiss,
And words whose parting tone
Lingers still in dreams of bliss,
That haunt young hearts alone.

LOVE IS A HUNTER-BOY.
Languedocian Air.

LOVE is a hunter-boy,
Who makes young hearts his prey,
And in his nets of joy
Ensnares them night and day.
In vain concealed they lie—
Love tracks them everywhere;
In vain aloft they fly—
Love shoots them flying there.

But 'tis his joy most sweet,
At early dawn to trace
The print of Beauty's feet,
And give the trembler chase.
And most he loves through snow
To trace those footsteps fair,
For then the boy doth know
None tracked before him there.

COME, CHASE THAT STARTING TEAR AWAY.
French Air.

COME, chase that starting tear away,
Ere mine to meet it springs;
To-night, at least, to-night be gay,
Whate'er to-morrow brings!

Like sunset gleams, that linger late
When all is darkening fast,
Are hours like these we snatch from Fate—
The brightest and the last.
Then, chase that starting tear, etc.

To gild our darkening life, if Heaven
But one bright hour allow,
Oh! think that one bright hour is given,
In all its splendour, now!
Let's live it out—then sink in night,
Like waves that from the shore
One minute swell—are touched with light—
Then lost for evermore.
Then, chase that starting tear, etc.

JOYS OF YOUTH, HOW FLEETING!
Portuguese Air.

WHISPERINGS, heard by wakeful maids,
To whom the night-stars guide us—
Stolen walks through moonlight shades,
With those we love beside us.
Hearts beating, at meeting,—
Tears starting, at parting;
Oh! sweet youth, how soon it fades!
Sweet joys of youth, how fleeting!

HEAR ME BUT ONCE.
French Air.

HEAR me but once, while o'er the grave,
In which our love lies cold and dead,
I count each flattering hope he gave,
Of joys now lost and charms now fled,
Who could have thought the smile he wore,
When first we met, would fade away?
Or that a chill would e'er come o'er
Those eyes so bright through many a day?

WHEN LOVE WAS A CHILD.
Swedish Air.

WHEN Love was a child, and went idling round,
'Mong flowers the whole summer's day,
One morn in the valley a bower he found,
So sweet, it allured him to stay.

O'erhead, from the trees, hung a garland fair,
A fountain ran darkly beneath—
'Twas Pleasure that hung the bright flowers up there;
Love knew it, and jumped at the wreath.

But Love didn't know—and at his weak years
What urchin was likely to know?—
That Sorrow had made of her own salt tears
That fountain which murmured below.

He caught at the wreath—but with too much haste,
As boys when impatient will do—
It fell in those waters of briny taste,
And the flowers were all wet through.

Yet this is the wreath he wears night and day;
And though it all sunny appears
With Pleasure's own lustre, each leaf, they say,
Still tastes of the Fountain of Tears.

SAY, WHAT SHALL BE OUR SPORT TO-DAY?
Sicilian Air.

SAY, what shall be our sport to-day?
There's nothing on earth, in sea or air,
Too bright, too bold, too high, too gay,
For spirits like mine to dare!
'Tis like the returning bloom
Of those days, alas! gone by,
When I loved each hour—I scarce knew whom,—
And was blest—I scarce knew why.

Ay, those were days when life had wings,
And flew—oh, flew so wild a height,
That, like the lark which sunward springs,
'Twas giddy with too much light;
And though of some plumes bereft,
With that sun, too, nearly set,
I've enough of light and wing still left
For a few gay soarings yet.

BRIGHT BE THY DREAMS!
Welch Air.

BRIGHT be thy dreams—may all thy weeping
Turn into smiles while thou art sleeping:
Those by death or seas removed,
Friends, who in thy spring-time knew thee,
All thou'st ever prized or loved,
In dreams come smiling to thee!

There may the child, whose love lay deepest,
Dearest of all, come while thou sleepest;
Still the same—no charm forgot—
Nothing lost that life had given;
Or, if changed, but changed to what
Thou'lt find her yet in Heaven!

GO, THEN—'TIS VAIN.
Sicilian Air.

Go, then—'tis vain to hover
Thus round a hope that's dead—
At length my dream is over,
'Twas sweet—'twas false—'tis fled!
Farewell; since nought it moves thee,
Such truth as mine to see,—

Some one, who far less loves thee,
Perhaps more blest will be.

Farewell, sweet eyes, whose brightness
New life around me shed!
Farewell, false heart, whose lightness
Now leaves me death instead!
Go, now, those charms surrender
To some new lover's sigh,
One who, though far less tender,
May be more blest than I.

THE CRYSTAL HUNTERS.
Swiss Air.

O'ER mountains bright with snow and light,
We Crystal Hunters speed along,
While grots and caves, and icy waves,
Each instant echo to our song;
And when we meet with stores of gems,
We grudge not kings their diadems.
O'er mountains bright with snow and light,
We Crystal Hunters speed along,
While grots and caves, and icy waves,
Each instant echo to our song.

No lover half so fondly dreams
Of sparkles from his lady's eyes,
As we of those refreshing gleams
That tell where deep the crystal lies;
Though, next to crystal, we too grant
That ladies' eyes may most enchant.
O'er mountains, etc.

Sometimes, when o'er the Alpine rose
The golden sunset leaves its ray,
So like a gem the floweret glows,
We thither bend our headlong way;
And though we find no treasure there,
We bless the rose that shines so fair.
O'er mountains, etc.

ROW GENTLY HERE.
Venetian Air.

Row gently here, my gondolier; so softly wake the tide,
That not an ear on earth may hear, but hers to whom we glide.
Had Heaven but tongues to speak, as well as starry eyes to see,
Oh! think what tales 'twould have to tell of wandering youths like me!

Now rest thee here, my gondolier; hush, hush, for up I go,
To climb yon light balcony's height, while thou keep'st watch below.
Ah! did we take for heaven above but half such pains as we
Take day and night for woman's love, what angels we should be!

2 D

OH! DAYS OF YOUTH.
French Air.

Oh! days of youth and joy, long clouded,
Why thus for ever haunt my view?
When in the grave your light lay shrouded,
Why did not Memory die there too?
Vainly doth Hope her strain now sing me,
Whispering of joys that yet remain—
No, no, never more can this life bring me
One joy that equals youth's sweet pain.

Dim lies the way to death before me,
Cold winds of Time blow round my brow;
Sunshine of youth that once fell o'er me,
Where is your warmth, your glory now?
'Tis not that then no pain could sting me—
'Tis not that now no joys remain;
Oh! it is that life no more can bring me
One joy so sweet as that worst pain.

WHEN FIRST THAT SMILE.
Venetian Air.

When first that smile, like sunshine, blessed my sight,
Oh! what a vision then came o'er me!
Long years of love, of calm and pure delight,
Seemed in that smile to pass before me.
Ne'er did the peasant dream, ne'er dream of summer skies,
Of golden fruit and harvests springing,
With fonder hope than I of those sweet eyes,
And of the joy their light was bringing.

Where now are all those fondly promised hours?
Oh! woman's faith is like her brightness,
Fading as fast as rainbows or day-flowers,
Or aught that's known for grace and lightness.
Short as the Persian's prayer, his prayer at close of day,
Must be each vow of Love's repeating;
Quick let him worship Beauty's precious ray—
Even while he kneels, that ray is fleeting!

PEACE TO THE SLUMBERERS!
Catalonian Air.

Peace to the slumberers!
  They lie on the battle plain,
With no shroud to cover them;
  The dew and the summer rain
Are all that weep over them.

Vain was their bravery!
  The fallen oak lies where it lay,
Across the wintry river;
But brave hearts, once swept away,
Are gone, alas! for ever.

Woe to the conqueror!
Our limbs shall lie as cold as theirs
Of whom his sword bereft us,
Ere we forget the deep arrears
Of vengeance they have left us!

WHEN THOU SHALT WANDER.
Sicilian Air.

When thou shalt wander by that sweet light
We used to gaze on so many an eve,
When love was new and hope was bright,
Ere I could doubt or thou deceive—
Oh! then remembering how swift went by
Those hours of transport, even thou may'st sigh.

Yes, proud one! even thy heart may own
That love like ours was far too sweet
To be, like summer garments thrown aside
When past the summer's heat;
And wish in vain to know again
Such days, such nights as bless'd thee then.

WHO'LL BUY MY LOVE-KNOTS?
Portuguese Air.

Hymen late, his love-knots selling,
Called at many a maiden's dwelling:
None could doubt who saw or knew them,
Hymen's call was welcome to them.
  'Who'll buy my love-knots?
  Who'll buy my love-knots?'
Soon as that sweet cry resounded,
How his baskets were surrounded!

Maids who now first dreamed of trying
These gay knots of Hymen's tying;
Dames, who long had sat to watch him
Passing by, but ne'er could catch him;—
  'Who'll buy my love-knots?
  Who'll buy my love-knots?'
All at that sweet cry assembled;
Some laughed, some blushed, and some trembled.

'Here are knots,' said Hymen, taking
Some loose flowers, 'of Love's own making;
Here are gold ones—you may trust 'em'—
(These, of course, found ready custom).
  'Come, buy my love-knots!
  Come, buy my love-knots!
Some are labelled "Knots to tie men"—
"Love the maker"—"Bought of Hymen."'

Scarce their bargains were completed,
When the nymphs all cried, 'We're cheated!
See these flowers—they're drooping sadly;
This gold-knot, too, ties but badly—

Who'd buy such love-knots?
Who'd buy such love-knots?
Even this tie, with Love's name round it—
All a sham—he never bound it.'

Love, who saw the whole proceeding,
Would have laughed, but for good-breeding;
While Old Hymen, who was used to
Cries like that these dames gave loose to—
'Take back our love-knots!
Take back our love-knots!'—
Coolly said, 'There's no returning
Wares on Hymen's hands—Good morning!'

SEE, THE DAWN FROM HEAVEN.

Sung at Rome on Christmas Eve.

SEE, the dawn from heaven is breaking o'er our sight,
And Earth, from sin awaking, hails the sight!
See, those groups of Angels, winging from the realms above,
On their sunny brows from Eden bringing wreaths of Hope and Love.

Hark—their hymns of glory pealing through the air,
To mortal ears revealing who lies there!
In that dwelling, dark and lowly, sleeps the heavenly Son,
He, whose home is in the skies—the Holy One!

NETS AND CAGES.

Swedish Air.

COME, listen to my story, while
Your needle's task you ply;
At what I sing some maids will smile,
While some perhaps may sigh.
Though Love's the theme, and Wisdom blames
Such florid songs as ours,
Yet Truth sometimes, like Eastern dames,
Can speak her thoughts by flowers.
Then listen, maids, come listen, while
Your needle's task you ply;
At what I sing there's some may smile,
While some perhaps will sigh.

Young Cloe, bent on catching Loves,
Such nets had learned to frame,
That none, in all our vales and groves,
Ere caught so much small game:
While gentle Sue, less given to roam,
When Cloe's nets were taking
These flights of birds, sat still at home,
One small, neat Love-cage making.
Come, listen, maids, etc.

Much Cloe laughed at Susan's task;
But mark how things went on:
These light-caught Loves, ere you could ask
Their name and age, were gone!
So weak poor Cloe's nets were wove,
That, though she charmed into them
New game each hour, the youngest Love
Was able to break through them.
Come, listen, maids, etc.

Meanwhile, young Sue, whose cage was wrought
Of bars too strong to sever,
One Love with golden pinions caught,
And caged him there for ever;
Instructing thereby, all coquettes,
Whate'er their looks or ages,
That though 'tis pleasant weaving Nets,
'Tis wiser to make Cages.
Thus, maidens, thus do I beguile
The task your fingers ply.—
May all who hear, like Susan smile,
Ah! not like Cloe sigh!

WHEN THROUGH THE PIAZZETTA.

Venetian Air.

WHEN through the Piazzetta
Night breathes her cool air,
Then, dearest Ninetta,
I'll come to thee there.
Beneath thy mask shrouded,
I'll know thee afar,
As Love knows, though clouded,
His own Evening Star.

In garb, then, resembling
Some gay gondolier,
I'll whisper thee, trembling,
'Our bark, love, is near:
Now, now, while there hover
Those clouds o'er the moon,
'Twill waft thee safe over
Yon silent Lagoon.'

GO, NOW, AND DREAM.

Sicilian Air.

Go, now, and dream o'er that joy in thy slumber—
Moments so sweet again ne'er shalt thou number.
Of Pain's bitter draught the flavour never flies,
While Pleasure's scarce touches the lip ere it dies!

That moon, which hung o'er your parting, so splendid,
Often will shine again, bright as she then did—
But, ah! never more will the beam she saw burn
In those happy eyes at your meeting return.

TAKE HENCE THE BOWL.
Neapolitan Air.

TAKE hence the bowl; though beaming
  Brightly as bowl e'er shone,
Oh! it but sets me dreaming
  Of days, of nights now gone.
There, in its clear reflection,
  As in a wizard's glass,
Lost hopes and dead affection,
  Like shades, before me pass.

Each cup I drain brings hither
  Some friend who once sat by—
Bright lips, too bright to wither,
  Warm hearts, too warm to die!
Till, as the dream comes o'er me
  Of those long vanished years,
Then, then the cup before me
  Seems turning all to tears.

FAREWELL, THERESA!
Venetian Air.

FAREWELL, Theresa! that cloud which over
  Yon moon this moment gathering we see,
Shall scarce from her pure orb have passed, ere thy lover
  Swift o'er the wide wave shall wander from thee.

Long, like that dim cloud, I've hung around thee,
  Darkening thy prospects, saddening thy brow;
With gay heart, Theresa, and bright cheek I found thee;
  Oh! think how changed, love, how changed art thou now!

But here I free thee: like one awaking
  From fearful slumber, this dream thou'lt tell;
The bright moon her spell too is breaking,
  Past are the dark clouds; Theresa, farewell!

HOW OFT, WHEN WATCHING STARS.
Savoyard Air.

How oft, when watching stars grow pale,
  And round me sleeps the moonlight scene,
To hear a flute through yonder vale
  I from my casement lean.
'Oh! come, my love!' each note it utters seems to say;
'Oh! come, my love!' the night wears fast away!'

No, ne'er to mortal ear
  Can words, though warm they be,
Speak Passion's language half so clear
  As do those notes to me!

Then quick my own light lute I seek,
  And strike the chords with loudest swell;
And though they nought to others speak,
  He knows their language well.
'I come, my love!' each sound they utter seems to say;
'I come, my love! thine, thine till break of day.
  Oh! weak the power of words,
  The hues of painting dim,
Compared to what those simple chords
  Then say and paint to him.

WHEN THE FIRST SUMMER BEE.
German Air.

WHEN the first summer bee
  O'er the young rose shall hover,
  Then, like that gay rover,
I'll come to thee.
He to flowers, I to lips, full of sweets to the brim—
What a meeting, what a meeting for me and him!

Then, to every bright tree
  In the garden he'll wander,
  While I, oh! much fonder,
Will stay with thee.
In search of new sweetness through thousands he'll run,
While I find the sweetness of thousands in one.

THOUGH 'TIS ALL BUT A DREAM.
French Air.

THOUGH 'tis all but a dream at the best,
  And still when happiest soonest o'er,
Yet, even in a dream to be blessed
  Is so sweet, that I ask for no more.
The bosom that opes with earliest hopes,
  The soonest finds those hopes untrue,
As flowers that first in spring-time burst,
  The earliest wither too!
    Ay—'tis all but a dream, etc.

By friendship we oft are deceived,
  And find the love we clung to past;
Yet friendship will still be believed,
  And love trusted to to the last.
The web in the leaves the spider weaves
  Is like the charm Hope hangs o'er men,
Though often she sees it broke by the breeze,
  She spins the bright tissue again.
    Ay—'tis all but a dream, etc.

'TIS WHEN THE CUP IS SMILING.
Italian Air.

'Tis when the cup is smiling before us,
  And we pledge round to hearts that are true,
    boy, true,
That the sky of this life opens o'er us,
  And Heaven gives a glimpse of its blue.
Talk of Adam in Eden reclining,
  We are better, far better off thus, boy, thus ;
For him but *two* bright eyes were shining—
  See what numbers are sparkling for us !

When ou one side the grape-juice is dancing,
  And on t'other a blue eye beams, boy. beams,
'Tis enough, 'twixt the wine and the glancing,
  To disturb even a saint from his dreams.
Though this life like a river is flowing,
  I care not how fast it goes on, boy, on,
While the grape on its bank still is growing,
  And such eyes light the waves as they run.

WHERE SHALL WE BURY OUR SHAME?
Neapolitan Air.

Where shall we bury our shame ?
  Where, in what desolate place,
Hide the last wreck of a name
  Broken and stained by disgrace ?
Death may dissever the chain,
  Oppression will cease when we're gone,
But the dishonour, the stain,
  Die as we may, will live on.

Was it for this we sent out
  Liberty's cry from our shore ?
Was it for this that her shout
  Thrilled to the world's very core ?

Thus to live cowards and slaves,
  Oh ! ye free hearts that lie dead !
Do you not, e'en in your graves,
  Shudder, as o'er you we tread ?

NE'ER TALK OF WISDOM'S GLOOMY
SCHOOLS.
Mahratta Air.

Ne'er talk of Wisdom's gloomy schools ;
  Give me the sage who's able
To draw his moral thoughts and rules
  From the sunshine of the table ;—
Who learns how lightly, fleetly pass
  This world and all that's in it,
From the bumper that but crowns his glass,
  And is gone again next minute.

The diamond sleeps within the mine,
  The pearl beneath the water ;
While Truth, more precious, dwells in wine,
  The grape's own rosy daughter !
And none can prize her charms like him,
  Oh ! none like him obtain her,
Who thus can, like Leander, swim
  Through sparkling floods to gain her !

HERE SLEEPS THE BARD!
Highland Air.

Here sleeps the Bard who knew so well
All the sweet windings of Apollo's shell,
Whether its music rolled like torrents near,
Or died, like distant streamlets, on the ear!
Sleep, mute Bard ! unheeded now.
The storm and zephyr sweep thy lifeless brow ;—
That storm, whose rush is like thy martial lay ;
That breeze which, like thy love-song, dies
  away !

IRISH MELODIES.

IRISH MELODIES.

ADVERTISEMENT.

Though the beauties of the National Music of Ireland have been very generally felt and acknowledged, yet it has happened, through the want of appropriate English words, and of the arrangement necessary to adapt them to the voice, that many of the most excellent compositions have hitherto remained in obscurity. It is intended, therefore, to form a Collection of the best Original Irish Melodies, with characteristic Symphonies and Accompaniments; and with Words containing as frequent as possible allusions to the manners and history of the country.

In the poetical part, the Publisher has had promises of assistance from several distinguished Literary Characters, particularly from Mr. Moore, whose lyrical talent is so peculiarly suited to such a task, and whose zeal in the undertaking will be best understood from the following extract of a letter which he has addressed to Sir John Stevenson (who has undertaken the arrangement of the airs) on the subject:—

'I feel very anxious that a Work of this kind should be undertaken. We have too long neglected the only talent for which our English neighbours ever deigned to allow us any credit Our National Music has never been properly collected; and while the composers of the Continent have enriched their operas and sonatas with melodies borrowed from Ireland—very often without even the honesty of acknowledgment—we have left these treasures in a great degree unclaimed and fugitive. Thus our airs, like too many of our countrymen, for want of protection at home, have passed into the service of foreigners. But we are come, I hope, to a better period both of politics and music; and how much they are connected, in Ireland at least, appears too plainly in the tone of sorrow and depression which characterizes most of our early songs.—The task which you propose to me, of adapting words to those airs, is by no means easy. The poet who would follow the various sentiments which they express, must feel and understand that rapid fluctuation of spirits, that unaccountable mixture of gloom and levity, which composes the character of my countrymen, and has deeply tinged their music. Even in their liveliest strains we find some melancholy note intrude—some minor third or flat seventh —which throws its shade as it passes, and makes even mirth interesting. If Burns had been an Irishman (and I would willingly give up all our claims upon Ossian for him), his heart would have been proud of such music, and his genius would have made it immortal.

'Another difficulty (which is, however, purely mechanical) arises from the irregular structure of many of those airs, and the lawless kind of metre which it will in consequence be necessary to adapt to them. In these instances the poet must write not to the eye, but to the ear; and must be content to have his verses of that description which Cicero mentions, "*Quos si cantu spoliaveris, nuda remanebit oratio.*" That beautiful air, *The Twisting of the Rope*, which has all the romantic character of the Swiss *Ranz des Vaches*, is one of those wild and sentimental rakes which it will not be very easy to tie down in sober wedlock with poetry. However, notwithstanding all these difficulties, and the very little talent which I can bring to surmount them, the design appears to me so truly national, that I shall feel much pleasure in giving it all the assistance in my power.

'Leicestershire, *Feb.* 1807.'

IRISH MELODIES.

No. I.
GO WHERE GLORY WAITS THEE.
Air—Maid of the Valley.

Go where glory waits thee,
But, while fame elates thee,
　Oh! still remember me.
When the praise thou meetest
To thine ear is sweetest,
　Oh! then remember me.
Other arms may press thee,
Dearer friends caress thee,
All the joys that bless thee
　Sweeter far may be;
But when friends are nearest,
And when joys are dearest,
　Oh! then remember me.

When at eve thou rovest
By the star thou lovest,
　Oh! then remember me.
Think, when home returning,
Bright we've seen it burning—
　Oh! thus remember me.
Oft as summer closes,
When thine eye reposes
On its lingering roses,
　Once so loved by thee—
Think of her who wove them,
Her who made thee love them—
　Oh! then remember me.

When, around thee dying,
Autumn leaves are lying,
　Oh! then remember me.
And at night, when gazing
On the gay hearth blazing,
　Oh! still remember me.
Then should music, stealing
All the soul of feeling,
To thy heart appealing,
　Draw one tear from thee;
Then let memory bring thee
Strains I used to sing thee—
　Oh! then remember me.

WAR SONG.
REMEMBER THE GLORIES OF BRIEN THE BRAVE.[1]
Air—Molly Macalpin.

REMEMBER the glories of Brien the brave,
Though the days of the hero are o'er;
Though lost to Mononia[2] and cold in the grave,
He returns to Kinkora[3] no more!
That star of the field, which so often has poured
Its beam on the battle, is set;
But enough of its glory remains on each sword
To light us to victory yet!

Mononia! when nature embellished the tint
Of thy fields and thy mountains so fair,
Did she ever intend that a tyrant should print
The footstep of Slavery there?
No, Freedom! whose smile we shall never resign,
Go, tell our invaders, the Danes,
That 'tis sweeter to bleed for an age at thy shrine,
Than to sleep but a moment in chains!

Forget not our wounded companions who stood[4]
In the day of distress by our side;
While the moss of the valley grew red with their blood,
They stirred not, but conquered and died!
The sun that now blesses our arms with his light,
Saw them fall upon Ossory's plain!—
Oh! let him not blush, when he leaves us to-night,
To find that they fell there in vain!

ERIN! THE TEAR AND THE SMILE IN THINE EYES.
Air—Aileen Aroon.

ERIN! the tear and the smile in thine eyes
Blend like the rainbow that hangs in thy skies!
　Shining through sorrow's stream,
　Saddening through pleasure's beam,
　Thy suns, with doubtful gleam,
　　Weep while they rise!

Erin! thy silent tear never shall cease,
Erin! thy languid smile ne'er shall increase,
　Till, like the rainbow's light,
　Thy various tints unite,
　And form, in Heaven's sight,
　　One arch of peace!

OH! BREATHE NOT HIS NAME.
Air—The Brown Maid.

OH! breathe not his name, let it sleep in the shade,
Where cold and unhonoured his relics are laid:

---

[1] Brien Boromhe, the great Monarch of Ireland, who was killed at the battle of Clontarf, in the beginning of the eleventh century, after having defeated the Danes in twenty-five engagements.

[2] Munster.

[3] The palace of Brien.

[4] This alludes to an interesting circumstance related of the Dalgais, the favourite troops of Brien, when they were interrupted in their return from the battle of Clontarf, by Fitzpatrick, Prince of Ossory. The wounded men entreated that they might be allowed to fight with the rest.—'*Let stakes* (they said) *be stuck in the ground, and suffer each of us, tied to and supported by one of these stakes, to be placed in his rank by the side of a sound man.*' 'Between seven and eight hundred wounded men (adds O'Halloran), pale, emaciated, and supported in this manner, appeared mixed with the foremost of the troops:—never was such another sight exhibited.'—*History of Ireland*, Book 12, chap. 1.

Sad, silent, and dark be the tears that we shed,
As the night-dew that falls on the grass o'er his head!

But the night-dew that falls, though in silence it weeps,
Shall brighten with verdure the grave where he sleeps;
And the tear that we shed, though in secret it rolls,
Shall long keep his memory green in our souls.

WHEN HE WHO ADORES THEE.

Air—The Fox's Sleep.

When he who adores thee has left but the name
Of his fault and his sorrows behind,
Oh! say, wilt thou weep when they darken the fame
Of a life that for thee was resigned?
Yes, weep, and however my foes may condemn,
Thy tears shall efface their decree;
For Heaven can witness, though guilty to them,
I have been but too faithful to thee!

With thee were the dreams of my earliest love—
Every thought of my reason was thine;
In my last humble prayer to the Spirit above,
Thy name shall be mingled with mine!
Oh! blest are the lovers and friends who shall live
The days of thy glory to see;
But the next dearest blessing that Heaven can give
Is the pride of thus dying for thee!

THE HARP THAT ONCE THROUGH TARA'S HALLS.

Air—Gramachree.

The harp that once through Tara's halls
The soul of music shed,
Now hangs as mute on Tara's walls
As if that soul were fled.
So sleeps the pride of former days,
So glory's thrill is o'er,
And hearts that once beat high for praise
Now feel that pulse no more!

No more to chiefs and ladies bright
The harp of Tara swells;
The chord alone, that breaks at night,
Its tale of ruin tells.
Thus Freedom now so seldom wakes,
The only throb she gives
Is when some heart indignant breaks,
To show that still she lives!

FLY NOT YET.

Air—Planxty Kelly.

Fly not yet, 'tis just the hour
When pleasure, like the midnight flower
That scorns the eye of vulgar light,
Begins to bloom for sons of night,
And maids who love the moon!
'Twas but to bless these hours of shade
That beauty and the moon were made;
'Tis then their soft attractions glowing
Set the tides and goblets flowing.
Oh! stay—oh! stay.—
Joy so seldom weaves a chain
Like this to-night, that oh! 'tis pain
To break its links so soon.

Fly not yet, the fount that played
In times of old through Ammon's shade,
Though icy cold by day it ran,
Yet still, like souls of mirth, began
To burn when night was near :
And thus should woman's heart and looks
At noon be cold as winter brooks,
Nor kindle till the night, returning,
Brings their genial hour for burning.
Oh! stay—oh! stay.—
When did morning ever break,
And find such beaming eyes awake
As those that sparkle here!

OH! THINK NOT MY SPIRITS ARE ALWAYS AS LIGHT.

Air—John O'Reilly the Active.

Oh! think not my spirits are always as light,
And as free from a pang, as they seem to you now;
Nor expect that the heart-beaming smile of to-night
Will return with to-morrow to brighten my brow.
No—life is a waste of wearisome hours,
Which seldom the rose of enjoyment adorns;
And the heart that is soonest awake to the flowers
Is always the first to be touched by the thorns!
But send round the bowl, and be happy awhile;
May we never meet worse, in our pilgrimage here,
Than the tear that enjoyment can gild with a smile,
And the smile that compassion can turn to a tear.

The thread of our life would be dark, Heaven knows,
If it were not with friendship and love intertwined;

And I care not how soon I may sink to repose,
When these blessings shall cease to be dear to my mind!
But they who have loved the fondest, the purest,
Too often have wept o'er the dream they believed;
And the heart that has slumbered in friendship securest
Is happy indeed if 'twas never deceived.
But send round the bowl—while a relic of truth
Is in man or in woman, this prayer shall be mine,—
That the sunshine of love may illumine our youth,
And the moonlight of friendship console our decline.

THOUGH THE LAST GLIMPSE OF ERIN WITH SORROW I SEE.

Air—*Coulin.*

Though the last glimpse of Erin with sorrow I see,
Yet wherever thou art shall seem Erin to me;
In exile thy bosom shall still be my home,
And thine eyes make my climate wherever we roam.

To the gloom of some desert or cold rocky shore,
Where the eye of the stranger can haunt us no more,
I will fly with my Coulin, and think the rough wind
Less rude than the foes we leave frowning behind.

And I'll gaze on thy gold hair, as graceful it wreathes,
And hang o'er thy soft harp, as wildly it breathes;
Nor dread that the cold-hearted Saxon will tear
One chord from that harp, or one lock from that hair.

RICH AND RARE WERE THE GEMS SHE WORE.[1]

Air—*The Summer is coming.*

Rich and rare were the gems she wore,
And a bright gold ring on her wand she bore;
But oh! her beauty was far beyond
Her sparkling gems or snow-white wand.

'Lady! dost thou not fear to stray,
So lone and lovely, through this bleak way?
Are Erin's sons so good or so cold
As not to be tempted by woman or gold?'

'Sir Knight! I feel not the least alarm,
No son of Erin will offer me harm—
For though they love woman and golden store,
Sir Knight! they love honour and virtue more!'

On she went, and her maiden smile
In safety lighted her round the green isle.
And blest for ever is she who relied
Upon Erin's honour and Erin's pride!

AS A BEAM O'ER THE FACE OF THE WATERS MAY GLOW.

Air—*The Young Man's Dream.*

As a beam o'er the face of the waters may glow
While the tide runs in darkness and coolness below,
So the cheek may be tinged with a warm sunny smile,
Though the cold heart to ruin runs darkly the while.

One fatal remembrance, one sorrow that throws
Its bleak shade alike o'er our joys and our woes,
To which life nothing darker or brighter can bring,
For which joy has no balm, and affliction no sting!—
Oh! this thought in the midst of enjoyment will stay,
Like a dead, leafless branch in the summer's bright ray;
The beams of the warm sun play round it in vain,—
It may smile in his light, but it blooms not again!

THE MEETING OF THE WATERS.[2]

Air—*The Old Head of Denis.*

There is not in the wide world a valley so sweet
As that vale in whose bosom the bright waters meet;[3]
Oh! the last rays of feeling and life must depart,
Ere the bloom of that valley shall fade from my heart.

---

[1] This ballad is founded upon the following anecdote: 'The people were inspired with such a spirit of honour, virtue, and religion, by the great example of Brien, and by his excellent administration, that, as a proof of it, we are informed that a young lady of great beauty, adorned with jewels and a costly dress, undertook a journey alone from one end of the kingdom to the other, with a wand only in her hand, at the top of which was a ring of exceeding great value; and such an impression had the laws and government of this monarch made on the minds of all the people, that no attempt was made upon her honour, nor was she robbed of her clothes or jewels.'—*Warner's History of Ireland*, vol. 1. book 10.

[2] 'The Meeting of the Waters' forms a part of that beautiful scenery which lies between Rathdrum and Arklow, in the county of Wicklow, and these lines were suggested by a visit to this romantic spot in the summer of 1807.

[3] The rivers Avon and Avoca.

Yet it *was* not that nature had shed o'er the scene
Her purest of crystal and brightest of green;
'Twas *not* the soft magic of streamlet or hill—
Oh! no—it was something more exquisite still.

'Twas that friends the beloved of my bosom were
  near,
Who made every dear scene of enchantment
  more dear,
And who felt how the best charms of nature improve,
When we see them reflected from looks that we
  love.

Sweet vale of Avoca! how calm could I rest
In thy bosom of shade, with the friends I love
  best,
Where the storms that we feel in this cold world
  should cease,
And our hearts, like thy waters, be mingled in
  peace.

No. II.

ST. SENANUS AND THE LADY.

AIR—*The Brown Thorn.*

ST. SENANUS.[1]

'Oh! haste, and leave this sacred isle,
Unholy bark, ere morning smile;
For on thy deck, though dark it be,
A female form I see;
And I have sworn this sainted sod
Shall ne'er by woman's feet be trod!'

THE LADY.

'Oh! Father, send not hence my bark
Through wintry winds and billows dark.
I come, with humble heart, to share
  Thy morn and evening prayer;
Nor mine the feet, oh! holy Saint,
The brightness of thy sod to taint.'

The lady's prayer Senanus spurned;
The winds blew fresh, the bark returned.
But legends hint, that had the maid
Till morning's light delayed,
And given the saint one rosy smile,
She ne'er had left his lonely isle.

HOW DEAR TO ME THE HOUR!

AIR—*The Twisting of the Rope.*

How dear to me the hour when daylight dies,
  And sunbeams melt along the silent sea!
For then sweet dreams of other days arise,
  And memory breathes her vesper sigh to thee.

And as I watch the line of light that plays
  Along the smooth wave toward the burning
    west,
I long to tread that golden path of rays,
  And think 'twould lead to some bright isle of
    rest!

TAKE BACK THE VIRGIN PAGE.

WRITTEN ON RETURNING A BLANK BOOK.

AIR—*Dermott.*

TAKE back the virgin page,
  White and unwritten still;
Some hand more calm and sage
  The leaf must fill.
Thoughts come as pure as light,
  Pure as even *you* require:
But oh! each word I write
  Love turns to fire.

Yet let me keep the book;
  Oft shall my heart renew,
When on its leaves I look,
  Dear thoughts of you!
Like you, 'tis fair and bright;
  Like you, too bright and fair
To let wild passion write
  One wrong wish there!

Haply, when from those eyes
  Far, far away I roam,
Should calmer thoughts arise
  Towards you and home,
Fancy may trace some line
  Worthy those eyes to meet;
Thoughts that not burn, but shine
  Pure, calm, and sweet!

And, as the records are,
  Which wandering seamen keep,
Led by their hidden star
  Through the cold deep—
So may the words I write
  Tell through what storms I stray,
You still the unseen light
  Guiding my way!

---

[1] In a metrical life of St. Senanus, taken from an old Kilkenny MS., and which may be found among the *Acta Sanctorum Hiberniæ*, we are told of his flight to the is and of Scattery, and his resolution not to admit any woman of the party; he refused to receive even a sister saint, St. Cannera, whom an angel had taken to the island for the express purpose of introducing her to him. According to Dr. Ledwich, St. Senanus was no less a personage than the river Shannon; but O'Connor, and other antiquarians, deny this metamorphose indignantly.

THE LEGACY.

Air—*Unknown.*

When in death I shall calm recline,
  O bear my heart to my mistress dear;
Tell her it lived upon smiles and wine
  Of the brightest hue while it lingered here:
Bid her not shed one tear of sorrow
  To sully a heart so brilliant and light;
But balmy drops of the red grape borrow,
  To bathe the relic from morn till night.

When the light of my song is o'er,
  Then take my harp to your ancient hall;
Hang it up at that friendly door,
  Where weary travellers love to call.[1]
Then if some bard, who roams forsaken,
  Revive its soft note in passing along,
Oh! let one thought of its master waken
  Your warmest smile for the child of song.

Keep this cup, which is now o'erflowing,
  To grace your revel when I'm at rest;
Never, oh! never its balm bestowing
  On lips that beauty hath seldom blest!
But when some warm devoted lover
  To her he adores shall bathe its brim,
Then, then my spirit around shall hover,
  And hallow each drop that foams for him.

HOW OFT HAS THE BENSHEE CRIED!

Air—*The Dear Black Maid.*

How oft has the Benshee cried!
How oft has Death untied
Bright links that Glory wove,
Sweet bonds, entwined by Love!
Peace to each manly soul that sleepeth!
Rest to each faithful eye that weepeth!
Long may the fair and brave
Sigh o'er the hero's grave.

We're fallen upon gloomy days,
Star after star decays,
Every bright name, that shed
Light o'er the land, is fled.
Dark falls the tear of him who mourneth
Lost joy, or hope that ne'er returneth;
But brightly flows the tear
Wept o'er a hero's bier!

Oh! quenched are our beacon lights—
Thou, of the hundred fights![2]
Thou, on whose burning tongue,
Truth, peace, and freedom hung!
Both mute—but long as valour shineth,
Or mercy's soul at war repineth,
So long shall Erin's pride
Tell how they lived and died.

WE MAY ROAM THROUGH THIS WORLD.

Air—*Garyone.*

We may roam through this world like a child at
  a feast,
Who but sips of a sweet and then flies to the
  rest;
And when pleasure begins to grow dull in the
  east,
We may order our wings and be off to the
  west:
But if hearts that feel, and eyes that smile,
  Are the dearest gifts that Heaven supplies,
We never need leave our own green isle,
  For sensitive hearts and for sun-bright eyes.
Then remember, wherever your goblet is
  crowned,
Through this world whether eastward or
  westward you roam,
When a cup to the smile of dear woman goes
  round,
Oh! remember the smile which adorns her at
  home.

In England, the garden of beauty is kept
  By a dragon of prudery placed within call;
But so oft this unamiable dragon has slept,
  That the garden's but carelessly watched after
  all.
Oh! they want the wild sweet briery fence,
  Which round the flowers of Erin dwells,
Which warms the touch while winning the
  sense,
  Nor charms us least when it most repels.
Then remember, wherever your goblet is
  crowned,
Through this world whether eastward or
  westward you roam,
When a cup to the smile of dear woman goes
  round,
Oh! remember the smile which adorns her at
  home.

In France, when the heart of a woman sets sail,
  On the ocean of wedlock its fortune to try,
Love seldom goes far in a vessel so frail,
  But just pilots her off, and then bids her
  good-bye!
While the daughters of Erin keep the boy,
  Ever smiling beside his faithful oar,
Through billows of woe and beams of joy,
  The same as he looked when he left the shore.

---

[1] 'In every house was one or two harps, free to all travellers, who were the more caressed the more they excelled in music.'—*O'Halloran.*

[2] This designation, which has been applied to Lord Nelson before, is the title given to a celebrated Irish hero in a poem by O'Gnive, the bard of O'Niel, which is quoted in the *Philosophical Survey of the South of Ireland*, p. 433. 'Con, of the hundred fights, sleep in thy grass-grown tomb, and upbraid not our defeats with thy victories!'

The white snow lay
On the narrow pathway
When the lord of the valley crost over the moor ;
And many a deep print
On the white snow's tint
Shew'd the track of his footstep to Eveleen's door.

Page 431.

Then remember, wherever your goblet is crowned,
Through this world whether eastward or westward you roam,
When a cup to the smile of dear woman goes round,
Oh! remember the smile which adorns her at home.

EVELEEN'S BOWER.

Air—*Unknown.*

Oh! weep for the hour,
 When to Eveleen's bower
The Lord of the valley with false vows came;
 The moon hid her light
 From the heavens that night,
And wept behind her clouds o'er the maiden's shame.
 The clouds passed soon
 From the chaste cold moon,
And Heaven smiled again with her vestal flame;
 But none will see the day,
 When the clouds shall pass away,
Which that dark hour left upon Eveleen's fame.

 The white snow lay
 On the narrow pathway,
Where the Lord of the valley crossed over the moor;
 And many a deep print
 On the white snow's tint
Showed the track of his footstep to Eveleen's door.
 The next sun's ray
 Soon melted away
Every trace on the path where the false Lord came;
 But there's a light above
 Which alone can remove
The stain upon the snow of fair Eveleen's fame.

LET ERIN REMEMBER THE DAYS OF OLD.

Air—*The Red Fox.*

Let Erin remember the days of old,
 Ere her faithless sons betrayed her;
When Malachi wore the collar of gold,[1]
 Which he won from her proud invader;
When her kings, with standard of green unfurled,
 Led the Red-Branch Knights to danger;[2]—
Ere the emerald gem of the western world
 Was set in the crown of a stranger.

On Lough Neagh's bank as the fisherman strays,[3]
 When the clear, cold eve's declining,
He sees the round towers of other days
 In the wave beneath him shining!
Thus shall memory often, in dreams sublime,
 Catch a glimpse of the days that are over;
Thus, sighing, look through the waves of time
 For the long-faded glories they cover!

THE SONG OF FIONNUALA.[4]

Air—*Arrah my dear Eveleen.*

Silent, oh Moyle! be the roar of thy water,
 Break not, ye breezes, your chain of repose,
While murmuring mournfully, Lir's lonely daughter
 Tells to the night-star her tale of woes.
When shall the swan, her death-note singing,
 Sleep with wings in darkness furled?
When will Heaven, its sweet bell ringing,
 Call my spirit from this stormy world?

Sadly, oh Moyle! to thy winter wave weeping,
 Fate bids me languish long ages away;
Yet still in her darkness doth Erin lie sleeping,
 Still doth the pure light its dawning delay!
When will that day-star, mildly springing,
 Warm our isle with peace and love?
When will Heaven, its sweet bell ringing,
 Call my spirit to the fields above?

---

[1] 'This brought on an encounter between Malachi (the monarch of Ireland in the tenth century) and the Danes, in which Malachi defeated two of their champions, whom he encountered successively hand to hand, taking a collar of gold from the neck of one, and carrying off the sword of the other, as trophies of his victory.'—*Warner's History of Ireland*, vol. i. book 9.

[2] 'Military orders of knights were very early established in Ireland. Long before the birth of Christ we find a hereditary order of chivalry in Ulster called *Curaidhe na Craoibhe ruadh*, or the knights of the Red Branch, from their chief seat in Emania, adjoining to the palace of the Ulster kings, called *Teagh na Craoibhe ruadh*, or the Academy of the Red Branch; and contiguous to which was a large hospital, founded for the sick knights and soldiers, called *Bron-bhearg*, or the house of the sorrowful soldier.'—*O'Halloran's Introduction*, etc., part i. chap. 5.

[3] 'It was an old tradition in the time of Giraldus, that Lough Neagh had been originally a fountain, by whose sudden overflowing the country was inundated, and a whole region, like the Atlantis of Plato, overwhelmed. He says that the fishermen, in clear weather, used to point out to strangers the tall ecclesiastical towers under the water.'—*Topogr. Hib. Dist.* 2, c. 9.

[4] To make this story intelligible in a song, would require a much greater number of verses than any one is authorized to inflict upon an audience at once. The reader must therefore be content to learn, in a note, that Fionnuala, the daughter of Lir, was by some supernatural power transformed into a swan, and condemned to wander for many hundred years over certain lakes and rivers in Ireland, till the coming of Christianity, when the first sound of the mass-bell was to be the signal of her release.—I found this fanciful fiction among some manuscript translations from the Irish, which were begun under the direction of that enlightened friend of Ireland, the late Countess of Moira.

COME, SEND ROUND THE WINE.

Air—*We brought the Summer with us.*

Come, send round the wine, and leave points of belief
To simpleton sages and reasoning fools;
This moment's a flower too fair and brief,
To be withered and stained by the dust of the schools.
Your glass may be purple and mine may be blue;
But while they are filled from the same bright bowl,
The fool who would quarrel for difference of hue
 Deserves not the comfort they shed o'er the soul.

Shall I ask the brave soldier, who fights by my side
In the cause of mankind, if our creeds agree?
Shall I give up the friend I have valued and tried,
If he kneel not before the same altar with me?
From the heretic girl of my soul shall I fly,
To seek somewhere else a more orthodox kiss?
No! perish the hearts and the laws that try
Truth, valour, or love, by a standard like this!

SUBLIME WAS THE WARNING.

Air—*The Black Joke.*

Sublime was the warning which Liberty spoke,
And grand was the moment when Spaniards awoke
Into life and revenge from the conqueror's chain!
Oh, Liberty! let not this spirit have rest,
Till it move, like a breeze, o'er the waves of the west—
Give the light of your look to each sorrowing spot,
Nor, oh! be the Shamrock of Erin forgot,
 While you add to your garland the Olive of Spain!

If the fame of our fathers bequeathed with their rights,
Give to country its charm, and to home its delights,
If deceit be a wound and suspicion a stain—
Then, ye men of Iberia! our cause is the same:
And oh! may his tomb want a tear and a name,
Who would ask for a nobler, a holier death,
Than to turn his last sigh into victory's breath
 For the Shamrock of Erin and Olive of Spain!

Ye Blakes and O'Donnels, whose fathers resigned
The green hills of their youth, among strangers to find
 That repose which at home they had sighed for in vain,
Join, join in our hope that the flame which you light,
May be felt yet in Erin, as calm and as bright,
And forgive even Albion, while blushing she draws,
Like a truant, her sword, in the long-slighted cause
 Of the Shamrock of Erin and Olive of Spain!

God prosper the cause!—oh! it cannot but thrive,
While the pulse of one patriot heart is alive,
 Its devotion to feel, and its rights to maintain.
Then how sainted by sorrow its martyrs will die!
The finger of Glory shall point where they lie,
While, far from the footstep of coward or slave,
The young Spirit of Freedom shall shelter their grave,
 Beneath Shamrocks of Erin and Olives of Spain.

BELIEVE ME, IF ALL THOSE ENDEARING YOUNG CHARMS.

Air—*My Lodging is on the cold Ground.*

Believe me, if all those endearing young charms,
 Which I gaze on so fondly to-day,
Were to change by to-morrow, and fleet in my arms,
 Like fairy-gifts fading away!
Thou wouldst still be adored, as this moment thou art,
 Let thy loveliness fade as it will,
And around the dear ruin, each wish of my heart
 Would entwine itself verdantly still!

It is not while beauty and youth are thine own,
 And thy cheeks unprofaned by a tear,
That the fervour and faith of a soul can be known,
 To which time will but make thee more dear!
Oh! the heart that has truly loved, never forgets,
 But as truly loves on to the close,
As the sun-flower turns on her god, when he sets,
 The same look which she turned when he rose!

No. III.

TO

THE MARCHIONESS DOWAGER OF DONEGAL.

While the Publisher of these Melodies very properly inscribes them to the Nobility and Gentry of Ireland in general, I have much pleasure in selecting *one* from that number to whom *my* share of the Work is particularly dedicated. Though your Ladyship has been so long absent from Ireland, I know that you remember it well and warmly—that you have not allowed the charm of English society, like the taste of the lotus, to produce oblivion of your country; but that even the humble tribute which I offer derives its chief claim upon your interest from the appeal which it makes to your patriotism. Indeed, absence, however fatal to some affections of the heart, rather strengthens our love for the land where we were born; and Ireland is the country, of all others, which an exile must remember with enthusiasm. Those few darker and less amiable traits, with which bigotry and misrule have stained her character, and which are too apt to disgust us upon a nearer intercourse, become softened at a distance, or altogether invisible; and nothing is remembered but her virtues and her misfortunes—the zeal with which she has always loved liberty, and the barbarous policy which has always withheld it from her—the ease with which her generous spirit might be conciliated, and the cruel ingenuity which has been exerted to 'wring her into undutifulness.'

It has often been remarked, and oftener felt, that our music is the truest of all comments upon our history. The tone of defiance, succeeded by the languor of despondency—a burst of turbulence dying away into softness—the sorrows of one moment lost in the levity of the next—and all that romantic mixture of mirth and sadness which is naturally produced by the efforts of a lively temperament to shake off or forget the wrongs which lie upon it,—such are the features of our history and character which we find strongly and faithfully reflected in our music; and there are many airs which I think it is difficult to listen to, without recalling some period or event to which their expression seems peculiarly applicable. Sometimes, when the strain is open and spirited, yet shaded here and there by a mournful recollection, we can fancy that we behold the brave allies of Montrose, marching to the aid of the royal cause, notwithstanding all the perfidy of Charles and his ministers, and remembering just enough of past sufferings to enhance the generosity of their present sacrifice. The plaintive melodies of Carolan take us back to the times in which he lived, when our poor countrymen were driven to worship their God in caves, or to quit for ever the land of their birth (like the bird that abandons the nest which human touch has violated); and in many a song do we hear the last farewell of the exile, mingling regret for the ties he leaves at home, with sanguine expectations of the honours that await him abroad—such honours as were won on the field of Fontenoy, where the valour of Irish Catholics turned the fortune of the day in favour of the French, and extorted from George the Second that memorable exclamation, 'Cursed be the laws which deprive me of such subjects!'

Though much has been said of the antiquity of our music, it is certain that our finest and most popular airs are modern; and perhaps we may look no further than the last disgraceful century for the origin of most of those wild and melancholy strains, which were at once the offspring and solace of grief, and which were applied to the mind, as music was formerly to the body, 'decantare loca dolentia.' Mr. Pinkerton is of opinion that none of the Scotch popular airs are as old as the middle of the sixteenth century; and though musical antiquaries refer us, for some of our melodies, to so early a period as the fifth century, I am persuaded that there are few of a *civilised* description (and by this I mean to exclude all the savage Ceanans, cries, etc.) which can claim quite so ancient a date as Mr. Pinkerton allows to the Scotch. But music is not the only subject upon which our taste for antiquity is rather unreasonably indulged; and however heretical it may be to dissent from these romantic speculations, I cannot help thinking that it is possible to love our country very zealously, and to feel deeply interested in her honour and happiness, without believing that Irish was the language spoken in Paradise; that our ancestors were kind enough to take the trouble of polishing the Greeks; or that Abaris the Hyperborean was a native of the North of Ireland.

By some of these archæologists, it has been imagined that the Irish were early acquainted with counterpoint; and they endeavour to support this conjecture by a well-known passage in Giraldus, where he dilates with such elaborate praise upon the beauties of our national minstrelsy. But the terms of this eulogy are too vague, too deficient in technical accuracy, to prove that even Giraldus himself knew anything of the artifice of counterpoint. There are many expressions in the Greek and Latin writers which might be cited, with much more plausibility, to prove that they understood the arrangement of music in parts; yet I believe it is conceded in general by the learned, that however grand and pathetic the melody of the ancients may have been, it was reserved for the ingenuity of modern Science to transmit the 'light of Song' through the variegating prism of Harmony.

Indeed, the irregular scale of the early Irish (in which, as in the music of Scotland, the interval of the fourth was wanting) must have furnished but wild and refractory subjects to the harmonist. It was only when the invention of Guido began to be known, and the powers of the harp were enlarged by additional strings, that our melodies took the sweet character which interests us at present; and while the Scotch persevered in the old mutilation of the scale,[1] our music became

---

[1] The Scotch lay claim to some of our best airs, but there are strong traits of difference between their melodies and ours. They had formerly the same passion for robbing us of our Saints, and the learned Dempster was, for this offence, called 'The Saint Stealer.' I suppose it was an Irishman who, by way of reprisal, stole Dempster's beautiful wife from him at Pisa.—See this anecdote in the *Pinacotheca of Erythræus*, part 1, page 25.

gradually more amenable to the laws of harmony and counterpoint.

In profiting, however, by the improvements of the moderns, our style still kept its originality sacred from their refinements; and though Carolan had frequent opportunities of hearing the works of Geminiani and other masters, we but rarely find him sacrificing his native simplicity to the ambition of their ornaments, or affectation of their science. In that curious composition, indeed, called his Concerto, it is evident that he laboured to imitate Corelli; and this union of manners, so very dissimilar, produces the same kind of uneasy sensation which is felt at a mixture of different styles of architecture. In general, however, the artless flow of our music has preserved itself free from all tinge of foreign innovation; and the chief corruptions of which we have to complain arise from the unskilful performance of our own itinerant musicians, from whom too frequently the airs are noted down, encumbered by their tasteless decorations, and responsible for all their ignorant anomalies. Though it be sometimes impossible to trace the original strain, yet, in most of them, 'auri per ramos *aura* refulget,' the pure gold of the melody shines through the ungraceful foliage which surrounds it; and the most delicate and difficult duty of a compiler is to endeavour as much as possible, by retrenching these inelegant superfluities, and collating the various methods of playing or singing each air, to restore the regularity of its form and the chaste simplicity of its character.

I must again observe, that in doubting the antiquity of our music, my scepticism extends but to those polished specimens of the art which it is difficult to conceive anterior to the dawn of modern improvement; and that I would by no means invalidate the claims of Ireland to as early a rank in the annals of minstrelsy as the most zealous antiquary may be inclined to allow her. In addition, indeed, to the power which music must always have possessed over the minds of a people so ardent and susceptible, the stimulus of persecution was not wanting to quicken our taste into enthusiasm; the charms of song were ennobled with the glories of martyrdom; and the acts against minstrels, in the reigns of Henry VIII. and Elizabeth, were as successful, I doubt not, in making my countrymen musicians, as the penal laws have been in keeping them Catholics.

With respect to the verses which I have written for these Melodies, as they are intended rather to be sung than read, I can answer for their sound with somewhat more confidence than their sense; yet it would be affectation to deny that I have given much attention to the task, and that it is not through want of zeal or industry if I unfortunately disgrace the sweet airs of my country by poetry altogether unworthy of their taste, their energy, and their tenderness.

Though the humble nature of my contributions to this work may exempt them from the rigours of literary criticisms, it was not to be expected that those touches of political feeling, those tones of national complaint, in which the poetry sometimes sympathizes with the music, would be suffered to pass without censure or alarm. It has been accordingly said that the tendency of this publication is mischievous, and that I have chosen these airs but as a vehicle of dangerous politics—as fair and precious vessels (to borrow an image of St. Augustin) from which the wine of error might be administered. To those who identify nationality with treason, and who see in every effort for Ireland a system of hostility towards England; to those, too, who, nursed in the gloom of prejudice, are alarmed by the faintest gleam of liberality that threatens to disturb their darkness (like that Demophon of old, who, when the sun shone upon him, shivered!),— to such men I shall not deign to apologize for the warmth of any political sentiment which may occur in the course of these pages. But as there are many among the more wise and tolerant, who, with feeling enough to mourn over the wrongs of their country, and sense enough to perceive all the danger of not redressing them, may yet think that allusions in the least degree bold or inflammatory should be avoided in a publication of this popular description—I beg of these respected persons to believe, that there is no one who deprecates more sincerely than I do any appeal to the passions of an ignorant and angry multitude; but that it is not through that gross and inflammable region of society a work of this nature could ever have been intended to circulate. It looks much higher for its audience and readers: it is found upon the pianofortes of the rich and the educated—of those who can afford to have their national zeal a little stimulated, without exciting much dread of the excesses into which it may hurry them; and of many whose nerves may be now and then alarmed with advantage, as much more is to be gained by their fears than could ever be expected from their justice.

Having thus adverted to the principal objection which has been hitherto made to the poetical part of this work, allow me to add a few words in defence of my ingenious coadjutor, Sir John Stevenson, who has been accused of having spoiled the simplicity of the airs by the chromatic richness of his symphonies and the elaborate variety of his harmonies. We might cite the example of the admirable Haydn, who has sported through all the mazes of musical science in his arrangement of the simplest Scottish melodies; but it appears to me that Sir John Stevenson has brought a national feeling to this task which it would be in vain to expect from a foreigner, however tasteful or judicious. Through many of his own compositions we trace a vein of Irish sentiment, which points him out as peculiarly suited to catch the spirit of his country's music; and, far from agreeing with those critics who think that his symphonies have nothing kindred with the airs which they introduce, I would say that, in general, they resemble those illuminated initials of old manuscripts, which are of the same character with the writing which follows, though more highly coloured and more curiously ornamented.

In those airs which are arranged for voices his skill has particularly distinguished itself; and though it cannot be denied that a single melody most naturally expresses the language of feeling and passion, yet often, when a favourite strain has been dismissed as having lost its charm of novelty for the ear, it returns in a harmonized shape, with new claims upon our interest and attention; and to those who study the delicate artifices of composition, the construction of the inner parts of these pieces must afford, I think, considerable satisfaction. Every voice has an air to itself, a flowing succession of notes, which might be heard with pleasure, independent of the rest, so artfully has the harmonist (if I may thus express it) *gavelled* the melody, distributing an equal portion of its sweetness to every part.

If your Ladyship's love of Music were not known to me, I should not have hazarded so long a letter upon the subject; but as probably may have presumed too far upon your partiality, the best revenge you can take is to write me just as long a letter upon Painting; and I promise to attend to your theory of the art, with a pleasure only surpassed by that which I have so often derived from your practice of it.—May the mind which such talents adorn, continue calm as it is bright, and happy as it is virtuous!

Believe me, your Ladyship's
Grateful Friend and Servant,
THOMAS MOORE.
DUBLIN, *January* 1810.

ERIN! OH ERIN!

AIR—*Thamama Halla.*

LIKE the bright lamp that shone in Kildare's holy fane,
 And burned through long ages of darkness and storm,
Is the heart that afflictions have come o'er in vain,
 Whose spirit outlives them, unfading and warm!
Erin! oh Erin! thus bright, through the tears
Of a long night of bondage, thy spirit appears!

The nations have fallen, and thou still art young,
 Thy sun is but rising, when others are set;
And though slavery's cloud o'er thy morning hath hung,
 The full moon of freedom shall beam round thee yet.

Erin! oh Erin! though long in the shade,
Thy star will shine out, when the proudest shall fade!

Unchilled by the rain, and unwaked by the wind,
 The lily lies sleeping through winter's cold hour,
Till spring with a touch her dark slumber unbind,
 And day-light and liberty bless the young flower.[1]
Erin! oh Erin! *thy* winter is past,
And the hope that lived through it shall blossom at last.

DRINK TO HER.

AIR—*Heigh oh! my Jackey.*

DRINK to her, who long
 Hath waked the poet's sigh;
The girl who gave to song
 What gold could never buy.
Oh! woman's heart was made
 For minstrel hands alone;
By other fingers played,
 It yields not half the tone.
Then here's to her, who long
 Hath waked the poet's sigh,
The girl who gave to song
 What gold could never buy!

At Beauty's door of glass
 When Wealth and Wit once stood,
They asked her '*which* might pass?'
 She answered, 'he who could.'
With golden key Wealth thought
 To pass—but 'twould not do;
While Wit a diamond brought,
 Which cut his bright way through!
So here's to her, who long
 Hath waked the poet's sigh,
The girl who gave to song
 What gold could never buy!

The love that seeks a home,
 Where wealth or grandeur shines,
Is like the gloomy gnome
 That dwells in dark gold mines.
But oh! the poet's love
 Can boast a brighter sphere;
Its native home's above,
 Though woman keeps it here!
Then drink to her, who long
 Hath waked the poet's sigh,
The girl who gave to song
 What gold could never buy!

---

[1] Mrs. H. Tighe, in her exquisite lines on the lily, has applied this image to a still more important subject.

OH! BLAME NOT THE BARD.[1]

Air—*Kitty Tyrrel.*

Oh! blame not the bard, if he fly to the bowers
  Where Pleasure lies carelessly smiling at Fame;
He was born for much more, and in happier hours
  His soul might have burned with a holier flame.
The string, that now languishes loose o'er the lyre,
  Might have bent a proud bow to the warrior's dart,[2]
And the lip, which now breathes but the song of desire,
  Might have poured the full tide of a patriot's heart.

But alas! for his country—her pride is gone by,
  And that spirit is broken which never would bend;
O'er the ruin her children in secret must sigh,
  For 'tis treason to love her, and death to defend.
Unprized are her sons, till they've learned to betray;
  Undistinguished they live, if they shame not their sires;
And the torch that would light them through dignity's way,
  Must be caught from the pile where their country expires!

Then blame not the bard, if in pleasure's soft dream
  He should try to forget what he never can heal;
Oh! give but a hope—let a vista but gleam
  Through the gloom of his country, and mark how he'll feel!
That instant his heart at her shrine would lay down
  Every passion it nursed, every bliss it adored;
While the myrtle, now idly entwined with his crown,
  Like the wreath of Harmodius, should cover his sword.

But though glory be gone, and though hope fade away,
  Thy name, loved Erin! shall live in his songs;
Not even in the hour when his heart is most gay
  Will he lose the remembrance of thee and thy wrongs!
The stranger shall hear thy lament on his plains;
  The sigh of thy harp shall be sent o'er the deep,
Till thy masters themselves, as they rivet thy chains,
  Shall pause at the song of their captive, and weep.

WHILE GAZING ON THE MOON'S LIGHT

Air—*Oonagh.*

While gazing on the moon's light,
  A moment from her smile I turned
To look at orbs that, more bright,
  In lone and distant glory burned.
    But, *too far*,
    Each proud star,
For me to feel its warming flame—
    Much more dear
    That mild sphere,
Which near our planet smiling came;[3]
Thus, Mary, be but thou my own—
While brighter eyes unheeded play,
I'll love those moonlight looks alone,
Which bless my home and guide my way!

The day had sunk in dim showers,
  But midnight now, with lustre meek,
Illumined all the pale flowers,
  Like hope, that lights a mourner's cheek.
    I said (while
    The moon's smile
Played o'er a stream in dimpling bliss),
    'The moon looks
    On many brooks,
The brook can see no moon but this;'[4]
And thus, I thought, our fortunes run,
For many a lover looks to thee,
While oh! I feel there is but *one*,
  One Mary in the world for me.

ILL OMENS.

Air—*Kitty of Coleraine; or, Paddy's Resource.*

When daylight was yet sleeping under the billow,
And stars in the heavens still lingering shone,

---

[1] We may suppose this apology to have been uttered by one of those wandering bards whom Spencer so severely, and perhaps truly, describes in his *State of Ireland*, and whose poems, he tells us, 'were sprinkled with some pretty flowers of their natural device, which gave good grace and comeliness onto them, the which it is great pity to see abused to the gracing of wickedness and vice, which with good usage would serve to adorn and beautify virtue.'

[2] It is conjectured by Wormius that the name of Ireland is derived from *Yr*, the Runic for a *bow*, in the use of which weapon the Irish were once very expert. This derivation is certainly more creditable to us than the following: 'So that Ireland (called the land of *Ire*, for the constant broils therein for 400 years) was now become the land of concord.'—*Lloyd's State Worthies, Art.* The Lord Grandison.

[3] 'Of such celestial bodies as are visible, the sun excepted, the single moon, as despicable as it is in comparison to most of the others, is much more beneficial than they all put together.'—*Whiston's Theory*, etc.

[4] This image was suggested by the following thought, which occurs somewhere in Sir William Jones' works: 'The moon looks upon many night-flowers, the night-flower sees but one moon.'

Young Kitty, all blushing, rose up from her
     pillow,
The last time she e'er was to press it alone.
For the youth, whom she treasured her heart
     and her soul in,
Had promised to link the last tie before noon;
And when once the young heart of a maiden is
     stolen,
The maiden herself will steal after it soon!

As she looked in the glass, which a woman ne'er
     misses,
Nor ever wants time for a sly glance or two,
A butterfly, fresh from the night-flower's kisses,
Flew over the mirror, and shaded her view.
Enraged with the insect for hiding her graces,
     She brushed him—he fell, alas! never to rise—
'Ah! such,' said the girl, 'is the pride of our
     faces,
For which the soul's innocence too often dies!'

While she stole through the garden, where
     heart's-ease was growing,
She culled some, and kissed off its night-fallen
     dew;
And a rose, further on, looked so tempting and
     glowing,
That, spite of her haste, she must gather it
     too;
But while o'er the roses too carelessly leaning,
     Her zone flew in two, and the heart's-ease
     was lost—
Ah! this means,' said the girl (and she sighed
     at its meaning),
'That love is scarce worth the repose it will
     cost!'

BEFORE THE BATTLE.

Air—*The Fairy Queen.*

By the hope within us springing,
    Herald of to-morrow's strife;
By that sun whose light is bringing
    Chains or freedom, death or life—
Oh! remember life can be
No charm for him who lives not free!
    Like the day-star in the wave,
    Sinks a hero to his grave,
'Midst the dew-fall of a nation's tears!
    Happy is he o'er whose decline
    The smiles of home may soothing shine,
And light him down the steep of years:—
    But oh! how grand they sink to rest
Who close their eyes on Victory's breast!

O'er his watchfire's fading embers
    Now the foeman's cheek turns white,
When his heart that field remembers,
    Where we dimmed his glory's light!
Never let him bind again
A chain like that we broke from then.

Hark! the horn of combat calls—
    Ere the golden evening falls,
May we pledge that horn in triumph round!
    Many a heart that now beats high,
    In slumber cold at night shall lie,
Nor waken even at victory's sound:—
    But oh! how blest that hero's sleep,
    O'er whom a wondering world shall weep!

AFTER THE BATTLE.

Air—*Thy Fair Bosom.*

Night closed around the conqueror's way,
    And lightnings showed the distant hill,
Where those who lost that dreadful day
    Stood, few and faint, but fearless still!
The soldier's hope, the patriot's zeal,
    For ever dimmed, for ever crossed—
Oh! who shall say what heroes feel,
    When all but life and honour's lost!

The last sad hour of freedom's dream,
    And valour's task, moved slowly by,
While mute they watched, till morning's beam
    Should rise, and give them light to die!—
There is a world where souls are free,
    Where tyrants taint not nature's bliss;
If death that world's bright opening be,
    Oh! who would live a slave in this?

OH! 'TIS SWEET TO THINK.

Air—*Thady, you Gander.*

Oh! 'tis sweet to think that, wherever we rove,
    We are sure to find something blissful and
    dear;
And that, when we're far from the lips we love,
    We have but to make love to the lips we are
    near!
The heart, like a tendril, accustomed to cling,
    Let it grow where it will, cannot flourish alone,
But will lean to the nearest and loveliest thing
    It can twine with itself, and make closely its
    own.
Then oh! what pleasure, where'er we rove,
    To be doomed to find something still that is
    dear,
And to know, when far from the lips we love,
    We have but to make love to the lips we are
    near.

'Twere a shame, when flowers around us rise,
    To make light of the rest, if the rose is not
    there;
And the world's so rich in resplendent eyes,
    'Twere a pity to limit one's love to a pair.
Love's wing and the peacock's are nearly alike,
    They are both of them bright, but they're
    changeable too,

And wherever a new beam of beauty can strike,
It will tincture Love's plume with a different hue!
Then oh! what pleasure, where'er we rove,
To be doomed to find something still that is dear,
And to know, when far from the lips we love,
We have but to make love to the lips we are near.

THE IRISH PEASANT TO HIS MISTRESS.

Air—— ——.

Through grief and through danger thy smile hath cheered my way,
Till hope seemed to bud from each thorn that round me lay;
The darker our fortune, the brighter our pure love burned,
Till shame into glory, till fear into zeal was turned:
Oh! slave as I was, in thy arms my spirit felt free,
And bless'd even the sorrows that made me more dear to thee.

Thy rival was honoured, while thou wert wronged and scorned;
Thy crown was of briers, while gold her brows adorned;
She wooed me to temples, while thou layest bid in caves;
Her friends were all masters, while thine, alas! were slaves;
Yet, cold in the earth, at thy feet I would rather be,
Than wed what I loved not, or turn one thought from thee.

They slander thee sorely, who say thy vows are frail—
Hadst thou been a false one, thy cheek had looked less pale!
They say, too, so long thou hast worn those lingering chains,
That deep in thy heart they have printed their servile stains—
Oh! do not believe them—no chain could that soul subdue—
Where shineth thy spirit, there liberty shineth too!

ON MUSIC.

Air—*Banks of Banna.*

When through life unblessed we rove,
Losing all that made life dear,
Should some notes we used to love
In days of boyhood meet our ear,

Oh how welcome breathes the strain!
Wakening thoughts that long have slept;
Kindling former smiles again,
In faded eyes that long have wept!

Like the gale that sighs along
Beds of oriental flowers,
Is the grateful breath of song,
That once was heard in happier hours.
Filled with balm the gale sighs on,
Though the flowers have sunk in death;
So, when Pleasure's dream is gone,
Its memory lives in Music's breath!

Music!—oh! how faint, how weak,
Language fades before thy spell!
Why should feeling ever speak,
When thou canst breathe her soul so well?
Friendship's balmy words may feign,
Love's are even more false than they;
Oh! 'tis only Music's strain
Can sweetly soothe, and not betray!

IT IS NOT THE TEAR AT THIS MOMENT SHED.[1]

Air—*The Sixpence.*

It is not the tear at this moment shed,
When the cold turf has just been laid o'er him,
That can tell how beloved was the friend that's fled,
Or how deep in our hearts we deplore him.
'Tis the tear, through many a long day wept,
Through a life by his loss all shaded;
'Tis the sad remembrance, fondly kept,
When all lighter griefs have faded!

Oh! thus shall we mourn, and his memory's light,
While it shines through our hearts, will improve them;
For worth shall look fairer, and truth more bright,
When we think how he lived but to love them!
And as buried saints have given perfume
To shrines where they've been lying,
So our hearts shall borrow a sweetening bloom
From the image he left there in dying!

THE ORIGIN OF THE HARP.

Air—*Gage Fane.*

'Tis believed that this harp, which I wake now for thee,
Was a Siren of old, who sung under the sea;
And who often at eve through the bright billow roved,
To meet on the green shore a youth whom she loved.

---

[1] These lines were occasioned by the death of a very near and dear relative.

But she loved him in vain, for he left her to weep,
And in tears all the night her gold ringlets to steep,
Till Heaven looked with pity on true love so warm,
And changed to this soft harp the sea-maiden's form!

Still her bosom rose fair—still her cheek smiled the same—
While her sea-beauties gracefully curled round the frame;
And her hair, shedding tear-drops from all its bright rings,
Fell over her white arm, to make the gold strings![1]

Hence it came, that this soft harp so long hath been known
To mingle love's language with sorrow's sad tone;
Till *thou* didst divide them, and teach the fond lay
To be love when I'm near thee, and grief when away!

The Airs of the last Number, though full of originality and beauty, were perhaps, in general, too curiously selected to become all at once as popular as we think they deserve to be. The public are remarkably reserved towards new acquaintances in music, which perhaps is one of the reasons why many modern composers introduce none but old friends to their notice. Indeed, it is natural that persons who love music only by association, should be slow in feeling the charms of a new and strange melody; while those who have a quick sensibility for this enchanting art, will as naturally seek and enjoy novelty, because in every variety of strain they find a fresh combination of ideas, and the sound has scarcely reached the ear before the heart has rapidly translated it into sentiment. After all, however, it cannot be denied that the most popular of our national Airs are also the most beautiful; and it has been our wish in the present Number, to select from those, Melodies only which have long been listened to and admired. The least known in the collection is the Air of *Love's Young Dream;* but it is one of those easy, artless strangers, whose merit the heart acknowledges instantly.

T. M.

Bury Street, St. James's,
Nov. 1811.

No. IV.

This Number of *The Melodies* ought to have appeared much earlier; and the writer of the words is ashamed to confess that the delay of its publication must be imputed chiefly, if not entirely, to him. He finds it necessary to make this avowal, not only for the purpose of removing all blame from the publisher, but in consequence of a rumour, which has been circulated industriously in Dublin, that the Irish Government had interfered to prevent the continuance of the Work. This would be, indeed, a revival of Henry the Eighth's enactments against Minstrels, and it is very flattering to find that so much importance is attached to our compilation, even by such persons as the inventors of the report. Bishop Lowth, it is true, was of this opinion, that *one* song, like the *Hymn to Harmodius,* would have done more towards rousing the spirit of the Romans than *all* the philippics of Cicero. But we live in wiser and less musical times; ballads have long lost their revolutionary powers, and we question if even a 'Lillibullero' would produce any very *serious* consequences at present. It is needless, therefore, to add, that there is no truth in the report; and we trust that whatever belief it obtained was founded more upon the character of *the Government* than of *the Work.*

LOVE'S YOUNG DREAM.

Air—*The Old Woman.*

Oh! the days are gone, when Beauty bright
    My heart's chain wove!
When my dream of life, from morn till night,
    Was love, still love!
New hope may bloom,
And days may come
Of milder, calmer beam,
But there's nothing half so sweet in life
    As love's young dream!
Oh! there's nothing half so sweet in life
    As love's young dream!

Though the bard to purer fame may soar,
    When wild youth's past;
Though he win the wise, who frowned before,
    To smile at last;
He'll never meet
A joy so sweet,
In all his noon of fame,
As when first he sung to woman's ear
    His soul-felt flame,
And at every close she blushed to hear
    The one loved name!

Oh! that hallowed form is ne'er forgot,
    Which first-love traced;
Still it lingering haunts the greenest spot
    On memory's waste!

---

[1] This thought was suggested by an ingenious design, prefixed to an ode upon St. Cecilia, published some years since, by Mr. Hudson of Dublin.

'Twas odour fled
  As soon as shed;
'Twas morning's wingèd dream;
Twas a light that ne'er can shine again
  On life's dull stream!
Oh! 'twas light that ne'er can shine again
  On life's dull stream.

But nothing can cloud its native ray;
  Each fragment will cast
  A light to the last!—
And thus, Erin, my country! though broken
  thou art,
There's a lustre within thee that ne'er will
  decay;
A spirit which beams through each suffering part,
And now smiles at their pain, on the Prince's
  Day!

THE PRINCE'S DAY.[1]

Air.—*St. Patrick's Day.*

Though dark are our sorrows, to-day we'll
  forget them,
And smile through our tears, like a sunbeam
  in showers;
There never were hearts, if our rulers would let
  them,
More formed to be grateful and blessed than
  ours!
    But just when the chain
    Has ceased to pain,
  And hope has enwreathed it round with
    flowers,
    There comes a new link
    Our spirit to sink—
Oh! the joy that we taste, like the light of the
  poles,
Is a flash amid darkness, too brilliant to stay;
But though 'twere the last little spark in our
  souls,
We must light it up now on our Prince's Day.

Contempt on the minion who calls you disloyal!
Though fierce to your foe, to your friends you
  are true;
And the tribute most high to a head that is royal
Is love from a heart that loves liberty too.
    While cowards who blight
    Your fame, your right,
  Would shrink from the blaze of the battle array,
    The Standard of Green
    In front would be seen—
Oh! my life on your faith! were you summoned
  this minute,
You'd cast every bitter remembrance away,
And show what the arm of old Erin has in it,
When roused by the foe, on her Prince's Day.

He loves the Green Isle, and his love is recorded
In hearts which have suffered too much to
  forget;
And hope shall be crowned, and attachment
  rewarded,
And Erin's gay jubilee shine out yet!
    The gem may be broke
    By many a stroke,

[1] This song was written for a fête in honour of the Prince of Wales' Birthday, given by my friend Major Bryan at his seat in the county of Kilkenny.

WEEP ON, WEEP ON.

Air.—*The Song of Sorrow.*

Weep on, weep on, your hour is past,
  Your dreams of pride are o'er;
The fatal chain is round you cast,
  And you are men no more!
In vain the hero's heart hath bled,
  The sage's tongue hath warned in vain;—
Oh, Freedom! once thy flame hath fled,
  It never lights again!

Weep on—perhaps in after days
  They'll learn to love your name;
When many a deed shall wake in praise
  That now must sleep in blame!
And when they tread the ruined isle,
  Where rest at length the lord and slave,
They'll wondering ask, how hands so vile
  Could conquer hearts so brave.

' 'Twas fate,' they'll say, 'a wayward fate
  Your web of discord wove;
And while your tyrants joined in hate,
  You never joined in love!
But hearts fell off that ought to twine,
  And man profaned what God had given,
Till some were heard to curse the shrine
  Where others knelt to Heaven!'

LESBIA HATH A BEAMING EYE.

Air.—*Nora Creina.*

Lesbia hath a beaming eye,
  But no one knows for whom it beameth;
Right and left its arrows fly,
  But what they aim at no one dreameth!
Sweeter 'tis to gaze upon
  My Nora's lid, that seldom rises;
Few its looks, but every one,
  Like unexpected light, surprises!
    Oh, my Nora Creina, dear!
    My gentle, bashful Nora Creina!
        Beauty lies
        In many eyes,
    But love in yours, my Nora Creina!

Lesbia wears a robe of gold,
But all so close the nymph hath laced it,
Not a charm of Beauty's mould
Presumes to stay where Nature placed it!
Oh! my Nora's gown for me,
That floats as wild as mountain breezes,
Leaving every beauty free
To sink or swell, as Heaven pleases!
Yes, my Nora Creina, dear!
My simple, graceful Nora Creina!
Nature's dress
Is loveliness—
The dress *you* wear, my Nora Creina!

Lesbia hath a wit refined,
But when its points are gleaming round us,
Who can tell if they're designed
To dazzle merely or to wound us?
Pillowed on my Nora's heart,
In safer slumber Love reposes—
Bed of Peace! whose roughest part
Is but the crumpling of the roses.
Oh, my Nora Creina, dear!
My mild, my artless Nora Creina!
Wit, though bright,
Hath not the light
That warms your eyes, my Nora Creina!

I SAW THY FORM IN YOUTHFUL PRIME.

Air—*Domhnall.*

I saw thy form in youthful prime,
Nor thought that pale decay
Would steal before the steps of time,
And waste its bloom away, Mary!
Yet still thy features wore that light
Which fleets not with the breath;
And life ne'er looked more truly bright
Than in thy smile of death, Mary!

As streams that run o'er golden mines,
Yet humbly, calmly glide,
Nor seem to know the wealth that shines
Within their gentle tide, Mary!
So, veiled beneath the simplest guise,
Thy radiant genius shone,
And that which charmed all other eyes
Seemed worthless in thy own, Mary!

If souls could always dwell above,
Thou ne'er hadst left that sphere;
Or, could we keep the souls we love,
We ne'er had lost thee here, Mary!
Though many a gifted mind we meet,
Though fairest forms we see,
To live with them is far less sweet
Than to remember thee, Mary!

BY THAT LAKE WHOSE GLOOMY SHORE.[1]

Air—*The Brown Irish Girl.*

By that lake whose gloomy shore
Skylark never warbles o'er,
Where the cliff hangs high and steep,
Young Saint Kevin stole to sleep.
'Here, at least,' he calmly said,
'Woman ne'er shall find my bed.'
Ah! the good saint little knew
What that wily sex can do.

'Twas from Kathleen's eyes he flew—
Eyes of most unholy blue!
She had loved him well and long,
Wished him hers, nor thought it wrong.
Wheresoe'er the saint would fly,
Still he heard her light foot nigh;
East or west, where'er he turned,
Still her eyes before him burned.

On the bold cliff's bosom cast,
Tranquil now he sleeps at last;
Dreams of heaven, nor thinks that e'er
Woman's smile can haunt him there.
But nor earth nor heaven is free
From her power, if fond she be:
Even now, while calm he sleeps,
Kathleen o'er him leans and weeps.

Fearless, she had tracked his feet
To this rocky wild retreat;
And when morning met his view,
Her mild glances met it too.
Ah! your saints have cruel hearts!
Sternly from his bed he starts,
And with rude, repulsive shock,
Hurls her from the beetling rock.

Glendalough! thy gloomy wave
Soon was gentle Kathleen's grave;
Soon the saint (yet, ah! too late)
Felt her love, and mourned her fate.
When he said, 'Heaven rest her soul!'
Round the lake light music stole;
And her ghost was seen to glide,
Smiling, o'er the fatal tide!

SHE IS FAR FROM THE LAND.

Air—*Open the Door.*

She is far from the land where her young hero sleeps,
And lovers are round her sighing;
But coldly she turns from their gaze, and weeps,
For her heart in his grave is lying!

---

[1] This ballad is founded upon one of the many stories related of St. Kevin, whose bed in the rock is to be seen at Glendalough, a most gloomy and romantic spot in the county of Wicklow.

She sings the wild song of her dear native
   plains,
Every note which he loved awaking.—
Ah! little they think, who delight in her strains,
How the heart of the Minstrel is breaking!

He had lived for his love, for his country he died,
   They were all that to life had entwined him;
Nor soon shall the tears of his country be dried,
   Nor long will his love stay behind him.

Oh! make her a grave where the sunbeams
   rest,
   When they promise a glorious morrow;
They'll shine o'er her sleep, like a smile from the
   West,
   From her own loved Island of Sorrow!

NAY, TELL ME NOT.

AIR—*Dennis, don't be threatening.*

NAY, tell me not, dear! that the goblet drowns
   One charm of feeling, one fond regret;
Believe me, a few of thy angry frowns
   Are all I've sunk in its bright wave yet.
      Ne'er hath a beam
      Been lost in the stream
That ever was shed from thy form or soul;
      The balm of thy sighs,
      The light of thine eyes,
Still float on the surface and hallow my bowl!
Then fancy not, dearest! that wine can steal
   One blissful dream of the heart from me!
Like founts that awaken the pilgrim's zeal,
   The bowl but brightens my love for thee!

They tell us that Love in his fairy bower
   Had two blush-roses, of birth divine;
He sprinkled the one with a rainbow's shower,
   But bathed the other with mantling wine.
      Soon did the buds,
      That drank of the floods
Distilled by the rainbow, decline and fade;
      While those which the tide
      Of ruby had dyed
All blushed into beauty, like thee, sweet maid!

Then fancy not, dearest! that wine can steal
   One blissful dream of the heart from me;
Like founts that awaken the pilgrim's zeal,
   The bowl but brightens my love for thee.

AVENGING AND BRIGHT.

AIR—*Crooghan a Venee.*

AVENGING and bright fall the swift sword of
   Erin [1]
On him who the brave sons of Usna betrayed!
For every fond eye he hath wakened a tear in,
   A drop from his heart-wounds shall weep o'er
      her blade.

By the red cloud that hung over Conor's dark
   dwelling,[2]
   When Ulad's three champions lay sleeping in
      gore[3]—
By the billows of war which, so often, high
   swelling,
   Have wafted these heroes to victory's shore!—

We swear to revenge them!—no joy shall be
   tasted,
The harp shall be silent, the maiden unwed;
Our halls shall be mute, and our fields shall lie
   wasted,
Till vengeance is wreaked on the murderer's
   head!

Yes, monarch! though sweet are our home recollections,
Though sweet are the tears that from tenderness fall;
Though sweet are our friendships, our hopes,
   our affections,
Revenge on a tyrant is sweetest of all!

WHAT THE BEE IS TO THE FLOWERET.

AIR—*The Yellow Horse.*

He.—WHAT the bee is to the floweret,
   When he looks for honey-dew
Through the leaves that close embower it,
   That, my love, I'll be to you!

---

[1] The words of this song were suggested by the very ancient Irish story, called 'Deirdri, or the lamentable ate of the sons of Usnach,' which has been translated literally from the Gaelic by Mr. O'Flanagan (see vol. 1. of *Transactions of the Gaelic Society of Dublin*), and upon which it appears that the 'Darthula' of Macpherson is founded. The treachery of Conor, King of Ulster, in putting to death the three sons of Usna, was the cause of a desolating war against Ulster, which terminated in the destruction of Eman. 'This story (says Mr. O'Flanagan) has been from time immemorial held in high repute as one of the three tragic stories of the Irish. These are, "The death of the children of Touran;" "The death of the children of Lear" (both regarding Tuatha de Danans); and this, "The death of the children of Usnach," which is a Milesian story.' In No. II. of these *Melodies* there is a ballad upon the story of the children of Lear or Lir, 'Silent, oh Moyle!' etc.

Whatever may be thought of those sanguine claims to antiquity which Mr. O'Flanagan and others advance for the literature of Ireland, it would be a very lasting reproach upon our nationality if the Gaelic researches of this gentleman did not meet with all the liberal encouragement which they merit.

[2] 'Oh Nalsi! view the cloud that I here see in the sky! I see over Eman green a chilling cloud of blood-tinged red.'—*Deirdri's Song.*

[3] Ulster.

She.—What the bank, with verdure glowing,
    Is to waves that wander near,
  Whispering kisses while they're going,
    That I'll be to you, my dear!

She.—But they say, the bee's a rover,
    That he'll fly when sweets are gone;
  And when once the kiss is over,
    Faithless brooks will wander on!

He.—Nay, if flowers *will* lose their looks,
    If sunny banks *will* wear away,
  'Tis but right that bees and brooks
    Should sip and kiss them while they may.

LOVE AND THE NOVICE.

AIR—*Cean Dubh Delish.*

'HERE we dwell, in holiest bowers,
  Where angels of light o'er our orisons bend;
Where sighs of devotion and breathings of flowers
  To Heaven in mingled odour ascend!
  Do not disturb our calm, oh Love!
  So like is thy form to the cherubs above,
It well might deceive such hearts as ours.'

Love stood near the Novice and listened,
  And Love is no novice in taking a hint;
His laughing blue eyes now with piety glistened;
  His rosy wing turned to heaven's own tint.
    'Who would have thought,' the urchin cries,
    'That love could so well, so gravely disguise
His wandering wings and wounding eyes?'

Love now warms thee, waking and sleeping,
  Young Novice; to him all thy orisons rise;
He tinges the heavenly fount with his weeping,
He brightens the censer's flame with his sighs.
  Love is the saint enshrined in thy breast,
  And angels themselves would admit such a guest,
If he came to them clothed in Piety's vest.

THIS LIFE IS ALL CHEQUERED WITH PLEASURES AND WOES.

AIR—*The Bunch of Green Rushes that grew at the Brim.*

THIS life is all chequered with pleasures and woes,
  That chase one another, like waves of the deep;
Each billow, as brightly or darkly it flows,
  Reflecting our eyes as they sparkle or weep.
So closely our whims on our miseries tread,
  That the laugh is awaked ere the tear can be dried;
And as fast as the rain-drop of Pity is shed,
  The goose-feathers of folly can turn it aside.
But pledge me the cup—if existence would cloy,
  With hearts ever happy, and heads ever wise,
Be ours the light Grief that is sister to Joy,
  And the short brilliant Folly that flashes and dies!

When Hylas was sent with his urn to the fount,
  Through fields full of sunshine, with heart full of play,
Light rambled the boy over meadow and mount,
  And neglected his task for the flowers on the way.
Thus some who, like me, should have drawn and have tasted
  The fountain that runs by Philosophy's shrine,
Their time with the flowers on the margin have wasted,
  And left their light urns all as empty as mine!
But pledge me the goblet—while Idleness weaves
  Her flowerets together, if Wisdom can see
One bright drop or two, that has fallen on the leaves
  From her fountain divine, 'tis sufficient for me!

No. V.

IT is but fair to those who take an interest in this Work, to state that it is now very near its termination, and that the Sixth Number, which shall speedily appear, will most probably be the last of the series.

It is not so much from a want of materials, and still less from any abatement of zeal or industry, that we have adopted the resolution of bringing our task to a close; but we feel so proud, for our country's sake and our own, of the interest which this purely Irish Work has excited, and so anxious lest a particle of that interest should be lost by any ill-judged protraction of its existence, that we think it wiser to take away the cup from the lip, while its flavour is yet, we trust, fresh and sweet, than to risk any longer trial of the charm, or give so much as not to leave some wish for more. In speaking thus, I allude entirely to the Airs, which are, of course, the main attraction of these Volumes; and though we have still many popular and delightful Melodies to produce,[1] yet

---

[1] Among these is *Savourna Deelish*, which I have hitherto only withheld, from the diffidence I feel in treading upon the same ground with Mr. Campbell, whose beautiful words to this fine air have taken too strong possession of all ears and hearts, for me to think of producing any impression after him. I suppose, however, I must attempt it for the next Number.

It cannot be denied that we should soon experience some difficulty in equalling the richness and novelty of the earlier Numbers, for which, as we had the choice of all before us, we naturally selected only the most rare and beautiful. The Poetry, too, would be sure to sympathize with the decline of the Music; and however feebly my words have kept pace with the *excellence* of the Airs, they would follow their *falling off*, I fear, with wonderful alacrity. So that, altogether, both pride and prudence counsel us to stop, while the Work is yet, we believe, flourishing and attractive, and in the imperial attitude, '*stantes mori*,' before we incur the charge either of altering for the worse, or, what is equally unpardonable, continuing too long the same.

We beg, however, to say, it is only in the event of our failing to find Airs as exquisite as most of those we have given, that we mean thus to anticipate the natural period of dissolution, like those Indians who put their relatives to death when they become feeble.

T. M.

MAYFIELD COTTAGE. ASHBOURNE,
December 1813.

OH, THE SHAMROCK!

AIR—*Alley Croker*.

Through Erin's Isle,
To sport awhile,
As Love and Valour wandered,
With Wit, the sprite,
Whose quiver bright
A thousand arrows squandered;
Where'er they pass,
A triple grass[1]
Shoots up, with dew-drops streaming,
As softly green
As emeralds seen
Through purest crystal gleaming!
Oh, the Shamrock, the green, immortal Shamrock!
Chosen leaf
Of bard and chief,
Old Erin's native Shamrock!

Says Valour, 'See,
They spring for me,
Those leafy gems of morning!'
Says Love, 'No, no,
For *me* they grow,
My fragrant path adorning!'

But Wit perceives
Three triple leaves,
And cries, 'Oh! do not sever
A type that blends
Three god-like friends,
Love, Valour, Wit, for ever!'
Oh, the Shamrock, the green, immortal Shamrock!
Chosen leaf
Of bard and chief,
Old Erin's native Shamrock!

So, firmly fond
May last the bond
They wove that morn together,
And ne'er may fall
One drop of gall
On Wit's celestial feather!
May Love, as shoot
His flowers and fruit,
Of thorny falsehood weed 'em!
May Valour ne'er
His standard rear
Against the cause of Freedom!
Oh, the Shamrock, the green, immortal Shamrock!
Chosen leaf
Of bard and chief,
Old Erin's native Shamrock!

AT THE MID HOUR OF NIGHT.

AIR—*Molly, my Dear*.

At the mid hour of night, when stars are weeping, I fly
To the lone vale we loved when life was warm in thine eye;
And I think that if spirits can steal from the regions of air
To revisit past scenes of delight, thou wilt come to me there,
And tell me our love is remembered, even in the sky!

Then I sing the wild song it once was rapture to hear,
When our voices, commingling, breathed like one on the ear;
And as Echo far off through the vale my sad orison rolls,
I think, oh, my love! 'tis thy voice from the kingdom of souls,[2]
Faintly answering still the notes once that were so dear.

---

[1] Saint Patrick is said to have made use of that species of the trefoil, in Ireland called the Shamrock, in explaining the doctrine of the Trinity to the pagan Irish. I do not know if there be any other reason for our adoption of this plant as a national emblem. Hope, among the ancients, was sometimes represented as a beautiful child, 'standing upon tiptoes, and a trefoil or three-coloured grass in her hand.'

[2] 'There are countries,' says Montaigne, 'where they believe the souls of the happy live in all manner of liberty, in delightful fields; and that it is those souls repeating the words we utter, which we call Echo.'

ONE BUMPER AT PARTING.

Air—*Moll Roe in the Morning.*

One bumper at parting!—though many
Have circled the boards since we met,
The fullest, the saddest of any
Remains to be crowned by us yet.
The sweetness that pleasure has in it
Is always so slow to come forth,
That seldom, alas, till the minute
It dies, do we know half its worth!
But fill—may our life's happy measure
Be all of such moments made up;
They're born on the bosom of pleasure,
They die 'midst the tears of the cup.

As onward we journey, how pleasant
To pause and inhabit awhile
Those few sunny spots, like the present,
That 'mid the dull wilderness smile!
But Time, like a pitiless master,
Cries, 'Onward!' and spurs the gay hours;
And never does time travel faster
Than when his way lies among flowers.
But, come—may our life's happy measure
Be all of such moments made up;
They're born on the bosom of pleasure,
They die 'midst the tears of the cup.

This evening, we saw the sun sinking
In waters his glory made bright—
Oh! trust me, our farewell of drinking
Should be like that farewell of light.
You saw how he finished, by darting
His beam o'er a deep billow's brim—
So fill up!—let's shine, at our parting,
In full liquid glory, like him.
And oh! may our life's happy measure
Of moments like this be made up;
'Twas born on the bosom of pleasure,
It dies 'mid the tears of the cup!

'TIS THE LAST ROSE OF SUMMER.

Air—*Groves of Blarney.*

'Tis the last rose of summer,
Left blooming alone;
All her lovely companions
Are faded and gone;
No flower of her kindred,
No rosebud is nigh,
To reflect back her blushes,
Or give sigh for sigh!

I'll not leave thee, thou lone one!
To pine on the stem;
Since the lovely are sleeping,
Go, sleep thou with them.
Thus kindly I scatter
Thy leaves o'er the bed,
Where thy mates of the garden
Lie scentless and dead.

So soon may *I* follow,
When friendships decay,
And from Love's shining circle
The gems drop away!
When true hearts lie withered,
And fond ones are flown,
Oh! who would inhabit
This bleak world alone?

THE YOUNG MAY-MOON.

Air—*The Dandy O!*

The young May-moon is beaming, love!
The glow-worm's lamp is gleaming, love!
How sweet to rove
Through Morna's grove,[1]
While the drowsy world is dreaming, love!
Then awake!—the heavens look bright, my dear!
'Tis never too late for delight, my dear!
And the best of all ways
To lengthen our days,
Is to steal a few hours from the night, my dear!

Now all the world is sleeping, love!
But the sage, his star-watch keeping, love!
And I, whose star,
More glorious far,
Is the eye from that casement peeping, love!
Then awake!—till rise of sun, my dear!
The sage's glass we'll shun, my dear!
Or, in watching the flight
Of bodies of light,
He might happen to take thee for one, my dear!

THE MINSTREL-BOY.

Air—*The Moreen.*

The Minstrel-Boy to the war is gone,
In the ranks of death you'll find him;
His father's sword he has girded on,
And his wild harp slung behind him.—
'Land of song!' said the warrior-bard,
'Though all the world betrays thee,
One sword at least thy rights shall guard,
One faithful harp shall praise thee!'

The Minstrel fell!—but the foeman's chain
Could not bring his proud soul under!
The harp he loved ne'er spoke again,
For he tore its chords asunder;

---

[1] 'Steals silently to Morna's Grove.'
See a translation from the Irish, in Mr. Bunting's collection, by John Brown, one of my earliest college companions and friends, whose death was as singularly melancholy and unfortunate as his life had been amiable, honourable, and exemplary.

And said, 'No chains shall sully thee,
　Thou soul of love and bravery!
Thy songs were made for the pure and free,
　They shall never sound in slavery!'

THE SONG OF O'RUARK, PRINCE OF BREFFNI.[1]

Air—*The pretty Girl milking her Cow.*

The valley lay smiling before me,
　Where lately I left her behind;
Yet I trembled, and something hung o'er me,
　That saddened the joy of my mind.
I looked for the lamp, which she told me
　Should shine when her pilgrim returned;
But though darkness began to enfold me,
　No lamp from the battlements burned!

I flew to her chamber—'twas lonely,
　As if the loved tenant lay dead!—
Ah! would it were death, and death only!
　But no—the young false one had fled.
And there hung the lute, that could soften
　My very worst pains into bliss,
While the hand that had waked it so often
　Now throbbed to a proud rival's kiss.

There *was* a time, falsest of women!
　When Breffni's good sword would have sought
That man, through a million of foemen,
　Who dared but to doubt thee *in thought!*
While now—oh, degenerate daughter
　Of Erin!—how fallen is thy fame!
And through ages of bondage and slaughter,
　Our country shall bleed for thy shame.

Already the curse is upon her,
　And strangers her valleys profane;
They come to divide—to dishonour,
　And tyrants they long will remain!
But, onward!—the green banner rearing,
　Go, flesh every sword to the hilt;
On *our* side is Virtue and Erin!
　On *theirs* is the Saxon and Guilt.

OH! HAD WE SOME BRIGHT LITTLE ISLE OF OUR OWN!

Air—*Sheela na Guira.*

Oh! had we some bright little isle of our own,
In a blue summer ocean, far off and alone,
Where a leaf never dies in the still-blooming bowers,
And the bee banquets on through a whole year of flowers;
　Where the sun loves to pause
　　With so fond a delay,
　That the night only draws
　　A thin veil o'er the day;
Where simply to feel that we breathe, that we live,
Is worth the best joy that life elsewhere can give!

There, with souls ever ardent and pure as the clime,
We should love, as they loved in the first golden time;
The glow of the sunshine, the balm of the air,
Would steal to our hearts, and make all summer there!
　With affection, as free
　　From decline as the bowers,
　And with Hope, like the bee,
　　Living always on flowers,
Our life should resemble a long day of light,
And our death come on, holy and calm as the night!

FAREWELL!—BUT WHENEVER YOU WELCOME THE HOUR.

Air—*Moll Roone.*

Farewell!—but whenever you welcome the hour
That awakens the night-song of mirth in your bower,
Then think of the friend who once welcomed it too,
And forgot his own griefs to be happy with you.
His griefs may return—not a hope may remain
Of the few that have brightened his pathway of pain—

---

[1] These stanzas are founded upon an event of most melancholy importance to Ireland, if, as we are told by our Irish historians, it gave England the first opportunity of profiting by our divisions and subduing us. The following are the circumstances as related by O'Halloran:—'The King of Leinster had long conceived a violent affection for Dearbhorgil, daughter to the King of Meath; and though she had been for some time married to O'Ruark, Prince of Breffni, yet it could not restrain his passion. They carried on a private correspondence, and she informed him that O'Ruark intended soon to go on a pilgrimage (an act of piety frequent in those days), and conjured him to embrace that opportunity of conveying her from a husband she detested to a lover she adored. Mac Murchad too punctually obeyed the summons, and had the lady conveyed to his capital of Ferns.'—The Monarch Roderick espoused the cause of O'Ruark, while Mac Murchad fled to England, and obtained the assistance of Henry II.

'Such,' adds Giraldus Cambrensis (as I find him in an old translation), 'is the variable and fickle nature of women, by whom all mischief in the world (for the most part) do happen and come, as may appear by Marcus Antonius, and by the destruction of Troy.'

But he ne'er will forget the short vision, that threw
Its enchantment around him, while lingering with you!

And still on that evening, when pleasure fills up
To the highest top sparkle each heart and each cup,
Where'er my path lies, be it gloomy or bright,
My soul, happy friends! shall be with you that night;
Shall join in your revels, your sports, and your wiles,
And return to me beaming all o'er with your smiles!—
Too blessed, if it tells me that, 'mid the gay cheer,
Some kind voice had murmured, 'I wish he were here!'

Let fate do her worst, there are relics of joy,
Bright dreams of the past, which she cannot destroy;
Which come, in the night-time of sorrow and care,
And bring back the features that joy used to wear.
Long, long be my heart with such memories filled!
Like the vase in which roses have once been distilled—
You may break, you may ruin the vase, if you will,
But the scent of the roses will hang round it still.

OH! DOUBT ME NOT.

Air—*Yellow Wat and the Fox.*

Oh! doubt me not—the season
Is o'er when folly made me rove,
And now the vestal Reason
Shall watch the fire awaked by Love.
Although this heart was early blown,
And fairest hands disturbed the tree,
They only shook some blossoms down,—
Its fruit has all been kept for thee.
Then doubt me not—the season
Is o'er when Folly made me rove,
And now the vestal Reason
Shall watch the fire awaked by Love.

And though my lute no longer
May sing of Passion's ardent spell,
Yet, trust me, all the stronger
I feel the bliss I do not tell.
The bee through many a garden roves,
And hums his lay of courtship o'er;
But when he finds the flower he loves,
He settles there, and hums no more.
Then doubt me not—the season
Is o'er when folly kept me free,
And now the vestal Reason
Shall guard the flame awaked by thee.

YOU REMEMBER ELLEN.[1]

Air—*Were I a Clerk.*

You remember Ellen, our hamlet's pride,
How meekly she blessed her humble lot,
When the stranger, William, had made her his bride,
And love was the light of their lowly cot.
Together they toiled through winds and rains,
Till William at length, in sadness, said,
'We must seek our fortunes on other plains;'
Then, sighing, she left her lowly shed.

They roamed a long and a weary way,
Nor much was the maiden's heart at ease,
When now, at close of one stormy day,
They see a proud castle among the trees.
'To-night,' said the youth, 'we'll shelter there;
The wind blows cold, the hour is late:'—
So he blew the horn with a chieftain's air,
And the porter bowed as they passed the gate.

'Now, welcome, Lady!' exclaimed the youth,—
'This castle is thine, and these dark woods all.'
She believed him wild, but his words were truth,
For Ellen is Lady of Rosna Hall!—
And dearly the Lord of Rosna loves
What William the stranger wooed and wed;
And the light of bliss, in these lordly groves,
Is pure as it shone in the lowly shed.

I'D MOURN THE HOPES.

Air—*The Rose-Tree.*

I'd mourn the hopes that leave me,
If thy smiles had left me too;
I'd weep when friends deceive me,
If thou wert, like them, untrue.
But while I've thee before me,
With heart so warm and eyes so bright,
No clouds can linger o'er me,—
That smile turns them all to light!

'Tis not in fate to harm me,
While fate leaves thy love to me;
'Tis not in joy to charm me,
Unless joy be shared with thee.
One minute's dream about thee
Were worth a long, an endless year
Of waking bliss without thee,
My own love, my only dear!

And though the hope be gone, love,
That long sparkled o'er our way,
Oh! we shall journey on, love,
More safely without its ray.

---

[1] This Ballad was suggested by a well-known and interesting story, told of a certain noble family in England.

Far better lights shall win me
Along the path I've yet to roam,—
The mind that burns within me,
And pure smiles from thee at home.

Thus, when the lamp that lighted
The traveller, at first goes out,
He feels awhile benighted,
And looks round, in fear and doubt.
But soon, the prospect clearing,
By cloudless starlight on he treads,
And thinks no lamp so cheering
As that light which Heaven sheds!

No. VI.

IN presenting this Sixth Number as our last, and bidding adieu to the Irish Harp for ever, we shall not answer very confidently for the strength of our resolution, nor feel quite sure that it may not prove, after all, to be only one of those eternal farewells which a lover takes of his mistress occasionally. Our only motive, indeed, for discontinuing the Work was a fear that our treasures were beginning to be exhausted, and an unwillingness to descend to the gathering of mere seed-pearl, after the very valuable gems it has been our lot to string together. But this intention, which we announced in our Fifth Number, has excited an anxiety in the lovers of Irish Music, not only pleasant and flattering, but highly useful to us; for the various contributions we have received in consequence have enriched our collection with so many choice and beautiful Airs, that, if we keep to our resolution of publishing no more, it will certainly be an instance of forbearance and self-command unexampled in the history of poets and musicians.

T. M.
MAYFIELD, ASHBOURNE,
March 1815.

COME O'ER THE SEA.

AIR—*Cuishlih ma Chree.*

COME o'er the sea,
Maiden! with me,
Mine through sunshine, storm, and snows!
Seasons may roll,
But the true soul
Burns the same, where'er it goes.
Let fate frown on, so we love and part not;
'Tis life where *thou* art, 'tis death where thou art not!

Then, come o'er the sea,
Maiden! with me,
Come wherever the wild wind blows;
Seasons may roll,
But the true soul
Burns the same, where'er it goes.

Is not the sea
Made for the free,
Land for courts and chains alone?
Here we are slaves,
But on the waves
Love and Liberty's all our own!
No eye to watch, and no tongue to wound us,
All earth forgot, and all heaven around us!—
Then, come o'er the sea,
Maiden! with me,
Mine through sunshine, storm, and snows!
Seasons may roll,
But the true soul
Burns the same, where'er it goes.

HAS SORROW THY YOUNG DAYS SHADED?

AIR—*Sly Patrick.*

HAS sorrow thy young days shaded,
As clouds o'er the morning fleet?
Too fast have those young days faded,
That even in sorrow were sweet?
Does Time with his cold wing wither
Each feeling that once was dear?—
Then, child of misfortune! come hither,
I'll weep with thee, tear for tear.

Has love to that soul, so tender,
Been like our Lagenian mine,[1]
Where sparkles of golden splendour
All over the surface shine—
But if in pursuit we go deeper,
Allured by the gleam that shone,
Ah! false as the dream of the sleeper,
Like Love, the bright ore is gone?

Has Hope, like the bird in the story,[2]
That flitted from tree to tree
With the talisman's glittering glory—
Has Hope been that bird to thee?
On branch after branch alighting,
The gem did she still display,
And when nearest and most inviting,
Then waft the fair gem away?

If thus the sweet hours have fleeted,
When Sorrow herself looked bright;

---

[1] Our Wicklow Gold Mines, to which this verse alludes, deserve, I fear, the character nere given of them.

[2] 'The bird having got its prize, settled not far off, with the talisman in his mouth. The prince drew near it, hoping it would drop it; but as he approached, the bird took wing, and settled again,' etc.—*Arabian Nights,* Story of Kummir al Zummaun and the Princess of China.

It thus the fond hope has cheated,
  That led thee along so light;
It thus, too, the cold world wither
  Each feeling that once was dear;—
Come, child of misfortune! come hither,
  I'll weep with thee, tear for tear.

NO, NOT MORE WELCOME.

Air—*Luggelaw.*

No, not more welcome the fairy numbers
  Of music fall on the sleeper's ear,
When, half-awaking from fearful slumbers,
  He thinks the full quire of Heaven is near,—
Than came that voice, when, all forsaken,
  This heart long had sleeping lain,
Nor thought its cold pulse would ever waken
  To such benign, blest sounds again.
Sweet voice of comfort! 'twas like the stealing
  Of summer wind through some wreathèd shell—
Each secret winding, each inmost feeling
  Of all my soul echoed to its spell!
'Twas whispered balm—'twas sunshine spoken!—
  I'd live years of grief and pain,
To have my long sleep of sorrow broken
  By such benign, blest sounds again!

WHEN FIRST I MET THEE.

Air—*O Patrick! fly from me.*

When first I met thee, warm and young,
  There shone such truth about thee,
And on thy lip such promise hung,
  I did not dare to doubt thee.
I saw thee change, yet still relied,
  Still clung with hope the fonder,
And thought, though false to all beside,
  From me thou couldst not wander.
    But go, deceiver! go,—
    The heart, whose hopes could make it
    Trust one so false, so low,
    Deserves that thou shouldst break it

When every tongue thy follies named,
  I fled the unwelcome story;
Or found, in even the faults they blamed,
  Some gleams of future glory.
I still was true, when nearer friends
  Conspired to wrong, to slight thee;
The heart that now thy falsehood rends,
  Would then have bled to right thee.
    But go, deceiver! go,—
    Some day perhaps thou'lt waken
    From pleasure's dream, to know
    The grief of hearts forsaken.

Even now, though youth its bloom has shed,
  No lights of age adorn thee;

The few who loved thee once have fled,
  And they who flatter scorn thee.
Thy midnight cup is pledged to slaves,
  No genial ties enwreathe it;
The smiling there, like light on graves,
  Has rank, cold hearts beneath it!
    Go—go—though worlds were thine,
    I would not now surrender
    One taintless tear of mine
    For all thy guilty splendour!

And days may come, thou false one! yet,
  When even those ties shall sever;
When thou wilt call, with vain regret,
  On her thou'st lost for ever!
On her who, in thy fortune's fall,
  With smiles had still received thee,
And gladly died to prove thee all
  Her fancy first believed thee.
    Go—go—'tis vain to curse,
    'Tis weakness to upbraid thee;
    Hate cannot wish thee worse
    Than guilt and shame have made thee.

WHILE HISTORY'S MUSE.

Air—*Paddy Whack.*

While History's Muse the memorial was keeping
  Of all that the dark band of Destiny weaves,
Beside her the Genius of Erin stood weeping,
  For hers was the story that blotted the leaves.
But oh! how the tear in her eyelids grew bright,
  When, after whole pages of sorrow and shame,
    She saw History write
    With a pencil of light
That illumed all the volume, her Wellington's name!

'Hail, Star of my Isle!' said the Spirit, all sparkling
  With beams, such as break from her own dewy skies;—
'Through ages of sorrow, deserted and darkling,
  I've watched for some glory like thine to arise.
For though heroes I've numbered, unblest was their lot,
  And unhallowed they sleep in the crossways of Fame;—
    But, oh! there is not
    One dishonouring blot
On the wreath that encircles my Wellington's name!

'Yet still the last crown of thy toils is remaining,
  The grandest, the purest even *thou* hast yet known;
Though proud was thy task, other nations unchaining,
  Far prouder to heal the deep wounds of thy own.

At the foot of that throne, for whose weal thou
  hast stood,
Go, p'ead for the land that first cradled thy
  fame—
    And, bright o'er the flood
    Of her tears and her blood,
Let the rainbow of Hope be her Wellington's
  name!'

THE TIME I'VE LOST IN WOOING.

AIR—*Peas upon a Trencher.*

The time I've lost in wooing,
In watching and pursuing
    The light that lies
    In Woman's eyes,
Has been my heart's undoing.
Though Wisdom oft has sought me,
I scorned the lore she brought me:
    My only books
    Were Woman's looks,
And folly's all they've taught me.

Her smile when Beauty granted,
I hung with gaze enchanted;
    Like him, the Sprite,[1]
    Whom maids by night
Oft meet in glen that's haunted.
Like him, too, Beauty won me;
But while her eyes were on me—
    If once their ray
    Was turned away,
Oh! winds could not outrun me.

And are those follies going?
And is my proud heart growing
    Too cold or wise
    For brilliant eyes
Again to set it glowing?
No—vain, alas! the endeavour
From bonds so sweet to sever;—
    Poor Wisdom's chance
    Against a glance
Is now as weak as ever!

WHERE IS THE SLAVE.

AIR—*Sios agus sios liom.*

Where is the slave, so lowly,
Condemned to chains unholy,
    Who, could he burst
    His bonds at first,
Would pine beneath them slowly?
What soul, whose wrongs degrade it,
Would wait till time decayed it,

When thus its wing
    At once may spring
To the throne of him who made it?
Farewell, Erin!—farewell all
Who live to weep our fall!

Less dear the laurel growing,
Alive, untouched, and blowing,
    Than that whose braid
    Is plucked to shade
The brows with victory glowing!
We tread the land that bore us,
Her green flag glitters o'er us,
    The friends we've tried
    Are by our side,
And the foe we hate before us!
Farewell, Erin!—farewell all
Who live to weep our fall!

COME, REST IN THIS BOSOM.

AIR—*Lough Sheeling.*

Come, rest in this bosom, my own stricken deer!
Though the herd have fled from thee, thy home
  is still here;
Here still is the smile, that no cloud can o'ercast,
And the heart and the hand all thy own to the
  last!

Oh! what was love made for, if 'tis not the same
Through joy and through torments, through
  glory and shame?
I know not, I ask not, if guilt's in that heart;
I but know that I love thee, whatever thou art!

Thou hast called me thy Angel in moments of
  bliss,
And thy Angel I'll be, 'mid the horrors of this,—
Through the furnace, unshrinking, thy steps to
  pursue,
And shield thee, and save thee, or—perish there
  too!

'TIS GONE, AND FOR EVER.

AIR—*Savournah Deelish.*

'Tis gone, and for ever, the light we saw
  breaking,
Like Heaven's first dawn o'er the sleep of the
  dead—
When man, from the slumber of ages awaking,
  Looked upward, and blessed the pure ray ere
  it fled!

---

[1] This alludes to a kind of Irish Fairy, which is to be met with, they say, in the fields at dusk. As long as you keep your eyes upon him, he is fixed and in your power; but the moment you look away (and he is ingenious in furnishing some inducement) he vanishes. I had thought that this was the sprite which we call the Leprechaun; but a high authority upon such subjects, Lady Morgan (in a note upon her national and interesting novel, *O'Donnel*), has given a very different account of that goblin.

'Tis gone—and the gleams it has left of its burning
But deepen the long night of bondage and mourning,
That dark o'er the kingdoms of earth is returning,
And, darkest of all, hapless Erin! o'er thee.

For high was thy hope, when those glories were darting
Around thee, through all the gross clouds of the world;
When Truth, from her fetters indignantly starting,
At once, like a sunburst, her banner unfurled.[1]
Oh, never shall earth see a moment so splendid!
Then, then, had one Hymn of Deliverance blended
The tongues of all nations, how sweet had ascended
The first note of Liberty, Erin, from thee!

But shame on those tyrants who envied the blessing!
And shame on the light race, unworthy its good,
Who at Death's reeking altar, like furies caressing
The young hope of Freedom, baptized it in blood!
Then vanished for ever that fair, sunny vision,
Which, spite of the slavish, the cold heart's derision,
Shall long be remembered, pure, bright, and elysian,
As first it arose, my lost Erin! on thee.

I SAW FROM THE BEACH.

Air—*Miss Molly.*

I saw from the beach, when the morning was shining,
A bark o'er the waters moved gloriously on;
I came, when the sun o'er that beach was declining,—
The bark was still there, but the waters were gone!

Ah! such is the fate of our life's early promise,
So passing the spring-tide of joy we have known:
Each wave that we danced on at morning ebbs from us,
And leaves us at eve on the bleak shore alone!

Ne'er tell me of glories, serenely adorning
The close of our day, the calm eve of our night;—
Give me back, give me back the wild freshness of Morning,
Her clouds and her tears are worth Evening's best light.

---

[1] 'The Sunburst' was the fanciful name given by the ancient Irish to the royal banner.

Oh, who would not welcome that moment's returning,
When passion first waked a new life through his frame,
And his soul—like the wood that grows precious in burning—
Gave out all its sweets to Love's exquisite flame!

FILL THE BUMPER FAIR.

Air—*Bob and Joan.*

Fill the bumper fair!
Every drop we sprinkle
O'er the brow of Care
Smoothes away a wrinkle.
Wit's electric flame
Ne'er so swiftly passes,
As when through the frame
It shoots from brimming glasses.
Fill the bumper fair!
Every drop we sprinkle
O'er the brow of Care
Smoothes away a wrinkle.

Sages can, they say,
Grasp the lightning's pinions,
And bring down its ray
From the starred dominions:—
So we, sages, sit,
And, 'mid bumpers brightening,
From the heaven of wit
Draw down all its lightning!
Fill the bumper, etc.

Wouldst thou know what first
Made our souls inherit
This ennobling thirst
For wine's celestial spirit?
It chanced upon that day,
When, as bards inform us,
Prometheus stole away
The living fires that warm us.
Fill the bumper, etc.

The careless Youth, when up
To Glory's fount aspiring,
Took nor urn nor cup
To hide the pilfered fire in :—
But oh his joy! when, round
The halls of heaven spying,
Amongst the stars he found
A bowl of Bacchus lying.
Fill the bumper, etc.

Some drops were in that bowl,
Remains of last night's pleasure
With which the Sparks of Soul
Mixed their burning treasure!
Hence the goblet's shower
Hath such spells to win us—
Hence its mighty power
O'er that flame within us.
Fill the bumper, etc.

DEAR HARP OF MY COUNTRY!

Air—*New Langolee.*

Dear Harp of my country! in darkness I found thee;
The cold chain of silence had hung o'er thee long,[1]
When proudly, my own Island Harp! I unbound thee,
And gave all thy chords to light, freedom, and song!
The warm lay of love and the light note of gladness
Have wakened thy fondest, thy liveliest thrill;
But so oft hast thou echoed the deep sigh of sadness,
That even in thy mirth it will steal from thee still.

Dear Harp of my Country! farewell to thy numbers,
This sweet wreath of song is the last we shall twine;
Go, sleep, with the sunshine of Fame on thy slumbers,
Till touched by some hand less unworthy than mine.
If the pulse of the patriot, soldier, or lover,
Have throbbed at our lay, 'tis thy glory alone;
I was *but* as the wind, passing heedlessly over,
And all the wild sweetness I waked was thy own.

No. VII.

If I had consulted only my own judgment, this Work would not have been extended beyond the Six Numbers already published; which contain perhaps the flower of our National Melodies, and have attained a rank in public favour, of which I would not willingly risk the forfeiture by degenerating in any way from those merits that were its source. Whatever treasures of our music were still in reserve (and it will be seen, I trust, that they are numerous and valuable), I would gladly have left to future poets to glean; and, with the ritual words '*tibi trado,*' would have delivered up the torch into other hands, before it had lost much of its light in my own. But the call for a continuance of the work has been, as I understand from the Publisher, so general, and we have received so many contributions of old and beautiful airs,[2] the suppression of which, for the enhancement of those we have published, would resemble too much the policy of the Dutch in burning their spices, that I have been persuaded, though not without considerable diffidence in my success, to commence a new series of the *Irish Melodies*.

T. M.

MY GENTLE HARP!

Air—*The Coina, or Dirge.*

My gentle Harp! once more I waken
The sweetness of thy slumbering strain;
In tears our last farewell was taken,
And now in tears we meet again.
No light of joy hath o'er thee broken,
But—like those harps whose heavenly skill
Of slavery, dark as thine, hath spoken—
Thou hang'st upon the willows still.

And yet, since last thy chord resounded,
An hour of peace and triumph came,
And many an ardent bosom bounded
With hopes—that now are turned to shame.
Yet even then, while Peace was singing
Her halcyon song o'er land and sea,
Though joy and hope to others bringing,
She only brought new tears to thee.

Then who can ask for notes of pleasure,
My drooping harp! from chords like thine?
Alas, the lark's gay morning measure
As ill would suit the swan's decline!
Or how shall I, who love, who bless thee,
Invoke thy breath for freedom's strains,
When even the wreaths in which I dress thee
Are sadly mixed—half flowers, half chains!

But come—if yet thy frame can borrow
One breath of joy—oh, breathe for me,
And show the world, in chains and sorrow,
How sweet thy music still can be;
How gaily, even 'mid gloom surrounding,
Thou yet canst wake at pleasure's thrill—
Like Memnon's broken image, sounding,
'Mid desolation, tuneful still!

---

[1] In that rebellious but beautiful song, 'When Erin first rose,' there is, if I recollect right, the following line:

'The dark chain of silence was thrown o'er the deep!'

The chain of silence was a sort of practical figure of rhetoric among the ancient Irish. Walker tells us of 'a celebrated contention for precedence between Finn and Gaul, near Finn's palace at Almhaim, where the attending bards, anxious if possible to produce a cessation of hostilities, shook the chain of silence, and flung themselves among the ranks.' See also the Ode to Gaul, the son of Morni, in Miss Brooke's *Reliques of Irish Poetry.*

[2] One gentleman in particular, whose name I shall feel happy in being allowed to mention, has not only sent us near forty ancient airs, but has communicated many curious fragments of Irish poetry, and some interesting traditions, current in the country where he resides, illustrated by sketches of the romantic scenery to which they refer; all of which, though too late for the present Number, will be of infinite service to us in the prosecution of our task.

AS SLOW OUR SHIP.

AIR—*The Girl I left behind me.*

As slow our ship her foamy track
Against the wind was cleaving,
Her trembling pennant still looked back
To that dear isle 'twas leaving.
So loth we part from all we love,
From all the links that bind us;
So turn our hearts, where'er we rove,
To those we've left behind us!

When round the bowl of vanished years
We talk, with joyous seeming,—
With smiles, that might as well be tears,
So faint, so sad their beaming;
While memory brings us back again
Each early tie that twined us,
Oh, sweet's the cup that circles then
To those we've left behind us!

And when, in other climes, we meet
Some isle or vale enchanting,
Where all looks flowery, wild, and sweet,
And nought but love is wanting;
We think how great had been our bliss,
If Heaven had but assigned us
To live and die in scenes like this,
With some we've left behind us!

As travellers oft look back, at eve,
When eastward darkly going,
To gaze upon that light they leave
Still faint behind them glowing,—
So, when the close of pleasure's day
To gloom hath near consigned us,
We turn to catch one fading ray
Of joy that's left behind us.

IN THE MORNING OF LIFE.

AIR—*The little Harvest Rose.*

In the morning of life, when its cares are unknown,
And its pleasures in all their new lustre begin,
When we live in a bright-beaming world of our own,
And the light that surrounds us is all from within;
Oh, it is not, believe me, in that happy time
We can love as in hours of less transport we may:—
Of our smiles, of our hopes, 'tis the gay sunny prime,
But affection is warmest when these fade away.

When we see the first glory of youth pass us by,
Like a leaf on the stream that will never return;

When our cup, which had sparkled with pleasure so high,
First tastes of the *other*, the dark flowing urn;
Then, then is the moment affection can away
With a depth and a tenderness joy never knew.
Love nursed among pleasures is faithless as they,
But the Love born of sorrow, like sorrow, is true!

In climes full of sunshine, though splendid their dyes,
Yet faint is the odour the flowers shed about;
'Tis the clouds and the mists of our own weeping skies
That call the full spirit of fragrancy out.
So the wild glow of passion may kindle from mirth,
But 'tis only in grief true affection appears;—
And even though to smiles it may first owe its birth,
All the soul of its sweetness is drawn out by tears.

WHEN COLD IN THE EARTH.

AIR—*Limerick's Lamentation.*

When cold in the earth lies the friend thou hast loved,
Be his faults and his-follies forgot by thee then;
Or if from their slumber the veil be removed,
Weep o'er them in silence, and close it again.
And, oh! if 'tis pain to remember how far
From the pathways of light he was tempted to roam,
Be it bliss to remember that thou wert the star
That arose on his darkness and guided him home.

From thee and thy innocent beauty first came
The revealings that taught him true Love to adore,
To feel the bright presence, and turn him with shame
From the idols he blindly had knelt to before.
O'er the waves of a life, long benighted and wild,
Thou camest, like a soft golden calm o'er the sea;
And if happiness purely and glowingly smiled
On his evening horizon, the light was from thee.

And though sometimes the shade of past folly would rise,
And though Falsehood again would allure him to stray,
He but turned to the glory that dwelt in those eyes,
And the folly, the falsehood, soon vanished away.

As the Priests of the Sun, when their altar grew
　　dim,
At the day-beam alone could its lustre repair,
So, if virtue a moment grew languid in him,
He but flew to that smile, and rekindled it
　　there.

REMEMBER THEE!

Air—*Castle Tirowen.*

Remember thee! yes, while there's life in this
　　heart,
It shall never forget thee, all lorn as thou art;
More dear in thy sorrow, thy gloom, and thy
　　showers,
Than the rest of the world in their sunniest
　　hours.

Wert thou all that I wish thee,—great, glorious,
　　and free—
First flower of the earth, and first gem of the
　　sea,—
I might hail thee with prouder, with happier
　　brow,
But, oh! could I love thee more deeply than now?

No, thy chains as they rankle, thy blood as it
　　runs,
But make thee more painfully dear to thy sons—
Whose hearts, like the young of the desert-bird's
　　nest,
Drink love in each life-drop that flows from thy
　　breast!

WREATHE THE BOWL.

Air—*Noran Kista.*

Wreathe the bowl
　　With flowers of soul,
The brightest wit can find us;
　　We'll take a flight
　　Towards heaven to-night,
And leave dull earth behind us!
　　Should Love amid
　　The wreaths be hid
That Joy, the enchanter, brings us,
　　No danger fear
　　While wine is near,
We'll drown him if he stings us.
　　Then wreathe the bowl
　　With flowers of soul,
The brightest wit can find us;
　　We'll take a flight
　　Towards heaven to-night,
And leave dull earth behind us!

'Twas nectar fed
　　Of old, 'tis said,
Their Junos, Joves, Apollos;
　　And man may brew
　　His nectar too,
The rich receipt's as follows:
　　Take wine like this,
　　Let looks of bliss
Around it well be blended;
　　Then bring wit's beam
　　To warm the stream,
And there's your nectar, splendid!
　　So, wreathe the bowl
　　With flowers of soul
The brightest wit can find us;
　　We'll take a flight
　　Towards heaven to-night,
And leave dull earth behind us!

Say, why did Time
　　His glass sublime
Fill up with sands unsightly,
　　When wine, he knew,
　　Runs brisker through,
And sparkles far more brightly!
　　Oh, lend it us,
　　And, smiling thus,
The glass in two we'd sever,
　　Make pleasure glide
　　In double tide,
And fill both ends for ever!
　　Then wreathe the bowl
　　With flowers of soul,
The brightest wit can find us;
　　We'll take a flight
　　Towards heaven to-night,
And leave dull earth behind us!

WHENE'ER I SEE THOSE SMILING EYES.

Air—*Father Quinn.*

Whene'er I see those smiling eyes,
　　All filled with hope, and joy, and light,
As if no cloud could ever rise
　　To dim a heaven so purely bright—
I sigh to think how soon that brow
　　In grief may lose its every ray,
And that light heart, so joyous now,
　　Almost forget it once was gay.

For Time will come with all his blights,
　　The ruined hope—the friend unkind—
The love that leaves, where'er it lights,
　　A chilled or burning heart behind!
While youth, that now like snow appears,
　　Ere sullied by the darkening rain,
When once 'tis touched by sorrow's tears,
　　Will never shine so bright again!

IF THOU'LT BE MINE.

Air—*The Winnowing Sheet.*

If thou'lt be mine, the treasures of air,
  Of earth and sea, shall lie at thy feet;
Whatever in Fancy's eye looks fair,
  Or in Hope's sweet music is *most* sweet,
    Shall be ours, if thou wilt be mine, love!

Bright flowers shall bloom wherever we rove,
  A voice divine shall talk in each stream,
The stars shall look like worlds of love,
  And this earth be all one beautiful dream
    In our eyes, if thou wilt be mine, love!

And thoughts, whose source is hidden and high,
  Like streams that come from heavenward hills,
Shall keep our hearts—like meads, that lie
  To be bathed by those eternal rills—
    Ever green, if thou wilt be mine, love!

All this and more the Spirit of Love
  Can breathe o'er them who feel his spells;
That heaven, which forms his home above,
  He can make on earth, wherever he dwells,
    And he *will*—if thou wilt be mine, love!

TO LADIES' EYES.

Air—*Fague a Ballagh.*

To ladies' eyes a round, boy,
  We can't refuse, we can't refuse;
Though bright eyes so abound, boy,
  'Tis hard to choose, 'tis hard to choose.
For thick as stars that lighten
  Yon airy bowers, yon airy bowers,
The countless eyes that brighten
  This earth of ours, this earth of ours.
But fill the cup—where'er, boy,
  Our choice may fall, our choice may fall,
We're sure to find Love there, boy,
  So drink them all! so drink them all!

Some looks there are so holy,
  They seem but given, they seem but given
As splendid beacons solely,
  To light to heaven, to light to heaven.
While some—oh! ne'er believe them—
  With tempting ray, with tempting ray,
Would lead us (God forgive them!)
  The other way, the other way.
But fill the cup—where'er, boy,
  Our choice may fall, our choice may fall,
We're sure to find Love there, boy,
  So drink them all! so drink them all!

In some, as in a mirror,
  Love seems portrayed, Love seems portrayed;
But shun the flattering error,
  'Tis but his shade, 'tis but his shade.
Himself has fixed his dwelling
  In eyes we know, in eyes we know,
And lips—but this is telling,
  So here they go! so here they go!
Fill up, fill up—where'er, boy,
  Our choice may fall, our choice may fall,
We're sure to find Love there, boy,
  So drink them all! so drink them all!

FORGET NOT THE FIELD.

Air—*The Lamentation of Aughrim.*

Forget not the field where they perished,
  The truest, the last of the brave,
All gone—and the bright hope they cherished
  Gone with them, and quenched in their grave

Oh! could we from death but recover
  Those hearts, as they bounded before,
In the face of high Heaven to fight over
  That combat for freedom once more;—

Could the chain for an instant be riven
  Which Tyranny flung round us then,
Oh! 'tis not in Man nor in Heaven
  To let Tyranny bind it again!

But 'tis past—and though blazoned in story
  The name of our Victor may be,
Accursed is the march of that glory
  Which treads o'er the hearts of the free.

Far dearer the grave or the prison,
  Illumed by one patriot name,
Than the trophies of all who have risen
  On liberty's ruins to fame!

THEY MAY RAIL AT THIS LIFE.

Air—*Noch bonin shin doe.*

They may rail at this life—from the hour I began it,
I've found it a life full of kindness and bliss;
And until they can show me some happier planet,
More social and bright, I'll content me with this.
As long as the world has such eloquent eyes,
  As before me this moment enraptured I see,
They may say what they will of their orbs in the skies,
  But this earth is the planet for you, love, and me.

In Mercury's star, where each minute can bring them
New sunshine and wit from the fountain on high,
Though the nymphs may have livelier poets to sing them,
They've none, even there, more enamoured than I.

And as long as this harp can be wakened to
    love,
And that eye its divine inspiration shall be,
They may talk as they will of their Edens above,
But this earth is the planet for you, love, and
    me.

In that star of the west, by whose shadowy
    splendour
At twilight so often we've roamed through the
    dew,
There are maidens, perhaps, who have bosoms
    as tender,
And look, in their twilights, as lovely as you.
But though they were even more bright than
    the queen
Of that isle they inhabit in heaven's blue sea,
As I never those fair young celestials have seen,
Why,—this earth is the planet for you, love,
    and me.

As for those chilly orbs on the verge of creation,
Where sunshine and smiles must be equally
    rare,
Did they want a supply of cold hearts for that
    station,
Heaven knows we have plenty on earth we
    could spare.
Oh! think what a world we should have of it
    here,
If the haters of peace, of affection, and glee,
Were to fly up to Saturn's comfortless sphere,
And leave earth to such spirits as you, love,
    and me.

OH FOR THE SWORDS OF FORMER
TIME!

AIR—*Name unknown.*

OH for the swords of former time!
    Oh for the men who bore them,
When, armed for Right, they stood sublime,
    And tyrants crouched before them!
When pure yet, ere courts began
    With honours to enslave him,
The best honours worn by Man
    Were those which Virtue gave him.
Oh for the swords of former time!
    Oh for the men who bore them,
When, armed for Right, they stood sublime,
    And tyrants crouched before them!

Oh for the kings who flourished then!
    Oh for the pomp that crowned them,
When hearts and hands of freeborn men
    Were all the ramparts round them!
When, safe built on bosoms true,
    The throne was but the centre
Round which Love a circle drew,
    That Treason durst not enter.

Oh for the kings who flourished then!
    Oh for the pomp that crowned them,
When hearts and hands of freeborn men
    Were all the ramparts round them!

No. VIII.

NE'ER ASK THE HOUR.

AIR—*My Husband's a Journey to Portugal gone.*

NE'ER ask the hour—what is it to us
    How Time deals out his treasures?
The golden moments lent us thus
    Are not *his* coin, but Pleasure's.
If counting them over could add to their blisses,
    I'd number each glorious second;
But moments of joy are, like Lesbia's kisses,
    Too quick and sweet to be reckoned.
Then fill the cup—what is it to us
    How Time his circle measures?
The fairy hours we call up thus
    Obey no wand but Pleasure's!

Young Joy ne'er thought of counting hours
    Till Care, one summer's morning,
Set up among his smiling flowers
    A dial, by way of warning.
But Joy loved better to gaze on the sun,
    As long as its light was glowing,
Than to watch with old Care how the shadow
    stole on,
    And how fast that light was going.
So fill the cup—what is it to us
    How Time his circle measures?
The fairy hours we call up thus
    Obey no wand but Pleasure's.

SAIL ON, SAIL ON.

AIR—*The Humming of the Ban.*

SAIL on, sail on, thou fearless bark—
    Wherever blows the welcome wind,
It cannot lead to scenes more dark,
    More sad, than those we leave behind.
Each wave that passes seems to say,
    'Though death beneath our smile may be,
Less cold we are, less false than they
    Whose smiling wrecked thy hopes and thee.'

Sail on, sail on—through endless space—
    Through calm—through tempest—stop no
    more;
The stormiest sea's a resting-place
    To him who leaves such hearts on shore.
Or—if some desert land we meet,
    Where never yet false-hearted men
Profaned a world that else were sweet—
    Then rest thee, bark, but not till then.

THE PARALLEL.

Air—*I would rather than Ireland.*

Yes, sad one of Sion,[1]—if closely resembling,
In shame and in sorrow, thy withered-up heart—
If drinking, deep, deep, of the same 'cup of trembling'
Could make us thy children, our parent thou art.

Like thee doth our nation lie conquered and broken,
And fallen from her head is the once royal crown;
In her streets, in her halls, Desolation hath spoken,
And 'while it is day yet, her sun hath gone down.'

Like thine doth her exile, 'mid dreams of returning,
Die far from the home it were life to behold;
Like thine do her sons, in the day of their mourning,
Remember the bright things that bless'd them of old!

Ah, well may we call her, like thee, 'the Forsaken,'
Her boldest are vanquished, her proudest are slaves;
And the harps of her minstrels, when gayest they waken,
Have breathings as sad as the wind over graves!

Yet hadst thou thy vengeance—yet came there the morrow,
That shines out at last on the longest dark night,
When the sceptre that smote thee with slavery and sorrow
Was shivered at once, like a reed, in thy sight.

When that cup, which for others the proud Golden City
Had brimmed full of bitterness, drenched her own lips,
And the world she had trampled on heard, without pity,
The howl in her halls and the cry from her ships.

When the curse Heaven keeps for the haughty came over
Her merchants rapacious, her rulers unjust,
And—a ruin, at last, for the earth-worm to cover—
The Lady of Kingdoms lay low in the dust.

[1] These verses were written after the perusal of a treatise by Mr. Hamilton, professing to prove that the Irish were originally Jews.

DRINK OF THIS CUP.

Air—*Paddy O'Rafferty.*

Drink of this cup—you'll find there's a spell in
Its every drop 'gainst the ills of mortality—
Talk of the cordial that sparkled for Helen,
Her cup was a fiction, but this is reality.

Would you forget the dark world we are in,
Only taste of the bubble that gleams on the top of it;
But would you rise above earth, till akin
To immortals themselves, you must drain every drop of it.

Send round the cup—for oh! there's a spell in
Its every drop 'gainst the ills of mortality—
Talk of the cordial that sparkled for Helen,
Her cup was a fiction, but this is reality.

Never was philtre formed with such power
To charm and bewilder as this we are quaffing!
Its magic began, when, in Autumn's rich hour,
As a harvest of gold in the fields it stood laughing.

There having by Nature's enchantment been filled
With the balm and the bloom of her kindliest weather,
This wonderful juice from its core was distilled,
To enliven such hearts as are here brought together!

Then drink of the cup—you'll find there's a spell in
Its every drop 'gainst the ills of mortality—
Talk of the cordial that sparkled for Helen,
Her cup was a fiction, but this is reality.

And though, perhaps—but breathe it to no one—
Like cauldrons the witch brews at midnight so awful,
In secret this philtre was first taught to flow on,
Yet—'tisn't less potent for being unlawful.

What though it may taste of the smoke of that flame
Which in silence extracted its virtue forbidden?
Fill up—there's a fire in some hearts I could name,
Which may work to its charm, though now lawless and hidden.

So drink of the cup—for oh! there's a spell in
Its every drop 'gainst the ills of mortality—
Talk of the cordial that sparkled for Helen,
Her cup was a fiction, but this is reality.

THE FORTUNE-TELLER.

Air—*Open the Door softly.*

Down in the valley come meet me to-night,
And I'll tell you your fortune truly
As ever 'twas told, by the new moon's light,
To young maidens shining as newly.

But, for the world, let no one be nigh,
  Lest haply the stars should deceive me;
These secrets between you and me and the sky
  Should never go farther, believe me.

If at that hour the heavens be not dim,
  My science shall call up before you
A male apparition—the image of him
  Whose destiny 'tis to adore you.

Then to the phantom be thou but kind,
  And round you so fondly he'll hover;
You'll hardly, my dear, any difference find
  'Twixt him and a true living lover.

Down at your feet, in the pale moonlight,
  He'll kneel, with a warmth of emotion—
An ardour, of which such an innocent sprite
  You'd scarcely believe had a notion.

What other thoughts and events may arise,
  As in Destiny's book I've not seen them,
Must only be left to the stars and your eyes
  To settle ere morning between them.

OH, YE DEAD!

Air—*Plough Tune.*

Oh, ye dead! oh, ye dead! whom we know by
  the light you give
From your cold gleaming eyes, though you move
  like men who live,
    Why leave you thus your graves,
    In far-off fields and waves,
Where the worm and the sea-bird only know
  your bed,
    To haunt this spot, where all
    Those eyes that wept your fall,
And the hearts that bewailed you, like your own,
  lie dead!

It is true—it is true—we are shadows cold and
  wan;
It is true—it is true—all the friends we loved are
  gone,
    But, oh! thus even in death,
    So sweet is still the breath
Of the fields and the flowers in our youth we
  wandered o'er,
    That, ere condemned we go
    To freeze 'mid Hecla's[1] snow,
We would taste it awhile, and dream we live
  once more!

O'DONOGHUE'S MISTRESS.[2]

Air—*The Little and Great Mountain.*

Of all the fair months, that round the sun
In light-linked dance their circles run,
  Sweet May, sweet May, shine thou for me!
For still, when thy earliest beams arise,
That youth who beneath the blue lake lies,
  Sweet May, sweet May, returns to me.

Of all the smooth lakes, where daylight leaves
His lingering smile on golden eves,
  Fair lake, fair lake, thou'rt dear to me;
For when the last April sun grows dim,
Thy Naiads prepare his steed for him
  Who dwells, who dwells, bright lake, in thee.

Of all the proud steeds, that ever bore
Young plumed chiefs on sea or shore,
  White steed, white steed, most joy to thee,
Who still, with the first young glance of spring,
From under that glorious lake dost bring,
  Proud steed, proud steed, my love to me.

While white as the sail some bark unfurls,
When newly launched, thy long mane[3] curls,
  Fair steed, fair steed, as white and free;
And spirits, from all the lake's deep bowers,
Glide o'er the blue wave scattering flowers,
  Fair steed, around my love and thee.

Of all the sweet deaths that maidens die,
Whose lovers beneath the cold wave lie,
  Most sweet, most sweet, that death will be,
Which under the next May-evening's light,
When thou and thy steed are lost to sight,
  Dear love, dear love, I'll die for thee.

ECHO.

Air—*The Wren.*

How sweet the answer Echo makes
  To Music at night,

---

[1] Paul Zeland mentions that there is a mountain in some part of Ireland where the ghosts of persons who have died in foreign lands walk about and converse with those they meet, like living people. If asked why they do not return to their homes, they say they are obliged to go to Mount Hecla, and disappear immediately.

[2] The particulars of the tradition respecting O'Donoghue and his white horse may be found in *Mr. Weld's Account of Killarney*, or more fully detailed in *Derrick's Letters*. For many years after his death, the spirit of this hero is supposed to have been seen on the morning of May-day gliding over the lake on his favourite white horse, to the sound of sweet, unearthly music, and preceded by groups of youths and maidens, who flung wreaths of delicate spring-flowers in his path.

Among other stories connected with this Legend of the Lakes, it is said that there was a young and beautiful girl, whose imagination was so impressed with the idea of this visionary chieftain, that she fancied herself in love with him, and at last, in a fit of insanity, on a May-morning threw herself into the lake.

[3] The boatmen at Killarney call those waves which come on a windy day, crested with foam, 'O'Donoghue's white horses.'

When, roused by lute or horn, she wakes,
And far away, o'er lawns and lakes,
   Goes answering light.

Yet Love hath echoes truer far,
   And far more sweet,
Than e'er, beneath the moonlight's star,
Of horn, or lute, or soft guitar,
   The songs repeat.

'Tis when the sigh in youth sincere,
   And only then,—
The sigh, that's breathed for one to hear,
Is by that one, that only dear,
   Breathed back again!

OH! BANQUET NOT.
Air—*Planxty Irwine.*

Oh! banquet not in those shining bowers
Where youth resorts, but come to me;
For mine's a garden of faded flowers,
More fit for sorrow, for age, and thee.
And there we shall have our feast of tears,
   And many a cup in silence pour—
Our guests, the shades of former years—
   Our toasts, to lips that bloom no more.

There, while the myrtle's withering boughs
   Their lifeless leaves around us shed,
We'll brim the bowl to broken vows,
   To friends long lost, the changed, the dead.
Or, as some blighted laurel waves
   Its branches o'er the dreary spot,
We'll drink to those neglected graves
   Where valour sleeps, unnamed, forgot!

THEE, THEE, ONLY THEE.
Air—*The Market-Stake.*

The dawning of morn, the day-light's sinking,
The night's long hours still find me thinking
   Of thee, thee, only thee.
When friends are met, and goblets crowned,
And smiles are near that once enchanted,
Unreached by all that sunshine round,
My soul, like some dark spot, is haunted
   By thee, thee, only thee.

Whatever in fame's high path could waken
My spirit once, is now forsaken
   For thee, thee, only thee.
Like shores, by which some headlong bark
To the ocean hurries—resting never—
Life's scenes go by me, bright or dark,
I know not, heed not, hastening ever
   To thee, thee, only thee.

I have not a joy but of thy bringing,
And pain itself seems sweet, when springing
   From thee, thee, only thee.

Like spells that nought on earth can break,
Till lips that know the charm have spoken,
This heart, howe'er the world may wake
Its grief, its scorn, can but be broken
   By thee, thee, only thee.

SHALL THE HARP THEN BE SILENT?
Air—*Macfarlane's Lamentation.*

Shall the Harp then be silent when he, who first gave
   To our country a name, is withdrawn from all eyes?
Shall a minstrel of Erin stand mute by the grave,
   Where the first, where the last of her patriots lies?[1]

No—faint though the death-song may fall from his lips,
   Though his harp, like his soul, may with shadows be crossed,
Yet, yet shall it sound, 'mid a nation's eclipse,
   And proclaim to the world what a star hath been lost![2]

What a union of all the affections and powers,
   By which life is exalted, embellished, refined,
Was embraced in that spirit, whose centre was ours,
   While its mighty circumference circled mankind!

Oh, who that loves Erin, or who that can see,
   Through the waste of her annals, that epoch sublime—
Like a pyramid raised in the desert—where he
   And his glory stand out to the eyes of all time!—

That *one* lucid interval snatched from the gloom
   And the madness of ages, when, filled with his soul,
A nation o'erleaped the dark bounds of her doom,
   And, for *one* sacred instant, touched liberty's goal!

Who, that ever hath heard him—hath drank at the source
   Of that wonderful eloquence, all Erin's own,
In whose high-thoughted daring, the fire, and the force,
   And the yet untamed spring of her spirit, are shown;—

An eloquence, rich—wheresoever its wave
   Wandered free and triumphant—with thoughts that shone through

---

[1] The celebrated Irish orator and patriot, Grattan.
[2] It is only these two first verses that are either fitted or intended to be sung.

As clear as the brook's 'stone of lustre,' and
  gave,
With the flash of the gem, its solidity too ;—

Who, that ever approached him, when, free from
  the crowd,
In a home full of love, he delighted to tread
'Mong the trees which a nation had given, and
  which bowed,
As if each brought a new civic crown for his
  head,—

That home, where—like him who, as fable hath
  told,
Put the rays from his brow, that his child
  might come near—
Every glory forgot, the most wise of the old
Became all that the simplest and youngest
  hold dear:—

Is there one who has thus, through his orbit of
  life,
But at distance observed him, through glory,
  through blame,
In the calm of retreat, in the grandeur of strife,
Whether shining or clouded, still high and
  the same?

Such a union of all that enriches life's hour,
Of the sweetness we love and the greatness we
  praise,
As that type of simplicity blended with power,
A child with a thunderbolt, only portrays.—

Oh no—not a heart that e'er knew him but
  mourns,
Deep, deep, o'er the grave where such glory is
  shrined—
O'er a monument Fame will preserve 'mong the
  urns
Of the wisest, the bravest, the best of mankind!

OH, THE SIGHT ENTRANCING.

AIR—*Planxty Sudley.*

Oh, the sight entrancing,
  When morning's beam is glancing
    O'er files arrayed
    With helm and blade,
  And plumes in the gay wind dancing!
When hearts are all high beating,
And the trumpet's voice repeating
    That song whose breath
    May lead to death,
  But never to retreating!
Oh, the sight entrancing,
  When morning's beam is glancing
    O'er files arrayed
    With helm and blade,
  And plumes in the gay wind dancing!

Yet 'tis not helm or feather—
For ask yon despot whether
    His plumèd bands
    Could bring such hands
  And hearts as ours together.
Leave pomps to those who need 'em—
Adorn but Man with Freedom,
    And proud he braves
    The gaudiest slaves
  That crawl where monarchs lead 'em.
The sword may pierce the beaver,
Stone walls in time may sever;
    'Tis heart alone,
    Worth steel and stone,
  That keeps men free for ever!
Oh, that sight entrancing,
  When morning's beam is glancing
    O'er files arrayed
    With helm and blade,
  And in Freedom's cause advancing!

No. IX.

SWEET INNISFALLEN.

AIR—*The Captivating Youth.*

SWEET Innisfallen, fare thee well,
  May calm and sunshine long be thine!
How fair thou art let others tell,
  While but to *feel* how fair is mine!

Sweet Innisfallen, fare thee well,
  And long may light around thee smile,
As soft as on that evening fell
  When first I saw thy fairy isle!

Thou wert *too* lovely then for one
  Who had to turn to paths of care—
Who had through vulgar crowds to run,
  And leave thee bright and silent there:

No more along thy shores to come,
  But on the world's dim ocean tost,
Dream of thee sometimes as a home
  Of sunshine he had seen and lost!

Far better in thy weeping hours
  To part from thee as I do now,
When mist is o'er thy blooming bowers,
  Like Sorrow's veil on Beauty's brow.

For though unrivalled still thy grace,
  Thou dost not look, as then, *too* blest,
But in thy shadows seem'st a place
  Where weary man might hope to rest—

Might hope to rest, and find in thee
  A gloom like Eden's, on the day
He left its shade, when every tree,
  Like thine, hung weeping o'er his way!

Weeping or smiling, lovely Isle!
And still the lovelier for thy tears—
For though but rare thy sunny smile,
'Tis heaven's own glance when it appears.

Like feeling hearts, whose joys are few,
But, when *indeed* they come, divine—
The steadiest light the sun e'er threw
Is lifeless to one gleam of thine!

'TWAS ONE OF THOSE DREAMS.

Air—*The Song of the Woods.*

'Twas one of those dreams that by music are brought,
Like a light summer haze, o'er the poet's warm thought,
When, lost in the future, his soul wanders on,
And all of this life but its sweetness is gone.

The wild notes he heard o'er the water were those
To which he had sung Erin's bondage and woes,
And the breath of the bugle now wafted them o'er
From Dinis' green isle to Glena's wooded shore.

He listened—while high o'er the eagle's rude nest
The lingering sounds on their way loved to rest;
And the echoes sung back from their full mountain quire,
As if loth to let song so enchanting expire.

It seemed as if every sweet note that died here
Was again brought to life in some airlier sphere,
Some heaven in those hills where the soul of the strain,
That had ceased upon earth, was awaking again!

Oh forgive, if, while listening to music whose breath
Seemed to circle his name with a charm against death,
He should feel a proud spirit within him proclaim—
'Even so shalt thou live in the echoes of Fame:

'Even so, though thy memory should now die away,
'T will be caught up again in some happier day,
And the hearts and the voices of Erin prolong,
Through the answering future, thy name and thy song!'

FAIREST! PUT ON AWHILE.

Air—*Cummilum.*

Fairest! put on awhile
These pinions of light I bring thee,
And o'er thy own green isle
In fancy let me wing thee.
Never did Ariel's plume,
At golden sunset, hover
O'er such scenes of bloom
As I shall waft thee over.

Fields, where the Spring delays,
And fearlessly meets the ardour
Of the warm Summer's gaze,
With but her tears to guard her.
Rocks, through myrtle boughs,
In grace majestic frowning—
Like some warrior's brows
That Love hath just been crowning.

Islets so freshly fair
That never hath bird come nigh them,
But, from his course through air,
Hath been won downward by them [1]—
Types, sweet maid, of thee,
Whose look, whose blush inviting,
Never did Love yet see
From heaven, without alighting

Lakes where the pearl lies hid,[2]
And caves where the diamond's sleeping
Bright as the gems that lid
Of thine lets fall in weeping.
Glens, where Ocean comes,
To 'scape the wild wind's rancour,
And harbours, worthiest homes
Where Freedom's sails could anchor.

Then if, while scenes so grand,
So beautiful, shine before thee,
Pride for thy own dear land
Should haply be stealing o'er thee,
Oh, let grief come first,
O'er pride itself victorious—
To think how man hath curst
What Heaven had made so glorious!

QUICK! WE HAVE BUT A SECOND.

Air—*Paddy Snap.*

Quick! we have but a second,
Fill round the cup while you may;
For Time, the churl, hath beckoned,
And we must away, away!

---

[1] In describing the Skelligs (Islands of the Barony of Forth), Dr. Keating says: 'There is a certain attractive virtue in the soil, which draws down all the birds that attempt to fly over it, and obliges them to light upon the rock.'

[2] 'Nennius, a British writer of the ninth century, mentions the abundance of pearls in Ireland. Their princes, he says, hung them behind their ears; and this we find confirmed by a present made, A.C. 1094, by Gilbert Bishop of Limerick to Anselm Archbishop of Canterbury, of a considerable quantity of Irish pearls.'—*O'Halloran.*

Grasp the pleasure that's flying,
  For oh! not Orpheus' strain
Could keep sweet hours from dying,
  Or charm them to life again.
    Then quick! we have but a second,
      Fill round, fill round, while you may;
    For Time, the churl, hath beckoned,
      And we must away, away!

See the glass, how it flushes,
  Like some young Hebe's lip,
And half meets thine, and blushes
  That thou shouldst delay to sip.
Shame, oh shame unto thee,
  If ever thou seest the day
When a cup or a lip shall woo thee,
  And turn untouched away!
    Then quick! we have but a second,
      Fill round, fill round, while you may;
    For Time, the churl, hath beckoned,
      And we must away, away!

AND DOTH NOT A MEETING LIKE THIS.

Air—*Unknown.*

And doth not a meeting like this make amends
  For all the long years I've been wandering away?
To see thus around me my youth's early friends,
  As smiling and kind as in that happy day!
Though haply o'er some of your brows, as o'er mine,
  The snow-fall of Time may be stealing—what then?
Like Alps in the sunset, thus lighted by wine,
  We'll wear the gay tinge of youth's roses again.

What softened remembrances come o'er the heart,
  In gazing on those we've been lost to so long!
The sorrows, the joys, of which once they were part,
  Still round them, like visions of yesterday, throng.
As letters some hand hath invisibly traced,
  When held to the flame will steal out on the sight,
So many a feeling, that long seemed effaced,
  The warmth of a meeting like this brings to light.

And thus, as in Memory's bark we shall glide
  To visit the scenes of our boyhood anew—
Though oft we may see, looking down on the tide,
  The wreck of full many a hope shining through—
Yet still, as in fancy we point to the flowers,
  That once made a garden of all the gay shore,
Deceived for a moment, we'll think them still ours,
  And breathe the fresh air of Life's morning once more.

So brief our existence, a glimpse, at the most,
  Is all we can have of the few we hold dear;
And oft even joy is unheeded and lost,
  For want of some heart, that could echo it, near.
Ah, well may we hope, when this short life is gone,
  To meet in some world of more permanent bliss;
For a smile, or a grasp of the hand, hastening on,
  Is all we enjoy of each other in this.

But come—the more rare such delights to the heart,
  The more we should welcome, and bless them the more:
They're ours when we meet—they are lost when we part,
  Like birds that bring summer, and fly when 'tis o'er.
Thus circling the cup, hand in hand, ere we drink,
  Let sympathy pledge us, through pleasure, through pain,
That fast as a feeling but touches one link,
  Her magic shall send it direct through the chain.

THE MOUNTAIN SPRITE.

Air—*The Mountain Sprite.*

In yonder valley there dwelt, alone,
A youth, whose life all had calmly flown,
Till spells came o'er him, and, day and night,
He was haunted and watched by a Mountain Sprite.

As he, by moonlight, went wandering o'er
The golden sands of that island shore,
A footprint sparkled before his sight,
'Twas the fairy foot of the Mountain Sprite.

Beside a fountain, one sunny day,
As, looking down on the stream, he lay,
Behind him stole two eyes of light,
And he saw in the clear wave the Mountain Sprite.

He turned—but lo, like a startled bird,
The Spirit fled—and he only heard
Sweet music, such as marks the flight
Of a journeying star, from the Mountain Sprite.

One night, pursued by that dazzling look,
The youth, bewildered, his pencil took,
And, guided only by memory's light,
Drew the fairy form of the Mountain Sprite.

'Oh thou, who lovest the shadow,' cried
A gentle voice, whispering by his side,
'Now turn and see,'—here the youth's delight
Sealed the rosy lips of the Mountain Sprite.

'Of all the Spirits of land and sea,'
Exclaimed he then, 'there is none like thee;
And oft, oh oft, may thy shape alight
In this lonely arbour, sweet Mountain Sprite.'

AS VANQUISHED ERIN.

Air—*The Boyne Water.*

As vanquished Erin wept beside
The Boyne's ill-fated river,
She saw where Discord, in the tide,
Had dropped his loaded quiver.
'Lie hid,' she cried, 'ye venomed darts,
Where mortal eye may shun you;
Lie hid—for oh! the stain of hearts
That bled for me is on you.'

But vain her wish, her weeping vain—
As Time too well hath taught her:
Each year the fiend returns again,
And dives into that water:
And brings triumphant, from beneath,
His shafts of desolation,
And sends them, winged with worse than death,
Throughout her maddening nation.

Alas for her who sits and mourns,
Even now beside that river—
Unwearied still the fiend returns,
And stored is still his quiver.
'When will this end? ye Powers of Good!'
She weeping asks for ever;
But only hears, from out that flood,
The demon answer, 'Never!'

DESMOND'S SONG.[1]

Air—*Unknown.*[2]

By the Feal's wave benighted,
Not a star in the skies,
To thy door by Love lighted,
I first saw those eyes.
Some voice whispered o'er me,
As the threshold I crossed,
There was ruin before me:
If I loved, I was lost.

Love came, and brought sorrow
Too soon in his train;
Yet so sweet, that to-morrow
'Twould be welcome again.
Were misery's full measure
Poured out to me now,
I would drain it with pleasure,
So the Hebe were thou.

You who call it dishonour
To bow to this flame,
If you've eyes, look but on her,
And blush while you blame.
Hath the pearl less whiteness
Because of its birth?
Hath the violet less brightness
For growing near earth?

No—Man, for his glory,
To history flies;
While Woman's bright story
Is told in her eyes.
While the monarch but traces
Through mortals his line,
Beauty, born of the Graces,
Ranks next to divine!

THEY KNOW NOT MY HEART.

Air—*Coolon Das.*

They know not my heart, who believe there can be
One stain of this earth in its feelings for thee;'
Who think, while I see thee in beauty's young hour,
As pure as the morning's first dew on the flower,
I could harm what I love—as the sun's wanton ray
But smiles on the dewdrop to waste it away!

No—beaming with light as those young features are,
There's a light round thy heart which is lovelier far:
It *is* not that cheek—'tis the soul dawning clear
Through its innocent blush makes thy beauty so dear—
As the sky we look up to, though glorious and fair,
Is looked up to the more, because heaven is there!

---

[1] 'Thomas, the heir of the Desmond family, had accidentally been so engaged in the chase, that he was benighted near Tralee, and obliged to take shelter at the Abbey of Feal, in the house of one of his dependants, called Mac Cormac. Catherine, a beautiful daughter of his host, instantly inspired the Earl with a violent passion, which he could not subdue. He married her, and by this inferior alliance alienated his followers, whose brutal pride regarded this indulgence of his love as an unpardonable degradation of his family.'—*Leland*, vol. ii.

[2] This air has been already so successfully supplied with words by Mr. Bayly, that I should have left it untouched if we could have spared so interesting a melody out of our collection.

I WISH I WAS BY THAT DIM LAKE.

Air—*I wish I was on yonder Hill.*

I wish I was by that dim lake,[1]
Where sinful souls their farewells take
Of this vain world, and half-way lie
In Death's cold shadow, ere they die.
There, there, far from thee,
Deceitful world, my home should be—
Where, come what might of gloom and pain,
False hope should ne'er deceive again!

The lifeless sky, the mournful sound
Of unseen waters, falling round—
The dry leaves quivering o'er my head,
Like man, unquiet even when dead—
These—ay—these should wean
My soul from Life's deluding scene,
And turn each thought, each wish I have,
Like willows, downward towards the grave.

As they who to their couch at night
Would welcome sleep, first quench the light,
So must the hopes that keep this breast
Awake, be quenched, ere it can rest.
Cold, cold, my heart must grow,
Unchanged by either joy or woe,
Like freezing founts, where all that's thrown
Within their current turns to stone.

SHE SUNG OF LOVE.

Air—*The Munster Man.*

She sung of love—while o'er her lyre
The rosy rays of evening fell,
As if to feed with their soft fire
The soul within that trembling shell.
The same rich light hung o'er her cheek,
And played around those lips that sung
And spoke, as flowers would sing and speak,
If love could lend their leaves a tongue.

But soon the West no longer burned,
Each rosy ray from heaven withdrew;
And when to gaze again I turned,
The minstrel's form seemed fading too.

As if *her* light and heaven's were one,
The glory all had left that frame;
And from her glimmering lips the tone,
As from a parting spirit, came.[2]

Who ever loved, but had the thought
That he and all he loved must part?
Filled with this fear, I flew and caught
That fading image to my heart—
And cried, 'Oh Love! is this thy doom?
Oh light of youth's resplendent day!
Must ye then lose your golden bloom,
And thus like sunshine die away?'

SING—SING—MUSIC WAS GIVEN.

Air—*The Humours of Ballamaguiry, or the Old Langoles.*

Sing—sing—Music was given
To brighten the gay, and kindle the loving;
Souls here, like planets in heaven,
By harmony's laws alone are kept moving.
Beauty may boast of her eyes and her cheeks,
But love from the lips his true archery wings;
And she who but feathers the dart when she speaks,
At once sends it home to the heart when she sings.
Then sing—sing—Music was given
To brighten the gay, and kindle the loving
Souls here, like planets in heaven,
By harmony's laws alone are kept moving.

When Love, rocked by his mother,
Lay sleeping as calm as slumber could make him,
'Hush, hush,' said Venus, 'no other
Sweet voice but his own is worthy to wake him.'
Dreaming of music he slumbered the while,
Till faint from his lips a soft melody broke,
And Venus, enchanted, looked on with a smile,
While Love to his own sweet singing awoke!
Then sing—sing—Music was given
To brighten the gay, and kindle the loving;
Souls here, like planets in heaven,
By harmony's laws alone are kept moving

---

[1] These verses are meant to allude to that ancient haunt of superstition called Patrick's Purgatory. 'In the midst of these gloomy regions of Donnegall (says Dr. Campbell) lay a lake, which was to become the mystic theatre of this fabled and intermediate state. In the lake were several islands; but one of them was dignified with that called the Mouth of Purgatory, which during the dark ages attracted the notice of all Christendom, and was the resort of penitents and pilgrims from almost every country in Europe.

'It was,' as the same writer tells us, 'one of the most dismal and dreary spots in the North, almost inaccessible, through deep glens and rugged mountains, frightful with impending rocks, and the hollow murmurs of the western winds in dark caverns, peopled only with such fantastic beings as the mind, however gay, is from strange association wont to appropriate to such gloomy scenes.'—*Strictures on the Ecclesiastical and Literary History of Ireland.*

[2] The thought here was suggested by some beautiful lines in Mr. Rogers's Poem of *Human Life*, beginning,

'Now in the glimmering, dying light she grows
Less and less earthly.'

I would quote the entire passage, but that I fear to put my own humble imitation of it out of countenance.

SACRED SONGS.

SACRED SONGS.

THOU ART, OH GOD!
Air—UNKNOWN.[1]

'The day is thine; the night also is thine; thou hast prepared the light and the sun.
'Thou hast set all the borders of the earth; thou hast made summer and winter.'—PSALM lxxiv. 16, 17.

THOU art, oh God! the life and light
  Of all this wondrous world we see;
Its glow by day, its smile by night,
  Are but reflections caught from Thee.
Where'er we turn, Thy glories shine,
And all things fair and bright are Thine!

When Day, with farewell beam, delays
  Among the opening clouds of Even,
And we can almost think we gaze
  Through golden vistas into heaven—
Those hues, that make the sun's decline
So soft, so radiant, Lord! are Thine.

When Night, with wings of starry gloom,
  O'ershadows all the earth and skies,
Like some dark, beauteous bird, whose plume
  Is sparkling with unnumbered eyes—
That sacred gloom, those fires divine,
So grand, so countless, Lord! are Thine.

When youthful Spring around us breathes,
  Thy Spirit warms her fragrant sigh;
And every flower the Summer wreathes
  Is born beneath that kindling eye.
Where'er we turn, Thy glories shine,
And all things fair and bright are Thine!

THIS WORLD IS ALL A FLEETING SHOW.
Air—STEVENSON.

THIS world is all a fleeting show,
  For man's illusion given;
The smiles of Joy, the tears of Woe,
Deceitful shine, deceitful flow—
  There's nothing true but Heaven!

And false the light on Glory's plume,
  As fading hues of Even;
And Love, and Hope, and Beauty's bloom,
Are blossoms gathered for the tomb,—
  There's nothing bright but heaven!

Poor wanderers of a stormy day,
  From wave to wave we're driven,
And Fancy's flash, and Reason's ray,
Serve but to light the troubled way—
  There's nothing calm but heaven!

FALLEN IS THY THRONE.
Air—MARTINI.

FALLEN is thy throne, oh Israel!
  Silence is o'er thy plains;
Thy dwellings all lie desolate,
  Thy children weep in chains.
Where are the dews that fed thee
  On Etham's barren shore?
That fire from heaven which led thee,
  Now lights thy path no more.

Lord! Thou didst love Jerusalem—
  Once she was all Thy own;
Her love Thy fairest heritage,
  Her power Thy glory's throne:
Till evil came, and blighted
  Thy long-loved olive-tree;—
And Salem's shrines were lighted
  For other Gods than Thee!

Then sunk the star of Solyma—
  Then passed her glory's day,
Like heath that, in the wilderness,
  The wild wind whirls away.
Silent and waste her bowers,
  Where once the mighty trod,
And sunk those guilty towers,
  While Baal reigned as God!

'Go,' said the Lord, 'ye conquerors!
  Steep in her blood your swords,

---

[1] I have heard that this air is by the late Mrs. Sheridan. It is sung to the beautiful old words, 'I do confess thou'rt smooth and fair.'

And raze to earth her battlements,
For they are not the Lord's!
Till Zion's mournful daughter
O'er kindred bones shall tread,
And Hinnom's vale of slaughter [1]
Shall hide but half her dead!'

WHO IS THE MAID?

ST. JEROME'S LOVE. [2]

Air—BEETHOVEN.

Who is the maid my spirit seeks,
Through cold reproof and slander's blight?
Has *she* Love's roses on her cheeks?
Is *hers* an eye of this world's light?
No,—wan and sunk with midnight prayer
Are the pale looks of her I love;
Or if at times a light be there,
Its beam is kindled from above.

I chose not her, my soul's elect,
From those who seek their Maker's shrine
In gems and garlands proudly decked,
As if themselves were things divine!
No—Heaven but faintly warms the breast
That beats beneath a broidered veil;
And she who comes in glittering vest
To mourn her frailty, still is frail.

Not so the faded form I prize
And love, because its bloom is gone;
The glory in those sainted eyes
Is all the grace her brow puts on.
And ne'er was Beauty's dawn so bright,
So touching as that form's decay,
Which, like the altar's trembling light,
In holy lustre wastes away!

THE BIRD, LET LOOSE.

Air—BEETHOVEN.

The bird, let loose in eastern skies,[3]
When hastening fondly home,
Ne'er stoops to earth her wing, nor flies
Where idle warblers roam.
But high she shoots through air and light,
Above all low delay,
Where nothing earthly bounds her flight,
Nor shadow dims her way.

So grant me, God! from every care
And stain of passion free,
Aloft, through Virtue's purer air,
To hold my course to Thee!
No sin to cloud—no lure to stay
My Soul, as home she springs;—
Thy sunshine on her joyful way,
Thy freedom in her wings!

OH! THOU WHO DRY'ST THE MOURNER'S TEAR!

Air—HAYDN.

'He healeth the broken in heart, and bindeth up their wounds.'—PSALM cxlvii. 3.

Oh! Thou who dry'st the mourner's tear,
How dark this world would be,
If, when deceived and wounded here,
We could not fly to Thee!
The friends who in our sunshine live,
When winter comes, are flown;
And he who has but tears to give,
Must weep those tears alone.
But Thou wilt heal that broken heart,
Which, like the plants that throw
Their fragrance from the wounded part,
Breathes sweetness out of woe.

When joy no longer soothes or cheers,
And even the hope that threw
A moment's sparkle o'er our tears,
Is dimmed and vanished too!
Oh! who would bear life's stormy doom,
Did not Thy wing of love
Come, brightly wafting through the gloom
Our peace-branch from above?
Then sorrow, touched by Thee, grows bright
With more than rapture's ray;
As darkness shows us worlds of light
We never saw by day!

WEEP NOT FOR THOSE.

Air—AVISON.

Weep not for those whom the veil of the tomb,
In life's happy morning, hath hid from our eyes,
Ere sin threw a blight o'er the spirit's young bloom,
Or earth had profaned what was born for the skies.

---

[1] 'Therefore, behold, the days come, saith the Lord, that it shall no more be called Tophet, nor the Valley of the Son of Hinnom, but the Valley of Slaughter; for they shall bury in Tophet till there be no place.'—JER. vii. 32.

[2] These lines were suggested by a passage in St. Jerome's reply to some calumnious remarks that had been circulated upon his intimacy with the matron Paula:—'Numquid me vestes sericæ, nitentes gemmæ, picta facies, aut auri rapuit ambitio? Nulla fuit alia Romæ matronarum, quæ meam possit edomare mentem, nisi lugens atque jejunans, fleta pene cæcata.'—*Epist.* 'Si tibi putem.'

[3] The carrier-pigeon, it is well known, flies at an elevated pitch, in order to surmount every obstacle between her and the place to which she is destined.

Death chilled the fair fountain, ere sorrow had stained it,
'Twas frozen in all the pure light of its course,
And but sleeps till the sunshine of heaven has unchained it,
To water that Eden where first was its source!
Weep not for those whom the veil of the tomb,
In life's happy morning, hath hid from our eyes,
Ere sin threw a blight o'er the spirit's young bloom,
Or earth had profaned what was born for the skies.

Mourn not for her, the young Bride of the Vale,[1]
Our gayest and loveliest, lost to us now,
Ere life's early lustre had time to grow pale,
And the garland of love was yet fresh on her brow!
Oh! then was her moment, dear spirit, for flying
From this gloomy world, while its gloom was unknown—
And the wild hymns she warbled so sweetly, in dying,
Were echoed in heaven by lips like her own!
Weep not for her,—in her spring-time she flew
To that land where the wings of the soul are unfurled,
And now, like a star beyond evening's cold dew,
Looks radiantly down on the tears of this world.

THE TURF SHALL BE MY FRAGRANT SHRINE.

Air—STEVENSON.

The turf shall be my fragrant shrine;
My temple, Lord! that Arch of Thine;
My censer's breath the mountain airs,
And silent thoughts my only prayers.

My choir shall be the moonlight waves,
When murmuring homeward to their caves,
Or when the stillness of the sea,
Even more than music, breathes of Thee!

I'll seek by day some glade unknown,
All light and silence, like Thy throne!
And the pale stars shall be at night
The only eyes that watch my rite.

Thy heaven, on which 'tis bliss to look,
Shall be my pure and shining book,
Where I shall read, in words of flame,
The glories of Thy wondrous name.

I'll read Thy anger in the rack
That clouds awhile the day-beam's track;
Thy mercy in the azure hue
Of sunny brightness breaking through!

There's nothing bright above, below,
From flowers that bloom to stars that glow,
But in its light my soul can see
Some feature of Thy Deity!

There's nothing dark below, above,
But in its gloom I trace Thy love,
And meekly wait that moment when
Thy touch shall turn all bright again!

SOUND THE LOUD TIMBREL!

MIRIAM'S SONG.

Air—AVISON.[2]

'And Miriam the prophetess, the sister of Aaron, took a timbrel in her hand; and all the women went out after her, with timbrels and with dances.'—EXOD xv. 20.

SOUND the loud timbrel o'er Egypt's dark sea!
Jehovah has triumphed,—His people are free.
Sing—for the pride of the tyrant is broken,
His chariots, his horsemen, all splendid and brave—
How vain was their boasting!—the Lord hath but spoken,
And chariots and horsemen are sunk in the wave.
Sound the loud timbrel o'er Egypt's dark sea!
Jehovah has triumphed,—His people are free.

Praise to the Conqueror, praise to the Lord!
His word was our arrow, His breath was our sword!
Who shall return to tell Egypt the story
Of those she sent forth in the hour of he pride?
For the Lord hath looked out from His pillar of glory,[3]
And all her brave thousands are dashed in the tide.
Sound the loud timbrel o'er Egypt's dark sea!
Jehovah has triumphed,—His people are free.

---

[1] This second verse, which I wrote long after the first, alludes to the fate of a very lovely and amiable girl, the daughter of the late Colonel Bainbrigge, who was married in Ashbourne church, October 31, 1815, and died of a fever in a few weeks after: the sound of her marriage-bells seemed scarcely out of our ears when we heard of her death. During her last delirium she sung several hymns, in a voice even clearer and sweeter than usual, and among them were some from the present collection (particularly, 'There's nothing bright but Heaven'), which this very interesting girl had often heard during the summer.

[2] I have so altered the character of this air, which is from the beginning of one of Avison's old-fashioned concertos, that, without this acknowledgment, it could hardly, I think, be recognised.

[3] 'And it came to pass, that in the morning watch the Lord looked unto the host of the Egyptians, through the pillar of fire and of the cloud, and troubled the host of the Egyptians.'—EXOD. xiv. 24.

SACRED SONGS.

GO, LET ME WEEP!
Air—STEVENSON.

Go, let me weep! there's bliss in tears,
  When he who sheds them inly feels
Some lingering stain of early years
  Effaced by every drop that steals.
The fruitless showers of worldly woe
  Fall dark to earth, and never rise;
While tears that from repentance flow,
  In bright exhalement reach the skies.
Go, let me weep! there's bliss in tears,
  When he who sheds them inly feels
Some lingering stain of early years
  Effaced by every drop that steals.

Leave me to sigh o'er hours that flew
  More idly than the summer's wind,
And while they passed, a fragrance threw,
  But left no trace of sweets behind.—
The warmest sigh that pleasure heaves
  Is cold, is faint to those that swell
The heart where pure repentance grieves
  O'er hours of pleasure loved too well!
Leave me to sigh o'er days that flew
  More idly than the summer's wind,
And while they passed, a fragrance threw,
  But left no trace of sweets behind.

COME NOT, OH LORD!
Air—HAYDN.

COME not, oh Lord! in the dread robe of splendour
  Thou worest on the Mount, in the day of Thine ire;
Come veiled in those shadows, deep, awful, but tender,
  Which Mercy flings over Thy features of fire!

Lord! Thou rememberest the night when Thy nation [1]
  Stood fronting her foe by the red-rolling stream;
On Egypt [2] Thy pillar frowned dark desolation,
  While Israel basked all the night in its beam.

So, when the dread clouds of anger enfold Thee,
  From us, in Thy mercy, the dark side remove;
While shrouded in terrors the guilty behold Thee,
  Oh, turn upon us the mild light of Thy Love!

---

[1] 'And it came between the camp of the Egyptians and the camp of Israel; and it was a cloud and darkness to them, but it gave light by night to these.'—EXOD. xiv. 20. My application of this passage is borrowed from some late prose writer, whose name I am ungrateful enough to forget.

WERE NOT THE SINFUL MARY'S TEARS.
Air—STEVENSON.

WERE not the sinful Mary's tears
  An offering worthy heaven,
When o'er the faults of former years
  She wept—and was forgiven?—

When, bringing every balmy sweet
  Her day of luxury stored,
She o'er her Saviour's hallowed feet
  The precious perfumes poured;—

And wiped them with that golden hair,
  Where once the diamond shone,
Though now those gems of grief were there
  Which shine for God alone!

Were not those sweets so humbly shed,—
  That hair,—those weeping eyes,—
And the sunk heart, that inly bled,—
  Heaven's noblest sacrifice?

Thou that hast slept in error's sleep,
  Oh wouldst thou wake in heaven,
Like Mary kneel, like Mary weep,
  'Love much' [3]—and be forgiven!

AS DOWN IN THE SUNLESS RETREATS.
Air—HAYDN.

As down in the sunless retreats of the ocean,
  Sweet flowers are springing no mortal can see,
So, deep in my soul the still prayer of devotion,
  Unheard by the world, rises silent to Thee,
    My God! silent to Thee—
    Pure, warm, silent, to Thee;
So, deep in my soul the still prayer of devotion,
  Unheard by the world, rises silent to Thee!

As still to the star of its worship, though clouded,
  The needle points faithfully o'er the dim sea,
So, dark as I roam, in this wintry world shrouded,
  The hope of my spirit turns trembling to Thee,
    My God! trembling to Thee—
    True, fond, trembling, to Thee:
So, dark as I roam, in this wintry world shrouded,
  The hope of my spirit turns trembling to Thee!

---

[2] Instead of 'On Egypt' here, it will suit the music better to sing 'On these;' and in the third line of the next verse, 'While shrouded' may, with the same view, be altered to 'While wrapped.'

[3] 'Her sins, which are many, are forgiven; for she loved much.'—LUKE vii. 47.

BUT WHO SHALL SEE.

Air—STEVENSON.

But who shall see the glorious day
When, throned on Zion's brow,
The Lord shall rend that veil away
Which hides the nations now!
When earth no more beneath the fear
Of His rebuke shall lie;
When pain shall cease, and every tear
Be wiped from every eye!

Then, Judah! thou no more shalt mourn
Beneath the heathen's chain;
Thy days of splendour shall return,
And all be new again.
The Fount of life shall then be quaffed
In peace by all who come!
And every wind that blows shall waft
Some long-lost exile home!

ALMIGHTY GOD!

CHORUS OF PRIESTS.

Air—MOZART.

Almighty God! when round Thy shrine
The palm-tree's heavenly branch we twine,[1]
(Emblem of Life's eternal ray,
And Love that 'fadeth not away,')
We bless the flowers, expanded all,[2]
We bless the leaves that never fall,
And trembling say, 'In Eden thus
The Tree of Life may flower for us!'

When round Thy cherubs, smiling calm
Without their flames,[3] we wreathe the palm,
Oh God! we feel the emblem true,—
Thy mercy is eternal too!
Those cherubs with their smiling eyes,
That crown of palm which never dies,
Are but the types of Thee above—
Eternal Life, and Peace, and Love!

OH FAIR! OH PUREST!

SAINT AUGUSTINE TO HIS SISTER.[4]

Air—MOORE.

Oh fair! oh purest! be thou the dove
That flies alone to some sunny grove,
And lives unseen, and bathes her wing,
All vestal white in the limpid spring.
There if the hovering hawk be near,
That limpid spring in its mirror clear
Reflects him ere he can reach his prey,
And warns the timorous bird away.
    Oh! be like this dove;
Oh fair! oh purest! be like this dove.

The sacred pages of God's own book
Shall be the spring, the eternal brook,
In whose holy mirror, night and day,
Thou wilt study Heaven's reflected ray:—
And should the foes of virtue dare,
With gloomy wing, to seek thee there,
Thou wilt see how dark their shadows lie
Between heaven and thee, and trembling fly!
    Oh! be like the dove;
Oh fair! oh purest! be like the dove.

ANGEL OF CHARITY.

Air—HANDEL.

Angel of Charity, who from above
Comest to dwell a pilgrim here,
Thy voice is music, thy smile is love,
And pity's soul is in thy tear!
When on the shrine of God were laid
    First-fruits of all most good and fair,
That ever grew in Eden's shade,
    Thine was the holiest offering there!

Hope and her sister, Faith, were given
    But as our guides to yonder sky;
Soon as they reach the verge of heaven,
    Lost in that blaze of bliss, they die.
But long as Love, almighty Love,
    Shall on his throne of thrones abide,
Thou shalt, oh! Charity, dwell above,
    Smiling for ever by his side.

---

[1] 'The Scriptures having declared that the Temple of Jerusalem was a type of the Messiah, it is natural to conclude that the *Palms*, which made so conspicuous a figure in that structure, represented that *Life* and *Immortality* which were brought to light by the Gospel.'—*Observations on the Palm as a sacred Emblem*, by W. Tighe.

[2] 'And he carved all the walls of the house round about with carved figures of cherubims, and palm-trees, and open flowers.'—1 KINGS vi. 29.

[3] 'When the passover of the tabernacles was revealed to the great lawgiver in the mount, then the cherubic images which appeared in that structure were no longer surrounded by flames; for the tabernacle was a type of the dispensation of mercy, by which Jehovah confirmed His gracious covenant to redeem mankind.'—*Observations on the Palm*.

[4] In St. Augustine's treatise upon the advantages of a solitary life, addressed to his sister, there is the following fanciful passage, from which the thought of this song was taken:—'Te, soror, nunquam nolo esse securam, sed timere, semperque tuam fragilitatem habere suspectam, ad instar pavidæ columbæ frequentare rivos aquarum et quasi in speculo accipitris cernere supervolantis effigiem et cavere. Rivi aquarum sententiæ sunt scripturarum, quæ de limpidissimo sapientiæ fonte profluentes,' etc. etc.—*De Vit. Eremit. ad Sororem.*

SACRED SONGS.

BEHOLD THE SUN.
Air—LORD MORNINGTON.

BEHOLD the sun, how bright
   From yonder east he springs,
As if the soul of life and light
   Were breathing from his wings.

So bright the gospel broke
   Upon the souls of men;
So fresh the dreaming world awoke
   In truth's full radiance then!

Before yon sun arose,
   Stars clustered through the sky—
But oh how dim, how pale were those,
   To his one burning eye!

So truth lent many a ray,
   To bless the Pagan's night—
But, Lord, how weak, how cold were they,
   To thy one glorious light!

LORD, WHO SHALL BEAR THAT DAY?
Air—DR. BOYCE.

LORD, who shall bear that day, so dread, so splendid,
When we shall see Thy angel hovering o'er
This sinful world, with hand to heaven extended,
And hear him swear by Thee that time's no more?
When earth shall feel Thy fast-consuming ray—
Who, mighty God, oh who shall bear that day?

When through the world Thy awful call hath sounded—
   'Wake, oh ye dead, to judgment wake, ye dead!'[1]
And from the clouds, by seraph eyes surrounded,
   The Saviour shall put forth His radiant head;
While earth and heaven before Him pass away—
Who, mighty God, oh who shall bear that day?

When, with a glance, the eternal Judge shall sever
Earth's evil spirits from the pure and bright,
And say to *those*, 'Depart from me for ever!'
   To *these*, 'Come, dwell with me in endless light!'
When each and all in silence take their way—
Who, mighty God, oh who shall bear that day?

OH! TEACH ME TO LOVE THEE.
Air—HAYDN.

OH! teach me to love thee, to feel what thou art,
   Till, filled with the one sacred image, my heart
Shall all other passions disown—
   Like some pure temple that shines apart,
Reserved for thy worship alone!

In joy and in sorrow, through praise and through blame,
Oh still let me, living and dying the same,
   In thy service bloom and decay—
Like some lone altar, whose votive flame
   In holiness wasteth away!

Though born in this desert, and doomed by my birth
To pain and affliction, to darkness and dearth,
   On thee let my spirit rely—
Like some rude dial, that, fixed on earth,
   Still looks for its light from the sky!

WEEP, CHILDREN OF ISRAEL.
Air—STEVENSON.

WEEP, weep for him, the Man of God—
   In yonder vale he sunk to rest,
But none of earth can point the sod
   That flowers above his sacred breast.
   Weep, children of Israel, weep!

His doctrines fell like heaven's rain,
   His words refreshed like heaven's dew—
Oh, ne'er shall Israel see again
   A chief, to God and her so true.
   Weep, children of Israel, weep!

Remember ye his parting gaze,
   His farewell song by Jordan's tide,
When, full of glory and of days,
   He saw the promised land—and died!
   Weep, children of Israel, weep!

Yet died he not as men who sink,
   Before our eyes, to soulless clay;
But, changed to spirit, like a wink
   Of summer lightning, passed away![1]
   Weep, children of Israel, weep!

LIKE MORNING, WHEN HER EARLY BREEZE.
Air—BEETHOVEN.

LIKE morning, when her early breeze
Breaks up the surface of the seas,

---

[1] 'Awake, ye dead, and come to judgment.'
[2] 'As he was going to embrace Eleazer and Joshua, and was still discoursing with them, a cloud stood over him on the sudden, and he disappeared in a certain valley, although he wrote in the Holy Books that he died, which was done out of fear, lest they should venture to say that, because of his extraordinary virtue, he went to God.'—*Josephus*, Book iv chap. viii.

That in their furrows, dark with night,
  Her hand may sow the seeds of light—

Thy grace can send its breathings o'er
  The spirit, dark and lost before,
And, freshening all its depths, prepare
  For truth divine to enter there!

Till David touched his sacred lyre,
  In silence lay the unbreathing wire;
But when he swept its chords along,
  Even angels stooped to hear that song.

So sleeps the soul, till Thou, O Lord,
  Shall deign to touch its lifeless chord—
Till, waked by Thee, its breath shall rise
  In music worthy of the skies!

COME, YE DISCONSOLATE.

Air—German.

Come, ye disconsolate, where'er you languish,
  Come, at the shrine of God fervently kneel;
Here bring your wounded hearts, here tell your anguish—
  Earth has no sorrow that Heaven cannot heal.

Joy of the desolate, light of the straying,
  Hope, when all others die, fadeless and pure,
Here speaks the Comforter, in God's name saying,
  'Earth has no sorrow that Heaven cannot cure.'

Go, ask the infidel what boon he brings us,
  What charm for aching hearts he can reveal,
Sweet as that heavenly promise Hope sings us—
  'Earth has no sorrow that God cannot heal.'

AWAKE, ARISE, THY LIGHT IS COME.

Air—Stevenson.

Awake, arise, thy light is come;
  The nations, that before outshone thee,
Now at thy feet lie dark and dumb—
  The glory of the Lord is on thee!

Arise—the Gentiles to thy ray
  From every nook of earth shall cluster;
And kings and princes haste to pay
  Their homage to thy rising lustre.

Lift up thine eyes around, and see,
  O'er foreign fields, o'er farthest waters,
Thy exiled sons return to thee,
  To thee return thy home-sick daughters.

And camels rich, from Midian's tents,
  Shall lay their treasures down before thee;
And Saba bring her gold and scents,
  To fill thy air, and sparkle o'er thee.

See who are these that, like a cloud,
  Are gathering from all earth's dominions,
Like doves, long absent, when allowed
  Homeward to shoot their trembling pinions.

Surely the isles shall wait for me,
  The ships of Tarshish round will hover,
To bring thy sons across the sea,
  And waft their gold and silver over.

And Lebanon, thy pomp shall grace—
  The fir, the pine, the palm victorious,
Shall beautify our Holy Place,
  And make the ground I tread on glorious.

No more shall discord haunt thy ways,
  Nor ruin waste thy cheerless nation;
But thou shalt call thy portals Praise,
  And thou shalt name thy walls Salvation.

The sun no more shall make thee bright,
  Nor moon shall lend her lustre to thee;
But God Himself shall be thy Light,
  And flash eternal glory through thee.

Thy sun shall never more go down;
  A ray, from heaven itself descended,
Shall light thy everlasting crown—
  Thy days of mourning all are ended.

My own, elect, and righteous Land!
  The Branch, for ever green and vernal,
Which I have planted with this hand—
  Live thou shalt in Life Eternal.

THERE IS A BLEAK DESERT.

Air—Crescentini.

There is a bleak Desert, where daylight grows weary
  Of wasting its smile on a region so dreary—
    What may that Desert be?
'Tis Life, cheerless Life, where the few joys that come
Are lost, like that daylight, for 'tis not their home.

There is a lone Pilgrim, before whose faint eyes
The water he pants for but sparkles and flies—
    Who may that Pilgrim be?
'Tis Man, hapless Man, through this life tempted on
By fair shining hopes, that in shining are gone.

There is a bright Fountain, through that Desert stealing,
To pure lips alone its refreshment revealing—
    What may that fountain be?
'Tis Truth, holy Truth, that, like springs under ground,
By the gifted of Heaven alone can be found.

There is a fair Spirit, whose wand hath the spell
To point where those waters in secrecy dwell—
　Who may that Spirit be?
'Tis Faith, humble Faith, who hath learned that, where'er
Her wand stoops to worship, the Truth must be there.

SINCE FIRST THY WORD.
Air—NICHOLAS FREEMAN.

SINCE first Thy word awaked my heart,
　Like new life dawning o'er me,
Where'er I turn mine eyes, Thou art,
　All light and love before me.
Nought else I feel, or hear, or see—
　All bonds of earth I sever—
Thee, oh God, and only Thee,
　I live for, now and ever.

Like him, whose fetters dropped away
　When light shone o'er his prison,
My spirit, touched by Mercy's ray,
　Hath from her chains arisen.
And shall a soul Thou bid'st be free
　Return to bondage?—never!
Thee, oh God, and only Thee,
　I live for, now and ever.

HARK! 'TIS THE BREEZE.
Air—ROUSSEAU.

HARK!—'tis the breeze of twilight calling
　Earth's weary children to repose;
While, round the couch of Nature falling,
　Gently the night's soft curtains close.
Soon o'er a world, in sleep reclining,
　Numberless stars, through yonder dark,
Shall look, like eyes of cherubs shining
　From out the veils that hid the Ark!

Guard us, oh Thou, who never sleepest,
　Thou who, in silence throned above,
Throughout all time, unwearied, keepest
　Thy watch of Glory, Power, and Love.
Grant that, beneath Thine eye, securely
　Our souls, awhile from life withdrawn,
May, in their darkness, stilly, purely,
　Like 'sealèd fountains,' rest till dawn.

WHERE IS YOUR DWELLING, YE SAINTED?
Air—HASSE.

WHERE is your dwelling, ye sainted?
　Through what Elysium more bright
Than fancy or hope ever painted,
　Walk ye in glory and light?

Who the same kingdom inherits?
　Breathes there a soul that may dare
Look to that world of spirits?
　Or hope to dwell with you there?

Sages who, even in exploring
　Nature through all her bright ways,
Went, like the seraphs, adoring,
　And veiled your eyes in the blaze—
Martyrs, who left for our reaping
　Truths you had sown in your blood—
Sinners, whom long years of weeping
　Chastened from evil to good—

Maidens who, like the young Crescent,
　Turning away your pale brows
From earth, and the light of the Present,
　Looked to your Heavenly Spouse—
Say, through what region enchanted
　Walk ye, in heaven's sweet air?
Or, oh, to whom is it granted,
　Bright souls, to dwell with you there?

HOW LIGHTLY MOUNTS THE MUSE'S WING.
Air—ANONYMOUS.

How lightly mounts the Muse's wing,
　Whose theme is in the skies—
Like morning larks, that sweeter sing
　The nearer heaven they rise!

Though Love his wreathèd lyre may tune,
　Yet ah! the flowers he round it wreathes
Were plucked beneath pale Passion's moon,
　Whose madness from their odour breathes.
How purer far the sacred lute,
　Round which Devotion ties
Sweet flowers that turn to heavenly fruit,
　And palm that never dies!

Though War's high-sounding harp may be
　Most welcome to the hero's ears,
Alas, his chords of victory
　Are bathed all o'er with tears.
How far more sweet their numbers run,
　Who hymn, like saints above,
No victor but the Eternal One,
　No trophies but of Love!

GO FORTH TO THE MOUNT.
Air—STEVENSON.

Go forth to the Mount—bring the olive-branch home,
And rejoice, for the day of our Freedom is come!
From that time, when the moon upon Ajalon's vale,
　Looking motionless down, saw the kings of the earth,

In the presence of God's mighty Champion,
  grow pale—
Oh never had Judah an hour of such mirth!
Go forth to the Mount—bring the olive-branch
  home,
And rejoice, for the day of our Freedom is come!

Bring myrtle and palm—bring the boughs of
  each tree
That is worthy to wave o'er the tents of the
  Free.
From that day, when the footsteps of Israel
  shone,
  With a light not their own, through the
    Jordan's deep tide,
Whose waters shrunk back as the Ark glided
  on—
Oh never had Judah an hour of such pride!
Go forth to the Mount—bring the olive-branch
  home,
And rejoice, for the day of our Freedom is come!

IS IT NOT SWEET TO THINK, HEREAFTER?

Air—HAYDN.

Is it not sweet to think, hereafter,
  When the spirit leaves this sphere,
Love, with deathless wing, shall waft her
  To those she long hath mourned for here?
Hearts, from which 'twas death to sever,
  Eyes, this world can ne'er restore,
There, as warm, as bright as ever,
  Shall meet us and be lost no more.

When wearily we wander, asking
  Of earth and heaven, where are they,
Beneath whose smile we once lay basking—
  Blest, and thinking bliss would stay!

Hope still lifts her radiant finger,
  Pointing to the eternal home,
Upon whose portal yet they linger,
  Looking back for us to come.

Alas! alas! doth Hope deceive us?
  Shall friendship—love—shall all those ties
That bind a moment, and then leave us,
  Be found again where nothing dies?
Oh! if no other boon were given,
  To keep our hearts from wrong and stain,
Who would not try to win a heaven
  Where all we love shall live again?

WAR AGAINST BABYLON.

Air—NOVELLO.

'War against Babylon!' shout we around,
  Be our banners through earth unfurled;
Rise up, ye nations, ye kings, at the sound—
  'War against Babylon!' shout through the
    world!
Oh thou, that dwellest on many waters,
  Thy day of pride is ended now;
And the dark curse of Israel's daughters
  Breaks, like a thunder-cloud, over thy brow!
    War, war, war against Babylon!

Make bright the arrows, and gather the shields,
  Set the standard of God on high—
Swarm we, like locusts, o'er all her fields,
  'Zion' our watchword, and 'vengeance' our
    cry!
Woe! woe!—the time of thy visitation
  Is come, proud Land, thy doom is cast—
And the bleak wave of desolation
  Sweeps o'er thy guilty head at last!
    War, war, war against Babylon!

THE END.

www.ingramcontent.com/pod-product-compliance
Lightning Source LLC
Chambersburg PA
CBHW021418300426
44114CB00010B/554